NEW AMERICAN CROSSWORD PUZZLE DICTIONARY

Edited by
ALBERT and LOY MOREHEAD

Introduction by Jack Luzzatto

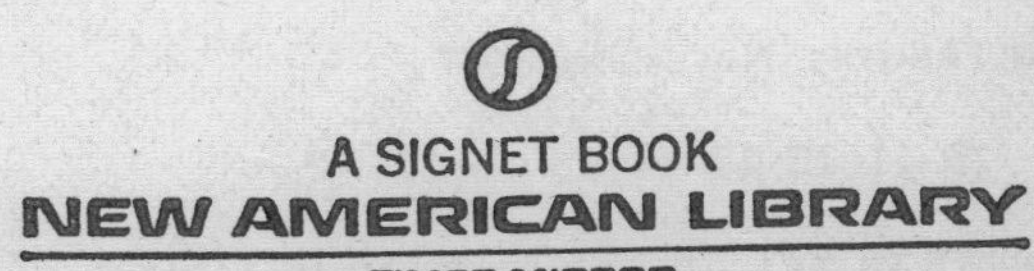

New American Crossword Puzzle Dictionary
Edited by: Albert and Loy Morehead
Chief Compiler: Gerard Mosler
Staff: Philip D. Morehead
Earle Pitts
Beverly Bowers
John Hechtlinger
Ronald Moore

SIGNET TRADEMARK REG. U.S. PAT. OFF. AND FOREIGN COUNTRIES
REGISTERED TRADEMARK—MARCA REGISTRADA
HECHO EN CHICAGO, U.S.A.

SIGNET, SIGNET CLASSICS, MENTOR, PLUME AND MERIDIAN BOOKS
are published by The New American Library, Inc.,
1301 Avenue of the Americas, New York, New York 10019

FIRST PRINTING, NOVEMBER, 1967

10 11 12 13 14 15 16 17

PRINTED IN THE UNITED STATES OF AMERICA

INTRODUCTION

It is my pleasure to introduce the only new and different Crossword Puzzle Dictionary to come along in years. Chock-full of information not even covered by many volumes of specialized scope, this book is the finest aid available for solving crossword puzzles and other word games. It is the largest and most compendious book of its type, as a glance at the richness and range of the contents pages will reveal.

Conceived by Albert H. Morehead, the well-known lexicographer, and worked on by a staff trained in the field, this book assures the confirmed puzzle solver of an authoritative and comprehensive guide to the world of words, and of crossword puzzles in particular. So complete are the various categories that even a person who is not primarily interested in crosswords could put it to use as a handy reference guide in various fields. Special stress has been laid on the unusual words, exactly the ones that baffle most solvers. (A dictionary that tells you what you already know is not only exasperating, but useless.) For the puzzle fan, this dictionary is the matchless source *par excellence*, a fount of information he cannot do without.

Mr. Morehead, before he created this book, had long and arduous experience in dictionary and encyclopedia making. In fact, lexicography was his lifework, by choice, so he could bring the advantages of more knowledge and trained techniques to a book like this, better than anyone else who ever tackled such a job. It is truly a labor of love, as the reader will find out as he enjoys this book. Mr. Morehead was also a pioneer in the crossword puzzle field, since he introduced the Puns and Anagrams type of puzzle to the American public, having created the first ever to appear in the United States, and the first complete book of them.

You can only learn what a complete puzzle guide this book is by browsing through it at your leisure, familiarizing yourself with all its qualities and quantities. Thus you will find it as up-to-date as the space age and as old as mythology and the Bible. Indispensable is the word that best describes this newest, largest, most useful and complete Crossword Puzzle Dictionary ever to appear in paperback or hard covers.

JACK LUZZATTO

CONTENTS

SECTION I

A

Aaron's rod MULLEIN
abacus SOROBAN, SUANPAN
abalone AWABI, ORMER, SEAEAR, U(H)LLO
abandoned CORRUPT, LORN
abase(ment) LOWER, MEIOSIS, SHAME
abash COW, DAUNT, HUMBLE, SHAME
abbe MONK, PRIEST
abbess AMMA
abbey (A)BADIA, FLY, NUNNERY, PRIORY
abbot ABBAS, COARB
abdomen BELLY, RUMEN, VENTER, VISCERA
abdominal C(O)ELIAC, HEMAL, VENTRAL
abecedary PRIMER, TYRO
abet EGG, FOMENT, INCITE
abigail MAID
ability CALIBER, TALENT
abject BASE, MENIAL, SCURVY, VILE
abjure DENY, RECANT, REJECT
ablution SIDU, WASH, WUZU
abode DAR, HABITAT, HUT
abode of bliss ARCADIA, EDEN, GOSHEN
abode of dead AALU, AARU, ARALU, HADES, ORCUS, SHEOL
abolitionist GARRISON, LUNDY, STEVENS
abominable snowman YETI
aboriginal BINGHI, NATIVE
abound(ing) RIFE, SNEE, SNY, SWARM, TEEM
about ANENT, CIRCA, INRE, NEAR, SOME
above ATOP, OER, OVER, SUPER, SUPRA, UPON
abrade CHAFE, FRET, RUB
abrasive CORUNDUM, EMERY, PUMICE
abridgment EPITOME, PRECIS
abrogate ANNUL, CANCEL, RESCIND
abrupt BLUNT, CURT, ICTIC, RUDE
abrupt flexure GENU
abscond ELOI(G)N, ELOPE, FLEE, LEVANT
absent ABROAD, AWOL, OFF
absolute CAPTAIN, FREE, TOTAL, VERY, ZERO
absolve CLEAR, FREE, SHRIVE
absorb DRINK, IMBIBE, OCCLUDE, SOAK, SUCK
absorbed LOST, RAPT, SUNK
abstruse ACROMATIC, ESOTERIC
abundance BOUNTY, GALORE, PLETHORA
abundant AMPLE, RIFE
abuse GALEE, GALI, RAIL, REVILE, SNASH, VIOLATE
abut BORDER, ADJOIN
abutment ALETTE
abyss CHASM, GULF, PIT, VORAGO
accelerate HASTEN, REV, SPRINT
accent ACUTE, ARSIS, BLAS, BROGUE, GRAVE, ICTUS, THESIS
access ADIT, ENTREE, ENTRY
acclivity SLANT, SLOPE, TALUS
accolade EMMY, OSCAR, TONY
accommodate BILLET, FAVOR, FIT, LEND, LODGE, OBLIGE
accordingly ERGO, HENCE, THUS
according to ALA, ALLA, AUX
accost GREET, HAIL, WAYLAY
account BATTEL, BILL, TAB, TALE, TOT
accountant AUDITOR, CPA, SIRCAR
accumulate ACCRUE, (A)MASS, FUND, HOARD
accurate JUST, LEAL, NICE
accuse DELATE, FRAME, INDICT, REPORT
accustomed USED, WONT
ace AONE, BASTO, JOT, ONE, PILOT, TIB, TOPS
acetone ACETOL, KETONE
acetylene ETHIN(E), TOLAN(E)
acid AMINO, BORIC, KEEN, NITRIC, OLEATE, OLEIC, TART
acid radical ACETYL, ACYL, ANION
acidity ACOR
acknowledge AVOW, NOD, OWN
acorn(s) BELOTE, CAMATA, MAST, OVEST
acquainted VERSANT
across OER, OVER, TRAN(S)
acrostic AGLA, PUZZLE
act ACTU(S), BILL, DEED, EMOTE, LAW, PLAY, WORK
action CONDUCT, DEED, FIGHT, WORKS
active AGILE, ALERT, BRISK, BUSY, NIMBLE, SPRY
actor AGENT, DOER, HAM, HISTORIO(N), MIME, STAGER, THESPIAN
actors' group AFTRA, CAST, TROOP, TROUPE

actress DIVA, INGENUE, STAR
actual, take as POSIT
acute KEEN, SHARP, SHREWD
adage DICT, MAXIM, SAW
adapt ADJUST, ATTUNE, SUIT
add AFFIX, ANNEX, APPEND, SUM, TOT(AL), TOTE
addict(ion) BUFF, DEVOTEE, FAN, FIEND, HABIT, HOOK, JUNKIE, MONKEY
addition(s) ADDEND(A), AFFIX, CODICIL, ELL, ENCORE, RIDER, TAB
addle(d) MIRE, MUDDLED
adenoids TONSILS
adept APT, EXPERT, VERSED
adequate AMPLE, DUE, FIT, MEET, PROPER
adhere CLEAVE, CLING, GLUE, HOLD
adherent AIDE, ALLY, IST, ITE, VOTARY
adhesive CEMENT, EPOXY, GLUE(Y), GUM(MY), PASTE, TAR
adjective ADNOUN
adjourn DEFER, DELAY, PROROGUE, SUSPEND
adjust ALIGN, FIT, FIX, SET(TLE), TRIM, TRUE
adjutant AIDE, ARGALA, HURGILA, STORK
adman HUCKSTER
admiral DEWEY, FARRAGUT, HALSEY, KING, LEAHY, NELSON, NIMITZ, PORTER, SPEE
admonish CHIDE, EXHORT, URGE
admonisher MONITOR, WARNER
ado FUSS, POTHER, STIR
adolescence NONAGE, PUBERTY, TEENS, YOUTH
adolescent CALLOW, MINOR, NUBILE, PREBETIC, SUBDEB, TEEN(AGER)
adorn BEDIZEN, BEGEM, DECK
adroit DEFT, HABILE
adulterate ALLOY, CORRUPT, DEACON, DEFILE, DILUTE, MIX
advance ABET, AID, LOAN, RAISE
advance slowly CREEP, INCH, NOSE
advantage AVAIL, BENEFIT, BOT(E), EDGE, PROFIT
adventure DARING, GEST(E), RISK
advertiser SPONSOR
advice AVISO, LORE, REDE
advocate ANGEL, BACK(ER), FAVOR, PRO
Aeneid poet VERGIL, VIRGIL
affected BELOVED, FALLAL
affectionate DOTING, FOND
affirm ASSERT, ATTEST, AVER, AVOW, VOUCH
affirmative AMEN, AY(E), YEA, YES
affix JOIN, PIN, SEAL, STAMP
afflict(ion) AIL, CURSE, DISTRESS, HURT, ONUS, PLY, TRY, WOE
affluence EASE, FLOW, PLENTY, RICHES
affray BRAWL, MELEE, RIOT
aforesaid DITTO, PRIOR, SUPRA
afraid (AD)RAD, REDDE
afreet GIANT, JINNI
African sectarian ABELITE, COPT
Afrikaans TAAL
aft ABAFT, ASTERN
aftermath ARRISH, EDDISH, EDGREW, ROWEN
again ANON, BIS, EFT, ENCORE, TWICE
agalloch AGAR, AGGUR, ALOES, GAROO, TAMBAC
age (A)ERA, ELD, EON, SENESCE
age, of same COEVAL
agency ARM, DESK, DINT, WING
agent AMIN, DOER, IST, MEDIUM, PROXY, SPY, WALLA(H)
agitation DITHER, FRET, GOG, POTHER, STIR
agnomen (NICK)NAME
agnostic ATHEOUS, INFIDEL, SKEPTIC
ago SINCE, SYNE, YORE
Agra tomb TAJ(MAHAL)
agree CONCUR, GEE, GIBE, GRANT, JIBE, TALLY
agreeable AMENE, LIEF, SUANT
agreement ACCORD, CARTEL, COVIN, ENTENTE, IKRAR, MISE
Aida role AMNERIS, AMONASRO, RADAMES, RAMPHIS
aim ACIES, BUTT, END, ETTLE, VISIE
air AER, AERATE, ARIA, AURA, ETHER, MIEN, OZONE, TELL, TUNE
air component ARGON, HELIUM, KRYPTON, NEON, NITROGEN, OXYGEN, XENON
air, pert. to AERO, AURAL
aircraft (AIR)PLANE, AVION, BIPLANE, BLIMP, BOMBER DRONE, FIGHTER, GYRO, JET, KITE, MIG, MONOPLANE, MUSTANG, PROPJET, SHIP, SPITFIRE
airplane carrier FLATTOP
airplane part AILERON, AIRFOIL, BAY, BLISTER, ELEVON, FLAP, HOOD, KEEL, NOSE, SKEW, SPONSOR, TAIL, WING
airplane runway STRIP, TARMAC
airplane shelter HANGAR

airport CROYDON, IDLEWILD, KENNEDY, LAGUARDIA, OHARE, ORLY, SCUTTLE, SHANNON
airship BALLOON, BOMBER, COPTER, GLIDER
airy AERIAL, ETHEREAL
ait EYOT, HOLM, ILE, ISLE(T)
akin AGNATE, COGNATE, GERMANE, SIB
alarm LARUM, PANIC, SIREN, SOS, TOCSIN
alas ACH, HEU, OCH, OCHONE, OHONE, OIME, OTOTOI, VAE
Albanian dialect G(H)EG, TOSK
Albanian king ZOG(U)
alcohol ETHAL, ETHYL, IDITE, IDITOL, TALITE
alcohol solid STERIN, STEROL
alcoholic BEERY, SOT, VINIC, WINY
Alcott heroine AMY, BETH, MEG
alcove BOWER, NICHE, RECESS
alderman BAILIE
alembic RETORT, STILL
Alexander victory ARBELA, ISSUS
Alexander, wife of ROXANA
Alexandrian priest ARIUS
alga ALARIA, DASYA, DESMID, DIATOM, FUCUS, NORI
Ali Baba's brother CASSIM
Ali Baba's password SESAME
Ali's descendants ALIDES, ALIDS
alien GER, METIC
alienate ESTRANGE, WEAN
align RANGE, TRAM, TRUE
alkali LYE, REH, SODA, USAR
alkaloid CERINE, CODEIN(E), CAFFEIN(E), ESERIN(E)
allay ASSUAGE, PALLIATE, SLAKE
allegiance FEALTY
allegory ANAGOGE, APOLOG(UE), EMBLEM, PARABLE
allergy ATOPY
alley LOKE, MIB, TEWER, WYND
alliance AXIS, ENTENTE, LEAGUE, NATO, SEATO, SHAPE
allied AGNATE, AKIN, COGNATE
allot CAVEL, DOLE, GRANT, METE
allotment see PORTION
allow ENDURE, GRANT, LET, LOW
allowance ARRAS, BOT(E), DOLE, ODDS, STINT, TARE, TRET
alloys see p. 233
allspice PIMENTO
allude ADVERT, HINT, IMPLY
allure DECOY, (EN)TICE, TEMPT, TOLE, TOLL
allusion INKLING, INNUENDO
almond emulsion AMARIN(E), ORGEAT
almost ANEAR, NIGH
alms CORBAN, DOLE, HANDOUT, MAUNDY
aloe substance ALOIN, PICRA
alone LORN, SOLA, SOLE, SOLO, SOLUS
aloof ABACK, COOL, REMOTE
alphabet ABC, FUTHORC, OG(H)AM, OGUM, SARADA; see p. 177
alphabet character RUNE
also DITTO, EKE, PLUS
altar ARA, BOMOS, CHANTRY, HAIKAL, VEDIKA
altar cloth DOSSAL, HAPLOMA, PALL(A)
altar part GRADIN, MENSA, PREDELLA, RETABLE
alter GELD, MUTATE, VARY
alter ego FRIEND, SELF
alternate OSCILLATE, OTHER, ROTATE, WAVER
although ALBEIT, EEN
alula SQUAMA
alumni GRADS, PUPILS
always AYE, E(V)ER
amadou PUNK, TINDER
amateur DABBLER, NOVICE, TYRO
ambassador ELCHEE, ELCHI, LEGATE, NUNCIO, VAKIL
amber ELECTRUM, LAMMER, MEDREGAL, RESIN, SUCCIN
ambit SCOPE, SPHERE
amble PADNAG
ambush BLIND, TRAP, WAYLAY
amend ATONE, BEETE, REPAIR, REVISE
amendment ATONEMENT, CODICIL, RIDER
ament CATKIN, CATTAIL, CHAT, GOSLING
amerce AFFEER, FINE, MULCT
American GRINGO, YANK(EE)
American Indian AMERIND, HOSTILE, RED(SKIN), ROJO, TAWNY
amide, pert. to AMIC
amino acid ALANIN(E), GLYCINE, LYSIN(E), SERIN(E), VALIN(E)
ammonia compound AMIDE, AMIN(E)
ammunition AMMO, AMMU, SHOT
amount FECK, MISE, RATAL, RISE
amour-propre VANITY
ampersand ALSO, AND, PLUS
Amphibia ANURA, APODA, CAUDATA, SALIENTIA, URODELA; see p. 218
amphitheater ARENA, CAVEA, CIRQUE, OVAL

ample COPIOUS, WALLY
amulet CHARM, FETISH, MERIAT, PERIAPT, SAFFI(E), SCARAB, TALISMAN
analyze ASSAY, DISSECT, PARSE
ancestor (BEL)SIRE, ELDER, MANU
ancestral AVAL, AVITAL
anchor (AF)FIX, DROGUE, GRAPNEL, KEDGE, KILLICK, MOOR
anchor lifter CAPSTAN, DANDY
anchor part CAT, FLUKE, PALM, PEE
anchor ring TORE, TOROID
anchorite HERMIT, STYLITE
and AMPERSAND, PLUS
and so on ETC, USW
andiron (FIRE)DOG, HESSIAN
anent ABOUT, BESIDE, (IN)RE, WITH
anesthetic CHLORAL, DULL, ETHER, GAS, NOVOCAIN
angel AZRAEL, BELIAL, CHERUB, EBLIS, MAH, SERAPH, SIJIL(L), URIEL
anger CHOLER, GALL, HUFF, IRE, PIQUE, RILE, ROIL
angle ARRIS, AXIL, CANT, ELBOW, ELL, HADE, WRO, ZIG
Anglo-Saxon letter EDH, ETH, WEN, WYN(N), YOGH, YOK
Anglo-Saxon official GEREFA, REEVE
Anglo-Saxon poem BEOWULF
angry HUFF, IRATE, IREFUL, MAD, RABID, SNUFFY, WROTH
angular EDGY, POINTED, ZIGZAG
animal life BIOTA, FAUNA
animal, many-footed DECAPOD, HEXAPOD, OCTOPOD
animal(s) BEASTS, BIPED, BRUTE, ZOON; see p. 209
animosity ENMITY, HATRED, RANCOR, VENOM
ankle, pert. to TALARIC, TARSAL
ankle(s) CUIT, HOCK, QUEET, TALI, TALUS, TARSI, TARSUS
annatto seeds ACHIOTE
anneal HEAT, TEMPER, TOUGHEN
annotate COMMENT, GLOSS
annotation APOSTIL, EXEGESIS, (FOOT)NOTE, RUBRIC
announce BRUIT, CERN, HERALD, STEVEN
announcement BAN(S), BLURB, BULLETIN, GAZETTE, TIDINGS
annoy BORE, FASH, FIKE, GALL, HARRY, IRK, MOLEST, NAG, NOY, PESTER, STURT, TRY, VEX
annual BOOK, ETESIAN, MASS, PLANT
annuity PENSION, RENTE, STIPEND, TONTINE
annul CANCEL, CASS, ELIDE, ERASE, REVOKE, UNDO, VOID
annular CYCLIC, RINGED
anoint ANELE, BALSAM, CHRISM, OIL, SALVE
anomalous ABERRANT, ODD
anon AGAIN, BEDENE, SOON
ante BLIND, KITTY, PAY, POT, STAKE
antecedent(s) ANCESTRY, PRIOR
antenna AERIAL, CERCUS, FEELER, HORN, PALP, TOUCH
antenna, end of CLAVA
anthelion ANTISUN, HALO
anther POLLEN, STAMEN
anthocyanin (O)ENIN
anthology ANA, CORPUS, GARLAND
antiaircraft ACKACK, FLACK
antic CAPER, DIDO, PRANK
antidote CACOON, EMETIC, REMEDY, SERUM, TOXIN
antiquity ELD, YORE
antiseptic BORAX, CRESOL, EGOL, IODIN(E), IODOL, SALOL, THYMOL
antitoxin ANTIGEN, SERA, SERUM
antler parts CROCHE, PRONG, ROYAL, TINE
antlers BEZ, BROW, DAG(UE), HORN, SNAG, TRESTINE
anvil AMBOS, INCUS, STITH(Y), TEEST
anxiety ANGOR, CARE, HOE, PANIC
any ALL, ARY, ONI, SOME
apart AROOM, ASIDE, ENISLED
apartment COOP, DINGLE, DUPLEX, FLAT, STANZA, SUITE
apartment house INSULA
apathy ACEDIA, DOLDRUMS, PHLEGM, TORPOR
ape COPY, MIME, MOCK, ORANG, PARROT, PONGIL, SIMIAN
aperture BOLE, BORE, CLEFT, PORE, RIMA, SLOT, STOMA, VENT
apex ACME, APOGEE, CACUMEN, CUSP
apex, belonging to APICAL
apex covering EPI
apex, rounded RETUSE
aphorism ADAGE, DICTUM, EPIGRAM, MAXIM, SAW, SUTRA
aplomb POISE, SURETY, TACT
Apochrpyha see p. 110
Apollo birthplace DELOS
Apollo instruments BOW, LYRE
Apollo, pert. to DELIAN

apoplexy ESCA, STROKE
apostate RAT, RECREANT, RENEGADE, TURNCOAT
apostle see p. 113
apostolic manual DIDACHE
apparatus DEVICE, GADGET, GEAR, TOOL
apparel GARB, RAIMENT
apparent EVIDENT, OVERT, PATENT. PLAIN
appear KITHE LOOM
appearance AIR, GUISE MIEN, OSTENT, PHASM
append ADD, AFFIX, ATTACH
appendage ADJUNCT, CAUDA, RIDER, TAB, TAIL
appetite GUSTO, OREXIS, ZEST
appetite, abnormal ASITIA, BULIMIA, PICA
apple acid MALIC
apple product CIDER, POMACE
apply APPOSE, IMPOSE, PERTAIN, RELATE, USE
appoint EQUIP, NAME, ORDAIN, SET
apportion DEAL, DOLE, METE, RATE
appraise ASSAY, ASSESS, (E)VALUE RATE
apprehend FEAR, GRASP, GRIPE, INTUE INTUIT, NAB
apprentice NEOPHYTE, SNOB, TRAINEE TYRO
approach ACCESS, ADIT, (A)NEAR, IMPEND, WAY
appropriate ALLOT, APT, MEET, USURP
apron BARVEL, BISHOP, RUNWAY, TIER
apropos FIT(TING), TIMELY
apteryx KIWI, MOA, RATITE
aptitude BENT, FLAIR, GIFT. TALENT
aquamarine BERYL, BLUE
aqueduct CANAL, CONDUIT
aqueduct of Sylvius ITER
Arab BROWN, GAMIN, HORSE, SEMITE, URCHIN
Arabian lyric G(H)AZEL
Arabian Nights characters see p. 181
Arabian poet and romance ANTAR(A)
Arabian script NESK(H)I
arable FERTILE, LAINE, TILLABLE
arachnids ACERATA; see p. 215
arbiter OVERMAN, REFEREE, UMPIRE
arbitrary DESPOTIC, THETIC
arbor BOWER, PERGOLA, RAMADA
arboreal DENDRAL, SYLVAN
arcade ARCATURE, LOGGIA, PORTICO

arch CHIEF, COY, HANCE, IMPISH, OGEE, OGIVE, SLY, VAULT
archangel GABRIEL, MICHAEL, RAPHAEL, SATAN, URIEL
archbishop BECKET, HATTO, PRIMATE, RAMSEY
archer BOWER, CLIM, CLYM, CUPID, TELL
archetype IDEA(L), MODEL, PATTERN, TYPE
architect ADAM, ALBERTI, BERNINI, BRAMANTE, BREUER, BULFINCH, EIFFEL, GROPIUS, KLENZE, MCKIM, MEAD, PAXTON, SAARINEN, SULLIVAN, WREN, WRIGHT
architecture, type of BAUHAUS, BAROQUE, BOURBON, CLASSIC, COPTIC, DORIC, EMPIRE, FLORID, GOTHIC, GREEK, IONIC, LANCET, LATIN, MOORISH, MOSLEM, NORMAN, RHENISH, ROCOCO, ROMAN, TUDOR, TUSCAN
arctic GALOSH, ICY, POLAR
ardor ELAN, FERVOR, FIRE, ZEAL
area AREOLA, PURLIEU, TREF
arena BOWL, DROME, LISTS, OVAL, RING, RINK, SAND, STADIUM, TURF
argonaut ACASTUS, JASON
argot see SLANG
argue MOOT, REBUT, WORD
argument AGON, DEBATE, FUSS, HASSLE, POLEMIC, TIFF, WORDS
aria AIR, SOLO, SONG
arid JEJUNE, STERILE, VAPID
arise APPEAR, MOUNT, REBEL
arista AWN, BEARD
Aristotle's father AMYNTAS
Aristotle's home town STAGIRA
Aristotle's teacher PLATO
Aristotle's work ETHICS, ORGANON, POETICS
ark ASYLUM, COFFER
ark landing place ARARAT
arm BRANCH, EQUIP, FORTIFY, GARDY, GIB, JIB, LIMB, OXTER, PINION, TENTACLE
arm of sea BAY, FIRTH, FJORD, FRITH, LOCH
arm, pert. to BRACHIAL
armadillo APAR(A), MATACO, PEBA, PELUDO, TAT(O)U
armed band HOST, POSSE
armful LOCK, YAFFLE
armor and arms see p. 108
armor, horse CHAMFRON, CRINIERE, CROUPIERE, POITREL
armor bearer ARMIGER, CUSTREL
army FERD, HERE, HOST, IMPI, LEGION, TROOPS

army division COHORT, COMPANY, INFANTRY, LEGION, MANIPLE, MORA, PLATOON, REGIMENT, SQUAD
army engineer PIONEER, SAPPER, SEABEE
aroid ARAD, ARUM, KONJAK, TANIA, TANIER, TARO
aroma BOUQUET, NIDOR, SAVOR
aromatic BALMY, PIQUANT, PUNGENT, SPICY
aromatic substance ARALIA, BALSAM, BUCCO, BUCHU, MYRRH, TOLU
around ABOUT, CIRCA, NEAR
arouse ACCITE, FIRE, PIQUE, STIR
arraign ACCUSE, (IM)PEACH, INDICT, INDITE
arrange DAIKER, DISPOSE, ETTLE, FIX, PLAT, SCORE, STAGE
arrangement FILE, INDEX, TAXIS
arrangement, pert. to TACTIC
arrant BAD, BRAZEN, VAGRANT
array ACIES, ADORN, (AP)PAREL, DECK
arrest COLLAR, DETAIN, HALT, NAB, PINCH, SIST, STUNT
arrive HENT, LAND, LIGHT
arrogance HUBRIS, HYBRIS
arrogant CAVALIER, HIGH, LORDLY, UPPISH
arrogate CLAIM, GRAB, USURP
arrow FLANE, FLO; see p. 109
arrow maker BOWYER, FLETCHER
arrow part NOCK, PILE, STELE
arrow poison ANTIAR, CURARE, INEE, UPAS, URALI, WOORALI, WOORARA
arrowroot ARARAO, ARARU, CANNA, MARANTA, MUSA, PIA, TACCA, TAPIOCA
arrow-shaped BELOID
arroyo BAYOU, BROOK, CREEK, GULLY, HONDO, RUN
arsenic mixture ERINITE, SPEISS
art ARS, KNACK, TRADE, WILE, WIT
art style DADA, GENRE, OP, POP
artery AORTA, ATERIA, AVENUE, CAROTID, WAY; see p. 106
artful DOWNY, POLITIC, SLY, WILY
arthritis help ACTH, CORTISONE
artichoke CANADA, CHOROGI, CYNARA, GIRASOL
articulate JOIN(TED), UTTER, VOCAL
artifice CRAFT, DODGE, FINESSE, GUILE, RUSE, TRICK
artificial ERSATZ, FAKE(D), SHAM
artillery man GUN(NER), TOPECHEE
artist(e) ADEPT, BRUSH, DAB, FICTOR, (SK)ETCHER
artless GAUCHE, NAIF, NAIVE, RUDE, SEELY
arum ARAD, AROID, CALLA, STARCH, TARO
as LIKE, QUA, SINCE, THUS, WHILE
asafetida FERULA, HING, LASER, NARTHEX
asbestos ABISTON, AMIANTH
ascent RIST, SLOPE, STEEP, STIPE, UPGO
ascetic AUSTERE, DERVISH, ESSENE, HERMIT, MUNI, SADHU, YATI, YOGI(N)
ash fruit KEY, SAMARA
ash(es) ARTER, CHAR, EMBER, ROWAN, SINTER, SORB, VAREC, WICKEN
Asiatic plague CHOLERA
aside APART, OFF, WHISPER
ask ENTREAT, FRAYN, SPEER, SPERE, SUE, THIG
askew AGEE, ALOP, (A)WRY
asp URAEUS
aspect ANGLE, FACET, MIEN, PHASE, SIDE, VULT
aspen POPLAR, TREMBLE
asperse LIBEL, MALIGN, SKIT, SLANDER, SLUR, VILIFY
asphyxia APN(O)EA
aspire AIM, COVET, CRAVE, HOPE
ass DOLT, DONKEY, LONGEAR, ONAGER
assail BESET, MOLEST, PELT
Assamese dialect AO, KHAMI, LHOTA
assassin CAIN, SICARIAN, THUG
assault BLITZ, BUFFET, ONSET, SIEGE, STORM, THRUST
assay ANALYSIS, TEST, TRY
assaying cup CUPEL, TEST
assemblage BODY, CAUCUS, HERD, LEVEE, LEVY, THRONG
assemble COLLECT, HUDDLE, MEET, MUSTER
assembly AGORA, BEVY, COVEN, COVINE, DIET, FORUM, GEMOT(E), HUI, PLENA, PLENUM, SABBAT, SESSION
assembly hall ESTUFA, KIVA
assembly, legislative BOULE, CHAMBERS, COMMONS, CONGRESS, CORTES, DAIL, DUMA, JUNTA, KNESSET, LAGTING, RAAD, RIGSDAG, RIKSDAG, SEIM, SEJM, SENATE, SEYM, STORTING, YUAN

assembly place **AGORA, PNYX**
assent **ACCEDE, AMEN, GRANT, NOD**
assert **AFFY, AVER, POSIT, THREAP, THREEP**
assess **BOTE, IMPOSE;** see **TAX**
assessor **JUDGE, MUFTI, RATER**
assign **ALLOT, CAVEL, REFER**
assignment **BEAT, JOB, ROUND**
assistance **ALMS, DOLE**
assistant(s) **AID(E), CAD, CREW, HAND, SECOND, STAFF**
assize **COURT, DECREE, WRIT**
associate **CRONY, HOBNOB, MIX, MONK, MOOP, SOCIUS**
association **BOND, BUND, (C)ARTEL, CONGER, GRANGE, G(U)ILD, HANSE, HONG LODGE, UNION**
association football **SOCCER**
assortment **BATCH, FONT, SUNDRIES**
assume **ARROGATE, ENDUE, FEIGN, INFER, USURP**
assurance **APLOMB, BRASS**
assure **PLEDGE, SICKER, WITTER**
Assyria(n) **ASSUR**
Assyrian king and queen **P(H)UL, SEMIRAMIS**
astern **ABAFT, (B)AFT, REAR**
asteroid **STARFISH;** see p. 277
Astolat, Lily Maid **ELAIN(E)**
astound **FERLY, SHOCK, STUN**
astral **SIDEREAL**
astray **AWRY, GLEED**
astringent **ALUM, CATECHU, COTO, KATH(A), STERN, STYPTIC(AL)**
astrologer **CHALDEAN, JOSHI, JOTI, JOTISI**
astrology term **ALMUTEN, ANARETA, APHETA**
astronauts see p. 278
astronomer **BRAHE, GALILEO, HALLEY, JEANS, KEPLER, NEWTON**
astronomical **URANIC**
astronomical instrument **ABA, ARMIL, ORRERY, SECTOR, SEXTANT**
asunder **APART, ATWAIN**
asylum **ARK, BEDLAM, HAVEN, HOME**
Athena epithet **ALEA, ARELA, ERGANE, HIPPIA, MINERVA, PALLAS**
Athenian **ATTIC, METIC**
Athenian ruler **ARCHON, CECROPS, CODRUS, DRACO, PERICLES**
athlete **GYMNAST, TURNER**
athletic event **AGON, GAME, MEET, OLYMPICS, RACE**

Atlas **BONE, MAPS, TITAN**
atmosphere **AURA, MAUVE, OZONE**
atmospheric pressure, of **BARIC**
atom **ISOBAR, ISOSTERE;** see **JOT**
atom part **ELECTRON, NEUTRON, NUCLEUS, PROTON**
atone **ABY(E), EXPIATE, REDEEM**
attach **(AF)FIX, (AP)PEND**
attache case **TASHIE**
attached **ADNATE, FOND, SESSILE**
attack **BESET, BLITZ, BRASH, FIT, FRAY, ONSET, RAID, SPASM**
attar **ITR, OIL, OTTO**
attempt **EFFORT, ESSAY, ETTLE, MIRD, OSSE, STAB**
attendant(s) **DONZEL, GILLIE, GILLY, SUITE, THANE, THEGN, TRAIN, VERGER**
attention **EAR, GAUM, HEED**
attentive **TENTIE, TENTY, WARY**
attenuate **DILUTE, RAREFY, THIN**
attest **CERTIFY, VOUCH, WITTEN**
attic **DORMER, GARRET, GRENIER, LOFT, SOLAR, SOLER, TALLET**
Attila **ATLI, ETZEL, HUN**
attitudinize **MINCE, POSE**
attorney **ADVOCATE, VAKEEL, VAKIL**
attraction **DAHLIA, MAGNET**
attribute **ASCRIBE, FEATURE, IMPUTE, OWE, TYPE**
attrition **GRIEF, REGRET, WEAR**
attune **ACCORD, ADAPT, KEY, PITCH**
auction **BRIDGE, CANT, HAMMER, ROUP, SALE, VEND(UE)**
audience **EAR, (H)EARING, PIT, PUBLIC**
audit **ACCOUNT, SCAN, VERIFY**
auditory **AURAL, OTIC**
auger **BORE(R), GIMLET, WIMBLE**
augment **ADD, EKE, SWELL, VOWEL**
augur **AUSPEX, BODE, SEER**
augury **OMEN, PORTENT**
August 1st **LAMMAS**
aunt **TIA, TANTA, TANTE**
aureate **GOLDEN, ORNATE**
aureole **GLORY, HALO, NIMBUS**
auric acid salt **AURATE**
auricle **ATRIUM, EAR, PINNA**
aurochs **BISON, TUR, URUS**
aurora **DAWN, EOS**
aurorian **EOAN, ROSEATE**
auspice **(A)EGIS, CARE, OMEN**
auspicious **BENIGN, DEXTER**
Australian cry **COOEE, COOEY**

Australian food KAI
autobiography MEMOIRS, VITA
automaton ANDROID, GOLEM, ROBOT
avalanche LA(U)WINE
avast CEASE, STAY, STOP
ave FAREWELL, HAIL
avenge REQUITE, RETALIATE, VISIT
avenger GOEL, NEMESIS
avenging spirit ALECTO, ERINYS, FURY, MAGAERA
average MEDIAL, NORM, PAR, SOSO
avert FEND, PARRY, SHEER, THWART
Avesta part GATHAS, VENDIDAD, VISPERED, YASNA, YASHTS
avifauna BIRDS, ORNIS
avocado CHININ, COYO, PEAR, PERSEA
avoid ESCHEW, EVITE, SHUN
await PEND, STAY, TARRY
awake(n) (A)DAW, ALERT, STIR
award BONUS, CONFER, DSC, DSM, DSO, EMMY, MEED, OSCAR, TONY
aware HEP, RECK, WISE
away ABSENT, GONE, HENCE, HYNE, OFF
aweather, opposed to ALEE
awkward CLUMSY, GAUCHE, GAWKY, INEPT, THUMBLESS
awkward one BUNGLER, GALOOT, LOUT
awl BROD, ELSIN, STABBER
awn(ed) ARISTA(TE), AVEL, BARB, ILE
awning CANOPY, SEMIAN, TILT, VELARIUM
awry AGEE, AGLEY, AJEE, CAM, GLEED
axes see p. 108
axilla, pert. to ALA(R)
axis, axle ARBOR, HUB, PIN, PIVOT
aye-aye LEMUR(OID)
Aztec hero(ine) NATA, NANA
Aztec temple TEOCALLI, TEOPAN

B

babble(r) BLAB, BLAT(E), GLAVER, HAVER(EL), JABBER
Babel DIN, SCHEME
Babel site SHINAR
Babul ACACIA, GARAD, GUM
baby HUMOR, TOTO, WEAN
Babylonian numeral SAROS
baccarat term BANCO
Bacchanal cry EVOE
Baccha(nt)e M(A)ENAD
bachelor AGAMIST, COELEBS
back ABET, AFT, AID, DORSUM, ENDORSE, FRO, HIND, NOTA, NOTUM, REAR, SPONSOR, STERN, TERGAL, TERGUM
back country BUSH, STICKS
back, lying on SUPINE
back, pert. to DORSAL, NOTAL, TERGAL
back, toward RETRAD, RETRAL
backbite MALIGN, SASS, VILIFY
backbone CHINE, GRID, NERVE, RIDGE, SPINE
backgammon TABLES, TRICTRAC
bacon JAMON, LARD, PRIZE, RASHER, SPECK
Bacon work NOVUM, ORGANUM
bacteria AEROBE, COCCUS, GERM, SARCINA, VIBRIO
badge INSIGNE, MON, PLAQUE
badge, shoulder EPAULET
badger CHEVY, FRET, HECKLE, PESTER
baffle BALK, ELUDE, FOIL, POSE
bag ASCUS, BOGUE, CHAGUL, CYST, DILLI, GRIP, KNAPSACK, MUSETTE, NAB, POCKY, POKE, PURSE, RETICULE, SAC(HET), SATCHEL, VALISE
bag net FIKE, FYKE
bagatelle TRIFLE
baggage DUNNAGE, SAMAN, WENCH
bagpipe hole LILL
bagpipe music PIBROCH
bail BOND, HOOP, LADE, SURETY
bailiff GEREFA, REEVE
bait BERLEY, CAPELIN, DECOY, HANK, SHRAP
bait, drop DAB, DIB
baker FLY, HORNERO, O(A)ST, OVEN
baking pit IMU, UMU
balance ATRY, POISE, REST, SANITY, SCALE
balance of sentence PARISON
balance weight BALLAST, RIDER
baldness ACOMIA, ALOPECIA
bale EVIL, PACK, PYRE
balk COND, FOIL, IMPEDE, REAR, REEST
ball CLEW, DANCE, GOLI, KNUR, ORB, PELLET, PINDA, PROM, TICE
ball, hit BOWL, BUNT, LOB, SWAT
ballad DERRY, LAI, LAY
ballet girl DAHLIA, FIGURANTE
ballet term BOURREE, CHAINE, CHASSE, COUPE, FOUETTE, JETE, PAS, PLIE, POSITION

balloon part CAR, GONDOLA, NACELLE
balm ANODYNE, BALSAM, SALVE
Baltimore heater LATROBE
balustrade PARAPET
Bambi DEER
Bambi author SALTEN
bamboo, pickled shoots ACHAR
banana ENSETE, MUSA, PLANTAIN
band BELT, CLAVUS, COMBO, FA(S)CIA, FESS, FILLET, LIGULA, MOB, PATTE, RADULA, REGULA, STRIA, TAENIA, ZONA
band leader(s) CHORAGI, MAESTRO, SOUSA, STRAUSS
bandage LIGATE, SPICA, STUPE
bandit CACO, CATERAN, HOOD, LADRONE, PAD, TORY, TULISAN
bane NEMESIS
bank BERM(E), BRAE, CAJA, DIGUE, DUNE, RELY, RIPA
bank, fishing HAAF
bank, pert. to RIPARIAN
banker BANYA, MELLON, MORGAN, SARAF, SHROFF
bankrupt BROKE, FAIL, QUISBY
banner LABRUM; see FLAG
banquet DIFFA, JUNKET, REGALE, SPREAD
banter ASTEISM, BORAK, CHAFF, JOSH, TWIT
Bantu language ILA, SUTO, VILI
bar BETTY, BISTRO, BLOCK, BRIDE, DETER, ESTOP, FID, HINDER, INGOT, JIMMY, LOOP, RAIL, REIN, ROSE, SESS, SHOAL, SNIB, STEEK, STRIPE, TAVERN, TIE
bar, door RISP, STANG
barb FLUE, JAG, NAG, SPINE
barb of feather HARL, HERL, RAMUS
Barbados native BIM
barbarian ALIEN, GOTH, HUN, VANDAL
Barbarossa FREDERICK
barbarous (C)RUDE, FELL, HEATHEN, SAVAGE
barber COMPOSER, FIGARO, FISH, SHAVE(R), TONSOR
bard DRUID, MINSTREL, RUNER, SAGAMAN, SCALD, SCOP, SKALD, VATES
bargain DEAL, DICKER, HAGGLE, HIGGLE, HUCK, KOOP, NIFFER, PALTER, PRIG, TROG
barge LUNGE, LURCH, PR(A)AM, SCOLD, SHREW
bark BAST(E), BAY, CORTEX, HIDE, RIND, ROSS, SKIN, YAP, YIP
bark, bitter CINCHONA, NIEPA, NIOTA, QUININE
bark, medicinal CANELLA, CASCA, COTO, MADAR, MUDAR
bark, mulberry KAPA, TA(P)PA
bark remover ROSSER, SPUD(DER)
barker PISTOL, SPIELER, TOUT
barking LATRANT
barley BEER, BIG(G), MALT, PTISAN, TISANE, TSAMBA
barn AMBAR, BYRE, LATHE, MEW, SKIPPER
barometric line ISOBAR
barony FIEF, HAN
barrack(s) BILLET, BIVOUAC, CAN(N)ABA
barrel CADE, KILDERKIN, KNAG, TIERCE, TUN
barrel-maker COOPER, TUBBER, TUBMAN
barrel part GA(U)NTRY, STAVE
barren DRAPE, DULL, EFFETE, GELD, HISTLE, SECK, STERILE
barren land DESERT, REH, USAR
barrier DAM, PALE, TREBLE
barrow KURGAN
bartender MIXER, SKINKER, TAPSTER
barter MONG, NIFFER, SWAP, TRAFFIC, TROG, TROKE
base BAD, BAG, CAITIFF, CAMP, (SER)VILE
base, architectural DADO, PATTEN, PLINTH, SOCLE
base, attached by SESSILE
baseball see also p. 138
baseball terms BAG, PLATE, RUBBER, SACK, SLAB, SLUGGER, STICK
bashful BLATE, COY, HELOE, SHY, VERECUND
basilica CANOPY, LATERAN
basin CUVETTE, FONT, HOLLOW, LAVABO, LAVER, LEKANE, MARINA, PAN, STOUP, TALA
basis AXIOM, FOND, PREMISE
basket CRESSET, DILLI, DOSSER, GABION, GRATE, HAMPER, HOPPET, JICARA, KIPSEY, KISH, MAUND, PANNIER, PED, PEGALL, SERON, SKEP
basket, fish CAUL, CAWL, CRAIL, CREEL, KIPE, WEEL
basket, fruit CABA(S), FRAIL, MOLLY, POTTLE, PUNNET, TAPNET
basket of coals CORB, CORF
basket, sports CESTA, GOAL
basketball player CAGE(STE)R, CENTER, GUARD, HOOPMAN
basketball term BUCKET, CAGE, DRIBBLE, DUNKER, FOUL, FREEZE, HOOP, JUMPER, KEYHOLE, LAYUP, NET, PALMING, WALKING, WEAVE

basketry rod OSIER, SCALLOM
basketwork SLA(R)TH, SLEW, TEE, WALE
Basque IBERIAN, SCOTER, WAIST
bast BARK, PHLOEM, RAMIE
baste CUDGEL, DRAB, LARD, SLEW
basto CARD, QUEEN
bat ALIPED, RACKET, VAMPIRE
batfish DIABOLO
bathe LAVE, TOSH
bath-house BAGNIO, CABANA
bathing suit BIKINI, MAILLOT, TRUNKS
bath(s) BAIN, SAUNA, STEW, THERM(AE)
baton ROD, SCEPTER, STICK
batten REEPER, RIB
batter FRUSH, PASTE, SLOPE
battering ram CORVUS, TEREBRA
battery CELL, PARAPET, PILE
battery term CHARGER, GRID, POST
battle (AF)FRAY, COPE, HOSTING
battle area CHAMP, SECTOR, TERRAIN
battle cry ABOO, ABU, BANZAI
battle formation ACIES, DEPLOY, HERSE, PHALANX
battle hymn author HOWE, JULIA, WARD
battle site ADOWA, ALAMO, ARBELA, BATAAN, BULGE, CANNAE, CRECY, CRESSY, HASTINGS, IPSUS, ISSUS, IVRY, JENA, MARENGO, MARNE, PLATAEA, SADOWA, SALAMIS, SEDAN, SHILOH, SKAGER(R)AK, SOMME, TRAFALGAR, VALMY, VERDUN, WATERLOO, YPRES, ZAMA
battlement CRENEL, MERLON, PINION
bauble GEWGAW, MAROTTE, TOY
bay BIGHT, COIL, COVE, INLET, LAUREL, VOE
bay window ORIEL
bazaar AGORA, FAIR, GINZA, SOOK, SOUK
beach PLAYA, SHILLA, SHORE, STRAND
beacon FANAL, PHAROS, PIKE
Beaconsfield DISRAELI
beads CHAPLET, ROSARY
beak NEB, NIB, TUTEL
beam CABER, GIRDER, RAFTER, RAY, SILE, TEMPLATE, TEMPLET
bean ADZUKI, HARICOT, LIMA, SOY, URD
bear DUBB, ENDURE, URSA, YIELD
beard ARISTA, AWN, BARBET, FUZZ, GOATEE, SHADOW
bearer SIRDAR, TOTER
bearing AIR, MIEN, ORLE, PORT
beast BRUTE, LOUT
beat BELABOR, CANE, CUDGEL, DRUB, LACE, LAM, LARRUP, LASH, POMMEL, PULSE, ROUND, RHYTHM, SWINGE, SWITCH, TAN, THRASH, WELT, WHIP; see ACCENT, DEFEAT, TACK
beater RAB
beaver CASTOR
beaver skin PLEW
beche-de-mer TREPANG
becket GROMMET
bed BUNK, COT, DONGA, DOSS, KIP, PALLET
bee APIS, DOR, DRONE
bee, pert. to APIAN
beechnuts MAST
beehive APIARY, SKEP
beer ALE, BOCK, CHANG, KVAS, KVASS, LAGER, PANGASI, POMBE, QUAS
beetle BORER, DOR, ELATER
beg CADGE, ENTREAT, SORN
beget EAN, SIRE
beggar FAKIR, LAZAR, RANDY
begin FANG, OPEN
beginning ALPHA, FRONT, INITIAL, NASCENT, ONSET, ORIGIN
begone AROINT, OUT, SCAT, VIA
beguile COZEN, LURE, VAMP, WILE, WISE
behave ACT, CONDUCT, DEPORT, KEEP
behest BID, MANDATE, ORDER
behind ABAFT, AFT, AREAR, ASTERN, SLOW, TARDY
behold ECCE, ESPY, LA, LO, SEE, VISE, VOILA
being(s) ANTEAL, ENS, ENTIA, ENTITY, ESSE, FRONT, HUMAN, LIFE
beldam(e) see HAG
belief CREDO, CREED, DEISM, DOGMA, DOXY, FAY, ISM, TENET, TROTH
believe DEEM, TROW
believer DEIST, IST, OMNIST
bell CAMPANA, CAMPANE, CODON, GONG, KNELL, SQUILLA, TOCSIN
bell town ADANO
belladonna ATROPIN(E), MANICON
belle DEB, MAJA, PERI
belly (MID)RIFF, PAUNCH, PLEON, THARM
belong INHERE, PERTAIN
below NEATH, SOTTO
belt CESTUS, CINGLE, CORDON, LACE, OBI, ZONE
bench BANC, BAR, DAIS, EXEDRA, PEW, SETTEE, THWART, ZYGA, ZYGON

bend BOW, BULGE, CROOK, CURVE, FLEX, KINK, LOUT, NID, SAG, WARP
benediction SHEMA
benefactor ANGEL, DONOR, PATRON, SPONSOR
benefice ANNAT, GLEBE
beneficiary DONEE, HEIR, LEGATEE, USER
benefit AVAIL, BOON, BOOT, PROFIT
benign GENIAL, GENTLE, SUAVE
bent BIAS, FLAIR, HOOK, KNACK, TASTE
bequest DOT, DOWRY, GIFT, LEGACY
berate CENSURE, CHIDE, JAW, REVILE, SCOLD, WIG
bereave DESPOIL, DIVEST, STRIP, WIDOW
berg BARROW, FLOE, ICE
berry BACCA, CUBEB, PASA
berserk AMOK, ENRAGED, MAD
berth BED, BILLET, BUNK, DOCK, JOB, SLIP
beseech ADJURE, APPEAL, BEG, ENTREAT, OBTEST, PRAY, SUE
beset HARRY, OBSESS, SIT
besides ALSO, AND, ELSE, EXCEPT, INBY, OVER, THEN, TOO, YET
besiege BESET, OBSIDE, PESTER, PLAGUE
besmear DAUB, SMOTTER, SOIL, TAINT
besom BROOM, HEATHER, MOP
bespangle (EN)STAR, STUD
best ACME, AONE, BEAT, CHOICE, CREAM, ELITE, MOST, OUTWIT, TOPS, UTMOST
bet ANTE, GO, HEDGE. MILIEU, PARLAY, POT, STAKE, WAGE(R)
bet, fail to pay WELCH WELSH
betray BLAB, PEACH, REVEAL, SELL, SILE, SNARE, SQUEAL, TRAP, TRICK
betrayer JUDAS, SEDUCER, TRAITOR
betroth AFFY, EARL, PLEDGE, PLIGHT, TOKEN
better (A)MEND, EMEND, REFORM, TOP
between AMELL, AMONG, INTER, MESNE
bevel ASLANT, CANT, EDGE, MITER, MITRE REAM, SNAPE
beverage ADE, ALE, BEER, CIDER, MORAT, NECTAR, NEGUS, POP, POSSET, POTABLE, SODA, TEA
bevy BATCH, BAZAAR, BROOD, CHARM, COVERT, COVEY, DESERT, DROVE, FLIGHT, FLOCK, GAGGLE, HERD, MUSTER, NYE, PACK, PLUMP, SIEGE, SKEIN, SPRING, SUITE, SWARM, WISP
bewail CRY, GRIEVE, LAMENT, WEEP, WEY
beware AVOID, ESCHEW, SHUN
bewildered ADDLED, AMAZED, ASEA, DAZED
bewitch CHARM, ENAMOR, ENCHANT, ENSORCEL, HEX, THRILL
beyond BY, PAST, ULTRA, YONDER
bezel EDGE, FACET, RIM, SEAL, TEMPLET
bias BENT, PLY, SLANT, SLOPE, SWAY
Bible BOOK, GOSPEL, TEXT, WORD, WRIT
Bible version DOUAY, HEXAPLA, ITALA, PESHITTA, REVISED, TARGUM, TETRAPLA, TYNDALE, VULGATE, WYCLIFFE
Biblical information see p. 110
bicker CAVIL, QUIBBLE, SPAT
bid ENJOIN, INVITE, TENDER
bier COFFIN, LITTER, PYRE, TABUT
bifurcation BRANCH, FORK, WYE
bight BAY, COVE, GULF, LOOP
bigot FANATIC, ZEALOT
bile CHOLER, GALL, SPLEEN, VENOM
bilk CHEAT, GYP, HOAX, TRICK
bill ACT, BEAK, CARD, DUN, LAW, MENU, NEB, NIB, NOTE, PEE, PLACARD, POSTER, TAB, TICKET
billet BERTH, JOB, LODGE, POST
billiards term CAROM, CUE, MASSE
billow ROLLER, SEA, SURGE, SWELL WAVE
bin ARK, CANCH, KENCH
bind COHERE, CONFINE LINK, SECURE, SWATHE, TAPE, TILE, TRUSS, UNITE, WAP
binding YAPP
bingo KENO, LOTTO
biography LIFE, MEMOIR, VITA
biological BIOTIC(AL)
biological term GENE, RIMA
birch BETULA, FLOG, STICK, TREE
bird house AVIARY, COTE, NEST
bird, mythological PH(O)ENIX, RUKH, SIMURG(H)
bird, pert. to AVIAN, AVIN(E), OSCINE
bird, talking CROW, MINA, MYNA, PARROT
bird(s) AVES, AVIFUNA, ORNIS; see p. 218
birth DELIVERY, GENESIS, LYINGIN, NATIVITY, ORIGIN

birth, before PRENATAL, PREPARTUM
birth, by NE(E)
birth, of one's NATAL
birthmark MOLE, N(A)EVUS
birthstones see p. 233
bis AGAIN, ENCORE, REPEAT, TWICE
biscuit BUN, PANAL, PANTILE, RATAFIA, RUSK, WAFER
bishop ABBA, ALFIN, ARIUS, POPE, PRELATE, PRIMATE
bishop's seat APSE, BEMA, DIOCESE, LAWN, SEE
bistro BAR, PUB, TAVERN
bit ACE, ATOM, FID, IOTA, JOT, MITE, MORSEL, MOTE, ORT, PALLION, PART, SIPPET, SNAP, SPECK, WEE, WHIT
bite CHAM, CHAMP, CHEW, GNAW, MORSEL, NIP, SNAP, WHEAL
biting ACRID, CAUSTIC, CRISP, MORDANT
bitter ACERB, ACRID, AIGRE, AMAR, BILE, HATE
bitterness ACOR, ACRIMONY, ATTER, MARAH, RUE
bitumen ASPHALT, PITCH, TAR
bivalve CLAM, MUSSEL, OYSTER
bizarre DAEDAL, ODD(ISH), OUTRE, QUEER
black DHU, EBON, JET, SABLE
blacken DEFAME, INK, JAPAN, SHINE, SOOT
blackguard GAMIN, KNAVE, VILIFY, VILLAIN
blackhead COMEDO, DUCK
blackheart CHERRY
Black Sea EUXINE, PONTUS
blacksmith FARRIER, LOHAR, SHOER, SMITHY, STITHY
blade BIT, DANDY, EDGE, LEAF, OAR, SPIRE, SWORD, TANG
blain BLISTER, BULLA, SORE
blame ASCRIBE, CENSURE, CHOP, FAULT, GUILT, ODIUM, ONUS, SNAPE
bland FLAT, MILD, SUAVE, URBANE
blandish CAJOLE, COAX, FLATTER, WHEEDLE
blanket BROT, CORONA, COTTA, MANTA, PONCHO, QUILT, SERAPE, SHEET, STROUD, TILPAH
blast ATTACK, BANG, BUB, FLAW, GALE
blatant COARSE, GLIB, GROSS, VOCAL
blaze FLARE, (G)LOW, MARK
bleach BLANCH, CHLORE, ETIOLATE, WHITEN
bleak ABLET, DREAR(Y), RAW
bleared DUSKY, INKY, RHEUMY
bleb BLISTER, BUBBLE, BULLA, PUSTULE
blemish AMPER, BRUISE, FLAW, MACULE, SLUR, STIGMA, TACHE, TASH
blench AVOID, ELUDE, FLINCH, PALE, QUAIL, RECOIL, SHIRK, SHUN
blend COALESCE, FUSE, MERGE, MIX, RUN, TINGE
bless BEATIFY, BENSH, EXTOL, HALLOW, PRAISE, SAIN
blessed DIVINE, HOLY, SACRE(D)
blessing BENEFICE, BENISON, BOON, GRACE, SAIN
blight MILDEW, NIP, ROT, RUIN, RUST, SMUT, SOKA
blind DECOY, SEEL, SHADE, SHUTTER
blind alley CULDESAC, DEADEND, IMPASSE
blind, printing for BRAILLE
blindness ANOPSIA, CECITY
blink NICTATE, PINK, TWINKLE, WINK
bliss ECSTASY, HEAVEN, KEF, KEIF, KIEF, KIF(F), RAPTURE
blissful ECSTATIC, HOLY, SEELY
blister BLAIN, BLEB, BLURE, BULLA(E)
blithe AIRY, GAY, JOVIAL
blizzard BURAN, PURGA
bloat DISTEND, INFLATE, SWELL, TUMEFY
blob BLEMISH, MASS, WEN
bloc CABAL, FACTION, RING
block BAR, BITT, CHECK, DAM, DENTEL, DENTIL, DOOK, FOIL, HINDER, MUTULE, NOG, PERCH, QUAD, STYMIE, VOL
blockhead ASS, DUNCE, MOKE, NINNY, OAF
blood CRUOR, GORE, ICHOR, PLASMA, SERA, SERUM
blood, lack of AN(A)EMIA
blood, pert. to H(A)EMAL, H(A)EMIC
blood emulsion CHYLE
blood money CRO, GALANAS
bloom DOWN, FLOWER, HEYDAY, PRIME
blooper ERROR, LAPSE, SLIP
blot BLUR; see STAIN
blot out DELE(TE), EFFACE
blotch BLAIN, BLEB, BULLA, MACULA, MOTTLE, SPLAT
blow CONK, COUP, CRIG, DINT, DISASTER, GALE, HIT, HUFF, ONER, PANT, SWAT, VAUNT, WAFT
blubber CRY, FAT, LIPPER, SPECK, WAIL

blubber, strip FLENSE
bludgeon BAT, CLUB, MACE
blue DISMAL, GLUM, LOW, SAD
Bluebeard's wife FATIMA
blueprint DRAFT, MAP, PLAN, PLOT, TRACE
blues DOLDRUMS, DUMPS, MEGRIMS, SADNESS
bluff BRAG, CLIFF, CRUSTY, CURT, HOAX, RUDE, STEEP
blunder BONER, BOTCH, BULL, BUNGLE, ERR(OR), GAFF, MISDO, SKEW, SLIP
blunt ASSUAGE, BLATE, DULL, GRUFF, OBTUND, OBTUSE, RUDE
blush FLUSH, MANTLE, REDDEN, TINGE
bluster BRAVADO, BULLY, RANT, ROAR, SWAGGER
board(s) COUNCIL, EATS, LODGE, MEALS, PANEL, PLANK, STAGE
boast BOG, BOMBAST, BRAG, CROW, FLAUNT, GAB, GLOAT, PREEN, RAVE, SWAGGER, VAUNT
boaster BRAGGART, BRAVADO, JINGO, RODOMONT
boastful air PARADO
boatman CHARON, PHAON
bob DUCK, FLOAT, JERK, PENDANT, SHILLING
bode AUGUR, PORTEND, PRESAGE
body BOLE, BULK, CADAVER, CARCASS, CORPSE, CORPUS, FORM, KHET, LICH(AM), MASS, RUPA, SOMA, STEM, TORSO
body of men ARMY, CORPS, FORCE, MASS, NAVY, POSSE
body, pert. to SOMAL, SOMATIC
body segment MEROSOME, METAMERE, SOMATOME, SOMITE
bodyguard THANE
body motion, pert. to GESTIC
bog FEN, GOG, MARSH, MIRE, MOOR, MORASS, OOZE, QUAG, SLOUGH, SWAMP, SYRT
boggle ALARM, BALK, JIB, SCARE, SHY
boil BUBBLE, (DE)COCT, ESTUATE, KYLE, RAGE, SEETHE, SORE, STEW, STY, TEEM
boiler ALEMBIC, CALDRON, COPPER, RETORT, YET
bold BRAZEN, DERF, HEROIC, MALAPERT, NERVY, PERT, RASH
bole CRYPT, DOSE, STEM, TRUNK
bolide METEOR, MISSILE
boll BULB, KNOB, ONION, POD, SWELL
boll weevil PICUDO
bolt BAR, CLOSE, ELOPE, FASTEN, FLASH, LOCK, PAWL, PIN, SCREEN, SIFT, SLOT, WINNOW
bolus CLOD, CUD, LUMP, MASS
bombard SHELL, STRAFE
bombardment RAFALE
bombast BLUSTER, BOAST, ELA, FUSTIAN, GAS, RANT, TUMOR
bombastic FLOWERY, OROTUND, POMPOUS, TUMID, TURGID
bombyx ERI(A), MOTH
bond BAIL, DUTY, ESCROW, GLUE, NEXUS, PLEDGE, TIE, VALENCE, VOW, YOKE
bondman CHURL, ESNE, HELOT, PEON, SERF, SLAVE, THRALL, VASSAL, VILLEIN
bond-stone PERPEND
bone, pert. to OSTEAL, ULNAR
bone(s) DICE, OS(SA); see p. 105
bonus AWARD, CUMSHAW, MEED, PREMIUM, PRESENT, TIP
bony HARD, LANK, LEAN, OSSEOUS, SKELETAL, STIFF
boob ASS, DUNCE, NITWIT
booby LOSER, PRIZE, STUPID
book ALDUS, BIBLE, CODEX, DIARY, FOLIO, HORA(E), LIBER, LOG, MANUAL, MISSAL, MO, MS(S), OPUS, PRIMER, PSALTER, TOME, VOL
book part JACKET, LEAF, PAGE, SPINE
boom DRUM, JIB, ROAR, SPAR, SPRIT
boomerang BACKFIRE, RECOIL, RESILE, RICOCHET
boon BENE, FAVOR, GAY, GRANT, JOVIAL
boor CARL(OT), CHURL, CLOD, LOUT, OAF
boorish GAWKY, RUDE, VULGAR
boost ABET, EXALT, HOIST, KITE, LIFT
boot KAMIK, KICK, RECRUIT, SHOE, SOCK
booth CRAME, LOGE, SOOK, SOUK, STALL, SUQ
bootlick FAWN, FLATTER, TOADY
booty FANG, GAIN, LOOT, PELF, PREY, SWAG
borax TINCAL
border ABUT, BRIM, BRINK, FLANK, FLOROON, FOREL, HEM, LINE, MARGE, MARGIN, MAT, PURFLE, RAND, SKIRT, TIP, VERGE
bore DRAG, EAGRE, ENNUI, IRK, PIERCE, PRICK, TIDE
boredom ENNUI, TEDIUM
born NASCENT, NATE, NE(E)
borough BORG, BURG
borrow ADOPT, COPY, KICK, STEAL

borrowed stock DAER
bosh END, JOKE, POOH, ROT, TRIVIA
boss BAAS, KNOB, KNOP, MASTER, STUD, UMBO
botanical terms see p. 231
botch BUNGLE, FLUB, MESS, MUX
bother AIL, FUSS, HARRY, MEDDLE, MOLEST, PESTER, TEASE, TODO
bottle CANTEEN, CARAFE, CARBOY, COSTREL, CRUET, CRUSE, FLAGON, FLASK, JUG, KIT, MAGNUM, PHIAL, PIG, VIAL
bottom BASE, BED, DREGS, FLOOR, GROUND, LEES, NADIR, PLAYA, SOLE
bough ARM, LIMB, SHOOT, SHROUD, SPRIG, TWIG
bounce EJECT, FIRE, LEAP, RECOIL, SACK, SPRING, VERVE
bound DART, (DE)LIMIT, HOP, LOPE, SCUD, SKIM, STEND
boundary AMBIT, LIMIT, LINE, MERE, METE
bounder CAD, CUB, RAKE, ROUE, SNOB
bounty BONUS, BOON, GIFT, GRANT, LARGESS, MEED, PRIZE
Bounty captain BLIGH
bouquet AROMA, NOSEGAY, ODOR, POS(E)Y
bout ESSAY, MATCH, ROUND, SETTO, TURN
bow ARC(H), BEND, CURTSY, CURVE, DEFER, NOD, PROW, SAL(A)AM, STEM, STOOP
bowed ARCATE ARCUATE(D)
bowels COLON PITY, RUTH
bower ANCHOR, ARBOR, GROTTO, KNAVE NOOK
bowl ACERRA, ARENA, BASIN, BEAKER, CENSER, CHAWAN, DEPAS, KITTY, MAZER, PAN, TANOA, THURIBLE
bowler DERBY, HAT, KEGLER
box ARCA, BIN(N), CADDY, CAISSON, CANISTER, CAPSA, CASE, CASKET, CHEST, CIST, COFFER, CRATE CUFF, ETUI, FIGHT, INRO, LOGE, PUNCH, SEAT, SLAP, SLUG, SPAR, SWAT, TILL, TRUMMEL
boxing term KAYO, TKO
boy BUB, GROOM, LAD, SHAVER, TAD, TOT, YOUTH
boycott BLACKBALL, BLACKLIST, OSTRACIZE, SHUN
boyish PUERILE
brace CRUTCH, GIRD, LEG, PAIR, PROP, SHORE, STAY, STIFFEN, TRUSS, TWO
brace and a half THREE, TIERCE, LEASH
bracket CLASS, CONSOLE, CORBEL, SHELF, STRUT
bract GLUME, PALEA PALET, SPADIX SPATHE
brag BOAST, CROW, PREEN, RAVE, SWAGGER, STRUT, VAPOR VAUNT, YELP
braid BREDE, CUE INKLE, LACET, ORRIS, PLA(I)T, QUEUE, TRESS TRIM
brain term ALBA, DURA, HARN, ITER, LURA, OBEX, PAN, PIA, PYLA, TELA UTAC
brake BLOCK, BUR(R), CURB, DELAY, DRAG
brake part DRUM SHOE
branch ARM, BROG, FORK LIMB, RAME, RAMIFY, RAMUS SPRIG, STOLON VIMEN
branched CLADOSE, RAMAL, RAMATE, RAMOSE, RAMOUS
branchia GILL
brand CHOP, FLAW, KIND, LABEL, MARK, SEAR, STAIN, STAMP, STIGMA TAINT
brash BOLD, HASTY, SAUCY
brass ALLOY, NERVE, OFFICER(S)
brave BOLD, DARE, DARING, DEFY, FACE GAME, HEROIC, INDIAN, MANLY, STIFF
bravo BIS, OLE RAH, THUG
brawl ROW, SHINDY; see FIGHT
bray CRUSH, GRIND, HEEHAW, MIX
brazen CHEEKY, NERVY, PERT, SASSY
breach CLEFT, CRACK GAP, RENT, RIFT, RUPTURE SLAP
bread BATCH, BREWIS BUN, CUSH, DIKA KISRA LOAF, MATZOS, MATZOTH PAIN, PANADA, PONE, ROLL, RUSK, SIPPET
break BOON, CAESURA, CRACK, HIATUS, HINT, RUIN, RUPTURE, SNAP
breaker BILLOW, COMBER, ROLLER
break in INITIATE, STAVE
breakwater COB, DAM DIKE, JETTY, MOLE, PIER QUAY
breastwork DICKEY, FORT, PARAPET, RAMPART, SCHERM
breath ANDE, HALITUS HUFF, LIFE, PECH, PNEUMA PRANA
breathe LIVE, PANT, PUFF, RESPIRE. WHEEZE
breathing GASP, PNEUMA, RALE, STRIDOR
breech BLOCK, BORE, BUTT, REAR

breechcloth MALO
breeches JODHPURS
breed BEGET, HATCH, ILK, KIND, PROGENY, RACE, RAISE, REAR, SIRE
breeze AIR, AURA, FLAW, GUST, PIRR, STIR, WIND, ZEPHYR
breve BRIEF, MARK, MINIM, NOTE, ORDER, WRIT
breviary COMPEND, DIGEST, EPITOME, ORDO, PORTAS(S)
brew CONCOCT, FOMENT, MIX, PLOT, STEW
brewing GAAL, GAIL, GYLE, MALTING
bribe BAIT, BOODLE, GRAFT, GRAVY, PAYOLA, SOP, SUBORN, SWAG, TEMPT
bric-a-brac BIBELOT, CURIO, VERTU, VIRTU
brick ADOBE, DOOK, MARL, NOG
brick carrier HOD
bricklayer MASON
bridal wreath SPIREA
bride KALLAH
Bridewell GAOL, JAIL, PRISON
bridge ARCH, LINK, MAGAS, PONS, PONT(OON), SPAN
bridge part CABLE, CAISSON, CROWN, DECK, HANGAR, PIER, PYLON, SHOE, SPANDREL, TRESSEL, TRESTLE, TRUSS
bridge game term BID, BOOK, BYE, DOUBLE, DUCK, LEG, OPEN, PASS, RAISE, RUBBER, SET, SLAM, SUIT, TENACE, TRICK, TRUMP, VOID
bridle BIT, BRANK(S), CAPER, CURB, PILLORY, SNAFFLE, STRUT
brief CONCISE, CURT, LACONIC, PITHY, SUMMARY, TERSE
brigand BANDIT, LATRON
bright ANIME, APT, GAY, GLEG, KEEN, LUCID, NAIF, NITID, SHARP, SHINING
brightness ACUMEN, NITOR, SHEEN
brilliance ECLAT, GLITTER, LUSTER, ORIENCY
brilliant DIAMOND, GEM, RADIANT, SIGNAL
brim POKE, SKIRT; see EDGE
brine BRACK, MAIN, OCEAN, PICKLE, SALT, SEA, TEARS
bring COMMAND, CONDUCT, FETCH, INCUR
bring forth BEAR, BEGET, HATCH, (Y)EAN
brink DITCH, END, EVE, MARGE, MARGIN
briny SALINE, SALTY
brisk ALERT, ALLEGRO, CHEERY, FLEET, KEDGE, LIVE, NIMBLE, PERK(Y), RAPID, SHARP, SPRY, YARE
bristle BRUSH, CHAETA, PALPUS, PREEN, PRIDE, RIB, RUFFLE, SETA, SPINE, STRUT
bristly HISPID, SETOSE
brittle CRISP, FICKLE, FRAIL, FROW(Y), WEAK
broach AIR, AWL, BEGIN, LAUNCH, PUBLISH, REAMER, RIMER, VENT, VOICE
brogan BOOT, SHOE, STOGY
broil FRACAS, GRILL, MELEE, ROW, SCORCH, SCRAP
broker AGENT, FACTOR, JOBBER, SCHATCHEN
brooch CAMEO, CLASP, FIBULA, OUCH, PECTORAL, PIN
brood BEVY, COVEY, FRY, HATCH, LITTER, MOPE, NEST, NID(E), NYE, SIT
brook ABIDE, BEAR, BECK, CREEK, RILL, RILLET, RUN(NEL), STAND
broom BESOM, COW, HIRSE, MOP, SWAB, WHISK
brother BILLY, CADET, FELLOW, FRA, FRATER, FRIAR, MONK, PAL, SIB(LING)
brotherhood SODALITY
brow BREE, CREST, EDGE, RIDGE, SNAP, TOP
brown COOK, SEAR, (SUN)TAN, TOAST
browned RISSOLE, TANNED
browse BRUT, CROP, FEED, GRAZE, NIBBLE, PASTURE
bruise BRAY, CONTUSE, CRUSH, DENT, HURT, ICTUS, MAUL, SHINER, SQUEEZE
bruised HUMBLE, HURT, LIVID
bruit HEARSAY, NOISE, RUMOR, TELL
brush CLEAN, COPSE, FIGHT, FITCH, FRAY, SCOPA(E), TIP
brusque ABRUPT, BLUFF, BLUNT, CURT, GRUFF, RUDE, TERSE
brutal BESTIAL, CARNAL, COARSE, CRUEL, FERAL, SAVAGE
Brythonic CORNISH
bubble AIR, BEAD, BLAIN, BLEB, BOIL, BOLL, CHEAT, GLOB, SEETHE
buccaneer CORSAIR, PICAROON, PIRATE, VIKING
buck DANDY, DOLLAR, DUDE, FOP, NOB, RESIST, STAG, SWELL, TOFF
bucket BOWK, PAIL, SCOOP, SKEEL, SOE, STOP, TUB
buckle BEND, CLASP, TACH(E), WARP

bucolic IDYL, PASTORAL, RURAL, RUSTIC
bud BEGIN(NING), CION, GEM(MA), GERM, GRAFT, IMP, KNOP, SPROUT
Buddha GAUTAMA, JATAKA
Buddha's wife AHALYA
budget BAG, BUNCH, PACK(ET), PLAN
buff FAN, POLISH, SHINE, TAN, TAWNY
buffet BOX, COUNTER, CUFF, PLAT, SLAP SMITE, TOSS
buffoon ANDREW, ANTIC, CLOWN, DROLL, FOOL, JAPE, JESTER, MIMER, ZANY
bugaboo GOGA, GOGO, JUMBO, MUMBO
bugle call RETREAT, REVEILLE, TANTARA, TAPS, TAT(T)OO
build COOT, ERECT, FORM, RAISE REAR
building ADOBE, EDIFICE, INSULA TAPIA
bulb BUD, CORM, GLOBE, KNOB, LAMP, TUBER
bulge BAG, BLOAT, BUG, HUMP, JUT, KNOB, SWELL
bulging CONVEX, FULL, GIBBOUS, TUMID
bulk BODY, BOUK, GROSS, MASS SHAPE, VOLUME
bull APIS, BLUNDER BOBBY, COP, ERROR, HAPI, OX, PEELER SLIP, SOLECISM
bulldoze BROWBEAT, BULLY, COW, DIG, FORCE RAM, SCOOP
bullet BALL, DUMDUM, PELLET, SHOT, SLUG, TRACER
bullfight CORRIDA
bullfight cry OLE
bullfighter MATADOR, PICADOR, TOREADOR, TORERO
bullion BAR, BILLOT, INGOT, MASS
bull-like TAURINE
bully COW, HECTOR, SCARE, SHANNY VAPOR
bulwark BAIL, BASTION, CITADEL, FORT, PARAPET, RAMPART, SCONCE
bum HOBO, IDLER, TRAMP
bumble BEADLE, BLUNDER, BUNGLE
bumper BUFFER, FACER, FINE, GLASS, GOBLET, TOAST
bun CAKE, JAG, ROLL, STEM, STALK, TAIL WIG
bunch BALE, CROWD, FAGOT, LOT, TUFT WISP
bund DAM, DIKE, LEAGUE QUAY
bundle BALE, BOLT, FADGE, FAGOT, HANK, PACK(ET), SHEAF
bung CORK, PLUG, SHIVE, STOPPER
bungle BOTCH, ERR, GOOF
bunk BERTH, COT, HOKUM, LODGE SLEEP
bunker ABRI, BIN, CRIB, HAZARD, SANDHOLE
buoy BELL, CAN, DAN, FLOAT, NUN, NUT, RAISE SPAR
buoyancy FLO(A)TAGE
burden BIRN, CARE, CARK, CARGO, CUMBER, FARDEL, LADE, LOAD, ONUS, TAX
bureau AGENCY, CHEST, DESK, DRESSER OFFICE
burgeon BUD, SHOOT, SPROUT
burial place AHU, BARROW, GRAVE, KURGAN, LOW, TUMULUS
buried HIDDEN, IMBEDDED, SUNKEN
burke MURDER
burl KNOT, LUMP, PIMPLE
burlesque COMEDY, FARCE, OVERDO, PARODY REVUE
burly BULKY, HUSKY, OBESE, STOUT
Burma chief BO(H), WOON, WUN
burn ASH, BROOK, CENSE, CHAR, CONSUME, CREMATE RILL, SCALD, SCORCH, SERE, SINGE
burning (A)FIRE, ARDENT, ARSON, CALID, EAGER, IRATE
burning bush WAHOO
burnisher AGATE, BUFFER, POLISHER
burr BRIAR, CIRCLE, CORONA, HALO, NUT, POD, RING, WHIRR
burrow DIG, HOLE, MINE, MOIL, NUZZLE, ROOT, TUBE, TUNNEL
bursa SAC
burst ERUPT, EXPLODE, POP, REAVE, REND, SPLIT, VOLLEY
bury CACHE, EARTH, INHUME, INTER, INURN
bush BOSCAGE, BOSH, CLUMP, SHRUB, TOD
bushing PINTLE
bushy DUMOSE, DUMOUS
business AFFAIR, CHORE, CRAFT, ERRAND, FEAT, FIRM GEAR, LINE, STINT TRADE
buss DECK, DRESS, KISS, SMACK
bustle ADO, DITHER, FISK, FLURRY, FUSS, HYPER, POTHER, TODO
busybody MEDDLER, QUIDNUNC, SNOOP
but BAR, MERE, ONLY, SAVE, STILL, YET
butler SERVANT, SPENCER, STEWARD
butt BUNT, CASK, GOAD, PUSH, RAM, STUB, STUMP, TUP

butter BEURRE, FULWA, GHEE, GHI, MAHUA, PHULWA
buttery LARDER, PANTRY, SPENCE
button BADGE, BOSS, BUD, FASTEN, HOOK, KNOB, KNOP, OLIVE, STUD
button part SHANK
buttress OUTCAST, PIER, PROP, STAY
buyer AGENT, CHAP, EMPTOR, VENDEE
buzzer ALARM, BEE, BELL, HOWLER, SIGNAL
by AGO, ASIDE, BESIDE, CAUSE, CLOSE, NEAR, PAST, PER, VIA, WITH
bygone FORMER, OLDEN, PAST, YORE

C

C mark CEDILLA
cab ARABA, HACK, TAXI
cabal BLOC, CLIQUE, INTRIGUE, JUNTO, PLOT
cabin BERTH, CABAN(A), COACH, HOVEL, HUT, SALOON, SHANTY, SHED
cabinet ALMIRAH, BAHUT, BUHL, BUREAU, CLOSET, ETAGERE, MINISTRY, WHATNOT
cable COAXIAL, CORD, GUY, PAINTER, WIRE
caboose CAB, CAR, GALLEY, HACK
cacao BROMA, COCKER
cache BURY, CONCEAL, HIDE, STORE, STOW, TROVE
cachet SEAL, STAMP, WAFER
cadence CLOSE, LILT, METER, PACE, RHYTHM, TONE
cadet JUNIOR, PLEB, SON
cadge BEG, MOOCH, SPONGE
caduceus SCEPTER, STAFF, WAND
Caesar foe BRUTUS, CASCA, CASSIUS, POMPEI
Caesar relative ATIA, AURELIA
caesura BREAK, PAUSE, REST
cafe BARROOM, BISTRO, CABARET
caffeine THEINA, THEIN(E)
cage GIG, HUTCH, MEW
cahoots LEAGUE, PARTNERS
caitiff BASE, MEAN, VILE
cajole BEGUILE, BUTTER, CHEAT, COAX, DECOY, ENTICE, FLATTER, PALP, TEASE, WHEEDLE
cake BATTY, FLOE, HARDEN, PONE, SCONE, TORTE, WAFER, WIG(G)
calamitous DIRE, EVIL, HAPLESS, SAD
calamity BLOW, DISASTER, MISERY, WOE, WRACK
calculate AIM, COMPUTE, FRAME, RATE, RECKON, TALLY
calculator ABACUS, LOG, TABLE
calendar ALMANAC, DIARY, DOCKET, JOURNAL, LOG, ORDO; see p. 255
calf, pert. to SURAL
caliber BORE, DIAMETER, GAUGE, METTLE
calico SALLO(O)
Caliph ALI, IMAM, OMAR, OTHMAN
calk CHINESE, CLOSE, COPY, NAP, STOP
call BAN, BID, CLEPE, CITE, CRY, DUB, ELICIT, INVITE, MUSTER, NAME, PHONE, ROUSE, SOOK, SUMMON, TERM, TITLE, VISIT, YELL
call to prayer ADAN, AZAN
calling (A)VOCATION, JOB, LINE, TRADE, METIER
callous HARD, HORNY, TOUGH, TORPID
calm ABATE, ALLAY, LOWN, LULL, PLACATE, PLACID, SERENE, STILL, STOIC
calorie THERM(E)
calumniate BELIE, DEFAME, MALIGN, REVILE, VILIFY
calumny LIBEL, SLANDER, SLUR
Calvinist BEREAN
calyx HUSK, SEPAL
cam CATCH, COG, LOBE, WIPER, TRIPPET
camp BIVOUAC, BOMA, ETAPE, LA(A)GER, POST, TABOR, ZAREBA
camp, pert. to CASTRAL
camphor ALANT, APIOL, BORNEOL, MENTHOL
campus FIELD, QUAD
can JAIL, JUG, MAY, PRESERVE
canal CHANNEL, CONDUIT, DUCT, ERIE, KIEL, MEATUS, PANAMA, RIO, SOO, STRAIT, SUEZ, ZANJA, ZELLAND
cancel ANNUL, BLOT, DELE(TE), EFFACE, ERASE, POSTMARK, REPEAL, REVOKE, VOID
candid ARTLESS, BLUNT, FRANK, HONEST, NAIVE
candle BOUGIE, CIERGE, DIP, TAPER, TEST, WAX
candlestick CRUSIE, GIRANDOLE, LAMPAD, LUSTRE, PRICKET, SCONCE
candy COMFIT, FONDANT, LOLLY, NOUGAT, PRALINE, SWEET, TAFFY

cane MALACCA, PUNISH, RATTAN, STEM, STICK
canine CUR, CUSPID, DOG, FANG, FICE, PUG, PUP
cannon see p. 108
canoe BUNGO, ROBROY
canon AXIOM, HYMN, LAUD, LAW, NODUS, RULE, SONG
canonical hour(s) COMPLIN, LAUDS, NONE, PRIME, SEXT, TIERCE, VESPERS
canopy AWNING, COPE, DAIS, SKY, TESTER, VAULT
cant see SLANG, TILT
canter PACE, RACK, RUN, WHINER
canticle ODE, HYMN, LAUD, SONG
canto AIR, FIT, PACE, PASSUS
canvas DUCK, SAIL, SCRIM, TARP, TENT, TEWKE, TUKE, WIGAN
canyon CANADA, GAP
canyon mouth ABRA
cap BERET, CORK, EXCEL, LID, PILEUS, TAJ, TOP
capacity BENT, KNACK, SIZE, SKILL
cape COD, MAY, NASE, NES(S), RAS, SCAW, SKAW
Capek play figure ROBOT, RUR
caper ANTIC, DIDO, FRISK, GAMBOL, HOP, PRANCE, PRANK, ROMP, TITTUP
capital BASIC, CITY, FATAL, LETTER, MAIN, PRIMAL, STOCK
caprice FAD, KINK, QUIRK, VAGARY, WHIM(SEY)
capstan DRUM, HOIST, LEVER
capsule CACHET, PEARL, PILL, POD, SHEATH, THECA
captain AHAB, BLIGH, RAIS, REIS, SOTNIK
caption HEADING, LEADER, LEGEND, TITLE
captious CARPING, TESTY
captivate ALLURE, CHARM, ENAMOR, ENCHANT, ENSLAVE
capture ARREST, BAG, COP, NAB, NET, PRIZE, SNARE
caput DOOMED, HEAD, TOP
Caradoc BALA
caravan CAFILA, SAFARI, TREK
caravansary see INN
carbohydrate STARCH, SUGAR
carbon COAL, COKE, COPY, LEAD, SOOT
card ACE, BASTO, BOWER, COMB, DAME, DEUCE, FOUR, JACK, JASZ, JOKER, KING, KNAVE, MENEL, NINE, NOBS, PAM, PEDRO, POSTAL, SIX, TAROC(CO), TAROT, TEASE, TEN, TREY, TUM, TWO, WAG
card term BID, BLIND, BLITZ, BRELAN, CAT, CHECK, CUT, DEAL, DECK, DROP, ENTRY, GIN, HAND, HONOR, KITTY, KNOCK, MELD, PACK, PASS, PIC, POT, RAISE, SMEAR, SUIT, TENACE, TRUMP, VOLE, WIDOW
cardinal CUSHING, DATARY, LEGER, MCGUIGAN, MCINTYRE, RITTER, ROY, SHEHAN, SPELLMAN
care CARK, HEED, RECK
careen CALK, CANT, HEEL, KEEL, LIST, TILT, TIP, YAW
careful CHARY, LEERY, WARY
careless CASUAL, LASH, LAX, RASH, REMISS
caress CODDLE, COSSET, DANDLE, HUG, NUZZLE, PET
cargo GOODS, LADING, LAST, LOAD, PORTAGE
caricature FARCE, PARODY, SKIT, TAKEOFF
carol LAY, NOEL
carom REBOUND, RICOCHET, SHOT
carousal BINGE, ORGY, JAMBOREE, REVEL, SPREE
carouse BIRLE, BOOZE, BOUSE
carp CAVIL, CENSURE, NAG, NIBBLE
carpel LEAF, PISTIL, SOREMA
carpenter ANT, FRAMER, JOINER, WRIGHT
carpet DRUGGET, MAT, TAPET(E), TAPIS; see p. 283
carriage GIG, MANNER, MIEN, POISE, PORT, SHAY
carrier HAMAL, PORTER, REDCAP
carry BEAR, FERRY, FETCH, HOLD, LUG, RIDE, TOTE
carry on CAPER, CONDUCT, CUTUP, WAGE
cartel PACT, POOL, TRUST
Carthage, of PUNIC
Carthage ruler BARCA, DIDO, HANNIBAL
cartoonist ARNO, BUELL, CAPP, KELLY, KIRBY, LOW, NAST, REA, SCHULZ, SOGLOW, STEIG
carve CHISEL, INCISE, SCULPT, SHAPE
carving in stone CAMEO, SCRIVE
case ABLATIVE, CARTON, DATIVE, ETUI, ETWEE, FOREL(L), INRO, LOCATIVE, PETARD, SHEATH, TRIAL, VOCATIVE
cash CLEAR, DARBY, DUST, HONOR, MONEY, SPECIE
cashier BURSAR, DROP, EXPEL, OUST, PURSER, TELLER
casing COVER, LINER, SHEATH(ING), SHOE

casino PINK, TEN
cask BARECA, BOSS, BUTT, CADE, FIRKIN, KEG, RIER, TIERCE, TUB, TUN, VAT
cask part BILGE, CHIMB, CHIME, LAG
casket BOX, COFFIN, PYX, SHRINE, TYE
casserole RAGOUT, STEW
cast FUSIL, JILT, JUNK, MOLD, MOLT, SHED, SLING, SPEW, TINT, TOSS, TOT
castaway DERELICT, MAROON, PARIAH, WAIF
caste AHIR, BANIAN, BRAHMAN, CHETTY, CLASS, DOM, GOLA, GRADE, JATI, KORI, KULI, LOHANA, MAGI, MAL(I), MEO, PARIAH, PASI, RAJPUT, RANK, SUDRA, TELI, VAISYA, VARNA
caster CRUET, HURLER, PHIAL, ROLLER, VIAL, WHEEL
castigate BEAT, CENSURE, LAMBASTE, PUNISH, REPROVE
castle ALCAZAR, CHATEAU, CITADEL, ELSINORE, FORTRESS, MORRO, ROOK, WINDSOR
castle part DONJON, KEEP, MOAT, TOWER
castor BEAN, BEAVER, CRUET, HAT, STAR
Castor and Pollux DIOSCURI, GEMINI, TWINS
casual(s) LOAFERS, OFFHAND
cat FELINE; see p. 211
catacomb CRYPT, LOCULUS, TOMB, VAULT
catafalque BIER, SCAFFOLD
catalog(ue) CANON, CENSUS, FILE, INDEX, LIST, ROSTER, ROTA
catapult BAL(L)ISTA, HURL, ONAGER, PROJECT, SCORPION
cataract CALIGO, CASCADE, CAST, FALLS, LINN
catarrh COLD, RHEUM
catch CLICK, DETENT, (EN)TRAP, GRAB, HAUL, HOOK, INCUR, KEP, NAB, NET, PAWL, PELVIS, RATCHET, SNAG, SNATCH
catchall BAG, BASKET, CLOSET
catchword CUE, SLOGAN, STARTER
category CASTE, CLASS, FAMILY, GENRE, GENUS, RUBRIC, SPECIES
cater FEED, PANDER, PROVIDE, PURVEY
catgut CORD, THARM, VIOLIN
cathedral CHURCH, DOM, LATERAN, MINSTER, SOBOR
Catholic, Greek UNIAT(A)
catkin AMENT, RAG, SPIKE
catnip CATMINT, NEP, NIP
cat's-paw CULLY, DUPE, GULL, STOOGE
cattle BEEVES, BOVINES, COWS, KINE, NOWT, OXEN, STOCK
cattle dealer DROVER, RANCHER
Caucasian language ADIGHE, ANDI, AVAR, LAZ, UDI
ca(u)ldron BOILER, KETTLE, POT, RED, VAT
causeuse SOFA, TETEATETE
caustic ACRID, ALUM, BITING, ERODENT, LIME, LYE, MORDANT, PHENOL, PUNGENT, PYROTIC, SEVERE
cautious CANNY, CHARY, FABIAN, SHY, WARY
cavalier HAUGHTY, KNIGHT, PROUD
cavalry LANCERS, TURM(A)
cavalryman DRAGOON, HUSSAR, SOWAR, SPAHEE, SPAHI, U(H)LAN
cave, inhabiting a SPEL(A)EAN
caveman TROGLODYTE
cave(rn) ANTRE, CAVITY, CROFT, CRYPT, DEN, GROT(TO), LAIR, RECESS, WEEM
caviar IKRA, ROE
caviar fish STERLET, STURGEON
cavil BICKER, CARP, CENSURE, HAFT, QUIBBLE
cavity ANTRUM, ATRIUM, DENT, DRUSE, FOSSA, GEODE, LUMEN, PIT, POCKET, SINUS, VOOG, VUG(G), VUGH
cavort CAPER, DIDO, PRANK
cayenne CANARY, CAPSICUM, COPEPOD, PEPPER, WHIST
cease AVAST, HALT, PETER, QUIT, STAY
cede ASSIGN, DEED, FORGO, GRANT, WAIVE, YIELD
celebrity ECLAT, LION, NAME, STAR, VIP
celestial ANGELIC, DIVINE, HOLY, URANIC
cell CYTODE, EGG, GAMETE, GERM, GROUP, KIL(L), NEURON(E), SPORE, VAULT
cell division SPIREM(E)
cell part ENERGID, LININ, PLASTID, VACUOLE
cella NAOS, SERDAB
Celtic ERSE, MANX, WELSH
cement GLUE, LUTE, MORTAR, PASTE, PUTTY, SOLDER
cenobite ESSENE, FRIAR, MONK, NUN
cenoby ABBEY, CONVENT, PRIORY
censure BLAME, CHIDE, FLAY, SLATE, TARGE

cent PENNY, SOU
center CORE, FOCUS, HEART, HUB, NAVE, NUCLEUS, PIVOT
center, away from DISTAL
center, toward ENTAD, MESIAL
centerpiece EPERGNE
central AXIAL, FOCAL, NUCLEAR, PIVOTAL
cerate LARD, SALVE, WAX
cereal BRAN, FARINA, GRITS, HOMINY, MAIZE, OATMEAL, SECALE
cerebrate COGITATE, PONDER, THINK
ceremony FORM, POMP, RITE, RITUAL
certain FIXED, ONE, SURE, TRUE, YEA
certificate DIPLOMA, SCRIP, STOCK, VOUCHER
certify ATTEST, DEPOSE, EVINCE, LICENSE, OKAY, VOUCH
cesspool SINK(ER), SUMP
cessation DEATH, DESITION, END, PAUSE, STAY, STOP(PING)
cetaceans see p. 214
chafe ABRADE, FRET, FROT, GALL, RUB, VEX
chaff BANTER, BRAN, HULLS, HUSK, PUG, TRASH
chaffer DICKER, HAGGLE, HIGGLE, SIEVE
chaffy ACEROSE, PALEATE, SCALY, TRIVIAL
chain ALBERT, CATENA, FETTER, FOB, GYVE, MANACLE, SHACKLE, TETHER, TORC, TORQUE, TYE
chair KAGO, ROCKER, SEAT, SEDAN, SPEAKER, STOOL
chair part RUNG, SPLAT
chalice AMA, AMULA, BOWL, CALIX, CUP GRAIL
challenge CARTEL, DARE, DEFY, GAGE, QUESTION
chamber CAMERA, KIVA, LOCULUS, ODA(H), ROOM
champion ACE, BACK, ESPOUSE, HERO, PALADIN, VICTOR
chance FATE, FORTUNE, HAP, HAZARD, KISMET, LOT, LUCK, OCCUR, ODDS, RANDOM, RISK
chancel BEMA, JUBE, SEDILE, SEDILIA
change ALTER, FLUX, MODIFY, MUTA, MUTATE, OBVERT, SHIFT, VARY
changeable FICKLE, PROTEAN, VARIANT
changeling DOLT, DOUBLE, DUNCE, ELF, OAF, RINGER
channel ALVEUS, BAND, CHUTE, CONDUIT, DIKE, DUCT, FLUME, FURROW, GAT, GROOVE, GUTTER, LEAF, MEDIUM, PIPE, RACE, SLUICE, STRAIT, STRIA, TUBE
chant CANTICLE, DRONE, INTONE, INTROIT, MELE, RESPONSE
chanticleer COCK ROOSTER
chantry ALTAR, CHAPEL, SHRINE
chaos ABYSS, APSU, BABEL, HAVOC, KORE, MESS, NU(N), PIE, VOID
chaotic MUDDLED, SNAFU
chap CHINK, COVE, CRACK, KEREL, KIBE, SPRAY
chapel BETHEL, CHANTRY, CHOIR, ORATORY SISTINE
chaperon DUE(N)NA ESCORT
chaplet ANADEM, FILLET, ROSARY, WREATH
chapped CRACKED, KIBED, KIBY, SPLIT
character ETHOS, NEUME, REPUTE, ROLE, RUNE
charge ADJURE, COST, DEBIT, FEE, INDICT, ONUS
charger MOUNT, PLATE, PLATTER, STEED
chariot BIGA, CURRE, ESSED(A), ESSEDE, RATH(A), WAIN
charioteer AURIGA, DRIVER, HUR, PILOT
charitable BENIGN, HUMANE
charity ALMS, DOLE, MERCY
charlatan EMPIRIC, FAKE(R), QUACK
Charlemagne's kin ORLANDO, PEPIN
charm AMULET, ENAMOR, ENCHANT, FETISH, GRIGRI, JUJU, MAGIC, MOJO, OBE, OBI, PERIAPT, SWASTIKA
chart DIAGRAM, GRAPH, MAP, MERCATOR, PLAT, PLOT, SCHEMA, TABLE
charter DEED, GRANT, HIRE, LEASE, LET, PATENT, RENT
Charybdis, rock opposite SCYLLA
chasm ABYSS, CLEFT, CREVAS, FLUME, GAP, GLUT, GORGE, GULF, HIATUS, RAVINE, REFT
chassis BODY, FRAME, NACELLE
chaste MODEST, PURE, VESTAL
chasten ABASH, HUMBLE, SMITE
chastise BLAME, CENSURE, SLATE, SWINGE, TAUNT, TRIM
chat CHIN, CONFAB, COZE, GAB, PRATE, TOVE
chatelaine BROOCH, CLASP, PIN
chattel EFFECTS, GOODS, SLAVE
chatter BABBLE, BLAT, CLAP, GAB, GAS, JABBER, PRATE, YAP
chatterer JAY, MAG, PIET
cheap NOMINAL, PALTRY, SHODDY, VILE

cheat BAM, BILK, CHISEL, CLIP, CON, COZEN, FOB, FUB, GIP, GULL, GYP, MUMP, RENEGE, RENIG, SHARK, SHARP(ER), STING, SWINDLE, SWIZ
check BLOCK, BRIDLE, CURB, NIP, REIN, STAY, STUNT, TAB
checkered MOSAIC, PIED, PLAID, VAIR
checkers DAM(E)S, DRAUGHTS
checkers term CROWN, DAM, KING
checking block SPRAG
checkmate BAFFLE, SCOTCH, STOP, STYMIE, THWART, UNDO
cheek(s) BRASS, BUCCA, CHAP, GALL, GENA, JAMP, JOLE, JOWL, NERVE, SAUCE
cheek, pert. to BUCCAL, GENAL, MALAR
cheer APPLAUD, BRAVO, CLAP, ELATE, ENCORE, HURRAH, LAUD, OLE, PRAISE, RAH, ROOT, VIVA
cheerful BLITHE, GLEG, HILARY, JOLLY, PE(A)RT, ROSY
cheerless DISMAL, DRAB, DREAR(Y), GLOOMY, GLUM
cheese BELPAESE, BRIE, CHEDDAR, DICK, DUNLOP, EDAM, GOUDA, GRATIN, GRUYERE, MYSOST, PARMESAN, RICOTTA, SAPSAGO, TILSITER
cheesy CASEOUS
chemical compound AMID(E), AMIN(E), AZIN(E), AZOLE, BORID(E), CERIA, ESTER, IMID(E), IMINE, IODIDE, ISOMER, INOSITE, LEUCINE, METAMER, STEARATE
chemical radical BENZOYL, BUTYL, CARBONYL, (M)ETHYL, OXALYL, TOLYL
chemical salt BORATE, ESTER, NITER, SAL
chemist ARRHENIUS, AVOGADRO, BECHER, BOYLE, BUCHNER, COUPER, CURIE, DALTON, FISCHER, HODGKIN, HOFF, KEKULE, KUHNE, LAVOISIER, LIEBIG, MILLIKAN, OSTWALD, PASTEUR, PAULING, PRIESTLEY, STAHL; see p. 244
cherish DOTE, ESTEEM, FOSTER, PET, PRIZE, REVERE
cherry CAPULIN, DUKE, GEAN, MARASCA, MOREL(L), OXHEART, RUDDY
chessman BISHOP, CASTLE, HORSE, KING, KNIGHT, PAWN, PIECE, QUEEN, ROOK
chess term CASTLE, CHECK, DEBUT, (EN)PRISE, FIDATE, GAMBIT, JADOUBE, MATE
chest ARCA, ARK, BAHUT, BOSOM, CASE, CIST, COFFER, KIST, LOCKER, THORAX
chevron ANGLE, RANK, STRIPE
chew BITE, CHAM(P), CHAVEL, GNAW, MUNCH, QUID
chic DAPPER, MODISH, NATTY, NIFTY, STYLISH
chicanery CAVIL, INTRIGUE, RUSE, WILE
chicken BROILER, COCK, FRYER, HEN, LAYER, POULT
chicle GUM, LATEX
chide (BE)RATE, REPROVE, SCOLD
chief(tain) AGA, ALDER, AMEER, AMIR, ARCH, ATAMAN, CAPITAL, DAT(T)O, DATU, ELDER, FRIST, HEAD, HETMAN, JAM, JARL, MIR, MORO, POMBO, PRIME, RAIS, RAJA(H), RANA, REIS, SUPREME, THANE, TYEE, VITAL, YARL, ZAIM
chilblain KIBE
child, foster DALT, NORRY, NURRY
childish ASININE, NAIVE, PUERILE
childlike DOCILE, MEEK, NAIVE, PUERILE
child(ren) ARAB, BABE, BABY, BATA, BRAT, CHIT, FUB, GAMIN, INFANT, KID, MOPPET, PROGENY, TIKE, TOT, TYKE
chill AGUE, ALGOR, FREEZE, GELID, ICE, NIP, RIGOR, SHIVER
chilly ALGID, BLEAK, COLD, COOL, GELID, ICY, RAW
chime AGREE, BELL, EDGE, HARMONY, RIM
chimney FLUE, LUM, TEWEL, VENT
chimney piece MANTEL, PAREL
china CATHAY, CERAMIC, CROCKERY, DELF(T), DRESDEN, EGGSHELL, FAIENCE, LIMOGES, PORCELAIN, SPODE
chine CREST, RIDGE, SILK, SPINE
Chinese CATAIA(N), JOHNNY, MIAO, MONGOL, SERIC, SINIC
chink BORE, CRACK, CRANNY, RIFT, RIMA, RIME
chinky RIMAL, RIMOSE, RIMOUS
chip BIT, CHECK, COUNTER, FLAKE, GALLET, NICK, NIG, SPALL
chipmunk CHIPPY, HACKEE
chipper COCKY, PERKY, SPRY
chirp CHEEP, PEEP, PEW, PIPE, PUE
chisel CELT, CHEAT, DROVE, GAD, PARE, POMMEL, SCULP, SLICK
chit INFANT, IOU, VOUCHER

chivy, chevy CHASE, CRY, GAME, HUNT, NAG, PURSUE
chock BLOCK, CLEAT, WEDGE
chocolate mixing stick MOLINET
chocolate powder PINOLE
choice AONE, CREAM, ELITE, OPT(ION), PICK(ED), PRIME, RARE, SELECT
choke BURKE, CLOG, DAM, GAG, STIFLE, WORRY
choler ANGER, BILE, FURY, IRE, RAGE, SPLEEN, WRATH
choleric FIERY, HUFFY, IRATE, TESTY
choose ADOPT, CULL, DESTINE, OPT(ATE), (S)ELECT, VOTE
chop AXE, CARVE, CHIP, DICE, HACK, HEW, JOWL, LOP, MINCE
chord HARMONY, TRIAD, TRINE
chore CHAR(E), DUTY, JOB, STINT
chorus ACCORD, BURDEN, CHOIR, REFRAIN, UNISON
chorus girl CHORINE, ROCKETTE
Chosen COREA, KOREA
christen CLEPE, NAME
Christmas NOEL, XMAS, YULE(TIDE)
chromosome IDANT
chronicle ACCOUNT, ANNAL(S), DIARY, RECORD
chrysalis AURELIA, COCOON, KELL, NYMPH, PUPA
chuck FOOD, GRUB, HURL
chuckle CACKLE, CHORTLE, CLUCK, GIGGLE, TITTER
chunk GOB(BET), WHANG, WHANK
chunky LUMPY, SQUAT, STOCKY, STOUT
church BASILICA, BETHEL, CATHEDRAL, CHAPEL, CRYPT, FANE, KIL, KIRK, MINSTER, MISSION, MOSQUE, PAGODA, SAMAJ, TEMPLE, TERA
church jurisdiction DEANERY, DIOCESE, PARISH, SEE
church leader ARIUS, HIERARCH, ORIGEN, PAPAS
church official BEADLE, ELDER, LECTOR, SACRIST(AN), SEXTON, VERGER
church, part of ALTAR, APSE, BEMA, NAVE, NEF, PEW
church property GLEBE
churchman ABBOT, BISHOP, CARDINAL, DEACON, DEAN, POPE, PRELATE, PRIEST, PRIMATE, RECTOR
churl BOOR, CARL, CEORL, KNAVE, LOUT, OAF, VILLEIN
churlish DOUR, SORDID, SOUR, SULKY, SULLEN, SURLY
ciborium CANOPY, COFFER, PYX
cider PERRY
cigar CHEROOT, CLARO, CORONA, CULEBRA, PANATELA, ROPE, SEGAR, STOGIE, STOGY, TOBY
cigarette BIRI, CIG, CUBES, FAG, GASPER
cinch BREEZE, FASTEN, GRIP
cinder(s) ASH(ES), CLINKER, DROSS, EMBER, SCAR, SCORIA, SLAG
cion BUD, GRAFT, SCION, SHOOT
cipher CODE, (N)AUGHT, NIL, NULL, OUGHT, ZERO
circle CIRC, CIRQUE, CLIQUE, CORDON, DISK, EDDY, GIRD(LE), GLOBE, HALO, HOOP, LOOP, NIMB, ORB, RHOMB, RING, ROTATE
circle part ARC, CENTER, CHORD, RADIUS, SECANT, SECTOR, SEGMENT, TANGENT
circuit AMBIT, CYCLE, (DE)TOUR, EYRE, LAP, ORBIT, ROUTE, ZONE
circuitous DEVIOUS, MAZY, SINUOUS
circular ANNULAR, BILL, DISCOID, ORBED, ROUND
circulate BRUIT, DEFUSE, ROTATE, SPREAD
circumference AMBIT, GIRT(H) VERGE
circumlocution AMBAGE, VERBIAGE
circumspect CHARY, DISCREET, WARY
circumstance DETAIL, EPISODE, FACT(OR), STATE, STRAIT
circus BIGTOP, CARNIVAL, CIRCLE, CIRQUE, COLISEUM
circus post META
cirque CORRIE, CWM, EROSION, RECESS
cistern BAC, SAC, SUMP, VAT, WELL
citadel ALAMO, ARX, CASTLE, FORT(RESS), TOWER
cite ADDUCE, CALL, MUSTER, QUOTE, SUBPOENA
citizen BURGHER, CIT, DENIZEN, NATIVE, OPPIDAN, RESIDENT, VOTER
citron CEDRAT, ET(H)ROG, LEMON, LIME
city BURGH, POLIS, STADT, URBS
city of the dead NECROPOLIS
city, pert. to CIVIC, URBAN
civet CAT, NANDINE, PERFUME
civic CIVIL, LAY, OPPIDAN, SECULAR, SUAVE, URBAN
civil CIVIC, HEND(E), LAY, POLITE, SUAVE, URBANE

Civil War commander BANKS, BARRON, BRAGG, BUELL, BUFORD, BUTLER, CANBY, COX, CROOK, CUSTER, EARLY, EWELL, FLOYD, FOOTE, FORREST, GRANT, HILL, HOOD, HOOKER, LEE, LOGAN, MCCLELLAN, MAURY, MEADE, MOSBY, PICKETT, POLK, PORTER, PRICE, SLOCUM, STUART, SUMNER, SYKES
claim ALLEGE, ARROGATE, EXACT, LIEN, TITLE, USURP
clamor BERE, DIN, NOISE
clamp BOLT, BRACE, CLASP, GLAND, VICE, VISE
clan AYLLU, CASTE, CLIQUE, FAMILY, GENOS, GEN(S), OBE, PHYLE, SEPT, SET, SIB, SIOL, TRIBE
clan, head of ALDER, TANIST
clandestine FURTIVE, PRIVY, SECRET, SLY
clang STROKE, TONK
clangor DIN, HUBBUB, UPROAR
clannish SECRET, TRIBAL
clarify CLEAR, DEPURATE, FREE, RENDER
clasp BUCKLE, CINCH, ENFOLD, HASP, HUG, INFOLD, MORSE, OUCH, TACH(E)
class CASTE, CLAN, FAMILY, GENERA, GENUS, HEIMIN, ILK, KIND, ORDER, RACE, RANK, SEMINAR, SORT, SPECIES, TYPE
classical ATTIC, CHASTE, PURE
classification CATEGORY, FILE, SYSTEM, TAXIS
classify CATALOG, GRADE, LABEL, LIST, RANK, RATE, (AS)SORT, TICKET, TYPE
clause PLANK, PROVISO
claw(s) CHELA(E), GRIFF, HOOK, NIPPER, SCRAPE, TALON, UNCI, UNCUS, UNGUIS, UNGULA
clay ADOBE, ARGIL, BOLE, BRICK, KAOLIN, LOAM, LOESS, MARL, OCHER, PUG, TASCO, TILE
clay bed GA(U)LT
clay layer SLOAM, SLOOM
clayey BOLAR, LUTOSE, MALMY
clean BREAM, CHASTE, DUST, EMPTY, FAY, KOSHER, TRIM
cleaner PURER, RAMROD, SCALER, SOAP, SWEEPER, VACUUM
cleanse DETERGE, PURGE, PURIFY
clear ACQUIT, AWEIGH, FAY, FREE, GRAPHIC, LIMPID, LUCENT, LUCID, NET, RID
clearing (AS)SART, MILPA
cleat BATTEN, BOLLARD, KEVEL, PITON, SPIKE, STRIP
cleave ADHERE, BISECT, CLING, REND, RIVE, SPLIT, SUNDER
cleft CLOVEN, FORKED, REFT, RIFT, RIMA, RIVA
clergyman ABBE, CANON, CLERIC, CLERK, CURATE, DEAN, DIVINE, PADRE, PARSON, PASTOR, PRIEST, PRIOR, RABBI, RECTOR, VICAR
clergyman residence MANSE, PARSONAGE, RECTORY, VICARAGE
clerk AGENT, SCRIBE, TELLER
clever ARTFUL, CANNY, DEFT, HABILE, HEND(E), SMART
clew BALL, CUE, HINT, SKEIN
click AGREE; see DETENT
cliff BLUFF, CLEVE, CRAG, KLIP, SCAR(P)
climax ACME, APEX, APOGEE, SUMMIT, ZENITH
climb ASCENT, CLAMBER, GRIMP, SCALE, SPEEL
climbing gear CARABINER, CLEAT, CRAMPON, PITON
clinch CLAMP, CLENCH, GRIP, HUG, NAIL, RIVET
cling ADHERE, COHERE, HANG, RELY, STICK, TRUST
clip BARB, CUT, MOW, PARE, PRUNE, SHEAR, SNIP, TRIM, WHACK
clique CABAL, CLUB, COTERIE, GANG, JUNTO, RING, SET
cloak BLIND, HIDE, MASK, PALL, SHIELD
clock BELL, DIAL, METER, NEF, TIME, VERGE
clod (C)LUMP, DOLT, EARTH, LOAM, SOD
clog(s) BALK, BETA, CHOKE, CHOPIN(E), CURB, DAGGLE, JAM, PATTEN, SABOT
cloister ABBEY, CELL, CLOSE, CONVENT, FRIARY, NUNNERY, PRIORY, STOA
close CALK, CHINSE, CODA, DAM, DENSE, ESTOP, FINAL(E), HUG, MUGGY, NIGH, NIGGARD, OCCLUDE, SEAL, SEAM, SEEL, STINGY, STIVY, STUFFY, TAUT
close ranks SERRY
closet AMBRY, EW(E)RY, LOCKER, WC
clot COAGULATE, CRUOR, GEL, GOB, JELL, LUMP, MASS, THICKEN
cloth BRIN, CHEYNEY, CRAPE, PATA, TAPET
cloth, blemish in AMPER, RIP, SNAG, TEAR

clothe ARRAY, DECK, DRAPE, ENDUE, GARB, GIRD, (IN)VEST, TOG
clothes BUREL, DUDS, REGALIA, TOGGERY, TOGS, VESTURE
clothing APPAREL, ARRAY, ATTIRE, COSTUME, DUDS, FINERY, FRIPPERY, GARB, GEAR, OUTFIT, RAGS, RAIMENT, RIG, TOGS; see p. 281
cloud(s) CIRRI, CIRRUS, COMA, CUMULI, CUMULUS, NEBULA, NIMBUS, NUBECULA, NUBIA, RACK(S), SCUD, SMUR, STRATI, STRATUS, VAPOR
cloudy FOGGY, FILMY, HAZY, LOWERY, OVERCAST
clout BUMP, CUFF, NAIL, PATCH, SLAP, SWAT
cloven-footed FISSIPED
clown BUFFOON, GOFF, HOB, JESTER, PUNCH, RUSTIC, ZANY
clownish GAWKY, LOUTISH
cloy CLOG, FILL, GLUT, GORGE, PALL, SATE, SATIATE, SURFEIT
club BRITH, DOES, ELKS, FRIARS, KIWANIS, LAMBS, LIONS, LODGE, MASONS, MOOSE, ORDER, ROTARY, SOCIETY, SORORITY, SOROSIS, TEAM, USO; see p. 108
clubfoot TALIPED, TALIPES
club-shaped CALVATE
clump BUNCH, MOTT(E), PATCH, TUFT
clumsy AWK(WARD), GAUCHE, OAFISH
cluster ANADEM, BUNCH, CLUMP, CYME, NEP, RACEME, SORUS, SPRIG, TUFT
coachman JEHU, PILOT, WHIP
coagulate CAKE, CLOT, CONGEAL, CURD(LE), GEL, JELL, POSSET, SET
coagulant RENNET, STYPTIC
coal BASS, CARBON, CINDER, COB, COKE, DUFF, EMBER, JET, LIGNITE, SMUT, SWAD
coal box DAN, HOD, SCUTTLE
coal refuse ASH, CINDER, CLINKER, COOM(B), CULM, SLAG, SMUT, SOOT
coal size EGG, NUT, PEA, STOVE
coalition AXIS, MERGER, UNION
coarse CRASS, CRUDE, GROSS, RIBALD, RUDE, VULGAR
coast BEACH, GLIDE, RIPA, SLIDE
coast, pert. to LITTORAL, ORARIAN, RIPARIAN
coat CLOAK, CRUST, FUR, GLAZE, HAIR, HIDE, LAYER, PATINA, PELAGE, PELT, PLATE, RIND, SKIN, TERNE, WOOL
coax CAJOLE, CANT, COG, EGG, ENTICE, LURE, WHEEDLE
cobble BOTCH, MEND, PATCH, PAVE
cobbler CRISPIN, SOUTER, SUTOR
cobweb NET, SNARE, TRAP
cock FAUCET, HEAP, RICK, PRIME, TAP
cockade KNOT, ROSETTE
cocker CODDLE, FONDLE, PAMPER, PET
cockle GITH, KILN, OAST, SHELL
cockpit ARENA, CAB(IN), NACELLE, NOSE
cocktail see p. 124
cocky JAUNTY, PERKY, PERT, PROUD
coconut COCO, COPRA, NARGIL, NOGGIN, PATE
coconut fiber COIR, COIRE, KOIR, KYAR
cocoon CLEW, KELL, POD
cod, pert. to GADOID
code CIPHER, CODEX, KEY, LAW, RULE
codger CHURL, MISER, NIGGARD
codicil DIPLOMA, RIDER, SEQUEL
coerce BULLY, COMPEL, COW, CURB, FORCE
coffee BRAZIL, JAVA, MOCHA, MUD, RIO, SANTOS, SUMATRA
coffee cup FINJAN
coffee cup holder ZARF
coffeepot BIGGIN
coffer ARK, CAISSON, CHEST, DAM
cog CHEAT, CHUCK, TENON, TOOTH, WHEEDLE
cognizance HEED, KEN, NOTICE
cognizant AWAKE, AWARE, HEP, ONTO
cognomen EPITHET, (SUR)NAME
coheir (CO)PARCENER
coil ANSA, CLUE, CURL, HELIX, LOOP, QUERL, ROLL, TWINE, TWIST, WHORL, WIND
coin BRASS, CASH, INVENT, JOE, MINT, SPECIE; see p. 189
coin box METER, PYX, TILL
coin edge (K)NURL, NIG
coincide AGREE, FIT, JIBE, TALLY
colander BOLTER, SIEVE, STRAINER
cold ALGID, GELID, ICY
collaborator QUISLING
collar CANG(UE), CATCH, NAB, RING, RUFF
collation LUNCHEON, MEAL, REPAST, TEA
collect (A)MASS, BAG, COMPILE, GARNER, GLEAN, LEVY, PRAYER, SHEAVE

collection ANA, CLAN, HEAP, RAFT, ROSARY, SET, SORITE(S), STACK
college ACADEMY, BREVET, GUILD, LYCEE, LYCEUM, SEMINARY, TOL
college grounds CAMPUS, LAWN, QUAD
college officer BEADLE, BURSAR, DEAN, DOCENT, DON, PROCTOR
collide BUMP, CRASH, HURTLE
colloquialism IDIOM
collude CONNIVE, PLOT, SCHEME
colonizer ANT, OECIST, SETTLER
colonnade PORTICO, STOA, TERRACE
color DYE, HUE, PAINT, SHADE, TINGE, TINT; see p. 119
colors BANNER, ENSIGN, FLAG
colorless ALBINO, ASHEN, CLEAR, DRAB, DULL, PALE, PALLID, WAN
Columbus' place GENOA, PALOS
column ANTA, DORIC, FUST, IONIC, LAT, PILASTER, PILLAR, STELE, TORSE, TORSO
column figure ATLANTES, CARYATID, TELAMON
column, ring of annulated BAGUE
comb CARD, CREST, CURRY, RAKE, RIDGE, TEASE
combat COPE, JOUST, SKIRMISH
combination CARTEL, FACTION, JUNTO, LEAGUE, MERGER, TRUST, UNION
combine BLEND, CARTEL, JOIN, MARRY, MIX, POOL, RING, SPLICE, WED
come ACCRUE, ADVENE, (A)RISE, ARRIVE, (EN)SUE, NEAR, REACH
come forth EMANATE, EMERGE, EMERSE, GUSH, ISSUE, JET, SPEW
comedian ANTIC, BUFF(OON), COMIC, FARCEUR, JESTER, JOKER, WAG, WIT
comedy FARCE, SLAPSTICK, TRAVESTY
comets see p. 277
comfit CANDY, CONFECT, PRALINE, SWEETMEAT
comfort CONSOLE, EASE, REPOSE, SOLACE, SOP
comfortable COSH, COZY, LITHE, PLEASING, SNUG
comforter PUFF, SCARF
comic DROLL, FUNNY, RISIBLE
coming ADVENT, ARRIVAL, DUE
command (BE)HEST, BID, DICTATE, ENJOIN, FIAT, MANDATE, ORDER
commander AG(H)A, ALCAIDE, CAID, CID, QAID, SIRDAR
commend COMMIT, EXTOL, KEN, LAUD
comment ASIDE, DESCANT, GLOSS, POSTIL
commentary EXEGESIS, GLOSS(ARY), REMARK
comminute CRUSH, GRIND, MILL
commiseration EMPATHY, PITY, RUTH
commission BREVET, CHARGE, DEPUTE, ORDAIN, PROXY
commit ASSIGN, CONSIGN, INTRUST
commodity GOODS, PRODUCT, STAPLE, WARE
common COARSE, CURRENT, GENERAL, JOINT, LOW, MUTUAL, ORNERY, PLAIN, PLEB(EIAN), TRITE, USUAL, VULGAR
commonplace BANAL, CLICHE, HUMDRUM, PROSAIC, PROSY, TRITE, TRUISM
commotion ADO, BUSTLE, CHOP, FUSS, HUBBUB, POTHER, STIR, TODO, WELTER
commune IMPART, KIBBUTZ, KOL(K)HOZ, MIR, SHARE, TOWNSHIP
communion EUCHARIST, HOST, MASS, RAPPORT, SECT, VIATICUM
community MIR, TOWN, VILLAGE
compact BOND, CARTEL, COVENANT, DENSE, ETUI, HARD, SOLID, TRIG, VANITY
companion ACHATES, (COM)PEER, CONSORT, CRONY, ESCORT, MATE, PAL, PARTNER, SPOUSE
company BAND, BATTERY, BODY, CIE, FERE, FIRM, PHALANX, TROOP, TROUPE
comparative EQUAL, RELATIVE, THAN
compare COLLATE, EVEN, LIKEN, SEMBLE
comparison ANALOGY, PARABLE, SIMILE
compartment BAY, BIN, CABIN, CELL, SECTION
compass AMBIT, ENCLOSE, GAMUT, GYRO, SWEEP, TRAMMEL
compass part AIRT(H), GIMBAL, RHUMB, VANE
compass point ENE, ESE, NNE, NNW, RHUMB, SSE, SSW, WNW, WSW
compassion GRACE, MERCY, PITY, RUE, RUTH
compel COERCE, FORCE, IMPEL, MAKE
compendium BRIEF, DIGEST, PRECIS, SUMMARY, SYLLABUS

compensate ATONE, (RE)PAY, TALLY
compensation BALM, REWARD, SALARY, UTU
compete COPE, EMULATE, MATCH, VIE
competent ADEPT, APT, CAPAX, SANE
competition FEIS, MATCH, RIVALRY, STRIFE
competitor OPPONENT, RIVAL
compile ARRANGE, COLLATE, EDIT, SELECT
complain CARP, FRET, FUSS, GRIPE, GRUMBLE, KICK, REPINE, WHINE
complaint GRAVAMEN
complaisant AFFABLE, CIVIL, LENIENT, POLITE, SUAVE
complete END, PLENARY, QUITE, TOTAL, UTTER
complex INTRICATE, KNOTTY, MANIFOLD, MAZE, MIXED, NETWORK, SYNDROME, TANGLED
complexion BLEE, HUE, TINGE, TINT
complicate INTORT, PERPLEX, TANGLE, WORSEN
complicated COMPLEX, KNOTTY, TANGLED
complication NODE, NODI, NODUS, SNARL
compliment EULOGY, EXTOL, LAUD
component ELEMENT, FACTOR, INTEGRAL
comport ACT, BEHAVE, DEMEAN, INVOLVE
composition CENTO, ESSAY, NOME, OPUS, PIECE, SCENA, THEME
compositor PRINTER, TYPO
composure BALANCE, MIEN, POISE, QUIET, REPOSE
compound AMIDE, FARRAGO, MIX(TURE), OLIO, OXIDE
comprehend GET, GRASP, LATCH, SENSE
compress ABRIDGE, BANDAGE, CONDENSE, CURTAIL, DEFLATE, DIGEST, PAD, PLEDGET, REDUCE, SHRINK, SQUEEZE, STUPE
comprise EMBODY, HOLD, INCLUDE
compulsion DURESS, FORCE, STRESS
compulsory service ANGARIA, ANGARY, DRAFT, SLAVERY
compunction QUALM, REGRET, SCRUPLE
compute ASSESS, FIGURE, RECKON, TALLY, TOTAL
comrade BILLY, BUDDY, CHUM, CRONY, PAL, TOVARICH
con ANTI, CHEAT, STUDY, VERSUS
concatenate CHAIN, CONNECT, JOIN, LINK, UNITE
conceal CACHE, CLOAK, ELOIGN, ELOIN, MASK, PALM, VEIL, WRY
concealed COVERT, INNER, LARVATE, LATENT, PERDU
conceit EGOTISM, FLAM, VANITY
conceive BRAIN, FRAME, IDEATE, IMAGINE, PLAN
concentrate AIM, CONDENSE, DISTILL, ELIXIR, ESSENCE, EXTRACT, FIX, FOCUS, SYRUP, UNIFY
conception FANCY, IDEA, IMAGE, NOTION
concern AFFAIR, CARE, FIRM, REGARD, RELATE, SAKE, WORRY
concerning ABOUT, ANEN(S)T, FOR, (IN)RE
concert hall ACADEMY, CARNEGIE, MASSEY
conciliate (APP)EASE, PACIFY, PLACATE
conciliatory GENTLE, IRENIC, WINNING
concise CURT, PITHY, TERSE
conclude DEDUCE, FINISH, INFER, REST, SETTLE
conclusion CODA, END, FINIS, RESULT
conclusive COGENT, FINAL, TELLING
concoct BREW, COOK, HATCH, MIX
concord AMITY, PACT, RAPPORT
concordat COMPACT, ENTENTE, TREATY
concrete ACTUAL, BETON, CEMENT, HARD, MORTAR
condemn BAN, BLAME, DECRY, DOOM, FILE
condense COMPRESS, CUT, DECOCT, DISTIL(L), SHRINK
condescend DEIGN, FAVOR, STOOP
condiment see p. 123
condition FACET, IF, PHASE, PLIGHT, PROVISO, STATUS, TERM
conduce AID, EFFECT, LEND, TEND
conduct CONVEY, CONVOY, DEMEAN, ESCORT, MANAGE, RUN
conductor BERNSTEIN, CARRIER, CICERONE, GUIDE, KARAJAN, LEADER, LEINSDORF, MAESTRO, SCHERCHEN, STOKOWSKI, SZELL, TOSCANINI, WALTER

conduit ADIT, CHANNEL, DRAIN, DUCT, MAIN
cone CONOID, COP, CORNET, FUNNEL, STROBILE
confection BONBON, CIMBAL, COMFIT, DULCE, FONDANT, NOUGAT, PRALINE, SWEET(MEAT)
confederate ABETTOR, ALLY, PARTNER, REB(EL), UNITE
confer AWARD, BESTOW, DUB, ENDOW, PARLEY
conference CONFAB, PALAVER, SYNOD
confess ADMIT, OWN, REVEAL, SHRIVE
confession AVOWAL, CREDO, CREED, SHRIFT
confide AFFY, COMMIT, (EN)TRUST, INTRUST
confidential ESOTERIC, PRIVY, SECRET
confine BORDER, BOX, CAGE, CHECK, COOP, CRAMP, DAM, HEM, INTERN, JAIL, LIMIT, PEN
confined ABED, ILL, PENT
confirm ENDORSE, RATIFY, VERIFY
conflict BOUT, FRAY, OPPOSE, WAR
confound BAFFLE, FAZE, NONPLUS, STUN
confront BRAVE, DEFY, FACE
confuse ABASH, BEMUSE, FLUSTER, FUDDLE, JUMBLE, NONPLUS
confused ADDLED, ASEA, MUZZY, WESTY
confusion BABEL, CHAOS, MESS, SNAFU
congeal GEL, HARDEN, JELL, PECTIZE, SET
congratulate LAUD, MACORIZE, SALUTE
congregation FLOCK, FOLD, PARISH, TEMPLE
congress DIET, DUMA, MAJLIS, MOD, RADA, SETAN, SOVIET
conifer CEDAR, FIR, LARCH, PINE, SPRUCE
conjecture ETTLE, POSIT, SURMISE, THEORY
conjunction AND, BUT, JOIN, NOR, SINCE, THAN, TIE, UNION
conjurer DOWSER, EXORCIST, MAGICIAN, SHAMAN, VOODOO
connect (AF)FIX, COUPLE, GLUE, JOIN, LINK
connection BOND, LINK, NEXUS
connubial CONJUGAL, MARITAL
conquer LICK, MASTER, SUBDUE
conscious AWAKE, (A)WARE, SENTIMENT
conscript DRAFT(EE), LEVY, MUSTER, RECRUIT
consecrate ANOINT, BLESS, HALLOW, SAIN, TABOO
consecrated OBLATE, SACRED
consent ACCEDE, COMPLY, CONCUR
consequence END, IMPORT, OUTCOME, RESULT, SEQUEL
conservative DIEHARD, SAFE, TORY
consider DEEM, MUSE, RATE, REFLECT, STUDY, TREAT
consignee BROKER, FACTOR, RECEIVER
consolation BOOBY, SOLACE, SOP
console BRACE, CABINET, CALM, CHEER, COMFORT
consolidate COMBINE, FUSE, KNIT, MERGE
consonant ATONIC, DENTAL, FORTIS, LENE, LENIS, SPIRANT, SURD
conspicuous BLATANT, OVERT, PATENT, SALIENT, SIGNAL
conspiracy CABAL, COUP, INTRIGUE, JUNTO
conspirator BRUTUS, CASSIUS, FAWKES, SABOTEUR
conspire CABAL, COLLUDE, COMPLOT, PLOT, SCHEME
constable BEADLE, BULL, COP, SLOP
constant FAST, LOYAL, STAUNCH, STILL
constellations see p. 277
constitution CHARTER, CODE, HEALTH, IRONSIDES, MAKEUP, NATURE
constraint BOND, DURESS, FORCE
constrict ASTRINGE, CHOKE, CRAMP, NARROW, SHRINK
constrictor BOA, SPHINCTER
construe INFER, PARSE
consume BURN, EAT, SPEND, USE, WASTE, WEAR
consummate ACHIEVE, ARRANT, END, SHEER, WHOLE
consumption PHTHISIS, USE, WASTE
contain CHECK, EMBODY, HOLD, SUBSUME
container BAG, BOTTLE, BOX, CAGE, CAN, CARTON, CASE, CUP, JAR, POUCH, TIN, TUB, URN, VAT
contaminate DEFILE, POISON, POLLUTE, SPOIL, SULLY, TAINT
contemporaneous COEVAL, CURRENT
contemptible ABJECT, BASE, LOW, MEAN, SORRY, VILE

contend ARGUE, CLAIM, COMPETE, COPE, DEAL, VIE, WAR
content GIST, REPLETE, SATED
contest (AF)FRAY, AGON, BOUT, DISPUTE, JOUST, ROLEO, TOURNEY
continent ATLANTIS, CASCADIA, CHASTE, LEMURIA, SOBER
continue ENDURE, LAST, PERDURE
continued CHRONIC, SERIAL
contort GNARL, TWIST, WRAP
contract CATCH, DEAL, INCUR, SHRINK
contradict BELIE, DENY, GAINSAY, IMPUGN, NEGATE, REBUT
contribution ALMS, BOON, GIFT, PRESENT, TAX, TITHE
contrite HUMBLE, RUEFUL, SORRY
contrive DEVISE, HATCH, MANAGE, PLOT
control CHECK, CURB, HANK, REIGN, STEER, SWAY
controversial ERISTIC, POLEMIC(AL)
controversy DEBATE, DISPUTE
conundrum ENIGMA, POSER, RIDDLE
convent ABBEY, CLOISTER, MATH, NUNNERY
conventional FORMAL, NOMIC, PROPER
conversation CAUSERIE, DIALOG, PALAVER
convert ALTER, ANSAR, GER, PROSELYTE
convex ARCHED, GIBBOUS
convey ASSIGN, CEDE, TRANSFER
conveyance CAR, DEED, DEMISE, WAFTAGE
convict CONDEMN, FELON, LIFER, TERMER
convivial FESTAL, GAY, GENIAL
convoy CONDUCT, ESCORT, PILOT
convulsion FIT, SPASM, THROE
cook CHEF, MAGIRIST, SHIR(R)
cooking, art of CUISINE, MAGIRICS
cool CALM, CHILL, GELID, ICE, NERVY
coop COTE, (EN)CASE, HUTCH, JAIL, MEW, PEN, STY
cop BOBBY, BULL, FLIC, GENDARME, PEELER
copal ANIME, RESIN
copious LUSH, PROFUSE, REPLETE
copper BOBBY, CENT, CUPRUM
copper alloy OROIDE, RHEOTAN
copse BOSK, COPPICE, HOLT
copy APE, CARBON, DRAFT, ECTYPE, ESTREAT, MODEL
cord AEA, AGAL, HEDDLE, LINE, RAIP, ROPE, TENDON, TORSADE, WELT
core AME, GIST, HEART, NAVE, NIFE, NOWEL, PITH
cork BOBBER, SHIVE, STOPPLE
corn CLAVUS, MAIZE, SALT
corn meal MASA, SOFK(I)
corner ANGLE, HERNE, INGLE, NICHE, NOOK, TREE
cornerstone COIGN(E), COIN, COYN, QUOIN
cornice ASTRAGAL, DRIP
Cornish prefix LAN, ROS, TRE
corolla PERIANTH, PETAL(S)
corona AUREOLA, AUREOLE, CIGAR, FILLET, SCYPHUS
corporeal BODILY, HYLIC, SOMATIC
corpse CADAVER, CARCASS, MUMMY, STIFF
corpulent BURLY, OBESE, PORTLY
corral ATAJO, PEN, POUND, STY
correct ADJUST, (A)MEND, (A)RIGHT, CHASTEN, EDIT, EMEND, OKAY, REVISE
corrode BURN, DECAY, EAT, ERODE, GNAW, RUST
corrosive ACID, CAUSTIC, MORDANT
corrupt DEBASE, SPOIL, VENAL, VILE, VITIATE
corsair PICAROON, PIRATE
corset BUSK, STAY(S)
cortex BARK, RIND
cosmetic CERUSE, HENNA, KOHL, MASCARA, ROUGE
cosmic order RITA
coterie CLIQUE, JUNTO, SET
cottage BARI, CABIN, CHALET
cotton measure HANK, LEA
couch DAVENPORT, DIVAN, HIDE, LAIR, SETTEE, SOFA
cough HACK, TUSSIS
council CABINET, FONO, SYNOD, WITAN
counsel(or) CHIDE, LAWYER, MENTOR, NESTOR, PROCTOR, REDE, WARN
count CENSUS, COMES, EARL, GRAF, RECKON, RELY, SCORE, TALLY, TOT(AL)
countenance ABET, FACE, VISAGE
counter BAR, CHECK, CHIP, CONTEND, GEIGER, SHELF
counterfeit BOGUS, FAKE, FORGE, PHONY, SHAM
countermand RESCIND, REVOKE
counterpart COPY, DOUBLE, PENDANT, REPLICA, TWIN

countersink BEVEL, CHAMFER, REAM
country LAND, PAIS, VALE, WEALD, WILD
country, pert. to AGRESTIC, RURAL, RUSTIC
county AMT, FYLKE, LAN, PARISH, SHIRE
coup BLOW, PUTSCH, SCOOP, STROKE
couple BRACE, DYAD, GEMINI, PAIR, SPAN, TWINS, TWO
coupled GEMEL(ED), WEDDED, YOKED
couplet DISTICH
courage GRIT, GUTS, METTLE, NERVE, PLUCK, SPUNK, VALOR
courier ESTAFET(TE), GUIDE
course CYCLE, ENTREE, LAP, LEG, ROAD, ROTE, ROUTE, TACK, WAY
court assistant AMALA, AMLAH, CLERK, CRIER, ELISOR, EYRE, JURY, TALESMAN
court president FOUD
courtly AULIC, ELEGANT, HEND(E)
court(s) BAR, CURIA, CURRY, DAIRO, DARI, FORA, FORUM, FAVOR, GEMOT(E), LEET, PALACE, PARVIS, PATIO, PROBATE, ROTA, SUE, TRIBUNAL, WOO, YARD
couturier BALMAIN, CARDIN, CHANEL, DIOR, PUCCI, RICCI
covered AWASH, FLOODED
cover(ing) CAP, CEIL, COSY, HIDE, HUSK, LID, PEEL, PELAGE, PELT, QUILT, RIND, SEAL, SKIN, TEG(U)MEN, THATCH
covet CRAVE, ENVY, PINE, YISSE
covey BEVY, BROOD, FLOCK
cow BOSSY, BOVINE, BULLY, KINE, VACHE
coward CRAVEN, POLTROON
cowboy GAUCHO, HERDER, LLANERO, VAQUERO
cowlike COUS
coxcomb FOP, NOB, SWELL, TOFF
coy ARCH, CHARY, DEMURE
coypu NUTRIA
cozy HOMEY, QUILT, SNUG
crack CHAP, CHINK, CLEFT, JOKE, KIBE, RIFT, SNAP
cradle CADER, CRECHE, SLEE
craft ART, METIER, POLICE, TALENT, TRADE
craftsman ARTISAN, NAVVY, WRIGHT
crafty FOXY, SLY, TRICKY, WILY
crag ARETE, BRACK, SCAR, TOR
cramp ART, KINK, STITCH
crane DAVIT, GIB, GRUS, JENNY, JIB
crank BRACE, HANDLE, WINCH
cranky CROSS, GROUCHY, TESTY
crash BURST, CLOTH, FAIL(URE), LINEN
crate CRADLE, ENCASE, HAMPER
crater CALDERA, CONE, LINNE, PIT
crave HANKER, LONG, PINE
craw CROP, MAW
crawl FAWN, GROVEL, INCH
crayon CHALK, PASTEL, PENCIL
craze FAD, FUROR, MADDEN, MANIA, RAGE
crazy AMOK, DAFFY, DAFT, DOTTY, LOCO, LOONY, LUNY, MANIC, POTTY, REE, WACKY
crease CRIMP, RUCK, SEAM, STRIA
creature BEING, MINION, WRETCH
credit ASCRIBE, IMPUTE, TICK, TRUST
credit transfer GIRO
creed CREDO, DOGMA, FAITH, ISM, NICENE, TENET
creek BAYOU, GEO, GIO, KILL, RIA, RITO, RUN, VLEI
creep CRAWL, FAWN, INCH, TINGLE
creeper IVY, SNAKE, VINE, WORM
creeping REPENT, REPTANT
cremate CALCINE
cremation SUTTEE
crescent(-shaped) CUSP, LUNAR, LUNATE, LUNE, LUNULA, MOON
crest ARETE, COMB, CROWN, PEAK, RIDGE, TOP, TOR, TUFT
crested CRISTATE(D), PILEATE
crevice CLEFT, CRANNY, RIME
crew BAND, GANG, HANDS, MEN, MOB, OARS, TEAM
crib BIN, CRECHE, PONY, TROT
cribbage term GO, HEELS, NOBS, PEG
cricket term BYE, EDGER, OFFS, ONS, TICE, YORK
crime ARSON, FELONY, SIMONY, SIN, VICE
criminal CONVICT, FELON, NOCENT
crimp CURL, FRIZ(Z), GOFFER
crimson CARMINE, LAC, RED
cripple(d) HALT, IMPAIR, LAME
critic BOOER, CARPER, CENSOR
criticism ZOILISM
criticize CARP, FLAY, PAN, ROAST, SLATE
crone BELDAM(E), EWE, HAG, WITCH
crook BEND, CROSIER, CURVE, PEDA, PEDUM, (POT)HOOK

crooked AGEE, AKIMBO, ASKEW, (A)WRY, BENT, CORRUPT
crop(s) CRAW, GEBBIE, HARVEST, MAW, RABI, REAP, ROWEN
cross ANKH, CELTIC, CRUX, FYLFOT, IRATE, LATIN, MALTESE, POTENT, ROOD, SALTIER, SALTIRE, SWASTIKA, TAU, TRIAL
crossbeam TRAVE, TREVE
crosspiece CLEAT, EVENER, RUNG
cross-stroke SERIF
crossthreads WEFT, WOOF
cross timber SPALE
crowbar JIMMY, PRY
crowd CRAM(P), MOB, RUCK, SERRY
crown BAY, CAP, CORONA(TE), CORONET, CREST, DIADEM, PATE, TAJ, TIARA
crucial point CRISIS, CRUX, PIVOT
crucible CRUSET, RETORT
crude COARSE, CRASS, RAW
cruel BESTIAL, FELL, FERAL, SAVAGE
cruet AMA, AMPULLA, CASTER, CRUSE, VIAL
crusade CAMPAIGN, JAHAD, JIHAD
crusader PILGRIM, TEMPLAR
crusader foe SALADIN, SARACEN, TURK
crush MASH, PRESS, SUBDUE
crust CORTEX, SCAB, SCALE
crustacean see p. 214
cry COOEE, COOEY, FAD, MEWL, OYES, OYEZ, PULE, RAGE, SNIVEL, WAIL, WEEP
crystal CLEAR, DIAMOND, ICE
crystal gaze SCRY
cube DICE, DIE, NASIK, TESSELLA, TESSERA
cubicle ALCOVE, CARREL, CELL, NICHE
cud BOLUS, CHEW, QUID, RUMEN
cudgel BASTE, BAT, CLUB, DRUB, STAVE, TOWEL
cue HINT, NOD, PRESA, ROD, SIGNAL, TAIL, TIP
cull DUPE, GLEAN, PLUCK, SELECT, WINNOW
culmination ACME, APEX, APOGEE, AUGE, CLIMAX, NOON, VERTEX, ZENITH
cult FAD, ISM, MANIA, SECT
cultivate EAR, FARM, HARROW, HOE, NURSE, PLOW, RATOON, TILL
cultivation JOOM, JUM, TILTH
culture AGAR, POLISH, TILLAGE
cunning ART(FUL), CALLID, CRAFTY, CUTE, D(A)EDAL, FOXY, GUILE, SLY, WILY
cup AMA, CHARK, COTULA, CRUSE, CUPEL, DEPAS, DOP, GODET, GRAIL, HOLMOS, LOTA(H), MAZER, NOGGIN, TASS, TIG, TROPHY, TYG
cupbearer HEBE, SAKI
Cupid AMOR, DAN, EROS, LOVE
curare OORALI, URALI
curd CASEIN(E), CONGEAL, CRUD
curdle CLABBER, POSSET, RENNET, SAM
cure CORN, HEAL, REMEDY, SMOKE
cure-all ELIXIR, PANACEA
Curia court ROTA, SIGNATURA
curio BIBELOT, VIRTU
curious NOSY, ODD, SNOOPY
curl BERGER, COIL, FEAK, FRIZ, KINK, RINGLET, TRESS
curling term BESOM, BUTTON, HACK, HOG, HOUSE, PATLID, PORT, SOOP, TEE, WICK
curly KINKY, OUNDY, UNDY, WAVY
current COURSE, EDDY, PRESENT, RAPID, RIFE, STREAM, TIDE
curse ANATHEM(A), HEX, MALISON, OATH, REVILE
curt BLUNT, BRUSK, BRUSQUE, GRUFF, SQUAB
curtail LOP, PARE, REDUCE
curtsy DIP, SALAAM, SCRAPE
curve ARC(H), BEND, BOW, CROOK, ELLIPSE, ESS, HOEK, OGEE, PARABOLA, SINUS, SNY
curved ADUNC, CONCAVE, CONVEX, NOWY
cushion BOLSTER, HASSOCK, PAD
custard apple ANNONA
custody CHARGE, DURANCE, TRUST
custom(s) CESS, DASTUR, DUTY, LEVY, MORES, RITUS, SUNNA(H), TARIFF, TAX, TOLL, URE, USAGE, WONT
cut CARVE, CLEAVE, DICE, DOCK, DOD, ESCARP(E), FELL, GASH, HACK, HEW, KERF, LESION, LOP, MOW, NIG, REAP, SCARP, SEVER, SHEAR, SLASH, SLICE, SLISH, SLIT, SNEE, SNIP, TREPAN, TRIM
cut down RASEE, RAZEE
cut in half BISECT, HALVE, SECANT
cut off ELIDE, ROACH, SNIP
cutting INCISAL, MORDANT, SCION, SECANT, SHARP
cycle BIKE, ROUND, SAROS
cyclone BAGUIO, TYPHOON

Cyclopes ARGES, BRONTES, POLYPHEMUS
cylinder BARREL, GAVION, INKER, PISTON, PLATEN
cylindrical TERETE
cyma GOLA, GULA, OGEE
Cymric WELSH
cyst BAG, POUCH, SAC, WEN

D

dabbler DUFFER, SCIOLIST, TRIFLER
Dadaist ARP, BALL, DUCHAMP, ERNST, GROSZ, PICABIA, TZARA
dado BASE, DIE, SOLIDUM
dagger see p. 108
daily ADAY, DIURNAL
dainty CATE, CHOICE, PETITE
dairy LACTARIUM
dais ESTRADE, ROSTRUM
dam DIKE, PARENT, PEN, SADD, SUDD, WAER, WEIR; see p. 167
damp DANK, MOIST, WET
dance BAL(L), PARTY, PROM
dance step CHASSE, GLISSADE, PAS
dancer ALMA, ALME, ALMEH, ASTAIRE, BOLGER, GEISHA, GRAHAM, KELLY, NIJINSKY, PAVLOVA, RASCH, SHAWN, STDENIS, ULANOVA, WIGMAN
dandruff SCURF
dandy BEAU, BUCK, DUDE, FINE, FOP, JAKE, SWELL, TOFF
Dane JUTLANDER
dank DAMP, HUMID, MOIST, WET
dapper CHIC, NATTY, NIFTY
dapple FLECK, PIED, SPOT
dare BRAVE, DEFY, FACE, OSSE, RISK, VENTURE
dark DISMAL, DUSKY, EBON, MIRKY, MURKY, SOMBRE, SWART, UNLIT
darkness GLOOM, MIRK, MURK
darling ACUSHLA, ASTHORE, CHERI(E), PET, ROON
dart ELANCE, FLIT, SCOOT
dash ELAN, HURTLE, HYPHEN, LACE, SOUPCON, TINGE, TOUCH, TRACE, VERVE
date CALENDS, COURT, IDES, NONE(S), OUTMODE, TRYST
daub APPLY, PLASTER, TEER
daunt AMATE, AWE, COW, DAW
davit CRANE, SPAR
dawn AURORA, DEW, EOS, SUNUP
dawn, pert. to EOAN
day DIES, YOM
dead (A)MORT, EXPIRED, FEY, FLAT, GONE, INERT, LATE, NAPOO
dead tree(s) DRIKI, RAMPIKE
deadlock DRAW, IMPASSE, TIE
deadly FATAL, LETHAL, MORT(AL)
deadly sins ANGER, COVETOUSNESS, ENVY, GLUTTONY, LUST, PRIDE, SLOTH
deafness AMUSIA, SURDITY
dealer AGENT, CO(O)PER, CUTLER, DRAPER, HOUSE, MERCER, MONGER, TRADER, VINTNER
dean DECAN, DOYEN(NE), ELDER
dean, pert. to DECANAL
dearth DROUGHT, FAMINE, PAUCITY, WANT
death DEMISE, FINIS, MORT
death notice OBIT
debase ALLOY, DEMEAN, LOWER
debate AGON, CANVASS, MOOT
debauchee RAKE, ROUE, SATYR
debility ATONY, FRAILTY
debris LITTER, RUBBISH, RUINS, SCREE
debt ARREARS, DUE, DUTY, IOU
decamp ABSCOND, BOLT, ELOPE, LAM, LEVANT, SCRAM, VAMO(O)SE
decanter CARAFE, CROFT, EWER
decay BLET, CARIES, CONK, PUTREFY
deceased DEFUNCT, GONE, LATE
deceit COVIN, FEINT, FRAUD, GUILE, SHAM, WILE
deceive BILK, COZEN, DUPE, FLAM, GAMMON, GULL, HUMBUG, ILLUDE, SILE, TRICK
deceiver FAKER, IMPOSTOR, LIAR, SHARPER, TRAPAN
decent MODEST, PROPER, SEEMLY
deception FAKE, HOAX, JAPE, RUSE, SHAM, WILE
deceptive HOLLOW, SERENIC, VAGUE
decide CERN, ELECT, RESOLVE
decimal REPETEND, TEN(TH)
deck ADORN, CARDS, DIZEN, ORLOP, PACK, POOP
declaim BLEEZE, ORATE, RANT, RAVE
declare AVER, AVOUCH, AVOW, BID, MELD, STATE
decline DEMUR, DIP, DROOP, EBB, FADE, REFUSE, SINK, SLUMP, SPURN, TABES
declivity CALADE, SCARP, SLANT, SLOPE
decorate ADORN, (BE)DECK, MINIATE

decoration DSC, DSM, DSO, MEDAL, PURFLE, RIBBON, TINSEL

decorous DEMURE, SEEMLY, STAID

decoy CAPPER, LURE, PLANT, TOLE

decrease ABATE, DWINDLE, EBB, LESSEN, RECEDE, WANE

decree ACT, ARRET, BULL, CANON, DICTUM, EDICT, FIAT, FIRMAN, IRADE, LAW, MANDATE, UKASE, WILL, WRIT

deduce DEEM, DERIVE, INFER

deduct BATE, FAIK, REBATE

deed(s) ACTA, CEDE, COUP, FACT, FAIT, FEAT, GEST(E), STROKE

deep BASS, SEA, WISE

deer, pert. to CERVINE, DAMINE

defame DECRY, LIBEL, MALIGN, SLANDER, VILIFY

default FAIL, MORA, WELCH

defeat BEST, FAILURE, FOIL, LICK, MATE, ROUT, WORST

defect BUG, DESERT, FLAW, SCOB, SNAG

defendant CHAMPION, REUS

defense ALIBI, PALISADE, SEPIMENT

deference FEALTY, HOMAGE, RESPECT

deficiency DEARTH, ULLAGE

deflect DIVERT, SWERVE, VEER

deform MAIM, MAR, WARP

defraud BILK, CHEAT, CHOUSE, COZEN, GULL, GYP

defy BEARD, DARE, FLOUT

degree(s) BSC, CLASS, DDS, DSC, EDD, LITTD, LLD, NTH, PHD, PITCH, RADIAN, RATE, STEP

dehydrate DRY, JERK, PARCH

deity GOD(DESS), NUMEN

delay ARREST, DEFER, DETAIN, LINGER, MORA(E), SLOW, STALL, WAIT

delegate AGENT, DEPUTY, ENVOY, LEGATE

deletion APOCOPE, DELE, EXCISION

delicacy CATE, FINESSE, TIDBIT

delight AMUSE, CHARM, GLEE, MIRTH, REVEL

delirious MAD, RAVING, REE

dell DALE, DINGLE, GLEN

deluge FLOOD, PLETHORA, SPATE

delusion MIRAGE, MOHA, VISION

delve DIG, DIP, GRUB, MINE, PROBE, SPADE

demand CLAIM, DUN, INSIST, NEED, SOLICIT

demeanor AIR, CARRIAGE, MIEN

demigod HERO, IDOL, SATYR

demolish LEVEL, RASE, RAZE, RUIN, UNDO, WRECK

demon(s) ABIGOR, AFREET, AFRIT(E), AITU, ANITO, ALP, ASURA, ATUA, DAEDAL, DAITYA, DEUCE, DEV(A), DEVIL, EBLIS, FIEND, GENIE, GHOUL, GOBLIN, IMP, JANN, JIN(N), JINNI, LAMIA, MARA, NAT, OGRE, RAHU, SHAITAN, SHEITAN, TROLL, WADE

demure COY, MIM, PRIM, SHY, STAID

den CAVEA, CAVE(RN), DIVE, LAIR, STUDY

denomination CLASS, SCHOOL, SECT

dense CLOSE, CRASS, DULL, HEAVY, OBTUSE, THICK

dent EFFECT, NICK, NOTCH

dental ODONTIC, ORAL

denture BRIDGE, PLATE, TEETH

deny ABJURE, DISOWN, GAINSAY, NEGATE, REFUSE

depart BEGONE, DECAMP, DIE, EXIT, SCRAM, VADE, VAMO(O)SE

departure EXIT, EXODUS, HEGIRA, OUTGANG

dependent MINION, SPONGER, SUBJECT

depict DRAW, LIMN, PORTRAY

depilate HUSK, PLUCK, SHAVE

depilatory RUSMA

deplore (BE)WAIL, GRIEVE, RUE

deport BAN(ISH), CARRY, EXILE, EXPEL

depose AVER, OUST, UNSEAT

deposit ALLUVIA, BED, CACHE, DELTA, DREGS, GEEST, LODE, MARL, PLACER, SILT, SINTER, TARTAR

depository CACHE, DEPOT, SAFE, VAULT

depress DAMPEN, DENT, SINK

depression BLUES, COL, DIP, DUMPS, ENNUI, FOVEA, GLOOM, PIT

deprived (BE)REFT, SHORN

deputy AGENT, ENVOY, FACTOR, PROXY, VICAR

derelict ASTRAY, CASTAWAY, SLACK, TRAMP, WAIF, WRECK

deride FLEER, GIBE, JEER, JIBE, MOCK, RAZZ, TAUNT

derrick CRANE, DAVIT, RIG, STEEVE

derrick part BOOM, GIN, LEG

descendants GENS, ISSUE, PROGENY, (S)CIONS, SONS

descent BIRTH, SCARP, SLOPE

descry BETRAY, ESPY, KEN

desert ABANDON, BARREN, DUE, LEAVE, QUIT, WASTE, WILD

desert, pert. to EREMIC
deserter RAT, RECREANT, RENEGADE, TURNCOAT
desiccated ARID, DRY, SERE
design AIM, END, INTENT(ION), MOTIF, PLAN
desire ASPIRE, COVET, CRAVE, LIBIDO, LUST, URGE, WANT, YEN
desirous EAGER, FAIN
desk, reading AMBO, LECTERN
desolate BLEAK, DREARY, LORN, RAZE, SACK
despise ABHOR, CONTEMN, SPURN
destiny DOOM, EURE, FATE, KARMA, KISMET, LOT
destroy RASE, SACK, UNDO, WRECK
destroyed KAPUT
destruction HAVOC, STR(O)Y, TALA
detach SEVER, SUNDER, WEAN
detail ITEM(IZE), NICETY, PATROL, SPECIFY
detain ARREST, CHECK, DELAY, INTERN, NAB
detecting device DOWSER, RADAR, SONAR
detective BEAGLE, DICK, HAWKSHAW, SLEUTH, TAILER, TEC
detent CATCH, CLICK, DOG, PAWL, RATCHET, STOP, STUD
deteriorate IMPAIR, WORSEN
determine DECIDE, FIX, JUDGE, RESOLVE
detonator CAP, EXPLODER, SQUIB
devastate RAZE, SACK, WASTE
deviate DIGRESS, ERR, HADE, MUTATE, SHIFT, STRAY, SWERVE, WARP, YAW
devil AZAZEL, BELIAL, BENG, CHORT, DEMON(ESS), DEUCE, DICKENS, DULE, EBLIS, FIEND, GOBLIN, HUGON, IMP, LUCIFER, OGRE, SATAN, SHAITAN
devise AIM, CONCOCT, FRAME, SCHEME, WILL
devotee BIGOT, BUFF, FAN, IST, VOTARY, ZEALOT
devotion ARDOR, FEALTY, FERVOR, NOVENA, PIETY
dewlap FOLD, PALEA, WATTLE
dewy MOIST, RORAL, RORIC
dexterity ART, FINESSE, KNACK
dexterous ADROIT, APT, DEFT, HANDY
diagram CHART, DRAFT, EPURE
dialect ARGOT, CANT, IDIOM, JARGON, LINGO, PATOIS
diameter BORE, CALIBER, MODULE
diamond CARBON, GEM, LOZENGE
diaphragm, pert. to PHRENIC
diary JOURNAL, LOG, RECORD
Diaspora GALUTH, GOLAH
diatribe HARANGUE, JEREMIAD, SCREED, TIRADE
dice CHOP, CUBE, MINCE
dice term AMBSACE, BONES, BOXCAR, COG, COME, CRAPS, DICK, FADE, FIELD, JOE, MISS, NATURAL, NICK, PHOEBE, POINT, ROLL, SHOOT, SICE, SISE
Dickens characters see p. 180
dictator CAESAR, FRANCO, HITLER, MIKADO, PERON, SALAZAR, SHOGUN, STALIN, SULLA, TRUJILLO, TYRANT
die CUBE, DADO, DOD, EXPIRE, PERISH, SICCA, STAMP, TAT, TESSERA
diet BANT, CONGRESS, FARE, REGIME(N)
difference EPACT, NUANCE, ODDS
different DIVERS(E), OTHER, SUNDRY
difficulty DILEMMA, FIX, JAM, KNOT, NODE, PICKLE, RUB, SCRAPE
dig DELVE, GRUB, JAB, PION
digest ABSORB, APERCU, EPITOME, PANDECT, PRECIS
digit CIPHER, FINGER, INTEGER, TOE
dike DITCH, JETTY, LEVEE
dilate DISTEND, SWELL, WIDEN
dilatory LAX, REMISS, SLOW, TARDY
dilemma FIX, JAM, PICKLE
dilettante AMATEUR, DABBLER
dill ANET, ANISE, FENNEL
dilute RAREFY, THIN, WEAKEN
dim BLEAR, DUSKY, FADE, FAINT
diminish (A)BATE, EBB, PETER, PLOY, SINK, TAPER, WANE
diminutive suffix (C)ULE, EL, ET(TE), IE, IN, ITA, KIN(S), LET, LING, OCK
dingle DALE, DELL, GLEN
dingy DRAB, GRIMY, OURIE
dining room CENACLE, MESS, OECUS, REFECTORY, SPENCE
diocese BISHOPRIC, SEE
Dioscuri ANACES, ANAX, CASTOR, POLLUX, TWINS
dip BAIL, DAP, DIB, DOPP, DOUSE, DUNK, LADE, MERSE
diplomacy FINESSE, PROTOCOL, TACT
diplomat ATTACHE, CONSUL, EMISSARY, ENVOY, LEGATE, MINISTER, NUNCIO, PROXENUS

direct AIM, CONN, LEVEL, OPEN, PILOT, POINT, STEER
directory BLUEBOOK, LIST, ORDO, REGISTER
dirge KEEN, LINOS, LINUS, THRENODY, TRENTAL
disable GRUEL, MAIM, SAP
disappear EVANESCE, VANISH
disavow DENY, DISOWN, RECANT
disbeliever ATHEIST, SKEPTIC, THOMAS
discard ABANDON, JUNK, MOLT, REJECT, SCRAP, SLUFF
discern DESCRY, DETECT, KEN
discernment ACUMEN, TACT
discharge DROP, EJECT, EMIT, EXPEL, FIRE, OUST, SACK
disciple CHELA, PUPIL; see p. 113
disciplinarian MARTINET, TYRANT
disclaim ABJURE, DENY, DISOWN
discolored DOTY, LIVID, USTULATE
discomfort DISTRESS, MALAISE
disconcert ABASH, FAZE, RATTLE
discount AGIO, BATTA, IGNORE, REBATE
discourse DESCANT, HOMILY, PR(A)ELECT, SERMON
discover DISCERN, (E)SPY, UNEARTH
discriminate SECERN
discuss DEBATE, DILATE, MOOT, TREAT
discussion group FORUM, PANEL, SEMINAR
disease, pert. to CLINIC, LOIMIC
diseases see p. 106
disease spreader CARRIER, VECTOR
disembark DEPLANE, DETRAIN, LAND
disencumber DETACH, FREE, RID
disengage FREE, PART, WEAN
disgrace ABASE, ODIUM, SCANDAL, SHEND, STIGMA
disguise MASK, MUMM, SHAM
dish BOWL, CHARGER, COMAL, COMPOTE, COMPOTIER, CRUSE, GIRL, LANX, PATEN, PATINA, PLATE, PLATTER, RAMEKIN, SAUCER, SERVE, TUREEN, VESSEL
dishearten AMATE, DAUNT, DETER
disinfectant CRESOL, IODIN(E), LYSOL, PEROXIDE, PHENOL
disinter EXHUME, UNBURY, UNEARTH
disk ATEN, DIAL, HARROW, PATEN, PLATE, PLATTER, PUCK, RECORD, SEQUIN, SPUT, WAFER
dislocate DISPLACE, LUXATE, SPLAY
dismal DREAR(Y), SOMBRE
dismantle RAZE, STRIP, UNRIG
dismay APPAL(L), DAUNT, FAZE
dismiss CASHIER, DEMIT, FIRE, IGNORE, OUST, REMUE
dismounted ALIT, DISLODGED
disorder CLUTTER, DERAY, JUMBLE, LITTER, MESS, SNARL
disparage DECRY, MALIGN, SLUR
dispatch CABLE, HASTE, KILL, NOTE, POST, SEND
dispel BANISH, EJECT, OUST
dispensation ABSOLUTION, EXEMPTION, PROVISION, RELEASE
dispense DOLE, EXEMPT, FOREGO
display ARRAY, EVINCE, EXHIBIT, FLAUNT, OSTENT, PARADE, POSE, SHEW, VAUNT
displease ANGER, ANNOY, MIFF, OFFEND, PIQUE, PROVOKE
disposed BENT, PRONE, READY, TENDING
dispossess DIVEST, EJECT, EVICT, OUST
disprove NEGATE, REBUT, REFUTE
dispute CARP, HAGGLE, HIGGLE
dissenter HERETIC, RECUSANT, SECTARY
dissertation ESSAY, SERMON, THESIS, TRACT, TREATISE
dissolute LEWD, LOOSE, RAKISH
dissolve DISBAND, MELT, VANISH
dissonant ATONAL
distant (A)FAR, ALOOF, AWAY, BEYOND, REMOTE, YON
distilling device ALEMBIC, MATRASS, RETORT, STILL
distortion TWIST, WARP, WRYNESS
distraint NAAM, POIND
distribute ALLOT, DEAL, DOLE, JOB, METE, RATION
district AREA, BELT, CANTON, CIRCUIT, DEMESNE, GAU, FIELT, MIAO, PALE, PRECINCT, SECTOR, SOC, SOKE, WARD, WICK, ZONE
disturb FAZE, MOLEST, ROIL
disturbance FRACAS, HUBBUB, RIOT, ROW, TUMULT
ditch DIKE, DRAIN, FLUME, FOSS(E), MOAT, RELAIS, RINE, SAP, SLUICE, TAJO, ZANJE
divan COURT, LEEWAN, SALOON, SETTEE, SOFA
dive BACKFLIP, DEN, DROP, GAINER, HEADER, SPIN
diverge DEVIATE, FORK, VARY
divert AMUSE, DECEIVE, PARRY
divest BARE, DENUDE, DEPRIVE, DOFF, STRIP, TIRL

divide BISECT, FORK, HALVE, REND, RIVE, SUNDER
divided APART, CLEFT, PARTITE, REFT, SPLIT
dividend BONUS, MELON, PLUM, SHARE
divider BUNTON, COMPASS, MERIST
divination AUGURY, DOWSING, OMEN, SORS, SORTES
divining rod DOWSER, WAND
divinity ADONAI, DEITY, ELOHIM, GODHEAD, IDOL, JAH, JEHOVAH, THEOLOGY, YAHWE
division COHORT, EOGAEA, FRACTION, H(S)IEN, MEER, MERE, MITOSIS, SCHISM, SEGMENT
divorce law GET(T), TALAK
dizziness SCOTOMY, VERTIGO
dizziness, pert. to DINIC(AL)
docile GENTLE, PLIANT, TAME
dock BASIN, BERTH, DEDUCT, FINE, JETTY, PEN, PIER, QUAY, SLIP, WHARF
doctor CORONER, FALSIFY, INTERN(E), LEECH, MEDICO, TREAT
doctrine CREED, CULT(US), DOGMA, ISM, MAXIM, RITE, SECT, TENET, THEORY
dodge DUCK, EVADE, PARRY
dog ARGUS, ASTA, BELKA, CATCH, CHECKERS, CLEO, FALA, FOOT, GARM(R), LAIKA, LASSIE, RASCAL, RINTINTIN, SHADOW, TIGE, TOBY, TRACK, TRAIL
dog chaps FLEWS
dogma CREED, DICTA, DOCTRINE, ISM, TENET
dole ALMS, GRIEF, METE, RELIEF
dollar BEAN, BILL, BUCK, SIMOLEON, TALER, WHEEL
dolt ASS, CLOD, COOT, DUNCE, LOUT, NINNY, NUMP(S), OAF
domain BARONY, BOURN(E), DEME(S)NE, ESTATE, REALM
dome CUPOLA, PATE, ROOF, THOLOS
domestic HOM(E)Y, LOCAL, MAID, NATIVE, SERVANT, TAME
domineer BOSS, BULLY, HECTOR
dominion COLONY, DUCHY, EMPERY, PROVINCE, REALM, SWAY
domino AMICE, BONE, CLOAK, HOOD, MASK
doom CONDEMN, FATE, RUIN
doomed KAPUT
door ENTRY, FUSUMA, GATE, HATCH, INLET, JANUA, PORTAL, POSTERN, TRAP
door part JAMB, KNOB, LINTEL, MULLION, PANEL, RAIL, SASH, SILL, STILE
doorkeeper CONCIERGE, HASP, JANITOR, OSTIARY, PORTER, TILER, TYLER
dormant ASLEEP, INERT, LATENT, TORPID
dorsal NOTAL, TERGAL
dosser DORSAL, PANNIER
dossier DATA, FILE, RECORD
dot DOWER, DOWRY, IOTA, PERIOD, SPECK(LE), STIPPLE
dote ADORE, DRIVEL, LIKE
dotted PIEBALD, PIED, PINTO, SEME
double BINATE, DUAL, DUPLEX, GEMEL, KA, TWIN
doubt DISTRUST, SCRUPLE
dough BATTER, DUFF, MONEY, PASTE, SPUD
doughnut BAGEL, BEIGNET, CRULLER, SIMBALL, SINKER
dovekie ALLE, ROTCH(E), ROTGE
dovetail FIT, JOIN, TENON
dower DOS, DOWRY, ENDOW, ENDUE
down ALOW, DUNE, DUVET, EIDER, FUZZ, NAP, PILE, PRONATE, SAD
downy LANATE, PILAR, VILLOUS
dowry DOS, DOT, DOWER, GIFT
doze (CAT)NAP, DORM, DROWSE, SNOOZE
drag BOTHER, HALE, HAUL, LUG, SNIG, TOW, TUG
dragnet TRAINEL, TRAWL, WEB
dragon DRAKE, DUENNA, FAFNIR, KETU, RAHU, WIVERN
drain CLOACA, CULVERT, DEPLETE, SAP, SEWER, SUMP, VITIATE
dram DRAFT, NIP, SLUG
drama AUTO, KABUKI, MIME, NOGAKU, NOH, PLAY, STAGE
draw DEPICT, HALE, LIMN, SIPHON, TIE, TOLE, TOW, WIN
draw back RESILE, WINCE
draw forth DERIVE, EDUCE, ELICIT
draw tight BIND, COUL, FRAP
dream FANCY, FANTASY, MUSE, REVE(RIE), VISION
dregs DRAFF, DROSS, FAEX, LEES, MAGMA, MARC, SALIN, SCUM, SILT, SORDES, VINASSE
drench DOUSE, SOAK, SOUSE
drenched ASOP, DEWED, WET
dress CLOTHE, DAB, DUB, NIG, PREEN, TAN, TAW, TOG
dresser BUREAU, CHEST, VANITY
drift COURSE, CURRENT, FLOAT, TENOR, TREND

drill BORE, PIERCE, TRAIN
drink ADE, ASSAI, BIB, BRACER, BOUSE, BOZA, BUMBO, CAUDLE, COLA, GULP, GUZZLE, IMBIBE, (K)AVA, KUMISS, MORAT, NECTAR, NEGUS, NIP(A), NOG, PEG, POP, POSSET, PTISAN, QUAFF, SIP, SLUG, SODA, SOT, SWIG, TIPPLE, TONIC, TOPE; see p. 123
drip CREEP, LEAK, OOZE, SEEP, SILE
drive FORCE, IMPEL, LANE, MOTOR, RIDE, STEER, URGE
drive back REPEL, REPULSE, ROUT
drive in HAMMER, TAMP
drivel DOTE, DROOL, SLAVER
driver CABBY, CHAUFFEUR, HAMMER, JEHU, SARWAN, WHIP
droll ODD, WAGGISH, ZANY
drone BEE, HUM, IDLER
droop LAG, SAG, SLOUCH, WILT
drop BEAD, DAP, DRIB, FALL, GLOBULE, GUTTA, PLOP, MINIM, SIE, SINK, SYE
dropsy EDEMA, HYDROPS
dross DREGS, SCORIA, SCUM, SINTER, SLAG, SPRUE, SULLAGE
drought ARIDITY, DEARTH, SOKA
drove ATAJO, HERD, PACK, RODE
drowse DOVER, DOZE, NAP, NOD
drudge FAG, GRUB, HACK, LABOR, MOIL, PLOD, SLAVE, TOIL
drug ALOES, ANODYNE, DILANTIN, DOPE, DOSE, JALAP, MECON, NARCOTIC, OPIATE, SINA, SULFA
drum BEAT, D(R)UB, REPEAT
drum call DIAN, RAPPEL, TAT(T)OO
drunk(ard) BARFLY, BLOTTO, HIGH, LIT, LUSH, POTTO, SOAK(ED), SOT, STONED, TIDDLY, TIPPLER, TOPER, TOSSPOT, WINO
drupe TRYMA
dry AREFY, ARID, BLOT, BRUT, SEC, SERE, SICCATE, WIPE
dub KNIGHT, NAME, TITLE
duck DIP, DODGE, EVADE, MERSE
duck-like ANATINE
duct AORTA, CANAL, CONDUIT, FLUE, LEMNA, MEATUS, VAS(A)
dude DANDY, FOP, MACARONI
due DEBT, DESERTS, FIT, HAK(H), OWED, PAYABLE, REWARD
duel HOLMGANG, TILT
dugout ABRI, FOXHOLE
dull BLUNT, BORING, DRAB, DRY, DUN, LOGY, MAT(TE), OBTUND, OBTUSE, PROSAIC, PROSY, STOGY, TERNE
dunce ASS, BOBBY, COOT, DOLT, DOPE, FRONT, LOUT, MORON, NINNY, OAF, PONTIC, PROXY
dupe BILK, COZEN, CULL(Y), GULL, HOAX, PAWN, SUCKER
dusky DARK, DIM, SWART(HY)
dust ASH, BRISS, COOM(B), POWDER, SOOT, STIVE, STOUR
duty CESS, CHORE, DEVOIR, DHARMA, EXCISE, IMPOST, LASTAGE, LEVY, TARIFF
dwarf BANTAM, CRILE, DROICH, DURGAN, ELF, FAY, GNOME, MANIKIN, MIDGET, NIX, PIGMY, PIXY, PUCK, RUNT, SHEE, SPRITE, STUNT, TROLL, URF
dwarfs, seven BASHFUL, DOC, DOPEY, GRUMPY, HAPPY, SLEEPY, SNEEZY
dwindle ABATE, EBB, PETER
dye AAL, ANIL, AN(N)ATTA, AN(N)ATTO, ANNOTTO, ARCHIL, ARNATTO, AURIN(E), EOSIN(E), MADDER, ORCHAL, ORCHIL, ORSELLE, STAIN, TINGE, TINT, WELD, WOAD, WOALD, WOLD

E

eager AGOG, ARDENT, AVID, FAIN, KEEN, YARE
eagle AQUILA, ERN(E), ETANA, GIER, HARPY
ear HANDLE, LUG, SPICA(E), SPIKE
ear, pert. to AURIC, (BIN)OTIC, (BIN)AURAL, LOBAR
earnest money ARRHA, HANDSEL
earth BYON, CLAY, DIRT, ERD, GEO, GLEBE, LOAM, SOIL, TERRA
earth, pert. to GEAL, TERRENE
earth surface EPIGENE, HORST, SIAL, SIMA
earthquake SEISM, TEMBLOR, TREMOR
earthquake site ALEPPO, ASSAM, CUTCH, ISCHIA, KANSU, LISBON, MESSINA, QUITO, TOKYO
earthwork AGGER, DIKE, FORT, MOUND, RIDGE
east LEVANT, ORIENT, SUNRISE
east, pert. to ASIAN, EOAN
Easter PAAS, PACE, PASCH(A)
easy job CINCH, SINECURE, SNAP
eat DEVOUR, ERODE, GNAW, INGEST, RUST

eat greedily BOLT, GOBBLE, GORGE, GULP, LAB, RAVEN, RAVIN(E)
eating away CAUSTIC, ERODENT
eccentric CRANK, ERRATIC, MISFIT, ODD, OUTRE, QUEER, UNICUM
echo APE, DITTO, ITERATE, RESOUND
eclipse DARKEN, DIM, SURPASS
edge ARRIS, BRIM, BRINK, HEM, LABRUM, LIP, MARGE, ODDS, PICOT, SELVAGE, SIDLE, SILL, VERGE
edict see DECREE
edit CORRECT, REDACT, REVISE
educated ERUDITE, LITERATE
educator ANGELL, BASCOM, BUTLER, DEWEY, ELIOT, FLEXNER, FROEBEL. GILMAN, HALL, HARPER. HOPKINS, JAMES, KERR, MANN, MATHER, NEILSON, PALMER, PEABODY, POUND, ROYCE, SETON
educe ELICIT, EVOKE, INFER
effervesce AERATE, BUBBLE, FIZZ, FOAM, FROTH
effort ASSAY, CONATUS, DINT, NISUS, TRIAL
egg collector OOLOGIST
egg on GOAD, INCITE, SPUR, URGE
egg(s) NIT, OVA, OVULE, OVUM, ROE
egg(s), part of ALBUMEN, GLAIR, LATEBRA, SHELL, WHITE, YOLK
egg-shaped OOID, OVAL, OVATE, OVOID
ego ATMAN, JIVATMA, SELF
Egypt, pert. to COPTIC
eject BOUNCE, EMIT, EVICT, OUST, SPEW, SPURT, VOID
elbow ANCON, ANGLE, BEND, CROWD, JOINT, JOSTLE, NUDGE
elder DEAN, PRIOR, SENIOR
eldest AINE(E), EIGNE, SENIOR
electric particle (AN)ION, CATION, KATION
electric unit AMP, AMPERE, BEL, DYNE, ELOD, FARAD, HENRY, MHO, OHM, PERM, REL, VOLT, WATT, WEBER
electrode ANODE, CATHODE
electronic tube KLYSTRON, MAGNETRON, PENTODE, TETRODE, THYRATRON, TRIODE
elegant FINE, POSH, RICH
elegy DIRGE, LAMENT, NENIA
element RECT; see p. 116
elementary BASIC, PRIMAL, PRIMARY, PRIMER, SIMPLE
elevation MESA, MOUND, MOUNT, RIDEAU
elf BROWNIE, ERLKING, FAY, FAIRY, GNOME, GOBLIN, HOB, IMP, KOBOLD, NIX, NIXIE, PERI, OUPHE, PIXIE, PIXY, PUCK, SPRITE
elfin FEY
elide DELE, OMIT
elixir AMRITA, ARCANUM, HAOMA, PANACEA, RASA, SOMA
elliptic OBLONG, OVAL, OVATE
elongated LINEAR, PROLATE
elude DODGE, EVADE, SHUN
elusive EELY, SLICK, SLIPPERY
emaciation ATROPHY, MACIES, TABES, WASTE
emanation(s) AURA(E), BLAS, NITON
emancipate MANUMIT, RELEASE
emancipator FREER, LINCOLN, MOSES
embankment BUND, DAM, DIGUE, DIKE, DYKE, LEVEE
ember ASH, CLINKER, CINDER, COAL, ISEL, IZLE, SPARK
embellish ADORN, (BE)DECK, GARNISH, GILD
emblem BADGE, BAR, DESIGN, EAGLE, FASCES, FLAG, INSIGNE, INSIGNIA, MACE, SIGN, SYMBOL. TOTEM
embrace ACCEPT, CARESS, CLASP, EMBODY, ENARM, HUB, INARM, WELCOME
embrocation ARNICA, LINIMENT
emerge EMANATE, ISSUE, RISE
emetic IPECAC, MUSTARD
emigree ALIEN, EXILE, REFUGEE
emit ERUCT, EXUDE, REEK, SHED
emmer SPELT, WHEAT
emotion ONDE, PASSION, PATHOS
emperor AKBAR, CZAR, KAISER, MIKADO, MOGUL, PADISHAH, TENNO, TSAR, TZAR
emphasis ACCENT, STRESS
employ ENGAGE, HIRE, PLACE, USE
employer BOSS, HIRER, JOSS, USER
emporium MARKET, MART, SHOP, STORE
empty BLANK, DEPLETE(D), (DE)VOID, DRAIN, INANE, VACANT, VACUOUS, VAIN
emulate APE, RIVAL, STRIVE, VIE
enchantress CIRCE, MEDEA, SIREN
encircle EMBAY, ENVIRON, GIRD, GIRT, HEM, ORB
enclose CAGE, (IN)CASE, CORRAL, ENCLAVE, FENCE, HEDGE, MEW, PEN, WRAP

enclosure ATAJO, CANCHA, COOP, CORRAL, SEKOS, STOCKADE, STY, YARD
encomium ELOGE, EULOGY, PANEGYRIC, PRAISE, TRIBUTE
encore BIS, REPEAT, TWICE
encourage ABET, BOOST, BRACE, EGG, ELATE, FOSTER, URGE
end AIM, BOURN, CODA, DIE, FINALE, FINE, FINIS, INTENT, OMEGA, REMNANT, RESULT, STUB, THIRTY, TIP
end, tending to TELIC
endeavor AIM, ESSAY, NISUS, TRY, VIE
endorse RATIFY, SANCTION, SIGN
endorsement VISA, VISE
endow BESTOW, GRACE, (IN)VEST
endowment BOON, DOWER, GRANT, TALENT
endue DIGEST, DOWER, (IN)VEST
endure (A)BIDE, BEAR, BROOK, DREE, LAST, PERSIST, WEAR
enemy FOE(MAN), RIVAL
energy BENT, ERGAL, METTLE, PEP, POWER, POTENCY, STHENIA, VIGOR, VIM, ZIP
energy, lack of ATONY, INERTIA
energy unit ERG(ON), JOULE, MEGERG, RAD
engage AFFIANCE, BETROTH, BOOK, CHARTER, ENLIST, HIRE, MESH, OCCUPY
engender BEGET, BREED, GENERATE, PROMOTE, SIRE
engine DIESEL, GIN, MACHINE, MOGUL, MOTOR, TURBINE, YARDER
engineer SAPPER, SEABEE
engrave CARVE, CHASE, CHISEL, ETCH, INCISE, INFIX, RIST, STIPPLE
engrossed ABSORBED, RAPT
enigma CONUNDRUM, PUZZLE, REBUS, RIDDLE, SECRET
enjoyment GUSTO, RELISH, ZEST
enlarge DILATE, DISTEND, EXPAND, REAM
enmity ANIMUS, MALICE, RANCOR
enough AMPLE, BASTA, BUS, ENOW
enrage ANGER, INCENSE, IRK, MADDEN, ROIL
enroll ENLIST, ENTER, IMPANEL, REGISTER
ensnare (BE)NET, DECOY, LURE, SNIGGLE, WEB
entangle (EN)MESH, ENTRAP, RAFFLE, SNARL
enter ADMIT, ENROL(L), INSERT, LIST, RECORD, START
entertain DIVERT, FETE, REGALE
entertainer(s) COURTESAN, HETAERA, HETAIRA, HOSTESS
enthusiasm ESTRO; see ZEAL
enthusiast ADDICT, BUFF, BUG, DEVOTEE, FAN, FANATIC, IST, ZEALOT
entice (AL)LURE, BAIT, CAJOLE, COAX, COZEN, INVEIGH, PIQUE, TEMPT, TOLE
entity BEING, ENS, ENTIA, ESSENCE
entomb BURY, INTER, INURN
entrance ACCESS, ADIT, DEBUT, DOOR, GATE, INGRESS, PORTAL, STILE
entreat ADJURE, HALSE(N), PLEAD, PRAY, SOLICIT
entry CREDIT, DEBIT, ITEM, MINUTE, NOTE
entwine ENLACE, WEAVE, WREATHE
envelop ENFOLD, INFOLD, (IN)WRAP, SHROUD, SWADDLE
envelope CAPSULE, POD, SACK, SHEATH, SHELL, WRAPPER
environment MILIEU, PURLIEU
environs EXURBS, LOCALE, OUTSKIRTS, SETTING, SUBURBS
envy COVET, GRUDGE, ONDE, SPITE
enzyme AMYLASE, ASE, DIASTASE, FICIN, INSULASE, KINASE, LOTASE, MALTASE, MUTASE, OLEASE, PAPAIN, PEPSIN, PTYALIN, RENNIN, TRYPSIN, ZYMASE
eon EPOCH, ERA, OLAM
epic (A)ENEID, BEOWULF, EDDA, EPOPEE, EPOS, HEROIC, HOMERIC, ILIAD, KALEVALA, ODYSSEY, POEM, RAMAYANA, SAGA, SAKUNTALA
epicure FRIAND, GOURMET, SYBARITE
epicurean APICIAN
epithet AGNOMEN, (BY)NAME, OATH
epoch AGE, ARENIG, BALA, CHAZY, ECCA, EON, ERA, ERIAN, FORMATION, KAIBAB, LIAS, MALM, MUAV, OOLITE, SERIES, UINTA
equal (A)LIKE, (COM)PEER, EVEN, FERE, ISO, MATCH, MEET, PARI, TIE(D)
equality ISONOMY, PAR(ITY)
equip ACCOUTRE, GIRD, (OUT)FIT, RIG
equivocate EVADE, FENCE, HEDGE
era AGE, CENOZOIC, CYCLE, EPOCH, GROUP, MESOZOIC, PALEOZOIC, PERIOD

eradicate EPILATE, LEVEL, (UP)ROOT
erase BLOT, CANCEL, DELE(TE), EFFACE
Erinyes ALECTO, MEGAERA, TISIPHONE
ermine FUR, STOAT, WEASEL
err MISTAKE, SIN, SLIP, WANDER
error(s) BONER, BULL, ERRATA, ERRATUM, GAFFE, MISCUE, SOLECISM, TYPO
escape ABSCOND, DECAMP, ELUDE, EVADE, LAM, LEAK
eschew ABSTAIN, FORGO, SHUN
escort BEAU, CONVOY, DUENNA, SQUIRE, USHER
esoteric ARCANE, INNER, MYSTIC, OCCULT
espalier PALISADE, TRELLIS
essay ATTEMPT, CHRIA, PAPER, TEST, THEME, THESIS, TRACT, TREATISE, TRY
essence AMRITA, ATTAR, BEING, ENS, EXTRACT, GIST, PERFUME, PITH, RASA, SCENT
establish BASE, FOUND, VERIFY
estate ALLOD(IUM), ALOD, ASSETS, DAIRA, DOMAIN, HOLDING, LEGACY, MANOR, RANK, TALUK
esteem ADMIRE, CHERISH, HONOR, PRIDE, PRIZE, REPUTE
ester ACETIN, ETHER, IODIDE, OLEATE, SILICATE, STEARIN
estimate APPRAISE, ASSAY, AUDIT, GAGE, METE, RATE, RECKON
estrade DAIS
estuary FIORD, FIRTH, FJORD, FRITH, INLET, LOCH, PARA, PLATA, RIA
etagere WHATNOT
eternity (A)EON, INFINITY, OLAM
ethereal AERIAL, AERY, AIRY, DELICATE, HEAVENLY
eulogy ELOGE, ENCOMIUM, PAEN
european FRANGI
evade AVOID, BILK, DODGE, ELUDE, FOIL, PALTER, PARRY SHIRK, SHUN(T)
evaluate APPRAISE, ASSAY, ASSESS, GA(U)GE, PRICE
evanescent AIR, EPHEMERAL, FLEETING
evangelist APOSTLE, GANTRY, GRAHAM, JOHN, LUKE, MCPHERSON, MARK, MATTHEW, PREACHER, SMITH, SUNDAY
even FLUSH, LEVEL, PLANE, PLUMB, SAME, SQUARE, UNIFORM
evening DEN, DUSK, GLOAMING, VESPER
everlasting AGELONG, ETERN(E), OLAMIC
evict EXPEL, OUST, SACK
evident CLEAR, PALPABLE, PATENT, PLAIN
evil BASE, HARM, MAL(A), MALIGN, VICE, VILE, WRONG
evil intent DOLUS
evolve (D)EDUCE, DERIVE, UNFOLD
exacerbate ENRAGE, IRK, PROVOKE
exact BLEED, DEMAND, ESTREAT, EXTORT, LEVY, LITERAL, WREST
exam GREATS
examination AUDIT, AUTOPSY, BIOPSY, CATECHISM, ORAL, PROBE, QUIZ, STUDY, TAT, TEST, TRIAL, TRIPOS, TRYOUT
examine APPOSE, CHECK, GRADE, PALPATE, PRY, SCAN, SPY, TRY
example PARADIGM, PINK, SPECIMEN
excavate DIG, DREDGE, GRUB, MUCK, PION, SCOOP, UNEARTH
excavation HOLE, HOLLOW, MINE, PIT, SHAFT, STOPE
excellence CLASS, MERIT, VIRTU
excellent AONE, DELUXE, PRIME, SELECT, TIPTOP, TOPS, WORTHY
except BAR, BUT, OMIT, SAVE
excess EPACT, GLUT, LUXUS, NIMIETY, PLETHORA, SURPLUS
exchange BANDY, BARTER, BOURSE, MARKET, PIT, SWAP
exchange medium SCHUIT, SHOE, SYCEE
exchequer FISC, FISK, TREASURY
excite AGITATE, ELATE, ROIL, ROUSE, WHET
excited AGOG, ASTIR, MANIC
excitement FRENZY, FUROR(E), FURY, PASSION
exclude BLACKBALL, (DE)BAR, DEPORT, OMIT
exclusive ONLY, POSH, SELECT, SOLE, UNIQUE
excoriate ABRADE, FLAY
excrete EGEST, EVACUATE, EXUDE
excursion JAUNT, JUNKET, OUTING, SALLY, TOUR, TREK
excuse ALIBI, ESSOIN(E), PLEA, REMIT
exemplar COPY, MODEL, PATTERN
exempt EXON, FREE, IMMUNE
exercise DRILL, EXERT, NISUS, PLY, PRAXIS, TASK, URE

exhaust DEPLETE, DRAIN, FAG, JADE, SAP, SPEND, TIRE, WASTE
exhausted BEAT, DONE, EFFETE, SPENT, WEAK, WEARY
existence BEING, CONDITION, ENS, ESSE
existence, pert. to NOUMENAL, ONTAL
existing ALIVE, BEING, EXTANT
exit DEATH, DEMISE, DEPART, EGRESS, END, LEAVE
exodus FLIGHT, HEGIRA
expand DILATE, DISTEND, FLAN, SWELL
expanse AREA, REACH, SCOPE, SEA, SWEEP, TRACT
expect (A)WAIT, HOPE, WEEN, WISH
expedition CARAVAN, CHASE, CRUSADE, JAUNT, QUEST, SAFARI, SHIKAR, SUFFARI
expert ACE, ADEPT, CRACK, DEFT, ONER, WHIZ
expiate ATONE, PURGE, SHRIVE
explain CLEAR, DEFINE, GLOSS, REDE, WISE
explicit CLEAR, LUCID, POSITIVE, PRECISE
explode BURST, DETONATE, FIRE, FULMINATE, POP
exploit CLIP, DEED, FEAT, GEST(E), MILK, TOUR
explorer BALBOA, BYRD, CORTES, DELEON, DELONG, DESOTO, HEDIN, LEWIS, LOGAN, PERRY, PIKE, SCOTT, WILKES
explosive AMATOL, AMMO, CAP, CORDITE, DYNAMITE, GAINE, FIERY, LYDDITE, MELINITE, NITRO, SOUP, TENSE, TONITE, TNT
expression ATTICISM, IDIOM, LOCUTION, PHRASE, SAYING, TERM
extend BEETLE, DEPLOY, EKE, JUT, LIE, REACH, WIDEN
exterior ECTAL, EXTRINSIC
extinguish DOUSE, QUELL, QUENCH, SNUFF, STIFLE
extirpate DELE, RAZE, STUB, (UP)ROOT
extort BLEED, EXACT, MILK, WREST, WRING
extra INSERT, ODD, OVER, SPARE, SUPE(R), (SUR)PLUS
extract AT(T)AR, DISTIL, DRAW, ELICIT, ESSENCE, ESTREAT, EVULSE, OTTAR, OTTO, PERICOPE, REMOVE
extracts ANALECTA, ANALECTS
extraneous ALIEN, EXOTIC, OUTER
extravagance ELA, WASTE
extravagant BAROQUE, FAROUT, LAVISH, OUTRE, (P)LUSH, PRODIGAL, ROCOCO
extreme DRASTIC, RADICAL, ULTRA
exudation AURA, GUM, LAC, PITCH, RESIN, SAP, SUDOR
exude EMIT, OOZE, REEK
eye GLIM, HILA, HILUM, OGLE, OPTIC, ORB, PEEPER, SEE, SIGHT, STARE, STEMMA, UTA
eye, black MOUSE, SHINER
eye protector BLINDER, BLINKER, GOGGLES, PATCH, VISOR
eyot AIT, ILE, ISLE(T)

F

fable ALLEGORY, APOLOG(UE), LEGEND, MYTH, PARABLE, YARN
fabrics see p. 282
fabricate COIN, CONCOCT, DEVISE, ERECT, FEIGN, MAKE, SCHEME
fabulist AESOP, ANDERSEN, GRIMM
face DARE, DIAL, FACADE, FACET, MAP, MUG, PHIZ, PUSS, REVET, VISAGE
face downward PRONATE, PRONE
facet BEZEL, BEZIL, COLLET, CULET
facile ADROIT, APT, DEFT, EASY
facility EASE, KNACK, MEANS
fact(s) DATA, DATUM, FACTO, FAIT
faction BLOC, CABAL, CLIQUE, JUNTO, SECT, SIDE
factor AGENT, BROKER, GENE
factory MILL, PLANT, WORKSHOP
faculty BENT, KNACK, SENSE, TALENT
fad CRAZE, CRY, FANCY, MODE, RAGE, STYLE
fade DIE, DIM, PALE, WILT, WITHER
fail FLOP, FLUNK, LOSE
failure BUST, DUD, FLOP
faint DIM, FADE, FEEBLE, SWELT, SWOON, WEAK
fair BAZA(A)R, BLONDE, CLEAR, FERIA, JUST, MELA, KERMESS, KERMIS, SOSO
fair-lead WAPP
fairy DRYAD, ELF, MAB, NIX(IE), OBERON, PERI, PIXIE, PIXY, PUCK, SHEE, SPRITE, SYLPH, TITANIA, TROLL, UNA, VILA, VILY

fairy fort LIS(S), SHEE
faith CULT, CREED, DOGMA, DOXY, TENET, TROTH
faith, pert. to PISTIC
faithful LEAL, LIEGE, LOYAL, STA(U)NCH, TRUE
fall(s) CASCADE, CATARACT, DROP, LIN(N), PLAP, PLOP, PLUNGE, SAG, SILE, SIN, SPILL, TOPPLE
fallacy IDOLA, IDOLUM, SOPHISM
false BOGUS, FAKE, PSEUD(O), SHAM, SPURIOUS
falter DODDER, TOTTER, WAVER
fame ECLAT, GLORY, HONOR, KUDOS, RENOWN, REPUTE
familiar BOLD, CLOSE, COSY, TRITE, VERSANT
family CINEL, CLAN, GEN(O)S, ILK, LINE(AGE), SEPT, STIRPS, STOCK, TRIBE
fan BUFF, DEVOTEE, FOMENT, OGI, PUNKA(H), ROOTER, VOTARY, ZEALOT
fanatic BIGOT, DEVOTEE, MANI(A)C, PARTISAN, RABID, ZEALOT
fancy CAPRICE, CHIMERA, FOIBLE, IDEA(TE), MEGRIM, NOTION, QUIRK, REVERIE, VAGARY, VISION, WHIM(SEY)
farce COMEDY, EXODE, MOCKERY, PARODY, SKIT, TRAVESTY
fare BOARD, DIET, MENU, PAY, THRIVE, TOKEN
farewell ADIEU, ADIOS, ANATH, AVE, CONGEE, LEAVE, VALE
farinaceous MEALY, STARCHY
farinaceous food SAGO, SALEP
farm BARTON, CHACRA, CROFT, HARAS, KOLKHOZ, MAINS, RANCH, TILL, TORP, WERF
farmer COTTER, GRANGER, KULAK, MEO, RYOT, SOWER, TILLER
fashion DESIGN, FAD, MOLD, MODE(L), SHAPE, STYLE, VOGUE
fast APACE, CARENE, DHARNA, EMBER, FLEET, LENT, RAMADAN
fasten BATTEN, BELAY, BOLT, GLUE, LOCK, NAIL, RIVET, SEAL, SNIB, TACK
fastidious FINICAL, FUSSY, GOURMET, QUEASY
fat ADEPS, ADIPOSE, ELAIN(E), ESTER, GREASE, LARD, LIPA, OBESE, OLEIN(E), PINGUID, PORCINE, STEARIN(E), SUET, TALLOW
fatal DEADLY, FUNEST, LETHAL, MORT(AL)
fate DOOM, KARMA, KISMET, LOT
father ABBA, ABOU, ABU, BEGET, PADRE, PAPA, PATER, PERE, POP, SIRE
father, relating to AGNATE, PATERNAL
fathom DELVE, GRASP, PLUMB, PROBE, SOUND
fatigue BORE, FAG, JADE, SAP, TIRE, WEARY
fatuous ASININE, INANE
faucet COCK, ROBINET, SPIGOT, TAP
fault CULPA, FLAW, FOIBLE
faultfind CARP, CAVIL
faultfinder MOMUS
faun SATYR
faux pas SLIP; see ERROR
favor BENEFIT, BIAS, BOON, OBLIGE
favorite HERO, IDOL, MINION, PET
favoritism BIAS, NEPOTISM
fawn CRINGE, GROVEL, TOADY
fear AWE, FUNK, PHOBIA
fearful CRAVEN, PAVID, TIMID, TREPID
fearless BOLD, BRAVE, DARING, HEROIC, IMPAVID
feast AHAAINA, ARVAL, BANQUET, FETE, LUAU, MAS, REGALE
feather(s) DOWN, EIDER, HULU, PENNA, PINION, PINNA, PLUMA, QUILL, REMEX, REMIGES, TECTRIX, TUFT
fee DUES, FIEF, RETAINER, TIP, TOLL
feeble ANILE, DEBILE, PUNY, WEAK
feed CATER, FODDER, GRAZE
feeding, forced GAVAGE
feel GROPE, PALP, SENSE, TOUCH
feeler ANTENNA, BARBEL, PALP(US), TACTOR, TENTACLE
feet, having PEDATE
feet, pert. to PEDAL, PEDARY, PODAL
feline CAT(TY), SLY, WILY
fellow BLADE, BOZO, CAD, CHAP(PIE), CHAPPY, DICK, GUY, LAD, PEER
fence FAGIN, HAHA, HAWHAW, HEDGE, OXER, PALING, PALISADE, PARR, RADDLE, RAIL, SCRIMP, STILE
fencer's cry HAI, HAY, SASA
fencing term APPEL, CARTE, EPEE, FOIL, LUNGE, OCTAVE, PARRY, PEL, PUNTO, QUARTE, QUINTE, REMISE, REPRISE, RIPOST(E), SECONDE, SEPTIME, SIXTE, TIERCE, TOUCHE

fend AVERT, PARRY, WARD
ferment BARM, FRET, LEAVEN, YEAST, ZYME
fern part SORI, SORUS, SPORE
ferryman CHARON
fertilizer COMPOST, GUANO, MARL
fervor ARDOR, ZEAL, ZEST
festival ALE, BON, BUSK, DASHAHARA, DELIA, DEWALI, FAIR, FERIA, FETE, FIESTA, GALA, HALOA, HOLI, HOOLEE, KERMESS, KERMIS, MELA, OPALIA, PESACH, PUJA, PURIM, SEDER, SUCCOS, SUKKOTH, VOTA
fetid FOUL, FUSTY, NOISOME, OLID, PUTRID, RANCID, RANK
fetish ANITO, CHARM, GRIGRI, JUJU, MASCOT, MOJO, OBEAH, OBI, OBIA, VOODOO, ZEME, ZEMI
fetter CUFF, GYVE, HOBBLE, IRON, MANACLE, SHACKLE
feud (AF)FRAY, BROIL, FIEF, VENDETTA
feudal land BENEFICE, FEOD, FEUD, FIEF
feudal, opposed to AL(L)OD, AL(L)ODIUM
feudal service AVERA
feudal tenant BORDAR, COTT(I)ER, LEUD, SOCAGER, VASSAL
fever AGUE, CAUMA, PYREXIA, TERTIANA
feverish FEBRILE, HECTIC
fiber NOIL, STAPLE, STRAND, THREAD; see p. 282
fickle ERRATIC, VOLATILE
fictitious BOGUS, FALSE, MYTHICAL, SPURIOUS, UNREAL
field ACRE, AGER, CROFT, DOMAIN, GLEBE, LEA, PADI, RANGE, ROWEN, WONG
fight (AF)FRAY, BARNEY, BOUT, BRAWL, CLEM, DUEL, FEUD, FRACAS, JOUST, MELEE, RUCTION, RUMPUS, SCRAP, SCUFFLE, SETTO, TILT
figure BOSH, COMPUTE, COUNT, DECAGON, DIGIT, HEXAGON, ISAGON, SOLID, STATUE, SYMBOL, TYPE
figure of speech IRONY, LITOTES, METAPHOR, SIMILE, (EPI)TROPE
filament BRIN, DOWL, ELATER, FIBER, FIBRIL, HAIR, HARL(E), STRAND
file CARLET, DOSSIER, QUANNET, RECORD
fillet LISTEL, ORLE, REGULA, SNOOD, TAENIA
film BRAT, CINEMA, LAYER, PATINA, SCUM, XRAY
fine ABWAB, AMERCE, CRO, GALANAS, IMPOST, LEVY, MINUTE, MULCT, RARE, SCONCE
Fingal's kingdom MORVEN
finger DACTYL, DIGIT, POINTER, POLLEX
fingerprint ARCH, LOOP, WHORL
finial APEX, EPI, TEE, TOP
finicky DAINTY, FUSSY, PRISSY
Finland, pert. to SUOMIC, SUOMISH
fire AGNI, CHAR, ELAN, IGNIS, IGNITE, KINDLE, SACK
fireman STOKER, VAMP
fireplace FOGON, GRATE, HEARTH, INGLE
fireplace part HOB, MANTEL, REREDOS
firewood FAG(G)OT, LENA
fireworks BOMB, FIZGIG, GERB(E), PETARD, RIPRAP, SALUTE, SQUIB, TORPEDO
fire worshiper GHEBER, PARSEE, PARSI
firm COMPANY, FAST, HARD, HUI, RIGID, STA(U)NCH, TIGHT
firmament SKY, VAULT, WELKIN
firn ICE, NEVE, SNOW
first CAPITAL, CHIEF, DEBUT, INITIAL, ORIGINAL, PRIMAL, PRIME
first-born AYNE, EIGNE
first-class ACE, AONE, DELUXE, PALMARY, TOPS
firth ARM, FIORD, FJORD, KYLE
fish ANGLE, DRAIL, FIN, TRAWL, TROLL; see p. 215
fish, fly for CAHILL, CLARET, HACKLE, HARL, HERL, SEDGE
fish line B(O)ULTER, SNELL, TRAWL, TROLL, TROT
fish measure MEASE
fish net SEINE, SPILLER, TRAWL
fish sauce ALEC, GARUM
fish trap FYKE, WEIR
fisherman ANGLER, EELER, NETTER, PISCATOR, SEINER, SQUAM, WALTONIAN, WEIRER
fishhook BARB, DRAIL, (FIZ)GIG, FLY, GAFF, KIRBY, SPROAT
fissure CHASM, CHINK, CLEFT, RENT, RIFT, RIMA, RIME, SLIT, SULCUS
fist MITT, MAULEY
fit (AD)APT, FADGE, FAY, HUFF, RIPE, SPELL, SPASM, SUIT, TANTRUM
fixed-income person RENTIER
flaccid FLABBY, LAX, LIMP
flag ALEM, BANDEROL(E), BANNER, BRUTE, BUNTING, BURGEE, COLORS, CORNET, ENSIGN, FANE, FANION,

GONFALON, GUIDON, IRIS, JACK, PENNANT, PENNON, ROGER, SINK, STANDARD
flagellants ALBI
flank LEER, LISK, LOIN, SIDE
flap FLUTTER, LAP(PET), LOMA, SLAT, TAB, TAG
flare BLAZE, FUSE(E), SIGNAL, SPLAY, TORCH
flash DAZZLE, LEVIN, SPEED, SPURT
flask BETTY, CANTEEN, FIASCO, FLACON, FLAGON, GIRBA, MATARA, MATRASS, OLPE
flat BROKE, EVEN, LEVEL, MOL(LE), PLANE, STALE, SUITE
flatten out CLAP, PLATTEN
flattened OBLATE, PLANATE, PLANE
flatter ADULATE, FAWN, PALP, TOADY
flattery BLARNEY, OIL, PALAVER
flavor AROMA, GUST, LACE, SAPOR, SAVOR, SEASON, TANG
flavoring see p. 123
flaxlike TOWY
flax, prepare RET
flee BOLT, DECAMP, DESERT, LAM
fleece ABB, NAP, PILE, SHEAR, SKIN, WOOL
fleet ARGOSY, ARMADA, ARMADO, FAST, FLOTILLA, NAVY
flexible LIMBER, LISSOM(E), LITHE, PLIANT, WITHY
flight EXODUS, HEGIRA, HOP; see BEVY
flippant BOLD, BRASSY, GLIB, PERT, SASSY, SAUCY
float BOB, BUOY, CORK, DRIFT, RAFT, SWIM, WAFT
floating ADRIFT, AWASH, NATANT
flock BROOD, DROVE, HERD, HIRSEL, HORDE, PACK, SHOAL, SWARM, TROOP; see BEVY
flog CAT, TROUNCE; see BEAT
flood BORE, DELUGE, EAGRE, FRESHET, SEA, SPATE, TIDE
floodgate CLOW, SLUICE
flora and fauna BIOTA
flour AT(T)A, FARINA
flourish FANFARE, FLAUNT, FUSTIAN, PARAPH, ROULADE, TANTARA, TANTIVY, THRIVE, WAX
flow FLUX, ISSUE, RUN, SPOUT
flower part AMENT, ANTHER, BRACT, CALYX, CARPEL, COROLLA, FILAMENT, OVARY, OVULE, PETAL, PISTIL, POLLEN, SEPAL, STAMEN, STEM, STIGMA, STYLE
flowers see p. 225
fluctuate VEER, VIBRATE, WAVE(R)
fluent COPIOUS, FACILE, FREE, GLIB
fluff DOWN, FLOC, FLOSS, LINT, MISCUE, NAP, PRIMP, PUFF
fluid FLUX, GAS, LIQUOR, SAP, SERUM
fluidity unit RHE
flume CHUTE, GORGE, RACE, SHUTE, SLUICE
flush BLUSH, DRENCH, GLOW, LAVISH, PLANE
flutter FLAP, FLIP, FLIT, HOVER, WAVE
fly AVIATE, DART, FLAP, FLIT, GLIDE, SCUD, SOAR, WHIR, WING
flying saucer UFO
foam BARM, FIZZ, FROTH, FUME, SCUM, SPUME, SUDS
focus AXIS, CORE, CRUX, HUB, NUCLEUS
fodder (EN)SILAGE, FORGE, STOVER
fog BEDIM, BRUME, HAZE, MIST, MURK, RAG, ROKE, SMOG
foghorn SIREN(E)
fold COTE, CREASE, CRIMP, DRAPE, (F)LAP, FLOCK, PEN, PLAIT, PLEAT, PLICA, PLIE, PLY, RUGA, TUCK
folded PLICATE
folkway(s) CUSTOM(S), MORES, MOS
follow DOG, ENSUE, HEEL, HOUND, OBEY, STALK, TAIL, TRACE, TRAIL
follower ADHERENT, APER, BUFF, HEELER, IST, ITE, VOTARY
folly FATUITY, LEVITY, LUNACY
foment ABET, BREW, SPUR
fondness GRA, LOVE
font BASIN, LAVER, ORIGIN, STOUP, TYPE
food ALIMENT, AMBROSIA, AMRITA, CATES, CHOW, CUISINE, DIET, EATS, FARE, FORAGE, GRUB, KAI, MANNA, MENU, MESS, PABLUM, SNACK, TABLE, TEREFA, TEREFE, VIANDS, VICTUALS; see p. 122
fool ASS, DOLT, DUNCE, JERK, JESTER, NINNY, OAF, RACA, SAP, SIMP, ZANY
foolish ASININE, DAFT, HARISH, INANE, SILLY, ZANY
foot ANAPEST, ARSIS, CHEK, CHORIAMB, DACTYL, IAMB(IC), IAMBUS, IONIC, PAD, PAW, PES, PUD, SPONDEE, TOTAL, TRIBRACH, TROCHEE

footless APOD(AL)
footlike PEDATE
footman FLUNKEY, LACKEY, MENIAL, VALET
footpad BANDIT, BRIGAND, HOOD, THUG, WHYO
footstalk PEDICEL, STRIG
footstool HASSOCK, MORA, OTTOMAN
forage FODDER, MARAUD, RAID, RUSSUD
foray INROAD, RAID, SALLY
forbid BAN, DEBAR, TABOO, TABU, VETO
force BIOD, COMPEL, DINT, DRIVE, DURESS, ELOD, ENERGY, IMPEL, ODYL, PANTOD, VIGOR, VIM, VIS
force, unit of DYNE
foreboding AUGURY, OMEN, PALL, PRESAGE
forecaster DOPESTER, TIPSTER, TOUT
for(e)go DENY, RESIGN, WAIVE
foreigner ALIEN, EMIGRE, GRINGO, HAOLE
foremost part ACRON, BOW, VAN, FRONT
forerun HERALD, PIONEER, PRELUDE, SCOUT
forest ARDEN, COPSE, GAPO, GROVE, GUBAT, SHERWOOD, SELVA, SILVA, TAIGA, WOLD
forest, pert. to NEMORAL, SILVAN, SYLVAN
foretell AUGUR, BODE, INSEE, SPAE
forever AKE, AYE, ETERN(E)
forfeit FINE, KEN, LAPSE, LOSE
forgetfulness AMNESIA, LETHE, OBLIVION
forgive ABSOLVE, REMIT
forked FURCATE, LITUATE
form BLANK, EIDOS, MODEL, MOLD, RITUAL, RUPA, TAILLE
form, pert. to MODAL
formation BIOME, ECHELON, FILE, HERSE, LINE
former(ly) ERST, NEE, ONCE, PRIOR
formless ARUPA
Formosa TAIWAN
formula LAW, LURRY, MANTRA, RECIPE
fort ALCAZAR, BASTILLE, CASTLE, CITADEL, COT(T)A, DONJON, DOON, DUN, KEEP, KOTA, PAH, POST
fortification ABATIS, BASTION, LIS(S), RAMPART, RAVELIN, REDAN, REDOUBT, TALUS
fortunate BLEST, DEXTER, FAUST, ROSY, SHREE, S(H)RI
fortune BAHI, FATE, HAP, LOT, RICHES, TYCHE
fortuneteller AUGUR, GYPSY, HARUSPEX, ORACLE, PALMIST, SEER, SIBYL, SPAEMAN
foundation BASE, BASIS, BED(ROCK)
fountain FONS, FONT, JET, SYKE, WELL
fracas see FIGHT
fraction DECIMAL, MOIETY, PART, SCRAP, SEGMENT
fragment ANA, ORT, SCRAP, SHARD, SHERD, SNIP, WISP
frailty FAULT, FLAW, FOIBLE, SIN
frame(work) CADRE, CHASSIS, HERSE, RACK, SESS, (S)TENTER, TRESSEL, TRESTLE, TRUSS
franchise LICENSE, SOC, SOKE, VOTE
frank BLUNT, EXEMPT, NAIVE
Franks, pert. to SALIC
fraud BUNCO, COVIN, COZENAGE, SHAM
fraught BESET, LADEN
fray CHAFE, RAVEL; see FIGHT
freckle LENTIGO
free CLEAR, EXEMPT, GRATIS, LOOSE(N), MANUMIT, RID
freedman LAET, LATIN
freeman CEORL, CHURL, THANE, THEGN, VILLEIN
frenzy AMOK, FUROR, MANIA
frequent HABITUAL, HAUNT, OFT
fresh FLIP, NOVEL, RAW, SASSY, SPICK, VIVID
freshet FLOOD, SPATE
freshman NOVICE, PLEBE
friar ABBOT, FRA, LISTER, MONK, SERVITE
Friday source FRIGGA
friend ACHATES, AMI(E), AMY, BUDDY, CHUM, CRONY, DOG, KITH, QUAKER
friendship AMITY, COMITY
fright(en) ALARM, AWE, FLEY, FUNK, GAST, PANIC
frill JABOT, RUCHE, RUFFLE
fringe EDGE, LOMA, TASSEL, THRUM
frisk CAPER, FROLIC, GAMBOL, SEARCH
frolic CAPER, DIDO, LARK, PLAY, SPORT, SPREE
front FACADE, FORE, VAN
frontiersman BOONE, BOWIE, CARSON, CLARK, CODY, EARP, HICKOK, LOGAN
frost HOAR, ICE, RIME
froth FOAM, LATHER, SCUM, SPUME, SUDS, YEAST
frown (G)LOWER, LOUR, SCOWL
frozen FRAPPE, GELID, GLACE

frugal CHARY, SPARE, THRIFTY
fruit ACHENE, BERRY, CROP, DRUPE, ETAERIO, LEGUME, LOMENT, NUT, PEPO, POME, PROFIT, SILICLE, SILIQUE, UTRICLE, YIELD; see p. 228
frustrate DASH, FOIL, SCOTCH, THWART
fuel COAL, COKE, GAS, LOG, OIL, PEAT, PEET
full OROTUND, PLENARY, REPLETE, SATED
fullness PLENUM, PLETHORA, SATIETY, SURFEIT
fume FRET, RAGE, RAVE, REEK, SMELL, SMOKE
function ACT, (CO)SINE, DUTY, ROLE, USE, WORK
fundamental BASAL, BASIC, PRIMAL, RADICAL, VITAL
fur HAIR, PELAGE, PELT(RY), SKIN, VAIR
furnace part BOSH, FAULD, GRATE, TEWEL, TUYERE
furnish CATER, ENDOW, EQUIP
furnishings DECOR, GEAR, RIG
furrowed RIVOSE, RUTTED
further ABET, AID, AND, MORE, YET
furtive SLY, SNEAKY, WARY
fury ERINYS, IRE, RAGE, WRATH
fuse ANNEAL, FRIT, MERGE, SMELT, SOLDER, WELD
fuss ADO, FANTOD, FIDGET, FIKE, POTHER, STIR, TODO

G

gable AILERON, PINION
gad PROWL, ROAM, ROVE
gadget DOODAD, GISMO, JIMJAM
Gael(ic) CELT(IC), ERSE, KELTIC, IRISH, MANX, SCOT(CH)
gaff FLEECE, GAMBLE, HOAX, SP(E)AR
gag CHOKE, MUFFLE, QUIP, RETCH
gain EARN, GET, LUCRE, NET, WIN
gainsay DENY, IMPUGN, REFUTE
gait CANTER, GALLOP, LOPE, PACE, RACK, RUN, (SH)AMBLE, TROT, VOLT, WALK
gallery ALURE, ARCADE, LOFT, LOGGIA, POY, PUBLIC, SALON, SOLLAR, VERANDA
gallop AUBIN, LOPE, TANTIVY
gallows GIBBET, YARDARM
gambler DICER, SHARK, SHILL(ABER)
gambol CAPER, CURVET, DIDO, FRISK
gamekeeper RANGER, WARDEN
game(s) BOLD, CONTEST, FROLIC, FUN, LAME, LUDI, PASTIME, SPORT, WILLING; see p. 137
gangster GOON, HOOD, MUG, THUG, WHYO, YEGG
gangway AISLE, PLANK, RAMP
gap HIATUS, LACUNA, MEUSE, MUSE(T), SHARD
gape OGLE, OSCITATE, YAWN
garden HERBARY, OLITORY
garland ANADEM, CHAPLET, FESTOON, FILLET, LEI
garment ROBIN(G), WRAP, WRIEL
garnish (BE)DECK, LARD, RELISH, TRIM
garnishment LIEN
garret ATTIC, LOFT, SOLER
gas ARGON, ARSINE, BENZENE, BRAG, BUTANE, DAMP, DRUG, ETHER, ETHYL, FLATUS, FREON, FUEL, HELIUM, KETONE, KRYPTON, (M)ETHANE, NEON, OXAN(E), PETROL, PHOSGENE, PROPANE, RADON, STIBINE, XENON
gate BAB, SPRUE; see DOOR
gateway DAR, PYLON, SLUICE, TORAN(A), TORII
gather AMASS, COLLATE, CULL, GARNER, GLEAN, LEK, MUSTER, PLAIT, SHE(A)VE, SHIRR
gaunt HAGGARD, SICKLY; see LEAN
gear CAM, COG, DUFFEL, GARB, KIT, PINION, TACKLE
gelastic RISIBLE
gelatin AGAR, ASPIC, COLLIN, COLLOID
gem ICE, JEWEL, MUFFIN
gem face BEZEL, CULET, FACET
gem setting BEZEL, CHATON, OUCH, PAVE
gender BEGET, NEUTER, SEX
genealogy LIN(E)AGE, PEDIGREE, TREE
general ANDERS, BOR, BRADLEY, GRANT, MACARTHUR, PERSHING, SHERIDAN, SHERMAN
gentle BALMY, DOCILE, PLACID, TAME
gentlemen BABOO, BABU, SENOR, SER, SIR, TOFF
genus see CLASS
geode CAVITY, DRUSE, NODULE, VOOG, VUG(G), VUGH
geographer APIANUS, BRUNHES, BUACHE, CLUVEL, HUMBOLDT, KANT, MELA, MERCATOR, MUNSTER, PTOLEMY, RITTER, STRABO, THALES, VAREN, VIDAL

geological formation IONE, TERRANE, TERRENE
geometric figure CUBE, CUSP, ELLIPSE, OBLONG, POLYGON, RHOMB, SQUARE, TRIGON
geometric solid CONE, CUBE, CYLINDER, LUNE, PRISM, PYRAMID, SPHERE
geometry term LOCI, LOCUS, SECANT, SINE, TANGENT, THEOREM, VERSOR
germ BACTERIA, BUG, MICROBE, SPORE, VIRUS; see SEED
germ-free ANTISEPTIC, ASEPTIC
German ALMAIN, BOCHE, HUN, JERRY, KRAUT, TEUTON
gesture MOTION, NOD, TOKEN, WAVE
get out! SCAT, SCRAM, SHOO, SKID(D)OO, VAMO(O)SE
ghastly LURID, MACABRE, PALLID
ghost BHUT, EIDOLON, HANT, JUBA, KER, LARVA, MANES, PHANTOM, SHADE, SHADOW, SPECTER, SPIRIT, SPOOK, UMBRA, WRAITH
giant(s) ANAK, BALOR, BANA, BUNYAN, ETEN, GOLIATH, GYGES, JUMBO, MAMMOTH, TITAN(IC)
gift ALMS, BONUS, BOON, DOLE, DOW, ENAM, HANDSEL, LEGACY, SOP, TIP
gig CHAISE, NAP, WHIM
gild, gilt AUREATE, DORE, ENRICH
gin RUMMY, SLOE, SNARE, TRAP
girder (I)BEAM, TBAR, TRUSS
girdle CEST(US), CINGLE, CORSET, OBI, SASH; see ENCLOSE
girl BELLE, CHIT, COLLEEN, DAME, DAMSEL, FRAIL, HOYDEN, LASS, MAID(EN), MINX, SIS, SKIRT, TOMBOY
gist CORE, CRUX, KERNEL, NUB, PITH
give BESTOW, CONFER, DONATE
glacial deposit AS(AR), ESCAR, ESKAR, ESKER, KAME, MORAINE, OS(AR), PAHA, PLACER
glacial ice FIRN, NEVE, SERAC
glaciation stage ACHEN, CARY, ELSTER, GUNZ, IOWAN, MANKATO, MINDEL, RISS, SAALE, VALDERS, WURM
glacier ICECAP, PIEDMONT
glacier, facing a STOSS
gladly FAIN, LIEF
gland, edible NOIX, RIS
gland secretion AUTACOID, BILE, CHALONE, GALL, SALIVA; see HORMONE
glands see p. 106
glass CALX, CRYSTAL, CULLET, FRIT(T), GOBLET, LENS, MIRROR, OPALINE, PANE, PARISON, PONY, RUMMER, SMALT, SNIFTER, STRASS, TUMBLER, UVIOL
glass ingredient ALKALI, LIME, POTASH, SAND, SILICA, SODA
glassmaker GLAZIER
glassy CRYSTAL, HYALINE, VITRIC
gleam GLINT, GLOZE
glide SKATE, SKI(D), SKIM, SKIP, SLIDE, SLIP
globe CLEW, EARTH, ORB, SPHERE
gloom BLUES, DUMPS, MURK
gloomy ADUSK, DARK, DOUR, DREAR(Y), MOROSE, WAN
gloss EXCUSE, EXEGESIS, SHEEN
glossary CLAVIS, LEXICON
glossy GLACE, GLIB, NITID, SLICK
glove CESTUS, MITT
glove shape TRANK
glow EXCEL, RUTILATE
glowing CANDENT, LAMBENT
glucoside ESTEVIN, GEIN, RUTIN
glue AGAR, MUCILAGE
glut CLOY, GORGE, SATE, SURFEIT
glutton HELLUO, CORMORANT
gnarl GROWL, KNUR(R), NUR(R), SNAG
gnome see ELF
go astray ABERRATE, ERR
go on! GARN, SCAT, SCRAM
goad ANKUS, EGG, GAD, PRICK, PROD, SPUR
goal AIM, BOURN(E), META, POST, THULE
goatish CAPRINE, HIRCINE
goblet CHALICE, HANAP, TASS
goblin BHUT, NIS(SE), POOK, PUCA, PUCK; see ELF
God ADONAI, ALLAH, ELOHIM, IAM, JAH, JEHOVAH, JHVH, YAHWEH, YHVH
god, false BAAL(IM), DAGON, MOLOCH
goddess DEA, STAR(LET)
god(s) DEI, DEITY, DEUS, DI(I), IDOL, PARAGON, TOTEM
gods, goddesses see p. 195
gold AU(RUM), CYME, GILT, ORO
golden AUREATE, AURIC, DURRY
golf club BRASSIE, CLEEK, DRIVER, MASHIE, (MID)IRON, NIBLICK, PUTTER, SPOON, WEDGE, WOOD
golf term BAFF, BIRDIE, BISQUE, BOGEY, BONE, CHIP, DIVOT, DORMIE, EAGLE, FORE, HOOK, LIE, LOFT, MULLIGAN, PAR, PITCH, PUT(T), SCLAFF, SLICE, TEE

golfer BOLT, CASPER, DUBBER, HOGAN, JONES, LITTLER, NICHOLS, PALMER, PLAYER, SANDERS, SNEAD, TEER, VENTURI, YANCEY
gone AGO, OUT, PAST, YORE
goods BONA, FEE, STOCK, WARES, WRACK
goods in sea FLOTSAM, JETSAM
goods sunk LAGAN, LAGEND, LIGAN
gore CRUOR, GUSSET; see STAB
gorge CHASM, CLOY, FLUME, GLUT, GULLY, RAVINE, STRID, TANGI
Gorgons EURYALE, MEDUSA, STHENO
gospel EVANGEL, EVANGILE, SYNOPTIC
gossip CAT, CLAVER, DIRT, EME, GUP, NORATE, ONDIT, TATTLE
Goth ALARIC, BERIG, EURIC, FILIMER, LEOVIGILD, RODERICK, THEODORIC
government POLITY, REGIME(N), STATE, SWAY
government control REGIE
governor BEY, DEY, DYNAST, HOSPODAR, KHEDIVE, PASHA, PILOT, REGENT, REGULATOR, SATRAP, SHEREEF, SHERIF, SHOGUN, TUCHUN, TUPAN, TYCOON, VAIVOD, VALI, VOIVOD(E), WALI
grace ADORN, CHARM, ESTE, MERCY, PARDON, TACT
graceful FEAT, GAINLY, GENT, SVELTE, SYLPHIC
Graces AGLAIA, EUPHROSYNE, THALIA
grade CLASS, LEVEL, MARK, RANK, RATE, SLANT, SORT, STEP
Graeae DEINO, ENYO, PEMPHREDO
graft BRIBE, CLAVE, (S)CION, SLIP
grain BIT, BRAN, CEREAL, GRIST, MEAL, SAMP, SEED, SPECK, TEMPER, WALE; see p. 228
grammatical term ACTIVE, ARTICLE, COPULA, FINITE, GENDER, JUSSIVE, MODE, MOOD, PARADIGM, PARSE, PARTICLE, PASSIVE, SUBJECT, SYLLEPSIS, SYNESIS, TELIC; see CASE, TENSE
granary BIN, CRIB, GOLA, GRANGE, GUNGE, GUNJ, SILO
grandchild OY(E)
grandparental AVAL
grant AWARD, CEDE, CHARTER, ENAM, MISE, PATENT, REMISE
grape disease APOPLEXY, ESCA
grape-like UVAL
graphite KISH, LEAD, PLUMBAGO
grasp EREPT, HENT, SEIZE
grassland LEA, MEAD, PAMPA, PASTURE, PRAIRIE, RANGE, SAVANNA, SWARD, VELD(T)
grate ABRADE, CHARK, GRIDE, JAR, RASP
gratify ARRIDE, PLEASE, SATE
gratinate BROWN, CRISP
grating GRID, GRILL(E), HOARSE, LATTICE, RASP(Y)
gratuity BOON, CUMSHA(W), FEE, PILON, TIP, VAIL
grave BARROW, CARVE, FOSSE, MOUND, SEDATE, SOBER, SOMBER, STAID, SUANT; see TOMB
gravestone MARKER, SLAB, STELA(E), STELAI, STELE
graze AGIST, BROWSE, FEED, NICK, RUB
grease AXUNGE, BRIBE, LARD, MORT, OIL, SUET
great AUGUST, BARO, SUPER, MICKLE
great number GALAXY, HEAP, HOST, LAC, LAKH, LEGION
Greece ACHAEA, ACHAIA, ATTICA, (H)ELLAS
greed AVIDITY, CUPIDITY, EDACITY
greedy GRIPPLE
green CALLOW, LEAFY, RAW, VERD(ANT)
greenhorn IKONA, ROOKIE, TYRO
greeting ACCOIL, ALOHA, AVE, CURTSY, HAIL, HELLO, NETOP, SALUTE
grief DOLE, DOLOR, MISERY, WOE
grill GRATING, GRID, QUIZ, RACK, TAVERN
grim DOUR, MACABRE, SET
grimace MOUE, MOW(E), SCOWL, SMIRK
grind BRAY, CHEW, CRAM, GRIT, MILL, WHET
grinder MILL, MOLAR, TOOTH
grindstone GRIT, HONE, MANO, METATE
grit GRAVEL, NERVE, PLUCK, SAND
grits KASHA
grommet BECKET, EYELET
groom BENEDICT, CURRY, EQUERRY, (H)OSTLER, PAGE, TRAIN, SAIS, SICE, SYCE
groove CHASE, CROZE, FLUTE, RABBET, RAGGLE, RUT, SCARF, STRIA, SULCUS
grooved LIRATE, STRIATE
grope FEEL, FUMBLE, PROBE

gross CRASS, CRUDE, RANK
grotto see CAVE
group BAND, BLOC, BODY, CADRE, CLASS, CORPS, CREW, ERA, GENUS, MUSTER, NYE, PHYLUM, TEAM; see BEVY
grove COPSE, NEMUS, TOPE
grow ACCRUE, BREED, MATURE, RAISE, THRIVE, WAX
growing out ENATE
growl GNAR, GURL, SNARL, YAR(R)
growth CANCER, CLAVUS, CORN, MOLE, POLYP, TUMOR, WART, WEN
grub ASSART, DIG, EATS, LARVA
grudge ENVY, PIQUE, SPITE
gruel ATOLE, CAUDLE
gruesome GRIM, GRISLY, MACABRE
guarantee AVAIL, BOND, GAGE, SCHOLIUM, SURETY, WARRANT
guard BANTAY, CONVOY, DRABANT, FENDER, GHAFIR, SENTRY, SHIELD, TILE(R)
guardhouse BRIG
guardian ARGUS, CERBERUS, CURATOR, TRUSTEE, WARDEN
guerrilla(s) MAQUI(S), REBEL
guide CLEW, CICERONE, CONVOY, KEY, LEAD(ER), PILOT, PIR, SCOUT, STEER
guidebook BAEDEKER, ORDO
guiding DIRIGENT, POLAR
Guido's scale see p. 191
guild EPIPHYTE, HANSE, HUI, LIANA, PARASITE, TONG
guilty CULPABLE, NOCENT
gulf ABYSS, BIGHT, CHASM
gullet CRAW, MAW, SWALLOW
gulls, pert. to LARINE
gully ARROYO, DONGA, SIKE
gum ACACIA, ACACIN(E), AMRA, BALATA, CAROB, CHICLE, GHATTI, KARAYA, KINO, LATEX, LOBAN, MATTI, MYRRH, WATTLE, XYLAN
gumbo OCRA, OKRA, SOUP
gums, pert. to GINGIVAL, ULETIC
gun part BARREL, BOLT, BORE, BREECH, BUTT, CHAMBER, COCK, CYLINDER, GOMER, HAMMER, LOCK, MAGAZINE, NAB, SIGHT, STOCK, TRIGGER
guns see p. 108
gunfire FUSILLADE, RAFALE, SALVO, VOLLEY
gusto PALATE, RELISH, ZEST
gutta DROP, MINIM, SIAK, SOH
guttural HUSKY, VELAR
guy-rope STAY, VANG
gym feat CROSS, KIP(P), LEVER, SCALE
gypsy CAIRD, CALE, CALO, CHAI, CHAL, GITANO, NOMAD, RANI, ROAMER, ROMANY, ROMI, ROM(NI), RYE

H

habit GARB, MODE, USAGE, WONT
habituate ADDICT, DRILL, ENURE, FREQUENT, INURE, USE
hack COUGH, DEVIL, DRUDGE, GRUB, NAG, TAXI, WRITER
hackneyed BANAL, STALE, TRITE
Hades ARALU, DIS, EREBUS, ORCUS, PLUTO, SHEOL, TARTARUS
hag BELDAM, CRONE, FURY, HARPY, HARRIDAN, SHREW, VECKE, VIRAGO, VIXEN
haggard DRAWN, GAUNT, WAN
haggle CAVIL, PALTER, PRIG
hail AHOY, AVAST, AVE, SALUTE
hair CRINE, DOWN, FUR, NAP, PILE, ROACH, SHAG, THATCH, TRESS
hair dressing POMADE
hair, fix COIF, MARCEL, PERM, SET, WAVE
hair, remove BOB, (D)EPILATE, TRIM
hair shirt CILICE
hairless BALD, GLABROUS, PELON
hairy CILIATE, COMATE, COMOSE, CRINATED, CRINITE, HIRSUTE, PILAR, PILOSE, VILLOSE, VILLOUS
half DEMI, HEMI, MOIETY, SEMI
half-breed GRIFF(E), LADINO, MESTEE, MESTIZO, METIS(SE), MULATTO, MULE, MUSTEE
half-moon ARC, CRESCENT, LUNE
hall(s) ATRIA, AULA, DORM, FOYER, ODEON, SAAL
halo AURA, AUREOLA, AUREOLE, BROUGH, CORONA, NIMB(US)
hamlet ALDEA, DORP, MIR, THORP, TREF
Hamlet site DENMARK, ELSINORE
hamper CRAMP, FETTER, PED, TRAMMEL
hand DEAL, MANUS, PUD, SCRIPT
hand, pert. to CHIRAL, MANUAL
handcuff DARBY, FETTER, MANACLE
handicap HINDER, ODDS, RACE
handle ANSA, BOOL, DEAL, EAR, HAFT, HANK, HELVE, HILT, LUG, PAW, SNATH(E), SNEAD, SWIPE, TOTE, TREAT

handled ANSATE, DEALT, PALMED
handstone MANO
handwriting on the wall MENE, TEKEL, UPHARSIN
hang DANGLE, DRAPE, DROOP, HOVER, (IM)PEND
hank COIL, LOOP, RAN, SKEIN
happen BEFALL, BETIDE, CHANCE, EVENE, OCCUR
happy BLITHE, COSH, FAUST
harangue DIATRIBE, ORATE, RANT, SCREED, TIRADE
harass BAIT, BESET, HECKLE, JADE, NAG, PESTER
harbor BAY, COVE, HAVEN, PIER, PORT
hard ARDUOUS, CALLOUS, FLINTY, STEELY, STERN
harden ENURE, GEL, INDURATE, INURE, KERN, SET, TEMPER
hardtack PANTILE, TOMMY
harem ODA, SERAGLIO, ZENANA
harm BALE, BANE, DAMAGE, DERE, INJURE, MAR, SCATHE
harmful ILL, NOCENT, NOXAL, NOISOME, NOXIOUS
harmful influence NOXA, UPAS
harmonize AGREE, ATTUNE, SET
harmony CONCORD, KEY, UNISON
harness ARMOR, EQUIP, GEAR, GRAITH, RIG, TAME
harness part BILLET, BLIND, CRUPPER, HAME, TERRET, TRACE, TUG
Harpies AELLO, CELAENO, OCYPETE
harrow CHIP, DRAG, TILL
harsh ACERB, CRUEL, DURE, STERN
harvest CROP, GARNER, KIRN, RAB(B)I, REAP, YIELD
hassock PESS, TU(F)T
hasty pudding MUSH, SEPON
hate ABHOR, AVERSION, DOSA, MALICE, MISO, ODIUM, RANCOR
haul BOOTY, BOUSE, LUG, SWAG, TRICE, TUG
haunt DEN, DIVE, NEST, OBSESS, PURLIEU, SPOOK
haven ASYLUM, HITHE, LEE, PORT, REFUGE
haystack COB, COIL, GOAF, MOW, PIKE, RICK
haze BRUME, FILM, FOG, GLIN, MIST, PALL, SMOG
head BEAN, CHIEF, LEAD, NODDLE, NOGGIN, NOODLE, PATE, POLL, VAN
head, membrane covering CAUL, OMENTUM
headland BLUFF, CAPE, NAZE, NESS, RAS
headman HETMAN, INDUNA
heap COB, PILE, RAFF, RAFT, STACK
hearing AUDIENCE, INQUEST, OYER, PROBE, TRIAL
h(e)arken ATTEND, HEAR, HEED, HIST, LIST(EN)
heart CARDIA, COR(E), GIST, PITH, TICKER
heat ARDOR, CALOR, CAUMA, FEVER, TEPOR, WARM, ZEAL
heat unit BTU, CALORIE, THERM
heath BENT, GRIG, MOOR
heathen INFIDEL, PAGAN, PAYNIM
heave FLING, KECK, SCEND, SWELL
heaven CIEL, EDEN, SION, SKY, URANO, VALHALLA, ZION
heavenly ANGELIC, DIVINE, EDENIC, SERAPHIC, SUPERNAL, URANIC
heavenly being AFA, ANGEL, CHERUB, SERAPH(IM)
Hebrew marginal note GRI, KERE, K(E)RI, QERE, Q(U)ERI
hedge RADDLE, REW, ROW
heed MIND, NOTE, OBEY, RECK
heel CAD, CALX, CAREEN, OBEY
height ACME, CLIMAX, PITCH, STATURE, SUMMIT
heir H(A)ERES, (IN)HERITOR, LEGATEE, PARCENER, SCION
helical SPIRAL, TORSE
hell ABADDON, ABYSS, AVERNUS, GEHENNA, INFERNO, NARAKA, PIT, TOPHET
helmet-shaped GALEATE
helmsman COX(ON), COXSWAIN, PILOT, TILLER
help ABET, REMEDY, SECOND, STAFF, SUCCOR, TIDE
helper AIDE, ASSIST(ER)
hem in BESET, FENCE
hence AWAY, ERGO, OFF, THEN
Henry VIII's wives ANNE, BOLEYN, CATHERINE, CLEVES, HOWARD, JANE, PARR
herald BLAZON, CRIER, USHER
herbs see p. 123
herd CAVIYA, CORRAL, DROVE, FLOCK, GAM, MOB, POD, SHOAL
herdsman COWBOY, GAUCHO, RANCHERO, SENN, VACHER, VAQUERO
hereditary factor DNA, GEN(E), RNA
heretic DISSENTER, PERVERT
heretofore ERENOW, ERST, QUONDAM
hermit ANCHORITE, ASCETIC, EREMITE, RECLUSE, SANTON, STYLITE

hero DEMIGOD, IDOL, LION, PALADIN
heroic EPIC(AL), GALLANT, VALIANT
heroic poem see EPIC
hesitate DEMUR, FALTER, HAW, HEM, TEETER, WAVER
hiatus CHASM, COL, GAP, LACUNA
hidden ARCANE, COVERT, INNER, LATENT, PERDU
hide(s) CACHE, FELL, JUFTI, KIP, MASK, PELT, SKIN, VEIL
high ALOFT, ALT, DEAR, DRUNK
highest point APEX, APOGEE, ZENITH
highlander GAEL, SCOT, TARTAN
highwayman BRIGAND, LADRONE, PAD
hike BOOST, DECAMP, TRAMP
hill BRAE, BULT, BUTTE, COP(PLE), DAGH, DENE, DOWN, DUNE, HOLT, KAME, KNAP, KNOLL, KOP(JE), LOMA, LOMITA, MESA, MORRO, MOUND, PAHA, RATH, TERTRE, TOR, TUMP
hilt HAFT, HANDLE, HELVE
hind BACK, REAR, ROE
hinder BALK, DETER, HAMPER
Hindu BABU, JAIN, JAINA, SEIK, HIKH, TAMIL
hinge AXIS, BUTT, JOINT, PIVOT
hint CLEW, C(L)UE, IMPLY, INKLE, TIP
hire CHARTER, ENGAGE, LEASE, LET, RENT, SALARY
hired labor TOGT
historian ANTIQUARY, ARCHIVIST, BOSWELL
history ANNALS, LORE, MEMOIRS, RECORD
hit CLOUT, LARRUP, POMMEL
Hittite ancestor HETH
hive(s) APIARY, GUM, SKEP, SWARM, UREDO
hoarder MISER, NIGGARD
hoarfrost RAG, RIME
hoax BAM, GULL, CANARD, HUMBUG, RUSE
hobgoblin BOG(E)Y, PUCK, SPRITE
hock GAMBREL, HAM, HOX, PAWN
hockey term BULLY, CAGE, CAMAN, CAMMOCK, FACEOFF, GOALIE, ICING, PUCK
hodgepodge CENTO, HASH, MESS, OLIO, OLLA
hoist DROP, HEAVE, JACK, LIFT, REAR
hold AVAST, BELAY, DETAIN, GRIP, HATCH, STAY, THINK
holder DOP(P), OWNER, TENANT
holding SEAT, TENURE
hole BORE, DENT, EYE, GEAT, GIME, LILL, PIT, PORE, SCYE, SIPAPU, SLOT, SPRUE, VOID
holiday(s) FERIA, FERIE, FIESTA; NONLEDAY, RECESS
hollow DENT, DIMPLE, FALSE, GORE, GULF, HOWE, PIT, SCOOP
holy man FAKIR, SADH(U)
home ABODE, ASTRE(R), HABITAT, HEARTH, NEST
honey DARLING, DEAR, MEL(L)
honey drink MEAD, MORAT
honeycombed FAVOSE, RIDDLED
hoodoo HEX, JINX, JONAH, JYNX
hoof CLEE, UNGUIS, UNGULA
hooked ADUNC(OUS), AQUILINE, CLEEKED, FALCATE(D), GAFFED, HAMATE, HAMOSE, HAMUS
hope ASPIRE, LONG, SPES
hopscotch stone PEEVER
horizontal FLUSH, PLANE, PRONE
horizontal timber LINTEL
hormone ANDROGEN, CORTISONE, ESTRADIOL, ESTRIOL, ESTROGEN, INSULIN, LIPOCAIC, PROGESTIN, PROLACTIN, SECRETIN, THYROXINE
horn ANTLER, CORNU, DAG, PRONG, RHYTON
horn tissue KERATIN, SCUR
hornless ACEROUS, DODDIE, NOT, POLEY, POLLED
horse BLOCK, FRAME, TRESTLE
horse, leg parts CANNON, CORONET, FETLOCK, GASKIN, HOCK, HOOF, INSTEP, PASTERN, SHANK, STIFLE
horse(s), command to GEE, GIDDAP, HAW, HUP, WHOA
horse disease HEAVES, NAGANA, SPAVIN, SURRA(H)
horseshoeing frame TRAVE, TREVE
host ARMY, HORDE, LEGION, PATEN, PYX, WAFER
hostel(ry) see INN
hot iron CAUTER(Y)
house ABODE, BAHAY, CASA, COTE, COTTAGE, ECO, GAZEBO, HOME, HUT, IGLOO, IGLU, MAISON, MANSION, ROOF, TEMBE, TUPEK, VILLA
household MENAGE
H-shaped ZYGAL
hub BOSTON, CENTER, NAVE
hubbub ADO, STIR, TUMULT
hue COLOR, CRY, TINGE
huge ENORM, GIANT, VAST
Huguenot leader ADRETS, COLIGNY, CONDE, MORNAY
hull CALYX, HUSK, POD, SHUCK
human BIPED, HOMO, MORTAL
humble ABASE, DEMEAN, MEEK

humid DANK, MOIST, SULTRY
humor BABY, CATER, FUN, MOOD, WIT
humorist ADAMS, ADE, ALLEN, BENCHLEY, COBB, NASH, NYE, ROGERS, THURBER
Hun ATLI, ATTILA, BOCHE, ETZEL, GERMAN, VANDAL
hundred CENTUM, HECTO
hunger ACORIA, CLEM, ITCH, PINE, YEN
hunt FERRET, POACH, SHIKAR, STALK, TRAIL, TRAP
hunter JA(E)GER, NIMROD, ORION, SHIKARI
huntress ATALANTA, DIANA
hurry DASH, HASTE(N), HIE, SESSA, TEAR
hurt ACHE, DERE, HARM, IMPAIR, LESION, MAR
hurtful MALEFIC, NOCENT, NOISOME
husband GOODMAN, GROOM, OLDMAN, SANNUP; see SPOUSE
husband's brother LEVIR
hush ALLAY, CALM, (H)SH, SHUSH
husk BRAN, HULL, LEAM, SHUCK
hut BARI, CABIN, COT(E), HOGAN, HOVEL, ISBA, JACAL, LEANTO, MIAM(IA), MIMI, SHACK, SHED, SKEO, TOLDO
hydrate SLAKE
hydrocarbon BUTANE, CYMENE, MELENE, (M)ETHANE, OCTANE, PINENE, PROPANE, RETENE, TERPENE, TOLAN, TOLUENE
hydroelectric plant see p. 167
hydrogen compound HYDRIDE, IMINE
hyperbole AUXESIS, ELA
hypnotic condition COMA, TRANCE

I

I EGO, IOTA, SELF
ice BERG, FLOE, GRUE, LOLLY, PAYOLA, SERAC, SHERBET, SISH
iced FROSTED, GELID, GLACE
idea EIDOS, FANCY, SCHEME
ideal HERO, IDOL, MODEL, UTOPIAN
ideal state EREWHON, ICARIA, OCEANA, UTOPIA
identical ALIKE, ONE, SAME
ideology DOGMA, ISM, THEORY
idiocy ANOESIA
idiom DIALECT, LOCUTION
idiot AMENT, CRETIN, MORON, OAF
idle GAMMER, LAZE, LAZY, LOAF, LOITER, OFF, OTIANT, OTIOSE, SORN; see INERT
idol (E)IDOLON, FETISH, IDOLUM, LION, PAGOD(A), SYMBOL, TERAPH, ZEMI
if not ELSE, NISI, UNLESS
ignorance TAMAS
ill ABED, EVIL, UNWELL, WICKED
ill will MALICE, RANCOR, SPITE, VENOM
illusion CHIMERA, FANTASY
image EFFIGY, FORM, ICON, IKON, RECEPT, REPLICA, SIGIL, STATUE; see IDOL
imagine IDEATE, SURMISE, WEEN, WIS
imbecile AMENT, ANILE, CRETIN, DOTARD, FATUOUS, FOOL, MORON
imbibe BIB, DRINK, GULP, SIP
imbue INFUSE, INSPIRE, PERVADE, TINGE
imitate APE, ECHO, MIME, MIMIC
imitation APISM, COPY, MIMESIS, MIMICRY
immature GREEN, NEANIC, PUERILE, RAW
immediately ANON, NOW, PROMPTLY
immerse DIP, DOUSE, DUCK, DUNK
immigrant ALIEN, METIC
immunizing substance HAPTEN(E), SERUM, VACCINE
impact BRUNT, JAR, SHOCK
impair DAMAGE, HARM, MAR, SPOIL, VITIATE
impasse CULDESAC, DEADLOCK
impassive PLACID, STOIC, STOLID
impede BLOCK, ESTOP, HAMPER, STYMIE, THWART
impertinent MALAPERT, PERT, SASSY, SAUCY
implant (EN)GRAFT, (EN)ROOT, FIX, INSPIRE, INSTILL
implement DEVICE, ENFORCE, EQUIP, GEAR, KIT, UTENSIL
implicit DEDUCED, INNATE, TACIT
impose ENTAIL, FOB, FOIST, IMPUTE, LAY, LEVY, OBTRUDE, PALM
impost see TAX
impostor CHARLATAN, FAKER, FRAUD, QUACK, RINGER, SHAM
impress DENT, MARK, PRINT, STAMP
imprison CAGE, CONFINE, IMMURE, QUAD
improve AMEND, EMEND, REVISE
improvise ADLIB, CONTRIVE, INVENT, PONG, VAMP

impudence BRASS, CHEEK, GALL, LIP, NERVE
impulse IMPETUS, MOTIVE, SPUR, URGE
impute (A)RET, ASCRIBE, IMPOSE
inactive DORMANT, FAINEANT; see IDLE, INERT
inadequate SCANT(Y), UNEQUAL
inane SILLY, VAPID, VOID
inarticulate APHONIC, DUMB, MUTE
inborn INNATE, NATIVE
incense ENRAGE, GUM, JOSS, MATTI, MYRRH, OLIBANUM, SPICE, STACTE
incentive IMPULSE, MOTIVE, SPUR
incidentally APROPOS, OBITER
incinerate (IN)CREMATE
incite ABET, EGG, FOMENT, GOAD, IMPEL, PROD, SPUR, SUBORN, URGE
inclination BEND, BENT, BIAS, SLANT, TASTE
incline CANT, DEVIATE, LEAN, RAMP, SLOPE, TEND, TILT, TREND, VERGE
inclined APT, PRONE, SKEW
income ANNUITY, PENSION, RENTE, USANCE
increase ACCRUE, DILATE, EKE, GREATEN, RISE, WAX
incubate BROOD, CONCOCT, HATCH
incubus NIGHTMARE, SPIRIT
incursion FORAY, INROAD, RAID
indeed AROO(N), ARU, (I)WIS
indentation CRENA(E), CRENELET, DINGE, MARGIN, NICK, NOTCH
index FIST, GNOMON, PIP, TABLE
Indian chief CACIQUE, CAZIQUE, INCA, SACHEM, SAGAMORE, TYEE
indicator ARROW, DIAL, GAUGE, POINTER, VANE
indict ARRAIGN, (IM)PEACH
indifferent BLASE, NEUTRAL, STOIC(AL)
indigenous EDAPHIC, ENDEMIC, INNATE, NATIVE
indite PEN, (IN)SCRIBE, WRITE
individual BEING, BION, ONE, SELF
Indo-European ARYA(N)
indolent LAZY, LISTLESS, OTIOSE, SORN, SUPINE, TORPID
induce LEAD, REASON, URGE
indulge CODDLE, PAMPER, PET(TLE)
inebriate SOT, SQUIFFY, TIGHT, TIPSY, TOPER
inert AMORT, DEAD, DULL, LATENT, SUPINE
infamy ODIUM, SHAME, VILLAINY
infant BABE, BAIRN, BRAT, CHIT, PAPOOSE, TOT, WEAN
infantryman ASKAR, CHASSEUR, DOGFACE, DOUGHBOY, ZOUAVE
infatuate BESOT, CHARM, ENAMOR
inference ILLATION, SURMISE
infidel ATHEIST, HEATHEN, HERETIC, KAFFIR, PAGAN, SARACEN
infinity ANATA, OLAM
infirm ANILE, SENILE, DECREPIT
inflame FAN, INCITE, IGNITE, RANKLE, RILE
inflammable PICEOUS
inflammable substance AMADOU, PUNK, TINDER
inflammation ANGINA, ITIS, RUBOR
inflexible ADAMANT, DOGGED, GRIM, IRON, RIGID, STARK
inflict DEAL, IMPOSE, WREAK
inflorescence AMENT, CYME, RACEME, SPADIX, WHORL
influence AFFECT, IMPEL, INDUCE, PULL, SWAY, WEIGHT
influenza CATARRH, CORYZA, FLU, GRIP(PE)
inform APPRIZE, RAT, SQUEAL
information DATA, DOPE, LORE, NEWS
informer DELATOR, NARK, STOOL
infusion TEA, TINCTURE, WORT
inhabitant CIT(IZEN), DENIZEN, INMATE, ITE, RESIDENT
inheritance BEQUEST, LEGACY, PATRIMONY
inheritor see HEIR
inhibit BAR, ENJOIN, REPRESS
inhuman BESTIAL, FELL, SAVAGE
initiate BEGIN, EPOPT(A), FOUND, HAZE, INDUCT, OPEN, START
injure HARM, IMPAIR, LAME, MAIM, MAR, SCATHE, TEEN
injury ILL, LESION, MAYHEM, TORT, TRAUMA WOUND
inlaid work BUHL, MOSAIC, NIELLO, TARSIA
inlet BAY(OU), BIGHT, COVE, FIORD, RIA, SLOUGH, VOE, ZEE
inn AUBERGE, CHOULTRY, FONDA, HOSPICE, HOSTEL(RY) HOTEL, IMARET, KHAN, LOCANDA, LODGE. MOTEL, POSADA, SERAI, TABARD, TAVERN
inner ENTAL, ESOTERIC
innkeeper BONIFACE, HOST, PADRONE, PUBLICAN
insanity AMENTIA, DEMENTIA, FOLIE, LUNACY, MADNESS, MANIA, VESANIA

insect body part ACRON, CLAVA, COXA, FEELER, LABIUM, NOTUM, OCELLUS, PALP(US), STEMMA, THORAX
insect stage COCOON, EGG, INSTAR, LARVA, NYMPH, (PRE)PUPA, REDIA, (SUB)IMAGO
insects see p. 221
insert GODET, IMMIT, INLAY, INSET, PANEL
insidious ARCH, CUNNING, SLY
insight ACUMEN, KEN
insipid FLAT, JEJUNE, PROSY
inspect AUDIT, OVERSEE, SCAN
inspire EXCITE, IMBUE, INHALE
install INSTATE, INVEST, ORDAIN
instant JIFFY, POP, TRICE
instead ELSE, LIEU, RATHER
instigate ABET, EGG, INCITE, PROMPT, PROVOKE, SPUR, SUBORN
instruct BRIEF, COACH, EDUCATE, IMPART
instructor COACH, LECTOR, LECTURER; see TEACHER
instrument AGENCY, AGENT, DEED, DEVICE, DOCUMENT, GADGET, MEANS, MEDIA, MEDIUM, ORGAN, WILL
insulate (EN)ISLE, ISOLATE
insult AFFRONT, CAG, FIG, RUFFLE, SLUR
integer NORM
intellect INWIT, MAHAT, MIND, NOESIS, NOUS, REASON, SENSE
intend AIM, ETTLE, INTEREST, MEAN, SUPPOSE, TRY
inter BURY, INHUME, INURN
interdict BAN, ENJOIN, TABOO, VETO
interest BEHALF, MOTIVE, WEAL
interference BLOOM, FLARE, GHOST, HUM, MUSH NOISE, RAIN, SNOW, STATIC
interim DIASTEM; see INTERVAL
interior CELLA, INLAND, INLY
interlace BRAID, PLEACH, WEAVE
interlude ENTRACTE, EPISODE, STASIMON; see INTERVAL
interpret CONSTRUE, EXPOUND, READ REDE
interpreter DRAGOMAN, EXEGETE, LATINER, LING(UI)STER
intersect CROSS CUT, DECUSSATE MEET
interstice AREOLA, AREOLE, PORE, SPIRACLE, STOMA
interval BREAK, CAESURA, GAP, HIATUS, INTERIM, LACUNA, LAPSE, REST
intervening MESNE
interweave MAT, PLA(I)T, PLASH, RADDLE, TWINE
intimidate ABASH, AWE, BULLY, COW, DAUNT
intone CHANT, CROON, RECITE
intricate D(A)EDAL, GORDIAN, MAZY
intrigue AFFAIR, AMOUR, BRIGUE, CABAL, WILE
introduce BROACH, IMMIT, INSERT, LAUNCH, PRESENT, USHER
introduction PREAMBLE, PRELUDE, PROEM
inundation see FLOOD
invalid DISABLED, FALSE, NULL, SICK VOID
inveigle COAX, ENTICE, LURE
invest CLOTHE, ENDOW, ENDUE, INDUE, ORDAIN
investigate INDAGATE, PROBE
invite ASK, BID, SOLICIT, SUE
involve COIL, ENTAIL, LAP
iodine source KELP
iota see JOT
ipecac source EVEA
irascible BRASH, EDGY, TESTY
irate ANGRY, MAD, PIQUED, WROTH
Ireland, Irish EIRANN, EIRE, ERIN, ERSE, HIBERNIA, IRENA
Irish party SINNFEIN
iron FERRUM, MANGLE, MASHIE, STEEL
iron, pert. to FERRIC, FERROUS
irons see FETTER
irony SARCASM, SATIRE
irrational number SURD
irritate CHAFE, GALL, HECTOR, IRE, IRK, NETTLE, RANKLE, RILE VEX
isinglass AGAR, KANTEN, MICA
island AIT, ATOLL, CAY, EYOT, HOLM, ILE, ILOT, INSULA, ISLE(T), IS(O)LA, KEY, REEF
isolate ENISLE
Israelites HEBREWS, JEWS, SION, ZION
issue DOLE, EGRESS, EMIT, ENSUE, FLUX, METE PROGENY
isthmus BALK, NECK, STRAIT
Italian family CENCI, DONATI, DORIA, ESTE MEDICI
itch CRAVE, ECZEMA, MANGE, PRURITUS, PSORA, SCABIES
ivory DENTINE, TUSH, TUSK

J

jack BOWER, HOIST, KNAVE, MULE, NOB(S), OPENER, PAM, RABBIT

jacket PEEL, RIND, SKIN
jagged EROSE, RAGGED, SERRATE(D), ZAG, ZIG
jai alai PELOTA
jai alai term BLE, CESTA, FRONTON, QUANTE, REBOTE
jail BRIG, CAGE, CELL, CLINK, COOLER, COOP, GAOL, JUG, LOCKUP, PEN, QUOD, STIR
janitor PORTER, SEXTON, SUPER
Japan(ese) AINO, AINU, CIPANGO, NIPPON
Japanese-American ISSEI, KIBEI, NISEI, SANSEI
Japanese painting school KANO, SESSHU, SHIJO, TOSA, UKIYOE
Japanese writing KANA
jar AMPHORA, BANGA, CADUS, CLASH, CROCK, CRUSE, DOLIUM, EWER, HYDRIA, JOLT, JUG, KALPIS, OLLA, PELIKE, TERRINE, URN
jargon see SLANG
jaunty CHIC, COCKY, DAPPER, MODISH, PERK(Y), SHOWY, SPRUCE
Javanese language KAVI, KAWI
javelin JEREED, JERID
jeer see MOCK
jejune ARID, BARREN, DRY, FLAT, INSIPID, STALE
jelly ASPIC, JAM, PECTIN
jest JAPE, JIBE, MOT, QUIP
jester GOLIARD; see BUFFOON
jet EBON, SABRE, SCORPION, SPOUT, STREAM
jet propulsion unit JATO
jetty MOLE, PIER, STARLING, WHARF
jewel BIJOU, GEM, LOUPE, PRIZE, TRINKET
jewelry, mock LOGIE, PASTE, STRASS
jinx HEX, HOODOO, JONAH
jittery EDGY, HECTIC, JUMPY
Job's comforters BILDAD, ELIHU, ELIPHAZ, ZOPHAR
jog DUNCH, HOD, NUDGE, REMIND, TROT
John EOAN, EOIN, HANS, I(V)AN, SEAN
join ATTACH, ENLIST, MERGE, MITER, MITRE, RABBET, SPLICE, UNITE, WELD, YOKE
joint DUAL, HINGE, LINK, NEXUS, NODE, SEAM, TENON; see p. 106
joke GAG, JAPE, JEST, JOSH, KID, MOT, PUN, QUIP, RIB, SALLY, TWIT
joker BUFFOON, CARD, CLOWN, DOR, FARCEUR, JESTER, WAG, WIT
jostle BUFFET, ELBOW, HUSTLE, JOG, MAUL
jot ACE, BIT, IOTA, MITE, MOTE, NOTE, TITTLE, WHIT
journalist ADAMS, BIERCE, BOK, BOWLES, BRISBANE, BROUN, CURTIS, DANA, DAVIS, FINLEY, GODKIN, GRADY, GREELEY, HARVEY, HEARST, HOWE, MCCLURE, MENCKEN, NOYES, OCHS, PYLE, REID, RICE, RUNYON, SWOPE, WEED, WHITE
journey EYRE, HIKE, ITER, JAUNT, JUNKET, ODYSSEY, RIDE, TOUR, TRAVEL, TREK, TRIP
joy BLISS, DELIGHT, GLEE, MIRTH, RAPTURE, ZEST
joyous BLITHE, GAY, ELATED, MERRY
judge(s) ALCALDE, ARBITER, CADI, CAZI, CAZY, CRITIC, DEEM, DOOM, FOUD, HAKIM, JUDEX, KADI, KAZI, KAZY, PUISNE, REFEREE, RATE, TRY, UMP(IRE)
judgment ARRET, DOOM, VIEW
jug BUIRE, EWER, LOCKUP, LOTA(H), OLPE, PITCHER, TOBY
juice MUST, RHOB, SAP(A), STUM, SURA
jumble MEDLEY, MESS, MIX, OLIO, PI(E)
jump BOUND, JERK, HOP, SKIP, VAULT
juncture JOINT, SEAM, SUTURE
junior CADET, FILS, PUISNE
jurisdiction SOC, SOKE, VENUE
jurist CARDOZA, DARROW, ERSKIN, GAIUS, HAND, HOLMES, KEY, LANDIS, SAVIGNY, SOLON, TANEY
jury PANEL, VENIRE
just BARELY, DUE, FAIR, MORAL
justice, chief CHASE, FULLER, HUGHES, JAY, STONE, TAFT, VINSON, WAITE, WARREN, WHITE

K

keel LIST, TILT, CAREEN, CARINA, FIN
keen ACRID, ACUTE, ASTUTE, DIRGE, GARE, SHARP, SNELL, TART, WAIL
keenness ACIES, ARDOR, ZEST
keeper CURATOR, MAHOUT, NAB, RANGER, TILER, WARDEN
keepsake MEMENTO, TOKEN
keg CADE, FIRKIN, TUN, VAT

kernel CORE, GIST, NUT, PIT
kettle CA(U)LDRON, POTHOLE
key CAY, CLAVIS, CLUE, CODE, COTTER, ISLE(T), PITCH, PONY, SPLINE, TAPPER, TONALITY
key part BIT, BOW, COLLAR, LOOP, PIN, STEM, WEB
key-shaped CLECHE, URDE, URDY
kid BANTER, JOSH, LAD, RIB, SUEDE
kidnap RAVISH, SHANGHAI
kidneys, pert. to RENAL
kiln LEER, LEHR, OAST, OST, OVEN, TILER(Y)
kind BENIGN. GENIAL, GENOS, GENRE, GENTLE, GENUS, ILK, SEELY, SPECIES TYPE
kindle IGNITE, TIND, WHET
kindness BOON, GRACE, LENITY
kindred (A)KIN, COGNATE, KITH, SIB
king KRAL, PADISHAH, REGULUS, REX, REY, ROI, SOPHY
king, pert. to REG(N)AL
kingdom DOMAIN, REALM
kinship AFFINITY, AGNATION, ENATION, NASAB
kiss BUSS, CARESS, OSCULATE, PECK, SMACK
kitchen COOKERY, CUISINE, GALLEY, SCULLERY
kitty ANTE, POOL, POT, WIDOW
knave BOWER, CHURL, JACK, LOREL, LOSEL, NOB(S), PAM ROGUE, SCAMP
knead ELT, MALAX, MASSAGE, PETRIE
knife BETRAY, SNEE, SNY, STAB
knight(s) BANNERET, BEVIS, DUB, EQUES EQUITES PALADIN, RITTER, SIR, TEMPLAR
knitting term GAUGE, PURL, SLEY, STITCH
knob BOSS, FINIAL, KNOP, STUD, UMBO
knobbed NODAL, NODOSE, TOROSE
knockout BASH, KAYO
knot AMORET, BEND, BURL, GNARL, GRANNY, HITCH, KNAR, KNOR, KNUR(L), MILE, NEP, NODE, NODI, NODUS, NOIL, SNAG
knot(s), remove ENODATE, UNRAVEL
know INTUIT, KEN, WIS(T), WOT
knowing GNOSTIC, SCIENT
knowledge KEN, KITH, LORE, NOESIS, OLOGY, SCIENTIA
Koran chapter SURA(H)
Korea CHOSEN
kosher, opposite of TREF(A)
Kubla Khan river ALPH

L

La Boheme character MIMI, MUSETTA, RODOLFO
label FILLET, INFULA, LAPPET, PASTER, STICKER, TAG
labor see WORK
labor union AFL, ARTEL, CIO, LOCAL
laborer COOLIE, FELLAH, HAND, NAVVY, PEON, SEGGON, TOTY
lace ADORN, A(I)GLET, ALENCON, BEAT, BRAID, CLUNY, EDGING, FILET, FILIGREE, GRILL(E), GUIPURE, LACIS, LASH, MACRAME, MALINES, ORRIS, SNARE, TATTING
lacerate LANIATE, RIP, TEAR
lacking DEVOID, SHORT, SHY
lacquer ENAMEL, JAPAN, VARNISH
ladder POMPIER, SCALE, STEE, STY
ladle BAIL, DIP, GEAT, SCOOP, SHANK
lady BEEBEE, BIBI, BURD, DAME; see MADAM
Lady of the Lake ELLEN, NIMUE, VIVIAN
lag DALLY, DRAG TARRY
lagoon HAFF, LIMAN
lake LAGOON, LOCH, LOUGH, MERE, SALINA, SHAT, SHOTT, TARN
lama DALAI, MONK, TESHU
lament (BE)WAIL DIRGE, GRIEVE, HONE, KEEN MOAN, (RE)PINE, RUE, WEY
lamentation LINOS, PLAINT, PLANGOR, TANGI
lamp ARGAND, CRUSIE DAVY, GEORDIE, LUCERNE, LUCIGEN
lamp, waving of ARATI
lancer HUSSAR, U(H)LAN
land ALIGHT, ALOD(IUM) ARADA, ARADO, ARDER, ASSART, DEBARK, DOAB DUAB FELI, GISH, GLEBE GORE, MULK, ODAL, SOLUM, TILTH, TRACT, UDAL WEALD
land, barren DESERT, GALL, WASTE
landholder THANE, THEGN, ZAMINDAR
landing DOCK, GAUT, GHAT, JETTY, KEY, LEVEE PIER, QUAI, QUAY, TARMAC, WHARF
landmark CAIRN, COPA, MEITH, SENAL

language DIALECT, DICTION, IDIOM, TONGUE; see p. 175
languish FLAG, PINE, WASTE
languor BLUES, ENNUI, KAIF, KE(E)F, KIEF, KIFF, TORPOR
lapel FLAP, REVER(S)
lapse ERR, SIN(K), VENALITY; see INTERVAL
lariat LASSO, LAZO, NOOSE, REATA, RIATA, ROPE
lariat eye HONDA, HONDO(O)
lash FLOG, KNUT, W(H)ALE, YERK; see BEAT, WHIP
lasso see LARIAT
last END(URE), FINAL(E), OMEGA
last but one PENULT
Last Mohican UNCAS
Last Supper C(O)ENA; see COMMUNION
latch(ing) BELAY, LASKET, SNECK
late DEAD, NEO, NEW, RECENT, SERO, TARDY
lath SLAT, SPALE, SPLINT
lather FOAM, FRENZY, FROTH, SCUM, SUDS, SPUME
lattice CANCELLI, TRELLIS
laugh(s) FLEER, GUFFAW, GIGGLE
laughable ABSURD, COMIC(AL), DROLL, RISIBLE
laughing RIANT
laughter, pert. to GELASTIC
lava ASH, BOMB, LAPILLUS, LATITE, MAGMA, SCORIA
law ACT, ADAT, CANON, CODE, DECALOG(UE), DROIT, EDICT, FAS, JURE, JUS, LEX, RULE, SALIC, STATUTE, TALION, TALMUD, TORA(H)
law, pert. to FORENSIC, LEGAL
lawful ENNOMIC, LEGAL, LICIT
lawyer ADVOCATE, ATTORNEY, COUNSEL(OR), JURIST, LEGIST, PORTIA
lay ASCRIBE, BET, DITTY, LAIC(AL), PLACE, SECULAR
layer COAT, LAMINA, PATINA, PLY, PROVINE, STRATA, STRATUM, VENEER
lazy (one) BUM, DRONE, LUSK, OTIOSE
lead HEAD, PILOT, PLUMB(UM), PRECENT, PRESA, SINKER, SOLDER, WAD
leader CANTOR, CAUDILLO, DUCE, DUX, FUHRER, GUIDE, SNELL, VAN
leading FORE(MOST), VAN
leaf BRACT, FOLIO, FROND, LAMINA, OLA(Y), OLE, OLLA, SEPAL, SHEET
leaf part BLADE, MIDRIB, PEN, PETIOLE, RIB, STIPEL, STIPULE, STOMA(TA), VEIN
leaflet PINNA, TRACT
league BLOC, BUND, HANSE
leak OOZE, SEEP, SPILL
lean BONY, GAUNT, LANK(Y), SCRAWNY, SPARE
lean-to LINTER, SHED
leap CURVET, FRIST, LOUP, LOWP, LUNGE, SALTO, SKIP, STEND, VAULT
learned ERUDITE, LETTERED, LITERATE
learned man see SAGE
learning KEN, LORE, WISDOM
lease CHARTER, CONVEY, DEMISE, HIRE, LET, RENT
leash CURB, JESS, LUNE, LYAM
leather ALUTA, BOCK, BULGAR, CALF, CHAMOIS, ELK, JUFTI, MOCHA, NAPA, ROAN, SHAGREEN, SKIVER, SUEDE, VELLUM, YUFT
leather, convert into TAN, TAW
leave ADIEU, CONGE, EXEAT, EXIT, FURLOUGH, QUIT, VACATE, WILL
leaven BARM, YEAST, ZYME
leavings CHAFF, DRAFF, DREGS, ORTS, RESIDUE; see REFUSE
ledge APRON, BERM(E), CAY, LODE, REEF, SHELF, SILL
ledger item CREDIT, DEBIT
leech PARASITE, SAIL, TOADY
lees DRAF, DREGS, DROSS
left KAY, LARBOARD, PORT, WENT
left-hand (page) LEVO, VERSO
leftover MORSEL, ORT
leg GAMB(E), GAMMON, PEG, PIN
leg, pert. to CRURAL, SURAL
legal JURAL, LEAL, LICIT, VALID
legal action CASE, (LAW)SUIT, LITIGATION, RES
legal delay(s) MORA(E)
legal term APPEAL, BILL, DEMURRER, PLEA, SUBPOENA, SUMMONS, VENUE, WRIT
legend CAPTION, FABLE, MOTTO, MYTH, SAGA
legislator DEPUTY, DRACO, MINOS, MOSES, SENATOR, SOLON
legislature see ASSEMBLY
leisure EASE, OTIUM, REPOSE, REST, TOOM
lens ADON, GLASS, MENISCUS, TORIC
leper LAZAR, OUTCAST, PARIAH
Lesbos poet ALCAEUS, ARION, LESCHES, SAPPHO
lessen (A)BATE, FADE, MINIFY, MITIGATE, REDUCE, THIN
let ALLOW, PERMIT; see LEASE
let it stand STA, STET

lethal see **FATAL**
lethargy **COMA, INERTIA, STUPOR, TORPOR**
letter **BILLET, BRIEF, DEMIT, EPISTLE, MEMO, MISSIVE, PARAPH, RUNE**
letter, Anglo-Saxon **EDH, ETH**
levee **DURBAR**; see **EMBANKMENT, LANDING**
level **AIM, EVEN, FLUSH, GRADE, PLANE, RASE, RAZE, STEADY**
lever **CANT, PEDAL, PRIZE, PRY**
levy **CESS, DRAFT, MUSTER**; see **TAX**
liar **ANANIAS, FIBBER, WERNARD**
liberate **MANUMIT, REDEEM**
license **GRANT, PATENT, READER**
lichen derivative **ARCHIL, CUDBEAR, LITMUS, PERSIS**
lie **FIB, INHERE, LIGE**
lie in wait **LURK, SKULK**
lieutenant **JEMADAR, LUFF, SHAVETAIL**
life **ANIMA, BIOS, VIE, VITA**
life, pert. to **BIOTIC(AL), VITAL**
life principle **ATMAN, JIVA, PRANA**
lifeless **AMORT, AZOIC, DEFUNCT, EXTINCT, FLAT, INERT**
lift(ed) **ELEVATOR, HEAVE, HEFT, HOIST, HOVE, PERK**
lifting engine **NORIA, SAKIEH, SHADOFF, RAM**
ligament **BOND, DESMO, TAENIA**
light **AIRY, ARC, CRESSET, FANAL, FLARE, FLASH, IGNITE, ILLUME, KLIEG, LAND, LEGER, LUNT, MATCH, TAPER, TORCH**; see **LAMP**
light unit **CARCEL, HEFNER, LUMEN, LUX, PHOT, PYR**
lighter **HOY, SCOW, SPILL**
lighthouse **PHARE, PHAROS**
lightning **FLASH, LAIT, LEVIN**
ligulate **LORATE**
like **AKIN, COGNATE, ENJOY**
likely **APT, PRONE, SEEMLY**
likeness **ANALOGY, EFFIGY, GUISE, ICON, IMAGE**
likewise **BESIDES, DITTO, ITEM**
limb **BOUGH, BRANCH, FIN, MEMBER, WING**
limber **LITHE, PLIABLE, SUPPLE**
lime **CALX**
limestone **CAEN, CALP, CHALK, MALM, OOLITE**
limit **BOURN(E), CONFINE, EDGE, STENT, STINT, TERM**
limp **FLABBY, FLIMSY, HALT**
line **AGONE, CERIF, CERIPH, CORD(ON), CUE, EARING, EDGE, CRY, FILE, MARLINE, PATTER, QUEUE, RANK, ROW, SECANT, SERIF, SNELL, STEAN, STEENE, STRIA(E), TROT, VECTOR, WAD**
lineage **DESCENT, PEDIGREE, STOCK, STRAIN**; see **FAMILY**
lines, marked by **RULED, STRAITE(D)**
linen **LINGERIE, NAPERY**
linen measure **CUT, HEER**
linger **DALLY, DAWDLE, LAG, TARRY**
lining **BUSHING, GASKET, WAINSCOT**
link(s) **CATENA(T)E, CHAIN, NEXUS, YOKE**
lip ornament **LABRET, PELELE**
lip, pert. to **LABIAL**
liquefied **FUSIL(E), POTATE**
liquefy **FUSE, MELT, RUN, THAW**
liqueurs see p. 124
liquidate **AMORTIZE, KILL, PURGE SETTLE**
lissome **LITHE, NIMBLE SVELTE**
list **AGENDA, ALBE, ALBUM, CANT, CAREEN, CATALOG HARK, HEEL, LEET, PANEL PLOW, ROSTER, ROTA, SLATE, TABLE**
listen **BUG, EAVESDROP, HARK(EN), HEAR, HEED, OBEY**
listlessness **ACEDIA, APATHY, ENNUI**
litany **EKTENE, ROGATION**
literature, characters in see p. 178
lithograph **CHROMO**
litter **BIER, BROOD, CABIN, FARROW, MULCH**
little **MINUTE, PALTRY, POCO, PUNY, WEE**
litus **COLONUS, SERF**
lively **AGILE, ANIMATO, BRISK, DESTO, KEEN, NIMBLE, PEART, PERK(Y), PERT, SPRY, VIR, VIVID, VIVO, YARE**
lively person **DYNAMO, GRIG**
liver, pert. to **HEPATIC**
livid **ASHEN, BLAE, PALE, WAN**
lixivium **LEACH, LYE**
lizardlike **SAURIAN**
load **CARGO, CARK, LADE, ONUS**
loaf **BAP, LOLL, LOUNGE, MIKE**
loam **LOESS, REGUR**
local **CHAPTER, EDAPHIC, TOPICAL**
locale **SCENE, SITE, VENUE**
locality **AREA, LOCUS, PLACE, PURLIEU, SPOT, ZONE**
lock **COTTER, CURL, DETENT, FRIB, HASP, JAM, TRESS**
lock part **BOLT, CYLINDER, STUMP, TUMBLER, WARD**
locks, Panama Canal **GATUN**
locomotive **BIGBOY, MIKADO, MOGUL, PACIFIC, PRAIRIE, SANTAFE, SWITCHER, TEXAS**

lode LEAD, LEDGE, REEF, RIDER, SCRIN, VEIN
lodge BILLET, BOARD, CABIN, QUARTER, ROOST
logarithm unit BEL
logic term ORGANON, PONENT, PREMISS, SALTUS, SUBALTERN
logroller BIRLER, DECKER
loincloth DHO(O)TI, LUNGI, MALO, PAGNE
loiter POKE, SAUNTER; see LINGER
London quarter ADELPHI, SOHO, MAYFAIR, HOLBORN, LAMBETH, CHELSEA
long ACHE, ASPIRE, COVET, CRAVE, HANKER, PANT, PINE, PROLIX, YEARN, YEN
long ago ELD, YORE(TIME)
long live (EV)VIVA, VIVE
look ASPECT, EYE, GAZE, HIST, KEN, LEER, MIEN, OGLE, PEEK, PEEP, PEER, PORE, PRY, SCAN, SKEW
loom APPEAR, TOOL, VESSEL, WEAVE
loom part BATTEN, BEAM, GRIFF, HEALD, HEDDLES, LAM, LINGOE, MAIL, PICKER, PIRN, REED, SHED, SHUTTLE, SLAY, TEMPLE, TREADLE, WARP, WEFT
loop ANSA, BIGHT, BRIDE, EYE, GROMMET, HONDA, NOOSE, PICOT, TERRY
loophole M(E)USE, PRETEXT
loose(n) BAGGY, EASE, LEWD, LIMP, (RE)LAX, REMISS, SLACKEN, UNDO, UNTIE, WANTON
loot BOOTY, PLUNDER, (RAN)SACK, RIFLE, SPOIL(S)
lop POLL, PRUNE, SNATHE, SNED, SNIP
lopsided ALIST, ALOP, ASKEW
lord LAIRD, MAR, KAAN, KAUN, KAWN, KHAN, LIEGE, PALATINE; see NOBLE
lose AMIT, FAIL, FORFEIT, MISS
lot FATE, HAP, PARCEL, SHARE
lotion see OINTMENT
lottery BINGO, LOTTO, RAFFLE, TOMBOLA
loud FORTE, SHOWY, WIGHT
loudspeaker CONE, TWEETER, WOOFER
lounge DIVAN, LAZE, LOBBY, LOLL, RECLINE, SETTEE, SOFA
love ADORE, AMOUR, DARLING, DEAR, DOAT, DOTE, (EN)AMOR, GRA, LOO, WOO, ZEAL
lover BEAU, FLAME, LEMAN, MINION, PARAMOUR, RATO, ROMEO, SWAIN
loving AMATIVE, AMATORY, DOTING, EROTIC
low BAS(E), BLUE, HUMBLE, MENIAL, MOO, ORRA, VILE
lower ABASE, DEBASE, LOOM, NETHER, VAIL
lowest point NADIR, PERIGEE
loyalty HOMAGE, PIETAS, TROTH
lozenge DIAMOND, PASTIL(E) PASTILLE, ROTULA, TROCHE
luck CESS, FATE, HAZARD, LOT
luck, stroke of FLUKE
lumberman GIRDLER, LOGGER, SAWYER, TOPPER
lump BURL, CLOD, CLOT, NODE, NUB, (S)WAD, TUMOR
luncheon TIFFIN, UNDERN
lurch CAREEN, JOLL, PITCH, ROLL, SWAB
lurk HIDE, SKULK, SNEAK
luster GLAZE, GLOSS, SCHILLER, SHEEN
lusterless DIM, MAT(TE)
lustrous NAIF, NITID, SILKY
luxuriant LAVISH, LUSH, ORNATE, RANK
luxuriate BASK, THRIVE, WALLOW
lyric(al) ALBA, MELIC, ODE

M

mace-bearer BEADLE, MACER
macerate PINE, RET, SOAK, STEEP, VEX
machine DEVICE, GADGET, PARTY, TOOL
madam DON(N)A, FRAU, MAAM, MILADY, MUM, SENORA
madhouse ASYLUM, BABEL, BEDLAM
madness FOLLY, FRENZY, FURY, LUNACY, MANIA, RABIES
Magi BALTHASAR, GASPAR, MELCHIOR
magic CONJURY, GOETIC, GOETY, HOODOO, JADOO, JADU, JUJU, MAYA, OBEAH, RUNE, VOODOO
magic word PRESTO, SESAME
magician CIRCE, HOUDINI, MAGE, MAGI, MAGIAN, MAGUS, MERLIN, SHAMAN, WITCH, WIZARD
magistrate (A)EDILE, AG(H)A, ARCHON, BAILIE, CADI, CENSOR, CONSUL, DOGE, EPHOR, FOUD, MAYOR, PR(A)ETOR, PREFECT, SYNDIC, TRIBUNE
magnate COB, MOGUL, NABOB, SHOGUN, TYCOON, VIP

mahatma AR(A)HAT, GANDHI
maid ABIGAIL, AMA(H), ANCILLA, AYAH, BONNE, EYAH, IYA, MATRANEE, SLAVEY, WENCH
maiden COLLEEN, DAMSEL, LASS(IE), MISS(Y), VIRGIN
mail ARMOR, DA(U)K, DAWK, POST, SEND
main DUCT, MIGHT, VITAL
maintain AVOW, CLAIM, (UP)HOLD
malice ENVY, EVIL, PIQUE, RANCOR, SPITE
malign ABUSE, ASPERSE, LIBEL, VILIFY
malignant EVIL, HEINOUS, VICIOUS
malleable DOCILE, DUCTILE, SOFT, TENSILE
mammals see p. 209
man BIPED, FORTIFY, HOMBRE, HOMO, HUMAN, MALE, SAHIB, SERVANT, STAFF, VALET
man, elderly CODGER, CRONE, DODO, DOTARD, FOGY, GAFFER, GEEZER, NESTOR, SENIOR
man, handsome ADONIS, APOLLO, BEAU, FOP
man of brass TALOS
manage DIGHT, TEND, WANGLE
manageable DOCILE, RULY, YARE
manager GERENT, GRIEVE, OPERATOR
mandarin's home YAMEN, YAMUN
mane BRUSH, JUBA, SHAG, STUBBLE
maned CRINED, JUBATE
manger BIN, CRATCH, CRECHE, CRIB
mangle CALENDAR, IRON, MAIM, MAUL
manifest ARRANT, ATTEST, EVINCE, OVERT, PATENT, SHOW
maniple FANO(N), FANUM
manner(s) AIR, AURA, METHOD, MIEN, MODE, MORES WONT
mantel LEDGE, LINTEL
manual training SLOID, SLOYD
manuscript(s) CODEX, CODICES, FOLIO, MSS, SCRIPT
Manxman CELT, GAEL
many GOBS, LOADS, LOT(S), MAINT, MYRIAD, REAMS. SCADS
map(s) ATLAS, CHART, GRAPH, INSET PLAT
marauder HUN, VANDAL VITI
marble AGGIE, ALAY, ALLEY, CARRARA, CIPOLIN, DUCK, MARL, MARMOR, MIB, MIG(G), RANCE, RANSE, SHOOTER, TAW
mark BRAND, SCAR, STAIN, STAMP, STIGMA(TA), SYMBOL, TALLY
mark, diacritical ACCENT, BREVE, CEDILLA, MACRON, PRIME, TIL(DE), UMLAUT
mark, printers' DELE, STET
mark, reference ASTERISK, ASTERISM, DAGGER, DIESIS, INDEX, OBELI(SK), OBELUS, SECTION, STAR
marker(s) CHIP, COUNTER, DAN, META, PYLON, SCORER, STELA(E), STELAI, STELE, TAB
market AGORA, BAZ(A)AR, FORA, FORUM, GUNGE, GUNJ, MART, PASAR, RIALTO, SOOK, SOUK, SUQ, TRONE. VEND
marriage MOTA, MUTA, NUPTIALS
marriage, absence of AGAMY
marriage notice BAN(NS)
marriage settlement DOS, DOT, DOW(E)RY, MAHR
marriageable NUBILE
marrow CORE, KEEST, MEDULLA, PITH
marry ESPOUSE, WED, WIVE
Mars, pert. to AREAN, MARTIAN
marsh BOG, FEN, LERNA LIMAN, MAREMMA, MIRE MOOR, MORASS, MOSS, MUSKEG, PINSK, PONTINE, PRIPET, QUAG, SLUE, SWALE
marsh fever HELODES
marsh gas METHANE
marshy PALUDAL, PALUDINE
marsupials see p. 214
mask DOMINO, LOUP, SCREEN, VISOR
mass BOLUS, BULK, GATHER, GOB, MATTER, TUMOR, WAD
Mass part COLLECT, CREDO, EPISTLE, FRACTION, GLORIA, GOSPEL, GRADUAL, INTROIT, KYRIE, LAVABO. PAX, PREFACE, SANCTUS, SECRETA
massacre CARNAGE POGROM
master BAAS, BOY, CAPTAIN, EMCEE, LEARN, LORD, RULE, SUBDUE; see TEACHER
master, pert. to a HERILE
mat BANIG, DOILY, MATRIX, PAD, PETATE, YAPA
match FIT, FUSEE, LUCIFER, MARRY, PEER, TALLY, VESTA
mathematical term CONSTANT, COSH, (CO)SINE, FACIEND, FACIENT, LOG, NABLA, QUADRANT, RADIX, SECH, SINH, SURD, TANH, TENSOR, VARIABLE, VECTOR, VESSOR
mathematician ALBIRUNI, ALKASHI, BOOLE, CARROLL, CREMONA, DESCARTES, EUCLID, EULER, FERMAT,

GAUSS, HUYGENS, KELVIN, LAPLACE, LEIBNITZ, NAPIER, NEWTON, PASCAL, PTOLEMY, RUSSELL, VERNIER, VIETA, WIENER
matrix CAST, GANGUE, MOLD
matter HYLE, IMPORT, PITH, PUS, RES
maudlin MUSHY, TIPSY, WEEPY
maul CLUB, MANGLE
maxim ADAGE, AXIOM, CLICHE, GNOME, MORAL, MOTTO, SAW, TRUISM
meadow HAUGH, LAWN, LEA, MEAD, VEGA
meager LEAN, LENTEN, PUNY, SCANT(Y), SPARSE
meal AT(T)A, BEVER, BRAN, CENA, FARINA, FLOUR, MASA, PINOLA, PINOLE, REPAST, TEA
mean(s) AGENT, BASE, IMPLY, INTEND, LOW, MEDIUM, SCURVY
meaning, pert. to LITERAL, SEMANTIC
meantime WHILST; see INTERVAL
measure EXTENT, GA(U)GE, METE, PAGE, SCAN; see p. 182
meat FLESH, KERNEL, MEAL
mechanics DYNAMICS, STATICS
meddle PRY, SNOOP, TAMPER
median AVERAGE, MEAN, MESNE, PAR
medical CURATIVE, IATRIC
medical group AMA
medicine man ANGEKOK, BASIR, KAHUNA, PEAI, PIACHE, PIAY, SHAMAN
medley FARRAGO, MELANGE, OLIO, PASTICCIO, POTPOURRI
meeting CAUCUS, GAM, INDABA, RALLY, SEANCE, SESSION, SYNOD, TRYST
melancholy BLUE(S), DOLOR, DREAR, MISERY
melee see FIGHT
melodious ARIOSE, ARIOSO, DULCET
melody MELISMA, MELOS, STRAIN, TUNE
melt FUSE, FUZE, RUN, SWALE, SWEAL
membrane CAUL, FILM, PIA, TELA, VELA, VELUM, WEB
memento BIBELOT, RELIC, TOKEN
memorandum BRIEF, CHIT, MINUTE, NOTE
memory, pert. to MNEMONIC, MNESIC
mender COBBLER, TINKER
mendicant BEGGAR, DANDI, DANDY, FAKEER, FAKIR, FRIAR
Mennonite sect AMISH, WISLER
mental PHRENIC
mercenary ARMATOLI, HESSIAN, HIRELING, VENAL
merchant COSTER, DEALER, MONGER, SETH, SUTLER, TRADER, VENDOR
mercy LENITY, PITY, RUTH
merge BLEND, FUSE, WED
merit EARN, MEED, WORTH
mescal PEYOTE, PEYOTL
Mesopotamia IRAK, IRAQ
mess BOTCH, BUNGLE, CHOW
metalworker SMITH, VULCAN, WELDER
metaphor SIMILE, TROPE
meteors see p. 277
meter CADENCE, RHYTHM
method MODE, ORDER, PLAN, SCHEME, SYSTEM, WAY
Mexican president ALEMAN, CALLES, DIAZ, GIL, HUERTA, JUAREZ, MADERO, MATEOS, ORDAZ
mezzanine ENTRESOL
microbe(s) BACTERIA, GERM, VIRUS
microspores POLLEN
middle HUB, MEDIAL, MES(I)AL, MESNE
middle, toward the MES(I)AD
midship, off ABEAM
midshipman REEFER
midwife DHAI, GAMP, GRANNY, HEBAMME, PARTERA
mien GUISE, OSTENT, POISE
mighty FELL, POTENT, PUISSANT, VALIANT
migration EXODUS, TREK
migratory worker ARKIE, OKIE, WETBACK
Mikado character KOKO, NANKIPOO, POOHBAH, YUMYUM
Mikado's court DAIRI
mild BLAND, MEEK, MOY, PLACID, SHY, SOFT
mildew BLIGHT, MO(U)LD, MUST
mile, naut. KNOT
milk BLEED, CLABBER, CURD, LAC(TOSE), LEBAN, LEBEN, SKYR, TAYIR, TYRE
milk part CASEIN, PLASMA, SERUM, WHEY
milk, pert. to LACTEAL, LACTIC
Milky Way GALAXY
mill ARRASTRA, (K)NURL, QUERN
millimeter, 1000th part MICRON
millstone support RYND
millwheel part AWE, LADE
mimic APE(R), MIMA, MIME, PSEUDO, QUASI, SHAM
mince DICE, SHRED, SIMPER
mind CARE, HEED, OBEY, NOUS, RECK, SOUL, TEND, WITS

mine LODE, PIT, SAP, VEIN
mine term ADIT, ASTEL, GOAF, GOB, LOB, NOG, PILE, RESUE, STOPE, STULL, STULM, SUMP, WINZE
miner COLLIER, SANDHOG, SAPPER
minerals see p. 232
minim DASH, DROP, MITE
minister AID, CATER, PREMIER, VIZI(E)R; see CLERGY
minstrel ARIOI, BARD, GLEEMAN, GOLIARD, JONGLEUR, RIMER, RUNER, SCOP, SKALD
mint COIN, FRESH, INVENT, STAMP
minute(s) ACTA, DETAIL, MEMO, RECORD, TINY, WEE
miracle ANOMY
miracle site CANA, FATIMA, LOURDES
mire see MUD
miscellany see MEDLEY
mischief DIDO, HAVOC, HOB, PRANK, WRACK
miser CHURL, NABAL, NIGGARD, SCROOGE
misery AGONY, CHAGRIN, DOLOR
Mishnah section ABOT(H), MOED, NASHIM, NEZIKIN, PERAKIM, SEDARIM, ZERAIM
misrepresent BELIE, GARBLE
missile see p. 278
missing AWOL, LOST, TRUANT
mist BRUME, FOG, HAZE, MISLE, RAG, SEREIN, SMOG, SMUR, VAPOR
mistake(s) BARNEY, BONER, BULL, ERRATA, ERRATUM, LAPSE, SLIP, TYPO
mister BABOO, BABU, DON, HERR, MIAN, MONSIEUR, PAN, SAHEB, SAHIB, SENOR, SIGNOR, SIR(E); see TITLE
mistress PARAMOUR
mite ATOM(Y), IOTA, MOTE
mitigate ABATE, ALLAY, ASSUAGE, EASE, TEMPER
mix ADDLE, KNEAD, SCRAMBLE, STIR
mixture HASH, MAGMA, MEDLEY, MELANGE, MONG, OLIO
moat DITCH, FOSS(E), GRAFF
mob CANAILLE, RABBLE, ROUT, RUCK
mock DERIDE, FLEER, GIBE, JAPE, JEER, JIBE, SCOFF, TAUNT
mode FAD, FLAIR, STYLE, VOGUE
model IDEAL, MANIKIN, NORM, PARADIGM, PARAGON, POSE, TYPE
modern LATE, NEO, NOVEL
modify ALTER, AMEND, REVISE, TEMPER, VARY
Mohammedan feast day ASHURA
Mohammedan(ism) HANIF, ISLAM(ITE), MOSLEM
Mohammedan principle IJMA
Mohammed's adopted son ALI
Mohammed's birthplace MECCA
Mohammed's burial place MEDINA
Mohammed's descendant SA(Y)ID, SEID
Mohammed's supporters ANSAR
Mohammed's uncle ABBAS
Mohammed's wife AISHA
moist DAMP, DANK, DEWY, HUMID, UVID
moisten BEDEW, DAMPEN, MOIL, SOAK
molasses TREACLE, TRIACLE
mold CAST, KNEAD, MATRIX, MUST
molding ASTRAGAL, CAVETTO, CONGE, CYMA, ECHINUS, FILLET, GULA, LISTEL, OGEE, OVOLI, OVOLO, REEDING, REGLET, REGULA, SCOTIA, SPLAY, TORI, TORUS
molding edge AR(R)IS
moldy FUSTY, MUSTY
mole JETTY, NEVUS, PIER, TALPA
molecule part (AN)ION, ATOM
mollusks see p. 224
molt CAST, MEW, SHED
molten rock see LAVA
mush SAMP, SEPON, SUPAWN; see PORRIDGE
moment IMPORT, JIFF(Y), TRICE
monad ATOM, ENTITY, UNIT
monastery ABBEY, CENOBY, FRIARY, LAMASERY, MANDRA, MATH, NUNNERY, PRIORY, RIBAT, TEKKE, TEKYA, TERA, VIHARA
money CASH, COIN, COWRIE, COWRY, CUSH, DOUGH, GELT, GRIGS, KALE, LARI(N), LETTUCE, LUCRE, MAZUMA, MOSS, PELF, SE(A)WAN, SHEKELS, SPENSE, TENDER, U(H)LLO, WAMPUM; see p. 189
moneylender MAHAJAN, SHYLOCK, USURER
mongrel CUR, HYBRID, MUT(T)
monk ABBE, ABBOT, AR(A)HAT, BHIKKU, BONZE, CALOYER, DERVISH, FAKIR, FRA, FRIAR, LAMA, LOHAN, PONGYI, PRIOR, SANTON, SUFI, TALAPOIN
monk settlement SCETE, SKETE
monkey puzzle PINON
monolith MENHIR, OBELISK
monopoly CARTEL, POOL, TRUST

monster BRUTE, ELLOPS, G(H)OUL, GOWL, OGRE, RAHAB, TERAS; see p. 208
month INST(ANT), ULT(IMO)
monument CA(I)RN, CENOTAPH, (CROM)LECH, DOLMEN, MENHIR, RECORD, STELE, TABUT
moon CRESCENT, GAZE, LUNA
moon, pert. to LUNAR, SELENIC
moon phase FULL, GIBBOUS, NEW
moon valley CLEFT, RILL(E)
moon's age EPACT
moor FEN, HEATH, LANDE
mooring place BERTH, DOCK, HARBOR, MARINA, PORT, SLIP
Moorish MORISCAN
mop MERKIN, SCOVEL, SWAB, SWOB
morass see MARSH
more BIS, ENCORE, EXCESS, EXTRA, PIU, PLUS, TOO
More's island UTOPIA
morning MATIN, UMAGA; see DAWN
moron AMENT, IDIOT
morose BLUE, DOUR, GLUM, GRUM, SOUR, SURLY
morsel BIT(E), ORT, SCRAP, SOP
mortar CANNON, COEHORN
mortuary CHARNEL, MORGUE
mosaic MUSIVE, TESSERA
Mosaic law TORA(H)
Moses' spies CALEB, GADDIEL, NAHBI
mosque JAMI, MASJID, OMAR
mosque part MIHRAB, MIMBAR, MINARET
mother ABBESS, AMMA, DAM, MATER
motion, pert. to KINETIC, MOTIVE
motion, producing MOTILE, MOTIFIC
motive CAUSE, IMPULSE, REASON, SPRING, SPUR, THEME
motor part CAPACITOR, COIL, ROTOR, STATOR
mottled PIED, PINTO, ROEY
motto ADAGE, BYWORD, MAXIM, SLOGAN
mound AHU, BARROW, KNOLL, TEE, TERP, TUMP, TUMULUS
Mount of Olives OLIVET
mountain(s) ALP, BERG, KAF, MERU, QAE, SIERRA
mountebank EMPIRIC, QUACK
mourn (BE)WAIL, GRIEVE, LAMENT, RUE, SIGH, WEEP
mouth(s) ABRA, BOC(C)A, CODON, DELTA, ESTUARY, FRITH, GOB, INLET, LADE, MUN, ORA, STOMA, VOICE
mouthpiece BOCAL
mouthward ORAD
move sidewise SIDLE, SLUE
move slowly EDGE, INCH, WORM
move to and fro FLAP, SWAY, WAG
movement MOTO, MUDGE, RHYTHM, TAXIS, TEMPO, THEME
mow DESS, GOAF, MATH
mud MIRE, MUCK, MURGEON, OOZE, SALSE, SILT, SLIME, SLOB, SLUDGE
muddle ADDLE, MESS, SNAFU, SOSS
muddy ROILY, SLIMY, TURBID
muffin COB, GEM
mug NOG(GIN), PUSS, STEIN, TOBY
mulct AMERCE, FINE, PUNISH
multitude HORDE, HOST, LEGION, MOB, MYRIAD
mundane COSMIC, EARTHLY, TERRENE
murder BURKE, HOMICIDE
murder fine BLOODWIT(E)
muscle BRAWN, LACERT, SINEW, THEW; see p. 106
musclelike MYOID
muscular BURLY, TOROSE
muse MULL, PONDER, REVE
Muses CALLIOPE, CLIO, ERATO, EUTERPE, MELPOMENE, POLYMNIA, TERPSICHORE, THALIA, URANIA
music hall ALHAMBRA, BIJOU, COLISEUM, EMPIRE, HIPPODROME, PALACE, PALLADIUM, WINDMILL
must MOLD, SAPA, STUM
musty FETID, FUSTY, MOLDY
mute LENE, MUFFLE, MUM, SURD
mutilate GARBLE, MAIM, MANGLE
mysterious ARCANE, CRYPTIC, ESOTERIC, OCCULT
mystery ARCANA, ARCANUM, ENIGMA, RUNE
mystic CABALIC, COVERT, ESOTERIC, OCCULT, SUFI(ST), TAOIST

N

nail(s) BRAD, CLAW, CLOUT, SPAD, SPRIG, TACK, TALON, TENTER, UNGUES, UNGUIS, UNGULA(E)
name (AG)NOMEN, ALIAS, CACONYM, CLEPE, COGNOMEN, DUB, (EN)TITLE, EPITHET, EPONYM, MONIKER, NOMINATE, NOUN, ONYM, TERM

named YCLEPED, YCLEPT
namely SCIL(ICET), TOWIT, VIDELICET, VIZ
naos CELLA
nap DOZE, DROWSE, SIESTA, WINK
nap, coarse GIG, PILE, SHAG, RAS, TEASEL, TEASLE, TEAZEL, TEAZLE
Napoleon's isle CORSICA, ELBA, HELENA
narcotic ANODYNE, B(H)ANG, CANNABIS, CHARAS, COCAINE, CODEINE, DOPE, DRUG, FAGINE, GANJA, HASHISH, HEMP, HEROIN, HORSE, KEF, KI(E)F, MARIJUANA, MORPHINE, OPIATE, OPIUM, POT, REEFER, SNOW
narrate RECOUNT, RELATE, SPIN
narrow ANGUST, LINEAL, STRAIT
nasal NARIAL, NARINE, RHINAL
native DENIZEN, ENDEMIC, (IN)BORN, INDIGENE, INNATE, ITE, NATAL, RAW, SON, TAO
naturalist AKELEY, ANDREWS, AUDUBON, BREHM, BURBANK, CARVER, DARWIN, DEVRIES, FRESIA, GRAY, JORDAN, LAMARCK, LINDLEY, LINNE, MENDEL, MUIR, PLINY, SARS, THOREAU
nature ESSENCE, ILK, OUSIA, TYPE
nautical MARINE, MARITIME, NAVAL, TARRISH
nautical equipment BINNACLE, CAPSTAN, COMPASS, GRAPNEL, HELM, NIGGER, PELORUS, SEXTANT, SONAR, TOGGLE
nautical term ABAFT, ABEAM, AFORE, AHOY, ALOW, ATRY, AVAST, OHOY
navigator BAFFIN, BERING, CABOT, COOK, DIAS, DRAKE, ERIC, GAMA, LEIF, RALEIGH, ROSS, TASMAN
nearsighted MYOPIC, PURBLIND
nearsighted person MYOPE
neat NATTY, PRIM, SPRUCE, TIDY, TOSH, TRIG, TRIM
necessitate COMPEL, ENTAIL
neck COLLUM, ISTHMUS, STRAIT
necklace BALDRIC, CHOKER, RIVIERE, SAUTOIR, TORQUE
need LACK, PENURY, REQUIRE, STRAIT(S), WANT
needle HECKLE, HYPO, OBELISK, SEW, STYLUS
needle-shaped ACERATE, ACEROSE, ACICULAR, ACUATE, SPICULAR
negative NAY, NEIN, NIX, NON, NOT, NYET
negative pole CATHODE
neglect DEFAULT, OMIT, SHIRK
negligent LAX, REMISS, SLACK
negotiate BARGAIN, PARLE(Y), TREAT
Negro BLACK, DARKY, HUBSHI, SAMBO
nephew NEPOTE, NEVE, VASU
nerve cell NEURON
nerve-cell process AXON(E), DENDRITE, NEURITE
nerve layer(s) ALVEI, ALVEUS
nerves see p. 106
nest AERIE, AERY, EYRIE, EYRY, DRAY, DREY, NID(E), NIDI, NIDUS
nestling EYAS, POULT, SQUAB
net CLEAR, FYKE, LACIS, RETICLE, SAGENE, SEINE, SNARE, SPILLER, STENT, TRAWL
netlike MESHY, RETIARY
network MESH, PLEXUS, RETE, RETIA, WEB
new LATE, NEOTERIC, NOVEL, RECENT
news agency ANETA, DOMEI, INS, REUTERS, TASS, UPI
next PROCHAIN, PROCHEIN
nibble GNAW, KNAB, KNAP
niche see NOOK
nicotinic acid NIACIN
niggard(ly) MISER, PIKER, STINGY
night DEATH, EVE, NATT, NOTT, NOX, NYX
nightmare ALP, INCUBUS, MARA
nimble AGILE, SPRY, SUPPLE, VOLANT
nimbus AUR(EOL)A, GLORIA, HALO
nip BITE, DRINK, PECK
nitrogen AZO(TE)
Noah, pert. to NOACHIAN, NOETIC
Nobel Prize winners see p. 243
noble(man) BARIN, BARON, COUNT, DAIMIO, DOGE, DON, DUKE, EARL, GRAF, GRANDEE, HIDALGO, KAMI, KUGE, LORD, MARQUIS, MURZA, PEER, RITTER, THANE
nod BECK, BOW, WINK
Nod, west of EDEN
nodding ANNUENT, NUTANT
node KNOB, KNOT, KNUR(L)
noise BABEL, CLAMOR, DIN
nomad ARAB, BEDOUIN, GYPSY, SARACEN, SCENITE
nominal PAR, TITULAR, TOKEN
nonconformist BEATNIK, HERETIC, REBEL, RECUSANT, SECTARY
nonentity CIPHER, NIL, NULLITY
nongypsy GAJO

non-Jew(s) GENTILE, GOI, GOY(IM)
non-Moslem GIAOUR, KAFFIR, RAIA, RAYAH, ZENDIK
non-professional LAIC, LAY
nonsense BLAH, DRIVEL, FLUMMERY, FOLDEROL, HOOEY, PISH, POOH, ROT, TRIPE, TWADDLE
nonsense creature GOLUK, GOOP, SMOO, SNARK
noodles MEIN, FARFEL, FERFEL, LAKSHEN; see PASTA
nook (AL)COVE, CANT, COVE, CRANNY, HERNE, NICHE, RECESS, WRO
noose HALTER, LEASH, LOOP
north(ern) ARCTIC, BOREAL, POLAR
nose BEAK, NEB, PUG, SCENT, SNIFF, SNOOP
nose, having large NASUTE
nose, having snub SIMOUS
nose part SEPTUM, VOMER
nostrils, of NARIAL, NARIC, NARINE
notch CRENA(E), DENT, DINT, KERF, NICK, NOCK, SCORE
notched CRENATE, SERRATE(D)
note APOSTIL(LE), BILLET, CHIT, IOU, LOAN, MEMO, POSTIL, RENOWN, SCHOLIUM
nothing CIPHER, NAUGHT, NI(HI)L, NIX, NUL(L), TRIFLE, ZERO
notion BEE, CURIO, IDEA, VIEW, WHIM
notorious ARRANT, INFAMOUS
notwithstanding THO, YET
noun APTOTE, GERUND, VERBAL
nourish FEED, FOSTER, SUCCOR
nourishing ALIBLE, ALMA, RICH
nourishment ALIMENT, FOOD, MANNA, NUTRI(M)ENT, PABULUM
novelty CURIOSITY, FAD, NEWNESS
now EXTANT, HERE, NOO, PRESENT
nozzle GIANT, TUYERE, VENT
nudge GOAD, JOG, KNUB, POKE, PROD
nuisance BORE, PEST, PLAGUE
nullify ABROGATE, CANCEL, NEGATE, REPEAL, UNDO, VETO, VOID
number ALIQUOT, AMOUNT, CIPHER, COMPUTE, COUNT, DIGIT, FIGURE, INTEGER, LAC, LAKH, SCALAR, (S)TEEN, SURD, UNIT
numerous GALORE, LOTS, MANIFOLD, MANY, MULTIPLE, MYRIAD
nun ABBESS, CLARE, MINORESS, SISTER, VOTARESS
nurse AMA(H), AYAH, BABA, BONNE, EYAH, FEED, FOSTER, IYA, LACTATE, NANNY, NUTRICE, REAR, SUCKLE, TEND
nursery CRECHE, HOTHOUSE
nut(s), pert. to NUCAL
nymph DRYAD, HOURI, KELPIE, LARVA, MAIA, NAIAD, NAIS, NEREID, NIXIE, OCEANID, ONDINE, OREAD, SYLPH, UNDINE

O

oaf BOOR, DOLT, GAWK, LOUT, RUBE
oak fruit ACORN, BELLOTE, CAMATA, MAST
oakum, seal with CA(U)LK
oar BLADE, PADDLE, PROPEL, ROW(ER), SCULL, SWEEP
oar holder (ROW)LOCK, THOLE
oar part LOOM, PALM, PEEL
oasis OJO, SPRING, WADI, WADY
oath AITH, BAN, CURSE, SERMENT, VOW
obeisance CONGEE, HOMAGE; see BOW
obese ADIPOSE, LIPAROUS, PORTLY, PUDGY, PURSY, PYKNIC
object AIM, CARP, CAVIL, DEMUR, KICK, MIND
object of art BIBELOT, CURIO
objection CAVIL, SCRUPLE
objects, biblical THUMMIM, URIM
obligation BOND, DEBT, DUTY, IOU, MUST, ONUS, TIE
oblique ASKEW, (A)SLANT, AWRY, BEVEL, CANT, SLOPE
obliterate ANNUL, RAZE; see ERASE
oblivion LETHE, LIMBO, NIRVANA
obscure (BE)DIM, CLOUD, CRYPTIC, DARK(EN), DARKLE, ECLIPSE, FOG, LOWLY, MURKY, OCCULT, OVERSILE, VAGUE
observatory AGASSIZ, CORDOBA, DUNLAP, HALE, HOOKER, LICK, PALOMAR, YERKES
observe ABIDE, BEHOLD, MARK, MENTION, NOTE, OBEY, REMARK
obsolete ARCHAIC, DISUSED, PASSE
obstinate HARD, MULISH, RENITENT, SET, STUBBORN
obstruct CLOG, DIT(T), FOIL
obtain FANG, SECURE
occasional ANTRIN, ODD, ORRA, SPORADIC

occidental HESPERIAN, PONENT
occultism CABALA, MAGIC
occupant RENTEE, RESIDENT, TENANT
oceanic DIPS(E)Y, MARINE, PELAGIC
octave UTAS, UTIS
odd AWK, AZYGOUS, DROLL, ORRA, QUEER, RUMMY
odd-job man JOEY, SWAMPER
odor AROMA, FETOR, FUME(T), NIDOR, NOSE, REEK, SCENT
odorless AOSMIC
offend CAB, CHAFE, INSULT, MIFF, NETTLE, OUTRAGE, PIQUE, SIN, VEX
offense CRIME, DELI(C)T, FELONY, INSULT, MALA, MALUM, SIN, TORT, UMBRAGE, WRONG
offer BID, PROFFER, PROPOSE, TENDER
offhand ADLIB, CASUAL, CAVALIER, INFORMAL
officer AVENER, BAILIE, BAILIFF, BEADLE, DEWAN, DEPUTY, DIWAN, ENS, EXON, LICTOR, MACER, NEO, PARNAS, SHERIFF, TINDAL
officer, military ADMIRAL, ATAMAN, CAPTAIN, CENTURION, COLONEL, COMMANDER, COMMODORE, CORNET, CORPORAL, ENSIGN, GENERAL, HETMAN, LIEUTENANT, MAJOR, MATE, MARSHAL, NAVARCH, NCO, PROVOST, SERGEANT, SGT, SIRDAR, SUBALTERN, YOEMAN
official (A)EDILE, HAJIB, KUAN, KWAN, SATRAP, TRIBUNE
oil ACEITE, AJOWAN, ANOINT, ARACHIS, ASARUM, ATTAR, BALM, BAY, BEN(NE), BUCHU, CADE, CARAPA, CASSIA, CASTOR, CETENE, CHIA, COSTUS, CURCAS, FAT, GHEE, HOP, KAPOK, LANOLIN, LARD, LINSEED, LOTION, LUBE, MACE, MADIA, NEROLI, OLEO, OLEUM, ORRIS, PERILLA, RAVISON, RUE, TANSY, TIL, TUNG, TUNNY; see FAT, GAS
oil, pert. to OLEIC
ointment BALM, CARRON, CERATE, NARD, POMADE, SALVE, UNGUENT
O.K. RIGHT, ROGER
old AGED, ANILE, ELD(ERLY), GRAY, HOARY, OGYGIAN, SENILE, WORN
old times ELD, QUONDAM, YORE
omen AUSPICE; see PRESAGE
omission DEFAULT, ELISION, SYNCOPE
omit DELE(TE), ELIDE, NEGLECT, PASS, SKIP, SLIGHT
one ACE, AIN, MONO, UNI(T)
only BUT, LONE, MERE, SAVE, SIMPLY, SOLE
ooze EXUD(AT)E, LEAK, SEEP, SEIP, SIPE, SYPE
open AGAPE, AJAR, BROACH, HONEST, OVERT, PATENT, PUBLIC, UNTIE, VACANT
opening BUR(R), CAVITY, EYELET, FORAMEN, GAMBIT, GAP, HIATUS, HOLE, MEATUS, ORIFICE, PORE, RIFT, RIMA, SINUS, SLIT, SLOT, STOMA(TA), VENT
opera house (LA)SCALA, MET
operas see p. 194
opinion CREDO, DOOM, DOXY, NOTION, TENET
opponent ANTI, FOE, RIVAL
opportune APROPOS, APT, TIMELY
opportunity HENT; see CHANCE
oppose DEFY, IMPUGN, OPPUGN
opposite ANTI(PODAL), CONTRA(RY), CONVERSE, COUNTER, POLAR
optical illusion MIRAGE
optimistic ROSEATE, ROSY, SANGUINE
oracle AUGUR, DELOS, DELPHI, DELPHOS, SEER, SIBYL, SPHINX
oral PAROL(E), SPOKEN, VOCAL
orator BRYAN, CATO, CICERO, CUSHING, EVERETT, HENRY, LYSIAS, OTIS, RHETOR
orbit point APOGEE, APSIS, PERIGEE
ordain DECREE, ENACT, FROCK
order (A)LINE, ARRAY, BID, EDICT, FIAT, LODGE, SYSTEM, WRIT
order of merit ALBERT, AVIZ, BATH, CHRIST, CROWN, LEOPOLD, STLOUIS, STOLAF, SWORD, VASA
ordinance ASSIZE, CANON, LAW
organ CALLIOPE; see p. 106
organ control COUPLER, (DRAW)KNOB, PEDAL, PISTON, STUD, TABLET
organ division ALTAR, ANTIPHONAL, CHANCEL, CHOIR ECHO, GALLERY, GREAT, PEDAL, SOLO, SWELL
organ part ACTION, BOX, CONSOLE, PALLET, PIPE, ROLLER, SHUTTER, SLIDER, TRACKER, WIND
organ stop BOMBARDE, BOURDON, CELESTA, DIAPASON, DOLCAN, DULCIANA, GAMBE, GEDEKT,

GEMSHORN, KRUMMHORN, LARIGOT, MELODIA, MIXTUR(E), MONTRE, NACHTHORN, NASARD, NASAT, POSAUNE, PRESTANT, PRINCIPAL, QUINT, RANKETT, REGISTER, SCHARF, SEXT, SUBBASS, TERZ, TIERCE, TREMOLO, UNDAMARIS, WALDFLOTE
organization CADRE, MORIM, OUTFIT, SETUP
organism AM(O)EBA, BODY, MONAD, MONAS
oriental ASIAN, EASTER(N), ORTIVE
orifice LURA, OSTIOLE, PORE, STOMA
origin BUD, GENESIS, GERM, OUTSET, SEED
original FONTAL, FRESH, PRISTINE, UNIQUE
original sin ADAM
ornament AMULET, (BE)DECK, DECOR, (EM)BOSS, EPAULET(TE), EPI, FINIAL, FRET, GUTTA, OUCH, SCROLL, SPANG(LE), STUD
ostentation ECLAT, GLOSS, STRUT
Ostrogoth see GOTH
otic AUDITORY, AURAL
Ottoman TURK
oust BOUNCE, CASHIER, EVICT
out AWAY, EGRESS, EXIT, FORTH, PASSE, UIT
out-and-out ARRANT, RANK, SHEER
outbreak BOUTADE, EMEUTE, RASH
outburst FLARE, SPATE, STORM
outcast CHANDALA, ETA, ISHMAEL, LEPER, PARIAH, RONIN, YETA
outcry GAFF, HUBBUB, POTHER
outer ECTAL, FOREIGN
outfit GARB, GEAR, GETUP, EQUIP, KIT, REGALIA, RIG, SUIT, UNIT
outlaw DESPERADO, RONIN
outlet EGRESS, SOCKET, VENT
outline CONTOUR, PROFILE, SHAPE, SILHOUETTE, SUMMARY, TRACE
outlook PURVIEW, SCOPE, VISTA
outmoded DATED, DESUETE, PASSE
outward ECTAD, EXTRINSIC
outwork LUNETTE, RAVELIN, TENAIL
oven HIBACHI, IMU, KILN, LEER, LEHR, OAST, OON, TILER, UMU
over ATOP, OER, SURPLUS
overact EMOTE, HAM, OUTDO
overdue ARREAR, REMISS, UNPAID
overflow DEBORD, SURPLUS; see FLOOD
overhang BEETLE, EAVES, LOOM
overlay CEIL, LAP
overseer BAILIFF, CAPORAL, CORK, STEWARD
overthrow DEPOSE, REVERSE, TOPPLE
oxide CALX
oxidize CALCINE, RUST
oxygen OXID(E), OZONE
oyster bed material CULCH, CU(L)TCH
oyster farm CLAIRE, PARK

P

pace RATE, STEP, TEMPO; see GAIT
pachyderm ELEPHANT, HIPPO, RHINO
pacify see CALM
pack (C)RAM, STEEVE, STOW, TAMP, WAD
package BALE, CEROON, FADGE, ROBBIN, SEROON
pact COMPACT, CONCORDAT, ENTENTE, TREATY
pad MAT, TABLET, TRAMP
paddle see OAR
pagan ETHNIC, HEATHEN, PAYNIM
page FOLIO, RECTO, RUBRIC, VERSO
Pagliacci character BEPPO, CANIO, NEDDA, TONIO, SILVIO
pagoda PON, TA(A)
pail BOUK, PIGGIN, SKEEL, SOE
pain ACHE, AGONY, PANG, THROE
painkiller ANODYNE, COCA, OPIATE
painlessness APONIA
paint FARD, LIMN, MINIATE, PARGET, ROUGE, STIPPLE
painting medium CASEIN, OIL, TEMPERA
painting method FRESCO, GOUACHE, GRISAILLE, SECCO
painting style ABSTRACT, CLASSIC, CUBIST, DADAIST, FAUVISM, FUTURIST, GENRE, IDEALIST, REALISTIC
pair BRACE, DIAD, DUAD, DUET, DUO, DYAD, MATE, SPAN, TEAM, YOKE
paired GEMEL, MATED, TEAMED, TWIN

palatable SAPID, TASTY
palate UVULA, VELUM
pale ASHEN, ASHY, DOUGHY, MEALY, PALLID, PALLOR, PASTEL, PASTY, SALLOW, WAN
Palestine ERETS, ISRAEL
palisade ESPALIER, HURDIS
palm CONCEAL, KUDOS, THENAR
palm off FOB, FOIST
palm juice SURA
palpitation PALMUS, THROB, TIRL
pamper CODDLE, COSHER, COSSET
pamphlet BROCHURE, CHAP(BOOK), TRACT
panacea CURE(ALL), ELIXIR
panel PANE, PLAQUE, VENIRE
pang ACHE, RACK, THROE
panic FEAR, FRAY, FUNK
pant GASP, HUFF, PUFF, YEARN
pantry AMBRY, BUTTERY, EWERY, LARDER, SPENCE
paper PAPIER, PAPYRUS, PELURE, TAPA, VELLUM
paper, imperfect CASSE, RETREE, SALLE
paper folding ORIGAMI
paper measure BUNDLE, QUIRE, REAM
paper size ATLAS, CROWN, DEMY, ELEPHANT, EMPEROR, FOLIO, FOOLSCAP, IMPERIAL, POST, POTT, ROYAL
parade ARRAY, FLAUNT, MARCH, STRUT
paradise EDEN, ELYSIUM, JODO, NIRVANA, UTOPIA, ZION
paradise-like EDENIC, ELYSIAN
paragraph CLAUSE, ITEM, PILCROW
parallelogram RHOMBOID, RHOMB(US)
paralysis PALSY, PARESIS, PLEGIA
parasite APHID, BINE, FAWNER, LEECH, TOADY, TRYP
parcel LOT, PACKET, PLAT
parchment FOR(R)EL, VELLUM
parchment roll PELL
pardon AMNESTY, CONDONE, MERCY, REMIT
parish head PASTOR, RECTOR
park COMMON, PRATER
parley CONFER, PALAVER, PARLANCE, POWWOW
parliament report HANSARD
parlor LOCUTORY, SALA, SALON
paroxysm AGONY, FIT, SPASM
parrot ECHO, MIMIC, POLLY; see p. 220
parry DEFLECT, FENCE, FEND, REPLY
parsonage see CLERGYMAN
part BREAK, CLEAVE, ELEMENT, PIECE, ROLE, SECTOR, SEVER, SOME, SUNDER
part of speech ADJECTIVE, (AD)VERB, CONJUNCTION, INTERJECTION, PREPOSITION, (PRO)NOUN
particle AFFIX, BIT, GRAIN, MESO(TRO)N, PALEA, RAMENTUM; see ATOM, JOT
particular FUSSY, ITEM, ODD, UNIQUE
partition SEPTA, SEPTUM
partnership CAHOOT, HOEY, HUI
party BASH, GALA, PROM, SECT, SHINDIG, SOCIAL, SOIREE, STAG, TEA
parvenu CLIMBER, SNOB, UPSTART
pass BYGO, COL, DEFILE, ELIDE, DIE, FADE, GAP, GHAT, GHAUT, HAND, (E)LAPSE, OMIT, REEVE, RELAY, SKIP, SKITTER, TICKET
passageway ADIT, AISLE, ALURE, ARCADE, CANAL, CLAUSE, DUCT, EGRESS, EXIT, GAT, GUT, HALL, ITER, SLYPE, STOPE, STULM, TRANSIT
passion RAGA
Passover PASCH(A), SEDAR, SEDER
pasta BUCATINI, DITALI, FUSILLI, LINGUINI, MAFALDE, MELONE, MEZZANI, PASTINA, RIGATI, ROTELLE, ZITI; see p. 122
paste BOND, GLUE, PAP, STRASS
pastel CRAYON, TINT, WOAD
paste-up COLLAGE
pastoral BUCOLIC, RURAL, RUSTIC
pasture AGIST, HEAF, HOGA, ING, LEA, SHIELING
pat APT, DAB, FIT, GLIB, TAP
patch BODGE, CLOUT, DARN
patchwork CENTO, MEDLEY, MONTAGE, MOSAIC
patella KNEEPAN, ROTULA
paten ARCA(E), DISC
patent BERAT, LICENSE
path BERM, CASAUN, LOCUS, ORBIT, RODDIN(G)
patriarch NASI, PATER, SIRE; see p. 112
patriot ALLEN, HALE, OTIS, REVERE
patron ANGEL, CLIENT, SAINT, SPONSOR
patronage (A)EGIS, AUSPICES, FAVOR, WING
pattern DAMIER, FORMAT, IDEAL, MODEL, NORM, PARAGON, SETT, STENCIL, TYPE

Paul's birthplace TARSUS
pause C(A)ESURA, LULL, SELAH, TRUCE
pavilion KIOSK, TELD, TENT
paving material ASPHALT, CONCRETE, MACADAM, TAR(MAC)
paving stone FLAG, PAVER, SETT
paw GAUM, FOOT, PUD
pawn GAGE, HOCK, PLEDGE, WAGER
pay ANTE, DEFRAY, REMIT, REWARD, SPEND, STIPEND, TIP WAGE
paymaster BAKSHI, BUXY, PURSER
payment ANNAT, CENS, CRO, ERIC, FEE, KIST, LABOLA, REBATE, SCOT
peace IRENE, LISS, NIRVANA, PAX
peaceful HALCYON, IRENIC
peak ACME, ALP, APEX. BEN, CLIMAX, CUSP, PITON, TOR, ZENITH
pear ANJOU, BOSC, COMICE, NOPAL, PYRUS, SECKEL SICKLE
pearl GEM, NACRE, OLIVET, ONION
pearlweed SAGINA
peasant CARL, CEORL, CHURL, COOLIE, COTTAR, COTTER, FELLAH, KULAK, MUZHIK, PAISANO, PEON, RAYAT, RYOT, TAO, TILLER
peat MOOR TURF
peck DAB, (K)NIP
pedal CELESTE, LEVER, TREADLE
peddle HAWK, SELL TOUT, TRANT VEND
peddler HAWKER; see MERCHANT
pedestal BASE GAINE
pedestal part DADO. ORLO, PLINTH, SOCLE, SUBBASE
peduncle SCAPE, STALK STEM
peel BARK, FLAY. HARL PARE. RIND, SKIN SKIVE
peep CHEEP, DEKKO, PULE, SKEG
peep show RAREE
peer FE(E)RE, GAZE, PEEK, PEEP, RIVAL
peevish GRUFF, TESTY, TOUCHY
peg DOWEL, KNAG, LEG NOB, TEE, THOLE, TRE(E)NAIL, TRUNNEL
pellet GOLI, PALLION
pellucid CLEAR, LIMPID, LUCENT
pelota see JAIALAI
pelt FELL, HIDE, SKIN, STONE
pen JAIL, SCRIPT, STY(LE), SWAN
pen point NEB, NIB
penalty CAIN, FINE, FORFEIT
penetrate BORE, ENTER, IMBUE, IMPALE
penmanship HAND, SCRIPT
pennant BURGEE, PENCEL, PENNON, WHIP
Pentateuch LAW, TORA(H)
people CLAN, CROWD, DAOINE, DEMOS, FOLK, GENTE, MEN, MOB, ONES, RABBLE, RACE, VOLK
per APIECE, VIA
perceive DESCRY, SENSE, SPOT
perception ACUMEN, EAR, ESP, TACT
perch AERIE, ROD, ROOST, SIT
percolate EXUDE, LEACH, OOZE, SEEP
perforate BORE, DRILL, PIERCE, PRICK, RIDDLE TREPAN
performer ACTOR, AGENT, ARTIST(E), DOER, PLAYER, SHINE
perfume AROMA, AT(T)AR, BOUQUET, CENSE, MUSK, OTTO, PASTIL SACHET
period AGE, CYCLE, DOT, EON, ERA, SPAN, STAGE, SYSTEM, TERM, TIME
period, geological CAMBRIAN, DEVONIAN, DYAS, EOCENE, ERIAN, JURA, KARROO, MIOCENE, SILURIAN, TRIAS, UINTA
periodic CYCLIC, ETESIAN
periphery AMBIT, EDGE LIMIT
perplex BAFFLE BEWILDER, CONFUSE, ELUDE MYSTIFY, NONPLUS STUMP
persist ENDURE LAST, PLOD
personage BIGWIG NIBS, VIP
personnel CREW, HANDS SQUAD, STABLE STAFF TROUPE
perspiration DEW. SUDOR SWEAT
pert FLIP, SASSY. SAUCY
pertinent ANENT. APT, FIT
perturb ALARM, HARASS RUFFLE
peruse CON, SCAN, STUDY, SURVEY
pervade IMBRUE, PERFUSE, PERMEATE
pest BANE, CURSE NAG, PLAGUE SCOURGE
pester ANNOY, BADGER, HARASS, NAG TEASE
pestle BRAY, PILUM PISTIL
pet CADE, CODDLE, COSSET, PIQUE
Peter Pan character HOOK, NANA, WENDY
petiole STALK, STEM, STIPE
petrol see GAS
petroleum derivative ASPHALT, BUTANE, COKE, NAPHTHA

peyote CACTUS, MESCAL
phantom(s) EIDOLA, EIDOLON
phase ASPECT, FACET, INSTAR, STAGE
philippic JOBATION, SCREED, TIRADE
philosopher BACON, BERGSON, BRUNO, COMTE, CYNIC, EDMAN, ELEATIC, ERISTIC, FICHTEAN, HEGEL, HUME, JOAD, KANT, LOCKE, MOTI, PLATO, RUSSELL, SARTRE, SENECA, SKEPTIC, SOCRATES, SPENCER, SPINOZA, THALES, ZENO, ZETETIC
philosopher's stone ELIXIR
philosophy ATOMISM, CASUISTRY, EGOISM, HEDONISM, IDEALISM, MONISM, PSYCHISM, REALISM, SENSISM, SOMATISM, SOPHISM, STOICISM, THOMISM, VITALISM, YOGA
phloem BARK, BAST, TISSUE
phonetic system IPA, ROMIC
photo(s) MUG, SHOT, SNAP, STAT, PIC, PIX
physical SOMAL, SOMATIC
physician CURER, DOCTOR, MEDIC, SURGEON
physicians CARREL, COLLES, DOOLEY, ERB, FINLAY, FINSEN, GALEN, HADEN, HALLER, HARVEY, JENNER, LISTER, MAYO, MESMER, MORTON, OSLER, PAGET, PARE, PARRAN, PERERA, POTT, REED, RHAZES, RUSK, SABIN, SALK; see p. 244
physicists ABBE, AMPERE, BOYLE, BUNSEN, ERMAN, HAHN, MACH, OHM, ROSSI, TELLER, VOLTA; see p. 244
pianist ANDA, ARRAU, BUSONI, CLIBURN, CURZON, GOULD, HESS, HOFMANN, HOROWITZ, ITURBI, KEMPF, LEVANT, LHEVINNE, PACHMANN, RICHTER, ROSEN, SERKIN, SOLOMON
pick CULL, ELITE, GLEAN, PLECTRUM
picket PALE, STAKE, TETHER
pickle ACHAR, ALEC, BRINE, CORN, CURE, GHERKIN, SOUSE
pickpocket DIP(PER), WIRE
picture CANVAS, DEPICT, EPITOME, FRESCO, ICON, MONTAGE, MURAL, PROFILE, TABLEAU; see PHOTO
piebald CALICO, PIED, PINTO
piece out CANTLE, EKE
pier ANTA, COB(B), PILASTER; see LANDING
pierce GORE, GOUGE, LANCE, STAB
pig INGOT, MOLD, SLOB
pigment-forming substance DOPA
pigtail CUE, PLAIT, QUEUE
pilaster ALETTE, ANTA
pile HOARD, NAP, RICK
pile driver FISTUCA, OLIVER, RAM, TUP
pilfer FILCH, SLOCK, STEAL
pilgrim HADJI, MIGRANT, PALMER, PIONEER
pilgrimage CRUSADE, HADJ, QUEST
Pilgrim's garb IHRAM
pill BOLUS, DOSE, GOLI, PELLET
pillage see PLUNDER
pillar HERMA, JAMB, LAT, NEWEL, OBELISK, PIER, PILASTER, PROP, SHAFT, STELE
pillory BRANK(S), CANG(UE), JOUG, STOCK, TRONE, YOKE
pillow BOLSTER, COD
pilot AVIATOR, GUIDE, STEER
pin ACUS, BROOCH, COTTER, DOWEL, FIBULA, FID, PINTLE, THOLE, TIGE, RIVET, SKEWER
pinafore APRON, TIER
pinch CRAMP, NIP, PUGIL, STRAIT, TWEAK
pinched CHITTY, URLED
pinnacle APEX, EPI, SERAC, ZENITH
pinniped SEAL, WALRUS
pinochle term BETE, DIX, KITTY, MELD, WIDOW
pip ACE, HIT, ROUP, SEED, SPOT
pipe BRIAR, BRIER, CALUMET, DUDEEN, FIFE, FLUE, HOOKAH, HUB(B), NARGILE, REED, RISER, STRAW, TEE, TUBE
pipelike TUBATE
piquant RACY, SHARP, ZESTY
pique NETTLE, PEEVE, STING
piquet term CAPOT, (RE)PIC, RUBICON, SINKING
pirate BRIGAND, CORSAIR, PICAROON, ROVER
pit ABYSS, FOSSA, FOVEA, HOLE, LACUNA, MINE, POCK, SEED, SUMP
pitch REEL, RESIN, TONE, TOSS
pitcher see JUG
pith GIST, JET, NUB, PULP
pithy CORKY, MEATY, TERSE
pitted ETCHED, FOVEATE, STONED
placard AFFICHE, BILL, POST(ER)
place(s) ASSIGN, JOB, LIEU, LOCALE, LOCI, LOCUS, NICHE, POSIT, RANK, SCENE, SE(A)T, SITUS, SPOT, STATUS, STEAD, VENUE
placid CALM, HALCYON, SUANT
plague see PEST, PESTER

plain BLUNT, CHASTE, CHOL, CLEAR, EVEN, HEATH, HOMELY, LLANO, LOWLAND, MERE, PAMPA, PRAIRIE, STEPPE, TUNDRA, VELDT, WEALD, WOLD
plait BRAID, MESH, PLEX, PLY
plan ETTLE, INTEND, PLOT
planetarium ORRERY
planets see p. 276
plank DECK, SLATE, TICKET
plant disease AECIUM, BLET, BLIGHT, BUNT, ERGOT, ERINOSE, ESCA, FUNGUS, GALL, RUST, SCALD, SMUT, STIPPEN
plant(s) FACTORY, FLORA, INSERT, MILL, SOW; see p. 225
plantation FINCA, HOLT, YERBAL
plaster ADOBE, GESSO, PARGET, STUCCO
plastic ACETATE, ACRYLIC, ALKYD, BAKELITE, BUNA, CASEIN, FICTILE, FORMICA, FURAN(E), LIGNIN, LUCITE, NITRATE, NYLON, PHENOLIC, RESINOID, TERPENE, UREA, VINYL
plate DISCUS, DOD, GRID, PATEN, SCUTE, SLAB, TAGGER
plateau KAR(R)OO, MESA, PLAT
platform BEMA, DAIS, DOLLY, ESTRADE, PERRON, ROSTRUM, SOLLAR, SOLLER, STAGE
Plato's Idea EIDE, EIDOS
platter ASHET, SALVER, TRENCHER
play COMEDY, DRAMA, (EN)ACT, FARCE, MASQUE, MIRACLE, MYSTERY, PAGEANT, SCOPE, SPIEL, SPORT, TRAGEDY
play part ACT, BIT, CURTAIN, EXODE, EXODOS, EXODUS, FINALE, ROLE, SCENA, SCENE, STANZA, WALKON
player(s) ACTOR, ACTRESS, CAST, DIVA, DUB, HAM, MIME, MUMMER, SHINE, STAR, THESPIAN, TROUPER
plea ABATER, DEMURRER
plead ENTREAT, PRESS, SUE
please ARRIDE, FANCY, SUIT
pleated PLICATE, PLISSE, SHIRRED
pledge BOND, (EN)GAGE, OATH, PAWN, SWEAR, TOAST, TROTH, VAS, VOW
Pleiades ALCYONE, CELAENO, ELECTRA, MAIA, MEROPE, STEROPE, TAYGETA
plenty UBERTY
pliable LITHE, PLASTIC, PLIANT, SUPPLE, WAXY
plinth BASE, ORLO
plot CABAL, CONSPIRE, LOT, SCENARIO, SCHEME, SITE
plow FURROW, ROVE, TILL
plow part CLEVIS, SHARE, SHEATH, SLADE, SOLE
plug BOOST, BOTT, BUNG, CAULK, CORK, QUID, SPILE, STOPPER, TAMPON
plume AIGRET, EGRET, PANACHE, PREEN
plunder BOOTY, LOOT, MARAUD, PILFER, PILLAGE, PREY, RANSACK, RAPINE, RAVAGE, RAVEN, RAVIN(E), REAVE, RIFLE, ROB, SACK, SPOIL, STRIP
plunge DIP, DIVE, DOUSE, DUNK, LUNGE
pocket CULDESAC, FOB, LODE, POCHE, SAC
pod(s) ARIL, BOLL, PIPI
Poe work GOLDBUG, RAVEN
poem AMHRAN, BALLAD, BUCOLIC, CANTO, DIT, DUAN, ECLOGUE, ELEGY, EPODE, GEORGIC, IDYL(L), LAI, (VIRE)LAY, ODELET, POESY, PSALM, RONDEAU, RUNES, SONNET, TRIOLET, VERSE; see EPIC
poet BARD, LYRIST, METRIST, ODIST, RIMER, SCALD, SCOP, SKALD
poi source TARO
point ACE, BARB, DOT, END, GOAL, JOT, NODE, ORD, PUNTA, PUNTO, SPIT, TIP
pointed ACUATE, OGIVAL, TERSE
pointer CLUE, FESCUE, ROD, WAND
poison ARSENIC, ATTER, BANE, BISH, CONINE, (C)URARE, (C)URARI, CYANIDE, DATURA, HEMP, INEE, LOCO, MESCAL, SUMAC, TAINT, TOXIN, UPAS, URALI, VENOM
poke DAWDLE, JAB, JOG, NUDGE, PROD
poker term ANTE, BLAZE, BOBTAIL, BUG, CAT, DOG, DRAW, FLASH, FLUSH, FOLD, HOLE, KICKER, KILTER, KITTY, PELTER, PIGEON, POT, RUNT, SEE, SKEET, STAY, STUD, TIGER
pole AXIS, CABER, MAST, PEW, PUNT, QUANT, SPRIT, STILT, THILL
pole to pole AX(I)AL
police CID, FBI, GESTAPO, MVD, NKVD, OGPU, SURETE
policeman BOBBY, BULL, COP, DICK, PEELER, ZARP
polish BUFF, GLAZE, GRACE, LEVIGATE, SHINE, WAX

polished ELEGANT, GLOSSY, SLEEK, URBANE
polisher BUFF, EMERY, PUMICE, RABAT
politician CONNIVER, HEELER
pond LOCHAN, LUM, TARN
pool CARR, DIB, DUB, KITTY, LAGOON, LINN, LLYN, MERE, PUDDLE, TARN
poor INFERIOR, NEEDY, SEELY
Pope ANGELO, MONTINI, PACELLI, PONTIFF, RATTI, RONCALLI; see p. 243
pony CAVY, CRIB, DRAM, NAG, TROT
poppy seed MAW
populace HOIPOLLOI; see PEOPLE
porcelain CELADON, CHINA, DERBY, GOMBROON, LIMOGES, MEISSEN, MING, MURRA, SEVRES, SPODE
porch GALILEE, LANAI, PARVIS, PIAZZA, PORTICO, STOA, STOOP, VERANDA(H)
pore(s) FORAMEN, OSTIOLE, PONDER, STOMA(TA)
porridge ATOLE, BROSE, GRUEL, MUSH, POB(S), POLENTA, POTTAGE
port LARBOARD; see HARBOR
portend, portent see PRESAGE
porter AKABO, ALE, BELLBOY, CARGADOR, COOLIE, DARWAN, (K)HAMAL, REDCAP, TAMEN
portico ARCADE, NARTHEX, PARVIS, PIAZZA, STOA, XYST(US)
portion BIT, DOLE, DOT, LOT, METE, QUOTA, RATION
portray DEPICT, DRAW, LIMN
pose FEIGN, MIEN, MODEL, SIT
position STAND, STANCE, UBIETY; see PLACE
positive ACTUAL, PLUS, THETIC
positive pole ANODE
post BOLLARD, CAMP, CAPSTAN, COLUMN, JAMB, JOB, MAIL, NEWEL
poster AFFICHE, BILL, PLACARD
postpone DEFER, SHELVE, TABLE
postulate AXIOM, CLAIM, POSIT, PREMISE
posture MIEN, STANCE
potassium ALUM, GROUGH, KALITE, MURIATE, NITER, POTASH
pottery BASALT, CHUN, CROUCH, DELFT, FAIENCE, JASPER, KUAN, LEEDS, TING, TUNG, YUEH
pottery, pert. to CERAMIC
pouch BURSA, POD, SAC(K), SPORRAN
pouch-shaped SACCATE
poultry disease GAPES, PIP, POX, ROUP
pound BRAY, BRUISE, DRUB, TAMP, THUMP, TUND
pour DECANT, GUSH, LIBATE, RAIN, SPEW, TEEM
powder ABIR, DUST, PICRA, POUNCE, TALC
power DINT, FORCE, MANA, OD(YL), SWAY
praise ECLAT, ELOGE, EXALT, EXTOL, KUDOS, LAUD
prance CAPER, CAVORT
prank ANTIC, CURVET, DIDO
prate BUKH, BUKK, GAB, YAP
pray BESEECH, DAVEN, SUE
prayer ALENU, AVE, BEAD, BENE, CREDO, GRACE, LITANY, MATIN, NOVENA, ORISON, PLEA, SALAT, SUIT, VESPER
prayerbook ORDO, PORTAS(S)
prayer place IDGAH
prayer stick BAHO(O), PAHO
praying figure ORANT
preacher see EVANGELIST, CLERGYMAN
precept(s) CODE, DICTA, TENET
precipice CRAG, LINN, PALI
preclude IMPEDE; see PREVENT
preconceive IDEATE, SCHEME
predicament DILEMMA, SCRAPE, STRAIT(S)
predict AUGUR, BODE, DIVINE, WEIRD
predisposed BIASED, PRONE
preen PLUME, PRIMP, PRINK
prefixes see p. 234
prelate ABBOT, BISHOP, CARDINAL, INGE, PONTIFF, POPE, PRIMATE
premium AGIO, BONUS
prepare ADAPT, EDIT, EQUIP, FIT, GIRD, PAVE, REDACT
preposition AFTER, FOR, FROM, INTO, ONTO, OUT, (UN)TO, UPON, WITH
presage AUGUR(Y), BODE, HERALD, OMEN, OSTENT, PORTEND, PORTENT, SIGN, TOKEN
prescribed THETIC
present DONATE, GIFT, GIVE, NONCE, TENDER, TODAY
presently ANON, (E)NOW, SOON
preserve CAN, CORN, CURE, JAM, KEEP, PROTECT, TIN
press CRAM, IRON, SERRY, STAMP, TAMP
pressure DURESS, STRESS
pressure unit BARAD, BARIE
pretend FAKE, FEIGN, SIMULATE
pretense(s) AIRS, FEINT, RUSE

pretentious POMPOUS, SIDY, TAWDRY
prevail OBTAIN, SWAY, WIN
prevalent EXTANT, RAMPANT, RIFE
prevent AVERT, BALK, (DE)BAR, DETER, (E)STOP, PRECLUDE, THWART
prey PRIZE, RAVIN(E), ROB
price COST, FARE, RATE, TOLL
prickle ACANTHA, ACULEUS, BUR(R), SETA, SPICULA
priest ABUNA, CALCHAS, DRUID, ELI, FLAMEN, FRA, LAMA, MOBED, MYST, PANDITA, PAPA, SARIP, SHAMAN; see CLERGYMAN
priestess AUGE, ENTUM, VESTAL
priesthood MAGI, SALII
primeval EARLY, NATIVE, OLD, PRISTINE
prince ATHELING, DAUPHIN, GAEKWAR, IMA(U)M, KHAN, NAWAB, RANA, RAS
principle BASIS, LOGOS, PRANA, TENET, YANG, YIN; see MAXIM
printer BRADFORD, CAXTON, DAY, FUST, GUTENBERG, JENSON, NUTHEAD, PLANTIN, SHORT, THOMAS, TORY, TYPO
prison see JAIL
prison camp DACHAU, STALAG
privilege CHARTER, FRANCHISE, LICENSE, OCTROI, PATENT
prize PRY, TERN; see AWARD
probe INQUEST, SOUND, STYLET
problem CRUX, NUT, POSER
proboscis ANTLIA, NEB, NOSE, SNOUT, TRUNK
proceed ISSUE, PRESS, WEND
proceedings ACTA, ACTION, ACTS
procession CORTEGE, FILE, PARADE, RETINUE, TRAIN
proclaim CRY, DECLARE, HERALD, KNELL, VOICE
prod EGG, GOAD, POKE
produce APPORT, BEGET, CAUSE, CREATE, ENGENDER, GENERATE, INWORK, YIELD
product EFFECT, OPUS, RESULT
profane DEFILE, NOA, VIOLATE
profession ART, AVOWAL, CALL(ING), CAREER, CRAFT, JOB, LINE, METIER, PURSUIT, TRADE, VOCATION
profit (A)VAIL, BOOT, BENEFIT, GAIN, NET
profit-taker PERNOR
profitable FAT, USEFUL, UTILE
progenitor SIRE, PARENT
progeny ISSUE, SCION, SEED
prohibit BAN, (DE)BAR, TABOO
prohibited ILLICIT, TABOO
prohibition EMBARGO, VETO
project IDEA, JUT, SCHEME
projecting piece ARM, FLANGE, RIM, TENDON
projection CAM, BARB, BULGE, EAR, FIN, HOB(B), KNOP, LEDGE, LOBE, PRONG, SHELF, SNAG
promenade ALAMEDA, MALL, MARINA, PASEAR, PRADO
promise (A)VOW, IOU, NOTE, OATH, PAROLE, PLEDGE, WORD
promontory CAPE, NASE, NAZE, NESS, NOUP, SKAW, SPIT, TOR
prompt CUE, SOON, URGE, YARE
prong ANTLER, FANG, NIB, PEG, TINE, TOOTH
pronoun HER(S), HIM, HIS, MINE, ONE, OUR(S), SHE, THAT, THEE, THEIR, THEM, THESE, THEY, THINE, THIS, THOSE, THOU, YOU(R)
pronounce BURR, SLUR, STRESS
proof GALLEY, REPRO, REVISE, SAFE, TRIAL
prop BOLSTER, BRACE, GIB, HOLD, RANGE, STAY
propeller BLADE, ROTOR, SCREW
properly APTLY, FEATLY
property AL(L)OD(IUM), ASSET, CHATTEL, DHAN, ESTATE, GOODS, LAND(S), WEALTH
property, hold on LIEN
property, receiver of ALIENEE
prophesy FORETELL; see PRESAGE
prophet(s) AUGUR, ORACLE, SEER, VATES; see p. 112
prophetess CASSANDRA, PYTHIA(N), PYTHONESS, SEERESS, SIBYL
prophetic ORACULAR, VATIC(AL)
proposition(s) LEMMA, PORISM, PREMISE, THEOREM, THESES, THESIS
proprietor PATROON
prosecute INTEND, LITIGATE, SUE
proselyte see CONVERT
prospect HOPE, MINE, VISTA
prosperity HAP, SONS(E), WEAL(TH), WELFARE
prostrate BOW, FELL, PRONE, REPENT, SUPINE
protection (A)EGIS, APRON, LEE, SHELTER, WING
protection right GRITH, MUND
protein ABRIN, ALBUMIN, CASEIN, FIBRIN, GLIADIN, GLOB(UL)IN, GLUT(EL)IN, HISTON(E), HORDEIN, MUCIN, PEPTIDE, PEPTONE, PROLAMIN, RICIN, ZEIN
protrude BEETLE, JUT, PROJECT

protuberance GNARL, HUMP, JAG, KNOB, KNOT, KNURL, LOBE, NODE, NUB, TORUS, UMBO, WART
protuberant STRUT, TOROSE
prove DERAIGN, EVINCE
proverb see MAXIM
provide CATER, ENDOW, ENDUE, PURVEY
provided BODEN, SOBEIT
provisioner SUTLER, VIVANDIER
provisions ANNONA, CATES
proviso CLAUSE, SALVO
provoke ANGER, ANNOY, IRE, NEEDLE, NETTLE, PEEVE, PIQUE, RILE, ROIL
prow BOW, PROA, STEM
prune LOP, PREEN, SNED, TRIM
pry JIMMY, LEVER, PRIZE, SNOOP
psalm(s) CANTATE, CANTICLE, HALLEL, LAUD(S), MISERERE, PRAISE
pseudonym ALIAS, NOM, SOBRIQUET
psyche MIND, PNEUMA, SPIRIT
psychiatrist ADLER, ALIENIST, ANALYST, BINET, BREUER, BRILL, CHARCOT, FREUD, HORNEY, JAMES, JANET, JUNG, MESMER, RANK, REIK, WARD, WUNDT
public CIVIC, COMMON, KNOWN, KUNG, OPEN, OVERT
publish AIR, BLAZON, DELATE, EDIT, ISSUE, REVEAL, SPREAD, VENT
pudding DUFF, HOY, SAGO
puff BLURB, ELATE, FLAM, SWELL, WAFF
pull BOUSE, DRAG, HALE, PLUCK, TOW, TUG, WRENCH, YANK
pulley SHEAVE, TACKLE
pulp CHYME, PAP, PITH, POMACE
pulpit AMBO, BEMA, MIMBAR, ROSTRUM
pulverize BRAY, MILL, MULL
punch BLOW, BORE, DOUSE, JAB, MATTOIR, POKE, PRITCHEL, STAMP
punctuation mark BRACE, BRACKET, CARET, COLON, COMMA, DASH, DOT, ELLIPSIS, HYPHEN, LEADERS, PARENS, PERIOD, POINT, QUOTES, SLANT, SOLIDUS, VIRGULE
pungent SPICY, TANGY, TEZ
punish AMERCE, FINE, FRAP
punishment FERULE, PENALTY, WRACK
punishment, pert. to PENAL
punt GAMBLE, KENT, QUANT
pupil GLENE; see STUDENT
puppet DOLL, EFFIGY, JUDY, KUKLA, MAUMET, OLLIE, PUNCH, TOOL
pure CHASTE, MERE, NEAT, PUTE, SHEER
purport FECK, GIST, TENOR
purpose AIM, ARTHA, END, GOAL, INTENT, MEANING, SAKE
purposive TELIC
pursue HOUND, HUNT, STALK, T(R)AIL
pursy PUDGY, PUFFY, STOUT
push BOOST, NUDGE, PING, PROD
put aside DAFF
put away BANK, CACHE, STORE
put off DEFER, DOFF, HAFT, STALL
put on ADORN, DON, FEIGN, PRODUCE, STAGE
put out DOUSE, EJECT, EVICT, FIRE, OUST, SACK
puzzle(s) AMAZE, BAFFLE, CRUCES, CRUX, ENIGMA, MYSTIFY, NONPLUS, POSE(R), REBUS, RIDDLE, TANGRAM
pygmy ATOMY, MINIM, RUNT; see DWARF
pyramid CHEOPS, KHAFRE, KHUFU, MENKAURE
pyromaniac ARSONIST, FIREBUG

Q

quack CHARLATAN, CROCUS, IMPOSTOR, SANGRADO
quadrant ARC, FOURTH, HENRY
quadrate AGREE, QUARTER, SQUARE
quaff see DRINK
quail BLENCH, COWER, WINCE
quake QUIVER, SHAKE, SHIVER, TREMBLE, TREMOR
Quaker FOX, FRIEND, HICKS
quaking ASPEN, TREMOR, TREPID
qualify ADAPT, EQUIP, FIT, LIMIT, PASS, PREPARE
quality CALIBER, GRADE, GUNA, METTLE, RAJAS, SATTVA, TAMAS, TIMBRE, TRAIT
qualm(s) NAUSEA, PANG, REGRET, SCRUPLE
quantity BULK, DOSE, MASS, SCALER, SOME, SPATE, VECTOR
quarrel BICKER, DISPUTE; see FIGHT
quarter of year RAITH
quarters BILLET, BIVOUAC, COMMONS, DIGS, ETAPE

quash ANNUL, CASS(ARE), QUELL, SQUELCH, VOID
quaternion TETRAD
quay see LANDING
queen ANNE, BASTA, BE(E)GUM, BESS, DIDO, (EL)ENA, MAB, MARIE, MARY, ORIANA, VICTORIA
queenly REG(IN)AL
quell CALM, CRUSH, QUASH, SPRING
quench ALLAY, SLAKE, STIFLE
question ASK, GRILL, NUT, POSE(R), QUERY, QUIZ
queue CUE, FILE, PIGTAIL
quibble CARP, CAVIL, EVADE, PUN, SOPHISM
quick ACTIVE, AGILE, (A)LIVE, FAST, FLEET, LISH, PROMPT, RAPID, SNAPPY, TOSTO, YARE
quickly ANON, APACE, CITO, INSTANTER, PRESTO, PRONTO
quicksand SYRT(IS), TRAP
quid CHAW, CHEW, CUD, FID, WAD
quiescent DORMANT, LATENT
quiet ALLAY, CALM, LULL, MUM, PST, SMOOTH, STILL, TST, TUT
quill(s) COP, PEN, REMEX, SPINA, SPINE
quilt CADDOW, DUVET, EIDER
quinine KINA, QUINA
quintessence ELIXIR, GIST, PITH
quirt ROMAL, WHIP
quivering see QUAKING
quoits JUKSKEI
quoits term DISCUS, HOB, MOT, SKEI, TEE
quotation CHRIA, CITAL
quote ADDUCE, CITE

R

rabbi AMORA, GAON, HAKAM
rabble DREGS, RIFFRAFF, SCUM; see MOB, PEOPLE
rabies LYSSA
race BREED, CONTEST, DASH, FLUME, HIE, LADE, LINE(AGE), PEDIGREE, REGATTA, RELAY, SPRINT, STIRPS
race, pert. to ETHNIC
racecourse AQUEDUCT, ASCOT, DOWNS, EPSOM, HIALEAH, JAMAICA, LAP, OVAL, PIMLICO, SARATOGA, TRACK, TURF
racket BABEL, BAT, GAME
Radames's love AIDA
radiation unit RAD
radical LEFTIST, LEFTWING, REBEL, RED, ULTRA; see ROOT
radius RANGE, SPOKE, SWEEP
rage FAD, FUME, FUROR, FURY, RAMP, RANT, RESE, STORM, TANTRUM, VOGUE
ragged FRAYED, SHABBY
ragout GOULASH, HARICOT, SALMI
raid COMMANDO, FORAY, INROAD, ONSET, RAZZIA
rail BAR, FENCE, RANT, REVILE, SCOLD, SEPTUM
railing GRATE, PARAPET
railroad car BOXCAR, BUGGY, CABOOSE, COACH, DINER, DINGHY, FLAT(CAR), GONDOLA, PULLMAN, RATTLER, REEFER, SLEEPER, SMOKER, TANK, TENDER
railroad terms CHAIR, (CROSS)TIE, CROW, FLARE, GAUGE, PEDESTAL, SEMAPHORE, SLEEPER
railroader BAKEHEAD, BRAKIE, CONDUCTOR, ENGINEER, FIREMAN, GUARD, MOTORMAN, PORTER, RAIL, YARDMAN
rain DAB, DRIZZLE, MISLE, MIST, MIZZLE, SEREIN, SHOWER, TEEM
rain, pert. to PLUVIAL
rainbow ARC, IRIS
rainbow, pert. to IRID(I)AL
rainy MISTY, PLUVIOUS, SHOWERY
rake COMB, ENFILADE, LOTHARIO, PEPPER, ROUE
ram ARIES, BUTT, STUFF, TAMP, TUP, WETHER
ramble GAD, ROVE, SAUNTER
rampart AGGER, PARAPET, REDAN, VALLUM
range AREA, DRIFT, GAMUT, ORBIT, ROAM, SCOPE
rank ARRANT, DEGREE, RATE, ROW, STATUS, TIER
rankle FESTER, IRRITATE
ransom RAIM, REDEEM
rap BOP, BOX, CUFF, THUMP, THWACK, WHACK
rapidly APACE, SKELP
rascal IMP, ROGUE, SCAMP, VARLET
rasp FILE, GRATE, SCRAPE
ratchet see DETENT
rate AGIO, ASSESS, BATTA, CESS, ESTIMATE, TAX
ratio DEGREE, QUOTA, RATE
rationalize REASON, THOB
ravage DESPOIL, RAZE, SACK
ravine ARROYO, DALE, DONGA, GAP, GORGE, GULCH, GULLY, LINN, NULLAH, WADI, WADY
raw BLEAK, DAMP, GREEN, SORE, UNRIPE

ray ACTINIC, ALPHA, ANODE, BEAM, BETA, CANAL, CATHODE, COSMIC, GAMMA, GLEAM, LENARD
rayon ACETATE, CELANESE, VISCOSE
rays, pert. to RADIAL
reaction REFLEX, RESPONSE, TAXIS, TROPISM
reactionary BIRCHER, DIEHARD, MISONEIST, RIGHTIST, RIGHTWING
read CONSTRUE, DECIPHER, PERUSE, PRELECT, SCAN
read, inability to ALEXIA
reader ANAGNOST, LECTOR, PRIMER
reading KERE, K(E)RI, LECTION
ready HANDY, RIPE, YARE
real thing MCCOY
really ARU, INDEED
realm DOMAIN, RICHE, SPHERE
rear(ing) ARRIERE, BREED, DERRIERE, ERECT, PESADE, STEND
rear, to the (AB)AFT, ASTERN
reason, deprive of DEMENT
reason(ing) APRIORI, ARGUE, LOGIC, MOTIVE, NOUS, SENSE
rebel DEFY, MUTINY, RESIST, REVOLT, RISE
rebellion PUTSCH, SEDITION
rebound BOUNCE, CAROM, ECHO, RESILE, RICOCHET
rebuff CENSURE, HIGHHAT, SLAP, SNUB, SPURN
recalcitrant PERVERSE, RENITENT, WAYWARD
recant ABJURE, RETRACT
recede EBB, REGRESS, RETREAT
receiver BAILEE, FENCE, TRUSTEE
recent LATE, MODERN, NEO(TERIC), NEW, NOVEL
receptacle ACERRA, BASIN, BASKET, BIN, BOX, BUCKET, CASE, CRATE, FONT, HAMPER, PAIL, POT, TRAY, URN, VESSEL
reception ACCUEIL, DURBAR, FETE, LEVEE, SALON, SOIREE
recess APSE, BAY, INTERVAL, NOOK; see CUBICLE
recession SETBACK, SLUMP
recipient DONEE, HEIR
recite QUOTE, RECOUNT, SCAN
reckon ARET, COUNT, GUESS, IMPUTE, TALLY
reclaim REDEEM, REFORM, RENEW
recline COUCH, LEAN, LOLL, LOUNGE
recoil KICK, RESILE, RICOCHET, SHRINK, SHY, WINCE
recompense (RE)PAY, WAGE; see REWARD
reconnaissance ESPIAL, RECCO, RECON
reconnoiter SCAN, SCOUT, SPY
record ACTA, AGENDA, ANNALS, BLOTTER, DIARY, DOCKET, DOSSIER, ENROL(L), ENTER, ENTRY, FASTI, FILE, HANSARD, LIST, LOG, MINUTE, NOTE, REGISTER, ROLL, TAB, TAPE
recording DISC, PLATTER, TAPE, WIRE
recover RALLY, RECOUP, SALVE
recovery SALVAGE, TROVER
recruit BOOT, CONSCRIPT, DRAFT(EE), ENLIST(EE), INDUCT, LEVY, MUSTER, RALLY, ROOKIE
rectifier DIODE
rectify REMEDY, SALVAGE; see CORRECT
red dye root CHAY, CHOY
redact DRAFT, EDIT, REVISE
redeem ATONE, FREE, RANSOM
redeemer GOEL, MESSIAH, SAVIO(U)R
reduce CURTAIL, DERATE, DIET, LESSEN, PARE, REEF, SHRINK, SLASH, SLIM, THIN
reef ATOLL, CAY, KAY, KEY, LEDGE, (SAND)BAR, SHOAL
reek FUG, FUME, SMELL
reel PIRN, SPIN, SWAY, TEETER, TOTTER
refer ADVERT, ALLUDE, ASCRIBE, CITE, HARP, PERTAIN
referee ARBITER, UMPIRE
reflection ECHO, GLARE, MUSING, SLUR
refractor LENS, PRISM, TELESCOPE
refrain BOB, BURDEN, DERRY, DESIST, FALA, FORBEAR, LALA, LUDDEN
refuge ARK, ASYLUM, HAVEN, SANCTUM, SHELTER
refugee EMIGREE, ESCAPEE
refuse COOM(B), COT, DENY, DROSS, LEES, MARC, OFFAL, POB, RECUSE, RUBBISH, SCORIA, SCRAP, SCUM, SLAG, TRASH
regale BANQUET, FEAST, FETE
regard ESTEEM, GAZE, RESPECT
regarding see CONCERNING
regimen DIET, DRILL
regiment ALAI, COSSACK, POLK, PULK
region BELT, CLIMATE, CLIME, LOCALE, PURLIEU, SECTOR, ZONE
register see RECORD
regret DEPLORE, REPENT, RUE

reign RAJ, REGIME, RULE, SWAY, TERM
reign, pert. to REGNAL, REGNANT
reinstate RESTORE, REVEST
reiterate see REPEAT
reject JILT, REBUFF, REPULSE
relate DETAIL, NARRATE, PERTAIN, RECITE, RECOUNT, REFER
related AGNATE, (A)KIN, COGNATE, ENATE, ENATIC, GERMAN(E)
relative AGNATE, AUNT, EME, ENATE, INLAW, KIN(DRED), KINSMAN, NIECE, PARENT, SIB(LING)
relative pronoun THAT, WHAT, WHO
relax(ing) DETENTE, EASE, LOOSEN, RELENT, SOFTEN
relay AGENT, RACE, REMUDA
release LOOSE, PUBLISH, REMISE
relent MODIFY, SOFTEN, THAW
relevant APROPOS, GERMAN(E)
relief AID, BAS, DOLE, FRET, REDRESS
relieve ALLAY, COMFORT, EASE, LIGHTEN, LISS(E)
religion BUDDHIST, CREED, CULT, FAITH, HINDU, JEWISH, ISLAM, PIETY, SHINTO, SIKHISM, TAOIST
relinquish CEDE, DEMIT, QUIT, WAIVE, YIELD
reliquary APSE, ARCA(E), CHEST, MEMORIA, SHRINE
relish ACHAR, DASH, GUSTO, SAVOR, TANG, ZEST
reluctant AVERSE, LO(A)TH
remainder (AR)REAR, RESIDUE, REST, UNITATE
remark CRACK, MOT, SALLY
remedy ANTIDOTE, BAL(SA)M, CURE(ALL), ELIXIR, FIX, NOSTRUM, PANACEA, PHYSIC, PLACEBO, SOP
remiss DILATORY, LAX, SLACK
remnant END, ORT, RESIDUE, REST, SHRED; see DREGS
remove CANCEL, DELETE, DEPOSE, DISBAR, DOFF, ELOIGN(E), ELOIN, GUT, OUST
rend RIVE, TEAR, WREST
render CLARIFY, TRANSLATE
rendezvous DATE, TRYST
renegade APOSTATE, TRAITOR; see DESERTER
renounce ABNEGATE, RENAY, RENEGE
renown NOTE, PRESTIGE; see FAME
rent AVENGE, HIRE, LEASE, LET, RIP, SPLIT, TEAR, TORN
repair DARN, IMP, MEND
repartee RETORT, RIPOST(E), SALLY
repast LUNCH, MEAL, SNACK, TIFFIN
repay MEED, REFUND, REQUITE
repeat BIS, DIN(G), ECHO, ENCORE, HARP, RAME, (RE)ITERATE, REPRISE, SEGNO
repetition ANAPHORA, ENCORE, MERISM, PLOCE, ROTE
replete FULL, GORGED, SATED
report BANG, BULLETIN, CAHIER, FAME, POP
repose CONFIDE, EASE, REST
representative AGENT, DELEGATE, DEPUTY, ENVOY, FACTOR, LEGATE, NUNCIO, PROXY
reproach (BE)RATE, BLAME, CENSURE, RACA, TAUNT
reproductive body EGG, GAMETE, SPERM
reptiles see p. 217
reptiles, pert. to OPHIDIAN, SAURIAN
reputation ESTEEM, NAME; see FAME
request BESEECH, PLEA, ROGATION
resentment CHOLER, DUDGEON, RANCOR, UMBRAGE
reserve BACKLOG, NESTEGG, STOCK, STORE
reservoir CENOTE, CISTERN
resident CIT(IZEN), INMATE, INTERN(E), ITE, TENANT
resign ABANDON, DEMIT, QUIT
resin ALK, AMBER, ANIME, BALSAM, COPAL, DAMMAR, ELEMI, ESERIN, EXUDATE, GAL(L)IPOT, GUGAL, GUM, JALAP, KAURI, LAC, MASTIC, MYRRH, PITCH, SANDARAC
resort REFER, SPA, USE
resource(s) ASSETS, CAPITAL, DEVICE, FUNDS, MEANS
respite LULL; see INTERVAL
respond FEEL, (RE)ACT, RISE
rest CAESURA, EASE, GAFFLE, LEAN, PAUSE, PERCH, REPOSE, SIESTA, SIT, SURPLUS
restaurant AUTOMAT, BEANERY, BISTRO, BUFFET, CAFE, DINER, EATERY, GRILL, ONEARM, PIZZERIA, SPA
resthouse see INN
restive BALKY, MULISH, SKITTISH, UNEASY, UNRULY
restore FIX, HEAL, STET
restrain CURB, DETER, ENJOIN, REIN, STINT, TETHER
restrict CENSOR, COERCE, CRAMP, LIMIT
restricted EXCLUSIVE, INSULAR

retaliate REPAY, REQUITE
retaliation REPRISAL, TALION
retard BRAKE, CHECK, STUNT; see DELAY
retinue CORTEGE, COURT, ESCORT, STABLE, STAFF, SUITE, TRAIN
retort ALEMBIC, REPARTEE, RIPOST(E), SALLY, VIAL
retract DISAVOW, DISOWN, RECANT
retreat DEN, NEST, NOOK, RECEDE; see REFUGE
retribution NEMESIS, REVENGE
retrograde EBB, RECEDE, (RE)LAPSE
return(s) ANSWER, EXCHANGE, RECUR, RESTORE, REVERT, RIPOST(E), VOTES, YIELD
returning REDIENT
reveal AIR, BARE, DIVULGE, EXPOSE, IMPART, UNVEIL
reveille DIAN, LEVET
revenue ANNAT(ES), RENTAL
reverberate BOUNCE, (RE)ECHO
reverberating REBOANT(IC)
reverse SETBACK, TRANSPOSE, VERSO
reversion ATAVISM, ESCHEAT
revile DEBASE, RAIL, VILIFY
revise AMEND, EDIT, REDACT, UPDATE
revoke ADEEM, RENEGE, REPEAL
revolution COUP, CYCLE, GYRE, REV
revolutionist CASTRO, FENIAN, LENIN, MARAT, PESTEL, SETTIMO
revolve BIRL, GYRATE, PIRL, ROLL, ROTATE, SPIN, TURN, TWIRL, WHIRL
reward CUP, GUERDON, PRIZE, TIP, UTU; see AWARD
rhythm BEAT, CADENCE, LILT, METRE, PULSE
ribbon COQUE, CORDON, FILLET, LISERE, TENE
ribs, pert. to COSTAL, COSTATE
rice DARAC, PALAY
rich person CROESUS, HAVE, MIDAS, NABOR, NAWAB
riddle LOGOGRIPH, REBUS, REE, SIFT; see PUZZLE
ridge(s) ARETE, BILO, CARINA, CREST. CUESTA. ESKER, GYRI, KAME, O(E)SAR, PARMA, RAND RAPHE, RIDEAU, S(I)ERRA, SPINE, SPUR, STRIA, WALE, WELT
ridicule BANTER, GUY, MOMUS, PAN, TWIT; see MOCK
rift CLEFT, FISSURE, GAP, RENT, SCHISM
right CLAIM, DEXTER, DROIT, RECTO, REDRESS
Rigoletto character BORSA, CEPRANO, GILDA, MARULLO
rim BRINK, EDGE, FELLOE, FELLY, FLANGE, LIP, ORLE, SOMMA, VERGE
ring(s) ANNULET, ARENA, CIRCLE(T), CLINK, CRIC, GASKET, GINNAL, GROMMET, HOOP, KNELL, LOOP, LUNET, LUTE, PEAL, SIGNET, TERRET, TERRIT, TOLL
ring part CHATON
ring-shaped ANNULAR, CIRCINATE
ripe(n) AUGUST; see MATURE
ripple LAP, PURL, RIFF(LE)
risible DROLL, GELASTIC
rite(s) ABDEST, AGAPE, CEREMONY, CULT, FORM, LITANY, LITURGY, NOVENA, PAX, RITUAL, SACRA(MENT)
river BAHR, ILOG, REE, RIO
river, pert. to a AMNIC
river bed CHANNEL, WADI, WADY
river mouth BOCA, DELTA, LADE
riverbank, of a RIPARIAN
rivers, Biblical ARNON, DRACO, HABOR, JABBOK, JORDAN, KISHON, TIGRIS, ULAI
rivers, underworld ACHERON, COCYTUS, LETHE, PHLEGETHON, STYX
road AGGER, AUTOBAHN, DRUN, EXPRESSWAY, FREEWAY, (HIGH)WAY, ITER, LANE, PARKWAY, PATH, PIKE, ROUTE, RTE, TARMAC, THRUWAY, VIA
roast BANTER, CALCINE, PARCH
rob FLEECE, REAVE, RIFLE
robot AUTOMATION, GOLEM
robots, play about RUR
rock CRAG, MINERAL, REEL, SCYLLA, SWAY, TOTTER, WHIN
rock salt AMOLE, EMOL
rockets see p. 278
rod BAR, CANE, CUE, FERULE, GUN, OSIER, PERCH, POLE, SPIT, STAFF, WAND
rogue CAD, CAITIFF, HELLION, IMP, KNAVE, PICARO, RASCAL, SCAMP, SCUM, SHARPER, VARLET, WAG
roguish ARCH, PAWKY, SLY
roister BRAG, REVEL, SPREE
Roland foe FERRAGUS, GAN(ELON), GANO
role BIT, HEAVY, INGENUE, LEAD, PART, WALKON
roll BAGEL, BAP, BIALY, BOLT, BUN, CAROTTE, FURL, LIST, ROSTER, ROTA, SCROLL, SLATE, TATTOO, TOSS

Roman hill AVENTINE, CAELIAN, CAPITOLINE, ESQUILINE, PALATINE, QUIRINAL, VIMINAL
romance AFFAIR, FABLE, GEST(E)
romance-teller ANTERI
Rome conqueror ALARIC, GAISERIC
Rome founder REMUS, ROMULUS
rood CRUCIFIX; see CROSS
roof CURB, FISH, GABLE, GAMBREL, HIP, HOWE, KINGPOST, MANSARD, PRATT, QUEENPOST, WARREN
roof part CLEAT, EAVE, FILLET, JOIST, PURLIN, RIDGE STRUT, TRUSS, VALLEW
roofing (PAN)TILE, RAG, SHINGLE, SLATE, THATCH
room ALA, ATRIA, ATRIUM, CHAMBER, DEN, EW(E)RY, LOFT, OECUS, PLAT(T), ROTUNDA, SALA, SPACE
roost (A)LIGHT, GARRET, NEST, PERCH
root BASE, ETYM(ON), GRUB, IMBED, RADICAL, RADIX, STEM, TUBER, WATAP; see CHEER
rootlet RADICEL, RADICLE
rope BIGHT, BRACE, CORD(AGE), JEFF, LARIAT, LASSO, LAZO, LONGE, MARLINE, REATA, REEVE, RIATA, TETHER
rope, naut. BRAIL, FAST, FOX, GASKET, HAWSER, LANIARD, LANYARD, LIFT, PAINTER, RATLIN(E), SENNIT, SHROUD, SNOTTER, SPAN, STAY, TACK, TYE, VANG, WAPP
Rosmunda's king ALBOIN
rosary BEADROLL, BEADS, CHAPLET
rosary bead AVE, GAUD(Y)
rose of Sharon ALTHEA
rosewood MOLOMPI
rosolic acid AURIN(E)
rotate see REVOLVE
rotating piece ARBOR, AXIS, AXLE, BOBBIN, CAM, MANDREL, REEL, ROTOR, SPINDLE
rotten FETID, PUTRID, RANK
rough COARSE, CRUDE, CURT, GRUFF, HARSH, HILLY, RUDE, RUGGED, UNEVEN
roughness LIPPER
roulette term BAS, (IM)PAIR, MANQUE, MILIEU, NOIR, PASSE, ROUGE, TOURNEUR
round CYCLE, GLOBATE, ORBED, PERIOD, ROT(UL)A, ROTUND
Round Table see p. 208
round-up RODEO
routine ROTE, RUT, WONT
row FILE, LINE, OAR, RANK, SCULL, TIER; see FIGHT
rowdy BHOY, RUFFIAN, THUG
rowlock POPPET, THOLE
royalty ALII, FEE
rub ABRADE, BUFF, BURNISH, CHAFE, SCRAPE, SHINE
rubber CAUCHO, CEARA, ELASTIC, ERASER, GALOSH, GUM, LATEX, PARA
rubbish CULCH, DEBRIS, DROSS, JUNK, ROT, SCREE, STENT; see REFUSE
rudiment ABC, ANLAGE, GERM
rue DEPLORE, REGRET, RUTA
ruff REE(VE), RUCHE, TIPPET, TRUMP
ruffer NAPPER
ruffle CRIMP, MUSS, PUCKER, RUCHE, SHIR(R)
rugby term FIVES, HEELING, KNOCKON, MARK, NOSIDE, PITCH, SCRUM(MAGE), TACKLE, TOUCH, TRY
rugs see p. 283
ruin DEBRIS, DOOM, WRACK
rule CANON, CODE, DOMINEER, HABIT, LAW, NORM
ruler CALIF, CALIPH, MONARCH, MPRET, NEGUS, NIZAM, SHAH, SULTAN(A)
rumen CUD, PAUNCH, STOMACH
ruminate CHEW, MULL, PONDER
rumor BRUIT, FAMA GOSSIP, HEARSAY, NORATE, REPORT
rumple MUSS, TOUSLE
run BROOK, ELOPE, FLOW, HIE, OPERATE, PANIC, SCUD
runner COURIER, MILER, RACER, SCARF, STOLO(N)
runway (AIR)STRIP, RAMP, TRAIL
rural AGRARIAN, BUCOLIC, GEORGIC, PASTORAL, RUSTIC
rush HASTE(N), HURTLE, ONSET, SPATE, SPEED, SPURT
Russia(n) MUSCOVY, RED, SOVIET
rust OXIDIZE
Rustam relative RUDABAH, SOHRAB, ZAL
rustic BOOR, BUCOLIC, CARL(E), PEASANT, RUBE, RURAL, SYLVAN, YOKEL
rustler ABACTOR, ABIGEUS

S

sac ASCUS, BURSA, CYST, POD, VENTER
saccharine source TAR
sack BAG, GUNNY, LOOT, POUCH
sacred HOLY, INVIOLATE, PIOUS, SACROSANCT

sacred object RELIC, ZOGO
sacred place ABATON, ALTIS, HIERON, SHRINE
sacrificial offering HIERA, SPHAGION
sacrificial rite SOMA
sad BLUE, DISMAL, DOLENT, MESTO, TRISTE
saddle part CANTLE, CINCH, GIRTH, HORN, JOCKEY, LATIGO, PAD, POMMEL, SKIRT, STIRRUP, SUDADERO
safe-conduct COWLE, PASSPORT
saga MYTH; see EPIC
sagacious ASTUTE, SAPIENT, WISE
sage NESTOR, SOLON; see SCHOLAR
sail JIB, KITE, LATEEN, LUFF, LUG, MIZZEN, ROYAL, SPANKER, VELA
sail part BUNTLINE, CLEW, CRINGLE, EARING, HORSE, IRON, LEECH, LIFT, REEF, TIE, WHIP, YOKE
sailor GOB, LASCAR, MARINE(R), MATELOT, SALT, SEABEE, SEADOG, SEAMAN, TAR
saint ALBAN, ALVAR, ARHAT, HOLY, PIR, STE
St. Francis' birthplace ASSISI
St. Vitus dance CHOREA
sale SELLOUT; see AUCTION
sally ERUPT, FORAY, QUIP, RAID, RIPOSTE, SORTIE
salt BORAX, BRINE, HALITE, NACL, SAL, SOUSE
salt factory SALTERN, SALTERY
salt, pert. to HALOID, SALINE
salt pond LICK, SALINA
saltpeter NITER, NITRE
salutation ACHARA, ALOHA, AVE, HAIL, SALAAM, TOAST
salve ANOINT, BALM, CERATE, LOTION, UNGUENT
salvia CHIA
same DITTO, IDEM, ILK
sanction AMEN, FIAT, OKAY, RATIFY
sanctuary ADYTUM, BAMAH, BEMA, FANE, NAOS, SHRINE
sand GRAVEL, GRIT, PAAR
sand bar see REEF
sand hill(s) AREG, DENE, DUNE
sandstorm HABOOB, SAMUM, SIMOOM
sandwich BLT, GRINDER, HERO, HO(A)GIE, SUBMARINE, TORPEDO
sandy ARENOSE, SABULOUS
sapodilla SAPOTA, SAPOTE
Saracen ARAB, MOOR, MOSLEM
sarcasm IRONY, JEERS, SATIRE
sash CASING, OBI
Satan ABADDON, AHRIMAN, APOLLYON, MEPHISTO; see DEVIL
satellites see pp. 276, 278
satiate see CLOY
satirical CAUSTIC, IRONIC, WRY
satisfaction AMENDS, CRO, UTU
saturate DRENCH, IMBUE, SOAK, STEEP
Saturday source SATURN
satyr FAUN, PANISC, SILENUS
sauces see p. 123
sausage BOLOGNA, CERVELAT, FRANK, SALAMI, SAVELOY, WIENER, WURST
savage FELL, FERAL, YAHOO
save BUT, HOARD, REDEEM, SPARE, STINT
savory PIQUANT, SAPID, SIPID, TASTY, YUMMY
sawlike part(s) SERRA(E)
saying(s) AGRAPHA, DIT, LOGIA, MOT, REDE; see MAXIM
scaffold GALLOWS, GIBBET, STAGING
scale CLIMB, GAMUT, LAMINA, PALE(A), PALET, SQUAMA
scallop CRENA, PINK, QUIN
scaly SCUTATE, TEGULAR
Scandinavian DANE, GEAT, LAPP, NORSE(MAN), ROS, RUS, SWEDE, VIKING
scar ARR, CATFACE, MAR(K)
scarce(ly) BARELY, RARE, VIX
scarlike ULOID
scatter DISPEL, LITTER, ROUT, SCOAD, SOW, STREW, TED
scattered DIFFUSE, SEME, SPORADIC
scenario LIBRETTO, SCRIPT
scene SCAPE, TABLEAU, VIEW, VISTA
scene of action ARENA, SPHERE
scent TRAIL; see ODOR
scented AROMATIC, (RED)OLENT, SPICY
schedule AGENDA, LIST, PLAN
scheme CABAL, CHART, PLAN, PLOT
scholar PANDIT, PEDANT, PUNDIT, SAVANT, ULEMA
scholarship BURSARY, BURSE, STIPEND
school ACADEMY, ECOLE, GAM, LYCEE, LYCEUM, MANEGE, PREP, SHOAL, TOL
school grounds CAMPUS
science OLOGY, SKILL, TECHNICS
scoff CARP, GIBE, JEER, JIBE, RAIL, SNEER, TAUNT
scold CARP, CHIDE, HARPY, JAW, NAG, RAIL, SHREW

scone FARL(E), SKON
scoop BEAT, DREDGE, LADLE
scope AMBIT, RANGE, SPAN
scorch CHAR, PARCH, SEAR, SERE, SINGE
score NOTCH, TAB, TALLY, TICK
scoria see DROSS, LAVA
Scotland ALBA, ECOSSE, SCOTIA
scout unit DEN, PACK, TROOP
scowl FROWN, (G)LOWER, MOUE
scrap BIT, ORT, RAZE
scrape ABRADE, DREDGE, GALL, GRAZE, RAKE, RASP
scrapings RAMENTA, SHAVINGS
scratch MAR, RASP, RIT
screed see DIATRIBE
screen PARAVENT, PAVIS, PURDAH, REREDOS, SHADE, SHOJI, TATTY; see SIEVE
script RONDE, SERTA
scripture AGAMA, ALCORAN, AVESTA, BIBLE, GEMARA, GRANTH, HAGGADA, HALAKAH, KORAN, MASORA(H), MIDRASH, MISHNA(H), PURANA, SMRITI, SRUTI, SUTRA, TALMUD, TANTRA, TORAH, VEDA
scrutinize CON, EYE, PROBE, SCAN
scum see DROSS
scuttle HOD, SINK, SWAMP
sea BAHR, BRINE, DEEP, MAIN, OCEAN
sea-ear ABALONE
sea, of the MARINE, MARITIME, NAUTICAL, NAVAL, OCEANIC, PELAGIC
seal BULLA, CACHET, SIGIL, SIGNET
seamark BEACON, MEITH, PHAROS
search DELVE, DOWSE, FERRET, FORAGE, FRISK, GROPE
season CORN, CURE, INURE, SALT, SELE, SPICE
seasonings see p. 123
seat(s) ASANA, BANC, CURULE, HOWDAH, PEW(AGE), POST, SEDILE, SEDILIA, SELLA, SETTEE
second ABET, MOMENT, TRICE
secondary BYE, LESS, MINOR
secret COVERT, LATENT, MYSTIC, OCCULT, PRIVY; see MYSTERY
secret society BLACKHAND, CAMORRA, EGBO, KKK, MAFIA, PORO, TONG
secretion AUTACOID, GUM, LAA(R)P, LATEX, LERP, SAP
sect CULT, FACTION, PARTY, WING
secure ANCHOR, BELAY, FAST(EN), FIX, MOOR, RIVET, SURE
security PLEDGE, STOCK; see SURETY
sedative ANODYNE, BROMIDE, DEMEROL, GOOFBALL, NARCOTIC, NEMBUTAL, OPIATE
sediment DREGS, LEES, LOESS, SILT(AGE)
see DESCRY, DIOCESE, (E)SPY, EYE, VIDE
seed GERM, KERNEL, MILT, NUCULE, NUT(LET), OVULE, PIP, PIT, PYRENE, SEMEN, SOW, SPERM, SPORE
seed coat ARIL, BUR(R), HULL, HUSK, TEG(U)MEN, TESTA(E)
seedless plant FERN
seeming LIKE(LY), QUASI
segment ARC, SECTOR, SOMITE, TELSON, TORE
segmental TORIC
seine NET, SAGENE, TRAWL
seize ARREST, COLLAR, GRAB, GRASP, HENT, NAB, REAVE, USURP
select CULL, ELITE, OPT
self EGO, ENTITY, SEITY
self-confidence APLOMB, POISE
self-defense JUDO, JUJITSU, KARATE
sell AUCTION, HAWK, MARKET, PEDDLE, SCALP, VEND
semblance COPY, FEINT, GUISE, IMAGE, MIEN
senility CADUCITY, DOTAGE
senior AINE, DEAN, ELDER
sense ACUMEN, ESP, FLAIR, HEARING, SIGHT, SMELL, TASTE, TOUCH
senseless ABSURD, FUTILE, INANE
sentence DOOM, RAP, TERM
sentence part CLAUSE, PHRASE, PREDICATE, SUBJECT
sentimentality BATHOS, MUSH
sentinel SENTRY, VEDETTE, VIGIL
separate APART, ISOLATE, SECERN, SIFT
separation APARTHEID, SCHISM
sequence SCALE, TIERCE; see SERIES
sequester CLOISTER, ENISLE, ISOLATE
seraglio HAREM, SERAI
serf COLONA, COLONUS, HELOT, LITUS, NEIF(E)
serially SERIATIM
series CATENA, CHAIN, GAMUT, SET, STRING
sermon HOMILY, KHUTBAH, REPROOF
serpent APEPI, ELOPS, SEPS; see p. 217
serpent worship OPHISM

serpentine OPHIDIAN, OPHIOID, OPHITE, SINUOUS
servant ALILA, BATA, BOY, BUTLER, FERASH, FLUNKY, HAMAL, MAN, MENIAL, PAGE, VALET; see MAID
server SALVER, TRAY, WAITER
service DEVOIR, MASS, RITE(S), USE
servile ABJECT, MENIAL, SLAVISH
set CLIQUE, GEL, JELL
settled ALIT, FIXED, SUNK
seven HEPTAD, PLEIAD, SEPTET(TE), SEPTUOR
sever CUT, LOP, REND, RIVE
sewing terms BASTE, BIND, CROCHET, FELL, KNIT, PURL, QUILT, RENTER, RUIN, SEAM, TACK, TAT, WHIP
sexes, common to both EPICENE
shabby DOWDY, SEEDY, SCURVY, WORN
shabby woman DOWD(Y), FRUMP, SLATTERN, SLOVEN, SLUT
shackle BOND, IRON; see CHAIN
shade HUE, NUANCE, SCREEN, VISOR
shadow UMBRA; see GHOST, TRAIL
shaft ARROW, AXIS, COLUMN, FUST, PILLAR, POLE, SCAPE, SPINDLE, SPIRE, STELE, THILL
shaggy BUSHY, HIRSUTE, NAPPY
shake JAR, JOLT, NIDGE, ROCK
Shakespeare characters see p. 179
Shakespeare relative ANNE, EDMUND, HAMNET, JOHN, JUDITH, SUSANNA
sham FEIGN, HOAX, MOCK
shank(s) CRURA, CRUS, GAM(B), SHIN
sharp ACERB, ACU(A)TE, CHEAT, KEEN
sharpen GRIND, HONE, WHET
sharpshooter JAGER, MARKSMAN
sheaf BALE, GAVEL, GERB
shear FLEECE, SHAVE, see CLIP
sheath OCREA, SPATHE, THECA
shed COTE, DOFF, MO(U)LT
sheep disease COE, GID, SHAB
sheepfold COTE, PEN, REE(VE)
sheeplike MEEK, OVINE
sheepskin BASIL, BOCK, BOND, DIPLOMA, ROAN, SKIVER
sheepwalk SLAIT
shelf BERM(E), GRADIN, LEDGE(R), MANTEL, RETABLE
shell BOMB(ARD), BURR, CONCH(A), SHOT, SHUCK, SKIN, TUNICA
shelter BIELD, COTE, LEE, SCREEN, SHEAL; see REFUGE
sheltered ALEE
shepherd DAPHNIS, PASTOR, THYRSIS
sheriff ELISOR, REEVE, SHRIEVE
shield AEGIS, BUCKLER, CLIPEUS, ECU, HIELAMAN, MULGA, PAVIS, PELTA, ROTELLA, ROUNDEL, SCUTE, SCUTUM, TARGE(T)
shield-shaped CLYPEATE, PELTATE, SCUTATE
shift DEVIATE, DODGE, GANG, GYBE, JIBE, VEER
shingle(s) CLIP, FACIA, SHIM, ZONA
ship crew ABLE, BUNGS, COOPER, HAND, MATE, PURSER, STEWARD, STOKER, YEOMAN
ship officer BOATSWAIN, BOSN, CAPTAIN, MASTER, MATE, PIPES, SKIPPER
ships see p. 265
shirk GOLDBRICK, MALINGER, SOLDIER
shoal DRAVE, HORDE, REEF
shoal-water deposit CULM
shock APPAL(L), STUN, TRAUMA
shod CALCED
shoe part EYELET, HEEL, INSOLE, LACING, LAST, RAND, SOLE, TOEBOY, UPPERS, VAMP, WELT
shoemaker BOTCHER, COBBLER, CRISPIN, SNOB, SUTOR
shoe(s) S(C)HOON, TALARIA
shoot BAG, BINE, BUD, CHIT, GEMMA, LIMB, RATOON, (S)CION, SNIPE, SPRIG, STOLO(N), TILLER, TURIO(N), TWIG, UDO, VIMEN
shooting match SHOOT, SKEET, TIR
shop ATELIER, BOUTIQUE, FACTORY, MART, TABERNA, TRADE
shore RIPA, STRAND, WARTH
short CURT, LACONIC, PUDGY, SCANTY, STUBBY, TERSE
short-winded PURSY, WHEEZY
shorten DELE, ELIDE, LOP
shorthand GREGG, PITMAN, STENOTYPE
shoulder BERM, EPAULE, SCAPULA
shoulder, of the ALAR, SCAPULAR
show EXPOSE, LEGIT, RAREE
showcase ETALAGE, VITRINE
shower SKEW, SPATE, SPRAY; see RAIN
showy GARISH, GAUDY, LOUD
shrew ERD, HARPY, KATE, TARTAR, VIRAGO, VIXEN
shrewd ARCH, CANNY, FOXY, PAWKY, SLY, WILY
shrill ACUTE, ARGUTE, PIPING, PIPY

shrine ALTAR, ARK, CHAITYA, CHASSE, DAGOBA, DARGAH, DURGAH, NAOS, PIR, SAMADH, STUPA, TOMB, TOPE
shrink CONTRACT, SHRIVEL, WIZEN
shrub(s) BOSCAGE, FRUTEX, TOD
shut up DAM, IMMURE, (S)HUSH, SILENCE
shy BALK, CHARY, COY, JIB, SKIT
sickle-shaped FALCATE
side AGREE, FACET, LATUS
side, pert. to COSTAL, LATERAL
sidetrack AVERT, DIVERT, SHUNT
sidewise ASKANCE, ASKEW, ASLANT
sidle CANT, CRAB, SKEW, SKIRT
sieve BOLT(ER), GRIZZLY, LAUN, PUREE, RIDDLE, SIFT(ER); see STRAINER
sift BOLT, LUE, REE, RIDDLE, SIE, WINNOW
sigh MOAN, SOB, SOUF, SOUGH
sight BEAD, KEN, SCENE, VISTA
sight, pert. to OCULAR, VISUAL
sign BADGE, MARK, MINUS, OMEN, PLUS, PRESA, RUNE, SEGNO, SEIN, TOKEN
sign, pert. to SEMIC
signal ALARM, CHAMADE, CUE, CURFEW, ENSIGN, FLARE, FUSEE, MOTION, PST
signet SIGIL
signify BODE, DENOTE, IMPLY
silence CALM, GAG, HUSH, LULL, PAX, REST, TACE(T)
silent GLUM, MUM, MUTE, TACIT
silk thread BAVE, FLOSS, TRAM(E)
silkworm disease UJI
silver ARGENT, COINS, STERLING, SYCEE
simper MINCE, SMIRK, TEEHEE
simpleton BOOB(Y), COOT, DAW, DUPE, GAUP, GOWK, NITWIT
simulate ACT, AFFECT, APE, FEIGN, INVENT, MOCK, SHAM
sin ERR(OR), EVIL, SLIP, TRESPASS, VICE
since AGO, HENCE, SYNE, YET
sinewy BRAWNY, ROPY, WIRY
sing CAROL, CHANT, CHIRP, CROON, HUM, LILT, TROLL
singer ALMA(H), ALME(H), CANTOR, CHANTEUR, CHORIST, DIVA, MINSTREL
singers ALDA, BORI, CALLAS, CALVE, CARUSO, GIGLI, GLUCK, LANZA, LEHMANN, LIND, LUCCA, MELBA, NILSSON, ONEGIN, PATTI, PINZA, PONS, PRICE, RUFFO, STEVENS, TAUBER, TEBALDI, TIBBETT, TRAUBEL
single ACE, (A)LONE, MONO, ONE ONLY, SOLO, UNAL, UNWED
sink BASIN, BOWL, DOLINA, FAIL, FLAG, SAG
sinning ERRANT, PECCANT
sinuous SNAKY, SPIRAL, WAVY
siren CIRCE, LORELEI, LURLEI
Sisera's killer JAEL
sister NUN, NURSE, SIB, SOROR
sitting ASTRIDE, CLUTCH, POSE, SEANCE, SEDENT, SESSION
six HEXAD, SENARY, SESTET, SEXTET
Six, Les AURIC, DUREY, HONEGGER, MILHAUD, POULENC, TAILLEFERRE
sizing GLAZE, GLUE, SEALER
skein HANK, MESH, RAP, WEB
skeleton BONES, CADRE, CORAL, FRAME, SPONGE
skeptic AGNOSTIC, APORETIC, CYNIC, THOMAS
sketch DOODLE, ESQUISSE, LIMN, OUTLINE, SKIT
ski part CAMBER, HEEL, SHOVEL, SOLE, TIP
ski term CHRISTY, INRUN, MOGUL, PASSGANG, SCHUSS, SITZMARK, SLALOM, SNOWPLOW, TELEMARK, VORLAGE
skillful ABLE, ADEPT, DEFT, HABILE
skim DART, FLIT, SCUD, SCUM
skin BARK, COAT, CORIUM, CUTIS, DERMA, FELL, FLAY, FUR, HIDE, PELT, STRIP
skin, pert. to DER(M)IC
skip CAPER, DAP, FLIT, OMIT, SALTO
skirmish TILT; see FIGHT
skirt DIRNDL, SAYA
skit CAPER, JIBE, NUMBER, PARODY
skittle(s) NINEPINS, PIN
skulk LURK, PROWL, SLINK
skull, pert. to CRANIAL, INIAL
sky AZURE, LANGI, TIEN, VAULT, WELKIN
slab DALLE, STELE, TABLET
slack LAX, LAZE, REMISS
slag see DROSS, LAVA
slam BANG, RAP, SHUT, VOLE
slander ASPERSE, DECRY, LIBEL, MALIGN, REVILE
slang ARGOT, CANT, DIALECT, FLASH, JARGON, JIVE, LINGO, PATOIS
slant ANGLE, BEVEL, BIAS, KEEL; see SLOPE
slanted ASKEW, AWRY, RAKISH, SKEW(Y)
slap CUFF, SNUB, SWAT
slash DAB, JAG, SLISH

slat(s) BATTEN, LATH, SPLINE, STRIP
slave ALIPIN, DASI, ESNE, MAROON, THRALL; see SERF
sleep DOZE, DROWSE, NAP, NOD, SIESTA, SNOOZE, SOPOR, WINK
slender LANK, LEAN, LITHE, REEDY, SLIM, THIN
sleuth see DETECTIVE
slice COL(LO)P, FLITCH, GASH, LAYER, RASHER, SLAB
slide CHUTE, SKID, SLUE
slight CUT, FAINT, SLIM, SLUR, SNUB
slip BONER, BULL, CUTTING, DOCK, (E)LAPSE, ERR(OR), GAFFE, GLIDE, SOLECISM
slippery EELY, SHIFTY, SLIMY, SLY
slope BRAE, CANT, (E)SCARP, GLACIS, GRADIENT, HADE, RAMP, RISE, SLANT, SPLAY, VERSANT
sluggish DOPEY, POKY, TORPID
sluice CLOW, FLUME, GOUT, SEWER
slush POSH, SLEECH, SLOSH
sly CAGEY, SLEE, SLOAN, WILY
smack BUSS, GUSTO, KISS, SAVOR, SLAP
small BANTAM, ELFIN, LIL, PETIT(E), PETTY, PUNY, WEE
smart CHIC, CLEVER, NATTY, POSH, STING, TRIG
smear DAUB; see STAIN
smell see ODOR
smelly see FETID
smile FLEER, GRIN, SIMPER, SMIRK
smith FORGER, MIME, VULCAN
smoke CURE, FLOC, FUME, REEK, SMAZE, SMOG
smoky FUMID, FUMOSE, REEKY, SOOTY
smokeless powder FILITE
smooth GLIB, GLOSS, IRON, LENE, LEVEL, PREEN
snack BITE, CANAPE, MORSEL
snake COLUBRID, OPHIDIAN, REPTILE, SERPENT
snake-bite aid CEDRON, GUACO
snake-haired woman see GORGON
snap up SNUP
snare DECOY, GIN, LURE, NET, SPRINGE, TRAP, WEB
snarl GNARL, GNAR(R), GROWL, TANGLE
snatch EREPT, FILCH, GRAB, PILFER
sneer see MOCK
snob BRAHMIN, PARVENU, PRIG
snoop LURK, PRY, SKULK
snoring STERTOR
snow FIRN, NEVE, PASH, SLEET, SNA
snowy NIVAL, NIVEOUS
snuff RAPPEE, SNIFF
snuffbox bean CACOON
snug COSY, COZY, TRIG
so ERGO, SAE, SIC, THUS, TRUE, VERY
soak FLEECE, RET, SOG, SOP, SOUSE, STEEP
soap AMOLE, CASTILE, DETERGENT, SAPO, SUDS
soap vine GOGO
soapstone TALC
sober GRAVE, SEDATE, STAID
social CIVIC, CIVIL, TEA
Socialist CABET, DEBS, ENGELS, FOURIER, JAURES, MARX, OWEN, PROUDHON, SAINTSIMON, SHAW, SUNYATSEN
society see ASSOCIATION
sod GLEBE, PEAT, SWARD, TURF
sodium NATRON, NITER, NITRE, SAL(T), SODA, TRONA
sofa CANAPE, COUCH, DIVAN, SETTEE, SETTLE
soft EASY, LOW, WAXY
Sohrab relative see RUSTAM
soil DEFILE, DIRTY, GOMBO, HUMUS, LOAM, LOESS, MARL, PEDOCAL, SOD,
soldier ANZAC, ASKAR, ATKINS, BUCKSKIN, CADET, CROAT, GALOOT, JA(E)GER, KERN(E), POILU, LANCER, NIZAM, REDIF, ROK, SEPOY, TOMMY, UHLAN, VET, ZOUAVE
solicit BEG, BID, CANVASS, COURT, DRUM, PLEA(D), TOUT, URGE
solidify OSSIFY, PETRIFY; see CONGEAL
solution strength TITER, TITRE
solvent ACETONE, ALCOHOL, ANILINE, BENZENE, CUMENE, DIOXANE, FURFURAL, GLYCEROL, GLYCOL, KETONE, LIGROIN, PHENOL, WATER
son ABSALOM, BAR, CADET, DAUPHIN, FILS, FITZ, MAC, SCION
son-in-law GENER
sonar ASDIC
song CANCION, CHANSON, CHANT(E)Y, DITE, LIED(ER), LYRIC, MATIN, MELE, MELOS, P(A)EAN, PSALM, STROUD, UTA; see p. 193
songlike ARIOSE, LYRIC, MELIC
sonship FILIETY
soon ANON, PRONTO, TITE
sooner ERE(R), RATHER
soot COOM, DIRT, SMUT, SOTE

soothe ALLAY, LULL, SALVE
soothing ANODYNE, DULCIT, LENITIVE
soothsayer AUSPEX, DIVINE, ORACLE, PALMIST, PYTHON, SPAER; see ORACLE
sorceress CIRCE, LAMIA, SIREN, USHA, WITCH
sorcery see MAGIC
sore ANGRY, LESION, SAIR
sorrow DOLOR, LAMENT, REMORSE, RUE
sorry PALTRY, POOR, SAD
sorter GRADER, STAPLER
sortie see SALLY
sortilege LOT; see MAGIC
soul AME, ANIMA, ATMA(N), JIVATMA, PNEUMA, PRANA, PSYCHE
sound AUDIO, BAY, FATHOM, FIRM, HALE, PLUMB, VALID
sound, pert. to SONANT, SONIC
soup BISK, POT(T)AGE, PUREE
sour ACERB, ACETOSE, ACID(IC), ACRID, BLEEZE, WRY
South AUSTER, DIXIE, SUR
sovereign IMPERIAL, QUID, SKIV
sovereignty DYNASTY, EMPERY, SWAY
sow PLANT, SCATTER, SEED, SOO
spa see SPRING
space AREOLA, AREOLE, HIATUS, LORA, LORE, METOPE
spade CARD, DIG, LOY, SPUD
Spain, Spaniard DIEGO, IBERIA(N)
spare EXTRA, GAUNT, LEAN, LENTEN, THIN
spasm CHOREA, CLONUS, CRAMP, FIT, ICTUS, THROE, TIC
spawn BEGET, EGGS, OVA, REDD, ROE
speak LISP, ORATE, UTTER
speak, inability to, ALALIA, APHASIA, MUTISM
speaker AUDIO, LOCUTOR, ORATOR, RHETOR
spear GAFF, GIG, GORE, PIERCE; see p. 109
spear-shaped HASTATE
spear thrower WOMERA
special KHAS(S), RARE, UNIQUE
species see CLASS
specimen SAMPLE, SLIDE, SWATCH
speck BIT, DOT, FLAW, FLECK, MOTE
spectacle(s) DRAMA, GOGGLES, PAGEANT, SPECKS
specter BOG(E)Y, EIDOLON, GHOST, PHANTOM, SHADE, SPOOK, SPIRIT, SPRITE, WRAITH
speech LECTURE, ORATION, SERMON, SPIEL
speech art ORATORY, RHETORIC
speech defect ALOGIA, LISP, STAMMER
speechless APHASIC, APHEMIC, APHONIC, DUMB, MUM, MUTE
speed HASTE(N), HIE, PACE, RACE, RUN, TEMPO
spell HEX, HOODOO, JYNX
spent EFFETE, FAGGED, WORN
sphere GLOBE, ORB(IT), SCOPE
spice DASH, GUSTO, SEASON, TANG; see p. 123
spice ball FAG(G)OT
spicule ACTINE, OXEA, TOXA
spicy AROMATIC, FIERY, RACY, RISQUE
spider ARACHNID, COP, GRIDDLE, TRIVET; see p. 215
spider fluid ARANEIN
spigot PLUG, SPILE; see FAUCET
spike BROB, DAG, EAR, GAD, SPICA, TINE
spiked SPICATE
spin BIRL, EDDY, REEL, TWIRL, WHIRL
spinal cord MYELON
spindle AXIS, AXLE, COP, HASP, MANDREL, PIRN, QUILL, ROD
spine ARETE, AXIS, AXON, CHINE, QUILL, RACHIS, SETA, VERTEBRA
spinning machine JENNY, MULE
spinning term BOBBIN, DISTAFF, FLYER, ROVING, SPINDLE, TRAVELER, WHARVE, WHORL
spiral HELICAL, HELICES, HELIX, SCROLLED, VOLUTE
spire FLECHE, STEEPLE; see TOWER
spirit AGIEL, ARIEL, BANSHEE, BANSHIE, D(A)EMON, DEVIL, ELAN, ELIXIR, ESPRIT, FAY, GEIST, GENIE, GENII, GHOST, HUACA, JIN(N), JINNEE, JINNI, KATCINA, KELPIE, KELPY, LARES, LEMURES, MANES, MANITO(U), METAL, MORALE, SOUL, UNDINE, YAKSHA, ZEMI
spirited EAGER, LIVELY, LUSTY, SPUNKY
splash DAUB, LAP, PURL, SPLATTER
splenic LIENAL, MILTY
splendid AUREATE, GRAND
splendor ECLAT, POMP, SHEEN
split BURST, RIT, TEAR; see SUNDER
spoil(s) BOTCH, CODDLE, DECAY, LOOT, MAR, PET, ROT, SOUR, UNDO
spoked RADIAL
spoken ORAL, PAROL(E)

sponge ASCON, ASCULA, CADGE, ERASE, LEUCON, MOOCH, MUMP, SWAB
sponge spicule ACTINE, OXEA, TOXA
sponsor ANGEL, PATRON, SURETY
sponsorship (A)EGIS
spool BOBBIN, COP, REEL, WHARVE, WHORL
spore case(s) ASCI, ASCUS, THECA
spore fruit AECIA, AECIUM, TELIA, TELIUM
spore(s) SORI, SORUS, ZYGOTE
sport ROMP, RUX; see p. 137
sport field COURSE, COURT, DIAMOND, GREEN, GRID(IRON), GROUND, LINKS, TRACK; see ARENA
spot FLAW, MACLE, MACULA, NEVUS, OCELLUS, PIP, TILAKA
spotted DAPPLED, NOTATE, PIED, PINTO
spouse CONSORT, MATE, PARTNER; see HUSBAND, WIFE
spray ATOMIZE, FOAM, LIPPER, SCUD, SPRIG, SPUME, SURF
spread BRUIT, DEPLOY, FAN, GOSSIP, NORATE, RANCH, RIVET, SCOPE, STREW, TED
sprightly BLITHE, PE(A)RT, TID
spring(s) AIN, BADEN, BALNEUM, BATH, BOUND, BUXTON, CASTALIA, EMS, FONT, GEYSER, KELD, (RE)COIL, RESILE, SARATOGA, SEEP, SPA, STEM, THERMAL
springboard BATULE
springlike VERNAL
sprinkle DEG, MOTTLE, SOW, SPARGE, SPRAY
sprite see ELF, SPIRIT
sprout BUD, CHIT, GROW, SCION
spruce DAPPER, NATTY, TRIG, TRIM
spur CALCAR, GOAD, ROWEL
spy ABEL, ANDRE, ARNOLD, BOND, CAVELL, FUCHS, GOLD, HALE, KEEK, PEEK, PEER, PINTO, SNOOP, SOBELL
squama ALULA, CALYPTER, TEGULA
squash CRUSH, FLATTEN, PEPO, QUELL, SQUELCH
squaw MAHALA, MAHALY
squeamish HELOE, QUEASY
stab GORE, IMPALE, PIERCE, PINK, SKEWER
stable BARN, BYRE, MEW, SOLID, STALL
stableman AVENER, GROOM, (H)OSTLER
stack FLUE, PILE, RICK, SCINTLE
stadium STANDS; see ARENA
staff ANKUS, BASTON, BATON, CADUCEUS, CROOK, CROSIER, CUDGEL, MACE, PEDUM, RETINUE, ROD, SCEPTER, SQUAD, THYRSUS
stag BUCK, DEER, HART, MALE
stage see also THEATER
stage direction ENTER, EXEUNT, EXIT, MANET, SENNET
stage equipment CLOTH, CURTAIN, DROP, FLAT, FLIPPER, FLOAT, FOOT, OLEO, PROP, RAG, SPOT, TAB, TEASER
stage part BOARDS, COULISSE, DOCK, FLIES, GRID(IRON), LOFT, PARADUS, PLATFORM, SKENAI, SKENE, WING
stagehand CALLBOY, CHIPS, FLYMAN, GAFFER, GRIP, JUICER, PITMAN, SCENIST
stagger LURCH, REEL, STOT
stagnation STASIS
stain BLOT, DYE, SMIRCH, SMUDGE, SMUTCH, SPOT, STIGMA, SULLY, T(A)INT, TASH
stair term FLIGHT, LANDING, NEWEL, NOSING, RISE(R), RUN, TREAD
stake ANTE, PALE, PALING, PALISADE, PEL, POT, WAGER
stakelike PALAR
stale BANAL, EFFETE, MUSTY, PASSE, RANCID, TRITE
stalk(s) CAULIS, CULM, PEDICEL, PEDICLE, PETIOLE, RATOON, SCAPE, STEM, STIPE
stall BOOTH, DELAY, LOGE, NICHE, PEW, STOG
stammer FAFFLE, HAW, HEM
stamp BRAND, CHOP, DIE, EMBOSS, PESTLE, SIGIL
stanch DAM, FIRM, LEAL, STEM
stand ABIDE, BASE, EASEL, ENDURE, RISE, TABORET, TEAPOY, TRIPOD, TRIVET, ZARF
standard LABARUM, NORM(A), PAR, TITER, TOUG, TYPE; see FLAG
standing PRESTIGE, STATIC, STATUS
stanza DISTICH, ENVOY, RUBAIYAT, STAVE, STEV, STROPHE
star cluster GALAXY, MILKYWAY, SPIRAL
starch AMYL, ARUM, CASSAVA, FARINA, MANIOC, SAGO, SALEP, STIFFEN
starlike ASTRAL, SIDEREAL, STARRY, STELLAR, STELLATE

star(s) ASTER(ISK), COR, NOVA, STELLA; see p. 276
starvation FAMINE, INEDIA
state AVER, ESTRE, ETAT, MOOD, STATUS
statement BILL, DICTUM, EDICT, PRECIS
statesmen GENRO; see p. 242
station DEPOT, POST, TERMINAL, TERMINUS
stationary FIXED, STATIC
statue EFFIGY, ICON, ORANT
stave BASH, LAG, STAP, VERSE
staylace AGLET
stead LIEU, PLACE
steal BONE, COP, CRIB, FILCH, GLOM, LIFT, LOOT, PILFER, ROB, RUSTLE, SNITCH
steam FUME, MIST, STUFA, VAPOR
steep BOWK, IMBUE, RET, SHEER, SOAK, SOP
steer COND, CONN, HELM, LUFF, PILOT, YAW
steersman COX(SWAIN), PILOT
stem (A)RISE, BASE, BINE, CANE, CORM, CULM, PROW, SHAFT, STALK, STIPE, STRAW, TUBER; see ROOT
step(s) CHASSE, GAIT, GRADE, PACE, PAS, PHASE, STAIR, STILE, TREAD
stern AFT, AUSTERE, GRIM, HARSH, REAR
stew BURGOO, COUSCOUS, FUME, OLIO, OLLA, POTTAGE, RAGOUT
steward DAPIFER, KHANSAMAH, REEVE
stick(s) ADHERE, BAR, BAT, BATON, BRIN, CAMAN, CANE, CLEAVE, COHERE, FAGOT, GAD, GLUE, MUNDLE, PASTE, POGO, STILT, WAND
stickler PURIST, TAPIST
sticky GOOEY, GUMMY, TACKY
stigma see STAIN
still BUT, COSH, PLACID, YET
stimulant AMMONIA, CAFFEIN(E), THEIN(E)
stimulate ELATE, GOAD, WHET
sting BARB, BITE, SMART
stint CHORE, SCRIMP, SKIMP, SKINCH
stipend ANNAT, PENSION, PREBEND
stir ADO, FUSS, INCITE, RILE, ROIL, TODO
stitch BASTE, PUNTO, SUTURE
stock BREED, GOODS, RACE, STORE
stock exchange BOURSE, CURB, MARKET
stockade BULWARK, ETAPE
stocky PLUMP, SQUAT, STUB
stoker FIREMAN, TEASER
stolen property HAUL, LOOT, PELF, SWAG
stomach BELLY, CRAW, OMASUM, RUMEN, TRIPE, VENTER
stone ASHLAR, FLAG, GEM, GEODE, HERMA, LAPIDATE, LAPILLUS, LAPIS, PIT, ROSETTA, SEED, STEAN, STEEN; see p. 232
stone heap AHU, CAIRN(E), KARN
stone, woman turned to NIOBE
stonecutter LAPICIDE
stonelike LITHOID
stoneware GRES
stop (AR)REST, AVAST, BALK, BELAY, CLOSE, CONK, DAM, DESIST, END, PAUSE, PLUG, QUIT, STALL, STEM, WHOA
stoppage CLOTURE, HALT, JAM
stopper BUNG, PLUG, SPILE, WAD
store CACHE, CANTEEN, COOP, ENSILE, GROCERY, POST, STOCK, SUPPLY, SUTLERY
storehouse BARN, DEPOT, ETAPE, GOLA, GRANARY, SILO
storm BURA(N), FUME, FURY, GALE, KHAMSIN, (O)RAGE, RANT, RAVE, SAMIEL, SHAITAN, TEMPEST, SIMOON, TORNADO, TYPHOON
stormy petrel ASSILAG
story CONTE, EPIC, FABLE, LORE, NOVEL, SAGA, TALE, YARN
stout ALE, BOCK, BURLY, HUSKY, PORTER, STANCH
stove COCKLE, ETNA, RANGE
strainer COLANDER, SCREEN, SIEVE, SILE, TAMIS, TAMMY
strand BEACH, FIBER, PLY
strange ODD, OUTRE, UNCO
strangle CHOKE, GARROT(TE)
strap JESS, LEASH, THONG
strap-shaped LORATE
strass GLASS, PASTE
stratagem COUP, SCHEME, WILE
stratum BED, FOLIUM, LAYER
stray DOGIE, ERR, GAD, WAIF
streak LINE, ROE, STRIA(E), TRAIT, VEIN
streaky LACED, LINY, ROWY
stream AAR, ARROYO, BOURN, BROOK, FLOW, RILL, RIO, RIVER, RUN(NEL), SIKE
street ARTERY, AVENUE, CALLE, RII, RIO, RUE, VIA
stretch DISTEND, EKE, STENT
stretched out PROLATE
stretcher LITTER, (S)TENTER
strife FEUD, STASIS, WAR

strike BAFF, BAT, CLOUT, CONK, LARRUP, PELT(ER), POMMEL, PUTT, RAP, SLAP, SLUG, SMITE, SOCK, SWAT, WHACK, WHAM
strikebreaker FINK, GOON, RAT, SCAB
strip BARE, BATTEN, DISROBE, DIVEST, FLAY, FILLET, FLENSE, LATH, PEEL, SPLINE, STRAKE
stripe BAND, BAR, PLAGA, STREAK, WALE, WEAL, WELT
stroke BAFF, COUP, FEAT, FIT, ICTUS
strong GAMY, MADURO
strong-arm man BOUNCER, GOON, THUG
strong man ATLAS, SAM(P)SON, TARZAN
strong point FORTE
strongbox COFFER, VAULT, SAFE
struggle COPE, FLOUNDER, PENIEL
stubborn MULISH, ORNERY
stud BOSS, KNOB, NAIL
student AGGIE, COED, DISCIPLE, ECOLIER, ELEVE, LEARNER, MONITOR, PLEBE, PUPIL, SCHOLAR, TYRO
studio ATELIER, WORKSHOP
study CON, DEN, PORE, READ
study group CLASS, SEMINAR
stuff CRAM, GORGE, PAD, RAM
stuffing DRESSING, FARCE, KAPOK
stum MUST, RENEW
stumble STOT, TRIP
stump BUTT, SNAG STUB
stupefy BESOT, DAZE, DOPE, MAZE, NUMB, STUN
stupid CRASS, DENSE, DUMB
stupid person ASS, CLOD, COOT, DOLT, GOOSE, LOON, LOUT, LOWN, MOKE, OAF
stupor COMA, SOPOR, TORPOR
style CHIC, FAD, GENRE, MODE, NAME, TON, VOGUE
stymie BALK, FOIL, IMPEDE
subject LIEGE, NOUN, PRONE, TEXT, THEME, VASSAL
sublet CONACRE
subside ABATE, EBB, FALL, LAPSE, WANE
substantiate BOLSTER, VERIFY, WARRANT
substitute ERSATZ, STANDIN
subtract see DEDUCT
subvert CORRUPT, RUIN, UPSET
subway METRO, TUBE
success ARTHA, HIT, LUCK
successive(ly) AROW, SERIATE
succinct CONCISE, LACONIC, PITHY, TERSE
sue APPEAL, COURT, LITIGATE, WOO
suet FAT, LARD, TALLOW
suffer BEAR, BIDE, CLEM, DREE, LET, STARVE
suffixes see p. 236
sugar (BI)OSE, CANE, DEXTROSE, GLUCOSE, GUR, KETOSE, LACTOSE, MALTOSE, PANELA, PANOCHA, SUCROSE
sugar cane disease ILIAU
sugar-molasses MELADA
sugar source BEET, CANE, CORN, FRUIT, GRAPE, MAPLE, MILK, SAP
suicide HARAKIRI, SEPPUKU, SUTTEE
suitcase see BAG
suite FLAT, RETINUE, SERIES
sullen DOUR, GLUM, GRUFF, MOPING, MOROSE, POUTY, SURLY, SULKY, TESTY
sultan MURAD, SELIM
sultanate KUWAIT, MAHRA, MUSCAT, OMAN
sultry EROTIC, HUMID, MUGGY, TORRID
summer, pert. to ESTIVAL
summit(s) ACME, APEX, APICES, CAP, CREST, DOD, KNAP, PEAK
summon BID, CITE, CLEPE, EVOKE, KNELL, PAGE, SIST, SUBPOENA
sun HELIOS, PHOEBUS, SOL, TITAN
sun, pert. to SOLAR
sunder CLEAVE, DIVIDE, REND, RIVE, SEVER, SPLIT
sunroom(s) SOLARIA, SOLARIUM
sundial part GNOMON, STYLE
sunspot(s) FACULA, FRECKLE, MACULA, (PEN)UMBRA(E)
superfluous DETROP, EXTRA, FUTILE
supernatural MAGIC, OCCULT, UNEARTHLY
supernatural power MAGIC, MANA, NGAI, ORENDA, WAKAN
superstition, object of FETICH, FETISH, TALISMAN
supply BACKLOG, CATER, ENDOW, EQUIP, RELAY, STOCK
support ABET, BACK, BRACE, FID, LEG, PEG, PROP, STAY, TRIPOD, UNIPOD
suppose ASSUME, GUESS, IMAGINE, SURMISE, TROW, WIS
suppress BAN, QUASH, QUELL, STIFLE
surety BAIL, BOND, GAGE, HOSTAGE, MAINPRISE
surface FACE(T), NAP(PE), VENEER

surfeit see CLOY
surfeited BLASE, REPLETE, SATED
surly see SULLEN
surmise GUESS, INFER, OPINE
surpass BEST, CAP, ECLIPSE, OUTDO, TOP
surrender CEDE, CESSION, DEDITION, REMISE, RESIGN, YIELD
surround AMBUSH, BESET, GIRD, INARM, RING
survey MAP, PLOT, POLL, REVIEW, SCAN
surveying instrument ALIDADE, CALIPER, LEVEL, ROD, TRANSIT, STADIA, VERNIER
surveyor's assistant RODMAN
suspend BAR, DEFER, DISBAR, HANG, STAY
suspenders BRACES, GALLOWS
suture RAPHE, SEAM, SEW
swab MALKIN, MOP, WIPE
swallow ABSORB, BOLT, EAT, GULP
swamp SLOO, SLUE, TERAI, VLEI; see MARSH
swarm BEVY, HIVE, HORDE, NEST, TEEM
swarthy DARK, DUN, DUSKY
swastika FYLFOT
sway ROCK, ROLL, RULE, WAVER, YAW
swear AVER, (A)VOW, CURSE, DEPONE, DEPOSE
sweat EXUDE, OOZE, SUDOR
sweep DUST, RANGE, SWATH
sweetmeat CANDY, CARAMEL, DRAGEE
swell BULGE, DILATE, HEAVE, PUFF, SURF, WAVE
swelling BUBO, EDEMA, GALL, LUMP, NODE, STRUMA, STY, WEN
swift CRAN, FAST, FLEET, FLIT
swimming NATANT
swindle(r) see CHEAT
swine feeding PANNAGE
swine fever ROUGET
swing music JAZZ, JIVE
swinish PORCINE, SUILLINE
swirl CURL, EDDY, GORCE, GURGE, TWIST, WHORL
Swiss, Switzerland HELVETIA, LADIN, SUISSE
Swiss patriot TELL
switch SHUNT, TWIG, TOGGLE
swollen BOLLEN, TUMID, TURGID
swoon FAINT, SWEB, SYNCOPE
swoop DESCEND, POUNCE
sword ASCALON, ASKELON, BALMUNG, EXCALIBUR, GRAM; see p. 108
syllable ARSIS, MORA(E), PENULT, SONANT, ULTIMA
symbolic figure ZOA
synagogue SHUL, TEMPLE
syncope ELISION, FAINT, SWOON
system CODE, ISM, METHOD, REGIME(N)

T

T-shaped TAU
tab BILL, FLAP, LABEL, PAN
table CREDENCE, DEFER, FARE, POUDREUSE, PYE, SHELVE, VANITY; see LIST, STAND
tableland MESA, KAROO, PLAT(EAU), PUNA
tablet BRED, FACIA, PILL, SLAB, SLATE, TROCHE
taboo, opposed to NOA
tack BASTE, BEAT, BUSK, SECURE; see NAIL
tackle CAT, GARNET, GEAR, GRASP, GUN, LUFF, OUTFIT, RUNNER
tag A(I)GLET, APPEND
tail BUN(T), CAUDA, CODA, FUD, QUEUE, SCUT, TAG, TRAIL, VERSO, WREATH
tail, pert. to CAUDAL, CAUDATE
tailor CLOTHIER, FIT, SARTOR
Taiwan FORMOSA
take GRAB, NAB, USURP
take away ADEEM, HEAVE, REVOKE
take off DOFF, FLEE, MIMIC, PARODY
take out DELE, ELIDE, EXPUNGE
tale GESTE, LAI, LEGEND; see STORY
talent DOWER, FLAIR, FORTE, KNACK
talisman see CHARM
talk BLAB, CHAT, CRACK, GAB, GAS, HARANGUE, KNAP, LECTURE, ORATE, PALAVER, PARLEY, PATTER, PRATE, RANT, RAVE, SASS, SPIEL, YAK
tally MATCH, NOTCH, SCORE
Talmud part GEMARA, MISHNAH
talon FANG, HALLUX, SPUR, STOCK, ZIPPER; see NAIL
tamarack LARCH
tan BEIGE, BUFF, DUN, ECRU, TAW
tan bark ROSS
tang SAVOR, STING, ZEST
tangle EMBROIL, FOUL, KNOT, MAT, SHAG, SLEAVE, SNARL
tantrum (CAT)FIT, CONNIPTION

tap DECANT, DRAFT; see SPIGOT, TAVERN
tapered CONOID, SPIRED, TERETE
tapestry ARRAS, BAYEUX, DORSAL, DOSSER, GOBELIN, TAPIS
tapioca source CAS(S)AVA
tar BREA, GOB, MALTHA, PITCH, SAILOR
target AIM, BULLSEYE, BUTT, MARK, OBJECTIVE
tarry BIDE, DALLY, DAWDLE, LAG, STAY, WAIT
tarsus ANKLE, HOCK, SHANK
tart ACERB, AC(R)ID, SAUCY
tartar ARGAL, ARGOL, TARTRE
task PENSUM; see CHORE
taste PALATE, SAVOR, SIP, SNACK, SUP, TANG
tasteless CRUDE, FLAT, GAUCHE, VAPID
tasty see SAVORY
tattooing MOKO
taunt JEER, MOCK, NEEDLE, SNEER, TWIT
taut EDGY, NERVOUS, RIGID, SNUG, STIFF, TENSE, TIGHT, TRIG
tavern BAR, BISTRO, CANTINA, INN, KHAN, PUB, SALOON, TAMBO, TAP(ROOM)
tax ABKARI, ANNALE, ANNATES, ASSESS, AVANIA, CESS, CRO, CUSTOM, DUTY, EXCISE, FEE, GELD, HIDAGE, IMPOST, LEVY, LIKIN, OCTROI, RATAL, SCAT(T), SCOT, SCUTAGE, SESS, STENT, TAILLE, TALLAGE, TARIFF, TITHE, TOLL, TRIBUTE
tea BOHEA, CHA(A), CONGOU, HYSON, KAT, KEEMUN, LAPSANG, LEDUM, MATE, OOLONG, OOPA(C)K, PEKOE, PTISAN, TCHA, TISANE, TSIA, YERBA
teacake LUNN, SCON(E)
teacher ALIM, DOCENT, DON, GURU, MASTER, MOLLA(H), MULLA(H), PEDAGOG, PROF(ESSOR), PUNDIT, RAB(BI), REB, TUTOR
team CREW, PAIR, RANDEM, SPAN, STRING
tear BEAD, DIVULSE, REND, RENT, RIP, TATTER
tearful MAUDLIN, MOIST
tease BOTHER, JOSH, RIB, RIDE, TWIT
teeter SEESAW, WOBBLE
teeth, false DENTURE, PLATE
teeth incrustation TARTAR
telegraph part ANVIL, KEY, TAPPER
telegraphic speed unit BAUD
television TELLY, VIDEO
television term ADDER, ENCODER, KINESCOPE, MIXER, ORTHICON, PICKUP, RELAY, SCAN, SCOPHONY, SCREEN, SIGNAL, TELECAST, TELEVISE, VIDICON
tell DIVULGE, IMPART, OWN; see RELATE
teller CAMBIST, POTDAR; see CASHIER
Tell's home URI
temper (AN)NEAL, DANDER, HUMOR, PET
temperament GEMUT, MOOD
temple CELLA, FANE, HUACA, KIACK, KOVIL, MOSK, NOAS, PAGODA, RATH(A), TAA, VAT, WAT
tempt see ENTICE
ten DECA(D), DENARY
Ten Commandments DECALOG(UE)
ten thousand MYRIAD
tenant CROFTER, INMATE, LESSEE, RENTER, SAER
tendon CORD, SINEW, THEW
tendril BINE, CAPREOL, CURL, SPRIG
tennis term ACE, ALLEY, COURT, CUT, DEUCE, DRIVE, FAULT, GAME, LET, LOB(B), LOVE, MATCH, RACKET, RALLY, SERVICE, SET, SMASH, STROKE, TOSS, VOLLEY
tenon COG, TUSK
tenor DRIFT, GIST, TREND
tense FLEX, FUTURE, PAST, (PLU)PERFECT, PRESENT, PRETERIT; see TAUT
tent BIGTOP, KIBITKA, MARQUEE, PAWL, TEPEE, TIPI, TUPEK, WIGWAM, WITU, YURT(A)
tentacle ANTENNA, FEELER, PALP
tent-dweller BEDOUIN, GYPSY, KEDAR, NOMAD, SCENITE, YURUK
tentmaker KHAYYAM, OMAR
tenth part DECI, TITHE
termagant see SHREW
terrace GALLERY, PATIO, PLATEAU, PORTICO, TIER
terrestrial GEAL, MUNDANE, TERRENE
territory DOMAIN, ENCLAVE, REALM
terrorist ALARMIST, APACHE, GOON, NIHILIST, THUG
terse see BRIEF
tessellated MOSAIC
test ASSAY, BOSE, DRYRUN, EXAM(INE), QUIZ, TEMPT, TRIAL, TRYOUT

texture GRAIN, NAP, WALE, WEB, WOOF
Thames estuary NORE
theater BROADWAY, DRAMA, FARNESE, GLOBE, HOUSE, LEGIT, ODEA, ODEON, ODEUM, OPERA, STAGE, SWAN, THEATRON
theater group ANTA, ASCAP, HABIMA
theater part BALCONY, BOX, CAVEA, CIRCLE, DIAZOMA, FRONT, GALLERY, LOGE, PARTERRE, PIT, STALL
theater sign SRO
theme (LEIT)MOTIF, STRAIN, TEMA, TOPIC
then ANON, NEXT, POI
theoretical ABSTRACT, ACADEMIC, PLATONIC, TITULAR
theory DOCTRINE, ISM, NOTION
therefore ARGAL, ARGO, ERGO, (W)HENCE, SINCE
thicket BOSK, BRAKE, COPSE, RONE, JUNGLE, SPINNEY, TOD, TUSSOCK
thick-lipped BLOBBER, LABROSE
thief BURGLAR, CHOR, FILCHER, GANEF, GANOF, GONOF, KLEPTO, PIKER, SANSI
thigh, of the FEMORAL
thin DILUTE, LANK, LEAN, PAPERY, RARE(FY), SHEER, SPAR(S)E, TENUOUS
thing(s) CHOSE, MATTER, RES
think DEEM, IDEATE, MULL, MUSE, OPINE, TROW, WIS
thirst-producing DIPSETIC
thirsty ARID, (A)DRY, PARCHED
thirty, series of TRENTAL
thither THERE, YON(D), YONDER
thong KNOUT, RIEM, ROMAL, STRAP
thorn BARB, BRIAR, BRIER, NETTLE, SPINE
thorn apple DATURA, METEL
thorny SPINATE
thousand MIL(LE)
thousand years CHILIAD, MILLENNIUM, MILLIAD
thrall see BONDMAN
thrash BLESS, TROUNCE, W(H)ALE, YERK; see BEAT
thread CLEW, CLUE, CORD, FIBER, LISLE, PURL, REEVE, RETICLE, STAMEN, TENOR, TRAM, TWINE, WARP, WEFT
threadlike FILAR, FILATE, FILOSE, NEMALINE
three DREI, LEASH, TER(N), TRIAD, TRIO
threefold TERNAL, TERNARY, TERNATE, TREBLE, TRINE
threshold EVE, LIMEN, SILL
thrifty FRUGAL, MISERLY, SAVING
thrill KICK, STIR, TIRL
thrive ADDLE, BATTEN, BOOM, SUCCEED, WAX
throat, pert. to (JU)GULAR
throe PANG, RACK, SPASM
throne ASANA, GADDI, GADHI, MUSNUD
throng HORDE, MOB, SWARM
through DONE, PER, VIA
throw CAST, FLING, HEAVE, HURL, KEST, PITCH, TOSS, WRAP
thrust BUTT, DART(LE), JAB, LUNGE, ONSET
thurible CENSER
Thursday source THOR
thus ERGO, SIC, YET
thwart see BAFFLE
ticket BALLOT, LABEL, PASS, SLATE
tidal flow BORE, EAGRE, EBB, FLOOD, NEAP
tidings EVANGEL, GOSPEL, NEWS
tidy KEMPT, NEAT, REDO, TRIG
tie BEAM, BIND, BOND, LASH, LIGATE, MOOR, NEXUS, SLEEPER, TACH(E), TRUSS
tighten FRAP, LACE, TAUTEN
tile FAVI, FAVUS, IMBREX, KASHI, PANTILE, TEGULA, TESSERA
tiller FARMER, HELM, PLOWMAN
tilt CANT, CAREEN, HEEL, JOUST, LEAN, LIST, SLANT, TIP
timber BATTEN, BEAM, BIBB, BITT, CAMBER, KEVEL, LOG(S), STUMPAGE
timber rot DOAT, DOTE
time (A)EON, BEAT, DATE, ELD, EPOCH, ERA, EVE, TEMPI, TEMPO, TENSE, YORE; see p. 255
time being NONCE
time, pert. to ERAL, TEMPORAL
timid PAVID, SHY, TREPID
tin CAN, COAT, STANNUM
tin foil TAIN
tin, pert. to STANNIC, STANNOUS
tinder AMADOU, PUNK
tine FANG, PRONG, SNAG, SPIKE, TYND
tinge DYE, DASH, IMBUE, TAINT, TOUCH
tingle THIRL, THRILL
tinkle CHINK, DINGLE, TING
tip APEX, CUE, END, KNAP; see GRATUITY, TILT
tipster INSIDER, TOUT(ER)
tirade SPATE; see DIATRIBE
tire BORE, CLOY, FAG, JADE, WEARY

tire part CASING, RIM, SHOE, TREAD, TUBE
tissue BAST, FASCIA, FIBER, PHLOEM, TELA
Titans see p. 208
title ABGAR, AG(H)A, ALI, AYA, BABA, BASHAW, BEY, CAPTION, COJA, DAME, DOM, EARL, EMEER, EMIR, GHAZI, GRAF, HEADING, HOJA, HUZOOR, KHAN, LORD, MA(D)AM, MME, MOLLA, MRS, MULLA, NAME, NAWAB, PACHA, PAN(I), PASHA, PRINZ, RAS, SAIYID, SAY(Y)ID, SHEREFF, SHERIF, SHREE, SIDI, SRI, TERM, TUAN, VON
toast BREDE, CHEERS, LEEP, SALUD, SALUTE, SANTE, SKOAL, PROSIT
tobacco BURLEY, CAPA, CAPORAL, PERIQUE, SANA, SHAG, VUELTA
tobacco ash DOTTEL, DOTTLE
toll KNEEL, PEAL, RING; see TAX
tomb BARROW, CIST(VAEN), CRYPT, DOKHMA, MASTABA, MOLE, TABUT, TUMULUS; see also SHRINE
tomboy HOIDEN, HOYDEN, ROMP
tone KEY, PITCH, TEAN, TIMBRE
tongue CHIB, GLOSSA, IDIOM, LINGUA, NEAP, TAB, TANG
tongue, pert. to APICAL, GLOSSAL
tonic ALOE, BRACER, CHIRATA, ELIXIR, PICKUP, ROBORANT, TANSY
tool(s) DEVICE, DUPE, GADGET, GEAR; see p. 257
tooth COG, GAM, IVORY, TINE, TUSH, TUSK
toothed DENTATE, SERRATE
toothless EDENTATE
top ACE, APEX, CAP, EPI, FINIAL, LIP, VERTEX, ZENITH
topknot CREST, ONKOS, PANACHE, TUFT
torch CRESSET, FLAMBEAU, LINK, MUSSAL
torment AGONY, ANNOY, BAIT, BANE, HARRY, ORDEAL
torn REFT, RENT, RIVEN, SPLIT
torture FLAY, GARBLE, MARTYR, RACK, STRAPPADO
toss BANDY, CAST, FLING, FLIP, PITCH, TAVE
touch ABUT, DASH, IMPINGE, PALP, TIG
touch, pert. to HAPTIC, TACTIC, TACTILE, TACTUAL
touchwood see TINDER
tough BULLY, CHEWY, HARDY, ROWDY, STURDY, WIRY, WITHY
tournament JOUST, MATCH, TILT
tower BABEL, BELFRY, CAMPANILE, DONJON, GAZEBO, GOPURA, MARTELLO, MINARET, PAGODA, RONDEL, SIK(H)ARA, SIKHRA, STUPA, TOPE, TOR(RION), TURRET, VIMANA; see also SPIRE, WATCHTOWER
town, of a CIVIC, OPPIDAN, URBAN
town(ship) BAYAN, BURG(H), DEME, MACHI, STAD(T), VILL; see VILLAGE
toy DALLY, FONDLE; see TRIFLE
trace HINT, SKETCH, SOUPCON, TINGE, VESTIGE
track RAILS, RUT, SCENT, SLOT, SPOOR, SPUR, TURF, WAKE
tracker PUGGI
trade BANDY; see BARTER, PROFESSION, SELL
trading site CANTEEN, MART, PIT
trail DOG, FOLLOW, HEEL, HOUND, SHADOW, TAIL, TRACE; see TRACK
train COACH, DRILL, EXPRESS, FLIER, FREIGHT(ER), INSTRUCT, LIMITED, LOCAL, MANIFEST, RETINUE, SHUTTLE, SPECIAL, SUITE, TUBE
tramp BUM, HIKE, HOBO, TRAIPSE
trample CHAMP, POACH, TREAD
trance DAZE, LUPA, SOPOR
transfer CEDE, CONVEY, DEED, DEMISE, DEPUTE, GRANT
transferer ALIENOR
transition CHANGE, FLUX, PASSAGE
trap (EN)SNARE, GIN, NET, TIPE, WEIR
trapdoor DROP, HATCH
trapshooting term PIGEON, SKEET
travel TOUR, TREK, WEND
travel, pert. to VIATIC
traveler ITINERANT, PILGRIM, TOURIST, VIATOR, WAYFARER
tray HOD, SALVER, SERVER
tread PAD, SNEAK, STEP, TRAMPLE, TIRE, VOLT
treasure CACHE, CHERISH, ROON, TROVE
treasurer BOUCHER, BURSAR, FISCAL, PURSER
treasury BURSARY, BURSE, FISC, FISK
treasury agents TMEN
treat DOCTOR, DOSE, REGALE, USE
treatise ESSAY, SUMMA, THESIS, TRACT
tree BOSCAGE, TIMBER, WOODS; see FOREST; see p. 226

tree, pert. to ARBOREAL
tremble DIDDER, DODDER, QUAKE
tremulous ASPEN, TREPID
trench see DITCH
trend BENT, DRIFT, TENOR
trespass ENCROACH, INTRUDE, INVADE, POACH, SIN, TROVER
triad TRIO, TRINARY, TRINITY
trial ASSIZE, CASE, HEARING, INQUEST, INQUIRY, (LAW)SUIT, ORDEAL; see TEST
triangle DELTA, GORE, GUSSET, SCALENE, TRIGON
tribute CARATCH, HOMAGE; see TAX
trick DIDO, DODGE, FICELLE, FLAM, GAWD, JEST, RUSE, STUNT, WILE
tricks won CAPOT, NULL(O), SLAM
trifle DALLY, DOIT, FICO, NIGGLE, PALTER, TOY
trill ROLL, SHAKE, TIRALEE, WARBLE
trim ADORN, DOCK, LOP, PREEN, SHRAG, TRIG
trimmed ADORNED, SNOD
trimming(s) FLOTS, GIMP, RUCHE
trinket BIBELOT, BIJOU, GAUD, GEWGAW
triple TREBLE, TRI
triplet(s) TERCET, TRIN(E)
trite BANAL, CORNY, DULL, INANE, JEJUNE
troche LOZENGE, PASTIL(E), ROTULA
Trojan DARDAN, ILIAN
trolley TRAM
troops ARMY, FORCES, MEN
trophy CUP, LAUREL, MEDAL, PALM, SCALP
trot AMBLE, DANCE, JOG, PACE, PONY
trouble ADO, AIL, EFFORT, ILLS, MOLEST, WOE, WORRY
trough GUTTER, STRAKE, TRUG; see CHANNEL
Troy ILLION, ILIUM, WEIGHT
Troy, pert. to ILIAC, ILIAN, TROJAN
truant LAGGARD, TRIVANT, TRONE, VAGRANT
trudge PACE, PLOD, SLOG
true GERMANE, LEAL, VERY
trundle CART, ROLL, RULL
trunk BOLE, CABER, CHEST, LOCKER, PROBOSCIS, TORSO
trust CUSTODY, RELY, TROW
truth FACT, FEALTY, TAO, UNA
truth drug PENTOTHAL
try ATTEMPT, CRACK, ESSAY, ETTLE, SHOT, STRIVE, TAX, TEST
tub COWL, GAAL, GYLE, HOGSHEAD, KEELER, KEEVE, KID, KIT, KNAP, KNOP, SKEEL, SOE; see VAT
tube DUCT, HOSE, PIPE, PIPET(TE), SIPPER, SNORKEL, SUBWAY
tuber EDDO, JALAP, OCA, SALEP, TARO, TRUFFLE, YAM
tuck FOLD, HIDE, LAP, PLEAT, RUCHE
Tuesday source TIU, TIW
tuft COMA, CREST
tumor CYST, MORO, OMA, WEN, YAW
tumult BABEL, DIN, LURRY, RIOT
tunnel ARLBERG, BURROW, CASCADE, CENIS, HOOSAC, MOFFAT, SEVERN, SIMPLON, TANNA, TUBE
tunnel term ADIT, HEADING, RISING, SHAFT, SINKING, SLOPE, STOPE
turban MANDIL, MUNDIL
turbid MURKY, ROILED, ROILY
turf DIVOT, PEAT, SOD, SWARD
Turkish government PORTE
turmoil HURLY, WELTER
turn BEND, BENT, DETOUR, EVERT, GYRE, HAW, PIVOT, (RE)VERT, ROTATE, SHUNT, VERTE, VOLTI, WHIRL; see VEER
turpentine derivative PINENE, ROSIN, TERPENE
turpentine resin ALK, GAL(L)IPOT
turtle delicacy CALIPASH, CALIPEE
tusk FANG, IVORY, RAZOR
tutor COACH, MENTOR, TUTE
twenty CORGE, SCORE
twenty-fourth part CARAT, KARAT
twice BIS, ENCORE
twig SCION, SLIP, WITHE
twigs, made of VIRGAL, WATTLED
twilight DUSK, EVE(NTIDE), GLOAM(ING)
twin CHANG, ENG, GEMEL
twin crystal MACLE
twine COIL, HEMP, TWIST, WIND
twinkle GLEAM, GLINT, WINK
twist COIL, CONTORT, FEAK, GNARL, GRIND, INTORT, KINK, SKEW, SLUB, SQUIRM, WARP
twisted (A)WRY, SKEW, TORSE, TORTILE
twitch JERK, TIC, TWEAK
two BRACE, DUO, PAIR, TWINS
twofold BINAL, BINARY, DUAL, TWIN
two-footed BIPED(AL)
two-month period BIMESTER
two-spot DEUCE
tycoon BARON, MOGUL, NABOB, SHOGUN

type BRAND, FONT, GENRE, ILK, NORM, SPECIES
type face AGATE, BEMBO, BODONI, BULMER, CASLON, CENTURY, CLOISTER, COCHIN, FUTURA, GOTHIC, GOUDY, GRANJON, HESS, IONIC, ITALIC, NEWS, PIE, ROMAN, RONDE, RUNIC, SCRIPT, STYMIE, TIMES, VOGUE
type part BEARD, BODY, COUNTER, FACE, FEET, GROOVE, NECK, NICK, SERIF, SHANK, SHOULDER, STEM
type size AGATE, BREVIER, CANON, DIAMOND, ELITE, ENGLISH, MINION, PARAGON, PEARL, PICA, PRIMER
typewriter part CARRIAGE, PLATEN, SHIFT, TAB(ULATOR)
tyrant CAESAR, DESPOT, NERO
Tyre royalty DIDO, HIRAM

U

umbrella CHATTA, CHUTE, GAMP, PARASOL
umpire ARBITER, REF(EREE), UMP
unadorned BALD, CHASTE, NAKED, STARK
unaspirated LENE
unbeliever AGNOSTIC, DOUBTER, SKEPTIC; see HEATHEN, INFIDEL
uncle EAM, NUNKA, NUNKS, NUNKY, OOM, SAM, (Y)EME
unclean DIRTY, IMMUND, TREF(A), VILE
unclothe DIVEST, STRIP, TIRL
uncommon EXOTIC, ODD, RARE, SPECIAL
unconscious state COMA, FAINT, SWOON, SYNCOPE
uncouth GAUCHE, RUDE, VULGAR
uncouth person BOOR, CAD, GALOOT, LOUT, YAHOO
unctuous OILY, PINGUID, SMUG, SUAVE
under ALOW, INFRA, NEATH, NETHER, SOTTO, SOUS, SUB
undergo DREE, ENDURE, SUFFER
underhand DERN, COVERT, SECRET, SLY
undersong TIERCE
undershirt(s) LINDER, SKIVVIES
understand DIG, GRASP, KEN, SAVVY
understanding ACCORD, ENTENTE, NOUS, SENSE
underworld see HADES, HELL
undeveloped BARREN, EMBRYO, LATENT
undulate PULSATE, RIPPLE, WAVE
undulation TREMOLO, WAVE
uneasiness ANXIETY, MALAISE, QUALMS
uneven EROSE, ODD, RAGGED
unfair BIASED, FOUL
unfair move FOUL, FULK
unfeeling CALLOUS, CRUEL, NUMB
unfold DEPLOY, EVOLVE, REVEAL
unguent BALM, CEROMA, CHRISM, CRATE, NARD, POMADE, SALVE
ungula see CLAW, HOOF
uniform EVEN, FLAT, FLOT, HABIT, LIVERY
union AFL, ARTEL, BLOC, CIO, FUSION, GUILD, HANSE, HUI, ILA, ILGWU, ITA, LEAGUE, MERGER, TWU, UAW
unite ALLY, BLEND, FUSE, JOIN, KNIT, MERGE, MIX, RABET, WED, WELD, YOKE
universal CATHOLIC, COSMIC, ECLECTIC, ECUMENIC, GLOBAL, PANDEMIC
universe COSMOS, LOKA, WORLD
unkeeled RATITE
unknown IGNOTE, INCOGNITO
unless BUT, EXCEPT, LEST, NISI, SAVE
unmarried CELIBATE, SINGLE, UNWED
unmarried state AGAMY
unplowed strip HADE
unprofitable BARREN, SECK
unravel FEAZE, SOLVE, TEASE
unrefined CRASS, CRUDE, EARTHY, RAW
unstable ASTATIC, ERRATIC, FICKLE, LABILE
untamed FERAL, FERINE, WILD
untidy DOWDY, MESSY, SLOPPY
until HENT, TILL, WHEN
unusual EXOTIC, OUTRE, STRANGE
unwilling AVERSE, LO(A)TH
unwillingness NILL
unworthy INDIGN, UNFIT, VILE
unyielding ADAMANT, FAST, FIRM, STANCH
Upanishad ISHA
upon ATOP, EPI, ONTO, OVER, SUR
uprising COUP, PUTSCH, REVOLT
uproar ADO, BABEL, DIN, HUBBUB, RACKET, RIOT
upstart PARVENU, SNOB
urchin ARAB, GAMIN, IMP, MUDLARK, TAD

urge ABET, COAX, EGG, GOAD, IMPEL, LUST, PLY, PROD, SPUR, YEN
urticaria HIVES, RASH, UREDO
urial SHA
urus AUROCHS, TUR
useless FUTILE, IDLE, INUTILE, NULL, OTIOSE, VOID
U.S. State information see p. 274
utter BID, SAY, SHEER, SPEAK, STARK, TOTAL, VENT
utterly FULLY, QUITE, STARK

V

vacant BLANK, (DE)VOID
vacillate REEL, TEETER, WAVER
vacuum CAVITY, HALLOW, VOID
vacuum, opposite of PLENUM
vagabond BUM, HOBO, LOREL, RODNEY, SHIRK, TRAMP, TRUANT, VAG(RANT); see WANDERER
vain EMPTY, IDLE, SMUG, VAPID
valance PALMETTE, PELMET
vale ADIEU, DELL, GLEN
valiant BRAVE, STALWART, WIGHT
valid COGENT, DEJURE, SOUND
valley ATRIO, COULEE, DALE, DELL, COOMB, DHOON, DINGLE, GEHENNA, GLADE, NEMEA, STRATH, SWALE, VAAL, VALE, WADI, WADY
valve CUSP, DAMPER, POPPET, VALV(UL)A, VENTIL; see FAUCET
vampire BAT, DRACULA, GHOUL, LAMIA
van FORE, LORRY, TRUCK
vandal GOTH, HUN, TEUTON
vanish EVANESCE, FADE, SINK
vanity AIRS, CONCEIT, EGO(T)ISM, PRIDE, VAINGLORY
vantage point COIGN(E)
vapid INANE, JEJUNE, STALE
vapor ATMO, BRUME, HAZE, MIST, ROKE, STEAM
Varangians ROS
variable FICKLE, PROTEAN, SHIFTY
variation LECTION, NUANCE, SHADE
variegated CALICO, MOTLEY, PIED, PINTO, SHOT
varnish GLOSS, JAPAN, SHELLAC(K)
varnish ingredient COPAL, ELEMI, LAC, RESIN
vassal LIEGE; see BONDMAN
vase AMPHORA, ASKOS, D(E)INOS, DIOTA, ECHEA, ECHEION, PELIKE, POTICHE, SITULA, TAZZA, URN
vat BAC, KEEVE, KEIR, KIER, KIVE, TUN
vault ARCH, CRYPT, CURVET, DOME, LEAP, SAFE
Vedic dialect PALI
veer SHEER, SHIFT, SHY, SKEW, SLUE, SWAY, SWERVE, TURN, YAW
vegetation FLORA; see p. 225
vehicle AGENT; see p. 264
veil CAUL, VELUM, YASHMAK
vein DRIFT, TENOR; see LODE; see p. 106
veneer ENAMEL, LAC, POLISH
venerable HOAR(Y), OLD, SAGE
veneration AWE, DULIA, ESTEEM, LATRIA, RESPECT
vent BUNG, EGRESS, FLUE
ventral HEMAD, HEMAL, STERNAL
venture DARE, FLING, FLYER, HAZARD, RISK
Venus, island of MELOS
veranda LOGGIA, PATIO, PYAL; see PORCH
verbal ORAL, SPOKEN, VOCAL
verbose DIFFUSE, PROLIX, WINDY, WORDY
verify (AT)TEST, AUDIT, PROVE
verily AMEN, INDEED, YEA
verity AXIOM, REALITY, TRUTH
vernier NONIUS
versatile DEFT, MOBILE
verse RANN, STICH; see POEM
verse form ANAPAEST, COUPLET, DACTYL, DIMETER, DIPODY, DISTICH, IAMB, OCTAVE, PANTUN, QUATRAIN, SESTINA, SPONDEE, TRISEME, TROCHEE
vertigo DINUS, MEGRIM, SCOTOMY
vesicle BLEB, BLISTER, BULLA, CYST, SAC
vessel AFTABA, AMA, AMULA, BASIN, BOCAL, BOTTLE, BOWL, CASK, CUP, DECANTER, ETNA, FLASK, FONT, GOURD, JAR, JUG, LOTA(H), MUG, PAN, PATERA, POT, STEIN, TANK, TUB, VASE, VAT
vestige RELIC, REMNANT, SURVIVAL, TRACE
vestry CHAPEL, SACRISTY
vetch AKRA, ERS, FITCH, TARE
vetiver BENA, CUSCUS
vex CARK, FASH, GALL, HARRY, IRK, NETTLE, RILE, ROIL
viand(s) see FOOD
vibrate JIGGLE, QUAVER, QUIVER, THRILL
vibration FREMITUS, TREMOLO

vice PIACLE, SIN, STEAD
viceroy EXARCH, NAWAB
victim CULLY, MARK, PREY, MARTYR
victory NIKE, PALM
victory cry ABU, ABOO
victual(s) see FOOD
view EYE, OGLE, SCENE, VISTA
vigor STAMINA, VIR; see ENERGY, FORCE
vilify ABUSE, MALIGN, REVILE
village BUSTEE, CASAL(E), CLACHAN, DESSA, GAV, KAIK(A), KRAAL, MURA, PUEBLO, RANCHO, REW, STAD, VILL; see HAMLET
villain BADDIE, BOOR, HEAVY, KNAVE, LEGREE, ROGUE
villein see SERF
vine GRAPE, HOP, IVY
vinegar ACETUM, ALEGAR, EISEL(L)
vinegar, pert. to ACETIC
violate ABUSE, ENCROACH, RAVISH
violin maker AMATI, GUARNERI, STRADIVARI
violinist AUER, ELMAN, GRUMIAUX, HEIFETZ, KREISLER, KREUTZER, MENUHIN, MILSTEIN, OISTRAKH, PAGANINI, STERN, SZIGETI, YSAYE
Virgil's hero(ine) (A)ENEAS, DIDO
virgin CHASTE, MADONNA, PIETA, PURE, VESTAL
visage ASPECT; see FACE
viscous GLUEY, LIMY, ROPY, SIZY, SLIMY, STICKY
Visigoth see GOTH
visionary AIRY, DREAMY, FEY, IDEAL, UNREAL, UTOPIAN
visit CALL, GAM, HAUNT, SEE, STAY
vital energy HORME
vitality SAP; see ENERGY
vitalize ANIMATE, VIVIFY
vitamin ADERMIN, ANEURIN, BIOTIN, CHOLINE, CITRIN, FLAVIN, NIACIN, THIAMINE, TORULIN
vitiate DEFILE, IMPAIR, SPOIL, TAINT, VOID
vitriols SORY
vivacity DASH, ELAN; see ENERGY
vocal ORAL, SONANT, TONIC, VERBAL
voice EMIT, SAY, SOUND, TONGUE, VOCE, VOTE, VOX
voiced SONANT, TONIC
voiceless ASONANT, SPIRATE, SURD
void INVALID, NUL(L), SPACE, VACANT, VACATE, VACUUM; see ANNUL
volcanic ejection BELCH, MOYA, PUMICE, SALSE, TUFF; see LAVA
volition CONATION, OPTION, WILL
voluble FLUENT, GLIB
volume BULK, LOUDNESS, RANGE; see BOOK
vomiting EMESIS
voodoo deity ZOMBI
vote AYE, BALLOT, ELECT, NAY, NOD, POLL, STRAW, YEA
voucher CHIT, NOTE, STUB

W

wade FORD, PLODGE, SLOG
wafer DISK, HOST, LAMINA, OBLEY, TROCHE
wag WAVE; see JOKER
wager HAZARD, RISK; see BET
wage(s) BATTA, FEE, HIRE, PAY, UTU
Wagnerian role ELSA, ERDA, ISOLDE, RIENZI, SENTA, TRISTAN
wagon part BLADE, CLEVIS, NEAP, POLE, THILL
wail KEEN, LAMENT, ULULATE
waiter CARHOP, SALVER, STEWARD
waive CEDE, DEFER, FOREGO
Wales CAMBRIA, CYMRU
walk ALAMEDA, AMBLE, HIKE, LIMP, MALL, MINCE, PACE, PAUP, PLOD, SAUNTER, SLOG, STEP, STROLL, STRUT
wall ESCARP, LEVEE, PARAPET, MUR(E), RAMPART, SEPTA, SEPTUM, SPINA
wall piece DADO, PANEL, TEMPLATE, TEMPLET, WAINSCOT
wallow GROVEL, WELTER, REVEL
wampum ROANOKE, SE(A)WAN, PEAG(E)
wan ASHEN, ASHY, SICKLY, WAXEN
wand BATON, MACE, ROD, SCEPTER, WATTLE, WITHE
wander DIGRESS, ERR, GAD, HAAK, HAIK, HAKE, MEANDER, MOON, ROAM, ROVE, STRAY
wanderer BEDOUIN, GYPSY, ITINERANT, MIGRANT, NOMAD, PALMER, ROVER, SCENITE, STRAY, VIATOR, WAIF; see VAGABOND
wandering BOHEMIAN, ERRANT NOMADIC, ODYSSEY, TRUANT, VAGABOND

want NEED, PENURY, YEARN
war BALKAN, BOER, CIVIL, CRIMEAN, CRUSADE, FIGHT, GALLIC, JEHAD, JIHAD, PUNIC, SAMNITE, WEER
war cry ALALA, WARISON, WHOOP
ward AVERT, CUSTODY, FEND, REPEL, PARRY
warden GUARD(IAN), RANGER
warehouse ARSENAL, DEPOT, ENTREPOT, ETAPE, GODOWN
warlike MARTIAL, MILITANT
warm BEEK, BALMY, CALID, (RE)HEAT, TEPID
warn CAUTION, FLAG, PREVISE, SIGNAL
warning ALARM, ALERT, CAVEAT
warp BIAS, BUCKLE, CRAM, DISTORT
warrant(s) BERAT, PLEVIN, WRIT
warrior AMAZON, COSSACK, HESSIAN, IMPI, SAMURAI, SANNUP, SPAHI; see SOLDIER
wary CAGY, CANNY, CHARY
wash ELUTE, LAUNDER, LAVE, LEACH, LOSH
washings ELUATE
waste ATROPHY, BARREN, DECAY, DREGS, DROSS, FRITTER, GARBAGE, GNAW, IDLE, LOSS, REFUSE, SCUM
waste fiber NOIL
waste silk FRISON, KNUB
watch EYE, GLOM, GUARD, MIND, SEE, SPY, TEND, VIGIL
watchman ARGUS, CHOKIDAR, SENTRY, SERENO, VEDETTE
watchtower ATALAYA, BARBICAN, MIRADOR
water AQUA, BROO, DILUTE, EAU(X), HTWOO, HYDROL, IRRIGATE, RAIN
water, living in LENITIC, LOTIC
water-raising device TABOOT, TABUT
water surface RYME
watercourse BROOK, FLUX, LADE, RACE, RIVER, STREAM
waterfall CASCADE, CATARACT, FORCE, FOSS, LIN(N), LYN, NIAGARA, SAULT
watering place OASIS, WELL; see SPRING
waterway CANAL, CHANNEL, RIVER, STRAIT, STREAM
watery AQUEOUS, SEROUS, THIN
wave see BILLOW
waver FALTER, SWAY, TEETER
wavy CRISP, NEBULE, ONDY, REPAND, UNDATE, UNDE, UNDOSE, UNDY
wax CERE(SIN), CERIN, CEROMA, CODE, GROW, PELA
wax, pert. to CERAL
wayside rest PARAO
weak DEBILE, EFFETE, FAINT, FEEBLE, FLAT, FRAIL, INFIRM, PUNY, WAN
weaken DILUTE, ENERVATE, ENFEEBLE, LABEFY, SAP, VITIATE
weakling PULER, SISSY
weakness ACRATIA, ATONY, FOIBLE
wealth AFFLUENCE, ASSETS, FORTUNE, LUCRE, MAMMON, OPULENCE, PELF
wealthy (F)LUSH, HEELED, RICH
weapon ARM(E), ARMS; see p. 108
wear away ABRADE, CORRODE, FRAY, USE
weathercock FANE, GIROUETTE, VANE
weave ENTWINE, KNIT, LOOM, PLAIT, PLASH, PLEACH
weaverbird BAYA, TAHA
weaving term BOBBIN, COP, LAPPET, LATHE, LAY, LEASE, LISSE, RAVEL, SLEY, UNI, WOOF; see LOOM
web GOSSAMER, NET, TELA
web, pert. to RETIARY, TELAR(Y)
wed ESPOUSE, MARRY, MERGE, WIVE
wedge CAM, CHOCK, COIGN, COTTER, CUNEUS, FROE, FROW, GLUT, GORE, GUSSET, JAM, QUOIN, SHIM, SPRAG
wedge-shaped CUNEATE
Wednesday source WODEN
weed CULL, HOE, PEST, TARE
week HEBDOMAD, OUK, SENNET, SENNIGHT
weep BOHO(O), BOOHOO, LAMENT, ORP, SOB; see CRY
weft WOOF, WOFT
weight BOB, HEFT, LOAD, PARI, PEISE, TRON(E), TROY, VALUE; see p. 187
weight, pert. to BARIC
weight system METRIC, TROY
weir DAM, GARTH, TRAP
weird EERIE, EERY, ODD, SPOOKY, UNCANNY, UNCO
welcome ACCOIL, GREET, HAIL
well AIN, BIEN, FONT, HALE
well curb PUTEAL
well done BRAVO, EUGE
well lining STEEN
Welsh CAMBRIAN, CYMRY, TAFFY
welt LASH, STRIP, WALE
wen CLYER, CYST, MOLE, TALPA
wend MEANDER, PASS, SORB
West Pointer CADET, PLEB(E), YEARLING
West Point mascot MULE

wet ASOP, DAMP, DANK, MOIST, SOAK, SOPPING, WAT
whale LEVIATHAN, MOBYDICK; see p. 214
whale hunter AHAB
whalebone BALEEN
whales, pert. to CETIC
wharf see LANDING
whatnot CABINET, ETAGERE, OMNIUM
wheat DURUM, EMMER, POULARD, SPELT
wheat disease BUNT, ERGOT, SMUT
wheedle CAJOLE, COAX, COG
wheel part ARBOR, AXLE, CAM, FELLY, HOB, HUB, NAVE, RIM, SPOKE, STRAKE
wheel(s) CASTER, DISK, GYRATE, HELM, NORIA, PULLEY, ROLL, ROTA(TE), ROWEL, SHEAVE, SPIN
whetstone BUHR, HONE, RIP
whey SERA, SERUM, WHIG
whiff GUST, PUFF, WAFT
while ALBEIT, DAWDLE, WHEN
whimper KEEN, WHINE; see CRY
whinny HINNY, NEIGH
whip AZOTE, CHICOTE, CROP, FLOG, KNOUT, KURBASH, PLET, QUIRT; see BEAT
whip mark WALE, WEAL
whipsocket SNEAD
whirlpool EDDY, GURGE, MAELSTROM, SWIRL, VORTEX, WEEL, WIEL
whiskey FIREWATER, HOOCH, POT(H)EEN, ROTGUT; see p. 124
whisper ASIDE, HINT, TUTEL
whist term GRAND, MISERE, MORT, SLAM, SOLO
whistle (CAT)CALL, FUTE, PIPE, SIREN
whit DOIT; see BIT
white BAWN, CHALKY, LABAN
white man CACHILA, PALEFACE
Whittier heroine MAUD, MOLL(Y)
whiz HUM, PIRR, WHIR
wick SNAST(E), SNUFF
wickerwork RATAN
wicket ARCH, HOOP, STUMP
widow RELICT, SKAT, SUTTEE
widow's share MITE, T(I)ERCE
wife BRIDE, FE(M)ME, FERE, FRAU, MATRON, RIB, SQUAW, UXOR; see SPOUSE
wife's property DOS
wig DIVOT, DOILY, JASEY, MAT, PERIWIG, PERUKE, RAMILLIE, RUG, TOUPEE
wild FERAL, FERINE, RABID
will BEHEST, CONATION, TESTAMENT, VELLEITY, VOLITION
will beneficiary DEVISEE
will maker DEVISOR
willing BAIN
willingly LIEF, READILY
willow EDDER, OSIER
wilt COWER, DROOP, FADE
wily FOXY, SUBTLE, SLY
wimple GORGET, WIMLUNGE
wince FLINCH, RECOIL, SHY
wind AFER, AUSTER, BISE, BORA, BOREAS, CYCLONE, FOEHN, GALE, GUST, K(H)AMSIN, KONA, LESTE, MONSOON, NOTUS, PAMPERO, PUNA, PUNO, SAMIEL, SARSAR, SIMOOM, SIMOON, SIROC(CO), TEMPEST, TRADE, TWINE, TWIST
wind indicator COCK, CONE, SLEEVE, SOCK, VANE
windborne AEOLIAN
windlass CRANK, REEL, WHIM, WHIN, WINCH, WINDLASS
windmill part AWE, CAP, CURB, SAIL, VANE
window DORMER, LUCARNE, ORIEL, OXEYE, ROUNDEL, SASH, SKYLIGHT, TRANSOM
window part CAME, LEADING, MULLION, MUNTIN, PANE, SASH, SILL, TRANSOM
window setter GLAZIER
windstorm BURA(N), TORNADO, TYPHOON
wine BRUT, CUIT, CUTE, GRAVE, MUST, SEC, VIN; see p. 123
wine disorder CASSE
wine, make VINT
wine quality SEVE
wine, pert. to VINIC, VINOUS
wine with honey MULSE
wing ALA(E), ALULA, ANNEX, ELL, ELYTRON, PENNA, PINION, PINNA, TEGMINA, TEGUMEN
wing part AILERON, FLANK
winged AILE, ALAR, ALATE
winged deity CUPID, EROS, NIKE
winged figure (E)IDOLON, IDOLUM
winged fruit SAMARA
wing-footed ALIPED
wingless APTERAL, DEALATE(D)
wink BAT, FLICKER, NICTATE
wintry ARCTIC, BOREAL, BRUMAL, HIBERNAL, HIEMAL, HYEMAL
wipe EFFACE, ERASE, RUB, SWAB
wire CABLE, CIRCUIT, CORD, LEAD, LINE, LITZ, RETICLE
wisdom GNOSIS, LORE, WIT
wise man GASPAR, MAGI, MAGUS, MENTOR, NESTOR, SAGE, SAVANT, SOLOMON, SOLON, WITAN

wisp TAIT, TATE, WASE
wit HUMOR, IRONY, WAG
witch ACRASIA, BELDAM(E), BRUJA, CIRCE, CRONE, DUESSA, HAG, HECAT(E), HEX, LAMIA, LILITH, WARLOCK
witch city ENDOR, SALEM
witch doctor BRUJO, GOOFER, SHAMAN, WIZARD
wither FADE, SEAR, WILT
without MINUS, OUTSIDE, SANS
witness ATTEST, DEPONENT, ONLOOKER, SEE, TESTE
witticism see JOKE
woe BANE, DOLOR, MISERY
wolfish LUPINE, RAVENOUS
woman BELLE, FEMALE, HAG, HOURI, M(A)ENAD, PARAMOUR, PERI, SHE, VIXEN; see HAG, MADAM, WIFE
wont CUSTOM, HABIT, USAGE
wood ALERCE, BALSA, BIRCH, CAHUY, VHERRY, CHESTNUT, EBONY, ELM, GUM, KOKRA, LANA, LUMBER, MAHOGANY, MAPLE, NARRA, OAK, ROSEWOOD, SYCAMORE, TIMBER, WALNUT
wood, bend in SNY
wood measure CORD, FATHOM
wood, piece of BOARD, BILLET, DEAL, PLANK, SLAT, SPRAG, STAVE
woody LIGNEUS, SYLVAN, TREEN, XYLOID
wool DOWN, FLEECE, FLOCCUS, FLOCK, GARE, HAIR, YARN
wool cluster NEP
wool measure HEER
wool package FADGE
woolly LANATE, LANOSE
word ANAGRAM, LOGOS, PAROL(E), PLEDGE, RHEMA, TERM
work CHARE, CHORE, ERGON, FAG, JOB, LABOR, MOIL, PLY, OPUS, POTTER, SLAVE, STINT, TOIL, TRAVAIL
work unit ERG(ON), KILERG
workman ARRY, ARTISAN, CAGER, CREW, HAND, OPERANT, OPERATOR, PEON, ROTO, VOLK
workshop ATELIER, FACTORY, LAB, MILL, PLANT, STUDIO
world COSMOS, LOKA, UNIVERSE
World War I group AEF, AMEX, BEF
World War II area CBI, ETO, MTO
worldwide see UNIVERSAL
worldly CARNAL, LAIC, LAY, MORTAL, MUNDANE, SECULAR
World's Fair sites BRUSSELS, CHICAGO, GHENT, LONDON, MONTREAL, NEWYORK, OSAKA, PARIS, SEATTLE, VIENNA
worm CRAWL, CREEP, INCH, SINUATE; see p. 224
worm track NEREITE
worn(out) ATTRITE, EFFETE, EROSE, JADED, MAGGED, SHABBY, SPENT, USED
worry CARE, FRET, RUX; see VEX
worship ADORE, DULIA, HOMAGE, LATRIA, PUJA, REVERE, RITUAL
worst BEAT, BEST, ROUT
worthless BAFF, PALTRY, RACA, TRASHY
wound LESION, TRAUMA, VULN
wrangle BICKER, HAGGLE, HASSLE, ROW, SPAR, SPAT
wrap FURL, LAP, SWADDLE, SWATHE
wrapper ENVELOPE, TILLOT
wrath see ANGER
wreath CIRCLET, INFULA, TORSE; see GARLAND
wreckage FLOTSAM
wrest ELICIT, JERK, PLUCK, REND, TWIST, WRING, YANK
wrestle GRAPPLE, TUSSLE; see FIGHT
wrestling term BACKHEEL, CHANCERY, CHIP, CLICK, FALL, GRAPEVINE, HANK, HIPE, HITCH, HYPE, LOCK, MARE, NELSON, PIN, SCISSORS
wriggling EELY
wrinkle ANGLE, RIMPLE, RUGA(E), RUCK, SEAM
wrinkled RUGOSE, RUGOUS
wrist guard BRACER
writ BREVE, CAPE, CAPIAS, ELEGIT, MANDAMUS, PR(A)ECIPE, PROCESS, SUBPOENA, SUMMONS, TALES, VENIRE
write PEN, SCRAWL, SCRIVE
writer AUTHOR, CLERK, COPYIST, NOVELIST, PENMAN, POET, PROSER, SCRIBE
writing instrument PEN(CIL), PLUME, QUILL, SNORKEL, STYLE, STYLUS
wrong(s) MALA, MALUM, TORT

X

X-shaped CHIASMAL, CRUCIATE, XED
xylophone GAMELAN(G), GIGELIRA, MARIMBA, STICCADO, VIBRAHARP

Y

Y('s) WIES, YOGH, YOK
yam HOI, KAAWI, UBE, UBI, UVE, UVI
yang, opposite of YIN
yard GARTH, PATIO, QUAD, SPAR
yarn ABB, CREWEL, FOX, GARN, INKLE, KNOP, SLUB, SPINEL, THREAD, THRUM; see STORY
yarn count TYPP
yarn measure CLEW, CLUE, COP, HANK, HEER, LEA, RAP, SKEIN
yawn GANE, OSCITATE
year HAAB
yearly ANNUAL, ETESIAN, PERANNUM
yearn FLAG, HANKER, PINE
yeast ANAMITE, BARM, BEES, FERMENT, KOJI, LEAVEN, LOB
yellow ocher SIL
yelp KIYI, YA(U)P, YAWP, YIP, YOUP
yoga BHAKTI, HATHA, JNANA, KARMA
yoga trance DHARANA, DHYANA, SAMADHI
yogi JNANI, SWAMI; see ASCETIC
yoke part BOW, RIEM(PIE), SKEY
young animal COLT, CUB, FILLY, GILT, JOEY, PUP(PY), SHOAT, STOT, WHELP
youngster GOSSOON, MINOR, TEEN(AGER); see BOY, CHILD, GIRL
youthful BOYISH, GIRLISH, NEANIC

Z

Zal relative see RUSTAM
zeal ARDOR, ELAN, FERVOR, GUSTO, RELISH, ZEST, VERVE
zealot see FAN, FANATIC
zenith ACME, HEYDAY, PEAK
zenith, opposite of NADIR
Zeno follower STOIC
zero see CIPHER
zest TANG; see ZEAL
Zeus epithet AMMON, SOTER, TELEIOS
zinc BLENDE, SPELTER, TUTENAG
zipper TALON
Zola novel DEBACLE, GERMINAL, NANA, REVE, TERRE, VERITE
zone BELT, CLIME, TRACT
Zoroastrian MAZDAIST, PARSEE, PARSI

SECTION II: CATEGORIES

ANATOMY AND HEALTH

PARTS OF THE BODY

Head, Neck, Trunk, Limbs

ARM
EAR
EYE
GUM
HIP
JAW
LEG
LID
LIP
ORA
ORB
TOE

ARCH
BACK
BILE
BONE
BREE
BUMP
BUST
CALF
CELL
CHAP
CHIN
CRUS
CUSP
DERM
DUCT
FACE
FIST
FOOT
GYRI
HAIR
HAND
HEAD
HEEL
IRIS
JOWL
KNEE
LENS
LIMB
LOBE
LOIN
LOOF
MANO
NAIL
NAPE
NECK
NOSE
PALM
PONS
ROOT
RUMP
SHIN
SKIN
SOLE
TUBE
UVEA
VEIN
VOLA

ANKLE
BELLY
BLOOD
BOSOM
BRAIN
CANAL
CAPUT
CHEEK
CHEST
CILIA
CROWN
CUTIS
DERMA
DIGIT
ELBOW
FRONS
GLAND
GROIN
GYRUS
INDEX
INION
JOINT
LYMPH
MANUS
MOUTH
NARES
NERVE
NUCHA
NUQUE
ORGAN
OXTER
PELMA
PENIS
PINNA
PUPIL
RUGAE
SCALA
SERUM
SHANK
SINUS
THIGH
THUMB
TORSO
TRUNK
UVULA
VELUM
WAIST
WRIST

ANTRUM

ARMPIT
ARTERY
AXILLA
BASION
BREAST
BREGMA
CERVIX
CORIUM
CORNEA
CORTEX
DACTYL
DORSUM
EYELID
FACIES
FINGER
GULLET
HAUNCH
LABIUM
LOBULE
LUNULA
LUNULE
MARROW
MEATUS
MEDIUS
MENTUM
OCULUS
PALATE
PAUNCH
PLANTA
POLLEX
RETINA
RICTUS
SCRUFF
TEMPLE
THENAR
THORAX
THROAT

TONGUE
TRAGUS
TRIGON
VERTEX

ABDOMEN
AURICLE
EARDRUM
ENDERON
EYEBALL
EYEBROW
EYELASH
FOREARM
GINGIVA
LOBULUS
METOPON
NOSTRIL
OCCIPUT
PAPILLA
TOENAIL

ANTINION
BRACHIUM
CALLOSUM
CALVARIA
CEREBRUM
FOREHEAD
OLFACTOR
OMPHALOS
PHILTRUM
PLECTRUM
SHOULDER
SINCIPUT
UNDERLIP
UPPERLIP

EPIDERMIS

Bones

OS

HIP
RIB

DENS
FANG
OSSA
ULNA

AMBON
AMBOS
ANCON
ANKLE
ANVIL
BLADE
COSTA

FEMUR
HYOID
ILIUM
INCUS
MALAR
MEROS
MOLAR
NASAL
PUBIS
RAMUS
SKULL
SPINE
TALUS
TEETH
TIBBY
TIBIA
TOOTH

VOMER

BICEPS
CANINE
CARPUS
COCCYX
CUBOID
CUSPID
CUTTER
DENTAL
DENTIN
DIPLOE
FIBULA
HALLUX
INSTEP
LUMBAR
MAGNUM

PELVIS
RACHIS
RADIUS
ROTULA
SACRUM
SPLINT
STAPES
TARSUS
ZYGOMA

BONELET
CARPAEL
COCHLEA
CRANIUM
DENTINE
ETHMOID
FRONTAL

GRINDER
HAMATUM
HIPBONE
HUMERUS
INCISOR
ISCHIUM
JAWBONE
JUGULUM
KNEECAP
KNUCKLE
LUNATUM
MALLEUS
MASTOID
MAXILLA
OSSELET
OSSICLE
OTOLITH

PATELLA
PHALANX
SCAPULA
SCIATIC
STERNUM
TRICEPS
WORMIAN

BACKBONE

BICUSPID
CLAVICLE
EYETOOTH
HEELBONE
LACERTUS
LACRIMAL
OTOSTEON
PHALANGE

SCAPHOID
SHINBONE
SIDEBONE
SPHENOID
TEMPORAL
UNCIFORM
VERTEBRA

CALCANEUM
CARTILAGE
CHEEKBONE
CUNEIFORM
LACHRYMAL
OCCIPITAL
TRICUSPID
VERTEBRAE

Organs and Glands

COR
GALL
LUNG
MAZA
NEER
TEAT
WOMB
ALVUS
BOWEL
CALYX
CECUM
COLON
GLANS
HEART
HEPAR
ILEUM
LIVER

MAMMA
METRA
OVARY
VALVE
ATRIUM
BOWELS
CAECUM
CARDIA
CARPUS
KIDNEY
LARYNX
MATRIX
NIPPLE
PLEURA
PLEXUS
RECTUM
SPLEEN

THYMUS
TONSIL
URETER
UTERUS
VISCUS
BLADDER
ENTERON
FIMBRIA
JEJUNUM
OMENTUM
PAROTID
PHARYNX
PYLORUS
SIGMOID
STOMACH
THYROID
TRACHEA

VISCERA
APPENDIX
BRONCHUS
DUODENUM
ENTRAILS
PANCREAS
PLACENTA
PROSTATE
TONSILLA
WINDPIPE
DIAPHRAGM
ENDOCRINE
ESOPHAGUS
INTESTINE
LYMPHATIC
PITUITARY
VENTRICLE

Arteries, Muscles, Joints, Nerves, Veins

CAVA
COXA
DURA
GENU
KNEE
TELA
VEIN
VENA
AORTA
CHORD
PSOAS
SINEW
SPALD
TENDO
TENIA
TERES
VAGUS

WRIST
ARTERY
DUCTUS
FLEXOR
MYELON
RECTUS
SOLEUS
TAENIA
TENDON
TENSOR
VASTUS
VENULA
ARTERIA
ARTHRON
CANINUS
CAROTID

DELTOID
DILATOR
ERECTOR
GLUTEUS
ILIACUS
JUGULAR
LEVATOR
MIDRIFF
NASALIS
ABDUCTOR
ADDUCTOR
EXTENSOR
GANGLION
LIGAMENT
MAMMILLA
MANDIBLE

MASSETTE
MENTALIS
MUSCULUS
PALMARIS
PECTORAL
PERONEUS
RISORIUS
SCALENUS
SERRATUS
SPINALIS
SPLENIUS
VENACAVA
LABYRINTH
SARTORIUS
SPHINCTER
TRAPEZIUS

DISEASES AND ACHES

POX
STY
TIC
UTA

ACNE
AGUE
BLEB
BUBA
BUBO
COLD

COMA
CYST
GOUT
ITCH
LATA
PICA
PUNA
RASH
VETA
YAWS
ZONA

AGRIA
AGROM
ATAXY
BENDS
BLAIN
BUBAS
BULLA
CAUMA
CHILL
COLIC
COUGH

CROUP
DINUS
EDEMA
FAINT
FAVUS
FEVER
GLEET
HIVES
INOMA
KAKKE
LEPRA

LUPUS
LYSSA
MANGE
MANIA
MUMPS
MYOMA
NENTA
NGANA
PALSY
PILES
POLIO
POLYP
PSORA
RAMEX
RHEUM
SHOCK
SPASM
SPRUE
TABES
TINEA
TUMOR
ULCER
ULCUS
UREDO

ABASIA
ABULIA
AINHUM
ALALIA
ALBUGO
ALEXIA
ALPHOS
ANEMIA
ANEPIA
ANGINA
ANOPIA
APHTHA
ASONIA
ASTHMA
ATAXIA
BRUISE
BUNION
CALIGO
CANCER
CANKER
CHILLS
CHOREA
COMEDO
CORYZA
COWPOX
CRAMPS
DENGUE
DROPSY
ECZEMA
EMESIS
GLIOMA
GOITER
GRIPPE
HERNIA
HERPES
HYDROA
IRITIS
LIPOMA
MACULA
MEGRIM
MYOPIA
NAUSEA
OMITIS
OTITIS
PALMUS
PESTIS
PIITIS
PLAGUE
PTOSIS
QUINSY
RABIES
SCURVY
SEPSIS
SPRAIN
STRUMA
SYCOMA
TETANY
TETTER
THRUSH
TUSSIS
TYPHUS
ULITIS
UREMIA
ZOSTER

ABSCESS
ACHOLIA
ADIPOMA
ALGESIA
ALLERGY
AMENTIA
AMNESIA
ANAPHIA
ANGIOMA
ANOPSIA
APHAGIA
APHASIA
APHONIA
APHORIA
ASTASIA
ATROPHY
BLISTER
CAISSON
CATARRH
CHOLERA
COLITIS
EARACHE
EMPYEMA
FIBROMA
FISTULA
HICCUPS
ICTERUS
ILEITIS
ISCHIAS
LEPROSY
LINITIS
LOCKJAW
LUMBAGO
MADNESS
MALARIA
MEASLES
MOROSIS
MYCOSIS
OSTEOMA
OSTEOME
OSTITIS
OTALGIA
PARESIS
PINKEYE
PODAGRA
POLYPUS
PRURIGO
PURPURA
RENITIS
RICKETS
ROSEOLA
RUBELLA
RUPTURE
SARCOMA
SCABIES
SPASMUS
STREMMA
SYCOSIS
TERTIAN
TETANIA
TETANUS
TORMINA
TOXEMIA
TRISMUS
TYPHOID
UVEITIS
VARIOLA
VERTIGO
WRYNECK

ACIDOSIS
ADENOIDS
AKINESIA
ALASTRIM
ALLERGIA
ALOPECIA
BERIBERI
BOTULISM
BURSITIS
CARDITIS
CATARACT
COPHOSIS
CORONARY
DEAFNESS
DEMENTIA
DIABETES
DIARRHEA
DIPLOPIA
DISCITIS
DIURESIS
EMBOLIUM
EPILEPSY
ERYTHEMA
EXANTHEM
FRACTURE
GANGRENE
GLAUCOMA
HEADACHE
HEMATOME
HOOKWORM
HYSTERIA
IMPETIGO
INSANITY
INSOMNIA
JAUNDICE
LEUKEMIA
LORDOSIS
MELANOMA
MIGRAINE
MYELITIS
MYOSITIS
MYXODEMA
NECROSIS
NEURITIS
NEUROSIS
OBTUSION
PARANOIA
PARAPHIA
PELLAGRA
PHLEGMON
PHTHISIS
PINWORMS
PLEURISY
PRURITUS
PYORRHEA
RACHITIS
RHINITIS
RINGWORM
SCIATICA
SHINGLES
SMALLPOX
STENOSIS
SYPHILIS
TAPEWORM
TOXAEMIA
TRACHOMA
VITILIGO

ARMS AND ARMOR

ARMS

Cannon and Gun

* Indicates gun

DAG*
GAT
ROD*
BREN*
COLT*
HAIK*
HAKE*
IRON*
KRAG
ROER*
STEN
ASPIC
BARIL*
DRAKE
LUGER*
MAXIM*
MINIE*
MOYEN
RIFLE*
SAKER
BARKER*
BERTHA
CULVER
DRAGON*
FALCON
FOWLER
HEATER*
JEZAIL*
JINGAL*
LICORN
MAUSER*
MINNIE
MORTAR
MUSKET*
PISTOL*
POMPOM
ROSCOE*
TREPAN
TUPERA*
BASTARD
BAZOOKA
BOMBARD
BULLDOG*
CARBINE*
DUNGEON*
GATLING*
HACKBUT
LANTACA
LOMBARD
MOYENNE
ROBINET
SHOTGUN*
TEREBRA
UNICORN
CULVERIN
FIRELOCK*
HOWITZER
PISTOLET*
TROMBONE*
AUTOMATIC*
CARRONADE
DERRINGER*
HARQUEBUS*
VEUGLAIRE
ZUMBOORUK
HARQUEBUSE*
SERPENTINE
BLUNDERBUSS*

Sword and Dagger

* Indicates dagger

SAX
BOLO
CHIV
CRIS*
DIRK*
EPEE
FALX
FOIL
KRIS
PATA
SEAX
TURK
BALAS*
BILBO
BOWIE
BRAND
CATAN
DIEGO
ESTOC
KATAR*
KUKRI
SABER
SKEAN*
ANDREW
ANLACE*
BANCAL
BARONG
BODKIN*
CREESE*
DUSACK
FLORET
GLAIVE
KHANDA
MACANA
PARANG
RAPIER
SPATHA
STYLET*
TOLEDO
VERDUN
WAFTER
BAYONET*
CUTLASS
ESPADON
ESTOQUE
FERRARA
KHANJAR*
MACHETE
PONIARD*
SLASHER
YASHMAC
BASELARD
CLAYMORE
DAMASCUS
FALCHION
SCHLAGER
SCIMITAR
STILETTO*
YATAGHAN
EXCALIBUR
SCHIAVONE
MISERICORDE*
SNICKERSNEE*

Club

KIRI
MACE
MERE
PATU
POLT
BILLY
STAFF
STICK
WADDY
CUDGEL
LIBBET
MACANA
MARREE
NULLAH
TAIAHA
BLUDGEON
BLACKJACK
BOOMERANG
KNOBKERRIE
SHILLALAH
TRUNCHEON
MAQUAHUITL
POGAMOGGAN
MORGENSTERN

Axe

BILL
CELT
HACHE
ONCIN
FASCES
MACANA
POLEAX
BOUCHER
HALBERD
TWIBILL
FRANCISC
LOCHABER
PARTISAN
TOMAHAWK

Bow and Arrow

* Indicates arrow

BOLT*	VIRE*	LONGBOW	CROSSBOW
DART*	ROVER*	QUARREL	MANGONEL
REED*	SHAFT*	ARBALEST	SUMPITAN*
RODD	ONAGER	BALLISTA	TREBUCHET
SELF*	SUMPIT*	CATAPULT	

Missile

BALL	ATLATL
BOLA	BULLET
BOLT	DUMDUM
BOMB	PELLET
DART	WOMERA
SHOT	GRENADE
SLUG	OUTCAST
GRAPE	TORPEDO
KILEY	SHRAPNEL
SHAFT	BOOMERANG
SHELL	PROJECTILE

Spear

DART	GIDGEE
FRAM	GLAIVE
PIKE	ASSAGAI
ACLYS	BAYONET
LANCE	BOURDON
ONCIN	HARPOON
PILUM	JAVELIN
SHAFT	LEISTER
VOUGE	TRIDENT
ATLATL	VERUTUM
ERAMEA	GAVELOCK

ARMOR

Full Suit

BARD	BARDE	JAZERANT	BRIGANDINE
MAIL	CUIRASS	PLACCATE	CATAPHRACT
WEED	PANOPLY		

Body

TACE	LORICA	SURCOAT	PLASTRON
ACTON	TASSET	DEMISUIT	BRAGUETTE
CULET	TONLET	DOSSIERE	ECREVISSE
TASSE	BROIGNE	GAMBESON	HABERGEON
BYRNIE	HAUBERK	PANSIERE	MAMELIERE
CORIUM	LAMBOYS		

Head and Neck

COIF	CASQUE	SECRET	BURGONET
HELM	GALERA	BASINET	CABASSET
ARMET	GORGET	GALERUM	GORGERIN
GALEA	HEAUME	GALERUS	COIFFETTE
VISOR	HELMET	VENTAIL	MENTONIERE
BEAVER	MORION	AVENTAIL	CERVELIERE
CAMAIL	SALLET		

Shoulder to Hand

ARMLET	VAMBRACE
AILETTE	CUBITIERE
ROUNDEL	EPAULIERE
BRASSARD	GARDEBRAS
BRASSART	REREBRACE
GAUNTLET	PASSEGARDE
PAULDRON	

Thigh to Foot

JAMB	CHAUSSE
CUISH	JAMBEAU
JAMBE	PALLETTE
CUISSE	SABBATON
GREAVE	SOLLERET
TUILLE	GENOUILLERE

THE BIBLE

BOOKS OF THE OLD TESTAMENT

King James Version	Abbr.	Douay Version	Abbr.
1. GENESIS	GEN	GENESIS	GEN
2. EXODUS	EX(OD)	EXODUS	EX(OD)
3. LEVITICUS	LEV(IT)	LEVITICUS	LEV(IT)
4. NUMBERS	NUM(B)	NUMBERS	NUM(B)
5. DEUTERONOMY	DEUT	DEUTERONOMY	DEUT
6. JOSHUA	JOS(H)	JOSUE	JOS
7. JUDGES	JUD(G)	JUDGES	JUD(G)
8. RUTH		RUTH	
9. SAMUEL I	SAM(L)	KINGS I	KI, KGS
10. SAMUEL II	SAM(L)	KINGS II	KI, KGS
11. KINGS I	KI, KGS	KINGS III	KI, KGS
12. KINGS II	KI, KGS	KINGS IV	KI, KGS
13. CHRONICLES I	CHRON	PARALIPOMENON I	PAR
14. CHRONICLES II	CHRON	PARALIPOMENON II	PAR
15. EZRA	EZ(R)	ESDRAS I	ESD
16. NEHEMIAH	NEH	ESDRAS II	NEH
17. ESTHER	ES(TH)	ESTHER	ES(TH)
18. JOB		JOB	
19. PSALMS	PS(A)	PSALMS	PS(A)
20. PROVERBS	PROV	PROVERBS	PROV
21. ECCLESIASTES	ECCL(ES)	ECCLESIASTES	ECCL(ES)
22. SONG OF SOLOMON	S OF SOL	CANTICLE OF CANTICLES	CANT
23. ISAIAH	IS(A)	ISAIAS	IS(A)
24. JEREMIAH	JER	JEREMIAS	JER
25. LAMENTATIONS	LAM	LAMENTATIONS	LAM
26. EZEKIEL	EZEK	EZECHIEL	EZECH
27. DANIEL	DAN(L)	DANIEL	DAN(L)
28. HOSEA	HOS	OSEE	
29. JOEL	JL, JO	JOEL	JL, JO
30. AMOS		AMOS	
31. OBADIAH	OB(AD)	ABDIAS	
32. JONAH		JONAS	
33. MICAH	MIC	MICHEAS	MICH
34. NAHUM	NAH	NAHUM	NAH
35. HABAKKUK	HAB	HABACUC	HAD
36. ZEPHANIAH	ZEPH	SOPHONIAS	SOPH
37. HAGGAI	HAG	AGGEUS	AGG
38. ZECHARIAH	ZECH	ZACHARIAS	ZACH
39. MALACHI	MAL	MALACHIAS	MAL

APOCRYPHA

* Indicates books in Douay Version

TOBIT
BARUCH*
ESDRAS I, II
ESDRAS III, IV*
ESTHER*
JUDITH*
SIRACH
TOBIAS

WISDOM*
SUSANNA
MACHABEES I, II*
ECCLESIASTICUS*
BELANDTHEDRAGON
PRAYEROFMANASSES
SUSANNAANDTHEELDERS
SONGOFTHETHREECHILDREN

BOOKS OF THE NEW TESTAMENT

	Abbr.
MATTHEW	MAT(T)
MARK	
LUKE	
JOHN	
THE ACTS	ACTS
ROMANS	ROM
CORINTHIANS I	COR
CORINTHIANS II	COR
GALATIANS	GAL
EPHESIANS	EPH(ES)
PHILIPPIANS	PHIL
COLOSSIANS	COL(OSS)
THESSALONIANS I	THESS
THESSALONIANS II	THESS
TIMOTHY I	TIM
TIMOTHY II	TIM
TITUS	TIT
PHILEMON	PHIL(EM)
HEBREWS	HEB(R)
JAMES	JA(S)
PETER I	PET
PETER II	PET
JOHN I	
JOHN II	
JOHN III	
JUDE	
REVELATION	REV

Note: All names as given above are also used in the Douay Version with the exception of Revelation, therein named APOCALYPSE (APOC).

BIBLICAL RULERS

OG
ASA
GOG
PUL
TOU
AGAG
AHAB
AHAZ
AMON
BERA
DOEG
ELAH
JEHU
NERO
OMRI
OREB
REBA
SAUL
AHIRA
BALAK
CYRUS
DAVID
HAMOR
HEROD
HIRAM
HOHAM
JABIN
JOASH
JOBAB
JORAM
MESHA
NADAB
PEKAH
PIRAM
REKEM
REZIN
REZON
SIHON
ZEBAH
ZIMRI
ABIJAH
ACHISH
ARETAS
BAASHA
CAESAR
DARIUS
HAZAEL
HEZION
HOSHEA
JOAHAZ
JOSIAH
JOSUAH
JOTHAM
LEMUEL
NAHASH
NECHOR
SARGON
SHINAB
SISERA
UZZIAH
AHAZIAH
AMAZIAH
JOHORAM
MENAHEM
PEKAIAH
SHALLUM
SHISHAK
SOLOMON
ATHALIAH
HEZEKIAH
HYRCANUS
JEROBOAM
REHOBOAM
SHESHONK
ZEDEKIAH

PRIESTS

ELI
IRA
EZRA
AARON
ANNAS
URIAH
ZADOK
ELIJAH
JADDUA
JOIADA
JOSHUA
SAMUEL
ALCIMUS
ANANIAS
ELEAZAR
HILIKAH
JOHANAN
JOIAKIM
SERAIAH
ABIATHAR
CAIAPHAS
ELIASHIB
JEHOIADA
AHIMELECH
ZEPHANIAH

PATRIARCHS

DAN	NOAH	PELEG	ISHMAEL
GAD	SETH	SERUG	JAPHETH
HAM	SHEM	TERAH	ZEBULUN
REU	ASHER	CAINAN	ARPHAXAD
CAIN	ENOCH	CANAAN	BENJAMIN
EBER	ISAAC	JOKTAN	ISSACHAR
ENOS	JACOB	JOSEPH	MAHALEEL
ESAU	JARED	LAMECH	MEHUJAEL
HETH	JUDAH	REUBEN	NAPHTALI
IRAD	KENAN	SIMEON	METHUSAEL
LEVI	NAHOR	ABRAHAM	METHUSELAH

PROPHETS

Major	Minor		Others
DANIEL	AMOS	HAGGAI	JEHU
ISAIAH	JOEL	MALACHI	MOSES
EZEKIEL	HOSEA	OBADIAH	ELIJAH
JEREMIAH	JONAH	HABAKKUK	ELISHA
	MICAH	ZECHARIAH	NATHAN
	NAHUM	ZEPHANIAH	SAMUEL

BIBLICAL NAMES

AHI	LAEL	ALVAN	LYCIA
BUZ	MARA	BEZER	MAHLI
ABBA	NAUM	CUSHI	REAIA
ABDA	OBAL	ETHAM	REUEL
AIAH	OBIL	HADAD	SARID
BELA	OREN	HADID	SHEAL
ERAN	PUAH	HAGAB	SILAS
ESLI	REBA	HAGGI	SIRAH
EZER	SEBA	HAMUL	TALAH
EZRI	SHOA	ISHOD	TIRIA
HORI	SUAH	ISHUI	UPHAZ
IDDO	UCAL	JAPHO	URIEL
IRAM	ADLAI	JARAD	ZABAD
ISUI	AHBAN	JERAH	ZAHAM
IVAH	AHLAI	KEDAR	ZELAH

QUEENS, QUEEN-MOTHERS

ABI	ZIBIAH	JERUSHA	NEHUSHTA
AZUBAH	AHINOAM	JEZEBEL	TAHPENES
ESTHER	BERNICE	MAACHAH	BATHSHEBA
NAAMAH	CANDACE	ZEBUDAH	JECHOLIAH
VASHTI	HAMUTAL	ATHALIAH	JEOHADDAM
ZERUAH	JEDIDAH	DRUSILLA	

TRIBES OF ISRAEL

Sons of Jacob	Mother	Sons of Jacob	Mother
DAN	Bilhah	REUBEN	Leah
GAD	Zilpah	SIMEON	Leah
LEVI	Leah	ZEBULUN	Leah
ASHER	Zilpah	BENJAMIN	Rachel
JUDAH	Leah	ISSACHAR	Leah
JOSEPH	Rachel	NAPHTALI	Bilhah

TRIBES

DAN
GAD
KIR
LUD
CUSH
EDOM
LEVI
MOAB
PHUT
SHOA
UZAL
ASHER
DUMAH
EMIMS
JUDAH
LUBIM
MEDES
MINNI
ANAKIM
ARKITE
HAMITE
HIVITE
HORITE
JOSEPH
KENITE
LEVITE
REUBEN
SEMITE
SIMEON
SINITE
AMORITE
DINAITE
DODANIM
EDOMITE
HITTITE
MINAEAN
MITANNI
MOABITE
REPHAIM
RODANIM
SABAEAN
ZEBULUN
BENJAMIN
GADARINE
ISSACHAR
MIRARITE
NAPHTALI
NAZARITE
CANAANITE
SAMARITAN
SHELANITE

JUDGES

ELI
EHUD
ELON
JAIR
TOLA
ABDON
BARAK
IBZAN
GIDEON
SAMSON
SAMUEL
DEBORAH
OTHNIEL
SHAMGAR
JEPHTHAH
ABIMELECH

WOMAN CHURCH WORKERS

LOIS
CHLOE
JULIA
LYDIA
PHEBE
RHODA
APPHIA
DORCAS
EUNICE
JOANNA
PERSIS
CLAUDIA
EUODIAS
SUSANNA
SAPPHIRA
SYNTYCHE
TRYPHENA
TRYPHOSA
PRISCILLA

APOSTLES AND DISCIPLES

JOHN	brother of James
JUDE	
LEVI	= MATTHEW
JAMES	brother of John
JAMES	
JUDAS	= JUDE
JUDAS	ISCARIOT
PETER	brother of Andrew
SIMON	= PETER
SIMON	the Canaanite or the Zealot
ANDREW	brother of Peter
CEPHAS	= PETER
PHILIP	
THOMAS	DIDYMUS
MATTHEW	
MATTHIAS	Judas' successor
THADDAEUS	= JUDE
BARTHOLOMEW	Nathanael

BIBLICAL TOWNS

DAN
LUZ
NOB
ONO
CANA
ETAM
GATH
GAZA
MAON
MARI
MYRA
TYRE
ZOAR
ACCAD
ARDER
BABEL
BARIS
BEREA
CALAH
DEBIR
DERBE
ELATH
ENDOR
ERECH
GEBAL
GERAR
GOLAN
HAZOR
JEBUS
JOPPA
PERGA
RESEN
SIDOM
SODOM
TROAS
ASHDOD
BETHEL
CYRENE
DOTHAN
EMMAUS
GADARA
GIBEAH
HEBRON
IBLEAM
KENATH
LIBNAH
MEDEBA
MIGDOL
PAPHOS
PISHON
RIBLAH
SARDIS
SHILOH
TARSUS
ANTIOCH
ASCALON
BABYLON
BEEROTH
BETHANY
CORINTH
EPHESUS
JERICHO
MEGIDDA
NINEVEH
ASHKALON
CAESAREA
NAZARETH
TIBERIAS

BIBLICAL SITES, MOUNTAINS, LANDS

Sites		Lands	Mountains
UR	AJALON	NOD	HOR
LUD	ATHLIT	EDOM	EBAL
TOB	BASHAN	ELAM	NEBO
ARAM	BOZRAH	MOAB	PEOR
EDEN	ENGEDI	SABA	SEIR
ELAH	HINNOM	EDREI	ZION
ELIM	KADESH	EKRON	HOREB
NAIN	KIDRON	JUDAH	MIZAR
SHUR	LAGASH	MYSIA	SENIR
AENON	MASSAH	PELLA	SINAI
GEZER	MIZPAH	SUMER	TABOR
HALAH	SHARON	ZOBAH	ARARAT
MOREH	BAALBEK	CANAAN	CARMEL
NEGEB	CALVARY	GOSHEN	HERMON
OPHIR	GALILEE	TADMOR	PISGAH
PARAN	GEHENNA	LEBANON	THANACH
SIRAH	SHITTIM		
	BETHESDA		

FAMILY RELATIONS

Father	Offspring
ELI	Hophni, Phinehas
HAM	Cush, Phut
JOB	Jemima, Kezia
NER	Abner
NUN	Joshua
ADAM	Abel, Cain, Seth
AHAB	Athaliah
AHAZ	Helekiah
AMON	Josiah
ARAM	Mash
BOAZ	Obed
BUZI	Ezekiel
CAIN	Enoch
CUSH	Nimrod
EBER	Peleg, Joktan
ELON	Bashemath, Adah
ESAU	Korah, Anah
JONA	Peter
KISH	Saul
LEVI	Gershon, Jochebed
NOAH	Ham, Shem, Japheth
OBED	Jesse
SAUL	Jonathan, Merab, Michal
SEIR	Timna
SETH	Enos
SHEM	Aram, Eber
SODI	Gaddiel
AARON	Nadab, Adihu, Eleazar, Ithamar
ABIEL	Kish, Ner
AMRAM	Aaron, Moses, Miriam
ASHER	Ara
BEERI	Judith
CALEB	Achsah
DAVID	Solomon, Tamar, Absalom, Amnon, Adonijah, Ithream, Maacah
ELIAM	Bathsheba
ENOCH	Methuselah, Irad
HARAN	Lot, Milcah, Ischa
HEBER	Shuah
HEROD	Antipas
ISAAC	Jacob, Esau
ITHRA	Amasa
JACOB	See Tribes of Israel; Dinah
JAMES	Jude
JARED	Enoch
JESSE	David, Abigail
JOASH	Gideon
JONAS	Peter
JUDAH	Er
LABAN	Leah, Rachel
MOSES	Gershom, Eliezer
NAHOR	Terah, Maacah, Huz
SERUG	Nahor
SIMON	Judas
TERAH	Haran, Abraham
ADAIAH	Jedidah
GILEAD	Jephthah
JETHRO	Zipporah
JOKTAN	Obal, Ebal
JOSEPH	Manasseh, Ephraim; Jesus, James, Jude
LAMECH	Noah, Naamah, Jabal, Jubal, Tubalcain
MACHIR	Gilead
MANOAH	Samson
PHAREZ	Tamar
SALMON	Boaz
SAMUEL	Abiah
TALMAI	Maacah
ABRAHAM	Isaac, Ishmael
ABSALOM	Maacah

Father	Offspring
DIBLAIM	Gomer
ELKANAH	Samuel
ETHBAAL	Jezebel
ISHMAEL	Massa
SHAPHAT	Elisha
SOLOMON	Rehoboam
ZEBEDEE	James, John
ALPHAEUS	James
HERODIAS	Salome
JEREMIAH	Hamutal
REHOBOAM	Abija
ZECHARIAH	Abi
METHUSELAH	Lamech

Mother	Offspring
ABI	Hezekiah
EVE	Abel, Cain, Seth
ADAH	Jabal, Jubal
ANNA	Mary
JAEL	Shua
LEAH	See Tribes of Israel; Dinah
LOIS	Eunice
MARY	Jesus; James, Joses
RUTH	Obed
ABIAH	Ashur
EGLAH	Ithream
HAGAR	Ishmael
NAOMI	Mahlon; Chilion
RAHAB	Boaz
SARAH	Isaac
TAMAR	Pharez
TIMNA	Amalek
ABITAL	Shephatiah
BILHAH	See Tribes of Israel
EUNICE	Timothy
HANNAH	Samuel
JUDITH	Korah
MAACAH	Asa; Absalom; Abijah
MILCAH	Haran; Rebekah, Huz
NAAMAH	Rehoboam
RACHEL	See Tribes of Israel
SALOME	James, John
TALMAI	Maachah, Absalom
ZERUAH	Jeroboam
ZIBIAH	Joash
ZILLAH	Naamah
ZILPAH	See Tribes of Israel
ABIGAIL	Amasa
AHINOAM	Jonathan, Amnon, Merab, Michal
HAMUTAL	Zedekiah
JEDIDAH	Josiah
JEZEBEL	Athaliah, Jehoram
REBECAH	Esau, Jacob
REBEKAH	Leah, Rachel
ZERUIAH	Joab, Asahel, Abishai
ATHALIAH	Ahaziah
JOCHEBED	Moses, Aaron, Miriam
ZIPPORAH	Gershom, Eliezer
BATHSHEBA	Solomon

Wife	Husband
ABI	Ahaz
ADAH	Lamech; Esau
ANAH	Esau
JAEL	Heber
LEAH	Jacob
MARY	Joseph, Cleophas
RUTH	Mahlon; Boaz
ABIAH	Hezron
EGLAH	David
EPHAH	Caleb
GOMER	Hosea
HAGAR	Abraham
HELAH	Ashur
MERAB	Adriel
NAOMI	Elimelech
ORPAH	Chilion
RAHAB	Salmon
SARAH	Abraham
SARAI	Abram
TAMAR	Er, Onan, Judah
ABITAL	David
AZUBAH	Asa; Caleb
BILHAH	Jacob
ESTHER	Ahasuerus
HANNAH	Elkanah
JUDITH	Esau
MAACAH	David; Rehoboam
MICHAL	Phalti; David
MILCAH	Nahor
MIRIAM	Hur
RACHEL	Jacob
RIZPAH	Saul
SALOME	Zebedee
VASHTI	Ahasuerus
ZERESH	Haman
ZIBIAH	Ahaziah
ZILLAH	Lemech
ZILPAH	Jacob
ABIGAIL	Nabal; David; Ithra
ABIHAIL	Rehoboam
AHINOAM	Saul; David
ASENATH	Joseph
CLAUDIA	Pilate
DEBORAH	Lapidoth
HAGGITH	David
HAMUTAL	Josiah
JEDIDAH	Amon
JEZEBEL	Ahab
KETURAH	Abraham
REBEKAH	Isaac
ELISHEBA	Aaron
HADASSAH	= ESTHER
HERODIAS	Herod
JOCHEBED	Amram
SAPPHIRA	Ananias
ZIPPORAH	Moses
BASHEMATH	Esau
BATHSHEBA	Uriah; David
AHOLIBAMAH	Esau

CHEMICAL ELEMENTS

Element	Symbol	Source
TIN	Sn	cassiterite
GOLD	Au	sylvanite
IRON	Fe	hematite
LEAD	Pb	galena
NEON	Ne	atmosphere
ZINC	Zn	sphalerite
ARGON	Ar or A	atmosphere
BORON	B	borax
RADON	Rn	radium
XENON	Xe	atmosphere
BARIUM	Ba	barite
CARBON	C	graphite
CERIUM	Ce	monazite
CESIUM	Cs	pollucite
COBALT	Co	smaltite
COPPER	Cu	cuprite
CURIUM	Cm	plutonium
ERBIUM	Er	gadolinite
HELIUM	He	natural gas
INDIUM	In	sphalerite
IODINE	I	Chile saltpeter
NICKEL	Ni	nickelite
OSMIUM	Os	iridosmine
OXYGEN	O	atmosphere
RADIUM	Ra	pitchblende
SILVER	Ag	argentite
SODIUM	Na	Chile saltpeter
SULFUR	S	limestone
ARSENIC	As	orpiment
BISMUTH	Bi	bismite
BROMINE	Br	sea water
CADMIUM	Cd	zinc ores
CALCIUM	Ca	gypsum
FERMIUM	Fm	plutonium
GALLIUM	Ga	bauxite
HAFNIUM	Hf	zircon
HOLMIUM	Ho	gadolinite
IRIDIUM	Ir	iridosmine
KRYPTON	Kr	atmosphere
LITHIUM	Li	spodumene
MERCURY	Hg	cinnabar
NIOBIUM	Nb	columbite
RHENIUM	Re	molybdenite
RHODIUM	Rh	platinum ores
SILICON	Si	silica
SULPHUR		= SULFUR
TERBIUM	Tb	monazite
THORIUM	Th	thorite
THULIUM	Tm	rare earth
URANIUM	U	pitchblende
WOLFRAM	W	= TUNGSTEN
YTTRIUM	Y	rare earth
ACTINIUM	Ac	pitchblende
ALUMINUM	Al	bauxite

Element	Symbol	Source
ANTIMONY	Sb	stibnite
ASTATINE	At	bismuth
CHLORINE	Cl	salt
CHROMIUM	Cr	chromite
EUROPIUM	Eu	monazite
FLUORINE	F	fluorite
FRANCIUM	Fr	actinium
HYDROGEN	H	atmosphere
LUTETIUM	Lu	rare earth
NITROGEN	N	sodium nitrate
NOBELIUM	No	curium
PLATINUM	Pt	alluvial
POLONIUM	Po	pitchblende
RUBIDIUM	Rb	pollucite
SAMARIUM	Sm	monazite
SCANDIUM	Sc	monazite
SELENIUM	Se	clausthalite
TANTALUM	Ta	tantalite
THALLIUM	Tl	crookesite
TITANIUM	Ti	rutile
TUNGSTEN	W	scheelite
VANADIUM	V	vanadinite
AMERICIUM	Am	uranium
BERKELIUM	Bk	americium
BERYLLIUM	Be	beryl
COLUMBIUM	Cb	= **NIOBIUM**
GERMANIUM	Ge	germanite
LANTHANUM	La	rare earth
MAGNESIUM	Mg	magnesite
MANGANESE	Mn	pyrolusite
NEODYMIUM	Nd	monazite
NEPTUNIUM	Np	uranium
PALLADIUM	Pd	gold ores
PLUTONIUM	Pu	pitchblende
POTASSIUM	K	potassium chloride
RUTHENIUM	Ru	iridosmine
STRONTIUM	Sr	celestite
TELLURIUM	Te	sylvanite
YTTERBIUM	Yb	rare earth
ZIRCONIUM	Zr	zircon
DYSPROSIUM	Dy	rare earth
GADOLINIUM	Gd	gadolinite
LAWRENCIUM	Lw	artificial
MOLYBDENUM	Mo	molybdenite
PHOSPHORUS	P	apatite
PROMETHIUM	Pm	rare earth
TECHNETIUM	Tc	uranium
CALIFORNIUM	Cf	curium
EINSTEINIUM	Es or E	plutonium
MENDELEVIUM	Md or Mv	einsteinium
PRASEODYMIUM	Pr	rare earth
PROTACTINIUM	Pa	uranium

COLLEGES

COE
MIT
NYU
VMI
VPI
CASE
DREW
DUKE
FENN
RICE
UCLA
YALE
BATES
BEREA
BROWN
CLARK
COLBY
DRAKE
DRURY
EMORY
LORAS
PRATT
RIDER
SMITH
TUFTS
AUSTIN
BAYLOR
BRYANT
BUTLER

CALVIN
DEPAUL
DEPAUW
DREXEL
FURMAN
GANNON
HARPUR
HOBART
HOWARD
HUNTER
LEHIGH
LOYOLA
MCGILL
MERCER
MORGAN
OLIVET
POMONA
PURDUE
TEMPLE
TULANE
UPSALA
VASSAR
WAGNER
XAVIER
ADELPHI
AMHERST
ANDREWS
ANTIOCH
BARNARD

BENTLEY
BETHANY
BOWDOIN
BRADLEY
CHAPMAN
CITADEL
COLGATE
CORNELL
DENISON
FORDHAM
GONZAGA
GOUCHER
HAMPTON
HARVARD
HOFSTRA
LASALLE
MCMURRY
NEWCOMB
OBERLIN
PARSONS
RUTGERS
STJOHNS
SIMMONS
STETSON
STEVENS
SUFFOLK
TRINITY
WILLIAM
YESHIVA

ALBRIGHT
AUGSBURG
BOBJONES
BRANDEIS
BRYNMAWR
BUCKNELL
CANISIUS
CARLETON
CARNEGIE
COLUMBIA
DUQUESNE
FRANKLIN
GRINNELL
HAMILTON
LAWRENCE
LYCOMING
MARSHALL
MARYWOOD
MILLIKEN
SKIDMORE
STANFORD
STEPHENS
WARTBURG
WASHBURN
WESLEYAN
WILLIAMS
WINTHROP
WOODBURY

COLLEGE NICKNAMES

DONS
ELIS
EPHS
NAVY
OWLS
RAMS
TARS
UTES
VOLS
ZIPS
BEARS
BULLS
DUKES
FORDS
HAWKS
HOYAS
LIONS
LOBOS
MULES
AGGIES
BIGRED
BISONS
BRAVES
BRUINS
CADETS
EAGLES
EPHMEN
FLYERS
FRIARS
GATORS

ILLINI
JUMBOS
REBELS
REDMEN
SAXONS
TIGERS
TITANS
UCLANS
BADGERS
BEAVERS
BENGALS
BOBCATS
BONNIES
BRONCOS
BULLETS
COUGARS
COWBOYS
DRAGONS
FALCONS
GOPHERS
HUSKIES
INDIANS
KEYDETS
LARRIES
MAROONS
PIRATES
QUAKERS
ROCKETS
SOONERS
SPIDERS

TARTANS
TROJANS
VANDALS
VIKINGS
VIOLETS
BEARCATS
BLUEHENS
BLUEJAYS
BUCKEYES
BULLDOGS
COLONELS
CYCLONES
DUTCHMEN
GENERALS
GOBBLERS
GRIFFINS
HAWKEYES
HOOSIERS
HORSEMEN
KINGSMEN
LEOPARDS
MARINERS
MUSTANGS
PANTHERS
PIONEERS
RAMBLERS
REDSKINS
SEAHAWKS
SHOCKERS
SPARTANS

TARHEELS
TERRIERS
WARRIORS
WEBFOOTS
WILDCATS
WOLFPACK
BILLIKENS
BUFFALOES
CARDINALS
CAVALIERS
COLONIALS
CRUSADERS
DIPLOMATS
ENGINEERS
EXPLORERS
GAMECOCKS
GREENWAVE
GRIZZLIES
HURRICANE
LONGHORNS
LORDJEFFS
MOCCASINS
ORANGEMEN
REDDEVILS
SEMINOLES
SIWASHERS
STATESMEN
SUNDEVILS
TERRAPINS

COLORS

ASH	gray
BAT	gray
BAY	brown
DOE	red/yellow
DUN	red/yellow
FOX	brown
IVY	green
JET	black
OAK	brown
RAT	yellow
RED	
SKY	blue
TAN	red/yellow
TEA	yellow/green
BARK	red/yellow
BICE	blue/green
BLUE	
BOLE	red/yellow
BRAN	red/yellow
BUFF	yellow/red
CLAY	yellow/red
CORK	brown
CORN	red/yellow
CUBA	brown
CYAN	blue
DEER	brown
DORE	yellow
DOVE	blue/gray
DRAB	brown
DUNE	red/yellow
DUSK	blue/red
DUST	red/yellow
EBON	black
ECRU	red/yellow
FAON	brown
FAWN	brown
FLAX	red/yellow
FLEA	red
GOLD	
GOYA	red
GRAY	
GULL	gray
HEBE	red
HOAR	gray
HOPI	brown
IRON	gray
JADE	green
LAKE	red
LAMA	brown
LAVA	yellow/red
LEAD	gray
LIME	yellow/red
MESA	brown
MILK	white
MOSS	green
MUSK	yellow/red
NAVY	blue
NILE	blue/green

NUDE	red/yellow
OPAL	varies
PINK	
PLUM	blue/red
PUCE	red
PURI	yellow
ROAN	yellow/red
ROSE	red
RUBY	red
RUST	red/yellow
SAGE	green
SAND	red/yellow
SAXE	blue
SEAL	brown
SIAM	brown
TEAK	brown
WINE	red
ZINC	blue/red
ACIER	gray
ACORN	red/yellow
AGATE	red/yellow
ALOMA	yellow/red
AMBER	yellow/red
ASHEN	gray
AZTEC	yellow/red
AZURE	blue
BAPHE	red
BEIGE	red/yellow
BERYL	blue/green
BLOND	yellow/red
BLUET	blue
BRICK	red/yellow
BROWN	
CACAO	red/yellow
CADET	blue
CAMEL	brown
CAMEO	varies
CEDAR	yellow/red
CEDRE	green
CHING	blue
COCOA	brown
CONGO	brown
CORAL	red
CREAM	red/yellow
DELFT	blue
DURRY	yellow
EMAIL	green/blue
EMBER	yellow/red
FAIRY	green
FLAME	red
FLESH	red/yellow
GREEN	
GYPSY	brown
HAZEL	brown
HENNA	brown
IVORY	white/yellow
KHAKI	brown
LEMON	yellow

LILAC	blue/red
LIVER	brown
MAIZE	yellow/red
MAPLE	red/yellow
MAUVE	blue/red
MELON	red/yellow
METAL	gray/blue
MOCHA	brown
MOUSE	gray
MUMMY	brown
NEGRO	brown
NIKKO	blue
OCHER	yellow
OLIVE	gray
PABLO	brown
PANSY	blue/red
PEACH	red/yellow
PEARL	gray/blue
PERSE	blue
PLOMB	gray
POPPY	red
PRUNE	blue/red
PUTTY	yellow/red
RAVEN	black
ROUGE	red
SABLE	black
SEDGE	brown
SEPIA	brown
SIENA	red
SIRUP	red/yellow
SLATE	blue/red
SMALT	blue
SNUFF	brown
SPRAY	blue/green
STEEL	gray
STRAW	red/yellow
SUDAN	red/yellow
SUEDE	brown
TAUPE	yellow
TAWNY	brown
TENNE	brown
TIVER	red
TOTEM	red/yellow
TWINE	red/yellow
UMBER	brown
VENUS	green

ACACIA	yellow
ACAJOU	brown
AFGHAN	yellow/red
ALESAN	red/yellow
ARGENT	white
AUBURN	red
AUTUMN	red/yellow
BEAVER	brown
BISTER	brown
BISTRE	brown
BRONZE	brown
CANARY	yellow
CANDID	white
CANNON	yellow/gray
CARROT	red/yellow
CASTOR	red/yellow
CERISE	red
CHERRY	red
CITRON	yellow
CLARET	red
COBALT	green/blue
COCHIN	brown
COFFEE	brown
CONDOR	brown
COPPER	brown
CYANIC	blue
DAHLIA	blue/red
DAMASK	red
DAMSON	blue/red
ERMINE	white
ESKIMO	brown
EVEQUE	blue/red
FALLOW	yellow
FUSTIC	yellow/red
GARNET	red
HATHOR	blue
HAVANA	brown
HUNTER	green
INDIGO	red/blue
JASPER	yellow/green
LIERRE	green
MADDER	blue/red
MALLOW	blue/red
MANILA	yellow/red
MARINE	blue
MAROON	brown
MASCOT	blue/red
MASTIC	yellow/red
MIKADO	red/yellow
MIMOSA	yellow
MINIUM	red
MODENA	blue/red
MOUSSE	green
MURREY	red
MYRTLE	green
NUTRIA	red/yellow
ONDINE	yellow/green
ORANGE	
ORCHID	blue/red
ORIENT	blue
ORIOLE	red/yellow
PAWNEE	red/yellow
PENSEE	blue/red
PONGEE	yellow/red
PURPLE	
PURREE	yellow
QUAKER	gray
RADDLE	red
RAISIN	blue/red
RESEDA	green
RUBRIC	red
RUDDLE	red/yellow
RUSSET	brown
SALMON	red/yellow
SEASAN	red/yellow
SEVRES	blue
SHRIMP	red
SIENNA	brown
SIERRA	red

SILVER	gray
SORREL	brown
STUCCO	red/yellow
SULFUR	yellow
SULTAN	red
TIFFIN	brown
TITIAN	red
TOMATO	red
TUSCAN	red
TYRIAN	blue/red
VESTAL	red/blue
VIOLET	
WALNUT	brown
YELLOW	
ZENITH	blue

ADMIRAL	blue
ANAMITE	red/yellow
ANEMONE	red/blue
ANNATTO	red/yellow
ANTIQUE	red/yellow
APRICOT	red/yellow
ARDOISE	red/blue
BEGONIA	red
BISCUIT	red/yellow
BITUMEN	brown
CALDRON	red
CARAIBE	brown
CARMINE	red
CELADON	green
CELESTE	blue
CHAMOIS	red/yellow
CITRINE	yellow
CORBEAU	green
CRIMSON	red
EMERALD	yellow/green
FEUILLE	brown
FILBERT	brown
FIREFLY	yellow/red
FUCHSIA	red
GAMBOGE	red/yellow
GLAIEUL	red
GOBELIN	blue
GRANITE	red
GRIZZLE	gray
HEATHER	blue/red
JONQUIL	yellow
LEATHER	red/yellow
LOBSTER	red/yellow
LOGWOOD	blue
MAGENTA	red/blue
MALABAR	brown
MASCARA	red
MATELOT	blue
MERMAID	yellow/green
MESANGE	green/blue
MUSTARD	red/yellow
NACARAT	red
OAKWOOD	brown
OLDWOOD	red
OPHELIA	red/blue
OXBLOOD	yellow/red
PEACOCK	blue
PERIDOT	green
PIMENTO	red
PONCEAU	red
PRAIRIE	yellow/red
PRALINE	brown
PRASINE	green
RAMESES	blue
ROSEATE	red
SAFFRON	yellow
SCARLET	red
SERPENT	green/yellow
TANBARK	brown
TEAROSE	yellow/red
THISTLE	blue/red
TILLEUL	green
TOBACCO	brown
TUSSORE	red

ABSINTHE	green
ALDERNEY	red/yellow
ALGERIAN	brown
BISMARCK	red/yellow
BORDEAUX	red
BRUNDORE	black/green
CAFENOIR	brown
CAPUCINE	yellow
CARDINAL	red
CERULEAN	blue
CHASSEUR	green
CHAUDRON	brown
CHESTNUT	brown
CINNABAR	red
CREVETTE	red
EMINENCE	blue/red
FUCHSINE	red
GENDARME	blue
GERANIUM	yellow/red
GLOWWORM	green/yellow
GUNMETAL	gray
HYACINTH	blue/red
LAVENDER	blue/red
MAHOGANY	brown
MANDARIN	red/orange
MARIGOLD	orange
MAUVETTE	blue/red
MAZARINE	blue
MOSSROSE	red
MULBERRY	red
MUSHROOM	brown
NOISETTE	brown
PALMETTO	yellow/green
PARAKEET	green
PERROCHE	green
PRIMROSE	red/yellow
RAWUMBER	brown
ROSEWOOD	red/yellow
SAPPHIRE	blue
SAUTERNE	red/yellow
SHAMROCK	green
TERRAPIN	brown
VIRIDIAN	yellow/green
WEDGWOOD	blue
WISTERIA	blue/red

FOOD AND DRINK

MENU AND COOKING TERMS

CUT
DIP
FRY
MIX

BAKE
BEAT
BOIL
BREE
CHOP
CUBE
DUST
FRIT
HASH
LARD
MASH
MELT
PARE
ROLL
ROUX
SEAR
SHIR
SIFT
SOAK
STEW
STIR
WHIP

ASPIC

AUJUS
BASTE
BLEND
BROIL
BRUSH
CHILL
COUPE
CREAM
CREPE
CURRY
DOUGH
FILET
FLAKE
FROST
GLACE
GLAZE
GRATE
GRILL
GRIND
KNEAD
MINCE
PASTE
PATTY
POACH
PUREE
ROAST
SAUTE
SCALD
SCORE

SHIRR
SIEVE
STALK
STEAM
STEEP
STOCK
TOAST
TRUSS

BATTER
BLANCH
BRAISE
CANAPE
CREOLE
DREDGE
FILLET
FLAMBE
FOLDIN
FRAPPE
GIBLET
MORTAR
OMELET
PANFRY
PESTLE
REDUCE
SIMMER
SKEWER
SPONGE
TIDBIT

ALAKING
ALAMODE
BOUQUET
CHOWDER
FILLING
FLAMAND
FONDANT
GARNISH
PARBOIL
PREHEAT
RAREBIT
RISSOLE
SCALLOP
SPATULA
VINTAGE

APERITIF
AUBEURRE
AUGRATIN
BARBECUE
BOUILLON
DEVILLED
FLAMANDE
JULIENNE
MARINADE
MARINATE
PANBROIL
STUFFING

MENU ITEMS AND DISHES

AME
BAP
BUN
JAM
KAI
PIE
POI

AGAR
BABA
CAKE
CHOU
FLAN
PATE
SABA
SOUP
TART

ASADO
BOMBE
BROSE
BROTH
CABOB
CANIN
GRAVY

GUMBO
KABOB
LACTO
PASTA
PILAF
PILAU
PILAW
PIZZA
PIZZE
SALAD
SALMI
SCONE
STEAK
TORTE
WAFER

BISQUE
BLINIS
BONBON
BORSCH
BORSHT
BOUDIN
CATSUP
COLLOP
CUSCUS

CUTLET
ECLAIR
ENTREE
FONDUE
GATEAU
HAGGIS
KNODEL
KUCHEN
MOUSSE
MUFFIN
NOUGAT
PANADA
PANADE
PASTRY
POSOLE
SUNDAE
TAMALE
TONGUE
TRIFLE

ABAISSE
BEIGNET
BLINTZE
BRIOCHE
CASSATA

COMPOTE
CROUTON
CUPCAKE
DESSERT
GARBURE
GNOCCHI
KETCHUP
LASAGNE
PANCAKE
PARFAIT
PEASOUP
POLENTA
POPOVER
PRALINE
PUDDING
RAVIOLI
RISOTTO
RISSOLE
SAVARIN
SHERBET
SOUFFLE
SPUMONI
TIMBALE
ZAKUSKA

AGARAGAR
CHOPSUEY
CHOWCHOW
COQUILLE
CRUSTADA
DUMPLING
FLAPJACK
FRICANDO
KEDGEREE
MARZIPAN
MEATBALL
MERINGUE
MIREPOIS
MIREPOIX
NAPOLEON
SANDWICH
SHASHLIK
TORTILLA
ANTIPASTO
CREAMPUFF
CROQUETTE
FRICANDEL
FRICASSEE
FROGSLEGS
HAMBURGER
MADRILENE
MINCEMEAT
SALLYLUNN
SCHNITZEL
SPAGHETTI
STIRABOUT
TOURNEDOS
VOLAUVENT

SAUCES

SOY
ALEC
CHILI
CURRY
GARUM
MELBA
GANSEL
MORNAY
MARENGO
SOUBISE
SUPREME
TABASCO
TARTARE
VELOUTE
BARBECUE
BECHAMEL
MARINARA
MATELOTE
MEUNIERE
BEARNAISE
MACEDOINE
REMOULADE
WORCESTER

HERBS, SPICES, FLAVORINGS

BAY
RUE
SOY

BALM
DILL
FILE
LEEK
MACE
MINT
SAGE
SALT

ANISE
BASIL
BENNE
BROOM
CAPER
CHILI
CHIVE
CIBOL
CLARY
CLOVE
COCOA
CUBEB
CUMIN
CURRY
DULSE

ONION
SUMAC
TANSY
THYME

BORAGE
BURNET
CASSIA
CATNIP
CELERY
CICELY
COMINO
FENNEL
GARLIC
GINGER
HYSSOP
LOVAGE
NUTMEG
PEPPER
PERSIL
ROCKET
SAVORY
SESAME
SORREL
SUMACH

ALECOST
ALKANET

ANCHUSA
BITTERS
BONESET
BUGLOSS
CALUMET
CANELLA
CARAWAY
CAYENNE
CHERVIL
COMFREY
COWSLIP
DITTANY
FIGWORT
GINSENG
JUNIPER
LAURIER
MILFOIL
MUGWORT
MUSTARD
OREGANO
PAPAVER
PAPRIKA
PARSLEY
PARSNIP
PIGNOLI
PIMENTO
SAFFRON
SHALLOT

VANILLA
VERBENA

ACHILLEA
ALLSPICE
ANGELICA
BERGAMOT
CAPSICUM
CARDAMON
CHARLOCK
CINNAMON
COLEWORT
COSTMARY
ESCHALOT
ESTRAGON
FINOCCHI
GALANGAL
LAVENDER
MARIGOLD
MARJORAM
ORIGANUM
ROQUETTE
ROSEMARY
SAMPHIRE
SERPOLET
TARRAGON
TURMERIC
VERONICA

WINES

AHR
AYL

ASTI
BUAL
GIRO
HOCK
NAHE
PORT
ROSE

SACK
SAKE
SAKI
SEKT

ANJOU
BADEN
BLANC
BYRRH
CAPRI

CORVO
FIXIN
MACON
MEDOC
PFALZ
PICON
ROUGE
SOAVE
TAVEL
TINTA

TOKAY
TRIER
XERES
YQUEM
ZUCCO

ALBANA
ALBANO
ALELLA
ALSACE

ARBOIS
AUSONE
BAROLO
BARSAC
BEAUNE
CANARY
CHINON
CLARET
GRAVES
LILLET
MALAGA
MASDEU
MONICA
MUSCAT
PATRAS
PERNOD
PINEAU
RUFINA
SAUMUR

SHERRY
VOLNAY
YVORNE

BANYULS
CALDARO
CATAWBA
CHABLIS
CHIANTI
CREMANT
DAGORED
EPERNAY
FALERNO
FRANKEN
INFERNO
MADEIRA
MALMSEY
MARGAUX
MARSALA

MAYWINE
MOSCATO
MOSELLE
OLOROSO
PASSITO
POMEROL
POMMARD
REDWINE
SEEWEIN
SERCIAL
SEYSSEL
VERDISO
VESUVIO
VINGRIS
VOUVRAY

ALEATICO
BORDEAUX
BURGUNDY

CABERNET
CALVADOS
CHABLAIS
CORONATA
DUBONNET
GRENACHE
MUSCADET
MUSCATEL
PIESPORT
RHEINGAU
RIESLING
RUBYPORT
SANCERRE
SAUTERNE
SYLVANER
TOURAINE
VERMOUTH

CORDIALS AND SPIRITS

ALE
GIN
RUM
RYE

BEER
BENO
BOCK
MEAD
MOKA

CACAO
KEFIR
LAGER
NOYAU
PEACH
PISCO
POMBE
SNAPS
STOUT
VODKA

ANANAS

ARRACK
ARROPE
BANANA
BARACK
BRANDY
CASSIS
CHERRY
COGNAC
FRAISE
GENEPI
KALUHA
KIRSCH
KUMISS
KUMMEL
MASTIC
MENTHE
PORTER
PULQUE
SCOTCH
SNAPPS
STREGA
TAFFIA
WHISKY

YVETTE

AQUAVIT
BACARDI
BITTERS
BOURBON
CURACAO
DAMIANA
NOYEAUX
PARFAIT
QUETSCH
RASPAIL
SLOEGIN
TEQUILA
VANILLE
WHISKEY

ABSINTHE
ADVOCAAT
ANISETTE
ARMAGNAC
CALVADOS
CLEANRUM
CORFINIO

DRAMBUIE
NEARBEER
PRUNELLE
SCHNAPPS
TIAMARIA
VIOLETTE

APPLEJACK
BOCACHICA
COINTREAU
FRAMBOISE
MANDARINE
METHEGLIN
MIRABELLE
SLIVOVITZ

APRICOTINE
BLACKBERRY
CHARTREUSE
CORNWHISKY
FIORDEALPI
GOLDWASSER
MARASCHINO

COCKTAILS AND MIXED DRINKS

BS

FIZZ
FLIP
GROG
PURL
SOUR

BRONX
DAISY
JULEP
NEGUS
PUNCH

SLING
SMASH
TODDY

BISHOP
CHASER
COOLER
EGGNOG
FRAPPE
GIBSON
GIMLET
POSSET
RICKEY

ROBROY
ROYALE
ZOMBIE

BACARDI
COBBLER
COLLINS
MARTINI
SIDECAR
STINGER
SWIZZLE
WASSAIL

DAIQUIRI
HIGHBALL
HOTTODDY
PINKLADY
SANGAREE
SPRITZER

ALEXANDER
CUBALIBRE
LAMBSWOOL
MANHATTAN
MARGARITA
PISCOSOUR

FOREIGN WORDS

SPANISH

aunt	TIA
be(ing)	SER
bear	OSO
because of	POR
bravo	OLE
by	POR
departure	IDA
estuary	RIA
eye	OJO
for	POR
garlic	AJO
give	DAR
gold	ORO
hither, here	ACA
inlet	RIA
king	REY
law	LEY
master	AMO
more	MAS
of the	DEL
owner	AMO
river	RIO
rum	RON
see	VER
south	SUR
there	AHI
through	POR
thus	ASI
time	VEZ
today	HOY
turn	VEZ
uncle	TIO
very	MUY

abbot	ABAD
after	TRAS
age	EDAD
all	TODO
annoy	ASAR
as	COMO
ass	ASNO
bad	MALO
ball	BOLA
bath	BANO
beak	PICO
bean	HABA
bed	CAMA
behind	TRAS
being	ENTE
blue	AZUL
box	CAJA
boy	NINO
broken	ROTO
bull	TORO
but	PERO
cape	CAPA
cash	CAJA
cat	GATO
chief	JEFE
child	NINO, HIJO
clothes	ROPA
cold	FRIO
construction	OBRA
cord	SOGA
cow	VACA
cut	TAJO
daughter	HIJA
dear	CARO
direction	LADO
donkey	ASNO
drygoods	ROPA
duck, drake	PATO
each	CADA
ear	OIDO
east	ESTE
elbow	CODO
event	ACTO
every	TODO
evil	MALO
face, facade	CARA
few	POCO
finger	DEDO
gait	PASO
girl	NINA
God	DIOS
grate, grille	REJA
hair	PELO
hall	SALA
hand	MANO
healthy	SANO
here	AQUI
high	ALTO
hill	LOMA
home	CASA
horn	ASTA
house	CASA
how?	COMO
idleness	OCIO
it	ELLO
jack	GATO
judge	JUEZ
kernel	HABA
kiss	BESO
laborer	PEON
lady	DAMA
lake	LAGO
lattice	REJA
lawsuit	ACTO
leisure	OCIO
like	COMO
little	POCO
living room	SALA
located	SITO
loud	ALTO
love, to	AMAR
low	BAJO
mast	ASTA
meadow	VEGA
mistress	DAMA
monkey	MONO
mouth	BOCA
nap	PELO
only	SOLO
pace	PASO
parlor	SALA
pastime	OCIO
peak	CIMA
peak	PICO
plain	VEGA
point	PICO
poor	MALO
ragged	ROTO
red	ROJO
repairs	OBRA
rich	RICO
roast, to	ASAR
room	LADO
rope	SOGA
short	BAJO
side	LADO
situated	SITO
son	HIJO
soul	ALMA
sound	SANO
spear	ASTA
step	PASO
summit	CIMA
sweetheart	ALMO
table	MESA
there	ALLA, ALLI
thing	COSA
toe	DEDO
top	CIMA
turkey	PAVO
under	BAJO
wave	ONDA
wax	CERA
white	ALBO
whole	TODO
why	COMO
work	OBRA
yesterday	AYER
young	NINO, NINA

ache	DOLER
afternoon	TARDE
agile	VELOZ
back	ATRAS
bay	BAHIA
be	ESTAR
beard	BARBA

beautiful	BELLO
before	ANTES
behind	ATRAS
black	NEGRA
boat	BARCA, BARCO
broth	CALDO
canyon	CANON
chair	SILLA
chance	ACASO
child	CHICO
chin	BARBA
cock	GALLO
convict	PRESO
cop	CUICO
dog	PERRO
dress	FALDA
egg	HUEVO
evening	TARDE
father	PADRE
fire	FUEGO
float	NADAR
fly	MOSCA
folks	GENTE
foothill	FALDA
formerly	ANTES
fox	ZORRO
friend	AMIGO
game	JUEGO
gentleman	SENOR
girl	CHICA
goat	CABRA
goddess	DIOSA
good-bye	ADIOS
grieve	DOLER
have	TOMAR, TENER
head	TESTA
heat	CALOR
heaven	CIELO
hurt	DOLER
hush	CHITO
inn	FONDA
kill	MATAR
landlady	DUENA
landlord	DUENO
landmark	SENAL
language	HABLA
lass	CHICA
lasso	REATA
late	TARDE
letter	CARTA, LETRA
little	CHICO, ENANO
mark	SENAL
master	SENOR, DUENO
maybe	ACASO
meat	CARNE
mister	SENOR
mother	MADRE
mouse	RATON
new	NUEVO
night	NOCHE
north	NORTE
nun	MONJA
only	UNICO
people	GENTE
perhaps	ACASO
plantation	FINCA
plate	PLATO
play	JUEGO
poor	POBRE
prairie	PAMPA
prisoner	PRESO
property	FINCA
purchase	MERCA
queen	REINA
quick	VELOZ
real estate	FINCA
restaurant	FONDA
ship	NAVIO
sidewalk	ACERA
sign	SENAL
silver	PLATA
sir	SENOR
skirt	FALDA
sky	CIELO
small	CHICO
so much	TANTO
soon	LUEGO
soul	ANIMO
spirit	ANIMO
strawberry	FRESA
strong	RECIO
summer	ESTIO
swim	NADAR
table	TABLA
then	LUEGO
token	SENAL
trace	SENAL
troops	GENTE
until	HASTA
vessel	NAVIO
village	ALDEA
warmth	CALOR
west	OESTE
where	DONDE
will	ANIMO
woman	MUJER

abbey	ABADIA
cellar	BODEGA
change	CAMBIO
chaperon	DUENNA
cheap	BARATO
city	CIUDAD
conflict	GUERRA
cowboy	RESERO
creek	ARROYO
dinner	COMIDA
dove	PALOMA
English	INGLES
exchange (rate)	CAMBIO
food	COMIDO
grocery store	BODEGA
gypsy	GITANO
head	CABEZA
height	ALTURA
herdsman	RESERO
Highness	ALTEZA
husband	ESPOSO
inn	POSADA
kitchen	COCINA
lady	SENORA
large	GRANDE
late	TARDIO
madam	SENORA
mail	CORREO
man	HOMBRE
meal	COMIDA
morning	MANANA
Mrs.	SENORA
paid	PAGADO
past	PASADO
pigeon	PALOMA
post office	CORREO
press	PRENSA
robber	LADRON
shirt	CAMISA
stream	ARROYO
thief	LADRON
tricky	GITANO
war	GUERRA
warm	CALIDO
watchword	ALERTA
when	CUANDO
white	BLANCO
wife	ESPOSA
winecellar	BODEGA

FRENCH

ass	ANE
back	DOS
ball (dance)	BAL
case	CAS
circumstance	CAS
corn	BLE
credit	FOI
crude	CRU
donkey	ANE
dry	SEC
duke	DUC
east	EST
event	CAS
evil	MAL
faith	FOI
fame	NOM
few	PEU
fire	TIR, FEU
fold	PLI
fool(ish)	FOU
friend	AMI

game	JEU
good	BON
goose	OIE
gravy	JUS
habit	PLI
heat	FEU
here	ICI
honor	FOI
ill, illness	MAL
iron	FER
is	EST
island	ILE
juice	JUS
king	ROI
level	UNI
liking	GRE
lily	LIS
little	PEU
lively	VIF
low	BAS
mt. pass	COL
name	NOM
neck	COL, COU
no	NON
nose	NEZ
noun	NOM
on	SUR
over	SUR
raw	CRU
rice	RIZ
said	DIT
salt	SEL
sea	MER
shooting	TIR
sickness	MAL
since	DES
soul	AME
south	SUD
spoken	DIT
sport	JEU
stocking	BAS
such	TEL
summer	ETE
sure	SUR
thread	FIL
united	UNI
upon	SUR, SUS
vineyard	CRU
wall	MUR
water	EAU
wheat	BLE
will	GRE
wine	VIN
wish	GRE
worse	PIS
wrinkle	PLI
yes	OUI

abbot	ABBE
act	ACTE
agreed!	SOIT
all	TOUT, TOUS
alone	SEUL
almost	PRES
already	DEJA
among	CHEZ
angel	ANGE
any	TOUT
arm	BRAS
at home with	CHEZ
baby	BEBE
bath	BAIN
beast	BETE
be(ing)	ETRE
bench	BANC
beware	GARE
beyond	DELA
bicycle	VELO
black	NOIR
blue	BLEU, AZUR
bread	PAIN
bridge	PONT
brown	BRUN
but	MAIS
cabbage	CHOU
care	SOIN
cloth	DRAP
comfort	AISE
cop	FLIC
cost	PRIX, COUT
country	PAYS
dare	OSER
dawn	AUBE
day	JOUR
dear	CHER
deed	FAIT
defiance	DEFI
doff	OTER
down with	ABAS
dream	REVE
drunk	IVRE
dugout	ABRI
ease	AISE
egg	OEUF
elder	AINE
equal	EGAL
evening	SOIR
every	TOUS, TOUT
exclamation	HEIN
expensive	CHER
eye	OEIL
eyes	YEUX
false	FAUX
fat	GRAS
father	PERE
fear	PEUR
foot	PIED
friend	AMIE
games	JEUX
gentle	DOUX
gilded, gilt	DORE
glove	GANT
God	DIEU
golden	DORE
gray	GRIS
green	VERT

grimace	MOUE
half mask	LOUP
hand	MAIN
handle	ANSE
head	TETE
heaven	CIEL
high	HAUT
honey	MIEL
hunger	FAIM
husband	MARI
hush!	CHUT
idea	IDEE
in	CHEZ, DANS
judge	JUGE
land	PAYS
late	TARD
laugh	RIRE
leather	CUIR
milk	LAIT
mother	MERE
mountain	MONT
nail	CLOU
nation	PAYS
near	PRES
new	NEUF
night	NUIT
noon	MIDI
north	NORD
nothing	RIEN
opinion	AVIS
out	HORS
peace	PAIX
people	GENS
petticoat	JUPE
pretty	JOLI
price	PRIX
prize	PRIX
quick	VITE
read	LIRE
ready	PRET
receipt	RECU
red	ROUX
remove	OTER
roast	ROTI
roof	TOIT
saw	SCIE
see	VOIR
sharp	AIGU
shell	OBUS
shelter	ABRI
silk	SOIE
skin	PEAU
skirt	JUPE
sky	CIEL
soft	DOUX
so much	TANT
son	FILS
state	ETAT
station	GARE
stupid	BETE
sweet	DOUX
then	PUIS, LORS
thirst	SOIF

tie	LIER
time	FOIS
true	VRAI
under	SOUS
very	TRES
warning	AVIS
wave	ONDE
weapon	ARME
well	BIEN
whole	TOUT
wing(ed)	AILE
with	AVEC, CHEZ
without	SANS
wolf	LOUP
wood	BOIS
worse	PIRE
yesterday	HIER

according	SELON
after	APRES
airplane	AVION
alas	HELAS
also	AUSSI
amid	PARMI
among	ENTRE
annuity	RENTE
arrest	ARRET
aunt	TANTE
avenue	ALLEE
beach	PLAGE
beef	BOEUF
beer	BIERE
before	AVANT
better	MIEUX
between	ENTRE
bizarre	OUTRE
blunder	GAFFE
book	LIVRE
bridegroom	MARIE
brother	FRERE
capture	PRISE
cheers	SALUT
chicken	POULE
cloud	NUAGE
cold	FROID
count	COMTE
cow	VACHE
coward(ly)	LACHE
cup	TASSE
daughter	FILLE
dear	CHERI, CHERE
debt	DETTE
dew	ROSEE
dream, to	REVER
drink, to	BOIRE
earl	COMTE
earth	TERRE
enamel	AMAIL
enough	ASSEZ
error	FAUTE
fame	BRUIT
farewell	ADIEU
fault	FAUTE
finally	ENFIN
finger	DOIGT
floor	ETAGE
flower	FLEUR
forward	AVANT
fresh	FRAIS
full	PLEIN
glass	VERRE
go	ALLER
grave	TOMBE
greeting	SALUT
hall	SALLE
have	AVOIR
health	SANTE
heavy	LOURD
hell	ENFER
here	VOICI
hire	LOUER
hold	TENIR
hot	CHAUD
hour	HEURE
I love	JAIME
income	RENTE
ink	ENCRE
kind	SORTE
lack	FAUTE
land	TERRE
large	GRAND
law	DROIT
less	MOINS
light	LEGER
like	COMME
love	AMOUR
love, to	AIMER
lover	AMANT
maid	BONNE
mail	POSTE
mamma	MAMAN
man	HOMME
manner	SORTE
marine	MARIN
mayor	MAIRE
meal	REPAS
miser	AVARE
mix	MELER
morning	MATIN
museum	MUSEE
new	NEUVE
noise	BRUIT
nurse	BONNE
obligation	DETTE
other	AUTRE
pain	PEINE
pause	ARRET
pear	POIRE
penalty	PEINE
pocket	POCHE
possess	TENIR
pupil	ELEVE
purchase	ACHAT
queen	REINE
rabbit	LAPIN
red	ROUGE
rain	PLUIE
rent, to	LOUER
reputation	BRUIT
rich	RICHE
right	DROIT
ring	BAGUE
room	SALLE
safety	SALUT
sailor	MARIN
school	LYCEE, ECOLE
sister	SOEUR
slang	ARGOT
slight	LEGER
small	PETIT
snow	NEIGE
soap	SAVON
soldier	POILU
sort	SORTE
square	CARRE
storm	ORAGE
straight	DROIT
subway	METRO
sum	SOMME
table	TABLE
thanks	MERCI
then	ALORS
there!	VOILA
thus	AINSI
tree	ARBRE
trouble	PEINE
uncle	ONCLE
warm	CHAUD
weight	POIDS
west	OUEST
when	QUAND
white	BLANC
winter	HIVER
world	TERRE, MONDE
yellow	JAUNE
young	JEUNE

again	ENCORE
around	AUTOUR
at first	DABORD
awkward	GAUCHE
bell	CLOCHE
beware	GAREDE
blank book	CAHIER
bride	MARIEE
butter	BEURRE
cake	GATEAU
carriage	FIACRE
chair	CHAISE
child	ENFANT
church	EGLISE
clumsy	GAUCHE
concession	OCTROI
copybook	CAHIER
customs	DOUANE, MOEURS
devil	DIABLE
dialect	PATOIS
dungeon	CACHOT

- equal PAREIL
- fall of stocks BAISSE
- false FAUSSE
- fly MOUCHE
- friendship AMITIE
- furniture MEUBLE
- future AVENIR
- gift CADEAU
- home MAISON
- horse CHEVAL
- house MAISON
- hungry AFFAME
- kiss BAISER
- know SAVOIR
- lamb AGNEAU
- language LANGUE
- left GAUCHE
- Lent CAREME
- lingo PATOIS
- mouse SOURIS
- notebook CARNET
- number NOMBRE
- open OUVERT
- penalty AMENDE
- police bureau SURETE
- poor PAUVRE
- prison CACHOT
- red ROUSSE
- reparation AMENDE
- rise of prices HAUSSE
- safety SURETE
- season SAISON
- security SURETE
- sheep MOUTON
- shepherd BERGER
- ship NAVIRE
- soldier SOLDAT
- speak PARLER
- star ETOILE
- stock exchange BOURSE
- strawberry FRAISE
- sun SOLEIL
- superfluous DETROP
- thirty TRENTE
- thought PENSEE
- toll OCTROI
- tongue LANGUE
- too much DETROP
- understand SAVOIR
- war GUERRE
- watch MONTRE
- well-groomed SOIGNE
- write ECRIRE

ITALIAN

- against CON
- age ETA
- always MAI
- aunt ZIA
- below GIU
- down GIU
- duration ORA
- ever MAI
- God DIO
- goose OCA
- grandfather AVO
- here QUA, QUI
- hour ORA
- many PIU
- more PIU
- never MAI
- now ORA
- ox BUE
- simpleton OCA
- south SUD
- there IVI
- time ORA
- uncle ZIO
- where OVE
- with CON

- act ATTO
- after DOPO
- afternoon SERA
- apple POMO, MELA
- art ARTE
- black NERO
- confidence FEDE
- dawn ALBA
- dear CARO, CARA
- deed ATTO
- drink, to BERE
- each OGNI
- east ESTE
- egg UOVO
- end CODA
- evening SERA
- every OGNI
- face VISO
- faith FEDE
- few POCO
- frost GELO
- gift DONO
- hair PELO
- hall SALA
- hand MANO
- hatred ODIO
- head CAPO
- husband UOMO
- ice GELO
- I see VEDO
- Jesus GESU
- lake LAGO
- light LUME
- little POCO
- lo! ECCO
- man UOMO
- matter COSA
- mountain peak CIMA
- night SERA
- north NORD
- nose NASO
- real VERO
- seat SEDE
- ship NAVE
- shore RIVA
- side LATO
- situated SITO
- so COSI
- sour AGRO
- summit CIMA
- swallow BERE
- tail CODA
- talent DONO
- thin POCO
- thing COSA
- thirst SETE
- thus COSI
- today OGGI
- tour GIRO, GITA
- true VERO
- voice VOCE
- wax CERA
- well BENE
- yesterday IERI

- account CONTO
- all TUTTI, TUTTO
- ardor ESTRO
- ass ASINO
- back TERGO
- ball PALLA
- beard BARBA
- bed LETTO
- beer BIRRA
- boiled LESSO
- bride SPOSA
- bridge PONTE
- cafe CAFFE
- camp CAMPO
- cat GATTA
- cathedral DUOMO
- chair SEDIA
- chest CASSA
- city CITTA
- course CORSA
- dad BABBO
- done FATTO
- donkey ASINO
- door PORTA
- dough PASTA
- dress ABITO
- enough BASTA
- excuse SCUSA
- farewell ADDIO
- father PADRE
- feast FESTA
- field CAMPO

force FORZA
fork FORCA
friend AMICA, AMICO
gate PORTA
get AVERE
good BUONO
good-bye ADDIO
harbor PORTO
have AVERE
head TESTA
heaven CIELO
holiday FESTA, FERIA
iron FERRO
isle ISOLA
kiss BACIO
lady DONNA
late TARDO
law LEGGE
leg GAMBA
love AMORE
love, to AMARE
many MOLTO
meal PASTO
mind MENTE
monk FRATE
mother MADRE
mouth BOCCA
much ASSI, MOLTO
night NOTTE
not at all PUNTO
other ALTRO
paper CARTA
please PREGO
power FORZA
race CORSA
red ROSSO
rich RICCO
said DETTO
sauce SALSA
sign SEGNO
skin PELLE
sky CIELO
sleep SONNO
so much TANTO
soul ANIMA
spirit ANIMA
spouse SPOSA, SPOSO
stamp BOLLO
star ASTRO
straight RETTO
street CALLE, CORSO
strength FORZA
sword SPADA
tailor SARTO
thief LADRO
tower TORRE
town CITTA
twisted TORTO
under SOTTO
very MOLTO
water ACQUA
west OVEST
without SENZA
women DONNE
wood LEGNO
world MONDO
wrong TORTO

again DACAPO
be(ing) ESSERE
canal CANALE
custom house DOGANA
daughter FIGLIA
day GIORNO
foreign ESTERO
forward AVANTI
from the beginning DACAPO
gentleman SIGNOR
hamlet CASALE
how much QUANTO
husband MARITO
key CHIAVE
large GROSS, GRANDE
lover AMANTE
money DENARO, MONETA
nothing NIENTE
now ADESSO
open APERTO
poor POVERO
queen REGINA
right DESTRO
road STRADA
same STESSO
self STESSO
shoe SCARPA
son FIGLIO
star STELLA
table TAVOLA
thanks GRAZIE
then ALLORA
tomorrow DOMANI
tree ALBERO
value VALUTA
village CASALE
when QUANDO
white BIANCO
yet ANCORA

GERMAN

abbot ABT
about BEI
alas ACH
among BEI
ancestor AHN
and UND
as ALS
at BEI
before VOR
clock UHR
cow KUH
dead TOT
ear OHR
east OST
eel AAL
from AUS, VON
gate TOR
how WIE
ice EIS
is IST
narrow ENG
near NAH
never NIE
new NEU
of VON, AUS, AUF
on AUF
out of AUS
path WEG
poor ARM
south SUD
than ALS
train ZUG
upon AUF
valley TAL
watch UHR
way WEG
with BEI, MIT

about ETWA
above OBEN, UBER
after NACH
age ALTE
air LIED, LUFT
all GANZ, ALLE
ass ESEL
band BUND
bank UFER
beard BART
because WEIL
bed BETT
beer BIER
behind NACH
be(ing) SEIN
besides NOCH
blood BLUT
blue BLAU
book BUCH
bread BROT
bundle BUND
but ABER
calm RUHE
cash GELD
chicken HUHN
clever KLUG
coin GELD
cold KALT

count	GRAF
couple	PAAR
deep	TIEF
dirty	FAUL
distant	WEIT
doctor	ARZT
dog	HUND
duck	ENTE
earl	GRAF
early	FRUH
earth	ERDE
elegant	FEIN
every	JEDE
eye	AUGE
far	WEIT
figure	BILD
fine	FEIN
first	WEAR
flight	FLUG
for	DENN
foul	FAUL
free	FREI
fruit	OBST
full	VOLL
gentleman	HERR
genuine	ECHT, WAHR
gift	GABE
gladly	GERN
glory	RUHN
God	GOTT
greatly	SEHR
hair	HAAR
hall	AULA, SAAL
heart	HERZ
here	HIER
high	HOCH
home	HEIM
host	WIRT
house	HAUS
humanity	WELT
if	WENN
image	BILD
lady	DAME, FRAU
language	REDE
late	SPAT
lazy	FAUL
league	BUND
leg	BEIN
lord	GOTT, HERR
man	MANN
many	VIEL
mind	SINN
mister	HERR
money	GELD
more	MEHR
much	SEHR, VIEL
murder	MORD
nation	VOLK
nearly	ETWA
neck	HALS
new	NEUE
no	NEIN
nobility	ADEL

noble	EDEL
nobleman	GRAF
north	NORD
old	ALTE
or	ODER
over	UBER
pair	PAAR
peace	RUHE
people	VOLK
perhaps	ETWA
picture	BILD
pure	ECHT
race	VOLK
real	ECHT, WAHR
repose	RUHE
residence	HAUS
rest	RUHE
room	SAAL, RAUM
sea	MEER
shore	UFER
sir	HERR
society	WELT
son	SOHN
song	LIED
space	RAUM
speech	REDE
still	DOCH
tall	HOCH
than	DENN
that	JENE
then	DANN, DENN
there	DORT
thief	DIEB
thing	DING
top	OBEN
tower	TURM
tree	BAUM
triumph	SIEG
true	WAHR
tune	LIED
upper	OBER
very	SEHR
victory	SIEG
village	DORF
visitor	GAST
viva!: salute	HOCH
well	WOHL
west	WEST
when	WENN
wide	WEIT
wife	WEIB, FRAU
willingly	GERN
without	OHNE
woman	DAME, FRAU, WEIB
world	WELT
yet	DOCH, NOCH
yonder	DORT

across	DURCH
affection	LIEBE
alley	GASSE
always	IMMER

apple	APFEL
aunt	TANTE
below, beneath	UNTER, UNTEN
beside	NEBEN
both	BEIDE
bride	BRAUT
broom	BESEN
carriage	WAGEN
chair	STUHL
cheers!	PROST
city	STADT
cost	PREIS
cross	KREUZ
dare, to	WAGEN
different	ANDER
east	OSTEN
eat	ESSEN
else	ANDER
empire	REICH
evening	ABEND
everything	ALLES
father	VATER
fear	ANGST
few	WENIG
fork	GABEL
game	SPIEL
give	GEBEN
go	GEHEN
harbor	HAFEN
have	HABEN
haven	HAFEN
hence	DAHER
hunter	JAGER
husband	GATTE
iron	EISEN
island	INSEL
ladies	DAMEN
lane	GASSE
leather	LEDER
letter	BRIEF
lightning	BLITZ
little	KLEIN, WENIG
love	LIEBE
mind	GEIST
move	GEHEN
new	NEUES, NEUER
night	NACHT
not	NICHT
once	EINST
orient	OSTEN
path	GASSE
play	SPIEL
people	LEUTE
persons	LEUTE
play	SPIEL
please	BITTE
price	PREIS
rain	REGEN
read	LESEN
request	BITTE
rich	REICH
small	KLEIN

soul	GEIST, SEELE
south	SUDEN
spirit	GEIST
spouse	GATTE
state	STAAT
steel	STAHL
street	GASSE
strife	KRIEG
sun	SONNE
table	TISCH, TAFEL
thanks	DANKE
thirst	DURST
through	DURCH
today	HEUTE
town	STADT
uncle	ONKEL
walk	GEHEN
war	KRIEG
why	WARUM

again	WIEDER
bell	GLOCKE
brother	BRUDER
cheap	BILLIG
cheers!	PROSIT
gentlemen	HERREN
heaven	HIMMEL
knife	MESSER
know(ledge)	WISSEN
labor	ARBEIT
ladies	FRAUEN
morning	MORGEN
mother	MUTTER
noon	MITTAG
north	NORDEN
once	EINMAL
plate	TELLER
school	SCHULE
self	SELBST
sky	HIMMEL
snow	SCHNEE
soldier	SOLDAT
spoon	LOFFEL
toil	ARBEIT
tomorrow	MORGEN
west	WESTEN
wife	GATTIN
work	ARBEIT

LATIN

alas	VAE, HEU
altar	ARA
anger	IRA
art	ARS
as	QUA
bronze	AES
but	SED
citadel	ARX
copper	AES
custom	MOS
divine law	GAS
edge	ORA
either	AUT
foot	PES
force	VIS
fortress	ARX
goddess	DEA
gods	DEI
heart	COR
husband	VIR
I love	AMO
is	EST
king	REX
law	LEX, JUS
lawful	FAS
leader	DUX
man	VIR
milk	LAC
not	NON
or	AUT
peace	PAX
pledge	VAS
power	VIS
pray	ORA
pyre	ARA
shore	ORA
strength	VIS
there	IBI
thing	RES
three times	TER
trade	ARS
twice	BIS
vessel	VAS
where	UBI
will	MOS
with	CUM
wrath	IRA

after	POST
alas	EHEU
all (in)	TOTO
at the same place	IBID
before	ANTE
behold!	ECCE
be(ing)	ESSE
beware	CAVE
bird	AVIS
birds	AVES
boy	PUER
bridge	PONS
child	PUER
city	URBS
culprit	REUS
day	DIEM
day(s)	DIES
defendant	REUS
dinner	CENA
egg	OVUM
except	NISI
field	AGER
fields	AGRI
go away!	VADE
grandfather	AVUS
he loves	AMAT
high	ALTA
hope	SPES
hour	HORA
hush!	TACE
I have spoken	DIXI
in the year	ANNO
knee	GENU
lambs	AGNI
life	VITA
lo!	ECCE
lot	SORS
mind	MENS
mountain	MONS
needle	ACUS
nobody	NEMO
note	NOTA
now	NUNC
observe!	NOTA
other	ALIA
others	ALII
palm: hand	VOLA
part	PARS
pin	ACUS
praise	LAUS
property	BONA
prophecy	SORS
proportion	RATA
road	ITER
same	IDEM
sea	MARE
see!	VIDE
share	RATA
soon	CITO
supper	CENA
thing done	ACTU
unless	NISI
was	ERAT
water	AQUA
well	BENE
wife	UXOR
without	SINE
wool	LANA
you love	AMAS

abbot	ABBAS
about	CIRCA
above	SUPER
abundance	COPIA
across	TRANS
air	ANIMA
all	TOTUM
all	OMNIA, OMNIS
alone	SOLUS
another thing	ALIUD
as far as	QUOAD

backward	RETRO
bad	MALUS
battle line	ACIES
behind	RETRO
blessed	BEATA
book	LIBER
broad	LATUS
brow	FRONS
cattle	PECUS
confidence	FIDES
cup	CALIX
daughter	FILIA
deceit	DOLUS
divine	DIVUS
door	PORTA, JANUA
earth	TERRA
ease	OTIUM
edge	ACTES
error	CULPA
evil	MALUM
faith	FIDES
fault	CULPA
fire	IGNIS
flock	PECUS
fodder	CIBUS
food	CIBUS
forehead	FRONS
form	MODUS
fraud	DOLUS
friend	AMICA
gate	PORTA
gentle	LENIS
goblet	CALIX
gold	AURUM
good	BONUM
ground	TERRA
happy	BEATA
healthy	SANUS
helmet	GALEA
herd	PECUS
keenness	ACIES
kings	REGES
lamb	AGNUS
land	TERRA
leisure	OTIUM
mass, the	MISSA
method	MODUS
more	SUPER
name	NOMEN
near by	JUXTA
negligence	CULPA
nothing	NIHIL
only	SOLUS
other	ALIUS
over	SUPER, TRANS
pardon	VENIA
place	LOCUS
plenty	COPIA
remains, it	MANET
resist!	OBSTA
rite	RITUS
sick	AEGER
side	LATUS
sinful	NEFAS
smooth	LENIS
soft	LENIS
soul	ANIMA
sound	SANUS
sour	VINUM
stars	ASTRA
supper	COENA
tail	CAUDA
that is	IDEST
thing done	ACTUS
trust	FIDES
unlawful	NEFAS
upon	SUPER
usage	RITUS
why	QUARE
wide	LATUS
wicked	MALUS
wind	ANIMA
wine	VINUM
within	INTRA
year	ANNUS

again	ITERUM
always	SEMPER
around	CIRCUM
authority	REGNUM
blessed	BEATUS
buying	EMPTIO
error	LAPSUS
fatherland	PATRIA
first	PRIMUM, PRIMUS
fish	PISCIS
fishes	PISCES
friend	AMICUS
gliding	LAPSUS
great	MAGNUS
Greece	ACHAIA
happy	BEATUS
iron	FERRUM
kingdom	REGNUM
learned	DOCTUS
lots	SORTES
otherwise	ALITER
partly	PARTIM
queen	REGINA
right	DEXTER
servant	SERVUS
slave	SERVUS
sliding	LAPSUS
son	FILIUS
summer	AESTAS
theft	FURTUM
therefore	IGITUR
tyranny	REGNUM
war	BELLUM
well-informed	DOCTUS
woman	FEMINA

ARTICLES, PRONOUNS, POSSESSIVES AND NUMERALS IN FIVE LANGUAGES

ARTICLES

Spanish	French	Italian	German	
EL	AU	I	DAS	EINEN
LA	DU	IL	DEM	EINER
LO	LA	LA	DEN	EINES
UN	LE	LE	DER	
LAS	UN	LO	DES	
LOS	AUX	UN	DIE	
UNA	DES	GLI	EIN	
UNAS	LES	UNA	EINE	
UNOS	UNE	UNO	EINEM	

PRONOUNS AND POSSESSIVES

* Indicates possessive pronouns or adjectives

Spanish

EL
LA
LE
LO
ME
MI*
OS
SE
SI
SU*
TE
TI
TU*
YO
ESA
ESE
ESO
LAS
LES
LOS
MIA*
MIO*

MIS*
NOS
QUE
SUS*
TAL
TUS*
UNA
UNO
VOS
ALGO
CADA
CUAL
CUYA
CUYO
ELLA
ELLO
ESAS
ESOS
ESTA
ESTE
ESTO
MIAS*

MIOS*
NADA
SUYA*
SUYO*
TUYA*
TUYO*
UNAS
UNOS
ALGUN
AQUEL
CUYAS
CUYOS
ELLAS
ELLOS
ESTAS
ESTOS
NADIE
USTED
QUIEN
SUYAS*
SUYOS*
TALES

TUYAS*
TUYOS*
ALGUNA
ALGUNO
CUALES
NINGUN
ALGUIEN
ALGUNAS
ALGUNOS
AQUELLA
AQUELLO
NINGUNA
NINGUNO
NUESTRA*
NUESTRO*
QUIENES
USTEDES
VUESTRA*
VUESTRO*

French

Y
CA
CE
EN
IL
JE
LA
LE
MA*
ME
ON
OU
SA*
SE
TA*
TE
TU
CES
CET
EUX
ILS

LES
LUI
MES*
MOI
MON*
NOS*
NUL
QUE
QUI
SES*
SOI
SON*
TEL
TES*
TOI
TON*
VOS*
CECI
CELA
CEUX
DONT

ELLE
LEUR*
MIEN*
NOUS
QUEL
QUOI
RIEN
SIEN*
TELS
TIEN*
VOUS
AUCUN
CELLE
CELUI
CETTE
ELLES
LEURS*
MIENS*
NOTRE*
NULLE
QUELS

SIENS*
TELLE
TIENS*
VOTRE*
AUCUNE
AUTRUI
CELLES
CHACUN
LEQUEL
MIENNE*
NOTRES*
QUELLE
SIENNE*
TELLES
TIENNE*
VOTRES*
CHACUNE
MIENNES*
QUELLES
SIENNES*
TIENNES*

Italian

CI
IO
LA
LE
LI
LO

ME
MI
NE
SE
SI
TE

TI
TU
VI
CHE
CHI
CIO

CUI
GLI
LEI
LUI
MIA*
MIE*

MIO*
NOI
SUA*
SUE*
SUO*
TAL
TUA*
TUE*
TUO*
VOI
EGLI
ELLA
ESSA
ESSE
ESSI
ESSO
LORO*
MIEI*
QUAL
QUEL
SUOI*
TALE
TALI
TUOI*
COLEI
COLUI
NIUNO
NULLA
QUALE
QUALI
ALCUNA
ALCUNE
ALCUNI
ALCUNO
ALTRUI
COLORO
COSTEI
COSTUI
NIENTE
NOSTRA*
NOSTRE*
NOSTRI*
NOSTRO*
OGNUNA
OGNUNO
QUEGLI
QUELLA
QUELLE
QUELLI
QUELLO
QUESTA
QUESTE
QUESTI
QUESTO
VOSTRA*
VOSTRE*
VOSTRI*
VOSTRO*
COSTORO
NESSUNA
NESSUNO
QUALCHE

German

DU
ER
ES
DAS
DEM
DEN
DER
DIE
ICH
IHM
IHN
IHR*
MAN
MIR
SIE
UNS
WAS
WEM
WEN
WER
WES
WIR
DEIN*
DICH
DIES
EUCH
EUER*
EURE*
IHRE*
JEDE
JENE
KEIN
MICH
MEIN*
SEIN*
SICH
DEINE*
DENEN
DEREN
DERER
DIESE
ETWAS
EUERE*
EUREM*
EUREN*
EURER*
EURES*
IHNEN
IHREM*
IHREN*
IHRER*
IHRES*
JEDEM
JEDEN
JEDER
JEDES
JENEM
JENEN
JENER
JENES
KEINE
MEINE*
SEINE*
UNSER*
DEINEM*
DEINEN*
DEINER*
DEINES*
DESSEN
DIESEM
DIESEN
DIESER
DIESES
EUEREM*
EUEREN*
EUERER*
EUERES*
JEMAND
KEINEM
KEINEN
KEINER
KEINES
MEINEM*
MEINEN*
MEINER*
MEINES*
NICHTS
SEINEM*
SEINEN*
SEINER*
SEINES*
UNSERE*
WELCHE
WESSEN
JEMANDS
NIEMAND
UNSEREM*
UNSEREN*
UNSERER*
UNSERES*
WELCHEM
WELCHEN
WELCHER
WELCHES

Latin

EA
EI
EO
HI
ID
IS
ME
SE
TE
TU
CUI
EAE
EAM
EAS
EGO
EIS
EOS
EUM
HAC
HAE
HAS
HIC
HIS
HOC
HOS
MEA*
MEI*
MEO*
NOS
QUA
QUI
QUO
SUA*
SUI*
SUO*
TOS*
TUA*
TUI*
TUO*
VOS
EIUS
HAEC
HANC
HUIC
HUNC
IDEM
ILLA
ILLE
ILLI
ILLO
IPSA
IPSE
IPSI
IPSO
ISTA
ISTE
ISTI
ISTO
MEAE*
MEAM*

MEAS*
MEIS*
MEOS*
MEUM*
MEUS*
MIHI
QUAE
QUAM
QUAS
QUEM
QUID
QUIS
QUOD
QUOS
SIBI
SUAE*
SUAM*
SUAS*
SUIS*
SUOS*
SUUM*
SUUS*
TIBI
TUAE*
TUAM*
TUAS*
TUIS*
TUUM*
TUUS*
CUIUS
EADEM
EARUM
EIDEM
EODEM
EORUM
HARUM
HORUM
HUIUS
ILLAE
ILLAM
ILLAS
ILLIS
ILLOS
ILLUD
ILLUM
IPSAE
IPSAM
IPSAS
IPSIS
IPSOS
IPSUM
ISTAE
ISTAM
ISTAS
ISTIS
ISTOS
ISTUD
ISTUM
NOBIS
VOBIS
ALICUI
ALIQUA
ALIQUI
ALIQUO
CUIDAM
CUIQUE
EAEDEM
EANDEM
EASDEM
EISDEM
EOSDEM
EUNDEM
ILLIUS
IPSIUS
ISTIUS
MEARUM*
MEORUM*
NOSTER*
NOSTRA*
NOSTRI*
NOSTRO*
QUADAM
QUARUM
QUIBUS
QUIDAM
QUIQUE
QUOQUE
QUOQUO
QUORUM
SUARUM*
SUORUM*
TUARUM*
TUORUM*
VESTER*
VESTRA*
VESTRI*
VESTRO*
ALIQUAE
ALIQUAM
ALIQUAS
ALIQUEM
ALIQUID
ALIQUIS
ALIQUOD
ALIQUOS
CUIQUAM
EIUSDEM
ILLARUM
ILLORUM
IPSARUM
IPSORUM
ISTARUM
ISTORUM
NOSTRAE*
NOSTRAM*
NOSTRAS*
NOSTRIS*
NOSTROS*
NOSTRUM*
QUAEDAM
QUAEQUE
QUANDAM
QUASDAM
QUASQUE
QUEMQUE
QUENDAM
QUIDDAM
QUIDQUE
QUISQUE
QUOQUAM
QUOSDAM
QUOSQUE
VESTRAE*
VESTRAM*
VESTRAS*
VESTRIS*
VESTROS*
VESTRUM*

NUMERALS

	Spanish	French	Italian	German	Latin
1	UNO	UN	UNO	EINS	UNUS
2	DOS	DEUX	DUE	ZWEI	DUO
3	TRES	TROIS	TRE	DREI	TRES
4	CUATRO	QUATRE	QUATTRO	VIER	QUATTUOR
5	CINCO	CINQ	CINQUE	FUNF	QUINQUE
6	SEIS	SIX	SEI	SECHS	SEX
7	SIETE	SEPT	SETTE	SIEBEN	SEPTEM
8	OCHO	HUIT	OTTO	ACHT	OCTO
9	NUEVE	NEUF	NOVE	NEUN	NOVEM
10	DIEZ	DIX	DIECI	ZEHN	DECEM
11	ONCE	ONZE	UNDICI	ELF	UNDECIM
12	DOZE	DOUZE	DODICI	ZWOLF	DUODECIM
20	VEINTE	VINGT	VENTI	ZWANZIG	VIGINTI
100	CIENTO	CENT	CENTO	HUNDERT	CENTUM
1000	MIL	MILLE	MILLE	TAUSEND	MILLE

GAMES AND SPORTS

GO

CAT
GIN
HEI
LOO
NAP
PAM
PIG
RUM
TAG

BRAG
DICE
FARO
FROG
GOLF
JASS
JUDO
KENO
LUDO
MILL
PICO
POLO
POOL
SKAT
SOLO
VINT

BANDY
BINGO
BOWLS
CATCH
CHESS
CINCH
CRAPS
DARTS
FARGO
FIVES
HALMA
JACKS
LOTTO
MACAO
MONTE
OHELL
OMBRE
PEDRO
PITCH
POKER
RUGBY
RUMMY

SALVO
SAMBA
SHOGI
STOPS
STUSS
TAROT
TRACK
WHIST

BOCCIE
BOSTON
BOXING
BRIDGE
CRAMBO
DISCUS
ECARTE
EIGHTS
EUCHRE
FANTAN
GHOSTS
GOBANG
GOFISH
HAMMER
HAZARD
HEARTS
HOCKEY
KARATE
MEMORY
MERELS
PELOTA
PIQUET
POCHEN
QUOITS
RACING
ROUNCE
SHINNY
SKIING
SLOUGH
SOCCER
SQUASH
TENNIS
TIVOLI

ARCHERY
AUTHORS
BARBUDI
BATBALL
BELOTTE
BEZIQUE
BOLIVIA
BOWLING

CANASTA
CASSINO
CRICKET
CROQUET
CURLING
FENCING
FISHING
HANGMAN
JAIALAI
LOWBALL
MARBLES
MUGGINS
OLDMAID
PACHISI
PALLONE
PLAFOND
SEVENUP
SHOTPUT
SKATING
SNOOKER
TENPINS
TILTING

ANAGRAMS
BACCARAT
BASEBALL
BOLOBALL
CHARADES
CHECKERS
CHOUETTE
CONQUIAN
CRAPETTE
CRIBBAGE
DOMINOES
DRAUGHTS
FOOTBALL
HANDBALL
HURDLING
IDOUBTIT
JACKPOTS
LACROSSE
LEAPFROG
MAHJONGG
MICHIGAN
MONOPOLY
NAPOLEON
NINEPINS
OKLAHOMA
PALLMALL
PATIENCE
PINGPONG

PINOCHLE
POPEJOAN
PYRAMIDS
ROULETTE
ROUNDERS
SCRABBLE
SIXTYSIX
SKITTLES
SLAPJACK
SOFTBALL
TUGOFWAR

ACEYDEUCY
BADMINTON
BAGATELLE
BILLIARDS
BLACKJACK
FORTYFIVE
HOPSCOTCH
ICEHOCKEY
PARCHEESI
SOLITAIRE
TEAKETTLE
TITTATTOE
TWENTYONE
WATERBALL
WATERPOLO
WRESTLING

BACKGAMMON
BASKETBALL
BATTLESHIP
CATEGORIES
DECKTENNIS
HORSESHOES
ICESKATING
LAWNTENNIS
PANGUINGUE
POSTOFFICE
TETHERBALL
VOLLEYBALL

BALLOONBALL
CHEMINDEFER
HIDEANDSEEK
RUSSIANBANK
TABLETENNIS
TIDDLYWINKS

CONSEQUENCES
SHUFFLEBOARD

TENNIS CHAMPIONS

FRY

ARTH
ASHE
BETZ
DOEG

FLAM
HARD
HART
HOAD
HUNT
KING

MAKO
WARD

BUDGE
BUENO
COOKE

FALES
LAVER
MOODY
MOORE
OSUNA
PERRY

RIGGS
ROCHE
SEARS
SMITH
VINES
WILLS

BOWREY
BROUGH
BROWNE
CASALS
COCHET
COOPER
DROBNY
DUPONT
EBBERN
FRASER
GIBSON

JACOBS
KRAMER
LARNED
LARSEN
LIZANA
MARBLE
MULLOY
MURRAY
PARKER
RICHEY
SEIXAS
STOLLE
SUSMAN
SUTTON
TILDEN
WRIGHT

ALLISON

BARTZEN
DOBERTY
EMERSON
LACOSTE
MALLORY
MCNEILL
NUTHALL
OSBORNE
RALSTON
SANTANA
SEDGMAN
TALBERT
TRABERT
WALLACH

ANDERSON
BROMWICH
CLOTHIER

CONNOLLY
GONZALES
GRAEBNER
JOHNSTON
MCKINLEY
MORTIMER
NEWCOMBE
ROSEWALL
VONCRAMM
WIGHTMAN
WILLIAMS

BJURSTEDT
HOTCHKISS
PASARELLE
SCHROEDER

MCLOUGHLIN

BASEBALL

* Indicates in the Hall of Fame

Famous Players

OTT*

COBB*
DEAN*
FORD
FOXX*
MAYS
MIZE
RICE*
RUTH*
WARD*

AARON
ANSON*
BAKER*
BANKS
BERRA
BROWN*
CAREY*
DUFFY*
EVERS*
EWING*
FABER*
FLICK*
GROVE*
KEEFE*
KELLY*
KINER
LYONS*

MARIS
PLANK*
RIXEY*
ROUSH*
TERRY*
VANCE*
WALSH*
WANER*
WHEAT*
WILLS
YOUNG*

BENDER*
CHANCE*
CLARKE*
DICKEY*
FELLER*
FRISCH*
GALVIN*
GEHRIG*
GRIMES*
KALINE
KEELER*
KOUFAX
LAJOIE*
MANTLE
MANUSH*
MUSIAL

SCHALK*
SISLER*
SNIDER
TINKER*
WAGNER*
WRIGHT*

APPLING*
BURKETT*
CHESBRO*
COLLINS*
HORNSBY*
HUBBELL*
HUGGINS*
JOHNSON*
NICHOLS*
OROURKE*
PENNOCK*
RIZZUTO
SIMMONS*
SPEAKER*
TRAYNOR*
WADDELL*
WALLACE*

BOUDREAU
BULKELEY*
CHADWICK*

CLARKSON*
COCHRANE*
CRAWFORD*
CUMMINGS*
DIMAGGIO*
DRYSDALE
HAMILTON*
HARTNETT*
HEILMANN*
JENNINGS*
ROBINSON*
SPALDING*
WILLIAMS*

ALEXANDER*
BRESNAHAN*
BROUTHERS*
DELAHANTY*
GEHRINGER*
GREENBERG*
KILLEBREW
MATHEWSON*
MCGINNITY*
RADBOURNE*

CAMPANELLA
CARTWRIGHT*
MARANVILLE*

Managers and Executives

DARK
HOUK
MACK*
MELE

FRICK
GRIMM
HANEY
KEANE
LOPEZ

TERRY
VEECK

ALSTON
BARROW*

CRONIN*
ECKERT
HARRIS
LANDIS*
MCGRAW*

RICKEY
YAWKEY

DRESSEN
HUGGINS

MCPHAIL
OMALLEY
STENGEL*

BOUDREAU

COCHRANE
COMISKEY*
DUROCHER
GRIFFITH*
MCCARTHY*

MURTAUGH
MCKECHNIE*

HUTCHINSON
SOUTHWORTH

Teams

National League

CUBS
METS
REDS
ASTROS
BRAVES

GIANTS
DODGERS
PIRATES
PHILLIES
CARDINALS

American League

TWINS
ANGELS
REDSOX
TIGERS
INDIANS

ORIOLES
YANKEES
SENATORS
WHITESOX
ATHLETICS

FAMOUS RACE HORSES

ZEV
NOOR
ALSAB
ARMED
KELSO
OMAHA
PAVOT
SWAPS
BUSHER
GUNBOW

NASHUA
PONDER
STYMIE
ASSAULT
MANOWAR
NEEDLES
SHUTOUT
TOMFOOL
BIMELICH
CITATION

CARRYBACK
CHALLEDON
DETERMINE
KAUAIKING
SIRBARTON
STAGEHAND
WHIRLAWAY
BUCKPASSER
CANDYSPOTS
COUNTFLEET

DEVILDIVER
GALLANTFOX
ROUNDTABLE
SEABISCUIT
WARADMIRAL
FIRSTFIDDLER
SWORDDANCER
COUNTERPOINT
NATIVEDANCER

BOXING

Heavyweight Champions

BAER
CLAY
HART
BURNS
LOUIS
LISTON

TUNNEY
CARNERA
CHARLES
CORBETT
DEMPSEY
JOHNSON

SHARKEY
WALCOTT
WILLARD
BRADDOCK
JEFFRIES
MARCIANO

SULLIVAN
JOHANSSON
PATTERSON
SCHMELING
FITZSIMMONS

FOOTBALL

Famous Players and Coaches

RAY

BELL
CARR
HEIN
MARA
OWEN

BAUGH
BLOOD
BROWN
BUREN
CLARK
GUYON
HALAS
HEALY
HENRY
LAYNE

LYMAN
NEALE
STAGG

ALBERT
DORAIS
DUBLEY
GRAHAM
GRANGE
HERBER
HESSER
HESTON
HEWITT
HINKLE
HUGHES
HUTSON
ISBELL
LITTLE

MCAFEE
NESSER
NEVERS
ROCKNE
ROONEY
STRONG
THORPE
TITTLE
TURNER
WALKER
WARNER
ZUPPKE

BATTLES
CONERLY
EDWARDS
HORNUNG
HORWEEN

HUBBARD
LAMBEAU
LEEMANS
LUCKMAN
MCNALLY
STANTON
TRAFTON

BROCKLIN
DRISCOLL
FLAHERTY
FORTMANN
KIESLING
MARSHALL
NAGURSKI
STYDAHAR
THOMPSON
VANBUREN

GEOGRAPHY

COUNTRIES AND CAPITALS

CAR	Bangui
UAR	Cairo
CHAD	Fort Lamy
CUBA	Havana
IRAK	Baghdad
IRAN	Teh(e)ran
IRAQ	Baghdad
LAOS	Vientiane
MALI	Bamako
OMAN	Muscat
PERU	Lima
SIAM	Bangkok
TOGO	Lome
USSR	Moscow
BURMA	Rangoon
CHILE	Santiago
CHINA	Peking
CHINA	Taipei
CONGO	Brazzaville
CONGO	Leopoldville
EGYPT	Cairo
GABON	Libreville
GHANA	Accra
HAITI	Port-au-Prince
INDIA	New Delhi
ITALY	Rome
JAPAN	Tokyo
KENYA	Nairobi
KOREA	Seoul
KOREA	Pyongyang
LIBYA	Tripoli
MALTA	Valetta
NEPAL	Katmandu
NIGER	Niamey
QATAR	Doha
SABAH	Jesselton
SPAIN	Madrid
SUDAN	Khartoum
SYRIA	Damascus
TIBET	Lhasa
WALES	Cardiff
YEMEN	Sana
BHUTAN	Tashi-chho (Thimbu)
BRAZIL	Brasilia
CANADA	Ottawa
CEYLON	Colombo
CYPRUS	Nicosia
FRANCE	Paris
GAMBIA	Bathurst
GREECE	Athens
GUINEA	Conakry
ISRAEL	Jerusalem
JORDAN	Amman
KUWAIT	Kuwait City
LATVIA	Riga
MALAWI	Zomba
MALAYA	George Town
MEXICO	Mexico City

MONACO	Monaco
NORWAY	Oslo
PANAMA	Panama City
POLAND	Warsaw
RWANDA	Kigali
SWEDEN	Stockholm
TOBAGO	Port of Spain
TURKEY	Ankara
UGANDA	Kampala
ULSTER	Dublin
ZAMBIA	Lusaka
ALBANIA	Tirana
ALGERIA	Algiers
ANDORRA	Andorra la Vella
AUSTRIA	Vienne
BAHRAIN	Manamah
BELGIUM	Brussels
BOLIVIA	Lapaz, Sucre
BRITAIN	
BURUNDI	Bujumbura
DAHOMEY	Porto Novo
DENMARK	Copenhagen
ECUADOR	Quito
ENGLAND	London
FINLAND	Helsinki
GERMANY	Bonn
GERMANY	East Berlin
HUNGARY	Budapest
ICELAND	Reykjavik
IRELAND	Dublin
JAMAICA	Kingston
LEBANON	Beirut
LIBERIA	Monrovia
MALDIVE (ISLANDS)	Male
MOROCCO	Rabat
NIGERIA	Lagos
RUMANIA	Bucharest
SARAWAK	Kuching
SENEGAL	Dakar
SOMALIA	Mogadishu
TRUCIAL (STATES)	
TUNISIA	Tunis
URUGUAY	Montivideo
VIETNAM	Saigon
VIETNAM	Hanoi
BULGARIA	Sofia
CAMBODIA	Phnom Penh
CAMEROON	Yaounde
COLOMBIA	Bogota
ETHIOPIA	Addis Ababa
HONDURAS	Tegucigalpa
MALAGASY	Tananarive
MALAYSIA	Kuala Lumpur
MONGOLIA	Ulan Bator
PAKISTAN	Rawalpindi
PARAGUAY	Asuncion
PORTUGAL	Lisbon
SCOTLAND	Edinburgh

SINKIANG	Tihwa (Urumchi)	NEWZEALAND	Wellington
TANZANIA	Dar es Salaam	TANGANYIKA	Dar es Salaam
THAILAND	Bangkok	UPPERVOLTA	Ouagadougou
TRINIDAD	Port of Spain	YUGOSLAVIA	Belgrade
ZANZIBAR	Zanzibar Town	AFGHANISTAN	Kabul
ARGENTINA	Buenos Aires	LUXEMBOURGH	Luxembourgh
AUSTRALIA	Canberra	NETHERLANDS	Amsterdam, The Hague
COSTARICA	San Jose	PHILIPPINES	Quezon City
DOMINICAN (REPUBLIC)	Santo Domingo	SAUDIARABIA	Riad (Riyadh)
GUATEMALA	Guatemala City	SIERRALEONE	Freetown
INDONESIA	(D)jakarta	SOUTHAFRICA	Capetown, Pretoria
NICARAGUA	Managua	SWITZERLAND	Bern(e)
SANMARINO	San Marino	GREATBRITAIN	London
SINGAPORE	Singapore	UNITEDSTATES	Washington
VENEZUELA	Caracas	LIECHTENSTEIN	Vaduz
ELSALVADOR	San Salvador	UNITEDKINGDOM	London
IVORYCOAST	Abidjan	CZECHOSLOVAKIA	Prague (Praha)
MADAGASCAR	Tananarive	NORTHERNIRELAND	Belfast
MAURITANIA	Nouakchott		

Canadian Provinces and Territories

	Abbr.	Capital
YUKON	YT	WHITEHORSE
QUEBEC	QUE	QUEBEC
ALBERTA	ALTA	EDMONTON
ONTARIO	ONT	TORONTO
MANITOBA	MAN	WINNIPEG
NORTHWEST	NWT	EDMONTON
NOVASCOTIA	NS	HALIFAX
NEWBRUNSWICK	NB	FREDERICTON
NEWFOUNDLAND	NEWF	STJOHNS
SASKATCHEWAN	SASK	REGINA
BRITISHCOLUMBIA	BC	VICTORIA

Union of Soviet Socialist Republics

UZBEK S.S.R.	Tashkent	ESTONIAN S.S.R.	Tallinn
KAZAKH S.S.R.	Alma-Ata	GEORGIAN S.S.R.	Tbilisi (Tiflis)
KIRGHIZ S.S.R.	Frunze	MOLDAVIAN S.S.R.	Kishinev
LATVIAN S.S.R.	Riga	UKRAINIAN S.S.R.	Kiev
RUSSIAN S.F.S.R.	Moscow	AZERBAIJAN S.S.R.	Baku
TADZHIK S.S.R.	Dushanbe	LITHUANIAN S.S.R.	Vilnius (Vilna)
TURKMEN S.S.R.	Ashkhabad	BYELORUSSIAN S.S.R.	Minsk
ARMENIAN S.S.R.	Erevan		

OTHER COUNTRIES OF EUROPE, ANCIENT AND MODERN

Former Independent Countries of Medieval and Modern Times

LEON	PSKOV	MODENA	SERBIA
BADEN	SAVOY	NAPLES	SICILY
GENOA	ARAGON	NASSAU	VENICE
HESSE	BOSNIA	RUSSIA	ARMENIA
PARMA	LATVIA	SAXONY	BATAVIA

BAVARIA
BOHEMIA
CASTILE
ESTONIA
GALICIA
GEORGIA
GRANADA
HANOVER
LIVONIA
MORAVIA
NAVARRE
PRUSSIA
SILESIA
TUSCANY
UKRAINE
VENETIA
ANATOLIA
ESTHONIA
HANNOVER
HOLSTEIN
LOMBARDY
MOLDAVIA
PIEDMONT
RUTHENIA
SLAVONIA
SLOVENIA
CIRCASSIA
DARMSTADT
KURDISTAN
LITHUANIA
OLDENBERG
POMERANIA
SCHLESWIG
WALLACHIA
BESSARABIA
MONTENEGRO
WESTPHALIA
BYELORUSSIA
MESOPOTAMIA
MECKLENBERG

Ancient Countries of British Isles

KENT
ESSEX
WALES
ANGLIA
MERCIA
SCOTIA
SUSSEX
WESSEX
DANELAW
IRELAND
DALRIADA
HIBERNIA
PICTLAND
EASTANGLIA
NORTHUMBRIA

Countries, Regions and Cities of Ancient Roman Times

GAUL
DACIA
GADES
HIPPO
NARBO
UTICA
APULIA
ARABIA
GALLIA
IBERIA
ISTRIA
LATIUM
MOESIA
RAETIA
SICILY
UMBRIA
ALBANIA
BAETICA
BELGICA
BRITAIN
CORDUBA
CORSICA
ETRURIA
GALICIA
GERMANY
LIGURIA
LUCANIA
LUTETIA
MESSANA
NORICUM
NUMIDIA
ODESSUS
PICENUM
POMPEII
SALONAE
SAMNIUM
SCANDIA
TOLETUM
VENETIA
BRUTTIUM
CAESAREA
CALABRIA
CAMPANIA
CARTHAGE
DALMATIA
EBORACUM
GERMANIA
HELVETIA
HIBERNIA
MASSILIA
PANNONIA
SARDINIA
SARGOSSA
SARMATIA
AQUITANIA
BRITANNIA
CALEDONIA
ILLYRICUM
LONDINIUM
LUSITANIA
PALESTINE
MAURETANIA

Ancient Greek and Eastern States and Cities

COS
IOS
ACTE
ARIA
CEOS
CIUS
CYME
DIAM
DURA
ELAM
ELIS
ELON
GAZA
ICUS
LATO
PISA
SIND
SOLI
SUSA
TEOS
TYRE
AEGAE
AENIS
AENUS
ARGOS
ASINE
BARCA
CARIA
CHIOS
DELOS
DORIS
GOLGI
ILIUM
IONIA
IPSUS
ISSUS
LAMIA
LEROS
LIBYA
LYDIA
MALIS
MEDIA
MELOS
MYSIA
NAXOS
NEMEA
PAROS
PELLA
PYDNA
PYLOS
RAGAE
SAMOS
SIDON
SYENE
SYRIA
TEGEA
TELOS
TEMPE
TENOS
THERA
TROAS
TYANA
ZIDON
ABDERA
ABYDUS
ACHAEA
AMASIA
ANAPHE
ANCORE
ANCYRA
ANDROS
APAMEA
ARBELA
ATHENS
ATTICA
CARDIA
CAUNUS
CITIUM
CNIDUS
CORONE
CUNAXA
CURIUM
CYRENE
DELPHI
DODONA
EPIRUS
EUBOEA
HYDREA
ICARIA
IMBROS
ITHACA
LEMNOS
LESBOS
LEUCAS
LINDUS
LISSUS

LOCRIS
MEGARA
MYLASA
MYRINE
PAPHOS
PARIUM
PATALA
PATRAE
PERSIA
PHASIS
PHERAE
PONTUS
PRIENE
RHODES
SAGALA
SARDES
SCIONE
SCYROS
SESTUS
SICYON
SINOPE
SKUDRA
SMYRNA
SPARTA
TARSUS
TAXILA
THASOS
THEBES
THRACE
TIRYNS
TYRONE
ZEUGMA
AETOLIA
AMATHUS
AMORGOS
AMYCLAE
ANTIOCH
ARCADIA
ARGOLIS
ARMENIA
ARSINOE
ASSYRIA
BABYLON
BACTRIA
BISITUN
BOEOTIA
CALYDON
CAMIRUS
CERYNIA
CHALCIS
CILICIA
CIMILOS
CLEONAE
CNOSSUS
CORCYRA
CORINTH
CYDONIA
CYNURIA
CYTHERA
DECELEA
ELEUSIS
EPHESUS
ERETRIA
GANDARA
GORDIUM
GORTYNA
IALYSUS
IDALIUM
LACONIA
LARISSA
LEUCTRA
MACEDON
MARONEA
MEMPHIS
MESSENE
METHONE
MILETUS
MYCENAE
MYCONOS
NISIBIS
NISYROS
OLYMPIA
PAEONIA
PAGASAE
PALLENE
PALMYRA
PARTHIA
PHOCAEA
PHRYGIA
PIRAEUS
PISIDIA
PRAESUS
SALAMIS
SAMARIA
SCYTHIA
SIPHNOS
STAGIRA
SUSIANA
TANAGRA
TENEDOS
THERMUM
TRALLAS
TROEZEN
XANTHUS
ACANTHUS
AMBRACIA
AMPHISSA
BERENICE
BITHYNIA
CALYMNOS
CARMANIA
CARPASIA
COLOPHON
DAMASCUS
ECBATANA
ERYTHRAE
GANDHARA
GEDROSIA
HYRCANIA
LAPETHUS
MAGNESIA
MARATHON
MARGIANA
MESSENIA
MYTILENE
OLYNTHUS
PELUSIUM
PERGAMUM
PHASELIS
PHILIPPI
PRIANSUS
SELENCIA
SERIPHOS
SITHONIA
SOGDIANA
TAMASSUS
THESSALY
TRAPEZUM
ZARIASPA
ACARNANIA
ARACHOSIA
BABYLONIA
BUCEPHALA
CALCHEDON
CARPATHOS
CHAERONEA
CHORASMIA
CTESIPHON
DASCYLIUM
DOLOPIANS
DRANGIANA
EPIDAURUS
JERUSALEM
MARACANDA
MESAMBRIA
NAUCRATIS
NICOMEDIA
PHARSALUS
PHOENICIA
PTOLOMAIS
THAPSACUS
ALEXANDRIA
CAPPADOCIA
CHALCIDICE
PERSEPOLIS
SAMOTHRACE
THERMOPYLAE

DEPARTMENTS, COMMUNES, PROVINCES, STATES, DISTRICTS, REGIONS, COUNTIES, CANTONS, COLONIES, POSSESSIONS

AIN	France
AKI	Japan
ANS	Belgium
AYR	Scotland
EDE	Netherlands
ELY	England
EPE	Netherlands
GOA	India
MOL	Belgium
PAU	France
RIF	Morocco
URI	Switzerland
VAR	France
ZUG	Switzerland
BAGO	Philippines
BAIA	Brazil
BIEL	Switzerland
BIRR	Ireland
BOGO	Philippines
BUTE	Scotland
CHUR	Switzerland
COMO	Italy
DOAB	India
ELIS	Greece

ENNA	Italy
ESTE	Italy
EURE	France
FANO	Italy
FARS	Iran
FIFE	Scotland
GAZA	Israel
GEEL	Belgium
GHOR	Afghanistan
HAUD	Ethiopia
ISSY	France
JAEN	Spain
JIND	India
KAFA	Ethiopia
KENT	England
LAON	France
LARA	Venezuela
LEON	Spain
LUGO	Italy, Spain
MAYO	Ireland
MONS	Belgium
NAGA	Philippines
NEJD	Saudi Arabia
OUDH	India
PARA	Brazil
PEGU	Burma
RAND	South Africa
REWA	India
RIFF	Morocco
RUHR	Germany
SAAR	France
SIND	India
SULU	Philippines
SWAT	Pakistan
VAUD	Switzerland
VICH	Spain
VIMY	France
AALST	Belgium
AARAU	Switzerland
ACQUI	Italy
ADIRA	Italy
AGRIA	Italy
AKYAB	Burma
ALAVA	Spain
ALBAY	Philippines
ALGAU	Germany
ALORA	Spain
ALOST	Belgium
ALWAR	India
ALWUR	India
AMAPA	Brazil
AMARA	Iran
ANGRI	Italy
ANGUL	India
ANGUS	Scotland
ANJOU	France
ANNAM	Viet Nam
AONIA	Greece
ARGAO	Philippines
ARLON	Belgium
ASOLO	Italy
ASSAM	India

ASSEN	Netherlands
ASWAN	Egypt
AUBIN	France
AUTUN	France
AVILA	Spain
BADEN	Germany
BAENA	Spain
BAHIA	Brazil
BAMRA	India
BALKH	Afghanistan
BANAT	Yugoslavia
BANAT	Rumania
BANFF	Canada
BEHAR	India
BENIN	Nigeria
BERAR	India
BERKS	England
BIHAR	India
BLYTH	England
BORNU	Nigeria
BOURG	France
BRAGA	Portugal
BREDA	Netherlands
BUCKS	England
CAPIZ	Philippines
CAPRI	Italy
CAVAN	Ireland
CEARA	Brazil
CHACO	South America
CHIAI	China
CLARE	Ireland
COORG	India
CUNEO	Italy
DELFT	Netherlands
DERBY	England
DEVON	England
DORIS	Greece
ESSEX	England
EUPEN	Belgium
EUTIN	Germany
EVERE	Belgium
EVORA	Portugal
FORLI	Italy
GALLA	Ethiopia
GANDO	Nigeria
GOIAS	Brazil
GOUDA	Netherlands
HANTS	England
HEJAZ	Saudi Arabia
HERAT	Afghanistan
HESSE	Germany
HONAN	China
HOPEH	China
HOPEI	China
HUNAN	China
HUNZA	India
HUPEH	China
IMOLA	Italy
IONIA	Greece
JEHOL	China
JHIND	India
KAFFA	Ethiopia

KALAT	Pakistan
KANSU	China
KEDAH	Malaysia
KERRY	Ireland
KIRIN	China
KUTCH	India
LECCE	Italy
LIPPE	Germany
LOUTH	Ireland
LUCCA	Italy
LUXOR	Egypt
MASSA	Italy
MEATH	Ireland
MEDOC	France
MONZA	Italy
NAIRN	Scotland
NATAL	South Africa
NEGEB	Israel
NEGEV	Israel
NUBIA	Sudan
PAVIA	Italy
PERAK	Malaysia
PIAUI	Brazil
POOLE	England
SAVOY	France
SIENA	Italy
SINDH	India
SLIGO	Ireland
SORIA	Spain
TERNI	Italy
TIGRE	Ethiopia
TIROL	Austria
TYROL	Austria
UDINE	Italy
WALES	United Kingdom
WILTS	England
AARGAU	Switzerland
ACADIA	Canada
ACHAEA	Greece
ALCAMO	Italy
ALCIRA	Spain
ALIAGA	Philippines
ALLGAU	Germany
ALMELO	Netherlands
ALPHEN	Netherlands
ALSACE	France
AMHARA	Ethiopia
ANCASH	Peru
ANDRIA	Italy
ANGELN	Germany
ANGOLA	Portugal
ANHALT	Germany
ANTRIM	Ireland
AOMORI	Japan
APULIA	Italy
ARAGON	Spain
ARAKAN	Burma
ARAUCO	Chile
ARCADY	Greece
AREZZO	Italy
ARMAGH	Ireland
ASHTON	England

ASSISI	Italy
ATHOLE	Scotland
ATTICA	Greece
BAYBAY	Philippines
BENGAL	India
BOSNIA	Yugoslavia
BRUGGE	Belgium
CARCAR	Philippines
CHAHAR	China
CHIHLI	China
COCHIN	India
CORATO	Italy
DORSET	England
EMILIA	Italy
EMPOLI	Italy
FUKIEN	China
FULHAM	England
GILGIT	India
GLARUS	Switzerland
GUIANA	South America
HAZARA	Pakistan
KARROO	South Africa
KUWAIT	Asia
LATIUM	Italy
MODENA	Italy
OAXACA	Mexico
OLDHAM	England
ORISSA	India
PAHANG	Malaysia
PAMIRS	Asia
PERLIS	Malaysia
PRIPET	USSR
PANJAB	India
PUNJAB	India
RAGUSA	Italy
SAXONY	Germany
SERBIA	Yugoslavia
SHANSI	China
SHARON	Israel
SHENSI	China
SIKKIM	India
SONORA	Mexico
STYRIA	Austria
SURREY	England
SUSSEX	England
SWABIA	Germany
TERUEL	Spain
THRACE	Greece
UMBRIA	Italy
VALAIS	Switzerland
VENDEE	France
YUNNAN	China
ALBERTA	Canada
ALMADEN	Spain
ALMANSA	Spain
ANDENNE	Belgium
ARCADIA	Greece
ASHANTI	Ghana
BAVARIA	Germany
BOEOTIA	Greece
BOHEMIA	Yugoslavia
BRABANT	Belgium

CASTILE	Spain	MASURIA	Poland
CHELSEA	England	MORAVIA	Czechoslovakia
CROATIA	Yugoslavia	MORELOS	Mexico
DURANGO	Mexico	NAVARRA	Spain
GALICIA	Spain	ORIENTE	Cuba
GALICIA	Poland	RIVIERA	France
GASCONY	France	SARAWAK	Indonesia
GWALIOR	India	SIBERIA	Asia
HOLBORN	England	SINALAO	Mexico
JALISCO	Mexico	SITSANG	Tibet
KARELIA	USSR	SURINAM	South America
LAMBETH	England	TABASCO	Mexico
LAPLAND	Sweden	TESCHEN	Poland
LIVONIA	Latvia	THURGAU	Switzerland

CITIES—UNITED STATES

* Indicates state capital

ADA	Ohio	OREM	Ut.	COLBY	Kan.
AJO	Ariz.	PANA	Ill.	CORRY	Pa.
AVA	Mo.	RENO	Nev.	CREWE	Va.
ELY	Minn.	RUSK	Tex.	CUERO	Tex.
OLA	Ark.	RUTH	Nev.	DANIA	Fla.
OPP	Ala.	RYAN	Okla.	DEPEW	N.Y.
ROY	Ut.	SACO	Me.	DERRY	N.H.
RYE	N.Y.	SPUR	Tex.	DIXON	Ill.
WAR	W.Va.	TAMA	Ia.	DONNA	Tex.
AIEA	Haw.	TROY	N.Y.	DOVER*	Del.
ALMA	Mich.	WACO	Tex.	EATON	Ohio
ARCO	Id.	WARE	Mass.	EDINA	Minn.
ARMA	Kan.	WEIR	Kan.	ELDON	Mo.
AYER	Mass.	WRAY	Col.	ELGIN	Ill.
BATH	Me.	YORK	Pa.	ENNIS	Tex.
BUHL	Id.	YUMA	Ariz.	ERWIN	Tenn.
DALE	Pa.	ZION	Ill.	FARGO	N.D.
DORA	Ala.	AIKEN	S.C.	FLINT	Mich.
DUNN	N.C.	AKRON	Ohio	FLORA	Ill.
DUPO	Ill.	ALAMO	Tex.	GALAX	Va.
EDNA	Tex.	ALBIA	Ia.	GALVA	Ill.
ELKO	Nev.	ALCOA	Tenn.	GREER	S.C.
ELMA	N.Y.	ALICE	Tex.	HAVRE	Mont.
ELOY	Ariz.	ALTON	Ill.	HOBBS	N.M.
ENID	Okla.	ANOKA	Minn.	HOUMA	La.
ERIE	Pa.	ASPEN	Col.	ILION	N.Y.
GARY	Ind.	BARRE	Vt.	IONIA	Mich.
HAYS	Kan.	BEREA	Ohio	IRWIN	Pa.
HILO	Haw.	BLAIR	Neb.	ISLIP	N.Y.
HOLT	Mich.	BOISE*	Ida.	KAPAA	Haw.
HUGO	Okla.	BOONE	Ia.	KEENE	N.H.
IOLA	Kan.	BRONX	N.Y.	KELSO	Wash.
KENT	Ohio	BRYAN	Tex.	LADUE	Mo.
LEHI	Ut.	BUTTE	Mont.	LAMAR	Col.
LIMA	Ohio	CAMAS	Wash.	LIHUE	Haw.
LODI	N.J.	CANEY	Kan.	LOGAN	Ut.
LYNN	Mass.	CAREY	Ohio	MACON	Ga.
MART	Tex.	CARMI	Ill.	MIAMI	Fla.
MAUD	Okla.	CASEY	Ill.	MINGO	Ohio
MENA	Ark.	CAYCE	S.C.	MINOT	N.D.
MESA	Ariz.	CHICO	Cal.	NAMPA	Id.
MILO	Me.	CHINO	Cal.	NILES	Ill.
MORA	Minn.	CLARE	Mich.	OCALA	Fla.
NAPA	Cal.	CLYDE	Ohio	OLNEY	Ill.
OMAK	Wash.	COCOA	Fla.	OMAHA	Neb.

ONAWA	Ia.	CANTON	Ohio	HOBART	Ind.
ORONO	Me.	CASPER	Wyo.	IDABEL	Okla.
OSSEO	Minn.	CELINA	Ohio	ITHACA	N.Y.
OWEGO	N.Y.	CICERO	Ill.	JASPER	Ala.
PAMPA	Tex.	CLOVIS	N.M.	JOLIET	Ill.
PAOLA	Kan.	COHOES	N.Y.	JOPLIN	Mo.
PAOLI	Pa.	COLTON	Cal.	JUNEAU*	Alas.
PARMA	Ohio	CONROE	Tex.	KENTON	Ohio
PASCO	Wash.	CONWAY	Ark.	KEOKUK	Ia.
PECOS	Tex.	CORBIN	Ky.	KOKOMO	Ind.
PEKIN	Ill.	CORONA	Cal.	LAREDO	Tex.
PELLA	Ia.	COSCOB	Conn.	LAUREL	Miss.
PHARR	Tex.	COVINA	Cal.	LAWTON	Okla.
PIQUA	Ohio	CRESCO	Ia.	LEMARS	Ia.
PRATT	Kan.	CUDAHY	Wis.	LENNOX	Cal.
PROVO	Ut.	DALLAS	Tex.	LENOIR	N.C.
PRYOR	Okla.	DALTON	Ga.	LINDEN	N.J.
RATON	N.M.	DARIEN	Conn.	LOMITA	Cal.
RAYNE	La.	DAWSON	Ga.	LORAIN	Ohio
RIPON	Wisc.	DAYTON	Ohio	LOWELL	Mass.
ROLFE	Ia.	DEKALB	Ill.	MCADOO	Pa.
ROLLA	Mo.	DELAND	Fla.	MCCOMB	Miss.
ROTAN	Tex.	DELANO	Cal.	MACOMB	Ill.
SALEM*	Ore.	DEMING	N.M.	MADERA	Cal.
SANDY	Ut.	DENVER*	Col.	MALDEN	Mass.
SAYRE	Pa.	DEPERE	Wis.	MARION	Ohio
SELMA	Ala.	DESOTO	Mo.	MARION	Ind.
STOWE	Pa.	DEXTER	Mo.	MERCED	Cal.
STOWE	Vt.	DILLON	S.C.	MILTON	Mass.
TAMPA	Fla.	DOLTON	Ill.	MOBILE	Ala.
TEMPE	Ariz.	DOWNEY	Cal.	MOLINE	Ill.
TOMAH	Wisc.	DRACUT	Mass.	MONACA	Pa.
TULSA	Okla.	DUBOIS	Pa.	MONROE	La.
TYLER	Tex.	DULUTH	Minn.	MONSON	Mass.
UKIAH	Cal.	EASTON	Pa.	MUNCIE	Ind.
UTICA	N.Y.	ECORSE	Mich.	NASHUA	N.H.
WAHOO	Neb.	ELDORA	Ia.	NATICK	Mass.
WELCH	W.Va.	ELKTON	Md.	NEWARK	N.J.
WYLIE	Tex.	ELMIRA	N.Y.	NEWTON	Mass.
WYNNE	Ark.	ELRENO	Okla.	NORMAN	Okla.
XENIA	Ohio	ELWOOD	Ind.	NUTLEY	N.J.
ADRIAN	Mich.	ELYRIA	Ohio	OWOSSO	Mich.
AGAWAM	Mass.	EMMAUS	Pa.	PALMER	Mass.
ALBANY*	N.Y.	EPPING	N.H.	PAWPAW	Mich.
ALGONA	Ia.	EUCLID	Ohio	PAXTON	Ill.
ANTIGO	Wis.	EUGENE	Ore.	PAYSON	Ut.
AUBURN	N.Y.	EUNICE	La.	PEORIA	Ill.
AURORA	Ill.	EUREKA	Cal.	PIERRE*	S.D.
AUSTIN*	Tex.	EUSTIS	Fla.	PUTNAM	Conn.
BANGOR	Me.	EXETER	N.H.	QUEENS	N.Y.
BARTOW	Fla.	FRESNO	Cal.	QUINCY	Mass.
BELOIT	Wis.	GALENA	Ill.	RACINE	Wisc.
BENTON	Ark.	GALION	Ohio	RAHWAY	N.J.
BETHEL	Pa.	GERING	Neb.	RANGER	Tex.
BILOXI	Miss.	GIRARD	Ohio	RENOVO	Pa.
BONHAM	Tex.	GOLDEN	Col.	RENTON	Wash.
BORGER	Tex.	GORHAM	Me.	REVERE	Mass.
BOSTON*	Mass.	GRETNA	La.	SALINA	Kan.
BREWER	Me.	GROTON	Conn.	SCOTIA	N.Y.
BUFORD	Ga.	HAMDEN	Conn.	SEGUIN	Tex.
BUNKIE	La.	HARLAN	Ky.	SENECA	S.C.
BURNET	Tex.	HELENA*	Mont.	SEWARD	Neb.
CAMDEN	N.J.	HINTON	W.Va.	SEWARD	Alas.

SHARON Pa.
SHELBY N.C.
SIDNEY Ohio
SKOKIE Ill.
SLAYTON Tex.
SNYDER Tex.
SOLVAY N.Y.
SONORA Cal.
SONORA Ariz.
SPARKS Nev.
STAMPS Ark.
STEGER Ill.
STPAUL* Minn.
STROUD Okla.
SUMTER S.C.
TACOMA Wash.
THROOP Pa.
TIFFIN Ohio
TIFTON Ga.
TIPTON Ind.
TOLEDO Ohio
TOPEKA* Kan.
TUCSON Ariz.
TULARE Cal.
TUPELO Miss.
UPLAND Cal.
URBANA Ill.
VERNAL Ut.
VERNON Tex.
VINITA Okla.
WALDEN N.Y.
WARREN Ohio
WAUSAU Wis.
WEISER Id.
WINONA Minn.
WOBURN Mass.
YAKIMA Wash.
YEADON Pa.
ABILENE Kan.
ALAMEDA Cal.
ALTOONA Pa.
AMHERST Mass.
ANDOVER Mass.
ANSONIA Conn.
ARDMORE Pa.
ASHLAND Ky.
ATLANTA* Ga.
ATTALLA Ala.
AUGUSTA Ga.
AUGUSTA* Me.
BASTROP La.
BAYCITY Mich.
BAYONNE N.J.
BEDFORD Ohio
BELMONT Mass.
BENICIA Cal.
BERKLEY Mich.
BETHANY Okla.
BEVERLY Mass.
BOONTON N.J.
BOULDER Col.
BOZEMAN Mont.
BRISTOL Conn.
BUFFALO N.Y.
CAMERON Tex.
CAMILLA Ga.
CHATHAM N.J.
CHELSEA Mass.
CHESTER Pa.
CHEVIOT Ohio
CHICAGO Ill.
CLAYTON Mo.
CLIFTON N.J.
CLINTON Ia.
CONCORD* N.H.
COOSBAY Ore.
CORDELE Ga.
CORINTH Miss.
CORNING N.Y.
COTULLA Tex.
CRAFTON Pa.
CROWLEY La.
CULLMAN Ala.
DECATUR Ill.
DECORAH Ia.
DELPHOS Ohio
DENISON Tex.
DETROIT Mich.
DICKSON Pa.
DORMONT Pa.
DOUGLAS Ariz.
DUBUQUE Ia.
DUNEDIN Fla.
DUNMORE Pa.
DURANGO Col.
ELKCITY Okla.
ELKHART Ind.
ENFIELD Conn.
EVERETT Mass.
FARRELL Pa.
FINDLAY Ohio
GADSDEN Ala.
GAFFNEY S.C.
GARDENA Cal.
GARRETT Ind.
GENESEO Ill.
GLENCOE Ill.
GRAFTON W.Va.
GREELEY Col.
GUTHRIE Okla.
HAMMOND Ind.
HAMPTON Va.
HIALEAH Fla.
HIBBING Minn.
HINGHAM Mass.
HOBOKEN N.J.
HOLYOKE Mass.
HORNELL N.Y.
HOUSTON Tex.
INKSTER Mich.
IRONTON Ohio
JACKSON* Miss.
KEARNEY N.J.
KENOSHA Wis.
KEWANEE Ill.
KEYWEST Fla.
KILGORE Tex.
KINSTON N.C.
KITTERY Me.
LACONIA N.H.
LANSING* Mich.
LAPORTE Ind.
LARAMIE Wyo.
LASALLE Ill.
LATROBE Pa.
LIBERAL Kan.
LINCOLN* Neb.
LIVONIA Mich.
LUBBOCK Tex.
LYNWOOD Cal.
MCALLEN Tex.
MADISON* Wis.
MANKATO Minn.
MATTOON Ill.
MAYWOOD Ill.
MEDFORD Mass.
MEMPHIS Tenn.
MENASHA Wis.
MILFORD Conn.
MINEOLA N.Y.
MOBERLY Mo.
MODESTO Cal.
MORENCI Ariz.
MULLINS S.C.
NATCHEZ Miss.
NEEDHAM Mass.
NEWPORT R.I.
NOGALES Ariz.
NORFOLK Va.
NORWALK Conn.
NORWOOD Ohio
OAKLAND Cal.
OAKPARK Ill.
OILCITY Pa.
OLDTOWN Me.
OLYMPIA* Wash.
ORLANDO Fla.
OSHKOSH Wis.
OTTUMWA Ia.
PADUCAH Ky.
PARAMUS N.J.
PARSONS Kan.
PASSAIC N.J.
PHOENIX* Ariz.
PULASKI Va.
QUITMAN Ga.
RALEIGH N.C.
RARITAN N.J.
READING Pa.
REDDING Cal.
ROANOKE Va.
ROSELLE N.J.
SAGINAW Mich.
SALINAS Cal.
SANFORD N.C.
SANJOSE Cal.
SANTAFE* N.M.
SAPULPA Okla.
SEATTLE Wash.

SEDALIA	Mo.
SHAWNEE	Okla.
SPENCER	Mass.
SPOKANE	Wash.
STURGIS	Mich.
SUFFOLK	Va.
SUNAPEE	N.H.
TARBORO	N.C.
TARRANT	Ala.
TEANECK	N.J.
TERRELL	Tex.
TRENTON*	N.J.
VALLEJO	Cal.
VANWERT	Ohio
VENTURA	Cal.
VISALIA	Cal.
WAREHAM	Mass.
WEBSTER	Mass.
WEIRTON	W.Va.
WESLACO	Tex.
WHEATON	Ill.
WICHITA	Kan.
WINDBER	Pa.
WINSTED	Conn.
WOOSTER	Ohio
YANKTON	S.D.
YONKERS	N.Y.
AMARILLO	Tex.
ANNARBOR	Mich.
ANNISTON	Ala.
BERKELEY	Cal.
BESSEMER	Ala.
BILLINGS	Mont.
BISMARCK*	N.D.
BOGALUSA	La.
BRAINERD	Minn.
BROCKTON	Mass.
BROOKLYN	N.Y.
BRYNMAWR	Pa.
CADILLAC	Mich.
CALDWELL	Id.
CALEXICO	Cal.
CARLISLE	Pa.
CARLSBAD	N.M.
CARTERET	N.J.
CHEYENNE*	Wyo.
COLUMBIA*	S.C.
COLUMBUS*	Ohio
CORTLAND	N.Y.
CRANSTON	R.I.
DANVILLE	Ill.
DANVILLE	Va.
DEARBORN	Mich.
DEERPARK	Ohio
EDINBURG	Tex.
EVANSTON	Ill.
FAIRMONT	W.Va.
FREDONIA	N.Y.
GASTONIA	N.C.
GLENDALE	Cal.
GREENBAY	Wis.
GULFPORT	Miss.
HANNIBAL	Mo.
HARTFORD*	Conn.
HASTINGS	Neb.
HAZLETON	Pa.
HONOLULU*	Haw.
KANKAKEE	Ill.
LACROSSE	Wis.
LAKEWOOD	N.J.
LASVEGAS	Nev.
LAWRENCE	Mass.
LEWISTON	Me.
LOCKPORT	N.Y.
MARIETTA	Ga.
MISSOULA	Mont.
MONTEREY	Cal.
MUSKEGON	Mich.
MUSKOGEE	Okla.
NEWBURGH	N.Y.
OAKRIDGE	Tenn.
OKMULGEE	Okla.
OSSINING	N.Y.
PALOALTO	Cal.
PASADENA	Cal.
PLYMOUTH	Mass.
PRESCOTT	Ariz.
RICHMOND*	Va.
ROCKFORD	Ill.
ROCKHILL	S.C.
SANDIEGO	Cal.
SANDUSKY	Ohio
SANMATEO	Cal.
SANTAANA	Cal.
SARASOTA	Fla.
SAVANNAH	Ga.
SCRANTON	Pa.
STAMFORD	Conn.
STAUNTON	Va.
STOCKTON	Cal.
SYRACUSE	N.Y.
TALLULAH	La.
TUSKEGEE	Ala.
VALDOSTA	Ga.
WATERLOO	Ia.
WAUKEGAN	Ill.
WAUKESHA	Wis.
WESTPORT	Conn.
WHEELING	W.Va.
WHITTIER	Cal.
WILMETTE	Ill.
WOODBURY	N.J.
ANNAPOLIS*	Md.
ARLINGTON	Va.
ASHEVILLE	N.C.
BALTIMORE	Md.
BARBERTON	Ohio
BELVEDERE	Cal.
BETHLEHEM	Pa.
BIDDEFORD	Me.
BRADENTON	Fla.
BRAINTREE	Mass.
BREMERTON	Wash.
BRUNSWICK	Ga.
CAMBRIDGE	Mass.
CHAMPAIGN	Ill.
CHARLOTTE	N.C.
CLEVELAND	Ohio
COVINGTON	Ky.
DESMOINES*	Ia.
ELIZABETH	N.J.
ENGLEWOOD	N.J.
FALLRIVER	Mass.
FLAGSTAFF	Ariz.
FONDULAC	Wis.
FORTDODGE	Ia.
FRANKFORT*	Ky.
HAMTRAMCK	Mich.
HOLLYWOOD	Cal.
JOHNSTOWN	Pa.
KALAMAZOO	Mich.
LANCASTER	Pa.
LEXINGTON	Ky.
MANHATTAN	N.Y.
MANHATTAN	Kan.
NASHVILLE*	Tenn.
PENSACOLA	Fla.
ROCHESTER	N.Y.
SALISBURY	N.C.
SANANGELO	Tex.
SOUTHBEND	Ind.
SOUTHGATE	Cal.
WATERBURY	Conn.
WESTALLIS	Wis.
WESTPOINT	N.Y.
WORCESTER	Mass.

FOREIGN CITIES

ABA	Nigeria
ABO	Finland
AIX	France
AUE	West Germany
AVA	Burma
BAM	Iran
BOR	Yugoslavia
DAX	France
DIR	Pakistan
EDE	Nigeria
EDO	Japan
EMS	West Germany
FES	Morocco
FEZ	Morocco
HOF	West Germany
HUE	South Viet-nam

ICA	Peru
IRI	South Korea
ITA	Paraguay
IWO	Nigeria
KEM	USSR
KUM	Iran
LAE	New Guinea
LEH	India
NIS	Yugoslavia
OYO	Nigeria
QUM	Iran
SAN	Mali
SPA	Belgium
TSU	Japan
UBE	Japan
UFA	USSR
ULM	West Germany
ACRE	Israel
ADEN	Aden
ADUA	Ethiopia
AGAR	India
AGEN	France
AGRA	India
AIUD	Rumania
ALBI	France
ALES	France
ALEY	Lebanon
AMOL	Iran
AMOY	China
AMUL	Iran
ANSI	China
APAM	Mexico
APIA	Western Samoa
APRA	Guam
ARAD	Rumania
ASCH	Czechoslovakia
AYAN	USSR
BAGE	Brazil
BAJA	Hungary
BAKU	USSR
BALE	Switzerland
BARI	Italy
BATH	England
BERN	Switzerland
BIDA	Nigeria
BIEL	Switzerland
BISK	USSR
BLED	Yugoslavia
BONE	Algeria
BONN	West Germany
BRNO	Czechoslovakia
BUDA	Hungary
BUEA	Cameroon
BUGA	Colombia
BUNA	New Guinea
BURG	East Germany
CAEN	France
CALI	Colombia
CEBU	Philippines
CHEB	Czechoslovakia
CHUR	Switzerland
CLUJ	Rumania
COBH	Ireland
CORK	Ireland
CORO	Venezuela
DHAR	India
DILI	Portuguese Timor
DOHA	Qatar
EGER	Hungary
ETAH	Greenland
FUYU	China
GAYA	India
GAZA	Israel
GENT	Belgium
GERA	East Germany
GIZA	Egypt
GRAZ	Austria
GYOR	Hungary
HAMM	West Germany
HILO	Hawaii
HOFU	Japan
HOKO	South Korea
HOMS	Libya; Syria
HULL	England
HUTT	New Zealand
IASI	Rumania
IFNI	Morocco
IPIN	China
IPOH	Malaysia
IRUN	Spain
JAEN	Spain
JENA	East Germany
KANO	Nigeria
KHOI	Iran
KIEL	West Germany
KIEV	USSR
KOBE	Japan
KOFU	Japan
KURE	Japan
LABE	Guinea
LIDO	Italy
LIMA	Peru
LINZ	Austria
LODI	Italy
LODZ	Poland
LOME	Togo
LOTA	Chile
LVOV	USSR
LWOW	USSR
METZ	France
MITO	Japan
MOJI	Japan
MONS	Belgium
NAHA	Ryukyu Is.
NARA	Japan
NAWA	Syria
NICE	France
NISH	Yugoslavia
OBAN	Scotland
OITA	Japan
OMSK	USSR
ORAN	Algeria
OREL	USSR
ORLY	France
ORSK	USSR
OSLO	Norway

OTSU	Japan
OULU	Finland
PARA	Brazil
PEGU	Burma
PERM	USSR
PILA	Poland
PISA	Italy
POLA	Yugoslavia
PORI	Finland
PRAG	Czechoslovakia
PULA	Yugoslavia
PUNO	Peru
RIAD	Saudi Arabia
RIGA	Latvia
RIVA	Italy
ROME	Italy
SAIS	Egypt
SANA	Yemen
SENS	France
SETE	France
SIAN	China
STLO	France
SUEZ	Egypt
SUMY	USSR
SUSA	Iran
SUVA	Fiji
TARA	Ireland
TULA	USSR
URFA	Turkey
VIGO	Spain
VILA	Scotland
WIEN	Austria
WUHU	China
YAFA	Israel
ACCRA	Ghana
ADANA	Turkey
ADONI	India
ADOWA	Ethiopia
ADUWA	Ethiopia
AGANA	Guam
AHLEN	West Germany
AHWAZ	Iran
AIGUN	China
AKITA	Japan
AKOLA	India
AKURE	Nigeria
ALLOA	Scotland
AMARA	Irak
AMBON	Indonesia
AMBUR	India
AMMAN	Jordan
ANAPA	USSR
ANCON	Panama
ANCUD	Chile
ANGOL	Chile
ANGUL	India
ANZIO	Italy
APAPA	Nigeria
ARCOT	India
ARICA	Chile
ARLES	France
ARRAH	India
ARRAS	France

ASHIO	Japan
ATAMI	Japan
AVILA	Spain
AVOLA	Italy
BABUL	Iran
BACAU	Rumania
BADEN	Austria
BAHIA	Brazil
BALLY	India
BALTA	USSR
BASEL	Switzerland
BASRA	Irak
BATUM	USSR
BAURU	Brazil
BEIRA	Portugal
BEKES	Hungary
BELEM	Brazil
BEPPU	Japan
BERNE	Switzerland
BIHAR	India
BLOIS	France
BOGOR	Indonesia
BREST	France
BULAN	Philippines
BUNDI	India
BURSA	Turkey
BYTOV	Poland
CADIZ	Spain
CAIRO	Egypt
CANEA	Greece
CAPUA	Italy
CAVAN	Ireland
CEARA	Brazil
CELLE	West Germany
CEUTA	Morocco
CHIBA	Japan
CHITA	USSR
CLEVE	.West Germany
COLON	Panama
COWES	England
DACCA	Pakistan
DAKAR	Senegal
DATIA	India
DAVAO	Philippines
DAVOS	Switzerland
DEHLI	India
DERNA	Libya
DIJON	France
DILLI	Portuguese Timor
DOORN	Netherlands
DOUAI	France
ELCHE	Spain
EMDEN	West Germany
ERLAU	Hungary
ESSEN	West Germany
FIUME	Yugoslavia
FUSAN	South Korea
GALLE	Ceylon
GATUN	Panama
GENOA	Italy
GHENT	Belgium
GIJON	Spain
GOMEL	USSR

GORKI	USSR	NIMES	France
GOTHA	East Germany	OGAKI	Japan
GREIZ	East Germany	OMURA	Japan
HAGEN	West Germany	OMUTA	Japan
HAIFA	Israel	OPOLE	Poland
HALLE	East Germany	ORURO	Bolivia
HAMAR	Norway	OSAKA	Japan
HANDA	Japan	OSTIA	Italy
HANOI	North Viet-nam	OTARU	Japan
HARAR	Ethiopia	PADUA	Italy
HERAT	Afghanistan	PALMA	Spain
HERNE	West Germany	PALOS	Spain
HORTA	Portugal	PARIS	France
HUBLI	India	PARMA	Italy
IJEBU	Nigeria	PASAY	Philippines
ISCHL	Austria	PATAN	Nepal
ITAMI	Japan	PATNA	India
IZMIR	Turkey	PENKI	China
IZMIT	Turkey	PENZA	USSR
JAFFA	Israel	PERAK	Malaysia
JEDDA	Saudi Arabia	PERTH	Australia
JEREZ	Spain	PINSK	USSR
JIDDA	Saudi Arabia	PLZEN	Czechoslovakia
KABUL	Afghanistan	PODOR	Senegal
KANDY	Ceylon	PONCE	Puerto Rico
KASUR	Pakistan	POONA	Afghanistan
KAZAN	USSR	POSEN	Poland
KEIJO	South Korea	PRAHA	Czechoslovakia
KERCH	USSR	PUSAN	South Korea
KHIVA	USSR	QUITO	Ecuador
KIMPO	South Korea	RABAT	Morocco
KIROV	USSR	RADOM	Poland
KIRYU	Japan	REIMS	France
KOCHI	Japan	RESHT	Iran
KONIA	Turkey	REVAL	Estonia
KONYA	Turkey	ROUEN	France
KOVNO	Lithuania	SAGAR	India
KOWNO	Lithuania	SAKAI	Japan
KYOTO	Japan	SALTA	Argentina
LAGOS	Nigeria	SEDAN	France
LAHTI	Finland	SEOUL	South Korea
LANUS	Argentina	SHASI	China
LAPAZ	Bolivia	SHOKA	Rep. China
LEEDS	England	SIDON	Lebanon
LHASA	Tibet	SIENA	Italy
LIEGE	Belgium	SIMLA	India
LILLE	France	SOFIA	Bulgaria
LOMAS	Argentina	SPLIT	Yugoslavia
LUTSK	Poland	SUCRE	Bolivia
LYONS	France	SURAT	India
MAINZ	West Germany	SUWON	South Korea
MALMO	Sweden	TAEGU	South Korea
MASAN	North Korea	TANTA	Egypt
MECCA	Saudi Arabia	TOKAY	Hungary
MEDAN	Indonesia	TOKYO	Japan
MEMEL	Lithuania	TOMSK	USSR
MILAN	Italy	TOURS	France
MINSK	USSR	TRANI	Italy
MOSUL	Irak	TRENT	Italy
NAMUR	Belgium	TRIER	West Germany
NANCY	France	TUNIS	Tunisia
NATAL	Brazil	TURIN	Italy
NIGEL	South Africa	TURKU	Finland

VAASA	Finland
VADUZ	Liechtenstein
VARNA	Bulgaria
VICHY	France
VILNA	Lithuania
VISBY	Sweden
WILNA	Lithuania
WORMS	West Germany
WUHAN	China
WUWEI	China
YALTA	USSR
ZOMBA	Malawi
AACHEN	West Germany
AARHUS	Denmark
ABADAN	Iran
ABUKIR	Egypt
AEGION	Greece
AEGIUM	Greece
AGADES	Nigeria
AGADIR	Morocco
AKASHI	Japan
ALATYR	USSR
ALBURY	Australia
ALEPPO	Syria
ALLADA	Dahomey
ALTONA	West Germany
ALTORF	Switzerland
AMALFI	Italy
AMBALA	India
AMBATO	Ecuador
AMIENS	France
ANCONA	Italy
ANGERS	France
ANGKOR	Cambodia
ANKARA	Turkey
ANNECY	France
ANSHAN	China
AOMORI	Japan
APATIN	Yugoslavia
APOLDA	East Germany
ARCOLE	Italy
ARNHEM	Netherlands
ASMARA	Ethiopia
ASTARA	USSR
ATHENS	Greece
BAGUIO	Philippines
BALBOA	Panama
BAMAKO	Mali
BANDRA	India
BARMEN	West Germany
BARODA	India
BASTIA	France
BATUMI	USSR
BEIRUT	Lebanon
BENONI	South Africa
BERGEN	Norway
BHOPAL	India
BILBAO	Spain
BINGEN	West Germany
BOCHUM	West Germany
BOGOTA	Columbia
BOLTON	England
BOMBAY	India
BOUGIE	Algeria
BRAILA	Rumania
BRASOV	Rumania
BREMEN	West Germany
BRIONI	Yugoslavia
BRUNEI	Indonesia
BURGAS	Bulgaria
CAGUAS	Puerto Rico
CALAIS	France
CALLAO	Peru
CAMBAY	India
CANNES	France
CANTON	China
CASSEL	West Germany
CAVITE	Philippines
CAXIAS	Brazil
CEGLED	Hungary
CHAPRA	India
CHOLON	South Viet-nam
CHOSHI	Japan
COLMAR	France
CRACOW	Poland
CUCUTA	Colombia
DAIREN	China
DANZIG	Poland
DELPHI	Greece
DODONA	Greece
DUBLIN	Ireland
DUMDUM	India
DUNDEE	Scotland
DURBAN	South Africa
EDESSA	Greece
ERFURT	East Germany
ERIVAN	USSR
EXETER	England
FUSHUN	China
GALATI	Rumania
GDYNIA	Poland
GENEVA	Switzerland
GONDAR	Ethiopia
GOSLAR	West Germany
GRASSE	France
GRODNO	USSR
GROZNY	USSR
GUNTUR	India
HAMELN	West Germany
HANKOW	China
HARBIN	China
HARRAR	Ethiopia
HAVANA	Cuba
HIMEJI	Japan
HOBART	Australia
IBADAN	Nigeria
ILOILO	Philippines
ILORIN	Nigeria
IMPHAL	India
INCHON	South Korea
INDORE	India
JAIPUR	India
JALAPA	Mexico
JOHORE	Malaysia
KALUGA	USSR
KANPUR	India

City	Country	City	Country
KAOLAN	China	OXFORD	England
KASHAN	Iran	PADANG	Indonesia
KASSEL	West Germany	PASSAU	West Germany
KAUNAS	Lithuania	PATRAS	Greece
KAZVIN	Iran	PEKING	China
KEDIRI	Indonesia	PILSEN	Czechoslovakia
KIGALI	Rwanda	PLAUEN	East Germany
KUNSAN	South Korea	POTOSI	Bolivia
KUWAIT	Kuwait	POZNAN	Poland
LAHORE	Pakistan	PRAGUE	Czechoslovakia
LEIDEN	Netherlands	QUEBEC	Canada
LEMANS	France	QUETTA	Pakistan
LERIDA	Spain	RAGUSA	Yugoslavia
LEYDEN	Netherlands	RAIPUR	India
LIDICE	Czechoslovakia	RAMPUR	India
LISBON	Portugal	RECIFE	Brazil
LONDON	England	RENNES	France
LUANDA	Angola	RIJEKA	Yugoslavia
LUBECK	West Germany	RIMINI	Italy
LUBLIN	USSR	RIYADH	Saudi Arabia
LUGANO	Switzerland	ROSTOV	USSR
MACEIO	Brazil	SAIGON	South Viet-nam
MADRAS	India	SANTOS	Brazil
MADRID	Spain	SASEBO	Japan
MADURA	India	SENDAI	Japan
MALAGA	Spain	SEVRES	France
MALANG	Indonesia	SPARTA	Greece
MANAUS	Brazil	STRESA	Italy
MANTUA	Italy	SUZUKA	Japan
MASQAT	Oman	SYDNEY	Australia
MEDINA	Saudi Arabia	TABRIZ	Iran
MENTON	France	TAIPEI	Rep. China
MERIDA	Mexico	TALIEN	China
MESHED	Iran	TEHRAN	Iran
MINDEN	West Germany	TETUAN	Morocco
MINHOW	China	THEBES	Greece
MODENA	Italy	TILSIT	USSR
MONACO	Monaco	TIRANA	Albania
MOSCOW	USSR	TOBRUK	Libya
MUKDEN	China	TOLEDO	Spain
MULTAN	Pakistan	TOULON	France
MUNICH	West Germany	TOYAMA	Japan
MURCIA	Spain	TRALEE	Ireland
MUSCAT	Oman	TSINAN	China
MYSORE	India	UPSALA	Sweden
NAGANO	Japan	VENICE	Italy
NAGOYA	Japan	VERDUN	France
NAGPUR	India	VERONA	Italy
NANTES	France	VIENNA	Austria
NAPLES	Italy	VYBORG	USSR
NARVIK	Norway	WARSAW	Poland
NIAMEY	Niger	YAHATA	Japan
NINGPO	China	YAWATA	Japan
NUMAZU	Greece	YANGKU	China
ODENSE	Denmark	ZAGREB	Yugoslavia
ODESSA	USSR	ZURICH	Switzerland
OPORTO	Portugal	ABIDJAN	Ivory Coast
ORADEA	Rumania	ALGIERS	Algeria
OREBRO	Sweden	ALLEPPI	India
ORENSE	Spain	ANDORRA	France
OSTEND	Belgium	ANTIBES	France
OTTAWA	Canada	ANTIGUA	Guatemala
OVIEDO	Spain	ANTWERP	Belgium

ARACAJU	Brazil	NITEROI	Brazil
AVIGNON	France	PALERMO	Italy
BAGHDAD	Iraq	PAPEETE	Tahiti
BANDUNG	Indonesia	POTSDAM	Germany
BANGKOK	Thailand	POLTAVA	USSR
BATAVIA	Indonesia	PUNAKHA	Bhutan
BELFAST	Ireland	RANGOON	Burma
BENARES	India	RAPALLO	Italy
BENGASI	Libya	RAVENNA	Italy
BERBERA	Somalia	ROSARIO	Argentina
BERGAMO	Italy	ROSTOCK	East Germany
BIZERTE	Tunisia	SALERNO	Italy
BOLOGNA	Italy	SANJOSE	Costa Rica
BRESCIA	Italy	SANTAFE	Argentina
BRESLAU	Poland	SAPPORO	Japan
BRISTOL	England	SARATOV	USSR
CALGARY	Canada	SEVILLA	Spain
CALICUT	India	SEVILLE	Spain
CARACAS	Venezuela	SIALKOT	Pakistan
CARDIFF	Wales	STALINO	USSR
CATANIA	Italy	STETTIN	Poland
CAYENNE	French Guiana	TAMPICO	Mexico
CHENGTU	China	TANGIER	Morocco
COLOGNE	West Germany	TARANTO	Italy
COLOMBO	Ceylon	TBILISI	USSR
CONAKRY	Guinea	TEHERAN	Iran
CORDOBA	Argentina	TELAVIV	Israel
CORDOVA	Spain	TILBURG	Netherlands
CREMONA	Italy	TORONTO	Canada
DRESDEN	East Germany	TORREON	Mexico
DUNKIRK	France	TRIESTE	Italy
FERRARA	Italy	TRIPOLI	Libya
GANGTOK	India	TUCUMAN	Argentina
GLASGOW	Scotland	UTRECHT	Netherlands
GRANADA	Spain	VILNYUS	Lithuania
HAARLEM	Netherlands	WINDSOR	Canada
HAMBURG	West Germany	WROCLAW	Poland
HANOVER	West Germany	YAOUNDE	Cameroon
HANYANG	China	ASUNCION	Paraguay
ISFAHAN	Iran	AUCKLAND	New Zealand
ISPAHAN	Iran	BATHURST	Gambia
IVANOVO	USSR	BRASILIA	Brazil
JAKARTA	Indonesia	BRUSSELS	Belgium
KALININ	USSR	BUDAPEST	Hungary
KAMPALA	Uganda	CALCUTTA	India
KARACHI	Pakistan	CANBERRA	Australia
KHARKOV	USSR	CAPETOWN	South Africa
KOWLOON	China	DAMASCUS	Syria
LAPLATA	Argentina	DJAKARTA	Indonesia
LATAKIA	Syria	DUISBURG	West Germany
LEGHORN	Italy	FORTLAMY	Chad
LEHAVRE	France	FREETOWN	Sierra Leone
LEIPZIG	East Germany	GOTEBORG	Sweden
LIMOGES	France	HANGCHOW	China
LOCARNO	Switzerland	HELSINKI	Finland
LUCERNE	Switzerland	KATMANDU	Nepal
MADEIRA	Portugal	KHARTOUM	Sudan
MANAGUA	Nicaragua	KINGSTON	Jamaica
MARSALA	Italy	MANNHEIM	West Germany
MESSINA	Italy	MONROVIA	Liberia
NAIROBI	Kenya	MONTREAL	Canada
NANKING	China	NAGASAKI	Japan
NICOSIA	Cyprus	NEWDELHI	India

PNOMPENH	Cambodia
PRETORIA	South Africa
SALONIKA	Greece
SANTIAGO	Chile
SARAJEVO	Yugoslavia
TASHKENT	USSR
VALLETTA	Malta
YOKOHAMA	Japan
AMSTERDAM	Netherlands
BUCHAREST	Rumania
BUJUMBURA	Burundi
JERUSALEM	Israel
MOGADISHU	Somalia
PHNOMPENH	Cambodia
PORTONOVO	Dahomey
PYONGYANG	North Korea
REYKJAVIK	Iceland
SANMARINO	San Marino
STOCKHOLM	Sweden
TASHICHHO	Bhutan
ULANBATOR	Mongolia
VIENTIANE	Laos

ISLANDS, PENINSULAS

RE	Atlantic
ALS	North Sea
ANN	North America
API	Pacific
ARU	Indonesia
CAT	Atlantic
COS	Greece
EPI	Pacific
FYN	North Sea
HOG	North America
HOY	Scotland
IKI	Japan
IOS	Greece
IZU	Japan
KAI	Indonesia
KEI	Indonesia
KOS	Greece
KRK	Yugoslavia
LAU	Pacific
MAN	England
OBI	Indonesia
OKI	Japan
PAG	Yugoslavia
RAB	Yugoslavia
REY	Panama
RUM	Scotland
SAL	Atlantic
UAP	Pacific
UEA	Pacific
VIS	Yugoslavia
WEH	Indonesia
YAP	Pacific
YEU	France
ARBE	Yugoslavia
ACTE	Mediterranean
ADAK	Bering
AERO	North Sea
AKUN	Bering
ALOR	Indian Ocean
AMOY	China
ANAA	Pacific
APEU	Atlantic
ARAN	Ireland
AROE	Indonesia
ATIU	Pacific
ATKA	Bering
ATTU	Bering
AVES	Caribbean
BALI	Indonesia
BATU	Indonesia
BIAK	Pacific
BUKA	Pacific
BURU	Indian Ocean
BUTE	Atlantic
CEBU	Philippines
COOK	Pacific
CORN	Caribbean
CRES	Yugoslavia
CUBA	Caribbean
CUYO	Philippines
DALL	Bering
EBON	Pacific
ELBA	Mediterranean
EYRE	Australia
FANO	Denmark
FARO	Baltic
FIJI	Pacific
FOGO	Atlantic
FOHR	North Sea
GIZO	Pacific
GOZO	Mediterranean
GUAM	Pacific
HERM	England
HILO	Atlantic
HVAR	Yugoslavia
IONA	Scotland
JAVA	Indian Ocean
JOLO	Philippines
KAIS	Iran
KEOS	Greece
KOJE	South Korea
KOLA	Arctic
KRIM	USSR
KURE	Pacific
LAUT	Indonesia
LEON	Mexico
LETI	Indonesia
LIFU	Pacific
MAHE	Indian Ocean
MAUI	Pacific
MILI	Pacific
MILO	Greece
MOEN	Denmark
MONA	Caribbean
MUHU	Baltic
MULL	Scotland
NIAS	Indonesia
NIUE	Pacific

OAHU	Pacific
ORRS	Caribbean
OSEL	Estonia
OTEA	New Zealand
PAGI	Indonesia
PICO	Atlantic
PLUM	Pacific
QAIS	Iran
RAPA	Pacific
RODI	Mediterranean
ROSS	Indian Ocean, Pacific
ROTI	Indonesia
SADO	Japan
SARK	England
SAVO	Pacific
SAWU	Indonesia
SCIO	Greece
SKYE	Scotland
SULA	Indonesia
SULU	Philippines
SYLT	North Sea
SYRA	Greece
TANA	Pacific
TRUK	Pacific
UIST	Scotland
UNST	Scotland
VATE	Pacific
WAKE	Pacific
WIST	Atlantic
ABACO	Caribbean
ALAND	Baltic
ALOFI	Pacific
ALSEN	North Sea
AMANI	Japan
AMLIA	Bering
AMMIN	China
AMRUM	North Sea
ARRAN	Scotland
ARROE	Indonesia
ARUBA	Caribbean
AWUDA	Pacific
BABAR	Indonesia
BAKER	North America
BALUT	Pacific
BANDA	Indian Ocean
BANKA	Indian Ocean
BANKS	Arctic
BATAN	Philippines
BICOL	Philippines
BONIN	Pacific
BOHOL	Philippines
BYLOT	Arctic
CALDY	Wales
CAPRI	Italy (Mediterranean)
CERAM	Indian Ocean, Pacific
CHEJU	South Korea
CHIOS	Greece
CIOVO	Mediterranean
COATS	Canada
COCOS	Indian Ocean
CORFU	Mediterranean
CRETE	Mediterranean
DAMAR	Indian Ocean

DELOS	Greece
DEVON	Arctic
DISKO	Arctic
DOMEL	Indian Ocean
DUCIE	Pacific
EFATE	Pacific
ELLIS	Pacific
EXUMA	Atlantic
FAYAL	Atlantic
FOULA	Atlantic
GASPE	Canada
GOUGH	Atlantic
HITRA	North Sea
HONDO	Japan
HOSTE	Chile
ISLAY	Scotland
IVIZA	Mediterranean
KASOS	Mediterranean
KATAR	Saudi Arabia
KAUAI	Pacific
KERCH	Black Sea
KISHM	Iran
KISKA	Bering
KUNIE	Pacific
KURIL	Pacific
LANAI	Pacific
LEROS	Greece
LETTI	Indonesia
LEYTE	Philippines
LIHOU	North Sea
LOBOS	Atlantic
LUZON	Philippines
MACAO	China
MAKIN	Pacific
MALTA	Mediterranean
MANUA	Pacific
MELOS	Greece
MISOL	Pacific
MOREA	Greece
NAURU	Pacific
NAXOS	Greece
NDENI	Pacific
NEVIS	Caribbean
OLAND	Baltic
PAGAI	Indonesia
PALAU	Pacific
PANAY	Philippines
PAPUA	Pacific
PAROS	Greece
PARRY	Arctic
PAXOI	Greece
PAXOS	Greece
PELEE	Canada
PELEW	Pacific
PEMBA	Indian Ocean
PSARA	Greece
QATAR	Saudi Arabia
QISHM	Iran
RAOUL	Pacific
ROCAS	Brazil
RUGEN	Baltic
SAMAR	Philippines
SAMOA	Pacific

SAMOS	Greece
SANGI	Indonesia
SINAI	Mediterranean
SOLTA	Yugoslavia
SUMBA	Indian Ocean
SUNDA	Indian Ocean
SYROS	Greece
TANNA	Pacific
TENOS	Greece
THERA	Greece
TIMOR	Indonesia
TONGA	Pacific
UMNAK	Bering
UPOLU	Pacific
WAKDE	Indian Ocean and Pacific
WHITE	Arctic
WIGHT	England
ZANTE	Greece
AALAND	Baltic
ACHILL	Atlantic
AEGEAN	Mediterranean
AEGINA	Mediterranean
AGATTU	Pacific
ALABAT	Pacific
AMAGER	Denmark
AMBRIM	Pacific
AMELIA	Atlantic
AMUKTA	Bering
ANDROS	Atlantic, Mediterranean
ANGAUR	Pacific
ARABIA	Asia
AVALON	Atlantic
AZORES	Atlantic
BAFFIN	Arctic
BAHAMA	Atlantic
BALKAN	Mediterranean
BATAAN	Philippines
BIKINI	Pacific
BINTAN	Indonesia
BORNEO	Indonesia
BOUVET	Atlantic
BURIAS	Philippines
CAMANO	North America
CANARY	Atlantic
CANDIA	Mediterranean
CARMEN	Atlantic, Mexico
CAYMAN	Caribbean
CERIGO	Mediterranean
CEYLON	Indian Ocean
CHALOS	Atlantic
CHILOE	Pacific
COMINO	Mediterranean
CRIMEA	Black Sea
CYPRUS	Mediterranean
EASTER	Pacific, Chile
ELLICE	Pacific
FLORES	Atlantic, Indian Ocean
FUTUNA	Pacific
GILLIS	Arctic
GOMERA	Atlantic
HAITAN	Pacific, China
HAWAII	Pacific
HONSHU	Japan
IBERIA	Atlantic, Mediterranean
INAGUA	Atlantic
ISTRIA	Mediterranean
JERSEY	Atlantic
KANAGA	Bering
KOMODO	Indonesia
KYOSAI	South Korea
KYUSHU	Japan
LABUAN	Indonesia
LANTAO	China
LEMNOS	Greece
LESBOS	Greece
LEUCAS	Greece
LIPARI	Italy
LOMBOK	Indonesia
MACTAN	Philippines
MADURA	Indonesia
MALDEN	Pacific
MARAJO	Brazil
MIDWAY	Pacific
NEGROS	Philippines
ORKNEY	Scotland
PARRIS	North America
PASCUA	Pacific; Chile
PENANG	Indonesia
POMONA	Scotland
PONAPE	Pacific
QUEMOY	Rep. China
RHODES	Mediterranean, Greece
ROTUMA	Atlantic
RYUKYU	Japan
SANDAY	Scotland
SAREMA	Estonia
SAVAII	Pacific
SCARBA	Atlantic
SCILLY	England
SHEMYA	Bering
SIBUTU	Philippines
SICILY	Mediterranean, Italy
TAHITI	Pacific
TAIWAN	Pacific (Nationalist China)
TANAGA	Bering
THASOS	Greece
TINIAN	Pacific
TOBAGO	Caribbean
TORTUE	Caribbean
TUBUAI	Pacific
TULAGI	Pacific
UNIMAK	Bering
USEDOM	Baltic
VIRGIN	Caribbean
WALLIS	Pacific
ACKLINS	Atlantic
AGALEGA	Indian Ocean
AMAKUSA	Japan
ANDAMAN	Indian Ocean
ANTIGUA	Caribbean
ARGOLIS	Greece
AUSTRAL	Pacific
BAHREIN	Indian Ocean
BARANOF	Pacific
BARENTS	Arctic
BERMUDA	Atlantic

CAYENNE	South America
CELEBES	Indonesia
CHATHAM	Pacific
CORSICA	Mediterranean
CURACAO	Caribbean
DIOMEDE	Bering
FAEROES	Atlantic
FALSTER	Denmark
FORMOSA	Rep. China
GILBERT	Pacific
GOTLAND	Baltic
IWOJIMA	Pacific
JAMAICA	Caribbean
JUTLAND	Denmark
KOLGUEV	Arctic
LAALAND	Denmark
LOFOTEN	Arctic
LOLLAND	Denmark
MADEIRA	Atlantic
MAJORCA	Mediterranean
MALACCA	Malaysia
MALDIVE	Indian Ocean
MARIANA	Pacific
MINDORO	Philippines
MINORCA	Mediterranean
MOLUCCA	Pacific
NICOBAR	Indian Ocean
OKINAWA	Pacific
PALAWAN	Philippines
REUNION	Indian Ocean
SALAMIS	Greece
SEMICHI	Bering
SOLOMON	Pacific
TERNATE	Indonesia
TORTOLA	Caribbean
TORTUGA	Caribbean
ALBERCHE	Spain
ALEUTIAN	Bering
AMCHITKA	Bering
ANTILLES	Caribbean
BALEARES	Mediterranean
BARBADOS	Caribbean
BERMUDAS	Atlantic
BORNHOLM	Baltic
CAROLINE	Pacific
CYCLADES	Mediterranean
DOMINICA	Caribbean
FALKLAND	Atlantic
GUERNSEY	England
HEBRIDES	Scotland
HOKKAIDO	Japan
LABRADOR	Canada
MARIANAS	Pacific
MARSHALL	Pacific
MELVILLE	Arctic
MINDANAO	Philippines
MOLUCCAS	Indonesia
SAKHALIN	Pacific
SARDINIA	Mediterranean, Italy
SHETLAND	Scotland
SOMERSET	Arctic
STHELENA	Atlantic
TASMANIA	Australia
TENERIFE	Atlantic
TRINIDAD	Caribbean
UNALASKA	Bering
VICTORIA	Arctic
ZANZIBAR	Indian Ocean
BALEARICS	Mediterranean
GALAPAGOS	Pacific
GREENLAND	Arctic
MARQUESAS	Pacific

LAKES, SEAS, GULFS, BAYS

ICA	Peru
ISE	Japan
RED	Saudi Arabia
REE	Ireland
SEG	USSR
VAN	Turkey
ZUG	Switerland
ARAL	USSR
AZOV	USSR
BAFA	Turkey
BALA	Wales
BIWA	Japan
CHAD	Africa
COMO	Italy
DEAD	Jordan
DEBO	Nigeria
ERIE	North America
ERNE	Ireland
ISEO	Italy
KARA	Arctic
KIVU	Congo
KORO	Pacific
MEAD	United States
MORO	Philippines
ROSS	Pacific
SAWU	Indonesia
SULU	Philippines
TAAL	Philippines
TANA	Ethiopia
THUN	Switzerland
TOTA	Colombia
ABAYA	Ethiopia
ALBAY	Philippines
AMMER	Germany
AMPER	Germany
ASNEN	Sweden
ATLIN	Canada
ATTER	Germany
BAKER	Canada
BALAH	Egypt
BELOE	USSR
CADDO	Caribbean
CHANY	USSR
CORAL	Pacific
DAVAO	Philippines
ELTON	USSR
ENARE	Finland
GARDA	Italy

GARRY Canada
HURON North America
ILMEN USSR
INARI Finland
JUNIN Peru
KIOGA Africa
KYOGA Africa
LANAO Philippines
LEMAN Switzerland
MAIPO Chile
MAIPU Chile
MERIN Uruguay
MINTO Canada
MIRIM Uruguay
MWERU Congo
NIRIZ Iran
NYASA Africa
ONEGA USSR
PETEN Guatemala
POOPO Bolivia
PSKOV Estonia
SAROS Mediterranean
SOGNE Norway
TABOR Israel
TAHOE United States
TAUPO New Zealand
TSANA Ethiopia
TUMBA Congo
URMIA Iran
ACHKEK Tunisia
AEGEAN Mediterranean
ALAKUL Turkey
ALBANO Greece
ALBERT Uganda
ANNECY France
APOPKA United States
BABINE Canada
BAIKAL USSR
BISCAY Atlantic
DONNER United States
GALWAY Ireland
IONIAN Mediterranean
IZABAL Guatemala
KHANKA USSR
LADOGA USSR
MAGADI Kenya
ONEIDA United States
ONTAKE Japan
PEIPUS Estonia
RUDOLF Kenya
SAGAMI Japan
SALTON North America
SCOTIA Atlantic
SIMCOE Canada
TASMAN Pacific
TONKIN Vietnam
UNGAVA Canada
VANERN Sweden
ARAFURA Australia
ATITLAN Guatemala
BALATON Hungary
BALKASH USSR
BARENTS Arctic
BOTHNIA Baltic
CASPIAN USSR
DONEGAL Ireland
DUBAWNT Canada
ILIAMNA Alaska
KOKONOR India
MARMARA Turkey
NIPIGON Canada
OKHOTSK Pacific
ONTARIO North America
ORESUND Sweden
OTRANTO Italy
SALERNO Italy
TEXCOCO Mexico
TORRENS Australia
VISAYAN Philippines
WEDDELL Atlantic
ADRIATIC Mediterranean
BALKHASH USSR
HOUGHTON United States
LIGURIAN Mediterranean
MANITOBA Canada
MICHIGAN North America
REINDEER Canada
SUPERIOR North America
TITICACA Peru
VICTORIA Africa

RIVERS OF THE UNITED STATES

DAN Va.
ELK Tenn.
ELK W. Va.
FOX Wisc.
NEW Va.
RED Okla.
EAST N.Y.
GILA N.M.
IOWA Ia.
KERN Cal.
LOUP Neb.
MILK Mont.
OHIO Mid-West
ROCK Wisc.
ALSEK Alas.
BLACK Mo., Ark.
BRONX N.Y.
CACHE Ark.
CEDAR Minn., Ia.
COOSA Ala., Ga.
FLINT Ga.
GRAND Mich.
GRAND Mo.
GRAND S.D.
GREEN Ill.
GREEN Ky., Ind.
GREEN Wyo., Col., Ut.
JAMES = DAKOTA
JAMES Va.
LLANO Tex.

MACON	La.
MIAMI	O.
NEUSE	N.C.
OSAGE	Kan., Mo.
PEARL	Miss.
PECOS	N.M., Tex.
ROGUE	Ore.
SNAKE	North-West
SNAKE	Minn.
WHITE	Ark.
WHITE	Col., Ut.
WHITE	S.D.
WHITE	Tex.
YAQUI	N.M.
YAZOO	Miss.
YUKON	Alas.
BARREN	Ky.
BEAVER	Pa.
BRAZOS	Tex.
CAHABA	Ala.
CLINCH	Tenn.
COPPER	Alas.
DAKOTA	N.D.
HUDSON	N.Y.
KANSAS	Kan.
MOHAWK	N.Y.
NECHES	Tex.
NEOSHO	Kan., Okla.
NOATAK	Alas.
NUECES	Tex.
OCONEE	Ga.
OWYHEE	Id., Ore.
PEEDEE	N.C., S.C.
PLATTE	Ia., Mo.
PLATTE	Neb.
POWDER	Ore.
POWDER	Wyo., Mont.
SABINE	Tex., La.
SALMON	Id.
SANTEE	S.C.
SCIOTO	O.
TANANA	Alas.
TONGUE	Wyo., Mont.
WABASH	Ind., Ill.
ALABAMA	Ala.
BIGHORN	Wyo., Mont.
CAHAWBA	= CAHABA
DOLORES	Col., Ut.
GENESEE	Pa., N.Y.
HOLSTON	Tenn.
JOHNDAY	Ore.
KLAMATH	Ore.
KOYUKUK	Alas.
LARAMIE	Col., Wyo.
LICKING	Ky.
POTOMAC	Mid-Atlantic
ROANOKE	Va., N.C.
SANJUAN	South-West
STCROIX	Wis., Minn.
STJOHNS	Fla.
SUWANEE	Ga., Fla.
TRINITY	Cal.
TRINITY	Tex.
WASHITA	Okla., Tex.
WASHITA	= OUACHITA
ALTAMAHA	Ga.
ARKANSAS	South-West
BIGBLACK	Miss.
CANADIAN	South-West
CAPEFEAR	N.C.
CHEYENNE	S.D.
CHIPPEWA	Wisc.
CIMARRON	N.M., Okla.
COLORADO	South-West
COLUMBIA	North-West
COLVILLE	Alas.
DELAWARE	Mid-Atlantic
GUNNISON	Col.
HUMBOLDT	Nev.
ILLINOIS	Ill.
KENNEBEC	Me.
KENTUCKY	Ky.
MISSOURI	Central
NIOBRARA	Wyo., Neb.
OUACHITA	Ark., La.
RIOBRAVO	= RIOGRANDE
RIOPECOS	= PECOS
SAVANNAH	Ga.
ALLEGHENY	Pa.
DESCHUTES	Ore.
DESMOINES	Ia.
KUSKOKWIM	Alas.
MERRIMACK	N.H., Mass.
MINNESOTA	Minn.
MUSKINGUM	O.
PENOBSCOT	Me.
PORCUPINE	Alas.
RIOGRANDE	South-West
SMOKYHILL	Col., Kan.
STFRANCIS	Mo., Ark.
TENNESSEE	South
TOMBIGBEE	Ala., Miss.
WISCONSIN	Wis.
CUMBERLAND	Ky., Tenn.

FOREIGN RIVERS

AA	Algeria
BO	Chile
OB	USSR
OM	USSR
PO	Italy
SI	China
WU	China
AAR	Switzerland
AIN	France
APA	Paraguay
ARO	Venezuela
BOW	Canada
BUG	Poland
CAM	England
CHU	USSR
COI	China
DAL	Sweden
DEE	Scotland, Wales, England

DON	USSR	**BOBR**	Poland
EMS	Germany	**CHER**	France
EXE	England	**CLUJ**	Rumania
FLY	New Guinea	**CRNA**	Yugoslavia
HAB	Pakistan	**DALY**	Australia
HAN	China	**DOCE**	Brazil
ICA	Peru	**DOON**	Scotland
ILI	USSR	**DRAU**	Austria
ILL	Austria	**DRIN**	Albania
ILL	France	**DUNA**	USSR
INN	Germany	**EBRO**	Spain
JIU	Rumania	**EDER**	Germany
JUR	Egypt	**EGER**	Czechoslovakia
KAN	China	**ELBE**	Germany
KEM	USSR	**EMBA**	USSR
KUM	Korea	**EMME**	Korea
LEE	Ireland	**ENNS**	Austria
LOA	Chile	**ERNE**	Ireland
LOT	France	**ESLA**	Spain
LYS	Belgium	**EURE**	France
MIN	China	**GEBA**	Africa
MUN	Thailand	**GERS**	France
MUR	Austria	**HRON**	Czechoslovakia
NAB	Germany	**HWAI**	China
NAN	Thailand	**HWEI**	China
OKA	USSR	**IBAR**	Gabon
OLT	Rumania	**ILEK**	USSR
OMO	Ethiopia	**IPEL**	Czechoslovakia
PEI	China	**ISAR**	Germany
RUR	Germany	**ISER**	Czechoslovakia
SAN	Poland	**IVAI**	Brazil
TAY	Scotland	**JARI**	Brazil
TZU	China	**JUBA**	Africa
UFA	USSR	**KAMA**	USSR
UME	Sweden	**KARA**	USSR
UNA	Yugoslavia	**KEMI**	Finland
URE	England	**KLAR**	Norway
USK	Wales, England	**KOSI**	India
VAH	Czechoslovakia	**KUPA**	Yugoslavia
VAR	France	**KURA**	USSR
WEI	China	**KUSI**	India
AARE	Switzerland	**KWEI**	China
ABRA	Philippines	**LAHN**	Germany
ADDA	Italy	**LENA**	USSR
AGNO	Philippines	**LIAO**	China
AIRE	England, France	**LOIR**	France
AKSU	Turkey	**LULE**	Sweden
ALLE	Germany	**LUNI**	India
ALMA	USSR	**LWAN**	China
ALTA	Norway	**MAAS**	Netherlands
AMGA	Iran	**MALI**	Burma
AMUR	Asia	**MAND**	Iran
ARAS	Turkey	**MAYA**	USSR
ARDA	Bulgaria	**MAYO**	Mexico
ARNO	Italy	**META**	Colombia
ARTA	Greece	**MONO**	Togo
ATHI	Kenya	**MSTA**	USSR
AUBE	France	**MUSI**	Indonesia
AUDE	France	**NAAB**	Germany
AVON	England	**NAPO**	Ecuador
AVRE	France	**NASS**	Canada
BANN	Ireland	**NERA**	Italy
BENI	Bolivia	**NEVA**	USSR

NILE	Africa
NMAI	Burma
NORE	Ireland
NYSA	Poland
ODER	Poland
OHRE	Czechoslovakia
OISE	France
ONON	USSR
ORNE	France
OUSE	England
OXUS	USSR
PARA	Brazil
PARU	Brazil
PING	Thailand
PITE	Sweden
PRUT	Rumania
RAAB	Austria
RABA	Austria
RAMU	New Guinea
RAVI	India
REMS	Germany
RENO	Italy
RIET	South Africa
ROER	Germany
RUHR	Germany
SAAR	France
SAMA	Peru
SAVA	Yugoslavia
SEIM	USSR
SPEY	Liechtenstein
STYR	USSR
SULA	USSR
SURA	USSR
SWAN	Australia
SWAT	Pakistan
TAJO	Spain
TANA	Kenya
TANA	Norway
TARN	France
TEJO	Spain
TISA	USSR
TOMO	Colombia
TURA	USSR
TYNE	England
UELE	Africa
URAL	USSR
VAAL	South Africa
VAKH	USSR
WAAL	Netherlands
YALU	Korea
YANA	USSR
YSER	France
YUAN	China
ABUNA	Bolivia
ADIGE	Italy
ADOUR	France
AGOUT	France
AGUAN	Honduras
AISNE	France
AKABA	Mongolia
AKOBO	Ethiopia
ALDAN	USSR
ALLER	Germany
ALLIA	Italy
ALUTA	Rumania
AMECA	Mexico
ANCRE	France
ANGAT	Philippines
ANNAN	Scotland
ANYUI	USSR
APURE	Venezuela
AQABA	Jordan
ARAKS	Turkey
ARGES	Rumania
ARGOS	Greece
ARGUN	USSR
ATRAK	Iran
ATREK	Iran
ATUEL	Argentina
BAKOY	Sudan
BANAS	India
BENIN	Nigeria
BENUE	Africa
BETWA	India
BHIMA	India
BOSNA	Yugoslavia
BOYNE	Ireland
BYTOM	Poland
CAMPO	Cameroon
CAUCA	Colombia
CAURA	Venezuela
CHARI	Africa
CLYDE	Scotland
CONGO	Africa
CUITO	Africa
DESNA	USSR
DNEPR	USSR
DOUBS	France
DOURO	Italy
DRAVA	Yugoslavia
DRAVE	Yugoslavia
DULCE	Argentina
DVINA	USSR
EIDER	Germany
ETSCH	Italy
ETSIN	China
FARAH	Afghanistan
FULDA	Germany
GANGA	India
GAUYA	Latvia
GOGRA	India
GUDEN	Denmark
GUMAL	Pakistan
HAVEL	Germany
HWANG	China
ILLER	Germany
INDRE	Colombia
INDUS	Pakistan
INGUL	USSR
IRIKI	Brazil
ISERE	France
ISHIM	USSR
ISKER	Bulgaria
JACUI	Brazil
JUMNA	India
JUTAI	Brazil

River	Location
KAFUE	Africa
KAJAN	Guatemala
KARUN	Iran
KASAI	Africa
KATUN	USSR
KHETA	USSR
KLONG	Thailand
KOBDO	Mongolia
KUBAN	USSR
KURSK	USSR
LAGAN	Sweden
LALIN	China
LEMPA	El Salvador
LIARD	Canada
LINDI	Congo
LIPPE	Germany
LOIRE	France
LULUA	Congo
MARNE	France
MEUSE	France
MEZEN	USSR
MINHO	Spain
MOSEL	Germany
MUTAN	China
NAMOI	Australia
NEMAN	USSR
NERIS	Poland
NIGER	Africa
NONNI	China
NOTEC	Poland
OGLIO	Italy
OGOKI	Canada
OGOWE	Gabon
ORTON	Peru
OSKOL	USSR
PALAR	India
PARDO	Brazil
PATIA	Colombia
PEACE	Canada
PERAK	Malaysia
PIAVE	Italy
PIBOR	Sudan
PIURA	Peru
PURUS	Peru
RAPTI	Nepal
REGEN	Germany
REUSS	Switzerland
RHEIN	Germany
RHINE	Europe
RHONE	France
ROPER	Australia
SAALE	Germany
SANGA	Congo
SAONE	France
SARRE	France
SEINE	France
SENNE	Belgium
SHARI	Africa
SHASI	China
SIANG	China
SIRET	Rumania
SOBAT	Ethiopia
SOMES	Hungary
SOSVA	USSR
SPREE	Germany
STOUR	England
SURMA	India
TAGUS	Rumania
TAPTI	India
TEREK	USSR
TIBER	Italy
TIETE	Brazil
TIGRE	Ecuador
TIMIS	Yugoslavia
TISTA	India
TISZA	USSR
TOBOL	USSR
TORNE	Finland
TRAUN	Austria
TRENT	England, Canada
VENTA	USSR
VESLE	France
VISLA	Poland
WARTA	Poland
WESER	Germany
WISLA	Poland
XINGU	Brazil
ABAKAN	USSR
AFRINE	Turkey
AGUSAN	Philippines
ALBANY	Canada
AMAZON	Brazil
ANGARA	USSR
ARAGON	Spain
ARAUCA	Colombia
ARIEGE	France
ATBARA	Sudan
BAFING	Sudan
BALIKH	Turkey
BARCOO	Australia
BARITO	Indonesia
BEAVER	Canada
BELAYA	USSR
BIOBIO	Chile
BRENTA	Italy
CARONI	Venezuela
CARROT	Canada
CHUBUT	Argentina
CHULYM	USSR
DANUBE	Europe
DAWSON	Australia
DELICE	Turkey
DNESTR	USSR
DONETS	USSR
ENISEI	USSR
FRASER	Canada
GALANA	Kenya
GANDAK	Nepal
GANGES	India
GILGIT	India
HAWASH	Ethiopia
HINGOL	Pakistan
IRTISH	Asia
IRTYSH	Asia
JAPURA	Colombia

KHILOK USSR
KOLIMA USSR
KOMATI South Africa
KURUME Japan
LIMMAT Switzerland
LOANGE Congo
LOPORI Congo
MADIDI Bolivia
MAMORE Bolivia
MEKONG Asia
MODDER South Africa
MOISIE Canada
MOLDAU Czechoslovakia
MOLOGA USSR
MOSKVA USSR
MURGAB USSR
MURRAY Australia
NECKAR Germany
NEISSE Poland
NELSON Canada
OLDMAN Canada
OLENEK USSR
OMOLON USSR
ORANGE South Africa
ORKHON Mongolia
PAHANG Malaysia
PARANA Brazil
PATUCA Honduras
PENNER India
PINEGA USSR
PREGEL USSR
PRIPET USSR
RAJANG Indonesia
SALADO Argentina
SALWIN Burma
SAMARA USSR
SEVERN Wales, England
SONORA Mexico
SOURIS Canada
STRUMA Bulgaria
SUTLEJ India
THAMES England
THEISS USSR
TICINO Switzerland
TIGRIS Turkey
TUGELA South Africa
UAUPES Colombia
VIENNE France
VITAVA Czechoslovakia
YALUNG China
YAPURA Colombia
YELLOW China
ABITIBI Canada
ALBERGA Canada
BERMEJO South America
DARLING Australia
DNIEPER USSR
GARONNE France
GLENELG Australia
LIMPOPO Africa
MADEIRA Brazil
MARITSA Turkey
MOSELLE France
ORINOCO Venezuela
PECHORA USSR
SALWEEN Burma
SHANNON Ireland
SITTANG Burma
SUNGARI China
VISTULA Poland
YANGTZE China
YENISEI USSR
ZAMBESI Africa
ZAMBEZI Africa
AMUDARYA USSR
HAMILTON Canada
RIONEGRO Argentina
SYRDARYA USSR
ATHABASCA Canada
EUPHRATES Asia
IRRAWADDY India
MACKENZIE Canada
MAGDALENA Colombia
RIOGRANDE Mexico

MOUNTAINS, PASSES, VOLCANOES

* Indicates volcanoes

ABU India
API Nepal
APO India
ASO* Japan
AWU* Denmark
DOM Switzerland
ERZ Germany
HOR Jordan
IDA Turkey
OMI China
OSO United States
TAI China
ADAM Saudi Arabia
AGUA Guatemala
AJAX United States
ALAI USSR
BACO Philippines
COOK Alaska
ETNA* Italy
FOGO* Atlantic
FUJI* Japan
GEDE* Indonesia
HARZ Germany
HENG China
HOOD United States
IJEN Indonesia
JURA Switzerland
KIBO Africa
MERU Africa
MIDI France
MUIR United States
NEBO Jordan

OETA	Greece	AJUSCO*	Mexico
OMEI	China	AKUTAN*	Alaska
OSSA	Greece	ALADAG	Turkey
RIGI	Switzerland	ALATAU	San Marino
TAAL	Philippines	ALUBLA	Switzerland
TAIF	Saudi Arabia	ALWAND	Iraq
TODI	Switzerland	AMPATO	Peru
URAL	USSR	ANADIR	USSR
VISO	Italy	ANTERO	United States
AETNA*	Italy	ANTUCO*	Chile
ALDAN	USSR	ARARAT	Turkey
ALLEN	United States	ARAYAT*	Philippines
ALTAI	USSR	ARDOST	Bulgaria
ALTAR	USSR	ARKONA	Germany
ALTYN	United States	BAIKAL	USSR
ANDES	Colombia	BANDAI	Japan
ARBER	Germany	BLANCA	United States
ASAMA*	Japan	BONETE	Argentina
ASKJA*	Iceland	CARMEL	Israel
ATHOS	Greece	CARNIC	Austria
ATLAS	North Africa	CHOKAI*	Japan
AZUMA*	Japan	COLIMA*	Mexico
BAKER	United States	DOMUYO*	Argentina
BALBI*	Solomon Is.	DONNER	United States
BLANC	Switzerland	DONREK	Thailand
BOLAN	India	EKBERT	United States
BROMO	Indonesia	ELBRUS	USSR
CACHI	Argentina	ELBRUZ	Iran
CENIS	Italy	EREBUS	Antarctica
CORNO	Italy	FREJUS	Italy
DICTE	Greece	GRAIAN	Italy
EIFEL	Germany	GUNTUR	Indonesia
EIGER	Switzerland	HERMON	Syria
ELGON	Uganda	KAILAS	Tibet
EOLUS	United States	KATMAI*	United States
EVANS	United States	KAZBEK	USSR
FUEGO*	Guatemala	KHYBER	India
GEDEH*	Indonesia	KOLIMA	USSR
GUMAL	India	KUNLUN	Tibet
GUYOT	United States	LASSEN*	United States
HATYA	Turkey	MAKALU	Nepal
HEKLA	Iceland	MERAPI	Indonesia
HOREB	Egypt	OLIVET	Israel
HUILA	Colombia	ORTLER	Italy
IDJEN	Indonesia	OSORNO*	Chile
IRAZU*	Costa Rica	PELION	Greece
KELUT*	Indonesia	POCONO	United States
LEONE	Switzerland	PURACE*	Colombia
LOGAN	Canada	ROBSON	Canada
LONGS	United States	SAHAMA	Bolivia
MAYON	Philippines	SANGAY*	Ecuador
NECOI	Rumania	SEGURA	Spain
OZARK	United States	SEMERU*	Indonesia
PASTO*	Colombia	SHASTA	United States
PELEE*	Martinique	SHIPKA	Bulgaria
POTRO	Argentina	TACANA	Guatemala
PULAR	Chile	TAUNUS	Germany
RATON	United States	TOLIMA	Colombia
RAUNG*	Indonesia	TRISUL	India
SIPKA	Bulgaria	ULAWUN	United States
SIANI	Egypt	VOSGES	France
TABOR	Israel	ZAGROS	Iran
TAHAN	Indonesia	ALBERES	Italy

ANTHONY	United States	SUDETEN	Czechoslovakia
ATITLAN*	Guatemala	TAMBORA*	Czechoslovakia
BERNINA	Switzerland	VIRGUNA	Uganda
BRENNER	Italy	CAUCASUS	USSR
DAPSANG	Nepal	COROPUNA	Peru
ELBORUS	USSR	DEMAVEND	Iran
EVEREST	Nepal	HIMALAYA	India
FORAKER	Alaska	ILLIMANI	Bolivia
HELICON	Greece	JUNGFRAU	Switzerland
HUBBARD	Alaska	KRAKATAO*	Indonesia
ILIAMNA*	Alaska	KRAKATAU*	Indonesia
KILAUEA*	Hawaii	MAUNALOA*	Hawaii
MUZTAGH	China	MCKINLEY	Alaska
NILGIRI	India	WRANGELL	Alaska
OMETEPE*	Nicaragua	ACONCAGUA	Argentina
OROHENA	Ecuador	ANNAPURNA	Nepal
PALOMAR	United States	DOLOMITES	Italy
RAINIER	United States	NANDADEVI	India
ROCKIES	United States	PIKESPEAK	United States
SEMENOV	USSR	TUPUNGATO	Chile
SHAVANO	United States	CHIMBORAZO	Ecuador
STELIAS	Canada	MATTERHORN	Switzerland

NATIONAL PARKS

ZION	Ut.	YOSEMITE	Cal.
PLATT	Okla.	HALEAKALA	Haw.
ACADIA	Me.	MESAVERDE	Col.
LASSEN	Cal.	CRATERLAKE	Ore.
SHILOH	Tenn.	CUMBERLAND	Ky., Tenn., Va.
BIGBEND	Tex.	EVERGLADES	Fla.
GLACIER	Mon.	GETTYSBURG	Pa.
OLYMPIC	Wash.	GRANDTETON	Wyo.
SEQUOIA	Cal.	HOTSPRINGS	Ark.
ANTIETAM	Md.	ISLEROYALE	Mich.
CARLSBAD	N.M.	SHENANDOAH	Va.
CHALMETE	La.	CANYONLANDS	Ut.
COLONIAL	Va.	GRANDCANYON	Ariz.
MANASSAS	Va.	KINGSCANYON	Cal.
PEARIDGE	Ark.	MAMMOTHCAVE	Ky.
SARATOGA	N.Y.	YELLOWSTONE	Wyo.
WINDCAVE	S.D.		

DAMS, HYDROELECTRIC PLANTS

*** Indicates hydroelectric plants**

GURI*	Venezuela	COUGAR	Oregon
OAHE	South Dakota	DALLES*	Oregon
ROSS*	Washington	DEGRAY	Arkansas
ASWAN*	Egypt	FRIANT	California
GATUN	Panama	FURNAS*	Brazil
GORKY	USSR	GRANBY	Colorado
KEBAN	Turkey	HOOVER*	Colorado
NUREK*	USSR	INGURI*	USSR
SWIFT*	Oregon	KARIBA	Africa
WYMAN	Maine	KUROBE	Japan
ASSUAN*	Egypt	MANGLA	Pakistan
BEKHME	Iran	MCNARY	Washington
BHAKRA	India	NAVAHO	California
BRATSK*	USSR	SAKUMA	Japan
BUFORD	Georgia	SHASTA	California
CONTRA	Switzerland	SULTAN	Washington

VAIONT	Italy
WINSOR	Massachusetts
WISHON	California
ASHOKAN	New York
BOULDER*	Colorado
BRIONES	California
CACHUMA	California
CARTERS	Georgia
CASITAS	California
CICEROZ	Turkey
CONCHAS	New Mexico
CURNERA	Switzerland
FONTANA	North Carolina
HIRAKUD	India
LUZZONE	Switzerland
PACTOLA	South Dakota
PAHLEVI	Iran
SANFORD	Texas
SANLUIS	California
TRINITY	California
WATAUGA	Tennessee
BLUEMESA	Colorado
COGSWELL	California
FORTPECK	Montana
GARRISON	Missouri
KAKHOVKA	USSR
KINGSLEY	Missouri
KREMASTA	Greece
MERRIMAN	New York
OROVILLE	California
PINEFLAT	California
TERMINUS	California
BEARCREEK	Pennsylvania
CALAVERAS	California
KUIBYSHEV*	USSR
LUCKYPEAK	Idaho
MAUVOISIN	Switzerland
MOSSYROCK	Washington
NEVERSINK	New York
PALISADES	Idaho
TWITCHELL	California
VOLGOGRAD*	USSR
WOLFCREEK	Kentucky
BONNEVILLE	Oregon
GLENCANYON	Colorado
HILLSCREEK	Oregon
TRESMARIAS	Brazil
YELLOWTAIL	Montana
GRANDCOULEE	Washington

FAMOUS BRIDGES

ELSA	Spain
FORTH	Scotland
MERIC	Greece
SANDO	Sweden
SIGHS	Italy
STORY	Australia
TOWER	England
HOBART	Australia
HOWRAH	India
LONDON	England
MTHOPE	N.Y., US
QUEBEC	Canada
RIALTO	Italy
VOULTE	France
BAYONNE	N.J., US
BIRECIC	Turkey
MIAPIMI	Mexico
NARROWS	Wash., US
OAKLAND	Cal., US
RAINBOW	N.Y., US
SEVERIN	Germany
STJOHNS	Ore., US
VECCHIO	Italy
WESTEND	Pa., US
ARRABIDA	Portugal
BROOKLYN	N.Y., US
BURDEKIN	Australia
CORNWALL	Canada
DEERISLE	Me., US
FORTPITT	Pa., US
HELLGATE	N.Y., US
LONGVIEW	Wash., US
MACKINAC	Mich., US
MIRABEAU	France
TRANSBAY	Cal., US
WATERLOO	England
HOODCANAL	Wash., US
LIONSGATE	Canada
SAVARIVER	Yugoslavia
TAPPANZEE	N.Y., US
WAALRIVER	Netherlands
AMBASSADOR	Mich., US
ARTHURKILL	N.Y., US
GOLDENGATE	Cal., US
NIBELUNGEN	West Germany
PLOUGASTEL	France
QUEENSBORO	N.Y., US
TRIBOROUGH	N.Y., US
VERRAZANNO	N.Y., US
VOLTARIVER	Ghana
WASHINGTON	N.Y., US
WHITESTONE	N.Y., US
BIRCHENOUGH	Rhodesia
GLADESVILLE	Wales
TANCARVILLE	France
WALTWHITMAN	Pa., US
BEARMOUNTAIN	N.Y., US

FAMOUS WATERFALLS

TWIN	Id., U.S.
ANGEL	Venezuela
BOWEN	New Zealand
DETTI	Iceland
KEGON	Japan
TOWER	Wyo., U.S.

FINCHA	Africa
GUAIRA	Brazil
HANDOL	Sweden
HELENA	New Zealand
HOWICK	Luxembourg
IGUAZU	Brazil
MARINA	South America
NARADA	Wash., U.S.
RIBBON	Nev., U.S.
TUGELA	South Africa
VERNAL	Nev., U.S.
VETTIS	Norway
VORING	Norway
YUDAKI	Japan
CAUVERY	India
GASTEIN	Austria
GOLLING	Austria
HANDEGG	Switzerland
IGUASSU	Brazil
KALAMBO	Tanzania
NIAGARA	Canada
PASSAIC	N.J., U..S
RUACANA	Africa
CHIROMBO	Zambia
GAVARNIE	France
GERSOPPA	India
KAIETEUR	South America
KRIMMLER	Austria
SLUISKIN	Wash., U.S.
STIRLING	New Zealand
TAKKAKAW	Canada
VICTORIA	Africa
YOSEMITE	Nev., U.S.
GIESSBACH	Switzerland
HARSPRANG	Sweden
HORSESHOE	Canada
MINNEHAHA	Minn., U.S.
MULTNOMAH	Ore., U.S.
SKYKJEFOS	Norway
STAUBBACH	Switzerland

FAMOUS DESERTS

GOBI	China
THAR	India
DAHNA	Yemen
NEFUD	Saudi Arabia
SHAMO	China
ARUNTA	Australia
GIBSON	Australia
DAHAMA	Yemen
LIBYAN	Libya
MOHAVE	Cal., US
NUBIAN	NE Africa
SAHARA	North Africa
SYRIAN	SW Asia
ANNAFUD	Saudi Arabia
ARABIAN	Saudi Arabia
ATACAMA	Chile
ELHAMAD	Syria
KARAKUM	USSR
QARAQUM	= KARAKUM
PAINTED	Ariz., US
SECHURA	Peru
COLORADO	Cal., US
KALAHARI	South Africa
KIZILKUM	USSR
KYZYLKUM	= KIZILKUM
MUYUNKUM	USSR
VIZCAINO	Mexico
BLACKROCK	Nev., US
DASHTILUT	Iran
ARALKARKUM	USSR
AUSTRALIAN	Australia
GREATSANDY	Australia
RUBALKHALI	Yemen
TAKLAMAKAN	China
DASHTIKAVIR	Iran
DEATHVALLEY	Cal., US
GREATVICTORIA	Australia

HERALDRY

BEARINGS

Charge Ordinary and Sub-ordinary

* Indicates roundels

BAR
BEND
COST
FESS
FRET
GORE
GUZE*
HURT*
ORLE
PALE
PALL
PILE
SYKE*
BATON
BENDY

CHIEF
CROSS
FESSE
FILET
FUSIL
GEMEL
GOLPE
GYRON
LABEL
PLATE*
POMEY*
SCARP
BEZANT*
BILLET
CANTON

CLOSET
COTISE
FILLET
GARTER
MASCLE
OGRESS*
ORANGE*
PALLET
PELLET*
RIBAND
RUSTRE
SCARPE
VIROLE*
ANNULET*
BORDURE

CHEVRON
ENDORSE
FLANCHE
QUARTER
ROUNDEL*
SALTIER
SALTIRE
TORTEAU*
BARRULET
DANCETTE
SALTOREL
TRESSURE
CHEVRONEL
SHAKEFORK

Cross (like)

CRUX
PATY
URDE
URDY
FLORY
POMME
URDEE

ANCREE
BOTONE
BOTONY
CLECHE
FITCHE
FLEURY
MOLINE

POTENT
AVELLAN
BOTONEE
CERCELE
CRUSILE
FITCHEE
FOURCHE

PATONCE
SALTIRE
CERCELEE
CRUSILEE
FOURCHEE
SARCELLE

CREATURES

GRAY	badger	TALBOT	hound
LOUP	wolf	WYVERN	dragon
ALAND	mastiff	ENFIELD	fox-wolf
BROCK	badger	GRIFFON	lion-eagle
HARPY	woman-bird	GRYPHON	= GRIFFON
GRICE	young boar	LIONCEL	little lion
TYGER	tiger	MARTLET	bird
WYVER	dragon	MUSIMON	goat-ram
ALANDT	mastiff	ALLERION	eagle
BAGWYN	antelope-horse	OPENICUS	lion-dragon
CANNET	duck	POPINJAY	parrot
CHOUGH	raven	SANGLIER	wild boar

Positions of Creatures

ASSIS	sitting	JESSANT	lying over
JACENT	lying over	PASSANT	walking
NAIANT	swimming	RAMPANT	reared up
SEJANT	sitting	ROUSANT	rising
VOLANT	flying	SALIENT	leaping
VORANT	eating	STATANT	standing
COURANT	running	URINANT	diving
DORMANT	lying down	COUCHANT	lying
FLOTANT	floating	HAURIENT	diving
FORCENE	rearing	TRIPPANT	tripping
ISSUANT	partly visible		

OBJECTS

VOL	two wings	TORSE	sheath
BREY	barnacle	GOUTTE	drop
SEAX	scimitar	MANCHE	sleeve
SYKE	fountain	MULLET	star
WEEI	fishtrap	TIRRET	manacle
BATON	staff	BOTEROL	sheath end
GERBE	sheaf	ESCROLL	scroll
LAVER	colter	ESTOILE	star
PHEON	arrowhead	LYMPHAD	boat

TINCTURES

OR	gold	TENNE	orange
VERT	green	ARGENT	silver
AZURE	blue	MURREY	dark red
GULES	red	PURPURE	purple
SABLE	black		

LINES OF PARTITION

NOWY
ONDE
UNDE
UNDY
URDY
WAVY
RAGULY
NEBULY
POTENTY
INDENTED
INVECTED
DANCETTY
EMBATTLED
ENGRAILED
RAYONNANT
DOVETAILED

FURS

PEAN
VAIR
ERMINE
POTENT

CADENCY
LINE OF SUCCESSION

LABEL	heir	ANNULET	5th son
CRESCENT	2nd son	FLEURDELIS	6th son
MULLET	3rd son	ROSE	7th son
MARTLET	4th son	MOLINE	8th son

OTHER TERMS

AILE	winged	TIERCE	in 3 parts
ENTE	grafted	TREFLE	three-lobed
PALY	divided vertically	APPAUME	showing palm
SEME	sprinkled, strewn	COMPONE	gobony
VULN	to wound	EMBOWED	bent
BARRY	with horizontal bars	ENFILED	passed through
CLOUE	nail-studded	FRACTED	broken
GUTTE	seme of drops	IMBRUED	blood-stained
GUTTY	= GUTTE	MASCULY	lozenged
NOWED	knotted	UNGULED	hoofed
ROMPU	broken	ADDORSED	back to back
ACCOLE	side by side	AFFRONTE	face to face
CHECKY	checkered	AVERSANT	showing back
COUPED	cut off	CABOSHED	showing head
DEXTER	right side (of wearer)	DEBRUISE	cover partly
GOBONY	divided into squares	ENGOULED	partly swallowed
GRINED	maned	SANGLANT	bleeding
GUSSET	abatement	SINISTER	left side (of wearer)

INDIANS–INDIAN TRIBES

I. NORTH OF MEXICO

LO

AHT
AUK
FOX
HOH
ITA
KAW
OFO
OTO
REE
SAC
SIA
UTE
WEA

ADAI
ATKA
COOS
CREE
CROW
DENE
ERIE
HANO
HARE
HOHE
HOPI
HUPA
IONI
IOWA
KASO
LOUP
MOKI
MONO
NOZI
OTOE
PIMA
PIRO
POMO
SAUK
SERI
TAKU
TANO
TAOS
TATU
TEWA
TIOU
UTAH
WACO
YANA
YUIT
YUKI
YUMA
ZUNI

ACOMA
ALEUT
ATNAH
BANAK
BLOOD
BRULE
CADDO
CHAUI
COMOX
CONOY
CREEK
HAIDA
HURON
KANSA
KASKA
KERES
KIOWA
KOROA
KWAPA
LIPAN
MAIDU
MAKAH
MIAMI
MINGO
MODOC
MOQUI
NAMBE
OMAHA
OSAGE
OZARK
PECOS
PIUTE
PONCA
SARSI
SIOUX
SITKA
SKIDI
SOOKE
TETON
TIGUA
TINNE
TONTO
TWANA
UCHEE
UINTA
UNAMI
WAPPO
WASCO
WASHO
WIYAT
WIYOT
YAMEL
YAMIL
YAZOO

YUCHI
YUROK

ABNAKI
AGAWAM
AHTENA
APACHE
ATUAMI
BABINE
BILOXI
CAHITA
CALUSA
CAYUGA
CAYUSE
CHATOT
COCOPA
COOSUK
DAKOTA
DOGRIB
EYEISH
FARAON
HAIDAH
HAINAI
HAISLA
INNUIT
ISLETA
KOSIMO
KUCHIN
LENAPE
MANDAN
MAYEYE
MICMAC
MOHAVE
MOHAWK
MOLALA
NAHANE
NASHUA
NAVAHO
NAVAJO
NAUSET
NEVOME
NIPMUC
NIPMUK
NOOTKA
OGLALA
ONEIDA
OTTAWA
PAIUTE
PAKAWA
PAPAGO
PATWIN
PAWNEE
PEORIA
PEQUOT

PERICU
PIEGAN
PUEBLO
QUAPAW
SALINA
SALISH
SAMISH
SANTEE
SEKANE
SEKANI
SENECA
SLAVEY
SPOKAN
SUTAIO
TAGISH
TENINO
TOLOWA
TONGAS
TUNICA
TUTELO
UMPQUA
WALAPI
WIKENO
WINTUN
YAKIMA
YAMASI
YOKUTS

ALIBAMU
AMERIND
ANDARKO
ARAPAHO
ARIKARA
BANNOCK
BEOTHUK
CAHOKIA
CARRIZO
CATAWBA
CHEHALI
CHILCAT
CHINOOK
CHIWERE
CHOCTAW
CHUMASH
CHUMAWI
CLALLAM
CLATSOP
COLCINE
DHEGIHA
ESSELEN
HELLELT
HIDATSA
HUCHNOM
KITAMAT

KITLOPE
KLAMATH
KOASATI
KOPRINO
KUTCHIN
KUTENAI
LLANERO
LUISENO
MAHICAN
MOHEGAN
MOHICAN
MONACHI
MONTAUK
NANAIMO
NATCHEZ
NIANTIC
NIPMUCK
OJIBWAY
PUJUNAN
SANETCH
SANPOIL
SANSARC
SERRANO
SHASTAN
SHAWNEE
SHUSWAP

SIKSIKA
STIKINE
TAHLTAN
TAKELMA
TEPEHUA
TIMICUA
TLINGIT
TONKAWA
TULALIP
TUTUTNI
WAICURI
WAILAKI
WALAPAI
WAMESIT
WISHOSK
WISHRAM
WYANDOT
YAKUTAT
YAMHILL
YANKTON
YAVAPAI
YONKALA

ALGONKIN
APALACHI
ARIKAREE

ARIVAIPA
ATFALATI
CAHUILLA
CHEROKEE
CHEYENNE
CHIMAKUM
CHIPPEWA
COLVILLE
COMANCHE
COWICHAN
COWICHIN
COYOTERO
DELAWARE
DIEGUENO
FLATHEAD
HITCHITI
HUNKPAPA
ILLINOIS
IROQUOIS
KENIPSIM
KICKAPOO
KIKATSIK
KLASKINO
KLIKITAT
KWAKIUTL
MALECITE

MASKEGON
MENOMINI
MIMBRENO
NESPELIM
NEZPERCE
NOTTOWAY
OKINAGAN
ONONDAGA
PANAMINT
POWHATAN
QUERECHO
QUILEUTE
SAHAPTIN
SEMINOLE
SHOSHONI
SIHASAPA
SISSETON
SNONOWAS
SOUHEGAN
TLAKLUIT
TUSKEGEE
UMATILLA
UNALASKA
WAHPETON
YAMASSEE
YONKALLA

II. SOUTH AMERICA

GES
ITE
ONA
URO
URU
YAO

AGAZ
ANDE
ANTA
ANTI
AUCA
BARE
BORO
CAME
CANE
CARA
CORA
DIAU
DUIT
GHES
INCA
INKA
IXIL
MAKU
MOJO
MOXO
MURO
MUSO
MUZO
PEBA
PIRO
PURU

TAMA
TAPA
TOBA
TRIO
TUPI
URAN
YNCA

ACROA
ARARA
ARAUA
ARUAC
AUCAN
BRAVO
BUGRE
CAITA
CAMPA
CHANE
CHIMU
CHOCO
CHOLO
COLAN
CUNZA
GESAN
GUANA
GUATO
HUARE
INERI
MBAYA
OYANA
PALTA
PAMPA
PASSE

PIOJE
PIOXE
QUITU
SAMBO
SENCI
SIUSI
UAUPE
VEJOZ
WAURA
YAGUA
YAMEO
YUNCA

AMORUA
APALAI
APIACA
APIBON
ARAUNA
ATORAI
AYMARA
BANIVA
BETOYA
BORORO
CANARI
CANCHI
CANELO
CARAHO
CARAJA
CARIRI
CAVINA
CAYAPA
CAYAPO
CHANCA

CHANGO
CHAYMA
CHORTI
COCAMA
COCOMA
COFANE
COROPO
COTOXO
GALIBI
GOYANA
HIBITO
IXIANA
JAPURA
JAVAHE
JAVAHI
JIVARO
JUCUNA
JUMANA
KECHUA
LAMANO
MACUSI
MIRANA
MUISCA
MUYACA
MUYSCA
NASCAN
NOCTEN
OMAGUA
OREJON
PIAROA
PURUHA
QUICHE
SALIVA

SAMUCU
SETIBO
SHUARA
SIPIBO
TACANA
TAHAMI
TAMOYO
TAPAJO
TAPUYA
TARUMA
TIMOTE
TOTORO
TUCANO
TUNEBO
VILELA
WARRAU
WITOTO
YAHGAN
YAHUNA
YARURO
YURUNA
ZAPARA
ZAPARO

ANDAQUI
APALAII
ARAUCAN
ARECUNA

AREKUNA
AYAHUCA
CABOCLO
CAINGUA
CAMACAN
CARANGA
CASHIBO
CHARRUA
CHATINO
CHIBCHA
CHIRINO
CHOROTE
CHOROTI
CHUNCHU
CHUROYA
CIBONEY
FUEGIAN
GOAJIRO
GUAHIBO
GUARANI
GUAYMIE
HUANUCO
HUANUCU
ITONAMA
JAVAHAI
LORENZO
MAIPURE
MAPUCHE

MARIANA
MIRANHA
MOLUCHE
PAMPEAN
PATAGON
PAUMARI
PAYAGUA
PUELCHE
PUINAVI
QUECHUA
SARIGUE
SATIENO
SINSIGA
TARIANA
TEHUECO
TERRABA
TIMBIRA
TOTONAC
UARAYCU
UGARONO
WOYAWAY
YUSTAGA

ALIKULUF
AMAHUACA
APOLISTA
ARAPAHOE
BARBACOA

BOTOCUDO
CADIUEIO
CAINGANG
CANAMARY
CARICUNA
CHAMBIOA
CHAVANTE
CHIQUITO
CHIRIANA
COCONUCO
CONCHULU
CORABECA
COVARECA
GUARAUNO
GUAYAQUI
JAVITERO
MAYORUNA
MOSETENA
PICUNCHE
PURUPURU
QUERENDI
TAMANACO
TOROMONA
TUMUPASA
YAMAMADI
YAUAPERY
YURUCARE
YURUCARI

III. MEXICO–CENTRAL AMERICA

MAM

BOTO
CHOL
CUNA
ITZA
JOVA
MAYA
MAYO
MIXE
PAME
PIMA
RAMA
SERI
SUMO
TECA
TECO
ULVA
VOTO
WABI
XOVA

AZTEC
CARIB
CHUJE
CUEVA
HUAVE
KICHE
LENCA
MOCOA

NAHUA
OLIVE
OPATA
OTOMI
PETEN
PINTO
PIPIL
SMOOS
TAINO
XINCA
YAQUI
ZOQUE

AMUSGO
ARAWAK
BORUCA
BRIBRI
BRUNCA
CAHITA
CARIBI
CHOCHO
DARIEN
DIRIAN
DORASK
EUDEVE
GUAYMI
GUETAC
KEKCHI
LUCAYO
MANGUE

MIXTEC
NEVOME
OTOMAC
PAKAWA
PAPAGO
PERICU
SABUJA
SERIAN
SUERRE
TARASC
TOLTEC
WOOLWA

AMISHGO
BAKAIRI
CARIBEE
CHONTAL
CHUMULU
COTONAM
GUALACA
GUATUSO
HUASTEC
HUATUSO
JICAQUE
MAZAHUA
MAZATEC
MIXTECA
MIXTECO
NAYARIT
NICARAO

OTOMACA
OTOMACO
PIRANDA
POKOMAM
TARASCO
TEPANEC
TEPEHUA
TIRRIBI
TZENTAL
TZOTZIL
WAICURI
ZACATEC
ZAPATEC

CHANABAL
CHAPANEC
JACALTEC
MAZATECA
MAZATECO
MELCHORA
MOSQUITO
OROTINAN
POKONCHI
POPOLOCA
POPOLOCO
TLASCALA
TOTONACA
TZUTUHIL
ZACATECO
ZAPOTECA

LANGUAGE

LANGUAGE FAMILIES AND GROUPS

ARYAN
BANTU
GREEK
INDIC
MUNDA
TAMIL
TATAR
YAKUT
ALTAIC
ARABIC
BALTIC
CELTIC
ITALIC
PAPUAN
SLAVIC
TELUGA
TURKIC
URALIC
ARAMAIC
CHUVASH

HAMITIC
IRANIAN
MALAYAN
ROMANCE
ROMANIC
SEMITIC
AKKADIAN
ALBANIAN
ARMENIAN
CUSHITIC
ETHIOPIC
GERMANIC
HELLENIC
KANARESE
MONGOLIC
MONKHMER
SLAVONIC
TEUTONIC
BRYTHONIC
CANAANITE

CAUCASIAN
DRAVIDIAN
INDOARYAN
MONGOLIAN
TASMANIAN
ANDAMANESE
AUSTRALIAN
FINNOURGIC
INDONESIAN
MELANESIAN
POLYNESIAN
HYPERBOREAN
INDOCHINESE
INDOIRANIAN
MICRONESIAN
SINOTIBETAN
INDOEUROPEAN
INDOGERMANIC
SCANDINAVIAN

AMERICAN INDIAN LANGUAGE FAMILIES

(See page 172; names of languages and tribes are often the same)

COOS
EYAK
POMO
YUKI
ZUNI
AYMAR
HAIDA
KAROK
KIOWA
MAYAN
OTOMI
WASHO
WIYOT

YUCHI
YUMAN
YUROK
MIXTEC
SHASTA
SIOUAN
TANOAN
CADDOAN
CARIBAN
CHINOOK
KERESAN
TLINGIT
ACHOMAWI

KOOTENAI
PENUTIAN
SALISHAN
WAKASHAN
ARAWAKAN
IROQUOIAN
TSIMSHIAH
ALGONQUIAN
ARAUCANIAN
ATHAPASCAN
UTOAZTECAN
ESKIMOALEUT
NATCHEZMUSKOGEAN

LANGUAGES

AO
MO
WA
WU

AKA
ANU
EWE
GEG
IBO

KUI
LAI
LAO
MIN
MRU
TAI
TWI

AINU
AMOY

AVAR
BHIL
BODO
BUGI
EFIK
ERSE
FULA
GARO
GEEZ
KAMI

KOMI
LAPP
LUBA
MANX
MAYA
MOLE
MORO
NAGA
PALA
PALI

RONG
SHAN
TAAL
THAI
TINO
TODA
TOSK
TULU
TUPI
URDU
XOSA
ZULU

ATTIC
BATAK
BIKOL
CARIB
CROAT
CZECH
DAYAK
DORIC
DUTCH
FANTI
GALLA
GANDA
GONDI
GREEK
HAKKA
HAUSA
IRISH
KAREN
KHOND
KOINE
LATIN
LIMBU
MAKUA
MALAY
MALTO
MAORI
MOSSI
MUONG
MURMI
NGAIA
ORAON
ORIYA
OSCAN
PAMIR
PARSI
PUNIC
SABIR
SHINA
SOTHO
TAGAL
TAINO
TAMIL
TATAR
TIGRE
UGRIC
UZBEK
VEDIC
VOGUL
WELSH
XHOSA
AEOLIC
AFGHAN
ARABIC
ARAWAK
AYMARA
BASQUE
BERBER
BIHARI
BISAYA
BRETON
CELTIC
COPTIC
CREOLE
CRETAN
CYMRIC
DANISH
FRENCH
GAELIC
GALCHA
GERMAN
GOTHIC
HARARI
HEBREW
IGOROT
IONIAN
KACHIN
KAFIRI
KALHIN
KAZAKH
KELTIC
KODAGU
KOREAN
KYMRIC
LEPCHA
LYDIAN
MAGYAR
MANGAR
MINOAN
NAVAJO
NEPALI
NEWARI
OSTYAK
PAHARI
PASHTO
PIDGIN
POLISH
PUSHTU
ROMANY
RUANDA
SAMOAN
SINDHI
SLOVAC
SOMALI
SYRIAC
TADJIK
TAGALA
TAJIKI
TELUGU
TONGAN
TSWANA
TUAREG
TUSCAN
UIGHUR
VISAYA
VOTYAK
YORUBA

AEOLIAN
AMHARIC
ARAMAIC
AVESTAN
BALUCHI
BASHKIR
BENGALI
BURMESE
CATALAN
CEBUANO
CHIBCHA
CHINESE
CHUVASH
CORNISH
CYPRIAN
ENGLISH
FAROESE
FINNISH
FLEMISH
FRISIAN
GAULISH
GUARANI
HITTITE
ILOCANO
IRANIAN
ITALIAN
KHALKHA
KIRGHIZ
KURDISH
LAPPISH
LATVIAN
LEONESE
LETTISH
LINGALA
LOMBARD
MARATHI
MOABITE
NAHUATL
OSSETIC
PAHLAVI
PERMIAN
PERSIAN
PRAKRIT
PUNJABI
QUECHUA
QUICHUA
ROMANSH
RUSSIAN
SANTALI
SERBIAN
SIAMESE
SLOVENE
SORBIAN
SPANISH
SWABIAN
SWAHILI
SWEDISH
TAGALOG
TIBETAN
TURKISH
TURKMEN
UMBRIAN
VISAYAN
WENDISH
YENISEI
YIDDISH
YUKAGIR

AKKADIAN
ALBANIAN
ANNAMESE
ARMENIAN
ASSAMESE
BALINESE
BAVARIAN
BOEOTIAN
ESTONIAN
FRANKISH
GALICIAN
GEORGIAN
GOIDELIC
GUJARATI
HAWAIIAN
ILLYRIAN
JAPANESE
JAVANESE
KANARESE
KASHMIRI
KHERWARI
KIMBUNDU
LESGHIAN
LIVONIAN
MADURESE
MALAGASY
MANDARIN
MANDINGO
PAMPANGO
PHRYGIAN
ROMANIAN
RUMANIAN
SAMARINO
SANSKRIT
SUMATRAN
SUMERIAN
TAHITIAN
THRACIAN
TURKOMAN
UKRANIAN

AFRIKAANS
ALEMANNIC
BULGARIAN
CAMBODIAN
CANTONESE
CHEREMISS
HOTTENTOT
ICELANDIC
KAMCHADAL
KASHUBIAN
MALAYALAM
NAVARRESE
NORWEGIAN

PROVENCAL
RUTHENIAN
SARDINIAN
SINHALESE
SUNDANESE
TOCHARIAN

TOKHARIAN
UKRAINIAN
YUGARITIC

ANDALUSIAN
CIRCASSIAN

CORINTHIAN
HINDUSTANI
LITHUANIAN
PHOENICIAN
PORTUGUESE
RAJASTHANI

SINGHALESE
VIETNAMESE

AZARBAIJANI
AZERBAIJANI
BYELORUSSIAN

ALPHABETS

ENGLISH	
A	1
E	5
I	9
O	15
U	21
AR	18
EF	6
EL	12
EM	13
EN	14
EX	24
WY	25
BEE	2
CEE	3
CUE	17
DEE	4
ESS	19
GEE	7
JAY	10
KAY	11
PEE	16
TEE	20
VEE	22
WYE	25
ZED	26
ZEE	26
AITCH	8
DOUBLEU	23

ARABIC	
BA	2
FA	20
HA	6, 26
RA	10
TA	3, 16
YA	28
ZA	17
DAD	15
DAL	8
AYN	18
JIM	5
KAF	22
KHA	7
LAM	23
MIM	24
NUN	25
SAD	14
SIN	12
THA	4
WAW	27
ZAY	11
ALIF	1
DHAL	9
SHIN	13
GHAYN	19

GREEK	
MU	12
NU	13
PI	16
XI	14
CHI	22
ETA	7
PHI	21
PSI	23
RHO	17
TAU	19
BETA	2
IOTA	9
ZETA	6
ALPHA	1
DELTA	4
GAMMA	3
KAPPA	10
OMEGA	24
SIGMA	18
THETA	8
LAMBDA	11
EPSILON	5
OMICRON	15
UPSILON	20

HEBREW	
HE	5
PE	17
AIN	16
MEM	13
NUN	14
SIN	21
TAV	23
TAW	23
VAU	6
WAW	6
ALEF	1
AYIN	16
BETH	2
CAPH	11
ELEF	1
KAPH	11
KOPH	19
QOPH	19
RESH	20
SADE	18
SHIN	22
TETH	9
YODH	10
ALEPH	1
CHETH	8
GIMEL	3
ZAYIN	7
DALETH	4
LAMEDH	12
SAMEKH	15

LITERATURE

FICTIONAL CHARACTERS

American Literature

EVA
JIM
RIP
TOM

AHAB
ANNA
BROM
CORA
DICK
DRED
DUER
FINN
HIST
MOBY
OMOO

ARTIE
CANTY
ELMER
GAMUT
HORNE
POLLY
TOPSY
TOZER
TRAUM
UNCAS

AYLMER
BUMPPO
GANTRY
JESSUP
LEGREE

MUNROE
PRYNNE
SAWYER
SHELBY
SMILEY
SNOPES
VENNER
WINKLE

AGAPIDA
ANTONIA
BABBITT
DOREMUS
FISCHER
HAWKEYE
SELLERS

ZENOBIA

DOCHORNE
GOTTLIEB
HOLGRAVE
REDROVER
STARBUCK
THATCHER
UNCLETOM

DODSWORTH
KENNICOTT
SNODGRASS
TOMSAWYER

ARROWSMITH

Literature of Great Britain and Ireland

AGG
BHO
DAN
DHU
FAG
JIM
KIM
LEW
MEG
PEW
UMA
UNA
WAT

ABEL
AMAL
BECK
BEDE
CASS
COAN
COXE
ENID
EYRE
GANN
GARM
GUNN
HATT
HOOK
HYDE
IPPS
JANE
KULU
LAWS
LYON
MEON

MOLL
NIBS
RIMA
TUCK
WAGG

AISSA
AKELA
ARDEN
ARGAN
BALOO
BARDI
BLANE
BONEY
BRACY
BRECK
BULBO
DEANS
EDGAR
FOKER
GARTH
GLEGG
SHAWE
SILAS
SNOWE
SORTI
TESSA
TINTO
TORRE
TROIL
TRYAN
VINCY
WAMBA

ABDIEL

ARIOCH
ASHTON
ATOSSA
BEETLE
BESSEE
BINNIE
BOLTON
BOURKE
CRUSOE
DECOUD
DEEVER
DOBBIN
ESMOND
FLORAC
FRIDAY
GRAEME
HELDAR
JACQUE
JEKYLL
LARSEN
MAISIE
MARLOW
MARNER
MELEMA
MOWGLI
ROMOLA
ROWENA
SEYTON
ZEPHON

ADONAIS
ALASTOR
BELINDA
BLUDYER
CRAWLEY

DERONDA
DINMONT
FENELLA
GIZELLE
HARLETH
IVANHOE
LATIMER
LORDJIM
LYDGATE
MATILDA
RODRIGO
SHAFTON
SHANDON
SHIRLEY
SWEENEY
TRAVERS
URFRIED
WILLEMS
ZOPHIEL

ABSOLUTE
CONACHAR
CRICHTON
FLANDERS
INJUNJOE
JELLICOT
MALAPROP
MARKHEIM
NEWCOMES
NOSTROND
ROBINSON
ELSHENDER
MANNERING

Literature of Continental Europe

ASE
BLY

ANNA
GOTZ
GYNT
NEMO
NORA
PEER
PERE
PONS

AOUDA
ARGAN
ATHOS
BAGOT
BRAND
BULBA
EYOLF
FAUST
HEDDA
HULAT
LELIE
MITYA
ORGON
SONIA
STIVA

TARAS
VANYA
WERLE

ALVING
ANITRA
ARAMIS
ARISTE
ASHLEY
BELINE
BUNGAY
CATHOS
COLLIN
DANTES
EGMONT
ESPARD
FEDORA
FROLLO
GABLER
GORIOT
HELMER
JAVERT
MARION
MARSAY
MIGNON
SHATOV

TRILBY

ALCESTE
ALOADIN
ALYOSHA
ANSELME
ARVALAN
CAMILLE
CLEANTE
COSETTE
DORANTE
GERONTE
GOBSEK
GRANDET
HERNANI
ISIDORE
KATUSHA
LEANDRE
MANDERS
MARTINE
MEISTER
MYSHKIN
POPINOT
PORTHOS
RESTAUD
SOLVEIG

VALJEAN
VAUTRIN
VRONSKI
WERTHER
WILHELM

ATHANAEL
BERGERET
CHRYSALE
DELORMES
FLORINDA
GORGIBUS
GRETCHEN
HARPAGON
KARENINA
LADURLAD
NASTASIA
RODERICK
SHIGALOV
TARTUFFE

CHICHIKOV
DARTAGNAN
ESMERALDA
KARAMAZOV
QUASIMODO

Shakespeare

NYM
SAY

ADAM
CADE
DAVY
DION
HERO
IAGO
IDEN
IRAS
JAMY
JOHN
LEAR
LUCE
PETO
PUCK
ROSS
SNUG
VAUX

ANGUS
ARIEL
BAGOT
BIRON
BOYET
BUSHY
CAIUS
CELIA
CORIN

CURAN
CURIO
EGEUS
ELBOW
FESTE
FLUTE
FROTH
GOBBO
GOFFE
GOWER
HENRY
JULIA
LAFEU
LOVEL
LUCIO
MELUN
MOPSA
OSRIC
PHEBE
PINCH
REGAN
ROBIN
ROMEO
RUGBY
SNOUT
SOSIA
SPEED
TIMON
TITUS

ADRIAN
AEGEON
ALONSO
ANGELO
ANTONY
BANQUO
BIANCA
BOLEYN
BOTTOM
CAESAR
CAPHIS
CLOTEN
DORCAS
DROMIO
DUNCAN
FABIAN
FENTON
GREMIO
GRUMIO
HAMLET
JULIET
JULIUS
LAUNCE
LENNOX
MUTIUS
OBERON
ORSINO
PISTOL
POMPEY
PORTIA

RUMOUR
SCROOP
SEYTON
SILVIA
SIWARD
TALBOT
TAMORA
THAISA
THURIO
TRANIO
TYBALT
VERGES
WOLSEY

AEMILIA
ANTONIO
BEROWNE
BERTRAM
CALIBAN
CAMILLO
CAPULET
CLAUDIO
CONRADE
CRANMER
DUMAINE
ESCALUS
ESCANES
FLEANCE
GATESBY
GONERIL

GONZALO
GREGORY
HORATIO
HOTSPUR
IACHIMO
JESSICA
LARTIUS
LAVACHE
LAVINIA
LEONATO
LEONTES
LUCETTA
LUCIANA
MACBETH
MACDUFF
MALCOLM
MARCADE
MARSIUS
MIRANDA
MONTANO
MOWBRAY
NERISSA
OPHELIA
ORLANDO
OTHELLO
PAULINA
PERDITA
PHRYNIA
PISANIO
PROTEUS
PUBLIUS
RICHARD

SALANIO
SAMPSON
SHALLOW
SHYLOCK
SIMPCOX
SLENDER
SOLINUS
TEMPEST
THESEUS
TITANIA
TROILUS
TYRRELL
URSWICK
VALERIA
VARRIUS

ABHORSON
ANNEPAGE
AVIRAGUS
BAPTISTA
BARDOLPH
BASSANIO
BELARIUS
BENEDICK
BENVOLIO
BERNARDO
BORACHIO
CAMPEIUS
CAPUCIUS
CLAUDIUS
COMINIUS

CORDELIA
CRESSIDA
DOGBERRY
DONPEDRO
EGLAMOUR
FALSTAFF
FASTOLFE
FLUELLEN
GADSHILL
GARDINER
GARGRAVE
GRATIANO
HARCOURT
LAURENCE
LODOVICO
LYSANDER
MENTEITH
MERCUTIO
MONTAGUE
PANTHINO
PAROLLES
PERICLES
PHILOTUS
POLONIUS
PROSPERO
RATCLIFF
REIGNIER
RODERIGO
SALARINO
STEPHANO
TRINCULO

VIOLENTA
VIRGILIA
VOLUMNIA

APEMANTUS
BALTHASAR
BASSIANUS
BOURCHIER
BRABANTIO
CAITHNESS
CLEOPATRA
CORNELIUS
CYMBELINE
DESDEMONA
DONALBAIN
ERPINGHAM
GLENDOWER
GUIDERIUS
MARCELLUS
ROTHERHAM
SEBASTIAN
TOBYBELCH
VALENTINE
VENTIDIUS
VINCENTIO
VOLTINAND

ANDRONICUS
CORIOLANUS
FORTINBRAS
LONGAVILLE

Dickens

AMY
BET
CLY
PIP
TOX

BAPS
BRAY
DORA
FANG
FIPS
FOGG
GAMP
HEEP
JOWL
KAGS
MELL
NELL
OMER
PEPS
POTT
PRIG
TIGG
VECK
WEGG

BALOO

BATES
BETSY
BEVAN
BRICK
CHOKE
CLARE
FAGIN
KROOK
MIGGS
NANCY
NOGGS
QUILP
RUDGE
SIKES
SMIKE
TWIST

BAILEY
BARKIS
BOFFIN
BUCKET
BUMBLE
BUZFUZ
CARKER
CARTON
DARNEY
DARTLE

DODSON
DOMBEY
DORRIT
HARMON
JARLEY
LAMMLE
MAYLIE
MERDLE
NIPPER
OLIVER
REDLAW
SLEARY
TAPLEY
WARDLE

BAILLIE
BLIMBER
BROWDIE
DEFARGE
ESTELLA
JAGGERS
JEDDLER
JELLYBY
MANETTE
MOWCHER
NADGETT
NUBBLES

PIPCHIN
PLUMMER
PODSNAP
SCROOGE
SLOWBOY
SLUMKEY
SNAGSBY
SNUBBIN
SPENLOW
STRYVER
TINYTIM
TROTTER

BAGSTOCK
CRATCHIT
CRUMMLES
CRUNCHER
HAVISHAM
HORTENSE
LIRRIPER
MAGWITCH
MICAWBER
NICKLEBY
PEGGOTTY
SKIMPOLE

CHADBAND

Characters in Arabian Nights

AGIB
AMINE
GANEM
FATIMA
HAROUN
SINBAD
ALADDIN
ALIBABA
BADOURA
HOUSSAIN
MORGIANA
SCHARIAH
BARMECIDE
SCHACABAC

Sleuths in Literature

BOND
CHAN
COOL
FELL
MAYO
MOTO
DUPIN
LUPIN
MASON
MCKEE
MORAN
NORTH
SAINT
VANCE
WOLFE
CARTER
HAMMER
HOLMES
JUSTUS
POIROT
PORTER
SHAYNE
WIMSEY
CHARLES
FREEMAN
MACLAIN
MERLINI
RAFFLES
VALCOUR
FUMANCHU
WESTLAKE
MERRIVALE

Unusual First Names in Literature

CLEM
DINK
EDEN
GYPO
MOTT
AGGIS
BINGO
COSMO
DISKO
GAVIN
LORNA
MANON
MATEO
NIKKI
PHILO
RHETT
TANIS
URIAH
ARSENE
BIGGER
CLOVIS
PENROD
PEYTON
SANCHO
SOAMES
YANERY
FLORIAN
HERCULE
ICHABOD
KIMBALL
MINIVER
MYCROFT
PEACHEY
PHILEAS
WILKINS
ZULEIKA
ALGERNON
EMMELINE
FANCOURT
SCARLETT
TRISTRAM
WACKFORD

Names in Nursery Rhymes

DAW
DUN
COLE
JILL
JUDY
POLT
ROSE
TROT
WREN
COLIN
GILES
JENNY
KITTY
MOREY
POLLY
PUNCH
SIMON
TAFFY
BOGGEN
BOPEEP
FOSTER
GRIGGS
GRUNDY
HORNER
JENNIE
MACKEY
MUFFET
PORGIE
SPRATT
TONSEY
TUCKER
WARLEY
WILLIE
WINKIE
BLUEBEN
BOLDERO
FAUSTUS
FINIKIN
HUBBARD
SHAFTOE
TERENCE
DAMETROT
ETTICOAT
FLINDERS
KINGCOLE
TOMTHUMB
BETTYBLUE
DANDYPRAT
MCDIDDLER
REDBREAST
TOMMYTROT

Animals in Literature

JIP
MEG
APIS
BABE
BIMI
BRAN
CHIL
EGAN
GHAO
GRIP
MANG
MOTI
MYSA
NANA
RAMA
RANN
TOBY
TYLO
ARGUS
BAMBI
BEVIS
DJALI
FADDA
GRANI
JUMBO
OSCAR
RUKSH
BAYARD
DAPPLE
FLOPIT
KATMIR
RAKUSH
ROLAND
WINNIE
ALBORAK
BAJARDO
BAVIECA
PEGASUS
RABICAN
REDWULL
XANTHUS
RABICANO
SLEIPNIR
BLACKBESS
BOATSWAIN
BRIGADORE
CAVALCADE
FERDINAND
GUNPOWDER
MARCHHARE
MEHITABEL
ROSINANTE
BLACKBEAUTY

MEASURES AND WEIGHTS

LINEAR MEASURES

Algeria	TERMIN
Arabia	BARID
	FARSAKH
	FARSANG
	MARHALA
Arabia, ancient	CABDA
	MILLE
	QASAB
	ASSBAA
	GHALVA
Argentina	VARA
	BRAZA
	LEGUA
Austria	FUSS
	LINIE
	MEILE
	PUNKT
	KLAFTER
Belgium	AUNE
	PIED
	PERCHE
Brazil	PE
	VARA
	BRACA
	LEGOA
	MILHA
	PALMO
	PASSO
	COVADO
Chile	VARA
	LEGUA
	LINEA
	CUADRA
China	LI
	TU
	FEN
	CHIH
	CHANG
Cyprus	PIK
Czechoslovakia	SAH
	LATRO
	LOKET
Denmark	FOD
	MIL
	ALEN
	FAVN
	RODE
	LINJE
	TOMME
	LANDMIL
Dominican Republic	ONA
Ecuador	CUADRA
Egypt	PIK
	ABDAT
Egypt, ancient	KHET
	THEB
	CUBIT
	SCHÈNE
	CHORYOS
Estonia	ELLE
	LIIN
	SULD
	TOLL
	FADEN
	SAGENE
Ethiopia	TAT
France	LIEUE
	LIGNE
	PERCHE
Germany	FUSS
	STAB
	ZOLL
	KETTE
	STRICH
	KLAFTER
Greece	PIK
	GRAMME
	PALAME
	STADION
Greece, ancient	BEMA
	POUS
	PYGON
	DICHAS
	ACAENA
	ORGYIA
	STADIUM
Hebrew	EZBA
	REED
	CUBIT
Holland	EL
	DUIM
	VOET
	ROEDE
	STREEP
Honduras	VARA
	MILLA
	TERCIA
Iceland	FET
	ALIN
	LINA
India	GUZ
	JOW
	KOS(S)
	HATH
	JAOB
	COVID
	CROSA
	HASTA
	GEERAH
	UNGLEE
Indonesia	KILAN
	TJENKAL
Iran	GUZ
	MOU
	ZAR
	MANSION
Ireland	BANDLE
	FATHMUR
Italy	CANNA
	PALMO
	PUNTO
	MIGLIO
	BRACCIO
Japan	BU
	JO
	MO
	RI
	BOO
	CHO
	RIN
	SUN
	HIRO
	SHAKU
Java	PAAL
Mexico	VARA
	LEGUA
	LINEA
	PULGADA
Norway	FOT
	ALEN
Paraguay	PIE
	VARA
	LEGUA
	CORDEL
	CUADRA
Poland	CAL
	MILA
	LINJA
	SAZEN
	STOPA
	LOKIEC
Portugal	PE
	VARA
	BRACA
	LEGOA
	LINHA
	MILHA
	PALMO
	COVADO
Rangoon	LAN
	DAIN
	TAUN
Rome, ancient	PES
	ACTUS
	CUBIT
	UNCIA

	GRADUS
	PALMUS
	PASSUS
	DIGITUS
Russia	FUT
	DUIM
	VERST
	ARSHIN
	PALETZ
	SAGENE
	TOTCHKA
	VERCHOK
Spain	CODO
	DEDO
	VARA
	BRAZA
	LEGUA
	PALMO
	SESMA
	CUARTA
	ESTADO
	PULGADA
Sweden	ALN
	FOT
	REF
	TUM
	FAMN
	LINJE
	NYMIL
Switzerland	AUNE
	FUSS
	PIED
	ZOLL
	LIEUE
	POUCE
	SCHUH
	STAAB
	TOISE
	PERCHE
	KLAFTER
Thailand	WA(H)
	KEN
	NIU
	SEN
	SOK
	YOT
	KEUP
Turkey	PIK
	HATT
	KHAT
	ZIRA
	BERRI
	ARSHIN
	PARMAK
Viet-Nam	LY
	GON
	NGU
	THUOC
	TRUONG
Yugoslavia	RIF
	KHVAT
	PALAZ
	STOPA

US Common Linear and Metric Equivalents

	1 INCH	= 2.54 cm.
12 in.	= 1 FOOT	= .3048 m.
3 ft.	= 1 YARD	= .9144 m.
5½ yd.	= 1 ROD	= 5.029 m.
40 rd.	= 1 FURLONG	= 200.15 m.
8 fur.	= 1 MILE	= 1.6093 km.
3 mi.	= 1 LEAGUE	= 4.8279 km.

Metric Measures and Equivalents

KILOMETER	= 1000 m.	= .62 mi.
HECTOMETER	= 100 m.	= 3937 in.
DECAMETER	= 10 m.	= 393.7 in.
METER	= 1 m.	= 39.37 in.
DECIMETER	= 0.1 m.	= 3.937 in.
CENTIMETER	= 0.01 m.	= .3937 in.
MILLIMETER	= 0.001 m.	= .03937 in.

US and UK Uncommon Linear Measures

CUT	300 yd.	POLE	5.5 in.
ELL	45 in.	ROOD	7 yd.
LEA	120 yd.	SPAN	9 in.
BOLT	40 yd.	CHAIN	22 yd.
HAND	4 in.	DIGIT	.75 in.
HANK	840 yd.	OUNCE	1/64 in.
HEER	600 yd.	PERCH	5.5 yd.
IRON	1/48 in.	PRIME	1 in.
LINE	1/12 in.	SKEIN	360 ft.
LINK	7.92 in.	FATHOM	6 ft.
NAIL	2.25 in.	SECOND	1/12 in.
PACE	30 in.	THREAD	1.5 yd.
PALM	3–4 in.		

SURFACE MEASURES

Arabia, ancient	FEDDAN
	QASABA
Argentina	QUADRA
	MANZANA
Austria	JOCH
Brazil	CUARTA
	TAREFA
Bulgaria	LEKHA
Chile	CUADRA
China	MU
	KISH
	CHING
Cuba	TAREA
	CORDEL
Czechoslovakia	LAN
	JITRO
	KOREC
	STRYCH
Denmark	ALBUM
Dominican Republic	TAREA
Egypt	SAHME
	AURURE
	FEDDAN
Estonia	TUN
Finland	TUNLAND
France	ARPENT
Germany	MORGEN
Greece	ACAENA
	STREMMA
Holland	BUNDER
Hungary	HOLD
	JOCH
	YOKE
Iceland	FERFET
	FERALIN
	FERMILA
India	BEGA
	BIGHA
Indonesia	BOUW
Iraq	MISHARA
Italy	TAVOLA
Japan	BU
	GO
	SE
	CHO
	TAN
	TSUBO
Libya	JABIA
Mexico	LABOR
	SITIO
Nicaragua	SUERTE
	ESTAJAL
	MANZANA
Norway	MA(A)L
Paraguay	LINE
	LINO
Peru	TOPO
Philippines	LOAN
	BRAZA
	BALITA
	QUINON
Poland	MORG(A)
	WIOKA
Portugal	GEIRA
	FERRADO
Rome	CLIMA
	JUGA
	UNCIO
	SALTUS
	VERSUS
Somalia	JARAT
	JUCHART
South Africa	MORGEN
Spain	YUGADA
	CELEMIN
	ESTADEL
Sweden	TUNLAND
Thailand	RAI
	NGAN
Turkey	DONUM
	DJERIB
United Kingdom	CHAIN
	COVER
	JUGUM
	VIRGATE
United States	ACRE
	BLOCK
	CHAIN
	LABOR
Uruguay	CUADRA
	SUERTE
Viet-Nam	MAU
	QUO
	SAO
Yugoslavia	RALO
	DONUM
	LANAZ
	RALICA
	MOTYKA

US Square Measures and Metric Equivalents

160 sq. rds.	= 1 ACRE	= .0407 ha.
640 acres	= 1 SQ. MILE	= 259 ha.
36 sq. mi.	= 1 TOWNSHIP	

Metric Measures and Equivalents

HECTARE	= 10,000 sq. m.	= 2.471 acres
ARE	= 100 sq. m.	= 119.6 sq. yd.
CENTIARE	= 1 sq. m.	= 1,550 sq. in.

LIQUID MEASURES

Arabia	CUDDY
	ZUDDA
	NUSFIAH
Arabia, ancient	DEN
	SAA
	FERK
	KIST
	CAFIZ
	CAPHITE
Argentina	GALON
	FRASCO
Austria	FASS
	MASS
	HALBE
	PFIFF
Brazil	PIPA
	ALMUD
	TONEL

Country	Measure
Burma	BYEE
	SEIT
China	KO
	QUEI
	SHIH
Cyprus	OKA
	CASS
	KOUZA
	KARTOS
Denmark	POT
	OLTONDE
	VIERTEL
Egypt	RO(U)B
	ROBHAN
	MALOUAH
Ethiopia	CUBA
	KUBA
Finland	KANNU
	TUNNA
France	POT
	PINTE
	CHOPINE
	POISSON
Germany	AAM
	FASS
	EIMER
	FUDER
	KANNE
	MAASS
Greece	BARILE
	COTULA
	KOILON
Greece, ancient	CHOUS
	AMPHORA
Hebrew	CAB
	HIN
	KOR
	LOG
	BATH
Holland	AAM
	AUM
	KAN
	STOOP
	MAATJE
	MUTSJE
Iceland	POTTUR
	OLTUNNA
India	DRONA
	MUSHTI
Indonesia	TAKAR
Japan	GO
	TO
	SHO
	KOKU
	SHAKU
Latvia	KANNE
	STOOF
Libya	BOZZE
	MATTARO
Mexico	BARIL
	JARRA
Peru	GALON
Philippines	CHUPA
	GANTA
	APATAN
Poland	CWIERC
	KWARTA
	GARNIEC
Portugal	BOTA
	MEIO
	PIPA
	ALMUD(E)
	OITAVA
Rome	URNA
	CULEUS
	DOLIUM
	CYATHUS
Russia	FASS
	STO(O)F
	CHARKA
	TCHAST
	BOTCHKA
Somalia	CABA
Spain	BUTT
	COPA
	MOYO
	ARROBA
	CANTARA
Sweden	AM
	KANNA
	KAPPE
	JUMFRU
	OXHUVUD
Switzerland	POT
	IMMI
	SAUM
	MAASS
	SETIER
Tangier	KULA
Thailand	KWIEN
	TANAN
Trieste	ORNA
	ORNE
United Kingdom	PIN
	PIPE
	FIRKIN
	RUNLET
United States	TUN
	BUTT
	DRAM
	DRUM
	PIPE
	MINIM
Viet-Nam	TAO
	SHITA
Yugoslavia	OKA
	AKOV

US Liquid Measures and Metric Equivalents

16	fl. oz.	= 1 PINT	= 0.4732 l.
4	gills	= 1 PINT	= 0.4732 l.
2	pt.	= 1 QUART	= 0.9463 l.
4	qt.	= 1 GALLON	= 3.7853 l.
31½	gal.	= 1 BARREL	
2	bbl.	= 1 HOGSHEAD	

Metric Measures and Equivalents

KILOLITER	= 1000 l.	= 264.2 gal.
HECTOLITER	= 100 l.	= 26.42 gal.
DECALITER	= 10 l.	= 2.642 gal.
LITER	= 1 l.	= 1.057 qt.
DECILITER	= 0.1 l.	= 0.211 pt.
CENTILITER	= 0.01 l.	= 0.338 fl. oz

DRY MEASURES

Algeria	TARRI
Arabia	TEMAN
Argentina	FENEGA
	LASTRE
Austria	MUTH
	METZE
	ACHTEL
	BECHER
	VIERTEL
Brazil	MOIO
	FANGA
	QUARTO
Bulgaria	KRINA
Burma	TENG
Calcutta	KUNK
	RAIK
Ceylon	PARAH
	AMUNAM
Channel Islands	CABOT
Chile	FANEGA
China	HO
	HU
	PU
	TOU
	SHENG
Costa Rica	FANEGA
	CAJUELA
Cyprus	MEDIMNO
Denmark	TONDE
	ACHTEL
Egypt	ARDEB
	FARDE
	KILAH
	KEDDAH
	DARIBAH
Egypt, ancient	ARTABA
France	MINOT
	HEMINE
Germany	KANNE
	MASSEL
	SCHEFFEL
Greece	BACHEL
Hebrew	CAB
	KAB
	KOR
	EPHA(H)
	OMER
	SEAH
	HOMER
Holland	KOP
	ZAK
	MUDDE
	SCHEPEL
Hungary	METZE
India	GARCE
Indonesia	GANTANG
Italy	STAIO
	MOGGIO
	RUBBIO
Japan	TO
	SHO
	KOKU
Latvia	KULMET
Malta	SALM(A)
Mexico	CARGA
	FANEGA
Norway	SKIEPPE
Philippines	CABAN
	CHUPA
	GANTA
	APATAN
Poland	KORZEC
Portugal	MEIO
	FANGA
	QUARTO
	SELAMIN
Rome	MODIUS
Russia	LOF
	OSMIN
	GARNETZ
Scotland	BOLL
	LIPPY
	FIRLOT
	CHALDER
Somalia	TABLA
South Africa	MUID
	SCHEPEL
Spain	ALMUD
	CAHIZ
	MEDIO
	FANEGA
	RACION
Sweden	FODER
	SPANN
	TUNNA
	KOLLAST
Switzerland	MUID
	VIERTEL
Syria	MAKUK
	GARAVA
Tangier	MUDD
Thailand	SAT
	TANG
	TANAN
Tunisia	SAA(H)
	UEBA
	CAFIZ
	WHIBA
Turkey	ALMUD
	KILEH
	FORTIN
United Kingdom	COOM(B)
United States	CORD
	BASKET

US Dry Measures and Metric Equivalents

2 pints	= 1 QUART	= 1.101 l.
8 qt.	= 1 PECK	= 8.809 l.
4 pk.	= 1 BUSHEL	= 35.24 l.
105 qt.	= 1 BARREL	

Metric Weights and Equivalents

KILOLITER	= 1.308 cu. yd.
HECTOLITER	= 2.838 bu.
DECALITER	= 1.135 pk.
LITER	= 0.9081 qt.
STERE	= KILOLITER

WEIGHTS

Algeria	UCKIA
Arabia	BAHAR
	CHEKI
	KELLA
	MAUND
	TOMAN
	MISKAL
	BOKARD
Arabia, ancient	ROTL
	NASCH
	NEVAT
	OCQUE
	OUKIA
Argentina	LIBRA
	QUINTAL
Austria	MARK
	SAUM
	UNZE
	DENAT
	KARCH
	STEIN
	PFUND
	PFENNIG
	CENTNER
Belgium	LIVRE
	CHARGE
	CHARIOT
Brazil	ONCA
	LIBRA
	ARROBA
	OITAVA
	ARRATEL
	QUILATE
	QUINTAL
Bulgaria	OKA
	OKE
	TOVAR
Burma	MOO
	VIS(S)
	KYAT
	TICAL
	ABUCCO
	PEIKTHA
Calcutta	DHAN
	PANK
China	LI
	FEN
	HAO
	KIN
	TAN
	YIN
	CHIN
	MACE
	SHIH
	TAEL
	CATTY
	PICUL
Colombia	SACO
	CARGA
	LIBRA
	QUILATE
	QUINTAL
Costa Rica	CAJA
Cyprus	OKA
	MOOSA
	KANTAR
Denmark	ES
	LOD
	ORT
	VOG
	MARK
	PUND
	UNZE
	KVINT
	CENTNER
	LISPUND
	QUINTIN
Egypt	OKA
	OKE
	HEML
	OKIA
	ROTL
	KERAT
	UCKIA
	KANTAR
	QUINTAL
Egypt, ancient	KAT
	KET
	KHAR
	DEBEN
	OKIEH
Estonia	NAEL
	PUUD
Ethiopia	KASM
	NATR
	OKET
	ALADA
	NETER
	WAKEA
	WOGIET
France	GROS
	MARC
	ONCE
	LIVRE
	TONNE
Germany	LOT
	PFUND
	STEIN
	CENTNER
Greece	MNA
	OKA
	MINA
	LITRA
	DRAMME
	OBULUS
	STATER
	DRACHMA
Greece, ancient	
	DIOBOL
	CHALCON
Guinea	AKEY
	PISO
	UZAN
	BENDA
	SERON
Hebrew	MINA
	BEKA(H)
	REBA(H)
	SHEKEL
Holland	ONS
	LOOD
	POND
	GREIN
	KORREL
	WICHTJE
India	SER
	DHAN
	PALA
	PICE
	RAT(T)I
	TOLA
	ADPAO
	BAHAR
	MAUND
	CHITTAK
Indonesia	TJI
	HOEN
	TALI
	WANG
	PICUL
	REAAL
	KOJANG
	KULACK
Iran	ZAR
	DRAM
	DUNG
	SANG
	ABBAS
	DINAR
	BATMAN
	GANDUM
	KARWAR
	NAKHOD
	ABBASSI
Italy	ONCIA
	DENARO
	GANDUM
	LIBBRA
	OTTAVA
Japan	MO
	FUN
	KIN
	RIN
	SHI
	KATI
	KWAN
	NIYO
	MOMME
	PICUL
Mexico	ONZA

	CARGA
	LIBRA
	MARCO
	ADARME
	ARROBA
	OCHAVA
	TERCIO
	QUINTAL
Morocco	ROTL
	GERBE
	KINTAR
Norway	LOD
	MARK
	PUND
Philippines	FARDO
	PICUL
	PUNTO
	LACHSA
	QUILATE
Poland	LUT
	FUNT
	UNCYA
	KAMIAN
	SKRUPUL
Portugal (see Brazil)	GRAO
ROME	AS
	BES
	LIBRA
	UNCIA
	DUELLA
	SEXTULA
	SOLIDUS
Russia	LOT
	PUD
	DOLA
	FUNT
	POOD
	KAMIAN
Scotland	BOLL
	DROP
Spain	ONZA
	LIBRA
	MARCO
	TOMIN
	ADARME
	ARROBA
	DINERO
	OCHAVA
Sweden	ASS
	ORT
	PUND
	STEN
	UNTZ
	NYLAST
	LISPUND
Syria	COLA
Thailand	PAI
	BAHT
	HAPH
	KLAM
	KLOM
	CHANG
	COYAN
	FUANG
	PICUL
	TICAL
	SALUNG
	SOMPAY
	TAMLUNG
Tunisia	UCKIA
	KANTAR
Turkey	OKA
	OKE
	KILE(H)
	CEQUI
	CHEKE
	KERAT
	BATMAN
	DIRHAM
	KANTAR
	MISKAL
	YUSDRUM
United Kingdom	KIP
	KEEL
	BARGE
	CLOVE
	FAGOT
	STONE
	CENTAL
	FIRKIN
	POCKET
United States	KEG
	KIP
	BARREL
	CENTAL
Viet-Nam	TA
	CAN
	BINH
	DONG
Yugoslavia	TOVAR
	WAGON
	DRAMMA
	SATLIJK
Zanzibar	GISLA

US Weights and Metric Equivalents

3.086 grains	= 1 CARAT	= 200 mg.
27 11/32 gr.	= 1 DRAM	= 1.772 g.
16 dr.	= 1 OUNCE	= 28.35 g.
16 oz.	= 1 POUND	= .4536 kg.
100 lb.	= 1 CWT.*	= 45.36 kg.
20 cwts.	= 1 TON	= .9072 M.T.

*Hundredweight

Metric Measures and Equivalents

Metric TON	= 2204.6 lb.
QUINTAL	= 220.46 lb.
KILO(GRAM)	= 2.2046 lb.
GRAM	= 15.432 gr.
MILLIGRAM	= .0154 gr.

MONEY AND COINS

ANCIENT AND MODERN

Afghanistan	PUL
	ABBASI
	AMANIA
	AFGHANI
Albania	LEK
	FRANC
	QINTAR
Angola	ESCUDO
	MACUTA
	ANGOLAR
	CENTAVO
Argentina	PESO
	CENTAVO
Austria	DUCAT
	KRONE
	FLORIN
	HELLER
	GROSCHEN
	SCHILLING
Belgium	BELGA
	FRANC
	CENTIME
Biblical	BEKA(H)
	MITE
	SHEKEL
	TALENT
Bolivia	CENTAVO
	BOLIVIANO
Brazil	REIS
	CONTO
	MILREIS
	MOIDORE
	CRUZEIRO
Bulgaria	LEV
	LEW
	DINAR
	STOTINKA
Burma	PYA
	KYAT
Ceylon	CENT
	TANG
	RUPEE
Chile	PESO
	COLON
	CONDOR
	LIBRA
	ESCUDO
	CENTAVO
China	LI
	PU
	CASH
	CENT
	TAEL
	TIAO
	YUAN
Colombia	PESO
	REAL
	CONDOR
	CENTAVO
Costa Rica	COLON
	CENTIMO
Czechoslovakia	DUCAT
	HALER
	HELLER
	KORUNA
Denmark	ORE
	KRONE
	SKILLING
Dutch East Indies	BONK
	DOIT
Ecuador	SUCRE
	CONDOR
	CENTAVO
Egypt	GIRSH
	POUND
	RIYAL
	PIASTER
	MILLIEME
El Salvador	COLON
	CENTAVO
Estonia	SENT
	KROON
	ESTMARK
Ethiopia	BESA
	GIRSH
	TALARI
	ASHRAFI
Finland	PENNI
	MARKKA
France	ECU
	SOL
	SOU
	AGNEL
	FRANC
	LIARD
	LOUIS
	OBOLE
	BESANT
	CENTIME
	SOLIDUS
	NAPOLEON
Genoa	JANE
German East Africa	PESA
	RUPIE
Germany	MARK
	TALER
	THALER
	PFENNIG
	BLAFFERT
Greece	OBOL
	LEPTON
	STATER
	DRACHMA
Guatemala	PESO
	QUETZAL
Haiti	FRANC
	GOURDE
Holland	DOIT
	OORD
	FLORIN
	GULDEN
	STIVER
	DAALDER
	GUILDER
Honduras	CENTAVO
	LEMPIRA
Hungary	GARA
	PENGO
	FILLER
Iceland	AURAR
	EYRIR
	KRONA
India	DAM
	LAC
	PIE
	ANNA
	DAWM
	FELS
	HOON
	LAKH
	PICE
	TARA
	CRORE
	MOHUR
	RUPEE
	PAGODA
Indonesia	RUPIAH
Iran	PUL
	KRAN
	POUL
	RIAL
	DARIC
	DINAR
	MOHUR
	SHAHI
	TOMAN
	ASHRAFI
	PAHLEVI
Iraq	DINAR
Ireland	RAP
	PENCE
	POUND
	SHILLING
Israel	POUND
	PRUTA
Italy	LIRA
	LIRE
	SCUDO
	SOLDO
	TESTON(E)
Japan	BU
	RIN

	SEN
	YEN
	OBAN
	ICHIBU
	ITZEBU
Korea	WON
	HWAN
Laos	AT
	ATT
	KIP
Latvia	LAT
	RUBLIS
	SANTIMS
	KAPEIKA
Lithuania	LIT
	MARKA
	CENTAS
	FENNIG
	OSTMARK
Macao	AVO
	PATACA
Malaya	TRA
	TRAH
Mexico	PESO
	AZTECA
	CENTAVO
Mongolia	TUGRIK
Montenegro	PARA
	FLORIN
	PERPERA
Morocco	OKIA
	RIAL
	DIRHAM
Nepal	MOHAR
	RUPEE
Nicaragua	CENTAVO
	CORDOBA
Norway	ORE
	KRONE
Oman	GAJ
	GOZ
	GHAZI
	MAHMUDI
Pakistan	ANNA
	PICE
	RUPEE
Panama	CENT
	BALBOA
Paraguay	GUARANI
Peru	SOL
	LIBRA
	DINERO
Poland	DUCAT
	GROSZ
	MARKA
	ZLOTY
	FENNIG
	HALERZ
Portugal	REI
	CONTO
	DOBRA
	DINERO
	ESCUDO
	TOSTAO
	CRUSADO
	JOHANNES
Rome	AS
	AES
	SEMIS
	DINDER
	SOLIDUS
	DENARIUS
	SESTERCE
Rumania	BAN
	LEI
	LEU
	LEY
	BANI
Russia	ALTIN
	KOPEK
	RUBLE
	CHERVONETS
Saudi-Arabia	POUND
	RIYAL
Somalia	BESA
	SOMALO
South Africa	CENT
	POND
	RAND
	FLORIN
	DAALDER
Spain	PESO
	REAL
	PESETA
	ALFONSO
	CENTIMO
	PISTOLE
Sweden	ORE
	KRONA
	RIGSDALER
Switzerland	BATZ
	FRANC
	RAPPE
	CENTIME
Thailand	AT
	ATT
	BAHT
	FUANG
	TICAL
	PYNUNG
	SALUNG
	SATANG
Tunisia	DINAR
Turkey	LIRA
	PARA
	ALTUN
	ASPER
	MAHBUB
	SEQUIN
	ALTILIK
	BESHLIK
	PIASTER
	ZECCHINO
Ukraine	GRIVNA
	SCHAGIV
United Kingdom	
	ANGEL
	BODLE
	CROWN
	DRAKE
	GROAT
	PENNY
	PLACK
	POUND
	BAWBEE
	FLORIN
	GUINEA
	CAROLUS
	JACOBUS
	UNICORN
	ATCHISON
	FARTHING
	SHILLING
	HALFCROWN
	SOVEREIGN
United States	CENT
	DIME
	MILL
	EAGLE
	PENNY
	DOLLAR
	NICKEL
	QUARTER
Venezuela	REAL
	MEDIO
	FUERTE
	BOLIVAR
	CENTIMO
	MOROCOTA
Venice	BETSO
	BEZZO
Viet-Nam	DONG
	PIASTER
Yugoslavia	PARA
	DINAR

Slang Terms

BIT	12½¢	QUID	pound	TANNER	sixpence
BOB	shilling	DEUCE	$2	TENNER	$10, £10
FIN	$5	FIVER	$5, £5	CENTURY	$100, £100
RED	penny	GRAND	$1,000	SAWBUCK	$10
PLUM	£100,000	MONKEY	£500	TWOBITS	quarter

MUSIC

MUSICAL TERMS

ALT
BIS
BAR
DOT
DUR
JUG
KEY
PES
TER
TIE

CLEF
FLAT
FUSA
HOLD
MODE
MOLL
NOTE
RAGA
REST
ROOT
SLUR
TAKT
TONE

ANCUS
BRACE
BREVE
CHORD
CLOSE
DUPLE
EPODE
FUSEE
GAMUT
GRACE
GUIDA

KLANG
LONGA
MAJOR
MAXIM
METER
MINIM
MINOR
MOTIF
NEUMA
NEUME
PAUSE
PEDAL
PIENA
PIENO
PITCH
PRESA
SCALE
SCORE
SHAKE
SHARP
SOLFA
SPACE
STAFF
STAVE
TEMPO
TONIC
TRIAD
TRILL
TROPE
VIRGA

BURDEN
CLIVIS
DEGREE
DITONE
DORIAN

ENCORE
GROUND
HOCKET
IONIAN
LYDIAN
MELODY
MOTIVE
OCTAVE
PARODY
PHRASE
PLAGAL
PNEUMA
QUAVER
RELISH
RENVOI
RHYTHM
SERIAL
TACTUS
TIERCE
TIMBRE
TRIPLE
UNISON

AEOLIAN
BARLINE
CADENCE
CLUSTER
FERMATA
HARMONY
HEMIOLA
INCIPIT
KEYNOTE
MEASURE
MEDIANT
MELISMA
MORDENT

NATURAL
ORISCUS
PODATUS
PRESSUS
PUNCTUM
PUNCTUS
RIPIENO
ROULADE
SALICUS
SIXFOUR
SOLFEGE
SYNCOPE
TREMOLO
TRIPLET
TRITONE
VIBRATO

ARPEGGIO
BASICSET
CAMBIATA
CLIMACUS
CROTCHET
DIAPASON
DOMINANT
DYNAMICS
HALFNOTE
HARMONIC
INTERVAL
LIGATURE
MODALITY
NOTATION
OSTINATO
PHRYGIAN
QUILISMA
SEMIFUSA
SEMITONE

NOTES OF THE SCALE

* Guido's scale

DI
DO
FA
FI
LA
LE
LI
ME
MI
RA

RE
RI
SE
SI
TE
TI
UT*
ARE*
DOH
ELA*

SOH
SOL
RAY
BEMI*
BEFA*
MESE
NETE
ELAMI*
MESON
TRITE

CEFAUT*
FEFAUT*
ALAMIRE*
CESOLFA*
DELASOL*
DESOLRE*
GAMMAUT*
CESOLFAUT*
DELASOLRE*
GESOLREUT*

MUSICAL DIRECTIONS

VIF
PIU
RIT

ADUE

ARCO
FINE
LENT
LOCO
MENO

MOTO
ZART

ANIME
DOLCE

FORTE
GRAVE
INNIG
LARGO
LENTO

MESTO
MOLTO
MOSSO
OSSIA
PIANO
SECCO
SEGUE
TACET
TARDO

ADAGIO
ARIOSO
ATEMPO
BELEBT
COMODO
DACAPO
GIUSTO

MASSIG
MUNTER
PRESTO
RUBATO
SUBITO
TENUTO
VELOCE
VIVACE

AGITATO
ALLEGRO
ALSEGNO
AMABILE
AMOROSO
ANDANTE
ANIMATO
ATTACCA

CALANDO
CONBRIO
CONMOTO
DETACHE
DOLENTE
GIOCOSO
GIOIOSO
LANGSAM
LEBHAFT
MARCATO
MARTELE
MORENDO
PORTATO
STRETTO

ABATTUTA
COLLARCO

COLLEGNO
CONANIMA
CONFUOCO
DALSEGNO
GRAZIOSO
LEGGIERO
MAESTOSO
MARZIALE
MODERATO
PIUMOSSO
RITENUTO
SPIANATO
SPICCATO
STACCATO
SULTASTO
TRECORDE
UNACORDA

MUSICAL INSTRUMENTS

String

GUE
KIT
UKE

ARPA
ASOR
BINA
CRUT
GIGA
GORA
HARP
KOTO
LUTE
LYRE
ROTE
TURR
VINA
VIOL

AMATI
BANJO
CANUN
CELLO
CROOD
CROWD
CRWTH
GAMBA
GEIGE
GORAH

GOURA
GRAND
GUDOK
GUIGE
GUMBE
GUMBY
GUSLA
JAMON
KITAR
NABLA
NANGA
NEBEL
PIANO
REBAB
REBEC
ROCTA
RUANA
SAROD
SITAR
STRAD
TARAU
TIPLE
VIOLA
VOYAL
VOYOL

CATGUT
CHELYS
CITOLE

FIDDLE
GOUSLE
GUITAR
KISSAR
KITTAR
REBECK
RIBIBE
SABECA
SANCHO
SANTIR
SATTAR
SPINET
TYMPAN
URHEEN
VIELLE
VIOLIN
ZITHER

BANDORE
CEMBALO
CHROTTA
CITHARA
CITTERN
CLAVIAL
CLAVIER
CREMONA
GITTERN
KANTELE
MANDOLA

PANDORA
PANDORE
PIANINO
PIANOLA
SAMBUKE
SAMISEN
SARANGI
SARINDA
THEORBO
UKULELE
UPRIGHT
VIHUELA

ARCHLUTE
AUTOHARP
BARITONE
BELLHARP
CLAVICIN
DULCIMER
JEWSHARP
MANDOLIN
PIANETTE
POCHETTE
PSALTERY
VIRGINAL
ZIMBALON

BALALAIKA
MONOCHORD

Wind

OAT

ALTO
BEME
BEEN
FIFE
HORN
LURE
OBOE

PIPE
REED
SANG
TUBA
ZINK

AULOS
BUGLE
CHENG

CODON
CORNO
FLUTE
KAZOO
ORGAN
REGAL
SHAWM
SHENG
TRUMP

ZINKE

ATABAL
CLARIN
CORNET
LITUUS
POMMER
SHOFAR
SYRNIX

TRIGON
TROMBA

ALTHORN
ANKLONG
BAGPIPE
BASSOON
BUCCINA
CLARION

DIAULOS
HAUTBOY
HELICON
MUSETTE
OCARINA
PANPIPE
PIBCORN
PICCOLO
RACKETT

SACKBUT
SAXHORN
SERPENT
SHOPHAR
TRUMPET

BARITONE
CALLIOPE
CLARINET

CROMORNE
MELODEON
NEHILOTH
PANPIPES
POSTHORN
RECORDER
SOURDINE
TROMBONE

Percussion

ZEL

DRUM
GONG
TAAR
TOPH

BELLS
BONES
BONGO
CHIME
DAIRA
DRONE
GRAND
PIANO

PUNGI
SARON
TABOR
TOMBE
ZANZE

CYMBAL
KETTLE
MARACA
NAGARA
RAPPEL
TABRET
TAMTAM
TIMBAL
TOMTOM

TYMPAN

ANACARA
BOMBARD
CELESTA
CLAVIAL
CYMBALS
MANDORE
MARIMBA
PIANINO
PIANOLA
SISTRUM
TABORET
TIMBREL
TIMPANI

TIMPANO
TYMPANO
UPRIGHT

CARILLON
CASTANET
CLAPPERS
CROTALUM
LAPIDEON
MELODION
PIANETTE
TABOURIN
TRIANGLE
ZAMBOMBA
XYLOPHONE

MUSICIANS AND MUSICAL PARTS

* indicates Musical Parts

DUO

ALTO*
BAND
BARD
BASS*
SOLO
TRIO
WAIT

BASSO*
CANTO*
CHOIR
FIFER
LUTER
MEZZO*
NONET
OCTET
PIPER
TENOR*
VOICE

AULETE
BUGLER
CANTOR
CHORUS
CORNET
HARPER
LEADER
LUTIST
LYRIST
MUSICO
OBOIST
SEPTET
SEXTET
SINGER
VIOLER

CAROLER
CHANTER
CELLIST
CROONER
DRUMMER
DUBADUB

FIDDLER
FLUTIST
GAMBIST
GLEEMAN
HARPIST
HORNIST
KAPELLE
MAESTRO
PIANIST
QUARTET
QUINTET
SOPRANO*
SOLOIST
VIOLIST
WARBLER
YODELER

BARITONE*
BARYTONE*
COMPOSER
CYMBALER
DUETTIST

FLAUTIST
GRIDDLER
LUTANIST
MELODIST
MINSTREL
ORGANIST
SONGSTER
STRUMMER
THRUMMER
TWANGLER
VIRTUOSO
VOCALIST

CHORISTER
CHANTEUSE
CONDUCTOR
CONTRALTO*
CORNETIST
ORCHESTRA
TIMPANIST
TRUMPETER
VIOLINIST

MUSICAL FORMS AND DANCES

* Indicates Dances

AIR
HAY*
HOP*
JIG*

LAY
ODE

ARIA

CODA
DUET
FADO
GLEE

HAKA*
HORA*
HULA*
HYMN

JOTA*
JUBA*
KOLO
LEED
LIED
MASS
NOEL
OPUS
POLO*
RAGA
REEL*
SHAG*
SIVA
SONG
TEMA
TRIO
TUNE

BLUES*
BOREE*
CANON
CAROL
CATCH
CHANT
CONGA*
CUECA
DERRY
DIRGE
DITTY
DOINA
ELEGY
ETUDE
FLING*
FUGUE
GALOP*
GAVOT*
GIGUE*
MAMBA*
MARCH
MELOS
MOTET
OCTET
OPERA
PAEAN
PAVAN*

POLKA*
REVUE
RONDO*
ROUND
RUMBA*
SAMBA*
SUITE
STUCK
TANGO*
THEME
TROLL
TWIST*
VALSE*
VOLTA*
WALTZ*

ALTHEA*
ANTHEM
ARIOSO
AUBADE
BALLAD
BALLET*
BOLERO*
BRANLE*
CANCAN*
CEBELL*
CHAUNT
CHORAL
DREHER*
HORMOS*
MAXIXE*
MINUET
MORRIS*
NAUTCH*
POLSKA
REDOWA*
RHUMBA*
SEPTET
SEXTET
SHIMMY*
SONATA
TRESCA*
VERSET

AURESCA*

BOURREE*
BRAVURA
CADENZA
CANTATA
CANTICO*
CANZONE
CHACCON*
CHACONA*
CHANSON
CHORALE
CONCERT
COURANT*
CZARDAS*
DESCANT
FANFARE
FORLANA*
FOXTROT*
FURIANT*
FURLANA*
GAVOTTA*
GAVOTTE*
HALLING*
HOEDOWN*
LANCERS*
LAVOLTA
LULLABY
MAZURKA*
MORISCO*
MUSETTE
MUSICAL
ONESTEP*
PARTITA
PIBROCH
PRELUDE
QUARTET
QUINTET
RAGTIME*
RECITAL
REQUIEM
ROMAIKA*
ROMANCE
SARDANA*
SCHERZO
SESTOLE
SHUFFLE*

TOCCATA
TWOSTEP*
WASSAIL

ANGLAISE*
ANTIPHON
BERCEUSE
BUNNYHUG*
CACHUCHA*
CAKEWALK*
CANTICLE
CAVATINA
CHACONNE*
CONCERTO
CORONACH
COTILLON*
COURANTE*
DUETTINO
FANDANGO*
FANTASIA
FOLKSONG
GALLIARD*
HABANERA*
HORNPIPE*
HULAHULA*
LANCIERS*
MADRIGAL
MATELOTE*
NOCTURNE
NOTTURNO
OPERETTA
ORATORIO
OVERTURE
PARLANDO
PARTSONG
PASTORAL
RHAPSODY
RIGADOON*
SARABAND*
SERENADE
SERENATA
SESTOLET
SONATINA
SYMPHONY
TONEPOEM

OPERAS, OPERETTAS, MUSICALS

AIDA
LULU
MONA
SARI
ZAZA
FAUST
LAKME
MANON
NORMA
OHKAY
SADKO
SALLY
SUNNY
THAIS
TOSCA

ARMIDE
CARMEN
CONSUL
EILEEN
ERNANI
JEWESS
LOUISE
MARTHA
MIGNON
MIKADO
NATOMA
OBERON
OTELLO
RIENZI
SALOME

THECID
UNDINE
ALCESTE
ELEKTRA
FIDELIO
FIREFLY
JUBILEE
KATINKA
MARINKA
MAZEPPA
MAYTIME
NEWMOON
PROPHET
ROBERTA
VANESSA

VOLPONE
WALKURE
WOZZECK
ARABELLA
CAROUSEL
COPPELIA
IOLANTHE
LABOHEME
OKLAHOMA
PARSIFAL
PATIENCE
SHOWBOAT
SHOWGIRL
TURNADOT

MYTHOLOGY

GODS AND GODDESSES

Greek Gods

PAN	fields, herds
ZAN	= ZEUS
ARES	war
EROS	love
ZEUS	chief
CHAOS	first god
COMUS	joy, mirth
HADES	underworld
HYMEN	marriage
MOMUS	ridicule
AEOLUS	winds
APOLLO	youth, sun
BOREAS	north wind
CABIRI	earth gods
CRONUS	Titan: crops
HELIOS	sun
HERMES	herds, science, herald
HYPNOS	sleep
KRONOS	= CRONUS
NEREUS	sea
PONTUS	sea
POTHOS	= EROS
TITANS	ancestors of gods
URANUS	heaven
ALASTOR	avenger
ANTEROS	Eros' foe
OCEANUS	waters
PHAETON	= HELIOS
PHOEBUS	= APOLLO
PRIAPUS	life power
PROTEUS	sea
SILENUS	woods
DIONYSUS	wine, drama
ENYALIUS	war
HYPERION	sun
MORPHEUS	sleep
POSEIDON	sea
THANATOS	death
ASCLEPIUS	medicine
HEPHAESTUS	fire

Greek Goddesses

GE	earth
ARA	vengeance
ATE	discord, infatuation
EOS	dawn
NOX	= NYX
NYX	night
CLIO	Muse: history
DICE	= DIKE
DIKE	Hora: justice
ENYO	war
ERIS	discord
GAEA	= GE
GAIA	= GE
HEBE	youth
HERA	queen
HORA	one of Horae
IRIS	rainbow; messenger
KORE	= PERSEPHONE
NIKE	victory
RHEA	gods' mother
UPIS	childbirth
ATTIS	vegetation
BAUBO	sensuality
COTYS	vegetation
DIONE	earth
ERATO	Muse: poetry
HERSE	dew
HORAE	seasons
HYGEA	health
IRENE	Hora: peace
MANES	dead spirits
MOIRA	fate
MUSES	arts
PARCA	Fate: birth
TYCHE	fortune
AGLAIA	Grace: brilliance
ATHENA	peace, arts
BENDIS	= ARTEMIS
CLOTHO	Fate: spinner
CYBELE	nature, earth
EIRENE	= IRENE
GRACES	gods' helpers
HECATE	moon, magic
HESTIA	hearth
HYGIEA	health
MOIRAI	Fates
PALLAS	= ATHENA
PHOBOS	fear
SELENA	= SELENE
SELENE	moon
SEMELE	earth
THALIA	Grace: bloom
THEMIS	earth, law
URANIA	Muse: astronomy
ANTHEIA	flowers
ARTEMIS	nature, moon
ASTARTE	= ARTEMIS
ATROPOS	Fate: thread
CHLORIS	flowers
COTYTTO	= COTYS
DEMETER	agriculture
EUNOMIA	Hora: law
EUTERPE	Muse: music
NEMESIS	retribution

CALLIOPE	Muse: eloquence
LACHESIS	Fate: disposer of lots
POLYMNIA	Muse: sacred song
APHRODITE	love, beauty
MELPOMENE	Muse: tragedy
MNEMOSYNE	memory
AMPHITRITE	sea
EUPHROSYNE	Grace: joy
PERSEPHONE	queen of underworld

Roman Gods

DIS	= PLUTO
SOL	= HELIOS
AMOR	= EROS
JOVE	= ZEUS
MARS	= ARES
MORS	= THANATOS
CUPID	= EROS
JANUS	gates
LARES	house gods
LIBER	= BACCHUS
ORCUS	= HADES
PICUS	agriculture
PLUTO	= HADES
CAELUS	sky
FAUNUS	= PAN
SATURN	= CRONUS
SOMNUS	= HYPNOS
VULCAN	fire
BACCHUS	wine
JUPITER	= ZEUS
MERCURY	= HERMES
NEPTUNE	= POSEIDON
PENATES	household
MULCIBER	= VULCAN
QUIRINUS	war
SILVANUS	woods
VERTUMNUS	season

Roman Goddesses

OPS	= RHEA
PAX	= IRENE
DIAN	= DIANA
JUNO	= HERA
LUNA	moon
MAIA	Vulcan's mate
NONA	= CLOTHO
SPES	hope
CERES	= DEMETER
DIANA	= ARTEMIS
EPONA	horses
FAUNA	fertility
FIDES	faith
FLORA	flowers
MORTA	= ATROPOS
PALES	herds
SALUS	= HYGEIA
TERRA	earth
VENUS	= APHRODITE
VESTA	= HESTIA
AESTAS	summer
ANNONA	crops
AURORA	= EOS
DECUMA	= LACHESIS
LUCINA	childbirth
MATUTA	dawn, birth
PARCAE	Fates
POMONA	fruit
TELLUS	earth
TRIVIA	= DIANA
VACUNA	hunting
BELLONA	war
FERONIA	fountain
FORTUNA	fortune
MINERVA	= ATHENA
JUVENTAS	= HEBE
LIBITINA	burials
PROSERPINA	queen of underworld

Egyptian Gods

NU	chaos
RA	sun, first god (black bull)
RE	= RA
SU	= SHU
BES	evil averter, pleasure
GEB	= KEB
KEB	earth
MIN	procreation
SEB	= KEB
SET	war, evil
SHU	atmosphere
TEM	sun, creator
TUM	= TEM
AMEN	gods' father
ATEN	solar disk
ATMU	= TEM
ATUM	= TEM
HAPI	Nile
KHEM	= MIN
MENT	= MENTU
PTAH	world shaper
SETH	= SET
SOKH	= SEBEK
AMMON	= AMEN
APUAT	old chief god
HORUS	day (hawk head)
KHNUM	builder (ram head)
MENTU	sun, war (falcon head)
SEBEK	evil (crocodile head)
SEKER	= SOKARI
THOTH	wisdom, magic (ibis head)
ANUBIS	judge of dead (jackal head)

DHOUTI	= THOTH
KHENSU	= KHONSU
KHNEMU	=KHNUM
KHONSU	Ra triad member
MNEVIS	= RA
OSIRIS	underworld (judge of dead)
SOKARI	night, sun (falcon head)
HERSHEF	= OSIRIS
IMHOTEP	learning
KHEPERA	morning sun, creator (beetle)
KHEPERI	= KHEPERA
SERAPIS	= OSIRIS
SOKARIS	= SOKARI
HARMACHIS	rising sun

Egyptian Goddesses

MA	= MAAT
MUT	Ra triad member
NUT	heavens
ANTA	war
APET	maternity (hippo body)
BAST	"Lady of Life" (lion head)
BUTO	serpent
ISIS	fertility
MAAT	truth, law
SATI	queen of gods
AMENT	gods' mother
ATHOR	= HATHOR
PACHT	= SEKHET
HATHOR	love, joy (cow head)
SEKHET	sun heat (cat head)
SESHAT	learning (lion head)
SPHINX	wisdom
NEPHTHYS	dead ritual

Assyrian, Babylonian, Persian, Phoenician Gods

EA	water, arts: triad member
ZU	storm
ANU	heavens: triad member
BEL	earth: triad member
EAR	= EA
HEA	= EA
SIN	moon, wisdom
UTU	sun
ADAD	wind
ADDA	= ADAD
ADDU	= ADAD
APSU	chaos
ASUR	= ASHUR
BAAL	fertility
ENKI	= EA
ENZU	= SIN
IRRA	war
NABU	wisdom
NEBO	= NABU
UTUG	= UTU
AHURA	= ORMAZD
ASHUR	chief, power
DAGAN	earth
DAGON	fish, fields
ELLIL	= BEL
ENLIL	= BEL
GIRRU	fire
MAZDA	= ORMAZD
NUSKU	fire, light
SAMAS	= SHAMASH
SIRIS	liquor
AMESHA	= SPENTA, Ormazd aid
ANSHAR	god's' father
ARIMAN	evil
BABBAR	sun
ESHMUN	healing
KISHAR	lower world
MARDUK	chief, sun
MOLOCH	sacrifice
NANNAR	= SIN
NERGAL	sun; pest
OANNES	wisdom
ORMAZD	creator, chief
RAMMAN	= ADAD
RIMMON	= ADAD
TAMMUZ	vegetation
AHRIMAN	= ARIMAN
MITHRAS	light, truth
MINURTA	sun
SHAMASH	sun, order
NINGIRSU	war, fields

Assyrian, Babylonian, Persian, Phoenician Goddesses

ERUA	mother goddess
GULA	healing
NAMA	= ARURU
NINA	watery deep
ANATH	war
ARURU	mother: earth
ISTAR	= ISHTAR
NANAI	earth
NINNI	= ISHTAR
NINTU	= ARURU
ALLATU	underworld
BELILI	lower world
INNINA	= ISHTAR
ISHTAR	earth, war, love
NINGAL	sun
ANAHITA	earth
ASTARTE	love, moon
DAMKINA	earth
ERESHKIGAL	= ALLATU

Celtic, Irish, British, Welsh, Gaulish Gods

LER	sea	**LLUDD**	= **NUDD**
LUG	light, sun	**MIDER**	underworld
BELI	= **BELENUS**	**NUADA**	= **NUDD**
BRAN	the blessed	**NUADU**	= **NUDD**
BRES	god king	**PWYLL**	dead
ESUS	vegetation	**AENGUS**	a Angus
GWYN	underworld	**ELATHA**	a Fomorian
LLEU	= **LLEW**	**HAFGAN**	chief
LLEW	sun	**NODENS**	= **NODONS**
LLYR	sea	**NODONS**	sun
LUGH	= **LUG**	**OENGUS**	a Angus
NUDD	sun	**OGMIUS**	eloquence
ANGUS	love, beauty	**BELENUS**	sun
ARAWN	Annwn's lord	**CAMULUS**	war
BALOR	Fomorian giant	**GWYDION**	sky, arts, magic
DAGDA	chief	**PRYDERI**	underworld
DOMNU	a Fomorian	**DIANCECHT**	medicine
DYLAN	waves		

Celtic, Irish, British, Welsh, Gaulish Goddesses

ANA	mother goddess	**BRIGIT**	Mary of the Gael; fire
DON	= **DANA**	**BRANWEN**	sea
BADB	= **BODB**	**MORRIGU**	war
BODB	battle	**BELISAMA**	beauty
DANA	fertility; ancestress	**ARIANRHOD**	rivers
EPONA	horses, mules	**BRIGANTIA**	mother goddess

Norse-Teutonic Gods

AS	Aesir (singular)	**AESIR**	chief gods
ER	= **TIU**	**ALCIS**	twin gods
TY	= **TIU**	**BALDR**	= **BALDUR**
VE	world creator, Odin's brother	**BRAGE**	= **BRAGI**
EAR	= **TIU**	**BRAGI**	poetry
LOK	= **LOKI**	**DONAR**	thunder
TIU	sky, war	**HODER**	= **HOTH**
TIW	= **TIU**	**HOTHR**	= **HOTH**
TYR	= **TIU**	**LODUR**	= **LOTHUR**
ULL	bow skill, beauty	**NJORD**	fertility
ZIO	= **TIU**	**VANIR**	early race of gods: crops, fertility
ASES	= **AESIR**		
BURI	father of gods	**WODAN**	= **ODIN**
FREY	fertility	**WODEN**	= **ODIN**
HLER	= **AEGIR**	**WOTAN**	= **ODIN**
HOTH	night; blind Balder slayer	**BALDER**	= **BALDUR**
LOKE	= **LOKI**	**BALDUR**	peace
LOKI	discord	**HOENIR**	creator of first human
ODIN	chief; war, wisdom; slays Ymir	**LOTHUR**	weather, crops
THOR	thunder, serpent slayer	**NJORTH**	= **NJORD**
VALI	Ragnarok survivor	**VITHAR**	Fenrir slayer
VANS	= **VANIR**	**FORSETI**	justice
VILI	world creator; Odin's brother	**VIDHARR**	= **VITHAR**
AEGIR	sea	**HEIMDALL**	Asgard guardian

Norse-Teutonic Goddesses

EIR	healing	**URD**	= **NORN**
HEL	dead; underworld	**ERDA**	earth
RAN	sea	**FREA**	= **FRIGG**
SIF	home	**FRIA**	= **FRIGG**

HELA = HEL
NORN fate; destiny
SAGA sorcery
URTH = NORN
FREYA beauty, love
FRIGG sky marriage; Friday source
SKULD = NORN
GEFJON = FRIGG
HERTHA = NERTHUS
ASYNJUR Aesirs' aid
NERTHUS peace
VERTHANDI = NORN

Hindu (Vedic) Gods

KA unknown god
AGNI fire
AKAL immortal one
CIVA = SIVA
DEVA = DEWA
DEWA angel
KALI "the black one"
KAMA love (parrot)
RAMA Vishnu avatar
SIVA supreme; destroyer: arts; miracles
SOMA ritual liquor
VASU = VISHNU
VAYU wind
YAMA judge of dead
BHAGA love, wealth
DYAUS sky, dawn, fire
GAURI "the brilliant"
INDRA thunder
KALKI Vishnu avatar
MARUT storm
MITRA sun
RUDRA storm
SHIVA = SIVA
SURYA sun
ASVINS dawn: twins
BRAHMA creator
GANESA wisdom
KALIKA = KALI
KUBERA wealth
PUSHAN roads, cattle
SKANDA war
VARUNA cosmic order
VISHNU supreme; preserver
GANESHA = GANESA
HANUMAN monkey king
PARVATI "mountaineer"
SAVITAR sun
BALARAMA = RAMA
PARJANYA rain
TRIMURTI trinity
KARTIKEYA = SKANDA

Hindu (Vedic) Goddesses

SRI beauty
UMA splendor
VAC speech
DEVI mother goddess
SHRI = SRI
USAS = USHAS
VACH = VAC
DURGA "the inaccessible" (on tiger)
SHREE = SRI
USHAS dawn
BRAHMI speech
CHANDI "the fierce"
SHAKTI mother goddess
BHAVANI = DEVI
CHANDRA moon
LAKSHMI = SRI
ANNAPURNA plenty
SARASVATI = SHAKTI

Miscellaneous Gods

ATAU god: Polynesian
CHAC -MOL: rain
JOSS home: Chinese
KANE chief: Hawaiian
MAUI chief culture hero: Polynesian
TANE forests: Hawaiian
TIKI man creator: Polynesian
ALLAH supreme being
AMIDA Jodo deity: Japanese
AMITA = AMIDA
EBISU happiness: Japanese
HOTEI happiness: Japanese
TINIA = ZEUS: Etruscan
WENTI literature: Chinese
BENTEN happiness: Japanese
JUMULA heavens: Finnish
TAAROA chief: Polynesian
TLALOC thunder: Aztec
DAIKOKU happiness: Japanese
HURAKAN thunder: Quiche
JUROJIN happiness: Japanese
KANALOA leading: Hawaiian
KWANNON mercy: Chinese
MANITOU great spirit
MICTLAN underworld: Aztec
BISHAMON happiness: Japanese
CENTEOTL agriculture: Aztec
KULULKAN creator: Mayan
MANABUSH creator: Algonquian (Great Hare)
TANGAROA chief: Polynesian
SVANTOVIT chief: Slavic

Miscellaneous Goddesses

MAMA	fertility: Peruvian
PELE	fire, volcano: Hawaiian
TARI	earth: Khond
ALLAT	mother goddess
SEDNA	culture: Eskimo
TANIT	moon: Carthage
TANITH	= TANIT
PERCHTA	earth, spinning: German

GODS AND GODDESSES

Listed by Specialties

* indicates goddesses

Chief Gods, Gods' Ancestors, Creators, Mother Goddesses

AS
EA
RA
RE
VE
ANA*
ANU
BEL
HEA
OPS*
ASES
ATMU
ATUM
BRES
BURI
CIVA
DEVI*
ENKI
ERUA*
HERA*
HLER
JOVE
JUNO*
KANE
MAUI
ODIN
PTAH
RAMA
RHEA*
SATI*
SIVA
VASU
VILI
ZEUS
AHURA
ALLAH
ALLAT*
AMENT*
APUAT
ARURU*
ASHUR
CHAOS
DAGDA
ELLIL
ENLIL
ISTAR*
MAZDA
NINNI*
NINTU*
VANIR
WODAN
WODEN
WOTAN
BRAHMA
HAFGAN
INNINA*
ISHTAR*
MARDUK
ORMAZD
SATURN
SHAKTI*
VISHNU
TAAROA
BHAVANI*
JUPITER
KANALOA
KUKULKAN
MANABUSH
TANGAROA

Sun, Light, Fire, Sky

ER
RA
RE
TY
ANU
EOS*
NUT*
SHU
SOL
TEM
TIU
TIW
TUM
TYR
UTU
AGNI
AMEN
AMON
ATEN
BELI
LLEU
LLEW
NUDD
PELE*
UTUG
DYAUS
FRIGG*
GIRRU
LLUDD
MITRA
NUADA
NUADU
NUSKU
SAMAS
SURYA
USHAS*
VESTA*
APOLLO
AURORA*
BABBAR
CAELUS
GEFJON*
HELIOS
HESTIA*
JUMALA
MARDUK
MATUTA*
NERGAL
NINGAL*
NODENS
SEKHET*
URANUS
VULCAN
BELENUS
KHEPERA
MITHRAS
NINURTA
PHAETON
PHOEBUS
SAVITAR
SHAMASH
SOKARIS
HYPERION
HARMACHIS

Earth, Fertility, Woods, Hunting, Fields, Nature

GE*
BEL
DON*
GEB
KEB
MIN
OPS*
PAN
SEB
BAAL
DANA*
DANU*

ERDA*
ESUS
FREY
GAEA*
GAIA*
ISIS*
MAMA*
NAMA*
TANE
TARI*
VANS
ATTIS*
ARURU*
CERES*
COTYS*
DAGON
DIANA*
DIONE*
FAUNA*
FLORA*
ISTAR*
NINTU*
NJORD
PALES*
PICUS
TERRA*
VANIR
ANNONA*
BENDIS*
CABIRI
CRONUS
CYBELE*
ISHTAR*
LOTHUR
POMONA*
PUSHAN
SATURN
SEMELE*
TELLUS*
VACUNA*
ANTHEIA*
ARTEMIS*
CHLORIS*
DEMETER*
PERCHTA*
SILENUS
SILVANUS
CENTEOTL

Underworld, Death, Sleep, Night, Magic, Moon

DIS
HEL*
NOX*
NYX*
SIN
ENZU
GWYN
HELA*
HOTH
KALI*
KORE*
LUNA*
MORS
SAGA*
YAMA
DIANA*
HADES
HODER
HOTHR
MANES
MIDER
ORCUS
PLUTO
PWYLL
SEKER
TANIT*
THOTH
ALLATU*
ANUBIS
BELILI*
BENDIS*
HECATE*
HYPNOS
KALIKA*
KISHAR
NANNAR
OSIRIS
SELENA*
SELENE*
SOKARI
SOMNUS
TANITH*
ARTEMIS*
ASTARTE*
CHANDRA
GWYDION
HERSHEF
MICTLAN
PRYDERI
SERAPIS
SOKARIS
LIBITINA*
MORPHEUS
NEPHTHYS*
THANATOS

Faith, Hope, Fate, Home, Happiness

URD*
JOSS
NONA*
NORN*
SPES*
URTH*
WYRD*
COMUS
EBISU
FIDES*
HOTEI
LARES
MOIRA*
MORTA*
TYCHE*
VESTA*
CLOTHO*
HATHOR*
HESTIA*
KUBERA
MOIRAI*
PARCAE*
ATROPOS*
DAIKOKU
FORTUNA*
JUROJIN
PENATES
BISHAMON
LACHESIS*
ANNAPURNA*

Medicine, Health, Arts, Science, Wisdom

EA
EIR*
HEA
SIN
VAC*
BELI
CIVA
ENKI
GULA*
NABU
NEBO
ODIN
SIVA
VACH*
BRAGE
BRAGI
HYGEA*
MUSES*
SALUS*
SEDNA*
SHIVA
THOTH
WENTI
ATHENA*
BRAHMI*
DHOUTI
ESHMUN
HERMES
HYGIEA*
GANESA
NANNAR
OGMIUS
SESHAT*
SPHINX*
BELENUS
GANESHA
IMHOTEP
MERCURY
MINERVA*
DIONYSUS
ASCLEPIUS
DIANCECHT

War, Discord, Vengeance, Evil

ER
TY
ARA*
ATE*
EAR
TIU
TIW
TYR
ZIO
ANTA*
ARES
BADB*
BODB*
ENYO*
ERIS*
FURY*
IRRA
LOKE
LOKI
MARS

MENT	MENTU	ISHTAR*	CAMULUS
ODIN	SEBEK	NERGAL	MORRIGU*
SETH	WODAN	PHOBOS	NEMESIS*
ANATH*	WODEN	SKANDA	ENYALIUS
ANATU*	WOTAN	ALASTOR	NINGIRSU
ISTAR*	ARIMAN	BELLONA*	QUIRINUS

Sea, Season, Wind, Weather

EA	LLYR	MARUT	CHACMOL
ZU	NINA*	RUDRA	HURAKAN
HEA	THOR	AEOLUS	NEPTUNE
LER	VAYU	AESTAS*	OCEANUS
RAN*	AEGIR	BOREAS	PROTEUS
ADAD	DONAR	LOTHUR	BELISAMA*
ADDA	DYLAN	NEREUS	PARJANYA
ADDU	EURUS	PONTUS	POSEIDON
ENKI	HERSE*	RAMMAN	VERTUMNUS
HAPI	HORAE*	TLALOC	AMPHITRITE
IRIS*	INDRA	BRANWEN*	

Beauty, Love, Youth, Joy, Marriage, Birth

BES	SHRI*	HYMEN	LUCINA*
SRI*	ULLR	PARCA*	MATUTA*
ULL	UPIS*	SHREE*	POTHOS
UMA*	ANGUS	VENUS*	THALIA*
AMOR	BHAGA	AENGUS	ASTARTE*
APET*	COMUS	AGLAIA*	LAKSHMI*
BAST*	CUPID	GEFJON*	JUVENTAS*
EROS	FREYA*	GRACES*	APHRODITE*
HEBE*	FRIGG*	HATHOR*	ARIANRHOD
KAMA			

Justice, Peace, Law, Truth

PAX*	BALDR	BALDUR	FORSETI
DICE*	IRENE*	EIRENE*	MITHRAS
DIKE*	ATHENA*	HERTHA*	NERTHUS*
MAAT*	BALDER	THEMIS*	

FAMILY RELATIONS

Father	Offspring
EA	Nina
RA	Shu, Maat
ANU	Nanai
BEL	Ninurta
GEB	Osiris, Set, Nephthys, Isis
SIF	Ull
SIN	Ishtar
AMEN	Khonsu
AMON	Bast
APSU	Mummu
ARES	Cycnus, Phobos, Alcippe
BANA	Usha
FINN	Ossian
ILUS	Laomedon
LLYR	Bran, Branwen, Manawyddan
LOKI	Hel, Fenris: wolf; Midgard: serpent

Father	Offspring
MARS	Romulus, Remus
ODIN	Balder, Vali: Vale, Vithar
SIVA	Skanda, Ganesha
VAYU	Hanuman
WADE	Wayland
ZEUS	Ate, Ares, Eris,Hebe, Kore, Helen, Irene, Muses, Aeacus, Apollo, Athena, Graces, Hermes, Amphion, Artemis, Epaphus, Dionysus, Hercules, Sarpedon, Aphrodite, Persephone, Hephaestus
AESON	Jason
ATLAS	Hyades, Pleiades
BELUS	Ninus, Danaus
CHAOS	Nyx
COEUS	Leto

Father	Offspring
CREON	Jocasta, Haemon
CREUS	Pallas
DAGDA	Aengus, Brigit
HOGNI	Hild
INDRA	Arjuna
IPHIS	Evadne
LAIUS	Oedipus
LLUDD	Gwynn
MINOS	Ariadne, Phaedra
PRIAM	Paris, Hector, Helenus, Troilus, Polydorus, Polyxena, Deiphobus, Cassandra
ACHEUS	Telamon
AEACUS	Telamon, Peleus
AEETES	Medea
AEGEUS	Theseus
AGENOR	Cadmus, Europa
APOLLO	Asclepius, Ion, Hymen
ATREUS	Menelaus, Agamemnon
BALDER	Forseti
BOREAS	Calais
BRAHMA	Daksha
CADMUS	Ino, Semele
CRONUS	Zeus, Hades, Hestia, Poseidon, Hera, Demeter
DEVAKI	Krishna
ELATHA	Bres
EREBUS	Charon
HELIOS	Circe
HELLEN	Aeolus, Dorus
HERMES	Pan, Silenus
IASION	Plutus
NEREUS	Amphitrite, Nereids
NJORTH	Frey
OILEUS	Ajax
OSIRIS	Horus, Anubis
PALLAS	Nike
PELEUS	Achilles
PELIAS	Alcestis, Acastus
PELOPS	Atreus
PENEUS	Daphne
RUSTUM	Sohrab
SATURN	= CRONUS
SIGURD	Swanhild
URANUS	Rhea, Themis, Cronus
CECROPS	Herse
CEPHEUS	Andromeda
DELLING	Dag
EURYTUS	Iole
GWYDION	Dylan
HIMAVAT	Devi, Parvati, Shakti
IAPETUS	Atlas, Prometheus
ICARIUS	Penelope, Erigone
LAERTES	Ulysses
OCEANUS	Styx, Doris
OEDIPUS	Ismene
PANDION	Procne
PHORCYS	Gorgons, Graeae
SIGMUND	Sigurd
TELAMON	Ajax
THAUMUS	Harpies

Father	Offspring
THESEUS	Hippolytus
ULYSSES	Telemachus
ANCHISES	Aeneas
DAEDALUS	Icarus
HYPERION	Eos, Helios
LAOMEDON	Priam
POSEIDON	Otus, Zetes, Pelias, Triton, Antaeus, Aloeus
SISYPHUS	Glaucus
TANTALUS	Niobe, Pelops
TITHONUS	Laomedon, Memnon
TYNDAEUS	Diomed
AGAMEMNON	Electra, Orestes
DEUCALION	Hellen
SCAMANDAR	Teucer

Mother	Offspring
GE	Uranus, Titans
IO	Epaphus
EOS	Memnon
INO	Melicertes, Palaemon
NUT	Osiris, Set, Nephthys, Isis
NYX	Thanatos
OPS	= RHEA
CETO	Gorgons, Graeae
ENYO	Ares
GAEA	Erechtheus, Cronus, Pontus, Phoebe, Anteus, Themis
HERA	Ares, Hebe, Eris, Hephaestus
ISIS	Horus
LEDA	Helen, Castor, Pollux
LETO	Artemis, Apollo
MAIA	Hermes
NOTT	Dag
RHEA	Zeus, Hades, Hera, Poseidon, Hestia, Demeter
STYX	Nike
ADITI	Aditya
AEGLE	Graces
CERES	= DEMETER
DANAE	Perseus
DIONE	Aphrodite
DORIS	Nereids
FRIGG	Balder
METIS	Zeus
NIOBE	Argus
SIGYN	Hel
THEIA	Eos
VENUS	Cupid
AEGINA	Aeacus
AETHRA	Hyades
CANACE	Aloeus
CREUSA	Ion
CYBELE	Zeus
EUROPA	Minos, Sarpedon
HECUBA	Paris, Helenus, Hector, Troilus, Polydorus, Polyxena, Deiphobus, Cassandra
LATONA	= LETO
PHOEBE	Leto

Mother	Offspring
SEMELE	Dionysus
TETHYS	Styx
THEMIS	Astraea, Irene, Prometheus
THETIS	Achilles
URANIA	Hymen
ALCMENE	Hercules
ANTIOPE	Amphion
CLYMENE	Atlas
CORONIS	Asclepius
DEMETER	Persephone, Plotos
ELECTRA	Dardanus, Harpies
EURYBIA	Pallas
JOCASTA	Oedipus
PARVATI	Ganesha
PLEIONE	Pleiades
CALLIOPE	Orpheus
CALLISTO	Arcas
MNEMOSYNE	Muses
AMPHITRITE	Triton
RHEASYLVIA	Remus, Romulus
CLYTEMNESTRA	Electra, Orestes

Husband (Lover)	Wife (Lover)
EA	Damkina
ANA	Anatum
BEL	Belit
GEB	Nut
LER	Aoife
SET	Nephthys
SHU	Tefnut
AMEN	Mut
APSU	Tiamat
ATLI	Gudrun
BAAL	Baalat(h)
BRES	Brigit
CEYX	Halcyone
EROS	Psyche
FREY	Gerth (Gerd)
HLER	Ran
IDAS	Marpessa
LOKI	Sigyn
NUDD	Morrigu
ODIN	Frigg = Frea = Fria; Rind(r)
PTAH	Sekhet
RAMA	Sita
SIVA	Devi, Shakti, Parvati
THOR	Sif
ZEUS	see page 208
AEGIR	Ran
ATLAS	Pleione, Aethra
ATTIS	Cybele
BRAGE	Ithun(n) = Idun
DAGDA	Boann
CONOR	Deirdre, Medb
HADES	Kore = Cora
JASON	Creusa, Medea
KINGU	Tiamat
LAIUS	Jocasta
LYCUS	Dirce

Husband (Lover)	Wife (Lover)
MINOS	Pasiphae
NOISE	Deirdre
NINUS	Semiramis
ORION	Eos
PARIS	Oenone, Helen
PHAON	Sappho
PRIAM	Hecuba
PWYLL	Rhiannon
ADONIS	Aphrodite
AENEAS	Creusa, Dido, Lavinia
AILILL	Medb
APOLLO	Creusa, Urania, Cassandra
ATREUS	Aerope
BALDER	Nanna
BRAHMA	Brahmi, Sarasvati
CADMUS	Harmonia
CRONUS	Rhea
GUNNAR	Brunhild
HAEMON	Antigone
HECTOR	Andromache
MARDUK	Sarpanitu, Zirbanit, Erua
NEREUS	Doris
NERGAL	Allatu
NJORTH	Thjazi
OENEUS	Althaea
OSIRIS	Isis
PALLAS	Styx
PELOPS	Hippodamia
PONTUS	Gaea
RAVANA	Sita
SIGURD	Gudrun
TAMMUZ	Ishtar
TEREUS	Procne
URANUS	Gaea
VARUNA	Aditi
VISHNU	Lakshmi
VULCAN	Maia
ADMETUS	Alcestis
AMPHION	Niobe
ATHAMAS	Ino
ATHAMUS	Nephele
GUNTHER	Brunhild
GWYDION	Arianrhod
IAPETUS	Clymene
LEANDER	Hero
NINURTA	Gula
ORPHEUS	Eurydice
PERSEUS	Andromeda
PROCRIS	Cephalus
SHAMASH	Ai = Aya
THESEUS	Antiope, Ariadne, Phaedra
TROILUS	Cressida
ULYSSES	Penelope
ASTRAEUS	Eos
CEPANEUS	Evadne
CEPHALUS	Eos
DIARMEIT	Brainne
ENDYMION	Selene
HERCULES	Hebe, Auge, Deianira
HYPERION	Theia
MENELAUS	Helen

Husband (Lover)	Wife (Lover)
MELEAGER	Atalanta
MILANION	Atalanta
PHILEMON	Baucis
POSEIDON	Cancace, Amphitrite, Gaea
TITHONUS	Eos
DEIPHOBUS	Helen
DEUCALION	Pyrrha

Husband (Lover)	Wife (Lover)
NARCISSUS	Echo
SIEGFRIED	Kriemhild
TYNDAREUS	Leda
AMPHITRYON	Alcmene
EPIMETHEUS	Pandora
HEPHAESTUS	Charis
HIPPOMENES	Atalanta

GREEK AND ROMAN TERMS AND NAMES

IO	became heifer
KER	doom spirit
AJAX	hero-suicide
ARGO	Jason ship
DIDO	Carthage queen
FAUN	wood deity
IDAS	Castor slayer
ILUS	Troy founder
NUMA	-POMPILIUS, king
OTUS	giant
AEAEA	Circe's isle
AEGIS	Zeus' shield
ALTIS	sacred grove
ARGOS	sacred city
ARGUS	Io guard: monster
ARION	poet saved by fish; horse
ATLAS	heaven supporter
AULIS	Iphigenia saved
CIRCE	sorceress
DRYAD	wood nymph
GYGES	magic ring king
HARPY	bird-woman
HELEN	Troy war cause
HELLE	fell into sea
HYADS	nymphs
HYDRA	9-head monster
ILIUM	Troy
IXION	wheel-bound king
JASON	gets Golden Fleece
LAMIA	vampire
LINUS	poet: lacerated
MEDEA	sorceress; Jason aide
MIDAS	ass-eared king
MINOS	king-judge
MORMO	bugbear
NAIAD	sea nymph
NAPEA	wood nymph
NIOBE	became stone
OREAD	mountain nymph
ORION	hunter
PARIS	apple awarder; slew Achilles
PHAON	Lesbos boatman
PRIAM	Troy king
REMUS	Romulus' brother
SATYR	man-horse
SINON	deceived Troy
SIREN	bird-woman lure
SYBIL	seeress
AENEAS	Troy war hero

ANANKE	ultimate fate
ANCILE	sacred shield
AUGEAS	Elis king (stables)
BAUCIS	Zeus' host
CHARON	Styx boatman
CREUSA	slain by Medea
DANAUS	Lynceus foe
DAPHNE	became tree
DELPHI	oracle site
DODONA	oracle seat
EGERIA	well nymph
EREBUS	dark site
EUROPA	abducted by bull
GEMINI	Castor, Pollux
GORGON	monster
IOLAUS	Hercules' pal
MAENAD	Nymph; Dionysus attendant
MEDUSA	slain by Perseus
NAPAEA	wood nymph
NEREID	sea nymph
NESSUS	slain Centaur
PELIAS	Tolcus king
SPHINX	winged-lion woman slain by Oedipus
TRITON	sea demigod
TURNUS	Aeneas' rival
TYPHON	monster
ACTAEON	became stag
AGANICE	witch
ALOADAE	giants
ARACHNE	became spider
AVERNUS	inferno
BRISEIS	Achilles' captive
CALCHAS	Greek seer
CALYPSO	nymph (Ulysses)
CECROPS	Athens founder
CENTAUR	man-horse
CHIMERA	monster slain by Bellerophon
CYCLOPS	one-eyed giant
CYTHERA	Aphrodite isle
ELEUSIS	mysteries site
ERINYES	avenging spirits
GALATEA	Pygmalion statue
GLAUCUS	Argo helmsman
HELICON	sacred mountain
INACHUS	Argos king
LAOCOON	priest warner
LEMURES	night spirits

LYNCEUS slew Danaus
MARSYAS lost Apollo duel
OEDIPUS Thebes king; slew father
OLYMPUS sacred mountain
ORESTES slew mother
PANDORA box opener
PEGASUS winged horse
ROMULUS slew Remus
THESEUS slew Minotaur
ULYSSES Ithaca king
ACHILLES Hector slayer; Patroclus pal
AGANIPPE Muses' fountain
AMBROSIA celestial food
ANTIGONE buried alive
ATALANTA huntress; picks golden apples
BRIAREUS 100-hand monster
CALLISTO huntress; became boar
CERBERUS Hades watchdog
DAEDALUS maze-wing maker
GANYMEDE gods' cupbearer
HELIADES became trees
HERACLES hero, strong
HERCULES hero, man
MELAMPUS seer
MINOTAUR man-beast slain by Theseus
MYRMIDON Achilles' ally
NAUSICAA Ulysses' friend
PLEIADES became stars
SISYPHUS stone roller
TANTALUS starving king
TIRESIAS blind seer
TITHONUS became butterfly
TIPHOEUS 100-head monster

HINDU AND VEDIC TERMS AND NAMES

AHI sky serpent
ATMA = ATMAN
BANA 100-arm giant
KALI evil genius; Agni's tongue
KETU Rahu's tail
MANU wise ancestor
MERU holy mountain
NAGA semihuman serpent
RAHU dragon: swallows sun
SURA angel
YUGA age of world
ASURA evil spirit
ATMAN universal ego
HANSA Asvin's swan, goose
GANGA holy river
KALPA aeon
NANDI Siva's bull
PITRI semi-divine ancestor
PRANA life breath
RISHI holy sage
SESHA = SHESHA
ARJUNA gets Krishna revelation
AMRITA life elixir
ANANTA infinity
AVATAR incarnation
BHRUGI gods' messenger
DAITYA evil spirit
DASYUS evil-demons
GARUDA man-bird Vishnu bearer
NARAKA hell
PATALA underworld series
RIBHUS artisans of the gods
SHESHA serpent king
SVARGA Indra's paradise
VASUKI Naga king
VRITRA dragon slain by Indra
YADAVA Krishna's race
APSARAS nymph, dancer
NIRVANA reunion with Brahma
PURUSHA male principle
SRADDHA ancestor rite
AIRAVATA Indra's elephant
LOKAPALA world guardian
MAHADEVA Siva title
NATARAJA Siva: cosmic dancer
RAKSHASA goblins
RAMAYANA sanskrit epic
TVASHTAR divine artificer

NORSE TERMS AND NAMES

ASK first man
DIS female spirit
DAG day; see Natt
LIF human survivor
NIX water sprite
ASKR = ASK
ATLI slain king
EGIL "Tell story" hero; Voland brother
GARM Hel's dog; slays Tyr
GERI Odin's wolf
GRAM Sigurd sword
NATT = NOTT: night
SURT fire demon: Frey's slayer
WADE = WATE: storm giant
YMIR "rime cold giant"
EGILL = EGIL
EMBLA first woman
ETZEL = ATLI
FREKI Odin's wolf
GIMLE home of blessed
GJOLL Hel's icy river
HAGEN Sigurd slayer; slain by Kriemhild
HOGNI Hethin foe
HYMIR sea giant
ITHUN keeps golden apples of youth
JOTUN giant
MIMIR well guarding giant
REGIN Sigurd's evil tutor

- SURTR = SURT
- TROLL giant; dwarf
- VOLVA seeress
- ALVISS dwarf
- ASGARD god's abode
- ITHUNN = ITHUN
- JOTUNN = JOTUN
- REGINN = REGIN
- SIGURD Volsunga saga hero
- VOLUND inventive smith
- ANDVARI ring guardian
- ALFHEIM Frey's home
- BIFROST rainbow bridge
- BALMUNG Sigurd's sword
- MIDGARD man's abode: earth
- NAGLFAR giant's ship
- NIFLHEL Hel's region
- VALHALL Odin's hall of heroes
- VINGOLF Asgard hall
- WAYLAND = VOLUND
- ALBERICH Nibelung dwarf
- BRUNHILD strong queen
- DRAUPNIR Odin's ring
- HRIMFAXI Nott's horse
- IRMINSUL sacred trees
- MJOLLNIR Thor's hammer
- NIBELUNG dwarf guarding treasure
- NIFLHEIM Hel's region
- RAGNAROK "twilight of gods"; Aesir giants fight
- SLEIPNER Odin's steed
- TARNHELM cap making invisible
- VALKYRIE Odin's messenger
- YGGDRASIL world tree

EGYPTIAN TERMS AND NAMES

- AB will, heart
- BA soul (bird-man)
- KA body
- RA sun-god
- AKH spirit of man
- GEB earth-god
- NUN chaos
- NUT sky-goddess
- SET god of evil
- SHU air-god
- AANI ape: dog-head
- AARU abode of dead
- AMON chief god
- ANKH sacred cross
- APIS sacred bull
- ATOM = RA
- ATUM = RA
- BAST cat-goddess
- BENU sarced heron
- DUAT underworld
- HAPI genius of Amenti
- HATI = AB
- ISIS nature-goddess (cow-head)
- PTAH thinker
- AMSET genius of Amenti
- APEPI great serpent
- HORUS solar-deity (falcon-head)
- KHNUM ram-god
- TAURT hippo-head
- THOTH ibis, patron of arts
- AMENTI abode of dead
- OPHOIS war-god

BABYLONIAN TERMS AND NAMES

- ROC giant bird
- AZHI -DAHAKA: dragon
- DEVA = DEAVA: demon
- YIMA king of man
- ADAPA first man
- AHURA benign genie
- ARALU underworld
- BELUS king
- ETANA eagle rider
- HAOMA sacred liquor
- IGIGI heavenly spirits
- KINGU slain by Marduk
- MUMMU Apsu's agent
- ALOROS king
- ALULIM = ALOROS
- ENGUDI wild man: Gilgamesh pal
- ENUKKI gods' servants
- RUSTAM = RUSTUM: hero
- SIMORG = ROC
- FEROHER disk symbol
- JAMSHID peri king
- NAMTARU Hades messenger
- SIMORGH = ROC
- FRAVASHI spiritual guardian
- GILGAMESH epic hero

CELTIC TERMS AND NAMES

- LUD king
- MIL MILEDH
- CROM -DUBH'S SUNDAY: feast
- MEDB Queen of Connault
- SHEE = SIDHE: fairy fort, folk
- DRUID sage, conjurer
- FOMOR sea robber; evil power
- KELPY water spirit
- POOKA marsh goblin
- AILILL king
- ANNWFN = ANNWN: Eden
- AVALON Arthur abode
- FIANNA Fenian heroes
- LUGNAS harvest feast
- MILEDH Irish ancestor
- OSSIAN hero

TUATHA	–DE DANNAN: gods	**SAMHAIN**	feast of dead
BANSHEE	warning spirit	**FIRBOLGS**	Fomor foes
BELTANE	Mayday rite	**TALIESIN**	bard
MORGAIN	fairy: sister of Arthur	**LEPRECHAUN**	tricky old man

TITANS

Gods		Goddesses	
ZEUS	**IAPETUS**	**LETO**	**PHOEBE**
ATLAS	**OCEANUS**	**MAIA**	**TETHYS**
COEUS	**HYPERION**	**RHEA**	**THEMIS**
CREUS	**EPIMETHEUS**	**DIONE**	**EURYNOME**
CRONUS	**PROMETHEUS**	**THEIA**	**MNEMOSYNE**

MONSTERS

OGRE	man-eater	**TYPHON**	flaming 100-headed
ARGUS	100-eyed	**CENTAUR**	half-man, half-horse
HARPY	predatory, winged dragon	**CHIMERA**	lion-goat; flame spewing
HYDRA	9-headed serpent	**GRIFFIN**	lion-eagle: gold guardian
LAMIA	woman-serpent	**LAMASSU**	bull with human head
SATYR	goat-man	**PEGASUS**	winged horse
BAGWYN	antelope-goat-horse	**PISTRIX**	sea monster
DRAGON	winged lizard	**UNICORN**	animal composite: 1 horn
GERYON	3 bodies, winged	**BASILISK**	dragon with fatal breath
GORGON	snake-haired woman	**MINOTAUR**	youth eating man-bull
KRAKEN	sea monster	**BUCENTAUR**	ox-man
SCYLLA	6 headed dog with 12 feet	**CHARYBDIS**	woman turned to whirlpool
SILENI	part man-part horse		
SPHINX	winged lion-woman; riddle poser	**MANTICORE**	horned lion-man
		SAGITTARY	Trojan ally

ROUND TABLE KNIGHTS AND RELATIONS

BORS	Lancelot's uncle	**MORGAN**	Arthur's sister
KAY	Arthur's foster brother	**GERAINT**	Enid's husband
BORT	= **BOHORT**: Lancelot's nephew	**GALAHAD**	Sir –: son of Lancelot
		MORDRED	= **MODRED**
BALAN	brother of Balin	**MORGAIN**	= **MORGAN**
BALIN	brother of Balan	**PELLEAS**	lover of Ettarre
ARTHUR	son of Uther, Igraine (Igerna)	**TRISTAN**	= **TRISTRAM**
		BEDIVERE	took Arthur's body to Avalon
ELAINE	Lancelot's love (Lily Maid)		
GARETH	nephew of Arthur	**LANCELOT**	son of Ban
GAWAIN	son of Morgain, Lancelot	**PERCIVAL**	= **PARSIFAL**: Grail seeker
ISOLDE	= **ISEULT**, beloved of Tristram; wife of Mark	**TRISTRAM**	Iseult's lover slain by Mark
MERLIN	magician	**GUINEVER**	Arthur's wife
MODRED	Arthur's slayer slain by him	**GUINEVERE**	= **GUINEVER**

WIVES AND LOVERS OF ZEUS (JUPITER)

IO	**AEGLE**	**EUROPA**	**ANTIOPE**
HERA	**CERES**	**LATONA**	**DEMETER**
JUNO	**DANAE**	**SEMELE**	**CALLISTO**
LEDA	**DIONE**	**THEMIS**	**EURYNOME**
LETO	**METIS**	**ALCMENE**	**MNEMOSYNE**
MAIA	**AEGINA**		

NATURAL HISTORY

* Indicates genus

MAMMALS

Oxen, Sheep, Goat Family (Bovidae)

ZO

BOB
BOS*
EWE
FAT
KEB
KEY
KID
KYL
MUG
MUL
NOT
OWE
PET
PUR
QUE
RAM
SHA
TAP
TEG
TIP
TUP
TUR
URE
YAK
YOE
YOW
ZAC
ZOH

AGNI
ANOA
APIS
ARNA
ARNI
ARUI
AVER
BOSS
BUCK
BUFF
BULL
BUSS
CADE
CALF
CAUR
CUSH
DOGY
DOWN
GAUR
GOUR
HAPI
HOGG
IBEX
KAIL
KINE
LAMB
LONK
MOIL
MUGS
MULL
NATA
NEAT
NOTT
OUSE
OVIS*
OXEN
QUEY
REEM
RUNT
SHIP
SOCK
TAGG
TAHR
TAIR
TEAP
TEGG
TEHR
THAR
TORO
TOUP
UDAD
UROY
VEAL
ZEBU
ZENU
ZOBO
ZOBU

AGNUS
AMMON
ANGUS
ARGAL
ARNEE
AUDAD
BEDEN
BILLY
BISON
BOBBY
BOSSY
BRAWN
BRAXY
CAPRA*
CAURE
CRONE
CRONY
CUSHA
DEVON
DOGIE
DUMBA
FLOCK
GAYAL
GEMSE
GORAL
GYALL
HEDER
JAELA
JAGLA
KAAMA
KERRY
KHAMA
KIDDY
MOLLY
NANNY
NIATA
PASAN
PESAH
PODDY
SANGA
SANGU
SLINK
SOOKY
STEER
STIRK
SUCKY
TAKIN
THAVE
URIAL
VACHE
WOOLY
YAKIN

AGNEAU
ANKOLI
AOUDAD
ARGALI
AUROCS
BANTIN
BARHAL
BARWAL
BHARAL
BIDENT
BOVOID
BRAMAN
BRAMIN
BUFFLE
BULKIN
BURHEL
CABREE
CABRIT
CALVER
CANNER
CAPRID
CATALO
CHAMAL
CHASER
COSSET
COTSOL
CREANE
CRUMMY
DEXTER
DINMAN
DODDIE
DUGHAM
EVICKE
EWETEG
EXMOOR
GIMMER
HAWKEY
HAWKIE
HEIFER
HIEDER
HOGGET
HOGGIE
HOGREL
HUMLIE
JERSEY
JHARAL
KIDDIE
KIDLET
LAMBER
LAMBIE
MAILLE
MAZAMA
MAZAME
MERINO
MOILEY
MOOLEY
MOOLLY
MOUTON
MUFLON
MULLEY
MUSKOX
MUSMON
MUTTON
NAHOOR
NAYAUR
OORIAL
OVIBOS*
OXFORD
PASANG
PASENG
PAULAR
PAULIE
PESACH
PUTTER
ROMNEY
SARLAK
SHEDER
SUCKER
SUSSEX
TAURUS
THEAVE
TUSKER
VEALER
WASTER
WEAVER
WEDDER
WETHER
WISENT
WOLLIE
WOOLLY

AUROCHS
BERENDO
BIGHORN
BLEATER
BRAHMAN
BRAHMIN
BUFFALO
BULLOCK
CARACUL
CHEVIOT
CHILVER
CRACKER
DELAINE
DISHLEY
EANLING
GRASSER
KARAKUL
LAMBKIN
LINCOLN
MOUFLON
MUFFLON
ROSELLA
SINGLER
SLINKER
TAURINE

Antelope Family (Antilocapridae)

AHO
DOE
DZO
GNU
GOA
KID
KOB
NIL

ADMI
ASSE
BISA
BUCK
CORA
DAMA
GEMS
GNOO
GUIB
KOBA
KUDU
MOHR
ORIX
ORYX
POKU

PUKU
TOPI
TORA

ADDAX
ARIEL
BEIRA
BEISA
BONGO
BUBAL
CAAMA
DODDY
ELAND
ETAAC
GAZEL
GEMSE
GORAL
GUIBA
IZARD
KOBUS*
KORIN
LICHI
MHORR
MUGGS

NAGOR
NUNNI
OREAS
ORIAS
ORIBL
PALLA
PEELE
SABLE
SAIGA
SASIN
SERAU
SERAW
SEROW
TAKIN
TIANG
YAKIN

BAGWYN
BUBALE
CABREE
CABRIT
CHUKER
DIGDIG
DIKDIK

DUIKER
DUYKER
DZEREN
DZERIN
DZERON
GOORAL
GRIMME
IMPALA
IMPOFO
IZZARD
KAINSI
KOKOON
KOODOO
KOUDOU
LECAMA
LECHEE
LECHWE
MAZAMA
MAZAME
NAKONG
NILGAI
NILGAU
OUREBI
OZANNA*

PALLAH
PASANG
PASENG
PYGARG
RHEBOC
RHEBOK
SAKEEN
SHAMMY
SHAMOY

BERENDO
BLAUBOK
BLESBOK
BUBALIS
CHAMOIS
CHIKARA
CONGONI
GAZELLA*
GEMSBOK
IMPALLA
REDBUCK
SASSABI
SASSABY

Swine Family (Suidae)

BEN
BOR
ELT
FAR
HOG
PIG
SEW
SOW
SUS*

APER
BENE

BOAR
FARE
GALT
GILT
KRAS
PORK
SHOT
SLIP
SUID
YELT
YILT

BONAV
DUROC
ESSEX
GRICE
PIGGY
SHEAT
SHOAT
SHOTE
SNORK
SUINA

BARROW

BONIVE
COCHON
FARROW
GUSSIE
JAVALI
PIGGIE
PIGLET
PORKER
PORKET
PORKIN
SUCKER
TITMAN

GRUNTER
PECCARY
PORCINE
ROASTER
SNORKER
SOUNDER
SUFFOLK
SUIDIAN
TANTANY
TANTONY
WARTHOG

Dog Family (Canidae)

CUR
GIP
GYP
JIP
MUT
POM
PUG
PUP
RUG
TOD
TOY
WAP
YAP

ALAN
ALCO
BICK
CHOW

CYON*
DANE
DIEB
FIST
GREW
HUND
LEAM
LIME
LOBO
LYAM
LYME
MUTT
PEKE
PULI
RACH
SKYE
THOS*
TYKE

WAPP

BAWTY
BITCH
BOXER
BRACH
CAAMA
CALEB
CANID
CANUS
COLLY
COOLY
DABUH
DHOLE
DINGO
DOGGY
DUMBY
ENTRY

FEIST
FYSTE
GUARA
HOUND
HUSKY
HYENA
KIOTE
LYOME
MASTY
MATIN
MERLE
PIDOG
POOCH
PUPPY
RACHE
RATCH
SHOCK
SWIFT

TRASY
VIXEN
ZERDA
ZORRO

AGUARA
ALAUNT
BAGMAN
BANDOG
BARBET
BARKER
BASSET
BAWTIE
BEAGLE
BOWWOW
BRATCH
BRIARD
BUFFER

CHANCO
COCKER
COLFOX
COLLIE
COLPEO
CORSAC
COYOTE
CUSSER
DOGGIE
FENNEC
FENRIP
HUNTER
HYAENA
ISGRIM
ISGRIN
JACKAL

JOWLER
KABERU
KELPIE
KOLSUN
KOULAN
KRATIM
LAPDOG
LOWRIE
LUCERN
LYCAON
MASTIS
MESSAN
MESSET
MESSIN
MOONER
MOPPET

MOPSIE
POODLE
RANGER
RATTER
RENARD
RUNNER
SALUKI
SAMOED
SAMOID
SCOTTY
SEIZER
SETTER
SHAKAL
SIGRIM
SIWASH
SLEUTH

SOMMER
SUNDOG
TALBOT
TANGUE
TANREC
TARRIE
TENREC
THOOID
TOLLER
TOWSER
TUFTER
VULPES
YAPPER
YAUPER
YAWPER
YELPER

BASTARD
BULLDOG
CHARLIE
CHARLEY
COURSER
GRIFFON
HARRIER
MASTIFF
MONGREL
POINTER
SAMOYED
SCOTTIE
TERRIER
WHIPPET
YAPSTER

Cat Family (Felidae)

CIT
GIB
KIT
LEO
PUS
TAB
TOM

BALU
EYRA
KITT
LION
PARD
PUMA
PUSS
SHER
SHIR
TIGE

TIKE

BERBE
CHATI
CHAUS
CHITA
CIVET
FELID
FELIS
FITCH
FOSSA
GALET
GENET
KITTY
MANUL
MEWER
MOGGY
OUNCE

PISHU
PUSSY
QUEEN
RASSE
SIMBA
SIVET
TABBY
TIGER
TILER
TOMMY
YOUSE
YOUZE
ZIBET

ANGOLA
ANGORA
BOBCAT
BONDAR

CHETAH
COUGAR
GIBCAT
JAGUAR
KITTEN
KITTIE
LIBARD
LIONEL
LIONET
MARGAY
MEWLER
MOUSER
MUSANG
NEUTER
OCELOT
PAGUMA
PAJERO
PAPION

PARDAL
POIANA
PURRER
PUSSIE
SERVAL
THOMAS
TIBERT
TOMCAT
ZIBETH

CARACAL
CHEETAH
GUEPARD
LEOPARD
LIONCEL
LIONESS
PANTHER
TIGRESS

Horse, Ass, Zebra (Equidae)

ASS
BAY
COB
CUT
DUN
FUS
GEE
GRI
GRY
HAN
JAD
JEE
JOB
NAG
PAT
POT
RAW
RIG
RIP
TAT
TIT
YAD

ARAB
BARB
COBB
COLT
FOAL
FUSS
GOER
GRAS
GRAY
GREY
GROG
HACK
HOSS
JADE
KOHL
MOKE
MULE
NAIG
PONY
PROD
PUCA
QUAD
RACE

RACK
RIDE
ROAN
RUCK
SCUT
SIRE
STOT
STUD
TATT
TATU
TURK
YABU
YAUD
YAWD
ZAIN

ARABY
BIDET
BRONC
BURRO
CAPLE
CAPUL
COBBE

CUDDY
DICKY
DUMMY
EQUID
EQUUS*
FAVEL
FILLY
HAIRY
HARAS
HINNY
HOBBY
JENNY
KIANG
KULAN
KYANG
LOPER
MILER
MOREL
MOUNT
NAGGY
NEDDY
PACER
PINTO

PIPER
PONEY
RACER
ROGUE
RUNSY
SHIER
SHIRE
SHYER
SHYRE
SKAIT
SKATE
SOMER
STEED
STIFF
TACKY
TATOO
WALER
WELSH
WIDGE
YABOO
ZEBRA

ALEZAN

AMBLER
AMEZEH
BANKER
BAYARD
BOLTER
BRONCO
BRUMBY
BUSSER
CABBER
CASTER
CAYUSE
CHEVAL
COOSER
CREAMY
CUDDIE
CURTAL
DAPPLE
DICKEY
DOBBIN
DONKEY
DRIVER
ENTIRE

EQUINE
EXMOOR
FENCER
FILLER
GALYAK
GANGER
GARRAN
GARRON
GEEGEE
GILLIE
GILLOT
GIRLIE
GLEYDE
GRASNI
HACKNY
HARACE
HUNTER
JENNET
KEFFEL
KIYANG
KUMRAH
LADINO

LEADER
MAIDEN
MORGAN
NACKER
NAIGIE
ONAGER
ORLOFF
PELTER
PLATER
PLOUGH
POLEYN
QUAGGA
REMUDA
RINGER
ROADER
ROARER
ROUNCY
RUNNER
SAVAGE
SHELTY
SORREL
STAGER

STONER
TACKEY
TANGAN
TANGLE
TANGUM
TANGUN
TARPAN
TATTOO
TRACER
TURKEY
VANNER
WEAVER

ARABIAN
BARBARY
BOBTAIL
BRONCHO
CAVALLO
CHARGER
CLIPPER
COACHER
COURSER

DRAFTER
FLEMISH
GELDING
HACKNEY
JACKASS
MONTURE
MUDLARK
MUSTANG
NEIGHER
PACOLET
PIEBALD
PRANCER
SADDLER
SHAFTER
SHELTIE
SLEDDER
SPANKER
SUMPTER
WHEELER
ZEBRASS
ZEBRULA

Camel, Llama (Camelidae)

LAMA
OUNT
PACO
GEMUL
OKAPI

ALPACA
DELOUL
HAGEEN
HAGEIN

HYGEEN
MEHARA
MEHARI
OKAPIA*

SERAPH
VICUNA
VIGONE
VIGUNA

CAMELUS*
GIRAFFA*
GIRAFFE
GUANACO

Deer, Moose (Cervidae)

DAE
DOE
ELK
ROE

ALCE
AXIS
DAUW
FAWN
HART
HIND
HINE
LOSH
MAHA

MORT
MUSK
NAPU
OLEN
PITA
PITO
PUDU
REIN
RUSA
SHOU
SHOW
SIKA
SPAY
STAG

ALCES*
KAKAR
KAKUR
LOSHE
MARAL
MOOSE
MUIST
PUDUA
RATWA
ROYAL
SABIR
SOWRE
SPADO
SURRE

CERVID
CERVUS
CHITAL
GUEMAC
GUEMUL
HANGUL
HAVIER
HEARST
KIDANG
MUNJAK
RASCAL
SAMBAR
SAMBOO
SAMBUR

SORREL
TARAND
THAMIN
VENADE
VENSON
WAPITI

BROCKET
CARIBOU
CERVINE
CERVOID
MOSCHUS*
VENISON

Rat Family (Rodentia)

BUN
TAN
WAT

BAUD
BAWD
CAVY
CONY
DEGU
GLIS
HARE
LOIR
MOLE

PACA
PIKA
TANA
TAWN
TUAN
TUZA
VOLE
WANT
WATT
WONT

AGUTI
BOBAC

BUNNY
CAVIA*
CONEY
COYPU
CUTTY
DAMAN
DASSY
GANAM
GUNDI
HIRAX
HYRAX
LABBA
LEPUS

LEROT
METAD
MOUDY
MOUSE
MOUSY
PORKY
RANNY
RATON
SHREW
SISEL
SOREX*
TALPA
URSON

XERUS*
ZAPUS*
ZEMMI
ZEMNI
ZOKOR

AGOUTI
AGOUTY
APEREA
BOBACK
CHIPPY
COYPOU
CRABER

CURURO
DASSIE
GEOMYS*
GERBIL
GNAWER
GOPHER
JERBOA
JUMPER
MALKIN
MARMOT

MAUKIN
MOUSEY
MYGALE
MYODES*
MYOXUS*
NUTRIA
OARLAP
OARLOP
PARKER
POLISH

RABBIT
RATTAN
RATTEN
ROTTAN
ROTTON
SUSLIK
TAGUAN
TALPID
TAMIAS*
TAPETI

TUPAIA*
WABBER
WARNER

ASSAPAN
BELGIAN
CHIPPIE
FLEMISH
HAMSTER
LEMMING

LEPORID
LEVERET
MUSKRAT
PEDETES
POTOROO
RATHARE
SANDRAT
SLEEPER
SONDELI

Primates

APE
KRA
LAR
PAN
PUG
SAI

AANI
BRUH
DOUC
HOMO
KAHA
LORI
MAHA
MAKI
MIAS
MICO
MONA
MONK
MONO
SAKI
SIME
TITI
TOTA
VARI
WAAG
WANA

ZATI

ACARI
AOTUS*
ARABA
AVAHI
CEBID
CEBUS*
DREEL
DRILL
INDRI
JACKO
JOCKO
KAHUA
KOKAM
LEMUR
LORIS
MACAC
MAGOT
MIDAS*
MUNGA
ORANG
PAPIO
PATAS
PIGMY
PONGO
POTTO

PYGMY
QUATA
RESUS
SAJOU
SATYR
SIFAC
SIMIA*
TOQUE
UNGKA
WAWAH
YARKE

ADAPID
ADAPIS*
APELET
ATELES*
AYEAYE
BABOON
BANDAR
CAMPER
CHACMA
COAITA
COLUGO
COUXIA
COUXIO
DOGAPE
GALAGO

GIBBON
GRIVET
GUENON
HAPALE*
HOGAPE
HOWLER
INDRIS*
LANGUR
MACACA*
MACACO
MACHIN
MAIMON
MARTIN
MOHOLI
MORMON
NCHEGA
NISNAS
OURANG
PIGMEW
PINCHE
RHESUS
RILAWA
SAGOIN
SAMIRI
SEACAT
SIFAKA
SIMIAN

SIMPAI
TEETEE
VERVET
WAUWAU
WEEPER
WISTIT
WOUWOU
YARKEE

COLOBIN
COLOBUS*
GUARIBA
HOOLOCK
LEMURID
MACACUS*
MACAQUE
NASALIS*
NOSEAPE
OUAKARI
ROLOWAY
SAIMIRI*
SAPAJOU
SIAMANG
STENTOR
TAMARIN
TARSIER
WISTITI

Marsupials

JOEY
ARIEL
BILBI
COALA
FLIER
FLYER
KOALA
QUICA
SELVA

SILVA
TAPOA
THILL
TUNGO
YAPOK
BOOMAH
BOOMER
CUSCUS
JERBOA

MONCAT
MONGAN
NUMBAT
POSSUM
WOMBAT
YAPOCK
DASYURE
KAPOUNE
MARMOSA*

MULGARA
OPOSSUM
WALLABY
ANTEATER
COESCOES
DASYURUS*
FORESTER
KANGAROO
MACROPUS*

TARSIPES*
WALLAROO
BANDICOOT
DIDELPHIS*
PADEMELON
PETAURIST
PHALANGER
PHILANDER
THYLACINE

Weasels, Beavers, Racoons

DAS
COON
FOIN
GULO*
MINK
PATE
VAIR
VARE

BRARO
BROCK
COATI
FITCH
HURON
LATAX*
LUTRA*
MELES*

NASUA*
NORSE
OTTER
PAHMI
PANDA
PEKAN
RATEL
SABLE

SKUNK
SOBOL
STOAT
TAXUS
TAYRA
TEJON
ZORIL
BADGER

BAUSON
BEAVER
BRAIRO
BRELAW
ERMINE
FERRET
FICHAT
FISHER

GALERA
GRISON
LASSET
MAPACH
MARTEN
MARTES*
MYDAUS*

NARICA
QUIQUE
RACOON
SEAAPE
TELEDU
WEASEL
CHINCHA

CHINCHE
ENHYDRA*
FITCHET
FITCHEW
GLUTTON
GORKHUS
ICTONYX*

MINIVER
MUSTELA*
POLECAT
RACCOON
SANDPIG
TAXIDEA*
ZORILLA

ZORRINO
BRAIREAU
CARCAJOU
KOLINSKY
MEPHITIS*
MUISHOND
ZORRILLO

Aquatic Mammals

Whale
ORC
CETE
HUSE*
HUSO*
ORCA
KRENG
OTARY
POGGY
SCRAG
BALEEN
BELUGA
BLOWER
FINNER
GIBBAR
KILLER
BALAENA*
BOWHEAD
FINBACK
FINFISH
GRAMPUS

MARSOON
ORCINUS*
RIPSACK
RORQUAL
SPOUTER
ZIPHIAN
BALAENID
CACHALOT
HUMPBACK
MUTILATE
ZALOPHUS*

Walrus
BRUTA*
MORSE
UNICORN
WALTRON
ODOBENUS

Dolphin
INIA*

SUSU
UNIE
BOUTO
DORADO
PALACH
PORPUS
SOOSOO
TURSIO
DELPHIN
NARWHAL
PELLOCK
PULLOCK
SNUFFER
GAIRFISH
NARWHALE
PHOCAENA*
PORPOISE
TURSIOPS*

Seal
WIG

SEAL
MATKA
PHOCA*
SWILE
URSAL
URSUK
USSUK
UTSUK
BEATER
JACKET
MAKLAK
MATKAH
OTARIA
PHOCID
FURSEAL
OTARIAN
OTARINE
PHOCOID
SADDLER
SEALKIE
HARPSEAL

OTARIINE
OTARIOID
PELAGIAN
PHOCIDAE*
PHOCINAE*
SEACATCH
SEECATCH
SEALCHIE

Others
DUGONG
MANATI
RYTINA
SEACOW
YUNGAN
COWFISH
MANATEE
SEALION
HALICORE
PINNIPED
SIRENIAN

Other Mammals

AI
BAT
APAR
BEAR
MUSS
PEBA
PEVA
TATU
UNAU
URVA
ABADA

APARA
BHALU
BRUIN
BRUTA
DANTA
HATHI
HATTY
JUMBO
MAKNA
MANID
MANIS

MUNGO
POYOU
RHINO
ROGUE
SLOTH
TATOU
ASWAIL
BOLITA
BORELE
DOTARD
JACKET

MAKHNA
MANGUE
MATACO
MATICO
MONGOE
NODIAK
OLDMAN
PELUDO
ANTBEAR
DASYPUS
ECHIDNA

ECHINUS
ELEPHAS*
GRIZZLY
ICEBEAR
LOXODON
SUNBEAR
TAMANDU*
TATOUAY
TOXODON*

CRUSTACEANS

DAD
UCA

CRAB
MAIA
MAYA
ZOEA

ACORN
ALIMA
AYUYU
CARID
ERYON
HIPPA
MAIAN

MYSID
MYSIS*
PRAWN
RACER
YABBI
YABBY
ZOAEA
ZOOEA

BUSTER
CANCER
CARIDA*
HOMARD
ISOPOD
MYSOID

PANDLE
PARTAN
PEELER
PUNGAR
PUNGER
SHRIMP
SLATER
SOWBUG
SPRITE
SQUILL
YABBER
YABBIE

ANATIFA
ANOMURA*

ARTEMIA
ASELLUS
ASTACUS*
BALANID
BUCKLER
BUCKLUM
BURSTER
CAMARON
CRAWDAD
CUMACEA*
FIDDLER
GRAPSUS*
GRIBBLE
INACHID
LIMULID

LIMULUS*
LOBSTER
MACRURA*
MUDCRAB
MYSIDAE*
OCIPODE*
ONISCUS*
PANFISH
PEACRAB
PILLBUG
SHEDDER
SQUILLA

ANATIFAE
BARNACLE

BLUECRAB
CAMBARUS*
CARIDEAN
CARIDOID
COPEPODA
CRABFISH
CRAWFISH
CRAYFISH
CREVETTE
CUMACEAN
EPICARID
FROGCRAB
GRAPSOID
INACHOID
KINGCRAB
LADYCRAB
LANDCRAB
LERNAEAN
LIMULOID
OCHIDORE
OCYPODAN
PILLWORM
PORTUNUS*
RANINIAN

ARACHNIDS

BUG
FAG
KED

MITE
TICK

ACARI
ARAIN
ARGAS
ATTID
BICHO
LOPPE
NANCY
NIGUA
PIQUE
SCREW
SCROW

ACARID
ACARUS*
ACERAE*
ANANSI
ARRAND
CARTER
CHEGOE
CHEGRE
CHIGGA
CHIGOE
CHIGRE
ENIGUA
GIGGER
IXODID
KATIPO
LEPTUS
LYCOSA*
MYGALE
REDBUG

SPIDER
TAMPAN
WEAVER

ACARIDA*
ACARINA*
AGALENA*
ALACRAN
ANNANCY
ARANEID
ARGASID
ARGIOPE*
ATTIDAE*
BDELLID
CHIGGER
CHIGGRE
DEMODEX
EGGMITE
IXODIAN

JAYHAWK
LYCOSID
MYGALID
OCTOPOD
PHOLCID
PHOLCUS*
PHRYNID
POKOMOO
RETIARY
SANDBOY
SPIDGER
SPINDER
SPINNER
STINGER

ACARAPIS*
ARANEIDA*
ARCTISCA

ATTERCOP
CARAPATO
FACEMITE
GAMAPATO
IXODIDAE*
LONGLEGS
ORBITELE
PEDIPALP
SANDWORM
SCORPION
SOLIFUGE
SOLPUGID
THOMISID
ULOBORID
ULOBORUS*
WANDERER

TARANTULA

FISH

AKU
AWA
AYU
BAR
BIB
COB
COD
DAB
EEL
FIN
FRY
GAG
GAR
GED
HAG
IDE
IHI
KOI
LAX
LOB
MAH
ORF
RAY
RUD
SMY
SUN
TAI

ALEC
AMIA
BANG
BARB
BASS
BLAY
BLOB
BOCE
BOGA
BOHO
BRET
BRIT
BUTT
CAJI
CARP
CAXI
CERO
CHAR
CHUB
CHUM
COHO
CONY
COOK
CUSK
DACE
DORE
DORN
DRUM
ESOX
GADE
GATA
GEDD
GOBY
GRIG
HAAK
HAGG
HAIK
HAKE
HAYE
HIKU
HIND
HUCH
HUSO
HUSS
JACK
JOCU
KELT
KETA
KIYI
LANT
LIJA
LING
LORO
LOTA*
LOTO
LUCE
MADO
MAKO
MAPO
MASU
MERO
MOKI
MOLA
MORT
OPAH
ORFE
PARR
PEGA
PENK
PETO
PIKE
PINK
POGY
POLE
POOR
POUT
PRIM
QUAB
RAAD
RAUN
RENA
ROCK
ROUD
RUDD
RUFF
SAMA
SAPO
SCAD
SCAR
SCUP
SESI
SHAD
SIER
SILE
SISI
SKIL
SNIG
SOLE
SPET
SPOT
TANG
TINK
TOPE
TORO
TUNA
ULUA
WELS
ZANT

ABOMA
ACARA
AGUJA
ALLIS
ALOSA*
ALOSE
ANGEL
APODA
BAGRE
BALAO
BARRY
BARSE
BECCO
BETTA
BLEAK
BLOAT
BOGUE
BOHOO
BOLTI
BOLTY
BREAM
BRILL
BULTI
CHARR
CHIRO
CHOPA
CISCO
COBIA

CRAVO
DICKY
DORAB
DORAD
DORAS*
DROUD
ELOPS
ELVER
FLAIR
FLATH
FLUKE
FRIAR
GADID
GADUS*
GAPER
GIBEL
GOBIO*
GOODY
GRUNT
GUASA
GUPPY
HADDO
HILSA
HITCH
HOUND
HUCHO
HURSE
JUREL
KANAE
KILLY
LAKER
LAMIA
LAUIA
LOACH
LONGE
LOOTA
LUCET
MANTA
MARAY
MATIE
MIDGE
MINIM
MINNY
MOLET
MORAY
MUGIL*
MURRY
MUSKY
OXEYE
PARGO
PATAO
PERCA*
PERCH
PIRAI
POGGE
POGGY
PORGY
POWAN
RAIAI*
REINA
RHINA
ROACH
ROKER

RONCO
ROVET
SARGO
SARPO
SAURY
SCAMP
SCROD
SEWEN
SEWIN
SHARK
SKATE
SLINK
SMELT
SMOLT
SMOOK
SMOUT
SPRAG
SPRAT
SPROD
SQUAT
SULEA
SUNNY
SWORD
TECON
TENCH
TOGUE
TONNY
TOPER
TORSK
TROUT
TRUBU
TRUFF
TUNNY
ULKEN
UMBRA
VIEJA
VIUVA
WAHOO
WHIFF
WHITY
WIRRA
WITCH
XUREL

ACOUPA
AGUAJI
AGUJON
ALAIHI
ALEVIN
ALLICE
ANABAS
ANGLER
APOGON
ARCHER
ATINGA
BAGGIE
BAGGIT
BALLAN
BALLAO
BARBEL
BATOID
BECUNA
BELONE*

BELUGA
BERVIE
BESHOW
BESUGO
BICHIR
BLENNY
BLOWER
BONACI
BONETA
BONITA
BONITO
BOOHOO
BOWFIN
BRASSE
BUNKER
BURBOT
BUTTER
CANDIL
CAPLIN
CARANX*
CARAPO
CARIBE
CHANOS*
CHAPIN
CHEBOG
CHERNA
CHERNE
CHEVIN
CHIVEY
COCUYO
COELHO
CONGER
COTORO
COTTID
CREOLE
CROCUS
CUBERA
CUCHIA
CUCUYO
CUNNER
DARTER
DARZEE
DENTEX
DIABLO
DIODON*
DIPNOI*
DOCMAC
DOCTOR
DORADO
ELLECK
ELLOPS
ESPADA
FAUSEN
FINNAC
FLATHE
FLIOMA
GADOID
GALEID
GALEUS*
GANOID
GARMON
GARVIE
GASCON

GERRES
GOBIID
GOLDNY
GORAMY
GRILSE
GRUBBY
GUNDIE
GUNNEL
HADDIE
HAMLET
HAPUKU
HASSAR
HEPPER
HILSAH
HUCHEN
HUSSAR
INANGA
INIOME
INIOMI*
ISURUS
JERKIN
JOHNNY
KELING
KIPPER
LAITHE
LAMNID
LAUNCE
LAWYER
LOOTAH
MAHSIR
MAHSUR
MAIGER
MAIGRE
MARLIN
MEAGER
MEAGRE
MENNOM
MENNON
MINNOW
MOLOID
MORGAY
MULLET
MULLID
MULVEL
MURENA
MURRAY
MUSKIE
MYKISS
MYXINE*
MYZONT
NATIVE
NONNAT
OBISPO
PAGRUS*
PARROT
PERCID
PICUDA
PIRAYA
PLAICE
POLLAN
POPEYE
PORGEE
PUFFER

PUNECA
QUASKY
RAMPER
REDEYE
REDFIN
REMORA
REQUIN
ROBALO
RONCHO
ROMERO
RUNNER
SABALO
SALELE
SALEMA
SALMON
SAMLET
SANDER
SARGUS
SAUGER
SAUQUI
SAUREL
SAVOLA
SCARUS
SENNET
SEPHEN
SHANNY
SHINER
SIERRA
SKELLY
SLIMER
SMOOTH
SPARID
SUCKER
TAILER
TAIMEN
TAMBOR
TAMURE
TANDAN
TARPON
TARPUM
TAUTOG
TESTAR
TETARD
TINKER
TINOSA
TOMCOD
TULIPE
TURBOT
TWAITE
ULCHEN
ULICON
ULIKAN
ULIKON
VENDIS
VOLIER
WACHNA
WALLER
WARSAW
WEEVER
WIRRAH
WOOHOO
WRASSE
ZANDER

ZINGEL

ABADEJO
ACHIGAN
ACRODUS
ALEWIFE
ALFIONA
ANADROM
ANCHOVY
ASPREDO
BACALAO
BARBUDO
BARFISH
BATFISH
BEARDIE
BERGALL
BERGYLT
BERYCID
BIGHEAD
BLOATER
BLUECAP
BONEDOG
BOWBACK
BOXFISH
BUGFISH
BUGHEAD
BURFISH
BURRITO
CANDIRU
CAPELIN
CATFISH
CAVALLA
CAVALLY
CHALACO
CHALDER
CHOGSET
CHROMID
CICHLID
CLUPEID
CODFISH
CORSAIR
COTTOID
COWFISH
CRAPPIE
CRAPPLE
CROAKER
CUCKOLD
CYCLOID
DIPNOAN
DOGFISH
DOLPHIN
EELPOUT
EGGFISH
ELLFISH
ESCOLAR
ESPADON
ESSLING
FATHEAD
FIDDLER
FLAPPER
FOXFISH
GARFISH
GARLOPA
GARPIKE
GEELBEC
GHOSTER
GILLING
GOBIOID
GOGGLER
GOLDNEY
GOURAMI
GRAMPUS
GRINDER
GROUPER
GRUNION
GUAPENA
GUAVINA
GUDGEON
GULARIS
GURNARD
GWINIAD
GWYNIAD
HADDOCK
HAGFISH
HALIBUT
HARMOOT
HARMOUT
HERRING
HOGFISH
HOMILYN
ICEFISH
INCONNU
ISUROID
JEWFISH
JUGULAR
KEELING
KILLING
LABROID
LAMPERN
LAMPRET
LAMPREY
LAVARET
LONGJAW
LOPHIID
MACHETE
MAHSEER
MAYFISH
MOJARRA
MONARRA
MOONEYE
MORWONG
MUDFISH
MURAENA*
OARFISH
OCHIGAN
OLDWIFE
OOLACAN
OOLAKAN
OQUASSA
PEGADOR
PEGASID
PEGASUS
PICAREL
PIGFISH
PINFISH
PINHEAD
PINTADO
PIRHANA
PLACOID
POISSON
POLLACK
POLLOCK
POMFRET
POMPANO
PRISTIS*
QUINNAT
RATTAIL
REDFISH
REQUIEM
ROCKEEL
ROVETTO
SANDEEL
SARDINE
SAWFISH
SCEGGER
SCULPIN
SEABASS
SERRANO
SILLAGO
SILURID
SKEGGER
SKIPPER
SLINKER
SNAPPER
SOCKEYE
SPARADA
SPAROID
SQUETTE
STERLET
SUNFISH
SURGEON
TAMBOUR
TELEOST
TIBURON
TOMTATE
TOPKNOT
TORPEDO
TOTUAVA
TREVALI
TRIGGER
TUBFISH
UMBRANA
UMBRINE
VENDACE
VIAJACA
VOLADIR
WALLEYE
WAREHOU
WHAPUKA
WHAPUKU
WHITING
WIDEGAB
WIDEGAP
XIPHIAS*
XYPHIAS*

REPTILES

ASP
BOA
BOM
DAB
GOA
NAG
UTA*

ADDA
BOID
CROC
DABB
DUBB
EMYD
EMYS*
GILA
IBID
IBIT
NAGA
NAJA*
NAKO
SEPS
TEJU
URAN

ABOMA
ADDER
AGAMA*
ANOLE
ANOLI
ARRAU
ASPIC
BITIS
CARET
COBRA
CRIBO
DHABB
DHOBB
DHUBB
DRACO*
ECHIS*
ELAPS*
GATOR
GECKO
GEKKO*
GUANO
KRAIT
MAMBA
NAKOO
RACER
SCINK
SKINK
SNECK
SWIFT
TIGER
TOKAY
TWEEG
VARAN
VIPER

AGAMID
AMEIVA*
ANGUID
ANGUIS*
ANOLIS*
ARBALO
BOIDAE*
BONGAR
CAIMAN
CAUSUS*
CAYMAN
CHELYS*
CHITAL
COODLE
COOTER
DABOIA
DABOYA
DIPSAS
DRAGON
ELAPID
EMYDEA
GAVIAL
GOPHER
HARDIM
HISSER
IGUANA
ILYSIA
JACARE
JESSUR
JURARA
KARAIT
KERRIL
LACERT
LEGUAN
MABUYA*
MOLOCH
MUGGAR
MUGGER
MUGGUR
NATRIX*
PYTHON
SAURIA*
SLIDER
PEIOID
WLAPHE*
WORRAL
YACARE
ZONURE

ANOLIAN
ATHECAE
ATHERIS
BOKADAM
CAMOODI
CARETTA*

CHEECHA
CHELONE*
COLUBER*
CRAWLER
CREEPER
CULEBRA
DIAPSID
ELAPINE
EUMECES*
GEITJIE
GEKKOTA*
HAGWORM
HOGNOSE
IGUANIA*
IGUANID
JUNIATA
LACERTA*
LAGARTO
LANGAHA
LOGHEAD
MEHELYA*
MONITOR
OPHIDIA*
PRESTER
PYGOPUS*
RATTLER
SANDBOA
SAURIAN
SCINCID
SCINCUS
SERPENT
SNAPPER
TARENTE
TEIIDAE*
TESTUDO*
TORTUGA
TREEBOA
TRIONYX*
TUATARA
TUCKTOO
TURTLET
VARANUS*
VIPERID
ZONURID*
ZONURUS*

AGAMIDAE
ANACONDA
ANGUIDAE
ARCHELON
BASILISK
BONETAIL
BOTHROPS*
BUNGARUM
BUNGARUS*
CASCAVEL
CERASTES
CHELONIA*
CHELYDRA*
COLUBRID*
CROTALUS*
CUNECTES*
DINOSAUR
EGGEATER
ELAPIDAE*
ELAPINAE*
EMYDIDAE
EMYDINAE*
FLAPJACK
GAVIALIS*
GEKKONID
HAWKBILL
HELODERM
IGUANOID
JARARACA
LACERATE*
LACHESIS
LORICATA*
LORICATE
LYGOSOMA*
MATAMATA
MICRURUS
MOCCASIN
MOKAMOKA
MOSASAUR
OPHIDIAN
PELUSIOS*
PITVIPER
RATSNAKE
RINGHALS
SAUROPOD
SCORPION
SHAGTAIL
SLOWWORM
SQUAMATA*
TERRAPIN
TORTOISE
VIPERINE
WATERDOG
WHIPTAIL
ZONUROID

ALLIGATOR
BLINDWORM
CHAMELEON
CHUNKHEAD
COACHWHIP
COLUBRINA
CORNSNAKE
EPICRATES
GALLIWASP
HELODERMA
HETERODON
IGUANODON
KINGCOBRA
KINGSNAKE
MILKSNAKE
MOLESNAKE
PUFFADDER
ROUGHTAIL
SERPENTES*
TERRAPENE*
TREESNAKE
WARTSNAKE
WHIPSNAKE

AMPHIBIANS

ASK
ESK
EFT
OLM
PAD
TAG

AGUA
BUFO
EVAT
EVET
FROG
HYLA
NEWT
PIPA
PODE
RANA
TAED
TAID
TOAD
TODE
TOOD

ANURA
ASKER
EFFET
FROSH
FROSK
PADDO
PADDY
PADOW
PIPAL
RONCO
SIREN
TOADY
TWEEG

ALYTES
ANURAN
CRAPON
MUDDER
PADDOW
PEEPER
TOGGLE
TRITON

AGLOSSA
AXOLOTL
CAUDATA
CAUDATE
COSTATA
CRAPAUD
CROAKER
DOGFISH
GANGREL
HOPTOAD
HYLIDAE
PADDOCK
PODDOCK
PROTEUS
QUILKIN
TADPOLE
URODELA

AMPHIUMA
BULLFROG
CAECILIA
FERREIRO
GANGEREL
LINGUATA
MUDPUDDY
NECTURUS
TREETOAD
TRITURUS

HELLBENDER
SALAMANDER

BIRDS

Prey, Hunting, Game

IO*

ERN
GOS
IOA
IWA
OWL

AURA
BUBO*
CHIL
CHIR
ERNE
EYAS
GLED
HAWK
KAHU
KEET
KITE
KUKU
KYAH
LOWA
LULU
OTIS*
PAPA
PERN
PISK
QUIS
RYPE
TYTO*
UTUM

AREND
ARGUS*
ASTUR
BESRA
BUTEO*
CHEER
COLIN
EAGLE
FALCO*
GANGA
GLEDE
HARPY
HOBBY
MADGE
MONAL
OWLET
PADGE
QUAIL
SAKER
URUBU
ALCEDO*
AQUILA*
AZIOLA
CHILLA
CHUKAR
CHUKOR
CONDOR
ELANET
FANNER
FORMEL
FULMAR
GENTLE
GORHEN

GROUSE
HOOTER
HOUTOU
HOWLET
HULLET
JAEGER
KEELIE
KETUPA*
LANNER
MERLIN
MEROPS*
MILVUS*

MOPOKE
MUCARO
NYCTEA*
OSPREY
PIPIRI
RAPTOR
SEESEE
SHAHIN
SHIKRA
TERCEL
TURNIX

AESALON
BOOBOOK
BULLBAT
BUSTARD
BUZZARD
CACICUS*
CHEEPER
COLINUS*
FLAPPER
FLOPPER
FRIGATE
GALEENY

GOSHAWK
HARRIER
KALEEGE
KALLEGE
KESTREL
PANDION*
PINTADO
PUDDOCK
PUTTOCK
SAKERET
SHAHEEN
STANNEL

TINAMOU
VULTURE
WOODHEN
WOOLERT

BOBWHITE
CARACARA
GUACHARO
MANOFWAR
MOREPORK
PHEASANT
WOODCOCK

Shore, Wading, Diving

AUK
COB
KIP
MEW
PEN
QUA

ALCA*
ALLE*
ANAS*
APUS*
CHEN*
CLEE
COBB
COOT
DARR
DOGY
DUCK
FALK
FUTE
GONY
GRUS
GULL
HERN
IBIS
KNOT
KOKO
KORA
KULM
LOON
LOWN
MALL
NOIO
OLOR*
PIRR
RAIL
RIXY
RUFF
SHAG
SKUA
SMEE
SMEW
SOCO
SORA
SULA
SWAN
TEAL
TERN

TITI
URIA*
WAEG

AIAIA
AJAJA
ALLAN
ANNET
ANSER*
ARDEA*
ARRIE
BOOBY
BRANT
BUNTY
CHAJA
CRAKE
CRANE
CUTTY
DILLY
DIVER
DRAKE
EGRET
EIDER
GAVIA*
GONEY
GOOSE
GORMA
GUARA
HARLE
HERLE
HERON
IMBER
LARID
MOLLY
MURRE
NELLY
NODDY
OMBER
OXEYE
PEARL
PEWEE
PEWIT
PRINE
PRION
QUAWK
REEVE
RODGE
ROTCH

SANDY
SCAUP
SCRAY
SHOOI
SKIRR
SKITE
SKURR
SNIPE
SOLAN
STILT
STINT
STORK
TIRMA
UMBER
WABBY
WAVEY
WHILK

AUKLET
AVOCET
BANTAM
BONXIE
CANARD
CHAUNA*
CHOUGH
CHUNGA
CURLEW
CYGNET
CYGNUS*
DARTER
DIPPER
DOPPER
DUIKER
DUNLIN
GANNET
GARROT
GAVIAE*
GENTOO
GODWIT
GOONEY
GORMAW
GUNNER
HAGDON
JABIRU
JACANA
JAEGER
KIALEE
KICKUP

KIRMEW
KITTLE
KOTUKU
KULANG
LUNGIE
MACUCA
NARECA*
MARLIN
MARROT
MUDHEN
PETREL
PLOTUS*
PLOVER
PUFFIN
QUANDY
ROTCHE
SCOTER
SICSAC
SIMBIL
STERNA*
STRANY
TEASER
TEETEE
TEETER
TRINGA*
WILLET
YOCKEL
ZUISIN

ANHINGA*
ASSILAG
BIGFOOT
BITTERN
BROWNIE
CANETON
CAPELLA
CICONIA*
CINCLUS*
COURLAN
COURSER
DOVEKIE
DOWITCH
DUNBIRD
DUNNOCK
FINFOOT
GADWALL
GOLIATH
GRALLAE*

GRAYLAG
ICEGULL
JACAMAR
JACKSAW
KAMICHI
LAPWING
LIMPKIN
MALLARD
MALMOCK
MARABOU
MOORHEN
OLDWIFE
PELICAN
PENGUIN
PIMLICO
PINTAIL
POCHARD
PODITTI
PYGOPOD*
RANTOCK
SAWBILL
SCAMELL
SKIMMER
SQUACCO
TARROCK
TATTLER
TOTANUS*
TWISTER
WAYBILL
WHOOPER
WIDGEON

ADJUTANT
BALDPATE
BOATBILL
DABCHICK
DOTTEREL
FLAMINGO
GARGANEY
JOHNDOWN
KILLDEER
OLDSQUAW
PEETWEET
SCREAMER
SHOEBILL
SHOVELER
UMBRETTE
WHIMBREL

Song Birds

ANI
ANO
DAW
IAO
KAE
TUE
TUI

BRAN
CHAT
CROW
FINK
HIAT
KALA
KATE
LARK
MERL
MIRO
MOHO
MORO
OMAO
PAPE
POPE
WREN
YENI
TUTU

AMMER
AMSEL
CUTTY
DAYAL
HOODY
IRENA*
JOREE
JUNCO
KAMAO
LINDO
MAVIS
MERLE
OUSEL
OUZEL
PIPIT
PIROL
ROBIN
SERIN
SHAMA
SPINK
TWITE
VEERY
VIREO

ANTHUS
BULBUL
BUNYAH

BURION
CANARY
CITRIL
CORBIE
DRONGO
GREENY
HOODIE
KOKAKO
LANIUS*
LINNET
LORIOT
MERUCA*
MOCKER
MUFFET
OLOMAO
ORIOLE
OSCINE*
OXBIRD
PALOLA
ROLLER
SHRIKE
SIALIA*
SISKIN
SOARER
SYLVIA*
THRUSH
TOWHEE

TURDUS*
VERDIN
WINNEL

BABBLER
BUNTING
BUSHTIT
CAPELLA
CARIAMA
CATBIRD
CHEWINK
CHIRPER
COWBIRD
ICTERUS*
JACKDAW
KINGLET
KIROMBO
MAYBIRD
MIMIDAE*
MIMINAE*
MINIVET
ORTALUS*
ORTOLAN
PIRANGA*
REDPOLL
REDWING
RUDDOCK

SCOLDER
SEIURUS*
SKYLARK
TANAGER
TIMALIA*
TITLARK
WAGTAIL
WARBLER
WIMBREL

BELLBIRD
BLUEBIRD
BOBOLINK
CARDINAL
CHIPCHAP
CHIPCHOP
GROSBEAK
HAWFINCH
LAZYBIRD
LONGSPUR
PHILOMEL
PINCPINC
REDSTART
SNOWBIRD
THRASHER
TITMOUSE
WHINCHAT

Tropical, Parrots

OO

ARA
KEA
POE

ANNA
COLY
CRAX*
GUAN
JACU
JYNX*
KAKA
KOAE
LORO
LORY
LUPE
MAKO
PEHO
PICI*

QUIT
RAYA
RURU
TAHA
TIWI
TOCK
TOCO
TODY

AGAMI
ARARA
BREVE
CAGIT
DAYAL
GALAH
HANNA
LOURI
LOWAN
LOXIA*
MACAW

MUNIA*
PIPRA*
PITTA*
SARUS
SYLPH
TURCO
VEUVE

ARGALA
BARBET
BECARD
BROLGA
CONURE
DIKKOP
HOAZIN
HOMRAI
KAKAPO
LEIPOA*
LIMOSA*
MANUAO

MOTMOT
PARROT
PICULE*
PIPILE*
QUELEA*
TOUCAN
TROGON
WELLAT
WHIDAH
WHYDAH
YETAPU
YNAMBU

ARACARI
COLIBRI
CORELLA
GANGANG
JACOBIN
KIROMBO
LORILET

MANAKIN
NAMAQUA
POEBIRD
QUETZAL
RASORES*
ROSELLA
SERIEMA
SIRGANG
SUNBIRD
TOURACO

CURASSOW
HORNBILL
KINGTODY
LORIKEET
LOVEBIRD
LYREBIRD
PARAKEET
POPINJAY
TOCORORO

Flightless, Extinct

EMU
IHI
MOA
ROC

DODO
EMEU
KAGU
KIWI

MAMO
RHEA
WEKA
DIDUS*

NANDU
MOORUP
RATITE

APTERYX
OSTRICH
NOTORNIS

Other Birds

GOR
HEN
JAY
MAG
MAO
NUN
OII
PIE
TIT

AVES
AVIS
BAYA
CHAB
COLK
DOVE
GORB
GRIG
HUIA
KOEL
MAGG
MITU
MYNA
NENE
PAVO*
PAWN
PICA

ROOK
STIB
WAMP
WEET

BIDDY
CAPON
COOEE
COOEY
GOURA*
HECCO
HUCCO
KOKIL
MALEO
MORUS
MYNAH
PIPER
PCTOO
RALPH
RAVEN
SPICK
SQUAE
STARN
SWIFT
TARIN
TERIN
UPUPA

BATARA
BRAHMA
CHEBEC
CHIPPY
COUCAL
CUCKOO
CUSHAT
DACELO
DRIVER
FUFFIT
GORBAL
GORBET
GORBIT
GORLIN
HOOPOE
HOUDAN
HUMMER
JERKIN
KOKILA
MAOMAO
MARTIN
NESTER
PASTOR
PEEPER
PEEWIT
PHOEBE
PIGEON

PULLET
PULLUS
REDLEG
SAPPHO
SULTAN
SWELLY
TIKLIN
TURBIT
TURKEY
TYRANT
WITTOL
YAFFLE
YELPER

ANTBIRD
CHICKEN
COLUMBA*
CREEPER
CUCULUS*
DORKING
FANTAIL
FLICKER
GOBBLER
GRACKLE
HIRUNDO*
LEGHORN

LOGCOCK
MARTLET
MEGAPOD
PEACOCK
PICULET
PUFFLEG
SNOWCAP
SPARROW
STINKER
SWALLOW
TOMFOOL
WARRIOR
WAXWING
WITWALL

BOATTAIL
COCKATOO
COQUETTE
KINGBIRD
KIWIKIWI
NIGHTJAR
POORWILL
RAINBIRD
RINGDOVE
STARLING
WHEATEAR

INSECTS

Bugs and Sucking Insects

BUG
NIT

AFIS
LAAP
LERP
NEPA*
PELA

ANASA*
APHID
APHIS*
BICHO
BORER
CHINK
CICAD
CIMEX

DORRE
EMESA
LOUSE
NEPID
PUNEE
PUNIE
SCALE
THRIP

ALTICA*
BEDBUG
BLIGHT
BUGGER
CHINCH
CHINTZ
CICADA

CIGALA
CIGALE
CIXIID
COCCID
COREID
CORIXA*
DIMERA*
DORBUG
ICERYA*
JARFLY
JASSID
JUGATE
PSYLLA*
PUNESE
PUNICE
SKATER

TAENIA*
TETRIX*
TETTIX*
THRIPS
TINGIS*

ADELGES*
APHIDID
BOATBUG
BOATMAN
CHERMES*
CICADID
CIMICID
CORSAIR
CRAWLER
DIMERAN

LACEBUG
LEAFBUG
LYGAEID
LYREMAN
NEPIDAE*
PSYLLID
PUCERON
PUNAISE
RANATRA*

HOGLOUSE
MEALYBUG
PLANTBUG
TAPEWORM
WATERBUG
WHEELBUG

Grasshoppers

CAGN
DRUM
GRIG
WETA

BRUKE
RACER

ROACH
STICK

BLATTA*
CHANGA
EARWIG
EMPUSA

LOCUST
MANTID
MANTIS
PHASMA

BLATTID

CATYDID
CRACKET
CRICKET
DRUMMER
GRYLLID
GRYLLUS*

KATYDID
KNOCKER
MANTOID
PROPHET

STICKBUG

Butterflies and Moths

ERI
PUG
WIT

CLEW
ERIA
HAWK
MAUL
MOCH
MOTE
MOTH
SLUG
WHIT

ARGUS
AWETO
COMMA
EGGER
ELFIN
ERUCA
GHOST
IMAGO
MICRO
NYMPH
OOBIT
OUBIT
PISKY
PLUME
SATYR
SWIFT
TINEA*
WHITE
WITCH
ZEBRA

APOLLO
ARCTIA*
BAGONG
BOGONG
CANKER
CODLIN
COLIAS*
COPPER
COSSID
DAGGER
DANAID
ERMINE
GRAPTA*
HERALD
HUMMER
IDALIA
IOMOTH
LAPPET
MILLER
MOODER
MORPHO*
NYMPHA
PIERIS*
PLUSIA*
PROGNE
PRUNER
PSYCHE
QUAKER
RISPER
RUSTIC
SPHINX
THECLA*
TINEAN

TINEID
TURNUS
TUSSAH
TUSSEH
TUSSER
URSULA
VIOLET
WOUBIT
YELLOW

ADMIRAL
AGROTIS*
ARCTIID
ATTACUS*
AURELIA
BAGWORM
BEEMOTH
BUDWORM
CODLING
CRAMBID
CRAMBUS
CRININE
CUTWORM
DANAINE
DELTOID
DIURNAL
DRINKER
EMPEROR
ERMELIN
ERMILIN
EURYMUS*
FIGWORM
FOOTMAN

HOPMOTH
JUGATAE*
JUNONIA
MONARCH
PSYCHID
PUGMOTH
PYRALID
PYRALIS*
TINEOID
TORTRIX
TUSSOCK
TUSSORE
URANIID
VANESSA
VICEROY
WAXMOTH
WEBWORM
YAMAMAI

ARMYWORM
BOLLWORM
FORESTER
GLOWWORM
GREYLING
HAWKMOTH
HESPERID
INCHWORM
KNOTHORN
LUNAMOTH
PLUTELLA
SILKWORM
SPANWORM
WANDERER

Flies and Mosquitoes

BOT
FAG
FLY
GAD
KEB
KED
LOP
MAD

BOTT
CLEG
FLEA
GLEG
KADE
KIVU
MAWK
TICK
ZIMB

AEDES*
CLEGG
CRIKE
CRUMB

CULEX*
DRAKE
FLECH
FLECK
MAGOT
MAITH
MATHE
MUSCA
OXBOT
OXFLY
PERLA
PHORA*
PULEX*
PUNKY
SALLY
WHAME
ZEBUB

ASILID
ASILUS*
BEEFLY
BLOWER
BOTFLY

BREEZE
CEPHID*
COOTIE
CRICKE
DAYFLY
FLEIGH
GADBEE
GADFLY
GENTIL
GENTLE
GORFLY
LEPTID
LEPTUS
MAGGOT
MAITHE
MIDGET
MUSCAE*
MUSCID
NITTER
PALMER
PERLID
PHORID
PODURA

PUNKIE
SALLIE
SAWFLY
SEROOT
TIPULA*
TORCEL
TSETSE
UJIFLY
WABBLE
WARBLE
WORMIL

BATTICK
BLOWFLY
BLUEFLY
CEPHOID
CHALCID
COLLIER
CONOPID
CORNFLY
CREEPER
CULICID

DIOPSIS*
DOLPHIN
EARTICK
FURCULA
GALLFLY
GLOWFLY
GOUTFLY
GRANNOM
GRAYFLY

GREYFLY
HORNFLY
HUZZARD
MADDOCK
MORPION
PULICID
TIPULID
WIGGLER

APPLEFLY
BEELOUSE
BIRDTRICK
BLACKFLY
CRANEFLY
DOGLOUSE
FRUITFLY
HORNTAIL

HOUSEFLY
MOSQUITO
ONIONFLY
PANORPID
PEARSLUG
STONEFLY
TATUKIRA

Beetles

DOR

BOUD
DOAR
DORE
DORR
GOGA
GOGO
IPID
POPE
TURK

AMARA*
CLOCK
FIDIA
GOGGA
HISPA
LARIA*
LYCID
MELOE
SAGRA*

BEETLE
CHAFER
CLERID
CLERUS*
CUCUYO
ELATER
GOLACH
GOLOCH
IPIDAE*
LAMIID
LARIID
LYCTID
LYCTUS*
MELOID
PICUDO
PIERID
PTINID
PTINUS*
SAWYER
SCARAB
SILPHA*

WEAVER
WEEVIL

ADELOPS*
AGRILUS*
BILLBUG
BUZZARD
CADELLE
CARABID
CARABUS
CUCUJID
DARDAOL
ELATRID
FIDDLER
FIREFLY
GIRDLER
GIRINID
GOLDBUG
GYRINID
GYRINUS*
HUMBUZZ

JUNEBUG
LADYBUG
LADYFLY
LAMPFLY
LUCANID
LUCANUS*
PTINOID
ROSEBUG
TUMBLER
VEDALIA*

CURCULIO
GRAYBACK
GREYBACK
HARDBACK
LADYBIRD
RUTELIAN
RUTILIAN
SEARCHER
SQUEAKER
WIREWORM

Wasps, Ants, Bees

ANT
BEE
DUN

ANAI
ANAY
APIS*
ATTA*
BIKE
CRAB
COON
COUN
GNAT
GYNE
HIVE
KING
SMUT
STUT
WAPS
WASP
WOPS

DRONE
EMMET
KARBI
KELEP
MASON

MAXIM
MIDGE
MINIM
NURSE
QUEEN
SAUBA
SLAVE
SPHEX
STOUT
VESPA*
WAPSE
WHAMP
WOPSE

AMAZON
APIDAE*
APINAE*
BEMBEX*
BEMBIX*
BOMBUS*
BOMBYX*
BUMBEE
BUMBLE
BUMMIE
CARDER
DAUBER
DIGGER

DINGAR
DRIVER
DRONEL
DRONER
DRONET
ECITON*
HORNET
LASIUS*
NASUTE
NEUTER
PONERA*
REDANT
TERMES*
TIPHIA*
VESPID
WORKER

ANDRENA
ANTLING
ANTLION
APOIDAE*
ARMYANT
BULLDOG
BUMBLER
BUMMLER
CYNIPID
DEBORAH

DESERET
EMMETTE
ERGATES
EUMENES*
EUMENID
FORAGER
FORMICA*
FORMICE
KOOTCHA
MASARID
MELISSA
MUDWASP
MUTILLA
PISMIRE
REPLETE
TERMITE
TRIGONA*
VESPINA

ACULEATA
ANGELITO
HONEYBEE
SANDWASP
SAUBAANT
WAXMAKER
WHITEANT

Other Insects

VEI
VERI
CADEW
CADIS
SEDGE
TAINT
CADDIS

CINURA*
DOBSON
DRAGON
PSOCID
SHINER
CADDICE

CINURAN*
CODWORM
LEPISMA*
PSOCINE
TERMITE
CHILOPOD

DIPLOPOD
FIREBRAT
LACEWING
MILLEPED
MYRIAPOD
PAUROPOD

LOW (MARINE) LIFE, WORMS & LARVAE

ERI
ESS
LOA
MAD

BOLL
BOUD
ERIA
GILL
GRUB
LURG
MAUK
MAWK
NAID
TURK
WORM

AMEBA
APODA
ARTER
BORER
CORAL
ERUCA
FLUKE
HYDRA
LARVA
LEECH
MATHE
MONAD
POLYP
REDIA
SALPA
TINEA
VELUM

AMOEBA
ANOPLA
APODAN
CADDIS
CRANIA
ENOPLA
EPHYRA
EUNICE
FUNGIA
GENTIL
GENTLE
HOPPER
LEPTUS
LOBOSA
LOOPER
MAGGOT
MEDUSA
NEREIS
PALOLO
PEDATA
PLAICE
PLOIMA
SEAFAN
SYLLID
TEREDO
TORCEL
TUSSAH
TUSSEH
TUSSER
WABBLE
WEEVIL
WORMIL

ACALEPH
ACTINIA

AMEBULA
ANNELID
ASCARID
ASCARIS
BRYOZOA
CADELLE
CARBORA
CILIATA
CRINOID
DISCINA
ENOPLAN
EUNICID
FILARIA
FLYBLOW
GORDIUS
LINGULA
LIPOPOD
OCULINA
PINWORM
PLANULA
PLUTEUS
PORPITA
PROTIST
ROTIFER
SABELLA
SAGITTA
SANGSUE
SEAMOSS
SERPULA
STENTOR
SUNSTAR
TAGTAIL
TREPANG
TUSSORE
VELELLA

VESTLET

ACALEPHE
ANNELIDA
ANNELOID
ANNULATA
ANNULATE
BDELLOID
CERCARIA
CLEPSINE
COMATULA
CURCULIO
GORGONIA
HELIOZOA
HELMINTH
INFUSORY
NEMATODA
NEMATODE
NEMATOID
ORBULINA
PHORONIS
PROTISTA
RETEPORA
RETEPORE
ROTIFERA
SABELLID
SEAMOUSE
SHIPWORM
STARFISH
SUCTORIA
TORNARIA
TUBEWORM
TUBICOLA
TUBIPORA
TUBIPORE

MOLLUSKS

MYA
TUN

CLAM
CONE
LEDA
LIMA
NAID
PIPI
PUPA
QUIN
SLUG

SPAT
UMBO
UNIO

AWABI
BULLA
CHAMA
CHANK
COHOG
CONCH
CONUS
COPIS

COWRY
DORIS
DRILL
HARPA
HELIX
JELLY
LIMAX
MITRA
MUREX
NACRE
NAIAD
OLIVA

ORMER
PEARL
PHYSA
PINNA
POLYP
POULP
QUARL
SHELL
SNAIL
SQUID
SQUIN
THAIS

TROCA
TURBO
UHLLO
VARIX
VASUM
VENUS
WHELK
WHORL

AEOLID
AEOLIS
ANOMIA
BYSSUS
CARVEL
CASSIS
CERION
CHITON
CLIONE
COCKLE
CONKER
COTUIT
COWRIE
DODMAN
DOLIUM
ELYSIA
GWEDUC
HUITRE
HYALEA
JINGLE
LIMPET
LIMPIN
MACTRA
MUCKET
MOUGAT
MOUKET
MUSCLE
MUSSEL
NATICA
NUCULA
OYSTER
PALOUR
PECTEN
PHOLAS
POULPE
PURPLE
PYRULA
QUAHOG
STROMB
TEREDO
TETHYS
TRITON
UMBONE
VOLUTA
VOLUTE
WINKLE

ABALONE
ASTARTE
AURELIA
BIVALVE
BLUBBER
CALAMAR
COQUINA
DECAPOD
ETHERIA
FLIDDER
GEODUCK
GLAUCUS
GOEDUCK
INKFISH
LIMNAEA
MEDUSAN
MYTILID
MYTILUS
NUCULID
OCTOPUS
OOTHECA
PANDORA
POLYPOD
POLYPUS
PURPURA
QUAHAUG
QUOHAUG
RISSOID
SCALLOP
SCUTTLE
SCYLLAE
SEPIOID
SERPULA
SHARPER
SLOBBER
SPIRULA
SPONDYL
SUNFISH
TELLINA
TEREBRA
TOHEROA
TOXIFER
TROCHID
TROCHUS
UNIONID
VALVATA
VARICES
VELIGER
VERTIGO
VITRINA

APLYSIAS
ARKSHELL
BULLNOSE
CALAMARY
CASSIDID
DITREMID
DEERHORN
DOGWHELK
EARSHELL
EARSNAIL
GEOPHILA
JANTHINA
MELANIAN
NAUTILUS
NERETINA
OPERCULA
SOLARIUM
STROBILA
STROMBUS
TOPSHELL
UNIVALVE
VELUTINA
VERMETID
VERMETUS

PLANTS

Flowers

BIK
GOB
GUL
LIN
LIS
LYS
MAW
MAY
MEU
MEW
MUM
NIL
PHU
PUA
RUE
SAK
SAN
SEG

ALOE
ANIL
ASSI
ATES
ATIS
ATTA
BELA
BETA
BIKH
BISH
BIXA
BLOB
BOLT
BUDA
CARL
CHES
DISA
FAAM
FLAG
FLAX
FLIX
FUJI
GEUM
GLAD
HAGI
HEMP
HOCK
HOYA
IMBY
INGA
IRID
IRIS
IXIA
KIKU
LILY
LISS
LOTE
LUCE
LUCY
MOXA
NAMA
PINK
PINY
POKE
POOA
POSY
PRIM
RINE
ROSA
ROSE
RUTA
SAMH
SANA
SANG
SARA
SEGG
SERI
SNOW
SUNN
ULEX
WABE
WABI
WELD
WHIN
WINK
WOAD
YAGE
YAJE
YARR
YUCA

ABACA
ABAKA
ABAMA
AGATI
AGAVE
ALTEA
AMOLE
ANIBA
ANILA
ASPIC
ASTER
ATEES
AVENS
BADAN
BEHEN
BESOM
BHANG
BLOBS
BLUET
BOCCA
BOOTS
BRIDE
BUCKY
BUGLE
CAJUN
CALLA
CAMAS
CAMPE
CARDO
CARLE

CASSY
CATHA
CEBIL
CHEIR
CHENA
CRAIN
CRAZY
CROCI
CUMAY
CUMBU
DAFFY
DAGGA
DAISY
DALEA
DATIL
DILLY
DRYAS
DWALE
ERICA
FAHAM
FURZE
GANJA
GAURA
GILIA
GILLY
GLAUX
GORSE
GOWAN
GUACO
HELIO
HENNA
HIPPO
HOLLY

HOSTA
HUBAM
HULDI
ILIMA
INULA
IREOS
IZOTA
JOWAR
JUVIA
KEIRI
KEITA
KOALI
KUSUM
LAYIA
LEDUM
LILAC
LINUM
LOTOS
LOTUS
LUPIS
MACAN
MALVA
MENDY
MESEM
MILLA
MILLY
MURGA
MURVA
NANCY
ORACH
ORPIN
ORYZA
OXEYE

OXLIP
PANSY
PEONY
PHLOX
PINEY
POCAN
POOAH
POPPY
PROSE
RUBIA
SARSA
SCOKE
SEDGE
SEDUM
SISAL
SIZAL
SOTOL
SULLA
TENAI
TUCKY
TULIP
VANDA
VINCA
VIOLA
WOCAS
WOKAS
YUCCA
YULAN

ADONIS
ALSIKE
ALTHEA
ANILLA

CASSIA
CLOVER
COLEUS
COLIMA
CORNUS
COSMOS
CROCUS
DAHLIA
FUNKIA
IBERIS
INDIGO
KISSME
LUPINE
LYCIUM
MADDER
MALLEE
MALLOW
MIMOSA
NALITA
ORCHID
POMPOM
PRIVET
RESEDA
SMILAX
SORREL
SPIREA
STOCKS
TEASEL
THRIFT
VIOLET
ZINNIA

ACONITE

ALTHAEA
ANEMONE
BEGONIA
BOXWOOD
CAMPION
COWSLIP
COXCOMB
DEWDROP
DOGBANE
FLYTRAP
FREEZIA
FUCHSIA
GENTIAN
GERBERA
HEATHER
HEMLOCK
HENBANE
HONESTY
IPOMOEA
JASMINE
JONQUIL
JUNIPER
LOBELIA
PAPAVER
PETUNIA
PRIMULA
RAMBLER
SOLANUM
SPIRAEA
SYRINGA
THISTLE
VERBENA

Trees and Shrubs

* Noted for Fruit, Sap, Useful Bark

IE
KI
TI

AAL
ACH
AGA
AIK
AKE
AMA
APA
ARN
ASH
ASP
ATA
AVE*
AWA*
BAY
BEL*
BEX*
BOX
BUR
CHE*
CYP
DAO*

DAR
DOM
DUM
EBO
ELB*
ELM
FEG
FIR
GAB*
GUM*
HAU
HAW*
HOP*
IBA*
IFE
IVA
JAK*
KAT*
KIO*
KOA
KOU
LIM
NIM
NYM
OAK

SAJ
SAL
TAY
TEA*
TIL*
TOA
TUA
TUI
TUN
UGH
ULE
YEW

ACER
ACLE
AKEE
AKIA
ALEM*
AMLA
AMLI
AMRA
ANAM
ANDA
ARAK*
ARAR

ASAK
ATAP*
ATLE
AULA
AULU*
AUSU*
AUTE*
AUZU*
BAGO
BAKU*
BANG
BARU
BIJA
BIRK
BITI
BITO
BOBO
BOGO
BOLA
BRAB
BREA
BROM
BURI
BURR
CADE*

CAJU*
CEBA
CHAA*
CHAW*
CHIA*
CHIL
CHIR
COCA*
COCO*
COLA*
COPA
CORK*
CUCA*
CUYA
DALI
DHAK
DILO
DITA
DOON*
DOUM*
DUKU*
EBOE
EBON
EJOO*
GAUB

GOAI
GUAO
HALA
HINO*
HOLM
HULE
HURA
ICHO*
IEIE
IFIL
ILEX*
IPIL
IROK
ITEA
JARA
JHOW*
JUTE*
KAAT*
KAIL
KAIO*
KAKI*
KARI*
KARO
KHAT*
KIKI*
KINO*
KIRI
KOKO*
KOPI
KOZO*
LAMA
LIAR
LIND
LING
LINN
MABA
MABI*
MAJO*
MAKO
MIRO
MOJO
MORA
MYXA*
NABK
NABO
NAGA
NAIO*
NEEM*
NIUG*
NIPA*
NUBK
ODUM*
OHIA
OLER
PALM
PAUM
PELU
PILI*
PINE
PINO
PIXY
POON
PUKA
PUNA
RATA*
RHUS
RIMU
ROKA*
SADR
SAGO*
SAIN
SALE
SAUF
SAUL
SHEA*
SHOQ
SIDA
SIPO
SOLA
SUGI
SUNT
SUPA*
TALA
TAPA
TARA
TAWA
TCHA*
TCHE*
TEAK
TEEL*
TEIL
THEA*
TITI*
TOOA
TOON
TORO
TORU
TSIA*
TULU
TUNG
TUNO*
TUNU*
TUTU*
TUUI
ULME
ULMO
UPAS*
VERA
WHAU
YATE
YAYA*

AALLI
ABELE
ABETO
ABIES
ABILO
ABURA
ACANA
ACAPU
ACOMA*
ADJAB*
AEGLE*
AFARA
AGLET*
AGOHO
AGOJO
AJARI
ALAMO
ALANI
ALDER
ALGUM
ALISO
ALLER
ALMON
ALMUG
ALNUS
ALPIN
AMAGA
AMAPA
AMATE
AMBAY
ANABO
ANANA
ANATO*
ANJAN
ANONA*
ARACA
ARECA
ARENG
ARJAN
ARTAR
ARUSA*
ASANA
ASOKA
ASPEN
ASSAI
ATTAP
BABUL
BACAO
BAHAN
BALAO
BALAU
BALSA
BALZA
BANAK
BARIA
BAROI
BATIS
BAYOK
BEALA
BELAH
BELAR
BETIS
BIABO
BILLA
BIRCH
BIRMA
BOGUM*
BOKOM
BOLDO*
BOLDU*
BONGA*
BONGO
BOREE
BUBBY*
BULAK*
BUMBO*
BUNYA
BURAO
BUXUS
CACAO*
CAJOU
CAOBA
CAROB
CEDAR
CEIBE*
CEIBO
CHICO
CLOVE*
COCOS
COOBA
COUMA*
COYOL
CURUA
CYPRE
DADAP
DALLI
DANLI
DAROO
DATIL
DHAVA*
DIRCA
DOMBA
DRAGO
DUALI
DURIO*
EBANO
EBONY
ELDER
FAGUS
GARAD*
GENIP*
GIDIA
GINEP*
GINKO*
GOKAN
GOUMI*
GUAVA*
GUIJO
HAKEA
HAZEL*
HEOAK
HEVEA*
HINAU*
HOWEA
ICACO*
ICICA
INAJA
IROKO
IXORA
JAGUA
JIQUE
JIQUI
JOCUM
JUNCO
KAPOR*
KAPUR*
KARRI*
KAURI
KAURY*
KEENA*
KHAIR*
KHAYA
KIAKI
KIKAR*
KOKAN
KOKIO
KONGU
LANSA*
LARCH
LARIX
LAWAN
LEHUA
LICCA
LICHI*
LIGAS*
LINGO
LITHI
MABEE
MAHOE
MAHUA*
MAHWA*
MAIRE
MAJOE*
MALOO
MALUS*
MAMET*
MANGI
MANIU
MAPAU
MAPLE
MAPOU
MAQUI
MARIA
MATAI
MATSU
MATTI*
MELIA
MESUA*
MUDAR
MULGA
MYALL
NABAX
NARAS*
NARRA
NEBUK
NIEPA
NIKAU
NIOTA
NJAVE*
NOGAL*
NONDA*
NURSE
NYSSA*
OADAL
OCHNA
OCOTE*
ODOOM
OSIER
PACAY*
PADUS*
PALAS
PALMA
PAVIA

PECAN*
PENDA
PICEA
PINON*
PIPAL*
PIPUL*
POLAK
POOLI
POONA
PULAS
PYRUS*
QUINA*
QUIRA
RAFIA
RATAN
RAULI
RETEM*
RHAMN
ROBLE
ROBUR
ROHAN*
ROHUN*
ROWAN*
ROWEN
RUBUS*
SABAL
SALAL*
SALIX
SAMAN

SAPIN
SASSY
SAVIN*
SCRAG
SEESU
SERON
SHOLA
SIMAL
SIRIS
SISSU
SORVA*
SPRUG
SUMAC
TABOG
TAPPA
TARFA
TAXUS
TECUM
TENIO
TERAP
THIEF
THUJA*
TIKUR*
TILIA
TIMBO
TINGI*
TOONA
TOWAI

TOYON
TREMA*
TSUGA
TUART
TUCUM
ULMUS
UMIRI
UNAMO
UNONA*
URENA*
URUCU*
UVITO
VACOA
VEREK
VITEX
WAHOO
WAMPI*
WICKY
WILGA
WITCH
WITHY
XYLIA
YACAL
YACCA
YAGUA
YARAI
YEARA
YEDDO

YOCCO*
ZAMAN
ZANTE
ZILLA*
ZORRO

ACACIA
ACAJOU*
ALMOND*
ANILAO
BALSAM
BANYAN
BOMBAX*
BRAZIL*
CACHOU*
CASHEW*
CASHIO*
CODLIN*
GEMUTI
GINGKO*
GOMUTI
GRIGRI*
GRUGRU
LAUREL
LICHEE*
LINDEN
LITCHI*
MISTLE

NUTMEG*
POPLAR
RATTAN
TUPELO*
WALNUT*
WILLOW

ARBUTUS
AVOCADO*
CASCARA*
CATECHU
COCONUT*
CONIFER
DOGWOOD
HICKORY
LINWOOD
PIASAVA
PIMENTO*
PLATANE
QUASSIA*
QUERCUS
REDWOOD
SANDBOX
SEQUOIA
SOLANUM*
TAMARIX
TARWOOD
TURTOSA

Cacti, Mosses, Fungi

BLEO
BUNT
CEPE
FERN
MOLD
MOSS
MYXO
PUFF
PULU
RUST
SMUT
WEKI
BANGA
BRAKE

BRYUM
CACTI
CYCAS
DUGAL
EKAHA
ERGOT
FILIX
FOMES
FUNGO
HYPHO
IRPEX
MEESE
MNIUM
MOREL

MORIL
MOULD
MUCOR
MUSCI
NARDU
NOPAL
PHOMA
PITAU
PONGA
PONGO
PONJA
PORIA
TODEA
ULUHI

UREDO
USNEA
VALSA
VERPA
WHEKI
YEAST
AGARIC
AMADOU
ARCHIL
CAEOMA
FUMAGO
LICHEN
MILDEW

NARDOO
ZYTHIA
AMANITA
BLEWITS
BOLETUS
CARDONA
PARELLA
PARELLE
STEREUM
STINKER
TORTULA
TRUFFLE
WOODSIA

Edible Fruit and Vegetables, Grains and Herbs

BON
COS
DAL
FEI
FIG
HAW
HIP
HOI
KEY
MUG
NEP
NIP
NUT
OAT

OCA
PEA
RYE
SLA
SOY
TOM
TUR
UBE
UBI
UME
URD
UVE
WOT
YAM

AIPI
AMMI
ANAY
ANET
ANGO
ANIS
ANSU
ANTA
ANZU
ARUM
ARVA
BAGA
BAHO
BALM

BEAN
BEET
BEHN
BENE
BENI
BIGG
BIWA
BOLE
BORO
BOSC
BUNK
BUYO
CALE
CANE

CEPA
CHAT
CHIT
CHOU
CHOW
CIVE
COLE
CORN
COUS
COYO
CRAB
CRAP
CUKE
DATE

DHAL
DILL
DUKE
EDDO
EKER
FABA
FARD
FICO
FIGO
FLAT
FUJI
GABE
GABI
GAGE
GEAN
GITH
GOBO
GUAR
HABA
HEVI
HING
IKMO
JAVA
JOBO
JUCA
KAIL
KALE
KALO
KAVA
KAWA
KERS
KIKI
KING
LEEK
LIMA
LIME
LINT
MAND
MANI
MATE
MEUM
MINT
MOLY
MUSA
NAPE
NEEP
NEPE
NOOP
OCRA
OKRA
OLAX
OLEA
PADI
PAGA
PAHO
PAJO
PALA
PAPA
PASA
PAUN
PAVY
PECO
PEPO
PINA
PITA
PITO
PLUM
POHA
POME
RAGI
RAMS
RAPE
RASP
RIBE
RICE
RIMA
ROME
SABA
SAGE
SEGO
SIRI
SITH
SIUM
SIVE
SKAG
SKEG
SLOE
SNAP
SOIA
SOJA
SORB
SOYA
SPUD
SUJI
TARE
TARO
TEFF
TRUB
TUNA
WORT
YAMP
YAVA
YUCA

ADLAI
ADLAY
AIPIM
AJAVA
AJUGA
AKALA
AKELA
AKPEK
AMINI
ANANA
ANDRE
ANISE
ANJOU
ANNIS
ANONA
APIUM
APPLE
ARARU
ARHAR
ARROZ
ARZAN
ARZUN
AVENA
BADAM
BAHOO
BASIL
BAUNO
BELLE
BENDY
BENNE
BENNI
BENNY
BETEL
BICHY
BIGAS
BOHEA
BREBA
BROMA
BUGLE
CAFFE
CAMAS
CANEL
CARUM
CEDRA
CHAIS
CHARD
CHAYA
CHILE
CHILI
CHINO
CHITS
CHIVE
CHOCO
CHOKO
CHOUX
CIBOL
CICER
CLARY
CLING
COCCO
COCOA
COLZA
COPEI
CRESS
CROUT
CUBEB
CUMIN
CUPAY
DHOLL
DOORA
DRIAS
DUHAT
DURRA
DURUM
EMMER
ERUCA
ERYUM
ETROG
FABES
FARDH
FICUS
GOBBE
GOURD
GRAPE
GUAVA
GUBBO
GUMBO
HAVER
HEDGE
HYSON
INGAN
ISLAY
JAMAN
JAMBO
JAMBU
JAMUN
JAWAR
JINKS
KAFIR
KAMAS
KANGA
KAROU
LEMON
LEXIA
LOOFA
LUFFA
MAIZE
MANGO
MAYES
MEBOS
MELON
METEL
MILLO
MOCHA
MOLKA
MOREL
MORON
MORUS
MUNGO
MYRRH
NAVET
NAVEW
NGAIO
NOGAL
OCHRO
OHELO
OLENA
OLIVE
ONION
OOPAK
OSAGE
OUABE
PADDY
PAGLE
PANGI
PAPAW
PAVIE
PEACH
PEKOE
PHACA
PINDA
PINTO
PISUM
PRUNE
PULSE
PUSSY
QUASH
RADIS
RAGEE
RAGGI
RAGGY
RAMPS
RHOEO
RIBES
RUNCH
RURAL
SABZI
SAIDI
SALAD
SALEB
SALEP
SANAI
SARAH
SCRAB
SHARD
SHIVE
SIEVA
SIRIH
SITAO
SITHE
SOLNE
SPELT
SPRUE
SUJEE
SWEDE
TANIA
TATER
TATIE
TERFA
THYME
TIROR
TOKAY
TONKA
TRIGO
TRUFF
TUGUI
TULSI
VITIS
WHEAT
YAMPA
YERBA
YUCCA

ALLIUM
ARALIA
ATIMON
BANANA
BAOBAB
BARLEY
BATATA
BORAGE
CAMMAS
CARROT
CASABA
CASSIS
CATNIP
CELERY
CEREAL
CHILLI
CHIVES
CITRON

CITRUS
COFFEA
COLANE
COLEUS
CUSHAW
DOUCIN
DURIAN
ENDIVE
ESOPUS
FENNEL
GARLIC
GINGER
GOOBER
HYSSOP
KANARI
LEGUME
LENTIL
LOQUAT
MARRON
MEDLAR
MUSKAT

OOLONG
ORANGE
PAPAYA
PAWPAW
PEANUT
PEPPER
PICKLE
PIPPIN
POMELO
POTATO
RADISH
RAISIN
RENNET
RUSSET
SALVIA
SAVORY
SORREL
SQUASH
TOMATO
TURNIP

APRICOT
AVOCADO
CABBAGE
CARAWAY
CARDOON
CASSABA
CATAWBA
CAYENNE
CHERVIL
CHICORY
COCONUT
COLLARD
CURRANT
GRANATE
HARICOT
KUMQUAT
LETTUCE
MUSTARD
OXHEART
PAPRIKA
PARSLEY

PARSNIP
PIMENTO
POMMELO
POPCORN
POTHERB
PUMPKIN
RAMPION
RHUBARB
RICINUS
ROMAINE
SALSIFY
SCALLOP
SHALLOT
SOLANUM
SOYBEAN
SPINACH
TANGELO
TAPIOCA
TARAGON
WINESAP

Grasses, Vines, Weeds, Other Herbs

AJI
AKA
BEN
BON
BUN
BUR
DOD
ERS
GIT
HAY
HEY
IFE
IVE
IVY
IYO
JIL
KEX
ORE
PIA
POA
RAG
RAY
REA
RIX
SEG
TOD
UDO
URE
WAD
ZEA

AGAR
AIRA
AKRA
ALFA
ALGA
AMIL
ARUM
BENA

BOHO
BOJO
CAPA
CHAY
CHOY
COCO
COIX
CUSH
CUVY
DARI
DESI
DISS
DION
DODD
DOOB
DOUB
DREW
DURA
DURR
FUCI
GERS
GILL
GILO
GOGO
GRIG
GUMI
HEII
HOLA
HOVE
ICHU
IVIN
JILL
JITI
JOAR
JUAR
KASA
KELP
KESH
KODA

KUSA
LASA
LIMU
LOCO
MILO
MOHA
MUNG
MUNJ
NARD
NETI
NITO
NORI
ODAL
OOZE
PILI
POLY
RAIT
RAND
REED
REEK
REIK
REIT
RESH
RHEA
RHIA
RISP
RUSA
RUSH
SASA
SION
TANG
TATH
TUIE
ULVA
ULUA
WAAR

AARON
ABRUS

ABUTA
ACUAN
ADOXA
ADRUE
AGSAM
AKEBI
AKEKI
ALGAE
ALGAL
ANKEE
APIOS
ARDOO
AWINI
BARID
BATAD
BATAK
BRIZA
BROME
BUAZE
CACUR
CAJAN
CALLA
CANNA
CAREX
CAROA
CARUA
CHARA
CHESS
CHUFA
CLITE
CLOTE
COGON
COUCH
CREAT
CUTCH
DASYA
DIOON
DONAX
DRABA

DRAWK
DRIFT
DRINN
DULSE
DURBA
DUTRA
EAVER
FITCH
FUCUS
FUNDI
GALAX
GLAGA
GOOMA
GRAMA
HALFA
HICHU
HIRSE
IVORY
JALAP
JEETE
KAINI
KLOPS
KODRO
KUSHA
KUTCH
LAVER
LEMNA
LIANA
LIANE
LIMON
LOASA
MANNA
MARAM
MATTA

MUNJA
NEELE
NONDO
OLONA
ORYZA
OSHAC
OTATE
PALAY
PANAX
PANIC
PICHI
PILEA
PIPER
PIPES
PLUSH
PYXIE
QUILA
RAMEE
RAMIE
RAUPO
REESK
REREE
REXEN
RHEUM
ROOSA
RUMEX
SABIA
SEAVE
SEDGE
SEGRA
SENNA
SEQUA
SIRKI
SLAKE

SLOKE
SORGO
SPART
SPIRE
SPRAT
SPRET
SPRIT
SPROT
STARR
STIPA
TACCA
TASCO
TAMUS
TANSY
TIBEY
TIMBO
TRAPA
TYPHA
URALI
URARE
URARI
VAREC
VETCH
VICIA
VIGNA
VIJAO
VRAIC
WRACK
XYRID
XYRIS

ACANTH
AGARUM
AMYRIS

AXWORT
BAMBOO
BORAGE
BRYONY
CATKIN
CURARE
CUSCUS
DARNEL
DATURA
FESCUE
LICHEN
NARDUS
QUITCH
REDTOP
TWITCH
URTICA
YARROW

ALFALFA
CATTAIL
ESPARTO
FIGWORT
GINSENG
LUCERNE
MATWEED
OREWEED
RAGWEED
SEATANG
SEAWEED
SORGHUM
TIMOTHY
TOCUSSO
TUSSOCK
VETIVER

Botanical Terms

ARIL
AXIL
CYME
NODE
POME
SPUR

AMENT
BERRY
BLADE
BRACT
CALYX
CLEFT
DRUPE
EROSE
HILUM
LATEX
LOBED
OVATE
OVOID
OVULE
PETAL
PINNA
RAPHE
SEPAL
SINUS

SPIKE
STOMA
UMBEL
WHORL

ADNATE
ANTHER
CARPEL
CORYMB
CYMOSE
HISPID
MIDRIB
NODOSE
NUTLET
PILOSE
PISTIL
POLLEN
RACEME
RACHIS
REPAND
RETUSE
RUGOSE
SAMARA
SECUND
SPATHE
STAMEN

STIGMA
STOLON
TERETE

ATHESIS
BACCATE
CAPSULE
CAUDATE
CILIATE
CLAVATE
CONNATE
CORDATE
COROLLA
CRENATE
CUNEATE
DENTATE
EXOCARP
FALCATE
FOLIATE
GLOBOSE
HABITAT
HASTATE
HYALINE
INCISED
LABIATE
LEAFLET

OBOVATE
OBOVOID
PALMATE
PANICLE
PEDICEL
PELTATE
PETIOLE
PILCATE
PINNATE
PLUMOSE
RADICLE
SEPTATE
SERRATE
SESSILE
SPICATE
SPINOSE
SPINULE
STIPULE
SULCATE
SYNCARP
TERNATE
THYRSUS
VALVATE
VEINLET
VILLOUS
VIRGATE

MINERALS AND STONES

* Indicates gemstones

ICE
JET*
ORE
WAD

ALUM
AUGE
BORT
CLAY
COAL
KNAR
LAVA
LIME
MICA
ONYX*
PACO
ROCK
SALT
SAND
SARD*
SIMA
SODA
TALC
TOPH
TUFA
TUFF
WADD
YESO

AGATE*
AMBER*
ARGIL
ARITE
BOART
BORAX
CHERT
CLINT
CRETA
EARTH
ELVAN
EMERY
FLINT
GESSO
GLASS
LAPIS
NITER
NITRE
OCHER
OCHRE
PRASE*
SHALE
SLATE
SMALT
STEEL
STONE
TABLE
TALUS
TOPHE

TRONA
YESSO

ACMITE
ALBITE
ANNITE
APLITE
AUGITE
BARITE
BASALT
BLENDE
CEMENT
CERUSE
DACITE
DIPYRE
DOMITE
EMERIL
GALENA
GNEISS
GRAVEL
GYPSUM
HELITE
HELVIN
HUMITE
JARCON
JASPER*
KAINIT
KAOLIN
LATITE
MARBLE
MORLOP
ORMULU
PEBBLE
PINITA
PLASMA*
POTASH
POTASS
PYRITE*
PYROPE*
RUBINE
RUTILE
SALITE
SCHIST
SILICA
SINTER
SMIRIS
SPHENE
STRASS

ALTAITE
ALUNITE
AMALGAM
ANATASE
APATITE
ASPHALT
AZURITE
BARYTES
BAUCITE

BAUXITE
BEEKITE
BIOTITE
BITUMEN
BOGIRON
BORNITE
BURMITE*
CALCITE
CALLAIS
CELSIAN
CITEINE*
CRYSTAL
CUPRITE
CYANITE
DANAITE
DESMINE
DIORITE
DRYBONE
EDENITE
EPIDOTE
FAHLERZ
FAHLORE
FELSPAR
GAHNITE
GEDRITE
GLIMMER
GRANITE
HELVINE
HESSITE
ICESPAR
ILVAITE
INYOITE
JADEITE
JARGOON
KAINITE
KAOLINE
KERNITE
KYANITE
LAURITE
MARTITE
ORTHITE
ORTHOSE
PETZIDE
PLASTER
PYRITES
RASPITE
REALGAR
SAHLITE
SENAITE
SYLVITE
THORITE
THULITE
TILEORE
TURGITE
ULEXITE
URALITE
WOLFRAM
WOODTIN

ZEOLITE
ZINCITE
ZOISITE
ZUNYITE

ACHROITE
ADULARIA
AIKINITE
ALLANITE
ANDESINE
ANKERITE
ASBESTOS
AUTUNITE
BORACITE
BRONZITE
BROOKITE
CALAMINE
CHLORITE
CHROMITE
CINNABAR
CORUNDUM
CROCOITE
CRYOLITE
DANALITE
DATOLITE
DIALLAGE
DIASPORE
DIOPSIDE
DOLOMITE
ELECTRUM
ELEOLITE
EMBOLITE
ENARGITE
EPSOMITE
FAYALITE
FELDSPAR
FLUORIDE
GALENITE
GANISTER
GIBBSITE
GOETHITE
GRAPHITE
HEMATITE*
IDOCRASE
ILMENITE
JAROSITE
LAZULITE
LAZURITE
LIMONITE
MEIONITE
MESITINE
MIMETITE
NOSELITE
OBSIDIAN*
ORPIMENT
ORANGITE
PERTHITE
PICOTITE

PISANITE	ROSELITE*	SMALTINE	SUNSTONE*
PLUMBAGO	SANIDINE	SMALTITE	TENORITE
PREHNITE	SARDONYX*	STANNITE	TITANITE
PYROXENE	SELENITE	STEATITE	TROILITE
ROCKMILK	SERICITE	STIBNITE	YENTNITE
ROCKSALT	SIDERITE	STILBITE	WURTZITE

Precious Stones

LASK	RUBIN	ANTHRAX	PRASINE
OPAL	VAJRA	BRIOLET	RUBELET
RUBY		CATSEYE	SMARAGD
	ADAMAS	DIAMOND	
BAHIA	LASQUE	EMERALD	HYACINTH
DORJE	LIGURE	JACINTH	SAPPHIRE
LASKE	TABLET		

Semiprecious Stones

JADE	QUARTZ	KUNZITE	ESSONITE
	SPINEL	OLIVINE	FIREOPAL
BERYL	ZIRCON	OVALINE	GIRASOLE
MACLE		PERIDOT	MELANITE
TOPAZ	AXINITE	TURCOIS	NEPHRITE
	EUCLASE	TURKOIS	SODALITE
GARNET	GIRASOL		TURQUOIS
IOLITE	HYALITE	AMETHYST	

Famous Diamonds

HOPE	HORNBY	REGENT	TENNANT
PITT	KOLLUR	CHAPADA	TIFFANY
MATAN	NASSAK	DEBEERS	CULLINAN
DUDLEY	ORLOFF	EUGENIE	KOHINOOR
DUTOIT	PIGOTT	STEWART	

Birthstones

ONYX	July	AMETHYST	Feb.
OPAL	Oct.	ROZIRCON	Oct.
RUBY	July, Dec.	SAPPHIRE	April, Sept.
AGATE	May, June	SARDONYX	Aug.
BERYL	Oct.	CARNELIAN	Aug.
PEARL	June	MOONSTONE	June
TOPAZ	Nov.	TURQUOISE	July, Dec.
GARNET	Jan.	BLOODSTONE	March
JASPER	March	AQUAMARINE	March, Oct.
ZIRCON	Dec.	TOURMALINE	Oct.
DIAMOND	April	CHRYSOLITE	Sept.
EMERALD	May, June	ALEXANDRITE	June
PERIDOT	Aug.		

Alloys

LAY	STEEL	BRONZE	TOMBAC	SPELTER
PIG	TERNE	GARBLE	AMALGAM	TOMBACK
AICH	VIDRY	LATTEN	BABBITT	TUTENAG
ASEM	ALBATA	NIELLO	BIDDERY	CARBOLOY
NIEL	ALNICO	OROIDE	DURIRON	ELECTRUM
TULA	ALUMEL	PEWTER	ELINVAR	HYPERNIK
BIDRI	BIDERY	SOLDER	INCONEL	NICHROME
BRASS	BIDREE	TAMBAC	MIXTURE	PACKTONG
INVAR	BILLON	TEMPER	PAKTONG	STELLITE

PREFIXES AND SUFFIXES

PREFIXES

AB	away from
AC	= AD
AD	to(ward)
AF	= AD
AG	= AD
AL	= AD
AP	= AD
BE	all around; excessively
BI	two, twice
CO	joint action
DE	off; down; wholly
DI	two
EC	= EX
EO	early
EU	well
EX	out (of)
FY	become, make
NE	= NEO
OB	to(ward)
OO	egg
PY	pus
UN	not; back
ZO	animal
ANA	up; back; again
APO	from, away
AZO	nitrogen
BIN	twice
BIO	life
BIS	twice
BLE	able
CIS	on this side
COM	with; jointly
DIA	through; apart
DIF	= DIS
DIS	not; apart
DYS	poor condition
EPI	on; over; among
EXO	outside
GEO	earth
GYN	female
HEM	blood
MAC	son of
MAL	bad
MIS	bad; wrong; not
MYO	muscle
NEO	new
NON	not
ORO	mountain
OTO	ear
OVI	egg
OXA	oxygen
OXY	oxygen; sharp
PED	feet
PRE	before
PYO	pus
PYR	fire; heat
SYN	with; at the same time

TOX	poisonous
TRI	three
URO	tail
UNI	one
ACRO	high
ENDO	within
EQUI	equal
ESCE	verb ending
GAMO	union
GONO	sex organs
GYNO	female
HAEM	blood
HEMI	half
HEMO	blood
HEXA	six
HOLO	whole
HOMO	same
HYLO	wood
IDEO	re ideas
IDIO	personal
INDO	Indian
KATA	down; away
KILO	thousand
LEVO	left
LIPO	fat
LITE	mineral; fossil
LOCO	re a place
LOGO	word; speech
LUNI	moon
MEGA	great
MESO	middle
META	along; after
MISO	hate
MONO	single
MUCO	mucous
MYCO	fungus
MYEL	marrow; spine
NASO	nose
NOSO	disease
NUCI	nut
NUDI	bare
NYCT	night
OCTA	eight
OCTO	eight
OLEO	oil
OLIG	few
OMNI	all
PARA	near; beyond; abnormal
PARI	equal
PEDI	foot
PEDO	children
PHEN	benzene deriv.
PHON	sound; voice
PILI	hair
POLY	much
PRAE	before
PYRO	fire; heat

RENI	kidney
RHEO	flow
RHIN	nose
SEMI	half
SEPT	seven
SINO	Chinese
SOLI	alone
TELE	far off
THEO	of God, gods
TOPO	place
TOXO	poisonous
VINI	wine
XENO	foreign
XERO	wax
XYLO	wood
ZYGO	yoke; pair
ZYMO	fermentation

ACETO	acid
ADENO	gland
AMPHI	around
AMYLO	starch
ANDRO	man
ANEMO	wind
ANGIO	vessel
ANGLO	English
ANISO	unequal
ANTHO	flower
ARCHI	chief
ASTRO	star
AVANT	before
BRADY	slow
BREVI	short
CARDI	heart
CARPO	fruit
CENTI	1/100
CHIRO	hand
CHOLO	gall; bile
CHROM	color
CHRON	time
CIRRO	curl
COENO	recent
COSTO	rib
CYANO	blue
DENTI	tooth
DERMO	skin
DICHO	in 2 parts
ETHNO	race; people
GALLO	Gallic
GRECO	Greek
HAEMO	blood
HAGIO	sacred
HAPLO	single
HECTO	hundred
HELIO	sun
HEPTA	seven
HIERO	sacred
HISTO	tissue
HOMEO	similar
HYALO	glass
HYDRO	water
HYGRO	water
HYPER	over; beyond

ICONO	image-like
INFRA	below
INTRA	within
INTRO	within
JUXTA	near; together
KARYO	cell nucleus
LACTO	milk
LEPTO	slender
LIGNO	wood
LITHO	stones
LUTEO	yellow
MACRO	large
MAGNI	large
MANCY	divination
MATRI	mother
METRO	measure
MEZZO	intermediate
MICRO	very small
MILLI	1/1000
MORPH	form
MULTI	many
MYRIA	many
MYTHO	myth
NEPHO	cloud
NEPHR	kidney
NEURO	nerve
NOCTI	night
OCULO	eye
ODONT	tooth
OLIGO	few
ORTHO	straight
OSTEO	bone
PAEDO	child
PALEO	remote
PANTO	all
PATHO	disease
PATHY	suffering
PATRI	father
PENNI	feather
PETRO	stone
PHENO	benzene deriv.
PHILO	loving
PHONO	sound
PHREN	diaphragm
PHYCO	seaweed
PHYLL	leaf
PHYLO	tribe
PHYTO	plant
PICRO	bitter
PISCI	fish
PLANI	plane
PLATY	broad
PLURI	several
PROTO	first
PTERO	wing; feather
RECTI	straight
RETRO	behind
RHIZO	root
RHODO	rose; red
RUSSO	Russian
SACRO	holy
SAPRO	rotten
SARCO	flesh

SAURO	lizard
SPIRO	breath; spiral
SPORO	seed
STENO	little
TAUTO	same
TETRA	four
TRANS	across
TURBO	turbine-driven
TURCO	Turkish
UTERO	womb
VERMI	worm
ACTINO	of rays
ANTERO	front
ARTHRO	joint
AUSTRO	Austrian
CENTRI	central
CERATO	horn; cornea
CHALCO	copper; brass
CHRONO	time
CRYPTO	hidden
DENDRO	tree
DEXTRO	right
DODECA	twelve
ENTERO	intestine
FRANCO	French
HELICO	spiral
HETERO	other
KERATO	horn, horny
KINETO	moving
MEGALO	very large
MELANO	black
NEMATO	thread
OBTUSI	blunt
PHRENO	diaphragm
PHYSIO	nature
PLEURO	side
PNEUMO	lung
PRETER	beyond
PSEUDO	false
PSYCHO	of mind
RRHAGE	abnormal flow
SANGUI	blood
SCHIZO	split
SCLERO	hard
SESQUI	1½
SOMATO	body
SPHENO	wedge-shaped
SPLENO	spleen
STETHO	chest
SUBTER	underneath
TRICHO	hair
TROPHO	nutrition
VARICO	enlarged vein
VENTRO	belly
VESICO	bladder
XANTHO	yellow

SUFFIXES

AC	relating to
AL	like
CY	quality
ED	past tense
ER	doer
IC	adjective
LY	like
MO	numerical
OL	chem. derivative
RY	= ERY
TH	numerical
TY	quality; tens
YL	radical form
ACY	quality
ANE	relating to
ARD	one who is too
ARY	relating to
DOM	domain
ENT	adj. ending
ERY	condition; state
EST	superlative
ETH	numerical
FIC	adj. ending
FID	divided
GEN	producing agent
GON	geom. figures
IAL	adj. ending
ICS	activity area
IDE	chem. compound
INE	fem. noun
ING	noun forming
ISE	cause to be
ISH	belonging to
ISM	doctrine
IST	believer
ITE	native; product; believer; fossil; salt; rock
ITY	condition
IVE	tendency
IZE	treat; act on
OCK	diminutive
OID	resembling
OLE	chem. compound
OMA	tumor
OPY	eye defect
ORY	pert. to
OSE	full of
OUS	full of; like
RIC	district
ULE	diminutive
URE	act, result of
ZOA	animal
ACEA	of the nature
ASIS	state; like
ATIC	of the kind
CENE	recent; new
CIDE	murder
CRAT	ruler

CRYO	cold, icy
CULE	diminutive
DERM	skin
EMIA	blood
ENCE	quality
FUGE	flight
GAMY	union
GENY	origin
GLOT	tongued
GONY	origin
GYNY	female
IBLE	able
ICAL	adj. ending
IOUS	adj. ending
ITIS	inflammation
LITH	stone
LOGY	science
MENT	action
MONY	state
NOMY	study
ODUS	toothed
OPIA	eye defect
OSIS	process
OTIC	of ear
PEDE	feet
PHYL	leaf
PODA	feet
PODE	foot
RHEA	discharge
SAUR	lizard
SION	action; result
STAT	stationary
STER	occupation
TEEN	plus ten
TION	action; result
TOMY	cutting
TRIX	fem. agent
TUDE	noun ending
URET	chem. ending
URGY	working of
URIA	urine disease
VASO	blood vessel
VORE	eating
XION	action; result
AEMIA	blood
ALGIA	pain
ARCHY	ruling
ATION	result of being
ATIVE	relative to
ATORY	produced by
CIDAL	to kill
COELE	body cavity
CRACY	rule
EDRAL	faced
ESQUE	like
GENIC	of origin
HEMIA	blood
IASIS	morbid state
IATRY	treatment
ICIAN	practitioner
ILITY	noun ending

ISTIC	adj. ending
ITION	action; result
LATRY	worship
LETTE	diminutive
LYSIS	disintegration
METRY	measurement
OIDEA	class name
OLOGY	science
OPSIS	sight
OSITY	noun ending
PHAGE	eating
PHAGY	eating
PHANE	resembling
PHANY	appearance
PHASY	speech
PHILE	loving
PHOBE	fear
PHORE	bearer
PHYTE	plant
PLAST	structure
PLASY	formation
PLEGY	paralysis
PLOID	number form
POLIS	city
RRHEA	discharge
SCOPY	science; viewing
SOPHY	knowledge
TIOUS	adj. ending
TROPE	turning
TROPY	turning
ULENT	full of
ULOSE	marked by
ULOUS	full of
AGOGUE	leading
BILITY	ability
CARPAL	fruit
CHROIC	color
CRATIC	ruling
FEROUS	bearing; yielding
GAMOUS	uniting
GRAPHY	science
GYNOUS	female
ISTICS	science of
LITHIC	stone
MYCETE	fungus
ODYNIA	pain
OLATRY	worship of
PAROUS	giving birth
PATHIC	disease; feeling
PHAGIA	eating
PHASIA	speech
PHILIA	loving
PHOBIA	fear
PHONIA	voice
PLASIA	formation
PLEGIA	paralysis
PODIUM	leg
PODOUS	feet
THERMY	heat
VOROUS	eating

PRESIDENTIAL INFORMATION

	Name	Age*	Party	Vice-Pres.
1	**WASHINGTON,** George	57		**ADAMS**
2	**ADAMS,** John	61	Fed.	**JEFFERSON**
3	**JEFFERSON,** Thomas	57	Dem.–Rep.	**BURR, CLINTON**
4	**MADISON,** James	57	Dem.–Rep.	**CLINTON, GERRY**
5	**MONROE,** James	58	Dem.–Rep.	**TOMPKINS**
6	**ADAMS,** John Quincy	57	Ind.	**CALHOUN**
7	**JACKSON,** Andrew	61	Dem.–Rep.	**CALHOUN, VAN BUREN**
8	**VAN BUREN,** Martin	54	Dem.–Rep.	**JOHNSON**
9	**HARRISON,** William Henry	68	Whig	**TYLER**
10	**TYLER,** John	51	Whig	
11	**POLK,** James Knox	49	Dem.	**DALLAS**
12	**TAYLOR,** Zachary	64	Whig	**FILLMORE**
13	**FILLMORE,** Millard	50	Whig	
14	**PIERCE,** Franklin	48	Dem.	**KING**
15	**BUCHANAN,** James	65	Dem.	**BRECKENRID**
16	**LINCOLN,** Abraham	52	Rep.	**HAMLIN, JOHNSON**
17	**JOHNSON,** Andrew	56	Dem.	
18	**GRANT,** Ulysses Simpson	46	Rep.	**COLFAX, WILSON**
19	**HAYES,** Rutherford Birchard	54	Rep.	**WHEELER**
20	**GARFIELD,** James Abram	49	Rep.	**ARTHUR**
21	**ARTHUR,** Chester Alan	50	Rep.	
22	**CLEVELAND,** Stephen Grover	47	Dem.	**HENDRICKS**
23	**HARRISON,** Benjamin	55	Rep.	**MORTON**
24	**CLEVELAND,** Stephen Grover	55	Dem.	**STEVENSON**
25	**MC KINLEY,** William	54	Rep.	**HOBART, ROOSEVELT**
26	**ROOSEVELT,** Theodore	42	Rep.	**FAIRBANKS**
27	**TAFT,** William Howard	51	Rep.	**SHERMAN**
28	**WILSON,** Thomas Woodrow	56	Dem.	**MARSHALL**
29	**HARDING,** Warren Gamaliel	55	Rep.	**COOLIDGE**
30	**COOLIDGE,** John Calvin	51	Rep.	**DAWES**
31	**HOOVER,** Herbert Clark	54	Rep.	**CURTIS**
32	**ROOSEVELT,** Franklin Delano	51	Dem.	**GARNER, WAL-LACE, TRUMAN**
33	**TRUMAN,** Harry S	60	Dem.	**BARKLEY**
34	**EISENHOWER,** Dwight David	62	Rep.	**NIXON**
35	**KENNEDY,** John Fitzgerald	43	Dem.	**JOHNSON**
36	**JOHNSON,** Lyndon Baines	55	Dem.	**HUMPHREY**

* at inauguration

PRESIDENTIAL INFORMATION

Sec'y of State	Def. Cand.	Winning Slogan
JEFFERSON, RANDOLPH, PICKERING		
PICKERING, MARSHALL	JEFFERSON	Peace and Prosperity
MADISON	BURR, PINCKNEY	
SMITH, MONROE	PINCKNEY, CLINTON	
ADAMS	KING, ADAMS	
CLAY	JACKSON, CLAY, CRAWFORD	
VAN BUREN, LIVINGSTON, MC LANE, FORSYTH	ADAMS, CLAY	Let the People Rule
FORSYTH	HARRISON	Tippecanoe and Tyler Too, Log Cabin and Hard Cider
WEBSTER	VAN BUREN	
WEBSTER, UPSHUR, CALHOUN		
CALHOUN, BUCHANAN	CLAY	The Northwest and the Southwest
BUCHANAN, CLAYTON	CASS	
CLAYTON, WEBSTER, EVERETT		
MARCY	SCOTT	
MARCY, CASS, BLACK	FREMONT	
BLACK, SEWARD	DOUGLAS, BRECKENRIDGE, BELL, MC CLELLAN	Free Territory for a Free People
SEWARD		
WASHBURNE, FISH	SEYMOUR, GREELEY	Let Us Have Peace
FISH, EVARTS	TILDEN	Waving the Bloody Shirt
EVARTS, BLAINE	HANCOCK	
BLAINE, FRELINGHUYSEN		
FRELINGHUYSEN, BAYARD	BLAINE	No More Seventy-Six
BAYARD, BLAINE, FOSTER	CLEVELAND	
GRESHAM, OLNEY	HARRISON, WEAVER	
OLNEY, SHERMAN, DAY, HAY	BRYAN	The Advance Agent of Prosperity
HAY, ROOT, BACON	PARKER	
BACON, KNOX	BRYAN	
KNOX, BRYAN, LANSING, COLBY	ROOSEVELT, TAFT, HUGHES	Stand Pat; He Kept Us Out of War
HUGHES	COX	Back to Normalcy
HUGHES, KELLOGG	DAVIS, LAFOLLETTE	Coolidge or Chaos
KELLOGG, STIMSON	SMITH	A Chicken in Every Pot and a Car in Every Garage
HULL, STETTINIUS	HOOVER, LANDON, WILLKIE, DEWEY	A New Deal for the Forgotten Man
STETTINIUS, BYRNES, MARSHALL, ACHESON	DEWEY	A Fair Deal
DULLES, HERTER	STEVENSON	Time for a Change
RUSK	NIXON	
RUSK	GOLDWATER	

	Name	Birthplace	Profession
1	**WASHINGTON**	Wakefield, Virginia	Farmer
2	**ADAMS**	Braintree, Massachusetts	Lawyer
3	**JEFFERSON**	Shadwell, Virginia	Farmer
4	**MADISON**	Port Conway, Virginia	Lawyer
5	**MONROE**	Westmoreland County, Virginia	
6	**ADAMS**	Braintree, Massachusetts	
7	**JACKSON**	Waxhaw, South Carolina	Lawyer
8	**VAN BUREN**	Kinderhook, New York	Lawyer
9	**HARRISON**	Berkeley, Virginia	Officer
10	**TYLER**	Greenway, Virginia	Lawyer
11	**POLK**	Mecklenburg County, North Carolina	Lawyer
12	**TAYLOR**	Orange County, Virginia	Officer
13	**FILLMORE**	Cayuga County, New York	Wool carder, lawyer
14	**PIERCE**	Hillsboro, New Hampshire	Lawyer
15	**BUCHANAN**	Mercersburg, Pennsylvania	Lawyer
16	**LINCOLN**	Hardin County, Kentucky	Storekeeper, postmaster, lawyer
17	**JOHNSON**	Raleigh, North Carolina	Tailor
18	**GRANT**	Point Pleasant, Ohio	Lawyer
19	**HAYES**	Delaware, Ohio	Officer
20	**GARFIELD**	Orange, Ohio	Bargeman, teacher
21	**ARTHUR**	Fairfield, Vermont	Teacher
22	**CLEVELAND**	Caldwell, New Jersey	Teacher, lawyer
23	**HARRISON**	North Bend, Ohio	Lawyer
24	**CLEVELAND**	Caldwell, New Jersey	
25	**MC KINLEY**	Niles, Ohio	Lawyer
26	**ROOSEVELT**	New York, New York	Police Head
27	**TAFT**	Cincinnati, Ohio	Lawyer
28	**WILSON**	Staunton, Virginia	Teacher
29	**HARDING**	Corsica, Ohio	Publisher
30	**COOLIDGE**	Plymouth, Vermont	Lawyer
31	**HOOVER**	West Branch, Iowa	Engineer
32	**ROOSEVELT**	Hyde Park, New York	Lawyer
33	**TRUMAN**	Lamar, Missouri	Storekeeper
34	**EISENHOWER**	Denison, Texas	Officer
35	**KENNEDY**	Brookline, Massachusetts	
36	**JOHNSON**	Stonewall, Texas	Teacher

PRESIDENTIAL ASSASSINS

BOOTH, John Wilkes	Lincoln
OSWALD, Lee Harvey [alleged]	Kennedy
GUITEAU, Charles J.	Garfield
CZOLGOSZ, Leon	McKinley

Nickname	Wife's Name
Old Fox	**CUSTIS,** Martha Dandridge
Duke of Braintree	**SMITH,** Abigail
Long Tom, Sage of Monticello	**SKELTON,** Martha Wayles
	TODD, Dorothea (Dolley) Payne
	KORTWRIGHT, Elizabeth
Accidental President	**JOHNSON,** Louisa Catherine
Old Hickory, Sharp Knife	**ROBARDS,** Rachel Donelson
Red Fox, Little Magician	**HOES,** Hannah
Hero of Tippecanoe	**SYMMES,** Anna
	CHRISTIAN, Letitia and **GARDINER,** Julia
Young Hickory	**CHILDRESS,** Sarah
	SMITH, Margaret
	POWERS, Abigail and **MC INTOSH,** Caroline Carmichael
	APPLETON, Jane Means
Old Buck, Ten-cent Jimmy	
Old Abe, Railsplitter	**TODD,** Mary
Sir Veto, King Andy	**MC CARDLE,** Eliza
Silent Man, Old Three-Stars	**DENT,** Julia
Old Eight to Seven, President de facto	**WEBB,** Lucy
Canal Boy, the Preacher	**RUDOLPH,** Lucretia
	HERNDON, Ellen Lewis
Old Veto, Stuffed Prophet	**FOLSOM,** Frances
Little Ben	**SCOTT,** Caroline Lavinia and **DIMMICK,** Mary Scott Lord
Perpetual Candidate	**FOLSOM,** Frances
Stocking-foot Orator	**SAXTON,** Ida
Bull Moose, Rough Rider	**LEE,** Alice Hathaway and **CAROW,** Edith Kermit
	HERRON, Helen
Woody	**AXSON,** Ellen Louise and **GALT,** Edith Bolling
	DE WOLFE, Florence Kling
	GOODHUE, Grace Ann
	HENRY, Lou
New Dealer	**ROOSEVELT,** Anna Eleanor
	WALLACE, Elizabeth (Bess) Virginia
Ike	**DOUD,** Mamie Geneva
	BOUVIER, Jacqueline
	TAYLOR, Claudia (Ladybird) Alta

PORTRAITS ON U. S. CURRENCY

CHASE	$10,000	**FRANKLIN**	$100
GRANT	$50	**HAMILTON**	$10
WILSON	$100,000	**MC KINLEY**	$500
JACKSON	$20	**CLEVELAND**	$1000
LINCOLN	$5	**JEFFERSON**	$2
MADISON	$5000	**WASHINGTON**	$1

PROMINENT PEOPLE

HEADS OF STATE, LEADERS

Roman
NERO
NUMA
OTHO
GALBA
NERVA
TITUS
DECIUS
GALLUS
JULIAN
TRAJAN
HADRIAN
SEVERUS
AUGUSTUS
CALIGULA
CLAUDIUS
COMMODUS
DOMITIAN
PERTINAX
TIBERIUS

English
ANNE
EDWY
JOHN
EDRED
HENRY
JAMES
ALFRED
CANUTE
EDMUND
EDWARD
EGBERT
GEORGE
HAROLD
CHARLES
RICHARD
STEPHEN
WILLIAM
VICTORIA
ETHELRED
ELIZABETH

German
OTTO
EBERT
ALBERT
CONRAD
HITLER
JOSEPH
RUDOLF
FRANCIS
LEOPOLD
LOTHAIR
RUDOLPH
THERESA
CONRADIN
MATTHIAS
FERDINAND
FREDERICK
SIGISMUND
BARBAROSSA
HINDENBURG
MAXIMILIAN

Russian
IVAN
LVOV
PAUL
BASIL
FEDOR
LENIN
PETER
ALEXIS
STALIN
MICHAEL
MOLOTOV
BREZHNEV
BULGANIN
KERENSKY
MALENKOV
NICHOLAS
ALEXANDER
CATHERINE
ELIZABETH
KHRUSHCHEV

French
ODO
COTY
HUGH
HENRY
LOUIS
AURIOL
DOUMER
LEBRUN
PETAIN
PHILIP
THIERS
CHARLES
FRANCIS
DEGAULLE
MACMAHON
POINCARE
DOUMERGUE
MILLERAND

Scandinavian
DAN
ERIC
GORM
INGE
OLAF
JOHAN
OSCAR
SWEYN
BIRGER
CANUTE
HAAKON
HAROLD
MAGNUS
SIGURD
SVERRE
ADOLPHUS
FREDERIK
MARGARET
WALDEMAR
CHRISTIAN

Egyptian
FUAD
NIKI
PEPI
SETI
ABBAS
KHUFU
MENES
NECHO
ZOSER
AHMOSE
APRIES
CHEOPS
HATASU
HOPHRA
KAPHRE
NAGUIB
NASSER
RAMSES
SHISAK
SNEFRU
HARMHAB
OSORKON
PSAMTIK
PTOLEMY
SHESHONK
THUTMOSE

STATESMEN

DAY
FOX
ITO
EDEN
BLUM
CATO
GREY
PEEL
PITT
TITO
BENES
BEVIN
CABOT
HENRY
MARAT
NENNI
NITTI
TISZA
ATTLEE
BRIAND
BUELOW
CAVOUR
CICERO
CURZON
FOUCHE
HORTHY
HUGHES
LYTTON
PELHAM
ASQUITH
BALDWIN
BALFOUR
CALHOUN
CLAYTON
COLBERT
HERRIOT
KELLOGG
KOSSUTH
LANSING
MASARYK
MAZARIN
PULASKI
STANLEY
TROTZKY
WALPOLE
ADENAUER
BISMARCK
CROMWELL
DISRAELI
GAMBETTA
HAMILTON
LITVINOV
MIRABEAU
POTEMKIN
RATHENAU
STANHOPE
CHURCHILL
ROOSEVELT

MILITARY LEADERS

COX
LEE
NEY
ORD
FOCH
GAGE
HAIG
KNOX
PIKE
SAXE
SIMS
ALLEN
BANKS
BRAGG
BUELL
CLARK
DEWEY
DRAKE
LEAHY
MEADE
MILNE
MURAT
PERRY
WOLFE
ARNOLD
CUSTER
HALSEY
HODGES
JOFFRE
MOLTKE
NELSON
PATTON
PICKEN
PUTNAM
RAEDER
ROMMEL
SUMTER
DECATUR
HOUSTON
SHERMAN
TIRPITZ
BLUECHER
BURGOYNE
BURNSIDE
CROCKETT
FARRAGUT
JELLICOE
JOHNSTON
LAWRENCE
MARSHALL
MITCHELL
PERSHING
SCHUYLER
SHERIDAN
STILWELL

LEADERS IN INDUSTRY AND RELIGION

* Indicates Religious Leaders

FOX*
EDDY*
FORD
HUSS*
KNOX*
ASTOR
BOOTH*
DAWES
FIELD
GOULD
GREEN
KRESS
KRUPP
SWIFT
YOUNG*
ABBOTT*
ARMOUR
BECKET*
CALVIN*
COOPER
DUPONT
FILENE
FUGGER
GRAHAM
LAMONT
LASKER
LEHMAN
LUTHER*
MACKAY
MATHER*
MELLON
MORGAN
SCHIFF
STRAUS
SUNDAY*
WESLEY*
WOLSEY*
BEECHER*
BELMONT
EDWARDS*
KNUDSEN
PEABODY
SEABURY*
THYSSEN
TYNDALL*
WARBURG
WHITNEY
ZWINGLI*
GARRISON*
HARKNESS
HARRIMAN
HARTFORD
TALMADGE*
WYCLIFFE*
ROTHSCHILD
ROCKEFELLER

POPES

LEO
JOHN
PAUL
PIUS
CONON
DONUS
FELIX
GAIUS
LANDO
LINUS
PETER
SOTER
URBAN
ADRIAN
AGATHO
ALBERT
FABIAN
JULIUS
LUCIUS
MARCUS
MARTIN
PHILIP
SIXTUS
VICTOR
ANTEROS
CLEMENT
DAMASUS
GREGORY
HYGINUS
MARINUS
PASCHAL
ROMANUS
SERGIUS
STEPHEN
URSINUS
ZOSIMUS
AGAPETUS
ANICETUS
BENEDICT
BONIFACE
CALIXTUS
EUGENIUS
EULALIUS
EUSEBIUS
FORMOSUS
GELASIUS
HILARIUS
HONORIUS
INNOCENT
LIBERIUS
NICHOLAS
NOVATIAN
PELAGIUS
SABINIAN
SIRICIUS
THEODORE
VIGILIUS
VITALIAN

NOBEL PRIZE WINNERS

Peace

IRC
ORR
HULL
KING
MOTT
PIRE
ROOT
ASSER
BAJER
BALCH
DAWES
FRIED
GOBAT
LAMAS
LANGE
PASSY

ADDAMS
ANGELL
BRIAND
BUNCHE
BUTLER
CREMER
DUNANT
MONETA
NANSEN
QUIDDE
UNICEF
WILSON
BUISSON
JOUHAUX
KELLOGG
LUTHULI
PAULING
PEARSON
RENAULT
SUTTNER
BRANTING
DUCOMMUN
MARSHALL
ARNOLDSON
BEERNAERT
BOURGEOIS
HENDERSON
NOELBAKER
OSSIETZKY
ROOSEVELT
SODERBLOM
LAFONTAINE
SCHWEITZER
STRESEMANN
CHAMBERLAIN
HAMMERSKJOLD

Chemistry

HAHN
HOFF
KUHN
TODD
UREY
ADLER
ASTON
BOSCH
CURIE
DEBYE
DIELS
HABER
LIBBY
NATTA
PREGL
SODDY
SYNGE
BAEYER
CALVIN
HARDEN
HEVESY
KARRER
MARTIN
NERNST
PERUTZ
RAMSEY
SANGER
SUMNER
WERNER
BERGIUS
BUCHNER
FISCHER
GIAUQUE
HAWORTH
HODGKIN
KENDREW
MOISSAN
OSTWALD
PAULING
RUZICKA
SEABORG
SEMENOV
STANLEY
WALLACH
WIELAND
WINDAUS
ZIEGLER
GRIGNARD
LANGMUIR
MCMILLAN
MULLIKAN
NORTHROP
RICHARDS
ROBINSON
SABATIER
SVEDBERG
TISELIUS
VIGNEAUD
VIRTANEN
WOODWARD
ARRHENIUS
BUTENANDT
HEYROVSKY
ZSIGMONDY

Medicine

DAM
CORI
DALE
HESS
HILL
KOCH
ROSS
ROUS
BLOCK
BOVET
CAJAL
CHAIN
CRICK
DOISY
GOLGI
HENCH
JACOB
KREBS
KROGH
LOEWI
LWOFF
LYNEN
MINOT
MONIZ
MONOD
OCHOA
TATUM
ADRIAN
BARANY
BEADLE
BEKESY
BORDET
BURNET
CARREL
DOMAGK
ECCLES
ENDERS
FINSEN
FLOREY
GASSER
HUXLEY
KOCHER
KOSSEL
MORGAN
MULLER
MURPHY
PAVLOV
RICHET
WATSON
WELLER
BANTING
BEHRING
EHRLICH
EIJKMAN
FIBIGER
FLEMING
HEYMANS
HODGKIN
HOPKINS
HOUSSAY
HUGGINS
JAUREGG
KENDALL
LAVERAN
LIPMANN
MACLEOD
MEDAWAR
MUELLER
NICOLLE
SPEMANN
THEILER
ROBBINS
WAKSMAN
WARBURG
WHIPPLE
WILKINS
COURNAND
ERLANGER
KORNBERG
MEYERHOF
RICHARDS
THEORELI
EINTHOVEN
FORSSMANN
LEDERBERG
GULLSTRAND
REICHSTEIN

Physics

LEE
BOHR
BORN
HESS
LAUE
RABI
TAMM
WIEN
YANG
BASOV
BLOCH
BOTHE
BRAGG
BRAUN
CURIE
DALEN
DIRAC
FERMI
FRANK
HERTZ
KUSCH
MAYER
PAULI
RAMAN
SEGRE
STARK
STERN
BARKLA

FRANCK
GLASER
JENSEN
LANDAU
LENARD
PERRIN
PLANCK
POWELL
TOWNES
WALTON
WIGNER
WILSON
YUKAWA

ZEEMAN
BARDEEN
COMPTON
FEYNMAN
KASTLER
LORENTZ
MARCONI
PURCELL
THOMSON
ZERNIKE
ANDERSON
APPLETON
BLACKETT

BRATTAIN
BRIDGMAN
CHADWICK
DAVISSON
EINSTEIN
LAWRENCE
LIPPMANN
MILLIKAN
RAYLEIGH
ROENTGEN
SHOCKLEY
SIEGBAHN
TOMONAGA

BECQUEREL
CHERENKOV
COCKCROFT
DEBROGLIE
GUILLAUME
MICHELSON
MOSSBAUER
PROKHOROV
SCHWINGER
HEISENBERG
HOFSTADTER
RICHARDSON
SCHROEDINGER

Literature

BUCK
GIDE
MANN
SHAW
AGNON
BUNIN
CAMUS
ELIOT
HESSE
HEYSE
LEGER
LEWIS
SACHS
YEATS
ANDRIC

DUGARD
EUCKEN
FRANCE
HAMSUN
JENSEN
ONEILL
SARTRE
TAGORE
UNDSET
BERGSON
DELEDDA
JIMINEZ
KIPLING
LAXNESS
MAURIAC

MISTRAL
MOMMSEN
REYMONT
ROLLAND
RUSSELL
BJORNSON
CARDUCCI
FAULKNER
LAGERLOF
MAURISAC
BENAVENTE
CHURCHILL
ECHEGARAY
GJELLERUP
HAUPTMANN

HEMINGWAY
KARLFELDT
PASTERNAK
PRUDHOMME
QUASIMODO
SHOLOKHOV
SILLANPAA
SPITTELER
STEINBECK
GALSWORTHY
HEIDENSTAM
LAGERKVIST
PIRANDELLO
SEFERIADES
SIENKIWICZ

CREATIVE CELEBRITIES

Authors, Poets, Dramatists

ADE
GAY
KEY
POE

ASCH
FORD
HUGO
HUME
INGE
LAMB
LIVY
MANN
OVID
POPE
SAND
SHAW
ZOLA

ALGER
ARLEN
AUDEN
BENET
BLAKE
BURNS
BYRON
CAMUS
CAPEK

CRANE
DANTE
DEFOE
DOYLE
DUMAS
ELIOT
FROST
GOGOL
GORKI
GRIMM
HARDY
HARTE
HEINE
HENRY
IBSEN
JAMES
JOYCE
KAFKA
KEATS
LEWIS
MOORE
ODETS
PEELE
PEPYS
PAINE
PATER
SCOTT
STAEL

STEIN
STOWE
SWIFT
TASSO
TWAIN
VERNE
WAUGH
WELLS
WILDE
WOLFE
WOOLF
WYLIE
YEATS
ZWEIG

ALCOTT
AUSTEN
BALZAC
BARRIE
BRECHT
BRONTE
BUNYAN
CATHER
CONRAD
COOPER
COWPER
CROUSE
DAUDET

DRYDEN
FERBER
FRANCE
GIBBON
GOETHE
HAMSUN
HEBBEL
HERSEY
HESIOD
HOLMES
HORACE
HUDSON
IBANEZ
IRVING
JONSON
LESAGE
LONDON
LOWELL
LYTTON
MILLAY
MILLER
MILTON
ONEILL
ORWELL
PINDAR
PORTER
PROUST
RACINE

SAPPHO
SARTRE
SENECA
SILONE
TAGORE
VILLON

ARIOSTO
BELLAMY
BENNETT
BOSWELL
CARLYLE
CHAUCER
CHEKHOV
CLEMENS
DICKENS
DREISER
EDWARDS
EMERSON
GAUTIER
GILBERT
GOLDONI
HAZLITT
HERRICK
KHAYYAM
KIPLING
MARLOWE
MASTERS
MOLIERE
PLAUTUS
PUSHKIN
ROLLAND
ROSTAND
SAROYAN
SHELLEY
SPENSER
TERENCE
THOREAU
THURBER
TOLSTOI
WEBSTER
WHARTON
WHITMAN

ANDERSEN
ANDERSON
ANNUNZIO
BROWNING
FAULKNER
FLAUBERT
HOFFMANN
LAGERLOF
LAWRENCE
MACAULAY
MELVILLE
MEREDITH
PETRARCH
RABELAIS
RINEHART
ROSSETTI
ROUSSEAU
SALINGER
SANDBURG
SCHILLER
SHERIDAN
SPENGLER
TENNYSON
TROLLOPE
TURGENEV
VOLTAIRE
WHITTIER

Painters, Sculptors

ARP

CIMA
COLE
DALI
DORE
DUFY
ETTY
GOYA
GRIS
HALS
KENT
KLEE
MARC
MIRO
OPIE
RENI
WOOD

BLAKE
COROT
CURRY
DAVID
DEGAS
DUFFY
DURER
ERNST
FLAGG
HOMER
INMAN
INNES
LEGER
LEONI
LIPPI
MANET
MARIN
MONET
MOSES
MYRON
ORPEN
PEALE
REDON
RODIN
RYDER
SARTO
STEEN
SULLY
WATTS
WYANT

ANDREA
BENTON
BRAQUE
CALDER
CANOVA
COPLEY
CRESPI
EAKINS
GIOTTO
GREUZE
HASSAM
HODLER
INGRES
LEBRUN
MENZEL
MILLET
PISANO
RENOIR
RIBERA
RIVERA
RUBENS
SAVAGE
SEURAT
SEWELL
SISLEY
STUART
TITIAN

BELLINI
BELLOWS
BERNINI
BOCKLIN
BONHEUR
BONNARD
BOUCHER
CELLINI
CEZANNE
CHAGALL
CHARDIN
CHIRICO
COURBET
CURRIER
DAUMIER
DAVINCI
ELGRECO
EPSTEIN
GAUGUIN
HOGARTH
HOKUSAI
HOLBEIN
MAILLOL
MATISSE
MESSINA
MURILLO
PHIDIAS
PICASSO
RAPHAEL
ROUAULT
SARGENT
UTRILLO
VANDYCK
VANEYCK
VANGOGH
VERMEER
WATTEAU

ANGELICO
BRANCUSI
BREUGHEL
CORREGIO
DAVIDSON
MANTEGNA
MONDRIAN
PISSARRO
REYNOLDS
ROUSSEAU
VERONESE
WHISTLER

Composers

ABT

ARNE
BACH
BERG
CAGE
FOSS
KERN
LALO
WOLF

ARLEN
AUBER
BALFE
BIZET
BLOCH
DINDY
DUKAS
ELGAR
FRIML
GLUCK
GRIEG
GUIDO
HAYDN
HOLST
IBERT
LEHAR
LISZT

LULLY
NEVIN
RAVEL
REGER
SOUSA
VERDI
WEBER
WEILL

BARBER
BARTOK
BERLIN
BOULEZ
BRAHMS
CARTER
CHOPIN
DELIUS
DVORAK

ENESCO
FOSTER
FRANCK
GOUNOD
HANDEL
KALMAN
MAHLER
MOZART
PORTER
ROGERS
SCHUTZ
WAGNER
WEBERN

ALBENIZ
BABBITT
BELLINI
BERLIOZ

BORODIN
COPLAND
CORELLI
DEBUSSY
DEFALLA
DELIBES
HERBERT
JOSQUIN
MACHAUT
MENOTTI
MILHAUD
POULENC
PUCCINI
PURCELL
RODGERS
ROMBERG
ROSSINI
SMETANA

STRAUSS
VIVALDI

BRUCKNER
CHAUSSON
COUPERIN
GERSHWIN
GRANADOS
MASCAGNI
MASSENET
MESSAIEN
RESPIGHI
SCHUBERT
SCHULLER
SCHUMANN
SIBELIUS
SULLIVAN
TELEMANN

Historians

LOT
BEDE
HUME
KNOX
LIVY
MORE
STOW
ADAMS
BACON

BEARD
CANTU
NEPOS
PARIS
PLINY
RANKE
RENAN
SEGUR
SKENE

STEIN
CAMDEN
DAUNOU
FROUDE
GIBBON
MIGNET
MOTLEY
OSGOOD
STUBBS

WILSON
BOSSUET
CARLYLE
LELEWEL
PSELLUS
SALLUST
TACITUS
TOYNBEE

Inventors, Discoverers

BELL
BENZ
COLT
DAVY
HOWE
IVES
KOCH
LONG
OTIS
SALK
SWAN
TAIT
VAIL
WATT

BAIRD
BRAHE
CURIE
FIELD
FISKE

FITCH
FREUD
HENRY
HERTZ
HYATT
LINDE
MORSE
NOBEL
TESLA
VOLTA

BUNSEN
DALTON
DARWIN
DIESEL
DOMAGK
DURYEA
EDISON
EUCLID
FULTON

HARVEY
JENNER
KEPLER
LISTER
MENDEL
MORTON
NEWTON
PASCAL
SPERRY
WRIGHT

BANTING
CURTISS
EASTMAN
EHRLICH
FARADAY
GALILEI
GATLING
LAENNEC
PASTEUR

PULLMAN
SIEMENS
SPRAGUE
WAKSMAN
WHITNEY

BERLINER
BESSEMER
BUSHNELL
DAGUERRE
MERCATOR
DEFOREST
EINSTEIN
FRANKLIN
GOODYEAR
HERSCHEL
LANGMUIR
ROENTGEN
THOMPSON
WATERMAN

FAMOUS NAMES

FIRST AND LAST NAMES

Abner	LIL	Ayers	LEW	Blas	GIL
Alfonso	DON	Baba	ALI	Brynner	YUL
Annabel	LEE	Beerbohm	MAX	Calloway	CAB
Arden	EVE	Ben	HUR	Carson	KIT

Chaney	LON
Cliburn	VAN
Dorothy	DIX
Durocher	LEO, LIP
Gehrig	LOU
Gershwin	IRA
Gould	JAY
Gray	ASA
Hammarskjold	DAG
Hogan	BEN
Houston	SAM
Hur	BEN
Hus	JAN
Jan	HUS
Jonson	BEN
Khan	ALI, AGA
Louis	JOE
Lowell	AMY
Masaryk	JAN
Mel	OTT
Neal	DOW
Ott	MEL
Paine	TOM
Rayburn	SAM
Rogers	ROY
Rohmer	SAX
Rutledge	ANN
Saud	IBN
Sawyer	TOM
Schmeling	MAX
Snead	SAM
Sumac	YMA
Tolstoy	LEO
Trygve	LIE
Turpin	BEN
Uncle	SAM
Vermeer	JAN
Whitney	ELI
Yutang	LIN

Aaron	HANK, BURR
Acheson	DEAN
Adam	BEDE
Adams	JOHN
Addams	JANE
Alden	JOHN
Alexander	POPE
Alfred	LUNT
Ali	KHAN
Aly	KHAN
Allen	FRED
Andre	GIDE
Anita	LOOS
Anna	HELD
Anthony	EDEN
Antony	MARK
Arnaz	DESI
Artemus	WARD
Asa	GRAY
Austen	JANE
Autry	GENE
Babe	RUTH
Bartok	BELA

Bede	ADAM
Bennett	CERF
Bernard	SHAW
Berra	YOGI
Billy	ROSE
Blum	LEON
Boleyn	ANNE
Bonheur	ROSA
Bradley	OMAR
Broz	TITO
Buffalo Bill	CODY
Burl	IVES
Captain	AHAB, NEMO
Carnegie	DALE
Cassius	CLAY
Catherine	PARR
Chagall	MARC
Chaplin	OONA
Chase	ILKA
Chico	MARX
Christian	DIOR
Christie	ANNA
Connie	MACK
Cooper	GARY
Crockett	DAVY
Coward	NOEL
Craig	RICE
Dean	RUSK
De La Roche	MAZO
Descartes	RENE
Dewey	JOHN
Disney	WALT
Dizzy	DEAN
Dorian	GRAY
Dow	NEAL
Drury	LANE
Dudevant	SAND
Edouard	LALO
Eleanora	DUSE
Elia	LAMB
Elias	HOWE
Elihu	ROOT, YALE
Elmer	RICE
Emile	ZOLA
Emily	POST
En-Lai	CHOU
Ericson	LEIF
Ernie	PYLE
Eugene	DEBS
Eyre	JANE
Ferber	EDNA
Flanders	MOLL
Frances	ALDA
Frans	HALS
Fritz	LANG
Gagarin	YURI
George	SAND
Geste	BEAU
Gil	BLAS
Goldberg	RUBE
Goriot	PERE
Gray	ZANE
Grey	JANE

Guido	RENI
Hamsun	KNUT
Harlow	JEAN
Harold	UREY
Harpo	MARX
Hart	MOSS
Harte	BRET
Held	ANNA
Helmer	NORA
Henry	CLAY, FORD
Heyerdahl	THOR
Hopkins	MARK
Horace	MANN
Huey	LONG
Hugo	WOLF
Ibn	SAUD
Immanuel	KANT
Iturbi	JOSE
Jacob	RIIS
Jane	GREY, EYRE
Jenny	LIND
Jerome	KERN
Jonas	SALK
Karl	MARX
Kalman	IMRE
Karenina	ANNA
Klee	PAUL
Khachaturian	ARAM
Khayyam	OMAR
Kreuger	IVAR
Lardner	RING
Laurel	STAN
Lazarus	EMMA
Leon	BLUM
Lily	PONS
Long	HUEY
Mamie	DOUD
Marco	POLO
Margaret	ROSE
Marquette	PERE
Marx	KARL
Mary	TODD
Mata	HARI
Maxwell	ELSA
Meitner	LISE
Mondrian	PIET
Montez	LOLA
Moss	HART
Muni	PAUL
Musial	STAN
Nathan	HALE
Niels	BOHR
O'Casey	SEAN
Ogden	NASH
Pacelli	PIUS
Paul —	MUNI, KLEE
Pavlova	ANNA
Perry	COMO
Peter	ARNO
Phileas	FOGG
Pinza	EZIO
Pons	LILY
Porter	COLE

Pound	**EZRA**
Rockwell	**KENT**
Rogers	**WILL**
Rusk	**DEAN**
Ruth	**BABE**
Saarinen	**EERO**
Sally	**LUNN**
Salvador	**DALI**
Schipa	**TITO**
Schulberg	**BUDD**
Shalom	**ASCH**
Sibelius	**JEAN**
Squire	**CASS**
Steven	**RISE**
Stravinsky	**IGOR**
Syngman	**RHEE**
The Red	**ERIC**
Thomas	**MANN**
Tilden	**BILL**
Tito	**BROZ**
Tunney	**GENE**
Tweed	**BOSS**
Ty	**COBB**
Tyler	**JOHN**
Uriah	**HEEP**
Vannevar	**BUSH**
Vincent Van	**GOGH**
Walter	**REED**
Warburg	**OTTO**
Warren	**EARL**
Waugh	**ALEC**
Webster	**NOAH**
Weill	**KURT**
Whiteman	**PAUL**
Wiley	**POST**
Willard	**EMMA**
Zane	**GRAY**
Zebulon	**PIKE**
Zeppo	**MARX**
Abigail	**SMITH**
Adams	**MAUDE**
Adelina	**PATTI**
Al(fred)	**SMITH**
Albert	**CAMUS**
Alec	**WAUGH**
Alessandro	**VOLTA**
Alexandre	**DUMAS**
Alighieri	**DANTE**
Allen	**STEVE, ETHAN**
Alma	**GLUCK**
Al Rashin	**HARUN**
Amundsen	**ROALD**
Anthony	**SUSAN**
Arden	**ENOCH**
Arsene	**LUPIN**
Arthur	**BOYLE**
Ataturk	**KEMAL**
Auguste	**RODIN**
Barkley	**ALBEN**
Barrymore	**ETHEL**
Barton	**CLARK**
Basie	**COUNT**
Beau	**GESTE**
Becky	**SHARP**
Ben	**HOGAN**
Benedetto	**CROCE**
Beniamino	**GIGLI**
Bergson	**HENRI**
Berling	**GOSTA**
Bernhardt	**SARAH**
Bette	**DAVIS**
Bolivar	**SIMON**
Booth	**EDWIN**
Boss	**TWEED**
Boswell	**JAMES**
Brahe	**TYCHO**
Brendan	**BEHAN**
Bret	**HARTE**
Brigham	**YOUNG**
Bruce	**CABOT**
Buchanan	**JAMES**
Buck	**PEARL**
Bunche	**RALPH**
Capek	**KAREL**
Carnera	**PRIMO**
Carpenter	**SCOTT**
Carroll	**LEWIS**
Casals	**PABLO**
Castle	**IRENE**
Cather	**WILLA**
Chauncey	**DEPEW**
Chekhov	**ANTON**
Chou	**ENLAI**
Clark	**GABLE**
Claude	**MONET**
Clay	**HENRY**
Como	**PERRY**
Copland	**AARON**
Count	**BASIE**
Daniel	**DEFOE, BOONE**
Davis	**BETTE**
Dean	**DIZZY**
De l'Enclos	**NINON**
De Leon	**PONCE**
Desi	**ARNAZ**
De Valera	**EAMON**
Dickinson	**EMILY**
Dionne	**MARIE, OLIVA**
Dodsworth	**BRENT**
Doone	**LORNA**
Doud	**MAMIE**
Dvorak	**ANTON**
Edouard	**MANET**
Edvard	**GRIEG**
Edward	**ELGAR**
Edwin	**BOOTH**
Elbridge	**GERRY**
Ellery	**QUEEN**
Emmet	**KELLY**
Enoch	**ARDEN**
Enrico	**FERMI**
Ethan	**FROME, ALLEN**
Eve	**CURIE**
Evita	**PERON**
Ezra	**POUND**
Ferde	**GROFE**
Fibber	**MCGEE**
Field	**CYRUS**
Ford	**EDSEL, HENRY**
Francis	**BACON, DRAKE**
Franck	**CESAR**
Franz	**LEHAR, LISZT**
Franz	**KAFKA**
Frome	**ETHAN**
Fulton	**SHEEN**
Gabler	**HEDDA**
Gantry	**ELMER**
Garbo	**GRETA**
Gene	**AUTRY**
George	**LLOYD**
Georges	**BIZET**
Gertrude	**STEIN**
Gherman	**TITOV**
Gide	**ANDRE**
Giordano	**BRUNO**
Goldoni	**CARLO**
Goodman	**BENNY**
Gorky	**MAXIM**
Graham	**BILLY**
Green	**HETTY**
Greta	**GARBO**
Grofe	**FERDE**
Guiseppe	**VERDI**
Guitry	**SACHA**
Hals	**FRANS**
Hank	**AARON**
Hanks	**NANCY**
Harold	**ICKES**
Hayes	**HELEN**
Heep	**URIAH**
Heinrich	**HEINE**
Helen	**HAYES**
Henrik	**IBSEN**
Hetty	**GREEN**
Hitler	**ADOLF**
Horatio	**ALGER**
Houdini	**HARRY**
Howe	**ELIAS**
Ichabod	**CRANE**
Ilka	**CHASE**
Janos	**KADAR**
James	**JESSE, JOYCE**
Jawaharlal	**NEHRU**
Jay	**GOULD**
Jean P.	**MARAT**
Jefferson	**DAVIS**
Jesse	**JAMES**
John	**ALDEN, DEWEY ADAMS, SMITH BROWN, TYLER**
Jonathan	**SWIFT**
Joyce	**JAMES**
Juan	**PERON**
Jules	**VERNE**
Kadar	**JANOS**
Kafka	**FRANZ**
Karel	**CAPEK**

Kazantakis	**NIKOS**
Keller	**HELEN**
Kreisler	**FRITZ**
Koussevitzky	**SERGE**
Kurt	**WEILL**
Lagerlof	**SELMA**
Lane	**DRURY**
Lanza	**MARIO**
Lawes	**LEWIS**
Legree	**SIMON**
Lehar	**FRANZ**
Lehmann	**LOTTE**
Lescaut	**MANON**
Levant	**OSCAR**
Lewis	**LAWES**
Lil	**ABNER**
Liszt	**FRANZ**
Loos	**ANITA**
Lonigan	**STUDS**
Lorna	**DOONE**
Lunn	**SALLY**
Maksim	**GORKI**
Manuel de	**FALLA**
Marie	**CURIE**
Marner	**SILAS**
Mario	**LANZA**
Marx	**CHICO, HARPO ZEPPO**
Maude	**ADAMS**
Maurice	**RAVEL**
Maurois	**ANDRE**
Maxim	**GORKI**
Meriwether	**LEWIS**
Miller	**GLENN**
Minuit	**PETER**
Mitchell	**MARIA**
Monroe	**JAMES**
Morini	**ERICA**
Nancy	**HANKS**
Nash	**OGDEN**
Nation	**CARRY**
Nero	**WOLFE**
Newton	**ISAAC**
Nikola	**TESLA**
Nikolai	**LENIN**
Onegin	**EUGEN**
Orlando	**LASSO**
Oscar	**WILDE**
Pancho	**VILLA**
Pasternak	**BORIS**
Pasteur	**LOUIS**
Patrick	**HENRY**
Pauling	**LINUS**
Perry	**MASON**
Philo	**VANCE**
Picasso	**PABLO**
Pierre	**CURIE**
Pirandello	**LUIGI**
Polo	**MARCO**
Post	**EMILY**
Priscilla	**ALDEN**
Pyle	**ERNIE**
Rainer	**RILKE**
Reni	**GUIDO**
Rhodes	**CECIL**
Rice	**CRAIG, ELMER**
Rickenbacker	**EDDIE**
Rivera	**DIEGO**
Rockne	**KNUTE**
Root	**ELIHU**
Rose	**BILLY**
Rosenblum	**MAXIE**
Rubinstein	**ANTON, ARTUR**
Runyon	**DAMON**
Salk	**JONAS**
Salmon	**CHASE**
Sam	**UNCLE**
Samuel	**MORSE, PEPYS**
Sancho	**PANZA**
Sharp	**BECKY**
Sigmund	**FREUD**
Sinclair	**LEWIS, UPTON**
Sklodowska	**CURIE**
Sonja	**HENIE**
Standish	**MILES**
Stengel	**CASEY**
Stephen	**CRANE**
Stevenson	**ADLAI**
Sunday	**BILLY**
Tamburlaine	**TIMUR**
Tarkington	**BOOTH**
Templar	**SIMON**
Thatcher	**BECKY**
Thomas	**WOLFE, MOORE**
Thomas	**HARDY, DYLAN**
Tom	**PAINE**
Torquato	**TASSO**
Truman	**HARRY**
Tycho	**BRAHE**
Varden	**DOLLY**
Virginia	**WOOLF**
Vladimir	**LENIN**
Walter	**BRUNO**
Walton	**IZAAK**
Welles	**ORSON**
Werner von	**BRAUN**
Wharton	**EDITH**
Wilde	**OSCAR**
Winslow	**HOMER**
Yale	**ELIHU**
Yogi	**BERRA**
Zola	**EMILE**
Albertus	**MAGNUS**
Aldous	**HUXLEY**
Alexis	**CARREL**
Ambrose	**BIERCE**
Anatole	**FRANCE**
Angelo	**GIOTTO**
Anne	**BOLEYN**
Anton	**DVORAK**
Arrhenius	**SVANTE**
Balzac	**HONORE**
Barrymore	**LIONEL**
Beatrice	**LILLIE**
Bela	**BARTOK**
Bell	**CURRER**
Ben	**JONSON, TURPIN**
Benedict	**ARNOLD**
Berlin	**IRVING**
Berlioz	**HECTOR**
Bernard	**BARUCH**
Bess	**TRUMAN**
Bill	**TILDEN**
Billy	**SUNDAY, GRAHAM**
Blaise	**PASCAL**
Boone	**DANIEL**
Breughel	**PIETER**
Bruno	**WALTER**
Burbank	**LUTHER**
Carnegie	**ANDREW**
Carrel	**ALEXIS**
Carry	**NATION**
Caruso	**ENRICO**
Castle	**VERNON**
Cecil	**RHODES**
Cesar	**FRANCK**
Cesare	**BORGIA**
Charlotte	**BRONTE, CORDAY**
Christie	**AGATHA**
Clara	**BARTON**
Clarence	**DARROW**
Cleveland	**GROVER**
Clement	**ATTLEE**
Cole	**PORTER**
Collins	**WILKIE**
Conrad	**JOSEPH**
Coolidge	**CALVIN**
Custis	**MARTHA**
Damon	**RUNYON**
Dantes	**EDMOND**
Debs	**EUGENE**
Defoe	**DANIEL**
Diego	**RIVERA**
Dionne	**CECILE, EMILIE**
Dodger	**ARTFUL**
Dolly	**VARDEN**
Donatello	**DONATO**
Dostoevsky	**FEODOR**
Dreyfus	**ALFRED**
Dylan	**THOMAS**
Eamon de	**VALERA**
Earhart	**AMELIA**
Edgar	**HOOVER**
Edmond	**DANTES**
Edna	**FERBER**
Einstein	**ALBERT**
Eleanor	**STEBER**
Elgar	**EDWARD**
Elmer	**GANTRY**
Emily	**BRONTE**
Enrico	**CARUSO**
Erhard	**LUDWIG**
Eric	**THERED, AMBLER**

Erica MORINI
Eugen ONEGIN
Eugene ONEILL
Ferenc MOLNAR
Fermi ENRICO
Franklin PIERCE
Frederic CHOPIN
Gary COOPER
Gene TUNNEY
Glenn JOHN
Giotto ANGELO
Graham GREENE, MARTHA
Gray DORIAN
Greeley HORACE
Gregor MENDEL
Grissom VIRGIL
Hale NATHAN
Harding WARREN
Harry S. TRUMAN
Hedda GABLER
Helen KELLER
Henry HUDSON
Hemingway ERNEST
Hercule POIROT
Herbert HOOVER, VICTOR
Hernando DESOTO, CORTES
Honore BALZAC
Horatio NELSON
Hugo VICTOR
Humphrey HUBERT, BOGART
Huxley ALDOUS
Ignazio SILONE
Imre KALMAN
Irene CASTLE
Irving BERLIN
Isadora DUNCAN
Isaac NEWTON
Izaak WALTON
Jack LONDON
Jackson ANDREW
Jane ADDAMS, AUSTEN
Jean HARLOW
Johannes KEPLER, BRAHMS
Johnson ANDREW, LYNDON
Jose ITURBI
Josef STALIN
Kern JEROME
Knut HAMSUN
Knute ROCKNE
Kodaly ZOLTAN
Lloyd GEORGE
Lombroso CESARE
Lorenzo de MEDICI
Lucrezia BORGIA
Ludwig ERHARD
Lupin ARSENE
Mack CONNIE

Mahler GUSTAV
Mailer NORMAN
Mann HORACE, THOMAS
Mantle MICKEY
Marcel PROUST
Marilyn MONROE
Martha GRAHAM, CUSTIS
Martin LUTHER
Mascagni PIETRO
Melville HERMAN
Mendel GREGOR
Menuhin YEHUDI
Mickey MANTLE
Mohandas GANDHI
Mussolini BENITO
Nielsson BIRGIT
Noel COWARD
Nora HELMER
Norman MAILER
OHenry PORTER
Orson WELLES
Orville WRIGHT
Pablo CASALS
Paganini NICOLO
Panza SANCHO
Pascal BLAISE
Pere GORIOT
Ponce DELEON
Priscilla MULLEN
Proust MARCEL
Pulitzer JOSEPH
Ralph BUNCHE
Richard WAGNER
Robinson CRUSOE
Rolland ROMAIN
Rudy VALLEE
Sax ROHMER
Schweitzer ALBERT
Silas MARNER
Sigrid UNDSET
Simon LEGREE
Skelton MARTHA
Spengler OSWALD
Spinoza BARUCH
Stalin JOSEPH
Strachey LYTTON
Sumner WELLES
Tebaldi RENATA
Thomas HOBBES
Thornton WILDER
Todd DOLLEY
Toqueville ALEXIS
Toscanini ARTURO
Ulanova GALINA
Undset SIGRID
Urey HAROLD
Van Buren MARTIN
Vecelli TITIAN
Vernon CASTLE
Villa PANCHO
Waksman SELMAN

Walt DISNEY
Webster DANIEL
Will ROGERS
Wolfe THOMAS
Wright WILBUR
Zanuck DARRYL
Zoltan KODALY

Aleksei KOSYGIN
Amelia EARHART
Andrew JOHNSON, JACKSON
Anna PAVLOVA
Arthur CHESTER
Baldwin STANLEY
Benvenuto CELLINI
Bierce AMBROSE
Caldwell ERSKINE
Carlo GOLDONI
Carroll DODGSON
Casey STENGEL
Chamberlain NEVILLE
Dionne ANNETTE
Dodgson CARROLL
Dolly MADISON
Eden ANTHONY
Fillmore MILLARD
Flagstad KIRSTEN
France ANATOLE
Galina ULANOVA
Gian-Carlo MENOTTI
Giacomo PUCCINI
Guglielmo MARCONI
Henri BERGSON
Hoover HERBERT
Horace GREELEY
Hull CORDELL
Kemal ATATURK
Laurence OLIVIER
Leif ERICSON
Leonardo DAVINCI
Lillian RUSSELL
Louis PASTEUR
Luther BURBANK
Macchiavelli NICCOLO
Marc CHAGALL
Mark ANTHONY
Mark Twain CLEMENS
Omar BRADLEY
Pablo PICASSO
Pike ZEBULON
Pius PACELLI
Primo CARNERA
Priscilla MULLINS
Prosper MERIMEE
Rembrandt VANRIJN
Ring LARDNER
Rosa BONHEUR
Russell LILLIAN
Simon BOLIVAR
TEMPLAR
Smith ABIGAIL
Susan ANTHONY

Taylor	**ZACHARY**
Titov	**GHERMAN**
Van Gogh	**VINCENT**
Victor	**HERBERT**
Von Braun	**WERNHER**
Walter	**RALEIGH**
Ward	**ARTEMUS**
Warren	**HARDING**
Wendell	**WILLKIE**
Willkie	**WENDELL**
Yuri	**GAGARIN**
Young	**BRIGHAM**

MIDDLE NAMES

Nasr—Din	**ED**
Abd—Krim	**EL**
John—Passos	**DOS**
Katherine—Porter	**ANN**
Louisa—Alcott	**MAY**
Mao—Tung	**TSE**
Mary—Evans	**ANN**
Sun—Sen	**YAT**
Chester—Arthur	**ALAN**
Claudia—Taylor	**ALTA**
Ermanno—Ferrari	**WOLF**
Henry—Beecher	**WARD**
James—Polk	**KNOX**
Jean—Sartre	**PAUL**
John—Jones	**PAUL**
Julia—Howe	**WARD**
William—Benet	**ROSE**
Arthur—Doyle	**CONAN**
Charles—Hughes	**EVANS**
Clare—Luce	**BOOTH**
David—George	**LLOYD**
Erich—Remarque	**MARIA**
Dwight—Eisenhower	**DAVID**
Francis—Key	**SCOTT**
Helen—Moody	**WILLS**
Henry—Thoreau	**DAVID**
Henry—Lodge	**CABOT**
Herbert—Hoover	**CLARK**
James—Garfield	**ABRAM**
John—Astor	**JACOB**
John—Garner	**NANCE**
Peter—Tchaikovsky	**ILICH**
Ralph—Emerson	**WALDO**
Richard—Lee	**HENRY**
William—Harrison	**HENRY**
Alexander—Bell	**GRAHAM**
Anne—Lindbergh	**MORROW**
Edward—Lytton	**BULWER**
Franklin—Roosevelt	**DELANO**
Franz—Haydn	**JOSEPH**
Gaius—Caesar	**JULIUS**
Herbert—Wells	**GEORGE**
John—Coolidge	**CALVIN**
John—Adams	**QUINCY**
John—Sousa	**PHILIP**
John—Mill	**STUART**
John—Dulles	**FOSTER**
John—Booth	**WILKES**
Leslie—Hope	**TOWNES**
Lyndon—Johnson	**BAINES**
Mamie—Doud	**GENEVA**
Nicholas—Butler	**MURRAY**
Nicolas—Korsakov	**RIMSKY**
Paul—White	**DUDLEY**
Percy—Shelley	**BYSSHE**
Samuel—Coleridge	**TAYLOR**
Steven—Cleveland	**GROVER**
William—Porter	**SYDNEY**
William—Taft	**HOWARD**
William—Bryant	**CULLEN**
William—Yeats	**BUTLER**
Dante—Rossetti	**GABRIEL**
Elizabeth—Browning	**BARRETT**
Erle—Gardner	**STANLEY**
George—Shaw	**BERNARD**
Harriet—Stowe	**BEECHER**
Hubert—Humphrey	**HORATIO**
John—Curry	**STEUART**
John—Rockefeller	**DAVISON**
Marcus—Cicero	**TULLIUS**
Mary—Rinehart	**ROBERTS**
Norman—Peale	**VINCENT**
Oliver—Holmes	**WENDELL**
Thomas—Eliot	**STEARNS**
Wolfgang—Mozart	**AMADEUS**
James—Cooper	**FENIMORE**
Johann—Goethe	**WOLFGANG**
John—Morgan	**PIERPONT**
John—North	**RINGLING**
Richard—Sheridan	**BRINSLEY**
William—Sherman	**TECUMSEH**
William—Bryan	**JENNINGS**

PEN NAMES

BOZ	Dickens
ELIA	Lamb
SAKI	Monroe
OUIDA	de la Ramee
OHENRY	Porter
VOLTAIRE	Arouet
MARKTWAIN	Clemens
SSVANDINE	Wright
NANCYBOYD	Millay
CURRERBELL	Bronte
GEORGESAND	Dudevant
PIERRELOTI	Viaud
ALICETOKLAS	Stein
ARTEMUSWARD	Browne
GEORGEELIOT	Evans
LEWISCARROLL	Dodgson
ANATOLEFRANCE	Thibault
PETROLEUMVNASBY	Locke

SOUNDS AND CRIES

* Indicates those of animals

BAY*
BOO
CAW*
CRY
DIN
HUM*
KEY
LOW*
MEW*
MOO*
POP
POW
RAP
SOB
TAP*
YAP*
ZIP

BANG
BARK*
BARR*
BELL*
BIRR
BLAT*
BONG
BOOM
BRAY*
BUST
CALL
CHUG
CLAP
CLOP
CRAW*
CROW
DING
ECHO
FIZZ
FLOP
GLUG
GOWL
HISS*
HONK*
HOWL*
JUCK*
JUKE*
LISP
MEWL*
MOAN
PEAL
PEEP*
PING
PUFF
PURL
RALE

RING
ROAR*
ROLL
SIGH
SING*
SLAM
TALK
TANG
THUD
TICK
TINK
TOLL
TONE
TOOT
TUCK
TUNE
WHAM
YARR
YAUP
YAWL
YAWP
YELL
YELP*
YOHO

ALARM
BINGO
BLARE
BLAST
BLEAT*
BINGO
CHEEP*
CHINK*
CHIRM*
CHIRP*
CHUCK*
CLANG
CLANK
CLICK
CLINK
CLOOP
CLUCK*
CLUMP
CLUNK
COOEE
COOEY
CRACK
CREAK
CRUMP
DRONE
FLUMP
GLUCK
GRIDE
GROAN

GROWL*
GRUNT*
HALLO
HOLLO
KNELL
LARUM
MIAOU*
MIAOW*
MUSIC
NEIGH*
NOISE
PLASH
PLUMP
QUACK*
SHOUT
SKIRL
SMACK
SNARL*
SNORE
SNORT*
SOUGH
SWISH
TRILL
TROAT
TWANG
TWEET*
VOICE
WHACK
WHANG
WHINE*
WHIRR
WHOOP
WOOSH

ACCENT
ALARUM
BELLOW*
BOOHOO
BOWWOW*
BUBBLE
CACKLE*
CANARY
CLAMOR
CRUNCH
FIZZLE
GAGGLE*
GOBBLE*
GUGGLE
GURGLE
HALLOA
HALLOO
HUBBUB
JANGLE
JINGLE

MELODY
MUFFLE
MURMUR
MUTTER
NICKER
OUTCRY
PATTER
PLAINT
RATTLE
REPORT
RUSTLE
SCREAM
SCROOP
SHRIEK
SHRILL
SIZZLE
SPEECH
SPLASH
SQUALL*
SQUAWK*
SQUEAK*
SQUEAL*
SQUISH
TATTOO
TIMBRE
TINGLE
TINKLE
UPROAR
WHEEZE
WHINNY*
WHOOSH
YOICKS

BLATTER
CADENCE
CHATTER
CHIRRUP
CLANGOR
CLATTER
DUBADUB
GRUMBLE
PITAPAT
RATATAT
RUBADUB
SCREECH
SONANCY
SQUELCH
STRIDOR
TALLYHO*
TIRALEE*
TRUMPET*
TWITTER
WHIMPER
WHISTLE

EXCLAMATIONS AND OATHS

AH
BO
EH
HA
HI
MY
OH
OW
UM

ACH
AHA
AUH
BAH
BAM
BAW
BOH
FIE
FOH
GEE
GRR
HAH
HAW
HEM
HEP
HEU
HEY
HIC
HIP
HOI
HOO
HOY
HUH
ODS
OHO
OUF
PAH
PEW
POH
PST
PUE
SOH
TCH
TCK
TST
TUT
UGH
WEE
WHY
WOW

AHEM
AHEY
AITH
ALAS
ARAH
ARRA
BOOH
CHUT
DANG
DRAT
EGAD
EHEU
EVOE
GOSH
HECK
HEIN
HOCH
HUSH
LAWK
NUTS
OONS
OUCH
OUGH
PHEW
PHUT
PISH
PSHA
SOOK
TUSH
WHAM
WHEW

ALACK
ARRHA
BEDAD
BEGAD
BLIMY
FAUGH
HELLO
HEUCH
HEUGH
HURRA
HUZZA
LAWKS
PSHAW
UHHUH
ZOOKS
ZOWIE

CRIKEY
CRIPES
HURRAH
HURROO
OCHONE
SBLOOD

ZOUNDS

TIME DIVISIONS

CALENDARS

No. of Month	JEWISH	MOHAMMEDAN	HINDU	EGYPTIAN
1	TISHRI, ETHANIM	MUHARRAN	BAISAKH	THOTH
2	HESHVAN, BUL	SAFAR	JETH	PAOPHI
3	KISLEV	RABIA 1	ASARH	HATHOR
4	TEBET(H)	RABIA 2	SA(RA)WAN	CHOIAK
5	SHEBAT	JUMADA 1	BHADON	TYBI
6	ADAR	JUMADA 2	ASIN, KUAR	MECHIR
7	NISAN, ABIB	RAJAB	KA(R)TIK	PHAMENOTH
8	IYAR, ZIF	SHABAN	AGHAN	PHARMUTHI
9	SIVAN	RAMADAN	PUS	PACHONS
10	TAMMUZ	SHAWWAL	MAGH	PAYNI
11	AB	ZULKADAH	PHA(L)GUN	APAR
12	ELUL	ZULHIJJAH	CHAIT	MESORE

No. of Month	FRENCH REVOLUTIONARY	1st DAY	ROMAN
1	VENDEMIAIRE (vintage)	Sept. 22, 23, 24	MARTIUS
2	BRUMAIRE (fog)	Oct. 22, 23, 24	APRILIS
3	FRIMAIRE (sleet)	Nov. 21, 22, 23	MAIUS
4	NIVOSE (snow)	Dec. 21, 22, 23	JUNIUS
5	PLUVIOSE (rain)	Jan. 20, 21, 22	JULIUS; QUINCTILIS
6	VENTOSE (wind)	Feb. 19, 20, 21	AUGUSTUS; SEXTILIS
7	GERMINAL (seed)	March 21, 22	SEPTEMBER
8	FLOREAL (blossom)	April 20, 21	OCTOBER
9	PRAIRIAL (pasture)	May 20, 21	NOVEMBRIS; NOVEMBER
10	MESSIDOR (harvest)	June 19, 20	DECEMBER
11	THERMIDOR (heat)	July 19, 20	JANUARIUS
12	FRUCTIDOR (fruit)	Aug. 18, 19	FEBRUARIUS

No. of Month	FRENCH	SPANISH	GERMAN	ITALIAN
1	JANVIER	ENERO	JANUAR	GENNAIO
2	FEVRIER	FEBRERO	FEBRUAR	FEBBRAIO
3	MARS	MARZO	MARZ	MARZO
4	AVRIL	ABRIL	APRIL	APRILE
5	MAI	MAYO	MAI	MAGGIO
6	JUIN	JUNIO	JUNI	GIUGNO
7	JUILLET	JULIO	JULI	LUGLIO
8	AOUT	AGOSTO	AUGUST	AUGUSTO
9	SEPTEMBRE	SEPTIEMBRE	SEPTEMBER	SETTEMBRE
10	OCTOBRE	OCTUBRE	OKTOBER	OTTOBRE
11	NOVEMBRE	NOVIEMBRE	NOVEMBER	NOVEMBRE
12	DECEMBRE	DICIEMBRE	DEZEMBER	DICEMBRE

ENGLISH	FRENCH	SPANISH	GERMAN	ITALIAN
Spring	PRINTEMPS	PRIMAVERA	FRUEHLING	PRIMAVERA
Summer	ETE	VERANO	SOMMER	ESTATE
Fall	AUTOMNE	OTONO	HERBST	AUTUNNO
Winter	HIVER	INVIERNO	WINTER	INVERNO
Monday	LUNDI	LUNES	MONTAG	LUNEDI
Tuesday	MARDI	MARTES	DIENSTAG	MARTEDI
Wednesday	MERCREDI	MIERCOLES	MITTWOCH	MERCOLEDI
Thursday	JEUDI	JUEVES	DONNERSTAG	GIOVEDI
Friday	VENDREDI	VIERNES	FREITAG	VENERDI
Saturday	SAMEDI	SABADO	SONNABEND	SABATO
Sunday	DIMANCHE	DOMINGO	SONNTAG	DOMENICA
Year	ANNEE	ANO	JAHR	ANNO
Month	MOIS	MES	MONAT	MESE
Week	SEMAINE	SEMANA	WOCHE	SETTIMANA
Day	JOUR	DIA	TAG	GIORNO
Hour	HEURE	HORA	STUNDE	ORA
Time	TEMPS	TIEMPO	ZEIT	TEMPO

	LATIN
Time	TEMPUS; pl. TEMPORA
Year	ANNUS; ANNO
Month	MENSIS
Day	DIES; DIE
Hour	HORA

First day of month, **CALENDS; KALENDS; CALENDIS**

7th day of March, May, July, October, 5th day of other months, **NONES; NONAS; NONIS**

15th day of March, May, July, October, 13th day of other months, **IDIBUS, IDES, IDUS**

Day before, **PRIDIE**

TOOLS, INSTRUMENTS, IMPLEMENTS (AND PARTS)

SHAPING, POLISHING, SEPARATING

BOB
DOD
MOP
RIP
RUB
ZAX

BUFF
BUNT
CARD
COMB
FILE
HARL
HONE
LAUN
MILL
PEEN
RAPE
RASP
RESP
RISP
SLIP
SPAT
SWAB
WISP

BROOM
BRUSH
CONER
CRIMP
DARBY

EDGER
FLUTE
GOOSE
GRAIL
HOWEL
JOLLY
LATHE
PAVER
PLANE
PRINT
PRUNT
PUNTY
PUPPY
QUIRK
QUIRL
RABAT
RICER
RIFLE
SABER
SABLE
SABRE
SIEVE
SIZER
SLICK
SNIPE
STEEP
STROP
STRUM
SWAGE
WAXER
WHISK

WHISP
WIPER

BADGER
BEADER
CAPPER
CARDEN
CARLET
CHUTER
COMBER
CURVER
DABBER
DAUBER
DUSTER
EVENER
FINNER
FLAKER
FLANCH
FLANGE
FLUTER
FORMER
GLAZER
GOFFER
GRADER
GRATER
HARROW
HEMMER
HICKEY
IRONER
JOLLEY
LASTER

MALKIN
MANGLE
MILLER
MOLDER
NAPPER
PALLET
PLANER
POMMEL
PONTIL
PUTOIS
RABBET
RAMROD
REAMER
REBATE
ROUTER
RUFFER
SANDER
SCREED
SCRIVE
SHAPER
SLOPER
SMOOTH
SOOTER
STRAIK
SWEDGE
TASTER
TENTER
VELURE
WAGWAG
WINNOW

LIFTING, LEVERING, PRYING

BAR
FID
GIN
GYN
PRY
TUG

BAIT
BEAM
CRAB
CROW
DART
DRAG
GAFF
GRAB
HAKE
HOCK
JACK
LIFT
LOOT
PALE

PEAL
PEEL
PUMP
WIND
WINK

BETTY
CRANE
DAVIT
DIDLE
FILCH
FLIRT
GRIFF
GRIPE
HELVE
JAMES
JEMMY
JIMMY
LADLE
LEASH
LEWIS

PEAVY
PEDAL
PINCH
PRIZE
QUOIN
STANG
SWAPE
SWEEP
SWELL
SWIPE
WEDGE
WINCH
WINZE

BAILER
BURTON
COUPER
DIPPER
DREDGE
FORCER
GAFFLE

GAGGER
GARNET
GARROT
GUNTER
HEAVER
KIBBLE
LADKIN
LADLER
LEAPER
LIFTER
LOWDER
OPENER
PEAVEY
PULLER
PUMPER
RIPPLE
SEEDER
STONER
TACKLE
TILLER
WRENCH

GRIPPING, HOLDING, CONNECTING

CAT
DAG
DOG
DOP
EAR
GAB
GAG
GIB
GIG
GUY
HOD
KEP
LUG
NOG
NUT
PEG
POT
RIB
SOW
TAB
TEE
TEW
TIE
TOO
TUB
TUN
TYE
WAD

ANSA
BAIL
BEAK
BIRN
BOLT
BOND
BOOM
BOOT
BOSS
BRAD
BRAG
BROB
BUCK
BUNG
CAGE
CALM
CAME
CASE
CAST
CAUL
CHUG
CLEP
CLEW
CLIP
CLOG
COAK
COPE
COPS
CRIB
CROC
CURB
DALE
DOPP
DRIP
DUCT
DULL
FANG
FLAN
FORM
FROG
GATE
GAWN
GIMP
GIRD
GRID
GYVE
HACK
HANK
HASP
HAWK
HEAD
HECK
HOOD
HOOK
HORN
KEEP
KEIR
KIER
KILP
KING
KNAG
KNOB
KNOP
LAST
LATH
LEAP
LILL
LINK
LULL
LUTE
MAIL
MOLD
NAIL
NOCK
PAWL
PECK
PIPE
POLE
RACK
RAKE
REST
RODE
ROSE
RUNG
SCAB
SCOB
SEAL
SEAT
SIME
SKID
SNAP
SOAM
SOGA
SPAD
SPAN
SPIT
STAY
STUB
STUD
TACK
TONG
TRAP
TUBE
VIAL
VICE
VISE
YARD
YOKE

ANGLE
ANVIL
APRON
APURN
ARIES
ARROW
BANGY
BASIN
BASON
BIPOD
BLOCK
BOCAL
BOWER
BRACE
BRANK
CAMEL
CAVEL
CAVIL
CHAIR
CHASE
CHECK
CHEEK
CHIMB
CHIME
CHINE
CHOCK
CHUCK
CHURN
CHUTE
CLAMP
CLASP
CLAUT
CLEAT
CLEEK
CLICK
CLINK
COPSE
CRAMP
CREEL
CROME
CROOK
DANDI
DANDY
DOWEL
DRAIL
DWANG
EASEL
FLASK
FLOAT
FLUME
FRAIL
FRAME
GIRSE
GIRTH
GLAND
GOMER
GRATE
GRILL
GROPE
GUIGE
HEART
HERSE
HONDA
HORSE
HOUND
IRONS
JINNY
JOUGS
KEDGE
KEEVE
KEVEL
KNOSP
LACER
LINER
LONGE
LUNET
MOULD
NEDDY
NIBBY
NOOSE
OILER
OLONA
ORRIS
PERCH
PIPET
PITON
PIVOT
PREEN
RAKER
RIBET
ROOVE
ROUGH
SARPE
SEINE
SETUP
SHAFT
SHAPE
SHIVE
SHORE
SKEET
SNARE
SNARL

SPANG
SPEED
SPELK
SPELL
SPIKE
SPILE
SPILL
SPOKE
SPOUT
SPANG
SPRIG
SQUIB
STALL
STAVE
TAMIS
TAMMY
TEEST
THIEF
THOLE
THONG
TONGS
TRAMP
TRAWL
ULLER
WADDY
WITHE
WRIST
WYTHE

AMPULE
ANCHOR
AXTREE
BANGHY
BEARER
BEATER
BECKET
BOWPIN
BRANCH
BRIDLE
BROACH
BROOCH
BUCCAN
BUCKET
BUCKLE
BULLET
BUTTON
CABLET
CANGUE
CANNEL
CANOPY
CAPLIN
CARCAN
CASING
CATENA
CHAFER
CHESIL
CLEVIS
CLINCH
CLUTCH
COLLAR
COLLET
CONVOY
COTTER
CRADLE
CRANCE
CRUTCH
DASHER
DETENT
DOGTIE
DROGUE
DUBBEH
ETALON
EXAMEN
EYEBAR
EYELET
FASCET
FETTER
FEUTER
FEWTER
FIBULA
FILLER
FRETTE
FUNNEL
GIMMER
GIMMOR
GIRDER
GRILLE
GROMET
GUSSET
HANGER
HANGLE
HILLER
HOLDER
HOPPER
HURTER
JANKER
KEDGER
KEEPER
LAGGEN
LAGGIN
LIKNON
LIMBER
LINPIN
LOCKER
MATRIX
MOOTER
MORTAR
MUSROL
MUZZLE
NORMAN
OLIVET
PACKER
POPPET
RABBLE
RACKAN
RUNDLE
RYPECK
SAGENE
SCATCH
SCAVEL
SEALER
SHEATH
SINKER
SKEWER
SOCKET
SPIDER
SPIGOT
SPIKER
STAPLE
STEADY
STRAKE
TACKET
TAPLET
TERRET
TINGLE
TOGGEL
TOGGLE
TUBULE
TUNNER
TURKIS
TURRET
UPHROE
VERVEL
VIROLE
WASHER
WELDER
ZIPPER

CUTTING, STRIKING, POUNDING

AX
SY

ADZ
AXE
BIT
DAB
DAH
DIG
FID
GAD
GUN
HOB
HOE
HOG
LEA
LIP
LOY
NIP
PEW
PIC
RAB
RAM
SAW
SAX
SEX
SUL
SYE
TUP
ULU

ADZE
BEAR
BENT
BROD
CELT
COCK
DAHO
EAWT
FROE
FROW
MACE
MALL
MASH
MAUL
MEAK
MELL
MERE
MOGO
MOON
NIPS
PLEW
PLOW
POLT
SEAR
SETT
SNIP
SOCK
SPUD
SUCK
SULL
TAMP

ADDIS
BLADE
BRIAR
BRUZZ
BURIN
CROZE
DOLLY
DRIFT
FACER
FLAIL
FRAZE
GAVEL
GOUGE
HACHE
HARDY
HOBBY
JERRY
KNIFE
KNURL
LANCE
LARRY
LATHE
LEWIS
MADGE
MATAX
PARER
PEGGY
PILUM
PLEWE

PLIER
PRESS
RAZOR
REEST
RIMER
ROWEL
SCOOP
SHARE
SHARP
SHAUL
SHAVE
SHEEL
SHOOL
SLANE
SLICE
SLING
SPADE
SPOON
STAMP
STYLE
THROE
WAGON

ADDICE
BARLOW
BEAMER
BEETLE
BENDER
BINDER
BLADER
BUNTER
BUSTER
CARVER
CATLIN
CHASER
CHISEL
CHONTA
CLEAVE
COLTER
COUTEL
CUTTER
CUTTLE
DAMSEL
DAPPER
DIGGER
DIPPER
DOCTOR
DREDGE
EOLITH
FASCES
FOLDER
FORFEX
FRAISE
FROWER
FULLER
GOUGER
GRAVER
GWEEON
HACKER
HAMMER
HEADER
HOGGER
HUGGER
JAGGER
JOGGER
JOINER
LABRYS
LANCET
LIPPER
MACHET
MAIDEN
MALLET
MARTEL
MASHER
MEADER
MEALER
METATE
MINCER
MUCKLE
NIBBER
NIDGET
NIPPER
OLIVER
PAVIOR
PEELER
PESTLE
PICKAX
PIOLET
PLEWCH
PLEWGH
PLIERS
PLOUGH
PODGER
POLEAX
PRIEST
PRUNER
PUDDLE
RAMMER
RANCER
RANDER
RAPPER
RASPER
RIMMER
RIPPER
RIPSAW
RUTTER
SAPPER
SCORER
SCUTCH
SCYTHE
SHAVER
SHEARS
SHOVEL
SICKLE
SKIVER
SLATER
SLEDGE
SLICER
SPADER
STADDA
STYLET
SULLOW
TAMPER
TEASEL
THIXLE
THRAIL
TILTER
TOOLER
TREPAN
TREVET
TRIVAT
TRIVET
TUBBAL
TUBBER
TUSKAR
TWIBIL
VEINER
WEEDER

MOVING, REVOLVING, FLEXIBLE

AWE
CAM
COG
FAN
FLY
FUR
JIB
KEY
LAP
OAR
POY
PUY
RAX
TOM
VAN

AXIS
AXLE
BEAD
CONE
CRIC
DISC
DRUM
FLAP
GEAR
HAIR
HARR
LEAF
LILY
LITZ
PALM
PIRN
PLET
PLUG
REEL
RING
ROLL
ROPE
ROVE
TRIG
VANE
VIOL
VIRL
WHIP
WING
WORM

AZOTE
BAGUE
BEVEL
CABLE
CANON
CLACK
CODER
CRANK
DITAL
FELLY
FLIER
FLYER
GEMEL
GUIDE
HEALD
HINGE
IDLER
INDEX
JENNY
KNOUT
LASSO
LATCH
LEVER
PILOT
PLETE
QUIRT
RATCH
REATA
RIATA
ROMAL
SCULL
SKEIF
SKIVE
SNELL
SPOOL
STILE
SWEPE
SWING
SWISH
THROW
TOMMY
TRACE
TROLL
TRULL
TWIST
VALVE
VERGE
VOYAL
VOYOL
WANTY
WAVER
WHANG
WHEEP

WHIRL
WIDDY
WINCE
WITHY
WOODY
WREST

BARREL
BEDKEY
BILOPE
BOBBIN
CANNON
CASTER
CHABUK
CHAMAR
CHOWRY
COILER
CURLER
CURPEL

CURPLE
CURSOR
DAMPER
DERAIL
DOFFER
DRIVEN
DRIVER
ENARME
FAUCET
FERULA
FERULE
FLIGHT
FUSEAU
GIMBAL
GIMMAL
GUIDER
HEDDLE
HINGLE
HORRAL

KILHIG
LAINER
LARIAT
LASKET
LEADER
LIGGER
LINGEL
LINGLE
MULLER
NORSEL
NOSSEL
PADDLE
PANTER
PINION
PULLEY
RABAND
RADDLE
RAFFLE

RATLIN
RATTLE
RIGGER
ROBAND
RODING
ROLLER
ROWLET
RUDDER
RUNNER
SHEAVE
SHIVER
SWIVEL
TAPPER
TETHER
TORQUE
TURNER
VERREL
WINDER

PIERCING, BORING

AWL
TAP

BROG
CALK
FORK
GOAD
MOLL
NILL
PICK
PIKE
POTE
PROG
PUGH
PYKE
SPUR
TANG
TINE

TING

ANKUS
AUGER
BLUNT
BORER
BRAND
CORER
DRILL
ELBOW
ELSIN
ELSON
FLUKE
FURCA
GRAIN
GRAIP
LATHE
MORNE

NOBBY
PIKEL
PIKLE
PRICK
PRONG
SOWEL
SPEAR
STING
STRAW
TRIER
VALET

BIDENT
BODKIN
BORREL
CALKER
CALKIN
CROTCH

CURATE
DIBBER
DIBBLE
ELSHIN
FERRET
FIZGAG
FRAMEA
GIMLET
GRAINS
JUMPER
NAUGER
PECKER
PROBER
RIPPON
SCRIBE
STYLUS
TWISEL
WIMBLE

PRINTING TOOLS AND TERMS

EM
EN
PI

BED
CUT
FAT
FLY
JOB
LAY
LOW
OUT
PIE
SUB

BANK
BITE
BODY
CASE
COPY

DELE
DRAG
DRAW
FACE
FEET
FIST
FONT
FORM
KERN
LEAD
LEAN
LINE
NICK
QUAD
RACK
RISE
ROLL
RULE
SLIP
SLUG

SLUR
SORT
STEM
STET
TAKE
TYPE

ALLEY
BELLY
BLOCK
BOXIN
BRACE
CARET
CHASE
COLON
COMMA
CUTIN
DUMMY
DWELL
FRAME

HORSE
INSET
PLATE
POINT
PROOF
QUOIN
RUNIN
SERIF
SETUP
SHAKE
SHANK
SHEET
SPACE
STAND
STICK
TITLE
TOKEN

ACCENT
BATTER

BEARER
BODKIN
BRAYER
CANCEL
CASTER
CERIPH
CHAPEL
CLICHE
COCKUP
DABBER
DAGGER
DELETE
DIESIS
DOCTOR
DOUBLE
EMBOSS
FINGER

GALLEY
IMPOSE
INDENT
ITALIC
LEADER
LETTER
LOCKUP
MACKLE
MAKEUP
MARGIN
MATRIX
MATTER
NIPPER
OFFCUT
OFFSET
PICKUP
PLATEN

POSTER
REGLET
REVISE
ROLLER
ROUNCE
SETOFF
THIRTY
TYMPAN

BASTARD
CLICKER
COLLATE
COMPOSE
COUNTER
FRISKET
GAGEPIN
GRIPPER

HEADING
HELLBOX
IMPRINT
JOBWORK
JUSTIFY
MEASURE
MORTISE
MOVABLE
OPENING
OVERLAY
OVERRUN
PACKING
PINMARK
PLANNER
QUADRAT
REPRINT

SURGICAL TOOLS AND TERMS

BUR

HYPO
SPUD
SWAB

AMPUL
CLAMP
FLEAM
LANCE
PROBE
SETON
SNARE
STAFF
STUPE
STYLE
SWATH

BILABE
BOUGIE

CATLIN
DOSSIL
GARROT
GORGET
LANCET
MATRIX
NEEDLE
PROBER
SCALER
SPLINT
STILET
STYLET
SUTURE
SWATHE
TAMPON
TREPAN
TROCAR
VELTIS
XYSTER

ABLATOR
AMPOULE
AMPULLA
CANNULA
CATLING
CAUTERY
CURETTE
EJECTOR
FORCEPS
LEVATOR
MANDREL
MANDRIN
PIPETTE
PLEDGET
PLESSOR
PLUGGER
PLUNGER
SCALPEL
SPATULA
SYRINGE

TRACTOR
TRILABE
TROCHAR

BISTOURY
CATHETER
CROTCHET
DENTAGRA
ECRASEUR
ELEVATOR
EXPLORER
FORCIPES
SPECULUM
SQUEEZER
TENACULA

EXCAVATOR
EXTRACTOR
PERCUSSOR
TEREBELLA

OTHERS

BOW
CAP
DIE
HUB
JET
JIG
LOG
PEN
PIN
ROD
SET
TIP
TOW

BALL
BAND
BELL
BULB
BUOY
COIL

CORD
CUFF
DENT
DIAL
DROP
FACE
FLUE
FRET
FUSE
FUZE
GAGE
HAAF
HOSE
IRON
LAMP
LENS
LINE
LOCK
LOOM
LOOP

MIKE
RAIL
RULE
SHOE
SLAB
SLUG
STOP
TRIP
WAND
WARP
WICK
WIRE

BOWET
BRAKE
BRICK
CHAIN
CHUMP
CODON
COVER

CROSS
CROWN
DEVIL
DIODE
DIPSY
DUMMY
FUSEE
FUZEE
GADGE
GAUGE
GUARD
HATCH
HELIX
INKER
LATHI
LEVEL
LINGO
LOUPE
MATCH
METER

METRE
MIXER
NICOL
NORMA
PEDUM
PEISE
PLUMB
POINT
POKER
POUND
PUNCH
QUILL
RANGE
RULER
SCALE
SCREW
SHADE
SHELL
SIGHT
STAFF
STAKE
STICK
STILT
STOCK
STONE
STOVE
STRAP
TABLE
TEWEL
TOLLY
TORCH
TUNER
TYPER
VESTA

ABACUS
ALINER
ANCONY
AUDION
BALLOW
BASTON
BATULE
BLOWER
BONNET
BOTTOM
BRIDGE
BUMPER
BUNSEN
BURNER
CANDLE
CENTER
CENTRE
CIERGE
CRAYON
CUPPER
CUTOFF
CUTOUT
DENTIN
DEVICE
DIACLE
DIMMER
DIPSEY
DIPSIE
DISCUS
DONKEY
DOTTER
DOUTER
DYNAMO
ENGINE
FEEDER
FEELER
FILTER
FINDER
FINGER
FLITCH
GADGET
HEATER
JIGGER
JIMJAM
KIPPIN
LADDER
LATHEE
LINGOE
LOOPER
MAGNET
MARKER
MODDLE
NEEDLE
NIPPLE
NONIUS
NOZZLE
PENCIL
POOLER
POPPER
PRIMER
PROKER
PUSHER
REEDER
RICKER
RIDGER
RIFFLE
ROCKER
ROOKER
ROUSER
SADDLE
SCREEN
SERVER
SETTER
SHAKER
SPACER
SPLINE
SPRING
STOKER
SUCKER
SWITCH
TEDDER
THIVEL
TONGUE
TROWEL
TUYERE
TWITCH
WEIGHT
WORKER

TRANSPORTATION
VEHICLES
Man-Animal Operated

FLY
GIG
RIG
RUT

ARBA
BIGA
BIKE
BUTT
BYKE
CART
CHAY
DRAG
DRAY
DUKE
EKKA
GOAT
HACK
LUGE
MAIL
PLOW
PRAM
PUTT
RATH
SADO
SHAY
TEAM
TODE
TRAP
WAIN

ARABA
BANDY
BRAKE
BREAK
BRETT
CYCLE
DANDY
DILLY
DOLLY
ESSED
GURRY

HURLY
JERRY
JUTKA
RATHA
SADOO
STAGE
SULKY
TONGA
WAGON

BARROW
BERLIN
CALASH
CALESA
CHAISE
CHARET
CISIUM
DENNET
DROSKY
ESSEDA
ESSEDE
FIACRE
GHARRI
GHARRY
GOCART
HANSOM
HEARSE
HERDIC
JINGLE
JINKER
KOSONG
LANDAU
LIMBER
RECKLA
SAFETY
SHOFUL
SPIDER
SURREY
TANDEM
TELEGA
TROIKA

BICYCLE
BOUNDER
BRITZKA
CAISSON
CALECHE
CARAVAN
CARIOLE
CAROCHE
CARRETA
CHARIOT
CONCORD
CROYDON
DOGCART
DOSADOS
DROSHKY
FOURGON
GONDOLA
GROWLER
HACKERY
HACKNEY
KIBITKA
MORFREY
PHAETON
RICKSHA
SCOOTER
TALLYHO
TARTANA
TILBURY
TRUCKLE
TUMBLER
TUMBREL
TUMBRIL
TURNOUT
UNICORN
VETTURA
VISAVIS
VOITURE
VOLANTE

BAROUCHE
BRANCARD
BROUGHAM

CAPECART
CARRIOLE
CARROZZA
CHARETTE
CLARENCE
CURRICLE
DEARBORN
DEMOCRAT
DORMEUSE
DROSCHKE
EQUIPAGE
HANDCART
MORPHREY
ORDINARY
PUSHCART
QUADRIGA
RICKSHAW
ROCKAWAY
RUNABOUT
SOCIABLE
STANHOPE
TARANTAS
TRICYCLE
VICTORIA

BUCKBOARD
CABRIOLET
CARROMATA
CHARIOTEE
CONESTOGA
DILIGENCE
STRETCHER
TARANTASS
WAGONETTE

FOURINHAND
GERMANTOWN
JINRICKSHA
JINRIKISHA
VELOCIPEDE
VOITURETTE
WHEELCHAIR

Automobiles

BUS
AUTO
DRAG
HACK
JEEP
TANK
TAXI
TRAM
WYNN
COACH
COUPE
LORRY
SEDAN

TRUCK
CAMION
HEARSE
JALOPY
JIGGER
JITNEY
LANDAU
TOURER
AUTOBUS
BERLINE
FLIVVER
JALLOPY

OMNIBUS
SCOOTER
SIDECAR
TAXICAB
TORPEDO
TRACTOR
TRAILER
TRAMCAR
TROLLEY
VOITURE
COUPELET
DUMPCART
MOTORBUS

MOTORCAB
MOTORCAR
ROADSTER
RUNABOUT
SUBURBAN
AMBULANCE
CABRIOLET
CHARABANC
LANDAULET
LIMOUSINE
AUTOMOBILE
BLACKMARIA
MOTORCYCLE

On Runners

BOB
SKI
PULK
PUNG
SLED
PALKI
PULKA
SKATE
TRAIN
CUTTER
HURDLE
JAMPAN
JUMPER
PALKEE
SLEDGE
SLEIGH
BOBSLED
COASTER
GODEVIL
TRAVOIS
SNOWSHOE
TOBOGGAN
TRAVOISE
BOBSLEIGH

Portable

JUAN
KAGO
DANDI
DANDY
DOOLI
SEDAN
DOOLEY
DOOLIE
HOWDAH
KURUMA
LITTER
TELEGA
TOMJON
TONJON
CACOLET
NORIMON
SKILIFT
MUNCHEEL
PALANKEEN
PALANQUIN
STRETCHER

Railroad

HOG
MULE
COACH
DINER
DINKY
DOLLY
DUMMY
LOCAL
MOGUL
TRAIN
WAGON
BOXCAR
DINKEY
DONKEY
ENGINE
HELPER
JOPPER
SMOKER
SUBWAY
TENDER
WAGGON
CABOOSE
CARAVAN
CLUBCAR
EXPRESS
FLATCAR
GIRAFFE
GONDOLA
LIMITED
PULLMAN
SLEEPER
SPEEDER
TANKCAR
BRAKEVAN
CABLECAR
DAYCOACH
ELEVATED
WAGONLIT
HOPPERCAR
PARLORCAR
LOCOMOTIVE

Parts of Vehicles

BOX
CAM
FAN
RIM
AXLE
GEAR
HOOD
PLUG
SHOE
TIRE
TUBE
BRAKE
MOTOR
PEDAL
REINS
SHAFT
SPOKE
THILL
WHEEL
WIPER
BONNET
BUMPER
CLUTCH
ENGINE
INTAKE
PILLAR
PISTON
RUMBLE
SADDLE
SPRING
BATTERY
CHASSIS
EXHAUST
MAGNETO
MUFFLER
STARTER
TONNEAU
CYLINDER
FLYWHEEL
IGNITION
MUDGUARD
OILGAUGE
RADIATOR
SPROCKET
THROTTLE
GEARSHIFT
HANDLEBAR
SPARKPLUG

SHIPS

Sailing Vessels

CAT
GIG
HOY

BARK
BRIG
BUSS
DHOW
DONI
JUNK
KOFF
PINK
PRAM
SAIC
SAIL
SNOW
TODE
TOUP
TROW
YAWL
ZULU

BARGE
BATEL
BOLIA
CASCO
DANDY
DHONI
DRAKE
FOIST
KETCH
PINKY
PRAAM
RASEE
RAZEE
SETEE
SHARP
SLOOP
SMACK
TJALK

XEBEC
YANKY
ZABRA

ARGOSY
BAIDAR
BARQUE
BAWLEY
BILALO
BOLIAH
BORLEY
BOUTRE
CAIQUE
CANGIA
CARVEL
DINGHY
DOGGER
DROMON
GALIOT
GAYYOU
HOGGIE
HOLCAD

HOOKER
LANCHA
LORCHA
LUGGER
MISTIC
PRAHAM
PULWAR
SAILER
SAMBUK
SAMPAN
SANDAL
SCAFFY
SETTEE
SHIBAR
SKAFFY
TARTAN
TOSHER
TRANKY

BAGGALA
BIRLING
BIRLINN

BUMBOAT
CARAVEL
CATBOAT
CLIPPER
FELUCCA
FLYBOAT
FOYBOAT
FRIGATE
GAIASSA
GALLEON
GALLIOT
HAGBOAT
ICEBOAT
PATAMAR
PIRAGUA
POLACCA
POLACRE
POOKAUN
SEASLED
SHALLOP
SHARPIE

SKAFFIE
TARTANE

BALINGER
BALLAHOO
BALLAHOU
BILANDER
BILLYBOY
DAHABEAH
ICEYACHT
MACKINAC
MACKINAW
PATTAMAR
PATTIMAR
SCHOONER
TONGKANG

CARAVELLE
MUMBLEBEE
SNEAKBOAT
TRABACOLO

Engine-Driven Vessels

TUG
AVISO
OILER
OOLAK
QBOAT
SHOUT
DROGER
LAUNCH
PADDLE

PONTIN
PUFFER
TENDER
CANALER
COASTER
COLLIER
DREDGER
DRIFTER

DROGHER
LIGHTER
PINNACE
STEAMER
TOWBOAT
CANALLER
INDIAMAN
CABLESHIP

GUARDSHIP
LIGHTSHIP
MOTORBOAT
PILOTBOAT
POWERBOAT
SPEEDBOAT
STEAMBOAT
STEAMSHIP

Warships

LST
RAM
BOYER
SCOUT
UBOAT
ANDREW
CARACK
CHASER

PTBOAT
CARRACK
CORSAIR
CRUISER
FLATTOP
GUNBOAT
LANTCHA
MONITOR

SNORKEL
WARSHIP
CORVETTE
FIRESHIP
FLAGSHIP
GALLEASS
GALLIASS
IRONCLAD

MANOFWAR
BOMBARDER
DESTROYER
EAGLEBOAT
FIRSTRATE
MINELAYER
SUBMARINE

Oared Vessels

BAC
BUM
COG
GIG
ACON
DINK
DORY
GUFA
KUFA
MULE
OARS
PAHI
PLAT
PRAH
PRAO

PRAU
PROA
PUNT
RAFT
SCOW
WAKA
ACCON
BALSA
BANCA
BARIS
BIDAR
BIRCH
BUNGO
CANOE
COBLE

DINGY
DONGA
DUNGA
FLOAT
FUNNY
GOOFA
JOLLY
KAYAK
KELEK
MOSES
PRAHU
PUNGY
SCULL
SHELL
SKIFF

UMIAK
VINTA
WAAPA
BAIDAK
BALLAM
BAROTO
BATEAU
BIREME
BUGEYE
CAYUCA
CAYUCO
CORIAL
DINGEY
DUGOUT
GALLEY

GOUPHA
JANGAR
KUPHAR
LERRET
NUGGAR
OOMIAK
OUMIAC
PITPAN
PUNGEY
RANDAN
ROBROY
SEXERN
TORPID
UMIACK
WHERRY
ALMADIA
ALMADIE
BIDARKA
BUCKEYE
CASCARA
CORACLE
CURRACH
CURRAGH
CURRANE
DROMOND
FOUROAR
GONDOLA
JANGADA
LAKATOI
MASOOLA
PAIROAR
PIROGUE
SCULLER
SKIPPET
TRIREME
UNIREME
BIDARKEE
BULLBOAT
COCKBOAT
DUCKBOAT
GUNDALOW
LONGBOAT
BIRCHBARK
BUCENTAUR
CATAMARAN
OUTRIGGER
TOOTHPICK

General

TOW
BOAT
HULK
KEEL
MAIL
MARD
MARN
NAVY
CRAFT
FERRY
FLEET
LINER
PRORE
RACER
YACHT
ARMADA
CUTTER
MARINE
PACKET
SEALER
SLAVER
TANKER
TONNER
VESSEL
WHALER
PONTOON
VEDETTE
DERELICT
FLOTILLA
LIFEBOAT
CANALBOAT
FERRYBOAT
FREIGHTER
PRIVATEER
TRANSPORT
WHALESHIP

Parts of Ships

AFT
BOW
BOX
FID
NEF
RIB
RUN
SNY
BACK
BEAK
BIBB
BITT
BOOM
BRIG
DECK
DOCK
GAFF
HEAD
HELM
HOLD
HULK
HULL
JACK
KEEL
LOOF
MAST
NOSE
POLE
POOP
PORT
PROW
RAIL
SKAG
SKEG
SPAR
SPIR
STEM
YARD
BILGE
BOWER
CABIN
DAVIT
HATCH
HAWSE
KEVEL
ORLOP
SNAPE
SPRIT
STERN
WAIST
BRIDGE
BUNKER
CANVAS
GALLEY
GUNNEL
ISLAND
RUDDER
STEEVE
STRAKE
TILLER
BOLLARD
BULWARK
BUMPKIN
COUNTER
FORETOP
FUTTOCK
GANGWAY
GUNWALE
JIBSTAY
KEELSON
KILLICK
KNUCKLE
MAINTOP
SCUPPER
SCUTTLE
SNORKEL
SPANKER
SPIRKET
TOPMAST
YARDARM
BEAKHEAD
BOWSPRIT
BULLSEYE
CASEMATE
CUTWATER
FOREFOOT
FOREJACK
FOREMAST
FOREYARD
MAINMAST
PORTHOLE
WATERWAY

Famous Ships

ARGO
FRAM
GJOA
NINA
AOTEA
ARAWA
MAINE
PINTA
BOUNTY
TAINUI
OREGON
ARIZONA
HOROUTA
MATATUA
MONITOR
OLYMPIA
PELICAN
REVENGE
SQUALUS
TITANIC
BISMARCK
BONHOMME
CLERMONT
ENDEAVOR
GRAFSPEE
HALFMOON
HARTFORD
MERRIMAC
MISSOURI
SAVANNAH
TAKITUNU
YORKTOWN
LUSITANIA
MAYFLOWER
BIRKENHEAD
SANTAMARIA

TRIBES, PEOPLE, NATIVES

EUROPE

GEG	Alb.
LAK	Russ.
LAZ	Russ.
VAN	Russ.
VOD	Finn
VOT	Finn
AVAR	Russ.
BALT	Lith.
BOII	Celt
CELT	Brit., Fr.
CHAM	Alb.
CHUD	Finn
DANE	
ESTH	
FINN	
FLEM	Belg.
GAEL	Celt
GAUL	Fr.
GEAT	Swed.
GHEG	Alb.
GOTH	Ger.
IMER	Russ.
JUTE	Ger.
KAMI	Russ.
KOMI	Russ.
KURI	Russ.
LAPP	Scan.
LAZE	Russ.
LAZI	Russ.
LETT	Lith.
MANX	Celt
PICT	Brit.
POLE	
REMI	Belg.
RUSS	
SCOT	Celt
SERB	Slav
SLAV	
SORB	Slav
SVAN	Russ.
TOSK	Alb.
UBII	Ger.
VEND	Slav
VEPS	Finn
VOTE	Finn
WEND	Slav
ZIPS	Ger.
AEQUI	It.
ALANI	
ALANS	
ALMAN	Ger.
ATTIC	Greek
AVARS	Russ.

BESSI	Greek
BOIKO	Russ.
CATTI	Ger.
CROAT	Slav
CYMRY	Celt
CZECH	Slav
DARGO	Russ.
DIGOR	Russ.
DUTCH	
ELYMI	It.
ERSAR	Russ.
FRANK	Ger.
GALGA	Russ.
GREEK	
GUZUL	Russ.
GYPSY	
IBERI	Spain
ICENI	Briton
IJORE	Finn.
IRISH	Celt
KAZAN	Russ.
KUMAN	Hung.
KUMYK	Turk.
KYMRY	Celt
LADIN	Swiss
MARSI	Ger.
MARSI	It.
MAZUR	Pole
MORDV	Russ.
NOGAI	Russ.
NORSE	Scan.
OSCAN	It.
OSSET	Russ.
PECHT	Celt
PISAN	It.
POLAB	Slav
POMAK	Bulg.
QUADI	Ger.
ROMAN	It.
SAXON	Ger.
SCIOT	Greek
SICEL	It.
SUEVI	Ger.
SVANE	Russ.
SWISS	
TAULI	Russ.
USKOK	Slav
VANNI	Russ.
VENED	Slav
VEPSE	Finn
VLACH	Rum.
VOGUL	Finn.
WELSH	Celt
ZHMUD	Lith.

ABKHAS	Russ.
ADIGHE	Russ.
ALEMAN	Ger.
ALMAIN	Ger.
ANGLES	Ger.
BASQUE	Sp., Fr.
BATAVI	Ger.
BOSHAS	Russ.
BRETON	Fr.
BRITON	
BULGAR	
CARIAN	Greek
CHATTI	Ger.
DORIAN	Greek
FRENCH	
GASCON	Fr.
GEATAS	Swed.
GERMAN	
GOIDEL	Celt
HANSAS	Ger.
HERULI	Ger.
HRVATI	Slav
IBERES	Spain
INGUSH	Russ.
IONIAN	Greek
KABARD	Russ.
KYURIN	Russ.
LADINO	Swiss
LITVAK	Lith.
MAGYAR	Hung.
MORDVA	Russ.
MOSCHI	Russ.
MOSCVA	Russ.
NEMEAN	Greek
NERVII	Celt
NORMAN	Scan.
NORMAN	Fr.
PADUAN	It.
PICARD	Fr.
POLACK	Pole
ROMANY	Gypsy
RUTULI	It.
SABINE	It.
SAFINI	It.
SALIAN	Dutch
SAMIAN	Greek
SATRAE	Greek
SICANI	It.
SICULI	It.
TAGAUR	Russ.
TAVAST	Finn.
TEUTON	Ger.
THEBAN	Greek
TUSCAN	It.
UGRIAN	Finn

VANDAL	Ger.
VANNAI	Russ.
VELIKA	Russ.
VENETI	It.
VOLCAE	Celt
VOLSKI	It.
VOTYAK	Finn
ZYRIAN	Russ.
AEOLIAN	Greek
AEQUIAN	It.
BASHKIR	Russ.
BELGIAN	
BOSNIAN	Slav
BRYTHON	Celt
BUKEYET	Russ.
CANDIOT	Greek
CATALAN	Spain
CHECHEN	Russ.
CHUVASH	Bulg.
CYPRIOT	Greek
DARDANI	Greek
DARGHIN	Russ.
FALISCI	It.
FAROESE	Dan.
FIRBOLG	Celt
FLEMING	Belg.
FRISIAN	Ger.
GADITAN	Spain
GALLEGO	Spain
GENOESE	It.
HELLENE	Greek
HESSIAN	Ger.
IBERIAN	Spain
ISTRIAN	It.
ITALIAN	
KARTHLI	Russ.
KARTVEL	Russ.
KASHUBE	Ger.
LATVIAN	Lith.
LEONESE	Spain
LESBAIN	Greek
LOMBARD	It.
MALTESE	
MANXMAN	Celt
MERCIAN	Eng.
MORDVIN	Russ.
OXONIAN	Eng.
PAPHIAN	Greek
PARMESE	It.
PATARIN	It.
PELASGI	Greek
PERMIAK	Finn
PERMIAN	Finn
RAURACI	Fr.
RAURICI	Fr.
RHODIAN	Greek
RUSSIAN	
RUTHENE	Russ.
SABELLI	It.
SAMNITE	It.
SENONES	Celt
SEQUANI	Celt
SERBIAN	Slav
SIENESE	It.
SILURES	Eng.
SLOVENE	Slav
SPARTAN	Greek
SUEVIAN	Ger.
SUIONES	Ger.
SULIOTE	Greek
SWABIAN	Ger.
TOLEDAN	Spain
UMBRIAN	It.
VAUDOIS	Swiss
VESTINI	It.
WALLOON	Belg.
ALBANIAN	
ANDORRAN	Spain
ARMENIAN	Russ.
ASTURIAN	Spain
AUSTRIAN	
BAVARIAN	Ger.
BISCAYAN	Spain
BOEOTIAN	Greek
BOHEMIAN	Slav
CHERUSCI	Ger.
CORSICAN	Fr.
CROATIAN	Slav
CYPRIOTE	Greek
ETRUSCAN	It.
FRIULIAN	It.
GALICIAN	Spain
GALLEGAN	Spain
ILLYRIAN	Alb.
KARELIAN	Russ.
KASUBIAN	Ger.
KHALDIAN	Finn
KONARIOT	Turk.
LEZGHIAN	Russ.
LIGURIAN	It.
LIVONIAN	Lith.
MAJORCAN	Spain
MAZOVIAN	Ger.
MEGARIAN	Greek
MILANESE	It.
MINORCAN	Spain
MORAVIAN	Slav
NORSEMAN	Scan.
NORTHMAN	Scan.
PANNONIC	Hung.
PARISIAN	Fr.
PARMESAN	It.
PATARINE	It.
PATAVIAN	It.
PELASGOI	Greek
PHRYGIAN	Greek
POLABIAN	Slav
POLANDER	Pole
PORTUGEE	
PRUSSIAN	Ger.
RHAETIAN	It.
RUMANIAN	
RUMELIAN	Bulg.
RUSSNIAK	Russ.
SALOPIAN	Eng.
SAVOYARD	Fr.
SEMNONES	Ger.
SICAMBRI	Ger.
SICILIAN	It.
SILESIAN	Ger.
SPAINARD	Spain
THRACIAN	Greek
TYROLESE	Aust.
ULTONIAN	Eng.
USIPETES	Ger.
VENETIAN	It.
VISIGOTH	Ger.
YUGOSLAV	Slav

AFRICA

GA
GI

ABO
ARO
EDO
EFE
EVE
EWE
FAN
FON
FUL
FUR
IBO
IJO
JUR
KRA
KRU
KUA
LUO
LVO
LWO
RUA
SAN
SUK
VAI
VEI
YAO

ABSI
AFAR
AKAN
AKIM
AKKA
AKRA
ALUR
ASHA
BARI
BAYA
BEJA
BENI
BERI
BINI
BOGO
BONI
BUBE
BUBI
DAGO
DAZA
DOKO
EBOE
EFIK

EGBA
EJAM
EKOI
FANG
FIOT
FONG
FULA
FUNG
FUNJ
GALA
GOGO
GOLO
GOMA
GUHA
HABE
HARB
HEHE
HIMA
HOVA
HUMA
IDJO
IDYO
IDZO
JAGA
KAFA
KORA
KROO
LUBA
LUOH
LURI
MABA
MADI
MARI
NAMA
NUBA
NUPE
QUNG
RAVI
RIFE
SAAN
SAHO
SARA
SERE
SHLU
SHOA
SOGA
SUKU
SUSU
SUTO
TEDA
TIBU
TOMA
VILI
VIRA
VITI
XOSA
YAKA
ZULU

AFIFI
AMADI
ATEBA
BALAO
BANDA
BANTU
BASSA
BATWA
BENIN
BONGO
BORAN
BRAVA
CHAGA
CONGO
DADJO
DINKA
DUALA
FANTI
FANWE
FULAH
FULBE
FUNJE
FUNJI
GABON
GALLA
GANDA
GIBBI
GREBO
HABAB
HABBE
HAUSA
IDDIO
IGARA
INKRA
JOLOF
KAFFA
KAMBA
KHUAI
KIOKO
KONDE
KONGO
KREPI
LANGO
LENDU
LUNDA
LUREM
MAKUA
MAKWA
MANDE
MARRI
MASAI
MAURI
MBUBA
MENDE
MENDI
MONGO
MOSGU
MOSSI
MUTER
NANDI
NEGRO
NILOT
NYORO
PONDO
PYGMY
RUNDI
SAKAI
SERER
SHLUH
SHONA
SONGO
SOTHO
SOTIK
SWAZI
TEMBU
TEMNE
TIBBU
TINNI
TONGA
VOLOF
WAASI
WARRI
WARUA
WAYAO
WOLOF
YOLOF
ZANDE

ABABUA
ABANTU
ABATOA
ABATUA
ABATWA
ABONGO
ACHIAS
AMHARA
ANTEVA
AZANDE
BAFIOT
BAHIMA
BAHUMA
BAHUTU
BAKELE
BAKUBA
BAKUTU
BALAWU
BALOLO
BALUBA
BANYAI
BASOGA
BASUTO
BATOKA
BEDUIN
BERBER
BERTAT
BORANA
BULLOM
CHAGGA
CHAWIA
DAMARA
DOROBO
FANTEE
FULANI
GABOON
GRIQUA
HAMITE
HARARI
HEIKUM
HERERO
IGBARA
IGBIRA
IKBERE
KABYLE
KAFFIR
KANURI
KIKUYU
KORANA
KPUESI
LATUKA
LIBYAN
LOBALE
LOTUKO
MAKARI
MARAVI
MBONDO
MBUNDA
MPONDO
MURREE
NUBIAN
NYAMBE
NZAMBI
OBONGA
OVAMPO
PANGWE
POKOMO
SENUSI
SESUTO
SHAGIA
SHILHA
SHUKRI
SOMALI
SONGOI
SUKUMA
SURHAI
THONGA
TIMNEH
TUAREG
WABENA
WABUMA
WAGOGO
WAGUHA
WAHABI
WAHEHE
WASOGA
WATUSI
WAVIRA
WOCHUA
YAKALA
YORUBA
ZARAMO
ZEHUGA
ZENAGA

ABABDEH
ACHANGO
AKWAPIM
AMAKOSA
AMAZULU
ANTAIVA
ASHANTI
BABONGO
BACONGO
BAGANDA

BAGARRA
BAGGARA
BAKALAI
BAKALEI
BAKONGO
BAKUNDA
BAKWIRI
BALANTA
BALANTE
BAMBARA
BAMBUBA
BAMBUTE
BANGALA
BANYORO
BARONGA
BAROTSE
BARUNDI
BASONGO
BATEKES
BATONGA
BATUSSI
BEDOUIN
BULANDA
BUNYORO
BUSHMAN
CABINDA
CUSHITE
DADSCHO
DAHOMAN
DANAGLA
DANAKIL
DANKALI
FALASHA
FELLATA
GAETULI

GETULAN
GUANCHE
GUHAYNA
HARATIN
IMOHAGH
KABINDA
KABONGA
KIRUNDI
KOLDAJI
KROOBOY
LOATUKO
LUGANDA
MACHOGO
MAIACCA
MAKONDE
MAREHAN
MASHONA
MOGRABI
MPANGWE
MUNANDI
NAMAQUA
NEGRITO
NEGROID
NILOTIC
PAHOUIN
SANDAWE
SANDAWI
SENOUSI
SHAIGIA
SHAMMAR
SHILLUH
SHILLUK
SHUKRIA
SONGHAI
SONGHAY

SONGHOI
SUKKIIM
SWAHILI
TUKULER
TURKANA
UGANDAN
WABUNGA
WACHAGA
WAGWENO
WAKAMBA
WAKWAFI
WAKWAVI
WAMBUBA
WAMBUGA
WANGONI
WANYASA
WASANGO
WASEGUA
WONGARA

ALGERIAN
AMATEMBU
ANDOROBO
ANGOLESE
ASHANTEE
AUXUMITE
BAGHIRMI
BAROLONG
BATETELA
BECHUANA
BISHARIN
CANGUELA
CONGOESE
EGYPTIAN

HADENDOA
HARRATIN
IMOSHAGH
KABABISH
KARAMOJO
KUKURUKU
LIBERIAN
MAGHRIBI
MAKARAKA
MALAGASY
MANDINGO
MATABELE
MOGREBEE
MOMBOTTU
MOROCCAN
NEGRILLO
NIAMNIAM
NIGERIAN
NYAMWEZI
RAHANVIN
SAKALAVA
SUDANESE
TUNISIAN
WAMBUTTI
WANGATTA
WAPOKOMO
WASAGARA

DANAGALEH
MANGBATTU
MATABELES
MAUGRABIN
OVAHERERO
WANDOROBO

ASIA, AUSTRONESIA

China, Mongolia, Siberia

HEH
HEI
YAO
CHUD
DAUR
GOLD
LOLO
MANS
MIAO
NOSU
SHIK
TOBA
USUN
UZUN
BURUT
CHUDE
DAURI
ELEUT
GOLDI
HAKKA
HOKLO

IGDYR
KALKA
KAZAK
LAMUT
MOGUL
OLCHA
OLCHI
SAGAI
SERES
SOYOT
TATAR
TURKI
UIGUR
USSUN
UZBEK
YAKUT
YURAK
ALTAIC
AMOYAN
BALKAR
BELTIR

BURIAT
DUNGAN
DURBAN
GILIAK
HAINAN
KALMUK
KALMYK
KASSAK
KHALKA
KOIBAL
KORIAK
MANCHU
MANTZU
MONGOL
OROKON
OSTYAK
SHARRA
TARTAR
TAVGHI
TELEUT
TUNGUS

UIGHUR
YAOMIN
ALTAIAN
AMOYESE
BOUROUT
BUKEYET
CHUKCHI
DZUNGAR
ITELMES
KALMUCK
KALMYCK
KAMASIN
KHALKHA
KIRGHIZ
OROCHON
SAMOYED
TURKMAN
YENISEI
YUKAGIR
TURKOMAN
YUKAGHIR

Japan, Australia, Philippines

ATA
ATI
GOA
AETA
AINO
AINU
FIJI
KOKO
MORO
SULU
ARAWA
BATAK
BATAN
BICOL
BIKOL
DIERI
ILOCO
ILOKO
KIWAI
LANAO
LUCHU
MACRI
NIUAN
TAGAL
YAKAN
APAYAO
ARUNTA
BALUGA
BILAAN
BISAYA
BONTOK
GADDAN
IBANAG
IBILAO
IFUGAO
IGOROT
ITALON
ITAVES
KANAKA
KOIARI
MANOBO
MONTES
PAPUAN
SAMBAL
SAMOAN
TAGALA
TONGAN
VISAYA
YAMATO
ZAMBAL
BISAYAN
BUSHMAN
CAGAYAN
DADAYAG
GADDANG
ILOCANO
ILOKANO
ILONGOT
ILPIRRA
JOLOANO
KALINGA
KOITAPU
LUCHUAN
MANGYAN
NABOLOT
NEGRITO
RINGATU
SANGGIL
SATSUMA
SUBANUM
TAGALOG
TIRURAI
VISAYAN
AWABAKAL
BUKIDNON
CHAMORRO
CHINHWAN
FORMOSAN
HAWAIIAN
IGORROTE
KANKANAI
MONTESCO
PAMPANGA
PAMPANGO
QUIANGAN
TAHITIAN
TINGGIAN

India, Pakistan, Tibet, Nepal

AO
HO
AKA
GOR
JAT
KHA
KOL
MEO
AHIR
AOUL
AWAN
BHAR
BHIL
DARD
GARO
GOND
KOCH
KOLI
KUKI
MAGH
MAGI
MARI
NAGA
NAIR
RAIS*
REKI
TODA
TULU
TURI
ANGKA
BALTI
CHANG
COORG
DAFLA
DARDI
DOGRA
DRUPA
GADDI
GUJAR
HINDI
HINDU
JUANG
KANDE
KHASI
KOERI
KONDH
KORWA
KOTAR
KUMNI
KUNBI
KURMI
LIMBU
MIKIR
MUNDA
MUREE
NEWAR
NURMI
ORAON
ORIYA
SAORA
SAURA
TAMIL
URIYA
VEDDA
WAKHI
AGHORI
ANGAMI
ARAINS
ARLENG
ARORAS
BADAGA
BALUCH
BEHARI
BHOTIA
BHUMIJ
BHUTIA
BIHARI
CHAMAR
CHAMPA
DROPKA
DRUKPA
GURKHA
HINDOO
HOLEYA
JHURIA
KALWAR
KANWAR
KHARIA
KHASIA
KODAGU
KOMATI
KONYAK
KURUBA
LEPCHA
LOHANA
MADIGA
MANGAR
MISHMI
PAHARI
PANJAB
RAJPUT
RAMUSI
SANTAL
SAVARA
SHERPA
SINDHI
TANGUT
TELUGU
TIPURA
YERAVA
YUECHI
BALUCHI
BANGASH
BAZIGAR
BENGALI
BHOTIYA
BHUTANI
DRAVIDA
GUJRATI
KACHARI
KHARWAR
KHASIYA
KURUMBA
LAMBADI
MADRASI
MARATHA
MARWARI
ORAKZAI
PUNJABI
SHERANI
TAGHLIK
TIBETAN

Middle East, Afghanistan

AUS
LUR
ARAB
GHUZ
IBAD
KURD
SAFI
SEID
SLEB
TURK
FARSI
IHLAT
IRAKI
IRAQI
KAFIR
KAJAR
KHUZI
MAHRI
MUKRI
NEJDI
OMANI
SHIAH
SUNNI
TAJIK
TAULI
TEKKE
YEZDI
YURUK
ZIRAK
AFGHAN
AFSHAR
AUSHAR
BRAHUI
DEHWAR
DUNGAN
DURANI
GALCHA
GHEBER
GILAKI
HAZARA
HEJAZI
KAFFIR
MYSIAN
PAMIRI
PATHAN
SELJUK
SHIITE
SULABA
SULAIB
SUNNEE
SYRIAN
TUNGAN
YEMINI
YEZIDI
BELUCHI
BELUCKI
DURZADA
GHILZAI
HADJEMI
IRANIAN
ISRAELI
KHOKANI
OSMANLI
OTTOMAN
PAKHTUN
PUKHTUN
PERSIAN
SARACEN
SOGDIAN
SUNNITE
VIDDHAL
ACHAZKAI
BACTRIAN
LEBANESE

Laos, Cambodia, Vietnam, Burma

WA
KAW
KHA
KUI
LAI
LAO
MEO
MON
MRU
TAI
THO
AHOM
AKHA
CHIN
KADU
KUKI
LOLO
SHAM
SHAN
THAI
TSIN
KAREN
KHMER
MUONG
BALAWA
BURMAN
KACHIN
KHAMTI
LUSHAI
PEGUAN
YAOYIN
ANAMESE
BURMESE
LAOTIAN
MEITHEI
PALAUNG
SIAMESE
ANNAMESE
TONKINESE

Indonesia, Malaya

BUGI
CHAM
DYAK
IBAN
BAJAU
BATTA
BUKAT
CHIAM
DAYAK
DUSUN
JAKUN
KAYAN
MALAY
MURUT
PUNAN
SAKAI
SAMAL
SASAK
TZAAM
ALFURO
BILAAN
KALANG
NESIOT
REJANG
SAMSAN
SASSAK
SELUNG
SEMANG
TORAJA
BAKATAN
BORNEAN
LAMPONG
MALAYAN
NIASESE
TORADJA
ACHINESE
BALINESE
JAVANESE
MACASSAR
MADURESE
MAKASSAR
SUDANESE
SUMATRAN
TAGBUANA
TIMORESE

THE UNITED STATES AT A GLANCE

	State	Abbr.	Capital	Flower
22	**ALABAMA**	Ala.	Montgomery	Camelia
49	**ALASKA***	Alas.	Juneau	Forget-me-not
48	**ARIZONA**	Ariz.	Phoenix	Saguaro-cactus
25	**ARKANSAS**	Ark.	Little Rock	Apple blossom
31	**CALIFORNIA**	Cal(if).	Sacramento	Golden poppy
38	**COLORADO**	Col(o).	Denver	Columbine
5	**CONNECTICUT**	Conn.	Hartford	Mountain laurel
1	**DELAWARE**	Del.	Dover	Peach blossom
27	**FLORIDA**	Fla.	Tallahassee	Orange blossom
4	**GEORGIA**	Ga.	Atlanta	Cherokee rose
50	**HAWAII**	Haw.	Honolulu	Hibiscus
43	**IDAHO**	Id.	Boise	Lewis mockorange
21	**ILLINOIS**	Ill.	Springfield	Butterfly violet
19	**INDIANA**	Ind.	Indianapolis	Peony
29	**IOWA**	Ia.	Des Moines	Wild rose
34	**KANSAS**	Kan(s).	Topeka	Sunflower
15	**KENTUCKY**	Ky.	Frankfort	Goldenrod
18	**LOUISIANA**	La.	Baton Rouge	Magnolia
23	**MAINE**	Me.	Augusta	Pine cone & tassel
7	**MARYLAND**	Md.	Annapolis	Black-Eyed Susan
6	**MASSACHUSETTS**	Mass.	Boston	Mayflower
26	**MICHIGAN**	Mich.	Lansing	Apple blossom
32	**MINNESOTA**	Minn.	St. Paul	Showy lady's-slipper
20	**MISSISSIPPI**	Miss.	Jackson	Magnolia
24	**MISSOURI**	Mo.	Jefferson City	Hawthorn
41	**MONTANA**	Mont.	Helena	Bitterroot
37	**NEBRASKA**	Neb(r).	Lincoln	Goldenrod
36	**NEVADA**	Nev.	Carson City	Sagebrush
9	**NEW HAMPSHIRE**	N.H.	Concord	Purple lilac
3	**NEW JERSEY**	N.J.	Trenton	Purple violet
47	**NEW MEXICO**	N.M.	Santa Fe	Yucca
11	**NEW YORK**	N.Y.	Albany	Rose
12	**NORTH CAROLINA**	N.C.	Raleigh	Dogwood
39	**NORTH DAKOTA**	N.D.	Bismarck	Wild prairie rose
17	**OHIO**	O.	Columbus	Scarlet carnation
46	**OKLAHOMA**	Okla.	Oklahoma City	Mistletoe
33	**OREGON**	Ore.	Salem	Oregon grape
2	**PENNSYLVANIA**	Penn(a).	Harrisburg	Mountain laurel
13	**RHODE ISLAND****	R.I.	Providence	Violet
8	**SOUTH CAROLINA**	S.C.	Columbia	Yellow jessamine
40	**SOUTH DAKOTA**	S.D.	Pierre	Pasqueflower
16	**TENNESSEE**	Tenn.	Nashville	Iris
28	**TEXAS**	Tex.	Austin	Bluebonnet
45	**UTAH**	Ut.	Salt Lake City	Sego lily
14	**VERMONT**	Vt.	Montpelier	Red clover
10	**VIRGINIA**	Va.	Richmond	American dogwood
42	**WASHINGTON**	Wash.	Olympia	Rhododendron
35	**WEST VIRGINIA**	W.Va.	Charleston	Rhododendron
30	**WISCONSIN**	Wis(c).	Madison	Wood violet
44	**WYOMING**	Wyo.	Cheyenne	Indian paintbrush

Numbers denote order of admission into the Union; 1–13 Original States
* Largest in area, smallest in population ** Smallest in area

THE UNITED STATES AT A GLANCE

Nickname	Motto
Heart of Dixie, Cotton	We Dare Defend Our Rights
The Last Frontier	None
Grand Canyon, Sunset Land	Ditat Deus: God Enriches
Land of Opportunity, Wonder	Regnat Populus: Let the People Rule
Golden, Grape	Eureka: I Have Found It
Centennial, Rover	Nil Sine Numine: Nothing Without
Constitution, Nutmeg	He Who Transplanted, Sustains /Deity
First, Diamond	Liberty and Independence
Sunshine, Everglade	In God We Trust
Empire State of the South	Wisdom, Justice, Moderation
Aloha	The Life of the Land is Perpetuated in Righteousness
Gem, Gem of the Mountains	Esto Perpetua: Exist Forever
Prairie, Sucker	State Sovereignty, National Union
Hoosier, Carnation	Cross-roads of America
Hawkeye, Beautiful Land	Our Liberties We Prize, And Our Rights We Will Maintain
Sunflower, Jayhawk	Ad Astra Per Aspera: To the Stars Through Difficulties
Blue Grass	United We Stand, Divided We Fall
Pelican, Sugar, Creole	Union, Justice, Confidence
Pine Tree, Lumber	Dirigo: I Direct
Old Line, Free	Manly Deeds, Womanly Words
Bay, Old Colony	By the Sword We Seek Peace, but Peace Only Under Liberty
Wolverine, Lake	If You Seek a Pleasant Peninsula Look About You
North Star, Gopher	L'Etoile du Nord: Star of the North
Magnolia, Bayou	Virtute et Armis: By Virtue and Arms
Show Me, Bullion	The Welfare of the People Shall Be the Supreme Law
Treasure, Bonanza	Oro y Plata: Gold and Silver
Beef, Cornhusker	Equality Before the Law
Sagebrush, Silver, Battle-Born	All for Our Country
Granite, White Mountain	Live Free or Die
Garden	Liberty and Prosperity
Land of Enchantment, Sunshine	Crescit Eundo: It Grows as It Goes
Empire, Excelsior	Excelsior: Ever Upward
Tar Heel, Old North	To be Rather Than To Seem
Sioux, Flickertail	Liberty and Union, Now and Forever One and Inseparable
Buckeye	With God All Things Are Possible
Sooner	Labor Conquers All Things
Beaver, Webfoot	The Union.
Keystone, Quaker, Steel	Virtue, Liberty and Independence
Little Rhody, Gun Flint	Hope
Palmetto	Dum Spiro, Spero: While I Breathe,
Coyote, Sunshine	Under God, The People Rule /I Hope
Volunteer, Big Bend	Agriculture, Commerce
Lone Star, Beef	Friendship
Beehive, Mormon	Industry
Green Mountain	Freedom and Unity
Old Dominion, Cavalier	Sic Semper Tyrannis: Thus Always to
Evergreen, Chinook	Bye and Bye /Tyrants
Mountain, Panhandle	Mountaineers Always Free
Badger, Cheese	Forward
Equality	Equal Rights

THE UNIVERSE

PLANETS AND SATELLITES

Planet	Satellite
Mars	DEIMOS
	PHOBOS
Earth	MOON
Pluto	
Venus	
Saturn	RHEA
	DIONE
	MIMAS
	TITAN
	PHOEBE
	THETYS
	IAPETUS
	HYPERION
	ENCELADUS
Uranus	ARIEL
	OBERON
	MIRANDA

Planet	Satellite
	TITANIA
	UMBRIEL
Jupiter	IO
	PAN
	HERA
	HADES
	EUROPA
	HESTIA
	DEMETER
	ADRASTEA
	AMALTHEA
	CALLISTO
	GANYMEDE
	POSEIDON
Mercury	
Neptune	NEREID
	TRITON

STARS

SUN
YED

ADIB
ALYA
ATIK
AZHA
BEID
CAPH
DUHR
ENIF
IZAR
JUGA
KAUS
KEID
KIDS
MAIA
MIRA
NAOS
PHAD
SADR
SALM
SKAT
UNUK
VEGA
WEGA
WEZN

ACRAB
ACRUX
AGENA

ALCOR
ALGOL
ALKES
ANCHA
ARKAB
ARNEB
ATLAS
BAHAM
BIHAM
CHARA
CUJAM
CURSA
DABIH
DELTA
DENEB
DIFDA
DUBHE
ERRAI
FURUD
GEMMA
HAMAL
HOMAN
KIFFA
MATAR
MEDIA
MERAK
MIRAC
MIRAK
MIZAR
NIHAL
NUNKI

PHACD
PHAET
RIGEL
SABIK
SAIPH
SPICA
TANIA
WEZEN
ZOSMA

ACAMAR
ADHARA
ALBALI
ALGEDI
ALHENA
ALIOTH
ALKAID
ALMACH
ALNASI
ALTAIR
ALTAIS
ALTARF
ALUDRA
ANCHAT
ARIDED
BOTEIN
CASTOR
DHENEB
ELNATH
ETAMIN

GIENAH
HYADES
KOCHAB
LESATH
MARFIK
MARKAB
MEGREZ
MEISSA
MENKAR
MENKIB
MERKEB
MEROPE
MIRACH
MIRFAK
MURZIN
NEKKAR
PHECDA
PLEIAD
POLLUX
PROPUS
SCHEAT
SIRIUS
SMYRNA
THUBAN
YILDUN
ZANIAH
ZAURAK

DOGSTAR
POLARIS

ASTEROIDS

HEBE
IRIS
JUNO
CERES
FLORA
IRENE
METIS
VESTA
EGERIA
HYGEIA
PALLAS
PSYCHE
THETIS
ASTRAEA
EUNOMIA
FORTUNA
LUTETIA
MASSALIA

COMETS AND METEORS

FAYE
WOLF
BIELA
ENCKE
KOPFF
SWIFT
BROOKS
COGGIA
DONATI
FINLAY
HALLEY
HOLMES
LYRIDS
OLBERS
TEMPEL
TUTTLE
URSIDS
BARNARD
BIELIDS
BORELLI
BRORSEN
DARREST
LEONIDS
LYRAIDS
PERRINE
TAURIDS
AQUARIDS
GEMINIDS
ORIONIDS
PERSEIDS
WESTPHAL
GIACOBINI

CONSTELLATIONS

ARA	altar
ARGO	ship
APUS	paradise bird
CRUX	cross
GRUS	crane
LYNX	lynx
URSA	bear
VELA	sails
CANIS	dog
DRACO	dragon
HYDRA	water monster
INDUS	Indian
LEPUS	hare
LUPUS	wolf
MALUS	mast
MENSA	table
MUSCA	fly
NORMA	square
ORION	hunter
PYXIS	compass
ANTLIA	pump
AQUILA	eagle
AURIGA	wagoner
BOOTES	herdsman
CAELUM	tool
CARINA	keel
CORVUS	crow
CRATER	cup
CYGNUS	swan
DORADO	swordfish
HYDRUS	watersnake
OCTANS	octant
PICTOR	easel
PUPPIS	stern
SCUTUM	shield
TUCANA	toucan
VOLANS	flying fish
CEPHEUS	monarch
COLUMBA	dove
LACERTA	lizard
PEGASUS	flying horse
PERSEUS	rescuer
SAGITTA	arrow
SERPENS	snake
SEXTANS	sextant

Zodiacal Constellations

LEO	Lion
ARIES	Ram
LIBRA	Scales
VIRGO	Virgin
CANCER	Crab
GEMINI	Twins
PISCES	Fishes
TAURUS	Bull
SCORPIO	Scorpion
AQUARIUS	Water-Bearer
CAPRICORN	Ram
SAGITTARIUS	Archer

MAN'S PROBES INTO OUTER SPACE

* Indicates USSR

Artificial Satellites and Spaceships

OAO
OGO
OSO
ECHO
ESSA
GREB
LUNA*
MARS*
SNAP
VELA
ZOND*
ARIEL
IDCSP
INJUN
LOFTI
LUNIK*
MIDAS
RELAY
SAMOS
TIROS
TOPSI
TRAAC
APOLLO
COSMOS*
GEMINI
NIMBUS
PAGEOS
POLYOT*
PROTON*
RANGER
SYNCOM
VOSTOK*
YANTAR*
COURIER
MARINER
MERCURY
MOLNIYA*
ORBITER
PIONEER
SPUTNIK*
TELSTAR
TRANSIT
VOSKHOD*
ALOUETTE
ELEKTRON*
EXPLORER
INTELSAT
LANIBIRD
SURVEYOR
VANGUARD
EARLYBIRD
DISCOVERER
FRIENDSHIP

Astronauts

SEE
GLENN
LAIKA*
SCOTT
TITOV*
WHITE
YOUNG
ALDRIN
BORMAN
CERNAN
CONRAD
COOPER
GORDON
LEONOV*
LOVELL
BASSETT
BLACKIE*
BREEZIE*
COLLINS
GAGARIN*
GRISSOM
KOMAROV*
SHEPARD
SCHIRRA
YEGOROV*
BIKOVSKY*
BELYAYEV*
MCDIVITT
POPOVICH*
STAFFORD
ARMSTRONG
CARPENTER
NIKOLAYEV*
FEOKTISTOV*
TERECHKOVA*

Missiles, Rockets

ABLE
NIKE
THOR
AGENA
ATLAS
DELTA
GENIE
GOLEM*
KOMET*
SCOUT
TITAN
FALCON
SATURN
BULLPUP
CENTAUR
JUPITER
POLARIS
SPARROW
TERRIER
CORPORAL
LACROSSE
HOUNDDOG
PERSHING
REDSTONE
MINUTEMAN
HONESTJOHN
LITTLEJOHN
SIDEWINDER

WEARING APPAREL

HISTORIC, ECCLESIASTIC

ALB

ALBA
CEST
COPE
COWL
FANO
HOOD
HUKE
PALL

AMICE
COTTA
EPHOD
FANON
FANUM
FROCK
MITER
MITRE
ORALE
PALLA

PHANO
SCARF
SIMAR
STOLA
STOLE
SYRMA
TALMA
TIARA
TUNIC
VAGAS

ABOLLA
ALMUCE
CASULA
CESTUS
CHIMER
CHITON
CYCLAS
FANNEL
JESUIT
LEVITE

MANTUA
ROCHET
TABARD
TIPPET
TUNICA
VAKASS

ARISARD
BIRETTA
BUSKINS
CALOTTE
CAPUCHE
CASSOCK
CHIMERE
CHLAMYS
CHRISOM
CUCULLA
MANIPLE
MOZETTA
ORARION
PAENULA

PALLIUM
PELLARD
PIANETA
PLANETA
SOUTANE
SPENCER
SULTANE
TUNICLE
ZIMARRA

BERRETTA
CAPUCHIN
CHASUBLE
CINCTURE
DALMATIC
GAMBESON
HIMATION
MANTEVIL
MOZZETTA
SCAPULAR
SURPLICE

NATIVE, LOCAL

ABA
OBI

BAJU
HAIK
IZAR
KILT
MALO
MINO
SARI
SAYA
TOGA

BURKA
CABAN
CHOGA
CHOLI
DHOTI

GREGO
HAORI
JELAB
JEMMY
JIBBA
LUNGI
PAGNE
PAREU
PARKA
SAGUM
TOOSH
TREWS

ANORAK
BARVEL
BIETLE
BYRRUS
CABAAN

CANDYS
CHAMMA
DIRNDL
DOLMAN
HUIPIL
JELICK
JELLAB
JIBBAH
JIBBEH
JUBBAH
KAROSS
KIMONO
LUNGEE
MOOCHA
NETCHA
PONCHO
RAILLY
SARONG

TEMIAK
TOUSER

BURNOUS
CHUDDAH
CHUDDAR
CHUDDER
FILIBEG
GALABIA
SARAFAN
TABLIER
ZAMARRA

BURNOOSE
CHAQUETA
CHARSHAF
JIRKINET

BODY

BRA
HAP
TOP
TUX

BELT
BRAT
CAPA
CAPE
COAT
DICK
ETON

GOWN
JUMP
JUPE
PALL
ROBE
SACK
SARK
SASH
SLIP
SUIT
TOBE
VEST

APRON
BENJY
BENNY
CAPOT
CLOAK
CYMAR
DICKY
DRESS
FICHU
FROCK
GANSY
GILET

HABIT
JEANS
JUMPS
JUPON
KHAKI
MIDDY
MUFTI
PANTS
PATTE
PLAID
POLKA
SHAWL

SHIFT
SHIRT
SKIRT
SLOPS
SMOCK
STAYS
STOLE
TALAR
TONGS
TUNIC
WAIST
WAMUS

BANIAN
BASQUE
BAVARY
BLAZER
BLOUSE
BODICE
BOLERO
BUSTLE
CAFTAN
CAMAIL
CAMISA
CAMISE
CAPOTE
COATEE
CORSET
DICKEY
GANSEY
GIRDLE
HALTER
JACKET
JERKIN

JOSEPH
KABAYA
KAFTAN
KIRTLE
LINDER
LIVERY
MANTLE
NAPRON
PEPLUM
PHAROS
RAGLAN
SKILTS
SLACKS
SLIPON
SONTAG
STEPIN
TIGHTS
TUXEDO
ULSTER
UNDIES
VESTEE
VISITE
WAMMUS
WAMPUS

BALDRIC
BANDEAU
BEDGOWN
CAMISIA
CHEMISE
CRISPIN
CUTAWAY
DESSOUS
DOUBLET

DRAWERS
GSTRING
HAPPING
HARNESS
NEGLIGE
NORFOLK
PAJAMAS
PALETOT
PALTOCK
PELISSE
PYJAMAS
RISTORI
ROMPERS
SHOOTER
SLICKER
SLIVERS
SPENCER
STAMMEL
SURCOAT
SURTOUT
SWEATER
TEAGOWN
UNIFORM
WRAPPER

BENJAMIN
BLOOMERS
BREECHES
CAMISOLE
CARDIGAN
CARDINAL
CEINTURE
CLEADING
CORSELET

JAQUETTE
KNICKERS
LINGERIE
MACKINAW
MANTILLA
NEGLIGEE
OILSKINS
OVERALLS
OVERCOAT
PEIGNOIR
PELERINE
PINAFORE
PULLOVER
TROUSERS
VESTMENT

BRASSIERE
BRUNSWICK
CRINOLINE
GABARDINE
GABERDINE
GARIBALDI
GREATCOAT
HOOPSKIRT
INVERNESS
LOINCLOTH
NIGHTGOWN
OVERSKIRT
PEAJACKET
PETTICOAT
PLUSFOURS
POMPADOUR
REDINGOTE
UNIONSUIT

Head and Neck

* Indicates Neckwear

BIB
BOA*
BOW
CAP
DIP
FEZ
HAT
HOW
LID
TAJ
TAM
TIE*

AGAL
BAKU
COIF
COWL
FELT
FLAT
FLOP
HOOD
HURA
JOAN
KEPI

MASK
MAUD*
PARE
RUFF*
TECK
TIAR
TILE
TOPI
VEIL

AMPYX
ASCOT*
BARBE*
BENJY
BERET
BOINA
BOXER
BUSBY
CADDY
CROWN
DERBY
DICER
FICHU*
GIBUS

JABOT*
JASEY
JERRY
KULAH
LAMBA*
LUNGI*
MILAN
MITER
MITRE
MUTCH
NUBIA*
PATTU*
RABAT*
RUCHE*
SCARF*
SHAKO
SNOOD
SQUAM
STOCK*
STRAW
TERAI
THROW
TIARA
TOPEE

TOQUE
TOZIE
TUQUE
VITTA
VOLET

AIGRET
ANALAV
ANGORA*
ASMACK
BARRAD
BARRET
BEAVER
BERTHA*
BIGGIN
BOATER
BONNET
BOWLER
BOWTIE*
BRUTUS
BURLET
CADDIE
CALASH
CALPAC

CAMAIL
CASTOR
CHOKER*
CLAQUE
CLOCHE
COCKUP
CRAVAT*
DIADEM
DOMINO
FAILLE
FEDORA
FILLET
GORGET*
GUIMPE*
HENNIN
KULLAH
LUNGEE*
MANDIL
MOBCAP
PANAMA
PEPLUM
PILEUS
PINNER
RABATO*
RABBAT*

RAFFIA
REBATO*
SAILOR
SARAPE*
SERAPE*
SLOUCH
TAENIA
TAPALO*
TIPPET*
TOPHAT
TRILBY
TUCKER*
TURBAN
UPARNA

ANLIKAR*
BANDANA
BANDEAU
BANDORE
BRIMMER
CALOTTE
CAUBEEN
CEREVIS
CHAPEAU
CHECHIA

COMMODE
DOPATTA*
FLANDAN
FORAGER
GALERUM
HOMBURG
LEGHORN
MOLOKER
MONTERO
MORTIER
MUFFLER*
NECKTIE*
PAISLEY*
PETASOS
PETASUS
PILLBOX
RAMILIE
SALACOT
SOWBACK
SUNDOWN
TALLITH
THERESE
TRESSON
TRICORN
TUTULUS

YASHMAC
YASHMAK

AIGRETTE
BALMORAL
BEARSKIN
BIGGONET
CAPELINE
CAPUTIUM
CARCANET
HAVELOCK
HEADGEAR
KERCHIEF
MAHARMAH
NIGHTCAP
OPERAHAT
RAMILLIE
REHOBOAM
SKULLCAP
STEPHANE
SOMBRERO
TARBOOSH
YARMULKA

STOVEPIPE

Legs and Feet

BAL

BOOT
CACK
CLOG
GETA
HOSE
MULE
PUMP
SHOE
SOCK
TABI

CAMIK
CHAPS
KAMIK
MOYLE
PUTTY
ROMEO
SABOT
SHAPS
SPATS
STOGA

STOGY

ANKLET
ARCTIC
BOOTEE
BROGAN
BROGUE
BUSKIN
CALIGA
CHOPIN
COBCAB
CRAKOW
CREOLE
GAITER
GALOSH
JULIET
KAMMIK
MOGGAN
MUKLUK
OXFORD
PATTEN
PEDULE
PINSON

PUTTEE
PUTTIE
RUBBER
SANDAL
SECQUE
STOGIE
SUEDES

BABOOSH
BLUCHER
BOTTINE
CHINELA
CHOPINE
COTHURN
CRUISER
GAMBADO
GARTERS
HESSIAN
HOSIERY
HUSHION
LEGGING
RULLION

SHINNER
SLIPPER
SLOGGER
TOPBOOT

BABOUCHE
BALMORAL
BOOTIKIN
BOTTEKIN
COLONIAL
FINNESKO
GAMASHES
HALFBOOT
HUARACHO
LARRIGAN
MOCCASIN
NAPOLEON
OVERSHOE
POULAINE
SABOTINE
SNEAKERS
STOCKING

Furs

CAT
DOG
FOX
KID

BEAR
CALF
FLIX
GOAT

HARE
LAMB
LYNX
MINK
MOLE
PONY
SEAL
VAIR
WOLF

CIVET
FITCH
GENET
KOALA
LLAMA
OTTER
PAHMI
PANDA
SABLE

SHEEP
SKUNK

ALPACA
BADGER
BEAVER
DESMAN
ERMINE
FISHER

JACKAL
JAGUAR
MARMOT
MARTEN
MONKEY
NUTRIA
OCELOT
PELTRY
RABBIT
SUSLIK
VICUNA

WEASEL
WOMBAT

CARACAL
CHEETAH
CRIMMER
FITCHEW
GUANACO
HAMSTER
KARAKUL
KRIMMER

LEOPARD
MINIVER
MUSKRAT
OPOSSUM
RACCOON
WALLABY

ANTELOPE
KANGAROO
KINKAJOU

KOLINSKY
REINDEER
SQUIRREL
VISCACHA

BASSARISK
WOLVERINE
WOODCHUCK

CHINCHILLA

FABRICS AND FIBERS

* indicates Cordage

MAT
NET
RAS
REP
SAK
TAT
WEB

ACCA
ADAD*
ALMA
BAFT
BAST*
BATT
COIR
CREA
CRIN
DRAB
DUCK
ERUC*
FELT
FERU*
FLAX*
GROS
HEMP*
HUCK
HUSI
IKAT
IMBE*
IXLE*
JEAN
JUSI
JUTE*
KELT
KEMP
LACE
LAME
LAWN
LENO
LINT
MACO
MAUD
MESH
MOFF
MUGA
MULL
PILE

PIMA
PINA
PITA*
REPP
RHEA*
SABA
SANA*
SILK
SUNN*
SUSI
TAPA
TASH
TASS
TRAM
WOOL

ABACA*
ADATI
ATLAS
BAIZE
BATIK
BEIGE
CADIS
CHINE
CRAPE
CRASH
CREPE
DATIL*
DENIM
DOREA
DORIA
DRILL
FILET
FLOSS
GAUZE
GULIX
GUNNY
ISTLE*
IXTLE*
KAPOK
KASHA
KHAKI
LACIS
LAINE
LINEN
LISLE
LLAMA

MANTA
MOIRE
MUNGO
OLONA*
PANNE
PEKIN
PIQUE
PLAID
PLUSH
RAMIE
ROMAL
RUMAL
SAKEL
SALLO
SATIN
SCRIM
SERGE
SHELA
SISAL*
SUEDE
SURAH
SURAT
SWISS
TABBY
TAMIS
TARSE
TERAP*
TERRY
TOILE
TULLE
TWEED
TWILL
TWIST*
UNION
VICHY
VOILE
WIGAN

ALACHA
ALPACA
AMBARY*
ANGORA
ARMURE
BATTIK
BEAVER
BOUCLE
BROCHE

BURLAP*
CADDIS
CALICO
CAMACA
CAMLET
CANVAS
CHINTZ
COTTON
COUTIL
COVERT
CRETON
DAMASK
DIMITY
DOMETT
DOWLAS
EPONGE
ETOILE
FAILLE
FLEECE
FRIEZE
FRISCA
GLORIA
GURRAH
KERSEY
LAMPAS
LINAGA*
LINENE
LINSEY
MADRAS
MALINE
MELTON
MERINO
MOHAIR
MOREEN
MUSLIN
NANKIN
OXFORD
PEELER
PENANG
POPLIN
RADIUM
RAFFIA*
RATINE
SALLOO
SAMITE
SATEEN
SAXONY

SELING
SHELAH
STAPLE*
TAMISE
TANJIB
TARTAN
THREAD*
TILLOT
TISSUE
TOBINE
TRICOT
TUSSAH
TUSSEH
VELOUR
VELURE
VELVET
VICUNA
WADMAL
WOOLEN
YACHAN
ZANANA
ZENANA
ZEPHYR

ALACHAH
ALLOVER
BATISTE
BROCADE
BUCKRAM
BUNTING
CAMBRIC
CHALLIS
CHAMOIS

CHEVIOT
CHIFFON
COATING
DOESKIN
DRUGGET
DUVETYN
EPINGLE
ESPARTO
ESTAMIN
ETAMINE
FILASSE
FLANNEL
FOULARD
FUSTIAN
GALATEA
GINGHAM
HABUTAI
HOLLAND
JACONET
MIXTURE
MOGADOR
NANKEEN
ORGANDY
ORGANZA
OTTOMAN
PAISLEY
PERCALE
SATINET
SILESIA
STAMMEL
SUITING
TABARET
TABINET

TAFFETA
TEXTILE
TICKING
TIFFANY
VEILING
VELOURS
WOOLLEN
WORSTED

BARATHEA
BIRDSEYE
BROCATEL
CASHMERE
CHAMBRAY
CHENILLE
CORDUROY
COUTELLE
COUTILLE
CRETONNE
DOMESTIC
DUNGAREE
DUVETINE
ESTAMENE
HOMESPUN
JACQUARD
LUSTRINE
MILANESE
MOGADORE
MOLESKIN
NAINSOOK
OILCLOTH
OSNABURG
PRUNELLA

SARSENET
SHANTUNG
SHEETING
SHIRTING
TAPESTRY
TARLATAN
TARLETAN
VALENCIA
WHIPCORD
ZIBELINE

ALBATROSS
ASTRAKHAN
BENGALINE
CASSIMERE
COTTONADE
EIDERDOWN
GABARDINE
GEORGETTE
GRENADINE
GROSGRAIN
HAIRCLOTH
HUCKABACK
LONGCLOTH
MATELASSE
MESSALINE
ORGANZINE
PARAMATTA
PERCALINE
SATINETTE
SHARKSKIN
TRICOTINE
VELVETEEN

Man-made Fabrics and Fibers

ARNEL
DYNEL
FIBRO
KODEL
LYCRA
NYLON
ORLON
RAYON

VELON
ARALAC
DACRON
DYNELO
LASTEX
TYCORA
VICARA
VINYON

ACETATE
ACRILAN
FORTREL
SARELON
SPANDEX
TREVIRA
CAPROLAN
CELANESE

FIBREFAX
FORTISAN
REVOLITE
REXENITE
FIBREGLAS
POLYESTER
POLYFIBRE
CHEMSTRAND

RUGS AND CARPETS

AGRA
BAKU
KUBA
CHILA
HERAT
KAZAK
KILIM
KULAH
LADIK
MECCA
MELAS
MELES
MOSUL
NAMDA
NUMDA
SARUK

SENNA
SUMAK
TAPET
TEKKE
USHAK
YOMUD
YORUK
AFGHAN
GELEEM
HERATI
KASHAN
KIRMAN
MOGHAN
NAMMAD
OUSHAK
RUNNER

SAROUK
SHIRAZ
TABRIZ
WILTON
BERGAMA
BERGAMO
BOKHARA
DERBEND
DRUGGET
FERAHAN
GIORDES
GUENDJE
HAMADAN
INGRAIN
ISFAHAN
SHIRVAN

AKHISSAR
BRUSSELS
DAGESTAN
FERAGHAN
GHIORDES
KABISTAN
KARABAGH
LESGHIAN
SERABEND
ANATOLIAN
AXMINSTER
BROADLOOM
CAUCASIAN
KHOROSSAN
KURDISTAN
SAMARKAND

SECTION III: WORD LOCATOR

EXPLANATION OF USE

This section lists words in easy-to-read columns and gives definitions for them. This method eliminates the need for cross-references and makes it possible to find the word you want very quickly.

The plan is based on letter-position of words. If you need a 2-letter word ending in — A meaning "Gold Coast Negro," run your eye down the 2-letter word list, where you will find the answer GA. The list is alphabetized starting with AA, giving all words with — A in the second position, then all words with — B in that position, and so on. Thus if you are looking for a word ending in — B meaning "river," you quickly find OB.

The 3-letter word list is based on the same plan. All words ending in — — A are listed in alphabetical order from ABA to ZOA, then all words ending in — — B from ABB to ZAB, and so on. As soon as one end-letter is finished, the next letter begins. This list concludes with the word YEZ. Then all words with — A — in the second position are listed (from BAA to TAZ), followed by — B — in the second position, and so on up to — Z — .

The 4-letter words are listed first in a straight alphabetical group, from A — — — to Z — — —. This enables you to find a word if you have only the *first* letter. This list goes from AALI to ZYME. Then the positional lists begin. All words with — A — — as a second letter are now listed, from BAAL to ZAZA; then all words with — B — — as a second letter; then — C — —; and all the way to — Z — —. When this entire second-letter group is complete, — — A — as a third letter, — — B — as a third letter, and so on to Z are listed. Finally, — — — A as a fourth letter is given, — — — B as a fourth letter, and so on.

The catchwords given in the upper left- and right-hand corners of each page direct you quickly to the letter-position you want.

Note: Puzzle makers vary their definitions, but you should recognize most words despite this variation.

TWO-LETTER WORDS

AA rough lava (opp. to pahoehoe)
BA soul (bird with human head); bleat; Bachelor of Arts (degree)
DA ambary (hemp); yes: Russ.; prosecutor; — Gama
EA Eridu's chief god; river
FA syllable of scale (mi — sol); 4th tone
GA Gold Coast Negro
HA exclamation; have
IA Iowa
JA yes: Ger.
KA genius, double (Egypt); unknown Hindu god (Brahma, Prajapati)
LA syllable of scale (sol — ti); 6th tone; Louisiana; article: Sp., Fr., It.; — Paz; — Plata; — Crosse
MA mother; — Bellona (goddess); Ra's daughter; Master of Arts (degree); Maritime Administration
NA continent
PA papa; N.Z. fort, village
RA sun god; Nut's son; mus. note
SA continent
TA pagoda; article: Scot.; mus. note; weight
VA it proceeds (mus.); comment ça — (how are you?): Fr.; Virginia; Veterans Administration
WA Burmese native, language; measure
YA Arabic Y; diphthong
ZA Tartini's B-flat; prefix: very

AB immortal heart; 11th Jewish month; prefix: from
BB chess move; rifle shot size
FB fullback (football)
HB halfback (football)
KB chess move
OB objection; — and sol; prefix: to, before, against; river
QB quarterback (football); chess move
RB chess move

AC alternating current
BC time
CC 200
DC direct current; 600; Washington
EC prefix: from, house
IC suffix
MC 1100; entertainer
OC yes; langue d'- (Fr. dialect)
XC 90

AD notice; toward: Lat.; — hoc; — lib; — infinitum
CD 400
DD Doctor of Divinity (degree)
ED verb ending; Jordan altar; nickname
ID fish; natural self; — est
MD Doctor of Medicine; Maryland
OD minced oath; alleged force
TD clay pipe

AE umlaut; Lat. plural; poet (G. W. Russell)
BE exist; subsist
CE Chemical, Civil Engineer; this: Fr.; n'est- pas?
DE prefix: from (Lat., Fr.); of, with: Sp.; — profundis
EE ye; eye: Scot.; Electrical Engineer
FE mus. syllable; Santa —
GE goddess; Gaea, Chaos's daughter, mother of Uranus, Titans; Tapuyan
HE man; anyone; Heb. letter, 5
IE screw pine (mat, basket); that is; diphthong
LE article: Fr.; mus. note; — Havre; — Bourget
ME pronoun; I; ego; mus. note; Maine
NE compass point; not
OE umlaut; whirlwind; islet
PE Heb. P, 80; weight; measure
RE regarding; syllable of scale (do — mi); Ra; Ile de —
SE compass point; mus. note; measure
TE right conduct (Tao — Ching); you: Sp.; thee: Fr.; mus. note; — Deum
UE umlaut
VE Odin's brother; Frigg's brother-in-law
WE pronoun; editorial, imperial I; Lindbergh book; island
YE you; yea

EF F; if
FF size of shot
IF provided; whether; condition; Chateau d'- (Monte Cristo's prison)
LF left field (baseball)
OF prep.; about
RF right field (baseball)

EG for example; that is
OG Bashan king; Whig poet Shadwell
UG feel fear, disgust

AH exclamation
CH digraph
EH exclamation
OH exclamation
PH digraph; Sorenson's symbol
RH digraph; — factor (blood substance)

SH digraph; hush!; quiet!
TH digraph; suffix
WH digraph

AI diphthong; exclamation; sloth; Shamash's wife; sweetfish
BI prefix: twice
CI 101
DI 501; gods: Lat.; prefix: away, twice, double
EI diphthong
FI mus. note; hi-
GI Liberian tribe; US Army enlisted man, woman (— Joe, — Jane)
HI salutation; -fi
II 2
LI 51; measure; weight; mus. note; propriety; — Tai-po (poet)
MI 1001; syllable of scale (re — fa)
OI diphthong; exclamation
PI Greek P, 80; math. ratio 3.1416; porcelain tokens; jumble(d type); mess
RI measure; note; Ir. king (ard-)
SI syllable of scale (sol la —); yes: Sp., It.; river
TI syllable of scale (si); palm
VI 6
WI with: Scot.
XI 11; Greek X, 60
YI — Pu (emperor)

AK mudar; fiber shrub
BK chess move
IK Isaac
KK chess move
OK correct; approve
QK chess move
RK chess move

AL Indian mulberry; nickname; according to
CL 150
DL 550
EL God; Syrian deity; L; elevated train; the: Sp.; measure; — Paso; — Capitan; — Alamein
IL the: It.; — Duce; prefix: not
ML 1050
OL suffix: alcohol, oil
XL 40

AM verb, part of "to be"; measure
CM 900
EM M; type measure; square elec unit; them; name; -cee
IM prefix not; contraction
MM 2000
OM assent; mystic sound; mantra (Hinduism); med. suffix
UM exclamation; word of hesitation

AN anyone; article; and; prefix not; -Najaf (Ali's shrine)
EN N; ½ em chief priest, in Fr.; — casserole, — passant; suffix: made of
IN among; at (home); nook; specially favored
ON cricket term; (proceeding) along; aware Heliopolis
UN prefix. not, negative word; United Nations

AO Assam tribe; personification of light (opp. to po)
BO buddy, tramp, monk, chief; boo! sacred tree (pipac); Song — (Papier river)
CO prefix together
DO perform syllable of scale (- re mi); Jap. district, stir; fare
EO prefix: dawn, early time
FO the Buddha
GO leave; move; energy; try; fashion; Jap. game
HO attend! tally-; Kol dialect tribe; measure yo-
IO Inachus's daughter; Jupiter moon; hawk; butterfly Iowa
JO sweetheart, nickname; measure; coin
KO Chin. porcelain, measure; knockout
LO behold!; Indian; St. —
MO book; instant; Mossi language; port; Missouri
NO denial; negative (vote); -gaku (drama); lake
OO bird; prefix: egg
PO realm of darkness (opp. to ao); river; P.I. title; Li Tai- (poet)
RO husband: Gypsy; Foster's language
SO king; thus; ever; if; very; sic!; mus. note
TO prep.; measure; takeout
UO diphthong; umlaut
WO falconer's cry; woo; woe
YO exclamation; -ho; Nan — (sacred mountain)
ZO zebra-yak hybrid; prefix: life

AP prefix: to; Associated Press
UP prep.; r(a)ise; United Press
XP monogram, symbol (Christ)

BQ chess move
IQ intelligence measure
KQ chess move
QQ chess move
RQ chess move

AR R; measure (100 sq. meters); critical point; city (Moab, Num)
BR chess move
ER stammering sound; he: Ger.; god; Judah's son
IR Benjamite
KR chess move
MR title
OR conjunction; alternative; tincture, gold: Her., Fr.; Cote d'-
QR chess move
RR chess move
UR Chaldean city (Abraham's home); primitive, original:

Ger.

AS like; thus; since; qua; glacial ridge; coin; weight; city
ES weight; elec. unit; suffix; it: Ger.
IS verb, part of "to be"; Ville d'- (King Gradlon's capital); Iraq city (Hit)
OS bone; mouth; signal; glacial ridge
SS shortstop (baseball); Nazi police
TS digraph
US pronoun; America

AT prep.: by, in, near; coin
ET and: Lat., Fr.; diminutive; coin; — cetera; — alii
IT pronoun; charm; player
ST quiet!; saint; street
TT rifle shot size
UT Guido's note; Utah
VT Vermont
XT Christ

AU with the: Fr.; — gratin; gold symbol
BU Jap. coin; measure
DU thou: Ger.; — Barry
EU prefix: good, true
FU Chin. department
HU Northerner; Tatar; Mongol
IU diphthong
JU Chin. porcelain; diphthong
LU perused: Fr.; nickname
MU Greek M, 40; measure; electronic term
NU Greek N, 80; primeval chaos; naked: Fr.
OU oh!; where, or: Fr.; diphthong
PU coin; measure; — Yi (emperor)
RU regret
SU Ra's son; known: Fr.
TU you: It.; thou: Fr.
VU seen: Fr.; deja — (paramnesia)
WU Chin. dialect; river
YU jade stone
ZU storm god

CV 105
DV 505
IV 4; birth of Christ
LV 55
MV 1005
XV 15

AW exclamation
NW compass point
OW exclamation
SW compass point
UW diphthong

AX cutting tool; fell; destroy; ask
CX 110
DX 510
EX X; expense; prefix: without, from; former
IX 9
LX 60
MX 1010
OX bovine; draft animal
XX 20

AY ah; alas!; champagne; always; yes (vote)
BY goal; pass; beside; in; near; with
EY exclamation
HY prefix: arch
IY diphthong
KY Kentucky
LY measure; suffix; prefix: to loose
MY poss. pronoun; exclamation
OY grandchild: Scot.; exclamation
PY prefix: suppurative
SY scythe; diminutive suffix
TY suffix: tens, state; god (Tiu, Tyr)
WY Y

UZ Job's home; Shem's grandson

THREE-LETTER WORDS

--A to --Z

ABA camel hair; Arab. cloak; altazimuth
ADA fem. name; city; (Java) canvas
AEA (candlenut) bark cord
AGA bark; rope; title; Turk. officer; ruler
AHA exclamation
AIA Rizpah's father
AKA Assam tribesman, language; N.Z. vine
ALA Alabama; (army) wing; petal; after, according to; — mode; — carte
AMA chalice; (nurse) maid; American Medical Association; tree
ANA collection; prefix: up, back; Irish gods' mother; coin
APA Braz. tree; wallaba
ARA constellation; altar; macaw; textile screw pine; measure; goddess
ASA masc. name; healer; king of Judah; Norse god
ATA Mindanao tribe, language; flour; sweetsop
AVA anc. Burma capital; pepper; shrub; kava; liquor
AWA kava; tenpounder; milkfish
AYA Brahman title; Shamash' consort; Ai
BAA sheep's bleat
BOA constrictor; python; anaconda; (fur, feather) scarf
BRA underwaist
CHA rolled tea; -cha (V.I. white, dance)

CIA Central Intelligence Agency
DEA goddess: Lat.
DHA measure, weight
DIA through; prefix: apart; day: Sp.
DRA measure
ECA Economic Cooperation Administration
ELA highest note; bombast; extravagance
ERA epoch; geol. time division
ESA Economic Stability Administration
ETA Jap. outcasts; Greek E, S; Negrito
EUA Tonga isle
EVA Evangeline; Little — (Uncle Tom's Cabin)
FHA Federal Housing, Farmers' Home Administration
FLA Florida
FRA brother; monk; — Angelo, Diavolo (Michele Pezza); Angelico, painter
GOA gazelle, mugger; crocodile; former Port. colony; Austral native
GRA love(r); fondness
HEA Eridu's chief god
HIA hawk parrot
HOA hallo!
IBA P.I. fruit tree
ICA river; city
IDA Idaho; Crete mountain; Princess — (opera); Countess —, heiress (Thackeray)
ILA Bantu language
IMA — Hogg (heiress)
INA fem. name suffix; mother
IOA iwa; frigate bird
IRA Bib. ruler; Irish Republican Army; masc. name: watchful
ITA Negrito; Eskimo; labor union; city
IVA yellow bugle; herb eve; marsh elder
IWA frigate bird; -iwa: fern stalks
IYA (nurse)maid; Koran verse; omen
KEA N.Z. parrot
KHA Nepalese; Laotian
KOA timber tree
KRA long-tailed ape
KUA Bantu tribe
LEA meadow; yarn measure; warp threads
LIA — Fail (crowning stone)
LOA worm; eye parasite; Lao; Mauna —
MAA sheep's cry; maw
MEA — culpa (my fault)
MFA Master of Fine Arts (degree)
MIA mine: It.
MNA mina (weight)
MOA flightless extinct bird
MYA long clam genus
NAA no
NEA National Education Association
NOA profane; common; no
NRA National Recovery Administration; FDR measure; Blue Eagle
OCA edible root; wood sorrel oxalis
ODA harem room, inmate
OKA weight; oca; river
OLA palm leaf
OMA suffix tumor
ONA measure; So. Amer. Indian
ORA Dan. money; mouths; — et labora (pray and work)
OVA eggs; Piman Indian
OXA prefix oxygen
PEA seed; plant; marble sweet —; — soup (fog); river
PIA arrowroot; — mater (brain part)
POA (blue)grass
PTA Parent-Teacher Association
PUA hemp cordage fiber
PWA Public Works Administration
PYA coin
QUA in so far as; sine — non (necessity)
REA turmeric; Rhea; Cybele, mother of the gods
RIA narrow inlet; creek; estuary
RUA Congo Bantu
SAA measure
SEA water(s); wave; vast area; at — (lost); naval; — horse
SHA Shinto temple; urial; sheep
SIA Keresan Indian
SLA sloe
SNA snow: Scot.
SOA tub; milk pail; cowl
SPA mineral spring; resort
SUA hers: Lat.
SWA so
TAA Chin. pagoda
TEA beverage; collation; — green; — ball; — wagon
THA thee; thou
TIA aunt: Sp.
TOA brave warrior; beefwood; Casuarina
TRA Malay coin
TUA dyewood tree
TVA Tennessee Valley Administration
TWA two
UCA fiddler crab
UEA island
UFA river
ULA the gums; diminutive
UMA Devi (goddess of splendor); Wiltshire's wife (Stevenson)
UNA river; Dan's sister (Kipling); Red Cross Knight's wife: Truth personified in "Faerie Queene"
UTA lizard; Jap. song
UVA grape
VIA way, vessel: Lat.; through; — Dolorosa
WEA Algonquian
WOA stop!
WPA Works Progress Administration
YEA yes (vote); — and Nay (Richard I)
ZEA Indian corn, maize
ZIA Gad's descendant; N.M. pueblo
ZOA Blake's symbol(s); suffix: animals

ABB warp yarn; poorest fleece

ALB church vestment

BAB Babism founder

BBB rifle shot size

BIB sip; apron part; fish; nozzle

BKB chess move

BOB cheat; mock; weight; curtsy; Scot. dance; shilling; haircut; Robert; -sled; — up

BQB chess move

BUB small boy; liquor

CAB (ride in) taxi; engineer's place; measure; Civil Aeronautics Board

COB swan; horse; seagull; excel; strike

CUB young animal; boy (scout); — reporter; light plane: grasshopper

DAB touch, tap; flounder; lizard; expert

DEB society girl; Deborah

DIB bob bait; dibble; dip

DOB dab; daub

DUB rub smooth; bestow title; play; do poorly; coin; add sound

EBB recede; delay; — tide; shallow

ELB jujube

FIB (tell white) lie; pummel

FOB pocket; cheat, trick; — chain

FUB plump child; cheat

GAB chatter; hook; notch; E.I. persimmon

GEB earth god; Osiris's father

GIB (tom)cat; salmon; prison; bearing plate; gut fish

GOB mouth(ful); mass; sailor; tar

HOB ferret; havoc; game pin; cut(ter); — and nob

HUB wheel center; nave; pipe; the — (Boston)

JAB punch; stab

JIB sail; mouth; crane arm; standstill

JOB (do odd) work; employment; OT book; patient sufferer; item

KAB measure

KEB earth god; Osiris's father

KOB Afr. antelope

KTB chess move

LAB rennet; study room

LIB castrate; ad —

LLB Bachelor of Laws (degree)

LOB go heavily; high curve (tennis); till; Puck

MAB fairy queen and midwife; Mabel

MIB marble

MOB crowd (about); masses; annoy; gang; cap

NAB lock keeper; arrest; river

NEB Nebraska; beak; mouth; kiss

NIB beak; pen(point); lint knot; scorer

NOB (blow on) head; knob(stick); hob and —

NUB knob; knot; gist

ORB disk; sphere; world; eye; encircle

PAB flax refuse (fuel)

POB porridge; post-office box

PUB inn; tavern

QKB chess move

QQB chess move

RAB teacher; mortar mixer; dog hero; Yugo. isle

REB rebel

RIB costa; meat cut; wife; vein; part of sock, ship, umbrella; tease; purl

RKB chess move

ROB steal; mine coal; juice; — Roy (outlaw)

RQB chess move

RUB polish; vex; chafe; hindrance; gibe

SEB earth god; Osiris's father

SIB brother; sister; litter mate; kinsman; congenial

SOB weep; wail(ing); — story; — sister

SUB pinch hitter; under: Lat.; — rosa

TAB flap; tag; account; Cambridge man; charges

TIB skip school

TOB anc. Syrian kingdom

TUB vessel; keg; wash

WEB gossamer; (en)mesh; membrane; network; rete

ZAB Great — (river)

ABC book; primer; rudiment

AEC Atomic Energy Commission

ARC curve part; light; rainbow

BAC ferryboat; cistern

BSC Bachelor of Chemical Science (degree)

CCC 300; Commodity Credit Corporation; Civilian Conservation Corps

CXC 190

DCC 700

DEC prefix: ten; December

DOC doctor; physician

DUC duke: Fr.

DXC 590

ETC and so on

FAC fact

FCC Federal Communications Commission

HIC hiccuping sound; — et ubique

HOC card game; — anno; ad —

ICC Interstate Commerce Commission

IHC Jesus symbol

LAC varnish component; resin; milk (pharm.); 100,000 rupees

MAC son of: Ir.; Scot; Irishman; coat

MCC 1200

MDC 1600

MMC 2100

MXC 1090

ORC grampus; whale

PAC moccasin; half-boot

PIC measure; very small

ROC fabled bird; simurg; bomb
SAC cavity; pouch; Sauk; Indian; — and soc
SEC second; dry (wine); Securities & Exchange Commission
SIC thus!; — transit gloria; chase; incite
SOC A.S. jurisdiction district; sac and —
TAC prefix: touch
TEC detective
TIC twitch(ing); spasm; funny habit; correct (slang)
VAC speech goddess; Sarasvati
WAC Women's Army Corps
ZAC Caucasian ibex

ADD (sub)join; augment; annex; total, foot
AID help(er); succor; Agency for International Development
AND conjunction; plus
ARD suffix: excessive doer
BAD evil; poor; ill; severe; faulty; wrong; river; — Ems
BED base; bottom; matrix; lodge
BID reveal; offer; order; invite; — fair; — price
BOD clay plug
BUD develop; immature one; lad; in the —; — stick
CAD (act as) bounder
CID the —; Sp. hero, epic; Diaz de Vivar
COD fish; hoax; Cape —
CUD something ruminated; tobacco quid
DAD father
DID performed; acted
DOD clip off; metal plate; annular die
DUD garment; faulty bomb; failure
EED Moslem Easter
ELD old time; age
END limit; death; extreme; phase; remnant; aim; finish; — man; — use; open —
ERD earth; land; — shrew
FAD custom; craze; polish
FED nourished; fattened
FID mast support; pin; tobacco quid
FOD measure
GAD rod; rove(r); -fly; oath; Jacob's son; Israel tribe; Syrian god
GED oath (God)
GID sheep disease
GOD Jehovah; deity; deify; gallery occupant
HAD possessed; tricked
HID concealed
HOD brick tray; coal scuttle; — carrier
IND India (poet.); Indiana
JOD yodh; Heb. Y, 10
KED sheep tick
KID young goat, child; fur; leather; tease
LAD boy; youth; stripling
LED guided; directed
LID (eye) cover; curb; hat
LLD Doctor of Laws (degree)
LOD weight
LTD limited (company)
LUD oath; legendary king
MAD crazy; vain; angry; river
MID among; central; half-way
MMD 2500
MOD Scot. artist congress; fashion fad
MUD abusive charge; — lark; — Cat State (Miss.)
MVD Soviet Ministry of Interior Affairs
NED Edgar; Edmund; Edward
NID nest; pheasant brood
NOD drowse; (show) assent; Land of —; East of Eden
ODD unpaired; queer; uneven; extra; fellow; — man wins
OID suffix: like
OLD stale; obsolete; passe; skilled; primeval; quondam; hoary; — hat
ORD mountain
PAD cushion; saddle; walk; tablet; robber; stuff; track; lodgings
PED basket; prefix: foot, boy, child
POD flock; socket; groove; bag; legume; suffix: foot
PUD paw; hand; weight
RAD afraid: Scot.; energy unit
RED color, dye; lurid; inflamed; golden; Communist; fowl; cent; river; sea; — Jacket (Seneca chief)
RID free; clear; dispose
ROD stick; race; bar; gum; scepter; 5½ yards
RUD redness; fish
SAD gloomy; dull; poor; depressed: grievous; — sack
SED but: Lat.
SID Sydney
SOD soil; turf; sward
SUD soapy water; foam
TAD small child; Theodore
TED spread for drying; scatter; waste
TID girl; woman
TOD wool weight; (ivy) bush; death: Ger.
UND and: Ger.
URD bean; woolly pyrol; Norn; Wyrd; — Verthandi, Skuld
VOD Baltic Finn
WAD lump; plug; roll; money; black ocher
WED marry; unite(d)
YOD Heb. Y, 10
ZED Z

ABE Lincoln; the Great Emancipator
ACE one-spot; card; bit; hole in one; air hero; game point; expert; first-rate

ADE soft drink; humorist
AGE period; generation; era; ripen; mellow
AKE forever: Maori; N.Z. tree; hopbush
ALE beverage; malt liquor; festival
AME wooden form; soul: Fr.; — damnee
ANE ass: Fr.; chem. suffix
APE monkey; anthropoid; mimic; Hawaiian herb; apii
ARE measure; verb form
ASE enzyme; Peer Gynt's mother (Ibsen)
ATE goddess of infatuation, folly, discord (Zeus's daughter); consumed
AUE Polynesian exclamation
AVE — atque vale (hail and farewell!); rosary bead
AWE reverence; intimidate; mill bucket, sail
AXE tool; fell; destroy
AYE always; yes (vote)
BEE B; Apis; drone; contest; crazy idea
BLE grain: Fr.
BYE run (cricket); aside; secondary; inactive
CEE C; em- (master of ceremonies)
CHE shrub; Chin. flute
CIE abbr., company: Fr.
CLE diminutive suffix
COE sheep disease; Ia. college
CUE Q; signal; hint; hair twist; waiting line; billiard rod
DAE do: Scot.
DEE D; river, mathematician
DIE expire; long; vanish; stop; cube; chance, tool; shape
DOE female animal; biscuit color; John —
DUE owed; just; debt; — date
DYE color; stain
EAE classifying suffix
EDE Dutch commune; Afr. city
EKE piece out; augment
ELE aisle; eel
EME uncle; friend; gossip
ENE suffix; compass point
EPE Dutch commune
ERE before; sooner; — long
ESE suffix; compass point
ETE summer: Fr.
EVE twilight; time before; woman; mother of mankind
EWE sheep; Negro tribe
EXE Devon river
EYE vision; view; scan; loop; spot; brood; — bank
FAE foe: Scot.
FEE land grant; charge; tip; reward
FIE exclamation
FOE enemy; adversary
GEE G; horse command; evade; agree; oath; haw and —
GIE give: Scot.
GUE Shetland viol
HAE have: Scot.
HIE hasten; speed
HOE tool; dig; scrape; inventor
HUE color; shout; — and cry
HYE hedge; hie
ICE frost(ing); chill; dessert; diamonds
IDE fish; chem. suffix
IFE hemp; cordage fiber
IKE Isaac; nickname (Eisenhower)
ILE isle: Fr.; suffix; -de-France; — de la Cite
INE suffix
IRE provoke; anger; choler; wrath
ISE suffix; fjord; bay (Atsuta)
ITE suffix: follower, resident; So. Amer. Indian
IVE contraction; suffix
IZE suffix
JOE coin; sweetheart; — Miller (joke); fat boy (Dickens)
KAE serve; oblige; jackdaw
LEE shelter; sediment; Annabel — (Poe); Lorelei — (Loos); Francis Lightfoot —; Henry — (Light-Horse Harry)
LIE fib; mislead; be; extend; slope; golf term; Trygve — (UN official)
LOE love: Scot.
LUE sift; bolt
LYE alkaline solution; lixivium
MAE — West (life preserver)
MME madame; My Lady
MOE masc. nickname
NAE no, not: Scot.
NEE born; by maiden name
NIE never: Ger.; eyes
NNE compass point
NYE pheasant brood; humorist
OBE Greek clan division; magic rite; fetish
ODE (Pindar) poem; song; canticle; hymn
OKE weight; measure
OLE palm leaf; old; Sp. victory cry
ONE single; unit(y); person; same; the absolute
OPE unlock (poet.)
ORE Oregon; seaweed; mineral; crude metal(lic rock); coin
OSE suffix: simple sugar
OTE suffix: resident
OVE egg-shaped ornament
OWE be obliged, indebted
OYE grandchild: Scot.
PEE P; turtle delicacy; calipee
PIE bird; mixed type; jumble; coin; tart
POE Edgar Allan — (Raven, Gold Bug); parson bird
PRE prefix: before
PUE pew
PYE poet; 1st engraver
QUE what, that: Fr.
RAE explorer; fem. name
REE sift; right!; Arikara; fem. ruff; sandpiper
RHE fluidity unit
RIE grass, cereal
ROE deer; doe; fish eggs; streaks in

wood
RUE herb; repent; regret; — de la Paix
RYE cereal; whisky; Gypsy; — and Indian (bread)
SAE so
SEE perceive; bishop's seat; curia; learn; call (bet); — red; — stars; astronomer
SHE woman; Haggard novel
SIE sye; you, she: Ger.
SOE tub; pail; cowl
SSE compass point
STE saint(e): Fr.
SUE urge; woo; plead; take court action
SYE scythe; drop; strain
TAE to; toe; take: Scot.
TEE T; game mark; golf term; top ornament; — beam, bar; to a —; -shirt
THE article
TIE bind; link; knot; duty; equal(ity); bond; beam; cravat, Ascot
TOE digit; drive aslant; golf club part; — the line; -hold
TRE prefix: town; three: It.
TSE Lao- (philosopher); Mao -tung
TUE parson bird
TYE mast chain
UBE P.I. yam
UKE ukulele; guitar
ULE caucho tree; rubber; diminutive suffix
UME Jap. apricot; river
UNE article, one: Fr.
URE suffix: chemist; river mist: Scot.
USE employ(ment); (ac)custom; treat(ment); gain; dupe; — and wont
UTE Shoshonean Indian; mountain
UVE P.I. yam
VAE alas! — victis
VEE V; $5; neckline; refusal
VIE emulate; strive; compete; life: Fr.
VOE inlet; creek
WEE little; pig's squeak; — Willie Winkle (Kipling)
WOE alas; sorrow(ful)
WYE Y; forked holder, track; river
YOE ewe
ZEE Z; zed

AEF American Expeditionary Force; WWI Amer. army; Pershing command
ALF Alfred; elf
AUF on, upon: Ger.
ELF fairy; sprite; dwarf
ERF ½-acre plot
HOF city
KAF myth. mountain, fabled bird abode; Arabic K
KEF hemp; languor
LIF — and Lifthrasir (myth. survivors)
LOF measure
NEF clock, vessel in form of ship; navicula; church nave
OAF elf's child; dolt; fool
OFF erring; away!; go; out; below par; — color; — stage
OLF bullfinch
ORF fish; yellow ide
OUF dog's bark; exclamation
QAF kaf
REF measure; referee
RIF measure
SIF Thor's wife; home guardian
VIF lively, animated: Fr.
ZIF Jewish month: Iyar

AGG carrier (Kipling)
BAG sac(k); measure; purse; seize; in the —
BEG ask; entreat; Turk. title; bey
BIG large; barley; — Bertha; — Ben; — Bend; — brother; — house; — Blue (river)
BOG mire; marsh; — down
BUG insect; defect; germ; fanatic; bulge (eyes); river
CAG offend; insult
CIG cigarette
COG cheat; (gear) tooth; (connect by) tenon; ship
DAG Nott and —, deities; antler; pistol; — Hammarskjold, UN chief
DEG sprinkle; dampen
DIG (verbal) thrust; dwell
DOG Canis; gripper; andiron; crampon; track
DUG delved; excavated
EGG ovum; germ cell; coal; bomb; fellow; incite
ENG Chang's Siamese twin
ERG work unit; desert area
FAG cigarette: drudge; tire; Capt. Absolute's servant; liar
FIG fruit; fico; zero; rig
FOG vapor; daze; blue; blur
FUG reek
GAG pry open; choke; joke; closure; fish; illustrator
GEG No. Albanian
GIG fish spear, hook; boat; chaise, carriage; nap
GOG — and Magog (statues)
HAG harpy; witch; urge; copse; bog
HOG pig, boar; sheep; dime, shilling; glutton; monopolize
HUG embrace; keep close; bear —
ING suffix; A.S. peace god
JAG pendant; barb; slash; drunken spree
JIG dance; prank; drill
JOG jostle; remind; trot
JUG ewer; jail; stew; nest(le); bird sound
KEG cask; — of nails: 100 lb.
LAG linger; slacken; stave; jailbird
LEG meat cut; support;

	run; lap; — art: cheesecake
LOG	cut timber; (ship) record
LUG	ear; loop; drag; worm, sail; measure god
MAG	chatter bird; Margaret, halfpenny (Brit.)
MEG	Margaret Princess —; Mag Alcott heroine horse (Burns); — Merrilies (Scott)
MIG	marble duck; plane
MOG	move slowly; depart
MUG	cup face; photograph; sheep; mungo assault; overact pose
NAG	horse annoy(ance); fret; snake; Nagaina's wife (Kipling)
NIG	dress (stone); cut coin edge revoke
NOG	egg drink peg; wood (block, fastener); pin
PAG	island
PEG	(cribbage) pin; support pretext; leg; hit, plod; Margaret
PIG	pork litter; glutton cushion; ingot; iron; The — Baby (Carroll)
PUG	dog; (mix) clay; boxer; - nose; footprint
RAG	shred scold; dance slate; fog; — doll
REG	desert region
RIG	equip(ment); swindle, tackle; ardri
ROG	shake pull; stir
RUG	mat. cozy
SAG	droop weaken; drift
SEG	sedge iris
SIG	signature
SOG	soak drowse
TAG	flap; tab lock; cue; story moral; join; follow game; label
TEG	young sheep
TOG	coat; dress up
TUG	pull; lug; effort; towboat; — of war
TYG	drinking vessel
VAG	(arrest as) vagabond
VEG	prank; wanderer
VOG	weight
VUG	lode cavity
WAG	sway; gossip; joker
WIG	hair(piece); peruke; judge
ZAG	jagged line angle
ZIG	part of a zigzag
ZOG	Albanian king
ZUG	Swiss canton, lake
AKH	spirit of man: Egypt
ASH	tree; residue burn pallor gray. - can: depth charge
AUH	exclamation
BAH	exclamation
BOH	Burmese chief; boo; — da Thone (Kipling)
DAH	Burmese knife
DOH	do (note)
EDH	A.S. letter: th
ETH	A.S. letter: th; suffix ordinal number
FOH	exclamation
HAH	exclamation
HEH	Chin. tribe; Hei; Miao
HOH	Quileute; Indian whaler
HSH	hush; exclamation
HUH	exclamation
ICH	I, ego: Ger.; fish dermatitis
ISH	adj. suffix
ITH	Irish ancestor
JAH	Jehovah god
LEH	Kashmir town
MAH	moon angel
NTH	any size, — degree; indefinite power
OCH	alas!; oh!
PAH	bah!; nasty; improper; N.Z. native fort
PEH	river
POH	bah!
RAH	(cheer with) hurrah
REH	salt mixture; alkali
SAH	measure
SOH	exclamation; gutta mixture
TCH	exclamation
UGH	assenting grunt
USH	usher
VAH	Danube tributary
WAH	panda; measure
YAH	yes; exclamation
ZOH	zobo; yak; zebu hybrid
ABI	Hezekiah's mother
ACI	chem. prefix
AHI	sky serpent; Vritra
AJI	Capsicum plant
ALI	Mohammed's son-in-law; Fatima's son; — Pasha: Lion of Janina
AMI	friend: Fr.
ANI	black bird; cuckoo
API	prefix: bee
ATI	P.I. Negrito
CCI	201
CDI	401
CHI	Greek letter, 600; fem. Gypsy. Gold Coast language; Tshi
CII	102
CLI	151
CMI	901
COI	river
CRI	cry: Fr.; dernier —
CUI	composer; engineer
CVI	106
CXI	111
DCI	601
DEI	the gods: Lat.; agnus —
DII	the gods; 502
DLI	551
DUI	duets; twosomes
DVI	506
DXI	511
EHI	Ahiram; Benjamin's son
ELI	high priest; Samuel's teacher; Yale; — Whitney
EPI	finial; grain ear: Fr.; prefix upon
ERI	silkworm; bombyx; Gad's son
EVI	Midianite king
FBI	Federal Bureau of Investigation
FEI	Yap stone money; banana
GHI	buffalo butter; ghee
GOI	non-Jew: Heb.
GRI	horse: Gypsy
HAI	Israelites defeat site
HEI	cat's cradle; Miss — (Greene)
HOI	yam; haw (as cattle)
HUI	guild; partnership

ICI here: Fr.
IHI stitchbird; fish; halfbeak; skipper
III 3
IKI island
ILI river
IMI measure
INI suffix: order
IRI Bela's son; city
KAI N.Z. food; apple; island
KEI apple; island
KOI Jap. carp
KRI read(ing substitute)
KUI Asian group; Lolo; Kandh
LAI medieval tale: Burmese
LEI wreath; coin
LII 52
LOI law: Fr.
LVI 56
LXI 61
MAI May: Ger.
MCI 1101
MDI 1501
MII 1002
MLI 1051
MMI 2001
MOI I: Fr.; Asian tribes
MUI — tsai: girl slave(ry)
MVI 1006
MXI 1011
NEI Eastern flute
OBI girdle; sash
OII N.Z. muttonbird
OKI evil spirit; archipelago
OMI sacred mountain
ONI any: Scot.
ORI prefix: mouth; limit
OVI prefix: egg
PAI money; weight
PEI river
PHI Greek letter PH, 500
POI Hawaiian food (taro)
PPI radarscope
PSI Greek letter PS, 700
QUI who, that: Fr.; — vive (watchword)
RAI measure
REI coin; David's friend
RII small streams; Venice canals
ROI fern rootstock; king: Fr.; vive le —
SAI Capuchin monkey; Cebus
SHI weight
SKI glide(r); runner; sport; — lift
SRI glorious; holy; Lakshmi (goddess)
SUI Chin. dynasty; — generis
TAI porgy; Laos; Shan; Siamese; Li -po (poet); — Shan (sacred mountain)
TJI river: Java; weight
TOI you, thou: Fr.
TRI prefix: three
TUI dyewood tree; parson bird
TWI prefix: double; Tshi
UBI where: Lat; white yam
UDI N. Caucasian language
UJI silkworm disease
UNI plainly woven; goddess (Juno); prefix: single
UPI news, wire service; United Press International
URI Swiss canton
UVI — yam (white yam)
VAI Liberian Negro
VEI Liberian Negro
VII 7
WEI Chin. dynasty, state; river
XCI 91
XII 12
XLI 41
XVI 16
XXI 21
YOI hunting cry

GAJ coin
GUJ Moti —: elephant (Kipling)
HAJ pilgrimage to Mecca
RAJ reign, rule: India
SAJ teak tree
TAJ (dervish) cap; — Mahal

ACK -ack (antiaircraft)
AIK oak: Scot
ALK — gum (turpentine)
ARK Arkansas; refuge; broadhorn; flatboat; wanigan; — of the covenant
ASK question; seek; need; invite; beg
AUK sea bird; Tlingit Indian
BIK poison; aconite
BOK Amer. editor
DAK India mail
ELK deer; wapiti; sambar; leather; color lama; river; city
HAK legal claim; share
HUK P.I. guerrilla
ICK fish dermatitis
ILK family; class, same
INK sepia; cuttlefish fluid; black; sign
IRK abhor; annoy; bore
KRK island
KTK chess move
LAK grouse's wooing strut
LEK gather(ing); coin; river
LOK god of discord; Balder slayer
NAK stigmatic point; mango
OAK Quercus; Casuarina; encina; — brown; poison —; — Park; — Ridge
OCK weight
ORK whale
OUK week: Scot.
PIK measure
ROK Korean soldier
SAK white cotton
SOK measure
SUK Nilotic Negro
TCK exclamation
USK river
YAK Tibet ox; beast of burden
YOK A.S. G; Middle English Y
ZAK measure

AAL Indian mulberry; red dye; morindin
AFL American Federation of Labor
AIL be ill
ALL whole; each; only; very; universe; according to; — out; — hands; — hours; — clear; — in one
AWL shoemaker's tool
BAL mine; ball: Fr.
BEL fruit, tree; Bengal quince; golden apple; power ratio; earth god; Marduk; — Affris (Shaw)
BUL Canaanite's 8th

month; Heshvan
CAL California; wolframite
CCL 250
CDL 450
CML 950
COL Colorado; mountain pass
CUL -de-sac; blind alley
CXL 140
DAL split pea; pigeon pea; Swedish river
DCL 650
DEL Delaware
DXL 540
EEL teleost fish: conger moray; elver lamprey; vinegar worm
ELL cloth measure; aune; building annex
FUL Hamitic Sudanese
GAL girl; speed unit
GEL jellify harden; set
GOL God (euphemistic form)
GUL rose: Persian
HAL Henry, Harry; Prince (Henry V); Bluff King — (Henry VIII)
HEL Loki's daughter; Niflheim goddess
HOL prefix complete
HUL Shem's descendant
HYL prefix wood
IAL adj. suffix
ILL Illinois sick; bad(ly) evil; river
KEL caul; net; film
KIL Ir. church; monk's cell
KOL Dravidian native; Munda Larka
KYL Himalayan ibex
LIL book, paper, letter: Gypsy little; — Abner
MAL — de mer (sea sickness); Sudra caste Hindu; prefix evil; measure
MCL 1150
MEL honey; prefix: limb, black
MIL 1/1000 inch (wire measure); coin; Ir. eponymous ancestor
MML 2050
MOL gram molecule
MUL measure
MXL 1040
NIL nothing; indigo dye; ipomoea; nilgai
NUL no, nothing (law)
OIL painting fuel; grease; flatter(y); bribe
OWL bird (of prey); night-
PAL partner; (to) chum
PEL prefix: mud, clay
PIL prefix: hair
POL degree without honors
PUL Tiglathpileser (king); coin; OT people
REL electric unit
SAL salt; - tree; tamarisk, rock; Sarah
SEL salt: Fr.; self: Scot.
SIL yellow ocher
SOL sun (god) tone G.; coin; fluid
TAL palm fiber hand clapping cymbals
TEL prefix: distant end
TIL tree; sesame, mark
TOL Sanskrit school
ULL chief god Sif's son; Thor's stepson
VOL wings (Her.); battery iron block
ZAL Rustam's father
ZEL Oriental cymbal

AAM liquid measure
AHM liquid measure
AIM direct(ion), design; scheme end
ARM branch, sleeve; bay; power; fortify
AUM measure
BAM hoax; Iranian town
BEM Pol. general; pasha
BIM Barbados man
BOM So. Amer serpent
BUM sponge upon; tramp; inferior; Levant ship
CAM awry; gear; rotating, sliding part; Ouse tributary
COM prefix: together, with
CUM summa — laude (with highest praise)
CWM cirque (geol. process)
DAM obstruct(ion); wall; weir; coin; female parent; Nobel biochemist
DEM Democrat: opp. to Rep(ublican)
DIM dark(en); dull; obscure; — view
DOM monastic title; church; low caste Hindu
DUM doom palm; gingerbread tree
EAM uncle; gossip
ELM tree; Ulmus; — City (New Haven)
FAM hand (slang)
FUM feng-huang; myth. bird
GAM whale school; visit; botanical suffix
GEM muffin; - State (Idaho); prize piece; jewel
GIM neat; spruce
GUM adhesive; exudate; resin; jaw tissue; overshoe; humbug
GYM sports hall
HAM Noah's son; Shem's brother; amateur radio; actor
HEM (cloth) edge; confine; surround; hesitate: haw
HIM pronoun; male
HUM buzz; sing; murmur; melody; hoax
ISM doctrine; system
JAM tight place; crush; interfere; preserve; native chief; — pack; — session
JEM James
JIM James; — Crow; -dandy; Lord — (Conrad); Sawyer's friend (Twain)
JUM cultivation method
KAM crooked
KEM river; port
KIM — O'Hara: waif (Kipling)
KUM Shiite pilgrim site; river
LAM beat; escape; loom lever
LIM blue pine; toon
LUM chimney; sink;

pond
MAM Mayan Indian
MCM 1900; fin de siecle; Boxer Rebellion
MEM Heb. letter M, 40
MIM (act) affectedly shy
MMM 3000
MOM mamma
MUM chrysanthemum; hush; beer; mask; madam
NAM distrain(t)
NIM steal; margosa tree
NOM name: Fr.; — de plume (pseudonym); — de guerre
NYM Falstaff follower
OHM electric unit; -'s law
OLM amphibian
OOM — Paul Kruger (Boer president)
PAM card game
POM Pomeranian (dog)
QUM Shiite pilgrim site
RAM sheep; batter(ing) —; weight; ship beak; pump; stuff; constellation: Aries
RIM border; edge; margin; wheel part
ROM Gypsy husband
RUM liquor; odd; tough; fine; dye
SAM unite; curdle; Uncle —
SEM Noah's son; Ham's brother
SIM Simeon; Simon
SUM total; amount; all; epitomize; in —; — up
TAM Scot. cap
TEM sun god; Atmu, (A)tum
TIM Tiny —: cripple (Dickens)
TOM male; Thomas; Ob tributary; — Thumb ("General" Charles Sherwood Stratton); -o' Bedlam (madman); — Alibi (Scott); — Canty (Twain); Aunt Chloe's husband
TUM sun god; Atmu; card (wool); banjo sound; The Rum — Tugger (Eliot)
ULM Danube city
VIM force; energy; spirit
VUM vow; swear
WEM spot; stain (in wood)
YAM sweet potato; batata; edible root; tuber; posthouse
YOM day: Heb.; — Kippur (Atonement Day); river

AIN well; spring; 16th Heb. letter, 70; Rhone tributary
ALN measure
ANN stipend; fem. name; Nancy; Nina; — Rutledge (Lincoln's fiancee)
ARN alder tree
AWN (remove grain) beard
BAN edict; forbid; curse; title; muslin; coin; kokumin (Jap. reserve); Lancelot's father
BEN son; Moringa seed, oil; Phaseolus; wild hog; — Lomond (mountain)
BIN box; crib; pungi (flute); Vina
BON good, bond: Fr.; bean; grass; Jap. festival (of lanters); Tibet religion; Cape —
BUN bread; roll; hair knot; boat; tipsiness
CAN vessel; preserve; tin; dismiss; jail; weight
CON learn; against; deceive; — game; — man; — amore
DAN title; Daniel; buoy; Jacob's (Bilhah's) son; tribe; from — to Beersheba; river; Una's brother (Kipling)
DEN retreat; lair; haunt; scout unit (pack part)
DIN noise; uproar; resound; Gunga —
DON Sir; tutor; put on; goddess; mother of Gwydion, Arianrhod; river
DUN urge payment; dingy (brown); May fly; cure fish
EAN bring forth; to lamb
EEN Ir. suffix; even (poet.)
EIN one, article: Ger.
EON time period; age; eternity
ERN sea eagle
FAN cool(er); vane; winnow; spread; stimulate; devotee; African; Pangwe; Pahouin; — dance
FEN marsh; weight; forbid, — Ho (river)
FIN (fish) appendage; part of keel, aircraft; kite
FON Dahomey Negro (Ewe)
FUN amusement; joke; weight
FYN island
GAN Roland's destroyer
GEN suffix: heredity factor
GIN liquor; snare; female (kangaroo); cotton —; — fizz; — rummy; — mill
GON measure; prefix: knee; suffix: angled figure
GUN firearm; pump; hunt; mug; — dog; speed up
GYN prefix: woman
HAN Chin. dynasty; Japanese barony; Yangtze tributary
HEN female bird, fish; fowl; coward; measure; — party
HIN measure
HUN vandal; invader; Boche
IAN John; — Fleming (James Bond author)
IBN — Saud (king)
INN ho(s)tel; lodge; river
ION charged particle; molecule; son of Apollo, Creusa
JAN — of Leiden, fanatic; — Hus, reformer
JIN Oriental demon(s)
KAN Kansas; measure; river
KEN insight; Japanese

measure, prefecture, games
KIN relative(s); zither; koto; Tatar dynasty
KON weight
KUN Bela —, revolutionary
LAN name prefix; measure; Swed. district
LIN linen; flax; linden; — Yutang (author); river
LON Alonso
LYN waterfall
MAN individual; homo; male; anyone; valet; game piece; fortify; tame; to a —; — of war; Isle of —
MEN crew; hands; people; troops; lunar god
MIN chief deity; ruler; river
MON my: Fr.; family badge; Pegu Burmese; prefix: one; — Dieu!
MUN must; mouth; roisterer; river
NAN fem. name; river
NEN river
NON not: Lat.; no: Fr.; prefix; sine qua —
NUN Niger mouth; convent woman; pigeon, smew; Heb. N, 50; Joshua's father; chaos
OON final syllable
OWN acknowledge; have
PAN tub; dish; ape; wash; result; betel leaf; sir; god: Faunus, Inuus (part goat); face; son of Hermes; prefix: all; Peter — (Barrie); dead-
PEN confine; jail; feather; style; write(r); fem. swan
PIN fasten(er); peg; badge; skittle; dowel; -curl; -up
PON pagoda; gold coin
PUN play on words; paronomasia
RAN twine hank; sea deity; Aegir's wife; sped
RIN Jap. coin, measure
RON King Arthur's lance
RUN hurry; operate; stretch; contest; flee; series; brook; trail
SAN Greek letter; Bushmen; hemp
SEN coin; measure; Sun Yat- (Chin. leader)
SIN (do) wrong; vice; err; Heb. S, 300; moon god; Enzu
SON male descendant; scion; — of Man; river
SUN star; shine; Apollo; Helios; Phoebus; — Yat-sen (Chin. leader)
SYN prefix: with
TAN make leather; brown; beat; Gypsy camp
TEN bill; card; X; many; denary; deca; big casino
TIN metal; element; stannium; can; preserve; inferior; 10th anniversary
TON weight; style: Fr.; bon —; suffix: town
TUN vat; cask; measure; guzzle; Mayan year
URN vessel; grave; bury
VAN (fore)front; lead; car; Urartu: Armenia; Turk. lake, town
VIN wine: Fr.; — blanc; — rouge
VON by noble birth: Ger.
WAN (grow) pale; dark; dim
WEN cyst; growth; coin; wyn
WIN gain; earn; persuade
WON obtained; conquered
WUN Burmese governor
WYN Old Eng. rune W
YEN desire; urge; Jap. money
YIN Shang dynasty; weight; female principle (opp. to yang)
YON at a distance; thither
YUN Laos tribesman
ZAN Zeus; Olympia statue
ZEN Buddhist sect, belief
ZIN Bib. wilderness

ABO Finn seaport; Turku
ADO do; trouble; fuss; stir
AGO past; since
AHO exclamation
AKO measure
AMO I love: Lat.
ANO blackbird; prefix: up
APO prefix: away; P.I. volcano; mil. address; Mount — (P.I.)
ARO Nigerian
ASO Jap. volcano
AZO nitrogenous
BOO ostrich tail; hoot; jeer; scary cry
CHO measure
CIO Congress of Industrial Organizations
COO dove cry; amorous talk
CRO -Magnon; homo sapiens; murder fine
DAO P.I. tree (fruit, fiber)
DIO Cassius — (historian)
DJO measure; Niger Negro
DSO Distinguished Service Order (Brit.)
DUO two; duet; pair
EBO tree; — oil; Niger Negro
ECO prefix: environment
EDO Nigerian: Ibo
EGO I; whole man; alter —; self(ishness)
ESO prefix: within
ETO European Theater of Operations (WW II)
EXO prefix: outside
FLO Florence; Flora; arrow
FOO Chin. prefecture
FRO from; away; to and —
GAO river

GEO Georgia; prefix: earth, soil
GOO sticky substance
HAO Chin dynasty
IAO honey eater bird; manuao
IBO Niger Negro
IDO artificial language: de Couturat, Jespersen
ILO International Labor Organization
INO Cadmus's daughter; Athamas's wife
ISO prefix equal
ITO Zionist (Zangwill's) group; Jap. admiral, statesman
IWO — Jima, island; Afr. city
IYO Afr. bass palm fiber; P.I. vine
KIO ngaio; N.Z. fruit tree
KOO Chin. statesman
LAO Tai native language; -tzu, -tse (philosopher)
LEO constellation Lion; composer; emperor; pope; — Tolstoy
LJO Niger delta Negro
LOO card game; halloo
LUO White Nile Negro
LWO White Nile Negro
MAO peacock; — Tse-tung (Chin leader); peacock (Kipling)
MEO Indian farmer caste
MHO unit of conductance
MIO my: Sp., It.; dio —
MOO cow's cry; low; weight
NEO advocate of new; prefix: recent
NOO now; new; prefix: mind
ODO William the Conqueror's half brother Eudes; Count of Paris
OFO Siouan language
OHO exclamation
OJO grassy spring; oasis
OMO prefix shoulder; river
ORO gold: Sp.; Tahiti god; mouth, prefix: mountain
OTO Siouan; prefix: ear
OVO ab — (from the egg, start)
OYO Nigerian town
PHO exclamation
POO Nanki —: Yum-Yum's husband
PRO for; expert; yes vote(r); quid — quo
QUO measure; quid pro —; status —
RHO Greek R, 100
RIO coffee; river; canal(e): It.; — Grande
ROO kangaroo
SAO measure; — Paulo (city)
SHO pshaw!; sure; measure
SOO murmur; sow
SRO box office sign
TAO man: P.I.; Chin. road, cosmic order, truth; — Te Ching: Lao-tse's work
THO Tonkin peasant
TIO uncle: Sp.
TKO boxing term
TOO also; excessively
TWO card; pair; in —: in half; little casino; — bits; -faced; -time
UDO Japanese herb; edible shoot
UFO flying saucer
ULO prefix: gums; shell money
UNO one: It., Sp.
URO So. Amer. Indian; Puqina
WHO rel. pronoun
WOO make love; court; sue
WRO angle; passage; nook
WYO Wyoming
YAO Chin. aborigines, emperor; Bantu; Indian
YEO officer; bodyguard
ZIO sky, war god; Tyr
ZOO animal collection; menagerie

ALP mountain; renegade (Byron)
AMP elec. unit of intensity; ampere
ASP adder; viper; uraeus: symbol; Cleo's snake
BAP bread loaf, roll
BOP bravura jazz
CAP top; cover; match; crown; explosive; detonator; paper size; capital; tread renewal
COP (wind) yarn; catch; thicket; policeman
CUP vessel; ½ pint; portion; prize; golf hole; crater; bloodletting —
CYP princewood tree
DAP dibble; drop bait; dip; rebound; skip
DIP immerse; lower; ladle; candle; pickpocket; hat; downturn
DOP diamond cup; — brandy
ESP 6th sense; extrasensory perception (Rhine, Duke); especially
FIP coin (four-, sixpence); picayune
FOP dandy; coxcomb; dude
GAP opening; breach; pass; hiatus; ravine
GIP gut fish
GOP Republican party
GUP gossip
GYP steal; swindle(r); bitch; college servant
HAP chance; befall; wrap
HEP wise to; informed; exclamation; -cat
HIP cheer; haunch; rose's false fruit (pseudocarp); bump
HOP leap; dance; limp; air trip; vine; bryony; opium; drug; stimulate
HUP command to horses
HYP make melancholy
IMP pretty demon; urchin; rascal; mock
JAP Nipponese
JIP dog (Dickens)
KEP catch; haul
KIP undressed hide; gym feat; sleeping place; weight
KOP hill; measure
KUP measure
LAP fold; wrap; cut; polish; circuit; drink; ripple; take

eagerly
LIP (saucy) speech; edge; spout; kiss; — service
LOP choppy sea; cut off; droop; act lazily
MAP chart; survey, image; Mercator; plan
MOP wipe(r); swab; hair; pout; — up
NAP doze; siesta; hairy surface; pile; game; seize
NEP catnip; cotton fiber knot; Soviet policy
NIP pinch; check; bite; sip; dram; Japanese
OLP blight; bullfinch
OOP up; bind; join: Scot.
ORP fret; weep: Scot.
PAP soft food; paste; dad; simple discourse
PEP energy; stimulate
PIP radar sign; disease; seed; chirp; break shell; spot on card; great!
POP sound; burst; sho(o)t; plant; protrude; ask; drink
PUP young dog, seal; bad security; silly fop
RAP coin; least bit; strike; knock; criticize; jail sentence
REP fabric; lewd one; Republican: opp. to Dem(ocrat)
RIP tear; (move full) speed; split; hay; basket; — van Winkle (Irving); — tide
SAP juice; vigor; money; fool; drain; trench; weaken
SIP drink; taste
SOP dip in; soak; ooze; wet food; bribe
SUP drink; eat; entertain; mouthful
TAP rap; signal; half sole; dance; spigot; liquor; ask money; draw
TIP tilt; upset; dump; apex; (apply) end; touch; hint; fee; bestow
TOP head; acme; best; cut off; cover; outdo; toy; upset; foremost; — secret
TUP ram; mallet; butt
UMP (act as) referee
VIP big shot (very important person)
WAP blow; wrap; truss
YAP yelp; gab; hoodlum; island
YEP yes
YIP yelp; squeal; outcry
ZEP zeppelin: airship
ZIP bullet sound; (move with) vim; energy

KTQ chess move
SUQ Moslem booth, market

AAR (underground) river
AER prefix: gas, air; chalice veil
AFR Africa
AIR ether; gas; breath; breeze; veil; tune; expose; manner; dismissal; — express; — lift
AYR Scot. county, port
BAR obstruct(ion); rod; gate; strip(e); counter; court; except; fish; maigre; mus. measure; son of; sandbank; rifle; — Cocheba (Heb. rebel)
BER jujube; elb
BKR chess move
BOR neighbor; Yugo. mine town
BQR chess move
BUR burr; seed coat; whirr; cut(ter)
CAR lift cage; chariot; for: Fr.; fish box; balloon basket; — Nicobar (island)
COR heart; main star; prefix: pupil
CUR mongrel dog; cad
DAR abode; gateway; tree; patriotic group
DER prefix: neck; the: Ger.
DIR to you: Ger.; Pakistan state
DOR beetle; bumblebee; Bongo; Sudanese; Le Coq —: opera; Cote — (Fr. dept.)
DUR C — (C major)
EAR sense; attention; grain spike; handle; front page box; god; Tiwaz; Tiu
EER ever (poet.); suffix
EIR healing goddess
EUR Europe
FAR greatly; widely; long; distant; advanced
FER iron: Fr.; chemin de — (railroad, baccarat)
FIR (ever)green; balsam; Douglas —; — Domnann (Ir. people)
FOR to; because; namely; pro; fur
FUR pelt; coat(ing); Negro
GAR needlefish
GER resident (Heb. law); Judaism convert
GOR Indus tribesman
GRR exclamation; growl
GUR raw sugar; massecuite
HAR chill fog: Scot.
HER pronoun; female
HIR her
HOR Edom mountain
HUR Ben —: hero (Wallace); Thamar's son; Tirzah's brother
IER noun suffix
IHR you: Ger.
IOR (comparative) ending
ITR attar; rose perfume
JAR grate; snake; drill; clash; shock; vessel; preserve
JUR Nile Negro; Luo; river
KER evil spirit; fate
KIR Bib. Syrian exile
KOR measure; homer
KTR chess move
LAR gibbon; house god; ancestral spirit
LER Brythonic god; Celtic Neptune; children of — (swans)
LUR Persian tribesman; trumpet

MAR	spoil; mutilate; — Ignatius (patriarch of Antioch)
MER	sea: Fr.; mal de —
MIR	chief, Eastern title; Russian communist; to me: Ger.; peace: Russ.
MOR	forest humus
MUR	wall: Fr.; Yugo. river
NAR	near(ly) Scot.
NER	Abner's father; Saul's uncle
NOR	conjunction and not
ORR	Nobel physiologist
PAR	value equality; average standard golf score by: Fr.
PER	through via; for each
PIR	Moslem saint, tomb
POR	push, kick; poke(r)
PUR	sound (cat motor)
PYR	prefix fire heat, fever; light unit
QKR	chess move
QQR	chess move
RKR	chess move
RQR	chess move
RUR	Rhine tributary
SAR	sixty sixties: 3,600 (Babylonian number)
SER	It. title, weight; exist: Sp.; prefix: serum
SIR	knight address
SUR	upon (law) prefix: over south Sp.; Tyre (Lebanon city)
TAR	pitch coal — (saccharine source); sailor lute, telegram river
TER	prefix thrice
TIR	shooting (match)
TOR	hill; peak, fool: Ger.
TUR	pigeon pea; aurochs urus; ibex; wild goat
TYR	god; Aesir Riu (Tuesday) Odin's son slain by Garm
VER	worm: Fr.
VIR	man: Lat.; vigor: Scot.
VOR	before: Ger.
WAR	strife; battle; fight; — bride; — cabinet
WER	who: Ger.; murder fine
WIR	we: Ger.
XER	prefix: dry
YAR	growl
YER	suffix: your
ZAR	measure
ZER	measure; weight
ABS	Bedouin tribesman
AES	Roman bronze; money
ALS	when, than: Ger.
ANS	Liege commune
ARS	art: Lat.; — Amandi (Ovid); — longa, vita brevis
ASS	Equus; donkey; kiang; weight; dolt
AUS	out of, finished: Ger.; Arab tribesman
BAS	low, stocking: Fr.; a — (down!); — relief; roulette bet
BES	pleasure god
BIS	twice; encore; replica
BOS	cow: Lat.; genus
BUS	vehicle; enough; — boy
CAS	en tout —: Fr.; vanity bag; umbrella
CES	these: Fr.
CIS	prefix: on this side
COS	lettuce; romaine; trigonometric function
DAS	cony; badger: Dutch; the: Ger.; — Kapital
DDS	Doctor of Dental Surgery (degree)
DES	of the: Ger., Fr.; from, since: Fr.; — Moines
DIS	Valkyrie; Norn; Freya; — pater (Pluto, Hades); prefix: apart
DOS	dowry; back: Fr. -a-dos; — Passos
EES	eyes: Scot.
EIS	ice: Ger.
EMS	Bad — (spa); river
ENS	being; essence, entity
EOS	goddess, dawn; Aurora; Tithonus's wife
ERS	bitter vetch
ESS	S; fem. suffix; worm; curve
FAS	divine law: Roman
FES	sacred city
GAS	fuel; anesthetic; chatter; boast; tear —, poison —, natural —, coal —
GBS	playwright: George Bernard Shaw
GES	Tapuyan Indian
GIS	soldiers; servicemen
GOS	goshawk bird: Scot.
GUS	Augustus; Gustavus
HAS	possesses; -been
HES	men; males
HIS	poss. pronoun
HMS	— Pinafore (G & S opera)
HUS	Jan — (reformer)
ICS	science suffix
IHS	symbol (Jesus)
ILS	they: Fr.
INS	International News Service
IOS	Hawaiian hawks
IRS	Internal Revenue Service
ITS	poss. pronoun
IUS	right, law: Lat.
JHS	symbol (Jesus)
JUS	law(s): Lat.; legal power; gravy, juice: Fr.
KAS	cupboard, wardrobe: Dutch
KOS	island
LAS	alas; the: Sp.; — Vegas
LES	the: Fr.; — Miserables
LIS	(fairy) fort; lily: Fr.; fleur-de-
LOS	the: Sp.; — Alamos; — Islands; — Negros (Admiralty I.)
LYS	prefix: loosening; fleur-de-lis; river
MAS	master; suffix: festival
MES	my: Fr.; prefix: middling, intermediate
MIS	prefix: wrong, evil
MOS	custom; folkway; mores (sing.)
MRS	title; address; — Grundy
MUS	mouse, rodent genus
NAS	has not, was not
NIS	goblin; kobold; Constantine's birthplace; Yugo. city

NOS we: Lat.; our: Fr.; prefix: disease
OAS Organization of American States
ODS minced oath
OES Os
ONS cricket field parts; weight
OPS goddess; Consus; Rhea; Saturn's wife; Cere's mother
OSS Office of Strategic Services
OUS suffix: abounding
PAS dance step; — de deux; n'est-ce-?
PES foot(like part)
PPS additional postscript
PUS suppuration; Hindu month
RAS fabric; prince; cape; Fascist leader
RES thing: Lat.; legal matter; in medias —
RIS — de veau (sweetbread)
RLS novelist; Robert Louis Stevenson
ROS prefix: Cornish names; rulers; Varangians
RUS rulers; Ros
SES his, her: Fr.
SIS girl; sweetheart; relative; Cecilia
SOS distress signal
SSS Selective Service System
SUS swine genus
TES your: Fr.
TIS contraction: it is
UNS us: Ger.
VAS pledge; surety; duct, vessel (anat.)
VIS force: Lat.; weight; -a-vis; Yugo. isle
WAS existed; the past
WIS Wisconsin; suppose; think
YES affirmative (vote)

ABT — system (mountain railroads); composer
ACT deed; decree; feign; do; play part; prayer; — of God, — of faith
AET of the age: Lat.
AFT astern; back; behind
AHT Wakashan Indian
AIT (river) islet
ALT high in pitch (octave); old: Ger.
AMT county: Dan.; public office: Ger.
ANT insect; formic acid source; emmet; pismire
APT fit; likely; ready
ART skill; science; trade; craft; wile; where — thou?; leg —: cheesecake
ATT coin
AUT prefix: self, same
BAT club; hit; brick; blow; flying mammal; wink; gray; bomb
BET stake; wager; Betsy — (Dickens)
BIT part of bridle, key; blade; check; drill; mite; morsel; 12½ cents
BKT chess move
BOT botfly larva
BUT conjunction: except, unless, yet, only
CAT feline; whip; shrew; fish; tripod; game; island; ship (tackle); jazz fan
CET that: Fr.
CIT townsman; civilian
COT hut; coop; small bed
CUT sever; carve; lower; cross; shorten; gash; slight; sarcasm
DDT insecticide
DIT poem, surnamed: Fr.; on —
DOT dowry; speck; point; scatter; mus. sign; — and dash (Morse)
EAT consume; gnaw; erode; rust; waste
EGT prefix: outside, without
EFT lizard; newt
ELT knead
ENT suffix; prefix: inner
ERT urge on: Scot.
EST suffix; is: Fr.; id —; n' -ce-pas? Eastern Standard Time

FAT oil(y); rich; gross; obese; stout; useful
FET measure
FIT suit(able); proper; ready; adjust(ment); attack; mood; spell
FOT measure
FUT measure
GAT channel; gun
GET obtain; reach; hit; persuade; divorce bill
GIT get; mold channel
GOT past tense of get
GUT intestine; eviscerate; destroy; good: Ger.
HAT headwear; cardinal's office; has: Ger.
HIT strike; reach; agree; impact; success
HOT torrid; burning; eager; violent; fresh; urgent; biting; exciting; stolen; contraband; — seat; — dog; -shot; -rod
HRT boiler
HUT hovel; cabin; hat: Ger.
INT anoint
IST adherent; practitioner; fanatic; is: Ger.
JAT Punjab Hindu
JET gush; spurt; gist; black; — set; — plane
JOT point; iota; tittle; brief note; — down
JUT project; extend
KAT weight; narcotic shrub
KET kat; rubbish: Scot.; Ob tributary
KIT violin; toolbox; young feline; Catherine; -cat (London club); — (Christopher) Carson
KUT -al-Imara (Brit. defeat)
LAT coin; Buddhist pillar
LET obstacle; allow(ed) to pass, be used; rent; tennis term
LIT coin; drunk;

ignited; bed: Fr.; wagon-
LOT fate; share; plot, parcel of land; great deal; river
LST landing ship tank
LUT weight
MAT fabric; door —; entangle; dull (finish); matrix; picture border; matador nickname
MET came upon; convened
MIT with: Ger.; therewith; glove
MOT pithy saying; quoits mark
MUT cur; doit; Amen's wife; courage: Ger.
NAT Siam nature spirit; hornless; — Blake (Alcott)
NET mesh; snare; web; pure; chain; line system; capture; profit; — income
NIT parasitic egg
NOT negation; hornless; smooth
NUT crank; fastener; kernel; head; guy; show investment; goddess, Geb's wife
OAT grain; Avena; feed; straw pipe
OCT prefix: eight
OFT frequently (poet.)
OLT Aluta; Danube tributary
OOT out: Scot.
OPT choose (citizenship)
ORT morsel; leftover; weight; place: Ger.
OST prefix: bone; oven; East(ern): Ger.
OUT absent; nook; game term; (at) odd(s); begone!; known; passe; wrong; on strike
PAT tap; flatten; stroke; jute; Irishman; foot; aptly
PET fondle(d); cosset; pet lamb; darling; favorite; sulk(iness)
PIT stone; hole; vat; hell; pocket; (rain) sound; floor of exchange, theater; river
POT drink; fish trap; sho(o)t; stake; much money; win; preserve; pepper —: soup
PST call for attention; quiet!
PUT lay; set; attach; throw; rustic; urge; golf shot; game; stay —; — and call; -in-Bay (Perry's victory site)
QKT chess move
RAT rodent; Mus; bandicoot; deserter; scab; hair pad; yellow; adviser: Ger.; -race
RET soak flax; macerate
RIT scratch; cut; pierce
RKT chess move
ROT ret; decay; die; nonsense; disease
RUT routine; groove; habit; oxcart; heat
SAT measure; Brahman bliss; conferred; Saturday
SET seat; fix(ed); established; direct; adjust; intent; series; group; rigid; descent; habit; harden; brood; scenery; young of plant, oyster; Osiris' evil brother
SIT rest; squat; fit; roost; press; confer; pose; -down
SOT guzzle(r); befool; waste; fixed; obstinate
SUT coal dust; smudge
TAT Indian(s); make lace; deed: Ger.; die; Hindu absolute
TIT horse; bird; return blow; twit
TNT explosive; toluene
TOT add; child; dead: Ger.
TST hissed sound; quiet!
TUT mild rebuke; rounders; game; staccato
TYT quickly; promptly
UIT out: Dutch
UST used to
VAT tub; measure; — dyes; salt pit; temple
VET (treat as) animal doctor; veterinarian
VOT Finn in Ingria
WAT temple; monument; Walter; hare; — the Devil (Scott)
WET moist(ure); rainy; not dried; fish; tipsy; soak; crazy; antiprohibitionist; — nurse
WIT know-how; to —; mind power; humor(ist); wag
YAT opening; that
YET but; though; besides; still; further; too
YOT measure
ZAT slate trimming tool

ABU battle cry; deity: Ninurta; father; — Hassan; Mount — (Jain temples)
ACU prefix: needle
AHU gazelle; waymark; burial place
AKU victorfish
ANU sky god; triad (—, Bel, Ea); Irish gods' mother; Danu
ARU indeed; really
AWU volcano
AYU sweetfish
CHU river
COU neck: Fr.
CRU tract of land; vineyard
DHU black; Roderick —, outlaw (Scott)
EAU water: Fr.; — de vie; — de Cologne; — Claire (river, city)
ECU shield; coin
EMU ostrichlike bird; Austral. tree, apple, millet
FEU fee; tenure; grant; fire: Fr.; pot au —
FLU grippe; 1918–19 pandemic
FOU full bushel: Scot.; fool(ish): Fr.
GAU Ger. region
GNU antelope; goat; takin
GRU practice: Scot.
HAU majagua; fiber tree
HEU alas!; hay: Ger.

HOU measure
IMU baking pit
IOU debt confirmation; note; I owe you
IRU Caleb's eldest son
ITU city
IZU peninsula
JAU city
JEU game: Fr.; — de mots (word play); — d'esprit (wit)
JIU river
KHU transfigured soul: Ka
KOU Hawaiian tree
KRU Liberian (language)
LAU islands
LEU Rumanian coin
LOU nickname
MAU measure; — Mau (Afr. rebels)
MEU spicknel herb; Meum
MOU measure
MRU Indo-Chinese native
NGU measure
NIU measure
PAU finished; measure; resort (Henry IV born); Edomite city
PEU little: Fr.; — a peu
PHU Cretan spikenard
PIU more: It.
REU Peleg's son
SHU deity; Ra's, Hathor's son; Geb's, Nut's father; Tefnut's husband
SOU small coin
SSU Chin. weight
TAU Greek T, 300; ankh; St. Anthony's cross
TEU strive; fuss; worry
TIU sky god; Tiwaz, Tyr (Tuesday source)
TOU measure
TSU Jap. seaport
TZU river
ULU Eskimo woman's knife
UMU Polynesian earth oven
URU Bolivian Indian
UTU sun god; Shamash; Babbar; Maori compensation; hoot
VAU Heb. letter, 6; digamma
YOU pronoun; — bet
ZIU Tiu, Tyr

CCV 205
CDV 405
CIV 104
CLV 155
CMV 905
CXV 115
DCV 605
DEV deity, angel, demon
DIV to do: Scot.; dev; 504
DLV 555
DXV 515
GAV village: Gypsy
LEV Bulgarian coin
LIV Finn(ic language); 54
LXV 65
MCV 1105
MDV 1505
MIV 1004
MLV 1055
MMV 2005
MXV 1015
NEV Nevada
REV step up motor
SOV gold coin: Br. slang; sovereign
TAV Heb. T, TH, 400
VAV Heb. letter, 6; digamma
XCV 95
XIV 14; death of Augustus
XLV 45
XXV 25

BAW exclamation: bah!
BOW weapon; archer; 6 feet; fiddlestick; Apollo's instrument; nod; yield; bend; prow; river
CAW crow's cry
COW bovine; Bos; tree raft; bogy; daunt; dolt
DAW bird; Corvus; grackle; eye color
DEW moist(ure); bloom; dawn liquor
DOW befit; Arab. sailboat; Burmese knife; Neal — (prohibitionist)
FAW fall: Scot.
FEW not many; quite a —
GAW drain, trench: Scot.
HAW tree; berry; command to horse; 3rd eyelid; hem and —; N.C. river
HEW chop; fell; stroke
HOW why; what; method; know-; Indian salute
JAW mandible; maxilla; scold(ing talk)
JEW Hebrew; Semite; Wandering —
JOW measure
KAW Burma tribe; Siouan
KEW London suburb
KOW bogy; goblin
LAW (body of) rules; code; ordinance; canon; jus; legal statute; decree; commandment; — officer; act
LEW shelter; coin; nickname; "Piggy": drummer boy (Kipling)
LOW moo; weak; inferior; plain; coarse; cheap(ly); soft(ly); cartoonist; Girl Scouts founder
MAW stomach; craw's gullet; seed of opium poppy
MEW gull; shed; molt; cage; conceal; cat's cry; spicknel
MOW cut down; (stack) hay
NAW know; no
NEW novel; (a)fresh; late; different; — look; — Deal; — Frontier
NNW compass point
NOW at this time; present(ly); admonition
PAW foot; hand(le fondly, clumsily); make fuss
PEW bench; rostrum; chirp; fishing prong
POW sound of blow; prisoner of war
RAW not cooked, spun, diluted; crude; sore; cold
REW series; pity
ROW brawl; propel; series; line; tier; file; Rotten —: Hyde Park; Skid —
SAW tool; cut; blade; disk; slice; fiddle; maxim; viewed
SEW stitch; close; — up; balk; swindle; cinch
SOW fem. swine; mold;

scatter; seed; — dragons teeth
SSW compass point
TAW marble; prepare with alum (tan); Heb. T, TH, 400
TEW fishing tackle
TIW sky god; Tiwaz; Tyr; Tiu (Tuesday source)
TOW draw; tug(boat); rope; flax fibers; spun yarn
VOW promise; dedicate
WAW Arab. W
WNW compass point
WOW sensational success; excite audience; sound distortion
WSW compass point
YAW deviate; steer widely; yes
YEW evergreen; Taxus; grief symbol; — green
YOW yelp; howl; miaow
ZIW Iyar; Heb. month

AEX (mandarin) duck genus
AIX aex; -les-Bains (spa); -la-Chapelle: Aachen
ARX citadel
AUX according to, a la: Fr.; — armes (to arms!)
BOX fight; spar; tree (topiary, Eucalyptus); mix paint; stow; gift; baseball term; — and Cox; -spring; — camera; — seat
CCX 210
CDX 410; 1st sack of Rome
CIX 109
CLX 160
CMX 910
COX steersman; Box and —; painter; reformer; politician (Pres. nominee)
CXX 120
DAX Fr. spa
DCX 610
DIX pinochle score; ten: Fr.; Dorothy — (Elizabeth Meriwether Gilmer); 509
DLX 560
DUX fugue theme; leader
DXX 520
FAX hair; suffix: maker
FIX fasten; set(tle); mend; arrange; determine; dilemma; limit; bribe; narcotic shot
FOX Vulpes; vixen; trick(ster); discolor; rope yarn; brown; river; orator; Quaker; educator; — Islands
HEX bewitch; jinx
HOX hamstring; pester
LAX loose; slack; salmon; remiss; vague
LEX law, statute: Lat.
LIX 59
LOX (smoked) salmon; — and bagels
LUX light unit
LXX 70; Septuagint; Temple at Jerusalem destroyed
MAX Maximilian; Maximus; Becky Sharp's love (Thackeray)
MCX 1110
MDX 1510
MIX mingle; cross; blend; prepared ingredients; 1009
MLX 1060
MMX 2010
MUX mess; botch
MXX 1020
NIX sprite; no(thing); undeliverable mail
NOX night goddess
NYX night goddess; Chaos's daughter; mother of day and night
PAX peace goddess; Irene; — Britannica; — vobiscum
PIX box; Eucharist case; ciborium; photos
POX infectious disease
PYX box; Eucharist case; ciborium
REX king: Lat.; Reginald; rabbit
RIX rush; reed
RUX worry; play; sport
SAX cutting tool; sword; wind instrument
SEX gender; — appeal; weaker —; — hormone
SIX card; die face; boat; — Hundred (Light Brigade)
TAX assess; censure; duty; charge; octroi
TEX Texas
TOX intoxicate
TUX men's evening dress
VEX afflict; annoy; harass
VOX voice: Lat.; — populi, — dei; — angelica
WAX grow; bee secretion; yellow; polish; rage; defeat
XIX 19
XXX 30; Crucifixion of Christ
YEX hiccup; cough
YOX hiccup; cough
ZAX slate trimmer

ABY endure; last; continue
ACY suffix: quality, state
ADY measure
AGY aged; old
ALY like malt drink
AMY female name; prochein — (nearest friend: law); (Little) — Dorrit: Dickens
ANY some; one; at all
ARY any; suffix: pert. to, engaged in
BAY inlet; compartment; dam; window; laurel; bark(ing); brown; horse; — State (Mass.); — City (Mich.); bomb —
BEY Tunis ruler; title
BLY Chief — (Saroyan); Nellie —, newspaperwoman
BOY youth; servant; act, treat as lad; office —; — orator: W. J. Bryan; Blue — (Gainsborough)

BUY (good) purchase; bribe; redeem
CAY key; islet
CLY seize; steal; servant (Dickens)
COY demure; bashful; shy; entice; hoax
CRY call; wail; weep; beg; summon; slogan; — wolf
DAY date; lifetime; solar, sidereal, lunar —; distance; — in court; educator; 1st printer
DEY Afr. ruler; (maid)servant
DRY hard; shrewd; arid; plain; dull; vapid; evaporate; — Tortugas (isles); dwindle(d); drought; — goods; — cell; — run; simulated
ELY cathedral city; mountain; island; Bishop of —
ERY suffix: conduct, art, place
FAY unite closely; fit; elf; cleanse; white man; name
FEY elfin; visionary
FLY leap; soar; vanish; pilot; tent canvas; printer's devil; keen; on the —; river
FOY feast; gift
FRY young brood; pan-cook; vex(ation); prison reformer
GAY merry; glad; John — (Beggar's Opera)
GEY considerable; very
GOY non-Jew: Heb.
GRY horse: Gypsy
GUY rope; chain; effigy; fellow; chaff; — Fawkes; Octavius — (Collins)
HAY fencer's cry; fodder; timothy; yellow; river; statesman, Lincoln's secretary
HEY call for attention
HOY barge; exclamation; Orkney Isle
ICY frosty; chilling
IVY vine; arbutus; creeper; overgrow
JAY J.; (chatter)bird; blue; stupid one; — Gatsby (Scott-Fitzgerald); 1st chief justice
JOY happiness; bliss; gaiety; exult; name
KAY K; islet; Catherine; Sir —; King Arthur's brother
KEY islet; bolt; clue; solution; pitch; style; fasten; attune; Francis Scott — (Star-Spangled Banner)
KUY Siamese; Shan group; Kandh language
LAY reclined; song; secular; unprofessional; superimpose; apply; bet; attach; plan; still; price; — of the land
LEY tax; Rumanian coin
LOY post-hole spade; a slick; name
MAY can; prime; heydey; hawthorn; spiraea; fem. name; Mary; month; Cape —
MUY very, greatly: Sp.
NAY no (vote); denial; refuse; Moslem flute
NEY Napoleonic marshal
ONY any
ORY like ore, seaweed; suffix: of
OXY of an ox; sharp; acute; prefix: oxygen
PAY tar vessel; wages; remit; reward(ing); punish(ment); satisfy
PLY fold; bend; strand (thickness); wield; practice; urge; paper web
POY boat pole
PRY lever(age); peep(er); gaze; Paul — (meddler)
PUY volcanic hill
RAY fish; torpedo; skate; sting —; father of natural history; particle; shine; radiance; vision; Raymond; Philip —: Annie Arden's husband (Tennyson)
REY king: Sp.
ROY name; Rob — (outlaw, canoe, Scott hero)
SAY tell; state; suggest; opinion, influence
SEY pollack; coalfish
SHY timid; wary; bashful; shrink; avoid; fling; trial
SKY heaven; firmament; blue; climate; raise
SLY shrewd; foxy; roguish; secretive; on the —; tinker (Shaks.)
SMY sprat
SNY abound; swarm; bend; curved plank
SOY bean; sauce
SPY watch(er); discover; search(ing); secret agent
STY pig enclosure; eyelid swelling
TAY river; Firth of —
THY poss. pronoun
TOY (diversionary) trifle; trinket; play(thing)
TRY attempt; test; prove; strain; annoy; essay; render fat; conduct court procedure
VLY low-land; marsh; creek; temporary lake
WAY route; means; distance; style; journey; point; scope; momentum; — out
WEY weight unit (40 bushels)
WHY reason; problem; enigma; for which; exclamation
WRY deflect; twist(ed); disgusted; askew
YOY yes

ADZ cutting tool
BIZ business (slang); show —
BOZ Dickens pseudonym
BUZ son of Nahor,

Mileah
COZ cousin
FEZ red tasseled cap; tarboosh; Morocco city
FIZ hiss(ing sound); fuss; champagne
GAZ coin; guz
GEZ guz
GIZ dialect; Ethiopic
GOZ coin
GUZ measure; zar; arshin
HUZ Abraham's nephew
LAZ Caucasian tribesman
LIZ Elizabeth
LUZ Bib. site; Bethel
NEZ nose: Fr.; — Perce (Shahaptian Indian); pince-
ODZ minced oath
PAZ peace: Sp.; La —: Bolivia
POZ positive(ly)
RIZ rice: Fr.
SUZ exclamation
TAZ river; — Bay
TEZ pungent; violent
VIZ namely
WIZ magician; genius
YEZ you

THREE-LETTER WORDS

–A– to –Z–

BAA sheep's bleat
MAA sheep's cry; maw
NAA no
SAA measure
TAA Chin. pagoda
BAB Babism founder
CAB (ride in) taxi; engineer's place; measure; Civil Aeronautics Board
DAB touch, tap; flounder; lizard; expert
GAB chatter; hook; notch; E.I. persimmon
JAB punch; stab
KAB measure
LAB rennet; study room
MAB fairy queen and midwife; Mabel
NAB lock keeper; arrest; river
PAB flax refuse (fuel)
RAB teacher; mortar mixer; dog hero; Yugo. isle
TAB flap; tag; account; Cambridge man; charges
ZAB Great — (river)
BAC ferryboat; cistern
FAC fact
LAC varnish component; resin; milk (pharm.); 100,000 rupees
MAC son of: Ir.; Scot; Irishman; coat
PAC moccasin; half-boot
SAC cavity; pouch; Sauk; Indian; — and soc
TAC prefix: touch
VAC speech goddess; Sarasvati
WAC Women's Army Corps
ZAC Caucasian ibex
BAD evil; poor; ill; severe; faulty; wrong; river; — Ems
CAD (act as) bounder
DAD father
FAD custom; craze; polish
GAD rod; rove(r); -fly; oath; Jacob's son; Israel tribe; Syrian god
HAD possessed; tricked
LAD boy; youth; stripling
MAD crazy; vain; angry; river
PAD cushion; saddle; walk; tablet; robber; stuff; track; lodgings
RAD afraid: Scot.; energy unit
SAD gloomy; dull; poor; depressed; grievous; — sack
TAD small child; Theodore
WAD lump; plug; roll; money; black ocher
DAE do: Scot.
EAE classifying suffix
FAE foe: Scot.
HAE have: Scot.
KAE serve; oblige; jackdaw
MAE — West (life preserver)
NAE no, not: Scot.
RAE explorer; fem. name
SAE so
TAE to; toe; take: Scot.
VAE alas! — victis
KAF myth. mountain, fabled bird abode; Arabic K
OAF elf's child; dolt; fool
QAF kaf
BAG sac(k); measure; purse; seize; in the —
CAG offend; insult
DAG Nott and —, deities; antler; pistol; — Hammarskjold, UN chief
FAG cigarette; drudge; tire; Capt. Absolute's servant; liar
GAG pry open; choke; joke; closure; fish; illustrator
HAG harpy; witch; urge; copse; bog
JAG pendant; barb; slash; drunken spree
LAG linger; slacken; stave; jailbird
MAG chatter; bird; Margaret; halfpenny (Brit.)
NAG horse; annoy(ance);

fret; snake; Nagaine's wife (Kipling)
PAG island
RAG shred; scold; dance; slate; fog; — doll
SAG droop; weaken; drift
TAG flap; tab; lock; cue; story moral; join; follow; game; label
VAG (arrest as) vagabond
WAG sway; gossip; joker
ZAG jagged line angle
BAH exclamation
DAH Burmese knife
HAH exclamation
JAH Jehovah; god
MAH moon angel
PAH bah!; nasty; improper; N.Z. native fort
RAH (cheer with) hurrah
SAH measure
VAH Danube tributary
WAH panda; measure
YAH yes; exclamation
HAI Israelites defeat site
KAI N.Z. food; apple; island
LAI medieval tale: Burmese
MAI May: Ger.
PAI money; weight
RAI measure
SAI Capuchin monkey; Cebus
TAI porgy; Laos; Shan; Siamese; Li -po (poet); — Shan (sacred mountain)
VAI Liberian Negro
GAJ coin
HAJ pilgrimage to Mecca
RAJ reign, rule: India
SAJ teak tree
TAJ (dervish) cap; — Mahal
DAK India mail
HAK legal claim; share
LAK grouse's wooing strut
NAK stigmatic point; mango
OAK Quercus; Casuarina; encina; — brown; poison —; — Park; — Ridge
SAK white cotton
YAK Tibet ox; beast of burden
ZAK measure
AAL Indian mulberry; red dye; morindin
BAL mine; ball: Fr.
CAL California; wolframite
DAL split pea; pigeon pea; Swedish river
GAL girl; speed unit
HAL Henry, Harry; Prince - (Henry V); Bluff King — (Henry VIII)
IAL adj. suffix
MAL — de mer (sea sickness); Sudra caste Hindu; prefix: evil; measure
PAL partner; (to) chum
SAL salt; - tree; tamarisk; rock; Sarah
TAL palm fiber; hand clapping cymbals
ZAL Rustam's father
AAM liquid measure
BAM hoax; Iranian town
CAM awry; gear; rotating, sliding part; Ouse tributary
DAM obstruct(ion); wall; weir; coin; female parent; Nobel biochemist
EAM uncle; gossip
FAM hand (slang)
GAM whale school; visit; botanical suffix
HAM Noah's son; Shem's brother; amateur radio; actor
JAM tight place; crush; interfere; preserve native chief; — pack; — session
KAM crooked
LAM beat; escape; loom lever
MAM Mayan Indian
NAM distrain(t)
PAM card game
RAM sheep; batter(ing) —; weight; ship beak; pump; stuff; constellation: Aries
SAM unite; curdle; Uncle —
TAM Scot. cap
YAM sweet potato; batata; edible root; tuber; posthouse
BAN edict; forbid; curse; title; muslin; coin; kokumin (Jap. reserve); Lancelot's father
CAN vessel; preserve; tin; dismiss; jail; weight
DAN title; Daniel; buoy; Jacob's (Bilhah's) son; tribe; from — to Beersheba; river; Una's brother (Kipling)
EAN bring forth; to lamb
FAN cool(er); vane; winnow; spread; stimulate; devotee; African; Pangwe; Pahouin; — dance
GAN Roland's destroyer
HAN Chin. dynasty; Japanese barony; Yangtze tributary
IAN John; — Fleming (James Bond author)
JAN — of Leiden, fanatic; — Hus, reformer
KAN Kansas; measure; river
LAN name prefix; measure; Swed. district
MAN individual; homo; male; anyone; valet; game piece; fortify; tame; to a —; — of war; Isle of —
NAN fem. name; river
PAN tub; dish; ape; wash; result; betel leaf; sir; god: Faunus, Inuus (part goat); face; son of Hermes; prefix: all; Peter — (Barrie); dead-
RAN twine hank; sea deity; Aegir's wife; sped
SAN Greek letter; Bushmen; hemp
TAN make leather; brown; beat; Gypsy camp
VAN (fore)front; lead;

car; Urartu: Armenia; Turk. lake, town
WAN (grow) pale; dark; dim
ZAN Zeus; Olympia statue
DAO P.I. tree (fruit, fiber)
GAO river
HAO Chin. dynasty
IAO honey eater bird; manuao
LAO Tai native, language; -tzu, -tse (philosopher)
MAO peacock; — Tse-tung (Chin. leader); peacock (Kipling)
SAO measure; — Paulo (city)
TAO man: P.I.; Chin. road, cosmic order, truth; — Te Ching: Lao-tse's work
YAO Chin. aborigines, emperor; Bantu; Indian
BAP bread loaf, roll
CAP top; cover; match; crown; explosive; detonator; paper size; capital; tread renewal
DAP dibble; drop bait; dip; rebound; skip
GAP opening; breach; pass; hiatus; ravine
HAP chance; befall; wrap
JAP Nipponese
LAP fold; wrap; cut; polish; circuit; drink; ripple; take eagerly
MAP chart; survey, image; Mercator; plan
NAP doze; siesta; hairy surface; pile; game; seize
PAP soft food; paste; dad; simple discourse
RAP coin; least bit; strike; knock; criticize; jail sentence
SAP juice; vigor; money; fool; drain; trench; weaken
TAP rap; signal; half sole; dance; spigot; liquor; ask money; draw
WAP blow; wrap; truss
YAP yelp; gab; hoodlum; island
AAR (underground) river
BAR obstruct(ion); rod; gate; strip(e); counter; court; except; fish; maigre; mus. measure; son of; sandbank; rifle; — Cocheba (Heb. rebel)
CAR lift cage; chariot; for: Fr.; fish box; balloon basket; — Nicobar (island)
DAR abode; gateway; tree; patriotic group
EAR sense; attention; grain spike; handle; front page box; god; Tiwaz; Tiu
FAR greatly; widely; long; distant; advanced
GAR needlefish
HAR chill fog: Scot.
JAR grate; shake; drill; clash; shock; vessel; preserve
LAR gibbon; house god; ancestral spirit
MAR spoil; mutilate; — Ignatius (patriarch of Antioch)
NAR near(ly): Scot.
PAR value; equality; average; standard golf score; by: Fr.
SAR sixty sixties: 3,600 (Babylonian number)
TAR pitch; coal — (saccharine source); sailor; lute; telegram; river
WAR strife; battle; fight; — bride; — cabinet
YAR growl
ZAR measure
BAS low, stocking: Fr.; a — (down!); — relief; roulette bet
CAS en tout —: Fr.; vanity bag; umbrella
DAS cony; badger: Dutch; the: Ger.; — Kapital
FAS divine law: Roman
GAS fuel; anesthetic; chatter; boast; tear —, poison —, natural —, coal —
HAS possesses; -been
KAS cupboard, wardrobe: Dutch
LAS alas; the: Sp.; — Vegas
MAS master; suffix: festival
NAS has not, was not
OAS Organization of American States
PAS dance step; — de deux; n'est-ce-?
RAS fabric; prince; cape; Fascist leader
VAS pledge; surety; duct, vessel (anat.)
WAS existed; the past
BAT club; hit; brick; blow; flying mammal; wink; gray; bomb
CAT feline; whip; shrew; fish; tripod; game; island; ship (tackle); jazz fan
EAT consume; gnaw; erode; rust; waste
FAT oil(y); rich; gross; obese; stout; useful
GAT channel; gun
HAT headwear; cardinal's office; has: Ger.
JAT Punjab Hindu
KAT weight; narcotic shrub
LAT coin; Buddhist pillar
MAT fabric; door —; entangle; dull (finish); matrix; picture border; matador nickname
NAT Siam nature spirit; hornless; — Blake (Alcott)
OAT grain; Avena; feed; straw pipe
PAT tap; flatten; stroke; jute; Irishman; foot; aptly
RAT rodent; Mus; bandicoot; deserter; scab; hair pad; yellow; adviser: Ger.; -race
SAT measure; Brahman

bliss; conferred; Saturday
TAT Indian(s); make lace; deed: Ger.; die; Hindu absolute
VAT tub; measure; — dyes; salt pit; temple
WAT temple; monument; Walter; hare; — the Devil (Scott)
YAT opening; that
ZAT slate trimming tool
EAU water: Fr.; — de vie; — de Cologne; — Claire (river, city)
GAU Ger. region
HAU majagua; fiber tree
JAU city
LAU islands
MAU measure; — Mau (Afr. rebels)
PAU finished; measure; resort (Henry IV born); Edomite city
TAU Greek T, 300; ankh; St. Anthony's cross
VAU Heb. letter, 6; digamma
GAV village: Gypsy
TAV Heb. T, TH, 400
VAV Heb. letter, 6; digamma
BAW exclamation: bah!
CAW crow's cry
DAW bird; Corvus; grackle; eye color
FAW fall: Scot.
GAW drain, trench: Scot.
HAW tree; berry; command to horse; 3rd eyelid; hem and —; N.C. river
JAW mandible; maxilla; scold(ing talk)
KAW Burma tribe; Siouan
LAW (body of) rules; code; ordinance; canon; jus; legal statute; decree; commandment; — officer; act
MAW stomach; craw's gullet; seed of opium poppy
NAW know; no
PAW foot; hand(le fondly, clumsily); make fuss
RAW not cooked, spun, diluted; crude; sore; cold
SAW tool; cut; blade; disk; slice; fiddle; maxim; viewed
TAW marble; prepare with alum (tan); Heb. T, TH, 400
WAW Arab. W
YAW deviate; steer widely; yes
DAX Fr. spa
FAX hair; suffix: maker
LAX loose; slack; salmon; remiss; vague
MAX Maximilian; Maximus; Becky Sharp's love (Thackeray)
PAX peace goddess; Irene; — Britannica; — vobiscum
SAX cutting tool; sword; wind instrument
TAX assess; censure; duty; charge; octrol
WAX grow; bee secretion; yellow; polish; rage; defeat
ZAX slate trimmer
BAY inlet; compartment; dam; window; laurel; bark(ing); brown; horse; — State (Mass.); — City (Mich.); bomb —
CAY key; islet
DAY date; lifetime; solar, sidereal, lunar —; distance; — in court; educator; 1st printer
FAY unite closely; fit; elf; cleanse; white man; name
GAY merry; glad; John — (Beggar's Opera)
HAY fencer's cry; fodder; timothy; yellow; river; statesman, Lincoln's secretary
JAY J; (chatter)bird; blue; stupid one; — Gatsby (Scott-Fitzgerald); 1st chief justice
KAY K; islet; Catherine; Sir —; King Arthur's brother
LAY reclined; song; secular; unprofessional; superimpose; apply; bet; attach; plan; still; price; — of the land
MAY can; prime; heydey; hawthorn; spiraea; fem. name; Mary; month; Cape —
NAY no (vote); denial; refuse; Moslem flute
PAY tar vessel; wages; remit; reward(ing); punish(ment); satisfy
RAY fish; torpedo; skate; sting —; father of natural history; particle; shine; radiance; vision; Raymond; Philip —: Annie Arden's husband (Tennyson)
SAY tell; state; suggest; opinion, influence
TAY river; Firth of —
WAY route; means; distance; style; journey; point; scope; momentum; — out
GAZ coin; guz
LAZ Caucasian tribesman
PAZ peace: Sp.; La —: Bolivia
TAZ river; — Bay

ABA camel hair; Arab. cloak; altazimuth
IBA P.I. fruit tree
ABB warp yarn; poorest fleece
BBB rifle shot size
EBB recede; delay; — tide; shallow
ABC book; primer; rudiment
ABE Lincoln; the Great Emancipator
OBE Greek clan division; magic rite; fetish
UBE P.I. yam
ABI Hezekiah's mother
FBI Federal Bureau of Investigation
OBI girdle; sash

UBI where: Lat; white yam
IBN — Saud (king)
ABO Finn seaport; Turku
EBO tree; — oil; Niger Negro
IBO Niger Negro
ABS Bedouin tribesman
GBS playwright: George Bernard Shaw
ABT — system (mountain railroads); composer
ABU battle cry; deity: Ninurta; father; — Hassan; Mount — (Jain temples)
ABY endure; last; continue

ECA Economic Cooperation Administration
ICA river; city
OCA edible root; wood sorrel; oxalis
UCA fiddler crab
CCC 300; Commodity Credit Corporation; Civilian Conservation Corps
DCC 700
FCC Federal Communications Commission
ICC Interstate Commerce Commission
MCC 1200
ACE one-spot; card; bit; hole in one; air hero; game point; expert; first-rate
ICE frost(ing); chill; dessert; diamonds
ACH alas; Indian mulberry
ICH I, ego: Ger.; fish dermatitis
OCH alas!; oh!
TCH exclamation
ACI chem. prefix
CCI 201
DCI 601
ICI here: Fr.
MCI 1101
XCI 91
ACK -ack (antiaircraft)
ICK fish dermatitis
OCK weight
TCK exclamation
CCL 250
DCL 650
MCL 1150
MCM 1900; fin de siecle; Boxer Rebellion
ECO prefix: environment
ICS science suffix
ACT deed; decree; feign; do; play part; prayer; — of God, — of faith
ECT prefix: outside, without
OCT prefix: eight
ACU prefix: needle
ECU shield; coin
CCV 205
DCV 605
MCV 1105
XCV 95
CCX 210
DCX 610
MCX 1110
ACY suffix: quality, state
ICY frosty; chilling

ADA fem. name; city; (Java) canvas
IDA Idaho; Crete mountain; Princess — (opera); Countess —, heiress (Thackeray)
ODA harem room, inmate
MDC 1600
ADD (sub)join; augment; annex; total, foot
ODD unpaired; queer; uneven; extra; fellow; — man wins
ADE soft drink; humorist
EDE Dutch commune; Afr. city
IDE fish; chem. suffix
ODE (Pindar) poem; song; canticle; hymn
EDH A.S. letter: th
CDI 401
MDI 1501
UDI N. Caucasian language
CDL 450
ADO do; trouble; fuss; stir
EDO Nigerian: Ibo
IDO artificial language: de Couturat, Jespersen
ODO William the Conqueror's half brother; Eudes; Count of Paris
UDO Japanese herb; edible shoot
DDS Doctor of Dental Surgery (degree)
ODS minced oath
DDT insecticide
CDV 405
MDV 1505
CDX 410; 1st sack of Rome
MDX 1510
ADY measure
ADZ cutting tool
ODZ minced oath

AEA (candlenut) bark cord
DEA goddess: Lat.
HEA Eridu's chief god
KEA N.Z. parrot
LEA meadow; yarn measure; warp threads
MEA — culpa (my fault)
NEA National Education Association
PEA seed; plant; marble; sweet —; — soup (fog); river
REA turmeric; Rhea; Cybele, mother of the gods
SEA water(s); wave; vast area; at — (lost); naval; — horse
TEA beverage; collation; — green; — ball; — wagon
UEA island
WEA Algonquian
YEA yes (vote); — and Nay (Richard I)
ZEA Indian corn; maize
DEB society girl; Deborah
GEB earth god; Osiris's father
KEB earth god; Osiris's father
NEB Nebraska; beak; mouth; kiss
REB rebel
SEB earth god; Osiris's father
WEB gossamer; (en)mesh; membrane; network; rete
AEC Atomic Energy Commission
DEC prefix: ten; December
SEC second; dry (wine);

Securities & Exchange Commission
TEC detective
BED base; bottom; matrix; lodge
EED Moslem Easter
FED nourished; fattened
GED oath (God)
KED sheep tick
LED guided; directed
NED Edgar; Edmund; Edward
PED basket; prefix: foot, boy, child
RED color, dye; lurid; inflamed; golden; Communist; fowl; cent; river; sea; — Jacket (Seneca chief)
SED but: Lat.
TED spread for drying; scatter; waste
WED marry; unite(d)
ZED Z
BEE B; Apis; drone; contest; crazy idea
CEE C; em- (master of ceremonies)
DEE D; river; mathematician
FEE land grant; charge; tip; reward
GEE G; horse command; evade; agree; oath; haw and —
LEE shelter; sediment; Annabel — (Poe); Lorelei — (Loos); Francis Lightfoot —; Henry — (Light-Horse Harry)
NEE born; by maiden name
PEE P; turtle delicacy; calipee
REE sift; right!; Arikara; fem. ruff; sandpiper
SEE perceive; bishop's seat; curia; learn; call (bet); — red; — stars; astronomer
TEE T; game mark; golf term; top ornament; — beam, bar; to a —; -shirt
VEE V; $5; neckline; refusal
WEE little; pig's squeak; — Willie Winkle (Kipling)
ZEE Z; zed
AEF American Expeditionary Force; WWI Amer. army; Pershing command
KEF hemp; languor
NEF clock, vessel in form of ship; navicula; church nave
REF measure; referee
BEG ask; entreat; Turk. title; bey
DEG sprinkle; dampen
GEG No. Albanian
KEG cask; — of nails: 100 lb.
LEG meat cut; support; run; lap; — art: cheesecake
MEG Margaret; Princess —; Mag, Alcott heroine; horse (Burns); — Merrilies (Scott)
PEG (cribbage) pin; support, pretext; leg; hit; plod; Margaret
REG desert region
SEG sedge; iris
TEG young sheep
VEG prank; wanderer
HEH Chin. tribe; Hei; Miao
LEH Kashmir town
PEH river
REH salt mixture; alkali
DEI the gods: Lat.; agnus —
FEI Yap stone money; banana
HEI cat's cradle; Miss — (Greene)
KEI apple; island
LEI wreath; coin
NEI Eastern flute
PEI river
REI coin; David's friend
VEI Liberian Negro
WEI Chin. dynasty, state; river
LEK gather(ing); coin; river
BEL fruit, tree; Bengal quince; golden apple; power ratio; earth god; Marduk; — Affris (Shaw)
DEL Delaware
EEL teleost fish: conger; moray; elver; lamprey; vinegar worm
GEL jellify; harden; set
HEL Loki's daughter; Niflheim goddess
KEL caul; net; film
MEL honey; prefix: limb, black
PEL prefix: mud, clay
REL electric unit
SEL salt: Fr.; self: Scot.
TEL prefix: distant, end
ZEL Oriental cymbal
BEM Pol. general; pasha
DEM Democrat: opp. to Rep(ublican)
GEM muffin; — State (Idaho); prize piece; jewel
HEM (cloth) edge; confine; surround; hesitate; haw
JEM James
KEM river; port
MEM Heb. letter M, 40
SEM Noah's son; Ham's brother
TEM sun god; Atmu, (A)tum
WEM spot; stain (in wood)
DEN retreat; lair; haunt; scout unit (pack part)
EEN Ir. suffix; even (poet.)
FEN marsh; weight; forbid; — Ho (river)
GEN suffix: heredity factor
HEN female bird, fish; fowl; coward; measure; — party
KEN insight; Japanese measure, prefecture, games
MEN crew; hands; people; troops; lunar god
NEN river
PEN confine; jail; feather; style; write(r); fem. swan
SEN coin; measure; Sun Yat- (Chin. leader)
TEN bill; card; X; many; denary; deca; big casino
WEN cyst; growth; coin;

YEN wyn desire; urge; Jap.
ZEN money Buddhist sect, belief
GEO Georgia; prefix: earth, soil
LEO constellation; Lion; composer; emperor; pope; — Tolstoy
MEO Indian farmer caste
NEO advocate of new; prefix: recent
YEO officer; bodyguard
HEP wise to; informed; exclamation; -cat
KEP catch; haul
NEP catnip; cotton fiber knot; Soviet policy
PEP energy; stimulate
REP fabric; lewd one; Republican: opp. to Dem(ocrat)
YEP yes
ZEP zeppelin: airship
AER prefix: gas, air; chalice veil
BER jujube; elb
DER prefix: neck; the: Ger.
EER ever (poet.); suffix
FER iron: Fr.; chemin de — (railroad, baccarat)
GER resident (Heb. law); Judaism convert
HER pronoun; female
IER noun suffix
KER evil spirit; fate
LER Brythonic god; Celtic Neptune; children of — (swans)
MER sea: Fr.; mal de —
NER Abner's father; Saul's uncle
PER through; via; for each
SER It. title; weight; exist: Sp.; prefix: serum
TER prefix: thrice
VER worm: Fr.
WER who: Ger.; murder fine
XER prefix: dry
YER suffix: your
ZER measure; weight
AES Roman bronze; money
BES pleasure god
CES these: Fr.
DES of the: Ger., Fr.; from, since: Fr.; — Moines
EES eyes: Scot.
FES sacred city
GES Tapuyan Indian
HES men; males
LES the: Fr.; — Miserables
MES my: Fr.; prefix: middling, intermediate
OES Os
PES foot(like part)
RES thing: Lat.; legal matter; in medias —
SES his, her: Fr.
TES your: Fr.
YES affirmative (vote)
AET of the age: Lat.
BET stake; wager; Betsy — (Dickens)
CET that: Fr.
FET measure
GET obtain; reach; hit; persuade; divorce bill
JET gush; spurt; gist; black; — set; — plane
KET kat; rubbish: Scot.; Ob tributary
LET obstacle; allow(ed) to pass, be used; rent; tennis term
MET came upon; convened
NET mesh; snare; web; pure; chain; line system; capture; profit; — income
PET fondle(d); cosset; pet lamb; darling; favorite; sulk(iness)
RET soak flax; macerate
SET seat; fix(ed); established; direct; adjust; intent; series; group; rigid; descent; habit; harden; brood; scenery; young of plant, oyster; Osiris' evil brother
VET (treat as) animal doctor; veterinarian
WET moist(ure); rainy; not dried; fish; tipsy; soak; crazy; antiprohibitionist; — nurse
YET but; though; besides; still; further; too
FEU fee; tenure; grant; fire: Fr.; pot au —
HEU alas!; hay: Ger.
JEU game: Fr.; — de mots (word play); — d'esprit (wit)
LEU Rumanian coin
MEU spicknel herb; Meum
PEU little: Fr.; — a peu
REU Peleg's son
TEU strive; fuss; worry
DEV deity, angel, demon
LEV Bulgarian coin
NEV Nevada
REV step up motor
DEW moist(ure); bloom; dawn liquor
FEW not many; quite a —
HEW chop; fell; stroke
JEW Hebrew; Semite; Wandering —
KEW London suburb
LEW shelter; coin; nickname; "Piggy": drummer boy (Kipling)
MEW gull; shed; molt; cage; conceal; cat's cry; spicknel
NEW novel; (a)fresh; late; different; — look; — Deal; — Frontier
PEW bench; rostrum; chirp; fishing prong
REW series; pity
SEW stitch; close; — up; balk; swindle; cinch
TEW fishing tackle
YEW evergreen; Taxus; grief symbol; — green
AEX (mandarin) duck genus
HEX bewitch; jinx
LEX law, statute: Lat.
REX king: Lat.; Reginald; rabbit
SEX gender; — appeal; weaker —; — hormone
TEX Texas
VEX afflict; annoy; harass
YEX hiccup; cough
BEY Tunis ruler; title

DEY Afr. ruler; (maid)servant
FEY elfin; visionary
GEY considerable; very
HEY call for attention
KEY islet; bolt; clue; solution; pitch; style; fasten; attune; Francis Scott — (Star-Spangled Banner)
LEY tax; Rumanian coin
NEY Napoleonic marshal
REY king: Sp.
SEY — pollack; coalfish
WEY weight unit (40 bushels)
FEZ red tasseled cap; tarboosh; Morocco city
GEZ guz
NEZ nose: Fr.; — Perce (Shahaptian Indian); pince-
TEZ pungent; violent
YEZ you

MFA Master of Fine Arts (degree)
UFA river
IFE hemp; cordage fiber
OFF erring; away!; go; out; below par; — color; — stage
AFL American Federation of Labor
OFO Siouan language
UFO flying saucer
AFR Africa
AFT astern; back; behind
EFT lizard; newt
OFT frequently (poet.)

AGA bark; rope; title; Turk. officer; ruler
AGE period; generation; era; ripen; mellow
AGG carrier (Kipling)
EGG ovum; germ cell; coal; bomb; fellow; incite
UGH assenting grunt
AGO past; since
EGO I; whole man; alter —; self(ishness)
NGU measure
AGY aged; old

AHA exclamation
CHA rolled tea; -cha (V.I. white, dance)
DHA measure, weight
FHA Federal Housing, Farmers' Home Administration
KHA Nepalese; Laotian
SHA Shinto temple; urial; sheep
THA thee; thou
IHC Jesus symbol
CHE shrub; Chin. flute
RHE fluidity unit
SHE woman; Haggard novel
THE article
AHI sky serpent; Vritra
CHI Greek letter Ch, 600; fem. Gypsy; Gold Coast language; Tshi
EHI Ahiram; Benjamin's son
GHI buffalo butter; ghee
IHI stitchbird; fish; halfbeak; skipper
PHI Greek letter PH, 500
SHI weight
AHM liquid measure
OHM electric unit; -'s law
AHO exclamation
CHO measure
MHO unit of conductance
OHO exclamation
PHO exclamation
RHO Greek R, 100
SHO pshaw!; sure; measure
THO Tonkin peasant
WHO rel. pronoun
IHR you: Ger.
IHS symbol (Jesus)
JHS symbol (Jesus)
AHT Wakashan Indian
AHU gazelle; waymark; burial place
CHU river
DHU black; Roderick —, outlaw (Scott)
KHU transfigured soul: Ka
PHU Cretan spikenard
SHU deity; Ra's, Hathor's son; Geb's, Nut's father; Tefnut's husband
SHY timid; wary; bashful; shrink; avoid; fling; trial
THY poss. pronoun
WHY reason; problem; enigma; for which; exclamation

AIA Rizpah's father
CIA Central Intelligence Agency
DIA through; prefix: apart; day: Sp.
HIA hawk parrot
LIA — Fail (crowning stone)
MIA mine: It.
PIA arrowroot; — mater (brain part)
RIA narrow inlet; creek; estuary
SIA Keresan Indian
TIA aunt: Sp.
VIA way, vessel: Lat.; through; — Dolorosa
ZIA Gad's descendant; N.M. pueblo
BIB sip; apron part; fish; nozzle
DIB bob bait; dibble; dip
FIB (tell white) lie; pummel
GIB (tom)cat; salmon; prison; bearing plate: gut fish
JIB sail; mouth; crane arm; standstill
LIB castrate; ad —
MIB marble
NIB beak; pen(point); lint knot; scorer
RIB costa; meat cut; wife; vein; part of sock, ship, umbrella; tease; purl
SIB brother; sister; litter mate; kinsman; congenial
TIB skip school
HIC hiccuping sound; — et ubique
PIC measure; very small
SIC thus!; — transit gloria; chase; incite
TIC twitch(ing); spasm; funny habit; correct (slang)
AID help(er); succor; Agency for International Development
BID reveal; offer; order; invite; — fair; —

price
CID the —; Sp. hero, epic; Diaz de Vivar
DID performed; acted
FID mast support; pin; tobacco quid
GID sheep disease
HID concealed
KID young goat, child; fur; leather; tease
LID (eye) cover; curb; hat
MID among; central; half-way
NID nest; pheasant brood
OID suffix: like
RID free; clear; dispose
SID Sydney
TID girl; woman
CIE abbr., company: Fr.
DIE expire, long; vanish, stop; cube; chance; tool; shape
FIE exclamation
GIE give: Scot.
HIE hasten speed
LIE fib; mislead; be; extend slope; golf term Trygve — (UN official)
NIE never Ger.; eyes
PIE bird; mixed type; jumble coin; tart
RIE grass cereal
SIE sye; you, she: Ger.
TIE bind; link, knot; duty; equal(ity); bond; beam; cravat, Ascot
VIE emulate; strive; compete life: Fr.
LIF — and Lifthrasir (myth. survivors)
RIF measure
SIF Thor's wife; home guardian
VIF lively, animated: Fr.
ZIF Jewish month: Iyar
BIG large; barley; — Bertha; - Ben; — Bend; - brother; — house; — Blue (river)
CIG cigarette
DIG (verbal) thrust; dwell
FIG fruit; fico; zero; rig
GIG fish spear, hook; boat; chaise, carriage, nap
JIG dance; prank; drill
MIG marble; duck; plane
NIG dress (stone); cut coin edge, revoke
PIG pork; litter; glutton cushion; ingot; - iron; The — Baby (Carroll)
RIG equip(ment); swindle; tackle; ardri
SIG signature
WIG hair(piece); peruke, judge
ZIG part of a zigzag
CII 102
DII the gods; 502
III 3
LII 52
MII 1002
OII N.Z. muttonbird
RII small streams; Venice canals
VII 7
XII 12
AIK oak: Scot
BIK poison; aconite
PIK measure
AIL be ill
KIL Ir. church; monk's cell
LIL book, paper, letter: Gypsy; little; Abner
MIL 1/1000 inch (wire measure), coin; Ir. eponymous ancestor
NIL nothing indigo dye; ipomoea; nilgai
OIL painting fuel; grease; flatter(y); bribe
PIL prefix: hair
SIL yellow ocher
TIL tree; sesame; mark
AIM direct(ion), design; scheme end
BIM Barbados man
DIM dark(en) dull; obscure; - view
GIM neat; spruce
HIM pronoun male
JIM James; - Crow; -dandy; Lord — (Conrad) Sawyer's friend (Twain)
KIM — O'Hara waif (Kipling)
LIM blue pine toon
MIM (act) affectedly shy
NIM steal; margosa tree
RIM border; edge; margin; wheel part
SIM Simeon; Simon
TIM Tiny —: cripple (Dickens)
VIM force; energy; spirit
AIN well; spring; 16th Heb. letter, 70; Rhone tributary
BIN box; crib; pungi (flute); Vina
DIN noise; uproar; resound; Gunga —
EIN one, article: Ger.
FIN (fish) appendage; part of keel, aircraft; kite
GIN liquor; snare; female (kangaroo); cotton —; — fizz; — rummy; — mill
HIN measure
JIN Oriental demon(s)
KIN relative(s); zither; koto; Tatar dynasty
LIN linen; flax; linden; — Yutang (author); river
MIN chief deity; ruler; river
PIN fasten(er); peg; badge; skittle; dowel; -curl; -up
RIN Jap. coin, measure
SIN (do) wrong; vice; err; Heb. S, 300; moon god; Enzu
TIN metal; element; stannium; can; preserve; inferior; 10th anniversary
VIN wine: Fr.; — blanc; — rouge
WIN gain; earn; persuade
YIN Shang dynasty; weight; female principle (opp. to yang)
ZIN Bib. wilderness
CIO Congress of Industrial Organizations
DIO Cassius — (historian)
KIO ngaio; N.Z. fruit tree
MIO my: Sp., It.; dio —
RIO coffee; river;

canal(e): It.; — Grande
TIO uncle: Sp.
ZIO sky, war god; Tyr
DIP immerse; lower; ladle; candle; pickpocket; hat; downturn
FIP coin (four-, sixpence); picayune
GIP gut fish
HIP cheer; haunch; rose's false fruit (pseudocarp); bump
JIP dog (Dickens)
KIP undressed hide; gym feat; sleeping place; weight
LIP (saucy) speech; edge; spout; kiss; — service
NIP pinch; check; bite; sip; dram; Japanese
PIP radar sign; disease; seed; chirp; break shell; spot on card; great!
RIP tear; (move full) speed; split; hay; basket; — van Winkle (Irving); — tide
SIP drink; taste
TIP tilt; upset; dump; apex; (apply) end; touch; hint; fee; bestow
VIP big shot (very important person)
YIP yelp; squeal; outcry
ZIP bullet sound; (move with) vim; energy
AIR ether; gas; breath; breeze; veil; tune; expose; manner; dismissal; — express; — lift
DIR to you: Ger.; Pakistan state
EIR healing goddess
FIR (ever)green; balsam; Douglas —; — Domnann (Ir. people)
HIR her
KIR Bib. Syrian exile
MIR chief; Eastern title; Russian communist; to me: Ger.; peace: Russ.
PIR Moslem saint, tomb
SIR knight; address
TIR shooting (match)
VIR man: Lat.; vigor: Scot.
WIR we: Ger.
BIS twice; encore; replica
CIS prefix: on this side
DIS Valkyrie; Norn; Freya; — pater (Pluto, Hades); prefix: apart
EIS ice: Ger.
GIS soldiers; servicemen
HIS poss. pronoun
LIS (fairy) fort; lily: Fr.; fleur-de-
MIS prefix: wrong, evil
NIS goblin; kobold; Constantine's birthplace; Yugo. city
RIS — de veau (sweetbread)
SIS girl; sweetheart; relative; Cecilia
TIS contraction: it is
VIS force: Lat.; weight; -a-vis; Yugo. isle
WIS Wisconsin; suppose; think
AIT (river) islet
BIT part of bridle, key; blade; check; drill; mite; morsel; 12½ cents
CIT townsman; civilian
DIT poem, surnamed: Fr.; on —
FIT suit(able); proper; ready; adjust(ment); attack; mood; spell
GIT get; mold channel
HIT strike; reach; agree; impact; success
KIT violin; toolbox; young feline; Catherine; -cat (London club); — (Christopher) Carson
LIT coin; drunk; ignited; bed: Fr.; wagon-
MIT with: Ger.; therewith; glove
NIT parasitic egg
PIT stone; hole; vat; hell; pocket; (rain) sound; floor of exchange, theater; river
RIT scratch; cut; pierce
SIT rest; squat; fit; roost; press; confer; pose; -down
TIT horse; bird; return blow; twit
UIT out: Dutch
WIT know-how; to —; mind power; humor(ist); wag
JIU river
NIU measure
PIU more: It.
TIU sky god; Tiwaz, Tyr (Tuesday source)
ZIU Tiu, Tyr
CIV 104
DIV to do: Scot.; dev; 504
LIV Finn(ic language); 54
MIV 1004
XIV 14; death of Augustus
TIW sky god; Tiwaz; Tyr; Tiu (Tuesday source)
ZIW Iyar; Heb. month
AIX aex; -les-Bains (spa); -la-Chapelle: Aachen
CIX 109
DIX pinochle score; ten: Fr.; Dorothy — (Elizabeth Meriwether Gilmer); 509
FIX fasten; set(tle); mend; arrange; determine; dilemma; limit; bribe; narcotic shot
LIX 59
MIX mingle; cross; blend; prepared ingredients; 1009
NIX sprite; no(thing); undeliverable mail
PIX box; Eucharist case; ciborium; photos
RIX rush; reed
SIX card; die face; boat; — Hundred (Light Brigade)
XIX 19

BIZ business (slang); show —
FIZ hiss(ing sound); fuss; champagne
GIZ dialect, Ethiopic
LIZ Elizabeth
RIZ rice: Fr.
VIZ namely
WIZ magician; genius

AJI Capsicum plant
TJI river: Java; weight
UJI silkworm disease
DJO measure, Niger Negro
LJO Niger delta Negro
OJO grassy spring; oasis

AKA Assam tribesman, language N.Z. vine
OKA weight oca; river
BKB chess move
QKB chess move
RKB chess move
AKE forever Maori; N.Z. tree hopbush
EKE piece out augment
IKE Isaac, nickname (Eisenhower)
OKE weight measure
UKE ukulele, guitar
AKH spirit of man: Egypt
IKI island
OKI evil spirit; archipelago
SKI glide(r) runner; sport, lift
AKO measure
TKO boxing term
BKR chess move
QKR chess move
RKR chess move
BKT chess move
QKT chess move
RKT chess move
AKU victorfish
SKY heaven firmament; blue; climate; raise

ALA Alabama; (army) wing; petal; after, according to; — mode, - carte
ELA highest note; bombast extravagance
FLA Florida
ILA Bantu language
OLA palm leaf
SLA sloe
ULA the gums; diminutive
ALB church vestment
ELB jujube
LLB Bachelor of Laws (degree)
ELD old time age
LLD Doctor of Laws (degree)
OLD stale; obsolete; passe; skilled. primeval quondam; hoary; hat
ALE beverage malt liquor; festival
BLE grain: Fr.
CLE diminutive suffix
ELE aisle; eel
ILE isle: Fr.; suffix; -de-France — de la Cite
OLE palm leaf old; Sp. victory cry
ULE caucho tree, rubber; diminutive suffix
ALF Alfred; elf
ELF fairy; sprite; dwarf
OLF bullfinch
ALI Mohammed's son-in-law, Fatima's son; - Pasha: Lion of Janina
CLI 151
DLI 551
ELI high priest; Samuel's teacher; Yale; — Whitney
ILI river
MLI 1051
XLI 41
ALK — gum (turpentine)
ELK deer; wapiti: sambar; leather; color lama; river; city
ILK family; class same
ALL whole; each only; very; universe according to - out; - hands; - hours; - clear; — in one
ELL cloth measure; aune; building annex
ILL Illinois sick; bad(ly), evil, river
ULL chief god Sif's son; Thor's stepson
ELM tree; Ulmus - City (New Haven)
OLM amphibian
ULM Danube city
ALN measure
FLO Florence; Flora; arrow
ILO International Labor Organization
ULO prefix: gums; shell money
ALP mountain; renegade (Byron)
OLP blight; bullfinch
ALS when, than: Ger.
ILS they: Fr.
RLS novelist; Robert Louis Stevenson
ALT high in pitch (octave); old: Ger.
ELT knead
OLT Aluta; Danube tributary
FLU grippe; 1918–19 pandemic
ULU Eskimo woman's knife
CLV 155
DLV 555
MLV 1055
XLV 45
CLX 160
DLX 560
MLX 1060
ALY like malt drink
BLY Chief — (Saroyan); Nellie —, newspaperwoman
CLY seize; steal; servant (Dickens)
ELY cathedral city; mountain; island; Bishop of —
FLY leap; soar; vanish; pilot; tent canvas; printer's devil; keen; on the —; river
PLY fold; bend; strand (thickness); wield; practice; urge; paper web
SLY shrewd; foxy; roguish; secretive; on the —; tinker (Shaks.)
VLY low-land; marsh; creek; temporary lake

AMA chalice; (nurse) maid; American Medical Association; tree
IMA — Hogg (heiress)
OMA suffix: tumor

UMA Devi (goddess of splendor); Wiltshire's wife (Stevenson)
MMC 2100
MMD 2500
AME wooden form; soul: Fr.; — damnee
EME uncle; friend; gossip
MME madame; My Lady
UME Jap. apricot; river
AMI friend: Fr.
CMI 901
IMI measure
MMI 2001
OMI sacred mountain
CML 950
MML 2050
MMM 3000
AMO I love: Lat.
OMO prefix: shoulder; river
AMP elec. unit of intensity; ampere
IMP petty demon; urchin; rascal; mock
UMP (act as) referee
EMS Bad — (spa); river
HMS — Pinafore (G & S opera)
AMT county: Dan.; public office: Ger.
EMU ostrichlike bird; Austral. tree, apple, millet
IMU baking pit
UMU Polynesian earth oven
CMV 905
MMV 2005
CMX 910
MMX 2010
AMY female name; prochein — (nearest friend: law); (Little) — Dorrit: Dickens
SMY sprat

ANA collection; prefix: up, back; Irish gods' mother; coin
INA fem. name, suffix; mother
MNA mina (weight)
ONA measure; So. Amer. Indian
SNA snow: Scot.
UNA river; Dan's sister (Kipling); Red Cross Knight's wife: Truth personified in "Faerie Queene"
AND conjunction; plus
END limit; death; extreme; phase; remnant; aim; finish; — man; — use; open —
IND India (poet.); Indiana
UND and: Ger.
ANE ass: Fr.; chem. suffix
ENE suffix; compass point
INE suffix
NNE compass point
ONE single; unit(y); person; same; the absolute
UNE article, one: Fr.
ENG Chang's Siamese twin
ING suffix; A.S. peace god
ANI black bird; cuckoo
INI suffix: order
ONI any: Scot.
UNI plainly woven; goddess (Juno); prefix: single
INK sepia; cuttlefish fluid; black; sign
ANN stipend; fem. name; Nancy; Nina; — Rutledge (Lincoln's fiancee)
INN ho(s)tel; lodge; river
ANO blackbird; prefix: up
INO Cadmus's daughter; Athamas's wife
UNO one: It., Sp.
ANS Liege commune
ENS being; essence, entity
INS International News Service
ONS cricket field parts; weight
UNS us: Ger.
ANT insect; formic acid source; emmet; pismire
ENT suffix; prefix: inner
INT anoint
TNT explosive; toluene
ANU sky god; triad (—, Bel, Ea); Irish gods' mother; Danu
GNU antelope; goat; takin
NNW compass point
WNW compass point
ANY some; one; at all
ONY any
SNY abound; swarm; bend; curved plank

BOA constrictor; python; anaconda; (fur, feather) scarf
GOA gazelle; mugger; crocodile; former Port. colony; Austral. native
HOA hallo!
IOA iwa; frigate bird
KOA timber tree
LOA worm; eye parasite; Lao; Mauna — (volcano)
MOA flightless extinct bird
NOA profane; common; no
POA (blue)grass
SOA tub; milk pail; cowl
TOA brave warrior; beefwood; Casuarina
WOA stop!
ZOA Blake's symbol(s); suffix: animals
BOB cheat; mock; weight; curtsy; Scot. dance; shilling; haircut; Robert; -sled; — up
COB swan; horse; seagull; excel; strike
DOB dab; daub
FOB pocket; cheat, trick; -chain
GOB mouth(ful); mass; sailor; tar
HOB ferret; havoc; game pin; cut(ter); — and nob
JOB (do odd) work; employment; OT book; patient sufferer; item
KOB Afr. antelope
LOB go heavily; high curve (tennis); till; Puck
MOB crowd (about); masses; annoy; gang; cap
NOB (blow on) head;

knob(stick); hob and —
POB porridge; post-office box
ROB steal; mine coal; juice; — Roy (outlaw)
SOB weep; wail(ing); — story; — sister
TOB anc. Syrian kingdom
DOC doctor; physician
HOC card game; — anno; ad —
ROC fabled bird; simurg; bomb
SOC A.S. jurisdiction district; sac and —
BOD clay plug
COD fish; hoax; Cape —
DOD clip off; metal plate; annular die
FOD measure
GOD Jehovah. deity; deify; gallery occupant
HOD brick tray; coal scuttle; — carrier
JOD yodh; Heb. Y, 10
LOD weight
MOD Scot. artist congress; fashion fad
NOD drowse; (show) assent; Land of —; East of Eden
POD flock; socket; groove; bag; legume; suffix: foot
ROD stick; race; bar; gun; scepter; 5½ yards
SOD soil; turf; sward
TOD wool weight; (ivy) bush death: Ger.
VOD Baltic Finn
YOD Heb. Y, 10
COE sheep disease; Ia. college
DOE female animal; biscuit color; John —
FOE enemy; adversary
HOE tool; dig scrape; inventor
JOE coin; sweetheart; — Miller (joke); fat boy (Dickens)
LOE love: Scot.
MOE masc. nickname
POE Edgar Allan — (Raven, Gold Bug); parson bird
ROE deer; doe; fish eggs; streaks in wood
SOE tub; pail; cowl
TOE digit; drive aslant; golf club part; — the line; -hold
VOE inlet; creek
WOE alas; sorrow(ful)
YOE ewe
HOF city
LOF measure
BOG mire; marsh; — down
COG cheat; (gear) tooth; (connect by) tenon; ship
DOG Canis; gripper; andiron; crampon; track
FOG vapor; daze; blue; blur
GOG — and Magog (statues)
HOG pig, boar, sheep; dime, shilling; glutton; monopolize
JOG jostle; remind; trot
LOG cut timber; (ship) record
MOG move slowly; depart
NOG egg drink; peg; wood (block, fastener); pin
ROG shake; pull; stir
SOG soak; drowse
TOG coat; dress up
VOG weight
ZOG Albanian king
BOH Burmese chief; boo; — da Thone (Kipling)
DOH do (note)
FOH exclamation
HOH Quileute; Indian whaler
POH bah!
SOH exclamation; gutta mixture
ZOH zobo; yak; zebu hybrid
COI river
GOI non-Jew: Heb.
HOI yam; haw (as cattle)
KOI Jap. carp
LOI law: Fr.
MOI I: Fr.; Asian tribes
POI Hawaiian food (taro)
ROI fern rootstock; king: Fr.; vive le —
TOI you, thou: Fr.
YOI hunting cry
BOK Amer. editor
LOK god of discord; Balder slayer
ROK Korean soldier
SOK measure
YOK A.S. G; Middle English Y
COL Colorado; mountain pass
GOL God (euphemistic form)
HOL prefix: complete
KOL Dravidian native; Munda, Larka
MOL gram molecule
POL degree without honors
SOL sun (god); tone G; coin; fluid
TOL Sanskrit school
VOL wings (Her.); battery iron block
BOM So. Amer. serpent
COM prefix: together, with
DOM monastic title; church; low caste Hindu
MOM mamma
NOM name: Fr.; — de plume (pseudonym); — de guerre
OOM — Paul Kruger (Boer president)
POM Pomeranian (dog)
ROM Gypsy husband
TOM male; Thomas; Ob tributary; — Thumb ("General" Charles Sherwood Stratton); -o' Bedlam (madman); — Alibi (Scott); — Canty (Twain); Aunt Chloe's husband
YOM day: Heb.; — Kippur (Atonement Day); river
BON good, bond: Fr.; bean; grass; Jap. festival (of lanterns); Tibet religion; Cape —
CON learn; against; deceive; — game;

— man; — amore
DON Sir; tutor; put on; goddess; mother of Gwydion, Arianrhod; river
EON time period; age; eternity
FON Dahomey Negro (Ewe)
GON measure; prefix: knee; suffix: angled figure
ION charged particle; molecule; son of Apollo, Creusa
KON weight
LON Alonso
MON my: Fr.; family badge; Pegu Burmese; prefix: one; — Dieu!
NON not: Lat.; no: Fr.; prefix; sine qua —
OON final syllable
PON pagoda; gold coin
RON King Arthur's lance
SON male descendant; scion; — of Man; river
TON weight; style: Fr.; bon —; suffix: town
VON by noble birth: Ger.
WON obtained; conquered
YON at a distance; thither
BOO ostrich tail; hoot; jeer; scary cry
COO dove cry; amorous talk
FOO Chin. prefecture
GOO sticky substance
KOO Chin. statesman
LOO card game; halloo
MOO cow's cry: low; weight
NOO now; new; prefix: mind
POO Nanki —; Yum-Yum's husband
ROO kangaroo
SOO murmur; sow
TOO also; excessively
WOO make love; court; sue
ZOO animal collection; menagerie
BOP bravura jazz
COP (wind) yarn; catch; thicket; policeman
DOP diamond cup; — brandy
FOP dandy; coxcomb; dude
GOP Republican party
HOP leap; dance; limp; air trip; vine; bryony; opium; drug; stimulate
KOP hill; measure
LOP choppy sea; cut off; droop; act lazily
MOP wipe(r); swab; hair; pout; — up
OOP up; bind; join: Scot.
POP sound; burst; sho(o)t; plant; protrude; ask; drink
SOP dip in; soak; ooze; wet food; bribe
TOP head; acme; best; cut off; cover; outdo; toy; upset; foremost; — secret
BOR neighbor; Yugo. mine town
COR heart; main star; prefix: pupil
DOR beetle; bumblebee; Bongo; Sudanese; Le Coq —: opera; Cote — (Fr. dept.)
FOR to: because; namely; pro; fur
GOR Indus tribesman
HOR Edom mountain
IOR (comparative) ending
KOR measure; homer
MOR forest humus
NOR conjunction: and not
POR push; kick; poke(r)
TOR hill; peak; fool: Ger.
VOR before: Ger.
BOS cow: Lat.; genus
COS lettuce; romaine; trigonometric function
DOS dowry; back: Fr. -a-dos; — Passos
EOS goddess; dawn; Aurora; Tithonus's wife
GOS goshawk bird: Scot.
IOS Hawaiian hawks
KOS island
LOS the: Sp.; — Alamos; — Islands; — Negros (Admiralty I.)
MOS custom; folkway; mores (sing.)
NOS we: Lat.; our: Fr.; prefix: disease
ROS prefix: Cornish names; rulers; Varangians
SOS distress signal
BOT botfly larva
COT hut; coop; small bed
DOT dowry; speck; point; scatter; mus. sign; — and dash (Morse)
FOT measure
GOT past tense of get
HOT torrid; burning; eager; violent; fresh; urgent; biting; exciting; stolen; contraband; — seat; — dog; -shot; -rod
JOT point; iota; tittle; brief note; — down
LOT fate; share; plot, parcel of land; great deal; river
MOT pithy saying; quoits mark
NOT negation; hornless; smooth
OOT out: Scot.
POT drink; fish trap; sho(o)t; stake; much money; win; preserve; pepper —: soup
ROT ret; decay; die; nonsense; disease
SOT guzzle(r); befool; waste; fixed; obstinate
TOT add; child; dead: Ger.
VOT Finn in Ingria
YOT measure
COU neck: Fr.
FOU full bushel: Scot.; fool(ish): Fr.
HOU measure
IOU debt confirmation; note; I owe you
KOU Hawaiian tree
LOU nickname
MOU measure
SOU small coin
TOU measure
YOU pronoun; — bet
SOV gold coin: Br. slang; sovereign
BOW weapon; archer; 6 feet; fiddlestick; Apollo's

instrument; nod; yield; bend; prow; river

COW bovine; Bos; tree raft; bogy; daunt; dolt

DOW befit; Arab. sailboat; Burmese knife. Neal — (prohibitionist)

HOW why; what. method; know-; Indian salute

JOW measure

KOW bogy; goblin

LOW moo; weak; inferior. plain; coarse. cheap(ly); soft(ly); cartoonist Girl Scouts founder

MOW cut down; (stack) hay

NOW at this time; present(ly); admonition

POW sound of blow; prisoner of war

ROW brawl; propel; series. line; tier; file; Rotten —: Hyde Park; skid —

SOW fem. swine; mold; scatter; seed; — dragons teeth

TOW draw; tug(boat); rope; flax fibers; spun yarn

VOW promise; dedicate

WOW sensational success. excite audience. sound distortion

YOW yelp; howl; miaow

BOX fight; spar; tree (topiary, Eucalyptus); mix paint; stow. gift; baseball term; — and Cox; -spring; — camera; — seat

COX steersman; Box and —; painter; reformer; politician (Pres. nominee)

FOX Vulpes, vixen; trick(ster); discolor; rope yarn; brown; river; orator; Quaker; educator; — Islands

HOX hamstring. pester

LOX (smoked) salmon; — and bagels

NOX night goddess

POX infectious disease

TOX intoxicate

VOX voice: Lat.; — populi, — Dei; — angelica

YOX hiccup; cough

BOY youth; servant; act, treat as lad; office —; — orator: W. J. Bryan; Blue — (Gainsborough)

COY demure, bashful; shy; entice. hoax

FOY feast; gift

GOY non-Jew: Heb.

HOY barge; exclamation; Orkney Isle

JOY happiness; bliss, gaiety; exult, name

LOY post-hole spade; a slick; name

POY boat pole

ROY name; Rob — (outlaw, canoe, Scott hero)

SOY bean; sauce

TOY (diversionary) trifle; trinket; play(thing)

YOY yes

BOZ Dickens pseudonym

COZ cousin

GOZ coin

POZ positive(ly)

APA Braz. tree; wallaba

SPA mineral spring; resort

WPA Works Progress Administration

APE monkey anthropoid; mimic. Hawaiian herb; apii

EPE Dutch commune

OPE unlock (poet.)

API prefix· bee

EPI final; grain, ear: Fr.; prefix: upon

PPI radarscope

UPI news, wire service; United Press International

APO prefix: away; P.I. volcano, mil. address; Mount — (P.I.)

OPS goddess; Consus; Rhea; Saturn's wife; Cere's mother

PPS additional postscript

APT fit; likely; ready

OPT choose (citizenship)

SPY watch(er); discover; search(ing); secret agent

BQB chess move

QQB chess move

RQB chess move

BQR chess move

QQR chess move

RQR chess move

ARA constellation; altar; macaw; textile screw pine; measure; goddess

BRA underwaist

DRA measure

ERA epoch; geol. time division

FRA brother; monk; — Angelo, Diavolo (Michele Pezza); — Angelico, painter

GRA love(r); fondness

IRA Bib. ruler. Irish Republican Army; masc. name: watchful

KRA long-tailed ape

NRA National Recovery Administration; FDR measure; Blue Eagle

ORA Dan. money; mouths; — et labora (pray and work)

TRA Malay coin

ORB disk; sphere; world; eye; encircle

ARC curve part; light; rainbow

ORC grampus (whale)

ARD suffix: excessive doer

ERD earth; land; -shrew

ORD mountain (Ariz.)

URD bean; woolly pyrol; Norn; Wyrd, — Verthandi, Skuld

ARE measure; verb form

ERE before; sooner; — long

IRE provoke; anger; choler; wrath

ORE Oregon; seaweed; mineral; crude metal(lic rock); coin

PRE prefix: before

TRE prefix: town; three: It.
URE suffix: chemist; river mist: Scot.
ERF ½-acre plot
ORF fish; yellow ide
ERG work unit; desert area
CRI cry: Fr.; dernier —
ERI silkworm; bombyx; Gad's son
GRI horse: Gypsy
IRI Bela's son; city
KRI read(ing substitute)
ORI prefix: mouth; limit
SRI glorious; holy; Lakshmi (goddess)
TRI prefix: three
URI Swiss canton
ARK Arkansas; refuge; broadhorn; flatboat; wanigan; — of the covenant
IRK abhor; annoy; bore
KRK island
ORK whale
ARM branch; sleeve; bay; power; fortify
ARN alder tree
ERN sea eagle
URN vessel; grave; bury
ARO Nigerian
CRO -Magnon; homo sapiens; murder fine
FRO from; away; to and —
ORO gold: Sp.; Tahiti god; mouth; prefix: mountain
PRO for; expert; yes vote(r); quid — quo
SRO box office sign
URO So. Amer. Indian; Puqina
WRO angle; passage; nook
ORP fret; weep: Scot.
GRR exclamation; growl
ORR Nobel physiologist
ARS art: Lat.; — Amandi (Ovid); — longa, vita brevis
ERS bitter vetch
IRS Internal Revenue Service
MRS title; address; — Grundy
ART skill; science; trade; craft; wile; where — thou?; leg —: cheesecake

ERT urge on: Scot.
HRT boiler
ORT morsel; leftover; weight; place: Ger.
ARU indeed; really
CRU tract of land; vineyard
GRU practice: Scot.
IRU Caleb's eldest son
KRU Liberian (language)
MRU Indo-Chinese native
URU Bolivian Indian
ARX citadel
ARY any; suffix: pert. to, engaged in
CRY call; wail; weep; beg; summon; slogan; — wolf
DRY hard; shrewd; arid; plain; dull; vapid; evaporate; — Tortugas (isles); dwindle(d); drought; — goods; — cell; — run; simulated
ERY suffix: conduct, art, place
FRY young brood; pan-cook; vex(ation); prison reformer
GRY horse: Gypsy
ORY like ore, seaweed; suffix: of
PRY lever(age); peep(er); gaze; Paul — (meddler)
TRY attempt; test; prove; strain; annoy; essay; render fat; conduct court procedure
WRY deflect; twist(ed); disgusted; askew

ASA masc. name; healer; king of Judah; Norse god
ESA Economic Stability Administration
BSC Bachelor of Chemical Science (degree)
ASE enzyme; Peer Gynt's mother (Ibsen)
ESE suffix; compass point
ISE suffix; fjord; bay (Atsuta)
OSE suffix: simple sugar
SSE compass point

TSE Lao- (philosopher); Mao -tung
USE employ(ment); (ac)custom; treat(ment); gain; dupe; — and wont
ASH tree; residue; burn; pallor; gray; — can: depth charge
HSH hush; exclamation
ISH adj. suffix
USH to usher
PSI Greek letter PS, 700
ASK question; seek; need; invite; beg
USK river
ISM doctrine; system
ASO Jap. volcano
DSO Distinguished Service Order (Brit.)
ESO prefix: within
ISO prefix: equal
ASP adder; viper; uraeus: symbol; Cleo's snake
ESP 6th sense; extrasensory perception (Rhine, Duke); especially
ASS Equus; donkey; kiang; weight; dolt
ESS S; fem. suffix; worm; curve
OSS Office of Strategic Services
SSS Selective Service System
EST suffix; is: Fr.; id —; n' -ce-pas?; Eastern Standard Time
IST adherent; practitioner; fanatic; is: Ger.
LST landing ship tank
OST prefix: bone; oven; East(ern): Ger.
PST call for attention; quiet!
TST hissed sound; quiet!
UST used to
SSU Chin. weight
TSU Jap. seaport
WSW compass point
SSW compass point

ATA Mindanao tribe, language; flour; sweetsop
ETA Jap. outcasts;

Greek E, 8; Negrito
ITA Negrito; Eskimo; labor union; city
PTA Parent-Teacher Association
UTA lizard; Jap. song
KTB chess move
ETC and so on
LTD limited (company)
ATE goddess of infatuation, folly, discord (Zeus's daughter); consumed
ETE summer: Fr.
ITE suffix: follower, resident; So. Amer. Indian
OTE suffix: resident
STE saint(e): Fr.
UTE Shoshonean Indian; mountain
ETH A.S. letter: th; suffix: ordinal number
ITH Irish ancestor
NTH any size; — degree; indefinite power
ATI P.I. Negrito
KTK chess move
ETO European Theater of Operations (WW II)
ITO Zionist (Zangwill's) group; Jap. admiral, statesman
OTO Sicuan; prefix: ear
KTQ chess move
ITR attar; rose perfume
KTR chess move
ITS poss. pronoun
ATT coin
ITU city
UTU sun god; Shamash; Babbar; Maori compensation; hoot
STY pig enclosure; eyelid swelling

EUA Tonga isle
KUA Bantu tribe
PUA hemp; cordage fiber
QUA in so far as; sine — non (necessity)
RUA Congo Bantu
SUA hers: Lat.
TUA dyewood tree
BUB small boy; liquor
CUB young animal; boy (scout); — reporter; light plane: grasshopper
DUB rub smooth; bestow title; play; do poorly; coin; add sound
FUB plump child; cheat
HUB wheel center; nave; pipe; the — (Boston)
NUB knob; knot; gist
PUB inn; tavern
RUB polish; vex; chafe; hindrance; gibe
SUB pinch hitter; under: Lat.; — rosa
TUB vessel; keg; wash
DUC duke: Fr.
BUD develop; immature one; lad; in the —; — stick
CUD something ruminated; tobacco quid
DUD garment; faulty bomb; failure
LUD oath; legendary king
MUD abusive charge; — lark; — Cat State (Miss.)
PUD paw; hand; weight
RUD redness; fish
SUD soapy water; foam
AUE Polynesian exclamation
CUE Q; signal; hint; hair twist; waiting line; billiard rod
DUE owed; just; debt; — date
GUE Shetland viol
HUE color; shout; — and cry
LUE sift; bolt
PUE pew
QUE what, that: Fr.
RUE herb; repent; regret; — de la Paix
SUE urge; woo; plead; take court action
TUE parson bird
AUF on, upon: Ger.
OUF dog's bark; exclamation
BUG insect; defect; germ; fanatic; bulge (eyes); river
DUG delved; excavated
FUG reek
HUG embrace; keep close; bear —
JUG ewer; jail; stew; nest(le); bird sound
LUG ear; loop; drag; worm; sail; measure; god
MUG cup; face; photograph; sheep; mungo; assault; overact; pose
PUG dog; (mix) clay; boxer; — nose; footprint
RUG mat; cozy
TUG pull; lug; effort; towboat; — of war
VUG lode cavity
ZUG Swiss canton, lake
AUH exclamation
HUH exclamation
CUI composer; engineer
DUI duets; twosomes
HUI guild; partnership
KUI Asian group; Lolo; Kandh
MUI — tsai: girl slave(ry)
QUI who, that: Fr.; — vive (watchword)
SUI Chin. dynasty; — generis
TUI dyewood tree; parson bird
GUJ Moti —: elephant (Kipling)
AUK sea bird; Tlingit Indian
HUK P.I. guerrilla
OUK week: Scot.
SUK Nilotic Negro
BUL Canaanite's 8th month; Heshvan
CUL -de-sac; blind alley
FUL Hamitic Sudanese
GUL rose: Persian
HUL Shem's descendant
MUL measure
NUL no, nothing (law)
PUL Tiglathpileser (king); coin; OT people
AUM measure
BUM sponge upon; tramp; inferior; Levant ship
CUM summa — laude (with highest praise)
DUM doom palm; gingerbread tree
FUM feng-haung; myth. bird
GUM adhesive; exudate; resin; jaw tissue; overshoe; humbug

HUM buzz; sing; murmur; melody; hoax
JUM cultivation method
KUM Shiite pilgrim site; river
LUM chimney; sink; pond
MUM chrysanthemum; hush; beer; mask; madam
QUM Shiite pilgrim site
RUM liquor; odd; tough; fine; dye
SUM total; amount; all; epitomize; in —; — up
TUM sun god; Atmu; card (wool); banjo sound; The Rum — Tugger (Eliot)
VUM vow; swear
BUN bread; roll; hair knot; boat; tipsiness
DUN urge payment; dingy (brown); May fly; cure fish
FUN amusement; joke; weight
GUN firearm; pump; hunt; mug; — dog; speed up
HUN vandal; invader; Boche
KUN Bela —, revolutionary
MUN must; mouth; roisterer; river
NUN Niger mouth; convent woman; pigeon, smew; Heb. N, 50; Joshua's father; chaos
PUN play on words; paronomasia
RUN hurry; operate; stretch; contest; flee; series; brook; trail
SUN star; shine; Apollo; Helios; Phoebus; — Yat-sen (Chin. leader)
TUN vat; cask; measure; guzzle; Mayan year
WUN Burmese governor
YUN Laos tribesman
DUO two; duet; pair
LUO White Nile Negro
QUO measure; quid pro —; status —
CUP vessel; ½ pint; portion; prize; golf hole; crater; bloodletting —
GUP gossip
HUP command to horses
KUP measure
PUP young dog, seal; bad security; silly fop
SUP drink; eat; entertain; mouthful
TUP ram; mallet; butt
SUQ Moslem booth, market
BUR burr; seed coat; whirr; cut(ter)
CUR mongrel dog; cad
DUR C — (C major)
EUR Europe
FUR pelt; coat(ing); Negro
GUR raw sugar; massecuite
HUR Ben —: hero (Wallace); Thamar's son; Tirzah's brother
JUR Nile Negro; Luo; river
LUR Persian tribesman; trumpet
MUR wall: Fr.; Yugo. river
PUR sound (cat, motor)
RUR Rhine tributary
SUR upon (law); prefix: over; south: Sp.; Tyre (Lebanon city)
TUR pigeon pea; aurochs; urus; ibex; wild goat
AUS out of, finished: Ger.; Arab tribesman
BUS vehicle; enough; — boy
GUS Augustus; Gustavus
HUS Jan — (reformer)
IUS right, law: Lat.
JUS law(s): Lat.; legal power; gravy, juice: Fr.
MUS mouse, rodent genus
OUS suffix: abounding
PUS suppuration; Hindu month
RUS rulers; Ros
SUS swine genus
AUT prefix: self, same
BUT conjunction: except, unless, yet, only
CUT sever; carve; lower; cross; shorten; gash; slight; sarcasm
FUT measure
GUT intestine; eviscerate; destroy; good: Ger.
HUT hovel; cabin; hat: Ger.
JUT project; extend
KUT -al-Imara (Brit. defeat)
LUT weight
MUT cur; dolt; Amen's wife; courage: Ger.
NUT crank; fastener; kernel; head; guy; show investment; goddess, Geb's wife
OUT absent; nook; game term; (at) odd(s); begone!; known; passe; wrong; on strike
PUT lay; set; attach; throw; rustic; urge; golf shot; game; stay —; — and call; -in-Bay (Perry's victory site)
RUT routine; groove; habit; oxcart; heat
SUT coal dust; smudge
TUT mild rebuke; rounders; game; staccato
AUX according to, a la: Fr.; — armes (to arms!)
DUX fugue theme; leader
LUX light unit
MUX mess; botch
RUX worry; play; sport
TUX men's evening dress
BUY (good) purchase; bribe; redeem
GUY rope; chain; effigy; fellow; chaff; — Fawkes; Octavius — (Collins)
KUY Siamese; Shan group; Kandh language
MUY very, greatly: Sp.
PUY volcanic hill
BUZ son of Nahor, Mileah
GUZ measure; zar; arshin
HUZ Abraham's nephew
LUZ Bib. site; Bethel
SUZ exclamation

AVA anc. Burma capital; pepper; shrub; kava; liquor
EVA Evangeline; Little — (Uncle Tom's Cabin)
IVA yellow bugle; herb eve; marsh elder
OVA eggs; Piman Indian
TVA Tennessee Valley Administration
UVA grape
MVD Soviet Ministry of Interior Affairs
AVE — atque vale (hail and farewell!); rosary bead
EVE twilight; time before; woman; mother of mankind
IVE contraction; suffix
OVE egg-shaped ornament
UVE P.I. yam
CVI 106
DVI 506
EVI Midianite king
LVI 56
MVI 1006
OVI prefix: egg
UVI — yam (white yam)
XVI 16
OVO ab — (from the egg, start)
IVY vine; arbutus; creeper; overgrow

AWA kava; tenpounder; milkfish
IWA frigate bird; -iwa: fern stalks
PWA Public Works Administration
SWA so
TWA two
AWE reverence; intimidate; mill bucket, sail
EWE sheep; Negro tribe
OWE be obliged, indebted
TWI prefix: double; Tshi
AWL shoemaker's tool
OWL bird (of prey); night-
CWM cirque (geol. process)

AWN (remove grain) beard
OWN acknowledge; have
IWO — Jima, island; Afr. city
LWO White Nile Negro
TWO card; pair; in —; in half; little casino; — bits; -faced; -time
AWU volcano

OXA prefix: oxygen
CXC 190
DXC 590
MXC 1090
AXE tool; fell; destroy
EXE Devon river
CXI 111
DXI 511
LXI 61
MXI 1011
XXI 21
CXL 140
DXL 540
MXL 1040
EXO prefix: outside
CXV 115
DXV 515
LXV 65
MXV 1015
XXV 25
CXX 120
DXX 520
LXX 70; Septuagint; Temple at Jerusalem destroyed
MXX 1020
XXX 30; Crucifixion of Christ
OXY of an ox; sharp; ocute; prefix: oxygen

AYA Brahman title; Shamash' consort; Al
IYA (nurse)maid; Koran verse; omen
MYA long clam genus
PYA coin
AYE always; yes (vote)
BYE run (cricket); aside; secondary; inactive
DYE color; stain
EYE vision; view; scan; loop; spot; brood; — bank
HYE hedge; hie
LYE alkaline solution; lixivium
NYE pheasant brood; humorist
OYE grandchild: Scot.
PYE poet; 1st engraver
RYE cereal; whisky; Gypsy; — and Indian (bread)
SYE scythe; drop; strain
TYE mast chain
WYE Y; forked holder, track; river
TYG drinking vessel
HYL prefix: wood
KYL Himalayan ibex
GYM sports hall
NYM Falstaff follower
FYN island
GYN prefix: woman
LYN waterfall
SYN prefix: with
WYN Old Eng. rune W
IYO Afr. bass; palm fiber; P. I. vine
OYO Nigerian town
WYO Wyoming
CYP princewood tree
GYP steal; swindle(r); bitch; college servant
HYP make melancholy
AYR Scot. county, port
PYR prefix: fire, heat, fever; light unit
TYR god; Aesir, Riu (Tuesday), Odin's son slain by Garm
LYS prefix: loosening; fleur-de-lis; river
TYT quickly; promptly
AYU sweetfish
NYX night goddess; Chaos's daughter; mother of day and night
PYX box; Eucharist case; ciborium

IZE suffix
AZO nitrogenous
IZU peninsula
TZU river

FOUR-LETTER WORDS

AA-- to ZY--

AALI pasha
AALU Hades; heaven
AANI ape
AARE river
AARU Hades; heaven
ABAC calculator
ABAS down: Fr.
ABBA father; title
ABBE priest; title; Amer. meteorologist
ABBY Abigail
ABCS first principles, alphabet
ABED in bed; bedridden
ABEL Adam's son; Cain's brother; — Magwitch (Dickens); letter A; monkey
ABET aid; incite
ABEY waive
ABIA Samuel's son
ABIB month
ABIE 's Irish Rose; name
ABIR red powder
ABLE fit; adept; suffix; -bodied
ABLY deftly
ABOO war cry
ABOT Mishnah
ABOU father; deity
ABOX braced
ABRA narrow pass; river
ABRI shelter
ABSI tribe
ABUT touch
ACCA fabric
ACER tree
ACHE pain; yearn
ACHT eight: Ger.
ACHY painful
ACID sour; biting
ACIS river; (Galatea's) lover
ACLE tree
ACME peak; crisis
ACNE disease
ACON boat
ACOR acidity
ACRE field; measure; city
ACTA deeds; records
ACTH hormone medicine
ACTO action: Sp.
ACTS NT book
ACTU act: Lat.
ACUS pin
ACYL acid part
ADAD fiber; god
ADAH wife of Lamech, Esau; fem. name
ADAI tribe
ADAK Aleut. island
ADAM first man; sin; composer; architect
ADAN prayer call
ADAR month
ADAT law
ADAY atomic attack date
ADDA god; river; skink
ADDU skink; fiber; god
ADDY Adeline
ADEN comb. form: gland; city; gulf; region
ADER Benjamite
ADES Hades
ADIB star
ADIN name
ADIT entrance
ADMI gazelle
ADRY thirsty
ADZE tool
AEON age
AERA age; era
AERI prefix: air
AERO go by aircraft
AERY ethereal; nest
AETA Negrito; native
AFAR far away; tribe
AFFA from off
AFFY join
AFRA name; union
AGAG king
AGAL cord
AGAO language
AGAR wood
AGAU language
AGAZ Indian
AGED old; oxygian
AGEE awry; Shammah's father; James (novelist)
AGER apparatus; field
AGHA officer; title
AGIB dervish
AGIO fee; commission
AGIS king
AGLA acrostic
AGNI god; lambs
AGNO Luzon river
AGOG eager
AGON contest; argument
AGRA comb. form; carpet; city (Taj Mahal site)
AGRI fields
AGRO prefix: soil
AGUA water; toad
AGUE fever
AHAB king; captain; prophet
AHAZ king
AHEM interjection
AHER Benjamite
AHET season (of inundation)
AHEY ho
AHIO Ark driver
AHIR caste
AHOM Assam native
AHOY call; ship —
AHUM humming
AIAH Edomite, Rizpah's father
AICH alloy
AIDA opera; Radames' lover
AIDE help; -de-camp; — memoire
AIEA town
AIEL writ of —
AILE winged
AINE elder
AINO Jap. aboriginal
AINT contraction
AINU Jap. aboriginal
AIPI cassava
AIRA grass
AIRE nobleman; river
AIRS pretensions; side
AIRT guide; turn
AIRY breezy; light
AITU god; demon
AJAR opened
AJAX hero (Telamon's son)
AJEE awry
AJOG jogging
AKAL deity
AKAN Negro
AKEE tree
AKEY weight
AKHA tribe; Burmese; Kaw

AKIA shrub (fish poison)
AKIM Negro; Tamiroff
AKIN related
AKKA Pygmy
AKOV measure
AKRA Negrito; vetch
AKTI peninsula
AKUA deity
AKUT ape man (Burroughs)
ALAE wings
ALAI regiment; mountain; jai —
ALAN dog; name
ALAR winglike; axillary
ALAS sad cry
ALAY marble
ALBA garb; poem; brain matter; duke
ALBE album
ALBI flagellants
ALBO prefix: white
ALCA auk
ALCO dog
ALDA soprano; hamlet: Sp.
ALEA Athena (war goddess)
ALEC fish; sauce; nickname
ALEE to shelter
ALEF letter
ALEM fruit
ALEN measure
ALEP city
ALES city
ALEY city
ALFA grass
ALGA plant
ALGY Algernon; suffix: pain
ALIA other: Lat.
ALIF letter
ALII royalty (Hawaiian)
ALIM teacher
ALIN measure
ALIT descended
ALIX fem. name
ALKY alcohol
ALLA by: It.
ALLE bird; all: Ger.
ALLO prefix: other, dissimilar
ALLY unite, confederate
ALMA girl; silk; river; city
ALME dancer
ALMS charity
ALOD estate
ALOE plant; tonic
ALOP lopsided
ALOR island
ALOW below
ALPH river (Coleridge, Kubla Khan)
ALPS mountains
ALSO besides
ALTA tall: Sp.
ALTE old: Ger.; Adenauer
ALTO hill: Sp.; voice
ALUM emetic; astringent; styptic
ALUR Negro
ALVA duke; city; Thomas — Edison
ALYA star
ALYS name: Alice
AMAH nurse
AMAN Ahasuerus's minister
AMAR measures
AMBA mountain
AMBI about; prefix: both
AMBO pulpit
AMEN assent; verily; deity; — Ra
AMER bitter
AMES author; city, college
AMEX Amer. Expeditionary Force
AMGA Siberian river
AMIA fish
AMIC amidic
AMID among
AMIE friend: Fr.
AMIL plant; remedy
AMIN agent
AMIR prince
AMIS friends: Fr.
AMIT headdress
AMLA tree
AMLI tree
AMMA abbess; god
AMMI herb
AMMO ammunition; prefix: sand
AMMU ammunition
AMOI mine: Fr.
AMOK frenzy
AMON deity; King of Judah
AMOR love; Cupid; — patriae
AMOS prophet
AMOY island
AMOZ Isaiah's father
AMRA plum
AMUN deity
AMUR river
AMYL starch; alcohol
ANAI termite
ANAK giant race
ANAL pert. to anus
ANAM tree; Viet Nam region
ANAN tree; interjection
ANAS duck
ANAT sky god; med. term
ANAX Castor, Pollux (Dioscuri)
ANAY fruit
ANBA title
ANCE suffix; — errand
ANCY suffix
ANDA tree
ANDE tribe
ANDI language
ANDY Andrew
ANEM prefix: wind; city
ANER city
ANES once
ANET dill
ANEW over again
ANGE angel: Fr.
ANGO herb; dye
ANIL shrub, indigo
ANIS fennel; birds
ANKH cross
ANNA coin; bird; name; — Christie (O'Neill); — Karenina (Tolstoi)
ANNE queen; Boleyn; Henry VIII wife; Elizabeth's mother; Shakespeare's wife; Dombey's maid (Dickens); Queen — style; Queen —'s lace
ANNI years: Lat.
ANNO — Domini (year of Our Lord)
ANOA ox
ANON again; now; soon; author unknown
ANSA handle; loop
ANSE handle: Fr.
ANSU Korean apricot
ANTA porch; nut; tapir; goddess; pier; theater group
ANTE stake; pay; before; -bellum
ANTI opposed; prefix: against; Indian
ANTU rat poison
ANUS end of alimentary canal
ANZU apricot
AONE first-rate
AOUL Nepalese
APAP month

APAR armadillo
APER imitator; boar
APET goddess
APEX summit; crisis
APIA port (Samoa)
APII plant
APIO celery: Sp.
APIS sacred bull (Ptah); bee; bull (Kipling)
APOD footless
APSE recess; throne
APSU primordial chaos
APUS bird; constellation
AQUA water; green-blue
ARAB Semite; horse; nomad; urchin
ARAD plant; city
ARAH exclamation
ARAK palm; spirit
ARAL lake
ARAM country (Syria); Eugene (murderer)
ARAN Seir's descendant; island
ARAR tree
ARAS river
ARBA cart
ARCA box; dish; shell
ARCH support; curve; chief; fingerprint; triumphal —
ARDU slave
AREA zone, region; scope; tract
AREG deserts
AREO prefix: Mars
ARES war; Mars; Zeus's, Hera's son; Eris' brother
ARGH timid
ARGO ship; therefore; constellation
ARGY argue
ARIA tune; city (Herat)
ARID dry; barren
ARIL seed covering
ARIS molding edge
ARME weapon: Fr.; — blanche (saber)
ARMS mil. science; ensigns weapons; branches limbs
ARMY multitude, force
ARNA buffalo
ARND theologian
ARNE composer; region
ARNI buffalo
ARNO river; cartoonist
ARNT contraction
AROA Venezuela copper center
AROD son of Gad
AROE islands, New Guinea
AROO indeed
AROW in a line
ARPA harp: It.
ARRA oath
ARRY cockney worker
ARTA Ionian gulf
ARTO prefix: bread
ARTS skills; sciences; fine —; — and crafts
ARTY artistic
ARUI sheep
ARUM herb; starch
ARYA Caucasian
ASAK tree
ASAR glacial ridges; eskers
ASCH Scholem (author)
ASCI spore sacs
ASEA at sea
ASEM alloy
ASER Jacob's son
ASHA tribe
ASHY gray, pale
ASIA continent; Orient; East
ASIN month
ASIR Arab. principate
ASKR — and Embla; Norse Adam and Eve
ASNO donkey: Sp.
ASOK tree
ASOP sopping
ASOR lyre
ASSE caama; fox
ASSI holly
ASTA measure; dog
ASTI city; — spumante
ASUR war god
ATAP palm
ATAR perfume; essence
ATEF crown (Osiris)
ATEN solar disk
ATEO Polynesian god
ATES sweetsop
ATHI Kenya river
ATIK star
ATIP expectant
ATIS monkshood; fruit
ATIU one of Cook Islands
ATKA fish; Aleut. island
ATLE tree
ATLI Gudrun's husband-king
ATMA soul
ATMO prefix: steam
ATMU sun god
ATOM whit; particle; nuclear complex
ATON solar disk
ATOP at the peak
ATRI It. town
ATRY lay to (naut.)
ATTA soul; native; flour; fruit; ant
ATTU Aleut. island
ATUA demon
ATUM sun god (Tem)
ATWO asunder
ATYS god (Cybele's lover)
AUCA Indian
AUDE Fr. dept.; river
AUER violinist
AUGE priestess
AULA hall; tree; brain part
AULD old; — lang syne
AULU tree
AUNE measure
AUNT parent's sister; tia: Sp.; tante: Fr., Ger.
AURA wind; emanation; bird
AURI prefix: gold, ear
AUSA Vich (Sp. commune)
AUSU tree
AUTE tree
AUTO prefix: same, self; drama: Sp.; (ride in) car
AUZU tree
AVAL grandparental
AVAR Caucasian language
AVEC with: Fr.
AVER assert; asseverate
AVES birds: Lat.
AVID eager; greedy
AVIS bird: Lat.
AVON river; Shakespeare home (Stratford)
AVOW declare; justify; confess
AVUS grandfather: Lat.
AWAG wagging
AWAN tribe
AWAY onward; hence; far; off; absent
AWNY bearded
AWOL absent without leave
AWRY distorted; perverse(ly)
AXAL around an axis
AXIL leaf angle
AXIS center line; spine; stem; deer; power alliance; partnership
AXLE spindle
AXON axis; cell process

AYAH nurse; sign
AYAN spruce
AYES yes votes
AYIN 16th Heb. letter; 70
AZAM sir: Persian
AZAN prayer call
AZEL Saul's descendant
AZHA star
AZID compound
AZIN chem. compound
AZOF town; sea
AZON bomb
AZOV town; sea
AZUL blue: Sp.
AZUN Hananiah's father
AZUR Cote d'— (Riviera); Hananiah's father

BAAL deity
BAAR weight
BAAS master
BABA nurse; title; cake
BABE baby; — Ruth; girl
BABI sect
BABU Hindu gentleman
BABY doll; indulge
BACH live alone; composer
BACK help; tub; past; retreat; kick-; dorsal, posterior; spine
BADB goddess
BADE waited; asked; invited; commanded
BAEL thorny (fruit) tree
BAER prizefighter, actor
BAEZ singer
BAFF strike; stroke
BAFT astern; cotton
BAGA turnip
BAGG heiress (Thackeray)
BAGO shrub
BAHI fortune
BAHO prayer stick
BAHR sea; — El Azrak
BAHT coin
BAIA state; city; resort; bay
BAIL bond; security; set free; dip out; hoop
BAIN bath: Fr.
BAIS caste
BAIT lure; harass; pest poison
BAJU jacket
BAKA devil
BAKE dry; roast; biscuit
BAKU hat; tree; rug; city; oil field
BALA geol. epoch
BALD naked; — eagle
BALE woe; bundle
BALI demon; monkey; offering; island
BALK thwart; signal
BALL game; confuse; dance; — bearing; good time; point; Amer. sculptor
BALM plant; soothe; — in Gilead
BALT Lithuanian; Esth; Latvian; Lett
BALU wildcat
BANA Titan
BANC (judge's) bench
BAND strip; group; orchestra; range; tie; sash
BANE woe; curse; poison
BANG beat; thump; hair; sardine; interjection
BANI coins
BANK mound; bench; deposit; bird flock; Left, Right —; blood —; eye —
BANS marriage notice
BANT diet
BAPS dancing master (Dickens)
BARA measure
BARB sharp point; fish; dog; mow; pigeon
BARD armor; poet; — of Avon (Shakespeare)
BARE expose(d); mere; Indian
BARI hut; Negro; city
BARK peel; tan; cough
BARM yeast
BARN storehouse; stable
BARO big; prefix: weight
BARR elephant's cry
BART man's name
BARU tree
BASE bottom; source; home; headquarters; found; diamond corner; ignoble
BASH smash; bruise
BASK luxuriate; warm
BASS fish; fiber; lowest part; singer; clef (F); musical instrument, viol
BAST (woody) fiber; goddess; phloem
BATA child; servant
BATE diminish; tanner's bath; restrain
BATH tub; measure; spa; order
BATT matted mass
BATZ coin
BAUD speed unit
BAUL mendicant
BAUM Vicki (novelist); Oz creator; tree: Ger.; — marten
BAUR joke
BAVE double silk thread
BAWD procurer(ess)
BAWL cry; howl; — out (chide)
BAWN mud enclosure; white
BAYA weaverbird; Bantu
BEAD globule; ball; drop; aim
BEAK bill; nose; judge
BEAL river mouth
BEAM bar; timber; breadth; ray; smile; on the —; broadcast
BEAN plant; trifle; head; strike
BEAR carry; yield; endure; relate; animal; Ursa; short-seller; pessimist
BEAS Punjab river
BEAT strike; defeat; mystify; throb; scoop; field; sphere; — the Dutch
BEAU dandy; lover; — Brummell, — Nash
BECK nod; bidding; dyeing vat; Pol., Ger. officer, statesman
BEDE Adam (Eliot); the Venerable (monk)
BEEF ox, steer, cow, bos; brawn; rage; complain(t)
BEEN charmer's clarinet; participle
BEEP radio sound
BEER beverage; ale; mead
BEES yeast

BEET vegetable; root; sugar —; — top
BEGA measure
BEHN herb; tree
BEID star
BEIN good; fine
BEJA Nile nomad
BEKA weight
BELA jasmine; Benjamin's 1st son; Hungarian king
BELI myth. Brit. king
BELL ringing cup; gong; time period; flower shape; helmet; Brontë pseudonym; — the cat; diving —
BELT strap; zone; beat
BEMA platform; altar; measure
BENA grass (vetiver)
BEND turn; curve; flex; bow
BENE wild hog; well: It. & Lat.
BENG devil (Gypsy)
BENI Bolivian river; sesame
BENJ hemp; narcotic
BENN seed
BENO alcoholic palm sap
BENT crooked; inclination; grass
BENU holy bird (Ra-Osiris)
BERA king of Sodom
BERG iceberg; mountain
BERI Sudanese (Fulah); -beri (disease)
BERM (l)edge; road shoulder
BERN Swiss capital
BERT nickname
BESA coin
BESS nickname; Mrs. Truman
BEST most (good); defeat
BETA Greek B, 2; star; ray
BETE beast, silly: Fr.; — noire
BETH Heb. B, 2; Alcott heroine (Little Women)
BEVY company; flock
BHAR Kolarian native
BHAT minstrel; scholar
BHEL thorny (fruit) tree
BHIL low-caste Indian
BHOY gang member; rowdy
BHUT Dravidian ghost
BIAS diagonal (incline); prejudice
BIBB mast's timber piece
BIBI title: Lady, Mrs. (India)
BICE blue, green pigment
BIDE wait; tarry; dwell
BIEN good, fine: Fr.; — aimee (well beloved)
BIER litter; coffin
BIFF (deal a) blow
BIGA two-horse chariot
BIGG barley
BIJA kino tree
BIKE bicycle
BIKH aconite; poison
BILE liver secretion; choler
BILK defraud
BILL beak; weapon; law; poster; invoice; debt; nickname: William; — and coo; Sikes (Dickens)
BILO Balkan karst area
BIMI orang-utang (Kipling)
BINA Hindu guitar
BIND tie; protect; sew; cohere
BINE (hop) stem
BING bed roll; sharp sound
BINH weight
BINI Nigerian
BINN box; frame; crib
BINO alcoholic pine sap
BINT daughter; woman
BIOD animal life force
BION physiological individual (morphon)
BIOS life: animal, plant
BIRD avian; flyer; fowl; shuttlecock; person; Blue —
BIRI cheap cigarette
BIRL revolve; spin
BIRN clarinet socket
BIRR wind force; sound
BISA antelope
BISE cold wind; winter
BISH aconite; poison
BISK soup; ice cream; red-yellow
BITE cut; pierce; grip; eat (into); sting; respond; snack
BITI blackwood
BITO tree; poison; oil
BITT naut. fastener
BIUR Heb. commentary
BIWA loquat
BIXA tree genus; achiote
BIZE cold wind; winter
BIZZ buzz
BKKT chess move
BLAA bunk
BLAB tattle
BLAE bleak
BLAH nonsense
BLAS Gil (Le Sage novel)
BLAT sheep's cry
BLAY bleak
BLEA bleak; livid
BLEB blister; bubble
BLED emitted or drew blood, sap; extorted
BLET fruit decay
BLEU blue, rookie: Fr.
BLEW stormed; puffed; sounded
BLIP radar screen sign
BLOB drop; daub; sound; fish; zero score
BLOC political unit; casting
BLOT stain; mar; dry
BLOW move (air); puff, pant; brag; expend; stroke; calamity; disappointment; — up (enlarge)
BLUB swell; puff out
BLUE color; ocean; sky; sailor; sad; -blood; puritanical
BLUP air bubble sound
BLUR obscure; stain
BLUT blood: Ger.
BNAI B'rith (Jewish society)
BOAR (wild) hog; male
BOAS Franz (anthropologist)
BOAT (go by) ship; gravy-
BOAZ Ruth's husband
BOBA chicken snake
BOBO owala tree; mullet
BOCA harbor mouth: Sp.
BOCE colored fish
BOCK beer; leather
BODB goddess

BODE presage; augur; omen
BODO Indo-Chin. language
BODY structure; anatomy; bulk; corpse; group
BOER So. Afr. Dutch
BOGA basslike fish
BOGO Eritrean Hamite
BOGY specter; bugbear
BOHO grass; weep; shout
BOHR Nils (Nobel physicist)
BOID of boas, anacondas
BOII Celtic tribe
BOIL heat; bubble; agitation; abscess
BOIS wood: Fr.; wine (cognac); — de Boulogne
BOJO grass
BOKO evil spirit (Haiti)
BOLA missile; majagua (tree)
BOLD valiant; brazen; strong, heavy (type)
BOLE trunk; clay; brown
BOLL (strip) plant pod
BOLO knife; Rafflesia (plant); pacifist
BOLT sift; refine; shaft; lightning; bar; plant; rifle part; flight; refusal
BOMA Afr. stockade; post
BOMB explosive; dispenser; A-; lead-lined container; buzz —
BONA good; Lat.; — fide
BOND adhesion; tie; covenant; paper; captivity; certificate
BONE study hard; plug; os
BONG bell sound
BONI African; Boschneger
BONK bar money (Dutch E.I.)
BONN city; Ger. capital
BONO Johnny (Briton); cui —
BONY skeletal; osseous; Napoleon
BOOB simpleton
BOOF stare; peach brandy
BOOH exclamation
BOOK tome; volume; Bible; libretto; (bet) record; register; throw the —
BOOL curved handle
BOOM hum; grow, push; beam
BOON benefit; convivial
BOOR rustic; lout; Boer
BOOT shoe; wader; sheath; torture; recruit; compartment; tube; kick; to — (in addition)
BORA north wind; rite
BORD -and-pillar (mining)
BORE pierce; hole; tire; dullard; tidal flow
BORG borough: Dan.
BORI Lucrezia (singer)
BORN given birth to; née; quantum physicist
BORO spring rice; Indian (Mirhana); — Budur (temple)
BORS king (Lancelot's uncle); Bohort (finder of Holy Grail)
BORT finder of Holy Grail; impure diamond
BOSA Arab. drink
BOSC best pear
BOSE test ground by sound
BOSH furnace part; nonsense (nothing: Turk.)
BOSK thicket
BOSS knob; pad; stud; master, employer
BOTA measure
BOTE house repair; amends
BOTH the two
BOTO Indian; Voto
BOTT clay plug; fly larva
BOUD malt weevil
BOUT contest; attack
BOUW measure
BOWK steep; soak in lime
BOWL basin; dish; (roll) ball
BOXY boxlike; squarish
BOZA Arab. drink
BOZO fellow
BQKT chess move
BRAB palm
BRAD nail
BRAE slope
BRAG boast; game
BRAJ basha
BRAM Abraham
BRAN god-king; seed coat; chaff
BRAS arm: Fr.
BRAT apron; child
BRAW handsome; fine
BRAY (donkey's) cry; grind; Mrs. Nickleby (Dickens)
BREA resin; tree; asphalt
BRED procreated; brought up
BREE (eye)brow
BREI soft tissue
BREN (machine) gun
BRER Rabbit (Harris; Uncle Remus)
BRES Elatha's beautiful son (Fomorian)
BREW beverage; plot; concoct
BREY barnacle
BRIE cheese
BRIG sailing ship; prison
BRIM rim; edge; swell
BRIN fan plate; silk thread
BRIO con — (with spirit)
BRIT young herring
BRIX scale (hydrometer)
BROB support spike
BROH macaque; monkey
BROM Bones (Ichabod's rival)
BROT bread: Ger.
BROW forehead; high-, low-
BROZ Josip (Tito)
BRUH pig-tailed macaque
BRUT dry: Fr.; Brit. king (New Troy, London)
BUAL wine
BUBA tropical sore
BUBE boy, jack: Ger.; Fernando Po Bantu
BUBI Fernando Po Bantu

BUBO horned —; eagle owl
BUCK deer; fop; butt; male; Pearl (novelist); pass the —
BUDA It. millet
BUDD Lanny (Sinclair)
BUDE light; burner
BUFF leather; coat; tan; ward off; polish; wheel; bare skin; enthusiast
BUFO toad genus; agua
BUGI Celebes Malay
BUHL inlaid decoration
BUHR whetstone
BUKA dried leaves
BUKH prate; talk
BUKK prate; talk
BULB bud; tuber; corm; lamp; swell
BULK mass, volume; loom; -head (stall)
BULL (bovine) male; stud; papal letter; optimist; Taurus; policeman; blunder; glib talk; -fight
BULT hill; ridge
BUMP coincide; hit; swelling; — off (kill)
BUNA synthetic rubber
BUND embankment; league
BUNG stop(per); throw
BUNK case; bed; nonsense
BUNN cake
BUNT sag (net, sail); (fungus) disease; butt (ball)
BUOY float; sustain; life-; channel marker
BURA steppe blizzard
BURD noble lady
BURE brown red-yellow
BURG (fortified) town
BURH (fortified) town
BURI palm (fiber); talipot
BURL (pick) knot; Ives (actor)
BURN (be on) fire; yearn; waste; speed; brand
BURP belch; — gun
BURR (prickly) nut, knob; reamer; banyan tree; Aaron (statesman)
BURT butt; gore; dent
BURY hide; inter; lose
BUSH shrub; thicket; tail
BUSK stir about; hasten; corset bone; Indian New Year
BUSS ship; kiss; calf
BUST bosom; statue; failure; break
BUSY (keep) active; in use
BUTE island; Scot. county; parson (Thackeray)
BUTO serpent goddess; Leto
BUTT cask; mound; target; ram; hinge; jut; halibut
BUXY paymaster
BUYO betel leaf; nut
BUZI Ezekiel's father
BUZZ hum; fly low (over); — bomb (V1, V2)
BYEE measure
BYGO pass by
BYKE nest of bees
BYON clayey earth
BYRD explorer; Va. statesman
BYRE cow house

CAAM loom; heddles
CABA measure
CABO Yubi
CACA goddess
CACO bandit
CADE cask; tree; pet; rebel
CADI judge
CADY golf boy
CAEN city
CAFE restaurant; coffee; -au-lait; society
CAGE confine; enclosure; elevator car; nor iron bars a —
CAGN mantis; deity
CAGY shrewd
CAID alcaide
CAIN tribute; (Abel's) slayer; mark of —
CAJA box; bank
CAJI snapper
CAJU fruit; mahogany
CAKE bar; dough; harden
CAKY crusty
CALE Gypsy; cabbage
CALF bovine, etc., young; fur; leather; skin; lower leg
CALI Colombian city
CALK tighten; stop; sleep; tool; copy
CALL summon; visit; cry; telephone; — girl; — money
CALM quiet; mold
CALO Gypsy
CALP limestone
CALX residue; heel: Lat.
CAME arrived; lead rod; Indian
CAMP tent(s); town; stay; boot —
CANA Indian
CANE stem; rattan; stick; walking —; sugar —; candy —
CANG wooden collar
CANO canal; Sp.
CANT angle; change course; log; tilt; whine; jargon; be unable
CAPA cloak: Sp.
CAPE cloak; promontory; — Cod, — Horn, — Good Hope
CAPH star, letter
CAPP Al, cartoonist (Abner, Dogpatch)
CARA dear (one): It.; Indian
CARD comb; pasteboard; menu; playing —; calling —
CARE grief; heed; responsibility; anxiety; foster; relief organization
CARF slit; notch
CARK trouble
CARL rustic; villain; Charles
CARN stone heap
CARO dear (one): It.; Caroline
CARP fish; complain
CARR pool
CART wagon; transport
CASA house, building: Sp., It.
CASE event; fact; record, problem (medical, etc.); legal action; argument;

grammar form; container, chest, box; queer phenomenon; inspect
CASH money; exchange; hemlock
CASK barrel; measure
CASO Dodecanese island
CASS treasure; Timberlane (Lewis); Squire (Eliot)
CAST throw; project; shed; deposit; form; found; actors; (assign) roles
CASY ex-preacher (Steinbeck)
CATA down; prefix: away
CATE delicacy
CATO the Censor (Roman statesman); foe of Carthage
CATS — cradle
CAUK (secure by a) tenon
CAUL basket; covering membrane
CAUP tribute: Scot.
CAVA pepper shrub, root; gum resin; vein
CAVE cavern; — in (collapse); — canem (beware of dog)
CAVY rodent; guinea pig; stray animal(s)
CAWK bird's cry; mineral
CAWL basket
CAXI snapper (fish)
CAYO island, reef: Sp.
CAZA Turkish district
CAZI Moslem judge
CAZY Moslem judge
CCIV 204; Septimus Severus reign
CCIX 209; Septimus Severus reign
CEBA tree; kapok source
CEBU Visayan island
CECH Czech
CEDE yield; grant; transfer
CEIL overlay, line, ceiling
CELA that: Fr.
CELL cubicle; group; elec. jar; organism
CELT Irish, Scot, Welsh, Breton; chisel
CENA (Last) supper
CENE suffix: recent
CENS payment due
CENT coin; penny; game
CEPA onion
CEPE boletus (edible fungus)
CERA prefix: horn, wax
CERE wax; (wrap in a) waxed cloth; beak part
CERN decide
CERO mackerel
CESS tax; luck
CEST girdle; belt (Venus)
CETE marine mammals
CETO prefix: whale
CEYX Halcyone's husband
CHAA tea
CHAB bird
CHAC -Mool (god); -chac (instr.)
CHAD lake; nation
CHAI person
CHAL man
CHAM tribe; title; bite
CHAN resthouse; lord; title
CHAO measure
CHAP fellow; crack; jaw
CHAR trout; burn; sandbank; -woman
CHAT talk; bird; spike
CHAW masticate
CHAY red dye plant
CHEE weight
CHEF head (cook); — d'oeuvre
CHEK Chin. foot (measure)
CHEN snow goose
CHER dear: Fr.
CHEW masticate; ruminate; — the cud; — the rag
CHEZ at home of, with: Fr.
CHIA salvia beverage, oil
CHIB tongue; language
CHIC stylish(ness)
CHIH Chin. foot (measure)
CHIL cher pine; kite (Kipling)
CHIN lower jaw; chatter; weight; dynasty; Burmese
CHIP fragment; cut; hew
CHIR pheasant; pine
CHIT child; sprout; memo; voucher; mind
CHIV knife
CHOB grain spike
CHOL desolate plain; Mayan
CHOP cut; crack; eat; barter; jaw
CHOR thief; steal (Gypsy)
CHOU cabbage, darling: Fr.; Chin. dynasty; En Lai (statesman)
CHOW food; dog
CHOY red dye root
CHUB fallfish; dace; chevin
CHUD Mongols; Vepse; Vote; Tavastian
CHUG pull; fish; (move with) vibration
CHUM friend, scrap fish
CHUN Chin. pottery
CHUR Swiss canton
CHUT nonsense!
CIEL ceiling; sky: Fr.
CIII 103; Trajan reign
CIMA mountain peak: It.
CINE movie: Sp.
CINQ five: Fr.
CION plant shoot
CIPO liana
CIRC circle; recess; corrie
CIRL bunting; bird
CISE dice term: six
CIST chest; roofed pit
CITE summon; quote
CITO quickly, soon: It.
CITS citizens; mufti
CITY urban place
CIVA Hindu deity
CIVE chive garlic
CIXO Ecuador Indian
CLAD dressed; plated
CLAM mollusk; hush
CLAN clique; family; group
CLAP rap; applaud; flatten
CLAT mess; chatter
CLAW nail; ungula; chela; scratch; hammer

CLAY earth; ceramic; pipe; — pigeon; color; Henry, statesman
CLEE redshank; bird
CLEF musical sign; roman a —; key
CLEM riot; suffer hunger; nickname
CLEO queen (Cleopatra)
CLEW yarn ball; sail loop; cocoon; hint
CLII 152; Hadrian reign
CLIM — of the Clough (archer outlaw)
CLIO history Muse; mollusk
CLIP clasp; cut(ting); gait
CLIV 254; Aemilianus reign
CLIX 159; Antoninus Pius reign
CLOD lump; soil; dolt
CLOE fem. name
CLOG block; sandal; stop; impede; choke
CLOP limp; hobble
CLOT mass; coagulate
CLOW sluice; floodgate
CLOY glut; surfeit
CLUB bat; beat; society; suit (cards)
CLUE hint; guide; thread
CLUM clutch roughly
CLYM — of the Clough (archer outlaw)
CMIV 904
CMIX 909
CNUT king; son of Magnus
COAD cushion
COAG dowel
COAK tenon
COAL ember; fuel
COAN pert. to Cos Island
COAT fur; skin; cover; — of arms
COAX flatterer; cajole
COBB Irvin S. (writer); Tyrus R. (baseball)
COBH Irish port
COCA cocaine source; shrub; leaf to chew; flavor
COCK male fowl; vane; leader; tap; tee; hay pile; cog
COCO palm; nut; grass
CODA finale; mark
CODE body of law (Julian, Justinian, Napoleon); signal system; cipher; — duello
CODO measure
CODY William (Buffalo Bill)
COED girl student
COEL cuckoo
COEN Jan (empire builder)
COHO silver salmon
COIF defensive skullcap; make up (hair)
COIL curl; wind; twist
COIN money; mint; invent; corner
COIR coconut fiber
COIX grass; Job's-tears
COJA title; teacher
COKE coal residue; fuel
COKY grimed; drug addict
COLA tree; nut; drink
COLD chill; frigid; indifferent; common —; coryza; — blood; — chisel
COLE brassica genus; Porter (composer)
COLI intestinal bacterium
COLL embrace; hug; Vincent (gangster; "mad dog")
COLP pasture; Irish acre
COLT young horse; pistol; — .45
COLY long-tailed bird
COMA torpor; blur; tuft
COMB crest; rake; scrape
COME arrive; chance; fare
COMO lake, resort (Italy)
COND direct helmsman
CONE geometric solid; pine fruit, strobile; peak; ice cream —; nose —
CONI It. commune
CONK nose; head; decay; fail; hit
CONN direct helmsman
CONY rabbit; daman; pika
COOK chef; concoct; falsify; James (explorer)
COOL chill; calm; unmoved
COOM coal dust; refuse
COON animal; fur; sly man
COOP pen; jail; confine; coöperative
COOS Bay (laurel); Indian
COOT rail; surf duck; dolt
COPA tree; yaya; landmark
COPE vestment; cover; bend; contend
COPT Egypt. Christian
COPY duplicate; mimic; follow; text
CORA gazelle; Indian; name; Persephone; Demeter's daughter
CORD string; twine; ribbed fabric; measure (wood)
CORE heart; nucleus; gist
CORI Carl, Gerty (Nobel winners)
CORK tree; bark; stop(per); brown; Irish city (Lee)
CORM bulblike stem (crocus)
CORN grain; ear, kernel; callus; whiskey; preserve; granulate(d); clavus; banality; red-yellow
COSE (friendly) chat
COSH snug; happy; math. term
COSO open space: Sp.
COSS measure
COSY snug; teapot cover
COTA P.I. fort
COTE birdhouse; sheep shed; Coast: Fr. (d'Or; d'Azur)
COTO bark; stomachic
COTY Fr. statesman; cosmetics
COUE psychotherapist ("Day by day . . .")
COUP blow; master stroke
COUS cowlike
COVE bay; recess; pass; chap; Gypsy
COWL hood; auto body front
COXA hip (joint)
COXE Capt. (Scott)
COYN corner(stone)
COYO avocado; chinin
COZE (friendly) chat

COZY snug; teapot cover
CRAB crustacean; apple; sign; anger
CRAG cliff; neck
CRAL hut; village
CRAM press; stuff; study
CRAN bird; measure
CRAP dregs; money; dice cast (crabs)
CRAW gullet; stomach
CRAX curassow (bird)
CREA linen, cotton fabric
CREE Indian
CREW company; gang; -cut
CREX corn crake (bird)
CRIB manger; hut; bin; box; steal "pony," "trot"
CRIC lamp condensing ring
CRIG blow
CRIN heavy silk
CRIS dagger; stab
CROC harquebus support; crocodile
CROM Cruaich (Irish idol)
CROP craw; harvest; trim
CROW raven; corvine bird; bar; black; Indian; Jim —; -bar
CRUS leglike part; shank
CRUX (Southern) Cross; crucial point
CUBA W.I. island; Pearl of Antilles; measure
CUBE square solid; 3rd power; die; plant poison
CUBI measure
CUCA cocaine source
CUFF slap; manacle; sleeve end; miser; on the —
CUIR leather; dorado
CUKE cucumber
CULE diminutive suffix
CULL pick out; assort
CULM grass stem; coal dust; shoal water deposit
CULT sect; worship system
CUNA Panama Indian
CUON wild dog (dhole)
CURA parish priest: Sp.
CURB restrain(t); sidewalk edge; market
CURD coagulated milk
CURE heal; remedy; preserve; priest: Fr.
CURL coil; twist; hair lock
CURR to murmur (as owlet)
CURT short; concise
CUSH sorghum; cow; money; Ham's son; country
CUSK fish; burbot; eel
CUSP (crescent) point; tooth edge
CUSS curse; person
CUTE clever; attractive
CUVY sea girdles; kelp
CUYA hardwood tree
CVII 107; Trajan reign
CXII 112; Trajan reign
CXIV 114; Trajan reign
CXIX 119; Hadrian reign
CYAN green-blue
CYKE cyclorama
CYLE brewing; beer; wort
CYMA cornice molding
CYME inflorescence
CYON wild dog (dhole)
CYST box; abnormal sac
CYTE prefix: hollow vessel
CZAR emperor; dictator

DACE fish
DADA father; cult
DADE support
DADO wall part; groove
DADU saint
DAER re borrowed stock
DAEZ daze
DAFF put aside
DAFT foolish; giddy
DAGG pistol
DAGH hill
DAGO tribe
DAIL legislature; — Eireann
DAIN Patusan chief (Conrad); — Curse (Hammett); measure
DAIS platform
DALE valley; share; trough
DALI tree; offering; Salvador —
DALL sheep
DAMA gazelle
DAME woman; title; — aux Camellas
DAMN curse; — the torpedoes
DAMP moist(ure); depress
DANA goddess; editor; author; lake
DANE Scandinavian; great — (dog); Hamlet
DANG curse (damn)
DANK moist; rank
DANS in: Fr.
DANU goddess
DARD language group
DARE venture; defy; fish; 1st Amer. child (Virginia)
DARI grain sorghum; carpet
DARK unlighted; wicked; dismal
DARN mend; interjection
DARR bird
DART missile; fish; seam; run
DASH sprint; smash; small portion
DASI concubine
DASS Durga, Ram (twins, Kipling)
DATA facts
DATE fruit; tree; brown; (make) appointment
DATO tribal chief
DATU tribal chief
DAUB plaster; besmear
DAUD dad
DAUK relay post
DAUN — stage (geol. period)
DAUR Manchu
DAUW zebra
DAVE David
DAVY David; lamp; affidavit; Jones' locker
DAWK relay transport; mail
DAWM coin
DAWN daybreak; Eos; Aurora; red
DAYE printer (Bay Psalm Book)
DAYS by day
DAZA Negro-Berber
DAZE stupefy; mica
DAZY confused
DDAY operation start
DEAD deceased; entire; absolute(ly); — reckoning
DEAF unhearing; inattentive; — and dumb, — mute
DEAL bargain;

transaction; unfinished wood; apportion(ment); policy: New —, Fair —
DEAN clergyman; educator; oldest member, doyen
DEAR costly; loved; loved one
DEBS Eugene (socialist)
DEBT fault; liability; obligation
DECA prefix: ten
DECI prefix: tenth
DECK ship floor; pack, cards; array; adorn
DEDO measure
DEED act; property transfer
DEEM consider; judge
DEEP profound; extensive; ocean
DEER ruminant; cervine; — Park (Buddha site)
DEFI challenge; defiance
DEFT skillful; trim
DEFY challenge; dare
DEGU rodent (Octodon)
DEHA body (theosophy)
DEIL devil; -s-bit (plant)
DEIN your(s): Ger.
DEJA already: Fr.
DELE omit; erase
DELF quarry; pottery; blue
DELL valley; dingle; wench
DEME Greek commune
DEMI prefix: half
DEMO prefix: populace
DEMY coin; scholar; paper size
DENE measure; dune; Indian
DENS tooth: Lat.
DENT depress(ion); notch
DENY refuse; contradict
DEPA measure
DERA suffix: neck types
DERE — Mable (Streeter book)
DERM prefix, suffix: skin layer
DESI jute; Arnaz
DESK table; lectern; department
DEUL Hindu temple
DEUM Te — (hymn)
DEUS god: Lat.; — ex machina
DEUX two: Fr.
DEVA deity (Indra); demon
DEVI goddess; Siva's wife (Shakti); title: Mrs., Lady
DEWA deity (Indra); demon
DEWY moist; refreshing
DHAI midwife
DHAK tree
DHAL split pea, lentil
DHAN wealth; loan
DHAO knife (Burma)
DHAR state; town (India)
DHAW billhook
DHER mound; land share
DHOW Arab. sailboat
DIAD pair
DIAL plate; face; call; sun-
DIAN reveille
DIAU Indian
DIAZ Bartholomeu (Port. navigator)
DIBS juice: grape, date
DICE (cut into) cubes; gamble; gaming implements
DICH you: Ger.
DICK Richard; whip; lad; detective; Whittington (London mayor)
DIDO trick; caper; Carthage queen, Aeneas' beloved
DIEB jackal
DIEM day: Lat.; per —
DIER one moribund
DIES day(s): Lat.; — irae; Cong. committee
DIET fare; food regimen; parliament
DIEU god: Fr.; mon —!
DIKA bread; fat; oil
DIKE levee; ditch; dig; goddess (Horae)
DILL flavoring herb; pickle
DILO poon tree
DIME coin; — novel
DINE eat; have dinner
DING thump; sound; urge
DINK small boat; cut out
DINO prefix: terrible
DINT blow; force; notch
DIOL chem. compound; suffix
DION lord in Winter's Tale
DIOS God: Sp.
DIRE evil; fatal; extreme
DIRK dagger; Theodoric
DIRT muck; earth; gossip; do one —; — cheap
DISA showiest orchid
DISC disk; record; — jockey
DISH receptacle; serve
DISK plate; harrow; puck
DISS reed grass
DITA tree; bark; upas
DITE mite; indict
DITT close up; obstruct
DIVA prima donna; blue
DIVE plunge; duck; low resort; — bomb(er)
DIVI divine ones
DIXI I have spoken: Lat.
DIXY camp pot
DOAB tract
DOAT drivel; be silly, overfond; wood rot
DOBE brick (house)
DOBY brick (house)
DOCE Brazil river
DOCK weed; rumex; (cur)tail; pier
DODD cut off (wool)
DODE nickname: Theodore
DODO extinct bird; reactionary
DOEG Saul's herdsman; poet's nickname; Indian
DOER performer; agent
DOES performs
DOFF put off; remove
DOGE Venice, Genoa ruler
DOGS scaup duck
DOGY calf; duck
DOIT coin; whit; bit
DOKO Afr. pygmy
DOLA weight
DOLE ration; (relief) alms; deal (out)
DOLI weights
DOLL plaything; puppet; dress up; girl
DOLT dunce; ignoramus
DOME edifice; cupola; roof
DOMN Rumanian ruler; lord
DOMY domelike

DONA lady; sapek (coin)
DONE agreed; exhausted
DONG sound; weight; ding-
DONI fishing boat
DONT contraction; prohibition
DOOB Bermuda grass
DOOK wooden brick; demon
DOOM (last) judgment; fate; condemn
DOON tree (varnish resin)
DOOR portal; entrance; open — policy
DOPA chemical (pigment test) crystalline
DOPE drug; information; guess; nitwit
DOPP diamond cup
DOPY sluggish
DORA Mrs. David Copperfield
DORE bullion; gold; pike; Paul Gustave (Fr. artist)
DORM dormitory; sleep
DORN thornback ray
DORP hamlet; city (So. Afr.)
DORR Rebellion (R.I.)
DORY John — (fish); boat
DOSA sheik's ritual ride; hatred
DOSE portion; (give) medicine
DOSS bed; sleep; — house
DOST (you) do: archaic
DOTE love to excess; drivel; timber rot
DOTH does
DOTO sea slug genus
DOTY discolored by rot
DOUB Bermuda grass
DOUC variegated monkey
DOUM palm
DOUP weaver's thread
DOUR sullen; gloomy
DOVE pigeon; — blue, gray; Columba; plunged
DOWD slovenly woman
DOWL feathery down
DOWN to below; reduce; defeat; feathers; eider-; dejected
DOXA religious stanzas
DOXY doctrine; hussy
DOZE drowse; timber rot
DOZY drowsy; decayed; doty
DRAA measure
DRAB dull; box; wench; cloth; drug
DRAG haul; harrow; obstacle; puff; auto race
DRAH measure
DRAM measure; drink
DRAP cloth
DRAT oath
DRAW drag; attract; gain; infer; extract; sketch; undecided contest
DRAY cart; squirrel's nest; — horse
DRED — Scott (slave)
DREE endure; tedious
DREG lees; residue
DREI three: Ger.
DREW sketched; pulled
DREY squirrel's nest
DRIB drop; a little
DRIN Balkan river
DRIP let fall
DROP globule; fall; discard; minim; trap door; die; pendant
DRUB (beat with) stick
DRUG medicine; dope; — on the market; — addict
DRUM spool; instrument: tympanum; beat
DRUN road (Gypsy)
DUAB tract
DUAD pair
DUAL double
DUAN canto; poem
DUAR mountain pass
DUAT Hades
DUBB Syrian bear; lizard
DUCE chief: It.; Mussolini
DUCK bird; webfoot; wild fowl; canvas; pet; plunge; evade; -soup; vehicle
DUCO pyroxylin lacquer
DUCT tube; vessel; pipe
DUDE dandy; fop; city fellow; — ranch
DUDS clothes; failures
DUEL combat; meeting
DUET music for two
DUFF pudding; cheat
DUFY Fr. artist
DUHR star
DUIM measure
DUIN demons
DUIT Chibchan Indian; coin
DUKE prince; cherry
DUKU lanseh tree fruit
DULL blunt(ed); dismal; inert; tedious; Shaks. character
DULY properly; timely
DUMA Russ. parliament
DUMB mute; stupid; — waiter; deaf and —
DUMP unload; junkyard; thud; mean place; holey dollar
DUNE sandhill; twine color
DUNG excrement; fertilize(r); weight
DUNK dip into; immerse
DUNS dull; stupid
DUNT split (ceramics)
DUNY having many dunes
DUOS duets
DUPE trick(ed one); copy
DURA — mater (spinal membrane)
DURN gatepost
DURO Sp. peso; dollar
DURR grain sorghum
DUSE incubus; Eleanora (actress)
DUSK twilight; gloom
DUST powdered matter; rubbish; clean; dust to —; gold —
DUTY obligation; task; tax
DYAD pair
DYAK Bornean
DYAS Permian (geol. period)
DYCE thus!: naut. command
DYCK Anthony Van (painter)
DYER tinter; Mary, Quaker martyr
DYKE levee; checkers opening
DYNA prefix: power
DYNE unit of force

EABA measure
EACH every(one)
EADS engineer; bridge
EARL nobleman; count; name
EARN gain; win; deserve
EASE repose; comfort;

moderate; facilitate
EAST direction; Asia; Orient
EASY simple; calm; soft; — Street
EATS food; consumes
EAUX waters: Fr.
EAVE roof edge
EBAL Mount (Joshua's altar)
EBED Gaal's father
EBEN Ebenezer
EBER Hebrew ancestor
EBOE tree; oil; Negrito
EBON ebony; black
EBRO Sp. river
EBUR ivory: Lat.
ECAD modified organism
ECCA geol. period (Karroo)
ECCE lo: Lat.; — homo
ECHO Narcissus's nymph; repeat; response; fruit tree (gingko)
ECHT genuine: Ger.
ECRU beige; unbleached
ECTO prefix: outside
EDAM city; cheese
EDAR Bib. site
EDDA Norse epic
EDDO taro root
EDDY whirlpool; Mary Morse (Baker) —: Christian Science
EDEA reproduction organs
EDEL noble: Ger.
EDEN paradise; West of Nod
EDER river
EDGE brink; sharpness; goad; advantage; — on
EDGY sharp; snappish
EDIT correct; redact; blue-pencil
EDNA female name; Ferber, novelist
EDOM Esau's country; Idumaea
EELY wriggling; slippery
EENY — meeny, miny, mo
EERY weird; uncanny; timid
EFIK Negro
EFOD priestly garb; image
EGAD oath
EGAL equal: Fr.
EGAN horse (Kipling)
EGBA Negro; Yoruba
EGBO secret society (Ogboni)
EGER river
EGGS ova; — and bacon, ham; — and butter (flowers)
EGGY egg-stained; yolky
EGIL Volund's (Wayland's) brother
EGIS protection; patronage; symbol of: Zeus, Athena; shield
EGMA enigma
EGOL antiseptic
EHEU alas
EHUD judge of Israel
EIDE ideas; forms
EINE one: Ger.
EILD barren; milkless
EIRE Ireland; Erin
EJAM Bantu
EJOO palm; fiber
EKER water cress
EKKA carriage
EKOI Bantu
ELAH king
ELAM kingdom
ELAN dash; ardor
ELBA Napoleon's exile isle
ELBE river
ELEF letter
ELIA Charles Lamb; essayist
ELIM Bib. oasis
ELIS Greek city state
ELLA Eleanor; she: Sp.; fem. suffix
ELLE measure; she: Fr.
ELMY rich in elms
ELOD alleged force
ELOI Eli; God
ELON Esau's father-in-law; college (N.C.)
ELSA — of Brabant (Lohengrin's bride)
ELSE other(wise); besides
ELUL month
EMER Cuchulainn's wife (ideal womanhood)
EMEU bird (ostrichlike)
EMIL man's name
EMIM Moabites; giants
EMIR ruler; title
EMIT eject; issue; voice
EMMA letter M; name; Austen novel; Bovary (Flaubert)
EMMY TV award; nickname
EMOL rock salt
EMPT empty
EMYD terrapin
EMYS tortoise
ENAM gift; land grant
ENAN Prince of Naphtali
ENCE suffix
ENDO prefix: within
ENID fem. name; Geraint's wife; city
ENIF star
ENIN blue grape pigment
ENKI Babylonian god
ENNA Sicilian resort
ENNE prefix: nine; fem. suffix
ENNS river
ENOL chem. suffix
ENON Paris's wife (nymph); John the Baptist site
ENOS Seth's son, Adam's grandson (905 years old); taken by God
ENOW enough
ENSE suffix
ENTE grafted (Her.); being: Sp.
ENTO prefix: inner
ENVY covet; grudge; 7th deadly sin
ENYO war goddess
ENZU moon god (Sin)
EOAN pert. to east; dawn
EOIN John; Sean
EPEE fencing sword
EPHA Hebrew dry measure
EPHI measure
EPIC heroic poem
EPOS epic poetry; events
EPPY Euphemia
EQUI prefix: equal, same
ERAL epochal
ERAN Ephraim's grandson
ERAT was: Lat.; quod — demonstrandum (Q.E.D.)
ERDA earth goddess; Wagner role
ERER sooner
ERGO hence; prefix: work
ERIA silk(worm)
ERIC male name; Viking; the Red
ERIE Iroquoian; lake; city

ERIN Eire; Ireland
ERIS goddess of discord, Ares' sister
ERMA Ermengarde
ERNE sea eagle
EROS (god of) love; Cupid; asteroid; Antony's friend
ERRA — Pater (almanac)
ERSE Irish; Gaelic
ERST former; first
ERUA mother goddess
ERUC cordage fiber
ERYX sand snake
ESAU Isaac's, Rebecca's son; Jacob's twin; hairy; red; Edom
ESAY Isaiah
ESCA apoplexy (plant disease)
ESCE suffix: begin to be
ESEK Isaac's well
ESER weight
ESNE slave
ESOP fable writer
ESOX fish (pike, pickerel, muskellunge)
ESPY behold; detect; meteorologist
ESSE existence; to be: Lat.
ESTA this: Sp.
ESTE It. family; this: Sp.
ESTH Balt; Estonian (Tallinn man)
ESUS Gaulish god (Mars)
ETAH Eskimo settlement; town
ETAL and others: Lat.
ETAT state: Fr.; L' — c'est moi!
ETCH eat into; engrave
ETES (you) are: Fr.
ETNA stove; volcano
ETON school, college; collar, jacket; playing field of —
ETRE exist; be: Fr.; raison d'—
ETTA Henrietta; Harriet
ETTE suffix: fem.
ETUI (vanity) case; box
ETYM Moabites, giants; abbr.: word sources
EUER your(s): Ger.
EUGE bravo!
EVAN name (Welsh)
EVAT eft
EVEA madder (tree); ipecac
EVEN evening; level; fair(ly); equal(ly); moderate; just; not odd; flush
EVER always; at anytime
EVET eft; newt
EVIL bad; sinful; injury; disease
EVOE bacchanals' wild cry; Punch editor
EWAN name (Welsh)
EWER pitcher; udder
EWRY linen storeroom
EXAM interrogation; test
EXES letters; expenses
EXIT depart(ure); die
EXON Exeter man
EYAH nurse; sign
EYAS nestling
EYED looked at; ogled
EYER needle maker
EYEY having holes
EYOT islet
EYRA wild cat
EYRE Jane (Bronte heroine); circuit (court)
EYRY bird's nest
EZAN prayer call
EZBA measure
EZEL juniper tree
EZRA prophet; OT book

FAAM tea; leaves
FABA bean; vetch
FACE surface; oppose; line
FACT deed; reality
FACY fresh
FADE weaken; flat; dissolve
FADO tune
FADY weakening
FAEX dregs
FAIL fall short; err
FAIN glad; eager
FAIR pleasing; ample; just; bazaar; — and square; — deal
FAIT fact; — accompli
FAKE loop; cheat; sham
FAKY spurious
FALA refrain; dog
FALL descend; ruin; autumn; — of Man
FALX weapon; — cerebri (brain fold)
FAMA rumor
FAME reputation
FAMN measure
FANA Sufistic concept
FANE temple
FANG tooth; measure; Dickens character
FANO cloth; cape
FAON fawn color
FARD face paint; date
FARE passenger; price; happen; food; travel
FARL cake (part)
FARM till; land; — out; club
FARO card game; Pharaoh
FASH rough edges; vex
FASS measure
FAST not eat; fixed(ly); quick(ly); wild; — and loose
FATA — Morgana (fairy, mirage)
FATE destiny (goddess); end; kismet
FAUN deity; satyr
FAUT comme il — (proper): Fr.
FAVI tiles; flagstones
FAVN measure
FAWN deer; cringe; toady; brown
FAZE disturb
FEAK twitch; wipe
FEAL conceal
FEAR fright; doubt
FEAT deed; accomplishment
FECK amount
FEED nourish; gratify; graze; fodder
FEEL sense; test; suffer
FEES charges; tips
FEET measure
FEIL comfortable; neat
FEIS convention; — of Tara
FEKE trick device
FELD field: Ger.
FELL skin; cut, sew (down); savage
FELS Eastern coin
FELT pressed fibers; hat; sensed
FEME wife; tribunal
FEND keep off; parry
FENT slit; cleft
FEOD feudal estate
FERK measure
FERN seedless plant
FERU bast fiber
FESS broad band (Her.); confess

FEST festive gathering
FETE festival; regale
FEUD strife; vendetta; fee
FIAT sanction; edict; money; automobile (It.)
FICO trifle
FIDE entrust; — et amore
FIDO fog evaporation; dog's name
FIEF feudal estate
FIFE flute; checkers opening
FIFO inventory method
FIJI islands (Lau, Yasawa)
FILE tool; rasp; smooth; march; column; folder; arrange
FILI learned poet
FILL pack; complete; glut; — the bill
FILM skin; coating; haze; photograph; picture
FILO silk thread
FILS son: Fr.; Dumas (Camille); Irak coin
FIND discover (y); (re)gain
FINE end; superior; thin; keen; well; (set) penalty; geil —, derb — (Irish clans)
FINK finch; derb; informer; strikebreaker
FINN man of Finland, Helsinki; Ugric; Mickey — (KO drops); Huckleberry — (Twain novel)
FIOT Congo tribe
FIPS Martin Chuzzlewit
FIRE combustion; ardor; discharge
FIRM fixed; solid; company
FIRN granular snow(field)
FISC exchequer
FISH piscine; angle; probe; search; tin — (torpedo)
FISK exchequer; Jim (speculator); tire
FIST grasp; effort; tightwad
FIVE number; basketball team; card
FIXE prix —
FIZZ hissing sound; drink
FLAG flower; standard; stone; signal; limp; reduce, dwindle
FLAK antiaircraft
FLAM trick; drum beat
FLAN tart; disk; net
FLAP slap; leaf; sway; -jack
FLAT level; (make) insipid, dull; wholly; — tire
FLAW crack; defect; wind
FLAX plant; fiber; thrash
FLAY (strip off) skin
FLEA insect; puce; — market
FLED ran away: shunned
FLEE run away; shun
FLEM Fleming; Belgian
FLEW aviated; winged
FLEX bend
FLEY fright(en)
FLIP toss; tap; drink; hop
FLIT flutter; move
FLIX down; fur; flax
FLOB move clumsily
FLOC flock(y mass); shreds
FLOE floating ice
FLOG whip
FLOP slump down; flap; change; fail(ure); bed; sleep
FLOT lateral ore deposit
FLOW gush; stream; flux; roll; ebb and —
FLUB blunder; botch
FLUE net; lint; barb; air passage; pipe
FLUX flow; change; melt
FOAL colt; equine young
FOAM froth; rage; rubber
FOCH Ferdinand (Fr. marshal; WW I commander)
FOCI center points
FOGG Phileas (Verne)
FOGO stench
FOGY dull, bigoted man
FOHN warm dry wind
FOIE liver: Fr.; — gras (pate)
FOIL balk; defeat; sword; leaf; sheet
FOLD plait; envelope; fail; quit; flock
FOLK people; — ways, laws, song, dance
FOND basis; fount; loving
FONG Ewe-speaking Negro
FONO Samoan council
FONT basin; spring; stoup; type
FONS fount; source
FOOD nutriment; victuals
FOOL dolt; jester; trick
FOOT pedal part; base; dance; trip; skip; pay; add
FORA meeting places; courts
FORB non-grassy herb
FORD crossing shallow; Henry (automobile); Shaks. character
FORE front; prior; golf cry
FORK implement (pronged); tuner; place of divergence
FORM shape; mold; fashion; school grade
FORT stronghold; trading post; dun
FOSS canal; ditch; moat
FOUD district magistrate
FOUL rotten; proor; illegal; invalid
FOUR number; card; boat
FOWL poultry; cock; hen
FOXY wily; brown; rank; sour
FRAB worry
FRAM spear
FRAP tighten
FRAT fraternity
FRAU Mrs., wife, Mme., woman: Ger.
FRAY contest; tumult; wear off
FREA Frigg; Odin's wife; goddess
FRED nickname
FREE independent; immune; rid; exempt; — and easy; — lance, port; trade, style
FRET gnaw; vex; worry; embroider; ridge;

ornament
FREY god (Njorth's son, Gerth's husband)
FRIA Frigg (Odin's wife)
FRIB dirty short wool
FRIM juicy; soluble
FRIT fuse; partly; fried: Fr.; waste
FRIZ curl; crisp; wig
FROE cleaver; steel wedge
FROG amphibian; hoarseness; loop; rail device
FROM out of
FROT rub; chafe
FROW Dutch woman; cleaver
FRUG modern dance
FUAD Arab king
FUCI rockweeds; algae
FUEL combustible matter
FUGA fugue: It.
FUGU poisonous fish
FUJI wisteria; cherry; volcano
FULA Sudanese
FULK unfair shove (marbles)
FULL filled; replete; quite; — dress; — house
FUME smoke; fit; rage
FUMY vaporous; smoky
FUND supply; finance; money; sinking —
FUNG Sennar Negroid
FUNJ Sennar Negroid
FUNK fear; coward; Casimir (vitamins); Isaac (lexicographer); — & Wagnalls
FUNT weight; Allen (TV)
FURL roll up (sail, flag)
FURY rage; avenging spirit; Erinys, Fate, Parca (Atropos)
FUSC dusky; somber
FUSE detonator; melt; unite
FUSS tumult; bustle; -budget
FUST pilaster; smell stale
FUTE Eskimo curlew
FUYE Jap. flute
FUZE detonator; melt; unite
FUZZ fine fibers; police
FYKE fish bag net
FYRD old English army

GAAL brewing
GABE taro
GABI taro
GABY fool
GADE fish; composer
GADS -hill (Dickens)
GAEA goddess; Titans' mother
GAEL Celt; Irishman
GAFF spear; ordeal; hoax
GAGE pledge; fruit; gauge; general; governor
GAGL sweet gale
GAIA goddess
GAIL Abigail; brewing
GAIN reach; earn; profit; notch
GAIT walk; pace
GAJO non-Gypsy
GALA festival; tribe
GALE storm, wind
GALI abuse
GALL bile; venom; wound; chafe; swelling; impudence
GALT clay bed
GAMA Vasco da — (navigator); grass
GAMB leg
GAME amusement; quarry; resolute; lame
GAMP umbrella; Sairey — (nurse: Dickens)
GANE yawn
GANG crew; associate; rock
GANO Count (Roland's destroyer)
GANT yawn; gaunt; gannet; Eugene (Wolfe character)
GANZ all, totally: Ger.
GAOL prison
GAON Jewish title
GAPA guided missile
GAPE yawn; stare; gap
GAPO (inundated) forest
GAPY yawning
GARA coin
GARB apparel; array
GARE wool; station: Fr.; beware: Fr.
GARM Hel's dog
GARN yarn; go on
GARO Assam native
GARY city, steel center
GASH (make) incision
GASP pant (eagerly)
GATA nurse shark
GATE entrance; pass; judgment; money
GATH Philistine city
GAUB persimmon (astringent)
GAUD ornament; bead
GAUE German regions
GAUL Celt, Frenchman; France
GAUM attention
GAUP gape
GAUR wild cattle
GAUS region: Ger.
GAUT range; pass; river bank stairs
GAVE donated
GAWD ornament; bead
GAWK lout; stare
GAWN gallon; tub
GAWP gape; simpleton
GAZA Israel (Philistine) seaport; Mozambique district; eyeless in — (Samson)
GAZE stare; wonder
GAZI warrior; title
GAZY gaping
GEAL pert. to earth
GEAN cherry
GEAR notched wheel; equipment; adjust; harmonize
GEAT channel in mold; Scandinavian (Beowulf)
GEBA Jonathan's victory site
GEEK carnival wild man
GEEZ Version (Ethiopic Bible)
GEIN glucoside (Geum urbanum)
GELD castrate; prune; tax
GELT money
GENA cheek; beak part
GENE hereditary factor; chromosome part; nickname
GENS clan: Lat.; people: Fr.
GENT gentleman; Belg. city
GENU knee: Lat.
GEON paradise river; Jerusalem spring
GERA city
GERB sheaf; firework
GERD Frey's wife
GERE Odin's wolf
GERI Odin's wolf

GERM bud; seed; microbe
GEST deed; romance tale, adventure
GESU Jesus: It.
GETA Jap. wooden clogs
GETT bill of divorce
GEUM plant (astringent)
GHAT range; bank; river bank stairs
GHEE butter
GHEG Albanian
GHES Tapuyan Indian
GHOR Dead Sea valley
GHOS Chin. dynasty
GHUZ Turkish invader
GIAN -Carlo (Menotti)
GIBE scoff; jeer; agree
GIDE Andre (author)
GIER eagle (vulture)
GIFT donation; talent
GIGA medieval fiddle
GILA — monster; lizard; Ariz. river
GILD lay gold on; adorn; — the lily; trade society
GILL measure; brook; breathing organ; wattle; coin; lass
GILO woody vine (tonic)
GILT gold; sow
GIMP silk fabric; vim
GINK eccentric one
GIRD encircle; clothe; brace
GIRL young female; maid; Gibson —; — Friday; — of the Golden West; chorus —
GIRO tour; round; credit system; aircraft (auto-)
GIRT encircled; prepared
GISH Moroccan public land; Lillian, Dorothy (actresses)
GIST main point; pith
GITA Bhagavad —; Indian scriptures (yoga)
GITE shelter: Fr.; mad
GIVE bestow; yield; grant
GIZA site: pyramids, Sphinx
GJOA ship (Northwest Passage; Amundsen)
GLAD pleased
GLED kite; buzzard
GLEN rival
GLIA neuroglia (nerve tissue)
GLIB flippant, smooth(ly)
GLIM light; eye
GLIS dormouse genus
GLOM watch; steal
GLOP look wildly; stare
GLOW shine; incandesce; flush; ardor; wax
GLUB make gulping sound
GLUE adhesive; stick
GLUG sound of liquids
GLUM moody; sullen
GLUT sate; surfeit; oversupply; wedge
GMAN U.S. police agent
GNAR growl
GNAT (biting) fly
GNAW bite; corrode
GOAD rod; decoy; urge
GOAF grain; rick
GOAI shrub
GOAL purpose, objective; score
GOAN pert. to Goa
GOAT ruminant; scape-; brown
GOBI Mongolian desert
GOBO burdock; okra; camera; mike shield
GOBY fish; passing
GOEL reclaimer; avenger
GOER runner
GOES walks; proceeds
GOFF clown; fool
GOGH Vincent van — (painter)
GOGO vine; bark soap; beetle; bugaboo; Bantu
GOLA storeroom; caste; cyma
GOLD metal; element; — dust, medal
GOLF game; blood-red; — links
GOLI musket ball; pill
GOLL Irish hero (Fenian)
GOLO Nilotic Sudanese
GOLP roundel purpore (Her.)
GOMA Bantu (Wagoma)
GONA New Guinea victory
GOND Dravidian Indian
GONE departed; enamored; lost; germ cell
GONG bell; tom-tom
GONY albatross
GOOD able; brave; sound; profit; happiness; welfare; benefit
GOOF dolt; blunder
GOOK trash; ooze; native
GOOM cultivation method
GOON thug; strikebreaker
GOOP nonsense creature
GOOR sugar; massecuite
GORA musical instrument
GORE stab; blood; triangular insert
GORY bloody; murderous
GOSH oath; -awful
GOTH Teuton (Theodoric, Alaric); barbarian; Ostro-, Visi-
GOUL monster; grave robber
GOUR cattle; koulan (onager)
GOUT drop; disease (arthritis); taste: Fr.
GOWK simpleton; fool
GOWL gad; defile; howl; monster
GOWN dress; toga; robe
GOYA Sp. painter; — red
GRAB grasp; capture; game
GRAD centesimal unit
GRAF nobleman: Ger.; — Spee (Zeppelin)
GRAM sword; plant; weight; —'s method; grandma
GRAN weight; grandma
GRAO weight
GRAS horse; foie — (paté)
GRAY dull; dismal; hoary; Dorian (Wilde); Asa, botanist; Elisha, inventor
GRAZ Austrian city (Mur)
GRES stoneware: Fr.
GREW increased
GREY color; neutral; dull; Zane (writer); Vivian (Disraeli novel)
GRID grating
GRIG dwarf; cricket; fowl
GRIM ruthless; ghastly
GRIN smile
GRIP grasp; power;

valise; Barnaby's raven (Dickens)
GRIS gray: Fr.
GRIT sand(stone); bravery; grate
GROG liquor (with water)
GROS coin; fabric; weight
GROT cave; Bremen coin
GROW expand; sprout; wax; develop
GRUB larva; food; dig(ger)
GRUE shiver; shudder
GRUM morose; guttural
GRUS constellation (Crane)
GUAD tree
GUAM Mariana Island
GUAN bird
GUAO tree
GUAR legume; cluster bean
GUEG Albanian
GUFA round boat
GUFF humbug; chaff
GUGU P.I. soldier, insurrecto
GUHA Bantu
GUHR earthy deposit
GUIB harnessed antelope
GULA upper throat; goddess (Ninurta's consort)
GULE of August (Lamma's Day)
GULF bay; chasm; eddy
GULL bird; cheat; dupe
GULO wolverine genus
GULP swallow; catch breath
GUMI shrub, flower, fruit
GUMP silly, stupid one; Andy, Chester, Min (cartoon family)
GUNA Sankhya term
GUNJ granary; market
GUNL gunwale
GUNK jilt; hoax
GUNN castaway (Stevenson)
GURU teacher
GUSH flow; spout; be effusive
GUST outburst of wind
GUTI Sumer settler; Kurd
GUZE red roundel (Her.)
GWYN Llud's son; deity
GYBE jibe; scoff; agree
GYLE brewing; wort; vat
GYNE prefix: female
GYPS gypsum
GYRE turn; ring; vortex
GYRI brain ridges
GYRO prefix: ring, spiral
GYVE fetter; shackle

HAAB year
HAAF fishing grounds
HAAK fish; wander
HAAR fog
HABA bean
HABE tribe
HABU pit viper
HACK chop; writer; horse
HADE angle; strip
HADJ pilgrimage
HAEC this one (fem.): Lat.
HAEM prefix: blood
HAFF lagoon
HAFT handle
HAGG demoness; hack; wood
HAGI clover; prefix: saint
HAHA laugh; fence
HAHN Otto (Nobel physicist)
HAIG soldier (Douglas)
HAIK garment; frame
HAIL ice pieces; salute; — fellow
HAIR filament; cilium, seta; fabric; -trigger
HAJE cobra
HAJI pilgrim
HAJJ pilgrimage
HAKA dance
HAKE fish; pester; frame
HAKH claim(er); legal claim; share
HAKO rite
HAKU fish
HALA pine tree
HALE healthy; Nathan — (patriot)
HALF moiety; -breed, -caste, -nelson, -shell
HALI prefix: sea, salt
HALL building; room; town —; guild-; astronomer; -Mills
HALM plant stems
HALO circle; glow; nimbus; prefix: sea, salt
HALS Frans — (painter)
HALT stop; lame
HAMI hooked processes
HAND control; aid; worker; measure; pass; player; cards; penmanship
HANG suspend; plan; bit; die on gallows
HANK coil; — Morgan (Twain)
HANO Indian
HANS John; Johannes; — Castorp (Mann)
HANT ghost
HAPH weight
HAPI bull; Nile (god)
HAPU clan
HARA Japanese statesman
HARB Bedouin
HARD solid; firm; close; severe; difficult
HARE leporid; rabbit; run
HARI river; Mata (spy)
HARK listen
HARL barb; filament
HARM hurt; evil; injury
HARP coin; seal; Lyra; constellation; Irishman; nag
HARR hinge
HART stag; deer
HARZ German mountains
HASH chop up; mixture; mess
HASP clasp
HASS throat; embrace
HAST contraction: havest
HATE detest; aversion
HATH contraction: haveth
HATI heart
HATT measure
HAUL drag; shift; loot
HAUT high: Fr.; — monde
HAVE possess; aux. verb; must; deceive
HAWK bird; predator; peddle; mortarboard
HAWM loiter
HAYA arrow poison
HAYZ zodiacal situation
HAZE mist; drizzle; harass
HAZY dim; obscure
HEAD skull; top; brain; chief; crux; source
HEAF pasture
HEAL cure; restore
HEAP pile; crowd; car
HEAR listen; perceive by ear
HEAT warmth; rage;

height; dead —; pressure; strain
HEBE cupbearer of gods; Zeus's daughter, Hercules' wife; color
HECK (weaving) frame; cough; oath
HEED notice; attention
HEEL back part; end; slant; follow; scoundrel
HEEP Uriah (Dickens villain)
HEER Mr., Sir: Dutch
HEFT weight; bulk; notebook: Ger.
HEGH exclamation; hey!
HEHE Bantu tribe
HEII Hawaiian fern
HEIL hail: Ger.
HEIN surprise!: Fr.
HEIR inherit(or); — apparent, presumptive
HELA goddess; Loki's daughter
HELD kept; retained
HELI prefix: sun, spiral
HELL Hades; state of misery; -bent
HELM steer (wheel); tiller
HELO squeamish
HELP relieve; avoid; wait on, aid(e); servants
HEMA prefix: blood
HEME reduced hematin
HEMI prefix: half
HEMO prefix: blood
HEMP herb; hashish; cannabis; rope (fiber)
HENS fowl; -foot (herb)
HERA Zeus's sister, wife
HERB plant; nickname
HERD crowd; feed together
HERE vicinity; present
HERL (feather) barb
HERO protagonist; demigod; — and Leander; Beatrice's cousin
HERR lord, Mister, Sir: Ger.
HERS fem., poss. pronoun
HEST command; precept
HETH son of Canaan; Hittite ancestor
HETT Hittite ancestor
HEVI apple (tree)
HEWN felled; squared
HICK hiccup; rube; jake
HIDE land measure; skin; conceal; shelter; — and hair
HIEL Jericho's rebuilder
HIEN Chin. government seat
HIER here: Ger.; yesterday: Fr.
HIFI faithful sound rendition
HIGH lofty; elevated; noble; expensive; shrill; tainted; tipsy
HIKE toss; tramp; raise
HIKU scabbard fish
HILA 'eyes' of bean
HILD Hethin's victim princess
HILL mound; Jenny (Shaw character); -billy
HILO grass; city (Hawaii)
HILT sword
HIMA Hamitic Negro
HIND fish; grouper; deer; posterior
HING asafetida (gum resin; antispasmodic)
HINO timber tree; dye
HINT suggestion; imply
HIPE wrestler's throw
HIRE engage; rent; wage
HIRO measure
HISH hiss; swish
HISS sibilant (of disapproval); goose; serpent; steam sound; Alger (Communist)
HIST call to attention; Indian girl (Cooper)
HIVE bees' swarm, house
HLER sea god (wife: Ran)
HOAR frost; gray; -hound
HOAX deceive; trick
HOBB havoc; fireplace ledge; pin; peg
HOBO vagrant worker
HOCH high: Ger.
HOCK leg joint; hamstring; wine; faro card; pawn
HOEK stream bend; — van Holland (Dutch cape, city)
HOEN weight
HOER scraper
HOEY partnership (Hawaii)
HOGA hill pasture
HOGG unshorn sheep
HOGO taint; stench
HOHE Siouan tribe
HOJA title; teacher
HOJU Jap. army reserve
HOLA fish poison; herb; hello
HOLD grasp; have; retain; believe; keep; bear; lair; prison
HOLE pit; cavity; flaw; — in one; — card; ace in the —
HOLI spring festival
HOLL ditch
HOLM holly; oak; islet
HOLT willow plantation; hill; lair; Eliot hero; actor
HOLY sacred; pious; — City; — Alliance; — Roller
HOMA sacred drink
HOME habitat; asylum; plate; natural
HOMO man; — sapiens; prefix: same
HOMY homey; intimate
HONE sharpen(er)
HONG Chin. trade guild
HONI — soit qui mal y pense; shamed
HONK goose cry; toot; ooga
HOOD cowl; cloak; seal; gangster; Thomas (poet)
HOOF ungula; foot; beast; walk; dance
HOOK trap; curve; catch; steal; — and eye; pirate: Peter Pan (Barrie)
HOON coin; gold pagoda
HOOP circle(t); wicket; — skirt
HOOT derisive (owl's) cry
HOPE trust, expect(ation); wish; -chest

HOPI French beige; Moqui Indian
HOPS beer
HORA book of hours; Israeli dance
HORN prong; antenna; trumpet; brasswind; cup; Cape —
HORS out of: Fr.; — d'oeuvre
HOSE stockings; pipe; drench
HOSS house; One — Shay (Holmes)
HOST army; throng; bread as Christ's body; innkeeper; person having guests
HOTH blind god (Balder slayer)
HOTI cause; reason
HOUR time unit; H- or zero —
HOVA Madagascar native; Malagasy
HOVE ground ivy; raised
HOWE hollow; empty; Elias (inventor); Julia Ward (Battle Hymn); Brit. general, admiral
HOWL (distress) cry; wail
HOYA honey plant (milkweed)
HSIA 1st Chin. dynasty
HUBB pipe end
HUCH Danube fish
HUCK towel fabric
HUED colored; tinged
HUEY Long (La. governor)
HUFF inflate; bully; anger
HUGE enormous; immense
HUGH name; saint (of Cluny)
HUGO name; Victor (novelist)
HUIA bird (starling)
HUIT eight: Fr.
HUKE hooded cape
HULA Hawaiian dance
HULE caucho source
HULK ship body; bulky thing
HULL husk; ship body; Cordell (statesman)
HULU o-o's feather tuft
HUMA Uganda Negro
HUME philosopher
HUMP protuberance; mound; crisis; Himalayan peaks; -back
HUND dog: Ger.
HUNG suspended; undecided (jury)
HUNH exclamation
HUNK pierce; lump; OK
HUNT seek; chase; Leigh (writer)
HUON pine; timber tree
HUPA Athapascan Indian
HUPP call to horse
HURA bishop's cap; sandbox tree; possumwood
HURE head of boar, wolf
HURI Abihail's father
HURL throw; pitch; rush
HURR to snarl
HURT harm(ed); pain
HUSE beluga; whale; huchen
HUSH quiet; silence; -hush; -puppy; — money
HUSI fine P. I. fiber
HUSK covering (of seed, corn); shell
HUSO beluga; whale; huchen
HUSS dogfish; John (religious leader)
HUZZ buzz; murmur
HYDE — Park; Dr. Jekyll and Mr. —; measure
HYKE cry to urge dogs
HYLA frog; toad
HYLE matter (philos.); demon
HYMN song (of praise)
HYPE wrestler's throw
HYPO photo solution; needle; injection
HYPS hypochondria

IAGO villain (Othello)
IALU Hades; heaven
IAMB verse foot
IBAD Hira Arab
IBAN dyak (Borneo)
IBEX wild goat; bouquetin
IBID P.I. lizard (tidbit); the same: abbr.
IBIS (sacred) wading bird
IBIT P.I. lizard (tidbit)
ICAL compound suffix
ICED frozen; chilled
ICER freezer; mixer
ICHO fruit tree (gingko)
ICHU valuable grass
ICON image; statue
IDAS Marpessa's lover; Castor's slayer
IDEA conception; fancy; key meaning; opinion
IDEE — fixe: Fr.
IDEM same: Lat.; semper —
IDEN Henry VI figure
IDEO prefix: idea
IDES Roman date; — of March (fateful day)
IDIC pert. to ids
IDIO prefix: one's own
IDJO Niger delta Negro
IDLE not working; empty; lazy; waste
IDLY vainly; lazily
IDOL god, deity; image; adored one
IDUN Bragi's wife (Norse)
IDYL pastoral poem
IDYO Niger delta Negro
IDZO Niger delta Negro
IFFY contingent
IFIL tree (brown dye)
IGAL Moses' spy
IGLU Eskimo hut; seal hole
IGOR Prince (opera)
IHVH God; Tetragrammaton
IISM egoism
IIWI bird (mamo)
IJMA Moslem principle (Sunna)
IKAT shrub; weight
IKMO betel palm, pepper
IKON image; statue
IKRA superior caviar
ILAI David's man
ILEX holm oak; holly
ILIA (hip)bones
ILLE that one: Lat.
ILLS troubles
ILLY badly; ill
ILOG river (Tagalog)
ILOT islet; ait; eyot
ILUS son of Tros; Priam's grandfather
IMAM priest; title
IMBE cordage fiber plant
IMER Caucasian
IMID chem. compound
IMLA Micaiah's father
IMMI measure

IMNA Asherites' chief
IMPI armed Kaffirs
IMPY impish
INBE be within
INCA Quechuan Indian (ruler)
INCH measure; move slowly
INDE blue (indigo)
INDY — pink (carnation)
INEE arrow poison
INEZ Don Juan's mother
INGA timber tree; mimosa
INGE prelate ("Gloomy Dean"); playwright (Bus Stop)
INIA Amazon cetacean
INKA Inca
INKY black; stained
INLY within; heartily
INRE concerning; actually
INRO Japanese receptacle
INTI Incas' deified sun; sun god
INTO penetrating; toward
IODO prefix: iodine
IOLA Kansas town
IOLE Eurytus' daughter (Hercules' captive)
IONA Scot. isle; Celt church; college
IONE Pompeii heroine (Bulwer-Lytton)
IONI Hainai; Chaddo Indian
IOTA Greek I, 10; jot
IOUS promissory notes; suffix
IOWA state; Indian
IPIL tree (brown dye)
IPSE himself: Lat.; — dixit
IPSO — jure, — facto
IRAD Enoch's son
IRAE Dies — (Day of Wrath)
IRAK country
IRAN Persia
IRAQ country
IRAS Cleopatra's maid
IRBM ballistics missile
IRID iris; crocus
IRIS rainbow; goddess; eye part; plant (flag); spirit (Shaks.); red-blue; March (Arlen)
IRMA name
IROK gomuti (palm)
IRON metal; element; weapon; instrument; club; shackle; press; strong; Age
IRRA war god
IRUS Odyssey beggar
ISAR river (Munich)
ISBA log hut
ISER river
ISHA Upanishad
ISIS goddess; Osiris's wife, sister; Horus's mother
ISLE ait; eyot; insulate; key
ISMY doctrinaire
ISUI Asher's son
ITCH skin irritation; desire
ITEA shrub; Virginia willow
ITEM also; article; bit; entry
ITEN So. Amer. Indian
ITER road; passage (brain)
ITIS suffix: inflammation, mania; Tereus' son
ITMO betel pepper
ITOL suffix: alcohol(ic)
ITYS Tereus' son
ITZA Mayan Indian
IUNO Jupiter's wife
IVAH Bib. city
IVAN John; — the Terrible
IVER ever
IVES inventor (photo-engr.)
IWIS certainly
IXIA corn lily; bulb
IXIL Mayan Indian
IXLE cordage fiber
IYAR month
IYNX wryneck (woodpecker)
IZAR Moslem garment; star

JAAL goat
JACA tree
JACK flag; tool; card; fruit; raise
JACU bird
JADE gem; horse; exhaust
JADU magic
JADY gemlike
JAEL Sisera's killer; Heber's wife
JAGA Bantu
JAGG pendant; tooth; slash
JAIL prison; gaol
JAIN sect (Indian)
JAKE Jacob; rube; money; satisfactory; ginger
JAKO parrot
JAMA tunic
JAMB leg armor; pillar; door part
JAMI mosque
JANE woman; false hair; cloth; — Eyre; Lady — Grey
JANN genii
JAOB measure
JAPE deride
JARA palm
JARL Norse chief; earl
JASS card game; jack
JATI caste
JATO jet-assisted take-off
JAUN palanquin
JAVA coffee; hood; (Indonesian) Sunda Isles; — man (Pithecanthropus)
JAVE Jehovah
JAWY talkative
JAZZ dance; music; banter
JEAN name; cotton cloth
JEEL pool; marsh
JEEP vehicle; automobile
JEER scoff; taunt
JEFE chief; leader
JEFF rope; nickname; Mutt and —
JEHU (chariot) driver; prophet, King (Israel)
JELL solidify; mature
JENA Ger. city (optical, Napoleonic victory); glass
JERK grab; twist; spasm; soda man; dullard; beef
JERL boat joint
JERM Levantine boat
JESS strap on hawk leg
JEST joke
JESU name: Jesus
JETE ballet jump
JETH Hindu month
JEUX cards, hands, games: Fr.

JEUZ chief Benjamite
JEWS -harp
JHOW tamarisk shrub
JHUM cultivation method
JHVH Jehovah; God; Tetragrammaton
JHWH Jahweh; God; Tetragrammaton
JIBE sneer; agree; coincide; shift course
JIBI extinct bird
JIFF instant
JILL girl; sweetheart; Jack and —
JILT betray in love
JINK prank
JINN demon; spirit
JINX hoodoo; bad luck
JITI Rajmahal creeper
JIVA life energy
JIVE dialect (dance, jazz)
JOAB (David's) captain
JOAD philosopher; Tom —: Grapes of Wrath (Steinbeck)
JOAH record keeper
JOAN lass; cap; — of Arc, the Maid, la Pucelia
JOAR durra; millet
JOBO hog plum; gumbo limbo
JOCH yoke, measure: Ger.
JOCK John; jockey; hobo
JOCU dog snapper
JODO Buddhist paradise (Gokaruku)
JOEL prophet, OT book
JOEY coin; clown; odd-job man; young kangaroo; Pal (O'Hara character)
JOGI yogi; ascetic
JOHN name; saint, evangelist; cop; man; — Bull (England); Long — Silver (Stevenson)
JOIE — de vivre (zest for life)
JOIN mix; unite; coalesce
JOKE jest; laughing stock
JOKY jocular
JOLE jowl; cheek
JOLI pretty, nice: Fr.
JOLL move clumsily; knock
JOLT shake; hard blow
JOMS Vikings Norse colony
JONK jonquil
JOOK perch; slumber
JOOM cultivation method
JORD Odin's wife; Thor's mother
JOSE Carmen lover
JOSH make fun; banter
JOSS Chin. deity
JOSY nickname
JOTA Sp. peasant dance
JOTI astrologer; astronomer
JOUG iron collar; pillory
JOUR day: Fr.
JOVA Opata; Pimian Indian
JOVE god; Jupiter; Zeus
JOWL jaw; cheek; wattle; gambler (Dickens)
JOZY Josepha; Josephine
JUAN John; Don —, Don Giovanni
JUAR durra; millet
JUBA ghost; dance; mane; river
JUBE chancel screen; lozenge
JUCA cassava; manioc
JUCK partridge call
JUDA James' brother
JUDE name; NT book, author; Jew: Ger.; — the Obscure (Hardy)
JUDO self-defense art
JUDY name; Punch and —; Judith; Kipling character
JUEZ judge, juror: Sp.
JUGA carrot ridges; yokes
JUGE judge: Fr.
JUJU Afr. magic, charm
JUKE partridge call; — box; sociological name (with Kallikak)
JULA suspension bridge
JULE name: Julian; Julius
JULY (5th Roman) month
JUMP leap; bounce; move; headstart; — the gun
JUNE month; beetle; — moon, bride
JUNG young: Ger.; Carl Gustave (psychologist)
JUNK ship; trash; scrap
JUNO goddess; Jupiter's wife, Hera; stately woman; missile
JUPE skirt
JURA rights; mountain range
JURE de — (by law)
JURY (court) panel; committee; grand —; hung —
JUSI fine P.I. fiber
JUST fair; virtuous; exact(ly)
JUTE fiber plant; Corchorus; Low German
JUZA star
JYNX wryneck; charm

KAAN inn; title
KAAT shrub; weight
KADA measure
KADE tick
KADI judge
KADU tribe
KAFA Ethiopian
KAGO conveyance
KAGS convict (Dickens)
KAGU bird
KAHA proboscis monkey
KAHN banker; test
KAHU harrier; bird
KAID chief; alcalde
KAIF languor; hemp
KAIK village
KAIL tree; ibex; kale
KAIN tribute
KAIO fruit
KAIR fiber
KAIS island
KAKA parrot
KAKI bird; tree
KALA bird
KALB de — (general)
KALE cabbage
KALI glasswort; carpet; evil genius; Agni's tongue; Siva's wife
KALO taro root
KAMA love god; desire; river
KAME hill
KAMI language; deity
KANA Japanese writing
KANE god
KANG — Hsi (Chinese emperor)
KANO painting school
KANT change course; Immanuel,

philosopher
KAPA cloth(es)
KAPH letter
KAPP measure
KAPU forbidden; taboo
KARA river
KARI gum tree
KARL Charles; — Marx
KARN stone heap
KARO plant
KASA grass
KASI tile work
KASM measure
KATE bird; Shaks. shrew; Greenaway
KATH astringent
KATI weight
KATY Catherine; -did
KAUN resthouse; lord; title
KAVA pepper shrub, root; gum resin; vein
KAVI Java language
KAWA pepper shrub, root; gum resin; vein
KAWI Java language
KAWN resthouse; lord; title
KAYO knock out
KAZI Moslem judge
KAZY Moslem judge
KEAL cabbage
KECK vomit; show disgust
KEEF hemp; languor
KEEK fashion spy
KEEL ship bottom; navigate; ocher; guinea fowl
KEEN sharp; acute; bewail
KEEP tend; retain; preserve; last
KEET guinea fowl
KEID star
KEIF hemp; languor
KEIR bleaching vat
KELA measures
KELD spring; fountain
KELE weight
KELK fish roe
KELL Gaul; net; film
KELP seaweed, iodine source
KELT Celt; cloth; trout
KEMP fur refuse
KENO lotto (game); prefix: empty
Eng. country,
KENT duchy; Lear's follower
KEPI military cap
KEPT retained; lasted
KERB gutter part
KERE read(ing substitute)
KERF cut; notch
KERI read(ing substitute)
KERN soldier; peasant; grain; type part; Jerome (composer)
KERR physicist
KERS cress
KETA dog salmon
KETU eclipse demon (Rahu)
KEUP measure
KEYS House of (Isle of Man legislature); cays: Florida —
KHAN resthouse; lord; title; Agha —
KHAR weight
KHAS special; noble
KHAT measure
KHEM chief god (Min)
KHET mortal body; measure
KHOR watercourse; gorge
KHOT farmer; contractor
KIAK canoe
KIBE chilblain crack
KIBO Afr. peak (Kilimanjaro)
KICK hit; die; object(ion); excitement; -back
KIDD William (privateer)
KIDS star (Auriga)
KIEF hemp; languor
KIEL ocher; ruddle; seaport; — Canal
KIER bleaching vat
KIEV Ukrainian city
KIFF languor
KIHO peacock butterfly
KIKI castor oil plant
KIKU chrysanthemum
KILE measure; weight
KILL slay; veto; creek
KILN (burn in) oven
KILO measure; -gram, -meter; prefix: 1000
KILT Scot's skirt
KINA quinine
KIND sort; species; gentle
KINE cattle
KING monarch; ruler; chief; chessman; card
KINK twist; loop; cramp
KINO gum (catechu); prefix: moving
KIPE basket
KIPP peak (Glacier National Park); gymnastic feat
KIRI paulownia tree; knobkerrie (missile)
KIRK church
KIRN harvest feast
KISH powder; basket; measure; Saul's father
KISS touch gently; caress; sweetmeat
KIST chest; installment; measure
KITE hawk; rogue; flying toy; banking fraud
KITH acquaintance; — and kin
KIVA ceremonial chamber
KIVE brewer's vat
KIVU tsetse fly
KIWI flightless bird; apteryx; non-flyer
KIYI herring; cisco; yelp
KLAM weight
KLAN Ku Klux —
KLEE Paul (painter)
KLIP rock; cliff
KLOM weight
KLOP hard sound
KMET Slav; tenant; mayor
KNAB nibble
KNAG spur; knot
KNAP summit; rap; talk; bite; button
KNAR knot; burr
KNEE joint; bend(ing)
KNEW understood; was aware
KNEZ Slavic prince
KNIP bite; crop; rap
KNIT looped, tie(d); unite; contract
KNOB lump; hill; antler; handle
KNOP button; finial; stud
KNOR knot (wood); gnarl
KNOT tie; loop; hitch; sandpiper; problem; blemish; stud; Gordian —
KNOW understand; recognize; -how;

-nothing (party)
KNUB waste silk
KNUR gnarl; knot; wood ball
KNUT king; son of Magnus
KOAE red-tailed bird
KOBA antelope
KOBE Honshu port
KOBI Japanese reserve duty (term)
KOBU seaweed food (kelp)
KOCH cook: Ger.; Robert (bacteriologist)
KOEL cuckoo
KOFF Dutch sailboat
KOHL eye shadow; horse
KOIL cuckoo
KOJI Jap. yeast cake
KOKO bird; palm; tribe; executioner (Mikado)
KOKU measure
KOLA caffeine nut; jackal; river; city; bay (Murmansk)
KOLI low-caste tribesman
KOLO folk dance
KOME Greenland geol. division
KOMI Soviet republic; Zyrians
KONA Hawaiian storm; weight
KONK conk
KOOP purchase; bargain
KOPH Heb. K, Q, 100
KOPI N.Z. tree (karaka)
KOPT Copt
KORA water cock; Hottentot dialect
KORE Persephone; Demeter's daughter; chaos (Maori myth.)
KORI bustard; low weaver
KOSO tree; cusso; Panamint Indian
KOSS measure
KOTA P.I. fort; Dravidian language
KOTO Jap. zither
KOZO paper mulberry
KRAG rifle
KRAL hut; village
KRAN coin
KRAS tahr (goat)
KRIS dagger; stab
KROO Liberian Negro
KTKB chess move
KTKR chess move
KTKT chess move
KTQB chess move
KTQR chess move
KUAN pottery; official
KUAR month
KUBA carpet; measure
KUDU Afr. antelope
KUEI disembodied spirit
KUFA round boat
KUGE Jap. courtier
KUHL eyelid cosmetic
KUKI Burma Mongol
KUKU N.Z. fruit pigeon; kukupa
KULA measure; gift exchange
KULI low-cast Indian
KULM crane; heron
KULU old woman (Kipling)
KUNG public
KUNK measure
KURD Sunnite Mohammedan; Iranian
KURE Jap. city; Hawaiian isle
KURI Lezhgian tribesman
KURK church: Scot.
KUSA ceremonial grass
KUSH Ham's son; country
KVAS sour beer, cider (Russian)
KWAN coin; weight
KWEI disembodied spirit
KYAH partridge
KYAK canoe
KYAR coconut fiber
KYAT weight; Burmese money
KYKE fashion spy
KYLE sore; ulcer; farmer

LAAP secretion; insect
LABE city
LACE cord; flavor; netting
LACK need
LACT prefix: milk
LACY netlike
LADE load; dip
LADY title; bird
LAEL Gershonite's father
LAET freedman
LAGO lake
LAHN river
LAIC secular
LAID put down; calmed
LAIN reclined
LAIR resting place
LAIS hetaera
LAIT milk: Fr.; cafe-au-
LAKE sea; pool; red (cochineal)
LAKH 100,000; coin
LAKY red
LALO composer
LAMA priest; llama; brown; Dalai, Panchen, Tashi —
LAMB amateur speculator; Charles — (Elia), essayist (roast pig)
LAME cripple(d); halt; plate; fabric
LAMP light; bulb
LANA wood; flannel
LAND ground; debark; state: Ger.
LANE (fixed) route; throat
LANG auld — syne; Fritz
LANK thin; lean(ness)
LANX platter
LAON Fr. city
LAOS country
LAPP N. Scandinavian
LARA Byron poem
LARD fat; stuff
LARI money; sea birds
LARK bird; frolic; yellow
LARP secretion; insect
LARS Porsena (conqueror)
LASH (whip) stroke; tie; eye part
LASI tribe
LASS girl; sweetheart
LAST block: final(ly); endure; measure
LATA jumping disease
LATE dead; tardy
LATH strip; slat
LATU gold coins
LAUD praise
LAUK exclamation
LAUN ceramic sieve
LAVA fluid rock; obsidian's source; red
LAVE pour; bathe
LAWK surprise!
LAWN fabric; grass plot; bishopric
LAWS rules; principles
LAZE idle(ness); tribesman

LAZI tribesman
LAZO lasso
LAZY idle
LEAD metal; element; plummet; bullets; color; guide; command
LEAF plant part; sheet; tea
LEAH fem. name; Laban's daughter; Jacob's wife
LEAK loss; ooze; crack
LEAL loyal: Scot.
LEAN be supported; incline; thin
LEAP jump, skip; — year
LEAR learning: Scot.; king; father of Goneril, Regan, Cordelia
LECH slab; capstone; river
LEDA mollusk; mother of Castor, Pollux, Helen, Clytemnestra; wooed by Zeus as swan
LEEK plant (onion; liliaceous); — green (Wales emblem)
LEER sly gaze; oven; loin
LEES dregs
LEET court; list
LEFT departed; blow; — of center (Liberals)
LEHI prophet
LEHR oven; Lew (comedian)
LEIF Ericson (explorer)
LEIL faithful, loyal (Land of the —)
LEIR sea god (Lear)
LELY Dutch painter
LENA firewood: Sp.; river; Conrad heroine
LEND make loan, grant; — an ear
LENE smooth; consonant
LENO (cotton, silk) fabric
LENS eye part; glass (optical); herb
LENT fasting period; slow; made loan
LEON country, city; Ponce de (explorer)
LERO Dodecanese isle
LERP secretion; insect
LESE — majesty (disrespect)
LESS shorter; fewer; inferior; minus
LEST for fear that
LETE quadrille set
LETI island off Timor
LETO mother of Apollo, Artemis
LETT Latvian, Balt (Riga man)
LEUD feudal tenant
LEVI Jacob's, Leah's son; tribe
LEVO prefix: left
LEVY assess; seize; tax
LEWD lecherous; obscene
LIAM O'Flaherty: "Informer"
LIAO Manchuria river
LIAR prevaricator; plant
LIAS geol. period
LICE insects (louse)
LICK tongue; stroke; whip; conquer; bit
LIDA Alida
LIDE March (month)
LIDO Venice beach
LIED fibbed; song: Ger.
LIEF gladly; freely
LIEN claim; attachment; garnishment
LIER rester; layer
LIEU place; stead
LIFE existence; vivacity; biography
LIFO inventory method
LIFT ra(i)se; exalt; steal; elevator
LIII 53; Claudius reign
LIIN measure
LIJA unicorn fish
LIKE as; similar(ly); love; prefer; probable
LILA deity manifestation
LILE little
LILL small pin; loll; Lillian
LILT (sing) lively tune
LILY flowers; Turk's-cap; pure; white
LIMA city; bean, yam; mollusk
LIMB leg; arm; member
LIME calcium oxide (mortar); snare; caustic; linden (tree); amber; citrus fruit
LIMN portray; delineate
LIMP halt; flaccid; loose
LIMU edible seaweed
LIMY viscous
LINA measure; Caroline
LIND Jenny (singer, Swedish Nightingale)
LINE thin mark; cable; cord; wire; piping; row; direction; cover; align; track; flax
LING fish; burbot; hake
LINK (chain) loop; connect; join; torch; measure
LINN waterfall; linden
LINO measure
LINT raveling, fiber (of linen); netting
LINY streaky
LINZ Austrian city
LION cat; king of beasts; celebrity
LIPA fat
LIRA money; lyre; hairlike ridge
LIRE coins; read: Fr.
LISA fem. name; nickname
LISK flank; loin
LISP speech defect
LISS (fairy) fort; release; peace; fleur-de-lis
LIST strip(e); roll; register; enter; inclination; careen
LITE suffix: mineral, rock
LITH prefix, suffix: stone
LITI medieval peasants
LITZ braided wire
LIVE exist; continue; vital; alert
LIVY Roman historian; Titus Livius
LLEW Celt deity (Gwydion's son)
LLYN lake; pool
LOAD burden; measure
LOAF bread; idle
LOAM clay; soil
LOAN lend
LOBB go heavily; tennis stroke; till
LOBE projection; ear part
LOBO timber wolf
LOCH lake, bay: Scot.
LOCI places; sites

LOCK gate (canal, dam); tuft; wool; fasten(ing); grapple; tie up; -out (labor)
LOCO (render) mad; weed
LODE ore deposit; vein; load
LODI city; Napoleon victory
LODZ Polish city
LOFT attic; warehouse floor; golf stroke
LOGE theater box
LOGY heavy; dull
LOIN body part; hips; meat cut
LOIR dormouse; river
LOIS name; Timothy's grandmother
LOJA bark (quinine)
LOKA sphere, universe
LOKE Loki; surprise!
LOKI god of discord; Aesir; Balder slayer
LOLA fem. name
LOLL droop; lounge; sprawl
LOLO Caucasian Chinese
LOMA fringe; lap; hill
LOME Togo seaport
LONE single; - Star
LONG lengthy; extended, yearn; — John Silver (Stevenson); Huey — (La. politician); — time no see
LONK black-faced sheep
LOOD weight
LOOF luff; sponge gourd
LOOK observe; appear(ance); eye (wink); care
LOOM auk; appear(ance); weaver's frame
LOON diving bird; lout
LOOP noose; catch; aerial stunt; Chicago area
LOOS Anita (writer: Gentlemen Prefer Blondes)
LOOT plunder; booty
LOPE go; move; gait
LORA thong; strap
LORD ruler; Jehovah; Jesus; duck; planet
LORE history; learning
LORI lemur; Afr. Negro
LORN forsaken; bereft
LORO monk parrot; fish
LORS exclamation: lord!
LORY parrot; touraco
LOSE miss; forfeit; fail; forget
LOSH wash leather
LOSS forfeiture; bereavement; waste; defeat; — leader
LOST not won; misplaced; confused; ruined; — cause
LOTA water pot; burbot genus
LOTE lotus (poetic); weights
LOTH averse; reluctant
LOTI Pierre (writer; Viaud)
LOTO pot; game
LOTS tracts; quantities; very much; chances
LOUD noisy; showy; vulgar
LOUN loon; lout
LOUP half mask; Skidi Indian; river; fish
LOUR frown; lower; scowl
LOUT boor; bumpkin; dolt
LOVE affection; like; Cupid; Eros; zero
LOWA bush quail
LOWN calm; quiet; dolt
LOWY banlieue; suburb
LOXA pale bark: quinine
LUAU feast; cook-out
LUBA Bantu; Bashilange
LUBE machine oil
LUBS of Lubeck (city)
LUCE fish, pike; Adriana's servant; Henry (editor); Clare (writer, stateswoman)
LUCK chance; event; fortune
LUCY fleur-de-lis; fem. name; camera lucida; Lemonade — (Mrs. Hayes); — Stone, suffragist
LUDI Roman public games
LUDO game; pachisi
LUES syphilis
LUFF sail nearer wind
LUFT air: Ger.; -waffe
LUGE lodge; small sled
LUGH Celtic light god
LUIF loof
LUKE name; evangelist; Paul's companion; author Acts; -warm
LULA name; Louisa
LULL (temporary) quiet
LULU barn owl; name; Louisa
LUMP mass; swelling; barge; like it or — it
LUNA moon goddess; silver
LUNE crescent; hawk leash
LUNG air bladder; iron —
LUNN Sally (teacake)
LUNT light; smoke; Alfred (actor)
LUNY crazy (man)
LUOH white Nile Negro
LUPE Samoan fruit pigeon; Velez (actress)
LURA brain opening
LURE entice; decoy; trumpet
LURG marine worm
LURI Lake Albert Negro
LURK lie in wait; skulk
LUSH luxurious; drunkard
LUSK lazy (fellow)
LUST sensual desire
LUTE cement; bricklayer's tool; Apollo's musical instrument; jar ring
LUXE elegance; de —
LVII 57; Nero reign
LWOW Polish city
LXII 62; Nero reign
LXIV 64; Nero reign
LYAM bloodhound
LYAS geol. period
LYME bloodhound
LYNX wildcat; fur; constellation
LYON Fr. city; bean
LYRA glockenspiel; constellation
LYRE harp; constellation
LYSE undergo lysis

MAAL measure
MAAM madam
MAAN city
MAAS river
MAAT goddess

MAAZ Judah's descendant
MABA Negro; tree
MABI tree
MACE staff; spice; weight; coin
MACK coat
MACO cotton
MADE successful; created; constructed
MADI Negro
MADO fish
MAFU stable boy
MAGE magician
MAGG bird; chatter
MAGH month
MAGI caste; priests; wise men; kings of Orient; Melchior, Gaspar, Balthazar
MAHA monkey; deer
MAHE island
MAHI river
MAHR marriage settlement
MAIA goddess; crab; star
MAID servant; — of Orleans
MAIL coin; tax; armor; post
MAIM disfigure; mutilate
MAIN conduit; first; river; Spanish —
MAIS but: Fr.
MAJA crab
MAJO dandy; shrub
MAKE produce, create; cause; reach; type; identify
MAKI lemur
MAKO shark
MAKU Indian
MALA evil(s), wrong(s): Lat.; jaw
MALE man(ly); tribe
MALI caste; nation; river
MALL mallet; game; bird; assembly (place)
MALM limestone
MALO loincloth
MALT barley; beer
MAMA mother; goddess
MAMO bird
MANA magic power; Chinese letter
MAND grass
MANE hair; in the morning: Lat.
MANG bat (Kipling)
MANI peanut; prefix: hand
MANN man: Ger.; Horace (educator); Thomas (writer)
MANO grindstone; hand: It.
MANS Chinese aborigine; Le — (city; auto race)
MANU prefix: hand; Laws (Hindu code book)
MANX pert. to Isle of Man; cat
MANY numerous
MAON Nabal's home
MAPO goby (fish)
MARA demon; aborigine; Naomi
MARC residue; name; weight
MARD spoil
MARE blues; sea; moon area; horse; shanks' —
MARI prefix: sea; husband: Fr.; native
MARK sign; aim; stamp; money; observe; evangelist; easy —; — time
MARL clayey soil; fertilizer; fiber
MARM ma'am; school-
MARO ship name: Jap.
MARS war god; planet
MART market; nickname
MARU ship name: Jap.
MARX Karl (economist)
MARY female name; queen; sister of Lazarus, Martha; Virgin; Lady
MASA corn meal
MASH crush; brew; mixture; hammer; flirt
MASK disguise; screen; domino
MASS rite, service; bulk; mob; populace; assemble
MAST pole; brown; nuts
MASU salmon
MATA Hari (spy)
MATE companion; match; tea; check-
MATH mowing; monastery; school course
MATT lusterless
MATY (assistant) servant
MAUD plaid; rug; name; Muller; Whittier, Tennyson heroine
MAUI Polynesian hero
MAUL hammer; bruise; mangle
MAUN must
MAWK maggot
MAYA weaverbird; (Mexican) Indian; magic; Buddha's mother
MAYO Indian; physicians, clinic (Rochester)
MAZE labyrinth; daze; perplex
MAZO de la Roche (novelist; Jalna)
MAZY perplexing
MCII 1102
MCIV 1104; First Crusade, conquest of Acre
MCIX 1109
MEAD drink; meadow; lake; Margaret, anthropologist
MEAH wall tower
MEAL grain; pulverize; repast
MEAN intend; denote; base; unkind; middle
MEAT flesh; kernel; food
MEDA secret Indian sect
MEDB Conchobor's wife; goddess; Queen Mab
MEDE ancient Asia
MEDI prefix: middle
MEED reward
MEEK mild; submissive
MEER sea: Ger.
MEET encounter; face; combat; fulfill; fit
MEGA prefix: great
MEIN Chinese noodles; chow —
MEIO measure
MELA festival; prefix: black
MELD announce (score); merge
MELE Hawaiian poem; chant
MELL (beat with) hammer; teacher (Dickens)
MELT liquefy
MEMO note; statement
MEND repair; improve
MENE — tekel upharsin

(handwriting on the wall)
MENG mix
MENO prefix: month
MENS mind: Lat.
MENT falcon-headed god
MENU bill of fare
MEOU cat's cry; measure
MEOW cat's cry; measure
MERE fen; lake; boundary; war club; bare; only; simple; mother: Fr.
MERL blackbird
MERO grouper (fish)
MERU fabled mountain
MESA flat hill; oakwood color
MESE Greek mus. term
MESH net; netting; entangle
MESS banquet; meal; muddle; disorder; botch
META goal post; river
METE measure; allot
METZ city, former fort
MEUM carrotlike herb, spicknel; mine: Lat.
MEWL whimper; miaou
MEWS (royal) stables
MIAM hut
MIAN sir; title
MIAO Chinese aborigine
MIAS orang-utan
MICA isinglass (silicate)
MICE rodents (mouse)
MICH me: Ger.
MICK Irishman
MICO marmoset
MIDE Ojibway secret order
MIDI south(ern France)
MIEN manner; bearing; air
MIFF quarrel; offend
MIGG marble (duck)
MIII 1003
MIKE Michael; Mick; microphone
MILA measure
MILD calm(ly); soft; tame
MILE measure; distance; 320 rods, 1,609.3 meters
MILK nutritious fluid; sap; white; exploit; drain
MILL grind(er); quern; box; John Stuart (economist)
MILO name; grain; sorghum; Venus (Melos)
MILT spleen; fish gland; nickname
MIMA woman actor
MIME drama; act; actor; clown; smith (Nibelungs)
MIMI nickname; opera heroine
MINA weight; money; myna; watchman
MIND intellect; brain; memory; wish; mood; plan; tend; dislike
MINE possessive pronoun; dig; pit; rich source; explosive
MING Chin. dynasty
MINK weasel-like animal
MINO Jap. straw coat
MINT herb; menthol; bonanza; coin; — julep
MINX pert girl
MINY of a mine
MIRA star
MIRE bog; (stick in) mud
MIRK dark(ness)
MIRO tree; wood robin
MIRY boggy; filthy
MISE levy; stake; tax; — en scene
MISS fail(ure); omit; want; girl; maiden
MIST dim; haze; gray
MITE arachnid; parasite; small (coin)
MITT glove; hand
MITU curassow; bird
MITY parasite-infested
MIXE Mexican Indian
MIXY confusedly mixed
MLII 1052
MLIV 1054; Catholic Church schism
MLIX 1059
MMIV 2004
MMIX 2009
MOAB kingdom; language; Lot's son
MOAN lament
MOAT trench
MOBY — Dick (whale; Melville)
MOCK jeer; taunt; sham; — apple, turtle
MODE manner; fashion; drab; a la —
MOED festivals (Mishnah)
MOFF Caucasian silk
MOGO stone hatchet
MOHA millet; delusion
MOHO bird; honey eater
MOHR gazelle; bezoar
MOIL toil; trouble; spot
MOIO measure
MOJI Jap. seaport
MOJO tree; majagua; voodoo charm; Indian
MOKE donkey; dolt
MOKI N.Z. raft
MOKO Maori tattoo; -moko (lizard)
MOLA sunfish genus
MOLD fungus; humus; die, matrix; shape; mix
MOLE nevus; birthmark; pier; burrow(ing animal); Mossi language
MOLL Mary; girl; — Flanders (Defoe)
MOLT shed (hair)
MOLY magic herb (Homer)
MOME buffoon; -rath
MOMO owl
MONA monkey; Lisa (La Gioconda, da Vinci)
MONG among; barter
MONK ascetic; friar; bird; fish; spot; ferret
MONO monkey; Indian; prefix: single, one
MONS mountain: Lat.; city (Belgium; WW I battle)
MONT mountain: Fr.; — Blanc (peak, Alps)
MOOD humor; temper; verb form
MOON satellite; crescent; month; Diana; Cynthia; languish
MOOR heath; anchor; Moslem; Moroccan; blacka-
MOOT arguable; ring gauge
MOPE be dull, listless (person)
MORA default; short syllable; Spartan army; stool
MORE greater; additional; St. Thomas (Utopia)
MORG measure
MORN A.M.; dawn; East

MORO finch; P.I. Moslem tribe
MORS deity; death
MORT nickname; woman; salmon; the kill; dead: Fr.
MOSE Moses
MOSK Moslem temple; Masjid
MOSS bryophyte; lichen; green; rose; Hart (writer)
MOST greatest; almost
MOSY moldy; rotten
MOTA Moslem marriage
MOTE speck; particle
MOTH lepidopterous insect; -ball; -eaten; gypsy —; page (Shakespeare)
MOTI elephant (Kipling)
MOTO movement: It.; con —
MOTT clump of trees; James, Lucretia (abolitionists)
MOUE pout; grimace: Fr.
MOVE impel; shift; excite; act; depart(ure); play
MOWN cut down; trimmed
MOXA cautery wormwood
MOXO Arawakan Indian
MOYO measure
MOZA manservant
MOZO manservant: Sp.
MUAV geol. epoch
MUCH great (deal); far; — Ado (Shaks.)
MUCK (rid of) manure; mess
MUDD measure; doctor of Booth (Lincoln assassin)
MUFF handwarmer; bungle
MUGA silk; moth
MUID measure
MUIR moor (Scot.)
MULE equine hybrid; spinning jenny; slipper
MULK freehold land
MULL muslin; ointment; ponder, humus
MUMM mask; disguise
MUMP beg; mumble; cheat
MUND protection right
MUNG grass
MUNJ tough grass: twine
MUNT sash bar
MURA Brazil Indian
MURE thrust against wall
MURK (make) gloomy
MUSA banana genus
MUSE meditate; goddess
MUSH meal; hasty pudding; flattery; proceed!
MUSK odor; aromatic secretion (of deer, ox, etc.)
MUSO Chibchan Indian
MUSS mess; rumple; row
MUST be obliged to; necessity; new wine; stum; staleness; frenzy
MUTA mus. change; Moslem marriage
MUTE silent; dumb; muffle
MUTH measure
MUTT cur; stupid one; — and Jeff
MVII 1007
MXII 1012
MXIV 1014; Brian Boru defeats Danes
MXIX 1019
MYAL cultic
MYNA talking bird: grackle
MYRA name; ancient city
MYSA buffalo (Kipling)
MYST Greek priest
MYTH (religious) legend; fiction
MYXA plum (geiger) tree; sebesten
MYXO slime mold
NAAB river
NAAM distrain
NABK shrub
NABO shrub
NABU god; mountain
NACH after: Ger.
NAEL weight
NAGA snake
NAGY Hungarian premier
NAHA city
NAHE river; near: Ger.
NAIA cobra
NAID worm
NAIF naive; of true luster
NAIK leader
NAIL fasten(er); claw; seize; expose
NAIO tree
NAIR native
NAIS nymph
NAJA cobra
NALA hero
NAMA Hottentot; herb
NAME title; reputation; clan; cite
NANA nurse; Aztec hero's wife; Zola novel; dog: Peter Pan (Barrie)
NANE own; none
NAOS star
NAPA leather; wine region; city; river
NAPE neck back
NAPU ruminant
NARD plant; ointment
NARE Loki's son
NARK informer; tease
NARY not one
NASA space-travel agency
NASE promontory; nose: Ger.
NASH soft; humorist
NASI prince; patriarch
NAST cartoonist
NATA Nana's hero
NATE born
NATH star
NATO international (Western) alliance; treaty organization
NATR weight
NAUT sea mile
NAVE hub; church part
NAVY fleet; blue; tobacco; — yard
NAZE promontory
NAZI fascist; Hitlerite
NEAL male name; novelist
NEAP wagon pole; tide
NEAR close(ly); approach
NEAT tidy; trim; straight
NEBO wisdom god; Moab mountain (Moses died)
NECK body part; violin part; isthmus; pet
NEED compulsion; lack; want
NEEM tree; Margosa
NEEP turnip
NEER never; kidney
NEIF serf; native; fist
NEIL male name
NEIN no: Ger.
NEIR kidney
NEJD kingdom
NELL Ellen; Helen; Little — (Dickens

girl)
NEMA eelworm; prefix: thread
NEMO nobody: Lat.; prefix: glade; Captain (Verne hero)
NEON gas(eous) element; lamp
NEPA water scorpion; needle bug
NERA Tiber tributary
NERI Blacks: It.
NERO emperor; fiddler; Agrippine's son; Wolfe (Stout)
NESH soft; juicy; dainty
NESS cape; promontory; suffix
NEST (make a) home
NETE Greek mus. term
NETI eulalia (thatch grass)
NETT undeductible
NEUE new
NEUF nine, new: Fr.
NEVA river (Leningrad)
NEVE snow; firn
NEWS intelligence; tidings
NEWT salamander; eft
NEXT nearest; following
NGAI spiritual power
NGAN measure
NIAS Ind. Ocean island(er)
NIBS personage (VIP); in Peter Pan (Barrie)
NICE good; kind; pleasing; delicate; dainty; quimper color; Riviera port
NICK notch; moment; cheat; cut; Old — (devil); Carter (detective)
NIDE pheasant's nest
NIDI breeding places
NIEL alloy
NIFE earth's core
NIGH near(ly); direct
NIKE victory goddess (Samothrace); missile
NILE river; green, blue
NILL refuse; negate
NILS Bohr (physicist)
NIMB nimbus; halo
NINA goddess (Ea's daughter); ship (Pinta, —, Santa Maria); girl: Sp.
NINE number (of Muses); baseball team
NINO boy: Sp.
NIOG coconut palm
NIOU measure
NIPA palm; juice; mat; atap
NISH Yugo. city
NISI unless: Lat.
NITO climbing fern
NIUE Savage Island language
NIXY undeliverable mail
NIZY fool
NKVD Soviet secret police
NOAH patriarch (Ark builder)
NOAP bullfinch
NOBS knave, jack (card, cribbage)
NOCK notch (in bow)
NODE knob; knot; orbit point; joint
NODI knots; difficulties
NOEL Christmas; carol; — Coward
NOGG egg drink
NOIL combing (wool fiber)
NOIO noddy tern
NOIR black: Fr.; bet
NOIX edible gland
NOLA fem. name; time
NOLI — me tangere
NOLL Oliver (Cromwell); head; noddle
NOLO — contendere
NOME city (Alaska)
NONA fate goddess; prefix: ninth
NONE not one; 9th hour
NONO ninth: It.
NOOK corner; retreat
NOON midday; meal; acme
NORA Helmer (Ibsen heroine)
NORE Thames estuary
NORI seaweed food
NORM type; standard; integer
NORN demigoddess (Urth, Skuld, Verthandi)
NOSE proboscis; smeller; scent; search; front; touch; — out (defeat); -dive
NOSU Lolo; Chin. Caucasian
NOSY fragrant; prying
NOTA insect backs; — bene (N.B.)
NOTE sign; tone; fame; heed; memo; IOU; record; see
NOTT Norse night (Dag)
NOUN speech part; name; substantive
NOUP steep promontory
NOUS mind; reason; wit; we: Fr.
NOVA star: new, temporary
NOVE nine: It.
NOWT neat cattle; dolt
NOWY having curvature
NOXA harmful thing
NOYL fiber knot
NOZI of Yanan tribe
NUBA Nubian; Berberi language
NUBK shrub
NUCI prefix: nut
NUDA ctenophore; Beroida
NUDD Brythonic god, king
NUDE naked; art work; color
NUIT night: Fr.
NULL nil; void; code filler
NUMA Pompilius (Roman king)
NUMB deaden(ed); helpless
NUNS sisters; veiling, fabric
NUPE Nigeria Negro
NURL wood knot; to mill
NUSS nurse
NUZO Chibchan Indian

OAHU (Hawaiian) island
OAKS horse race; trees
OAKY oaklike
OARY oarlike
OAST kiln
OATH appeal; pledge; vow; curse
OATY full of oats
OBAN coin
OBED David's grandfather
OBEX brain matter
OBEY submit; comply
OBIA Ashanti religion
OBIT death notice
OBOE woodwind; chanter
OBOL 1/16 drachma (coin)
OBRA works: Sp.
OBUS howitzer shell
OCHA weight

OCHS Adolph (publisher)
OCRA vegetable; gumbo
OCTA prefix: eight
OCTO prefix: eight
ODAL land; vine
ODAX rock whiting (fish)
ODDS inequality; advantage; at —; -on
ODEA theaters; halls; galleries
ODED prophet or his father
ODEL vine; land ownership
ODER river
ODIC pert. to ode, od
ODIN one-eyed Norse god: Frigg's husband, Thor's father
ODIO hatred: It.
ODOR smell; repute
ODUM tree (iroko)
ODYL alleged force
OEIL eye: Fr.; — de boeuf
OENO prefix: wine
OESE bacteriologist's wire
OEUF egg: Fr.
OFFA Angles' hero (Beowulf)
OFFS cricket-field sides
OGAM Irish alphabet
OGEE arch; molding
OGLE gaze (amorously)
OGOR early Turkic man
OGPU Soviet police body
OGRE giant; monster
OGUM Irish alphabet
OHAD Simeon's son
OHEL Zerubabbel's son
OHIA timber tree; apple
OHIO Buckeye state
OHNE without: Ger.
OHOY ahoy; call
OILY unctuous; bland; suave
OIME alas
OINT apply oil
OISE Fr. river
OKAY approve; all right
OKEE evil spirit
OKEH all right; O.K.
OKET ounce
OKIA Moroccan money
OKIE migratory worker
OKRA vegetable; gumbo
OKRO plant; stew; soup; gumbo
OLAF (Vi)king
OLAM infinity; — haba (life after death)
OLAN Wang Lung's wife (Pearl Buck; The Good Earth)
OLAX tree
OLAY palm
OLEA shrub; olive
OLEO margarine
OLGA fem. name
OLIC chem. suffix
OLID smelly; fetid
OLIO medley; olla-podrida
OLLA jar; meat dish; -podrida (medley)
OLOR swan genus; Cygnus
OLPE oil flask; pitcher
OLPH bullfinch
OMAN Arabian state; sultanate; Muscat
OMAO thrush
OMAR Khayyam; tentmaker; caliph
OMEI Buddhist mountain
OMEN presage; portent; sign
OMER measure; sheaf; undertaker (Dickens)
OMIT leave out; neglect
OMNI prefix: all
OMRI king of Israel
OMSK Siberian city
ONAN Indian; Judah's son
ONCA ounce
ONCE one time; if ever; former(ly)
ONDE wave: Fr.: wavy (Her.)
ONDY wavy (Her.)
ONER ace; blow; individual
ONES individuals
ONLY alone; but; single; exclusively
ONTO upon; wise to
ONUS burden; duty
ONYM technical name (biol.)
ONYX cameo stone; quartz; gem
ONZA Sp. ounce (1/16 libra); coin
OOAA Hawaiian bird
OOFY rich (Eng. slang)
OOID egg-shaped
OONS mild oath
OONT camel; mole
OORD coin (double doit, ¼ stiver)
OOZE exude; slime; liquor
OOZY muddy; slimy
OPAH fish
OPAL birthstone (Oct.); girasol
OPEN undefended; plain; frank; -end; uncertain; bare; start; unfold; public; — sesame
OPIE Eng. painter
OPUS work
ORAD mouthward
ORAL spoken; of the mouth
ORAN seaport
ORAS Danish money
ORBY revolving
ORCA killer whale
ORDO order: Lat.; feast list
ORDU Turk. military district, army corps
OREB Midianite defeated by Gideon
OREL Russian City
OREN Judah's descendant
ORFE fish; yellow ide
ORGY carousal; Saturnalia, Bacchanalia
ORLE shield border; fillet
ORLO smooth surface; plinth
ORLY Paris airport
ORNA measure
ORNE measure; river (Caen)
ORRA oddly; laborer
ORYX antelope, gemsbok
OSAR glacial ridges; eskers
OSER dare: Fr.
OSID suffix: sugar
OSLO city (Norway); Christiania
OSSA bones; Mt. (Olympus)
OSTE prefix: bone
OTEA Great Barrier Island
OTHO Roman emperor
OTIC of the ear; auditory
OTIS bustard genus; general; inventor (elevator)
OTOE Sioux Indian
OTRA other: Sp.
OTRO other, another: Sp.

OTTO name; palindrome; perfume; Ger. ruler
OTUS giant slain by Apollo
OUCH exclamation
OUGH exclamation
OURS possessive pronoun
OUSE Great — (river)
OUST eject; discharge
OVAL egg-shaped; elliptic; arena
OVEN (bake in) stove; kiln
OVER above; across; beyond; again; surplus; ended; Roger and —
OVID poet (Metamorphoses); P.O.N.; Naso
OVIS sheep genus
OVUM germ cell; egg
OWEN (Welsh) name; socialist; zoologist
OWER debtor
OWSE tan liquor
OXAN gas
OXEA sponge spicule
OXEN bovines; draft animals
OXER hedge (fox hunting)
OXID oxygen compound
OXIM chem. compound
OXYL oxygen radical
OYER hearing (law); — and terminer
OYES court crier's cry
OYEZ court crier's cry
OZEM David's brother
OZNI Gad's son

PAAL measure
PAAN town
PAAR sand
PAAS Easter
PABA vitamin
PACA rodent
PACE step; speed; peace: It.
PACK bundle; cosmetic paste; cards; crowd; animal(s)
PACO alpaca
PACT agreement
PADI rice
PAGA rice
PAGE young attendant; call, summon; leaf
PAGO -Pago (city)
PAHA hill
PAHI ship
PAHO prayer stick
PAID recompensed; discharged; satisfied
PAIL bucket
PAIN ache; trouble; forfeit
PAIR couple; brace
PAIS country
PAJO prayer stick
PALA weight; antelope; vine; rice
PALE wan; pallid; ashy; picket; stake; beyond the —
PALI slope; coral parts; Buddhist language
PALL cloak; covering; cloy
PALM tree; measure; hand part; paddle; conceal; grease the —
PALO pole, wood: Sp.
PALP appendage; feeler
PALY wan; heraldic design
PANA city
PANE glass; panel
PANG agony
PANI madam: Polish
PANK weight
PANT gasp; yearn
PAON peacock blue
PAPA father; Pope; potato: Sp.; baboon; clay
PAPE bunting (bird)
PARA coin; weight; river; city (Belem)
PARC park; oyster farm: Fr.
PARD chum; leopard
PARE cut off; peel
PARI weight; prefix: equal
PARK (common) grounds; green; deposit; Hyde, Central, etc.
PARR young fish; skegger; Catherine (Henry VIII wife)
PARS part: Lat.
PART portion; duty; role; separate; split; go
PASA raisin
PASH hurl; smash
PASI low-caste Hindu
PASO measure
PASS opening; go through; by; license; abstention; condition; amatory gesture
PAST tense; ago; after
PATA painting; turban; sword
PATE head; paste
PATH track; route
PATO Muscovy duck
PATT stalemate(d)
PATU weapon
PAUL click; detent; Apostle; Bunyan; Revere; — VI (pope)
PAUN betel leaf
PAUP walk idly
PAVE cover firmly; — the way; jewel setting
PAVO peacock; constellation
PAVY peach
PAWA weight
PAWL click; detent; tent
PAWN chessman; pledge
PEAG money
PEAI medicine man
PEAK point; top; summit
PEAL ring; loud sound; fish
PEAN panegyric; praise; fur
PEAR fruit, tree
PEAT darling; turf; fuel
PEAU skin: Fr.
PEAY medicine man
PEBA armadillo; Indian
PECA coin
PECK measure; nip; bite; kiss
PECO black tea
PEDA pastoral staffs
PEDI prefix: foot
PEDO child
PEEK sly glance; pry; chirp
PEEL pare; tower; spade
PEEN hammer head
PEEP chirp; bird; peer slyly; Bo —; jeep
PEER gaze; equal; nobleman
PEET darling; turf; fuel
PEGA remora fish
PEGU Burmese language, city
PEHO morepork (bird)
PEKE (Pekinese) dog
PELA wax (secreting

insect)
PELE fire goddess
PELF booty; riches
PELO hair: It.
PELT skin; hurl; strike
PELU hardwood tree
PEND hang; be delayed
PENE (hammer) head
PENK minnow
PENN William (Penna. founder)
PENT confined; -house
PEON laborer
PEOR Bib. mountain
PEPO pumpkin; squash; melon; cucumber
PERA Istanbul district
PERE father, priest: Fr. — Goriot (Balzac)
PERI fairy; elf; beauty
PERK lift up; preen; cocky; percolate
PERM elec. unit; hair wave
PERN honey buzzard
PERO but: Sp.
PERT bold; lively; sandpiper
PERU country
PESA coin
PESO coin; Sp. dollar
PESS hassock
PEST plague; insect; nuisance
PETE strongbox; Peter
PETO wahoo (fish); Henry IV figure
PEUL Fulah (Sudanese)
PEUR fear: Fr.
PEVA Peru Indian
PEVY lumberman's hook
PFUI exclamation
PHAD star
PHAG comb. form: eating
PHAN measure
PHAO wolf (Kipling)
PHEW exclamation
PHIL nickname; Philip; prefix: loving
PHIT bullet sound
PHIZ physiognomy; face
PHON loudness measure
PHOO disgusting!
PHOS phosphorus
PHOT light unit
PHUD bullet sound; exclamation
PHUT (bullet) sound; OT people
PIAN tumor
PIAT magpie; antitank gun
PIAY medicine man
PICA type size; magpies
PICE coin; weight
PICI birds (woodpeckers)
PICK tool; scratch; choose; rob; eat; best
PICO peak; game; weight
PICT British aborigine
PIED variegated; Piper; -a-terre
PIEN arris (sharp edge)
PIER mole; dock; pillar
PIET magpie
PIFF bullet sound; exclamation
PIKA little chief hare
PIKE fish; weapon; pierce; highway; farmer, gamble; Zebulon (explorer; peak)
PIKI maize bread; pik
PIKY full of fish
PILE hair; heap (up); awn; atomic —
PILI nut; grass; hairs
PILL medicine tablet
PILY pilelike
PIMA Ariz. Indian; cotton
PIMP procurer; bawd; maquereau
PINA pineapple; silver cone
PINE tree; conifer; evergreen; yearn; mourn
PING (bullet, striking) sound
PINK color (red); ship; cut; hunter's coat; carnation; in the — (healthy)
PINO pine tree
PINT measure
PINY pinelike; peony
PION dig; excavate
PIOT magpie
PIPA toad; measure
PIPE tube; flute; cask (measure); -dream; — down
PIPI astringent; mollusk
PIPY tubular; weepy
PIRN reed; bobbin; nose ring
PIRO Tanoan Indian
PIRR wind gust; whiz; gull
PISA city (leaning tower)
PISE building material
PISH reject; nonsense!
PISK nighthawk
PISO weight
PIST attention!; track
PITA fiber; flax; hemp; brocket (deer)
PITH marrow; kernel; gist
PITO fiber; flax; hemp; brocket (deer)
PITT statesman (Commoner, Chatham); diamond
PITY sympathy; mercy
PIUS Pope: X (St.; Sarto); XI (Ratti); XII (Pacelli)
PIXY impish sprite
PLAN design; scheme
PLAP fall loudly
PLAT plait; map; plot; fish
PLAY frolic; act; drama; contend; sport; game
PLEA excuse; prayer; request; pretext; allegation
PLEB freshman cadet; common man
PLED pleaded
PLET three-lash whip
PLEW beaver skin
PLEX form a network
PLIM swell; swollen
PLOD trudge; drudge
PLOP sound of fall
PLOT tract; ground; press (soap); scheme; intrigue
PLOW implement; till; cut; stars
PLOY make column; frolic; coup
PLUG stop(per); plod; shoot; spark —; horse; praise
PLUM fruit (damson; greengage); tree; raisin; choice job
PLUP sound of (soft) fall
PLUS and; more; extra; — fours
PNYX Greek voting site
POBS porridge; pap
POCK pustule
POCO slightly; old-clothes man
PODA suffix: foot
PODE suffix: foot
POEM verse creation
POET writer of verse;

artist
POGO springy stick
POGY menhaden; trout
POHA gooseberry (jelly)
POIL raw silk thread
POKE thrust; prod; pry; sack; potter; herb
POKU antelope
POKY shabby; dull; bonnet
POLA Yugo. city (Pulj)
POLE rod; tail; terminal: axis, battery; — Star; Polish, Polack
POLK Cossack regiment; James Knox (President)
POLL head; register, survey; cut off; Mary; parrot; vote
POLO game; Marco —
POLT knock; trump; club
POLY herb; Teucrium; prefix: many
POMA rosa (rose apple)
POME fruit; ball; globe
POMO California Indian
POMP pageant(ry); splendor
POND lake; pool; weight
PONE corn bread; writ
PONG sound; improvise
PONS bridge: Lat.; — asinorum; Lily (singer)
PONT ferry(boat); bridge: Fr.
PONY small equine (Shetland, polo); glass (1 oz.); translation
POOA pua hemp
POOD weight
POOF exclamation
POOH pshaw! — Bah (Mikado); Winnie (bear; Milne)
POOK hobgoblin; disk
POOL pond; puddle; game; stake; fund; Thames
POON tree (mastwood)
POOP deck; cabin; dickey; exhaust; tire
POOR indigent; scanty; feeble; lowgrade; lean; ill; hapless; cod (fish)
POOT disgusting!
POPE pontiff; Holy Father; — Joan (game); Alexander (poet); bird
PORE gaze; ponder; opening
PORK meat; swine; — barrel
PORO Sierra Leone secret society
PORR push; poke; kick
PORT harbor; haven; wine; blue-red; left side; tune; demeanor
PORY porous; permeable
POSE posture; affectation; baffle; propound
POSH slush; elegant
POST pillar; advertise; mil. station; mail; inform; record
POSY flower; nosegay; poem
POTE poker; stick
POTT paper size; editor (Dickens)
POUF puff; ottoman; bang!
POUL Russ. coin
POUR (make) flow; for: Fr.; emit; — le merite
POUS measure
POUT sulk(iness); fish
POWE weight
PRAD horse
PRAH canoe
PRAM carriage
PRAO canoe
PRAT buttock
PRAU swift canoe
PRAY ask; beseech; please
PREP prepare; student
PRES near: Fr.
PRET measure
PREX (college) president
PREY victim; pillage; booty
PRIG precisian; steal; thief; fop
PRIX price: Fr.; — fixe (table d'hôte)
PROA Malay outrigger
PROD reminder; goad; horse; prodigy
PROG (steal) food; forage
PROM dance, ball (college)
PROO slow up! (horse call)
PROP support; shore; theater equipment
PROW ship's bow; stem; beak
PRUT exclamation; river
PSHA exclamation
PTAH god
PUAN latex
PUCA goblin; specter
PUCE flea: Fr.; eureka red
PUCK sprite; Robin Goodfellow; Shaks. character; hockey disk
PUDU Chilean deer
PUFF blow; pastry; distend; hair roll; adder; powder —
PUGH pshaw!; fish prong
PUJA worship; festival
PUKA rare N.Z. tree
PUKE cloth; vomit
PUKU Afr. antelope
PUKY nauseated
PULE cheep; whimper
PULI coins
PULK (Cossack) regiment
PULL drag; influence
PULP pith; tissue; paper; magazine
PULU tree fern
PULY whining; complaining
PUMA cougar; catamount
PUME Yarura(n language)
PUMP force; draw out; slipper
PUNA high Andes; wind; sickness (soroche)
PUND weight
PUNG (drive) box sleigh; mah jong term
PUNK touchwood; tinder; conch; tramp; bad
PUNO Pacific trade wind; city (Peru)
PUNT (propel) flatboat; kick; bet
PUNY weak; slight
PUPA chrysalis; snail; instar
PURE unmixed; chaste; sheer; free; Simon —
PURI Indian yellow
PURL knitting stitch; beer; murmur; spin; swirl
PURR cat's sound
PURU of Arawakan
PUSH shove; thrust; strive; -button
PUSS cat; lip; face

PUTT golf stroke
PUUD weight
PUXY ill-tempered
PUYA pineapple genus
PYAL veranda
PYAT magpie
PYET magpie
PYIC purulent
PYLA brain opening
PYLE Ernie (journalist); Howard (artist)
PYOT piebald; chatty
PYRE funeral pile, fire
PYRO prefix: fire, fever

QAID alcaide
QAIS island
QERE read(ing substitute)
QERI read(ing substitute)
QKKT chess move
QOPH Heb. K, Q, 100
QQKT chess move
QUAB fish
QUAD type; four; -rangle, -ruplet, etc.
QUAE — vide (which see)
QUAG morass
QUAI pier
QUAN money
QUAR fill; choke
QUAS sour beer, cider (Russian)
QUAT squat
QUAY pier
QUEI measure
QUID cud; essence; pound; — pro quo
QUIP witty sally; jest
QUIT abandon; yield; stop; free
QUIZ test; odd one; hoax
QUNG So. Afr. Bushman
QUOD prison; — erat demonstrandum (Q.E.D.)

RAAB river
RAAD assembly; fish
RABA river
RABI crop; physicist
RACA reproach; fool
RACE run; contest; people; speed; Cape —; rat-
RACK framework; clouds; gait; torture
RACY smart
RADA legislature
RADE elated
RAFF Raphael
RAFT collection; float
RAGA state of nirvana
RAGE fury; storm; fad
RAGI grass
RAHU demon
RAIA ottman; fish
RAID attack; foray
RAIK weight; measure
RAIL bird; scold; paling
RAIN shower; scratch; — check
RAIP rope
RAIS chief (Nepalese)
RAJA prince; fish
RAKE incline; tool; collect; roue; —'s Progress
RAKH hayfield
RAKI spirits
RAKU -ware
RALE rattling sound
RALO measure
RAMA Indian; Vishnu incarnation; bull (Kipling)
RAME branch
RAMI branches
RAMP inclined way; rear
RANA frog; prince; Aegir's wife
RAND border; ridge; strip; So. Afr. gold mine
RANG sounded
RANI princess; wife
RANK luxuriant; gross; fetid; grade; array
RANN verse; stanza; kite (Kipling)
RANT scold; rave; frolic
RANZ — des vaches (Alpine melodies)
RAPE herb; ravish
RAPT engrossed; rapture
RARA — avis (rare bird)
RARE underdone; thin; uncommon
RASA essence; tabula —
RASE rub; demolish
RASH hasty; careless
RASP grate; file
RATA tree; chestnut; rate; pro —
RATE censure; ratio; charge; estimate; rank; tax
RATH chariot; fort; temple; early; mome-
RATI weight
RATS bah!
RAVE rant, rage; enthusiasm; rod
RAVI tribesman
RAYA broadbill
RAZE scrape; demolish
RAZZ chaff; ridicule
READ interpret; learn; study; understand
REAL coin; true; genuine; very
REAM 500 (paper) quantity; bevel; enlarge
REAP cut; harvest
REAR back; raise; — admiral
REBA weight
RECK heed; concern
RECT element (philos.)
REDD make tidy; free of; scold
REDE interpret; counsel
REDO make over
REED woody grass; pipe; mouthpiece; Walter (doctor, hospital)
REEF shoal; lode; reduce sail
REEK cloud; exude; smell
REEL wind(er); dance; waver; sway
REEM ox; unicorn
REFT cleft; rift; deprived
REIM oxhide strap
REIN strap; check; direct; kidney
REIS money; (boat) captain; effendi (state officer)
REJA screen, grille: Sp.
REKE rick; pile
REKI Baluchistan nomad
RELY trust; depend
REMI Gaul people; prefix: oar
REMS river
RENA rockfish
REND tear; rupture; bark trees
RENI It. painter; prefix: kidney
RENO Nev. city ("biggest little"; divorce, gambling)
RENT torn; schism; let, lease; payment, income
REPP silk or wool fabric
RESE shake; rush
RESH Heb. 20th letter, 200; plant

REST pause; stop; peace; prop; stay; rely; mus. sign; remainder; set; found
RETE network
REUS defendant: Lat.
REVE (muse in) dream: Fr.
REVS rotations per minute
RHEA Cybele, mother of the gods; Gaea's daughter; Cronos's wife; ostrich; satellite; grass
RHIA China grass
RHIN Rhine: Fr.
RHOB juice; jelly
RHUM alcoholic drink
RHUS sumac genus
RIAL coin
RICE cereal; use ricer; Elmer (playwright)
RICH wealthy; vivid; full; fragrant; fat
RICK pile (up); haystack
RIDD Lorna Doone's rescuer
RIDE be borne; float; endure; manage; mount; journey
RIEL Canadian (Indian) rebel
RIEM oxhide strap
RIEN nothing: Fr.; — ne va plus
RIER oil cask (whaling)
RIFE abundant; prevalent
RIFF Berber; Kabyle; ripple
RIFI Riffs
RIFT split; divide; cleft
RIGA Latvian city, gulf
RIGI Swiss mountain
RIIS Jacob (journalist)
RIKK tambourine
RILE irritate; vex
RILL (run in a) brook
RILY turbid; irritated
RIMA fissure; breadfruit; child heroine (Hudson)
RIME frost; (make) rhymes; chink; rung
RIMU red pine; imou pine
RIMY frosty; rhyming
RIND bark; peel; Vali's mother, Odin's wife
RINE hemp; ditch
RING gird; arena; prizefighting; gang; atomic order; sound (bell); Vienna landmark; Nibelungen cycle (Wagner)
RINK skating arena
RIOT tumult; success; — act, squad
RIPA river bank
RIPE mature; fit; tipsy
RIRE to laugh: Fr.
RISE climb; grow(th); begin; emerge(nce); thrive; retort
RISK peril; hazard; subject of insurance
RISP metal bar
RISS glaciation stage
RIST engrave; scratch
RITA cosmic order (Vedic); Rio —; fem. name
RITE ceremony; liturgy
RIVA shore: It.
RIVE tear; split; — droite (right bank), — gauche (left bank)
RIVO stream: It.
RKKT chess move
ROAD (rail)way; track; anchorage
ROAM wander
ROAN horse; yellow-red
ROAR loud sound; laugh
ROBE gown; mantle; Douglas novel
ROCH Saint (14th cent.)
ROCK stone; Gibraltar; cliff; staunch support; diamond; candy; sway, lull; — the boat
RODA Nile island
RODD crossbow
RODE anchor rope; measure; was borne; cross
RODI Medit. island
ROED filled with roe
ROER hunting gun
ROEY of mottled grain
ROIL disturb; muddy; vex
ROJO redskin: Sp.
ROKA mafura (tree)
ROKE vapor; smoke
ROKY misty; hoarse
ROLE actor's part
ROLL wrap; trill; drumbeat; rotate; list; bank-
ROMA Rome: It.
ROME city (Eternal); Church; beauty (apple)
ROMI Gypsy wife
ROMP girl; gambol, frolic
RONE brushwood
RONG Sikkimese language
ROOD crucifix; measure
ROOF cover; house; top
ROOK bird; cheat; dupe; chessman (tower)
ROOL crumple; ruffle
ROOM space; apartment; lodge; — and board
ROON treasure; darling
ROOS Ger. painter
ROOT underlying source; rhizome; base; dig; applaud; plant; eradicate
ROPE cord; cable; noose; bind; chain
ROPY viscous; stringy
RORI Bantu tribe
RORY O'More (Irish novel)
ROSA shrub genus; name; sub —
ROSE stood up; got up; flower; tree; wood; red; pink; window; Abie's Irish —; Eng. emblem
ROSS rough bark; seal; island; navigator; Harold (editor)
ROSY blushing; optimistic
ROTA roster; curia tribunal; a round; hurdy-gurdy
ROTE surf noise; routine
ROTI roasted: Fr.
ROTL Afr. weight
ROTO ragged: Sp.; printing
ROUB measure
ROUD fish
ROUE dissolute man; rake
ROUP a cold; hoarseness
ROUT defeat; tumult; mob; the brant;

snare
ROUX (soup, sauce) thickener; physician
ROVE wander; ramble; draw through an eye
ROWY streaked
ROXY name: Roxana; Rothafel (impresario); theater
RYOT Indian peasant
RQKT chess move
RSVP please reply: Fr.
RUAY weight
RUBE Reuben; rustic; yokel
RUBY gem; corundum; bird; name; Oswald killer
RUCK crowd; rake; wrinkle
RUDD carplike fish
RUDE rough; boorish; vulgar
RUER repenter
RUFF collar; bird; fish; plait; trump
RUGA stomach membrane
RUGG pull
RUHR Ger. industrial area
RUIN destroy; destruction; violate
RUKH fabled bird; jungle
RULE law; guide; reign; method; control; — Britannia; ruler; line
RULL to wheel; trundle
RUMB compass point
RUMP sirloin part; remnant; — Parliament
RUNE Teutonic sign; magic
RUNG wheel spoke; hooped
RUNT small animal, man
RUPA body form (Buddhism)
RURU N.Z. morepork
RUSA deer; sambar; grass; oil
RUSE trick; deceit; slip
RUSH haste(n); attack; red (mace); cattail
RUSK bread; biscuit; Dean (statesman)
RUSS Russian; Slav
RUST oxidize; corrode; inaction; reddish-brown
RUTA herb genus; rue
RUTE measure
RUTH pity; grief; name; OT book, heroine (Moabitess); wife of Boaz
RYAL coin
RYAN peak, Idaho
RYAZ coin
RYEL coin
RYME water surface
RYND millstone support
RYPE ptarmigan

SAAH measure
SAAL hall: Ger.
SAAN Bushmen
SAAR river; region
SABA fiber; kingdom; island
SABE know
SACK dismiss; plunder; wine; bag; gown; sad —
SACO weight; river
SADD dam; waste matter
SADE letter; Marquis
SADH holy man
SADI poet
SADO carriage; island; river
SADR tree
SAER tenant
SAFE secure; box
SAFI Afghan
SAGA legend; story; goddess; weight
SAGE herb; wise; Russell — (financier)
SAGO palm; starch
SAGY wise
SAHA measure
SAHH measure
SAHO language
SAHU spiritual body
SAIC Near East ketch
SAID before-mentioned; Port —; city; name
SAIL canvas; rigging; journey; travel
SAIM grease
SAIN consecrate; tree
SAIR savor
SAIS groom; city; know: Fr.
SAKA era; Scythians
SAKE purpose; beer
SAKI monkey; Munro
SALA dining room: Sp.
SALE bargain; auction; willow; salted: Fr.
SALM star
SALP marine animal
SALT sodium chloride, NaCl; sailor; season; — away; — Lake City; — Sea
SAMA fish; trance-inducing music
SAME identical
SAMH bread plant
SAMP maize
SANA Yemen's capital; fiber
SAND grit; silica; polish, smooth; red-yellow; George, novelist (Dudevant)
SANE rational
SANG Hindu group; herb; weight; did sing
SANK descended
SANS without: Fr.; — culotte (radical); — gene
SAPA grape juice
SAPH giant (Philistine)
SAPO soap; toadfish
SARA native
SARD carnelian; gem; Sardinian
SARG Toni (puppeteer)
SARI Hindu garment
SARK Channel island
SART Iranian Turk
SARY sorry
SASA fencer's cry
SASH casement; scarf; belt
SASS sauce
SATE gratify; glut
SATI queen of the gods
SAUD ibn (king)
SAUF safe: Fr.; — conduit
SAUK Indian; Mont. river
SAUL tree; king (son of Kish); — of Tarsus (Paul)
SAUM weight
SAUR prefix, suffix: lizard
SAVA Yugo. river
SAVE rescue; avoid; lay by; but; — face
SAWK measure
SAWN sawed; cut
SAXE Saxony; blue
SAYA outer skirt
SCAB crust; strikebreaker

SCAD fish; large amount
SCAN examine; measure poetry
SCAP skull
SCAR rock; cicatrix; mar(k); fish
SCAT buffet; scatter; begone!; tax; skat
SCAW promontory
SCIO prefix: sky
SCOB fabric defect
SCON teacake
SCOP bard; poet
SCOT Celt; Highlander; taxi; — free
SCOW flat-bottomed boat
SCUD run fast; wind-driven clouds; skim; flea
SCUG squirrel: Brit.
SCUM dross; refuse; rabble
SCUP pan fish; porgy
SCUR horn tissue
SCUT rabbit's tail; fur
SEAH measure
SEAL otarian; pinniped; fur; fasten; brown; ratify; stamp
SEAM fold; crevice; join; ornament; measure
SEAN John
SEAR burn; dried up; gun-lock catch
SEAT chair; fundament; site; membership; install; hot —
SEBA Bib. country; Ham's grandson
SEBI prefix: tallow
SECH such
SECK unprofitable (rent)
SECT group; denomination
SEED fertile germ; progeny; decay; plant; extract
SEEK ask; try; hunt
SEEL shut eyes of; blind
SEEM look; appear
SEEN observed
SEEP ooze; small spring
SEER prophet
SEGO herb; bulb; lily; Utah state flower
SEHR very: Ger.
SEID tribe; lord; chief; Mohammed's descendant
SEIK Hindu sectarian
SEIL rope: Ger.
SEIM Polish assembly
SEIN poss. pronoun, be, being: Ger.
SEIP seep; ooze
SEIR Bib. mountain (Hor), Edom (Esau's home)
SEIS six: Sp.
SEIT measure
SEJM Polish assembly
SELA Dead Sea town
SELF identity; ego; one
SELL vend; betray; persuade; hoax; — short
SEME (sprinkling) pattern
SEMI half
SEMO Sancus (deity); Dius Fidius
SEND transmit; dispatch; propel; swing; enthrall
SENN Swiss herdsman
SEPS snake; lizard
SEPT social unit; screen; seven: Fr.
SERA antitoxins; blood parts; whey; evening: It.
SERB Servian; Yugo(slav)
SERE wither(ed); Negroid
SERF slave; peasant
SERI betel; Indian
SERO prefix: thin; late pupil
SERT Sp. painter
SESI black-fin snapper
SESS soap frame bar
SETA caterpillar's hair; spine
SETH banker; Adam's son; Osiris' evil brother
SETI river; pharaoh
SETT tool; paving stone
SEVE wine delicacy: Fr.
SEWN stitched
SEXT canonical hour (noon); organ stop; sixth
SEXY sexually appealing
SHAB paltry guy
SHAD fish
SHAG hair; tobacco; bird; rascal; dance step
SHAH ruler
SHAM deceit; fake
SHAN Thai
SHAP silk yarn
SHAT saline lake
SHAW thicket; pshaw; playwright (George Bernard)
SHAY chaise; carriage
SHEA tree; butter
SHED cast off; abandon; drop; hut; shelter
SHEE Irish fairyfolk
SHEM Noah's son; Semite
SHEN Christian God (China)
SHER tiger
SHEW show: Brit.; -bread
SHIH weight; measure
SHIK Arabian Turkoman
SHIM leveling slip; shingle; knife
SHIN leg, calf front; run; climb
SHIP vessel; send; — of state
SHIR cook; gathers; tiger
SHIV bit of husk; fluff; blade
SHLU Moroccan Berber
SHOA Abyssinian
SHOD wearing shoes
SHOE foot covering; crakow; wheel drag; tire
SHOG shake; jog
SHOO scare away; begone!
SHOP store; buy; buying place; talk —; window-
SHOQ tree (tanning); chogak
SHOR salt lake; Tatar tribe
SHOT missile; pellet; guess; range; marksman; film record; long —; big —
SHOU Tibetan deer
SHOW exhibit(ion); reveal; appear(ance); 3rd place; no — (airline term)
SHRI glorious; holy; Lakshmi (goddess)
SHUA Abraham's son
SHUE Tibetan deer
SHUL synagogue
SHUN avoid; abstain (from)
SHUT close; refine
SIAK latex
SIAL earth's outer part

SIAM Thailand; Anna's king (The King and I)
SICE number 6 on die
SICK urge (dog); ill; weak
SIDA herb; shrub; hemp
SIDE region; part(y); oblique; aspect; support; lateral
SIDI Moslem title; Negro
SIDY pretentious
SIEG victory: Ger.
SIER pintado (fish)
SIFT screen; separate; bolt
SIGH lament(ing sound)
SIGN symbol; signal; subscribe; ratify; hire
SIKA Jap. deer
SIKH Hindu soldier
SILK fiber; thread; -worm
SILL beam (door, window)
SILO fodder pit; ensile
SILT sediment; scum; drift
SIMA igneous rock
SIME monkey
SIMI Dodecanese isle
SIMP simpleton
SINA drug; mountain (Moses)
SIND river; Pakistan province; are: Ger.
SINE math. ratio; without: Lat.; — qua non; — die
SING vocalize; warble; tell
SINH hyperbolic function
SINK fall; droop; conceal; basin
SINN — Fein (Irish society)
SINO prefix: Chinese
SIOL great Irish clan
SION purple seaweed; Zion
SIPO liana
SIRE father; beget; king
SIRI betel
SIRS gentlemen
SISE six (dice)
SISH slushy ice
SISI porkfish
SISS hiss; shame!; girl
SIST stay; delay; summon
SITA Ramachandra's wife (Sanskrit Ramayana)
SITE location; scene
SITO prefix: grain
SIUM water parsnip
SIVA Hindu deity; cosmic dancer (Nataraja)
SIVE sickle; knife
SIZE bulk; quality; glue; filler; — up
SIZY viscous
SIZZ hiss(ing sound)
SKAG boat; keel part
SKAL health toast
SKAT card game; star
SKEE ski
SKEG keel part; plum; tear
SKEN squint
SKEO fisherman's hut
SKEP basket; measure; beehive
SKEW twist; swerve; distort(ed); slant(ing)
SKEY yoke bar
SKID clog; slide; — Road, Row
SKIL candlefish; beshow
SKIM scoop off; scud; brush
SKIN hide; pelt; peel; fleece; — and bones
SKIP jump; escape; mess; captain; -tracer
SKIR fly; scurry; skim
SKIT comedy sketch; jest
SKIV sovereign (coin)
SKUA bird; great —; jaeger
SKUN skinned
SKYE isle; dog, terrier
SKYR sour curdled milk
SKYT move fast; dart; slip
SLAB slice; road
SLAG dross; lava
SLAM bang; criticize; grand —
SLAP strike; — bang
SLAT lath; slab; sheep's hide; flap
SLAV Eastern European
SLAW cabbage
SLAY kill; overwhelm
SLEB nomadic Arab
SLED vehicle, snow or ice
SLEE sly
SLEW killed; twist; swamp; large number
SLEY weaver's reed
SLID glided; slipped
SLIM slight; scanty; sly; slenderize
SLIP slide; err(or); escape; pier; leash; garment; memo; cut
SLIT cut; slash; opening
SLOB slovenly one
SLOE blackthorn; plum; blueblack
SLOG hit (hard); slug; slam
SLOO swamp
SLOP slush; gush; mash
SLOT (cut) opening; bolt; deer; track; — machine
SLOW dilatory; tardy; inert; boring; hinder
SLUB twisted wool roll
SLUE swamp; twist; lot
SLUG snail; idle; metal spacer; small drink; bullet; strike
SLUM dilapidated district
SLUR pass over; mumble; defame; stigma; glide (mark)
SLUT slattern; harlot
SMEE pintail duck; widgeon; Peter Pan pirate
SMEW merganser; duck
SMIT struck; destroyed
SMOG fog and smoke; haze
SMUG tidy; neat; priggish
SMUR mist; cloud
SMUT soot; coal dust; plant disease; obscenity
SNAB hill part; girl
SNAG stump; cut; obstacle; tangle
SNAP seize; break; click; shut; photo; vigor; easy task; — out
SNED lop; prune
SNEE cut; snick(er) —

SNIB escape logging work
SNIG chop off; drag; pilfer
SNIP cut; shred; slip
SNOB social climber; game
SNOD trim; snug; plausible
SNOT wick end; blow nose
SNOW ice crystals; white hair; cocaine; — goose; TV spots
SNUB rebuke; slight; stumpy
SNUG cozy; trim; Shaks. character
SNUP snap up cheaply
SNUR snort
SOAK absorb; sot
SOAP cleanser; detergent; money; soft —; -box; — opera
SOAR fly high; glide
SOBK evil deity
SOCK beat; wind cone; stocking
SOCO heron; bittern
SODA carbonated water; Vichy; drink; sodium compound (bicarbonate)
SODI Gaddiel's father (spy)
SOFA couch; divan
SOFT giving way; easy; light(ly); mild; tractable
SOGA grass rope: Sp.; Bantu
SOHO exclamation; London district
SOIA food plant
SOIE silk
SOIL earth, ground; land; stain; pollute
SOIR evening: Fr.
SOJA bean; Glycine
SOKA drought blight
SOKE jurisdiction
SOLA herb (topee source); alone; holla!
SOLD vended; persuaded; cheated
SOLE pelma (bottom); flatfish; single; only
SOLI single performances; prefix: sun, alone
SOLO song; (fly) alone
SOMA vine; sacred drink; body
SOME various; any; somewhat; part
SONG poem (music); pittance
SOOK Moslem market; hog call
SOOL pull, tousle about
SOON promptly; willingly
SOOT powdery carbon smudge
SOPH 2nd year student
SOPT Dog Star; Isis
SORA bird; rail
SORB wild apple; Slav
SORE painful; vexed; sensitive; deer
SORI clusters; spores
SORS lot: Lat.; divination
SORT type; kind; quality; classify
SORY vitriolic earth
SOSH jag; drunk; dash
SOSO middling; passably
SOSS hog call for food
SOTO Hernando de (explorer)
SOTS yeast
SOUD pay
SOUF sigh
SOUK Moslem market
SOUL spirit; inspirer; force; psyche; person
SOUP broth; stew; — and fish; duck —; step (up); explosive; fog
SOUR acid(ify); tart; disagreeable
SOUS coins; under: Fr.
SOWN scattered; seeded
SOYA bean; dill; fennel
SPAD nail
SPAE prophecy
SPAN stretch; team; measure; dog
SPAR mineral; mast; gaff; box
SPAT mollusk; gaiter; snap; tiff
SPAY deer; castrate
SPEC speculation
SPED hastened
SPEE Graf — (ship, admiral)
SPES (goddess of) hope
SPET spit; barracuda
SPEW eject; scatter; gush
SPEX spectacles
SPEY river
SPIN whirl; twist; aerial stunt; — a yarn
SPIR prefix: coiled
SPIT land point; rod; impale; expectorate; — and image
SPIV slacker: Brit.
SPOT stain; point, place; fish; small amount; espy
SPRY nimble; brisk; smart
SPUD scrape(r); potato; dig
SPUN twisted; whirled
SPUR point; good; kick; otter track; ridge
SPUT boiler plate
STAB pierce; trial
STAD town
STAG deer; men's party; warn
STAR sun; heavenly body; asterisk; hummingbird; excel
STAT photocopy
STAY rope; fasten; prop, endure; wait; remain; stop(ping); — put
STEM shaft; trunk; stock; axis; dam; check; derive; turn skis
STEN weight; gun
STEP pace; foot rest; rank; act; dance; crush; — on it
STER suffix: agent
STET let it stand!
STEV stanza
STEW boil; steep; hash; worry; study; oyster bed
STIB sandpiper (dunlin)
STIR agitate; rouse; ado; jail
STLO WW II battle site
STOA portico; poikile (Zeno)
STOD Danish speech
STOF measure
STOG stall in mud
STOM prefix: mouth
STOP halt; discontinue; arrest; close; instrument part; period

STOT stumble; stutter
STOW pack; hide; hold; skiing resort
STUB stump; penpoint; short, stocky; extirpate; ticket part; bump
STUD breeding stock; knob; stump; dot; poker
STUM grape juice; must; renew wine
STUN stupefy; daze
STYX Hades river; nymph: daughter of Oceanus, Tethys
STUT horsefly
STYE eyelid swelling
SUAN — pan: Chin. abacus
SUCH of this kind; same
SUCK draw in; bleed; drink
SUDD Nile waste matter; dam
SUDS lather; froth; beer
SUER prosecutor; suitor
SUET hard fat
SUEZ canal; seaport
SUFI mystic ascetic
SUGI Jap. cedar
SUIT costume; card set, legal action; please; (out)fit
SUJI wheat; semolina
SUKE Susan; teakettle
SUKU Bantu
SUKY Susan; teakettle
SULA genus; booby; gannet
SULD measure
SULK mope; be sullen
SULU Moro
SUMO Ulvan
SUMP dig pit; tank; cistern
SUNG chanted; Chin. dynasty
SUNK immersed; overcome
SUNN hemp: fiber plant
SUNT babul: gum tree; pod; were: Lat.
SUPA P.I. tree: lamp oil
SUPE stage extra; supercharge
SURA Koran section; deva
SURD irrational; mute
SURE safe; firm; certain
SURF swell of sea; foam
SURT Frey's slayer
SUSA Elam city (Esther story)
SUSI fine cotton
SUSU blind dolphin; Congo
SUSY name: Susan; Susanna
SUUM hum; — cuique
SUZY name: Susanna
SVAN Caucasian
SWAB mop; lout
SWAD mass; soldier
SWAG bag; booty; sway; sag
SWAM floated
SWAN constellation; dive; — song
SWAP barter; exchange
SWAT hit (hard); river, state (Pakistan); sultan of — (Ruth)
SWAY oscillate; veer; rule
SWIG gulp; hoist; tackle
SWIM move in water; float; teem
SWIZ swindle
SWOB sponge; wipe; mop
SWOP trade
SWOT hard work; grind; hit
SWOW I — (oath)
SWUM swim participle
SYCE groom
SYED Moslem chief
SYKE fountain (Her.)
SYNC synchronize
SYPE ooze
SYRA Aegean island
SYRT quicksand
SYUD Moslem prince; title

TAAL lake; volcano; language
TAAR tambourine
TABI sock
TABU forbidden
TACE steel splint
TACK hook; rope; course; attach
TACT diplomacy; perception
TAEL weight; coin
TAEN taken
TAFT President; Republican; rower's seat; — Hartley Act
TAHA bird
TAHR goat
TAIL end; cue; follow; high-
TAIN plate
TAIR goat
TAIT marsupial
TAJO trench
TAKE acquire, seize; scene part; receipts
TAKT beat(s); tempo
TAKU Indian
TAKY taking
TALA tree; basin; ruin
TALC soapy mineral
TALE story; — of Two Cities; count
TALI gold piece; weight
TALK speak; converse; conference; empty words; dialect; — turkey
TALL high; incredible
TAMA Indian
TAME gentle; subdue
TAMP fill up; pound down; tool
TANA shrew; rabbi; police station; lake (Blue Nile)
TANE Polynesian god
TANG spur; flavor; sound; seaweed; dynasty
TANH math. term
TANK basin; store; war vehicle; panzer
TANO Indian
TAOS Indian
TAPA bark; cloth
TAPE band; tie; Indian; record; red —; ticker —
TAPS lights-out signal; bugle call
TAPU taboo
TARA fern; goddess; palm
TARE vetch; allowance (weight)
TARI coin; goddess
TARN lake
TARO rootstock; poi; elephant's ear
TARP canvas; sailor; hat
TARR tease
TART sour; pastry; harlot
TASH fabric
TASK labor; assignment; take to — (censure)
TASS Soviet News Agency
TASU measure

TATE wool; hair lock
TATH dung
TATT knot lace
TATU Indian; armadillo; tattoo
TAUN measure
TAUR Taurus (bull)
TAUT snug; tense
TAVE Octavia
TAVY Octavia
TAWA tree
TAWN tawny
TAXI (ride a) cab; prefix: arrangement
TAXO prefix: arrangement
TCHA (rolled) tea
TCHE fruit tree; Chin. flute
TCHI measure
TCHU exclamation
TEAK tree; dark
TEAL duck (blue)
TEAM group; yoke
TEAN tone: Scot.
TEAP ram
TEAR drop; weep; rip; glass defect
TEAT nipple
TEBJ Negro Berber
TECA teak; Indian
TECH technical school
TECK readymade tie
TECO Indian
TEDA Negro Berber
TEEL sesame
TEEM abound
TEEN 13–19; injury; pain
TEER golfer; mix colors
TEES river (North Sea)
TEFF grain plant
TEGG sheep in 2nd year
TEHR wild goat
TEIG Teague; Thaddeus; Timothy; dough: Ger.
TEIL linden tree; lime
TEJU lizard
TELA tissue; web; banana port
TELE prefix: far, complete
TELI low (merchant) caste
TELL inform; discern; chat; William (Swiss hero)
TEMA musical theme; Arab
TEMS sieve; sift
TEND serve; incline
TENE suffix: ribbon
TENG measure
TENT cloth shelter; pup —; wine; frame
TEOS Ionian city
TERA Buddhist monastery
TERM phrases; word; condition; time, period
TERN gull; threefold; ship
TERP prehistoric mound
TESA Indian buzzard
TESS Theresa, Hardy heroine
TEST shell; cupel; examination; try
TETE head: Fr.; — a tete; hairdo
TETH Heb. J, 9
TEWA N.M. Indian
TEXT (literary) substance; topic; Scripture passage; type
TEYL linden; lime tree
THAI Siamese
THAN in comparison with; conjunction
THAR goat
THAT so; which; pronoun; connective; that's —
THAW melt; unbend
THEA tea source; name
THEB measure
THEE you
THEM pronoun
THEN at a time; therefore
THEO prefix: god
THEW muscle; sinew
THEY pronoun; people; men
THIN lean; dim; rare; dilute; — ice
THIO prefix: brimstone
THIS pronoun, demonstrative
THOB rationalize
THOR thunder god (Thursday); Midgard slayer; Odin's son; missile
THOS jackal genus
THOU 2nd pers. pronoun
THUD dull sound; blow
THUG assassin; hoodlum
THUS in this way; hence
TIAM language
TIAO Chinese money
TIAR crown; shrub
TIBS — eve (never-never)
TIBU Negro-Berber
TICE lure; yorker (bowled ball)
TICK parasite; mattress; count; tic
TIDE ocean's rise, fall; season; drift; endure; current; help
TIDY (make) neat
TIED bound; knotted; drawn
TIEN sky: Chin.; — Chu (Lord of Heaven); your(s): Fr.
TIER row; layer; pinafore
TIFF (petty) quarrel
TIGE rifle steel pin; dog
TIGG swindler (Dickens)
TIKE child
TIKI god; first man; image
TILE ceramic slab; drain pipe; domino; tessera; slate
TILL until; plow; cultivate; tray, cash box
TILT cover; incline; tip; joust; sport
TIME period; moment; credit term; speed rate; meter, rhythm; Father —; space —
TINA fem. nickname
TIND kindle
TINE tooth; prong; pain; grass
TING sound; Chin. pottery
TINO Sambal language
TINT color; shade; tinge
TINY small; -tim (herb); Tim (Dickens)
TION suffix
TIOU Indian (Tonikan)
TIPE rabbit trap
TIPI wigwam
TIRE fatigue; bore; wheel covering; rubber; shoe
TIRO amateur; novice
TITI monkey; tree; petrel
TITO Yugo. leader (Broz)
TIVY huntsman's cry
TIZA ulexite mineral
TLAC coin

TMAN U.S. Treasury agent
TMEN Treasury agents
TOAD amphibian; anuran; fawn
TOAG Indian
TOAT plane handle
TOBA Tatar; Chaco Indian
TOBE cotton cloth; future
TOBY cigar; mug; dog; rob
TOCK hornbill
TOCO toucan
TODA Ceylon aborigine
TODE (haul with) sled
TODO bustle; stir; ado
TODY green — (bird)
TOED stepped (gingerly)
TOFF dandy
TOFT — and croft (house)
TOGA Roman garb; gown; senatorship
TOGO Afr. republic; Jap. admiral and statesman
TOGS clothes
TOGT trading enterprise
TOHO halt! (to dogs)
TOHU -bohu (confusion)
TOIL work; drudge(ry); snare
TOKO Chin. store; flogging
TOLA weight
TOLD narrated; counted
TOLE entice; told; tinware
TOLL tax; lure; sound
TOLT writ; isolated peak
TOLU balsam (rose odor)
TOMA Liberian Negro
TOMB grave; monument; bury
TOME book; papal letter
TONE pitch; accent; Wolfe (Ir. rebel)
TONG secret society
TONK (cow bell) clang; honky-; game
TONY nickname (Anthony); stylish
TOOA hero; beefwood
TOOK seized; caught; endured; supposed
TOOL instrument; polish; dupe
TOON tree (dye); mahogany
TOOP measure
TOOT sound horn; carousal
TOPE drink; shark; stupa; orchard
TOPH drum; porous rock
TOPI antelope; pith hat
TOPO prefix: place
TOPS most superior
TORA hartebeest; law (of Moses); Pentateuch
TORE ripped; geom. surface
TORI moldings
TORN ripped; damaged
TORO N.Z. tree
TORP croft; Swed. small farm
TORT wrongful act
TORU N.Z. tree
TORY conservative
TOSH bath(tub)
TOSK Albanian
TOSS throw; fling; change
TOTA grivet monkey
TOTE carry; haul; total
TOTO baby (animal); all
TOTY low-caste worker
TOUG horsetail standard
TOUP Malay lugger
TOUR trip; circuit; — de force
TOUT tip(ster); praise; all: Fr.; — a fait; — de suite
TOWN city; Hamlet; — hall; man about —
TOWY like flax fibers
TOXA sponge spicule
TRAM trolley; gauge
TRAP snare; mouth; net; catch; clothe; basalt; — shooting
TRAY salver; platter; old dog
TREE wood, plant; family —; boot; shoe —
TREF homestead
TREK migrate; journey
TRES very: Fr.; three: Sp.
TRET weight allowance
TREY three(spot)
TRIG trim; sound; prim; math. course
TRIM shear; adjust; adorn; rebuke; defeat; neat
TRIN one of triplets
TRIO set of 3; So. Amer. Indian
TRIP move; slip; journey; (mis)step
TRIS prefix: thrice
TRIT prefix: third
TRIX fem. suffix
TROD walked; track
TROP too much: Fr.
TROT jog; gait; race; translation; fishing line
TROW believe; fishing boat
TROY weight system; Ilium, Ilion (Troas); city
TRUE factual; loyal; align
TRUK islands (Carolines)
TRYP parasite in blood (sleeping sickness, nagana, surra)
TSAO Chinese state
TSAR emperor; dictator
TSHI Gold Coast language
TSIA tea
TSIN Chin. dynasty
TSUN measure (1/10 ch'ih)
TUAN measure; sir; title
TUBA saxhorn; tree; nut; fish poison; palm sap
TUBE cylinder; tunnel; subway; radio, TV part; Audion (DeForest)
TUCK draw up; fold (in); eat; Friar (Robin Hood)
TUEL furnace
TUFA porous rock
TUFF volcanic rock
TUFT crest; clump; tassle
TUKE fabric; canvas
TULA metal; niello; city; Toltec ruins
TULE bulrush; cattail
TULU Dravidian Indian
TUMP drag slain deer
TUNA fish; pear: opuntia
TUND pound; bruise
TUNE song; pitch; harmony
TUNG tree; oil
TUNK rap; thump; game
TUNO rubber tree; gum
TUNU rubber tree; gum
TUNY melodious
TUPI Amazon Indian
TUPY Amazon Indian
TURB crowd; clump
TURF sod; grassy ground; peat;

racing
TURI Pathan tribesman
TURK Mongoloid; Seljuk; Ottoman; Osmanli; horse
TURM troop; company
TURN bending; corner; revolve; reverse; change; shape; act; movement
TURP turpentine
TUSH tooth; Georgian; pshaw!
TUSK long tooth
TUTE to tutor
TUTU N.Z. shrub; poison; ballet skirt
TUUM thin: Lat.
TUWI P.I. dyewood tree
TUZA pocket gopher
TWEE bird's cry
TWIG discover; branch; beat
TWIN double; match; — Cities
TWIT taunt; yarn snarl
TYBI 1st Egypt. spring month
TYEE chief
TYER binder
TYKE dog; child
TYLO dog (Maeterlinck)
TYMP blast furnace stone
TYNE Eng. river
TYPE kind, sort; class(ify); printer's letter; use typewriter, produce copy
TYPO printing error
TYPP yarn count unit
TYPY typical
TYRE Phoenician city; Sur
TYRO beginner; novice
TYRR Odin's son; war god
TYTO barn owl; Strix; Aluco
TYTY farmer of God's Little Acre
TZAR emperor; dictator

UANG beetle
UBER over: Ger.
UBII Teutonic tribe
UDAD sheep
UDAL land
UDIC Caucasian language
UEBA measure
UFER fir pole; shore: Ger.
UGLY badlooking; unpleasant; plug-
ULAM Gilead's descendant
ULAN lancer; — Bator
ULEX spine shrub (furze)
ULLA grass; paper pulp
ULLO Indian shell money
ULLR chief god; Sif's son; Thor's stepson
ULME elm
ULMO muermo; hardwood
ULNA elbow bone; ell
ULUA cavalla; fish; caranx
ULVA sea lettuce; laver
UMBO shield boss; shell beak
UMPH grunt
UNAL land
UNAU sloth
UNBE cease to be
UNCA 8th note
UNCI hooks; claws
UNCO strange; very: Scot.
UNDE waving, wavy (Her.)
UNDO untie; unfasten; ruin
UNDY waving, wavy (Her.)
UNIE unicorn fish
UNIO mussel
UNIS Etats — (USA)
UNIT single thing; basic amount; one; monad
UNTO to; for; toward
UNTZ weight
UNUK star; — al Hay
UNZE weight
UPAS tree (juice); arrow poison
UPDO upswept hair
UPGO ascend
UPIS Artemis, Nemesis
UPLA cow dung; fuel
UPON prep: above; against
UPSY -daisy
URAL -Altaic; mountains; hypnotic
URAN lizard; Indian
URAO trona (mineral)
URBS (capital) city
URDE key shaped (Her.)
URDU Hindustani language
URDY key shaped (Her.)
UREA chemical compound
UREY Nobel physicist
URFA Turkish city (Edessa)
URGA Outer Mongolia
URGE prod; impel; impulse
URIA Bathsheba's husband; auk
URIM — and Thummim (sacred instruments)
URNA measure
URSA bear; stars: — Major, Minor; Great, Little Bear (Dipper)
URTH Norn; Wyrd (with Verthandi, Skuld); Weird Sister
URUS wild ox
URVA mongoose
USAR salt; grass
USAS dawn goddess
USED accustomed; secondhand
USEE future user
USER employer
USES law of — (beneficiary)
USHA Bana's daughter; sorceress
USUN ancient North Chinese
USUS user, use: Lat.
UTAH state; Indian; Deseret (Mormon)
UTAI no songs (yo-kyoku)
UTAS 8 day feast; Jap. songs
UTCH "I"
UTIA rodent
UTOR to use: Lat.
UTUG horsetail standard
UTUM small owl
UVAL grapelike
UVEA iris layer
UVIC grapelike; acid
UVID moist; wet
UZAI Palal's father
UZAL Shem's descendant
UZAN weight
UZUN ancient North Chinese

VAAL river
VACH goddess
VADE leave; — mecum
VADY vade mecum; summons
VAGI nerves
VAIL inventor
VAIN empty, idle; futile; proud
VAIR fur
VALE valley; — of tears; farewell:

Lat.
VALI Odin's son; viceroy
VALL valley
VAMP sock; shoe part; fireman; ghost; flirt
VANE weathercock; feather; blade
VANG rope
VANS race of gods
VARA measure
VARE weasel
VARI lemur; prefix: diverse
VARY alter; differ
VASA ducts; Swedish dynasty
VASE vessel
VASO vase: It; prefix: blood vessel
VAST huge (space)
VASU deity (Vishnu); nephew
VAUX village; fort (Verdun battle)
VAYU wind god
VEAL calf; meat
VEAU veal, calf: Fr.
VEDA sacred Hindu books
VEEP vice-president
VEER shift (course); waver
VEGA meadow
VEHM medieval tribunal
VEIL screen; facial garment; cloistered life
VEIN channel; streak; blood vessel
VELA membranes; soft palates; the Sails (Argo constellation)
VELD So. Afr. grassland
VELO speed unit
VELT measure
VENA vein: Lat.
VEND Slav; sell; sale
VENI prefix: vein; —, vidi, vici (I came, I saw, I conquered)
VENO prefix: vein
VENT hole; let out; issue
VEPS Finnish tribe (Chud); Dog Star (Isis); Horus
VERA tree; measure; name
VERB action word
VERD green(leafed)
VERI centipede
VERT green (Her.); veer; convert
VERY true; same; extremely; light signals; flare
VEST waistcoat; clothe; empower
VETA mountain sickness
VETO prohibit(ion); no
VIAL vessel
VIBO gulf (Italy)
VICA Pota (goddess)
VICE sin; fault; vise; proxy; — versa
VIDA feminine of David
VIDE see: Lat., for example; quae —
VIER striver; four: Ger.
VIEW sight; see; aim; opinion; scene
VIGA rafter; log
VIII 8; Augustus reign
VILA fairy; New Hebrides
VILE base; evil; odious
VILI brother of Odin; Ve
VILL village; township
VILY fairies
VINA harp; guitar; wines
VINE creeping plant
VINO palm liquor
VINT card game
VINY entwining
VIOL string instrument
VIRA Bantu
VIRE feathered arrow
VISA endorse(ment); -vis
VISE tool; clamp; endorse
VISS weight
VITA life: Lat.
VITE quick, lively: Fr.
VITI East African
VIVA salute (long live); — voce (spoken aloud)
VIVE — le roi!; long live!: Fr.
VIVO spirited
VLEI marsh; lake; creek
VLEY marsh; swamp; creek
VOCE voice: It.; sotto —
VOET measure
VOGT medieval official
VOID empty; vacuum; cancel
VOIR see: Fr.
VOLA palm (hand, foot)
VOLE rodent; slam (cards)
VOLK people: Ger.; workmen (So. Afr.)
VOLT sideways gait; fencing leap; elec. unit
VONE robot bomb
VOOG lode cavity
VOTA Roman festivals
VOTE ballot; suffrage; voice; enact; propose; Ingrian Finn
VOTH Ingrian Finn
VOTO So. Amer. Indian
VTWO robot bomb
VUGG lode cavity
VUGH lode cavity
VULN wound (Her.)

WAAC fem. soldier
WAAG monkey
WABE tree
WABI Indian; tree
WACO city
WADD mineral
WADE pass; demon; Hampton
WADI valley; river; oasis
WADY valley; river; oasis
WAEG bird; kittiwake
WAER dam
WAFD Egyptian
WAFF flapping; paltry
WAFT float; flag; whiff
WAGE carry on; -earner; pay, salary
WAGH interjection
WAHA lake trout
WAHR true: Ger.
WAIF stray
WAIL lament
WAIN wagon; Charles's —
WAIT attend; defer; serenader; lie in —
WAKA canoe
WAKE track; arouse; vigil; island
WAKF trust fund
WAKY alert
WALE streak; texture; ridge; welt
WALI prefect
WALK go on foot; path; pass, base on balls; — the plank
WALL barrier; fence; enclose; knot; Berlin —
WALT Whitman
WAMP eider
WAND rod; staff; magic —
WANE ebb; lessen
WANG weight; meadow; prince
WANT lack; desire
WANY diminished

WAPP rope guide
WAQF trust fund
WARD (safe)guard; parry; district; charge; Artemus (Browne)
WARE merchandise; beware
WARF warp
WARM hot; genial; newly made; heat; — Springs
WARN caution; give notice
WARP threads; twist; falsify
WART protuberance; -hog
WARY watchful
WASH bathe; laundry; tint
WASP yellow jacket; hornet; fem. flyer: WW II
WAST were
WATE sea demon
WATT inventor, elec. unit (volt-ampere); hare
WAUK wake: Scot.
WAUL wail
WAVE billow; swell; undulation, flutter; signal; — length; navy woman
WAVY fluctuating; undulating
WAWA gibbon
WAXY viscid; pliable
WAYS wise; — and means
WEAK feeble; pliable; light
WEAL body politic; stripe
WEAN withdraw; alienate
WEAR be clothed in; impair; endure; deteriorate
WEBB Beatrice Potter (writer)
WEED plant; tobacco; remove
WEEK time unit; sennight; squeak
WEEL fish basket, trap; pool
WEEP cry; bend; leak
WEET bird; cry of bird
WEFT yarn; mist; (weave) web
WEGA star
WEGG Silas (ballad seller: Dickens)
WEIN wine: Ger.
WEIR dam; fish trap
WEKA flightless bird
WEKI fern
WELD unite; junction
WELF ducal family
WELK (gather) snail; Lawrence (musician)
WELL (water) pit; shaft; eddy; flow; rightly; very; sound; healthy
WELS sheatfish
WELT ridge; wale; strip; sew; beat; universe: Ger.
WEND Slav; go; travel
WENT departed
WEPT cried; Jesus —
WERE prefix: metamorphosed human
WERF farmyard
WERI aweto (caterpillar)
WERT were: archaic, poetic
WESE we shall
WEST wind; painter, author; occident; go —; Mae —
WETA wingless locust
WEVE contraction
WHAM exclamation
WHAT interrogative; pronoun; what's —
WHAU why; tree
WHEE whistle sound
WHEN whereas; how soon
WHET sharpen; excite; edge
WHEW whistle; exclamation
WHEY milk serum; thin; pale; curds and —
WHIG U.S., Brit. party
WHIM fancy; caprice
WHIN gorse; restharrow; rock; winch
WHIP lash; urge; defeat
WHIR fly; hurry; buzz
WHIT bit; jot; dull sound
WHIZ hum; bargain; corker
WHOA stop!; opp. of giddap
WHOO exclamation
WHOM pronoun
WHOP dash; beat; bump
WHUN gorse; restharrow
WHYO gangster; footpad
WICK part of candle, lamp
WIDE broad; far; lax; astray
WIDU Moslem ablution
WIEL whirlpool
WIES Ys
WIFE spouse; marry
WIGG peruke; long hair
WIGS — on the green (fray)
WILD rough; savage; mad; eager; unruly; wilderness
WILE trick; guile; lure
WILK (gather) snail
WILL volition; choice; decree; bequeath; testament
WILT droop; lose spirit
WILY artful; subtle
WIND turn; coil; blowing air; mere talk
WINE fermented juice
WING alar appendage; faction; annex; fly
WINK blink; signal
WINY vinous; drunken
WIPE rub off; beat
WIRE cable; snare
WIRY tough; sinewy
WISE sage; learned
WISH desire; request
WISP torch; shred; flock; brush; ignis fatuus
WIST know; knew; measure
WITH prep.: including, and
WIVE marry; act as wife
WOAD herb
WOKE stirred; roused
WOLD upland plain
WOLF canid (dog); Lupus; larva; devour; dissonance; cry —; flirtatious man
WONG field; meadow
WONT custom; contraction
WOOD timber; forest; Grant (painter); Leonard (general)
WOOF crossthreads; texture; weft; bark
WOOL (sheep) fleece; down
WOON Burmese governor
WORD term; news; promise; order; phrase
WORE had on (clothes); tired
WORK labor; mental product; act; operate; function; needlework

WORM crawler; maggot; screw; insinuate
WORN used (as clothing); shabby; tired
WORT plant; (pot)herb
WOTE Ingrian Finn
WOVE entwined; spun
WRAC women's army corp
WRAF air force; aviatrix
WRAP cloak; blanket; coat
WREN bird; navy woman; architect
WRIG wriggle
WRIT legal order; Holy —
WROX rot
WUDU Moslem ablution
WUFF gruff bark sound
WUKF trust fund
WURD Norn; Urth
WURM glacial period
WUZU Moslem ablution
WYCH -hazel; — elm
WYND alley; small court
WYNN timber truck; Ed (actor, Perfect Fool)
WYRD Norn; Urth

XEMA artic gull
XENO guest; prefix: foreign
XERO prefix: dry
XIII 13; Augustus reign
XINA nickname: Christina
XIPE -totec (Aztec god)
XMAS Christmas
XOSA Kaffir
XOVA Opata; Pimian Indian
XXIV 24; Tiberius reign

YABA bark; cabbage tree
YABU Afghan pony
YAGE plant
YAGI antenna
YAHO tribesman
YAJE plant
YAKA Bantu
YAKI cayman
YALE university; lock; Eli, Elihu —; myth. antelope
YALI mansion
YALU river (Korean War)
YAMA first mortal (Judge of Dead)
YAMP herb; tuber
YANA tribe
YANG honk; male or positive principle
YANK jerk; New Englander; Union soldier; American
YAPA leaf mat
YAPP (bookbinding) style
YARD 3 feet; grounds; enclosure; spar
YARE prompt; ready
YARK yerk
YARL Norse chief; earl
YARM scream; wail
YARN spun wool; story
YARR growl; snarl; herb
YARU Hades; heaven
YATE eucalyptus
YATI ascetic; devotee
YAUP yap; yawn
YAVA weight
YAWL (sail)boat
YAWN open wide; gape; chasm
YAWP yap; yawn
YAWS skin disease
YAYA copa, lancewood (tree)
YEAH yes
YEAN to lamb
YEAR time period; twelve month; leap —; calendar, fiscal —
YEAS yes votes
YEDO Tokyo
YEGG safecracker; tramp
YELD barren; milkless
YELK yolk
YELL cry; cheer
YELP shrill bark
YELT gilt (sow)
YENI So. Amer. tanager
YERK wrench; kick; trump
YESO plaster of Paris; gypsum
YETA Jap. outcast
YETI abominable snowman
YGUN antisub gun
YHVD God, Yahveh, Tetragrammaton
YHVH God, Yahweh, Tetragrammaton
YIMA Avestan demigod
YIPE howl; cry
YIRM fret; whine: Scot., Ir.
YIRN whine; grimace; smirk: Scot., Ir.
YIRR growl; snarl: Scot.
YITE bird (yellowhammer)
YMCA welfare organization
YMER myth. giant
YMIR rime-cold giant
YNCA Quechuan Indian (ruler); Inca
YOBI Jap. military service
YODH Hebrew Y, 10
YOGA mental discipline
YOGH Middle English G, Y
YOGI ascetic; yoga disciple
YOKE join; link; slavery
YOKY coupled
YOLK egg yellow; essence
YOND past; beyond
YOOP sobbing sound
YORE ancient (times); long ago
YORK city; archbishopric; imperial (apple); Sgt. Alvin (WWI)
YOUP yelp; scream; yawn
YOUR possessive pronoun
YOWL howl(ing); yell
YPIL tree (brown dye)
YSER river
YUAN dynasty; money
YUCA cassava; manioc
YUFT Russ. leather
YUGA Hindu age cycle
YUIT Asian Eskimo
YUKI Cal. Indian
YULE Christmas
YUMA Indian (Calif.); city
YUNX woodpecker genus
YURT Kirghiz tent
YUTU Peru tinamou; bird
YWCA welfare organization

ZACH name
ZAIN horse
ZAMA Hannibal's defeat
ZANT fish
ZANY clown(ish)
ZARA city; Judah's son
ZARF holder for cup
ZARP policeman
ZATI bonnet monkey
ZAZA opera (Leoncavallo)
ZEAL ardor; enthusiasm
ZEBU ox; Brahman bull
ZEIN protein
ZEKE Ezekiel
ZEME (abode of) spirit; fetish
ZEMI (abode of) spirit; fetish
ZEND — Avesta (holy text)

ZENO philosopher (Stoic, Cynic); emperor
ZENU Afr. sheep
ZERO nothing; cipher; nullity; — hour; Japanese plane
ZEST orange peel; relish; gusto
ZETA Greek Z, 7
ZEUS chief god; Jupiter; Hera's husband; son of Cronus, Rhea
ZIMB Ethiopian fly
ZINC metal; element; color
ZING sharp thrill; vim
ZION Israelites; heaven
ZIPA Chibcha chief
ZIPS Czech
ZIRA measure
ZITA Austrian empress
ZIZA Rehoboam's son
ZIZZ whirring sound
ZOAR town; Bela; city of Lot
ZOAS symbolic figures (Blake)
ZOBO mongrel yak
ZOEA crab larva
ZOGO sacred object
ZOIC pert. to animals
ZOID organic body cell
ZOLA author (J'accuse: Dreyfus case; Nana)
ZOLL measure
ZONA girdle; shingles
ZONE area; band; partition
ZOOM buzz; climb; approach suddenly
ZOON developed compound animal
ZOOT — suit: extreme style
ZULU Bantu; Kaffir; ship; artificial fly
ZUNI Indian; reservation
ZUPA Yugo. district
ZUPH Samuel's ancestor
ZUZA weight
ZWEI two: Ger.
ZYGA rowers' benches; brain fissures
ZYME ferment

FOUR-LETTER WORDS

-AA- to -ZU-

BAAL deity
BAAR weight
BAAS master
CAAM loom; heddles
FAAM tea; leaves
GAAL brewing
HAAB year
HAAF fishing grounds
HAAK fish; wander
HAAR fog
JAAL goat
KAAN inn; title
KAAT shrub; weight
LAAP secretion; insect
MAAL measure
MAAM madam
MAAN city
MAAS river
MAAT goddess
MAAZ Judah's descendant
NAAB river
NAAM distrain
PAAL measure
PAAN town
PAAR sand
PAAS Easter
RAAB river
RAAD assembly; fish
SAAH measure
SAAL hall: Ger.
SAAN Bushmen
SAAR river; region
TAAL lake; volcano; language
TAAR tambourine
VAAL river
WAAC fem. soldier
WAAG monkey
BABA nurse; title; cake
BABE baby; — Ruth; girl
BABI sect
BABU Hindu gentleman
BABY doll; indulge
CABA measure
CABO Yubi
EABA measure
FABA bean; vetch
GABE taro
GABI taro
GABY fool
HABA bean
HABE tribe
HABU pit viper
LABE city
MABA Negro; tree
MABI tree
NABK shrub
NABO shrub
NABU god; mountain
PABA vitamin
RABA river
RABI crop; physicist
SABA fiber; kingdom; island
SABE know
TABI sock
TABU forbidden
WABE tree
WABI Indian; tree
YABA bark; cabbage tree
YABU Afghan pony

BACH live alone; composer
BACK help; tub; past; retreat; kick-; dorsal, posterior; spine
CACA goddess
CACO bandit
DACE fish
EACH every(one)
FACE surface; oppose; line
FACT deed; reality
FACY fresh
HACK chop; writer; horse
JACA tree
JACK flag; tool; card; fruit; raise
JACU bird
LACE cord; flavor; netting
LACK need
LACT prefix: milk
LACY netlike
MACE staff; spice; weight; coin
MACK coat
MACO cotton
NACH after: Ger.
PACA rodent

PACE step; speed; peace: It.
PACK bundle; cosmetic paste; cards; crowd; animal(s)
PACO alpaca
PACT agreement
RACA reproach; fool
RACE run; contest; people; speed; Cape —; rat-
RACK framework; clouds; gait; torture
RACY smart
SACK dismiss; plunder; wine; bag; gown; sad —
SACO weight; river
TACE steel splint
TACK hook; rope; course; attach
TACT diplomacy; perception
VACH goddess
WACO city
ZACH name
BADB goddess
BADE waited; asked; invited; commanded
CADE cask; tree; pet; rebel
CADI judge
CADY golf boy
DADA father; cult
DADE support
DADO wall part; groove
DADU saint
EADS engineer; bridge
FADE weaken; flat; dissolve
FADO tune
FADY weakening
GADE fish; composer
GADS -hill (Dickens)
HADE angle; strip
HADJ pilgrimage
JADE gem; horse; exhaust
JADU magic
JADY gemlike
KADA measure
KADE tick
KADI judge
KADU tribe
LADE load; dip
LADY title; bird
MADE successful; created; constructed
MADI Negro
MADO fish
PADI rice

RADA legislature
RADE elated
SADD dam; waste matter
SADE letter; Marquis
SADH holy man
SADI poet
SADO carriage; island; river
SADR tree
VADE leave; — mecum
VADY vade mecum; summons
WADD mineral
WADE pass; demon; Hampton
WADI valley; river; oasis
WADY valley; river; oasis
BAEL thorny (fruit) tree
BAER prizefighter, actor
BAEZ singer
CAEN city
DAER re borrowed stock
DAEZ daze
FAEX dregs
GAEA goddess; Titans' mother
GAEL Celt; Irishman
HAEC this one (fem.): Lat.
HAEM prefix: blood
JAEL Sisera's killer; Heber's wife
LAEL Gershonite's father
LAET freedman
NAEL weight
SAER tenant
TAEL weight; coin
TAEN taken
WAEG bird; kittiwake
WAER dam
BAFF strike; stroke
BAFT astern; cotton
CAFE restaurant; coffee; -au-lait; society
DAFF put aside
DAFT foolish; giddy
GAFF spear; ordeal; hoax
HAFF lagoon
HAFT handle
KAFA Ethiopian
MAFU stable boy
RAFF Raphael
SAFI collection; float
RAFT secure; box
SAFE Afghan
TAFT President; Republican; rower's seat; — Hartley Act
WAFD Egyptian
WAFF flapping; paltry

WAFT float; flag; whiff
BAGA turnip
BAGG heiress (Thackeray)
BAGO shrub
CAGE confine; enclosure; elevator car; nor iron bars a —
CAGN mantis; deity
CAGY shrewd
DAGG pistol
DAGH hill
DAGO tribe
GAGE pledge; fruit; gauge; general; governor
GAGL sweet gale
HAGG demoness; hack; wood
HAGI clover; prefix: saint
IAGO villain (Othello)
JAGA Bantu
JAGG pendant; tooth; slash
KAGO conveyance
KAGS convict (Dickens)
KAGU bird
LAGO lake
MAGE magician
MAGG bird; chatter
MAGH month
MAGI caste; priests; wise men; kings of Orient; Melchior, Gaspar, Balthazar
NAGA snake
NAGY Hungarian premier
PAGA rice
PAGE young attendant; call, summon; leaf
PAGO Pago (city)
RAGA state of nirvana
RAGE fury; storm; fad
RAGI grass
SAGA legend; story; goddess; weight
SAGE herb; wise; Russell — (financier)
SAGO palm; starch
SAGY wise
VAGI nerves
WAGE carry on; -earner; pay; salary
WAGH interjection
YAGE plant
YAGI antenna
BAHI fortune
BAHO prayer stick
BAHR sea; — El Azrak
BAHT coin
HAHA laugh; fence
HAHN Otto (Nobel physicist)
KAHA proboscis monkey

KAHN banker; test
KAHU harrier; bird
LAHN river
MAHA monkey; deer
MAHE island
MAHI river
MAHR marriage settlement
NAHA city
NAHE river; near: Ger.
OAHU (Hawaiian) island
PAHA hill
PAHI ship
PAHO prayer stick
RAHU demon
SAHA measure
SAHH measure
SAHO language
SAHU spiritual body
TAHA bird
TAHR goat
WAHA lake trout
WAHR true: Ger.
YAHO tribesman
BAIA state; city; resort; bay
BAIL security; bond; set free; dip out; hoop
BAIN bath: Fr.
BAIS caste
BAIT lure; harass; pest poison
CAID alcaide
CAIN tribute; (Abel's) slayer; mark of —
DAIL legislature; — Eireann
DAIN Patusan chief (Conrad); — Curse (Hammett); measure
DAIS platform
FAIL fall short; err
FAIN glad; eager
FAIR pleasing; ample; just; bazaar; — and square; — deal
FAIT fact; — accompli
GAIA goddess
GAIL Abigail; brewing
GAIN reach; earn; profit; notch
GAIT walk; pace
HAIG soldier (Douglas)
HAIK garment; frame
HAIL ice pieces; salute — fellow
HAIR filament; cilium, seta; fabric; -trigger
JAIL prison; gaol
JAIN sect (Indian)
KAID chief; alcaide
KAIF languor; hemp
KAIK village
KAIL tree; ibex; kale
KAIN tribute
KAIO fruit
KAIR fiber
KAIS island
LAIC secular
LAID put down; calmed
LAIN reclined
LAIR resting place
LAIS hetaera
LAIT milk: Fr.; cafe-au-
MAIA goddess; crab; star
MAID servant; — of Orleans
MAIL coin; tax; armor; post
MAIM disfigure; mutilate
MAIN conduit; first; river; Spanish —
MAIS but: Fr.
NAIA cobra
NAID worm
NAIF native; of true luster
NAIK leader
NAIL fasten(er); claw; seize; expose
NAIO tree
NAIR native
NAIS nymph
PAID recompensed; discharged; satisfied
PAIL bucket
PAIN ache; trouble; forfeit
PAIR couple; brace
PAIS country
QAIS island
QAID alcaide
RAIA ottoman; fish
RAID attack; foray
RAIK weight; measure
RAIL bird; scold; paling
RAIN shower; scratch; — check
RAIP rope
RAIS chief (Nepalese)
SAIC Near East ketch
SAID before-mentioned; Port —; city; name
SAIL canvas; rigging; journey, travel
SAIM grease
SAIN consecrate; tree
SAIR savor
SAIS groom; city; know: Fr.
TAIL end; cue; follow; high-
TAIN plate
TAIR goat
TAIT marsupial
VAIL inventor
VAIN empty, idle; futile; proud
VAIR fur
WAIF stray
WAIL lament
WAIN wagon; Charles's —
WAIT attend; defer; serenader; lie in —
ZAIN horse
BAJU jacket
CAJA box; bank
CAJI snapper
CAJU fruit; mahogany
GAJO non-Gypsy
HAJE cobra
HAJI pilgrim
HAJJ pilgrimage
MAJA crab
MAJO dandy; shrub
NAJA cobra
PAJO prayer stick
RAJA prince; fish
TAJO trench
YAJE plant
BAKA devil
BAKE dry; roast; biscuit
BAKU hat; tree; rug; city; oil field
CAKE bar; dough; harden
CAKY crusty
FAKE loop; cheat; sham
FAKY spurious
HAKA dance
HAKE fish; pester; frame
HAKH claim(er); legal claim; share
HAKO rite
HAKU fish
JAKE Jacob; rube; money; satisfactory; ginger
JAKO parrot
KAKA parrot
KAKI bird; tree
LAKE sea; pool; red (cochineal)
LAKH 100,000; coin
LAKY red
MAKE produce, create; cause; reach; type; identify
MAKI lemur
MAKO shark
MAKU Indian
OAKS horse race; trees

OAKY oaklike
RAKE incline; tool; collect; roue; —'s Progress
RAKH hayfield
RAKI spirits
RAKU -ware
SAKA era; Scythians
SAKE purpose; beer
SAKI monkey; Munro
TAKE acquire, seize; scene part; receipts
TAKT beat(s); tempo
TAKU Indian
TAKY taking
WAKA canoe
WAKE track; arouse; vigil; island
WAKF trust fund
WAKY alert
YAKA Bantu
YAKI cayman
AALI pasha
AALU Hades; heaven
BALA geol. epoch
BALD naked; — eagle
BALE woe; bundle
BALI demon; monkey; offering; island
BALK thwart; signal
BALL game; confuse; dance; — bearing; good time; -point; Amer. sculptor
BALM plant; soothe; — in Gilead
BALT Lithuanian; Esth; Latvian; Lett
BALU wildcat
CALE Gypsy; cabbage
CALF bovine, etc., young; fur; leather; skin; lower leg
CALI Colombian city
CALK tighten; stop; sleep; tool; copy
CALL summon; visit; cry; telephone; — girl; — money
CALM quiet; mold
CALO Gypsy
CALP limestone
CALX residue; heel: Lat.
DALE valley; share; trough
DALI tree; offering; Salvador —
DALL sheep
FALA refrain; dog
FALL descend; ruin; autumn; — of Man
FALX weapon; — cerebri (brain fold)
GALA festival; tribe
GALE storm, wind
GALI abuse
GALL bile; venom; wound; chafe; swelling; impudence
GALT clay bed
HALA pine tree
HALE healthy; Nathan — (patriot)
HALF moiety; -breed, -caste, -nelson, -shell
HALI prefix: sea, salt
HALL building; room; town —; guild-; astronomer; -Mills
HALM plant stems
HALO circle; glow; nimbus; prefix: sea, salt
HALS Frans — (painter)
HALT stop; lame
IALU Hades; heaven
KALA bird
KALB de — (general)
KALE cabbage
KALI glasswort; carpet; evil genius; Agni's tongue; Siva's wife
KALO taro root
LALO composer
MALA evil(s), wrong(s): Lat.; jaw
MALE man(ly); tribe
MALI caste; nation; river
MALL mallet; game; bird; assembly (place)
MALM limestone
MALO loincloth
MALT barley; beer
NALA hero
PALA weight; antelope; vine; rice
PALE wan; pallid; ashy; picket; stake; beyond the —
PALI slope; coral parts; Buddhist language
PALL cloak; covering; cloy
PALM tree; measure; hand part; paddle; conceal; grease the —
PALO pole, wood: Sp.
PALP appendage; feeler
PALY wan; heraldic design
RALE rattling sound
RALO measure
SALA dining room: Sp.
SALE bargain; auction; willow; salted: Fr.
SALM star
SALP marine animal
SALT sodium chloride, NaCl; sailor; season; — away; — Lake City; — Sea
TALA tree; basin; ruin
TALC soapy mineral
TALE story; — of Two Cities; count
TALI gold piece; weight
TALK speak, converse; conference; empty words; dialect; — turkey
TALL high; incredible
VALE valley; — of tears; farewell: Lat.
VALI Odin's son; viceroy
VALL valley
WALE streak; texture; ridge; welt
WALI prefect
WALK go on foot; path; pass, base on balls; — the plank
WALL barrier; fence; enclose; knot; Berlin —
WALT Whitman
YALE university; lock; Eli, Elihu —; myth. antelope
YALI mansion
YALU river (Korean War)
CAME arrived; lead rod; Indian
CAMP tent(s); town; stay; boot —
DAMA gazelle
DAME woman; title; — aux Camelias
DAMN curse; — the torpedoes
DAMP moist(ure); depress
FAMA rumor
FAME reputation
FAMN measure
GAMA Vasco da — (navigator); grass
GAMB leg
GAME amusement; quarry; resolute; lame
GAMP umbrella; Sairey — (nurse: Dickens)
HAMI hooked processes

IAMB verse foot
JAMA tunic
JAMB leg armor; pillar; door part
JAMI mosque
KAMA love god; desire; river
KAME hill
KAMI language; deity
LAMA priest; llama; brown; Dalai, Panchen, Tashi —
LAMB amateur speculator; Charles — (Elia), essayist (roast pig)
LAME cripple(d); halt; plate; fabric
LAMP light; bulb
MAMA mother; goddess
MAMO bird
NAMA Hottentot; herb
NAME title; reputation; clan; cite
RAMA Indian; Vishnu incarnation; bull (Kipling)
RAME branch
RAMI branches
RAMP inclined way; rear
SAMA fish; trance-inducing music
SAME identical
SAMH bread plant
SAMP maize
TAMA Indian
TAME gentle; subdue
TAMP fill up; pound down; tool
VAMP sock; shoe part; fireman; ghost; flirt
WAMP eider
YAMA first mortal (Judge of Dead)
YAMP herb; tuber
ZAMA Hannibal's defeat
AANI ape
BANA Titan
BANC (Judge's) bench
BAND strip; group; orchestra; range; tie; sash
BANE woe; curse; poison
BANG beat; thump; hair; sardine; interjection
BANI coins
BANK mound; bench; deposit; bird flock; Left, Right —; blood —; eye —
BANS marriage notice
BANT diet
CANA Indian
CANE stem; rattan; stick; walking —; sugar —; candy —
CANG wooden collar
CANO canal: Sp.
CANT angle; change course; log; tilt; whine; jargon; be unable
DANA goddess; editor; author; lake
DANE Scandinavian; great — (dog); Hamlet
DANG curse (damn)
DANK moist; rank
DANS in: Fr.
DANU goddess
FANA Sufistic concept
FANE temple
FANG tooth; measure; Dickens character
FANO cloth; cape
GANE yawn
GANG crew; associate; rock
GANO Count (Roland's destroyer)
GANT yawn; gaunt; gannet; Eugene (Wolfe character)
GANZ all, totally: Ger.
HAND control; aid; worker; measure; pass; player; cards; penmanship
HANG suspend; plan; bit; die on gallows
HANK coil; — Morgan (Twain)
HANO Indian
HANS John; Johannes; — Castorp (Mann)
HANT ghost
JANE woman; false hair; cloth; — Eyre; Lady — Grey
JANN genii
KANA Japanese writing
KANE god
KANG — Hisi (Chinese emperor)
KANO painting school
KANT change course; Immanuel, philosopher
LANA wood; flannel
LAND ground; debark; state: Ger.
LANE (fixed) route; throat
LANG auld — syne; Fritz
LANK thin; lean(ness)
LANX platter
MANA magic power; Chinese letter
MAND grass
MANE hair; in the morning: Lat.
MANG bat (Kipling)
MANI peanut; prefix: hand
MANN man: Ger.; Horace (educator); Thomas (writer)
MANO grindstone; hand: It.
MANS Chinese aborigine; Le — (city; auto race)
MANU prefix: hand; Laws (Hindus code book)
MANX pert. to the Isle of Man; cat
MANY numerous
NANA nurse; Aztec hero's wife; Zola novel; dog: Peter Pan (Barrie)
NANE own; none
PANA city
PANE glass; panel
PANG agony
PANI madam: Polish
PANK weight
PANT gasp; yearn
RANA frog; prince; Aegir's wife
RAND border; ridge; strip; So. Afr. gold mine
RANG sounded
RANI princess; wife
RANK luxuriant; gross; fetid; grade; array
RANN verse; stanza; kite (Kipling)
RANT scold; rave; frolic
RANZ — des vaches (Alpine melodies)
SANA Yemen's capital; fiber
SAND grit; silica; polish, smooth; red-yellow; George, novelist (Dudevant)
SANE rational
SANG Hindu group; herb; weight; did sing
SANK descended

SANS without: Fr.; — culotte (radical); — gene
TANA shrew; rabbi; police station; lake (Blue Nile)
TANE Polynesian god
TANG spur; flavor; sound; seaweed; dynasty
TANH math. term
TANK basin; store; war vehicle; panzer
TANO Indian
UANG beetle
VANE weathercock; feather; blade
VANG rope
VANS race of gods
WAND rod; staff; magic —
WANE ebb; lessen
WANG weight; meadow; prince
WANT lack; desire
WANY diminished
YANA tribe
YANG honk; male or positive principle
YANK jerk; New Englander; Union soldier; American
ZANT fish
ZANY clown(ish)
FAON fawn color
GAOL prison
GAON Jewish title
JAOB measure
LAON Fr. city
LAOS country
MAON Nabal's home
NAOS star
PAON peacock blue
TAOS Indian
BAPS dancing master (Dickens)
CAPA cloak; Sp.
CAPE cloak; promontory; — Cod, — Horn, — Good Hope
CAPH star, letter
CAPP Al, cartoonist (Abner, Dogpatch)
GAPA guided missile
GAPE yawn; stare; gap
GAPO (inundated) forest
GAPY yawning
HAPH weight
HAPI bull; Nile (god)
HAPU clan
JAPE deride
KAPA cloth(es)
KAPH letter
KAPP measure
KAPU forbidden; taboo
LAPP N. Scandinavian
MAPO goby (fish)
NAPA leather; wine region; city; river
NAPE neck back
NAPU ruminant
PAPA father; Pope; potato: Sp.; baboon; clay
PAPE bunting (bird)
RAPE herb; ravish
RAPT engrossed; rapture
SAPA grape juice
SAPH giant (Philistine)
SAPO soap; toadfish
TAPA bark; cloth
TAPE band; tie; Indian; record; red —; ticker —
TAPS lights-out signal; bugle call
TAPU taboo
WAPP rope guide
YAPA leaf mat
YAPP (bookbinding) style
WAQF trust fund
AARE river
AARU Hades; heaven
BARA measure
BARB sharp point; fish; dog; mow; pigeon
BARD armor; poet; — of Avon (Shakespeare)
BARE expose(d); mere; Indian
BARI hut; Negro; city
BARK peel; tan; cough
BARM yeast
BARN storehouse; stable
BARO big; prefix: weight
BARR elephant's cry
BART man's name
BARU tree
CARA dear (one): It.; Indian
CARD comb; pasteboard; menu; playing —; calling —
CARE grief; heed; responsibility; anxiety; foster; relief organization
CARF slit; notch
CARK trouble
CARL rustic; villain; Charles
CARN stone heap
CARO dear (one): It.; Caroline
CARP fish; complain
CARR pool
CART wagon; transport
DARD language group
DARE venture; defy; fish; 1st Amer. child (Virginia)
DARI grain sorghum; carpet
DARK unlighted; wicked; dismal
DARN mend; interjection
DARR bird
DART missile; fish; seam; run
EARL nobleman; count; name
EARN gain; win; deserve
FARD face paint; date
FARE passenger; price; happen; food; travel
FARL cake (part)
FARM till; land; — out; club
FARO card game; Pharaoh
GARA coin
GARB apparel; array
GARE wool; station: Fr.; beware: Fr.
GARM Hel's dog
GARN yarn; go on
GARO Assam native
GARY city, steel center
HARA Japanese statesman
HARB Bedouin
HARD solid; firm; close; severe; difficult
HARE leporid; rabbit; run
HARI river; Mata (spy)
HARK listen
HARL barb; filament
HARM hurt; evil; injury
HARP coin; seal; Lyra; constellation; Irishman; nag
HARR hinge
HART stag; deer
HARZ German mountains
JARA palm
JARL Norse chief; earl
KARA river
KARI gum tree
KARL Charles; — Marx
KARN stone heap
KARO plant
LARA Byron poem
LARD fat; stuff
LARI money; sea birds
LARK bird; frolic; yellow
LARP secretion; insect
LARS Porsena

(conqueror)
MARA demon; aborigine; Naomi
MARC residue; name; weight
MARD spoil
MARE blues; sea; moon area; horse; shanks' —
MARI prefix: sea; husband: Fr.; native
MARK sign; aim; stamp; money; observe; evangelist; easy —; — time
MARL clayey soil; fertilizer; fiber
MARM ma'am; school-
MARO ship name: Jap.
MARS war god; planet
MART market; nickname
MARU ship name: Jap.
MARX Karl (economist)
MARY female name; queen; sister of Lazarus, Martha; Virgin; Lady
NARD plant; ointment
NARE Loki's son
NARK informer; tease
NARY not one
OARY oarlike
PARA coin; weight; river; city (Belem)
PARC park; oyster farm: Fr.
PARD chum; leopard
PARE cut off; peel
PARI weight; prefix: equal
PARK (common) grounds; green; deposit; Hyde, Central, etc.
PARR young fish; skegger; Catherine (Henry VIII wife)
PARS part: Lat.
PART portion; duty; role; separate; split; go
RARA — avis (rare bird)
RARE underdone; thin; uncommon
SARA native
SARD carnelian; gem; Sardinian
SARG Toni (puppeteer)
SARI Hindu garment
SARK Channel Island
SART Iranian Turk
SARY sorry
TARA fern; goddess; palm
TARE vetch; allowance (weight)
TARI coin; goddess
TARN lake
TARO rootstock; poi; elephant's ear
TARP canvas; sailor; hat
TARR tease
TART sour; pastry; harlot
VARA measure
VARE weasel
VARI lemur; prefix: diverse
VARY alter; differ
WARD (safe)guard; parry; district; charge; Artemus (Browne)
WARE merchandise; beware
WARF warp
WARM hot; genial; newly made; neat; — Springs
WARN caution; give notice
WARP threads; twist; falsify
WART protuberance; -hog
WARY watchful
YARD 3 feet; grounds; enclosure; spar
YARE prompt; ready
YARK yerk
YARL Norse chief; earl
YARM scream; wail
YARN spun wool; story
YARR growl; snarl; herb
YARU Hades; heaven
ZARA city; Judah's son
ZARF holder for cup
ZARP policeman
BASE bottom; source; home; headquarters; found; diamond corner; ignoble
BASH smash; bruise
BASK luxuriate; warm oneself
BASS fish; fiber; lowest part; singer; musical instrument
BAST (woody) fiber; goddess; phloem
CASA house, building: Sp., It.
CASE event; fact; record, problem (medical, etc.); legal action; argument; grammar form; container, chest, box; queer phenomenon; inspect
CASH money; exchange; hemlock
CASK barrel; measure
CASO Dodecanese island
CASS treasure; Timberlane (Lewis); Squire (Eliot)
CAST throw; project; shed; deposit; form; found; actors; (assign) roles
CASY ex-preacher (Steinbeck)
DASH sprint; smash; small portion
DASI concubine
DASS Durga, Ram (twins, Kipling)
EASE repose; comfort; moderate; facilitate
EAST direction; Asia; Orient
EASY simple; calm; soft; — Street
FASH rough edges; vex
FASS measure
FAST not eat; fixed(ly); quick(ly); wild; — and loose
GASH (make) incision
GASP pant (eagerly)
HASH chop up; mixture; mess
HASP clasp
HASS throat; embrace
HAST contraction: havest
JASS card game
KASA grass
KASI tile work
KASM measure
LASH (whip) stroke; tie; eye part
LASI tribe
LASS girl; sweetheart
LAST block, final(ly); endure; measure
MASA corn meal
MASH brew; mixture; hammer; flirt
MASK disguise; screen; domino
MASS rite; bulk; populace; assemble
MAST pole; brown; nuts
MASU salmon
NASA space-travel agency

NASE promontory; nose: Ger.
NASH soft; humorist
NASI prince; patriarch
NAST cartoonist
OAST kiln
PASA raisin
PASH hurl; smash
PASI low-caste Hindu
PASO measure
PASS opening; go through; by; license; condition; amatory gesture
PAST tense; ago; after
RASA essence; tabula
RASE rub; demolish
RASH hasty; careless
RASP grate; file
SASA fencer's cry
SASH casement; scarf; belt
SASS sauce
TASH fabric
TASK labor; assignment; take to — (censure)
TASS Soviet News Agency
TASU measure
VASA ducts; Swedish dynasty
VASE vessel
VASO vase: It.; prefix: blood vessel
VAST huge (space)
VASU deity (Vishnu); nephew
WASH bathe; laundry; tint
WASP yellow jacket; hornet; fem. flyer: WW II
WAST were
BATA child; servant
BATE diminish; tanner's bath; restrain
BATH tub; measure; spa; order
BATT matted mass
BATZ coin
CATA down; prefix: away
CATE delicacy
CATO the Censor (Roman statesman); foe of Carthage
CATS — cradle
DATA facts
DATE fruit; tree; brown; (make) appointment
DATO tribal chief
DATU tribal chief
EATS food; consumes
FATA — Morgana (fairy, mirage)
FATE destiny (goddess); end; kismet
GATA nurse shark
GATE entrance; pass; judgment; money
GATH Philistine city
HATE detest; aversion
HATH contraction: haveth
HATI heart
HATT measure
JATI caste
JATO jet-assisted take-off
KATE bird; Shaks. shrew; Greenaway
KATH astringent
KATI weight
KATY Catherine; -did
LATA jumping disease
LATE dead; tardy
LATH strip; slat
LATU gold coins
MATA Hari (spy)
MATE companion; match; tea; check-
MATH mowing; monastery; school course
MATT lusterless
MATY (assistant) servant
NATA Nana's hero
NATE born
NATH star
NATO International (Western) alliance; treaty organization
NATR weight
OATH appeal; pledge; vow; curse
OATY full of oats
PATA painting; turban; sword
PATE head; paste
PATH track; route
PATO Muscovy duck
PATT stalemate(d)
PATU weapon
RATA tree; chestnut; rate; pro —
RATE censure; ratio; charge; estimate; rank; tax
RATH chariot; fort; temple; early; mome-
RATI weight
RATS bah!
SATE gratify; glut
SATI queen of the gods
TATE wool; hair lock
TATH dung
TATT knot lace
TATU Indian; armadillo; tattoo
WATE sea demon
WATT inventor, elec. unit (volt-ampere); hare
YATE eucalyptus
YATI ascetic; devotee
ZATI bonnet monkey
BAUD speed unit
BAUL mendicant
BAUM Vicki (novelist); Oz creator; tree: Ger.; — marten
BAUR joke
CAUK (secure by a) tenon
CAUL basket; covering membrane
CAUP tribute: Scot.
DAUB plaster; besmear
DAUD dad
DAUK relay post
DAUN — stage (geol. period)
DAUR Manchu
DAUW zebra
EAUX waters: Fr.
FAUN deity; satyr
FAUT comme il — (proper): Fr.
GAUB persimmon (astringent)
GAUD ornament; bead
GAUE German regions
GAUL Celt, Frenchman; France
GAUM attention
GAUP gape
GAUR wild cattle
GAUS region: Ger.
GAUT range; pass; river bank stairs
HAUL drag; shift; loot
HAUT high: Fr.; — monde
JAUN palanquin
KAUN resthouse; lord; title
LAUD praise
LAUK exclamation
LAUN ceramic sieve
MAUD plaid; rug; name; Muller; Whittier, Tennyson heroine
MAUI Polynesian hero
MAUL hammer; bruise; mangle
MAUN must
NAUT sea mile
PAUL click; detent; Apostle; Bunyan; Revere; — VI

(pope)
PAUN betel leaf
PAUP walk idly
SAUD ibn (king)
SAUF safe Fr.; — conduit
SAUK Indian, Mont. river
SAUL tree; king (son of Kish); — of Tarsus (Paul)
SAUM weight
SAUR prefix, suffix: lizard
TAUN measure
TAUR Taurus (bull)
TAUT snug; tense
VAUX village; -fort (Verdun battle)
WAUK wake: Scot.
WAUL wail
YAUP yap; yawn
BAVE double silk thread
CAVA pepper shrub, root; gum resin; vein
CAVE cavern; — in (collapse); — canem (beware of dog)
CAVY rodent; guinea pig; stray animal(s)
DAVE David
DAVY David; lamp; affidavit; Jones' locker
EAVE roof edge
FAVI tiles; flagstones
FAVN measure
GAVE donated
HAVE possess; aux. verb, must; deceive
JAVA coffee; hood; (Indonesian) Sunda isles; — man (Pithecanthropus)
JAVE Jehovah
KAVA pepper shrub, root; gum resin; vein
KAVI Java language
LAVA fluid rock; obsidian's source; red
LAVE pour; bathe
NAVE hub; church part
NAVY fleet; blue; tobacco; — yard
PAVE cover firmly; — the way; jewel setting
PAVO peacock; constellation
PAVY peach
RAVE rant, rage; enthusiasm; rod
RAVI tribesman
SAVA Yugo. river
SAVE rescue; avoid; lay by; but; — face
TAVE Octavia
TAVY Octavia
WAVE billow, swell; undulation flutter; signal; - length; Navy woman
WAVY fluctuating; undulating
YAVA weight
BAWD procurer(ess)
BAWL cry; howl; — out (chide)
BAWN mud enclosure; white
CAWK bird's cry; mineral
CAWL basket
DAWK relay transport; mail
DAWM coin
DAWN daybreak; Eos; Aurora red
FAWN deer; cringe; toady, brown
GAWD ornament; bead
GAWK lout; stare
GAWN gallon tub
GAWP gape simpleton
HAWK bird. predator; peddle. mortarboard
HAWM loiter
JAWY talkative
KAWA pepper shrub, root; gum resin vein
KAWI Java language
KAWN resthouse; lord; title
LAWK surprise!
LAWN fabric; grass plot; bishopric
LAWS rules; principles
MAWK maggot
PAWA weight
PAWL click; detent; tent
PAWN chessman; pledge
SAWK measure
SAWN sawed; cut
TAWA tree
TAWN tawny
WAWA gibbon
YAWL (sail)boat
YAWN open wide; gape; chasm
YAWP yap; yawn
YAWS skin disease
CAXI snapper (fish)
SAXE Saxony; blue
TAXI (ride a) cab; prefix:
arrangement
TAXO prefix: arrangement
WAXY viscid; pliable
BAYA weaverbird; Bantu
CAYO island reef: Sp.
DAYE printer (Bay Psalm Book)
DAYS by day
HAYA arrow poison
HAYZ zodiacal situation
KAYO knock out
MAYA weaverbird (Mexican) Indian; magic; Buddha's mother
MAYO Indian; physicians, clinic (Rochester)
RAYA broadbill
SAYA outer skirt
VAYU wind god
WAYS wise; — and means
YAYA copa, lancewood (tree)
CAZA Turkish district
CAZI Moslem judge
CAZY Moslem judge
DAZA Negro-Berber
DAZE stupefy; mica
DAZY confused
FAZE disturb
GAZA Israel (Philistine) seaport; Mozambique district; eyeless in — (Samson)
GAZE stare; wonder
GAZI warrior; title
GAZY gaping
HAZE mist; drizzle; harass
HAZY dim; obscure
JAZZ dance; music; banter
KAZI Moslem judge
KAZY Moslem judge
LAZE idle(ness); tribesman
LAZI tribesman
LAZO lasso
LAZY idle
MAZE labyrinth; daze; perplex
MAZO de la Roche (novelist; Jalna)
MAZY perplexing
NAZE promontory
NAZI fascist; Hitlerite
RAZE scrape; demolish
RAZZ chaff; ridicule
ZAZA opera (Leoncavallo)
ABAC calculator

ABAS down: Fr.
EBAL Mount (Joshua's altar)
IBAD Hira Arab
IBAN dyak (Borneo)
OBAN coin
ABBA father; title
ABBE priest; title; Amer. meteorologist
ABBY Abigail
ABCS first principles; alphabet
ABED in bed; bedridden
ABEL Adam's son; Cain's brother; — Magwitch (Dickens); letter A; monkey
ABET aid; incite
ABEY waive
EBED Gaal's father
EBEN Ebenezer
EBER Hebrew ancestor
IBEX wild goat; bouquetin
OBED David's grandfather
OBEX brain matter
OBEY submit; comply
UBER over: Ger.
ABIA Samuel's son
ABIB month
ABIE 's Irish Rose; name
ABIR red powder
IBID P.I. lizard (tidbit); the same: abbr.
IBIS (sacred) wading bird
IBIT P.I. lizard (tidbit)
OBIA Ashanti religion
OBIT death notice
UBII Teutonic tribe
ABLE fit; adept; suffix; -bodied
ABLY deftly
ABOO war cry
ABOT Mishnah
ABOU father; deity
ABOX braced
EBOE tree; oil; Negrito
EBON ebony; black
OBOE woodwind; chanter
OBOL 1/16 drachma (coin)
ABRA narrow pass; river
ABRI shelter
EBRO Sp. river
OBRA works: Sp.
ABSI tribe
ABUT touch
EBUR ivory: Lat.
OBUS howitzer shell

ECAD modified organism

ICAL compound suffix
SCAB crust; strikebreaker
SCAD fish; large amount
SCAN examine; measure poetry
SCAP skull
SCAR rock; cicatrix; mar(k); fish
SCAT buffet; scatter; begone!; tax; skat
SCAW promontory
ACCA fabric
ECCA geol. period (Karroo)
ECCE lo: Lat.; — homo
ACER tree
ICED frozen; chilled
ICER freezer; mixer
ACHE pain; yearn
ACHT eight: Ger.
ACHY painful
ECHO Narcissus's nymph; repeat; response; fruit tree (ginko)
ECHT genuine: Ger.
ICHO fruit tree (ginko)
ICHU valuable grass
OCHA weight
OCHS Adolph (publisher)
TCHA (rolled) tea
TCHE fruit tree; Chin. flute
TCHI measure
TCHU exclamation
ACID sour; biting
ACIS river; (Galatea's) lover
CCIV 209; Septimus Severus reign
CCIX 209; Septimus Severus reign
MCII 1102
MCIV 1104; First Crusade, conquest of Acre
MCIX 1109
SCIO prefix: sky
ACLE tree
ACME peak; crisis
ACNE disease
ACON boat
ACOR acidity
ICON image; statue
SCOB fabric defect
SCON teacake
SCOP bard; poet
SCOT Celt; Highlander; tax; - free
SCOW flat-bottomed boat
ACRE field; measure; city
ECRU beige; unbleached
OCRA vegetable; gumbo

ACTA deeds; records
ACTH hormone medicine
ACTO action: Sp.
ACTS NT book
ACTU act: Lat.
ECTO prefix: outside
OCTA prefix: eight
OCTO prefix: eight
ACUS pin
SCUD run fast; wind-driven clouds; skim; flea
SCUG squirrel: Brit.
SCUM dross; refuse; rabble
SCUP pan fish; porgy
SCUR horn tissue
SCUT rabbit's tail; fur
ACYL acid part

ADAD fiber; god
ADAH wife of Lamech, Esau; fem. name
ADAI tribe
ADAK Aleut. island
ADAM first man; sin; composer; architect
ADAN prayer call
ADAR month
ADAT law
ADAY date atomic attack
DDAY operation start
EDAM city; cheese
EDAR Bib. site
IDAS Marpessa's lover; Castor's slayer
ODAL land; vine
ODAX rock whiting (fish)
UDAD sheep
UDAL land
ADDA god; river; skink
ADDU skink; fiber; god
ADDY Adeline
EDDA Norse epic
EDDO taro root
EDDY whirlpool; Mary Morse (Baker) —: Christian Science
ODDS inequality; advantage; at —; -on
ADEN comb. form: gland; city; gulf; region
ADER Benjamite
ADES Hades
EDEA reproduction organs
EDEL noble: Ger.
EDEN paradise; West of Nod
EDER river
IDEA conception; fancy; key meaning; opinion

IDEE — fixe: Fr.
IDEM same: Lat.; semper —
IDEN Henry VI figure
IDEO prefix: idea
IDES Roman date; — of March (fateful day)
ODEA theaters; halls; galleries
ODED prophet or his father
ODEL vine; land ownership
ODER river
EDGE brink; sharpness; goad; advantage; — on
EDGY sharp; snappish
ADIB star
ADIN name
ADIT entrance
EDIT correct; redact; blue-pencil
IDIC pert. to ids
IDIO prefix: one's own
ODIC pert. to ode, od
ODIN one-eyed Norse god: Frigg's husband, Thor's father
ODIO hatred: It.
UDIC Caucasian language
IDJO Niger delta Negro
IDLE not working; empty; lazy; waste
IDLY vainly; lazily
ADMI gazelle
EDNA female name; Ferber, novelist
EDOM Esau's country; Idumaea
IDOL god, deity; image; adored one
ODOR smell; repute
ADRY thirsty
IDUN Bragi's wife (Norse)
ODUM tree (iroko)
IDYL pastoral poem
IDYO Niger delta Negro
ODYL alleged force
ADZE tool
IDZO Niger delta Negro

BEAD globule; ball; drop; aim
BEAK bill; nose; judge
BEAL river mouth
BEAM bar; timber; breadth; ray; smile; on the —; broadcast
BEAN plant; trifle; head; strike
BEAR carry; yield; endure; relate; animal; Ursa; short-seller; pessimist
BEAS Punjab river
BEAT strike; defeat; mystify; throb; scoop; field; sphere; — the Dutch
BEAU dandy; lover; — Brummell, — Nash
DEAD deceased; entire; absolute(ly); — reckoning
DEAF unhearing; inattentive; — and dumb, — mute
DEAL bargain; transaction; unfinished wood; apportion(ment); policy; New —, Fair —
DEAN clergyman; educator; oldest member, doyen
DEAR costly; loved; loved one
FEAK twitch; wipe
FEAL conceal
FEAR fright; doubt
FEAT deed; accomplishment
GEAL pert. to earth
GEAN cherry
GEAR notched wheel; equipment; adjust; harmonize
GEAT channel in mold; Scandinavian (Beowulf)
HEAD skull; top; brain; chief; crux; source
HEAF pasture
HEAL cure; restore
HEAP pile; crowd; car
HEAR listen; perceive by ear
HEAT warmth; rage; height; dead —; pressure; strain
JEAN name; cotton cloth
KEAL cabbage
LEAD metal; element; plummet; bullets; color; guide; command
LEAF plant part; sheet; tea
LEAH fem. name; Laban's daughter; Jacob's wife
LEAK loss; ooze; crack
LEAL loyal: Scot.
LEAN be supported; incline; thin
LEAP jump, skip; — year
LEAR learning: Scot.; king; father of Goneril, Regan, Cordelia
MEAD drink; meadow; lake; Margaret, anthropologist
MEAH wall tower
MEAL grain; pulverize; repast
MEAN intend; denote; base; unkind; middle
MEAT flesh; kernel; food
NEAL male name; novelist
NEAP wagon pole; tide
NEAR close(ly); approach
NEAT tidy; trim; straight
PEAG money
PEAI medicine man
PEAK point; top; summit
PEAL ring; loud sound; fish
PEAN panegyric; praise; fur
PEAR fruit, tree
PEAT darling; turf; fuel
PEAU skin: Fr.
PEAY medicine man
READ interpret; learn; study; understand
REAL coin; true; genuine; very
REAM 500 (paper) quantity; bevel; enlarge
REAP cut; harvest
REAR back; raise; — admiral
SEAH measure
SEAL otarian; pinniped; fur; fasten; brown; ratify; stamp
SEAM fold; crevice; join; ornament; measure
SEAN John
SEAR burn; dried up; gun-lock catch
SEAT chair; fundament; site; membership;

install; hot —
TEAK tree; dark
TEAL duck (blue)
TEAM group; yoke
TEAN tone: Scot.
TEAP ram
TEAR drop; weep; rip; glass defect
TEAT nipple
VEAL calf; meat
VEAU veal, calf: Fr.
WEAK feeble; pliable; light
WEAL body politic; stripe
WEAN withdraw; alienate
WEAR be clothed in; impair; endure; deteriorate
YEAH yes
YEAN to lamb
YEAR time period; twelve month; leap —; calendar, fiscal —
YEAS yes votes
ZEAL ardor; enthusiasm
CEBA tree; kapok source
CEBU Visayan Island
DEBS Eugene (socialist)
DEBT fault; liability; obligation
GEBA Jonathan's victory site
HEBE cupbearer of gods; Zeus's daughter, Hercules' wife; color
NEBO wisdom god; Moab mountain (Moses died)
PEBA armadillo; Indian
REBA weight
SEBA Bib. country; Ham's grandson
SEBI prefix: tallow
TEBJ Negro Berber
UEBA measure
WEBB Beatrice Potter (writer)
ZEBU ox; Brahman bull
BECK nod; bidding; dyeing vat; Pol., Ger. officer, statesman
CECH Czech
DECA prefix: ten
DECI prefix: tenth
DECK ship floor; pack, cards; array; adorn
FECK amount
HECK (weaving) frame; cough; oath
KECK vomit; show disgust
LECH slab; capstone; river
NECK body part; violin part; isthmus; pet
PECA coin
PECK measure; nip; bite; kiss
PECO black tea
RECK heed; concern
RECT element (philos.)
SECH such
SECK unprofitable (rent)
SECT group; denomination
TECA teak; Indian
TECH technical school
TECK readymade tie
TECO Indian
BEDE Adam (Eliot); the Venerable (monk)
CEDE yield; grant; transfer
DEDO measure
LEDA mollusk; mother of Castor, Pollux, Helen, Clytemnestra; wooed by Zeus as swan
MEDA secret Indian sect
MEDB Conchobor's wife; goddess; Queen Mab
MEDE ancient Asian
MEDI prefix: middle
PEDA pastoral staffs
PEDI prefix: foot
PEDO child
REDD make tidy; free of; scold
REDE interpret; counsel
REDO make over
TEDA Negro Berber
VEDA sacred Hindu books
YEDO Tokyo
BEEF ox, steer, cow, bos; brawn; rage; complain(t)
BEEN charmer's clarinet; participle
BEEP radio sound
BEER beverage; ale; mead
BEES yeast
BEET vegetable; root; sugar —; — top
DEED act; property transfer
DEEM consider; judge
DEEP profound; extensive; ocean
DEER ruminant; cervine; — Park (Buddha site)
FEED nourish; gratify; graze; fodder
FEEL sense; test; suffer
FEES charges; tips
FEET measure
GEEK carnival wild man
GEEZ Version (Ethiopic Bible)
HEED notice; attention
HEEL back part; end; slant; follow; scoundrel
HEEP Uriah (Dickens villain)
HEER Mr., Sir: Dutch
JEEL pool; marsh
JEEP vehicle; automobile
JEER scoff; taunt
KEEF hemp; languor
KEEK fashion spy
KEEL ship bottom; navigate; ocher; guinea fowl
KEEN sharp; acute; bewail
KEEP tend; retain; preserve; last
KEET guinea fowl
LEEK plant (onion; liliaceous); — green (Wales emblem)
LEER sly gaze; oven; loin
LEES dregs
LEET court; list
MEED reward
MEEK mild; submissive
MEER sea: Ger.
MEET encounter; face; combat; fulfill; fit
NEED compulsion; lack; want
NEEM tree; Margosa
NEEP turnip
NEER never; kidney
PEEK sly glance; pry; chirp
PEEL pare; tower; spade
PEEN hammer head
PEEP chirp; bird; peer slyly; Bo —; jeep
PEER gaze; equal; nobleman
PEET darling; turf; fuel
REED woody grass; pipe; mouthpiece; Walter (doctor, hospital)
REEF shoal; lode;

reduce sail
REEK cloud; exude; smell
REEL wind(er); dance; waver; sway
REEM ox; unicorn
SEED fertile germ; progeny; decay; plant; extract
SEEK ask; try; hunt
SEEL shut eyes of; blind
SEEM look; appear
SEEN observed
SEEP ooze; small spring
SEER prophet
TEEL sesame
TEEM abound
TEEN 13–19; injury; pain
TEER golfer; mix colors
TEES river (North Sea)
VEEP vice-president
VEER shift (course); waver
WEED plant; tobacco; remove
WEEK time unit; sennight; squeak
WEEL fish basket, trap; pool
WEEP cry; bend; leak
WEET bird; cry of bird

DEFI challenge; defiance
DEFT skillful; trim
DEFY challenge; dare
HEFT weight; bulk; notebook: Ger.
JEFE chief; leader
JEFF rope; nickname; Mutt and —
LEFT departed; blow; — of center (Liberals)
REFT cleft; rift; deprived
TEFF grain plant
WEFT yarn; mist; (weave) web
BEGA measure
DEGU rodent (Octodon)
HEGH exclamation; hey!
MEGA prefix: great
PEGA remora fish
PEGU Burmese language, city
SEGO herb; bulb; lily; Utah state flower
TEGG sheep in 2nd year
VEGA meadow
WEGA star
WEGG Silas (ballad seller: Dickens)

YEGG safecracker; tramp
BEHN herb; tree
DEHA body (theosophy)
HEHE Bantu tribe
JEHU (chariot) driver; prophet, king (Israel)
LEHI prophet
LEHR oven; Lew (comedian)
PEHO morepork (bird)
SEHR very: Ger.
TEHR wild goat
VEHM medieval tribunal
BEID star
BEIN good; fine
CEIL overlay; line; ceiling
DEIL devil; -s-bit (plant)
DEIN your(s): Ger.
FEIL comfortable; neat
FEIS convention; — of Tara
GEIN glucoside (Geum urbanum)
HEII Hawaiian fern
HEIL hail: Ger.
HEIN surprise!: Fr.
HEIR inherit(or); — apparent, presumptive
KEID star
KEIF hemp; languor
KEIR bleaching vat
LEIF Ericson (explorer)
LEIL faithful, loyal (Land of the —)
LEIR sea god (Lear)
MEIN Chinese noodles; chow —
MEIO measure
NEIF serf; native; fist
NEIL male name
NEIN no: Ger.
NEIR kidney
OEIL eye: Fr.; — de boeuf
REIM oxhide strap
REIN strap; check; direct; kidney
REIS money; (boat) captain; effendi (state officer)
SEID tribe; lord; chief; Mohammed's descendant
SEIK Hindu sectarian
SEIL rope: Ger.
SEIM Polish assembly
SEIN poss. pronoun, be, being: Ger.
SEIP seep; ooze
SEIR Bib. mountain (Hor), Edom (Esau's home)
SEIS six: Sp.
SEIT measure
TEIG Teague; Thaddeus; Timothy; dough: Ger.
TEIL linden tree; lime
VEIL screen; facial garment; cloistered life
VEIN channel; streak; blood vessel
WEIN wine: Ger.
WEIR dam; fish trap
ZEIN protein
BEJA Nile nomad
DEJA already: Fr.
NEJD kingdom
REJA screen, grille: Sp.
SEJM Polish assembly
TEJU lizard
BEKA weight
FEKE trick device
PEKE (Pekinese) dog
REKE rick; pile
REKI Baluchistan nomad
WEKA flightless bird
WEKI fern
ZEKE Ezekiel
BELA jasmine; Benjamin's 1st son; Hungarian king
BELI myth. Brit. king
BELL ringing cup; gong; time period; flower shape; helmet; Brontë pseudonym; — the cat; diving —
BELT strap; zone; beat
CELA that: Fr.
CELL cubicle; group; elec. jar; organism
CELT Irish, Scot, Welsh, Breton; chisel
DELE omit; erase
DELF quarry; pottery; blue
DELL valley; dingle; wench
EELY wriggling; slippery
FELD field: Ger.
FELL skin; cut, sew (down); savage
FELS Eastern coin
FELT pressed fibers; hat; sensed
GELD castrate; prune; tax
GELT money

HELA goddess; Loki's daughter
HELD kept; retained
HELI prefix: sun, spiral
HELL Hades; state of misery; -bent
HELM steer (wheel); tiller
HELO squeamish
HELP relieve; avoid; wait on, aid(e); servants
JELL solidify; mature
KELA measures
KELD spring; fountain
KELE weight
KELK fish roe
KELL Gaul; net; film
KELP seaweed, iodine source
KELT Celt; cloth; trout
LELY Dutch painter
MELA festival; prefix: black
MELD announce (score); merge
MELE Hawaiian poem; chant
MELL (beat with) hammer; teacher (Dickens)
MELT liquefy
NELL Ellen; Helen; Little — (Dickens girl)
PELA wax (secreting insect)
PELE fire goddess
PELF booty; riches
PELO hair: It.
PELT skin; hurl; strike
PELU hardwood tree
RELY trust; depend
SELA Dead Sea town
SELF identity; ego; one
SELL vend; betray; persuade; hoax; — short
TELA tissue; web; banana port
TELE prefix: far, complete
TELI low (merchant) caste
TELL inform; discern; chat; William (Swiss hero)
VELA membranes; soft palates; the Sails (Argo constellation)
VELD So. Afr. grassland
VELT measure
VELO speed unit
WELD unite; junction
WELF ducal family
WELK (gather) snail; Lawrence (musician)
WELL (water) pit; shaft; eddy; flow; rightly; very; sound; healthy
WELS sheatfish
WELT ridge; wale; strip; sew; beat; universe: Ger.
YELD barren; milkless
YELK yolk
YELL cry; cheer
YELP shrill bark
YELT gilt (sow)
BEMA platform; altar; measure
DEME Greek commune
DEMI prefix: half
DEMO prefix: populace
DEMY coin; scholar; paper size
FEME wife; tribunal
HEMA prefix: blood
HEME reduce hematin
HEMI prefix: half
HEMO prefix: blood
HEMP herb; hashish; cannabis; rope (fiber)
KEMP fur refuse
MEMO note; statement
NEMA eelworm; prefix: thread
NEMO nobody: Lat.; prefix: glade; Captain (Verne hero)
REMI Gaul people; prefix: oar
REMS river
SEME (sprinkling) pattern
SEMI half
SEMO Sancus (deity); Dius Fidius
TEMA musical theme; Arab
TEMS sieve; sift
XEMA arctic gull
ZEME (abode of) spirit; fetish
ZEMI (abode of) spirit; fetish
BENA grass (vetiver)
BEND turn; curve; flex; bow
BENE wild hog; well: It. & Lat.
BENG devil (Gypsy)
BENI Bolivian river; sesame
BENJ hemp; narcotic
BENN seed
BENO alcholic palm sap
BENT crooked; inclination; grass
BENU holy bird (Ra-Osiris)
CENA (Last) supper
CENE suffix: recent
CENS payment due
CENT coin; penny; game
DENE measure; dune; Indian
DENS tooth: Lat.
DENT depress(ion); notch
DENY refuse; contradict
EENY — meeny, miny, mo
FEND keep off; parry
FENT slit; cleft
GENA cheek; beak part
GENE hereditary factor; chromosome part; nickname
GENS clan: Lat.; people: Fr.
GENT gentleman; Belg. city
GENU knee: Lat.
HENS fowl; -foot (herb)
JENA Ger. city (optical, Napoleonic victory); glass
KENO lotto (game); prefix: empty
KENT Eng. country, duchy; Lear's follower
LENA firewood: Sp.; river; Conrad heroine
LEND make loan, grant; — an ear
LENE smooth; consonant
LENO (cotton, silk) fabric
LENS eye part; glass (optical); herb
LENT fasting period; slow; made loan
MEND repair; improve
MENE — tekel upharsin (handwriting on the wall)
MENG mix
MENO prefix: month
MENS mind: Lat.
MENT falcon-headed god
MENU bill of fare
OENO prefix: wine

PEND hang; be delayed
PENE (hammer) head
PENK minnow
PENN William (Penna. founder)
PENT confined; -house
RENA rockfish
REND tear; rupture; bark trees
RENI It. painter; prefix: kidney
RENO Nev. city ("biggest little"; divorce, gambling)
RENT torn; schism; let, lease; payment, income
SEND transmit; dispatch; propel; swing; enthrall
SENN Swiss herdsman
TEND serve; incline
TENE suffix: ribbon
TENG measure
TENT cloth shelter; pup —; wine; frame
VENA vein: Lat.
VEND Slav; sell; sale
VENI prefix: vein; —, vidi, vici (I came, I saw, I conquered)
VENO prefix: vein
VENT hole; let out; issue
WEND Slav; go; travel
WENT departed
XENO guest; prefix: foreign
YENI So. Amer. tanager
ZEND — Avesta (holy text)
ZENO philosopher (Stoic, Cynic); emperor
ZENU Afr. sheep
AEON age
FEOD feudal estate
GEON paradise river; Jerusalem spring
LEON country, city; Ponce de (explorer)
MEOU cat's cry; measure
MEOW cat's cry; measure
NEON gas(eous) element; lamp
PEON laborer
PEOR Bib. mountain
TEOS Ionian city
CEPA onion
CEPE boletus (edible fungus)
DEPA measure
KEPI military cap
KEPT retained; lasted
NEPA water scorpion; needle bug
PEPO pumpkin; squash; melon; cucumber
REPP silk or wool fabric
SEPS snake; lizard
SEPT social unit; screen; seven: Fr.
VEPS Finnish tribe (Chud); Dog Star (Isis); Horus
WEPT cried; Jesus —
AERA age; era
AERI prefix: air
AERO go by aircraft
AERY ethereal; nest
BERA king of Sodom
BERG iceberg; mountain
BERI Sudanese (Fulah); -beri (disease)
BERM (l)edge; road shoulder
BERN Swiss capital
BERT nickname
CERA prefix: horn, wax
CERE wax; (wrap in a) waxed cloth; beak part
CERN decide
CERO mackerel
DERA suffix: neck types
DERE — Mable (Streeter book)
DERM prefix, suffix: skin layer
KERY weird; uncanny; timid
FERK measure
FERN seedless plant
FERU bast fiber
GERA city
GERB sheaf; firework
GERD Frey's wife
GERE Odin's wolf
GERI Odin's wolf
GERM bud; seed; microbe
HERA Zeus's sister, wife
HERB plant; nickname
HERD crowd; feed together
HERE vicinity; present
HERL (feather) barb
HERO protagonist; demigod; — and Leander; Beatrice's cousin
HERR lord, Mister, Sir: Ger.
HERS fem., poss. pronoun
JERK grab; twist; spasm; soda man; dullard; beef
JERL boat joint
JERM Levantine boat
KERB gutter part
KERE read(ing substitute)
KERF cut; notch
KERI read(ing substitute)
KERN soldier; peasant; grain; type part; Jerome (composer)
KERR physicist
KERS cress
LERO Dodecanese isle
LERP secretion; insect
MERE fen; lake; boundary; war club; bare; only; simple; mother: Fr.
MERL blackbird
MERO grouper (fish)
MERU fabled mountain
NERA Tiber tributary
NERI Blacks: It.
NERO emperor; fiddler; Agrippine's son; Wolfe (Stout)
PERA Istanbul district
PERE father, priest: Fr. — Goriot (Balzac)
PERI fairy; elf; beauty
PERK lift up; preen; cocky; percolate
PERM elec. unit; hair wave
PERN honey buzzard
PERO but: Sp.
PERT bold; lively; sandpiper
PERU country
QERE read(ing substitute)
QERI read(ing substitute)
SERA antitoxins; blood parts; whey; evening: It.
SERB Servian; Yugo(slav)
SERE wither(ed); Negroid
SERF slave; peasant
SERI betel; Indian
SERO prefix: thin; late pupil
SERT Sp. painter
TERA Buddhist monastery
TERM phrase; word; condition; time, period
TERN gull; threefold; ship
TERP prehistoric mound

VERA tree; measure; name
VERB action word
VERD green(leafed)
VERI centipede
VERT green (Her.); veer; convert
VERY true; same; extremely; light signals; flare
WERE prefix: metamorphosed human
WERF farmyard
WERI aweto (caterpillar)
WERT were: archaic, poetic
XERO prefix: dry
YERK wrench; kick; trump
ZERO nothing; cipher; nullity; — hour; Japanese plane
BESA coin
BESS nickname; Mrs. Truman
BEST most (good); defeat
CESS tax; luck
CEST girdle; belt (Venus)
DESI jute; Arnaz
DESK table; lectern; department
FESS broad band (Her.); confess
FEST festive gathering
GEST deed; romance tale, adventure
GESU Jesus: It.
HEST command; precept
JESS strap on hawk leg
JEST joke
JESU name: Jesus
LESE — majesty (disrespect)
LESS shorter; fewer; inferior; minus
LEST for fear that
MESA flat hill; oakwood color
MESE Greek mus. term
MESH net; netting; entangle
MESS banquet; meal; muddle; disorder; botch
NESH soft; juicy; dainty
NESS cape; promontory; suffix
NEST (make a) home
OESE bacteriologist's wire
PESA coin
PESO coin; Sp. dollar
PESS hassock
PEST plague; insect; nuisance
RESE shake; rush
RESH Heb. 20th letter, 200; plant
REST pause; stop; peace; prop; stay; rely; mus. sign; remainder; set; found
SESI black-fin snapper
SESS soap frame bar
TESA Indian buzzard
TESS Theresa, Hardy heroine
TEST shell; cupel; examination; try
VEST waistcoat; clothe; empower
WESE we shall
WEST wind; painter, author; occident; go —; Mae —
YESO plaster of Paris; gypsum
ZEST orange peel; relish; gusto
AETA Negrito; native
BETA Greek B, 2; star; ray
BETE beast, silly: Fr.; — noire
BETH Heb. B, 2; Alcott heroine (Little Women)
CETE marine mammals
CETO prefix: whale
FETE festival; regale
GETA Jap. wooden clogs
GETT bill of divorce
HETH son of Canaan; Hittite ancestor
HETT Hittite ancestor
JETE ballet jump
JETH Hindu month
KETA dog salmon
KETU eclipse demon (Rahu)
LETE quadrille set
LETI island off Timor
LETO mother of Apollo, Artemis
LETT Latvian, Balt (Riga man)
META goal post; river
METE measure; allot
METZ city, former fort
NETE Greek mus. term
NETI eulalia (thatch grass)
NETT undeductible
PETE strongbox; Peter
PETO wahoo (fish); Henry IV figure
RETE network
SETA caterpillar's hair; spine
SETH banker; Adam's son; Osiris' evil brother
SETI river; pharaoh
SETT tool; paving stone
TETE head: Fr.; — a tete; hairdo
TETH Heb. J, 9
VETA mountain sickness
VETO prohibit(ion); no
WETA wingless locust
YETA Jap. outcast
YETI abominable snowman
ZETA Greek Z, 7
DEUL Hindu temple
DEUM Te — (hymn)
DEUS god: Lat.; — ex machina
DEUX two: Fr.
FEUD strife; vendetta; feo
GEUM plant (astringent)
JEUX cards, hands, games: Fr.
JEUZ chief Benjamite
KEUP measure
LEUD feudal tenant
MEUM carrotlike herb, spicknel; mine: Lat.
NEUE new
NEUF nine, new: Fr.
OEUF egg: Fr.
PEUL Fulah (Sudanese)
PEUR fear: Fr.
REUS defendant: Lat.
ZEUS chief god; Jupiter; Hera's husband; son of Cronus, Rhea
BEVY company; flock
DEVA deity (Indra); demon
DEVI goddess; Siva's wife (Shakti); title: Mrs., Lady
HEVI apple (tree)
LEVI Jacob's, Leah's son; tribe
LEVO prefix: left
LEVY assess; seize; tax
NEVA river (Leningrad)
NEVE snow; firn
PEVA Peru Indian
PEVY lumberman's hook

REVE (muse in) dream: Fr.
REVS rotations per minute
SEVE wine delicacy: Fr.
WEVE contraction
DEWA deity (Indra); demon
DEWY moist; refreshing
HEWN felled; squared
JEWS -harp
LEWD lecherous; obscene
MEWL whimper; miaou
MEWS (royal) stables
NEWS intelligence; tidings
NEWT salamander; eft
SEWN stitched
TEWA N.M. Indian
NEXT nearest; following
SEXT canonical hour (noon); organ stop; sixth
SEXY sexually appealing
TEXT (literary) substance; topic; Scripture passage; type
CEYX Halcyone's husband
KEYS House of (Isle of Man legislature); cays; Florida —
TEYL linden; lime tree

AFAR far away; tribe
UFER fir pole; shore: Ger.
AFFA from off
AFFY join
IFFY contingent
OFFA Angles' hero (Beowulf)
OFFS cricket-field sides
EFIK Negro
IFIL tree (brown dye)
EFOD priestly garb; image
AFRA name; union
PFUI exclamation

AGAG king
AGAL cord
AGAO language
AGAR wood
AGAU language
AGAZ Indian
EGAD oath
EGAL equal: Fr.
EGAN horse (Kipling)
IGAL Moses' spy
NGAI spiritual power
NGAN measure

OGAM Irish alphabet
EGBA Negro; Yoruba
EGBO secret society (Ogboni)
AGED old; oxygian
AGEE awry; Shammah's father; James (novelist)
AGER apparatus; field
EGER river
OGEE arch; molding
EGGS ova; — and bacon, ham; — and butter (flowers)
EGGY egg-stained; yolky
AGHA officer; title
AGIB dervish
AGIO fee; commission
AGIS king
EGIL Volund's (Wayland's) brother
EGIS protection; patronage; symbol of: Zeus, Athena; shield
AGLA acrostic
IGLU Eskimo hut; seal hole
OGLE gaze (amorously)
UGLY badlooking; unpleasant; plug-
EGMA enigma
AGNI god; lambs
AGNO Luzon river
AGOG eager
AGON contest; argument
EGOL antiseptic
IGOR Prince (opera)
OGOR early Turkic man
OGPU Soviet police body
AGRA comb. form; carpet; city (Taj Mahal site)
AGRI fields
AGRO prefix: soil
OGRE giant; monster
AGUA water; toad
AGUE fever
OGUM Irish alphabet
YGUN antisub gun

AHAB king; captain; prophet
AHAZ king
BHAR Kolarian native
DHAT minstrel; scholar
CHAA tea
CHAB bird
CHAC -Mool (god); -chac (instr.)
CHAD lake; nation
CHAI person
CHAL man
CHAM tribe; title; bite
CHAN resthouse; lord; title
CHAO measure
CHAP fellow; crack; jaw
CHAR trout; burn; sandbank; -woman
CHAT talk; bird; spike
CHAW masticate
CHAY red dye plant
DHAI midwife
DHAK tree
DHAL split pea, lentil
DHAN wealth; loan
DHAO knife (Burma)
DHAR state; town (India)
DHAW billhook
GHAT range; bank; river bank stairs
KHAN resthouse; lord; title; Agha —
KHAR weight
KHAS special; noble
KHAT measure
OHAD Simeon's son
PHAD star
PHAG comb. form: eating
PHAN measure
PHAO wolf (Kipling)
SHAB paltry guy
SHAD fish
SHAG hair; tobacco; bird; rascal; dance step
SHAH ruler
SHAM deceit; fake
SHAN Thai
SHAP silk yarn
SHAT saline lake
SHAW thicket; pshaw; playwright (George Bernard)
SHAY chaise; carriage
THAI Siamese
THAN in comparison with; conjunction
THAR goat
THAT so; which; pronoun; connective; that's —
THAW melt; unbend
WHAM exclamation
WHAT interrogative; pronoun; what's —
WHAU why; tree
AHEM interjection
AHER Benjamite
AHET season (of inundation)
AHEY ho
BHEL thorny (fruit) tree

CHEE weight
CHEF head (cook); — d'oeuvre
CHEK Chin. foot (measure)
CHEN snow goose
CHER dear: Fr.
CHEW masticate; ruminate; — the cud; — the rag
CHEZ at home of, with: Fr.
DHER mound; land share
EHEU alas
GHEE butter
GHEG Albanian
GHES Tapuyan Indian
KHEM chief god (Min)
KHET mortal body; measure
OHEL Zerubabbel's son
PHEW exclamation
RHEA Cybele, mother of the gods; Gaea's daughter; Cronos's wife; ostrich; satellite; grass
SHEA tree; butter
SHED cast off; abandon; drop; hut; shelter
SHEE Irish fairyfolk
SHEM Noah's son; Semite
SHEN Christian God (China)
SHER tiger
SHEW show: Brit.; -bread
THEA tea source; name
THEB measure
THEE you
THEM pronoun
THEN at a time; therefore
THEO prefix: god
THEW muscle; sinew
THEY pronoun; people; men
WHEE whistle sound
WHEN whereas; how soon
WHET sharpen; excite; edge
WHEW whistle; exclamation
WHEY milk serum; thin; pale; curds and —
AHIO Ark driver
AHIR caste
BHIL low-caste Indian
CHIA salvia beverage, oil
CHIB tongue; language
CHIC stylish(ness)
CHIH Chin. foot (measure)
CHIL cheer pine; kite (Kipling)
CHIN lower jaw; chatter; weight; dynasty; Burmese
CHIP fragment; cut; hew
CHIR pheasant; pine
CHIT child; sprout; memo; voucher; mind
CHIV knife
OHIA timber tree; apple
OHIO Buckeye state
PHIL nickname; Philip; prefix: loving
PHIT bullet sound
PHIZ physiognomy; face
RHIA China grass
RHIN Rhine: Fr.
SHIH weight; measure
SHIK Arabian Turkoman
SHIM leveling slip; shingle; knife
SHIN leg, calf front; run; climb
SHIP vessel; send; — of state
SHIR cook; gathers; tiger
SHIV bit of husk; fluff; blade
THIN lean; dim; rare; dilute; — ice
THIO prefix: brimstone
THIS pronoun, demonstrative
WHIG U.S., Brit. party
WHIM fancy; caprice
WHIN gorse; restharrow; rock; winch
WHIP lash; urge; defeat
WHIR fly; hurry; buzz
WHIT bit; jot; dull sound
WHIZ hum; bargain; corker
SHLU Moroccan Berber
OHNE without: Ger.
AHOM Assam native
AHOY call; ship —
BHOY gang member; rowdy
CHOB grain spike
CHOL desolate plain; Mayan
CHOP cut; crack; eat; barter; jaw
CHOR thief; steal (Gypsy)
CHOU cabbage; darling: Fr.; Chin. dynasty; En Lai (statesman)
CHOW food; dog
CHOY red dye root
DHOW Arab. sailboat
GHOR Dead Sea valley
GHOS Chin. dynasty
JHOW tamarisk shrub
KHOR watercourse; gorge
KHOT farmer; contractor
OHOY ahoy; call
PHON loudness measure
PHOO disgusting!
PHOS phosphorus
PHOT light unit
RHOB juice; jelly
SHOA Abyssinian
SHOD wearing shoes
SHOE foot covering; crackow; wheel drag; tire
SHOG shake; jog
SHOO scare away; begone!
SHOP store; buy; buying place; talk —; window-
SHOQ tree (tanning); chogak
SHOR salt lake; Tatar tribe
SHOT missile; pellet; guess; range; marksman; film record; long —; big —
SHOU Tibetan deer
SHOW exhibit(ion); reveal; appear(ance); 3rd place; no — (airline term)
THOB rationalize
THOR thunder god (Thursday); Midgard slayer; Odin's son; missile
THOS jackal genus
THOU 2nd pers. pronoun
WHOA stop!; opp. of giddap
WHOM pronoun
WHOO exclamation
WHOP dash; beat; bump
SHRI glorious; holy; Lakshmi (goddess)
AHUM humming
BHUT Dravidian ghost
CHUB fallfish; dace; chevin
CHUD Mongols; Vepse; Vote; Tavastian
CHUG pull; fish; (move with) vibration
CHUM friend; scrap fish

CHUN Chin. pottery
CHUR Swiss canton
CHUT nonsense!
EHUD judge of Israel
GHUZ Turkish invader
JHUM cultivation method
PHUD bullet sound; exclamation
PHUT (bullet) sound; OT people
RHUM alcholic drink
RHUS sumac genus
SHUA Abraham's son
SHUE Tibetan deer
SHUL synagogue
SHUN avoid; abstain
SHUT close; refine
THUD dull sound; blow
THUG assassin; hoodlum
THUS in this way; hence
WHUN gorse; restharrow
IHVH God; Tetragrammaton
JHVH Jehova; God; Tetragrammaton
YHVH God, Yahveh, Tetragrammaton
JHWH Jahweh; God; Tetragrammaton
YHWH God, Yahweh, Tetragrammaton
WHYO gangster; footpad

AIAH Edomite, Rizpah's father
BIAS diagonal (incline); prejudice
DIAD pair
DIAL plate; face; call; sun-
DIAN reveille
DIAU Indian
DIAZ Bartholomeu (Port. navigator)
FIAT sanction; edict; money; automobile (It.)
GIAN -Carlo (Menotti)
KIAK canoe
LIAM O'Flaherty: "Informer"
LIAO Manchuria river
LIAR prevaricator; plant
LIAS geol. period
MIAM hut
MIAN sir; title
MIAO Chinese aborigine
MIAS orang-utan
NIAS Ind. Ocean island(er)
PIAN tumor
PIAT magpie; antitank gun
PIAY medicine man
RIAL coin
SIAK latex
SIAL earth's outer part
SIAM Thailand; Anna's king (The King and I)
TIAM language
TIAO Chinese money
TIAR crown; shrub
VIAL vessel
BIBB mast's timber piece
BIBI title: Lady, Mrs. (India)
DIBS juice: grape, date
GIBE scoff; jeer; agree
JIBE sneer; agree; coincide; shift course
JIBI extinct bird
KIBE chilblain crack
KIBO Afr. peak (Kilimanjaro)
NIBS personage (VIP); Peter Pan (Barrie)
TIBS — eve (never-never)
TIBU Negro-Berber
VIBO gulf (Italy)
AICH alloy
BICE blue, green pigment
DICE (cut into) cubes; gamble; gaming implements
DICH you: Ger.
DICK Richard; whip; lad; detective; Whittington (London mayor)
FICO trifle
HICK hiccup; rube; jake
KICK hit; die; object(ion); excitement; -back
LICE insects (louse)
LICK tongue; stroke; whip; conquer; bit
MICA isinglass (silicate)
MICE rodents (mouse)
MICH me: Ger.
MICK Irishman
MICO marmoset
NICE good; kind; pleasing; delicate; dainty; quimper color; Riviera port
NICK notch; moment; cheat; cut; Old — (devil); Carter (detective)
PICA type size; magpies
PICE coin; weight
PICI birds (woodpeckers)
PICK tool; scratch; choose; rob; eat; best
PICO peak; game; weight
PICT British aborigine
RICE cereal; use ricer; Elmer (playwright)
RICH wealthy; vivid; full; fragrant; fat
RICK pile (up); haystack
SICE number 6 on die
SICK urge (dog); ill; weak
TICE lure; yorker (bowled ball)
TICK parasite; mattress; count; tic
VICA Pota (goddess)
VICE sin; fault; vise; proxy; — versa
WICK part of candle, lamp
AIDA opera; Radames' lover
AIDE help; -de-camp; — memoire
BIDE wait; tarry; dwell
DIDO trick; caper; Carthage queen, Aeneas' beloved
EIDE ideas; forms
FIDE entrust; — et amore
FIDO fog evaporation; dog's name
GIDE Andre (author)
HIDE land measure; skin; conceal; shelter; — and hair
KIDD William (privateer)
KIDS star (Auriga)
LIDA Alida
LIDE March (month)
LIDO Venice beach
MIDE Ojibway secret order
MIDI south(ern France)
NIDE pheasant's nest
NIDI breeding places
RIDD Lorna Doone's rescuer
RIDE be borne; float; endure; manage; mount; journey
SIDA herb; shrub; hemp
SIDE region, part(y); oblique; aspect; support; lateral

SIDI Moslem title; Negro
SIDY pretentious
TIDE ocean's rise, fall; season; drift; endure; current; help
TIDY (make) neat
VIDA feminine of David
VIDE see: Lat.; for example; quae —
WIDE broad; far; lax; astray
WIDU Moslem ablution
AIEA town
AIEL writ of —
BIEN good, fine: Fr.; — aimee (well beloved)
BIER litter; coffin
CIEL ceiling; sky: Fr.
DIEB jackal
DIEM day: Lat.; per —
DIER one moribund
DIES day(s): Lat.; — irae; Cong. committee
DIET fare; food regimen; parliament
DIEU god: Fr.; mon —!
FIEF feudal estate
GIER eagle (vulture)
HIEL Jericho's rebuilder
HIEN Chin. government seat
HIER here: Ger.; yesterday: Fr.
KIEF hemp; languor
KIEL ocher; ruddle; seaport; — Canal
KIER bleaching vat
KIEV Ukrainian city
LIED fibbed; song: Ger.
LIEF gladly; freely
LIEN claim; attachment; garnishment
LIER rester; layer
LIEU place; stead
MIEN manner; bearing; air
NIEL alloy
PIED variegated; Piper; -a-terre
PIEN arris (sharp edge)
PIER mole; dock; pillar
PIET magpie
RIEL Canadian (Indian) rebel
RIEM oxhide strap
RIEN nothing: Fr.; — ne va plus
RIER oil cask (whaling)
SIEG victory: Ger.
SIER pintado (fish)
TIED bound; knotted; drawn
TIEN sky: Chin.; — Chu (Lord of Heaven); your(s): Fr.
TIER row; layer; pinafore
VIER striver; four: Ger.
VIEW sight; see; aim; opinion; scene
WIEL whirlpool
WIES Ys
BIFF (deal a) blow
FIFE flute; checkers opening
FIFO inventory method
GIFT donation; talent
HIFI faithful sound rendition
JIFF instant
KIFF languor
LIFE existence; vivacity; biography
LIFO inventory method
LIFT ra(i)se; exalt; steal; elevator
MIFF quarrel; offend
NIFE earth's core
PIFF bullet sound; exclamation
RIFE abundant; prevalent
RIFF Berber; Kabyle; ripple
RIFI Riffs
RIFT split; divide; cleft
SIFT screen; separate; bolt
TIFF (petty) quarrel
WIFE spouse; marry
BIGA two-horse chariot
BIGG barley
GIGA medieval fiddle
HIGH lofty: elevated; noble; expensive; shrill; tainted; tipsy
MIGG marble (duck)
NIGH near(ly); direct
RIGA Latvian city, gulf
RIGI Swiss mountain
SIGH lament(ing sound)
SIGN symbol; signal; subscribe; ratify; hire
TIGE rifle steel pin; dog
TIGG swindler (Dickens)
VIGA rafter; log
WIGG peruke; long hair
WIGS — on the green (fray)
KIHO peacock butterfly
CIII 103; Trajan reign
LIII 53; Claudius reign
LIIN measure
MIII 1003
RIIS Jacob (journalist)
VIII 8; Augustus reign
XIII 13; Augustus reign
BIJA kino tree
FIJI islands (Lau, Yasawa)
LIJA unicorn fish
BIKE bicycle
BIKH aconite; poison
DIKA bread; fat; oil
DIKE levee; ditch; dig; goddess (Horae)
HIKE toss; tramp; raise
HIKU scabbard fish
KIKI castor oil plant
KIKU chrysanthemum
LIKE as; similar(ly); love; prefer; probable
MIKE Michael; Mick; microphone
NIKE victory goddess (Samothrace); missile
PIKA little chief hare
PIKE fish; weapon; pierce; highway; farmer; gamble; Zebulon (explorer; peak)
PIKI maize bread; pik
PIKY full of fish
RIKK tambourine
SIKA Jap. deer
SIKH Hindu soldier
TIKE child
TIKI god; first man; image
AILE winged
BILE liver secretion; choler
BILK defraud
BILL beak; weapon; law; poster; invoice; debt; nickname: William; — and coo; Sikes (Dickens)
BILO Balkan karst area
DILL flavoring herb; pickle
DILO poon tree
EILD barren; milkless
FILE tool; rasp; smooth; march; column; folder; arrange
FILI learned poet
FILL pack; complete; glut; — the bill
FILM skin; coating;

haze; photograph; picture
FILO silk thread
FILS son: Fr.; Dumas (Camille); Irak coin
GILA — monster; lizard; Ariz. river
GILD lay gold on; adorn; — the lily; trade society
GILL measure; brook; breathing organ; wattle; coin; lass
GILO woody vine (tonic)
GILT gold; sow
HILA 'eyes' of bean
HILD Hethin's victim princess
HILL mound; Jenny (Shaw character); -billy
HILO grass; city (Hawaii)
HILT sword
JILL girl; sweetheart; Jack and —
JILT betray in love
KILE measure; weight
KILL slay; veto; creek
KILN (burn in) oven
KILO measure; -gram, -meter; prefix: 1000
KILT Scot's skirt
LILA deity manifestation
LILE little
LILL small pin; loll; Lillian
LILT (sing) lively tune
LILY flower; Turk's-cap; pure; white
MILA measure
MILD calm(ly); soft; tame
MILE measure; distance; 320 rods, 1,609.3 meters
MILK nutritious fluid; sap; white; exploit; drain
MILL grind(er); quern; box; John Stuart (economist)
MILO name; grain; sorghum; Venus (Melos)
MILT spleen; fish gland; nickname
NILE river; green, blue
NILL refuse; negate
NILS Bohr (physicist)
OILY unctuous; bland; suave
PILE hair; heap (up); awn; atomic —
PILI nut; grass; hairs
PILL medicine tablet
PILY pilelike
RILE irritate; vex
RILL (run in a) brook
RILY turbid; irritated
SILK fiber; thread; -worm
SILL beam (door, window)
SILO fodder pit; ensile
SILT sediment; scum; drift
TILE ceramic slab; drain pipe; domino; tessera; slate
TILL until; plow; cultivate; tray, cash box
TILT cover; incline; tip; joust; sport
VILA fairy; New Hebrides
VILE base; evil; odious
VILI brother of Odin; Ve
VILL village; township
VILY fairies
WILD rough; savage; mad; eager; unruly; wilderness
WILE trick; guile; lure
WILK (gather) snail
WILL volition; choice; decree; bequeath; testament
WILT droop; lose spirit
WILY artful; subtle
BIMI orang-utang (Kipling)
CIMA mountain peak: It.
DIME coin; — novel
GIMP silk fabric; vim
HIMA Hamitic Negro
LIMA city; bean, yam; mollusk
LIMB leg; arm; member
LIME calcium oxide (mortar); snare; caustic; linden (tree); amber; citrus fruit
LIMN portray; delineate
LIMP halt; flaccid; loose
LIMU edible seaweed
LIMY viscous
MIMA woman actor
MIME drama; act; actor; clown; smith (Nibelungs)
MIMI nickname; opera heroine
NIMB nimbus; halo
OIME alas
PIMA Ariz. Indian; cotton
PIMP procurer; bawd; maquereau
RIMA fissure; breadfruit; child heroine (Hudson)
RIME frost; (make) rhymes; chink; rung
RIMU red pine; imou pine
RIMY frosty; rhyming
SIMA igneous rock
SIME monkey
SIMI Dodecanese isle
SIMP simpleton
TIME period; moment; credit term; speed rate; meter, rhythm; Father —; space-
YIMA Avestan demigod
ZIMB Ethiopian fly
AINE elder
AINO Jap. aboriginal
AINT contraction
AINU Jap. aboriginal
BINA Hindu guitar
BIND tie; protect; sew; cohere
BINE (hop) stem
BING bed roll; sharp sound
BINH weight
BINI Nigerian
BINN box; frame; crib
BINO alcoholic pine sap
BINT daughter; woman
CINE movie: Sp.
CINQ five: Fr.
DINE eat; have dinner
DING thump; sound; urge
DINK small boat; cut out
DINO prefix: terrible
DINT blow; force; notch
EINE one: Ger.
FIND discover(y); (re)gain
FINE end; superior; thin; keen; well; (set) penalty; geil —, derb — (Irish clans)
FINK finch; derb; informer; strikebreaker
FINN man of Finland, Helsinki; Ugric; Mickey — (KO drops); Huckleberry — (Twain novel)

GINK eccentric one
HIND fish; grouper; deer; posterior
HING asafetida (gum resin; antispasmodic)
HINO timber tree; dye
HINT suggestion; imply
JINK prank
JINN demon; spirit
JINX hoodoo; bad luck
KINA quinine
KIND sort; species; gentle
KINE cattle
KING monarch; ruler; chief; chessman; card
KINK twist; loop; cramp
KINO gum (catechu); prefix: moving
LINA measure; Caroline
LIND Jenny (singer, Swedish Nightingale)
LINE thin mark; cable; cord; wire; piping; row; direction; cover; align; track; flax
LING fish; burbot; hake
LINK (chain) loop; connect; join; torch; measure
LINN waterfall; linden
LINO measure
LINT raveling, fiber (of linen); netting
LINY streaky
LINZ Austrian city
MINA weight; money; myna; watchman
MIND intellect; brain; memory; wish; mood; plan; tend; dislike
MINE possessive pronoun; dig; pit; rich source; explosive
MING Chin. dynasty
MINK weasel-like animal
MINO Jap. straw coat
MINT herb; menthol; bonanza; coin; — julep
MINX pert girl
MINY of a mine
NINA goddess (Ea's daughter); ship (Pinta, —, Santa Maria); girl: Sp.
NINE number (of Muses); baseball team
NINO boy: Sp.
OINT apply oil
PINA pineapple; silver cone
PINE tree; conifer; evergreen; yearn; mourn
PING (bullet, striking) sound
PINK color (red); ship; cut; hunter's coat; carnation; in the — (healthy)
PINO pine tree
PINT measure
PINY pinelike; peony
RIND bark; peel; Vali's mother, Odin's wife
RINE hemp; ditch
RING gird; arena; prizefighting; gang; atomic order; sound (bell); Vienna landmark; Nibelungen cycle (Wagner)
RINK skating arena
SINA drug; mountain (Moses)
SIND river; Pakistan province; are: Ger.
SINE math. ratio; without: Lat.; — qua non; — die
SING vocalize; warble; tell
SINH hyperbolic function
SINK fall; droop; conceal; basin
SINN — Fein (Irish society)
SINO prefix: Chinese
TINA fem. nickname
TIND kindle
TINE tooth; prong; pain; grass
TING sound; Chin. pottery
TINO Sambal language
TINT color; shade; tinge
TINY small; -tim (herb); Tim (Dickens)
VINA harp; guitar; wines
VINE creeping plant
VINO palm liquor
VINT card game
VINY entwining
WIND turn; coil; blowing air; mere talk
WINE fermented juice
WING alar appendage; faction; annex; fly
WINK blink; signal
WINY vinous; drunken
XINA nickname: Christina
ZINC metal; element; color
ZING sharp thrill; vim
BIOD animal life force
BION physiological individual (morphon)
BIOS life: animal, plant
CION plant shoot
DIOL chem. compound; suffix
DION lord in Winter's Tale
DIOS God: Sp.
FIOT Congo tribe
LION cat; king of beasts; celebrity
NIOG coconut palm
NIOU measure
PION dig; excavate
PIOT magpie
RIOT tumult; success; — act, squad
SIOL great Irish clan
SION purple seaweed; Zion
TION suffix
TIOU Indian (Tonikan)
VIOL string instrument
ZION Israelites; heaven
AIPI cassava
CIPO liana
FIPS Martin Chuzzlewit
HIPE wrestler's throw
KIPE basket
KIPP peak (Glacier National Park); gymnastic feat
LIPA fat
NIPA palm; juice; mat; atap
PIPA toad; measure
PIPE tube; flute; cask (measure); -dream; — down
PIPI astringent; mollusk
PIPY tubular; weepy
RIPA river bank
RIPE mature; fit; tipsy
SIPO liana
TIPE rabbit trap
TIPI wigwam
WIPE rub off; beat
XIPE -totec (Aztec god)
YIPE howl; cry
ZIPA Chibcha chief
ZIPS Czech
AIRA grass

AIRE nobleman; river
AIRS pretensions; side
AIRT guide; turn
AIRY breezy, light
BIRD avian; flyer; fowl; shuttlecock; person; Blue —
BIRI cheap cigarette
BIRL revolve spin
BIRN clarinet socket
BIRR wind force; sound
CIRC circle; recess; corrie
CIRL bunting; bird
DIRE evil; fatal; extreme
DIRK dagger; Theodoric
DIRT muck; earth; gossip; do one —; — cheap
EIRE Ireland; Erin
FIRE combustion; ardor; discharge
FIRM fix; solid; company
FIRN granular snow(field)
GIRD encircle; clothe; brace
GIRL young female; maid; Gibson —; — of the Golden West; chorus —; — Friday
GIRO tour; round; credit system; aircraft (auto-)
GIRT encircled; prepared
HIRE engage; rent; wage
HIRO measure
KIRI paulownia tree; knobkerrie (missile)
KIRK church
KIRN harvest feast
LIRA money; lyre; hairlike ridge
LIRE coins; read: Fr.
MIRA star
MIRE bog; (stick in) mud
MIRK dark(ness)
MIRO tree; wood robin
MIRY boggy; filthy
PIRN reed; bobbin; nose ring
PIRO Tanoan Indian
PIRR wind gust; whiz; gull
RIRE to laugh: Fr.
SIRE father; beget; king
SIRI betel
SIRS gentlemen
TIRE fatigue; bore; wheel covering; rubber; shoe
TIRO amateur; novice
VIRA Bantu
VIRE feathered arrow
WIRE cable; snare
WIRY tough; sinewy
YIRM fret; whine: Scot., Ir.
YIRN whine; grimace; smirk: Scot., Ir.
YIRR growl; snarl: Scot.
ZIRA measure
BISA antelope
BISE cold wind; winter
BISH aconite; poison
BISK soup; ice cream; red-yellow
CISE dice term: six
CIST chest; roofed pit
DISA showiest orchid
DISC disk; record; — jockey
DISH receptacle; serve
DISK plate; harrow; puck
DISS reed grass
FISC exchequer
FISH piscine, angle; probe; search; tin — (torpedo)
FISK exchequer; Jim (speculator); tire
FIST grasp; effort; tightwad
GISH Moroccan public land; Lillian, Dorothy (actresses)
GIST main point; pith
HISH hiss; swish
HISS sibilant (of disapproval); goose; serpent; steam sound; Alger (Communist)
HIST call to attention; Indian girl (Cooper)
IISM egoism
KISH powder; basket; measure; Saul's father
KISS touch gently; caress, sweetmeat
KIST chest; installment; measure
LISA fem. name; nickname
LISK flank; loin
LISP speech defect
LISS (fairy) fort; release; peace; fleur-de-lis
LIST strip(e); roll; register; enter; inclination; careen
MISE levy; stake; tax; — en scene
MISS fail(ure); omit; want; girl; maiden
MIST dim; haze; gray
NISH Yugo. city
NISI unless; Lat.
OISE Fr. river
PISA city (leaning tower)
PISE building material
PISH reject; nonsense!
PISK nighthawk
PISO weight
PIST attention!; track
RISE climb; grow(th); begin; emerge(nce); thrive; retort
RISK peril; hazard; subject of insurance
RISP metal bar
RISS glaciation stage
RIST engrave; stretch
SISE six (dice)
SISH slushy ice
SISI porkfish
SISS hiss; shame!; girl
SIST stay; delay; summon
VISA endorse(ment); — vis
VISE tool; clamp; endorse
VISS weight
WISE sage; learned
WISH desire; request
WISP torch; shred; flock; brush; ignis fatuus
WIST know; knew; measure
AITU god; demon
BITE cut; pierce; grip; eat (into); sting; respond; snack
BITI blackwood
BITO tree; poison; oil
BITT naut. fastener
CITE summon; quote
CITO quickly, soon: It.
CITS citizens; mufti
CITY urban place
DITA tree; bark; upas
DITE mite; indict
DITT close up; obstruct

GITA Bhagavad —; Indian scriptures (yoga)
GITE shelter: Fr.; mad
JITI Rajmahal creeper
KITE hawk; rogue; flying toy; banking fraud
KITH acquaintance; — and kin
LITE suffix: mineral, rock
LITH prefix, suffix: stone
LITI medieval peasants
LITZ braided wire
MITE arachnid; parasite; small (coin)
MITT glove; hand
MITU curassow; bird
MITY parasite-infested
NITO climbing fern
PITA fiber; flax; hemp; brocket (deer)
PITH marrow; kernel; gist
PITO fiber; flax; hemp; brocket (deer)
PITT statesman (Commoner, Chatham); diamond
PITY sympathy; mercy
RITA cosmic order (Vedic); Rio —; fem. name
RITE ceremony; liturgy
SITA Ramachandra's wife (Sanskrit Ramayana)
SITE location; scene
SITO prefix: grain
TITI monkey; tree; petrel
TITO Yugo. leader (Broz)
VITA life: Lat.
VITE quick, lively: Fr.
VITI East African
WITH prep.: including, and
YITE bird (yellowhammer)
ZITA Austrian empress
BIUR Heb. commentary
NIUE Savage Island language
PIUS Pope: X (St.; Sarto); XI (Ratti); XII (Pacelli)
SIUM water parsnip
CIVA Hindu deity
CIVE chive garlic
DIVA prima donna; blue
DIVE plunge; duck; low resort; — bomb(er)
DIVI divine ones
FIVE number; basketball team; card
GIVE bestow; yield; grant
HIVE bees' swarm, house
JIVA life energy
JIVE dialect (dance, jazz)
KIVA ceremonial chamber
KIVE brewer's vat
KIVU tsetse fly
LIVE exist; continue; vital; alert
LIVY Roman historian; Titus Livius
RIVA shore: It.
RIVE tear; split; — droite (right bank), — gauche (left bank)
RIVO stream: It.
SIVA Hindu deity; cosmic dancer (Nataraja)
SIVE sickle; knife
TIVY huntsman's cry
VIVA salute (long live); — voce (spoken aloud)
VIVE — le roi!; long live!: Fr.
VIVO spirited
WIVE marry; act as wife
BIWA loquat
IIWI bird (mamo)
KIWI flightless bird; apteryx; non-flyer
BIXA tree genus; achiote
CIXO Ecuador Indian
DIXI I have spoken: Lat.
DIXY camp pot
FIXE prix —
MIXE Mexican Indian
MIXY confusedly mixed
NIXY undeliverable mail
PIXY impish sprite
KIYI herring; cisco; yelp
BIZE cold wind; winter
BIZZ buzz
FIZZ hissing sound; drink
GIZA site: pyramids, Sphinx
NIZY fool
SIZE bulk; quality; glue; filler; — up
SIZY viscous
SIZZ hiss(ing sound)
TIZA ulexite mineral
ZIZA Rehoboam's son
ZIZZ whirring sound

AJAR opened
AJAX hero (Telamon's son)
EJAM Bantu
AJEE awry
IJMA Moslem principle (Sunna)
AJOG jogging
EJOO palm; fiber
GJOA ship (Northwest Passage; Amundsen)

AKAL deity
AKAN Negro
IKAT shrub; weight
OKAY approve; all right
SKAG boat; keel part
SKAL health toast
SKAT card game; star
AKEE tree
AKEY weight
EKER water cress
OKEE evil spirit
OKEH all right; O.K.
OKET ounce
SKEE ski
SKEG keel part; plum; tear
SKEN squint
SKEO fisherman's hut
SKEP basket; measure; beehive
SKEW twist; swerve; distort(ed); slant(ing)
SKEY yoke bar
AKHA tribe; Burmese; Kaw
AKIA shrub (fish poison)
AKIM Negro; Tamiroff
AKIN related
OKIA Moroccan money
OKIE migratory worker
SKID clog; slide; — Road, Row
SKIL candlefish; beshow
SKIM scoop off; scud; brush
SKIN hide; pelt; peel; fleece; — and bones
SKIP jump; escape; mess; captain; -tracer
SKIR fly; scurry; skim

SKIT comedy sketch; jest
SKIV sovereign (coin)
AKKA Pygmy
BKKT chess move
EKKA carriage
QKKT chess move
RKKT chess move
IKMO betel palm, pepper
AKOV measure
EKOI Bantu
IKON image; statue
AKRA Negrito; vetch
IKRA superior caviar
OKRA vegetable; gumbo
OKRO plant; stew; soup; gumbo
AKTI peninsula
AKUA deity
AKUT ape man (Burroughs)
SKUA bird; great —; jaeger
SKUN skinned
NKVD Soviet secret police
SKYE isle; dog, terrier
SKYR sour curdled milk
SKYT move fast; dart; slip

ALAE wings
ALAI regiment; mountain; jai —
ALAR winglike; axillary
ALAN dog; name
ALAS sad cry
ALAY marble
BLAA bunk
BLAB tattle
BLAE bleak
BLAH nonsense
BLAS Gil (Le Sage novel)
BLAT sheep's cry
BLAY bleak
CLAD dressed; plated
CLAM mollusk; hush
CLAN clique; family; group
CLAP rap; applaud; flatten
CLAT mess; chatter
CLAW nail; ungula; chela; scratch; hammer
CLAY earth; ceramic; pipe; pigeon; color; Henry, statesman
ELAH king
ELAM kingdom
ELAN dash; ardor
FLAG flower; standard; stone; signal; limp; reduce, dwindle
FLAK antiaircraft
FLAM trick; drum beat
FLAN tart; disk; net
FLAP slap; leaf; sway; -jack
FLAT level; (make) insipid, dull; wholly; — tire
FLAW crack; defect; wind
FLAX plant; fiber; thrash
FLAY (strip off) skin
GLAD pleased
ILAI David's man
KLAM weight
KLAN Ku Klux —
OLAF (Vi)king
OLAM infinity; — haba (life after death)
OLAN Wang Lung's wife (Pearl Buck; The Good Earth)
OLAX tree
OLAY palm
PLAN design; scheme
PLAP fall loudly
PLAT plait; map; plot; fish
PLAY frolic; act; drama; contend; sport; game
SLAB slice; road
SLAG dross; lava
SLAM bang; criticize; grand —
SLAP strike; — bang
SLAT lath; slab; sheep's hide; flap
SLAV Eastern European
SLAW cabbage
SLAY kill; overwhelm
TLAC coin
ULAM Gilead's descendant
ULAN lancer; — Bator
ALBA garb; poem; brain matter; duke
ALBE album
ALBI flagellants
ALBO prefix: white
ELBA Napoleon's exile isle
ELBE river
ALCA auk
ALCO dog
ALDA soprano; hamlet: Sp.
ALEA Athena (war goddess)
ALEC fish; sauce; nickname
ALEE to shelter
ALEF letter
ALEM fruit
ALEN measure
ALEP city
ALES city
ALEY city
BLEA bleak; livid
BLEB blister; bubble
BLED emitted or drew blood, sap; extorted
BLET fruit decay
BLEU blue, rookie: Fr.
BLEW stormed; puffed; sounded
CLEE redshank; bird
CLEF musical sign; roman a —; key
CLEM riot; suffer hunger; nickname
CLEO queen (Cleopatra)
CLEW yarn ball; sail loop; cocoon; hint
ELEF letter
FLEA insect; puce; — market
FLED ran away; shunned
FLEE run away; shun
FLEM Fleming; Belgian
FLEW aviated; winged
FLEX bend
FLEY fright(en)
GLED kite; buzzard
GLEN rival
HLER sea god (wife: Ran)
ILEX holm oak; holly
KLEE Paul (painter)
LLEW Celt deity (Gwydion's son)
OLEA shrub; olive
OLEO margarine
PLEA excuse; prayer; request; pretext; allegation
PLEB freshman cadet; common man
PLED pleaded
PLET three-lash whip
PLEW beaver skin
PLEX form a network
SLEB nomadic Arab
SLED vehicle, snow or ice
SLEE sly
SLEW killed; twist; swamp; large number
SLEY weaver's reed

ULEX spine shrub (furze)
VLEI marsh; lake; creek
VLEY marsh; swamp; creek
ALFA grass
ALGA plant
ALGY Algernon; suffix: pain
OLGA fem. name
ALIA other: Lat.
ALIF letter
ALII royalty (Hawaiian)
ALIM teacher
ALIN measure
ALIT descended
ALIX fem. name
BLIP radar screen sign
CLII 152; Hadrian reign
CLIM — of the Clough (archer outlaw)
CLIO history Muse; mollusk
CLIP clasp; cut(ting); gait
CLIV 254; Aemilianus reign
CLIX 159; Antoninus Pius reign
ELIA Charles Lamb; essayist
ELIM Bib. oasis
ELIS Greek city state
FLIP toss; tap; drink; hop
FLIT flutter; move
FLIX down; fur; flax
GLIA neuroglia (nerve tissue)
GLIB flippant, smooth(ly)
GLIM light; eye
GLIS dormouse genus
ILIA (hip)bones
KLIP rock; cliff
MLII 1052
MLIV 1054; Catholic Church schism
MLIX 1059
OLIC chem. suffix
OLID smelly; fetid
OLIO medley; olla-podrida
PLIM swell; swollen
SLID glided; slipped
SLIM slight; scanty; sly; slenderize
SLIP slide; err(or); escape; pier; leash; garment; memo; cut
SLIT cut; slash; opening
ALKY alcohol
ALLA by: It.
ALLE bird; all: Ger.
ALLO prefix: other, dissimilar
ALLY unite, confederate
ELLA Eleanor; she: Sp.; fem. suffix
ELLE measure; she: Fr.
ILLE that one: Lat.
ILLS troubles
ILLY badly; ill
OLLA jar; meat dish; -podrida (medley)
ULLA grass; paper pulp
ULLO Indian shell money
ULLR chief god; Sif's son; Thor's stepson
ALMA girl; silk; river; city
ALME dancer
ALMS charity
ELMY rich in elms
ULME elm
ULMO muermo; hardwood
ULNA elbow bone; ell
ALOD estate
ALOE plant; tonic
ALOP lopsided
ALOR island
ALOW below
BLOB drop; daub; sound; fish; zero score
BLOC political unit; casting
BLOT stain; mar; dry
BLOW move (air); puff, pant; brag; expend; stroke; calamity; disappointment; — up (enlarge)
CLOD lump; soil; dolt
CLOE fem. name
CLOG block; sandal; stop; impede; choke
CLOP limp; hobble
CLOT mass; coagulate
CLOW sluice; floodgate
CLOY glut; surfeit
ELOD alleged force
ELOI Eli; God
ELON Esau's father-in-law; college (N.C.)
FLOB move clumsily
FLOC flock(y mass); shreds
FLOE floating ice
FLOG whip
FLOP slump down; flap; change; fail(ure); bed; sleep
FLOT lateral ore deposit
FLOW gush; stream; flux; roll; ebb and —
GLOM watch; steal
GLOP look wildly; stare
GLOW shine; incandesce; flush; ardor; wax
ILOG river (Tagalog)
ILOT islet; ait; eyot
KLOM weight
KLOP hard sound
OLOR swan genus; Cygnus
PLOD trudge; drudge
PLOP sound of fall
PLOT tract; ground; press (soap); scheme; intrigue
PLOW implement; till; cut; stars
PLOY make column; frolic; coup
SLOB slovenly one
SLOE blackthorn; plum; blueblack
SLOG hit (hard); slug; slam
SLOO swamp
SLOP slush; gush; mash
SLOT (cut) opening; bolt; deer; track; — machine
SLOW dilatory; tardy; inert; boring; hinder
ALPH river (Coleridge, Kubla Khan)
ALPS mountains
OLPE oil flask; pitcher
OLPH bullfinch
ALSO besides
ELSA — of Brabant (Lohengrin's bride)
ELSE other(wise); besides
ALTA tall: Sp.
ALTE old: Ger.; Adenauer
ALTO hill: Sp.; voice
ALUM emetic; astringent; styptic
ALUR Negro
BLUB swell; puff out
BLUE color; ocean; sky; sailor; sad; -blood; puritanical
BLUP air bubble sound
BLUR obscure; stain
BLUT blood: Ger.
CLUB bat; beat; society; suit (cards)
CLUE hint; guide; thread

CLUM clutch roughly
ELUL month
FLUB blunder; botch
FLUE net; lint; barb; air passage; pipe
FLUX flow; change; melt
GLUB make gulping sound
GLUE adhesive; stick
GLUG sound of liquids
GLUM moody; sullen
GLUT sate; surfeit; oversupply; wedge
ILUS son of Tros; Priam's grandfather
PLUG stop(per); plod; shoot; spark —; horse; praise
PLUM fruit (damson; greengage); tree; raisin; choice job
PLUP sound of (soft) fall
PLUS and; more; extra; — fours
SLUB twisted wool roll
SLUE swamp; twist; lot
SLUG snail; idle; metal spacer; small drink; bullet; strike
SLUM dilapidated district
SLUR pass over; mumble; defame; stigma; glide (mark)
SLUT slattern; harlot
ULUA cavalla; fish; caranx
ALVA duke; city; Thomas — Edison
ULVA sea lettuce; laver
ALYA star
ALYS name: Alice
CLYM — of the Clough (archer outlaw)
LLYN lake; pool

AMAH nurse
AMAN Ahasuerus's minister
AMAR measures
GMAN U.S. police agent
IMAM priest; title
OMAN Arabian state; sultanate; Muscat
OMAO thrush
OMAR Khayyam; tentmaker; caliph
TMAN U.S. Treasury agent
XMAS Christmas
AMBA mountain
AMBI about; prefix: both
AMBO pulpit
IMBE cordage fiber plant
UMBO shield boss; shell beak
YMCA welfare organization
AMEN assent; verily; deity; — Ra
AMER bitter
AMES author; city, college
AMEX Amer. Expeditionary Force
EMER Cuchulainn's wife (ideal womanhood)
EMEU bird (ostrichlike)
IMER Caucasian
KMET Slav; tenant; mayor
OMEI Buddhist mountain
OMEN presage; portent; sign
OMER measure; sheaf; undertaker (Dickens)
SMEE pintail duck; widgeon; Peter Pan pirate
SMEW merganser; duck
TMEN Treasury agents
YMER myth. giant
AMGA Siberian river
AMIA fish
AMIC amidic
AMID among
AMIE friend: Fr.
AMIL plant; remedy
AMIN agent
AMIR prince
AMIS friends: Fr.
AMIT headdress
CMIV 904
CMIX 909
EMIL man's name
EMIM Moabites; giants
EMIR ruler; title
EMIT eject; issue; voice
IMID chem. compound
MMIV 2004
MMIX 2009
OMIT leave out; neglect
SMIT struck; destroyed
YMIR rime-cold giant
AMLA tree
AMLI tree
IMLA Micaiah's father
AMMA abbess; god
AMMI herb
AMMO ammunition; prefix: sand
AMMU ammunition
EMMA letter M; name; Austen novel; Bovary (Flaubert)
EMMY TV award; nickname
IMMI measure
IMNA Asherites' chief
OMNI prefix: all
AMOI mine: Fr.
AMOK frenzy
AMON deity; King of Judah
AMOR love; Cupid; — patriae
AMOS prophet
AMOY island
AMOZ Isaiah's father
EMOL rock salt
SMOG fog and smoke; haze
EMPT empty
IMPI armed Kaffirs
IMPY impish
UMPH grunt
AMRA plum
OMRI king of Israel
OMSK Siberian city
AMUN deity
AMUR river
SMUG tidy; neat; priggish
SMUR mist; cloud
SMUT soot; coal dust; plant disease; obscenity
AMYL starch; alcohol
EMYD terrapin
EMYS tortoise

ANAI termite
ANAK giant race
ANAL pert. to anus
ANAM tree; Viet Nam region
ANAN tree; interjection
ANAS duck
ANAT sky god; med. term
ANAX Castor, Pollux (Dioscuri)
ANAY fruit
BNAI B'rith (Jewish society)
ENAM gift; land grant
ENAN Prince of Naphtali
GNAR growl
GNAT (biting) fly
GNAW bite; corrode
KNAB nibble
KNAG spur; knot
KNAP summit; rap; talk; bite; button
KNAR knot; burr
ONAN Indian; Judah's son
SNAB hill part; girl

SNAG stump; cut; obstacle; tangle
SNAP seize; break; click; shut; photo; vigor; easy task; — out
UNAL land
UNAU sloth
ANBA title
INBE be within
UNBE cease to be
ANCE suffix; — errand
ANCY suffix
ENCE suffix
INCA Quechuan Indian (ruler)
INCH measure; move slowly
ONCA ounce
ONCE one time; if ever; former(ly)
UNCA 8th note
UNCI hooks; claws
UNCO strange; very: Scot.
YNCA Quechuan Indian (ruler); Inca
ANDA tree
ANDE tribe
ANDI language
ANDY Andrew
ENDO prefix: within
INDE blue (indigo)
INDY — pink (carnation)
ONDE wave: Fr.; wavy (Her.)
ONDY wavy (Her.)
UNDE waving, wavy (Her.)
UNDO untie; unfasten; ruin
UNDY waving, wavy (Her.)
ANEM prefix: wind; city
ANER city
ANES once
ANET dill
ANEW over again
INEE arrow poison
INEZ Don Juan's mother
KNEE joint; bend(ing)
KNEW understood; was aware
KNEZ Slavic prince
ONER ace; blow; individual
ONES individuals
SNED lop; prune
SNEE cut; snick(er) —
ANGE angel: Fr.
ANGO herb; dye
INGA timber tree; mimosa
INGE prelate ("Gloomy Dean"); playwright (Bus Stop)
ANIL shrub, indigo
ANIS fennel; birds
ENID fem. name; Geraint's wife; city
ENIF star
ENIN blue grape pigment
INIA Amazon cetacean
KNIP bite; crop; rap
KNIT looped, tie(d); unite; contract
SNIB escape logging work
SNIG chop off; drag; pilfer
SNIP cut; shred; slip
UNIE unicorn fish
UNIO mussel
UNIS Etats — (USA)
UNIT single thing; basic amount; one; monad
ANKH cross
ENKI Babylonian god
INKA Inca
INKY black; stained
INLY within; heartily
ONLY alone; but; single; exclusively
ANNA coin; bird; name; — Christie (O'Neill); — Karenina (Tolstoi)
ANNE Queen; Boleyn; Henry VIII wife; Elizabeth's mother; Shakespeare's wife; Dombey's maid (Dickens); Queen — style; Queen —'s lace
ANNI years: Lat.
ANNO — Domini (Year of our Lord)
ENNA Sicilian resort
ENNE prefix: nine; fem. suffix
ENNS river
ANOA ox
ANON again; now; soon; author unknown
ENOL chem. suffix
ENON Paris's wife (nymph); John the Baptist site
ENOS Seth's son, Adam's grandson (905 years old); taken by God
ENOW enough
KNOB lump; hill; antler; handle
KNOP button; finial; stud
KNOR knot (wood); gnarl
KNOT tie; loop; hitch; sandpiper; problem; blemish; stud; Gordian —
KNOW understand; recognize; -how; -nothing (party)
SNOB social climber; game
SNOD trim; snug; plausible
SNOT wick end; blow nose
SNOW ice crystals; white hair; cocaine; — goose; TV spots
INRE concerning; actually
INRO Japanese receptacle
ANSA handle; loop
ANSE handle: Fr.
ANSU Korean apricot
ENSE suffix
ANTA porch; nut; tapir; goddess; pier; theater group
ANTE stake; pay; before; -bellum
ANTI opposed; prefix: against; Indian
ANTU rat poison
ENTE grafted (Her.); being: Sp.
ENTO prefix: inner
INTI Incas' deified sun; sun god
INTO penetrating; toward
ONTO upon; wise to
UNTO to; for; toward
UNTZ weight
ANUS end of alimentary canal
CNUT king; son of Magnus waste silk
KNUB gnarl; knot; wood ball
KNUR gnarl; knot; wood ball
KNUT king; son of Magnus
ONUS burden; duty
SNUB rebuke; slight; stumpy
SNUG cozy; trim; Shaks. character

SNUP snap up cheaply
SNUR snort
UNUK star; — al Hay
ENVY covet; grudge; 7th deadly sin
ENYO war goddess
ONYM technical name (biol.)
ONYX cameo stone; quartz; gem
PNYX Greek voting site
ANZU apricot
ENZU moon god (Sin)
ONZA Sp. ounce (1/16 libra); coin
UNZE weight

BOAR (wild) hog; male
BOAS Franz (anthropologist)
BOAT (go by) ship; gravy-
BOAZ Ruth's husband
COAD cushion
COAG dowel
COAK tenon
COAL ember; fuel
COAN pert. to Cos Island
COAT fur; skin; cover; — of arms
COAX flatter; cajole
DOAB tract
DOAT drivel; be silly, overfond; wood rot
EOAN pert. to east; dawn
FOAL colt; equine young
FOAM froth; rage; rubber
GOAD rod; decoy; urge
GOAF grain; rick
GOAI shrub
GOAL purpose, objective; score
GOAN pert. to Goa
GOAT ruminant; scape-; brown
HOAR frost; gray; -hound
HOAX deceive; trick
JOAB (David's) captain
JOAD philosopher; Tom —: Grapes of Wrath (Steinbeck)
JOAH record keeper
JOAN lass; cap; — of Arc, the Maid; la Pucelle
JOAR durra; millet
KOAE red-tailed bird
LOAD burden; measure
LOAF bread; idle
LOAM clay; soil
LOAN lend
MOAB kingdom; language; Lot's son
MOAN lament
MOAT trench
NOAH patriarch (Ark builder)
NOAP bullfinch
OOAA Hawaiian bird
ROAD (rail)way; track; anchorage
ROAM wander
ROAN horse; yellow-red
ROAR loud sound; laugh
SOAK absorb; sot
SOAP cleanser; detergent; money; soft —; -box; — opera
SOAR fly high; glide
TOAD amphibian; anuran; fawn
TOAG Indian
TOAT plane handle
WOAD herb
ZOAR town; Bela; city of Lot
ZOAS symbolic figures (Blake)
BOBA chicken snake
BOBO owala tree; mullet
COBB Irvin S. (writer); Tyrus R. (baseball)
COBH Irish port
DOBE brick (house)
DOBY brick (house)
GOBI Mongolian desert
GOBO burdock; okra; camera; mike shield
GOBY fish; passing
HOBB havoc; fireplace ledge; pin; peg
HOBO vagrant worker
JOBO hog plum; gumbo limbo
KOBA antelope
KOBE Honshu port
KOBI Japanese reserve duty (term)
KOBU seaweed food (kelp)
LOBB go heavily; tennis stroke; till
LOBE projection; ear part
LOBO timber wolf
MOBY — Dick (whale; Melville)
NOBS knave, jack (card, cribbage)
POBS porridge; pap
ROBE gown; mantle; Douglas novel
SOBK evil deity
TOBA Tatar; Chaco Indian
TOBE cotton cloth; future
TOBY cigar; mug; dog; rob
YOBI Jap. military service
ZOBO mongrel yak
BOCA harbor mouth: Sp.
BOCE colored fish
BOCK beer; leather
COCA cocaine source; shrub; leaf to chew; flavor
COCK male fowl; vane; leader; tap; tee; hay pile; cog
COCO palm; nut; grass
DOCE Brazil river
DOCK weed; rumex; (cur)tail; pier
FOCH Ferdinand (Fr. marshal; WW I commander)
FOCI center points
HOCH high: Ger.
HOCK leg joint; hamstring; wine; faro card; pawn
JOCH yoke, measure: Ger.
JOCK John; jockey; hobo
JOCU dog snapper
KOCH cook: Ger.; Robert (bacteriologist)
LOCH lake, bay: Scot.
LOCI places; sites
LOCK gate (canal, dam); tuft; wool; fasten(ing); grapple; tie up; -out (labor)
LOCO (render) mad; weed
MOCK jeer; taunt; sham; — apple, turtle
NOCK notch (in bow)
POCK pustule
POCO slightly; old-clothes man
ROCH Saint (14th cent.)
ROCK stone; Gibraltar; cliff; staunch support; diamond; candy; sway, lull; — the boat

SOCK beat; wind cone; stocking
SOCO heron; bittern
TOCK hornbill
TOCO toucan
VOCE voice: It.; sotto —
BODB goddess
BODE presage; augur; omen
BODO Indo-Chin. language
BODY structure; anatomy; bulk; corpse; group
CODA finale; mark
CODE body of law (Julian, Justinian, Napoleon); signal system; cipher; — duello
CODO measure
CODY William (Buffalo Bill)
DODD cut off (wool)
DODE nickname: Theodore
DODO extinct bird; reactionary
IODO prefix: iodine
JODO Buddhist paradiso (Gokaruku)
LODE ore deposit; vein; load
LODI city; Napoleon victory
LODZ Polish city
MODE manner; fashion; drab; a la —
NODE knob; knot; orbit; point; joint
NODI knots; difficulties
PODA suffix: foot
PODE suffix: foot
RODA Nile island
RODD crossbow
RODE anchor rope; measure; was borne; cross
RODI Medit. island
SODA carbonated water; Vichy; drink; sodium compound (bicarbonate)
SODI Gaddiel's father (spy)
TODA Ceylon aborigine
TODE (haul with) sled
TODO bustle; stir; ado
TODY green — (bird)
YODH Hebrew Y, 10
BOER So. Afr. Dutch
COED girl student
COEL cuckoo
COEN Jan (empire builder)
DOEG Saul's herdsman; poet's nickname; Indian
DOER performer; agent
DOES performs
GOEL reclaimer; avenger
GOER runner
GOES walks; proceeds
HOEK stream bend; — van Holland (Dutch cape, city)
HOEN weight
HOER scraper
HOEY partnership (Hawaii)
JOEL prophet, OT book
JOEY coin; clown; odd-job man; young kangaroo; Pal (O'Hara character)
KOEL cuckoo
MOED festivals (Mishnah)
NOEL Christmas; carol; — Coward
POEM verse creation
POET writer of verse; artist
ROED filled with roe
ROER hunting gun
ROEY of mottled grain
TOED stepped (gingerly)
VOET measure
ZOEA crab larva
DOFF put off; remove
GOFF clown; fool
KOFF Dutch sailboat
LOFT attic; warehouse floor; golf stroke
MOFF Caucasian silk
OOFY rich (Eng. slang)
SOFA couch; divan
SOFT giving way; easy; light(ly); mild; tractable
TOFF dandy
TOFT — and croft (house)
BOGA basslike fish
BOGO Eritrean Hamite
BOGY specter; bugbear
DOGE Venice, Genoa ruler
DOGS scaup duck
DOGY calf; duck
FOGG Phileas (Verne)
FOGO stench
FOGY dull, bigoted man
GOGH Vincent van — (painter)
GOGO vine; bark soap; beetle; bugaboo; Bantu
HOGA hill pasture
HOGG unshorn sheep
HOGO taint; stench
JOGI yogi; ascetic
LOGE theater box
LOGY heavy; dull
MOGO stone hatchet
NOGG egg drink
POGO springy stick
POGY menhaden; trout
SOGA grass rope: Sp.; Bantu
TOGA Roman garb; gown; senatorship
TOGO Afr. republic; Jap. admiral and statesman
TOGS clothes
TOGT trading enterprise
VOGT medieval official
YOGA mental discipline
YOGH Middle English G, Y
YOGI ascetic; yoga disciple
ZOGO sacred object
BOHO grass; weep; shout
BOHR Nils (Nobel physicist)
COHO silver salmon
FOHN warm dry wind
HOHE Siouan tribe
JOHN name; saint, evangelist; cop; man; — Bull (England); Long — Silver (Stevenson)
KOHL eye shadow; horse
MOHA millet; delusion
MOHO bird; honey eater
MOHR gazelle; bezoar
POHA gooseberry (jelly)
SOHO exclamation; London district
TOHO halt! (to dogs)
TOHU -bohu (confusion)
BOID of boas, anacondas
BOII Celtic tribe
BOIL heat; bubble; agitation; abscess
BOIS wood: Fr.; wine (cognac); — de Boulogne
COIF defensive skullcap; make up (hair)
COIL curl; wind; twist
COIN money; mint; invent; corner
COIR coconut fiber
COIX grass; Job's-tears
DOIT coin; whit; bit
EOIN John; Sean

FOIE liver: Fr.; — gras (pate)
FOIL balk; defeat; sword; leaf; sheet
JOIE — de vivre (zest for life)
JOIN mix; unite; coalesce
KOIL cuckoo
LOIN body part; hips; meat cut
LOIR dormouse; river
LOIS name; Timothy's grandmother
MOIL toil; trouble; spot
MOIO measure
NOIL combing (wool fiber)
NOIO noddy tern
NOIR black: Fr.; bet
NOIX edible gland
OOID egg-shaped
POIL raw silk thread
ROIL disturb; muddy; vex
SOIA food plant
SOIE silk
SOIL earth, ground; land; stain; pollute
SOIR evening: Fr.
TOIL work; drudge(ry); snare
VOID empty; vacuum; cancel
VOIR see: Fr.
ZOIC pert. to animals
ZOID organic body cell
BOJO grass
COJA title; teacher
HOJA title; teacher
HOJU Jap. army reserve
KOJI Jap. yeast cake
LOJA bark (quinine)
MOJI Jap. seaport
MOJO tree; majagua; voodoo charm; Indian
ROJO redskin: Sp.
SOJA bean; Glycine
BOKO evil spirit (Haiti)
COKE coal residue; fuel
COKY grimed; drug addict
DOKO Afr. pygmy
JOKE jest; laughing stock
JOKY jocular
KOKO bird; palm; tribe; executioner (Mikado)
KOKU measure
LOKA sphere; universe
LOKE Loki; surprise!
LOKI god of discord; Aesir; Balder slayer
MOKE donkey; dolt
MOKI N.Z. raft
MOKO Maori tattoo; -moko (lizard)
POKE thrust; prod; pry; sack; potter; herb
POKU antelope
POKY shabby; dull; bonnet
ROKA mafura (tree)
ROKE vapor; smoke
ROKY misty; hoarse
SOKA drought blight
SOKE jurisdiction
TOKO Chin. store; flogging
WOKE stirred; roused
YOKE join; link; slavery
YOKY coupled
BOLA missile; majagua (tree)
BOLD valiant; brazen; strong, heavy (type)
BOLE trunk; clay; brown
BOLL (strip) plant pod
BOLO knife; Rafflesia (plant); pacifist
BOLT sift; refine; shaft; lightning; bar; plant; rifle part; flight; refusal
COLA tree; nut; drink
COLD chill; frigid; indifferent; common —; coryza; — blood; — chisel
COLE brassica genus; Porter (composer)
COLI intestinal bacterium
COLL embrace; hug; Vincent (gangster; "mad dog")
COLP pasture; Irish acre
COLT young horse; pistol; — .45
COLY long-tailed bird
DOLA weight
DOLE ration; (relief) alms; deal (out)
DOLI weights
DOLL plaything; puppet; dress up; girl
DOLT dunce; ignoramus
FOLD plait; envelop; fail; quit; flock
FOLK people; — ways, laws, song, dance
GOLA storeroom; caste; cyma
GOLD metal; element; — dust, medal
GOLF game; blood-red; — links
GOLI musket ball; pill
GOLL Irish hero (Fenian)
GOLO Nilotic Sudanese
GOLP roundel purpure (Her.)
HOLA fish poison; herb; hello
HOLD grasp; have; retain; believe; keep; bear; lair; prison
HOLE pit; cavity; flaw; — in one; — card; ace in the —
HOLI spring festival
HOLL ditch
HOLM holly; oak; islet
HOLT willow plantation; hill; lair; Eliot hero; actor
HOLY sacred; pious; — City; — Alliance; — Roller
IOLA Kansas town
IOLE Eurytus' daughter (Hercules' captive)
JOLE jowl; cheek
JOLI pretty, nice: Fr.
JOLL move clumsily; knock
JOLT shake; hard blow
KOLA caffeine nut; jackal; river; city; bay (Murmansk)
KOLI low-caste tribesman
KOLO folk dance
LOLA fem. name
LOLL droop; lounge; sprawl
LOLO Caucasian Chinese
MOLA sunfish genus
MOLD fungus; humus; die, matrix; shape; mix
MOLE nevus; birthmark; pier; burrow(ing animal); Mossi language
MOLL Mary; girl; — Flanders (Defoe)
MOLT shed (hair)
MOLY magic herb (Homer)
NOLA fem. name; time

NOLI — me tangere
NOLL Oliver (Cromwell); head; noddle
NOLO — contendere
POLA Yugo. city (Pulj)
POLE rod; tail; terminal: axis, battery; — Star; Polish, Polack
POLK Cossack regiment; James Knox (President)
POLL head; register; survey; cut off; Mary; parrot; vote
POLO game; Marco —
POLT knock; trump; club
POLY herb; Teucrium; prefix: many
ROLE actor's part
ROLL wrap; trill; drumbeat; rotate; list; bank-
SOLA herb (topee source); alone; holla!
SOLD vended; persuaded; cheated
SOLE pelma (bottom); flatfish; single; only
SOLI single performances; prefix: sun, alone
SOLO song; (fly) alone
TOLA weight
TOLD narrated; counted
TOLE entice; told; tinware
TOLL tax; lure; sound
TOLT writ; isolated peak
TOLU balsam (rose odor)
VOLA palm (hand, foot)
VOLE rodent; slam (cards)
VOLK people: Ger.; workmen (So. Afr.)
VOLT sideways gait; fencing leap; elec. unit
WOLD upland plain
WOLF canid (dog); Lupus; larva; devour; dissonance; cry —; flirtatious man
YOLK egg yellow; essence
ZOLA author (J'accuse: Dreyfus case; Nana)
ZOLL measure
BOMA Afr. stockade; post
BOMB explosive; dispenser; A-; lead-lined container; buzz —
COMA torpor; blur; tuft
COMB crest; rake; scrape
COME arrive; chance; fare
COMO lake, resort (Italy)
DOME edifice; cupola; roof
DOMN Rumanian ruler; lord
DOMY domelike
GOMA Bantu (Wagoma)
HOMA sacred drink
HOME habitat; asylum; plate; natural
HOMO man; — sapiens; prefix: same
HOMY homey; intimate
JOMS Vikings Norse colony
KOME Greenland geol. division
KOMI Soviet republic; Zyrians
LOMA fringe; lap; hill
LOME Togo seaport
MOME buffoon; -rath
MOMO owl
NOME city (Alaska)
POMA rosa (rose apple)
POME fruit; ball; globe
POMO California Indian
POMP pageant(ry); splendor
ROMA Rome: It.
ROME city (Eternal); Church; beauty (apple)
ROMI Gypsy wife
ROMP girl; gambol, frolic
SOMA vine; sacred drink; body
SOME various; any; somewhat; part
TOMA Liberian Negro
TOMB grave; monument; bury
TOME book; papal letter
AONE first-rate
BONA good: Lat.; — fide
BOND adhesion; tie; covenant; paper; captivity; certificate
BONE study hard; plug; os
BONG bell sound
BONI African; Boschneger
BONK bar money (Dutch E.I.)
BONN city; Ger. capital (Beethoven born)
BONO Johnny (Briton); cui —
BONY skeletal; osseous; Napoleon
COND direct helmsman
CONE geometric solid; pine fruit, strobile; peak; ice cream —; nose —
CONI It. commune
CONK nose; head; decay; fail; hit
CONN direct helmsman
CONY rabbit; daman; pika
DONA lady; sapek (coin)
DONE agreed; exhausted
DONG sound; weight; ding-
DONI fishing boat
DONT contraction; prohibition
FOND basis; fount; loving
FONG Ewe-speaking Negro
FONO Samoan council
FONS fount; source
FONT basin; spring; stoup; type
GONA New Guinea victory
GOND Dravidian Indian
GONE departed; enamored; lost; germ cell
GONG bell; tom-tom
GONY albatross
HONE sharpen(er)
HONG Chin. trade guild
HONI — soit qui mal y pense; shamed
HONK goose cry; toot; ooga
IONA Scot. isle; Celt church; college
IONE Pompeii heroine (Bulwer-Lytton)
IONI Hainai; Chaddo Indian
JONK jonquil
KONA Hawaiian storm; weight
KONK conk
LONE single; — Star
LONG lengthy; extended; yearn; — John Silver (Stevenson);

Huey — (La. politician); — time no see
LONK black-faced sheep
MONA monkey; Lisa (La Gioconda, da Vinci)
MONG among; barter
MONK ascetic; friar; bird; fish; spot; ferret
MONO monkey; Indian; prefix: single, one
MONS mountain: Lat.; city (Belgium; WW I battle)
MONT mountain: Fr.; — Blanc (peak, Alps)
NONA fate goddess; prefix: ninth
NONE not one; 9th hour
NONO ninth: It.
OONS mild oath
OONT camel; mole
POND lake; pool; weight
PONE corn bread; writ
PONG sound; improvise
PONS bridge: Lat.; — asinorum; Lily (singer)
PONT ferry(boat); bridge: Fr.
PONY small equine (Shetland, polo); glass (1 oz.); translation
RONE brushwood
RONG Sikkimese language
SONG poem (music); pittance
TONE pitch; accent; Wolfe (Ir. rebel)
TONG secret society
TONK (cow bell) clang; honky-; game
TONY nickname (Anthony); stylish
VONE robot bomb
WONG field; meadow
WONT custom; contraction
YOND past; beyond
ZONA girdle; shingles
ZONE area; band; partition
BOOB simpleton
BOOF stare; peach brandy
BOOH exclamation
BOOK tome; volume; Bible; libretto; (bet) record; register; throw the —
BOOL curved handle
BOOM hum; grow, push; beam
BOON benefit; convivial
BOOR rustic; lout; Boer
BOOT shoe; wader; sheath; torture; recruit; compartment; tube; kick; to —; addition
COOK chef; concoct; falsify; James (explorer)
COOL chill; calm; unmoved
COOM coal dust; refuse
COON animal; fur; sly man
COOP pen; jail; confine; coöperative
COOS Bay (laurel); Indian
COOT rail; surf duck; dolt
DOOB Bermuda grass
DOOK wooden brick; demon
DOOM (last) judgment; fate; condemn
DOON tree (varnish resin)
DOOR portal; entrance; open — policy
FOOD nutriment; victuals
FOOL dolt; jester; trick
FOOT pedal part; base; dance; trip; skip; pay; add
GOOD able; brave; sound; profit; happiness; welfare; benefit
GOOF dolt; blunder
GOOK trash; ooze; native
GOOM cultivation method
GOON thug; strikebreaker
GOOP nonsense creature
GOOR sugar; massecuite
HOOD cowl; cloak; seal; gangster; Thomas (poet)
HOOF ungula; foot; beast; walk; dance
HOOK trap; curve; catch; steal; — and eye; pirate: Peter Pan (Barrie)
HOON coin; gold pagoda
HOOP circle(t); wicket; — skirt
HOOT derisive (owl's) cry
JOOK perch; slumber
JOOM cultivation method
KOOP purchase; bargain
LOOD weight
LOOF luff; sponge gourd
LOOK observe appear(ance); eye (wink); care
LOOM auk; appear(ance); weaver's frame
LOON diving bird; lout
LOOP noose; catch; aerial stunt; Chicago area
LOOS Anita (writer: Gentlemen Prefer Blondes)
LOOT plunder; booty
MOOD humor; temper; verb form
MOON satellite; crescent; month; Diana; Cynthia; languish
MOOR heath; anchor; Moslem; Moroccan; blacka-
MOOT arguable; ring gauge
NOOK corner; retreat
NOON midday; meal; acme
POOA pua hemp
POOD weight
POOF exclamation
POOH pshaw!; — Bah (Mikado); Winnie (bear; Milne)
POOK hobgoblin; disk
POOL pond; puddle; game; stake; fund; Thames
POON tree (mastwood)
POOP deck; cabin; dickey; exhaust; tire
POOR indigent; scanty; feeble; lowgrade; lean; ill; hapless; cod (fish)
POOT disgusting!
ROOD crucifix; measure
ROOF cover; house; top
ROOK bird; cheat; dupe; chessman (tower)
ROOL crumple; ruffle
ROOM space; apartment; lodge; — and board
ROON treasure; darling
ROOS Ger. painter
ROOT underlying source;

rhizome; base; dig; applaud; plant; eradicate
SOOK Moslem market; hog call
SOOL pull, tousle about
SOON promptly; willingly
SOOT powdery carbon smudge
TOOA hero; beefwood
TOOK seized; caught; endured; supposed
TOOL instrument; polish; dupe
TOON tree (dye); mahogany
TOOP measure
TOOT sound horn; carousal
VOOG lode cavity
WOOD timber; forest; Grant (painter); Leonard (general)
WOOF crossthreads; texture; weft; bark
WOOL (sheep) fleece; down
WOON Burmese governor
YOOP sobbing sound
ZOOM buzz; climb; approach suddenly
ZOON developed compound animal
ZOOT — suit: extreme style
COPA tree; yaya; landmark
COPE vestment; cover; bend; contend
COPT Egypt. Christian
COPY duplicate; mimic; follow; text
DOPA chemical (pigment test) crystalline
DOPE drug; information; guess; nitwit
DOPP diamond cup
DOPY sluggish
HOPE trust, expect(ation); wish; -chest
HOPI French beige; Moqui Indian
HOPS beer
KOPH Heb. K, Q, 100
KOPI N.Z. tree (karaka)
KOPT Copt
LOPE go; move; gait
MOPE be dull, listless (person)
POPE pontiff; Holy Father; — Joan (game); Alexander (poet); bird
QOPH Heb. K, Q, 100
ROPE cord; cable; noose; bind; chain
ROPY viscous; stringy
SOPH 2nd year student
SOPT Dog Star; Isis
TOPE drink; shark; stupa; orchard
TOPH drum; porous rock
TOPI antelope; pith hat
TOPO prefix: place
TOPS most superior
BORA north wind; rite
BORD -and-pillar (mining)
BORE pierce; hole; tire; dullard; tidal flow
BORG borough: Dan.
BORI Lucrezia (singer)
BORN given birth to; nee; quantum physicist
BORO spring rice; Indian (Mirhana); — Budur (temple)
BORS king (Lancelot's uncle); Bohort (finder of Holy Grail)
BORT finder of Holy Grail; impure diamond
CORA gazelle; Indian; name; Persephone; Demeter's daughter
CORD string; twine; ribbed fabric; measure (wood)
CORE heart; nucleus; gist
CORI Carl, Gerty (Nobel winners)
CORK tree; bark; stop(per); brown; Irish city (Lee)
CORM bulblike stem (crocus)
CORN grain; ear, kernel; callus; whisky; preserve; granulate(d); clavus; banality; red-yellow
DORA Mrs. David Copperfield
DORE bullion; gold; pike; Paul Gustave (Fr. artist)
DORM dormitory; sleep
DORN thornback ray
DORP hamlet; city (So. Afr.)
DORR Rebellion (R.I.)
DORY John — (fish); boat
FORA meeting places; courts
FORB non-grassy herb
FORD crossing shallow; Henry (automobile); Shaks. character
FORE front; prior; golf cry
FORK implement (pronged); tuner; place of divergence
FORM shape; mold; fashion; school grade
FORT stronghold; trading post; dun
GORA musical instrument
GORE stab; blood; triangular insert
GORY bloody; murderous
HORA book of hours; Israeli dance
HORN prong; antenna; trumpet; brasswind; cup; Cape —
HORS out of: Fr.; — d'oeuvre
JORD Odin's wife; Thor's mother
KORA water cock; Hottentot dialect
KORE Persephone; Demeter's daughter; chaos (Maori myth.)
KORI bustard; low weaver
LORA thong; strap
LORD ruler; Jehovah; Jesus; duck; planet
LORE history; learning
LORI lemur; Afr. Negro
LORN forsaken; bereft
LORO monk parrot; fish
LORS exclamation: lord!
LORY parrot; touraco
MORA default; short syllable; Spartan army; stool
MORE greater; additional; St. Thomas (Utopia)
MORG measure
MORN A.M.; dawn: East
MORO finch; P.I. Moslem tribe
MORS deity; death
MORT nickname; woman; salmon; the kill;

dead: Fr.
NORA Helmer (Ibsen heroine)
NORE Thames estuary
NORI seaweed food
NORM type; standard; integer
NORN demigoddess (Urth, Skuld, Verthandi)
OORD coin (double doit, ¼ stiver)
PORE gaze; ponder; opening
PORK meat; swine; — barrel
PORO Sierra Leone secret society
PORR push; poke; kick
PORT harbor; haven; wine; blue-red; left side; tune; demeanor
PORY porous; permeable
RORI Bantu tribe
RORY O'More (Irish novel)
SORA bird; rail
SORB wild apple; Slav
SORE painful; vexed; sensitive; deer
SORI clusters; spores
SORS lot: Lat.; divination
SORT type; kind; quantity; classify
SORY vitriolic earth
TORA hartebeest; law (of Moses); Pentateuch
TORE ripped; geom. surface
TORI moldings
TORN ripped; damaged
TORO N.Z. tree
TORP croft; Swed. small farm
TORT wrongful act
TORU N.Z. tree
TORY conservative
WORD term; news; promise; order; phrase
WORE had on (clothes); tired
WORK labor; mental product; act; operate; function; needlework
WORM crawler; maggot; screw; insinuate
WORN used (as clothing); shabby; tired
WORT plant; (pot)herb
YORE ancient (times); long ago
YORK city; archbishopric; imperial (apple); Sgt. Alvin (WWI)
BOSA Arab. drink
BOSC best pear
BOSE test ground by sound
BOSH furnace part; nonsense (nothing: Turk.)
BOSK thicket
BOSS knob; pad; stud; master, employer
COSE (friendly) chat
COSH snug; happy; math. term
COSO open space: Sp.
COSS measure
COSY snug; teapot cover
DOSA sheik's ritual ride; hatred
DOSE portion; (give) medicine
DOSS bed; sleep; — house
DOST (you) do: archaic
FOSS canal; ditch; moat
GOSH oath; -awful
HOSE stockings; pipe; drench
HOSS house; One — Shay (Holmes)
HOST army; throng; bread as Christ's body; innkeeper; person having guests
JOSE Carmen lover
JOSH make fun; banter
JOSS Chin. deity
JOSY nickname
KOSO tree; cusso; Panamint Indian
KOSS measure
LOSE miss; forfeit; fail; forget
LOSH wash leather
LOSS forfeiture; bereavement; waste; defeat; — leader
LOST not won; misplaced; confused; ruined; — cause
MOSE Moses
MOSK Moslem temple; Masjid
MOSS bryophyte; lichen; green; rose; Hart (writer)
MOST greatest; almost
MOSY moldy; rotten
NOSE proboscis; smeller; scent; search; front; touch; — out (defeat); -dive
NOSU Lolo; Chin. Caucasian
NOSY fragrant; prying
POSE posture; affectation; baffle; propound
POSH slush; elegant
POST pillar; advertise; mil. station; mail; inform; record
POSY flower; nosegay; poem
ROSA shrub genus; name; sub —;
ROSE stood up; got up; flower; tree; wood; red; pink; window; Abie's Irish —; Eng. emblem
ROSS rough bark; seal; island; navigator; Harold (editor)
ROSY blushing; optimistic
SOSH jag; drunk; dash
SOSO middling; passably
SOSS hog call for food
TOSH bath(tub)
TOSK Albanian
TOSS throw; fling; change
XOSA Kaffir
BOTA measure
BOTE house repair; amends
BOTH the two
BOTO Indian; Voto
BOTT clay plug; fly larva
COTA P.I. fort
COTE birdhouse; sheep shed; Coast: Fr. (d'Or; d'Azur)
COTO bark; stomachic
COTY Fr. statesman; cosmetics
DOTE love to excess; drivel; timber rot
DOTH does
DOTO sea slug genus
DOTY discolored by rot
GOTH Teuton (Theodoric, Alaric); barbarian; Ostro-, Visi-
HOTH blind god

(Balder slayer)
HOTI cause; reason
IOTA Greek I, 10; jot
JOTA Sp. peasant dance
JOTI astrologer; astronomer
KOTA P.I. fort; Dravidian language
KOTO Jap. zither
LOTA water pot; burbot genus
LOTE lotus (poetic); weights
LOTH averse; reluctant
LOTI Pierre (writer; Viaud)
LOTO pot; game
LOTS tracts; quantities; very much; chances
MOTA Moslem marriage
MOTE speck, particle
MOTH lepidopterous insect. -ball; -eaten, gypsy —; page (Shakespeare)
MOTI elephant (Kipling)
MOTO movement: It.; con —
MOTT clump of trees; James. Lucretia (abolitionists)
NOTA insect backs; — bene (N.B.)
NOTE sign; tone; fame; heed; memo; IOU; record see
NOTT Norse night (Dag)
POTE poker stick
POTT paper size; editor (Dickens)
ROTA roster; curia tribunal; a round; hurdy-gurdy
ROTE surf noise; routine
ROTI roasted: Fr.
ROTL Afr. weight
ROTO ragged: Sp.; printing
SOTO Hernando de (explorer)
SOTS yeast
TOTA grivet monkey
TOTE carry. haul; total
TOTO baby (animal); all
TOTY low-caste worker
VOTA Roman festivals
VOTE ballot suffrage; voice, enact; propose; Ingrian Finn
VOTH Ingrian Finn
VOTO So. Amer. Indian
WOTE Ingrian Finn
AOUL Nepalese
BOUD malt weevil
BOUT contest; attack
BOUW measure
COUE psychotherapist ("Day by day . . ." physician
COUP blow; master stroke
COUS cowlike
DOUB Bermuda grass
DOUC variegated monkey
DOUM palm
DOUP weaver's thread
DOUR sullen; gloomy
FOUD district magistrate
FOUL rotten; poor; illegal: invalid
FOUR number. card; boat
GOUL monster grave robber
GOUR cattle; koulan (onager)
GOUT drop; disease (arthritis); taste: Fr.
HOUR time unit; H- or zero —
IOUS promissory notes; suffix
JOUG iron collar; pillory
JOUR day: Fr.
LOUD noisy; showy; vulgar
LOUN loon; lout
LOUP half mask; Skidi Indian; river; fish
LOUR frown; lower; scowl
LOUT boor; bumpkin; dolt
MOUE pout; grimace: Fr.
NOUN speech part; name; substantive
NOUP steep promontory
NOUS mind; reason; wit; we: Fr.
POUF puff; ottoman; bang!
POUL Russ. coin
POUR (make) flow; for: Fr.; emit; — le merite
POUS measure
POUT sulk(iness); fish
ROUB measure
ROUD fish
ROUE dissolute man; rake
ROUP a cold; hoarseness
ROUT defeat; tumult; mob; the brant; snare
ROUX (soup, sauce) thickener;
SOUD pay
SOUF sigh
SOUK Moslem market
SOUL spirit; inspirer; force; psyche; person
SOUP broth; stew; — and fish; duck —; step (up); explosive; fog
SOUR acid(ify); tart; disagreeable
SOUS coins; under: Fr.
TOUG horsetail standard
TOUP Malay lugger
TOUR trip; circuit; — de force
TOUT tip(ster); praise; all: Fr.; — a fait; — de suite
YOUP yelp; scream; yawn
YOUR possessive pronoun
COVE bay; recess; pass; chap; Gypsy
DOVE pigeon; blue, gray; Columba; plunged
HOVA Madagascar native; Malagasy
HOVE ground ivy; raised
JOVA Opata; Pimian Indian
JOVE god; Jupiter; Zeus
LOVE affection; like; Cupid; Eros; zero
MOVE impel; shift; excite; act; depart(ure); play
NOVA star; new, temporary
NOVE nine: It.
ROVE wander; ramble; draw through an eye
WOVE entwined; spun
XOVA Opata; Pimian Indian
BOWK steep; soak in lime
BOWL basin; dish; (roll) ball
COWL hood; auto body front
DOWD slovenly woman
DOWL feathery down
DOWN to below. reduce; defeat; feathers; elder-; dejected
FOWL poultry; cock; hen
GOWK simpleton; fool

GOWL gad; defile; howl; monster
GOWN dress; toga; robe
HOWE hollow; empty; Elias (inventor); Julia Ward (Battle Hymn); Brit. general, admiral
HOWL (distress) cry; wail
IOWA state; Indian
JOWL jaw; cheek; wattle; gambler (Dickens)
LOWA bush quail
LOWN calm; quiet; dolt
LOWY banlieue; suburb
MOWN cut down; trimmed
NOWT neat cattle; dolt
NOWY having curvature
POWE weight
ROWY streaked
SOWN scattered; seeded
TOWN city; Hamlet; — hall; man about -
TOWY like flax fibers
YOWL howl(ing); yell
BOXY boxlike; squarish
COXA hip (joint)
COXE Capt. (Scott)
DOXA religious stanzas
DOXY doctrine; hussy
FOXY wily; brown; rank; sour
LOXA pale bark: quinine
MOXA cautery wormwood
MOXO Arawakan Indian
NOXA harmful thing
ROXY name: Roxana; Rothafel (impresario); theater
TOXA sponge spicule
COYN corner(stone)
COYO avocado; chinin
GOYA Sp. painter; — red
HOYA honey plant (milkweed)
MOYO measure
NOYL fiber knot
SOYA bean; dill; fennel
BOZA Arab. drink
BOZO fellow
COZE (friendly) chat
COZY snug; teapot cover
DOZE drowse; timber rot
DOZY drowsy; decayed; doty
JOZY Josepha; Josephine
KOZO paper mulberry
MOZA manservant
MOZO manservant: Sp.

NOZI of Yanan tribe
OOZE exude; slime; liquor
OOZY muddy; slimy

APAP month
APAR armadillo
OPAH fish
OPAL birthstone (Oct.); girasol
SPAD nail
SPAE prophecy
SPAN stretch; team; measure; dog
SPAR mineral; mast; gaff; box
SPAT mollusk; gaiter; snap; tiff
SPAY deer; castrate
UPAS tree (juice); arrow poison
UPDO upswept hair
APER imitator; boar
APET goddess
APEX summit; crisis
EPEE fencing sword
OPEN undefended; plain; frank; — end; uncertain; bare; start; unfold; public; — sesame
SPEC speculation
SPED hastened
SPEE Graf — (ship, admiral)
SPES (goddess of) hope
SPET spit; barracuda
SPEW eject; scatter; gush
SPEX spectacles
SPEY river
UPGO ascend
EPHA Hebrew dry measure
EPHI measure
APIA port (Samoa)
APII plant
APIO celery: Sp.
APIS sacred bull (Ptah); bee; bull (Kipling)
EPIC heroic poem
IPIL tree (brown dye)
OPIE Eng. painter
SPIN whirl; twist; aerial stunt; — a yarn
SPIR prefix: coiled
SPIT land point; rod; impale; expectorate; — and image
SPIV slacker: Brit.

UPIS Artemis, Nemesis
YPIL tree (brown dye)
UPLA cow dung; fuel
APOD footless
EPOS epic poetry; events
SPOT stain; point, place; fish; small amount; espy
UPON prep.: above; against
EPPY Euphemia
SPRY nimble; brisk; smart
APSE recess; throne
APSU primordial chaos
IPSE himself: Lat.; — dixit
IPSO — jure, — facto
UPSY -daisy
APUS bird; constellation
OPUS work
SPUD scrape(r); potato; dig
SPUN twisted; whirled
SPUR point; good; kick; otter track; ridge
SPUT boiler plate

BQKT chess move
QQKT chess move
RQKT chess move
AQUA water; green-blue
EQUI prefix: equal, same

ARAB Semite; horse; nomad; urchin
ARAD plant; city
ARAH exclamation
ARAK palm; spirit
ARAL lake
ARAM country (Syria); Eugene — (murderer)
ARAN Seir's descendant; island
ARAR tree
ARAS river
BRAB palm
BRAD nail
BRAE slope
BRAG boast; game
BRAJ basha
BRAM Abraham
BRAN god-king; seed coat; chaff
BRAS arm: Fr.
BRAT apron; child
BRAW handsome; fine
BRAY (donkey's) cry; grind; Mrs. Nickleby (Dickens)

CRAB crustacean; apple; sign; anger
CRAG cliff; neck
CRAL hut; village
CRAM press; stuff; study
CRAN bird; measure
CRAP dregs; money; dice cast (crabs)
CRAW gullet; stomach
CRAX curassow (bird)
DRAA measure
DRAB dull; box; wench; cloth; drug
DRAG haul; harrow; obstacle; puff; auto race
DRAH measure
DRAM measure; drink
DRAP cloth
DRAT oath
DRAW drag; attract; gain; infer; extract; sketch; undecided contest
DRAY cart; squirrel's nest; — horse
ERAL epochal
ERAN Ephraim's grandson
ERAT was: Lat.; Q[uod] — D[emonstrandum]
FRAB worry
FRAM spear
FRAP tighten
FRAT fraternity
FRAU Mrs., wife, Mme., woman: Ger.
FRAY contest; tumult; wear off
GRAB grasp; capture; game
GRAD centesimal unit
GRAF nobleman: Ger.; — Spee (Zeppelin)
GRAM sword; plant; weight; —'s method; grandma
GRAN weight; grandma
GRAO weight
GRAS horse; foie — (paté)
GRAY dull; dismal; hoary; Dorian (Wilde); Asa, botanist; Elisha, inventor
GRAZ Austrian city (Mur)
IRAD Enoch's son
IRAE Dies — (Day of Wrath)
IRAK country
IRAN Persia
IRAQ country
IRAS Cleopatra's maid
KRAG rifle
KRAL hut; village
KRAN coin
KRAS tahr (goat)
ORAD mouthward
ORAL spoken; of the mouth
ORAN seaport
ORAS Danish money
PRAD horse
PRAH canoe
PRAM carriage
PRAO canoe
PRAT buttock
PRAU swift canoe
PRAY ask; beseech; please
TRAM trolley; gauge
TRAP snare; mouth; net; catch; clothe; basalt; — shooting
TRAY salver; platter; old dog
URAL -Altaic; mountains; hypnotic
URAN lizard; Indian
URAO trona (mineral)
WRAC women's army corp
WRAF air force; aviatrix
WRAP cloak; blanket; coat
ARBA cart
IRBM ballistics missile
ORBY revolving
URBS (capital) city
ARCA box; dish; shell
ARCH support; curve; chief; fingerprint; triumphal —
ORCA killer whale
ARDU slave
ERDA earth goddess; Wagner role
ORDO order: Lat.; feast list
ORDU Turk. military district, army corps
URDE key shaped (Her.)
URDU Hindustani language
URDY key shaped (Her.)
AREA zone, region; scope; tract
AREG deserts
AREO prefix: Mars
ARES war; Mars; Zeus's, Hera's son; Eris' brother
BREA resin; tree; asphalt
BRED procreated; brought up
BREE (eye)brow
BREI soft tissue
BREN (machine) gun
BRER Rabbit (Harris; Uncle Remus)
BRES Elatha's beautiful son (Fomorian)
BREW beverage; plot; concoct
BREY barnacle
CREA linen, cotton fabric
CREE Indian
CREW company; gang; -cut
CREX corn crake (bird)
DRED Scott (slave)
DREE endure; tedious
DREG lees; residue
DREI three: Ger.
DREW sketched; pulled
DREY squirrel's nest
ERER sooner
FREA Frigg; Odin's wife; goddess
FRED nickname
FREE independent; immune; rid; exempt; — and easy; — lance, port, trade, style
FRET gnaw; vex; worry; embroider; ridge; ornament
FREY god (Njorth's son, Gerth's husband)
GRES stoneware: Fr.
GREW increased
GREY color; neutral; dull; Zane (writer); Vivian (Disraeli novel)
OREB Midianite defeated by Gideon
OREL Russian city
OREN Judah's descendant
PREP prepare; student
PRES near: Fr.
PRET measure
PREX (college) president
PREY victim; pillage; booty
TREE wood, plant; family —; boot, shoe —
TREF homestead
TREK migrate; journey
TRES very: Fr.; three: Sp.

TRET weight allowance
TREY three(spot)
UREA chemical compound
UREY Nobel physicist
WREN bird; navy woman; architect
ORFE fish; yellow ide
URFA Turkish city (Edessa)
ARGH timid
ARGO ship; therefore; constellation
ARGY argue
ERGO hence; prefix: work
ORGY carousal; Saturnalia, Bacchanalia
URGA Outer Mongolia
URGE prod; impel; impulse
ARIA tune; city (Herat)
ARID dry; barren
ARIL seed covering
ARIS molding edge
BRIE cheese
BRIG sailing ship; prison
BRIM rim; edge; swell
BRIN fan plate; silk thread
BRIO con — (with spirit)
BRIT young herring
BRIX scale (hydrometer)
CRIB manger; hut; bin; box; steal "pony," "trot"
CRIC lamp condensing ring
CRIG blow
CRIN heavy silk
CRIS dagger; stab
DRIB drop; a little
DRIN Balkan river
DRIP let fall
ERIA silk(worm)
ERIC male name; Viking; the Red
ERIE Iroquoian; lake; city
ERIN Eire; Ireland
ERIS goddess of discord, Ares' sister
FRIA Frigg (Odin's wife)
FRIB dirty short wool
FRIM juicy; soluble
FRIT fuse; partly; fried: Fr.; waste
FRIZ curl; crisp; wig
GRID grating
GRIG dwarf; cricket; fowl
GRIM ruthless; ghastly
GRIN smile
GRIP grasp; power; valise; Barnaby's raven (Dickens)
GRIS gray: Fr.
GRIT sand(stone); bravery; grate
IRID iris; crocus
IRIS rainbow; goddess; eye part; plant (flag); spirit (Shaks.); red-blue; March (Arlen)
KRIS dagger; stab
PRIG precisian; steal; thief; fop
PRIX price: Fr.; — fixe (table d'hôte)
TRIG trim; sound; prim; math. course
TRIM shear; adjust; adorn; rebuke; defeat; neat
TRIN one of triplets
TRIO set of 3; So. Amer. Indian
TRIP move; slip; journey; (mis)step
TRIS prefix: thrice
TRIT prefix: third
TRIX fem. suffix
URIA Bathsheba's husband; auk
URIM — and Thummim (sacred instruments)
WRIG wriggle
WRIT legal order; Holy —
ORLE shield border; fillet
ORLO smooth surface; plinth
ORLY Paris airport
ARME weapon: Fr.; — blanche (saber)
ARMS mil. science; ensigns; weapons; branches; limbs
ARMY multitude; force
ERMA Ermengarde
IRMA name
ARNA buffalo
ARND theologian
ARNE composer; region
ARNI buffalo
ARNO river; cartoonist
ARNT contraction
ERNE sea eagle
ORNA measure
ORNE measure; river (Caen)
URNA measure
AROA Venezuela copper center
AROD son of Gad
AROE Islands, New Guinea
AROO indeed
AROW in a line
BROB support spike
BROH macaque; monkey
BROM Bones (Ichabod's rival)
BROT bread: Ger.
BROW forehead; high-, low-
BROZ Josip (Tito)
CROC harquebus support; crocodile
CROM Cruaich (Irish idol)
CROP craw; harvest; trim
CROW raven; corvine bird; bar; black; Indian; Jim —; -bar
DROP globule; fall; discard; minim; trap door; die; pendant
EROS (god of) love; Cupid; asteroid; Antony's friend
FROE cleaver; steel wedge
FROG amphibian; hoarseness; loop; rail device
FROM out of
FROT rub; chafe
FROW Dutch woman; cleaver
GROG liquor (with water)
GROS coin; fabric; weight
GROT cave; Bremen coin
GROW expand; sprout; wax; develop
IROK gomuti (palm)
IRON metal; element; weapon; instrument; club; shackle; press; strong; Age
KROO Liberian Negro
PROA Malay outrigger
PROD reminder; goad; horse; prodigy
PROG (steal) food; forage
PROM dance, ball (college)
PROO slow up! (horse call)

PROP support; shore; theater equipment
PROW ship's bow; stem; beak
TROD walked; footstep; track
TROP too much: Fr.
TROT jog; gait; race; translation; fishing line
TROW believe; fishing boat
TROY weight system; Ilium, Ilion (Troas); city
WROX rot
ARPA harp: It.
ARRA oath
ARRY cockney worker
ERRA — Pater (almanac)
IRRA war god
ORRA oddly; laborer
ERSE Irish; Gaelic
ERST former; first
URSA bear; stars: — Major, Minor; Great, Little Bear (Dipper)
ARTA Ionian gulf
ARTO prefix: bread
ARTS skills; sciences; fine —; — and crafts
ARTY artistic
URTH Norn; Wyrd (with Verthandi, Skuld); Weird Sister
ARUI sheep
ARUM herb; starch
BRUH pig-tailed macaque
BRUT dry: Fr.; Brit. king (New Troy, London)
CRUS leglike part; shank
CRUX (Southern) Cross; crucial point
DRUB (beat with) stick
DRUG medicine; dope; — on the market; — addict
DRUM spool; instrument: tympanum; beat
DRUN road (Gypsy)
ERUA mother goddess
ERUC cordage fiber
FRUG modern dance
GRUB larva; food; dig(ger)
GRUE shiver; shudder
GRUM morose; guttural
GRUS constellation (Crane)
IRUS Odyssey beggar
PRUT exclamation; river

TRUE factual; loyal; align
TRUK islands (Carolines)
URUS wild ox
URVA mongoose
ARYA Caucasian
ERYX sand snake
ORYX antelope, gemsbok
TRYP parasite in blood (sleeping sickness, nagana, surra)

ASAK tree
ASAR glacial ridges; eskers
ESAU Isaac's, Rebecca's son; Jacob's twin; hairy; red; Edom
ESAY Isaiah
ISAR river (Munich)
OSAR glacial ridges; eskers
TSAO Chinese state
TSAR emperor; dictator
USAR salt; grass
USAS dawn goddess
ISBA log hut
ASCH Scholem (author)
ASCI spore sacs
ESCA apoplexy (plant disease)
ESCE suffix: begin to be
ASEA at sea
ASEM alloy
ASER Jacob's son
ESEK Isaac's well
ESER weight
ISER river
OSER dare: Fr.
USED accustomed; secondhand
USEE future user
USER employer
USES law of — (beneficiary)
YSER river
ASHA tribe
ASHY gray, pale
ISHA Upanishad
PSHA exclamation
TSHI Gold Coast language
USHA Bana's daughter; sorceress
ASIA continent; Orient; East
ASIN month
ASIR Arab. principate
HSIA 1st Chin. dynasty
ISIS goddess; Osiris's wife, sister; Horus's mother
OSID suffix: sugar

TSIA tea
TSIN Chin. dynasty
ASKR — and Embla; Norse Adam and Eve
ISLE ait; eyot; insulate; key
OSLO city (Norway); Christiania
ISMY doctrinaire
ASNO donkey: Sp.
ESNE slave
ASOK tree
ASOP sopping
ASOR lyre
ESOP fable writer
ESOX fish (pike, pickerel, muskellunge)
ESPY behold; detect; meteorologist
ASSE caama; fox
ASSI holly
ESSE existence; to be: Lat.
OSSA bones; Mt. (Olympus)
ASTA measure; dog
ASTI city; — spumante
ESTA this: Sp.
ESTE It. family; this: Sp.
ESTH Balt; Estonian (Tallinn man)
OSTE prefix: bone
ASUR war god
ESUS Gaulish god (Mars)
ISUI Asher's son
TSUN measure (1/10 ch'ih)
USUN ancient North Chinese
USUS user, use: Lat.
RSVP please reply: Fr.

ATAP palm
ATAR perfume; essence
ETAH Eskimo settlement; town
ETAL and others: Lat.
ETAT state: Fr.; L' — c'est moi!
PTAH god
STAB pierce; trial
STAD town
STAG deer; men's party; warn
STAR sun; heavenly body; asterisk; hummingbird; excel
STAT photocopy
STAY rope; fasten; prop, endure; wait;

remain; stop(ping); — put
UTAH state; Indian; Deseret (Mormon)
UTAI no songs (yo-kyoku)
UTAS 8 day feast; Jap. songs
ETCH eat into; engrave
ITCH skin irritation; desire
UTCH "I"
ATEF crown (Osiris)
ATEN solar disk
ATEO Polynesian god
ATES sweetsop
ETES (you) are: Fr.
ITEA shrub; Virginia willow
ITEM also; article; bit; entry
ITEN So. Amer. Indian
ITER road; passage (brain)
OTEA Great Barrier island
STEM shaft; trunk; stock; axis; dam; check; derive; turn skis
STEN weight; gun
STEP pace; foot rest; rank; act; dance; crush; — on it
STER suffix: agent
STET let it stand!
STEV stanza
STEW boil; steep; hash; worry; study; oyster bed
ATHI Kenya river
OTHO Roman emperor
ATIK star
ATIP expectant
ATIS monkshood; fruit
ATIU one of Cook Islands
ITIS suffix: inflammation, mania; Tereus' son
OTIC of the ear; auditory
OTIS bustard genus; general; inventor (elevator)
STIB sandpiper (dunlin)
STIR agitate; rouse; ado; jail
UTIA rodent
ATKA fish; Aleut. island
KTKB chess move
KTKR chess move
KTKT chess move
ATLE tree
ATLI Gudrun's husband-king
STLO WW II battle site
ATMA soul
ATMO prefix: steam
ATMU sun god
ITMO betel pepper
ETNA stove; volcano
ATOM whit; particle; nuclear complex
ATON solar disk
ATOP at the peak
ETON school, college; collar; jacket; playing field of —
ITOL suffix: alcohol(ic)
OTOE Sioux Indian
STOA portico; poikile (Zeno)
STOD Danish speech
STOF measure
STOG stall in mud
STOM prefix: mouth
STOP halt; discontinue; arrest; close; instrument part; period
STOT stumble; stutter
STOW pack; hide; hold; skiing resort
UTOR to use: Lat.
KTQB chess move
KTQR chess move
ATRI It. town
ATRY lay to (naut.)
ETRE exist; be; Fr.; raison d'—
OTRA other: Sp.
OTRO other, another: Sp.
ATTA soul; native; flour; fruit; ant
ATTU Aleut. island
ETTA Henrietta; Harriet
ETTE suffix: fem.
OTTO name; palindrome; perfume; Ger. ruler
ATUA demon
ATUM sun god (Tem)
ETUI (vanity) case; box
OTUS giant slain by Apollo
STUB stump; penpoint; short, stocky; extirpate; ticket part; bump
STUD breeding stock; knob; stump; dot; poker
STUM grape juice; must; renew wine
STUN stupefy; daze
STUT horsefly
UTUG horsetail standard
UTUM small owl
ATWO asunder
VTWO robot bomb
ATYS god (Cybele's lover)
ETYM Moabites, giants; abbr.: word sources
ITYS Tereus' son
STYE eyelid swelling
STYX Hades river; nymph: daughter of Oceanus, Tethys
ITZA Mayan Indian

BUAL wine
DUAB tract
DUAD pair
DUAL double
DUAN canto; poem
DUAR mountain pass
DUAT Hades
FUAD Arab king
GUAD tree
GUAM Mariana island
GUAN bird
GUAO tree
GUAR legume; cluster bean
JUAN John; Don —; Don Giovanni
JUAR durra; millet
KUAN pottery; official
KUAR month
LUAU feast; cook-out
MUAV geol. epoch
PUAN latex
QUAB fish
QUAD type; four; -rangle, -ruplet, etc.
QUAE — vide (which see)
QUAG morass
QUAI pier
QUAN money
QUAR fill; choke
QUAS sour beer, cider (Russian)
QUAT squat
QUAY pier
RUAY weight
SUAN — pan: Chin. abacus
TUAN measure; sir; title
YUAN dynasty; money
BUBA tropical sore
BUBE boy; jack: Ger.; Fernando Po Bantu
BUBI Fernando Po Bantu
BUBO horned —; eagle owl
CUBA W.I. island; Pearl of Antilles; measure

CUBE square solid; 3rd power; die; plant poison
CUBI measure
DUBB Syrian bear; lizard
HUBB pipe end
JUBA ghost; dance; mane; river
JUBE chancel screen; lozenge
KUBA carpet; measure
LUBA Bantu; Bashilange
LUBE machine oil
LUBS of Lubeck (city)
NUBA Nubian; Berberi language
NUBK shrub
RUBE Reuben; rustic; yokel
RUBY gem; corundum; bird; name; Oswald killer
TUBA saxhorn; tree; nut; fish poison; palm sap
TUBE cylinder; tunnel; subway; radio, TV part; Audion (DeForest)
AUCA Indian
BUCK deer; fop; butt; male; Pearl (novelist); pass the —
CUCA cocaine source
DUCE chief: It.; Mussolini
DUCK bird; webfoot; wild fowl; canvas; pet; plunge; evade; — soup; vehicle
DUCO pyroxylin lacquer
DUCT tube; vessel; pipe
FUCI rockweeds; algae
HUCH Danube fish
HUCK towel fabric
JUCA cassava; manioc
JUCK partridge call
LUCE fish, pike; Adriana's servant; Henry (editor); Clare (writer, stateswoman)
LUCK chance; event; fortune
LUCY fleur-de-lis; fem. name; camera lucida; Lemonade — (Mrs. Hayes); — Stone, suffragist
MUCH great (deal); far; — Ado (Shaks.)
MUCK (rid of) manure; mess
NUCI prefix: nut
OUCH exclamation
PUCA goblin; specter
PUCE flea: Fr.; eureka red
PUCK sprite; Robin Goodfellow; Shaks. character; hockey disk
RUCK crowd; rake; wrinkle
SUCH of this kind; same
SUCK draw in; bleed; drink
TUCK draw up; fold (in); eat; Friar (Robin Hood)
YUCA cassava; manioc
AUDE Fr. dept.; river
BUDA It. millet
BUDD Lanny (Sinclair)
BUDE light; burner
DUDE dandy; fop; city fellow; — ranch
DUDS clothes; failures
JUDA James' brother
JUDE name; NT book, author; Jew: Ger.; — the Obscure (Hardy)
JUDO self-defense art
JUDY name; Punch and —; Judith; Kipling character
KUDU Afr. antelope
LUDI Roman public games
LUDO game; pachisi
MUDD measure; doctor of Booth (Lincoln assassin)
NUDA ctenophore; Beroida
NUDD Brythonic god, king
NUDE naked; art work; color
PUDU Chilean deer
RUDD carplike fish
RUDE rough; boorish; vulgar
SUDD Nile waste matter; dam
SUDS lather; froth; beer
WUDU Moslem ablution
AUER violinist
DUEL combat; meeting
DUET music for two
EUER your(s): Ger.
FUEL combustible matter
GUEG Albanian
HUED colored; tinged
HUEY Long (La. governor)
JUEZ judge, juror: Sp.
KUEI disembodied spirit
LUES syphilis
QUEI measure
RUER repenter
SUER prosecutor; suitor
SUET hard fat
SUEZ canal; seaport
TUEL furnace
BUFF leather; coat; tan; ward off; polish; wheel; bare skin; enthusiast
BUFO toad genus; agua
CUFF slap; manacle; sleeve end; miser; on the —
DUFF pudding; cheat
DUFY Fr. artist
GUFA round boat
GUFF humbug; chaff
HUFF inflate; bully; anger
KUFA round boat
LUFF sail nearer wind
LUFT air: Ger.; -waffe
MUFF handwarmer; bungle
PUFF blow; pastry; distend; hair roll; adder; powder —
RUFF collar; bird; fish; plait; trump
SUFI mystic ascetic
TUFA porous rock
TUFF volcanic rock
TUFT crest; clump; tassle
WUFF gruff bark sound
YUFT Russ. leather
AUGE priestess
BUGI Celebes Malay
EUGE bravo!
FUGA fugue: It.
FUGU poisonous fish
GUGU P.I. soldier, insurrecto
HUGE enormous; immense
HUGH name; saint (of Cluny)
HUGO name; Victor (novelist)
JUGA carrot ridges; yokes
JUGE judge: Fr.
KUGE Jap. courtier
LUGE lodge; small sled
LUGH Celtic light god
MUGA silk; moth

OUGH exclamation
PUGH pshaw!; fish prong
RUGA stomach membrane
RUGG pull
SUGI Jap. cedar
VUGG lode cavity
VUGH lode cavity
YUGA Hindu age cycle
BUHL inlaid decoration
BUHR whetstone
DUHR star
GUHA Bantu
GUHR earthy deposit
KUHL eyelid cosmetic
RUHR Ger. industrial area
CUIR leather; dorado
DUIM measure
DUIN demons
DUIT Chibchan Indian; coin
GUIB harnessed antelope
HUIA bird (starling)
HUIT eight: Fr.
LUIF loof
MUID measure
MUIR moor (Scot.)
NUIT night: Fr.
QUID cud; essence; pound; — pro quo
QUIP witty sally; jest
QUIT abandon; yield; stop; free
QUIZ test; odd one; hoax
RUIN destroy; destruction; violate
SUIT costume; card set, legal action; please; (out)fit
YUIT Asian Eskimo
FUJI wisteria; cherry; volcano
JUJU Afr. magic, charm
PUJA worship; festival
SUJI wheat; semolina
BUKA dried leaves
BUKH prate; talk
BUKK prate; talk
CUKE cucumber
DUKE prince; cherry
DUKU lanseh tree fruit
HUKE hooded cape
JUKE partridge call; — box; sociological name (with Kallikak)
KUKI Burma Mongol
KUKU N.Z. fruit pigeon; kukupa
LUKE name; evangelist; Paul's companion; author Acts; -warm
PUKA rare N.Z. tree
PUKE cloth; vomit
PUKU Afr. antelope
PUKY nauseated
RUKH fabled bird; jungle
SUKE Susan; teakettle
SUKU Bantu
SUKY Susan; teakettle
TUKE fabric; canvas
WUKF trust fund
YUKI Cal. Indian
AULA hall; tree; brain part
AULD old; — lang syne
AULU tree
BULB bud; tuber; corm; lamp; swell
BULK mass, volume; loom; -head (stall)
BULL (bovine) male; stud; papal letter; optimist; Taurus; policeman; blunder; glib talk; -fight
BULT hill; ridge
CULE diminutive suffix
CULL pick out; assort
CULM grass stem; coal dust; shoal water deposit
CULT sect; worship system
DULL blunt(ed); dismal; inert; tedious; Shaks. character
DULY properly; timely
FULA Sudanese
FULK unfair shove (marbles)
FULL filled; replete; quite; — dress; — house
GULA upper throat; goddess (Ninurta's consort)
GULE of August (Lamma's Day)
GULF bay; chasm; eddy
GULL bird; cheat; dupe
GULO wolverine genus
GULP swallow; catch breath
HULA Hawaiian dance
HULE caucho source
HULK ship body; bulky thing
HULL husk; ship body; Cordell (statesman)
HULU o-o's feather tuft
JULA suspension bridge
JULE name: Julian; Julius
JULY (5th Roman) month
KULA measure; gift exchange
KULI low-caste Indian
KULM crane; heron
KULU old woman (Kipling)
LULA name; Louisa
LULL (temporary) quiet
LULU barn owl; name; Louisa
MULE equine hybrid; spinning jenny; slipper
MULK freehold land
MULL muslin; ointment; ponder; humus
NULL nil; void; code filler
PULE cheep; whimper
PULI coins
PULK (Cossack) regiment
PULL drag; influence
PULP pith; tissue; paper; magazine
PULU tree fern
PULY whining; complaining
RULE law; guide; reign method; control; — Britannia; ruler; line
RULL to wheel; trundle
SULA genus; booby; gannet
SULD measure
SULK mope; be sullen
SULU Moro
TULA metal; niello; city; Toltec ruins
TULE bulrush; cattail
TULU Dravidian Indian
VULN wound (Her.)
YULE Christmas
ZULU Bantu; Kaffir; ship; artificial fly
BUMP coincide; hit; swelling; — off (kill)
DUMA Russ. parliament
DUMB mute; stupid; — waiter; deaf and —
DUMP unload; junkyard; thud; mean place; holey dollar
FUME smoke; fit; rage
FUMY vaporous; smoky
GUMI shrub, flower, fruit
GUMP silly, stupid one; Andy, Chester, Min (cartoon family)
HUMA Uganda Negro
HUME philosopher

HUMP protuberance; mound; crisis; Himalayan peaks; -back
JUMP leap; bounce; move; headstart; — the gun
LUMP mass; swelling; barge; like it or — it
MUMM mask; disguise
MUMP beg; mumble; cheat
NUMA Pompilius (Roman king)
NUMB deaden(ed); helpless
PUMA cougar; catamount
PUME Yarura(n language)
PUMP force; draw out; slipper
RUMB compass point
RUMP sirloin part; remnant; — Parliament
SUMO Ulvan
SUMP dig pit; tank; cistern
TUMP drag slain deer
YUMA Indian (Calif.); city
AUNE measure
AUNT parent's sister; tia: Sp.; tante: Fr., Ger.
BUNA synthetic rubber
BUND embankment; league
BUNG stop(per); throw
BUNK case; bed; nonsense
BUNN cake
BUNT sag (net, sail); (fungus) disease; butt (ball)
CUNA Panama Indian
DUNE sandhill; twine color
DUNG excrement; fertilize(r); weight
DUNK dip into; immerse
DUNS dull; stupid
DUNT split (ceramics)
DUNY having many dunes
FUND supply; finance; money; sinking —
FUNG Sennar Negroid
FUNJ Sennar Negroid
FUNK fear; coward; Casimir (vitamins) Isaac (lexicographer); — & Wagnalls
FUNT weight; Allen (TV)
GUNA Sankhya term
GUNJ granary; market
GUNK jilt; hoax
GUNL gunwale
GUNN castaway (Stevenson)
HUND dog: Ger.
HUNG suspended; undecided (jury)
HUNH exclamation
HUNK pierce; lump; OK
HUNT seek; chase; Leigh (writer)
IUNO Jupiter's wife
JUNE month; beetle; — moon, bride
JUNG young: Ger.; Carl Gustave (psychologist)
JUNK ship; trash; scrap
JUNO goddess; Jupiter's wife, Hera; stately woman; missile
KUNG public
KUNK measure
LUNA moon goddess; silver
LUNE crescent; hawk leash
LUNG air bladder; iron —
LUNN Sally (teacake)
LUNT light; smoke; Alfred (actor)
LUNY crazy (man)
MUND protection right
MUNG grass
MUNJ tough grass: twine
MUNT sash bar
NUNS sisters; veiling, fabric
PUNA high Andes; wind; sickness (soroche)
PUND weight
PUNG (drive) box sleigh; mah jong term
PUNK touchwood; tinder; conch; tramp; bad
PUNO Pacific trade wind; city (Peru)
PUNT (propel) flatboat; kick; bet
PUNY weak; slight
QUNG So. Afr. Bushman
RUNE Teutonic sign; magic
RUNG wheel spoke; hooped
RUNT small animal, man
SUNG chanted; Chin. dynasty
SUNK immersed; overcome
SUNN hemp: fiber plant
SUNT babul: gum tree; pod; were: Lat.
TUNA fish; pear: opuntia
TUND pound; bruise
TUNE song; pitch; harmony
TUNG tree; oil
TUNK rap; thump; game
TUNO rubber tree; gum
TUNU rubber tree; gum
TUNY melodious
YUNX woodpecker genus
ZUNI Indian; reservation
BUOY float; sustain; life-; channel marker
CUON wild dog (dhole)
DUOS duets
HUON pine; timber tree
LUOH white Nile Negro
QUOD prison; — erat demonstrandum (Q.E.D.)
DUPE trick(ed one); copy
HUPA Athapascan Indian
HUPP call to horse
JUPE skirt
LUPE Samoan fruit pigeon; Velez (actress)
NUPE Nigeria Negro
PUPA chrysalis; snail; instar
RUPA body form (Buddhism)
SUPA P.I. tree: lamp oil
SUPE stage extra; supercharge
TUPI Amazon Indian
TUPY Amazon Indian
ZUPA Yugo district
ZUPH Samuel's ancestor
AURA wind; emanation; bird
AURI prefix: gold, ear
BURA steppe blizzard
BURD noble lady
BURE brown red-yellow
BURG (fortified) town
BURH (fortified) town
BURI palm (fiber); talipot
BURL (pick) knot; Ives (actor)
BURN (be on) fire; yearn; waste; speed; brand
BURP belch; — gun
BURR (prickly) nut, knob;

reamer; banyan tree; Aaron (statesman)
BURT butt; gore; dent
BURY hide; inter; lose
CURA parish priest: Sp.
CURB restrain(t); sidewalk edge; market
CURD coagulated milk
CURE heal; remedy; preserve; priest: Fr.
CURL coil; twist; hair lock
CURR to murmur (as owlet)
CURT short; concise
DURA — mater (spinal membrane)
DURN gatepost
DURO Sp. peso; dollar
DURR grain sorghum
FURL roll up (sail, flag)
FURY rage; avenging spirit; Erinys, Fate, Parca (Atropos)
GURU teacher
HURA bishop's cap; sandbox tree; possumwood
HURE head of boar, wolf
HURI Abihail's father
HURL throw; pitch; rush
HURR to snarl
HURT harm(ed); pain
JURA rights; mountain range
JURE de — (by law)
JURY (court) panel; committee; grand —; hung —
KURD Sunnite Mohammedan; Iranian
KURE Jap. city; Hawaiian isle
KURI Lezhgian tribesman
KURK church: Scot.
LURA brain opening
LURE entice; decoy; trumpet
LURG marine worm
LURI Lake Albert Negro
LURK lie in wait; skulk
MURA Brazil Indian
MURE thrust against wall
MURK (make) gloomy
NURL wood knot; to mill
OURS possessive pronoun
PURE unmixed; chaste; sheer; free; Simon —
PURI Indian yellow
PURL knitting stitch; beer; murmur; spin; swirl
PURR cat's sound
PURU of Arawakan
RURU N.Z. morepork
SURA Koran section; deva
SURD irrational; mute
SURE safe; firm; certain
SURF swell of sea; foam
SURT Frey's slayer
TURB crowd; clump
TURF sod; grassy ground; peat; racing
TURI Pathan tribesman
TURK Mongoloid; Seljuk; Ottoman; Osmanli; horse
TURM troop; company
TURN bending; corner; revolve; reverse; change; shape; act; movement
TURP turpentine
WURD Norn; Urth
WURM glacial period
YURT Kirghiz tent
AUSA Vich (Sp. commune)
AUSU tree
BUSH shrub; thicket; tail
BUSK stir about; hasten; corset bone; Indian New Year
BUSS ship; kiss; calf
BUST bosom; statue; failure; break
BUSY (keep) active; in use
CUSH sorghum; cow; money; Ham's son; country
CUSK fish; burbot; eel
CUSP (crescent) point; tooth edge
CUSS curse; person
DUSE incubus; Eleanora (actress)
DUSK twilight; gloom
DUST powdered matter; rubbish; clean; dust to —; gold —
FUSC dusky; somber
FUSE detonator; melt; unite
FUSS tumult; bustle; -budget
FUST pilaster; smell stale
GUSH flow; spout; be effusive
GUST outburst of wind
HUSE beluga; whale; huchen
HUSH quiet; silence; -hush; -puppy; — money
HUSI fine P.I. fiber
HUSK covering (of seed, corn); shell
HUSO beluga; whale; huchen
HUSS dogfish; John (religious leader)
JUSI fine P.I. fiber
JUST fair; virtuous; exact(ly)
KUSA ceremonial grass
KUSH Ham's son; country
LUSH luxurious; drunkard
LUSK lazy (fellow)
LUST sensual desire
MUSA banana genus
MUSE meditate; goddess
MUSH meal; hasty pudding; flattery; proceed!
MUSK odor; aromatic secretion (of deer, ox, etc.)
MUSO Chibchan Indian
MUSS mess; rumple; row
MUST be obliged to; necessity; new wine; stum; staleness; frenzy
NUSS nurse
OUSE Great — (river)
OUST eject; discharge
PUSH shove; thrust; strive; -button
PUSS cat; lip; face
RUSA deer; sambar; grass; oil
RUSE trick; deceit; slip
RUSH haste(n); attack; red (mace); cattail
RUSK bread; biscuit; Dean (statesman)
RUSS Russian; Slav
RUST oxydize; corrode; inaction; reddish-brown
SUSA Elam city (Esther story)
SUSI fine cotton
SUSU blind dolphin; Congo
SUSY name: Susan; Susanna

TUSH tooth; Georgian; pshaw!
TUSK long tooth
AUTE tree
AUTO prefix: same, self; drama: Sp.; (ride in) car
BUTE island; Scot. county; parson (Thackeray)
BUTO serpent goddess; Leto
BUTT cask; mound; target; ram; hinge; jut; halibut
CUTE clever; attractive
DUTY obligation; task; tax
FUTE Eskimo curlew
GUTI Sumer settler; Kurd
JUTE fiber plant; Corchorus; Low German
LUTE cement; bricklayer's tool; Apollo's musical instrument; jar ring
MUTA mus. change; Moslem marriage
MUTE silent; dumb; muffle
MUTH measure
MUTT cur; stupid one; — and Jeff
PUTT golf stroke
RUTA herb genus; rue
RUTE measure
RUTH pity; grief; name; OT book, heroine (Moabitess); wife of Boaz
TUTE to tutor
TUTU N.Z. shrub; poison; ballet skirt
YUTU Peru tinamou; bird
PUUD weight
SUUM hum; — cuique
TUUM thin: Lat.
CUVY sea girdles; kelp
TUWI P.I. dyewood tree
BUXY paymaster
LUXE elegance; de —
PUXY ill-tempered
BUYO betel leaf; nut
CUYA hardwood tree
FUYE Jap. flute
PUYA pineapple genus
AUZU tree
BUZI Ezekiel's father
BUZZ hum; fly low (over); — bomb (V1, V2)
FUZE detonator; melt; unite
FUZZ fine fibers; police
GUZE red roundel (Her.)
HUZZ buzz; murmur
JUZA star
NUZO Chibchan Indian
SUZY name: Susanna
TUZA pocket gopher
WUZU Moslem ablution
ZUZA weight

AVAL grandparental
AVAR Caucasian language
EVAN name (Welsh)
EVAT eft
IVAH Bib. city
IVAN John; — the Terrible
KVAS sour beer, cider
OVAL egg-shaped; elliptic; arena
SVAN Caucasian
UVAL grapelike
AVEC with: Fr.
AVER assert; asseverate
AVES birds: Lat.
EVEA madder (tree); ipecac
EVEN evening; level; fair(ly); equal(ly), moderate; just; not odd; flush
EVER always; at anytime
EVET eft; newt
IVER ever
IVES inventor (photo-engr.)
OVEN (bake in) stove; kiln
OVER above; across; beyond; again; surplus; ended; Roger and —
UVEA iris layer
AVID eager; greedy
AVIS bird: Lat.
CVII 107; Trajan reign
EVIL bad; sinful; injury; disease
LVII 57; Nero reign
MVII 1007
OVID poet (Metamorphoses); P.O.N.; Naso
OVIS sheep genus
UVIC grapelike; acid
UVID moist; wet
AVON river; Shakespeare home (Stratford)
AVOW declare; justify; confess
EVOE bacchanals' wild cry; Punch editor
AVUS grandfather: Lat.
OVUM germ cell; egg

AWAG wagging
AWAN tribe
AWAY onward; hence; far; off; absent
EWAN name (Welsh)
KWAN coin; weight
SWAB mop; lout
SWAD mass; soldier
SWAG bag; booty; sway; sag
SWAM floated
SWAN constellation; dive; — song
SWAP barter; exchange
SWAT hit (hard); river, state (Pakistan); Sultan of — (Ruth)
SWAY oscillate; veer; rule
YWCA welfare organization
EWER pitcher; udder
KWEI disembodied spirit
OWEN (Welsh) name; socialist; zoölogist
OWER debtor
TWEE bird's cry
ZWEI two: Ger.
IWIS certainly
SWIG gulp; hoist; tackle
SWIM move in water; float; teem
SWIZ swindle
TWIG discover; branch; beat
TWIN double; match; — Cities
TWIT taunt; yarn snarl
AWNY bearded
AWOL absent without leave
LWOW Polish city
SWOB sponge; wipe; mop
SWOP trade
SWOT hard work; grind; hit
SWOW I — (oath)
AWRY distorted; perverse(ly)
EWRY linen storeroom
OWSE tan liquor
SWUM swim participle
GWYN Llud's son; deity

AXAL around an axis
EXAM interrogation; test

OXAN gas
EXES letters; expenses
OXEA sponge spicule
OXEN bovines; draft animals
OXER hedge (fox hunting)
AXIL leaf angle
AXIS center line; spine; stem; deer; power alliance; partnership
CXII 112; Trajan reign
CXIV 114; Trajan reign
CXIX 119; Hadrian reign
EXIT depart(ure); die
IXIA corn lily; bulb
IXIL Mayan Indian
LXII 62; Nero reign
LXIV 64; Nero reign
MXII 1012
MXIV 1014; Brian Boru defeats Danes
MXIX 1019
OXID oxygen compound
OXIM chem. compound
XXIV 24; Tiberius reign
AXLE spindle
IXLE cordage fiber
AXON axis; cell process
EXON Exeter man
OXYL oxygen radical

AYAH nurse; sign
AYAN spruce
CYAN green-blue
DYAD pair
DYAK Bornean
DYAS Permian (geol. period)
EYAH nurse; sign
EYAS nestling
IYAR month
KYAH partridge
KYAK canoe
KYAR coconut fiber
KYAT weight; Burmese money
LYAM bloodhound
LYAS geol. period
MYAL cultic
PYAL veranda
PYAT magpie
RYAL coin
RYAN peak, Idaho
RYAZ coin
GYBE jibe; scoff; agree
TYBI 1st Egypt. spring month
DYCE thus!: naut. command
DYCK Anthony Van (painter)
SYCE groom
WYCH -hazel; — elm
HYDE — Park; Dr. Jekyll and Mr. —; measure
AYES yes votes
BYEE measure
DYER tinter; Mary, Quaker Martyr
EYED looked at; ogled
EYER needle maker
EYEY having holes
OYER hearing (law); — and terminer
OYES court crier's cry
OYEZ court crier's cry
PYET magpie
RYEL coin
SYED Moslem chief
TYEE chief
TYER binder
BYGO pass by
ZYGA rowers' benches; brain fissures
AYIN 16th Heb. letter; 70
PYIC purulent
BYKE nest of bees
CYKE cyclorama
DYKE levee; checkers opening
FYKE fish bag net
HYKE cry to urge dogs
KYKE fashion spy
SYKE fountain (Her.)
TYKE dog, child
CYLE brewing; beer; wort
GYLE brewing; wort; vat
HYLA frog; toad
HYLE matter (philos.); demon
KYLE sore; ulcer; farmer
PYLA brain opening
PYLE Ernie (journalist); Howard (artist)
TYLO dog (Maeterlinck)
CYMA cornice molding
CYME inflorescence
HYMN song (of praise)
LYME bloodhound
RYME water surface
TYMP blast furnace stone
ZYME ferment
DYNA prefix: power
DYNE unit of force
GYNE prefix: female
IYNX wryneck (woodpecker)
JYNX wryneck; charm
LYNX wildcat; fur; constellation
MYNA talking bird: grackle
RYND millstone support
SYNC synchronize
TYNE Eng. river
WYND alley; small court
WYNN timber truck; Ed (actor, Perfect Fool)
BYON clayey earth
CYON wild dog (dhole)
EYOT islet
LYON Fr. city; bean
PYOT piebald; chatty
RYOT Indian peasant
GYPS gypsum
HYPE wrestler's throw
HYPO photo solution; needle; injection
HYPS hypochondria
RYPE ptarmigan
SYPE ooze
TYPE kind, sort; class(ify); printer's letter; use typewriter, produce copy
TYPO printing error
TYPP yarn count unit
TYPY typical
BYRD explorer; Va. statesman
BYRE cow house
EYRA wild cat
EYRE Jane (Bronte heroine); circuit (court)
EYRY bird's nest
FYRD old English army
GYRE turn; ring; vortex
GYRI brain ridges
GYRO prefix: ring, spiral
LYRA glockenspiel; constellation
LYRE harp; constellation
MYRA name; ancient city
PYRE funeral pile, fire
PYRO prefix: fire, fever
SYRA Aegean island
SYRT quicksand
TYRE Phoenician city; Sur
TYRO beginner; novice
TYRR Odin's son; war god
WYRD Norn; Urth
CYST box; abnormal sac
LYSE undergo lysis
MYSA buffalo (Kipling)
MYST Greek priest
CYTE prefix: hollow vessel
MYTH (religious) legend; fiction
TYTO barn owl; Strix;

Aluco
TYTY farmer of God's Little Acre
SYUD Moslem prince; title
GYVE fetter; shackle
MYXA plum (geiger) tree; sebesten
MYXO slime mold

AZAM sir: Persian
AZAN prayer call
CZAR emperor; dictator
EZAN prayer call
IZAR Moslem garment; star
TZAR emperor; dictator
UZAI Palal's father
UZAL Shem's descendant
UZAN weight
EZBA measure
AZEL Saul's descendant
EZEL juniper tree
OZEM David's brother
AZHA star
AZID compound
AZIN chem. compound
OZNI Gad's son
AZOF town; sea
AZON bomb
AZOV town; sea
EZRA prophet; OT book
AZUL blue: Sp.
AZUN Hananiah's father
AZUR Cote d'— (Riviera); Hananiah's father
UZUN ancient North Chinese

FOUR-LETTER WORDS

--AA to --ZZ

BLAA bunk
CHAA tea
DRAA measure
OOAA Hawaiian bird
AHAB king; captain; prophet
ARAB Semite; horse; nomad; urchin
BLAB tattle
BRAB palm
CHAB bird
CRAB crustacean; apple; sign; anger
DOAB tract
DRAB dull; box; wench; cloth; drug
DUAB tract
FRAB worry
GRAB grasp; capture; game
HAAB year
JOAB (David's) captain
KNAB nibble
MOAB kingdom; language; Lot's son
NAAB river
QUAB fish
RAAB river
SCAB crust; strikebreaker
SHAB paltry guy
SLAB slice; road
SNAB hill part; girl
STAB pierce; trial
SWAB mop; lout
ABAC calculator
CHAC -Mool (god); -chac (instr.)
TLAC coin
WAAC fem. soldier
WRAÇ women's army corps
ADAD fiber; god
ARAD plant; city
BEAD globule; ball; drop; aim
BRAD nail
CHAD lake; nation
CLAD dressed; plated
COAD cushion
DEAD deceased; entire; absolute(ly); — reckoning
DIAD pair
DUAD pair
DYAD pair
ECAD modified organism
EGAD oath
FUAD Arab king
GLAD pleased
GOAD rod; decoy; urge
GRAD centesimal unit
GUAD tree
HEAD skull; top; brain; chief; crux; source
IBAD Hira Arab
IRAD Enoch's son
JOAD philosopher; Tom —: Grapes of Wrath (Steinbeck)
LEAD metal; element; plummet; bullets; color; guide; command
LOAD burden; measure
MEAD drink; meadow; lake; Margaret, anthropologist
OHAD Simeon's son
ORAD mouthward
PHAD star
PRAD horse
QUAD type; four; -rangle, -ruplet, etc.
RAAD assembly; fish
READ interpret; learn; study; understand
ROAD (rail)way; track; anchorage
SCAD fish; large amount
SHAD fish
SPAD nail
STAD town
SWAD mass; soldier
TOAD amphibian; anuran; fawn
UDAD sheep
WOAD herb
ALAE wings
BLAE bleak
BRAE slope
IRAE Dies — (Day of Wrath)
KOAE red-tailed bird
QUAE — vide (which see)
SPAE prophecy
DEAF unhearing; inattentive; — and dumb, — mute
GOAF grain; rick
GRAF nobleman: Ger.; — Spee (Zeppelin)
HAAF fishing grounds
HEAF pasture
LEAF plant part; sheet; tea
LOAF bread; idle

OLAF (Vi)king
WRAF air force; aviatrix
AGAG king
AWAG wagging
BRAG boast; game
COAG dowel
CRAG cliff; neck
DRAG haul; harrow; obstacle; puff; auto race
FLAG flower; standard; stone; signal; limp; reduce, dwindle
KNAG spur; knot
KRAG rifle
PEAG money
PHAG comb. form: eating
QUAG morass
SHAG hair; tobacco; bird; rascal; dance step
SKAG boat; keel part
SLAG dross; lava
SNAG stump; cut; obstacle; tangle
STAG deer; men's party; warn
SWAG bag; booty; sway; sag
TOAG Indian
WAAG monkey
ADAH wife of Lamech, Esau; fem. name
AIAH Edomite, Rizpah's father
AMAH nurse
ARAH exclamation
AYAH nurse; sign
BLAH nonsense
DRAH measure
ELAH king
ETAH Eskimo settlement; town
EYAH nurse; sign
IVAH Bib. city
JOAH record keeper
KYAH partridge
LEAH fem. name; Laban's daughter; Jacob's wife
MEAH wall tower
NOAH patriarch (Ark builder)
OPAH fish
PRAH canoe
PTAH god
SAAH measure
SEAH measure
SHAH ruler
UTAH state; Indian; Deseret (Mormon)

YEAH yes
ADAI tribe
ALAI regiment; mountain; Jal —
ANAI termite
BNAI B'rith (Jewish Society)
CHAI person
DHAI midwife
GOAI shrub
ILAI David's man
NGAI spiritual power
PEAI medicine man
QUAI pier
THAI Siamese
UTAI no songs (yo-kyoku)
UZAI Palal's father
BRAJ basha
ADAK Aleut. island
ANAK giant race
ARAK palm; spirit
ASAK tree
BEAK bill; nose; judge
COAK tenon
DHAK tree
DYAK Bornean
FEAK twitch; wipe
FLAK antiaircraft
HAAK fish; wander
IRAK country
KIAK canoe
KYAK canoe
LEAK loss; ooze; crack
PEAK point; top; summit
SIAK latex
SOAK absorb; sot
TEAK tree; dark
WEAK feeble; pliable; light
AGAL cord
AKAL deity
ANAL pert. to anus
ARAL lake
AVAL grandparental
AXAL around an axis
BAAL deity
BEAL river mouth
BUAL wine
CHAL man
COAL ember; fuel
CRAL hut; village
DEAL bargain; transaction; unfinished wood; apportion(ment); policy: New —, Fair —
DHAL split pea, lentil
DIAL plate; face; call; sun-
DUAL double
EBAL Mount (Joshua's altar)

EGAL equal: Fr.
ERAL epochal
ETAL and others: Lat.
FEAL conceal
FOAL colt; equine young
GAAL brewing
GEAL pert. to earth
GOAL purpose; objective; score
HEAL cure; restore
ICAL compound suffix
IGAL Moses' spy
JAAL goat
KEAL cabbage
KRAL hut; village
LEAL loyal: Scot.
MAAL measure
MEAL grain; pulverize; repast
MYAL cultic
NEAL male name; novelist
ODAL land; vine
OPAL birthstone (Oct.); girasol
ORAL spoken; of the mouth
OVAL egg-shaped; elliptic; arena
PAAL measure
PEAL ring; loud sound; fish
PYAL veranda
REAL coin; true; genuine; very
RIAL coin
RYAL coin
SAAL hall: Ger.
SEAL otarian; pinniped; fur; fasten; brown; ratify; stamp
SIAL earth's outer part
SKAL health toast
TAAL lake; volcano; language
TEAL duck (blue)
UDAL land
UNAL land
URAL -Altaic; mountains; hypnotic
UVAL grapelike
UZAL Shem's descendant
VAAL river
VEAL calf; meat
VIAL vessel
WEAL body politic; stripe
ZEAL ardor; enthusiasm
ADAM first man; sin; composer; architect
ANAM tree; Viet Nam

region
ARAM country (Syria); Eugene (murderer)
AZAM sir: Persian
BEAM bar; timber; breadth; ray; smile; on the —; broadcast
BRAM Abraham
CAAM loom; heddles
CHAM tribe; title; bite
CLAM mollusk; hush
CRAM press; stuff; study
DRAM measure; drink
EDAM city; cheese
EJAM Bantu
ELAM kingdom
ENAM gift; land grant
EXAM interrogation; test
FAAM tea; leaves
FLAM trick; drum beat
FOAM froth; rage; rubber
FRAM spear
GRAM sword; plant; weight; —'s method; grandma
GUAM Mariana island
IMAM priest; title
KLAM weight
LIAM O'Flaherty: "Informer"
LOAM clay; soil
LYAM bloodhound
MAAM madam
MIAM hut
NAAM distrain
OGAM Irish alphabet
OLAM infinity; — haba (life after death)
PRAM carriage
REAM 500 (paper) quantity; bevel; enlarge
ROAM wander
SEAM fold; crevice; join; ornament; measure
SHAM deceit; fake
SIAM Thailand; Anna's king (The King and I)
SLAM bang; criticize; grand —
SWAM floated
TEAM group; yoke
TIAM language
TRAM trolley; gauge
ULAM Gilead's descendant
WHAM exclamation
ADAN prayer call
AKAN Negro
ALAN dog; name
AMAN Ahasuerus's minister
ANAN tree; interjection
ARAN Seir's descendant; island
AWAN tribe
AYAN spruce
AZAN prayer call
BEAN plant; trifle; head; strike
BRAN god-king; seed coat; chaff
CHAN resthouse; lord; title
CLAN clique; family; group
COAN pert. to Cos Island
CRAN bird; measure
CYAN green-blue
DEAN clergyman; educator; oldest member, doyen
DHAN wealth; loan
DIAN reveille
DUAN canto; poem
EGAN horse (Kipling)
ELAN dash; ardor
ENAN Prince of Naphtali
EOAN pert. to east; dawn
ERAN Ephraim's grandson
EVAN name (Welsh)
EWAN name (Welsh)
EZAN prayer call
FLAN tart; disk; net
GEAN cherry
GIAN -Carlo (Menotti)
GMAN U.S. police agent
GOAN pert. to Goa
GRAN weight; grandma
GUAN bird
IBAN dyak (Borneo)
IRAN Persia
IVAN John; the Terrible
JEAN name; cotton cloth
JOAN lass; cap; — of Arc, the Maid, la Pucelle
JUAN John; Don —; Don Giovanni
KAAN inn; title
KHAN resthouse; lord; title; Agha —
KLAN Ku Klux —
KRAN coin
KUAN pottery; official
KWAN coin; weight
LEAN be supported; incline; thin
LOAN lend
MAAN city
MEAN intend; denote; base; unkind; middle
MIAN sir; title
MOAN lament
NGAN measure
OBAN coin
OLAN Wang Lung's wife (Pearl Buck; The Good Earth)
OMAN Arabian state; sultanate; Muscat
ONAN Indian; Judah's son
ORAN seaport
OXAN gas
PAAN town
PEAN panegyric; praise; fur
PHAN measure
PIAN tumor
PLAN design; scheme
PUAN latex
QUAN money
ROAN horse; yellow-red
RYAN peak, Idaho
SAAN Bushmen
SCAN examine; measure poetry
SEAN John
SHAN Thai
SPAN stretch; team; measure; dog
SUAN — pan: Chin. abacus
SVAN Caucasian
SWAN constellation; dive; — song
TEAN tone: Scot.
THAN in comparison with; conjunction
TMAN U.S. Treasury agent
TUAN measure; sir; title
ULAN lancer; — Bator
URAN lizard; Indian
UZAN weight
WEAN withdraw; alienate
YEAN to lamb
YUAN dynasty; money
AGAO language
CHAO measure
DHAO knife (Burma)
GRAO weight
GUAO tree
LIAO Manchuria river
MIAO Chinese aborigine
OMAO thrush
PHAO wolf (Kipling)
PRAO canoe
TIAO Chinese money
TSAO Chinese state
URAO trona (mineral)

APAP month
ATAP palm
CHAP fellow; crack; jaw
CLAP rap; applaud; flatten
CRAP dregs; money; dice cast (crabs)
DRAP cloth
FLAP slap; leaf; sway; -jack
FRAP tighten
HEAP pile; crowd; car
KNAP summit; rap; talk; bite; button
LAAP secretion; insect
LEAP jump, skip; — year
NEAP wagon pole; tide
NOAP bullfinch
PLAP fall loudly
REAP cut; harvest
SCAP skull
SHAP silk yarn
SLAP strike; — bang
SNAP seize; break; click; shut; photo; vigor; easy task; — out
SOAP cleanser; detergent; money; soft —; -box; — opera
SWAP barter; exchange
TEAP ram
TRAP snare; mouth; net; catch; clothe; basalt; — shooting
WRAP cloak; blanket; coat
IRAQ country
ADAR month
AFAR far away; tribe
AGAR wood
AJAR opened
ALAR winglike; axillary
AMAR measures
APAR armadillo
ARAR tree
ASAR glacial ridges; eskers
ATAR perfume; essence
AVAR Caucasian language
BAAR weight
BEAR carry; yield; endure; relate; animal; Ursa; short-seller; pessimist
BHAR Kolarian native
BOAR (wild) hog; male
CHAR trout; burn; sandbank; -woman
CZAR emperor; dictator
DEAR costly; loved; loved one
DHAR state; town (India)
DUAR mountain pass
EDAR Bib. site
FEAR fright; doubt
GEAR notched wheel; equipment; adjust; harmonize
GNAR growl
GUAR legume; cluster bean
HAAR fog
HEAR listen; perceive by ear
HOAR frost; gray; -hound
ISAR river (Munich)
IYAR month
IZAR Moslem garment; star
JOAR durra; millet
JUAR durra; millet
KHAR weight
KNAR knot; burr
KUAR month
KYAR coconut fiber
LEAR learning: Scot.; king; father of Goneril, Regan, Cordelia
LIAR prevaricator; plant
NEAR close(ly); approach
OMAR Khayyam; tentmaker; caliph
OSAR glacial ridges; eskers
PAAR sand
PEAR fruit, tree
QUAR fill; choke
REAR back; raise; — admiral
ROAR loud sound; laugh
SAAR river; region
SCAR rock; cicatrix; mar(k); fish
SEAR burn; dried up; gun-lock catch
SOAR fly high; glide
SPAR mineral; mast; gaff; box
STAR sun; heavenly body; asterisk; hummingbird; excel
TAAR tambourine
TEAR drop; weep; rip; glass defect
THAR goat
TIAR crown; shrub
TSAR emperor; dictator
TZAR emperor; dictator
USAR salt; grass
WEAR be clothed in; impair; endure; deteriorate
YEAR time period; twelve month; leap —; calendar, fiscal —
ZOAR town; Bela; city of Lot
ABAS down: Fr.
ALAS sad cry
ANAS duck
ARAS river
BAAS master
BEAS Punjab river
BIAS diagonal (incline); prejudice
BLAS Gil (Le Sage novel)
BOAS Franz (anthropologist)
BRAS arm: Fr.
DYAS Permian (geol. period)
EYAS nestling
GRAS horse; foie — (paté)
IDAS Marpessa's lover; Castor's slayer
IRAS Cleopatra's maid
KHAS special; noble
KRAS tahr (goat)
KVAS sour beer, cider (Russian)
LIAS geol. period
LYAS geol. period
MAAS river
MIAS orang-utan
NIAS Ind. Ocean island(er)
ORAS Danish money
PAAS Easter
QUAS sour beer, cider (Russian)
UPAS tree (juice); arrow poison
USAS dawn goddess
UTAS 8 day feast; Jap. songs
XMAS Christmas
YEAS yes votes
ZOAS symbolic figures (Blake)
ADAT law
ANAT sky god; med. term
BEAT strike; defeat; mystify; throb; scoop; field; sphere; — the Dutch
BHAT minstrel; scholar
BLAT sheep's cry

BOAT (go by) ship; gravy-
BRAT apron; child
CHAT talk; bird; spike
CLAT mess; chatter
COAT fur; skin; cover; — of arms
DOAT drivel; be silly, overfond; wood rot
DRAT oath
DUAT Hades
ERAT was: Lat.; quod — demonstrandum (Q.E.D.)
ETAT state: Fr.; L' — c'est moi!
EVAT eft
FEAT deed; accomplishment
FIAT sanction; edict; money; automobile (It.)
FLAT level; (make) insipid, dull; wholly; — tire
FRAT fraternity
GEAT channel in mold; Scandinavian (Beowulf)
GHAT range; bank; river bank stairs
GNAT (biting) fly
GOAT ruminant; scape-; brown
HEAT warmth; rage; height; dead —; pressure; strain
IKAT shrub; weight
KAAT shrub; weight
KHAT measure
KYAT weight; Burmese money
MAAT goddess
MEAT flesh; kernel; food
MOAT trench
NEAT tidy; trim; straight
PEAT darling; turf; fuel
PIAT magpie; antitank gun
PLAT plait; map; plot; fish
PRAT buttock
PYAT magpie
QUAT squat
SCAT buffet; scatter; begone!; tax; skat
SEAT chair; fundament; site; membership; install; hot —
SHAT saline lake
SKAT card game; star
SLAT lath; slab; sheep's hide; flap
SPAT mollusk; gaiter; snap; tiff
STAT photocopy
SWAT hit (hard); river, state (Pakistan); Sultan of — (Ruth)
TEAT nipple
THAT so; which; pronoun; connective; that's —
TOAT plane handle
WHAT interrogative; pronoun; what's —
AGAU language
BEAU dandy; lover; — Brummell, — Nash
DIAU Indian
ESAU Isaac's, Rebecca's son; Jacob's twin; hairy; red; Edom
FRAU Mrs., wife, Mme., woman: Ger.
LUAU feast; cook-out
PEAU skin: Fr.
PRAU swift canoe
UNAU sloth
VEAU veal, calf: Fr.
WHAU why; tree
MUAV geol. epoch
SLAV Eastern European
BRAW handsome; fine
CHAW masticate
CLAW nail; ungula; chela; scratch; hammer
CRAW gullet; stomach
DHAW billhook
DRAW drag; attract; gain; infer; extract; sketch; undecided contest
FLAW crack; defect; wind
GNAW bite; corrode
SCAW promontory
SHAW thicket; pshaw; playwright (George Bernard)
SLAW cabbage
THAW melt; unbend
AJAX hero (Telamon's son)
ANAX Castor, Pollux (Dioscuri)
COAX flatter; cajole
CRAX curassow (bird)
FLAX plant; fiber; thrash
HOAX deceive; trick
ODAX rock whiting (fish)
OLAX tree
ADAY atomic attack date
ALAY marble
ANAY fruit
AWAY onward; hence; far; off; absent
BLAY bleak
BRAY (donkey's) cry; grind; Mrs. Nickleby (Dickens)
CHAY red dye plant
CLAY earth; ceramic; pipe; — pigeon; color; Henry, statesman
DDAY operation start
DRAY cart; squirrel's nest; — horse
ESAY Isaiah
FLAY (strip off) skin
FRAY contest; tumult; wear off
GRAY dull; dismal; hoary; Dorian (Wilde); Asa, botanist; Elisha, inventor
OKAY approve; all right
OLAY palm
PEAY medicine man
PIAY medicine man
PLAY frolic; act; drama; contend; sport; game
PRAY ask; beseech; please
QUAY pier
RUAY weight
SHAY chaise; carriage
SLAY kill; overwhelm
SPAY deer; castrate
STAY rope; fasten; prop, endure; wait; remain; stop(ping); — put
SWAY oscillate; veer; rule
TRAY salver; platter; old dog
AGAZ Indian
AHAZ king
BOAZ Ruth's husband
DIAZ Bartholomeu (Port. navigator)
GRAZ Austrian city (Mur)
MAAZ Judah's descendant
RYAZ coin

ABBA father; title
ALBA garb; poem; brain matter; duke
AMBA mountain
ANBA title

ARBA cart
BABA nurse; title; cake
BOBA chicken snake
BUBA tropical sore
CABA measure
CEBA tree; kapok source
CUBA W.I. Island; Pearl of Antilles; measure
EABA measure
EGBA Negro; Yoruba
ELBA Napoleon's exile isle
EZBA measure
FABA bean; vetch
GEBA Jonathan's victory site
HABA bean
ISBA log hut
JUBA ghost; dance; mane; river
KOBA antelope
KUBA carpet; measure
LUBA Bantu; Bashilange
MABA Negro; tree
NUBA Nubian; Berberi language
PABA vitamin
PEBA armadillo; Indian
RABA river
REBA weight
SABA fiber; kingdom; island
SEBA Bib. country; Ham's grandson
TOBA Tatar; Chaco Indian
TUBA saxhorn; tree; nut; fish poison; palm sap
UEBA measure
YABA bark; cabbage tree
BIBB mast's timber piece
COBB Irvin S. (writer); Tyrus R. (baseball)
DUBB Syrian bear; lizard
HOBB havoc; fireplace ledge; pin; pig
HUBB pipe end
LOBB go heavily; tennis stroke; till
WEBB Beatrice Potter (writer)
ABBE priest; title; Amer. meteorologist
ALBE album
BABE baby; — Ruth; girl
BUBE boy, jack: Ger.; Fernando Po Bantu
CUBE square solid; 3rd power; die; plant poison
DOBE brick (house)
ELBE river
GABE taro
GIBE scoff; jeer; agree
GYBE jibe; scoff; agree
HABE tribe
HEBE cupbearer of gods; Zeus's daughter, Hercules' wife; color
IMBE cordage fiber plant
INBE be within
JIBE sneer; agree; coincide; shift course
JUBE chancel screen; lozenge
KIBE chilblain crack
KOBE Honshu port
LABE city
LOBE projection; ear part
LUBE machine oil
ROBE gown; mantle; Douglas novel
RUBE Reuben; rustic; yokel
SABE know
TOBE cotton cloth; future
TUBE cylinder; tunnel; subway; radio, TV part; Audion (DeForest)
UNBE cease to be
WABE tree
COBH Irish port
ALBI flagellants
AMBI about; prefix: both
BABI sect
BIBI title: Lady, Mrs. (India)
BUBI Fernando Po Bantu
CUBI measure
GABI taro
GOBI Mongolian desert
JIBI extinct bird
KOBI Japanese reserve duty (term)
MABI tree
RABI crop; physicist
SEBI prefix: tallow
TABI sock
TYBI 1st Egypt. spring month
WABI Indian; tree
YOBI Jap. military service
TEBJ Negro Berber
NABK shrub
NUBK shrub
SOBK evil deity
IRBM ballistic missile
ALBO prefix: white
AMBO pulpit
BOBO owala tree; mullet
BUBO horned —; eagle owl
CABO Yubi
EGBO secret society (Ogboni)
GOBO burdock; okra; camera; mike shield
HOBO vagrant worker
JOBO hog plum; gumbo limbo
KIBO Afr. peak (Kilimanjaro)
LOBO timber wolf
NABO shrub
NEBO wisdom god; Moab mountain (Moses died)
UMBO shield boss; shell beak
VIBO gulf (Italy)
ZOBO mongrel yak
DEBS Eugene (socialist)
DIBS juice: grape, date
LUBS of Lubeck (city)
NIBS personage (VIP); Peter Pan (Barrie)
NOBS knave, jack (card, cribbage)
POBS porridge; pap
TIBS — eve (never-never)
URBS (capital) city
DEBT fault, liability; obligation
BABU Hindu gentleman
CEBU Visayan island
HABU pit viper
KOBU seaweed food (kelp)
NABU god; mountain
TABU forbidden
TIBU Negro-Berber
YABU Afghan pony
ZEBU ox; Brahman bull
ABBY Abigail
BABY doll; indulge
DOBY brick (house)
GABY fool
GOBY fish; passing
MOBY — Dick (whale; Melville)
ORBY revolving
RUBY gem; corundum; bird; name; Oswald killer
TOBY cigar; mug; dog; rob

ACCA fabric
ALCA auk
ARCA box; dish; shell
AUCA Indian
BOCA harbor mouth: Sp.
CACA goddess
COCA cocaine source; shrub; leaf to chew; flavor
CUCA cocaine source
DECA prefix: ten
ECCA geol. period (Karroo)
ESCA apoplexy (plant disease)
INCA Quechuan Indian (ruler)
JACA tree
JUCA cassava; manioc
MICA isinglass (silicate)
ONCA ounce
ORCA killer whale
PACA rodent
PECA coin
PICA type size; magpies
PUCA goblin; specter
RACA reproach; fool
TECA teak; Indian
UNCA 8th note
VICA Pota (goddess)
YMCA welfare organization
YNCA Quechuan Indian (ruler); Inca
YUCA cassava; manioc
YWCA welfare organization
ANCE suffix; — errand
BICE blue, green pigment
BOCE colored fish
DACE fish
DICE (cut into) cubes; gamble; gaming implements
DOCE Brazil river
DUCE chief: It.; Mussolini
DYCE thus!: naut. command
ECCE lo: Lat.; — homo
ENCE suffix
ESCE suffix: begin to be
FACE surface; oppose; line
LACE cord; flavor; netting
LICE insects (louse)
LUCE fish, pike; Adriana's servant; Henry (editor); Clare (writer, stateswoman)
MACE staff; spice; weight; coin
MICE rodents (mouse)
NICE good; kind; pleasing; delicate; dainty; quimper color; Riviera port
ONCE one time; if ever; former(ly)
PACE step; speed; peace: It.
PICE coin; weight
PUCE flea: Fr.; eureka red
RACE run; contest; people; speed; Cape —; rat-
RICE cereal; use ricer; Elmer (playwright)
SICE number 6 on die
SYCE groom
TACE steel splint
TICE lure; yorker (bowled ball)
VICE sin; fault; vise; proxy; — versa
VOCE voice: It.; sotto —
AICH alloy
ARCH support; curve; chief; fingerprint; triumphal —
ASCH Scholem (author)
BACH live alone; composer
CECH Czech
DICH you: Ger.
EACH every(one)
ETCH eat into; engrave
FOCH Ferdinand (Fr. marshal; WW I commander)
HOCH high: Ger.
HUCH Danube fish
INCH measure; move slowly
ITCH skin irritation; desire
JOCH yoke, measure: Ger.
KOCH cook: Ger.; Robert (Bacteriologist)
LECH slab; capstone; river
LOCH lake, bay: Scot.
MICH me: Ger.
MUCH great (deal); far; — Ado (Shaks.)
NACH after: Ger.
OUCH exclamation
RICH wealthy; vivid; full; fragrant; fat
ROCH Saint (14th cent.)
SECH such
SUCH of this kind; same
TECH technical school
UTCH "I"
VACH goddess
WYCH -hazel; — elm
ZACH name
ASCI spore sacs
DECI prefix: tenth
FOCI center points
FUCI rockweeds; algae
LOCI places; sites
NUCI prefix: nut
PICI birds (woodpeckers)
UNCI hooks; claws
BACK help; tub; past; retreat; kick-; dorsal, posterior; spine
BECK nod; bidding; dyeing vat; Pol., Ger. officer, statesman
BOCK beer; leather
BUCK deer; fop; butt; male; Pearl (novelist); pass the —
COCK male fowl; vanes; leader; tap; tee; hay pile, cog
DECK ship floor; pack, cards; array; adorn
DICK Richard; whip; lad; detective; Whittington (London mayor)
DOCK weed; rumex; (cur)tail; pier
DUCK bird; webfoot; wild fowl; canvas; pet; plunge; evade; — soup; vehicle
DYCK Anthony Van (painter)
FECK amount
HACK chop; writer; horse
HECK (weaving) frame; cough; oath
HICK hiccup; rube; jake
HOCK leg joint; hamstring; wine; faro card; pawn
HUCK towel fabric
JACK flag; tool; card; fruit; raise
JOCK John; jockey; hobo
JUCK partridge call
KECK vomit; show disgust
KICK hit; die; object(ion); excitement; -back
LACK need

LICK tongue; stroke; whip; conquer; bit
LOCK gate (canal, dam); tuft; wool; fasten(ing), grapple; tie up; -out (labor)
LUCK chance; event; fortune
MACK coat
MICK Irishman
MOCK jeer; taunt; sham; — apple, turtle
MUCK (rid of) manure; mess
NECK body part; violin part; isthmus; pet
NICK notch; moment; cheat; cut; Old — (devil); Carter (detective)
NOCK notch (in bow)
PACK bundle; cosmetic; cards; crowd; animal(s)
PECK measure; nip; bite; kiss
PICK tool; scratch; choose; rob; eat; best
POCK pustule
PUCK sprite; Robin Goodfellow; Shaks. character; hockey disk
RACK framework; clouds; gait; torture
RECK heed; concern
RICK pile (up); haystack
ROCK stone; Gibraltar; cliff; staunch support; diamond; candy; sway, lull; — the boat
RUCK crowd; rake; wrinkle
SACK dismiss; plunder; wine; bag; gown; sad —
SECK unprofitable (rent)
SICK urge (dog); ill; weak
SOCK beat; wind cone; stocking
SUCK drawn in; bleed; drink
TACK hook; rope; course; attach
TECK readymade tie
TICK parasite; mattress; count; tic
TOCK hornbill
TUCK draw up; fold (in); eat; Friar (Robin Hood)
WICK part of candle, lamp
ALCO dog
CACO bandit
COCO palm; nut; grass
DUCO pyroxylin lacquer
FICO trifle
LOCO (render) mad; weed
MACO cotton
MICO marmoset
PACO alpaca
PECO black tea
PICO peak; game; weight
POCO slightly; old-clothes man
SACO weight; river
SOCO heron; bittern
TECO Indian
TOCO toucan
UNCO strange; very: Scot.
WACO city
ABCS first principles; alphabet
DUCT tube; vessel; pipe
FACT deed; reality
LACT prefix: milk
PACT agreement
PICT British aborigine
RECT element (philos.)
SECT group; denomination
TACT diplomacy; perception
JACU bird
JOCU dog snapper
ANCY suffix
FACY fresh
LACY netlike
LUCY fleur-de-lis; fem. name; camera lucida; Lemonade — (Mrs. Hayes); — Stone, suffragist
RACY smart
ADDA god; river; skink
AIDA opera; Radames' lover
ALDA soprano; hamlet: Sp.
ANDA tree
BUDA It. millet
CODA finale; mark
DADA father; cult
EDDA Norse epic
ERDA earth goddess; Wagner role
JUDA James' brother
KADA measure
LEDA mollusk; mother of Castor, Pollux, Helen, Clytemnestra; wooed by Zeus as swan
LIDA Alida
MEDA secret Indian sect
NUDA ctenophore; Beroida
PEDA pastoral staffs
PODA suffix: foot
RADA legislature
RODA Nile island
SIDA herb; shrub; hemp
SODA carbonated water; Vichy; drink; sodium compound (bicarbonate)
TEDA Negro Berber
TODA Ceylon aborigine
VEDA sacred Hindu books
VIDA feminine of David
BADB goddess
BODB goddess
MEDB Conchobor's wife; goddess; Queen Mab
BUDD Lanny (Sinclair)
DODD cut off (wool)
KIDD William (privateer)
MUDD measure; doctor of Booth (Lincoln assassin)
NUDD Brythonic god, king
REDD make tidy; free of; scold
RIDD Lorna Doone's rescuer
RODD crossbow
RUDD carplike fish
SADD dam; waste matter
SUDD Nile waste; dam
WADD mineral
AIDE help; -de-camp; — memoire
ANDE tribe
AUDE Fr. dept.; river
BADE waited; asked; invited; commanded
BEDE Adam (Eliot); the Venerable (monk)
BIDE wait; tarry; dwell
BODE presage; augur; omen
BUDE light; burner
CADE cask; tree; pet; rebel
CEDE yield; grant; transfer
CODE body of law (Julian, Justinian, Napoleon); signal

system; cipher; — duello
DADE support
DODE nickname: Theodore
DUDE dandy; fop; city fellow; — ranch
EIDE ideas; forms
FADE weaken; flat; dissolve
FIDE entrust; — et amore
GADE fish; composer
GIDE Andre (author)
HADE angle; strip
HIDE land measure; skin; conceal; shelter; — and hair
HYDE — Park; Dr. Jekyll and Mr. —; measure
INDE blue (indigo)
JADE gem; horse; exhaust
JUDE name; NT book, author; Jew: Ger.; — the Obscure (Hardy)
KADE tick
LADE load; dip
LIDE March (month)
LODE ore deposit; vein; load
MADE successful; created; constructed
MEDE ancient Asian
MIDE Ojibway secret order
MODE manner; fashion; drab; a la —
NIDE pheasant's nest
NODE knob; knot; orbit point; joint
NUDE naked; art work; color
ONDE wave: Fr.; wavy (Her.)
PODE suffix: foot
RADE elated
REDE interpret; counsel
RIDE be borne; float; endure; manage; mount; journey
RODE anchor rope; measure; was borne; cross
RUDE rough; boorish; vulgar
SADE letter; Marquis
SIDE region; part(y); oblique; aspect; support; lateral
TIDE ocean's rise, fall; season; drift; endure; current; help
TODE (haul with) sled
UNDE waving, wavy (Her.)
URDE key shaped (Her.)
VADE leave; — mecum
VIDE see: Lat.; for example; quae —
WADE pass; demon; Hampton
WIDE broad; far; lax; astray
SADH holy man
YODH Hebrew Y, 10
ANDI language
CADI judge
KADI judge
LODI city; Napoleon victory
LUDI Roman public games
MADI Negro
MEDI prefix: middle
MIDI south(ern France)
NIDI breeding places
NODI knots; difficulties
PADI rice
PEDI prefix: foot
RODI Medit. island
SADI poet
SIDI Moslem title; Negro
SODI Gaddiel's father (spy)
WADI valley; river; oasis
HADJ pilgrimage
BODO Indo-Chin. language
CODO measure
DADO wall part; groove
DEDO measure
DIDO trick; caper; Carthage queen, Aeneas' beloved
DODO extinct bird; reactionary
EDDO taro root
ENDO prefix: within
FADO tune
FIDO fog evaporation; dog's name
IODO prefix: iodine
JODO Buddhist paradise (Gokaruku)
JUDO self-defense art
LIDO Venice beach
LUDO game; pachisi
MADO fish
ORDO order: Lat.; feast list
PEDO child
REDO make over
SADO carriage; island; river
TODO bustle; stir; ado
UNDO untie; unfasten; ruin
UPDO upswept hair
YEDO Tokyo
SADR tree
DUDS clothes; failures
EADS engineer; bridge
GADS -hill (Dickens)
KIDS star (Auriga)
ODDS inequality; advantage; at —; -on
SUDS lather; froth; beer
ADDU skink; fiber; god
ARDU slave
DADU saint
JADU magic
KADU tribe
KUDU Afr. antelope
ORDU Turk. military district, army corps
PUDU Chilean deer
URDU Hindustani language
WIDU Moslem ablution
WUDU Moslem ablution
ADDY Adeline
ANDY Andrew
BODY structure; anatomy; bulk; corpse; group
CADY golf boy
CODY William (Buffalo Bill)
EDDY whirlpool; Mary Morse (Baker) —: Christian Science
FADY weakening
INDY — pink (carnation)
JADY gemlike
JUDY name; Punch and —; Judith; Kipling character
LADY title; -bird
ONDY wavy (Her.)
SIDY pretentious
TIDY (make) neat
TODY green — (bird)
UNDY waving, wavy (Her.)
URDY key shaped (Her.)
VADY vade mecum; summons
WADY valley; river; oasis
LODZ Polish city

AIEA town
ALEA Athena (war goddess)
AREA zone, region; scope; tract
ASEA at sea
BLEA bleak; livid
BREA resin; tree; asphalt
CREA linen, cotton fabric
EDEA reproduction organs
EVEA madder (tree); ipecac
FLEA insect; puce; — market
FREA Frigg; Odin's wife; goddess
GAEA goddess; Titans' mother
IDEA conception; fancy; key meaning; opinion
ITEA shrub; Virginia willow
ODEA theaters; halls; galleries
OLEA shrub; olive
OTEA Great Barrier Island
OXEA sponge spicule
PLEA excuse; prayer; request; pretext; allegation
RHEA Cybele; mother of the gods; Gaea's daughter; Cronos's wife; ostrich; satellite; grass
SHEA tree; butter
THEA tea source; name
UREA chemical compound
UVEA iris layer
ZOEA crab larva
BLEB blister; bubble
DIEB jackal
OREB Midianite defeated by Gideon
PLEB freshman cadet; common man
SLEB nomadic Arab
THEB measure
ALEC fish; sauce; nickname
AVEC with: Fr.
HAEC this one (fem.): Lat.
SPEC speculation
ABED in bed; bedridden
AGED old; oxygian
BLED emitted or drew blood, sap; extorted
BRED procreated; brought up
COED girl student
DEED act; property transfer
DRED — Scott (slave)
EBED Gaal's father
EYED looked at; ogled
FEED nourish; gratify; graze; fodder
FLED ran away; shunned
FRED nickname
GLED kite; buzzard
HEED notice; attention
HUED colored; tinged
ICED frozen; chilled
LIED fibbed; song: Ger.
MEED reward
MOED festivals (Mishnah)
NEED compulsion; lack; want
OBED David's grandfather
ODED prophet or his father
PIED variegated; Piper; -a-terre
PLED pleaded
REED woody grass; pipe; mouthpiece; Walter (doctor, hospital)
ROED filled with roe
SEED fertile germ; progeny; decay; plant; extract
SHED cast off; abandon; drop; hut; shelter
SLED vehicle, snow or ice
SNED lop; prune
SPED hastened
SYED Moslem chief
TIED bound; knotted; drawn
TOED stepped (gingerly)
USED accustomed; secondhand
WEED plant; tobacco; remove
AGEE awry; Shammah's father; James (novelist)
AJEE awry
AKEE tree
ALEE to shelter
BREE (eye)brow
BYEE measure
CHEE weight
CLEE redshank; bird
CREE Indian
DREE endure; tedious
EPEE fencing sword
FLEE run away; shun
FREE independent; immune; rid; exempt; — and easy; — lance, port, trade, style
GHEE butter
IDEE — fixe: Fr.
INEE arrow poison
KLEE Paul (painter)
KNEE joint; bend(ing)
OGEE arch; molding
OKEE evil spirit
SHEE Irish fairyfolk
SKEE ski
SLEE sly
SMEE pintail duck; widgeon; Peter Pan pirate
SNEE cut; snick(er) —
SPEE Graf — (ship, admiral)
THEE you
TREE wood, plant; family —; boot, shoe —
TWEE bird's cry
TYEE chief
USEE future user
WHEE whistle sound
ALEF letter
ATEF crown (Osiris)
BEEF ox, steer, cow, bos; brawn; rage; complain(t)
CHEF head (cook); — d'oeuvre
CLEF musical sign; roman a —; key
ELEF letter
FIEF feudal estate
KEEF hemp; languor
KIEF hemp; languor
LIEF gladly; freely
REEF shoal; lode; reduce sail
TREF homestead
AREG deserts
DOEG Saul's herdsman; poet's nickname; Indian
DREG lees; residue
GHEG Albanian
GUEG Albanian
SIEG victory: Ger.
SKEG keel part; plum; tear
WAEG bird; kittiwake
OKEH all right, O.K.
BREI soft tissue
DREI three: Ger.
KUEI disembodied spirit

KWEI disembodied spirit
OMEI Buddhist mountain
QUEI measure
VLEI marsh; lake; creek
ZWEI two: Ger.
CHEK Chin. foot (measure)
ESEK Isaac's well
GEEK carnival wild man
HOEK stream bend; — van Holland (Dutch cape, city)
KEEK fashion spy
LEEK plant (onion; liliaceous); — green (Wales emblem)
MEEK mild; submissive
PEEK sly glance; pry; chirp
REEK cloud; exude; smell
SEEK ask; try; hunt
TREK migrate; journey
WEEK time unit; sennight; squeak
ABEL Adam's son; Cain's brother; — Magwitch (Dickens); letter A; monkey
AIEL writ of —
AZEL Saul's descendant
BAEL thorny (fruit) tree
BHEL thorny (fruit) tree
CIEL ceiling; sky; Fr.
COEL cuckoo
DUEL combat; meeting
EDEL noble: Ger.
EZEL juniper tree
FEEL sense; test; suffer
FUEL combustible matter
GAEL Celt; Irishman
GOEL reclaimer; avenger
HEEL back part; end; slant; follow; scoundrel
HIEL Jericho's rebuilder
JAEL Sisera's killer; Heber's wife
JEEL pool; marsh
JOEL prophet, OT book
KEEL ship bottom; navigate; ocher; guinea fowl
KIEL ocher; ruddle; seaport; — Canal
KOEL cuckoo
LAEL Gershonite's father
NAEL weight
NIEL alloy
NOEL Christmas; carol; — Coward
ODEL vine; land ownership
OHEL Zerubabbel's son
OREL Russian city
PEEL pare; tower; spade
REEL wind(er); dance; waver; sway
RIEL Canadian (Indian) rebel
RYEL coin
SEEL shut eyes of; blind
TAEL weight; coin
TEEL sesame
TUEL furnace
WEEL fish basket, trap; pool
WIEL whirlpool
AHEM interjection
ALEM fruit
ANEM prefix: wind; city
ASEM alloy
CLEM riot; suffer hunger; nickname
DEEM consider; judge
DIEM day: Lat.; per —
FLEM Fleming; Belgian
HAEM prefix: blood
IDEM same: Lat.; semper —
ITEM also; article; bit; entry
KHEM chief god (Min)
NEEM tree; Margosa
OZEM David's brother
POEM verse creation
REEM ox; unicorn
RIEM oxhide strap
SEEM look; appear
SHEM Noah's son; Semite
STEM shaft; trunk; stock; axis; dam; check; derive; turn skis
TEEM abound
THEM pronoun
ADEN comb. form: gland; city; gulf; region
ALEN measure
AMEN assent; verily; deity; — Ra
ATEN solar disk
BEEN charmer's clarinet; participle
BIEN good, fine: Fr.; — aimee (well beloved)
BREN (machine) gun
CAEN city snow goose
CHEN Jan (empire
COEN builder)
EBEN Ebenezer
EDEN paradise; West of Nod
EVEN evening; level; fair(ly); equal(ly); moderate; just; not odd; flush
GLEN rival
HIEN Chin. government seat
HOEN weight
IDEN Henry VI figure
ITEN So. Amer. Indian
KEEN sharp; acute; bewail
LIEN claim; attachment; garnishment
MIEN manner; bearing; air
OMEN presage; portent; sign
OPEN plain; frank; undefended; uncertain; bare; start; unfold; public; — sesame
OREN Judah's descendant
OVEN (bake in) stove; kiln
OWEN (Welsh) name; socialist; zoölogist
OXEN bovines; draft animals
PEEN hammer head
PIEN arris (sharp edge)
RIEN nothing: Fr.; — ne va plus
SEEN observed
SHEN Christian God (China)
SKEN squint
STEN weight; gun
TAEN taken
TEEN 13–19; injury; pain
THEN at a time; therefore
TIEN sky: Chin.; — Chu (Lord of Heaven); your(s): Fr.
TMEN Treasury agents
WHEN whereas; how soon
WREN bird; navy woman; architect
AREO prefix: Mars
ATEO Polynesian god
CLEO queen (Cleopatra)
IDEO prefix: idea
OLEO nargarine
SKEO fisherman's hut
THEO prefix: god
ALEP city
BEEP radio sound

DEEP profound; extensive; ocean
HEEP Uriah (Dickens villain)
JEEP vehicle; automobile
KEEP tend; retain; preserve; last
NEEP turnip
PEEP chirp; bird; peer slyly; Bo —; jeep
PREP prepare; student
SEEP ooze; small spring
SKEP basket; measure; beehive
STEP pace; foot rest; rank; act; dance; crush; — on it
VEEP vice-president
WEEP cry; bend; leak
ACER tree
ADER Benjamite
AGER apparatus; field
AHER Benjamite
AMER bitter
ANER city
APER imitator; boar
ASER Jacob's son
AUER violinist
AVER assert; asseverate
BAER prizefighter, actor
BEER beverage; ale; mead
BIER litter; coffin
BOER So. Afr. Dutch
BRER Rabbit (Harris; Uncle Remus)
CHER dear: Fr.
DAER re borrowed stock
DEER ruminant; cervine; — Park (Buddha site)
DHER mound; land share
DIER one moribund
DOER performer; agent
DYER tinter; Mary, Quaker martyr
EBER Hebrew ancestor
EDER river
EGER river
EKER water cress
EMER Cuchulainn's wife (ideal womanhood)
ERER sooner
ESER weight
EUER your(s): Ger.
EVER always; at any time
EWER pitcher; udder
EYER needle maker
GIER eagle (vulture)
GOER runner
HEER Mr., Sir: Dutch
HIER here: Ger.; yesterday: Fr.
HLER sea god (wife: Ran)
HOER scraper
ICER freezer; mixer
IMER Caucasian
ISER river
ITER road; passage (brain)
IVER ever
JEER scoff; taunt
KIER bleaching vat
LEER sly gaze; oven; loin
LIER rester; layer
MEER sea: Ger.
NEER never; kidney
ODER river
OMER measure; sheaf; undertaker (Dickens)
ONER ace; blow; individual
OSER dare: Fr.
OVER above; across; beyond; again; surplus; ended; Roger and —
OWER debtor
OXER hedge (fox hunting)
OYER hearing (law); — and terminer
PEER gaze; equal; nobleman
PIER mole; dock; pillar
RIER oil cask (whaling)
ROER hunting gun
RUER repenter
SAER tenant
SEER prophet
SHER tiger
SIER pintado (fish)
STER suffix: agent
SUER prosecutor; suitor
TEER golfer; mix colors
TIER row; layer; pinafore
TYER binder
UBER over: Ger.
UFER fir pole; shore: Ger.
USER employer
VEER shift (course); waver
VIER striver; four: Ger.
WAER dam
YMER myth. giant
YSER river
ADES Hades
ALES city
AMES author; city, college
ANES once
ARES war; Mars; Zeus's, Hera's son; Eris' brother
ATES sweetsop
AVES birds: Lat.
AYES yes votes
BEES yeast
BRES Elatha's beautiful son (Formorian)
DIES day(s): Lat.; — irae; Cong. committee
DOES performs
ETES (you) are: Fr.
EXES letters; expenses
FEES charges; tips
GHES Tapuyan Indian
GOES walks; proceeds
GRES stoneware: Fr.
IDES Roman date; — of March (fateful day)
IVES inventor (photo-engr.)
LEES dregs
LUES syphilis
ONES individuals
OYES court crier's cry
PRES near: Fr.
SPES (goddess of) hope
TEES river (North Sea)
TRES very: Fr.; three: Sp.
USES law of — (beneficiary)
WIES Ys
ABET aid; incite
AHET season (of inundation)
ANET dill
APET goddess
BEET vegetable; root; sugar —; — top
BLET fruit decay
DIET fare; food regimen; parliament
DUET music for two
EVET eft; newt
FEET measure
FRET gnaw; vex; worry; embroider; ridge; ornament
KEET guinea fowl
KHET mortal body; measure
KMET Slav; tenant; mayor
LAET freedman
LEET court; list
MEET encounter; face; combat; fulfill; fit
OKET ounce
PEET darling; turf; fuel
PIET magpie
PLET three-lash whip
POET writer of verse;

artist
PRET measure
PYET magpie
SPET spit; barracuda
STET let it stand!
SUET hard fat
TRET weight allowance
VOET measure
WEET bird; cry of bird
WHET sharpen; excite; edge
BLEU blue, rookie: Fr.
DIEU god: Fr.; mon —!
EHEU alas
EMEU bird (ostrichlike)
LIEU place; stead
KIEV Ukrainian city
STEV stanza
ANEW over again
BLEW stormed; puffed; sounded
BREW beverage; plot; concoct
CHEW masticate; ruminate; — the cud; — the rag
CLEW yarn ball; sail loop; cocoon; hint
CREW company; gang; cut
DREW sketched; pulled
FLEW aviated; winged
GREW increased
KNEW understood; was aware
LLEW Celt deity (Gwydion's son)
PHEW exclamation
PLEW beaver skin
SHEW show: Brit.; bread
SKEW twist; swerve; distort(ed); slant(ing)
SLEW killed; twist; swamp; large number
SMEW merganser; duck
SPEW eject; scatter; gush
STEW boil; steep; hash; worry; study; oyster bed
THEW muscle; sinew
VIEW sight; see; aim; opinion; scene
WHEW whistle; exclamation
AMEX Amer. Expeditionary Force
APEX summit; crisis
CREX corn crake (bird)
FAEX dregs
FLEX bend
IBEX wild goat; bouquetin
ILEX holm oak; holly
OBEX brain matter
PLEX form a network
PREX (college) president
SPEX spectacles
ULEX spine shrub (furze)
ABEY waive
AHEY ho
AKEY weight
ALEY city
BREY barnacle
DREY squirrel's nest
EYEY having holes
FLEY fright(en)
FREY god (Njorth's son, Gerth's husband)
GREY color; neutral; dull; Zane (writer); Vivian (Disraeli novel)
HOEY partnership (Hawaii)
HUEY Long (La. governor)
JOEY coin; clown; odd-job man; young kangaroo; Pal (O'Hara character)
OBEY submit; comply
PREY victim; pillage; booty
ROEY of mottled grain
SKEY yoke bar
SLEY weaver's reed
SPEY river
THEY pronoun; people; men
TREY three(spot)
UREY Nobel physicist
VLEY marsh; swamp; creek
WHEY milk serum; thin; pale; curds and —
BAEZ singer
CHEZ at home of, with: Fr.
DAEZ daze
GEEZ Version (Ethiopic Bible)
INEZ Don Juan's mother
JEUZ chief Benjamite
JUEZ judge, juror: Sp.
KNEZ Slavic prince
OYEZ court crier's cry
SUEZ canal; seaport

AFFA from off
ALFA grass
GUFA round boat
KAFA Ethiopian
KUFA round boat
OFFA Angles' hero (Beowulf)
SOFA couch; divan
TUFA porous rock
URFA Turkish city (Edessa)
WAFD Egyptian
CAFE restaurant; coffee; -au-lait; society
FIFE flute; checkers opening
JEFE chief; leader
LIFE existence; vivacity; biography
NIFE earth's core
ORFE fish; yellow ide
RIFE abundant; prevalent
SAFE secure; box
WIFE spouse; marry
BAFF strike; stroke
BIFF (deal a) blow
BUFF leather; coat; tan; ward off; polish; wheel; bare skin; enthusiast
CUFF slap; manacle; sleeve end; miser; on the —
DAFF put aside
DOFF put off; remove
DUFF pudding; cheat
GAFF spear; ordeal; hoax
GOFF clown; fool
GUFF humbug; chaff
HAFF lagoon
HUFF inflate; bully; anger
JEFF rope; nickname; Mutt and —
JIFF instant
KIFF languor
KOFF Dutch sailboat
LUFF sail nearer wind
MIFF quarrel; offend
MOFF Caucasian silk
MUFF handwarmer; bungle
PIFF bullet sound; exclamation
PUFF blow; pastry; distend; hair roll; adder; powder —
RAFF Raphael
RIFF Berber; Kabyle; ripple
RUFF collar; bird; fish; plait; trump
TEFF grain plant
TIFF (petty) quarrel
TOFF dandy
TUFF volcanic rock
WAFF flapping; paltry
WUFF gruff bark sound

DEFI challenge; defiance
FUFI wisteria; cherry; volcano
HIFI faithful sound rendition
RIFI Riffs
SAFI Afghan
SUFI mystic ascetic
BUFO toad genus; agua
FIFO inventory method
LIFO inventory method
OFFS cricket-field sides
BAFT astern; cotton
DAFT foolish; giddy
DEFT skillful; trim
GIFT donation; talent
HAFT handle
HEFT weight; bulk; notebook: Ger.
LEFT departed; blow; — of center (Liberals)
LIFT ra(i)se; exalt; steal; elevator
LOFT attic; warehouse floor; golf stroke
LUFT air: Ger.; -waffe
RAFT collection; float
REFT cleft; rift; deprived
RIFT split; divide; cleft
SIFT screen; separate; bolt
SOFT giving way; easy; light(ly); mild; tractable
TAFT President; Republican; rower's seat; — Hartley Act
TOFT — and croft (house)
TUFT crest; clump; tassle
WAFT float; flag; whiff
WEFT yarn; mist; (weave) web
YUFT Russ. leather
MAFU stable boy
AFFY join
DEFY challenge; dare
DUFY Fr. artist
IFFY contingent
OOFY rich (Eng. slang)

ALGA plant
AMGA Siberian river
BAGA turnip
BEGA measure
BIGA two-horse chariot
BOGA basslike fish
FUGA fugue: It.
GIGA medieval fiddle
HOGA hill pasture
INGA timber tree; mimosa
JAGA Bantu
JUGA carrot ridges; yokes
MEGA prefix: great
MUGA silk; moth
NAGA snake
OLGA fem. name
PAGA rice
PEGA remora fish
RAGA state of nirvana
RIGA Latvian city, gulf
RUGA stomach membrane
SAGA legend; story; goddess; weight
SOGA grass rope: Sp.; Bantu
TOGA Roman garb; gown; senatorship
URGA Outer Mongolia
VEGA meadow
VIGA rafter; log
WEGA star
YOGA mental discipline
YUGA Hindu age cycle
ZYGA rowers' benches; brain fissures
ANGE angel: Fr.
AUGE priestess
CAGE confine; enclosure; elevator car; nor iron bars a —
DOGE Venice, Genoa ruler
EDGE brink; sharpness; goad; advantage; — on
EUGE bravo!
GAGE pledge; fruit; gauge; general
HUGE enormous; immense
INGE prelate ("Gloomy Dean"); playwright (Bus Stop)
JUGE judge: Fr.
KUGE Jap. courtier
LOGE theater box
LUGE lodge; small sled
MAGE magician
PAGE young attendant; call, summon; leaf
RAGE fury; storm; fad
SAGE herb; wise; Russell — (financier)
TIGE rifle steel pin; dog
URGE prod; impel; impulse
WAGE carry on; -earner; pay, salary
YAGE plant
BAGG heiress (Thackeray)
BIGG barley
DAGG pistol
FOGG Phileas (Verne)
HAGG demoness; hack; wood
HOGG unshorn sheep
JAGG pendant; tooth; slash
MAGG bird; chatter
MIGG marble (duck)
NOGG egg drink
RUGG pull
TEGG sheep in 2nd year
TIGG swindler (Dickens)
VUGG lode cavity
WEGG Silas (ballad seller: Dickens)
WIGG peruke; long hair
YEGG safecracker; tramp
ARGH timid
DAGH hill
GOGH Vincent van — (painter)
HEGH exclamation; hey!
HIGH lofty; elevated; noble; expensive; shrill; tainted; tipsy
HUGH name; saint (of Cluny)
LUGH Celtic light god
MAGH month
NIGH near(ly); direct
OUGH exclamation
PUGH pshaw!; fish prong
SIGH lament(ing sound)
VUGH lode cavity
WAGH interjection
YOGH Middle English G, Y
BUGI Celebes Malay
HAGI clover; prefix: saint
JOGI yogi; ascetic
MAGI caste; priests; wise men; kings of Orient; Melchior, Gaspar, Balthazar
RAGI grass
RIGI Swiss mountain
SUGI Jap. cedar
VAGI nerves
YAGI antenna
YOGI ascetic; yoga disciple
GAGL sweet gale
CAGN mantis; deity
SIGN symbol; signal; subscribe; ratify; hire
ANGO herb; dye
ARGO ship; therefore; constellation
BAGO shrub

BOGO Eritrean Hamite
BYGO pass by
DAGO tribe
ERGO hence; prefix: work
FOGO stench
GOGO vine; bark soap; beetle; bugaboo; Bantu
HOGO taint; stench
HUGO name; Victor
IAGO villain (Othello)
KAGO conveyance
LAGO lake
MOGO stone hatchet
PAGO -Pago (city)
POGO springy stick
SAGO palm; starch
SEGO herb; bulb; lily; Utah state flower
TOGO Afr. republic; Jap. admiral and statesman
UPGO ascend
ZOGO sacred object
DOGS scaup duck
EGGS ova; — and bacon, ham; — and butter (flowers)
KAGS convict (Dickens)
TOGS clothes
WIGS — on the green (fray)
TOGT trading enterprise
VOGT medieval official
DEGU rodent (Octodon)
FUGU poisonous fish
GUGU P.I. soldier; insurrecto
KAGU bird
PEGU Burmese language; city
ALGY Algernon; suffix: pain
ARGY argue
BOGY specter; bugbear
CAGY shrewd
DOGY calf; duck
EDGY sharp; snappish
EGGY egg-stained; yolky
FOGY dull, bigoted man
LOGY heavy; dull
NAGY Hungarian premier
ORGY carousal; Saturnalia, Bacchanalia
POGY menhaden; trout
SAGY wise

AGHA officer; title
AKHA tribe; Burmese; kaw
ASHA tribe
AZHA star
DEHA body (theosophy)
EPHA Hebrew dry measure
GUHA Bantu
HAHA laugh; fence
ISHA Upanishad
KAHA proboscis monkey
MAHA monkey; deer
MOHA millet; delusion
NAHA city
OCHA weight
PAHA hill
POHA gooseberry (jelly)
PSHA exclamation
SAHA measure
TAHA bird
TCHA (rolled) tea
USHA Bana's daughter; sorceress
WAHA lake trout
ACHE pain; yearn
HEHE Bantu tribe
HOHE Siouan tribe
MAHE island
NAHE river; near: Ger.
TCHE fruit tree; Chin. flute
SAHH measure
ATHI Kenya river
BAHI fortune
EPHI measure
LEHI prophet
MAHI river
PAHI ship
TCHI measure
TSHI Gold Coast language
BUHL inlaid decoration
KOHL eye shadow; horse
KUHL eyelid cosmetic
VEHM medieval tribunal
BEHN herb; tree
FOHN warm dry wind
HAHN Otto (Nobel physicist)
JOHN name; saint, evangelist; cop; man; — Bull (England); Long — Silver (Stevenson)
KAHN banker; test
LAHN river
BAHO prayer stick
BOHO grass; weep; shout
COHO silver salmon
ÉCHO Narcissus's nymph; repeat; response; fruit tree (gingko)
ICHO fruit tree (gingko)
KIHO peacock butterfly
MOHO bird; honey eater
OTHO Roman emperor
PAHO prayer stick
PEHO morepork (bird)
SAHO language
SOHO exclamation; London district
TOHO halt! (to dogs)
YAHO tribesman
BAHR sea; — El Azrak
BOHR Nils (Nobel physicist)
BUHR whetstone
DUHR star
GUHR earthy deposit
LEHR oven; Lew (comedian)
MAHR marriage settlement
MOHR gazelle; bezoar
RUHR Ger. industrial area
SEHR very: Ger.
TAHR goat
TEHR wild goat
WAHR true: Ger.
OCHS Adolph (publisher)
ACHT eight: Ger.
BAHT coin
ECHT genuine: Ger.
ICHU valuable grass
JEHU (chariot) driver; prophet, king (Israel)
KAHU harrier; bird
OAHU (Hawaiian) island
RAHU demon
SAHU spiritual body
TCHU exclamation
TOHU -bohu (confusion)
ACHY painful
ASHY gray, pale

ABIA Samuel's son
AKIA shrub (fish poison)
ALIA other: Lat.
AMIA fish
APIA port (Samoa)
ARIA tune; city (Herat)
ASIA continent; Orient; East
BAIA state; city; resort; bay
CHIA salvia beverage, oil
ELIA Charles Lamb; essayist
ERIA silk(worm)
FRIA Frigg (Odin's wife)
GAIA goddess
GLIA neuroglia (nerve tissue)
HSIA 1st Chin. dynasty
HUIA bird (starling)
ILIA (hip) bones
INIA Amazon cetacean

IXIA corn lily; bulb
MAIA goddess; crab; star
NAIA cobra
OBIA Ashanti religion
OHIA timber tree; apple
OKIA Moroccan money
RAIA ottoman; fish
RHIA China grass
SOIA food plant
TSIA tea
URIA Bathsheba's husband; auk
UTIA rodent
ABIB month
ADIB star
AGIB dervish
CHIB tongue; language
CRIB manger; hut; bin; box; steal; "pony," "trot"
DRIB drop; a little
FRIB dirty short wool
GLIB flippant, smooth(ly)
GUIB harnessed antelope
SNIB escape logging work
STIB sandpiper (dunlin)
AMIC amidic
CHIC stylish(ness)
CRIC lamp condensing ring
EPIC heroic poem
ERIC male name; Viking; the Red
IDIC pert. to ids
LAIC secular
ODIC pert. to ode, od
OLIC chem. suffix
OTIC of the ear; auditory
PYIC purulent
SAIC Near East ketch
UDIC Caucasian language
UVIC grapelike; acid
ZOIC pert. to animals
ACID sour; biting
AMID among
ARID dry; barren
AVID eager; greedy
AZID compound
BEID star
BOID of boas, anacondas
CAID alcaide
ENID fem. name; Geraint's wife; city
GRID grating
IBID P.I. lizard (tidbit); the same: abbr.
IMID chem. compound
IRID iris; crocus
KAID chief; alcaide
KEID star
LAID put down; calmed
MAID servant; — of Orleans
MUID measure
NAID worm
OLID smelly; fetid
OOID egg-shaped
OSID suffix: sugar
OVID poet (Metamorphoses); P.O.N.; Naso
OXID oxygen compound
PAID recompensed; discharged; satisfied
QAID alcaide
QUID cud; essence; pound; — pro quo
RAID attack; foray
SAID before-mentioned; Port —, city; name
SEID tribe; lord; chief; Mohammed's descendant
SKID clog; slide; — Road, Row
SLID glided; slipped
UVID moist; wet
VOID empty; vacuum; cancel
ZOID organic body cell
ABIE 's Irish Rose; name
AMIE friend: Fr.
BRIE cheese
ERIE Iroquoian; lake; city
FOIE liver: Fr.; — gras (pate)
JOIE — de vivre (zest for life)
OKIE migratory worker
OPIE Eng. painter
SOIE silk
UNIE unicorn fish
ALIF letter
COIF defensive skullcap; make up (hair)
ENIF star
KAIF languor; hemp
KEIF hemp; languor
LEIF Ericson (explorer)
LUIF loof
NAIF naive; of true luster
NEIF serf; native; fist
WAIF stray
BRIG sailing ship; prison
CRIG blow
GRIG dwarf; cricket; fowl
HAIG soldier (Douglas)
PRIG precisian; steal; thief; fop
SNIG chop off; drag; pilfer
SWIG gulp; hoist; tackle
TEIG Teague; Thaddeus; Timothy
TRIG trim; sound; prim; math. course
TWIG discover; branch; beat
WHIG U.S., Brit. party
WRIG wriggle
CHIH Chin. foot (measure)
SHIH weight; measure
ALII royalty (Hawaiian)
APII plant
BOII Celtic tribe
CIII 103; Trajan reign
CLII 152; Hadrian reign
CVII 107; Trajan reign
CXII 112; Trajan reign
HEII Hawaiian fern
LIII 53; Claudius reign
LVII 57; Nero reign
LXII 62; Nero reign
MCII 1102
MIII 1003
MLII 1052
MVII 1007
MXII 1012
UBII Teutonic tribe
VIII 8; Augustus reign
XIII 13; Augustus reign
ATIK star
EFIK Negro
HAIK garment; frame
KAIK village
NAIK leader
RAIK weight; measure
SEIK Hindu sectarian
SHIK Arabian Turkoman
AMIL plant; remedy
ANIL shrub; indigo
ARIL seed covering
AXIL leaf angle
BAIL security; bond; set free; dip out; -hoop
BHIL low-caste Indian
BOIL heat; bubble; agitation; abscess
CEIL overlay; line; ceiling
CHIL cheer pine; kite (Kipling)
COIL curl; wind; twist
DAIL legislature; — Eireann
DEIL devil; -'s-bit (plant)
EGIL Volund's (Wayland's) brother
EMIL man's name

EVIL bad; sinful; injury; disease
FAIL fall short; err
FEIL comfortable; neat
FOIL balk; defeat; sword; leaf; sheet
GAIL Abigail; brewing
HAIL ice pieces; salute; — fellow
HEIL hail: Ger.
IFIL tree (brown dye)
IPIL tree (brown dye)
IXIL Mayan Indian
JAIL prison; gaol
KAIL tree; ibex; kale
KOIL cuckoo
LEIL faithful, loyal (Land of the —)
MAIL coin; tax; armor; post
MOIL toil; trouble; spot
NAIL fasten(er); claw; seize; expose
NEIL male name
NOIL combing (wool fiber)
OEIL eye: Fr.; — de boeuf
PAIL bucket
PHIL nickname; prefix: loving
POIL raw silk thread
RAIL bird; scold; paling
ROIL disturb; muddy; vex
SAIL canvas; rigging; journey; travel
SEIL rope: Ger.
SKIL candlefish; beshow
SOIL earth, ground; land; stain; pollute
TAIL end; cue; follow; high-
TEIL linden tree; lime
TOIL work; drudge(ry); snare
VAIL inventor
VEIL screen; facial garment; cloistered life
WAIL lament
YPIL tree (brown dye)
AKIM Negro; — Tamiroff
ALIM teacher
BRIM rim; edge; swell
CLIM — of the Clough (archer outlaw)
DUIM measure
ELIM Bib. oasis
EMIM Moabites; giants
FRIM juicy; soluble
GLIM light; eye
GRIM ruthless; ghastly
MAIM disfigure; mutilate
OXIM chem. compound
PLIM swell; swollen
REIM oxhide strap
SAIM grease
SEIM Polish assembly
SHIM leveling slip; shingle; knife
SKIM scoop off; scud; brush
SLIM slight; scanty; sly; slender
SWIM move in water; float; teem
TRIM shear; adjust; adorn; rebuke; defeat; neat
URIM — and Thummim (sacred instruments)
WHIM fancy; caprice
ADIN name
AKIN related
ALIN measure
AMIN agent
ASIN month
AYIN 16th Heb. letter; 70
AZIN chem. compound
BAIN bath: Fr.
BEIN good; fine
BRIN fan plate; silk thread
CAIN tribute; (Abel's) slayer; mark of —
CHIN lower jaw; chatter; weight; dynasty; Burmese
COIN money; mint; invent; corner
CRIN heavy silk
DAIN Patusan chief (Conrad); — Curse (Hammett); measure
DEIN your(s): Ger.
DRIN Balkan river
DUIN demons
ENIN blue grape pigment
EOIN John; Sean
ERIN Eire; Ireland
FAIN glad; eager
GAIN reach; earn; profit; notch
GEIN glucoside (Geum urbanum)
GRIN smile
HEIN surprise!: Fr.
JAIN sect (Indian)
JOIN mix; unite; coalesce
KAIN tribute
LAIN reclined
LIIN measure
LOIN body part; hips; meat cut
MAIN conduit; first; river; Spanish —
MEIN Chinese noodles; chow —
NEIN no: Ger.
ODIN one-eyed Norse god: Frigg's husband, Thor's father
PAIN ache; trouble; forfeit
RAIN shower; scratch; — check
REIN strap; check; direct; kidney
RHIN Rhine: Fr.
RUIN destroy; destruction; violate
SAIN consecrate; tree
SEIN poss. pronoun, be, being: Ger.
SHIN leg, calf front; run; climb
SKIN hide; pelt; peel; fleece; — and bones
SPIN whirl; twist; aerial stunt; — a yarn
TAIN plate
THIN lean; dim; rare; dilute; — ice
TRIN one of triplets
TSIN Chin. dynasty
TWIN double; match; — Cities
VAIN empty, idle; futile; proud
VEIN channel; streak; blood vessel
WAIN wagon; Charles's —
WEIN wine: Ger.
WHIN gorse; restharrow; rock; winch
ZAIN horse
ZEIN protein
AGIO fee; commission
AHIO Ark driver
APIO celery: Sp.
BRIO con — (with spirit)
CLIO history Muse; mollusk
IDIO prefix: one's own
KAIO fruit
MEIO measure
MOIO measure
NAIO tree
NOIO noddy tern
ODIO hatred: It.

OHIO Buckeye state
OLIO medley; olla-podrida
SCIO prefix: sky
THIO prefix: brimstone
TRIO set of 3; So. Amer. Indian
UNIO mussel
ATIP expectant
BLIP radar screen sign
CHIP fragment; cut; hew
CLIP clasp; cut(ting); gait
DRIP let fall
FLIP toss; tap; drink; hop
GRIP grasp; power; valise; Barnaby's raven (Dickens)
KLIP rock; cliff
KNIP bite; crop; rap
QUIP witty sally; jest
RAIP rope
SEIP seep; ooze
SHIP vessel; send; — of state
SKIP jump; escape; mess; captain; -tracer
SLIP slide; err(or); escape; pier; leash; garment; memo; cut
SNIP cut; shred; slip
TRIP move; slip; journey; (mis)step
WHIP lash; urge; defeat
ABIR red powder
AHIR caste
AMIR prince
ASIR Arab. principate
CHIR pheasant; pine
COIR coconut fiber
CUIR leather; dorado
EMIR ruler; title
FAIR pleasing; ample; just; bazaar; — and square; — deal
HAIR filament; cilium, seta; fabric; -trigger
HEIR inherit(or); — apparent, presumptive
KAIR fiber
KEIR bleaching vat
LAIR resting place
LEIR sea god (Lear)
LOIR dormouse; river
MUIR moor (Scot.)
NAIR native
NEIR kidney
NOIR black: Fr.; bet
PAIR couple; brace
SAIR savor
SEIR Bib. mountain (Hor), Edom (Esau's home)
SHIR cook; gather; tiger
SKIR fly; scurry; skim
SOIR evening: Fr.
SPIR prefix: coiled
STIR agitate; rouse; ado; jail
TAIR goat
VAIR fur
VOIR see: Fr.
WEIR dam; fish trap
WHIR fly; hurry; buzz
YMIR rime-cold giant
ACIS river; (Galatea's) lover
AGIS king
AMIS friends: Fr.
ANIS fennel; birds
APIS sacred bull (Ptah); bee; bull (Kipling)
ARIS molding edge
ATIS monkshood; fruit
AVIS bird: Lat.
AXIS center line; spine; stem; deer; power alliance; partnership
BAIS caste
BOIS wood: Fr.; wine (cognac); — de Boulogne
CRIS dagger; stab
DAIS platform
EGIS protection; patronage; symbol of: Zeus, Athena, shield
ELIS Greek city state
ERIS goddess of discord, Ares' sister
FEIS convention; — of Tara
GLIS dormouse genus
GRIS gray: Fr.
IBIS (sacred) wading bird
IRIS rainbow; goddess; eye part; plant (flag); spirit (Shaks.); red-blue; March (Arlen)
ISIS goddess; Osiris's wife, sister; Horus's mother
ITIS suffix: inflammation, mania; Tereus' son
IWIS certainly
KAIS island
KRIS dagger; stab
LAIS hetaera
LOIS name; Timothy's grandmother
MAIS but: Fr.
NAIS nymph
OTIS bustard genus; general; inventor (elevator)
OVIS sheep genus
PAIS country
QAIS island
RAIS chief (Nepalese)
REIS money; (boat) captain; effendi (state officer)
RIIS Jacob (journalist)
SAIS groom; city; know: Fr.
SEIS six: Sp.
THIS pronoun, demonstrative
TRIS prefix: thrice
UNIS Etats — (USA)
UPIS Artemis, Nemesis
ADIT entrance
ALIT descended
AMIT headdress
BAIT lure; harass; pest poison
BRIT young herring
CHIT child; sprout; memo; voucher; mind
DOIT coin; whit; bit
DUIT Chibchan Indian; coin
EDIT correct; redact; blue-pencil
EMIT eject; issue; voice
EXIT depart(ure); die
FAIT fact; — accompli
FLIT flutter; move
FRIT fuse; fried: Fr.; waste
GAIT walk; pace
GRIT sand(stone); bravery; grate
HUIT eight: Fr.
IBIT P.I. lizard (tidbit)
KNIT looped, tie(d); unite; contract
LAIT milk: Fr.; cafe-au-
NUIT night: Fr.
OBIT death notice
OMIT leave out; neglect
PHIT bullet sound
QUIT abandon; yield; stop; free

SEIT measure
SKIT comedy sketch; jest
SLIT cut; slash; opening
SMIT struck; destroyed
SPIT land point; rod; impale; expectorate; — and image
SUIT costume; card set, legal action; please; (out)fit
TAIT marsupial
TRIT prefix: third
TWIT taunt; yarn snarl
UNIT single thing; basic amount; one; monad
WAIT attend; defer; serenader; lie in —
WHIT bit; jot; dull sound
WRIT legal order; Holy —
YUIT Asian Eskimo
ATIU one of Cook Islands
CCIV 204; Septimus Severus reign
CHIV knife
CLIV 254; Aemilianus reign
CMIV 904
CXIV 114; Trajan reign
LXIV 64; Nero reign
MCIV 1104; First Crusade, conquest of Acre
MLIV 1054; Catholic church schism
MMIV 2004
MXIV 1014; Brian Boru defeats Danes
SHIV bit of husk; fluff; blade
SKIV sovereign (coin)
SPIV slacker: Brit.
XXIV 24; Tiberius reign
ALIX fem. name
BRIX scale (hydrometer)
CCIX 209; Septimus Severus reign
CLIX 159; Antoninus Pius reign
CMIX 909
COIX grass; Job's-tears
CXIX 119; Hadrian reign
FLIX down; fur; flax
MCIX 1109
MLIX 1059
MMIX 2009
MXIX 1019
NOIX edible gland
PRIX price: Fr.; — fixe (table d'hôte)
TRIX fem. suffix
FRIZ curl; crisp; wig
PHIZ physiognomy; face
QUIZ test; odd one; hoax
SWIZ swindle
WHIZ hum; bargain; corker

BEJA Nile nomad
BIJA kino tree
CAJA box; bank
COJA title; teacher
DEJA already: Fr.
HOJA title; teacher
LIJA unicorn fish
LOJA bark (quinine)
MAJA crab
NAJA cobra
PUJA worship; festival
RAJA prince; fish
REJA screen, grille: Sp.
SOJA bean; Glycine
NEJD kingdom
HAJE cobra
YAJE plant
CAJI snapper
FIJI islands (Lau, Yasawa)
FUJI wisteria; cherry; volcano
HAJI pilgrim
KOJI Jap. yeast cake
MOJI Jap. seaport
SUJI wheat; semolina
HAJJ pilgrimage
SEJM Polish assembly
BOJO grass
GAJO non-Gypsy
IDJO Niger delta Negro
MAJO dandy; shrub
MOJO tree; majagua; voodoo charm; Indian
PAJO prayer stick
ROJO redskin: Sp.
TAJO trench
BAJU jacket
CAJU fruit; mahogany
HOJU Jap. army reserve
JUJU Afr. magic, charm
TEJU lizard

AKKA Pygmy
ATKA fish; Aleut. Island
BAKA devil
BEKA weight
BUKA dried leaves
DIKA bread; fat; oil
EKKA carriage
HAKA dance
KAKA parrot
LOKA sphere; universe
PIKA little chief hare
PUKA rare N.Z. tree
ROKA mafura (tree)
SAKA era; Scythians
SIKA Jap. deer
SOKA drought blight
WAKA canoe
WEKA flightless bird
YAKA Bantu
KTKB chess move
BAKE dry; roast; biscuit
BIKE bicycle
BYKE nest of bees
CAKE bar; dough; harden
COKE coal residue; fuel
CUKE cucumber
CYKE cyclorama
DIKE levee; ditch; dig; goddess (Horae)
DUKE prince; cherry
DYKE levee; checkers opening
FAKE loop; cheat; sham
FEKE trick device
FYKE fish bag net
HAKE fish; pester; frame
HIKE toss; tramp; raise
HUKE hooked cape
HYKE cry to urge dogs
JAKE Jacob; rube; money; satisfactory; ginger
JOKE jest; laughing stock
JUKE partridge call; — box; sociological name (with Kallikak)
KYKE fashion spy
LAKE sea; pool; red (cochineal)
LIKE as; similar(ly); love; prefer; probable
LOKE Loki; surprise!
LUKE name; evangelist; Paul's companion; author Acts; -warm
MAKE produce, create; cause; reach; type; identify
MIKE Michael; Mick; microphone
MOKE donkey; dolt
NIKE victory goddess (Samothrace); missile
PEKE (Pekinese) dog
PIKE fish; weapon; pierce; highway; farmer; gamble;

Zebulon (explorer; peak)
POKE thrust; prod; pry; sack; potter; herb
PUKE cloth; vomit
RAKE incline; tool; collect; roue; —'s Progress
REKE rick; pile
ROKE vapor; smoke
SAKE purpose; beer
SOKE jurisdiction
SUKE Susan; teakettle
SYKE fountain (Her.)
TAKE acquire, seize; scene part; receipts
TIKE child
TUKE fabric; canvas
TYKE dog, child
WAKE track; arouse; vigil; island
WOKE stirred; roused
YOKE join; link; slavery
ZEKE Ezekiel
WAKF trust fund
WUKF trust fund
ANKH cross
BIKH aconite; poison
BUKH prate; talk
HAKH claim(er); legal claim; share
LAKH 100,000; coin
RAKH hayfield
RUKH fabled bird; jungle
SIKH Hindu soldier
ENKI Babylonian god
KAKI bird; tree
KIKI castor oil plant
KUKI Burma Mongol
LOKI god of discord; Aesir; Balder slayer
MAKI lemur
MOKI N.Z. raft
PIKI maize bread; pik
RAKI spirits
REKI Baluchistan nomad
SAKI monkey; Munro
TIKI god; first man; image
WEKI fern
YAKI cayman
YUKI Cal. Indian
BUKK prate; talk
RIKK tambourine
BOKO evil spirit (Haiti)
DOKO Afr. pygmy
HAKO rite
JAKO parrot
KOKO bird; palm; tribe; executioner (Mikado)
MAKO shark
MOKO Maori tattoo; -moko (lizard)
TOKO Chin. store; flogging
ASKR — and Embla: Norse Adam and Eve
KTKR chess move
OAKS horse race; trees
BKKT chess move
BQKT chess move
KTKT chess move
QKKT chess move
QQKT chess move
RKKT chess move
RQKT chess move
TAKT beat(s); tempo
BAKU hat; tree; rug; city; oil field
DUKU lanseh tree fruit
HAKU fish
HIKU scabbard fish
KIKU chrysanthemum
KUKU N.Z. fruit pigeon; kukupa
MAKU Indian
POKU antelope
PUKU Afr. antelope
RAKU -ware
SUKU Bantu
TAKU Indian
ALKY alcohol
CAKY crusty
COKY grimed; drug addict
FAKY spurious
INKY black; stained
JOKY jocular
LAKY red
OAKY oaklike
PIKY full of fish
POKY shabby; dull; bonnet
PUKY nauseated
ROKY misty; hoarse
SUKY Susan; teakettle
TAKY taking
WAKY alert
YOKY coupled

AGLA acrostic
ALLA by: It.
AMLA tree
AULA hall; tree; brain part
BALA geol. epoch
BELA jasmine; Benjamin's 1st son; Hungarian king
BOLA missile; majagua (tree)
CELA that: Fr.
COLA tree; nut; drink
DOLA weight
ELLA Eleanor; she: Sp.; fem. suffix
FALA refrain; dog
FULA Sudanese
GALA festival; tribe
GILA — monster; lizard; Ariz. river
GOLA storeroom; caste; cyma
GULA upper throat; goddess (Ninurta's consort)
HALA pine tree
HELA goddess; Loki's daughter
HILA 'eyes' of bean
HOLA fish poison; herb; hello
HULA Hawaiian dance
HYLA frog; toad
IMLA Micaiah's father
IOLA Kansas town
JULA suspension bridge
KALA bird
KELA measures
KOLA caffeine nut; jackal; river; city; bay (Murmansk)
KULA measure; gift exchange
LILA deity manifestation
LOLA fem. name
LULA name; Louisa
MALA evil(s), wrong(s): Lat.; jaw
MELA festival; prefix: black
MILA measure
MOLA sunfish genus
NALA hero
NOLA fem. name; tune
OLLA jar; meat dish; -podrida (medley)
PALA weight; antelope; vine; rice
PELA wax (secreting insect)
POLA Yugo. city (Pulj)
PYLA brain opening
SALA dining room: Sp.
SELA Dead Sea town
SOLA herb (topee source); alone; holla!
SULA genus; booby; gannet
TALA tree; basin; ruin
TELA tissue; web; banana port
TOLA weight
TULA metal; niello; city; Toltec ruins
ULLA grass; paper pulp

UPLA cow dung; fuel
VELA membranes; soft palates; the Sails (Argo constellation)
VILA fairy; New Hebrides
VOLA palm (hand, foot)
ZOLA author (J'accuse: Dreyfus case; Nana)
BULB bud; tuber; corm; lamp; swell
KALB de — (general)
TALC soapy mineral
AULD old; — lang syne
BALD naked; — eagle
BOLD valiant; brazen; strong, heavy (type)
COLD chill; frigid; indifferent; common —; coryza; — blood; — chisel
EILD barren; milkless
FELD field: Ger.
FOLD plait; envelop; fail; quit; flock
GELD castrate; prune; tax
GILD lay gold on; adorn — the lily; trade society
GOLD metal; element; — dust, medal
HELD kept; retained
HILD Hethin's victim princess
HOLD grasp; have; retain; believe; keep; bear; lair; prison
KELD spring; fountain
MELD announce (score); merge
MILD calm(ly); soft; tame
MOLD fungus; humus; die, matrix; shape; mix
SOLD vended; persuaded; cheated
SULD measure
TOLD narrated; counted
VELD So. Afr. grassland
WELD unite; junction
WILD rough; savage; mad; eager; unruly; wilderness
WOLD upland plain
YELD barren; milkless
ABLE fit; adept; suffix; -bodied
ACLE tree
AILE winged
ALLE bird; all: Ger.
ATLE tree
AXLE spindle
BALE woe; bundle
BILE liver secretion; choler
BOLE trunk; clay; brown
CALE Gypsy; cabbage
COLE brassica genus; Porter (composer)
CULE diminutive suffix
CYLE brewing; beer; wort
DALE valley; share; trough
DELE omit; erase
DOLE ration; (relief) alms; deal out
ELLE measure; she: Fr.
FILE tool; rasp; smooth; march; column; folder; arrange
GALE storm, wind
GULE of August (Lamma's Day)
GYLE brewing; wort; vat
HALE healthy; Nathan — (patriot)
HOLE pit; cavity; flaw; — in one; — card; ace in the —
HULE caucho source
HYLE matter (philos.); demon
IDLE not working; empty; lazy; waste
ILLE that one: Lat.
IOLE Eurytus' daughter (Hercules' captive)
ISLE ait; eyot; insulate; key
IXLE cordage fiber
JOLE jowl; cheek
JULE name: Julian; Julius
KALE cabbage
KELE weight
KILE measure; weight
KYLE sore; ulcer; farmer
LILE little
MALE man(ly); tribe
MELE Hawaiian poem; chant
MILE measure; distance; 320 rods, 1,609.3 meters
MOLE nevus; birthmark; pier; burrow(ing animal); Mossi language
MULE equine hybrid; spinning jenny; slipper
NILE river; green, blue
OGLE gaze (amorously)
ORLE shield border; fillet
PALE wan; pallid; ashy; picket; stake; beyond the —
PELE fire goddess
PILE hair; heap (up); awn; atomic —
POLE rod; tail; terminal: axis, battery; — Star; Polish, Polack
PULE cheep; whimper
PYLE Ernie (Journalist); Howard (artist)
RALE rattling sound
RILE irritate; vex
ROLE actor's part
RULE law; guide; reign method; control; — Britannia; ruler; line
SALE bargain; auction; willow; salted: Fr.
SOLE pelma (bottom); flatfish; single; only
TALE story; — of Two Cities; count
TELE prefix: far, complete
TILE ceramic slab; drain pipe; domino; tessera; slate
TOLE entice; told; tinware
TULE bulrush; cattail
VALE valley; — of tears; farewell: Lat.
VILE base; evil; odious
VOLE rodent; slam (cards)
WALE streak; texture; ridge; welt
WILE trick; guile; lure
YALE university; lock; Eli, Elihu —; myth. antelope
YULE Christmas
CALF bovine, etc., young; fur; leather; skin; lower leg
DELF quarry; pottery; blue
GOLF game; blood-red; — links
GULF bay; chasm; eddy
HALF moiety; -breed -caste, -nelson, -shell
PELF booty; riches
SELF identity; ego; one
WELF ducal family
WOLF canid (dog); Lupus; larva; devour;

dissonance; cry —; flirtatious man
AALI pasha
AMLI tree
ATLI Gudrun's husband-king
BALI demon; monkey; offering; island
BELI myth. Brit. king
CALI Colombian city
COLI intestinal bacterium
DALI tree; offering; Salvador —
DOLI weights
FILI learned poet
GALI abuse
GOLI musket ball; pill
HALI prefix: sea, salt
HELI prefix: sun, spiral
HOLI spring festival
JOLI pretty, nice: Fr.
KALI glasswort; carpet; evil genius; Agni's tongue; Siva's wife
KOLI low-caste tribesman
KULI low-caste Indian
MALI caste; nation; river
NOLI — me tangere
PALI slope; coral parts; Buddhist language
PILI nut; grass; hairs
PULI coins
SOLI single performances; prefix: sun, alone
TALI gold piece; weight
TELI low (merchant) caste
VALI Odin's son; viceroy
VILI brother of Odin; Ve
WALI prefect
YALI mansion
BALK thwart; signal
BILK defraud
BULK mass, volume; loom; -head (stall)
CALK tighten; stop; sleep; tool; copy
FOLK people; — ways, laws, song, dance
FULK unfair shove (marbles)
HULK ship body; bulky thing
KELK fish roe
MILK nutritious fluid; sap; white; exploit; drain
MULK freehold land
POLK Cossack regiment; James Knox (President)
PULK (Cossack) regiment
SILK fiber; thread; -worm
SULK mope; be sullen
TALK speak; converse; conference; empty words; dialect; — turkey
VOLK people: Ger.; workmen (So. Afr.)
WALK go on foot; path; pass, base on balls; — the plank
WELK (gather) snail; Lawrence (musician)
WILK (gather) snail
YELK yolk
YOLK egg yellow; essence
BALL game; confuse; dance; — bearing; good time; -point; Amer. sculptor
BELL ringing cup; gong; time period; flower shape; helmet; Brontë pseudonym; — the cat; diving —
BILL beak; weapon; law; poster; invoice; debt; nickname: William; — and coo; Sikes (Dickens)
BOLL (strip) plant pod
BULL (bovine) male; stud; papal letter; optimist; Taurus; policeman; blunder; glib talk; -fight
CALL summon; visit; cry; telephone; — girl; — money
CELL cubicle; group; elec. jar; organism
COLL embrace; hug; Vincent (gangster; "mad dog")
CULL pick out; assort
DALL sheep
DELL valley; dingle; wench
DILL flavoring herb; pickle
DOLL plaything; puppet; dress up; girl
DULL blunt(ed); dismal; inert; tedious; Shaks. character
FALL descend; ruin; autumn; — of Man
FELL skin; cut, sew (down); savage
FILL pack; complete; glut; — the bill
FULL filled; replete; quite; — dress; — house
GALL bile; venom; wound; chafe; swelling; impudence
GILL measure; brook; breathing organ; wattle; coin; lass
GOLL Irish hero (Fenian)
GULL bird; cheat; dupe
HALL building; room; town —; guild-; astronomer; -Mills
HELL Hades; state of misery; -bent
HILL mound; Jenny (Shaw character); -billy
HOLL ditch
HULL husk; ship body; Cordell (statesman)
JELL solidify; mature
JILL girl; sweetheart; Jack and —
JOLL move clumsily; knock
KELL Gaul; net; film
KILL slay; veto; creek
LILL small pin; loll; Lillian
LOLL droop; lounge; sprawl
LULL (temporary) quiet
MALL mallet; game; bird; assembly (place)
MELL (beat with) hammer; teacher (Dickens)
MILL grind(er); quern; box; John Stuart (economist)
MOLL Mary; girl; — Flanders (Defoe)
MULL muslin; ointment; ponder; humus
NELL Ellen; Helen; Little — (Dickens girl)
NILL refuse; negate
NOLL Oliver (Cromwell); head; noddle
NULL nil; void; code filler
PALL cloak; covering;

cloy
PILL medicine tablet
POLL head; register, survey; cut off; Mary; parrot; vote
PULL drag; influence
RILL (run in a) brook
ROLL wrap; trill; drumbeat; rotate; list; bank-
RULL to wheel; trundle
SELL vend; betray; persuade; hoax; — short
SILL beam (door, window)
TALL high; incredible
TELL inform; discern; chat; William (Swiss hero)
TILL until; plow; cultivate; tray, cash box
TOLL tax; lure; sound
VALL valley
VILL village; township
WALL barrier; fence; enclose; knot; Berlin —
WELL (water) pit; shaft; eddy; flow; rightly; very; sound, healthy
WILL volition; choice; decree; bequeath; testament
YELL cry; cheer
ZOLL measure
BALM plant; soothe; — in Gilead
CALM quiet; mold
CULM grass stem; coal dust; shoal water deposit
FILM skin; coating; haze; photograph; picture
HALM plant stems
HELM steer (wheel); tiller
HOLM holly; oak; islet
KULM crane; heron
MALM limestone
PALM tree; measure; hand part; paddle; conceal; grease the —
SALM star
KILN (burn in) oven
VULN wound (Her.)
ALLO prefix: other, dissimilar
BILO Balkan karst area
BOLO knife; Rafflesia (plant); pacifist
CALO Gypsy
DILO poon tree
FILO silk thread
GILO woody vine (tonic)
GOLO Nilotic Sudanese
GULO wolverine genus
HALO circle; glow; nimbus; prefix: sea, salt
HELO squeamish
HILO grass; city (Hawaii)
KALO taro root
KILO measure; -gram, -meter; prefix: 1000
KOLO folk dance
LALO composer
LOLO Caucasian Chinese
MALO loincloth
MILO name; grain; sorghum; Venus (Melos)
NOLO — contendere
ORLO smooth surface; plinth
OSLO city (Norway); Christiania
PALO pole, wood: Sp.
PELO hair: It.
POLO game; Marco —
RALO measure
SILO fodder pit; ensile
SOLO song; (fly) alone
STLO WW II battle site
TYLO dog (Maeterlinck)
ULLO Indian shell money
VELO speed unit
CALP limestone
COLP pasture; Irish acre
GOLP roundel purpure (Her.)
GULP swallow; catch breath
HELP relieve; avoid; wait on, aid(e); servants
KELP seaweed, iodine source
PALP appendage; feeler
PULP pith; tissue; paper; magazine
SALP marine animal
YELP shrill bark
ULLR chief god; Sif's son; Thor's stepson
FELS Eastern coin
FILS son: Fr.; Dumas (Camille); Irak coin
HALS Frans — (painter)
ILLS troubles
NILS Bohr (physicist)
WELS sheatfish
BALT Lithuanian; Esth; Latvian; Lett
BELT strap; zone; beat
BOLT sift; refine; shaft; lightning; bar; plant; rifle part; flight; refusal
BULT hill; ridge
CELT Irish, Scot, Welsh, Breton; chisel
COLT young horse; pistol; — .45
CULT sect; worship system
DOLT dunce; ignoramus
FELT pressed fibers; hat; sensed
GALT clay bed
GELT money
GILT gold; sow
HALT stop; lame
HILT sword
HOLT willow plantation; hill; lair; Eliot hero; actor
JILT betray in love
JOLT shake; hard blow
KELT Celt; cloth; trout
KILT Scot's skirt
LILT (sing) lively tune
MALT barley; beer
MELT liquefy
MILT spleen; fish gland; nickname
MOLT shed (hair)
PELT skin; hurl; strike
POLT knock; trump; club
SALT sodium chloride, NaCl; sailor; season; — away; — Lake City; — Sea
SILT sediment; scum; drift
TILT cover; incline; tip; joust; sport
TOLT writ; isolated peak
VELT measure
VOLT sideways gait; fencing leap; elec. unit
WALT Whitman
WELT ridge; wale; strip; sew; beat; universe: Ger.
WILT droop; lose spirit
YELT gilt (sow)
AALU Hades; heaven

AULU tree
BALU wildcat
HULU o-o's feather tuft
IALU Hades; heaven
IGLU Eskimo hut; seal hole
KULU old woman (Kipling)
LULU barn owl; name; Louisa
PELU hardwood tree
PULU tree fern
SHLU Moroccan Berber
SULU Moro
TOLU balsan (rose odor)
TULU Dravidian Indian
YALU river (Korean War)
ZULU Bantu; Kaffir; ship artificial fly
CALX residue heel: Lat
FALX weapon - cerebri (brain fold)
ABLY deftly
ALLY unite, confederate
COLY long-tailed bird
DULY properly timely
EELY wriggling slippery
HOLY sacred pious; - City; - Alliance; -- Roller
IDLY vainly lazily
ILLY badly ill
INLY within heartily
JULY (5th Roman) month
LELY Dutch painter
LILY flower Turk's-cap; pure, white
MOLY magic herb (Homer)
OILY unctuous; bland; suave
ONLY alone; but; single; exclusively
ORLY Paris airport
PALY wan; heraldic design
PILY pilelike
POLY herb; Teucrium; prefix many
PULY whining, complaining
RELY trust; depend
RILY turbid, irritated
UGLY badlooking; unpleasant; plug-
VILY fairies
WILY artful; subtle

ALMA girl; silk; river; city
AMMA abbess; god
ATMA soul
BEMA platform; altar; measure
BOMA Afr. stockade; post
CIMA mountain peak It.
COMA torpor, blur; tuft
CYMA cornice molding
DAMA gazelle
DUMA Russ parliament
EGMA enigma
EMMA letter M name, Austen novel; Bovary (Flaubert)
ERMA Ermengarde
FAMA rumor
GAMA Vasco da — (navigator), grass
GOMA Bantu (Wagoma)
HEMA prefix blood
HIMA Hamite Negro
HOMA sacred drink
HUMA Ugand. Negro
IJMA Moslem principle (Sunna)
IRMA name
JAMA tunic
KAMA love god; desire; river
LAMA priest llama; brown Dalai, Panchen Tashi -
LIMA city; bean, yam mollusk
LOMA fringe lap, hill
MAMA mother goddess
MIMA woman actor
NAMA Hottentot herb
NEMA eelworm prefix thread
NUMA Pompilius (Roman king)
PIMA Ariz. Indian; cotton
POMA rosa (rose apple)
PUMA cougar catamount
RAMA Indian Vishnu incarnation bull (Kipling)
RIMA fissure, breadfruit; child heroine (Hudson)
ROMA Rome: It.
SAMA fish; trance-inducing music
SIMA igneous rock
SOMA vine; drink; body
TAMA Indian
TEMA musical theme; Arab
TOMA Liberian Negro
XEMA arctic gull
YAMA first mortal (Judge of Dead)
YIMA Avestan demigod
YUMA Indian (Calif.); city
ZAMA Hannibal's defeat

BOMB explosive; dispenser; A-; lead-lined container, buzz —
COMB crest rake, scrape
DUMB mute, stupid; — waiter; deaf and —
GAMB leg
IAMB verse foot
JAMB leg armor; pillar; door part
LAMB amateur speculator; Charles (Elia), essayist (roast pig)
LIMB leg; arm member
NIMB nimbus halo
NUMB deaden(ed); helpless
RUMB compass point
TOMB grave monument; bury
ZIMB Ethiopian fly
ACME peak crisis
ALME dancer
ARME weapon Fr.; — blanche (saber)
CAME arrived lead rod; Indian
COME arrive, chance; fare
CYME inflorescence
DAME woman title; — aux Camelias
DEME Greek commune
DIME coin; - novel
DOME edifice; cupola; roof
FAME reputation
FEME wife tribunal
FUME smoke fit; rage
GAME amusement; quarry resolute; lame
HEME reduced hematin
HOME habitat asylum; plate natural
HUME philosopher
KAME hill
KOME Greenland division
LAME cripple(d), halt; plate; fabric
LIME calcium oxide (mortar) snare; caustic linden (tree) amber; citrus fruit
LOME Togo seaport
LYME bloodhound
MIME drama; act; actor; clown; smith

(Nibelungs)
MOME buffoon; -rath
NAME title; reputation; clan; cite
NOME city (Alaska)
OIME' alas
POME fruit; ball; globe
PUME Yarura(n language)
RAME branch
RIME frost; (make) rhymes; chink; rung
ROME city (Eternal); Church; beauty (apple)
RYME water surface
SAME identical
SEME (sprinkling) pattern
SIME monkey
SOME various; any; somewhat; part
TAME gentle; subdue
TIME period; moment; credit term; speed rate; meter, rhythm; Father —; space —
TOME book; papal letter
ULME elm
ZEME (abode of) spirit; fetish
ZYME ferment
SAMH bread plant
ADMI gazelle
AMMI herb
BIMI orang-utang (Kipling)
DEMI prefix: half
GUMI shrub, flower, fruit
HAMI hooked processes
HEMI prefix: half
IMMI measure
JAMI mosque
KAMI language; deity
KOMI Soviet republic; Zyrians
MIMI nickname; opera heroine
RAMI branches
REMI Gaul people; prefix: oar
ROMI Gypsy wife
SEMI half
SIMI Dodecanese isle
ZEMI (abode of) spirit; fetish
MUMM mask; disguise
DAMN curse; — the torpedoes
DOMN Rumanian lord
FAMN measure
HYMN song (of praise)
LIMN portray; delineate
AMMO ammunition; prefix: sand
ATMO prefix: steam
COMO lake, resort (Italy)
DEMO prefix: populace
HEMO prefix: blood
HOMO man; — sapiens; prefix: same
IKMO betel palm, pepper
ITMO betel pepper
MAMO bird
MEMO note; statement
MOMO owl
NEMO nobody: Lat.; prefix: glade; Captain (Verne hero)
POMO California Indian
SEMO Sancus (deity); Dius Fidius
SUMO Ulvan
ULMO muermo; hardwood
BUMP coincide; hit; swelling; — off (kill)
CAMP tent(s); town; stay; boot —
DAMP moist(ure); depress
DUMP unload; junkyard; thud; mean place; holey dollar
GAMP umbrella; Sairey — (nurse: Dickens)
GIMP silk fabric; vim
GUMP silly, stupid one; Andy, Chester, Min (cartoon family)
HEMP herb; hashish; cannabis; rope (fiber)
HUMP protuberance; mound; crisis; Himalayan peaks; -back
JUMP leap; bounce; move; headstart; — the gun
KEMP fur refuse
LAMP light; bulb
LIMP halt; flaccid; loose
LUMP mass; swelling; barge; like it or — it
MUMP beg; mumble; cheat
PIMP procurer; bawd; maquereau
POMP pageant(ry); splendor
PUMP force; draw out; slipper
RAMP inclined way; rear
ROMP girl; gambol, frolic
RUMP sirloin part; remnant; — Parliament
SAMP maize
SIMP simpleton
SUMP dig pit; tank; cistern
TAMP fill up; pound down; tool
TUMP drag slain deer
TYMP blast furnace stone
VAMP sock; shoe part; fireman; ghost; flirt
WAMP eider
YAMP herb; tuber
ALMS charity
ARMS mil. science; ensigns; weapons; branches; limbs
JOMS Vikings; Norse colony
REMS river
TEMS sieve; sift
AMMU ammunition
ATMU sun god
LIMU edible seaweed
RIMU red pine; imou pine
ARMY multitude; force
DEMY coin; scholar; paper size
DOMY domelike
ELMY rich in elms
EMMY TV award; nickname
FUMY vaporous; smoky
HOMY homey; intimate
ISMY doctrinaire
LIMY viscous
RIMY frosty; rhyming

ANNA coin; bird; name; — Christie (O'Neill); — Karenina (Tolstoi)
ARNA buffalo
BANA Titan
BENA grass (vetiver)
BINA Hindu guitar
BONA good: Lat.; — fide
BUNA synthetic rubber
CANA Indian
CENA (Last) supper
CUNA Panama Indian
DANA goddess; author; editor; lake
DONA lady; sapek (coin)
DYNA prefix: power
EDNA female name; Ferber, novelist

ENNA Sicilian resort
ETNA stove; volcano
FANA Sufistic concept
GENA cheek; beak part
GONA New Guinea victory
GUNA Sankhya term
IMNA Asherites' chief
IONA Scot. isle; Celt church; college
JENA Ger. city (optical, Napoleonic victory) glass
KANA Japanese writing
KINA quinine
KONA Hawaiian storm; weight
LANA wood; flannel
LENA firewood: Sp.; river; Conrad heroine
LINA measure; Caroline
LUNA moon goddess; silver
MANA magic power; Chinese letter
MINA weight; money; myna; watchman
MONA monkey; Lisa (La Gioconda, da Vinci)
MYNA talking bird: grackle
NANA nurse; Aztec hero's wife; Zola novel; dog: Peter Pan (Barrie)
NINA goddess (Ea's daughter) ship (Pinta, —, Santa Maria); girl: Sp.
NONA fate goddess; prefix: ninth
ORNA measure
PANA city
PINA pineapple; silver cone
PUNA high Andes; wind; sickness (soroche)
RANA frog; prince; Aegir's wife
RENA rockfish
SANA Yemen's capital; fiber
SINA drug; mountain (Moses)
TANA shrew; rabbi; police station; lake (Blue Nile)
TINA fem. nickname
TUNA fish; pear: opuntia
ULNA elbow bone; ell
URNA measure
VENA vein: Lat.
VINA harp; guitar; wines
XINA nickname: Christina
YANA tribe
ZONA girdle; shingles
BANC (judge's) bench
SYNC synchronize
ZINC metal; element; color
ARND theologian
BAND strip; group; orchestra; range; tie; sash
BEND turn; curve; flex; bow
BIND tie; protect; sew; cohere
BOND adhesion; tie; covenant; paper; captivity; certificate
BUND embankment; league
COND direct helmsman
FEND keep off; parry
FIND discover(y); (re)gain
FOND basis; fount; loving
FUND supply; finance; money; sinking —
GOND Dravidian Indian
HAND control; aid; worker; measure; pass; player; cards; penmanship
HIND fish; grouper; deer; posterior
HUND dog: Ger.
KIND sort; species; gentle
LAND ground; debark; state: Ger.
LEND make loan; grant; — an ear
LIND Jenny (singer, Swedish Nightingale)
MAND grass
MEND repair; improve
MIND intellect; brain; memory; wish; mood; plan; tend; dislike
MUND protection right
PEND hang; be delayed
POND lake; pool; weight
PUND weight
RAND border; ridge; strip; So. Afr. gold mine
REND tear; rupture; bark trees
RIND bark; peel; Vali's mother, Odin's wife
RYND millstone support
SAND grit; silica; polish, smooth; red-yellow; George, novelist (Dudevant)
SEND transmit; dispatch; propel; swing; enthrall
SIND river; Pakistan province; are: Ger.
TEND serve; incline
TIND kindle
TUND pound; bruise
VEND Slav; sell; sale
WAND rod; staff; magic —
WEND Slav; go; travel
WIND turn; coil; blowing air; mere talk
WYND alley; small court
YOND past; beyond
ZEND — Avesta (holy text)
ACNE disease
AINE elder
ANNE queen; Boleyn; Henry VIII wife; Elizabeth's mother; Shakespeare's wife; Dombey's maid (Dickens); Queen — style; Queen —'s lace
AONE first-rate
ARNE composer; region
AUNE measure
BANE woe; curse; poison
BENE wild hog; well: It. & Lat.
BINE (hop) stem
BONE study hard; plug; os
CANE stem; rattan; stick; walking —; sugar —; candy —
CENE suffix: recent
CINE movie: Sp.
CONE geometric solid; pine fruit, strobile; peak; ice cream —; nose —
DANE Scandinavian; great — (dog); Hamlet
DENE measure; dune; Indian
DINE eat; have dinner
DONE agreed; exhausted
DUNE sandhill; twine

color
DYNE unit of force
EINE one: Ger.
ENNE prefix: nine; fem. suffix
ERNE sea eagle
ESNE slave
FANE temple
FINE end; superior; thin; keen; well; (set) penalty; geil —, derb — (Irish clans)
GANE yawn
GENE hereditary factor; chromosome part; nickname
GONE departed; enamored; lost; germ cell
GYNE prefix: female
HONE sharpen(er)
IONE Pompeii heroine (Bulwer-Lytton)
JANE woman; false hair; cloth; — Eyre; Lady — Grey
JUNE month; beetle; — moon, bride
KANE god
KINE cattle
LANE (fixed) route; throat
LENE smooth; consonant
LINE thin mark; cable; cord; wire; piping; row; direction; cover; align; track; flax
LONE single; — Star
LUNE crescent; hawk leash
MANE hair; in the morning: Lat.
MENE — tekel upharsin (handwriting on the wall)
MINE possessive pronoun; dig; pit; rich source; explosive
NANE own; none
NINE number (of Muses); baseball team
NONE not one; 9th hour
OHNE without: Ger.
ORNE measure; river (Caen)
PANE glass; panel
PENE (hammer) head
PINE tree; conifer; evergreen; yearn; mourn
PONE corn bread; writ
RINE hemp; ditch
RONE brushwood
RUNE Teutonic sign; magic
SANE rational
SINE math. ratio; without: Lat.; — qua non; — die
TANE Polynesian god
TENE suffix: ribbon
TINE tooth; prong; pain; grass
TONE pitch; accent; Wolfe (Ir. rebel)
TUNE song; pitch; harmony
TYNE Eng. river
VANE weathercock; feather; blade
VINE creeping plant
VONE robot bomb
WANE ebb; lessen
WINE fermented juice
ZONE area; band; partition
BANG beat; thump; hair; sardine; interjection
BENG devil (Gypsy)
BING bed roll; sharp sound
BONG bell sound
BUNG stop(per); throw
CANG wooden collar
DANG curse (damn)
DING thump; sound; urge
DONG sound; weight; ding-
DUNG excrement; fertilize(r); weight
FANG tooth; measure; Dickens character
FONG Ewe-speaking Negro
FUNG Sennar Negroid
GANG crew; associate; rock
GONG bell; tom-tom
HANG suspend; plan; bit; die on gallows
HING asefetida (gum resin; antispasmodic)
HONG Chin. trade guild
HUNG suspended; undecided (jury)
JUNG young: Ger.; Carl Gustave (psychologist)
KANG — Hsi (Chinese emperor)
KING monarch; ruler; chief; chessman; card
KUNG public
LANG auld — syne; Fritz
LING fish; burbot; hake
LONG lengthy; extended; yearn; — John Silver (Stevenson); Huey — (La. politician); — time nc see
LUNG air bladder; iron —
MANG bat (Kipling)
MENG mix
MING Chin. dynasty
MONG among; barter
MUNG grass
PANG agony
PING (bullet, striking) sound
PONG sound; improvise
PUNG (drive) box sleigh; mah jong term
QUNG So. Afr. Bushman
RANG sounded
RING gird; arena; prizefighting; gang; atomic order; sound (bell); Vienna landmark; Nibelungen cycle (Wagner)
RONG Sikkimese language
RUNG wheel spoke; hooped
SANG Hindu group; herb; weight; did sing
SING vocalize; warble; tell
SONG poem (music); pittance
SUNG chanted; Chin. dynasty
TANG spur; flavor; sound; seaweed; dynasty
TENG measure
TING sound; Chin. pottery
TONG secret society
TUNG tree; oil
UANG beetle
VANG rope
WANG weight; meadow; prince
WING alar appendage; faction; annex; fly
WONG field; meadow
YANG honk; male or

positive principle
ZING sharp thrill; vim
BINH weight
HUNH exclamation
SINH hyperbolic function
TANH math. term
AANI ape
AGNI god; lambs
ANNI years: Lat.
ARNI buffalo
BANI coins
BENI Bolivian river; sesame
BINI Nigerian
BONI African; Boschneger
CONI It. commune
DONI fishing boat
HONI — soit qui mal y pense; shamed
IONI Hainai; Chaddo Indian
MANI peanut; prefix: hand
OMNI prefix: all
OZNI Gad's son
PANI madam: Polish
RANI princess; wife
RENI It. painter; prefix: kidney
VENI prefix: vein; —, vidi, vici (I came, I saw, I conquered)
YENI So. Amer. tanager
ZUNI Indian; reservation
BENJ hemp; narcotic
FUNJ Sennar Negroid
GUNJ granary; market
MUNJ tough grass: twine
BANK mound; bench; deposit; bird flock; Left, Right —; blood —; eye —
BONK bar money (Dutch E.I.)
BUNK case; bed; nonsense
CONK nose; head; decay; fail; hit
DANK moist; rank
DINK small boat; cut out
DUNK dip into; immerse
FINK finch; derb; informer; strikebreaker
FUNK fear; coward; Casimir (vitamins) Isaac (lexicographer); — & Wagnalls
GINK eccentric one
GUNK jilt; hoax
HANK coil; — Morgan (Twain)
HONK goose cry; toot; ooga
HUNK piece; lump; OK
JINK prank
JONK jonquil
JUNK ship; trash; scrap
KINK twist; loop; cramp
KONK conk
KUNK measure
LANK thin; lean(ness)
LINK (chain) loop; connect; join; torch; measure
LONK black-faced sheep
MINK weasel-like animal
MONK ascetic; friar; bird; fish; spot; ferret
PANK weight
PENK minnow
PINK color (red); ship; cut; hunter's coat; carnation; in the — (healthy)
PUNK touchwood; tinder; conch; tramp; bad
RANK luxuriant; gross; fetid; grade; array
RINK skating arena
SANK descended
SINK fall; droop; conceal; basin
SUNK immersed; overcome
TANK basin; store; war vehicle; panzer
TONK (cow bell) clang; honky-; game
TUNK rap; thump; game
WINK blink; signal
YANK jerk; New Englander; Union soldier; American
GUNL gunwale
BENN seed
BINN box; frame; crib
BONN city; Ger. capital (Beethoven born)
BUNN cake
CONN direct helmsman
FINN man of Finland, Helsinki; Ugric; Mickey — (KO drops); Huckleberry — (Twain novel)
GUNN castaway (Stevenson)
JANN genii
JINN demon; spirit
LINN waterfall; li[illegible]
LUNN Sally (teacake)
MANN man: Ger.; Horace (educator); Thomas (writer)
PENN William (Penna. founder)
RANN verse, stanza; kite (Kipling)
SENN Swiss herdsman
SINN — Fein (Irish society)
SUNN hemp: fiber plant
WYNN timber truck; Ed (actor, Perfect Fool)
AGNO Luzon river
AINO Jap. aboriginal
ANNO — Domini (year of our Lord)
ARNO river; cartoonist
ASNO donkey: Sp.
BENO alcoholic palm sap
BINO alcoholic pine sap
BONO Johnny (Briton); cui —
CANO canal: Sp.
DINO prefix: terrible
FANO cloth; cape
FONO Samoan council
GANO Count (Roland's destroyer)
HANO Indian
HINO timber tree; dye
IUNO Jupiter's wife
JUNO goddess; Jupiter's wife, Hera; stately woman; missile
KANO painting school
KENO lotto (game); prefix: empty
KINO gum (catechu); prefix: moving
LENO (cotton, silk) fabric
LINO measure
MANO grindstone; hand: It.
MENO prefix: month
MINO Jap. straw coat
MONO monkey; Indian; prefix: single, one
NINO boy: Sp.
NONO ninth: It.
OENO prefix: wine
PINO pine tree
PUNO Pacific trade wind; city (Peru)
RENO Nev. city ("biggest little"; divorce, gambling)
SINO prefix: Chinese
TANO Indian
TINO Sambal language

TUNO rubber tree; gum
VENO prefix: vein
VINO palm liquor
XENO guest; prefix: foreign
ZENO philosopher (Stoic, Cynic); emperor
CINQ five: Fr.
BANS marriage notice
CENS payment due
DANS in: Fr.
DENS tooth: Lat.
DUNS dull; stupid
ENNS river
FONS fount; source
GENS clan: Lat.; people: Fr.
HANS John; Johannes; — Castorp (Mann)
HENS fowl; -foot (herb)
LENS eye part; glass (optical); herb
MANS Chinese aborigine; Le — (city; auto race)
MENS mind: Lat.
MONS mountain: Lat.; city (Belgium; WW I battle)
NUNS sisters; veiling, fabric
OONS mild oath
PONS bridge: Lat.; — asinorum; Lily (singer)
SANS without: Fr.; — culotte (radical); — gene
VANS race of gods
AINT contraction
ARNT contraction
AUNT parent's sister; tia: Sp.; tante: Fr., Ger.
BANT diet
BENT crooked; inclination; grass
BINT daughter; woman
BUNT sag (net, sail); (fungus) disease; butt (ball)
CANT angle; change course; log; tilt; whine; jargon; be unable
CENT coin; penny; game
DENT depress(ion); notch
DINT blow; force; notch
DONT contraction; prohibition
DUNT split (ceramics)
FENT slit; cleft
FONT basin; spring; stoup; type
FUNT weight; Allen (TV)
GANT yawn; gaunt; gannet; Eugene (Wolfe character)
GENT gentleman; Belg. city
HANT ghost
HINT suggestion; imply
HUNT seek; chase; Leigh (writer)
KANT change course; Immanuel, philosopher
KENT Eng. county, duchy; Lear's follower
LENT fasting period; slow; made loan
LINT raveling, fiber (of linen); netting
LUNT light; smoke; Alfred (actor)
MENT falcon-headed god
MINT herb; menthol; bonanza; coin; — julep
MONT mountain: Fr.; — Blanc (peak, Alps)
MUNT sash bar
OINT apply oil
OONT camel; mole
PANT gasp; yearn
PENT confined; -house
PINT measure
PONT ferry(boat); bridge: Fr.
PUNT (propel) flatboat; kick; bet
RANT scold; rave; frolic
RENT torn; schism; let, lease; payment, income
RUNT small animal, man
SUNT babul: gum tree; pod; were: Lat.
TENT cloth shelter; pup —; wine; frame
TINT color; shade; tinge
VENT hole; let out; issue
VINT card game
WANT lack; desire
WENT departed
WONT custom; contraction
ZANT fish
AINU Jap. aboriginal
BENU holy bird (Ra-Osiris)
DANU goddess
GENU knee: Lat.
MANU prefix: hand; Laws (Hindu code book)
MENU bill of fare
TUNU rubber tree; gum
ZENU Afr. sheep
IYNX wryneck (woodpecker)
JINX hoodoo; bad luck
JYNX wryneck; charm
LANX platter
LYNX wildcat; fur; constellation
MANX pert. to Isle of Man; cat
MINX pert girl
YUNX woodpecker genus
AWNY bearded
BONY skeletal; osseous; Napoleon
CONY rabbit; daman; pika
DENY refuse; contradict
DUNY having many dunes
EENY — meeny, miny, mo
GONY albatross
LINY streaky
LUNY crazy (man)
MANY numerous
MINY of a mine
PINY pinelike; peony
PONY small equine (Shetland, polo); glass (1 oz.); translation
PUNY weak; slight
TINY small; -tim (herb); Tim (Dickens)
TONY nickname (Anthony); stylish
TUNY melodious
VINY entwining
WANY diminished
WINY vinous; drunken
ZANY clown(ish)
GANZ all, totally: Ger.
LINZ Austrian city
RANZ — des vaches

ANOA ox
AROA Venezuela copper center
GJOA ship (Northwest Passage; Amundsen)
POOA pua hemp
PROA Malay outrigger
SHOA Abyssinian
STOA portico; poikile (Zeno)
TOOA hero; beefwood
WHOA stop!; opp. of giddap
BLOB drop; daub; sound; fish; zero score

BOOB simpleton
BROB support spike
CHOB grain spike
DOOB Bermuda grass
FLOB move clumsily
JAOB measure
KNOB lump; hill; antler; handle
RHOB juice; jelly
SCOB fabric defect
SLOB slovenly one
SNOB social climber; game
SWOB sponge; wipe; mop
THOB rationalize
BLOC political unit; casting
CROC harquebus support; crocodile
FLOC flock(y mass); shreds
ALOD estate
APOD footless
AROD son of Gad
BIOD animal life force
CLOD lump; soil; dolt
EFOD priestly garb; image
ELOD alleged force
FEOD feudal estate
FOOD nutriment; victuals
GOOD able; brave; sound; profit; happiness; welfare; benefit
HOOD cowl; cloak; seal; gangster; Thomas (poet)
LOOD weight
MOOD humor; temper; verb form
PLOD trudge; drudge
POOD weight
PROD reminder; goad; horse; prodigy
QUOD prison; — erat demonstrandum (Q.E.D.)
ROOD crucifix; measure
SHOD wearing shoes
SNOD trim; snug; plausible
STOD Danish speech
TROD walked; track
WOOD timber; forest; Grant (painter); Leonard (general)
ALOE plant; tonic
AROE islands, New Guinea
CLOE fem. name
EBOE tree; oil; Negrito
EVOE bacchanals' wild cry; Punch editor
FLOE floating ice
FROE cleaver; steel wedge
OBOE woodwind; chanter
OTOE Sioux Indian
SHOE foot covering; crakow; wheel drag; tire
SLOE blackthorn; plum; blueblack
AZOF town; sea
BOOF stare; peach brandy
GOOF dolt; blunder
HOOF ungula; foot; beast; walk; dance
LOOF luff; sponge gourd
POOF exclamation
ROOF cover; house; top
STOF measure
WOOF crossthreads; texture; weft; bark
AGOG eager
AJOG jogging
CLOG block; sandal; stop; impede; choke
FLOG whip
FROG amphibian; hoarseness; loop; rail device
GROG liquor (with water)
ILOG river (Tagalog)
NIOG coconut palm
PROG (steal) food; forage
SHOG shake; jog
SLOG hit (hard); slug; slam
SMOG fog and smoke; haze
STOG stall in mud
VOOG lode cavity
BOOH exclamation
BROH macaque; monkey
LUOH white Nile Negro
POOH pshaw!; — Bah (Mikado); Winnie (bear; Milne)
AMOI mine: Fr.
EKOI Bantu
ELOI Eli; God
AMOK frenzy
ASOK tree
BOOK tome; volume; Bible; libretto, (bet) record; register; throw the —
COOK chef; concoct; falsify; James (explorer)
DOOK wooden brick; demon
GOOK trash; ooze; native
HOOK trap; curve; catch; steal; — and eye; pirate: Peter Pan (Barrie)
IROK gomuti (palm)
JOOK perch; slumber
LOOK observe; appear(ance); eye(wink); care
NOOK corner; retreat
POOK hobgoblin; disk
ROOK bird; cheat; dupe; chessman (tower)
SOOK Moslem market; hog call
TOOK seized; caught; endured; supposed
AWOL absent without leave
BOOL curved handle
CHOL desolate plain; Mayan
COOL chill; calm; unmoved
DIOL chem. compound; suffix
EGOL antiseptic
EMOL rock salt
ENOL chem. suffix
FOOL dolt; jester; trick
GAOL prison
IDOL god, deity; image; adored one
ITOL suffix: alcohol(ic)
OBOL 1/16 drachma (coin)
POOL pond; puddle; game; stake; fund; Thames
ROOL crumple; ruffle
SIOL great Irish clan
SOOL pull, tousle about
TOOL instrument; polish; dupe
VIOL string instrument
WOOL (sheep) fleece; down
AHOM Assam native
ATOM whit; particle; nuclear complex
BOOM hum; grow, push; beam
BROM Bones (Ichabod's rival)
COOM coal dust; refuse
CROM Cruaich (Irish idol)
DOOM (last) judgment; fate; condemn

EDOM Esau's country; Idumaea
FROM out of
GLOM watch; steal
GOOM cultivation method
JOOM cultivation method
KLOM weight
LOOM auk; appear(ance); weaver's frame
PROM dance, ball (college)
ROOM space; apartment; lodge; — and board
STOM prefix: mouth
WHOM pronoun
ZOOM buzz; climb, approach suddenly
ACON boat
AEON age
AGON contest; argument
AMON deity; King of Judah
ANON again; now; soon; author unknown
ATON solar disk
AVON river; Shakespeare home (Stratford)
AXON axis; cell process
AZON bomb
BION physiological individual (morphon)
BOON benefit; convivial
BYON clayey earth
CION plant shoot
COON animal; fur; sly man
CUON wild dog (dhole)
CYON wild dog (dhole)
DION lord in Winter's Tale
DOON tree (varnish resin)
EBON ebony; black
ELON Esau's father-in-law; college (N.C.)
ENON Paris's wife (nymph); John the Baptist site
ETON school, college; collar, jacket; playing fields of —
EXON Exeter man
FAON fawn color
GAON Jewish title
GEON paradise river; Jerusalem spring
GOON thug; strikebreaker
HOON coin; gold pagoda
HUON pine; timber tree
ICON image; statue
IKON image; statue
IRON metal; element; weapon; instrument; club; shackle; press; strong; Age
LAON Fr. city
LEON country, city; Ponce de (explorer)
LION cat; king of beasts; celebrity
LOON diving bird; lout
LYON Fr city; bean
MAON Nabal's home
MOON satellite; crescent; month; Diana; Cynthia; languish
NEON gas(eous) element; lamp
NOON midday; meal; acme
PAON peacock blue
PEON laborer
PHON loudness measure
PION dig; excavate
POON tree (mastwood)
ROON treasure; darling
SCON teacake
SION purple seaweed; Zion
SOON promptly; willingly
TION suffix
TOON tree (dye); mahogany
UPON prep.: above; against
WOON Burmese governor
ZION Israelites; heaven
ZOON developed compound animal
ABOO war cry
AROO indeed
EJOO palm; fiber
KROO Liberian Negro
PHOO disgusting!
PROO slow up! (horse call)
SHOO scare away; begone!
SLOO swamp
WHOO exclamation
ALOP lopsided
ASOP sopping
ATOP at the peak
CHOP cut; crack; eat; barter; jaw
CLOP limp; hobble
COOP pen; jail; confine; coöperative
CROP craw; harvest; trim
DROP globule; fall; discard; minim; trap door; die; pendant
ESOP fable writer
FLOP slump down; flap; change; fail(ure); bed; sleep
GLOP look wildly; stare
GOOP nonsense creature
HOOP circle(t); wicket; — skirt
KLOP hard sound
KNOP button; finial; stud
KOOP purchase; bargain
LOOP noose; catch; aerial stunt; Chicago area
PLOP sound of fall
POOP deck; cabin; dickey; exhaust; tire
PROP support; shore; theater equipment
SCOP bard; poet
SHOP store; buy; buying place; talk —; window-
SLOP slush; gush; mash
STOP halt; discontinue; arrest; close; instrument part; period
SWOP trade
TOOP measure
TROP too much: Fr.
WHOP dash; beat; bump
YOOP sobbing sound
SHOQ tree (tanning); chogak
ACOR acidity
ALOR island
AMOR love; Cupid; — patriae
ASOR lyre
BOOR rustic; lout; Boer
CHOR thief; steal (Gypsy)
DOOR portal; entrance; Open — policy
GHOR Dead Sea valley
GOOR sugar; masseculte
IGOR Prince (opera)
KHOR watercourse; gorge
KNOR knot (wood); gnarl
MOOR heath; anchor; Moslem; Moroccan; blacka-
ODOR smell; repute
OGOR early Turkic man
OLOR swan genus; Cygnus
PEOR Bib. mountain
POOR indigent; scanty; feeble; lowgrade; lean; ill; hapless;

cod (fish)
SHOR salt lake; Tatar tribe
THOR thunder god (Thursday) Midgard slayer; Odin's son; missile
UTOR to use: Lat.
AMOS prophet
BIOS life: animal, plant
COOS Bay (laurel); Indian
DIOS God: Sp.
DUOS duets
ENOS Seth's son, Adam's grandson (905 years old); taken by God
EPOS epic poetry; events
EROS (god of) love; Cupid; asteroid; Antony's friend
GHOS Chin. dynasty
GROS coin; fabric; weight
LAOS country
LOOS Anita (writer: Gentlemen Prefer Blondes)
NAOS star
PHOS phosphorus
ROOS Ger. painter
TAOS Indian
TEOS Ionian city
THOS ackal genus
ABOT Mishnah
BLOT stain; mar; dry
BOOT shoe; wader; sheath; torture; recruit; compartment; tube; kick; to — (in addition)
BROT bread: Ger.
CLOT mass; coagulate
COOT rail; surf duck; dolt
EYOT islet
FIOT Congo tribe
FLOT lateral ore deposit
FOOT pedal part; base; dance; trip; skip; pay; add
FROT rub; chafe
GROT cave; Bremen coin
HOOT derisive (owl's) cry
ILOT islet; ait; eyot
KHOT farmer; contractor
KNOT tie; loop; hitch; sandpiper; problem; blemish; stud; Gordian —
LOOT plunder; booty
MOOT arguable; ring gauge
PHOT light unit
PIOT magpie
PLOT tract; ground; press (soap); scheme; intrigue
POOT disgusting!
PYOT piebald; chatty
RIOT tumult; success; act, squad
ROOT underlying source; rhizome; base; dig; applaud; plant; eradicate
RYOT Indian peasant
SCOT Celt; Highlander; tax; — free
SHOT missile; pellet; guess; range; marksman; film record; long —; big —
SLOT (cut) opening; bolt; deer; track; — machine
SNOT wick end; blow nose
SOOT powdery carbon smudge
SPOT stain; point, place; fish; small amount; espy
STOT stumble; stutter
SWOT hard work; grind; hit
TOOT sound horn; carousal
TROT jog; gait; race; translation; fishing line
ZOOT — suit: extreme style
ABOU father; deity
CHOU cabbage, darling: Fr.; Chin. dynasty; En Lai (statesman)
MEOU cat's cry; measure
NIOU measure
SHOU Tibetan deer
THOU 2nd pers. pronoun
TIOU Indian (Tonikan)
AKOV measure
AZOV town; sea
ALOW below
AROW in a line
AVOW declare; justify; confess
BLOW move (air); puff, pant; brag; expend; stroke; calamity; disappointment; — up (enlarge)
BROW forehead; high-, low-
CHOW food; dog
CLOW sluice; floodgate
CROW raven; corvine; black; Indian; Jim —; -bar
DHOW Arab. sailboat
ENOW enough
FLOW gush; stream; flux; roll; ebb and —
FROW Dutch woman; cleaver
GLOW shine; incandesce; flush; ardor; wax
GROW expand; sprout; wax; develop
JHOW tamarisk shrub
KNOW understand; recognize; -how; nothing (party)
LWOW Polish city
MEOW cat's cry; measure
PLOW implement; till; cut; stars
PROW ship's bow; stem; beak
SCOW flat-bottomed boat
SHOW exhibit(ion); reveal; appear(ance); 3rd place; no — (airline term)
SLOW dilatory; tardy; inert; boring; hinder
SNOW ice crystals; white hair; cocaine; — goose; TV spots
STOW pack; hide; hold; skiing resort
SWOW I – (oath)
TROW believe; fishing boat
ABOX braced
ESOX fish (pike, pickerel, muskellunge)
WROX rot
AHOY call; ship —
AMOY island
BHOY gang member; rowdy
BUOY float; sustain; life-; channel marker
CHOY red dye root
CLOY glut; surfeit
OHOY ahoy; call
PLOY make column; frolic; coup
TROY weight system;

Ilium, Ilion (Troas); city
AMOZ Isaiah's father
BROZ Josip (Tito)

ARPA harp: It.
CAPA cloak: Sp.
CEPA onion
COPA tree; yaya; landmark
DEPA measure
DOPA chemical (pigment test)
GAPA guided missile
HUPA Athapascan Indian
KAPA cloth(es)
LIPA fat
NAPA leather; wine region; city; river
NEPA water scorpion; needle bug
NIPA palm; juice; mat; atap
PAPA father; Pope; potato: Sp.; baboon; clay
PIPA toad; measure
PUPA chrysalis; snail; instar
RIPA river bank
RUPA body form (Buddhism)
SAPA grape juice
SUPA P.I. tree: lamp oil
TAPA bark; cloth
YAPA leaf mat
ZIPA Chibcha chief
ZUPA Yugo. district
CAPE cloak; promontory, — Cod, — Horn, — Good Hope
CEPE boletus (edible fungus)
COPE vestment; cover; bend; contend
DOPE drug; information; guess; nitwit
DUPE trick(ed one); copy
GAPE yawn; stare; gap
HIPE wrestler's throw
HOPE trust, expect(ation); wish; -chest
HYPE wrestler's throw
JAPE deride
JUPE skirt
KIPE basket
LOPE go; move; gait
LUPE Samoan fruit pigeon; Velez (actress)
MOPE be dull, listless (person)
NAPE neck back
NUPE Nigeria Negro
OLPE oil flask; pitcher
PAPE bunting (bird)
PIPE tube; flute; cask (measure); -dream; — down
POPE pontiff; Holy Father; — Joan (game); Alexander (poet); bird
RAPE herb; ravish
RIPE mature; fit; tipsy
ROPE cord; cable; noose; bind; chain
RYPE ptarmigan
SUPE stage extra; supercharge
SYPE ooze
TAPE band; tie; Indian; record; red —; ticker —
TIPE rabbit trap
TOPE drink; shark; stupa; orchard
TYPE kind, sort; class(ify); printer's letter; use typewriter, produce copy
WIPE rub off; beat
XIPE -totec (Aztec god)
YIPE howl; cry
ALPH river (Coleridge, Kubla Khan)
CAPH star, letter
HAPH weight
KAPH letter
KOPH Heb. K, Q, 100
OLPH bullfinch
QOPH Heb. K, Q, 100
SAPH giant (Philistine)
SOPH 2nd-year student
TOPH drum; porous rock
UMPH grunt
ZUPH Samuel's ancestor
AIPI cassava
HAPI bull; Nile (god)
HOPI French beige; Moqui Indian
IMPI armed Kaffirs
KEPI military cap
KOPI N.Z. tree (karaka)
PIPI astringent; mollusk
TIPI wigwam
TOPI antelope; pith hat
TUPI Amazon Indian
CIPO liana
GAPO (inundated) forest
HYPO photo solution; needle; injection
MAPO goby (fish)
PEPO pumpkin; squash; melon; cucumber
SAPO soap; toadfish
SIPO liana
TOPO prefix: place
TYPO printing error
CAPP Al, cartoonist (Abner; Dogpatch)
DOPP diamond cup
HUPP call to horse
KAPP measure
KIPP peak (Glacier National Park); gymnastic feat
LAPP N. Scandinavian
REPP silk or wool fabric
TYPP yarn count unit
WAPP rope guide
YAPP (bookbinding) style
ALPS mountains
BAPS dancing master (Dickens)
FIPS Martin Chuzzlewit
GYPS gypsum
HOPS beer
HYPS hypochondria
SEPS snake; lizard
TAPS lights-out signal; bugle call
TOPS most superior
VEPS Finnish tribe (Chud); Dog Star (Isis); Horus
ZIPS Czech
COPT Egypt. Christian
EMPT empty
KEPT retained; lasted
KOPT Copt
RAPT engrossed; rapture
SEPT social unit; screen; seven: Fr.
SOPT Dog Star; Isis
WEPT cried; Jesus —
HAPU clan
KAPU forbidden; taboo
NAPU ruminant
OGPU Soviet police body
TAPU taboo
COPY duplicate; mimic; follow; text
DOPY sluggish
EPPY Euphemia
ESPY behold; detect; meteorologist
GAPY yawning
IMPY impish
PIPY tubular; weepy
ROPY viscous; stringy
TUPY Amazon Indian
TYPY typical

KTQB chess move
WAQF trust fund
KTQR chess move

ABRA narrow pass; river
AERA age; era
AFRA name; union
AGRA comb. form; carpet; city (Taj Mahal site)
AIRA grass
AKRA Negrito; vetch
AMRA plum
ARRA oath
AURA wind; emanation; bird
BARA measure
BERA king of Sodom
BORA north wind; rite
BURA steppe blizzard
CARA dear (one): It.; Indian
CERA prefix: horn, wax
CORA gazelle; Indian; name; Persephone; Demeter's daughter
CURA parish priest: Sp.
DERA suffix: neck types
DORA Mrs. David Copperfield
DURA — mater (spinal membrane)
ERRA — Pater (almanac)
EYRA wild cat
EZRA prophet; OT book
FORA meeting places; courts
GARA coin
GERA city
GORA musical instrument
HARA Japanese statesman
HERA Zeus's sister, wife
HORA book of hours; Israeli dance
HURA bishop's cap; sandbox tree; possumwood
IKRA superior caviar
IRRA war god
JARA palm
JURA rights; mountain range
KARA river
KORA water cock; Hottentot dialect
LARA Byron poem
LIRA money; lyre; hairlike ridge
LORA thong; strap
LURA brain opening
LYRA glockenspiel; constellation
MARA demon; aborigine; Naomi
MIRA star
MORA default; short syllable; Spartan army; stool
MURA Brazil Indian
MYRA name; ancient city
NERA Tiber tributary
NORA Helmer (Ibsen heroine)
OBRA works: Sp.
OCRA vegetable; gumbo
OKRA vegetable; gumbo
ORRA oddly; laborer
OTRA other: Sp.
PARA coin; weight; river; city (Belem)
PERA Istanbul district
RARA — avis (rare bird)
SARA native
SERA antitoxins; blood parts; whey; evening: It.
SORA bird; rail
SURA Koran section; deva
SYRA Aegean island
TARA fern; goddess; palm
TERA Buddhist monastery
TORA hartebeest; law (of Moses); Pentateuch
VARA measure
VERA tree; measure; name
VIRA Bantu
ZARA city; Judah's son
ZIRA measure
BARB sharp point; fish; dog; mow; pigeon
CURB restrain(t); sidewalk edge; market
FORB non-grassy herb
GARB apparel; array
GERB sheaf; firework
HARB Bedouin
HERB plant; nickname
KERB gutter part
SERB Servian; Yugo(slav)
SORB wild apple; Slav
TURB crowd; clump
VERB action word
CIRC circle; recess; corrie
MARC residue; name; weight
PARC park; oyster farm: Fr.
BARD armor; poet; — of Avon (Shakespeare)
BIRD avian; flyer; fowl; shuttlecock; person; Blue — -and-pillar (mining)
BORD
BURD noble lady
BYRD explorer; Va. statesman
CARD comb; pasteboard; menu; playing —; calling —
CORD string; twine; ribbed fabric; measure (wood)
CURD coagulated milk
DARD language group
FARD face paint; date
FORD crossing shallow; Henry (automobile); Shaks. character
FYRD old English army
GERD Frey's wife
GIRD encircle; clothe; brace
HARD solid; firm; close; severe; difficult
HERD crowd; feed together
JORD Odin's wife; Thor's mother
KURD Sunnite Mohammedan; Iranian
LARD fat; stuff
LORD ruler; Jehovah; Jesus; duck; planet
MARD spoil
NARD plant; ointment
OORD coin (double doit, ¼ stiver)
PARD chum; leopard
SARD carnelian; gem; Sardinian
SURD irrational; mute
VERD green(-leafed)
WARD (safe)guard; parry; district; charge; Artemus (Browne)
WORD term; news; promise; order; phrase
WURD Norn; Urth
WYRD Norn; Urth
YARD 3 feet; grounds; enclosure; spar
AARE river
ACRE field; measure; city
AIRE nobleman; river
BARE expose(d); mere; Indian
BORE pierce; hole; tire; dullard; tidal flow
BURE brown red-yellow
BYRE cow house

CARE grief; heed; responsibility; anxiety; foster; relief organization
CERE wax; (wrap in a) waxed cloth; beak part
CORE heart; nucleus; gist
CURE heal; remedy; preserve; priest: Fr.
DARE venture; defy; fish; 1st Amer. child (Virginia)
DERE — Mable (Streeter book)
DIRE evil; fatal; extreme
DORE bullion; gold; pike; Paul Gustave (Fr. artist)
EIRE Ireland; Erin
ETRE exist; be: Fr.; raison d'—
EYRE Jane (Bronte heroine); circuit (court)
FARE passenger; price; happen; food; travel
FIRE combustion; ardor; discharge
FORE front; prior; golf cry
GARE wool; station: Fr.; beware: Fr.
GERE Odin's wolf
GORE stab; blood; triangular insert
GYRE turn; ring; vortex
HARE leporid; rabbit; run
HERE vicinity; present
HIRE engage; rent; wage
HURE head of boar, wolf
INRE concerning; actually
JURE de — (by law)
KERE read(ing substitute)
KORE Persephone; Demeter's daughter; chaos (Maori myth.)
KURE Jap. city; Hawaiian isle
LIRE coins; read: Fr.
LORE history; learning
LURE entice; decoy; trumpet
LYRE harp; constellation
MARE blues; sea; moon area; horse; shanks' —
MERE fen; lake; boundary; war club; bare; only; simple; mother: Fr.
MIRE bog; (stick in) mud
MORE greater; additional St. Thomas (Utopia)
MURE thrust against wall
NARE Loki's son
NORE Thames estuary
OGRE giant; monster
PARE cut off; peel
PERE father, priest: Fr.; — Goriot (Balzac)
PORE gaze; ponder; opening
PURE unmixed; chaste; sheer; free; Simon —
PYRE funeral pile, fire
QERE read(ing substitute)
RARE underdone; thin; uncommon
RIRE to laugh: Fr.
SERE wither(ed); Negroid
SIRE father; beget; king
SORE painful; vexed; sensitive; deer
SURE safe; firm; certain
TARE vetch; allowance (weight)
TIRE fatigue; bore; wheel covering; rubber; shoe
TORE ripped; geom. surface
TYRE Phoenician city; Sur
VARE weasel
VIRE feathered arrow
WARE merchandise; beware
WERE be (past tense); prefix: metamorphosed human
WIRE cable; snare
WORE had on (clothes); tired
YARE prompt; ready
YORE ancient (times); long ago
CARF slit; notch
KERF cut; notch
SERF slave; peasant
SURF swell of sea; foam
TURF sod; grassy ground; peat; racing
WARF warp
WERF farmyard
ZARF holder for cup
BERG iceberg; mountain
BORG borough: Dan.
BURG (fortified) town
LURG marine worm
MORG measure
SARG Toni (puppeteer)
BURH (fortified) town
ABRI shelter
AERI prefix: air
AGRI fields
ATRI It. town
AURI prefix: gold, ear
BARI hut; Negro; city
BERI Sudanese (Fulah); -beri (disease)
BIRI cheap cigarette
BORI Lucrezia (singer)
BURI palm (fiber); talipot
CORI Carl, Gerty (Nobel winners)
DARI grain sorghum; carpet
GERI Odin's wolf
GYRI brain ridges
HARI river; Mata (spy)
HURI Abihail's father
KARI gum tree
KERI read(ing substitute)
KIRI paulownia tree; knobkerrie (missile)
KORI bustard; low weaver
KURI Lezhgian tribesman
LARI money; sea birds
LORI lemur; Afr. Negro
LURI Lake Albert Negro
MARI prefix: sea; husband: Fr.; native
NERI Blacks: It.
NORI seaweed food
OMRI king of Israel
PARI weight; prefix: equal
PERI fairy; elf; beauty
PURI Indian yellow
QERI read(ing substitute)
RORI Bantu tribe
SARI Hindu garment
SERI betel; Indian
SHRI glorious; holy; Lakshmi (goddess)
SIRI betel
SORI clusters; spores
TARI coin; goddess
TORI moldings
TURI Pathan tribesman
VARI lemur; prefix:

diverse
VERI centipede
WERI aweto (caterpillar)
BARK peel; tan; cough
CARK trouble
CORK tree; bark; stop(per); brown; Irish city (Lee)
DARK unlighted; wicked; dismal
DIRK dagger; Theodoric
FERK measure
FORK implement (pronged); tuner; place of divergence
HARK listen
JERK grab; twist; spasm; soda man; dullard; beef
KIRK church
KURK church: Scot.
LARK bird; frolic; yellow
LURK lie in wait; skulk
MARK sign; aim; stamp; money; observe; evangelist; easy —; — time
MIRK dark(ness)
MURK (make) gloomy
NARK informer; tease
PARK (common) grounds; green; deposit; Hyde, Central, etc.
PERK lift up; preen; cocky; percolate
PORK meat; swine; — barrel
SARK Channel Island
TURK Mongoloid; Seljuk; Ottoman; Osmanli; horse
WORK labor; mental product; act; operate: function; needlework
YARK yerk
YERK wrench; kick; trump
YORK city; archbishopric; Imperial (apple); Sgt. Alvin (WW I)
BIRL revolve; spin
BURL (pick) knot; Ives (actor)
CARL rustic; villain; Charles
CIRL bunting; bird
CURL coil; twist; hair lock
EARL nobleman; count; name
FARL cake (part)
FURL roll up (sail, flag)
GIRL young female; maid; Gibson —; — Friday; — of the Golden West; chorus —
HARL barb; filament
HERL (feather) barb
HURL throw; pitch; rush
JARL Norse chief; earl
JERL boat joint
KARL Charles; — Marx
MARL clayey soil; fertilizer; fiber
MERL blackbird
NURL wood knot; to mill
PURL knitting stitch; beer; murmur; spin; swirl
YARL Norse chief; earl
BARM yeast
BERM (l)edge; road shoulder
CORM bulblike stem (crocus)
DERM prefix, suffix: skin layer
DORM dormitory; sleep
FARM till; land; — out; club
FIRM fixed; solid; company
FORM shape; mold; fashion; school grade
GARM Hel's dog
GERM bud; seed; microbe
HARM hurt; evil; injury
JERM Levantine boat
MARM ma'am; school-
NORM type; standard; integer
PERM elec. unit; hair wave
TERM phrase; word; condition; time, period
TURM troop; company
WARM hot; genial; newly made; heat; — Springs
WORM crawler; maggot; screw; insinuate
WURM glacial period
YARM scream; wail
YIRM fret; whine: Scot., Ir.
BARN storehouse; stable
BERN Swiss capital
BIRN clarinet socket
BORN given birth to; née; quantum physicist
BURN (be on) fire; yearn; waste; speed; brand
CARN stone heap
CERN decide
CORN grain; ear, kernel; callus; whisky; preserve; granulate(d); clavus; banality; red-yellow
DARN mend; interjection
DORN thornback ray
DURN gatepost
EARN gain; win; deserve
FERN seedless plant
FIRN granular snow(field)
GARN yarn; go on
HORN prong; antenna; trumpet; brasswind; cup; Cape —
KARN stone heap
KERN soldier; peasant; grain; type part; Jerome (composer)
KIRN harvest feast
LORN forsaken; bereft
MORN A.M.; dawn; East
NORN demigoddess (Urth, Skuld, Verthandi)
PERN honey buzzard
PIRN reed; bobbin; nose ring
TARN lake
TERN gull; threefold; ship
TORN ripped; damaged
TURN bending; corner; revolve; reverse; change; shape; act; movement
WARN caution; give notice
WORN used (as clothing); shabby; tired
YARN spun wool; story
YIRN whine; grimace; smirk: Scot., Ir.
AERO go by aircraft
AGRO prefix: soil
BARO big; prefix: weight
BORO spring rice; Indian (Mirhana); — Budur (temple)
CARO dear (one): It.; Caroline
CERO mackerel
DURO Sp. peso; dollar

EBRO Sp. river
FARO card game; Pharaoh
GARO Assam native
GIRO tour; round; credit system; aircraft (auto-)
GYRO prefix: ring, spiral
HERO protagonist; demigod; — and Leander; Beatrice's cousin
HIRO measure
INRO Japanese receptacle
KARO plant
LERO Dodecanese isle
LORO monk parrot; fish
MARO ship name: Jap.
MERO grouper (fish)
MIRO tree; wood robin
MORO finch; P.I. Moslem tribe
NERO emperor; fiddler; Agrippine's son; Wolfe (Stout)
OKRO plant; stew; soup; gumbo
OTRO other, another: Sp.
PERO but: Sp.
PIRO Tanoan Indian
PORO Sierra Leone secret society
PYRO prefix: fire, fever
SERO prefix: thin; late pupil
TARO rootstock; pol; elephant's ear
TIRO amateur; novice
TORO N.Z. tree
TYRO beginner; novice
XERO prefix: dry
ZERO nothing; cipher; nullity; — hour; Japanese plane
BURP belch; — gun
CARP fish; complain
DORP hamlet; city (So. Afr.)
HARP coin; seal; Lyra; constellation; Irishman; nag
LARP secretion, insect
LERP secretion; insect
TARP canvas; sailor; hat
TERP prehistoric mound
TORP croft; Swed. small farm
TURP turpentine
WARP threads; twist; falsify
ZARP policeman
BARR elephant's cry
BIRR wind force; sound
BURR (prickly) nut, knob; reamer; banyan tree; Aaron (statesman)
CARR pool
CURR to murmur (as owlet)
DARR bird
DORR Rebellion (R.I.)
DURR grain sorghum
HARR hinge
HERR lord, Mister, Sir: Ger.
HURR to snarl
KERR physicist
PARR young fish; skegger; Catherine (Henry VIII wife)
PIRR wind gust; whiz; gull
PORR push; poke; kick
PURR cat's sound
TARR tease
TYRR Odin's son; war god
YARR growl; snarl; herb
YIRR growl; snarl: Scot.
AIRS pretensions; side
BORS king (Lancelot's uncle); Bohort (finder of Holy Grail)
HERS fem., poss. pronoun
HORS out of: Fr.; — d'oeuvres
KERS cress
LARS Porsena (conqueror)
LORS exclamation: lord!
MARS war god; planet
MORS deity; death
OURS possessive pronoun
PARS part: Lat.
SIRS gentlemen
SORS lot: Lat.; divination
AIRT guide; turn
BART man's name
BERT nickname
BORT finder of Holy Grail; impure diamond
BURT butt; gore; dent
CART wagon; transport
CURT short; concise
DART missile; fish; seam; run
DIRT muck; earth; gossip; do one —; — cheap
FORT stronghold; trading post; dun
GIRT encircled; prepared
HART stag; deer
HURT harm(ed); pain
MART market; nickname
MORT nickname; woman; salmon; the kill; dead: Fr.
PART portion; duty; role; separate; split; go
PERT bold; lively; sandpiper
PORT harbor; haven; wine; blue-red; left side; tune; demeanor
SART Iranian Turk
SERT Sp. painter
SORT type; kind; quantity; classify
SURT Frey's slayer
SYRT quicksand
TART sour; pastry; harlot
TORT wrongful act
VERT green (Her.); veer; convert
WART protuberance; -hog
WERT were: archaic, poetic
WORT plant; (pot)herb
YURT Kirghiz tent
AARU Hades; heaven
BARU tree
ECRU beige; unbleached
FERU bast fiber
GURU teacher
MARU ship name: Jap.
MERU fabled mountain
PERU country
PURU of Arawakan
RURU N.Z. morepork
TORU N.Z. tree
YARU Hades; heaven
MARX Karl (economist)
ADRY thirsty
AERY ethereal; nest
AIRY breezy; light
ARRY cockney worker
ATRY lay to (naut.)
AWRY distorted; perverse(ly)
BURY hide; inter; lose
DORY John — (fish); boat
EERY weird; uncanny; timid
EWRY linen storeroom
EYRY bird's nest
FURY rage; avenging spirit; Erinys, Fate, Parca (Atropos)
GARY city, steel center
GORY bloody; murderous

JURY (court) panel; committee; grand —; hung —
LORY parrot; touraco
MARY female name; queen; sister of Lazarus, Martha; Virgin; Lady
MIRY boggy; filthy
NARY not one
OARY oarlike
PORY porous; permeable
RORY O'More (Irish novel)
SARY sorry
SORY vitriolic earth
SPRY nimble; brisk; smart
TORY conservative
VARY alter; differ
VERY true; same; extremely; light signals; flare
WARY watchful
WIRY tough; sinewy
HARZ Ger. mountains

ANSA handle; loop
AUSA Vich (Sp. commune)
BESA coin
BISA antelope
BOSA Arab. drink
CASA house, building: Sp., It.
DISA showiest orchid
DOSA sheik's ritual ride; hatred
ELSA — of Brabant (Lohengrin's bride)
KASA grass
KUSA ceremonial grass
LISA fem. name; nickname
MASA corn meal
MESA flat hill; oakwood color
MUSA banana genus
MYSA buffalo (Kipling)
NASA space-travel agency
OSSA bones; Mt. (Olympus)
PASA raisin
PESA coin
PISA city (leaning tower)
RASA essence; tabula —
ROSA shrub genus; name; sub —; Bonheur (artist)
RUSA deer; sambar; grass; oil
SASA fencer's cry
SUSA Elam city (Esther story)
TESA Indian buzzard
URSA bear; stars: — Major, Minor; Great, Little Bear (Dipper)
VASA ducts; Swedish dynasty
VISA endorse(ment); -vis
XOSA Kaffir
BOSC best pear
DISC disk; record; — jockey
FISC exchequer
FUSC dusky; somber
ANSE handle: Fr.
APSE recess; throne
ASSE caama; fox
BASE bottom; source; home; headquarters; found; diamond corner; ignoble
BISE cold wind; winter
BOSE test ground by sound
CASE event; fact; record, problem (medical, etc.); legal action; argument; grammar form; container, chest, box; queer phenomenon; inspect
CISE dice term: six
COSE (friendly) chat
DOSE portion; (give) medicine
DUSE incubus; Eleanora (actress)
EASE repose; comfort; moderate; facilitate
ELSE other(wise); besides
ENSE suffix
ERSE Irish; Gaelic
ESSE existence; to be: Lat.
FUSE detonator; melt; unite
HOSE stockings; pipe; drench
HUSE beluga; whale; huchen
IPSE himself: Lat.; — dixit
JOSE Carmen lover
LESE — majesty (disrespect)
LOSE miss; forfeit; fail; forget
LYSE undergo lysis
MESE Greek mus. term
MISE levy; stake; tax; — en scene
MOSE Moses
MUSE meditate; goddess
NASE promontory; nose: Ger.
NOSE proboscis; smeller; scent; search; front; touch; — out (defeat); -dive
OESE bacteriologist's wire
OISE Fr. river
OUSE Great — (river)
OWSE tan liquor
PISE building material
POSE posture; affectation; baffle; propound
RASE rub; demolish
RESE shake; rush
RISE climb; grow(th); begin; emerge(nce); thrive; retort
ROSE stood up; got up; flower; tree; wood; red; pink; window; Abie's Irish —; Eng. emblem
RUSE trick; deceit; slip
SISE six (dice)
VASE vessel
VISE tool; clamp; endorse
WESE we shall
WISE sage; learned
BASH smash; bruise
BISH aconite; poison
BOSH furnace part; nonsense (nothing: Turk.)
BUSH shrub; thicket; tail
CASH money; exchange; hemlock
COSH snug; happy; math. term
CUSH sorghum; cow; money; Ham's son; country
DASH sprint; smash; small portion
DISH receptacle; serve
FASH rough edges; vex
FISH piscine; angle; probe; search;

tin — (torpedo)
GASH (make) incision
GISH Moroccan public land; Lillian, Dorothy (actresses)
GOSH oath; -awful
GUSH flow; spout; be effusive
HASH chop up; mixture; mess
HISH hiss; swish
HUSH quiet; silence; -hush; -puppy; — money
JOSH make fun; banter
KISH powder; basket; measure; Saul's father
KUSH Ham's son; country
LASH (whip) stroke; tie; eye part
LOSH wash leather
LUSH luxurious; drunkard
MASH crush; brew; mixture; hammer; flirt
MESH net; netting; entangle
MUSH meal; hasty pudding; flattery; proceed!
NASH soft; humorist
NESH soft; juicy; dainty
NISH Yugo. city
PASH hurl; smash
PISH reject; nonsense!
POSH slush; elegant
PUSH shove; thrust; strive; button
RASH hasty; careless
RESH Heb. letter, 200; plant
RUSH haste(n); attack; red (mace); cattail
SASH casement; scarf; belt
SISH slushy ice
SOSH jag; drunk; dash
TASH fabric
TOSH bath(tub)
TUSH tooth; Georgian; pshaw!
WASH bathe; laundry; tint
WISH desire; request
ABSI tribe
ASSI holly
DASI concubine
DESI jute; Arnaz
HUSI fine P.I. fiber
JUSI fine P.I. fiber
KASI tile work
LASI tribe
NASI prince; patriarch
NISI unless: Lat.
PASI low-caste Hindu
SESI black-fin snapper
SISI porkfish
SUSI fine cotton
BASK luxuriate; warm
BISK soup; ice cream; red-yellow
BOSK thicket
BUSK stir about; hasten; corset bone; Indian New Year
CASK barrel; measure
CUSK fish; burbot; eel
DESK table; lectern; department
DISK plate; harrow; puck
DUSK twilight; gloom
FISK exchequer; Jim (speculator); tire
HUSK covering (of seed, corn); shell
LISK flank; loin
LUSK lazy (fellow)
MASK disguise; screen; domino
MOSK Moslem temple; Masjid
MUSK odor; aromatic secretion (of deer, ox, etc.)
OMSK Siberian city
PISK nighthawk
RISK peril; hazard; subject of insurance
RUSK bread; biscuit; Dean (statesman)
TASK labor; assignment; take to — (censure)
TOSK Albanian
TUSK long tooth
IISM egoism
KASM measure
ALSO besides
CASO Dodecanese Island
COSO open space: Sp.
HUSO beluga; whale; huchen
IPSO — jure, — facto
KOSO tree; cusso; Panamint Indian
MUSO Chibchan Indian
PASO measure
PESO coin; Sp. dollar
PISO weight
SOSO middling; passably
VASO vase: It.; prefix: blood vessel
YESO plaster of Paris; gypsum
CUSP (crescent) point; tooth edge
GASP pant (eagerly)
HASP clasp
LISP speech defect
RASP grate; file
RISP metal bar
WASP yellow jacket; hornet; fem. flyer: WW II
WISP torch; shred; flock; brush; ignis fatuus
BASS fish; fiber; lowest part; singer; clef (F); musical instrument, viol
BESS nickname; Mrs. Truman
BOSS knob; pad; stud; master; employer
BUSS ship; kiss; calf
CASS treasure; Timberlane (Lewis); Squire (Eliot)
CESS tax; luck
COSS measure
CUSS curse; person
DASS Durga, Ram (twins, Kipling)
DISS reed grass
DOSS bed; sleep; — house
FASS measure
FESS broad band (Her.); confess
FOSS canal; ditch; moat
FUSS tumult; bustle; budget
HASS throat; embrace
HISS sibilant (of disapproval); goose; serpent; steam sound; Alger (Communist)
HOSS horse; One — Shay (Holmes)
HUSS dogfish; John (religious leader)
JASS card game; jack
JESS strap on hawk leg
JOSS Chin. deity
KISS touch gently; caress; sweetmeat
KOSS measure
LASS girl; sweetheart
LESS shorter; fewer; inferior; minus
LISS (fairy) fort; release; peace;

fleur-de-lis
LOSS forfeiture; bereavement; waste; defeat; — leader
MASS rite, service; bulk; mob, populace; assemble
MESS banquet; meal; muddle; disorder; botch
MISS fail(ure); omit; want; girl; maiden
MOSS bryophyte; lichen; green; rose; Hart (writer)
MUSS mess; rumple; row
NESS cape; promontory; suffix
NUSS nurse
PASS opening; go through; by; license; abstention; condition; amatory gesture
PESS hassock
PUSS cat; lip; face
RISS glaciation stage
ROSS rough bark; seal; island; navigator; Harold (editor)
RUSS Russian; Slav
SASS sauce
SESS soap frame bar
SISS hiss; shame!; girl
SOSS hog call for food
TASS Soviet News Agency
TESS Theresa; Hardy heroine
TOSS throw; fling; change
VISS weight
BAST (woody) fiber; goddess, phloem
BEST most (good); defeat
BUST bosom; statue; failure; break
CAST throw; project; shed; deposit; form; found; actors; (assign) roles
CEST girdle; belt (Venus)
CIST chest; roofed pit
CYST box; abnormal sac
DOST (you) do: archaic
DUST powdered matter; rubbish; clean; dust to —; gold —
EAST direction; Asia; Orient
ERST former; first
FAST not eat; fixed(ly); quick(ly); wild; — and loose
FEST festive gathering
FIST grasp; effort; tightwad
FUST pilaster; smell stale
GEST deed; romance tale, adventure
GIST main point; pith
GUST outburst of wind
HAST contraction: havest
HEST command; precept
HIST call to attention; Indian girl (Cooper)
HOST army; throng; bread as Christ's body; innkeeper; person having guests
JEST joke
JUST fair; virtuous; exact(ly)
KIST chest; installment; measure
LAST block; final(ly); endure; measure
LEST for fear that
LIST strip(e); roll; register; enter; inclination; careen
LOST not won; misplaced; confused; ruined; — cause
LUST sensual desire
MAST pole; brown; nuts
MIST dim; haze; gray
MOST greatest, almost
MUST be obliged to; necessity; new wine; stum; staleness; frenzy
MYST Greek priest
NAST cartoonist
NEST (make a) home
OAST kiln
OUST eject; discharge
PAST tense; ago; after
PEST plague; insect; nuisance
PIST attention!; track
POST pillar; advertise; mil. station; mail; inform; record
REST pause; stop; peace; prop; stay; rely; mus. sign; remainder; set; found
RIST engrave; scratch
RUST oxydize; corrode; inaction; reddish-brown
SIST stay; delay; summon
TEST shell; cupel; examination; try
VAST huge (space)
VEST waistcoat; clothe; empower
WAST were
WEST wind; painter, author; occident; go —; Mae —
WIST know; knew; measure
ZEST orange peel; relish; gusto
ANSU Korean apricot
APSU primordial chaos
AUSU tree
GESU Jesus: It.
JESU name: Jesus
MASU salmon
NOSU Lolo; Chin. Caucasian
SUSU blind dolphin; Congo
TASU measure
VASU deity (Vishnu); nephew
BUSY (keep) active; in use
CASY ex-preacher (Steinbeck)
COSY snug; teapot cover
EASY simple; calm; soft; — Street
JOSY nickname
MOSY moldy; rotten
NOSY fragment; prying
POSY flower; nosegay; poem
ROSY blushing; optimistic
SUSY name: Susan; Susanna
UPSY -daisy

ACTA deeds; records
AETA Negrito; native
ALTA tall: Sp.
ANTA porch; nut; tapir; goddess; pier; theater group
ARTA Ionian gulf
ASTA measure; dog
ATTA soul; native; flour; fruit; ant

BATA child; servant
BETA Greek B, 2; star; ray
BOTA measure
CATA down; prefix: away
COTA P.I. fort
DATA facts
DITA tree; bark; upas
ESTA this: Sp.
ETTA Henrietta; Harriet
FATA — Morgana (fairy, mirage)
GATA nurse shark
GETA Jap. wooden clogs
GITA Bhagavad —; Indian scriptures (yoga)
IOTA Greek I, 10; jot
JOTA Sp. peasant dance
KETA dog salmon
KOTA P.I. fort; Dravidian language
LATA jumping disease
LOTA water pot; burbot genus
MATA Hari (spy)
META goal post; river
MOTA Moslem marriage
MUTA change; Moslem marriage
NATA Nana's hero
NOTA insect backs; — bene (N.B.)
OCTA prefix: eight
PATA painting; turban; sword
PITA fiber; flax; hemp; brocket (deer)
RATA tree; chestnut; rate; pro —
RITA cosmic order (Vedic); Rio —; fem. name
ROTA roster; curia tribunal; round; hurdy-gurdy
RUTA herb genus; rue
SETA caterpillar's hair; spine
SITA Ramachandra's wife (Sanskrit Ramayana)
TOTA grivet monkey
VETA mountain sickness
VITA life: Lat.
VOTA Roman festivals
WETA wingless locust
YETA Jap. outcast
ZETA Greek Z, 7
ZITA Austrian empress
ALTE old: Ger.; Adenauer
ANTE stake; pay; before; -bellum
AUTE tree
BATE diminish; tanner's bath; restrain
BETE beast, silly: Fr.; — noire
BITE cut; pierce; grip; eat (into); sting; respond; snack
BOTE house repair; amends
BUTE island; Scot. county; parson (Thackeray)
CATE delicacy
CETE marine mammals
CITE summon; quote
COTE birdhouse; sheep shed; Coast: Fr. (d'Or; d'Azur)
CUTE clever; attractive
CYTE prefix: hollow vessel
DATE fruit; tree; brown; (make) appointment
DITE mite; indict
DOTE love to excess; drivel; timber rot
ENTE grafted (Her.); being: Sp.
ESTE It. family; this: Sp.
ETTE suffix: fem.
FATE destiny (goddess); end; kismet
FETE festival; regale
FUTE Eskimo curlew
GATE entrance; pass; judgment; money
GITE shelter: Fr.; mad
HATE detest; aversion
JETE ballet jump
JUTE fiber plant; Corchorus; Low German
KATE bird; Shaks. shrew; Greenaway
KITE hawk; rogue; flying toy; banking fraud
LATE dead; tardy
LETE quadrille set
LITE suffix: mineral, rock
LOTE lotus (poetic); weights
LUTE cement; bricklayer's tool; Apollo's musical instrument; jar ring
MATE companion; match; tea; check-
METE measure; allot
MITE arachnid; parasite; small (coin)
MOTE speck; particle
MUTE silent; dumb; muffle
NATE born
NETE Greek mus. term
NOTE sign; tone; fame; heed; memo; IOU; record; see
OSTE prefix: bone
PATE head; paste
PETE strongbox; Peter
POTE poker; stick
RATE censure; ratio; charge; estimate; rank; tax
RETE network
RITE ceremony; liturgy
ROTE surf noise; routine
RUTE measure
SATE gratify; glut
SITE location; scene
TATE wool; hair lock
TETE head: Fr.; — a tete; hairdo
TOTE carry; haul; total
TUTE tutor
VITE quick, lively: Fr.
VOTE ballot; suffrage; voice; enact; propose; Ingrian Finn
WATE sea demon
WOTE Ingrian Finn
YATE eucalyptus
YITE bird (yellowhammer)
ACTH hormone medicine
BATH tub; measure; spa; order
BETH Heb. B, 2; Alcott heroine (Little Women)
BOTH the two
DOTH does
ESTH Balt; Estonian (Tallinn man)
GATH Philistine city
GOTH Teuton (Theodoric, Alaric); barbarian; Ostro-. Visi-
HATH contraction: haveth
HETH son of Canaan; Hittite ancestor
HOTH blind god (Balder slayer)
JETH Hindu month
KATH astringent
KITH acquaintance; — and kin
LATH strip; slat
LITH prefix, suffix: stone

LOTH averse; reluctant
MATH mowing; monastery; school course
MOTH lepidopterous insect; -ball; -eaten; gypsy —; page (Shakespeare)
MUTH measure
MYTH (religious) legend; fiction
NATH star
OATH appeal; pledge; vow; curse
PATH track; route
PITH marrow; kernel; gist
RATH chariot; fort; temple; early; mome-
RUTH pity; grief; name; OT book, heroine (Moabitess); wife of Boaz
SETH banker; Adam's son; Osiris' evil brother
TATH dung
TETH Heb. T, 9
URTH Norn; Wyrd (with Verthandi, Skuld); Weird Sister
VOTH Ingrian Finn
WITH prep.: including, and
AKTI peninsula
ANTI opposed; prefix: against; Indian
ASTI city; — spumante
BITI blackwood
GUTI Sumer settler; Kurd
HATI heart
HOTI cause; reason
INTI Incas' deified sun; sun god
JATI caste
JITI Rajmahal creeper
JOTI astrologer; astronomer
KATI weight
LETI island off Timor
LITI medieval peasants
LOTI Pierre (writer; Viaud)
MOTI elephant (Kipling)
NETI eulalia (thatch grass)
RATI weight
ROTI roasted: Fr.
SATI queen of the gods
SETI river; pharaoh
TITI monkey; tree; petrel
VITI East African
YATI ascetic; devotee
YETI abominable snowman
ZATI bonnet monkey
ROTL Afr. weight
ACTO action: Sp.
ALTO hill: Sp.; voice
ARTO prefix: bread
AUTO prefix: same, self; drama: Sp.; (ride in) car
BITO tree; poison; oil
BOTO Indian; Voto
BUTO serpent goddess; Leto
CATO the Censor (Roman statesman); foe of Carthage
CETO prefix: whale
CITO quickly, soon: It.
COTO bark; stomachic
DATO tribal chief
DOTO sea slug genus
ECTO prefix: outside
ENTO prefix: inner
INTO penetrating; toward
JATO jet-assisted take-off
KOTO Jap. zither
LETO mother of Apollo, Artemis
LOTO pot; game
MOTO movement: It.; con —
NATO international (Western) alliance; treaty organization
NITO climbing fern
OCTO prefix: eight
ONTO upon; wise to
OTTO name; palindrome; perfume; Ger. ruler
PATO Muscovy duck
PETO wahoo (fish); Henry IV figure
PITO fiber; flax; hemp; brocket (deer)
ROTO ragged: Sp.; printing
SITO prefix: grain
SOTO Hernando de (explorer)
TITO Yugo. leader (Broz)
TOTO baby (animal); all
TYTO barn owl; Strix; Aluco
UNTO to; for; toward
VETO prohibit(ion); no
VOTO So. Amer. Indian
NATR weight
ACTS NT book
ARTS skills; sciences; fine —; — and crafts
CATS — cradle
CITS citizens; mufti
EATS food; consumes
LOTS tracts; quantities; very much; chances
RATS bah!
SOTS yeast
BATT matted mass
BITT naut. fastener
BOTT clay plug; fly larva
BUTT cask; mound; target; ram; hinge; jut; halibut
DITT close up; obstruct
GETT bill of divorce
HATT measure
HETT Hittite ancestor
LETT Latvian, Balt (Riga man)
MATT lusterless
MITT glove; hand
MOTT clump of trees; James, Lucretia (abolitionists)
MUTT cur; stupid one; — and Jeff
NETT undeductible
NOTT Norse night (Dag)
PATT stalemate(d)
PITT statesman (Commoner, Chatham); diamond
POTT paper size; editor (Dickens)
PUTT golf stroke
SETT tool; paving stone
TATT knot lace
WATT inventor, elec. unit (volt-ampere); hare
ACTU act: Lat.
AITU god; demon
ANTU rat poison
ATTU Aleut. island
DATU tribal chief
DETU eclipse demon (Rahu)
LATU gold coins
MITU curassow; bird
PATU weapon
TATU Indian; armadillo; tattoo
TUTU N.Z. shrub; poison; ballet skirt
YUTU Peru tinamou; bird
ARTY artistic
CITY urban place

COTY Fr. statesman; cosmetics
DOTY discolored by rot
DUTY obligation; task; tax
KATY Catherine; -did
MATY (assistant) servant
MITY parasite-infested
OATY full of oats
PITY sympathy; mercy
TOTY low-caste worker
TYTY farmer of God's Little Acre
BATZ coin
LITZ braided wire
METZ city, former fort
UNTZ weight

AGUA water; toad
AKUA deity
AQUA water; green-blue
ATUA lemon
ERUA mother goddess
SHUA Abraham's son
SKUA bird; great —; jaeger
ULUA cavalla; fish; caranx
BLUB swell; puff out
CHUB fallfish; dace; chevin
CLUB bat; beat; society; suit (cards)
DAUB plaster; besmear
DOUB Bermuda grass
DRUB (beat with) stick
FLUB blunder; botch
GAUB persimmon (astringent)
GLUB make gulping sound
GRUB larva; food; dig(ger)
KNUB waste silk
ROUB measure
SLUB twisted wool roll
SNUB rebuke; slight; stumpy
STUB stump; penpoint; short, stocky; extirpate; ticket part; bump
DOUC variegated monkey
ERUC cordage fiber
BAUD speed unit
BOUD malt weevil
CHUD Mongols; Vepse; Vote; Tavastian
DAUD dad
EHUD judge of Israel
FEUD strife; vendetta; fee
FOUD district magistrate
GAUD ornament; bead
LAUD praise
LEUD feudal tenant
LOUD noisy; showy; vulgar
MAUD plaid; rug; name; Muller; Whittier, Tennyson heroine
PHUD bullet sound; exclamation
PUUD weight
ROUD fish
SAUD Ibn (king)
SCUD run fast; wind-driven clouds; skim; flea
SOUD pay
SPUD scrape(r); potato; dig
STUD breeding stock; knob; stump; dot; poker
SYUD Moslem prince; title
THUD dull sound; blow
AGUE fever
BLUE color; ocean; sky; sailor; sad; -blood; puritanical
CLUE hint; guide; thread
COUE psychotherapist ("Day by day . . .")
FLUE net; lint; barb; air passage; pipe
GAUE German regions
GLUE adhesive; stick
GRUE shiver; shudder
MOUE pout; grimace: Fr.
NEUE new
NIUE Savage Island language
ROUE dissolute man; rake
SHUE Tibetan deer
SLUE swamp; twist; lot
TRUE factual; loyal; align
NEUF nine, new: Fr.
OEUF egg: Fr.
POUF puff; ottoman; bang!
SAUF safe: Fr.; — conduit
SOUF sigh
CHUG pull; fish; (move with) vibration
DRUG medicine; dope; — on the market; — addict
FRUG modern dance
GLUG sound of liquids
JOUG iron collar; pillory
PLUG stop(per); plod; shoot; spark —; horse; praise
SCUG squirrel: Brit.
SLUG snail; idle; metal spacer; small drink; bullet; strike
SMUG tidy; neat; priggish
SNUG cozy; trim; Shaks. character
THUG assassin; hoodlum
TOUG horsetail standard
UTUG horsetail standard
BRUH pig-tailed macaque
ARUI sheep
EQUI prefix: equal, same
ETUI (vanity) case; box
ISUI Asher's son
MAUI Polynesian hero
PFUI exclamation
CAUK (secure by a) tenon
DAUK relay post
LAUK exclamation
SAUK Indian; Mont. river
SOUK Moslem market
TRUK Islands (Carolines)
UNUK star; — al Hay
WAUK wake: Scot.
AOUL Nepalese
AZUL blue: Sp.
BAUL mendicant
CAUL basket; covering membrane
DEUL Hindu temple
ELUL month
FOUL rotten; poor; illegal; invalid
GAUL Celt, Frenchman; France
GOUL monster; grave robber
HAUL drag; shift; loot
MAUL hammer; bruise; mangle
PAUL click; detent; Apostle; Bunyan; Revere; — VI (pope)
PEUL Fulah (Sudanese)
POUL Russ. coin
SAUL tree; king (son of Kish); — of Tarsus (Paul)
SHUL synagogue
SOUL spirit; inspirer; forces; psyche; person
WAUL wail
AHUM humming
ALUM emetic; astringent; styptic
ARUM herb; starch
ATUM sun god (Tem)

BAUM Vicki (novelist); Oz creator; tree: Ger.; — marten
CHUM friend; scrap fish
CLUM clutch roughly
DEUM Te — (hymn)
DOUM palm
DRUM spool; instrument; tympanum; beat
GAUM attention
GEUM plant (astringent)
GLUM moody; sullen
GRUM morose; guttural
JHUM cultivation method
MEUM carrotlike herb, spicknel, mine: Lat.
ODUM tree (iroko)
OGUM Irish alphabet
OVUM germ cell; egg
PLUM fruit (damson; greengage); tree; raisin; choice job
RHUM alcoholic drink
SAUM weight
SCUM dross; refuse; rabble
SIUM water parsnip
SLUM dilapidated district
STUM grape juice, must; renew wine
SUUM hum — cuique
SWUM swim participle
TUUM thin: Lat.
UTUM small owl
AMUN deity
AZUN Hananiah's father
CHUN Chin. pottery
DAUN stage (geol. period)
DRUN roar (Gypsy)
FAUN deity; satyr
IDUN Bragi's wife (Norse)
JAUN palanquin
KAUN resthouse; lord; title
LAUN ceramic sieve
LOUN loon; lout
MAUN must
NOUN speech part; name; substantive
PAUN betel leaf
SHUN avoid; abstain (from)
SKUN skinned
SPUN twisted; whirled
STUN stupefy; daze
TAUN measure
TSUN measure (1/10 ch'ih)
USUN ancient North Chinese
UZUN ancient North Chinese
WHUN gorse; restharrow
YGUN antisub gun
BLUP air bubble sound
CAUP tribute: Scot.
COUP blow; master stroke
DOUP weaver's thread
GAUP gape
KEUP measure
LOUP half mask; Skidi Indian; river; fish
NOUP steep promontory
PAUP walk idly
PLUP sound of (soft) fall
ROUP a cold; hoarseness
SCUP pan fish; porgy
SNUP snap up cheaply
SOUP broth; stew; — and fish; duck —; step (up); explosive; fog
TOUP Malay lugger
YAUP yap; yawn
YOUP yelp; scream; yawn
ALUR Negro
AMUR river
ASUR war god
AZUR Cote d'— (Riviera); Hananiah's father
BAUR joke
BIUR Heb. commentary
BLUR obscure; stain
CHUR Swiss canton
DAUR Manchu
DOUR sullen; gloomy
EBUR ivory: Lat.
FOUR number; card; boat
GAUR wild cattle
GOUR cattle; koulan (onager)
HOUR time unit; H- or zero —
JOUR day: Fr.
KNUR gnarl; knot; wood ball
LOUR frown; lower; scowl
PEUR fear: Fr.
POUR (make) flow; for: Fr.; emit; — le merite
SAUR prefix, suffix: lizard
SCUR horn tissue
SLUR pass over; mumble; defame; stigma; glide (mark)
SMUR mist; cloud
SNUR snort
SOUR acid(ify); tart; disagreeable
SPUR point; good; kick; otter track; ridge
TAUR Taurus (bull)
TOUR trip; circuit; — de force
YOUR poss. pronoun
ACUS pin
ANUS end of alimentary canal
APUS bird; constellation
AVUS grandfather: Lat.
COUS cowlike
CRUS leglike part; shank
DEUS god: Lat.; — ex machina
ESUS Gaulish god (Mars)
GAUS region: Ger.
GRUS constellation (Crane)
ILUS son of Tros; Priam's grandfather
IOUS promissory notes; suffix
IRUS Odyssey beggar
NOUS mind; reason; wit; we: Fr.
OBUS howitzer shell
ONUS burden; duty
OPUS work
OTUS giant slain by Apollo
PIUS Pope: X (St.; Sarto); XI (Ratti); XII (Pacelli)
PLUS and; more; extra; — fours
POUS measure
REUS defendant: Lat.
RHUS sumac genus
SOUS coins; under: Fr.
THUS in this way; hence
URUS wild ox
USUS user, use: Lat.
ZEUS chief god; Jupiter; Hera's husband; son of Cronus, Rhea
ABUT touch
AKUT ape man (Burroughs)
BHUT Dravidian ghost
BLUT blood: Ger.
BOUT contest; attack
BRUT dry: Fr.; Brit. king (New Troy, London)
CHUT nonsense!
CNUT king; son of Magnus
FAUT comme il —

(proper): Fr.
GAUT range; pass; river bank stairs
GLUT sate; surfeit; oversupply; wedge
GOUT drop; disease (arthritis); taste: Fr.
HAUT high: Fr.; — monde
KNUT king; son of Magnus
LOUT boor; bumpkin; dolt
NAUT sea mile
PHUT (bullet) sound; OT people
POUT sulk(iness); fish
PRUT exclamation; river
ROUT defeat; tumult; mob; the brant; snare
SCUT rabbit's tail; fur
SHUT close; refine
SLUT slattern; harlot
SMUT soot; coal dust; plant disease; obscenity
SPUT boiler plate
STUT horsefly
TAUT snug; tense
TOUT tip(ster); praise; all: Fr.; — a fait; — de suite
BOUW measure
DAUW zebra
CRUX (Southern) Cross; crucial point
DEUX two: Fr.
EAUX waters: Fr.
FLUX flow; change; melt
JEUX cards, hands, games: Fr.
ROUX (soup, sauce) thickener; physician
VAUX village; fort (Verdun battle)
GHUZ Turkish invader
JEUZ chief Benjamite

ALVA duke; city; Thomas — Edison
CAVA pepper shrub, root; gum resin; vein
CIVA Hindu deity
DEVA deity (Indra); demon
DIVA prima donna; blue
HOVA Madagascar native; Malagasy
JAVA coffee; hood; (Indonesian) Sunda Isles; — man (Pithecanthropus)
JIVA life energy
JOVA Opata; Pimian Indian
KAVA pepper shrub, root; gum resin; vein
KIVA ceremonial chamber
LAVA fluid rock; obsidian's source; red
NEVA river (Leningrad)
NOVA star: new, temporary
PEVA Peru Indian
RIVA shore: It.
SAVA Yugo. river
SIVA Hindu deity; cosmic dancer (Nataraja)
ULVA sea lettuce; laver
URVA mongoose
VIVA salute (long live); — voce (spoken aloud)
XOVA Opata; Pimian Indian
YAVA weight
NKVD Soviet secret police
BAVE double silk thread
CAVE cavern; — in (collapse); — canem (beware of dog)
CIVE chive garlic
COVE bay; recess; pass; chap; Gypsy
DAVE David
DIVE plunge; duck; low resort; — bomb(er)
DOVE pigeon; blue, gray; Columba; plunged
EAVE roof edge
FIVE number; basketball team; card
GAVE donated
GIVE bestow; yield; grant
GYVE fetter; shackle
HAVE possess; aux. verb; must; deceive
HIVE bees' swarm, house
HOVE ground ivy; raised
JAVE Jehovah
JIVE dialect (dance, jazz)
JOVE god; Jupiter; Zeus
KIVE brewer's vat
LAVE pour; bathe
LIVE exist; continue; vital; alert
LOVE affection; like; Cupid; Eros; zero
MOVE impel; shift; excite; act; depart(ure); play
NAVE hub; church part
NEVE snow; firn
NOVE nine: It.
PAVE cover firmly; — the way; jewel setting
RAVE rant, rage; enthusiasm; rod
REVE (muse in) dream: Fr.
RIVE tear; split; — droite (right bank), — gauche (left bank)
ROVE wander; ramble; draw through an eye
SAVE rescue; avoid; lay by; but; — face
SEVE wine delicacy: Fr.
SIVE sickle; knife
TAVE Octavia
VIVE — le roi!; long live!: Fr.
WAVE billow; swell; undulation, flutter; signal; — length; navy woman
WEVE contraction
WIVE marry; act as wife
WOVE entwined; spun
IHVH God; Tetragrammaton
JHVH Jehovah; God; Tetragrammaton
YHVH God, Yaheveh, Tetragrammaton
DEVI goddess; Siva's wife (Shakti); title: Mrs., Lady
DIVI divine ones
FAVI titles; flagstones
HEVI apple (tree)
KAVI Java language
LEVI Jacob's, Leah's son; tribe
RAVI tribesman
FAVN measure
LEVO prefix: left
PAVO peacock; constellation
RIVO stream: It.
VIVO spirited
RSVP please reply: Fr.
REVS rotations per minute
KIVU tsetse fly

BEVY company; flock
CAVY rodent; guinea pig; stray animal(s)
CUVY sea girdles; kelp
DAVY David; lamp; affidavit; Jones' locker
ENVY covet; grudge; 7th deadly sin
LEVY assess; seize; tax
LIVY Roman historian; Titus Livius
NAVY fleet; blue; tobacco; — yard
PAVY peach
PEVY lumberman's hook
TAVY Octavia
TIVY huntsman's cry
WAVY fluctuating; undulating

BIWA loquat
DEWA deity (Indra); demon
IOWA state; Indian
KAWA pepper shrub, root; gum resin; vein
LOWA bush quail
PAWA weight
TAWA tree
TEWA N.M. Indian
WAWA gibbon
BAWD procurer(ess)
DOWD slovenly woman
GAWD ornament; bead
LEWD lecherous; obscene
HOWE hollow; empty; Elias (inventor); Julia Ward (Battle Hymn); Brit. general, admiral
POWE weigh
JHWH Jahweh; God; Tetragrammaton
YHWH God, Yahweh, Tetragrammaton
IIWI bird (mamo)
KAWI Java language
KIWI flightless bird; apteryx; non-flyer
TUWI P.I. dyewood tree
BOWK steep; soak in lime
CAWK bird's cry; mineral
DAWK relay transport; mail
GAWK lout; stare
GOWK simpleton; fool
HAWK bird; predator; peddle; mortarboard
LAWK surprise!
MAWK maggot
SAWK measure
BAWL cry; howl; — out (chide)
BOWL basin; dish; (roll) ball
CAWL basket
COWL hood; auto body front
DOWL feathery down
FOWL poultry; cock; hen
GOWL gad; defile; howl; monster
HOWL (distress) cry; wail
JOWL jaw; cheek; wattle; gambler (Dickens)
MEWL whimper; miaou
PAWL click; detent; tent
YAWL (sail)boat
YOWL howl(ing); yell
DAWM coin
HAWM loiter
BAWN mud enclosure; white
DAWN daybreak; Eos; Aurora; red
DOWN to below; reduce; defeat; feathers; eider-; dejected
FAWN deer; cringe; toady; brown
GAWN gallon; tub
GOWN dress; toga; robe
HEWN felled; squared
KAWN resthouse; lord; title
LAWN fabric; grass plot; bishopric
LOWN calm; quiet; dolt
MOWN cut down; trimmed
PAWN chessman; pledge
SAWN sawed; cut
SEWN stitched
SOWN scattered; seeded
TAWN tawny
TOWN city; hamlet; — hall; man about —
YAWN open wide; gape; chasm
ATWO asunder
VTWO robot bomb
GAWP gape; simpleton
YAWP yap; yawn
JEWS -harp
LAWS rules; principles
MEWS (royal) stables
NEWS intelligence; tidings
YAWS skin disease
NEWT salamander; eft
NOWT neat cattle; dolt
DEWY moist; refreshing
JAWY talkative
LOWY banlieue; suburb
NOWY having curvature
ROWY streaked
TOWY like flax fibers

BIXA tree genus; achiote
COXA hip (joint)
DOXA religious stanzas
LOXA pale bark: quinine
MOXA cautery wormwood
MYXA plum (geiger) tree; sebesten
NOXA harmful thing
TOXA sponge spicule
COXE Capt. (Scott)
FIXE prix —
LUXE elegance; de —
MIXE Mexican Indian
SAXE Saxony; blue
CAXI snapper (fish)
DIXI I have spoken: Lat.
TAXI (ride a) cab; prefix: arrangement
CIXO Ecuador Indian
MOXO Arawakan Indian
MYXO slime mold
TAXO prefix: arrangement
NEXT nearest; following
SEXT canonical hour (noon); organ stop; sixth
TEXT (literary) substance; topic; Scripture passage; type
BOXY boxlike; squarish
BUXY paymaster
DIXY camp pot
DOXY doctrine; hussy
FOXY wily; brown; rank; sour
MIXY confusedly mixed
NIXY undeliverable mail
PIXY impish sprite
PUXY ill-tempered
ROXY name: Roxana; Rothafel (impresario); theater
SEXY sexually appealing
WAXY viscid; pliable

ALYA star
ARYA Caucasian
BAYA weaverbird; Bantu
CUYA hardwood tree
GOYA Sp. painter; — red
HAYA arrow poison
HOYA honey plant

(milkweed)
MAYA weaverbird; (Mexican) Indian; magic; Buddha's mother
PUYA pineapple genus
RAYA broadbill
SAYA outer skirt
SOYA bean; dill; fennel
YAYA copa, lancewood (tree)
EMYD terrapin
DAYE printer (Bay Psalm Book)
FUYE Jap. flute
SKYE Isle; dog, terrier
STYE eyelid swelling
KIYI herring; cisco; yelp
ACYL acid part
AMYL starch; alcohol
IDYL pastoral poem
NOYL fiber knot
ODYL alleged force
OXYL oxygen radical
TEYL linden; lime tree
CLYM — of the Clough (archer outlaw)
ETYM Moabites, giants; abbr.: word sources
ONYM technical name (biol.)
COYN corner(stone)
GWYN Llud's son; deity
LLYN lake; pool
BUYO betel leaf; nut
CAYO island, reef: Sp.
COYO avocado; chinin
ENYO war goddess
IDYO Niger delta Negro
KAYO knock out
MAYO Indian; physicians, clinic (Rochester)
MOYO measure
WHYO gangster; footpad
TRYP parasite in blood (sleeping sickness, nagana, surra)
SKYR sour curdled milk
ALYS name: Alice
ATYS god; Cybele's lover
DAYS by day
EMYS tortoise
ITYS Tereus' son
KEYS House of (Isle of Man legislature); cays: Florida —
WAYS wise; — and means
SKYT move fast; dart; slip
VAYU wind god
CEYX Halcyone's husband
ERYX sand snake
ONYX cameo stone; quartz; gem
ORYX antelope; gemsbok
PNYX Greek voting site
STYX Hades river; nymph: daughter of Oceanus, Tethys
HAYZ zodiacal situation
BOZA Arab. drink
CAZA Turkish district
DAZA Negro-Berber
GAZA Israel (Philistine) seaport; Mozambique district; eyeless in — (Samson)
GIZA site: pyramids, Sphinx
ITZA Mayan Indian
JUZA star
MOZA manservant
ONZA Sp. ounce (1/16 libra); coin
TIZA ulexite mineral
TUZA pocket gopher
ZAZA opera (Leoncavallo)
ZIZA Rehoboam's son
ZUZA weight
ADZE tool
BIZE cold wind; winter
COZE (friendly) chat
DAZE stupefy; mica
DOZE drowse; timber rot
FAZE disturb
FUZE detonator; melt; unite
GAZE stare; wonder
GUZE red roundel (Her.)
HAZE mist; drizzle; harass
LAZE idle(ness); tribesman
MAZE labyrinth; daze; perplex
NAZE promontory
OOZE exude; slime; liquor
RAZE scrape; demolish
SIZE bulk; quality; glue; filler; — up
WNZE weight
BUZI Ezekiel's father
CAZI Moslem judge
GAZI warrior; title
KAZI Moslem judge
LAZI tribesman
NAZI fascist; Hitlerite
NOZI of Yanan tribe
BOZO fellow
IDZO Niger delta Negro
KOZO paper mulberry
LAZO lasso
MAZO de la Roche (novelist; Jalna)
MOZO manservant: Sp.
NUZO Chibchan Indian
ANZU apricot
AUZU tree
ENZU moon god (Sin)
WUZU Moslem ablution
CAZY Moslem judge
COZY snug; teapot cover
DAZY confused
DOZY drowsy; decayed; doty
GAZY gaping
HAZY dim; obscure
JOZY Josepha; Josephine
KAZY Moslem judge
LAZY idle
MAZY perplexing
NIZY fool
OOZY muddy; slimy
SIZY viscous
SUZY name: Susanna
BIZZ buzz
BUZZ hum; fly low (over); — bomb (V1, V2)
FIZZ hissing sound; drink
FUZZ fine fibers; police
HUZZ buzz; murmur
JAZZ dance; music; banter
RAZZ chaff; ridicule
SIZZ hiss(ing sound)
ZIZZ whirring sound

FOUR-LETTER WORDS

A--A to Z--Z

ABBA father; title
ABIA Samuel's son
ABRA narrow pass; river
ACCA fabric
ACTA deeds; records
ADDA god; river; skink
AERA age; era
AETA Negrito; native
AFFA from off
AFRA name; union
AGHA officer; title
AGLA acrostic
AGRA comb. form; carpet; city (Taj Mahal site)
AGUA water; toad
AIDA opera; Radames' lover
AIEA town
AIRA grass
AKHA tribe; Burmese; Kaw
AKIA shrub (fish poison)
AKKA Pygmy
AKRA Negrito; vetch
AKUA deity
ALBA garb; poem; brain matter; duke
ALCA auk
ALDA soprano; hamlet: Sp.
ALEA Athena (war goddess)
ALFA grass
ALGA plant
ALIA other: Lat.
ALLA by: It.
ALMA girl; silk; river; city
ALTA tall: Sp.
ALVA duke; city; Thomas — Edison
ALYA star
AMBA mountain
AMGA Siberian river
AMIA fish
AMLA tree
AMMA abbess; god
AMRA plum
ANBA title
ANDA tree
ANNA coin; bird; name; — Christie (O'Neill); — Karenina (Tolstoi)
ANOA ox
ANSA handle; loop
ANTA porch; nut; tapir; goddess; pier; theater group
APIA port (Samoa)
AQUA water; green-blue
ARBA cart
ARCA box; dish; shell
AREA zone, region; scope; tract
ARIA tune; city (Herat)
ARNA buffalo
AROA Venezuela copper center
ARPA harp: It.
ARRA oath
ARTA Ionian gulf
ARYA Caucasian
ASEA at sea
ASHA tribe
ASIA continent; Orient; East
ASTA measure; dog
ATKA fish; Aleut. island
ATMA soul
ATTA soul; native; flour; fruit; ant
ATUA demon
AUCA Indian
AULA hall; tree; brain part
AURA wind; emanation; bird
AUSA Vich (Sp. commune)
AZHA star
ABIB month
ADIB star
AGIB dervish
AHAB king; captain; prophet
ARAB Semite; horse; nomad; urchin
ABAC calculator
ALEC fish; sauce; nickname
AMIC amidic
AVEC with: Fr.
ABED in bed; bedridden
ACID sour; biting
ADAD fiber; god
AGED old; oxygian
ALOD estate
AMID among
APOD footless
ARAD plant; city
ARID dry; barren
ARND theologian
AROD son of Gad
AULD old; — lang syne
AVID eager; greedy
AZID compound
AARE river
ABBE priest; title; Amer. meteorologist
ABIE —'s Irish Rose; name
ABLE fit; adept; suffix; -bodied
ACHE pain; yearn
ACLE tree
ACME peak; crisis
ACNE disease
ACRE field; measure; city
ADZE tool
AGEE awry; Shammah's father; James (novelist)
AGUE fever
AIDE help; -de-camp; — memoire
AILE winged
AINE elder
AIRE nobleman; river
AJEE awry
AKEE tree
ALAE wings
ALBE album
ALEE to shelter
ALLE bird; all: Ger.
ALME dancer
ALOE plant; tonic
ALTE old: Ger.; Adenauer
AMIE friend: Fr.
ANCE suffix; — errand
ANDE tribe
ANGE angel: Fr.
ANNE queen; Boleyn; Henry VIII wife; Elizabeth's mother; Shakespeare's wife; Dombey's maid (Dickens); Queen — style; Queen —'s lace
ANSE handle: Fr.
ANTE stake; pay; before;

-bellum
AONE first-rate
APSE recess; throne
ARME weapon: Fr.; — blanche (saber)
ARNE composer; region
AROE islands, New Guinea
ASSE caama; fox
ATLE tree
AUDE Fr. dept.; river
AUGE priestess
AUNE measure
AUTE tree
AXLE spindle
ALEF letter
ALIF letter
ATEF crown (Osiris)
AZOF town; sea
AGAG king
AGOG eager
AJOG jogging
AREG deserts
AWAG wagging
ACTH hormone medicine
ADAH wife of Lamech, Esau; fem. name
AIAH Edomite, Rizpah's father
AICH alloy
ALPH river (Coleridge, Kubla Khan)
AMAH nurse
ANKH cross
ARAH exclamation
ARCH support; curve; chief; fingerprint; triumphal —
ARGH timid
ASCH Scholem (author)
AYAH nurse; sign
AALI pasha
AANI ape
ABRI shelter
ABSI tribe
ADAI tribe
ADMI gazelle
AERI prefix: air
AGNI god; lambs
AGRI fields
AIPI cassava
AKTI peninsula
ALAI regiment; mountain; Jai —
ALBI flagellants
ALII royalty (Hawaiian)
AMBI about; prefix: both
AMLI tree
AMMI herb
AMOI mine: Fr.
ANAI termite
ANDI language
ANNI years: Lat.
ANTI opposed; prefix: against; Indian
APII plant
ARNI buffalo
ARUI sheep
ASCI spore sacs
ASSI holly
ASTI city; — spumante
ATHI Kenya river
ATLI Gudrun's husband-king
ATRI It. town
AURI prefix: gold, ear
ADAK Aleut. island
AMOK frenzy
ANAK giant race
ARAK palm; spirit
ASAK tree
ASOK tree
ATIK star
ABEL Adam's son; Cain's brother; — Magwitch (Dickens); letter A; monkey
ACYL acid part
AGAL cord
AIEL writ of —
AKAL deity
AMIL plant; remedy
AMYL starch; alcohol
ANAL pert. to anus
ANIL shrub, indigo
AOUL Nepalese
ARAL lake
ARIL seed covering
AVAL grandparental
AWOL absent without leave
AXAL around an axis
AXIL leaf angle
AZEL Saul's descendant
AZUL blue: Sp.
ADAM first man; sin; composer; architect
AHEM interjection
AHOM Assam native
AHUM humming
AKIM Negro; Tamiroff
ALEM fruit
ALIM teacher
ALUM emetic; astringent; styptic
ANAM tree; Viet Nam region
ANEM prefix: wind; city
ARAM country (Syria); Eugene (murderer)
ARUM herb; starch
ASEM alloy
ATOM whit; particle; nuclear complex
ATUM sun god (Tem)
AZAM sir: Persian
ACON boat
ADAN prayer call
ADEN comb. form: gland; city; gulf; region
ADIN name
AEON age
AGON contest; argument
AKAN Negro
AKIN related
ALAN dog; name
ALEN measure
ALIN measure
AMAN Ahasuerus's minister
AMEN assent; verily; deity; — Ra
AMIN agent
AMON deity; King of Judah
AMUN deity
ANAN tree; interjection
ANON again; now; soon; author unknown
ARAN Seir's descendant; island
ASIN month
ATEN solar disk
ATON solar disk
AVON river; Shakespeare home; (Stratford)
AWAN tribe
AXON axis; cell process
AYAN spruce
AYIN 16th Heb. letter; 70
AZAN prayer call
AZIN chem. compound
AZON bomb
AZUN Hananiah's father
ABOO war cry
ACTO action: Sp.
AERO go by aircraft
AGAO language
AGIO fee; commission
AGNO Luzon river
AGRO prefix: soil
AHIO Ark driver
AINO Jap. aboriginal
ALBO prefix: white
ALCO dog
ALLO prefix: other, dissimilar
ALSO besides
ALTO hill: Sp.; voice
AMBO pulpit
AMMO ammunition; prefix: sand
ANGO herb; dye
ANNO — Domini (year of our Lord)
APIO celery: Sp.

AREO prefix: Mars
ARGO ship; therefore; constellation
ARNO river; cartoonist
AROO indeed
ARTO prefix: bread
ASNO donkey: Sp.
ATEO Polynesian god
ATMO prefix: steam
ATWO asunder
AUTO prefix: same, self: drama: Sp.; (ride in) car
ALEP city
ALOP lopsided
APAP month
ASOP sopping
ATAP palm
ATIP expectant
ATOP at the peak
ABIR red powder
ACER tree
ACOR acidity
ADAR month
ADER Benjamite
AFAR far away; tribe
AGAR wood
AGER apparatus; field
AHER Benjamite
AHIR caste
AJAR opened
ALAR winglike; axillary
ALOR island
ALUR Negro
AMAR measures
AMER bitter
AMIR prince
AMOR love; Cupid; — patriae
AMUR river
ANER city
APAR armadillo
APER imitator; boar
ARAR tree
ASAR glacial ridges; eskers
ASER Jacob's son
ASIR Arab. principate
ASKR — and Embla; Norse Adam and Eve
ASOR lyre
ASUR war god
ATAR perfume; essence
AUER violinist
AVAR Caucasian language
AVER assert; asseverate
AZUR Cote d'— (Riviera); Hananiah's father
ABAS down: Fr.
ABCS first principles; alphabet
ACIS river; (Galatea's) lover
ACTS NT book
ACUS pin
ADES Hades
AGIS king
AIRS pretensions; side
ALAS sad cry
ALES city
ALMS charity
ALPS mountains
ALYS name: Alice
AMES author; city, college
AMIS friends: Fr.
AMOS prophet
ANAS duck
ANES once
ANIS fennel; birds
ANUS end of alimentary canal
APIS sacred bull (Ptah); bee; bull (Kipling)
APUS bird; constellation
ARAS river
ARES war; Mars; Zeus's, Hera's son; Eris' brother
ARIS molding edge
ARMS mil. science; ensigns; weapons; branches; limbs
ARTS skills; sciences; fine —; — and crafts
ATES sweetsop
ATIS monkshood; fruit
ATYS god (Cybele's lover)
AVES birds: Lat.
AVIS bird: Lat.
AVUS grandfather: Lat.
AXIS center line; spine; stem; deer; power alliance; partnership
AYES yes votes
ABET aid; incite
ABOT Mishnah
ABUT touch
ACHT eight: Ger.
ADAT law
ADIT entrance
AHET season (of inundation)
AINT contraction
AIRT guide; turn
AKUT ape man (Burroughs)
ALIT descended
AMIT headdress
ANAT sky god; med. term
ANET dill
APET goddess
ARNT contraction
AUNT parent's sister; tia: Sp.; tante: Fr., Ger.
AALU Hades; heaven
AARU Hades; heaven
ABOU father; deity
ACTU act: Lat.
ADDU skink; fiber; god
AGAU language
AINU Jap. aboriginal
AITU god; demon
AMMU ammunition
ANSU Korean apricot
ANTU rat poison
ANZU apricot
APSU primordial chaos
ARDU slave
ATIU one of Cook Islands
ATMU sun god
ATTU Aleut. island
AULU tree
AUSU tree
AUZU tree
AKOV measure
AZOV town; sea
ALOW below
ANEW over again
AROW in a line
AVOW declare; justify; confess
ABOX braced
AJAX hero (Telamon's son)
ALIX fem. name
AMEX Amer. Expeditionary Force
ANAX Castor, Pollux (Dioscuri)
APEX summit; crisis
ABBY Abigail
ABEY waive
ABLY deftly
ACHY painful
ADAY atomic attack date
ADDY Adeline
ADRY thirsty
AERY ethereal; nest
AFFY join
AHEY ho
AHOY call; ship —
AIRY breezy; light
AKEY weight
ALAY marble
ALEY city
ALGY Algernon; suffix: pain
ALKY alcohol
ALLY unite, confederate

AMOY island
ANAY fruit
ANCY suffix
ANDY Andrew
ARGY argue
ARMY multitude; force
ARRY cockney worker
ARTY artistic
ASHY gray, pale
ATRY lay to (naut.)
AWAY onward; hence; far; off; absent
AWNY bearded
AWRY distorted; perverse(ly)
AGAZ Indian
AHAZ king
AMOZ Isaiah's father

BABA nurse; title; cake
BAGA turnip
BAIA state; city; resort; bay
BAKA devil
BALA geol. epoch
BANA Titan
BARA measure
BATA child; servant
BAYA weaverbird; Bantu
BEGA measure
BEJA Nile nomad
BEKA weight
BELA jasmine; Benjamin's 1st son; Hungarian king
BEMA platform; altar; measure
BENA grass (vetiver)
BERA king of Sodom
BESA coin
BETA Greek B, 2; star; ray
BIGA two-horse chariot
BIJA kino tree
BINA Hindu guitar
BISA antelope
BIWA loquat
BIXA tree genus; achiote
BLAA bunk
BLEA bleak; livid
BOBA chicken snake
BOCA harbor mouth: Sp.
BOGA basslike fish
BOLA missile; majagua (tree)
BOMA Afr. stockade; post
BONA good: Lat.; — fide
BORA north wind; rite
BOSA Arab. drink
BOTA measure
BOZA Arab. drink

BREA resin; tree; asphalt
BUBA tropical sore
BUDA It. millet
BUKA dried leaves
BUNA synthetic rubber
BURA steppe blizzard
BADB goddess
BARB sharp point; fish; dog; mow; pigeon
BIBB mast's timber piece
BLAB tattle
BLEB blister; bubble
BLOB drop; daub; sound; fish; zero score
BLUB swell; puff out
BODB goddess
BOMB explosive; dispenser; A-; lead-lined container; buzz —
BOOB simpleton
BRAB palm
BROB support spike
BULB bud; tuber; corm; lamp; swell
BANC (judge's) bench
BLOC political unit; casting
BOSC best pear
BALD naked; — eagle
BAND strip; group; orchestra; range; tie; sash
BARD armor; poet; — of Avon (Shakespeare)
BAUD speed unit
BAWD procurer(ess)
BEAD globule; ball; drop; aim
BEID star
BEND turn; curve; flex; bow
BIND tie; protect; sew; cohere
BIOD animal life force
BIRD avian; flyer; fowl; shuttlecock; person; Blue —
BLED emitted or drew blood, sap; extorted
BOID of boas, anacondas
BOLD valiant; brazen; strong, heavy (type)
BOND adhesion; tie; covenant; paper; captivity: certificate
BORD -and-pillar (mining)

BOUD malt weevil
BRAD nail
BRED procreated; brought up
BUDD Lanny (Sinclair)
BUND embankment; league
BURD noble lady
BYRD explorer; Va. statesman
BABE baby; — Ruth; girl
BADE waited; asked; invited; commanded
BAKE dry; roast; biscuit
BALE woe; bundle
BANE woe; curse; poison
BARE expose(d); mere; Indian
BASE bottom; source; home; headquarters; found; diamond corner; ignoble
BATE diminish; tanner's bath; restrain
BAVE double silk thread
BEDE Adam (Eliot); the Venerable (monk)
BENE wild hog; well: It. & Lat.
BETE beast, silly: Fr.; — noire
BICE blue, green pigment
BIDE wait; tarry; dwell
BIKE bicycle
BILE liver secretion; choler
BINE (hop) stem
BISE cold wind; winter
BITE cut; pierce; grip; eat (into); sting; respond; snack
BIZE cold wind; winter
BLAE bleak
BLUE color; ocean; sky; sailor; sad; -blood; puritanical
BOCE colored fish
BODE presage; augur; omen
BOLE trunk; clay; brown
BONE study hard; plug; os
BORE pierce; hole; tire; dullard; tidal flow
BOSE test ground by sound
BOTE house repair; amends

BRAE slope
BREE (eye)brow
BRIE cheese
BUBE boy, jack: Ger.; Fernando Po Bantu
BUDE light; burner
BURE brown red-yellow
BUTE island; Scot. county; parson (Thackeray)
BYEE measure
BYKE nest of bees
BYRE cow house
BAFF strike; stroke
BEEF ox, steer, cow, boss; brawn; rage; complain(t)
BIFF (deal a) blow
BOOF stare; peach brandy
BUFF leather; coat; tan; ward off; polish; wheel; bare skin; enthusiast
BAGG heiress (Thackeray)
BANG beat; thump; hair; sardine; interjection
BENG devil (Gypsy)
BERG iceberg; mountain
BIGG barley
BING bed roll; sharp sound
BONG bell sound
BORG borough: Dan.
BRAG boast; game
BRIG sailing ship; prison
BUNG stop(per); throw
BURG (fortified) town
BACH live alone; composer
BASH smash; bruise
BATH tub; measure; spa; order
BETH Hebrew B, 2; Alcott heroine (Little Women)
BIKH aconite; poison
BINH weight
BISH aconite; poison
BLAH nonsense
BOOH exclamation
BOSH furnace part; nonsense (nothing: Turk.)
BOTH the two
BROH macaque; monkey
BRUH pig-tailed macaque
BUKH prate; talk
BURH (fortified) town
BUSH shrub; thicket; tail
BABI sect
BAHI fortune
BALI demon; monkey; offering; island
BANI coins
BARI hut; Negro; city
BELI myth. Brit. king
BENI Bolivian river; sesame
BERI Sudanese (Fulah); -beri (disease)
BIBI title: Lady, Mrs. (India)
BIMI orang-utang (Kipling)
BINI Nigerian
BIRI cheap cigarette
BITI blackwood
BNAI B'rith (Jewish Society)
BOII Celtic tribe
BONI African; Boschneger
BORI Lucrezia (singer)
BREI soft tissue
BUBI Fernando Po Bantu
BUGI Celebes Malay
BURI palm (fiber); talipot
BUZI Ezekiel's father
BENJ hemp; narcotic
BRAJ basha
BACK help; tub; past; retreat; kick-; dorsal, posterior; spine
BALK thwart; signal
BANK mound; bench; deposit; bird flock; Left, Right —; blood —; eye —
BARK peel; tan; cough
BASK luxuriate; warm
BEAK bill; nose; judge
BECK nod; bidding; dyeing vat; Pol., Ger. officer, statesman
BILK defraud
BISK soup; ice cream; red-yellow
BOCK beer; leather
BONK bar money (Dutch E.I.)
BOOK tome; volume; Bible; libretto; (bet) record; register; throw the —
BOSK thicket
BOWK steep; soak in lime
BUCK deer; fop; butt; male; Pearl (novelist); pass the —
BUKK prate; talk
BULK mass, volume; loom; -head (stall)
BUNK case; bed; nonsense
BUSK stir about; hasten; corset bone; Indian New Year
BAAL deity
BAEL thorny (fruit) tree
BAIL security; bond; set free; dip out; hoop
BALL game; confuse; dance; — bearing; good time; -point; Amer. sculptor
BAUL mendicant
BAWL cry; howl; — out (chide)
BEAL river mouth
BELL ringing cup; gong; time period; flower shape; helmet; Brontë pseudonym; — the cat; diving —
BHEL thorny (fruit) tree
BHIL low-caste Indian
BILL beak; weapon; law; poster; invoice; debt; nickname: William; — and coo; Sikes (Dickens)
BIRL revolve; spin
BOIL heat; bubble; agitation; abscess
BOLL (strip) plant pod
BOOL curved handle
BOWL basin; dish; (roll) ball
BUAL wine
BUHL inlaid decoration
BULL (bovine) male; stud; papal letter; optimist; Taurus; policeman; blunder; glib talk; -fight
BURL (pick) knot; Ives (actor)
BALM plant; soothe; — in Gilead
BARM yeast
BAUM Vicki (novelist); Oz creator; tree: Ger.; — marten
BEAM bar; timber; breadth; ray; smile; on the —;

broadcast
BERM (l)edge; road shoulder
BOOM hum; grow, push; beam
BRAM Abraham
BRIM rim; edge; swell
BROM Bones (Ichabod's rival)
BAIN bath: Fr.
BARN storehouse; stable
BAWN mud enclosure; white
BEAN plant; trifle; head; strike
BEEN charmer's clarinet; participle
BEHN herb; tree
BEIN good; fine
BENN seed
BERN Swiss capital
BIEN good, fine: Fr.; — aimee (well beloved)
BINN box; frame; crib
BION physiological individual (morphon)
BIRN clarinet socket
BONN city; Ger capital (Beethoven born)
BOON benefit, convivial
BORN given birth to; nee; quantum physicist
BRAN god-king; seed coat; chaff
BREN (machine) gun
BRIN fan plate; silk thread
BUNN cake
BURN (be on) fire; yearn; waste; speed; brand
BYON clayey earth
BAGO shrub
BAHO prayer stick
BARO big; prefix: weight
BENO alcoholic palm sap
BILO Balkan karst area
BINO alcoholic pine sap
BITO tree; poison; oil
BOBO owala tree; mullet
BODO Indo-Chin. language
BOGO Eritrean Hamite
BOHO grass; weep; shout
BOJO grass
BOKO evil spirit (Haiti)
BOLO knife; Rafflesia (plant); pacifist
BONO Johnny (Briton); cui —
BORO spring rice; Indian (Mirhana); — Budur (temple)
BOTO Indian; Voto
BOZO fellow
BRIO con — (with spirit)
BUBO horned —; eagle owl
BUFO toad genus; agua
BUTO serpent goddess; Leto
BUYO betel leaf; nut
BYGO pass by
BEEP radio sound
BLIP radar screen sign
BLUP air bubble sound
BUMP coincide; hit; swelling; — off (kill)
BURP belch; — gun
BAAR weight
BAER prizefighter, actor
BAHR sea; — El Azrak
BARR elephant's cry
BAUR joke
BEAR carry; yield; endure; relate; animal; Ursa; short-seller; pessimist
BEER beverage; ale; mead
BHAR Kolarian native
BIER litter; coffin
BIRR wind force; sound
BIUR Heb. commentary
BLUR obscure, stain
BOAR (wild) hog; male
BOER So. Afr. Dutch
BOHR Nils (Nobel physicist)
BOOR rustic; lout; Boer
BRER Rabbit (Harris; Uncle Remus)
BUHR whetstone
BURR (prickly) nut, knob; reamer; banyan tree; Aaron (statesman)
BAAS master
BAIS caste
BANS marriage notice
BAPS dancing master (Dickens)
BASS fish; fiber; lowest part; singer; clef (F), musical instrument, viol
BEAS Punjab river
BEES yeast
BESS nickname; Mrs. Truman
BIAS diagonal (incline); prejudice
BIOS life: animal, plant
BLAS Gil (Le Sage novel)
BOAS Franz (anthropologist)
BOIS wood: Fr.; wine (cognac); — de Boulogne
BORS king (Lancelot's uncle); Bohort (finder of Holy Grail)
BOSS knob; pad; stud; master; employer
BRAS arm: Fr.
BRES Elatha's beautiful son (Fomorian)
BUSS ship; kiss; calf
BAFT astern; cotton
BAHT coin
BAIT lure; harass; pest poison
BALT Lithuanian; Esth; Latvian; Lett
BANT diet
BART man's name
BAST (woody) fiber; goddess, phloem
BATT matted mass
BEAT strike; defeat; mystify, throb; scoop; field; sphere; — the Dutch
BEET vegetable; root; sugar —; — top
BELT strap; zone; beat
BENT crooked; inclination; grass
BERT nickname
BEST most (good); defeat
BHAT minstrel; scholar
BHUT Dravidian ghost
BINT daughter; woman
BITT naut. fastener
BKKT chess move
BLAT sheep's cry
BLET fruit decay
BLOT stain; mar; dry
BLUT blood: Ger.
BOAT (go by) ship; gravy-
BOLT sift; refine; shaft; lightning; bar; plant; rifle part; flight; refusal
BOOT shoe; wader; sheath; torture; recruit; compartment; tube; kick; to — (in

addition)
BORT finder of Holy Grail; impure diamond
BOTT clay plug; fly larva
BOUT contest; attack
BQKT chess move
BRAT apron; child
BRIT young herring
BROT bread: Ger.
BRUT dry: Fr.; Brit. king (New Troy, London)
BULT hill; ridge
BUNT sag (net, sail); (fungus) disease; butt (ball)
BURT butt; gore; dent
BUST bosom; statue; failure; break
BUTT cask; mound; target; ram; hinge; jut; halibut
BABU Hindu gentleman
BAJU jacket
BAKU hat; tree; rug; city; oil field
BALU wildcat
BARU tree
BEAU dandy; lover; — Brummell, — Nash
BENU holy bird (Ra-Osiris)
BLEU blue, rookie: Fr.
BLEW stormed; puffed; sounded
BLOW move (air); puff, pant; brag; expend; stroke; calamity; disappointment; — up (enlarge)
BOUW measure
BRAW handsome; fine
BREW beverage; plot; concoct
BROW forehead; high-, low-
BRIX scale (hydrometer)
BABY doll; indulge
BEVY company; flock
BHOY gang member; rowdy
BIZZ buzz
BLAY bleak
BODY structure; anatomy; bulk; corpse; group
BOGY specter; bugbear
BONY skeletal; osseous; Napoleon
BOXY boxlike; squarish
BRAY (donkey's) cry; grind; Mrs. Nickleby (Dickens)
BREY barnacle
BUOY float; sustain; life-; channel marker
BURY hide; inter; lose
BUSY (keep) active; in use
BUXY paymaster
BAEZ singer
BATZ coin
BOAZ Ruth's husband
BROZ Josip (Tito)
BUZZ hum; fly low (over); — bomb (V1, V2)

CABA measure
CACA goddess
CAJA box; bank
CANA Indian
CAPA cloak: Sp.
CARA dear (one): It.; Indian
CASA house, building: Sp., It.
CATA down; prefix: away
CAVA pepper shrub, root; gum resin; vein
CAZA Turkish district
CEBA tree; kapok source
CELA that: Fr.
CENA (Last) supper
CEPA onion
CERA prefix: horn, wax
CHAA tea
CHIA salvia beverage, oil
CIMA mountain peak: It.
CIVA Hindu deity
COCA cocaine source; shrub; leaf to chew; flavor
CODA finale; mark
COJA title; teacher
COLA tree; nut; drink
COMA torpor; blur; tuft
COPA tree; yaya; landmark
CORA gazelle; Indian; name; Persephone; Demeter's daughter
COTA P.I. fort
COXA hip (joint)
CREA linen, cotton fabric
CUBA W.I. island; Pearl of Antilles; measure
CUCA cocaine source
CUNA Panama Indian
CURA parish priest: Sp.
CUYA hardwood tree
CYMA cornice molding
CHAB bird
CHIB tongue; language
CHOB grain spike
CHUB fallfish; dace; chevin
CLUB bat; beat; society; suit (cards)
COBB Irvin S. (writer); Tyrus R. (baseball)
COMB crest; rake; scrape
CRAB crustacean; apple; sign; anger
CRIB manger; hut; bin; box; steal; "pony," "trot"
CURB restrain(t); sidewalk edge; market
CHAC -Mool (god); -chac (instr.)
CHIC stylish(ness)
CIRC circle; recess; corrie
CRIC lamp condensing ring
CROC harquebus support; crocodile
CAID alcalde
CARD comb; pasteboard; menu; playing —; calling —
CHAD lake; nation
CHUD Mongols; Vepse; Vote; Tavastian
CLAD dressed; plated
CLOD lump; soil; dolt
COAD cushion
COED girl student
COLD chill; frigid; indifferent; common —; coryza; — blood; — chisel
COND direct helmsman
CORD string; twine; ribbed fabric; measure (wood)
CURD coagulated milk
CADE cask; tree; pet; rebel
CAFE restaurant; coffee; -au-lait; society
CAGE confine; enclosure; elevator car; nor iron bars a —
CAKE bar; dough; harden
CALE Gypsy; cabbage
CAME arrived; lead rod; Indian
CANE stem; rattan; stick; walking —; sugar —; candy —
CAPE cloak; promontory;

— Cod, — Horn, — Good Hope
CARE grief; need; responsibility; anxiety; foster; relief organization
CASE event; fact; record; problem (medical, etc.); legal action; argument; grammar form; container, chest, box; queer phenomenon; inspect
CATE delicacy
CAVE cavern; — in (collapse); — canem (beware of dog)
CEDE yield; grant; transfer
CENE suffix: recent
CEPE boletus (edible fungus)
CERE wax; (wrap in a) waxed cloth; beak part
CETE marine mammals
CHEE weight
CINE movie: Sp.
CISE dice term: six
CITE summon; quote
CIVE chive garlic
CLEE redshank; bird
CLOE fem. name
CLUE hint; guide; thread
CODE body of law (Julian Justinian, Napoleon); signal system; cipher; — duello
COKE coal residue; fuel
COLE brassica genus; Porter (composer)
COME arrive; chance; fare
CONE geometric solid; pine fruit, strobile; peak; ice cream —; nose —
COPE vestment; cover; bend; contend
CORE heart; nucleus; gist
COSE (friendly) chat
COTE birdhouse; sheep shed; Coast: Fr. (d'Or; d'Azur)
COUE psychotherapist ("Day by day . . .")
COVE bay; recess; pass; chap; Gypsy
COXE Capt. (Scott)
COZE (friendly) chat
CREE Indian
CUBE square solid; 3rd power; die; plant poison
CUKE cucumber
CULE diminutive suffix
CURE heal; remedy; preserve; priest: Fr.
CUTE clever; attractive
CYKE cyclorama
CYLE brewing; beer; wort
CYME inflorescence
CYTE prefix: hollow vessel
CALF bovine, etc., young; fur; leather; skin; lower leg
CARF slit; notch
CHEF head (cook); — d'oeuvre
CLEF musical sign; roman a —; key
COIF defensive skullcap; make up (hair)
CUFF slap; manacle; sleeve end; miser; on the —
CANG wooden collar
CHUG pull; fish; (move with) vibration
CLOG block; sandal; stop; impede; choke
COAG dowel
CRAG cliff; neck
CRIG blow
CAPH star; letter
CASH money; exchange; hemlock
CECH Czech.
CHIH Chin. foot (measure)
COBH Irish port
COSH snug; happy; math. term
CUSH sorghum; cow; money; Ham's son; country
CADI judge
CAJI snapper
CALI Colombian city
CAXI snapper (fish)
CAZI Moslem judge
CHAI person
CIII 103; Trajan reign
CLII 152; Hadrian reign
COLI intestinal bacterium
CORI It. commune
CONI Carl, Gerty (Nobel winners)
CUBI measure
CVII 107; Trajan reign
CXII 112; Trajan reign
CALK tighten; stop; sleep; tool; copy
CARK trouble
CASK barrel; measure
CAUK (secure by a) tenon
CAWK bird's cry; mineral
CHEK Chin. foot (measure)
COAK tenon
COCK male fowl; vane; leader; tap; tee; hay pile; cog
CONK nose; head; decay; fail, hit
COOK chef; concoct; falsify; James (explorer)
CORK tree; bark; stop(per); brown; Irish city (Lee)
CUSK fish; burbot; eel
CALL summon; visit; cry; telephone; — girl; — money
CARL rustic; villain; Charles
CAUL basket; covering membrane
CAWL basket
CEIL overlay; line; ceiling
CELL cubicle; group; elec. jar; organism
CHAL man
CHIL cheer pine; kite (Kipling)
CHOL desolate plain; Mayan
CIEL ceiling; sky: Fr.
CIRL bunting; bird
COAL ember; fuel
COEL cuckoo
COIL curl; wind; twist
COLL embrace; hug; Vincent (gangster; "mad dog")
COOL chill; calm; unmoved
COWL hood; auto body front
CRAL hut; village
CULL pick out; assort
CURL coil; twist; hair lock
CAAM loom; heddles
CALM quiet; hold
CHAM tribe; title; bite
CHUM friend; scrap fish
CLAM mollusk; hush
CLEM riot; suffer hunger;

nickname
CLIM — of the Clough (archer outlaw)
CLUM clutch roughly
CLYM — of the Clough (archer outlaw)
COOM coal dust; refuse
CORM bulblike stem (crocus)
CRAM press; stuff; study
CROM Cruaich (Irish idol)
CULM grass stem; coal dust; shoal water deposit
CAEN city
CAGN mantis; deity
CAIN tribute; (Abel's) slayer; mark of —
CARN stone heap
CERN decide
CHAN resthouse; lord; title
CHEN snow goose
CHIN lower jaw; chatter; weight; dynasty; Burmese
CHUN Chin. pottery
CION plant shoot
CLAN clique; family; group
COAN pert. to Cos Island
COEN Jan (empire builder)
COIN money; mint; invent; corner
CONN direct helmsman
COON animal; fur; sly man
CORN grain; ear, kernel; callus; whisky; preserve; granulate(d); clavus; banality; red-yellow
COYN corner(stone)
CRAN bird; measure
CRIN heavy silk
CUON wild dog (dhole)
CYAN green-blue
CYON wild dog (dhole)
CABO Yubi
CACO bandit
CALO Gypsy
CANO canal: Sp.
CARO dear (one): It.; Caroline
CASO Dodecanese Island
CATO the Censor (Roman statesman); foe of Carthage
CAYO island, reef: Sp.
CERO mackerel
CETO prefix: whale
CHAO measure
CIPO liana
CITO quickly, soon: It.
CIXO Ecuador Indian
CLEO queen (Cleopatra)
CLIO history Muse; mollusk
COCO palm; nut; grass
CODO measure
COHO silver salmon
COMO lake, resort (Italy)
COSO open space: Sp.
COTO bark; stomachic
COYO avocado; chinin
CALP limestone
CAMP tent(s); town; stay; boot —
CAPP Al, cartoonist (Abner, Dogpatch)
CARP fish; complain
CAUP tribute Scot.
CHAP fellow; crack; jaw
CHIP fragment; cut; hew
CHOP cut; crack; eat; barter; jaw
CLAP rap; applaud; flatten
CLIP clasp; cut(ting); gait
CLOP limp; hobble
CLOP pasture; Irish acre
COOP pen; jail; confine; coöperative
COUP blow; master stroke
CRAP dregs; money; dice cast (crabs)
CROP craw; harvest; trim
CUSP (crescent) point; tooth edge
CINQ five: Fr.
CARR pool
CHAR trout; burn; sandbank; -woman
CHER dear: Fr.
CHIR pheasant; pine
CHOR thief; steal (Gypsy)
CHUR Swiss canton
COIR coconut fiber
CUIR leather; dorado
CURR to murmur (as owlet)
CZAR emperor; dictator
CASS treasure; Timberlane (Lewis); Squire (Eliot)
CATS — cradle
CENS payment due
CESS tax; luck
CITS citizens; mufti
COOS Bay (laurel); Indian
COSS measure
COUS cowlike
CRIS dagger; stab
CRUS leglike part; shank
CUSS curse; person
CANT angle; change course; log; tilt; whine; jargon; be unable
CART wagon; transport
CAST throw; project; shed; deposit; form; found; actors; (assign) roles
CELT Irish, Scot, Welsh, Breton; chisel
CENT coin; penny; game
CEST girdle; belt (Venus)
CHAT talk; bird; spike
CHIT child; sprout; memo; voucher; mind
CHUT nonsense!
CHEW masticate; ruminate; — the cud; — the rag
CIST chest; roofed pit
CLAT mess; chatter
CLOT mass; coagulate
CNUT king; son of Magnus
COAT fur; skin; cover; — of arms
COLT young horse; pistol; — .45
COOT rail; surf duck; dolt
COPT Egypt. Christian
CULT sect; worship system
CURT short; concise
CYST box; abnormal sac
CAJU fruit; mahogany
CEBU Visayan Island
CHOU cabbage, darling: Fr.; Chin dynasty; En Lai (statesman)
CCIV 204; Septimus Severus reign
CHIV knife
CLIV 254; Aemilianus reign
CMIV 904
CXIV 114; Trajan reign
CHAW masticate
CHOW food; dog
CLAW nail; ungula; chela; scratch; hammer
CLEW yarn ball; sail loop; cocoon; hint
CLOW sluice; floodgate
CRAW gullet; stomach
CREW company; gang; -cut
CROW raven; corvine;

black; Indian; Jim —; -bar
CALX residue; heel: Lat.
CCIX 209; Septimus Severus reign
CEYX Halcyone's husband
CLIX 159; Antoninus Pius reign
CMIX 909
COAX flatter; cajole
COIX grass; Job's-tears
CRAX curassow (bird)
CREX corn crake (bird)
CRUX (Southern) Cross; crucial point
CXIX 119; Hadrian reign
CADY golf boy
CAGY shrewd
CAKY crusty
CASY ex-preacher (Steinbeck)
CAVY rodent; guinea pig; stray animal(s)
CAZY Moslem judge
CHAY red dye plant
CHOY red dye root
CITY urban place
CLAY earth; ceramic; pipe; - pigeon; color; Henry, statesman
CLOY glut; surfeit
CODY William (Buffalo Bill)
COKY grimed; drug addict
COLY long-tailed bird
CONY rabbit; daman; pika
COPY duplicate; mimic; follow; test
COSY snug; teapot cover
COTY Fr. statesman; cosmetics
COZY snug; teapot cover
CUVY sea girdles; kelp
CHEZ at home of, with: Fr.

DADA father; cult
DAMA gazelle
DANA goddess; author; editor; lake
DATA facts
DAZA Negro-Berber
DECA prefix: ten
DEHA body (theosophy)
DEJA already: Fr.
DEPA measure
DERA suffix; neck types
DEVA deity (Indra); demon
DEWA deity (Indra); demon
DIKA bread; fat; oil
DISA showiest orchid
DITA tree; bark; upas
DIVA prima donna; blue
DOLA weight
DONA lady; sapek (coin)
DOPA chemical (pigment test)
DORA Mrs. David Copperfield
DOSA sheik's ritual ride; hatred
DOXA religious stanzas
DRAA measure
DUMA Russ. parliament
DURA — mater (spinal membrane)
DYNA prefix: power
DAUB plaster; besmear
DIEB jackal
DOAB tract
DOOB Bermuda grass
DOUB Bermuda grass
DRAB dull; box; wench; cloth; drug
DRIB drop; a little
DRUB (beat with) stick
DUAB tract
DUBB Syrian bear; lizard
DUMB mute; stupid; — waiter; deaf and —
DISC disk; record; — jockey
DOUC variegated monkey
DARD language group
DAUD dad
DEAD deceased; entire; absolute(ly); — reckoning
DEED act; property transfer
DIAD pair
DODD cut off (wool)
DOWD slovenly woman
DRED — Scott (slave)
DUAD pair
DYAD pair
DACE fish
DADE support
DALE valley; share; trough
DAME woman; title; — aux Camelias
DANE Scandinavian; great — (dog); Hamlet
DARE venture; defy; fish; 1st Amer. child (Virginia)
DATE fruit; tree; brown; (make) appointment
DAVE David
DAYE printer (Bay Psalm Book)
DAZE stupefy; mica
DELE omit; erase
DEME Greek commune
DENE measure; dune; Indian
DERE — Mable (Streeter book)
DICE (cut into) cubes; gamble; gaming implements
DIKE levee; ditch; dig; goddess (Horae)
DIME coin; - novel
DINE eat; have dinner
DIRE evil; fatal; extreme
DITE indite; indict
DIVE plunge; duck; low resort; - bomb(er)
DOBE brick (house)
DOCE Brazil river
DODE nickname: Theodore
DOGE Venice, Genoa ruler
DOLE ration; (relief) alms; deal (out)
DOME edifice; cupola; roof
DONE agreed; exhausted
DOPE drug; information; guess; nitwit
DORE bullion; gold; pike; Paul Gustave (Fr. artist)
DOSE portion; (give) medicine
DOTE love to excess; drivel; timber rot
DOVE pigeon; blue, gray; Columba; plunged
DOZE drowse; timber rot
DREE endure; tedious
DUCE chief: It.; Mussolini
DUDE dandy; fop; city fellow; - ranch
DUNE sandhill; twine color
DUPE trick(ed one); copy
DUSE incubus; Eleanora (actress)
DYCE thus!: naut. command
DYKE levee; checkers opening
DYNE unit of force
DAFF put aside
DEAF unhearing; inattentive; — and dumb, — mute
DELF quarry; pottery;

blue
DOFF put off; remove
DUFF pudding; cheat
DAGG pistol
DANG curse (damn)
DING thump; sound; urge
DOEG Saul's herdsman; poet's nickname; Indian
DONG sound; weight; ding-
DRAG haul; harrow; obstacle; puff; auto race
DREG lees; residue
DRUG medicine; dope; — on the market; — addict
DUNG excrement; fertilize(r); weight
DAGH hill
DASH sprint; smash; small portion
DICH you: Ger.
DISH receptacle; serve
DOTH does
DRAH measure
DALI tree; offering; Salvador —
DARI grain sorghum; carpet
DASI concubine
DECI prefix: tenth
DEFI challenge; defiance
DEMI prefix: half
DESI jute; Arnaz
DEVI goddess; Siva's wife (Shakti); title: Mrs., Lady
DHAI midwife
DIVI divine ones
DIXI I have spoken: Lat.
DOLI weights
DONI fishing boat
DREI three: Ger.
DANK moist; rank
DARK unlighted; wicked; dismal
DAUK relay post
DAWK relay transport; mail
DECK ship floor; pack, cards; array; adorn
DESK table; lectern; department
DHAK tree
DICK Richard; whip; lad; detective; Whittington (London mayor)
DINK small boat; cut out
DIRK dagger; Theodoric
DISK plate; harrow; puck
DOCK weed; rumex; (cur)tail; pier
DOOK wooden brick; demon
DUCK bird; webfoot; wild fowl; canvas; pet; plunge; evade; — soup; vehicle
DUNK dip into; immerse
DUSK twilight; gloom
DYAK Bornean
DYCK Anthony Van (painter)
DAIL legislature; — Eireann
DALL sheep
DEAL bargain; transaction; unfinished wood; apportion(ment); policy: New —, Fair —
DEIL devil; -'s-bit (plant)
DELL valley; dingle; wench
DEUL Hindu temple
DHAL split pea, lentil
DIAL plate; face; call; sun-
DILL flavoring herb; pickle
DIOL chem. compound; suffix
DOLL plaything; puppet; dress up; girl
DOWL feathery down
DUAL double
DUEL combat; meeting
DULL blunt(ed); dismal; inert; tedious; Shaks. character
DAWM coin
DEEM consider; judge
DERM prefix, suffix: skin layer
DEUM Te — (hymn)
DIEM day: Lat.; per —
DOOM (last) judgment; fate; condemn
DORM dormitory; sleep
DOUM palm
DRAM measure; drink
DRUM spool; instrument: tympanum; beat
DUIM measure
DAIN Patusan chief (Conrad); — Curse (Hammett); measure
DAMN curse; — the torpedoes
DARN mend; interjection
DAUN stage (geol. period)
DAWN daybreak; Eos; Aurora; red
DEAN clergyman; educator; oldest member, doyen
DEIN your(s): Ger.
DHAN wealth; loan
DIAN reveille
DION lord in Winter's Tale
DOMN Rumanian lord
DOON tree (varnish resin)
DORN thornback ray
DOWN to below; reduce; defeat; feathers; eider-; dejected
DRIN Balkan river
DRUN road (Gypsy)
DUAN canto; poem
DUIN demons
DURN gatepost
DADO wall part; groove
DAGO tribe
DATO tribal chief
DEDO measure
DEMO prefix: populace
DHAO knife (Burma)
DIDO trick; caper; Carthage queen, Aeneas' beloved
DILO poon tree
DINO prefix: terrible
DODO extinct bird; reactionary
DOKO Afr. pygmy
DOTO sea slug genus
DUCO pyroxylin lacquer
DURO Sp. peso; dollar
DAMP moist(ure); depress
DEEP profound; extensive; ocean
DOPP diamond cup
DORP hamlet; city (So. Afr.)
DOUP weaver's thread
DRAP cloth
DRIP let fall
DROP globule; fall; discard; minim; trap door; die; pendant
DUMP unload; junkyard; thud; mean place; holey dollar
DAER re borrowed stock
DARR bird
DAUR Manchu
DEAR costly; loved; loved one
DEER ruminant; cervine;

— Park (Buddha site)
DHAR state; town (India)
DHER mound; land share
DIER one moribund
DOER performer; agent
DOOR portal; entrance; Open - policy
DORR Rebellion (R.I.)
DOUR sullen; gloomy
DUAR mountain pass
DUHR star
DURR grain sorghum
DYER tinter; Mary, Quaker martyr
DAIS platform
DANS in: Fr.
DASS Durga, Ram (twins, Kipling)
DAYS by day
DEBS Eugene (socialist)
DENS tooth: Lat.
DEUS god: Lat.; — ex machina
DIBS juice: grape, date
DIES day(s): Lat.; — Irae; Cong. committee
DIOS God: Sp.
DISS reed grass
DOES performs
DOGS scaup duck
DOSS bed; sleep; — house
DUDS clothes; failures
DUNS dull; stupid
DUOS duets
DYAS Permian (geol. period)
DAFT foolish; giddy
DART missile; fish; seam; run
DEBT fault; liability; obligation
DEFT skillful; trim
DENT depress(ion); notch
DIET fare; food regimen; parliament
DINT blow; force; notch
DIRT muck; earth; gossip; do one —; — cheap
DITT close up; obstruct
DOAT drivel; be silly, overfond; wood rot
DOIT coin; whit; bit
DOLT dunce; ignoramus
DONT contraction; prohibition
DOST (you) do: archaic
DRAT oath
DUAT Hades
DUCT tube; vessel; pipe
DUET music for two
DUIT Chibchan Indian; coin
DUNT split (ceramics)
DUST powdered matter; rubbish; clean; dust to —; gold —
DADU saint
DANU goddess
DATU tribal chief
DEGU rodent (Octodon)
DETU eclipse demon (Rahu)
DIAU Indian
DIEU god: Fr. mon —:
DUKU lanseh tree fruit
DAUW zebra
DHAW billhook
DHOW Arab. sailboat
DRAW drag; attract; gain; infer; extract; sketch; undecided contest
DREW sketched; pulled
DEUX two: Fr.
DAVY David; lamp; affidavit; Jones' locker
DAZY confused
DDAY operation start
DEFY challenge; dare
DEMY coin; scholar; paper size
DENY refuse; contradict
DEWY moist; refreshing
DIXY camp pot
DOBY brick (house)
DOGY calf; duck
DOMY domelike
DOPY sluggish
DORY John — (fish); boat
DOTY discolored by rot
DOXY doctrine; hussy
DOZY drowsy; decayed; doty
DRAY cart; squirrel's nest; horse
DREY squirrel's nest
DUFY Fr. artist
DULY properly; timely
DUNY having many dunes
DUTY obligation; task; tax
DAEZ daze
DIAZ Bartholomeu (Port. navigator)

EABA measure
ECCA geol. period (Karroo)
EDDA Norse epic
EDEA reproduction organs
EDNA female name; Ferber, novelist
EGBA Negro; Yoruba
EGMA enigma
EKKA carriage
ELBA Napoleon's exile isle
ELIA Charles Lamb; essayist
ELLA Eleanor; she: Sp.; fem. suffix
ELSA — of Brabant (Lohengrin's bride)
EMMA letter M; name; Austen novel; Bovary (Flaubert)
ENNA Sicilian resort
EPHA Hebrew dry measure
ERDA earth goddess; Wagner role
ERIA silk(worm)
ERMA Ermengarde
ERRA — Pater (almanac)
ERUA mother goddess
ESCA apoplexy (plant disease)
ESTA this: Sp.
ETNA stove; volcano
ETTA Henrietta; Harriet
EVEA madder (tree); ipecac
EYRA wild cat
EZBA measure
EZRA prophet; OT book
EPIC heroic poem
ERIC male name; Viking; the Red
ERUC cordage fiber
EBED Baal's father
ECAD modified organism
EFOD priestly garb; image
EGAD oath
EHUD judge of Israel
EILD barren; milkless
ELOD alleged force
EMYD terrapin
ENID fem. name; Geraint's wife; city
EYED looked at; ogled
EASE repose; comfort; moderate; facilitate
EAVE roof edge
EBOE tree; oil; Negrito
ECCE lo: Lat.; — homo
EDGE brink; sharpness; goad; advantage; — on
EIDE ideas; forms

EINE one: Ger.
EIRE Ireland; Erin
ELBE river
ELLE measure; she: Fr.
ELSE other(wise); besides
ENCE suffix
ENNE prefix: nine; fem. suffix
ENSE suffix
ENTE grafted (Her.); being: Sp.
EPEE fencing sword
ERIE Iroquoian; lake; city
ERNE sea eagle
ERSE Irish; Gaelic
ESCE suffix: begin to be
ESNE slave
ESSE existence; to be: Lat.
ESTE It. family; this: Sp.
ETRE exist; be: Fr.; raison d'—
ETTE suffix: fem.
EUGE bravo!
EVOE bacchanals' wild cry; Punch editor
EYRE Jane (Bronte heroine); circuit (court)
ELEF letter
ENIF star
EACH every(one)
ELAH king
ESTH Balt; Estonian (Tallinn man)
ETAH Eskimo settlement; town
ETCH eat into; engrave
EYAH nurse; sign
EKOI Bantu
ELOI Eli; God
ENKI Babylonian god
EPHI measure
EQUI prefix: equal, same
ETUI (vanity) case; box
EFIK Negro
ESEK Isaac's well
EARL nobleman; court; name
EBAL Mount (Joshua's altar)
EDEL noble: Ger.
EGAL equal: Fr.
EGIL Volund's (Wayland's) brother
EGOL antiseptic
ELUL month
EMIL man's name
EMOL rock salt
ENOL chem. suffix
ERAL epochal
ETAL and others: Lat.
EVIL bad; sinful; injury; disease
EZEL juniper tree
EDAM city; cheese
EDOM Esau's country; Idumaea
EJAM Bantu
ELAM kingdom
ELIM Bib. oasis
EMIM Moabites; giants
ENAM gift; land grant
ETYM Moabites, giants; abbr.: word sources
EXAM interrogation; test
EARN gain; win; deserve
EBEN Ebenezer
EBON ebony; black
EDEN paradise; West of Nod
EGAN horse (Kipling)
ELAN dash; ardor
ELON Esau's father-in-law; college (N.C.)
ENAN Prince of Naphtali
ENIN blue grape pigment
ENON Paris's wife (nymph); John the Baptist site
EOAN pert. to east; dawn
EOIN John; Sean
ERAN Ephraim's grandson
ERIN Eire; Ireland
ETON school, college; collar; jacket; playing fields of —
EVAN name (Welsh)
EVEN evening; level; fair(ly); equal(ly), moderate, just; not odd; flush
EWAN name (Welsh)
EXON Exeter man
EZAN prayer call
EBRO Sp. river
ECHO Narcissus's nymph; repeat; response. fruit tree (gingko)
ECTO prefix: outside
EDDO taro root
EGBO secret society (Ogboni)
EJOO palm; fiber
ENDO prefix: within
ENTO prefix: inner
ENYO war goddess
ERGO hence; prefix: work
ESOP fable writer
EBER Hebrew ancestor
EBUR ivory: Lat.
EDAR Bib. site
EDER river
EGER river
EKER water cress
EMER Cuchulainn's wife (ideal womanhood)
EMIR ruler; title
ERER sooner
ESER weight
EUER your(s): Ger.
EVER always; at any time
EWER pitcher; udder
EYER needle maker
EADS engineer; bridge
EATS food; consumes
EGGS ova; — and bacon, ham; — and butter (flowers)
EGIS protection; patronage; symbol of: Zeus, Athena, shield
ELIS Greek city state
EMYS tortoise
ENNS river
ENOS Seth's son, Adam's grandson (905 years old); taken by God
EPOS epic poetry; events
ERIS goddess of discord, Ares' sister
EROS (god of) love; Cupid; asteroid; Antony's friend
ESUS Gaulish god (Mars)
ETES (you) are: Fr.
EXES letters; expenses
EYAS nestling
EAST direction; Asia; Orient
ECHT genuine: Ger.
EDIT correct; redact; blue-pencil
EMIT eject; issue; voice
EMPT empty
ERAT was: Lat.; quod — demonstrandum (Q.E.D.)
ERST former; first
ETAT state: Fr.; L'— c'est moi!
EVAT eft
EVET eft; newt
EXIT depart(ure); die
EYOT islet
ECRU beige; unbleached
EHEU alas
EMEU bird (ostrichlike)
ENZU moon god (Sin)
ESAU Isaac's, Rebecca's son; Jacob's twin; hairy; red, Edom
ENOW enough

EAUX waters: Fr.
ERYX sand snake
ESOX fish (pike, pickerel, muskellunge)
EASY simple; calm; soft; — Street
EDDY whirlpool; Mary Morse (Baker) —: Christian Science
EDGY sharp; snappish
EELY wriggling; slippery
EENY — meeny, miny, mo
EERY weird; uncanny; timid
EGGY egg-stained; yolky
ELMY rich in elms
EMMY TV award; nickname
ENVY covet; grudge; 7th deadly sin
EPPY Euphemia
ESAY Isaiah
ESPY behold; detect; meteorologist
EWRY linen storeroom
EYEY having holes
EYRY bird's nest

FABA bean; vetch
FALA refrain; dog
FAMA rumor
FANA Sufistic concept
FATA — Morgana (fairy, mirage)
FLEA insect; puce; — market
FORA meeting places; courts
FREA Frigg; Odin's wife; goddess
FRIA Frigg (Odin's wife)
FUGA fugue: It.
FULA Sudanese
FLOB move clumsily
FLUB blunder; botch
FORB non-grassy herb
FRAB worry
FRIB dirty short wool
FISC exchequer
FLOC flock(y mass); shreds
FUSC dusky; somber
FARD face paint; date
FEED nourish; gratify; graze; fodder
FELD field: Ger.
FEND keep off; parry
FEOD feudal estate
FEUD strife; vendetta; fee
FIND discover(y); (re)gain
FLED ran away; shunned
FOLD plait; envelop; fail; quit; flock
FOND basis; fount; loving
FOOD nutriment; victuals
FORD crossing shallow; Henry (automobile); Shaks. character
FOUD district magistrate
FRED nickname
FUAD Arab king
FUND supply; finance; money; sinking —
FYRD old English army
FACE surface; oppose; line
FADE weaken; flat; dissolve
FAKE loop; cheat; sham
FAME reputation
FANE temple
FARE passenger; price; happen; food; travel
FATE destiny (goddess); end; kismet
FAZE disturb
FEKE trick device
FEME wife; tribunal
FETE festival; regale
FIDE entrust; — et amore
FIFE flute; checkers opening
FILE tool; rasp; smooth; march; column; folder; arrange
FINE end; superior; thin; keen; well; (set) penalty; geil —, derb — (Irish clans)
FIRE combustion; ardor; discharge
FIVE number; basketball team; card
FIXE prix —
FLEE run away; shun
FLOE floating ice
FLUE net; lint; barb; air passage; pipe
FOIE liver: Fr.; — gras (pate)
FORE front; prior; golf cry
FREE independent; immune; rid; exempt; — and easy; — lance, port, trade, style
FROE cleaver; steel wedge
FUME smoke; fit; rage
FUSE detonator; melt; unite
FUTE Eskimo curlew
FUYE Jap. flute
FUZE detonator; melt; unite
FYKE fish bag net
FIEF feudal estate
FANG tooth; measure; Dickens character
FLAG flower; standard; stone; signal; limp; reduce, dwindle
FLOG whip
FOGG Phileas (Verne)
FONG Ewe-speaking Negro
FROG amphibian; hoarseness; loop; rail device
FRUG modern dance
FUNG Sennar Negroid
FASH rough edges; vex
FISH piscine; angle; probe; search; tin — (torpedo)
FOCH Ferdinand (Fr. marshal; WW I commander)
FAVI tiles; flagstones
FIJI islands (Lau, Yasawa)
FILI learned poet
FOCI center points
FUCI rockweeds; algae
FUJI wisteria; cherry; volcano
FUNJ Sennar Negroid
FEAK twitch; wipe
FECK amount
FERK measure
FINK finch; derb; informer; strikebreaker
FISK exchequer; Jim (speculator); tire
FLAK antiaircraft
FOLK people; — ways, laws, song, dance
FORK implement (pronged); tuner; place of divergence
FULK unfair shove (marbles)
FUNK fear; coward; Casimir (vitamins) Isaac (lexicographer); — & Wagnalls
FAIL fall short; err
FALL descend; ruin;

autumn; — of Man
FARL cake (part)
FEAL conceal
FEEL sense; test; suffer
FEIL comfortable; neat
FELL skin; cut, sew (down); savage
FILL pack; complete; glut; — the bill
FOAL colt; equine young
FOIL balk; defeat; sword; leaf; sheet
FOOL dolt; jester; trick
FOUL rotten; poor; illegal; invalid
FOWL poultry; cock; hen
FUEL combustible matter
FULL filled; replete; quite; — dress; — house
FURL roll up (sail, flag)
FAAM tea; leaves
FARM till; land; — out; club
FILM skin; coating; haze; photograph; picture
FIRM fixed; solid; company
FLAM trick; drum beat
FLEM Fleming; Belgian
FOAM froth; rage; rubber
FORM shape; mold; fashion; school grade
FRAM spear
FRIM juicy; soluble
FROM out of
FAIN glad; eager
FAMN measure
FAON fawn color
FAUN deity; satyr
FAVN measure
FAWN deer; cringe; toady; brown
FERN seedless plant
FINN man of Finland, Helsinki; Ugric; Mickey - (KO drops); Huckleberry — (Twain novel)
FIRN granular snow(field)
FLAN tart; disk; net
FOHN warm dry wind
FADO tune
FANO cloth; cape
FARO card game; Pharaoh
FICO trifle
FIDO fog evaporation; dog's name
FIFO inventory method
FILO silk thread
FOGO stench
FONO Samoan council
FLAP slap; leaf; sway; -jack
FLIP toss; tap; drink; hop
FLOP slump down; flap; change; fail(ure); bed; sleep
FRAP tighten
FAIR pleasing; ample; just; bazaar; — and square; — deal
FEAR fright; doubt
FOUR number; card; boat
FASS measure
FEES charges; tips
FEIS convention; — of Tara
FELS Eastern coin
FESS broad band (Her.); confess
FILS son: Fr.; Dumas (Camille); Irak coin
FIPS Martin Chuzzlewit
FONS fount; source
FOSS canal; ditch; moat
FUSS tumult; bustle; -budget
FACT deed; reality
FAIT fact; - accompli
FAST not eat; fixed(ly); quick(ly); wild; — and loose
FAUT comme il — (proper): Fr.
FEAT deed; accomplishment
FEET measures
FELT pressed fibers; hat; sensed
FENT slit; cleft
FEST festive gathering
FIAT sanction; edict; money; automobile (It.)
FIOT Congo tribe
FIST grasp; effort; tightwad
FLAT level; (make) insipid; dull; wholly; — tire
FLIT flutter; move
FLOT lateral ore deposit
FONT basin; spring; stoup; type
FOOT pedal part; base; dance; trip; skip; pay; add
FORT stronghold; trading post; dun
FRAT fraternity
FRET gnaw; vex; worry; embroider; ridge; ornament
FRIT fuse; fried: Fr.; waste
FROT rub; chafe
FUNT weight; Allen (TV)
FUST pilaster; smell stale
FERU bast fiber
FRAU Mrs. wife, Mme., woman: Ger.
FUGU poisonous fish
FLAW crack; defect; wind
FLEW aviated; winged
FLOW gush; stream; flux; roll; ebb and —
FROW Dutch woman; cleaver
FAEX dregs
FALX weapon; — cerebri (brain fold)
FLAX plant; fiber; thrash
FLEX bend
FLIX down; fur; flax
FLUX flow; change; melt
FACY fresh
FADY weakening
FAKY spurious
FLAY (strip off) skin
FLEY fright(en)
FOGY dull, bigoted man
FOXY wily; brown; rank; sour
FRAY contest; tumult; wear off
FREY god (Njorth's son, Gerth's husband)
FUMY vaporous smoky
FURY rage; avenging spirit; Erinys, Fate, Parca (Atropos)
FIZZ hissing sound; drink
FRIZ curl; crisp; wig
FUZZ fine fibers; police

GAEA goddess; Titans' mother
GAIA goddess
GALA festival; tribe
GAMA Vasco da — (navigator); grass
GAPA guided missile
GARA coin
GATA nurse shark
GAZA Israel (Philistine) seaport; Mozambique district; eyeless

in — (Samson)
GEBA Jonathan's victory site
GENA cheek; beak part
GERA city
GETA Jap. wooden clogs
GIGA medieval fiddle
GILA — monster; lizard; Ariz. river
GITA Bhagavad —; Indian scriptures (yoga)
GIZA site: pyramids, Sphinx
GJOA ship (Northwest Passage; Amundsen)
GLIA neuroglia (nerve tissue)
GOLA storeroom; caste; cyma
GOMA Bantu (Wagoma)
GONA New Guinea victory
GORA musical instrument
GOYA Sp. painter; — red
GUFA round boat
GUHA Bantu
GULA upper throat; goddess (Ninurta's consort)
GUNA Sankhya term
GAMB leg
GARB apparel; array
GAUB persimmon (astringent)
GERB sheaf; firework
GLIB flippant, smooth(ly)
GLUB make gulping sound
GRAB grasp; capture; game
GRUB larva; food; dig(ger)
GUIB harnessed antelope
GAUD ornament; bead
GAWD ornament; bead
GELD castrate; prune; tax
GERD Frey's wife
GILD lay gold on; adorn; — the lily; trade society
GIRD encircle; clothe; brace
GLAD pleased
GLED kite; buzzard
GOAD rod; decoy; urge
GOLD metal; element; — dust, medal
GOND Dravidian Indian
GOOD able; brave; sound; profit; happiness; welfare; benefit
GRAD centesimal unit
GRID grating
GUAD tree
GABE taro
GADE fish; composer
GAGE pledge; fruit; gauge; general; governor
GALE storm, wind
GAME amusement; quarry; resolute; lame
GANE yawn
GAPE yawn; stare; gap
GARE wool; station: Fr.; beware: Fr.
GATE entrance; pass; judgment; money
GAUE German regions
GAVE donated
GAZE stare; wonder
GENE hereditary factor; chromosome part; nickname
GERE Odin's wolf
GHEE butter
GIBE scoff; jeer; agree
GIDE Andre (author)
GITE shelter: Fr.; mad
GIVE bestow; yield; grant
GLUE adhesive; stick
GONE departed; enamored; lost; germ cell
GORE stab; blood; triangular insert
GRUE shiver; shudder
GULE of August (Lamma's Day)
GUZE red roundel (Her.)
GYBE jibe; scoff; agree
GYLE brewing; wort; vat
GYNE prefix: female
GYRE turn; ring; vortex
GYVE fetter; shackle
GAFF spear; ordeal; hoax
GOAF grain; rick
GOFF clown; fool
GOLF game; blood-red; — links
GOOF dolt; blunder
GRAF nobleman: Ger.; — Spee (Zeppelin)
GUFF humbug; chaff
GULF bay; chasm; eddy
GANG crew; associate; rock
GHEG Albanian
GLUG sound of liquids
GONG bell; tom-tom
GRIG dwarf; cricket; fowl
GROG liquor (with water)
GUEG Albanian
GASH (make) incision
GATH Philistine city
GISH Moroccan public land; Lillian, Dorothy (actresses)
GOGH Vincent van — (painter)
GOSH oath; -awful
GOTH Teuton (Theodoric, Alaric); barbarian; Ostro-; Visi-
GUSH flow; spout; be effusive
GABI taro
GALI abuse
GAZI warrior; title
GERI Odin's wolf
GOAI shrub
GOBI Mongolian desert
GOLI musket ball; pill
GUMI shrub, flower, fruit
GUTI Sumer settler; Kurd
GYRI brain ridges
GUNJ granary; market
GAWK lout; stare
GEEK carnival wild man
GINK eccentric one
GOOK trash; ooze; native
GOWK simpleton; fool
GUNK jilt; hoax
GAAL brewing
GAEL Celt; Irishman
GAGL sweet gale
GAIL Abigail; brewing
GALL bile; venom; wound; chafe; swelling; impudence
GAOL prison
GAUL Celt, Frenchman; France
GEAL pert. to earth
GILL measure; brook; breathing organ; wattle; coin; lass
GIRL young female; maid; Gibson —; — Friday; — of the Golden West; chorus —
GOAL purpose; objective; score
GOEL reclaimer; avenger
GOLL Irish hero (Fenian)
GOUL monster; grave robber
GOWL gad; defile; howl; monster
GULL bird; cheat; dupe
GUNL gunwale
GARM Hel's dog
GAUM attention
GERM bud; seed; microbe

GEUM plant (astringent)
GLIM light; eye
GLOM watch; steal
GLUM moody; sullen
GOOM cultivation method
GRAM sword; plant; weight; —'s method; grandma
GRIM ruthless; ghastly
GRUM morose; guttural
GUAM Mariana Island
GAIN reach; earn; profit; notch
GAON Jewish title
GARN yarn; go on
GAWN gallon; tub
GEAN cherry
GEIN glucoside (Geum urbanum)
GEON paradise river; Jerusalem spring
GIAN -Carlo (Menotti)
GLEN rival
GMAN U.S. police agent
GOAN pert. to Goa
GOON thug; strikebreaker
GOWN dress; toga; robe
GRAN weight; grandma
GRIN smile
GUAN bird
GUNN castaway (Stevenson)
GWYN Llud's son; deity
GAJO non-Gypsy
GANO Count (Roland's destroyer)
GAPO (Inundated) forest
GARO Assam native
GILO woody vine (tonic)
GIRO tour; round; credit system; aircraft (auto-)
GOBO burdock; okra; camera; mike shield
GOGO vine; bark soap; beetle; bugaboo; Bantu
GOLO Nilotic Sudanese
GRAO weight
GUAO tree
GULO wolverine genus
GYRO prefix: ring, spiral
GAMP umbrella; Sairey — (nurse: Dickens)
GASP pant (eagerly)
GAUP gape
GAWP gape; simpleton
GIMP silk fabric; vim
GLOP look wildly; stare
GOLP roundel purpure (Her.)
GOOP nonsense creature
GRIP grasp; power; valise; Barnaby's raven (Dickens)
GULP swallow; catch breath
GUMP silly, stupid one; Andy, Chester, Min (cartoon family)
GAUR wild cattle
GEAR notched wheel; equipment; adjust; harmonize
GHOR Dead Sea valley
GIER eagle (vulture)
GNAR growl
GOER runner
GOOR sugar; massecuite
GOUR cattle; koulan (onager)
GUAR legume; cluster bean
GUHR earthy deposit
GADS -hill (Dickens)
GAUS region: Ger.
GENS clan: Lat.; people: Fr.
GHES Tapuyan Indian
GHOS Chin. dynasty
GLIS dormouse genus
GOES walks; proceeds
GRAS horse; foie — (paté)
GRES stoneware: Fr.
GRIS gray: Fr.
GROS coin; fabric; weight
GRUS constellation (Crane)
GYPS gypsum
GAIT walk; pace
GALT clay bed
GANT yawn; gaunt; gannet; Eugene (Wolfe character)
GAUT range; pass; river bank stairs
GEAT channel in mold; Scandinavian (Beowulf)
GELT money
GENT gentleman; Belg. city
GEST deed; romance tale, adventure
GETT bill of divorce
GHAT range; bank; river bank stairs
GIFT donation; talent
GILT gold; sow
GIRT encircled; prepared
GIST main point; pith
GLUT sate; surfeit; oversupply; wedge
GNAT (biting) fly
GOAT ruminant; scape-; brown
GOUT drop; disease (arthritis); taste: Fr.
GRIT sand(stone); bravery; grate
GROT cave; Bremen coin
GUST outburst of wind
GENU knee: Lat.
GESU Jesus: It.
GUGU P.I. soldier; Insurrecto
GURU teacher
GLOW shine; incandesce; flush; ardor; wax
GNAW bite; corrode
GREW increased
GROW expand; sprout; wax; develop
GABY fool
GAPY yawning
GARY city, steel center
GAZY gaping
GOBY fish; passing
GONY albatross
GORY bloody; murderous
GRAY dull; dismal; hoary; Dorian (Wilde); Asa, botanist; Elisha, inventor
GREY color; neutral; dull; Zane (writer); Vivian (Disraeli novel)
GANZ all, totally: Ger.
GEEZ Version (Ethiopic Bible)
GHUZ Turkish invader
GRAZ Austrian city (Mur)

HABA bean
HAHA laugh; fence
HAKA dance
HALA pine tree
HARA Japanese statesman
HAYA arrow poison
HELA goddess; Loki's daughter
HEMA prefix: blood
HERA Zeus's sister, wife
HILA 'eyes' of bean
HIMA Hamitic Negro
HOGA hill pasture
HOJA title; teacher
HOLA fish poison; herb; hello
HOMA sacred drink
HORA book of hours; Israeli dance
HOVA Madagascar native; Malagasy

HOYA honey plant (milkweed)
HSIA 1st Chin. dynasty
HUIA bird (starling)
HULA Hawaiian dance
HUMA Uganda Negro
HUPA Athapascan Indian
HURA bishop's cap; sandbox tree; possumwood
HYLA frog; toad
HAAB year
HARB Bedouin
HERB plant; nickname
HOBB havoc; fireplace ledge; pin; peg
HUBB pipe end
HAEC this one (fem.): Lat.
HAND control; aid; worker; measure; pass; player; cards; penmanship
HARD solid; firm; close; severe; difficult
HEAD skull; top; brain; chief; crux; source
HEED notice; attention
HELD kept; retained
HERD crowd; feed together
HILD Hethin's victim princess
HIND fish; grouper; deer; posterior
HOLD grasp; have; retain; believe; keep; bear; lair; prison
HOOD cowl; cloak; seal; gangster; Thomas (poet)
HUED colored; tinged
HUND dog: Ger.
HABE tribe
HADE angle; strip
HAJE cobra
HAKE fish; pester; frame
HALE healthy; Nathan — (patriot)
HARE leporid; rabbit; run
HATE detest; aversion
HAVE possess; aux. verb; must; deceive
HAZE mist; drizzle; harass
HEBE cupbearer of gods; Zeus's daughter, Hercules' wife; color
HEHE Bantu tribe
HEME reduced hematin
HERE vicinity; present
HIDE land measure; skin; conceal; shelter; — and hair
HIKE toss; tramp; raise
HIPE wrestler's throw
HIRE engage; rent; wage
HIVE bees' swarm, house
HOHE Siouan tribe
HOLE pit; cavity; flaw; — in one; — card; ace in the —
HOME habitat; asylum; plate; natural
HONE sharpen(er)
HOPE trust, expect(ation); wish; -chest
HOSE stockings; pipe; drench
HOVE ground ivy; raised
HOWE hollow; empty; Elias (inventor); Julia Ward (Battle Hymn); Brit. general, admiral
HUGE enormous; immense
HUKE hooked cape
HULE caucho source
HUME philosopher
HURE head of boar, wolf
HUSE beluga; whale; huchen
HYDE — Park; Dr. Jekyll and Mr. —; measure
HYKE cry to urge on dogs
HYLE matter (philos.): demon
HYPE wrestler's throw
HAAF fishing grounds
HAFF lagoon
HALF moiety; -breed, -caste, -nelson, -shell
HEAF pasture
HOOF ungula; foot; beast; walk; dance
HUFF inflate; bully; anger
HAGG demoness; hack; wood
HAIG soldier (Douglas)
HANG suspend; plan; bit; die on gallows
HING asafetida (gum resin; antispasmodic)
HOGG unshorn sheep
HONG Chin. trade guild
HUNG suspended; undecided (jury)
HAKH claim(er); legal claim; share
HAPH weight
HASH chop up; mixture; mess
HATH contraction: haveth
HEGH exclamation; hey!
HETH son of Canaan; Hittite ancestor
HIGH lofty; elevated; noble; expensive; shrill; tainted; tipsy
HISH hiss; swish
HOCH high: Ger.
HOTH blind god (Balder slayer)
HUCH Danube fish
HUGH name; saint (of Cluny)
HUNH exclamation
HUSH quiet; silence; -hush; -puppy; — money
HAGI clover; prefix: saint
HAJI pilgrim
HALI prefix: sea, salt
HAMI hooked processes
HAPI bull; Nile (god)
HARI river; Mata (spy)
HATI heart
HEII Hawaiian fern
HELI prefix: sun, spiral
HEMI prefix: half
HEVI apple (tree)
HIFI faithful sound rendition
HOLI spring festival
HONI —soit qui mal y pense; shamed
HOPI French beige; Moqui Indian
HOTI cause; reason
HURI Abihail's father
HUSI fine P.I. fiber
HADJ pilgrimage
HAJJ pilgrimage
HAAK fish; wander
HACK chop; writer; horse
HAIK garment; frame
HANK coil; — Morgan (Twain)
HARK listen
HAWK bird; predator; peddle; mortarboard
HECK (weaving) frame; cough; oath
HICK hiccup; rube; jake
HOCK leg joint; hamstring; wine; faro card; pawn
HOEK stream bend; — van Holland (Dutch cape, city)

HONK goose cry; toot; ooga
HOOK trap; curve; catch; steal; — and eye; pirate: Peter Pan (Barrie)
HUCK towel fabric
HULK ship body; bulky thing
HUNK piece; lump; OK
HUSK covering (of seed, corn); shell
HAIL ice pieces; salute; — fellow
HALL building; room; town —; guild-; astronomer; -Mills
HARL barb; filament
HAUL drag; shift; loot
HEAL cure; restore
HEEL back part; end; slant; follow; scoundrel
HEIL hail: Ger.
HELL Hades; state of misery; -bent
HERL (feather) barb
HIEL Jericho's rebuilder
HILL mound; Jenny (Shaw character); -billy
HOLL ditch
HOWL (distress) cry; wail
HULL husk; ship body; Cordell (statesman)
HURL throw; pitch; rush
HAEM prefix: blood
HALM plant stems
HARM hurt; evil; injury
HAWM loiter
HELM steer (wheel); tiller
HOLM holly; oak; islet
HAHN Otto (Nobel physicist)
HEIN surprise!: Fr.
HEWN felled; squared
HIEN Chin. government seat
HOEN weight
HOON coin; gold pagoda
HORN prong; antenna; trumpet; brasswind; cup; Cape —
HUON pine; timber tree
HYMN song (of praise)
HAKO rite
HALO circle; glow; nimbus; prefix: sea, salt
HANO Indian
HELO squeamish
HEMO prefix: blood
HERO protagonist; demigod; — and Leander; Beatrice's cousin
HILO grass; city (Hawaii)
HINO timber tree; dye
HIRO measure
HOBO vagrant worker
HOGO taint; stench
HOMO man; — sapiens; prefix: same
HUGO name; Victor (novelist)
HUSO beluga; whale; huchen
HYPO photo solution; needle; injection
HARP coin; seal; Lyra; constellation; Irishman; nag
HASP clasp
HEAP pile; crowd; car
HEEP Uriah (Dickens villain)
HELP relieve; avoid; wait on, aid(e); servants
HEMP herb; hashish; cannabis; rope (fiber)
HOOP circle(t); wicket; — skirt
HUMP protuberance; mound; crisis; Himalayan peaks; -back
HUPP call to horse
HAAR fog
HAIR filament; cilium, seta; fabric; -trigger
HARR hinge
HEAR listen; perceive by ear
HEER Mr., Sir: Dutch
HEIR inherit(or); — apparent, presumptive
HEER lord, Mister, Sir: Ger.
HIER here: Ger.; yesterday: Fr.
HLER sea god (wife: Ran)
HOAR frost; gray; -hound
HOER scraper
HOUR time unit; H- or zero —
HURR to snarl
HALS Frans — (painter)
HANS John; Johannes; — Castorp (Mann)
HASS throat; embrace
HENS fowl; -foot (herb)
HERS fem., poss. pronoun
HISS sibilant (of disapproval); goose; serpent; steam sound; Alger (Communist)
HOPS beer
HORS out of: Fr.; — d'oeuvres
HOSS horse; One — Shay (Holmes)
HUSS dogfish; John (religious leader)
HYPS hypochondria
HAFT handle
HALT stop; lame
HANT ghost
HART stag; deer
HAST contraction: havest
HATT measure
HAUT high: Fr.; — monde
HEAT warmth; rage; height; dead —; pressure; strain
HEFT weight; bulk; notebook: Ger.
HEST command; precept
HETT Hittite ancestor
HILT sword
HINT suggestion; imply
HIST call to attention; Indian girl (Cooper)
HOLT willow plantation; hill; lair; Eliot hero; actor
HOOT derisive (owl's) cry
HOST army; throng; bread as Christ's body; innkeeper; person having guests
HUIT eight: Fr.
HUNT seek; chase; Leigh (writer)
HURT harm(ed); pain
HABU pit viper
HAKU fish
HAPU clan
HIKU scabbard fish
HOJU Jap. army reserve
HULU o-o's feather tuft
HOAX deceive; trick
HAZY dim; obscure
HOEY partnership (Hawaii)
HOLY sacred; pious; — City; — Alliance; — Roller

HOMY homey intimate

HUEY Long (La governor)

HARZ Ger mountains

HAYZ zodiacal situation

HUZZ buzz; murmur

IDEA conception; fancy; key meaning; opening

IJMA Moslem principle (Sunna)

IKRA superior caviar

ILIA (hip) bones

IMLA Micaiah's father

IMNA Asherite chief

INCA Quechuan Indian (ruler)

INGA timber tree; mimosa

INIA Amazon cetacean

INKA Inca

IOLA Kansas town

IONA Scot isle Celt church college

IOTA Greek I, 10; jot

IOWA state Indian

IRMA name

IRRA war god

ISBA log hut

ISHA Upanishad

ITEA shrub Virginia willow

ITZA Mayan Indian

IXIA corn lily bulb

IAMB verse foot

IDIC pert to ids

IBAD Hira Arab

IBID P.I. lizard (tidbit) the same abbr

ICED frozen chilled

IMID chem compound

IRAD Enoch's son

IRID iris; crocus

IDEE - fixe Fr.

IDLE not working; empty lazy; waste

ILLE that one Lat.

IMBE cordage fiber plant

INBE be within

INDE blue (indigo)

INEE arrow poison

INGE prelate ("Gloomy Dean") playwright (Bus Stop)

INRE concerning; actually

IOLE Eurytus' daughter (Hercules captive)

IONE Pompei heroine (Bulwer-Lytton)

IPSE himself: Lat.; — dixit

IRAE Dies — (Day of Wrath)

ISLE ait; eyot; insulate; key

IXLE cordage fiber

ILOG river (Tagalog)

IHVH God; Tetragrammaton

INCH measure; move slowly

ITCH skin irritation; desire

IVAH Bib. city

IIWI bird (mamo)

ILAI David's man

IMMI measure

IMPI armed Kaffirs

INTI Incas' deified sun sun god

IONI Hainai; Chaddo Indian

ISUI Asher's son

IRAK country

IROK gomuti (palm)

ICAL compound suffix

IDOL god, deity image adored one

IDYL pastoral poem

IFIL tree (brown dye)

IGAL Moses spy

IPIL tree (brown dye)

ITOL suffix alcohol(ic)

IXIL Mayan Indian

IDEM same: Lat.; semper —

IISM egoism

IMAM priest; title

IRBM ballistic missile

ITEM also; article; bit; entry

IBAN dyak (Borneo)

ICON image statue

IDEN Henry VI figure

IDUN Bragi's wife (Norse)

IKON image; statue

IRAN Persia

IRON metal; element; weapon instrument; club shackle press; strong; Age

ITEN So. Amer Indian

IVAN John the Terrible

IAGO villain (Othello)

ICHO fruit tree (gingko)

IDEO prefix idea

IDIO prefix one's own

IDJO Niger delta Negro

IDYO Niger delta Negro

IDZO Niger delta Negro

IKMO betel palm; pepper

INRO Japanese receptacle

INTO penetrating; toward

IODO prefix iodine

IPSO - jure - facto

ITMO betel pepper

IUNO Jupiter's wife

IRAQ country

ICER freezer mixer

IGOR Prince (opera)

IMER Caucasian

ISAR river (Munich)

ISER river

ITER road; passage (brain)

IVER ever

IYAR month

IZAR Moslem garment; star

IBIS (sacred) wading bird

IDAS Marpessa's lover; Castor's slayer

IDES Roman date; — of March (fateful day)

ILLS troubles

ILUS son of Tros; Priam's grandfather

IOUS promissory notes; suffix

IRAS Cleopatra's maid

IRIS rainbow goddess; eye part plant (flag) spirit (Shaks.) red-blue; March (Arlen)

IRUS Odysse: beggar

ISIS goddess Osiris's wife, sister; Horus's mother

ITIS suffix: inflammation, mania; Tereus' son

ITYS Tereus' son

IVES inventor (photo-engr.)

IWIS certainly

IBIT P.I. lizard (tidbit)

IKAT shrub, weight

ILOT islet; ait eyot

IALU Hades heaven

ICHU valuable grass

IGLU Eskimo hut; seal hole

IBEX wild goat; bouquetin

ILEX holm oak; holly

IYNX wryneck

	(woodpecker)
IDLY	vainly; lazily
IFFY	contingent
ILLY	badly; ill
IMPY	impish
INDY	- pink (carnation)
INKY	black; stained
INLY	within; heartily
ISMY	doctrinaire
INEZ	Don Juan's mother
JACA	tree
JAGA	Bantu
JAMA	tunic
JARA	palm
JAVA	coffee; hood; (Indonesian) Sunda Isles; man (Pithecanthropus)
JENA	Ger. city (optical, Napoleonic victory); glass
JIVA	life energy
JOTA	Sp. peasant dance
JOVA	Opata; Pimian Indian
JUBA	ghost; dance; mane; river
JUCA	cassava; manioc
JUDA	James' brother
JUGA	carrot ridges; yokes
JULA	suspension bridge
JURA	rights; mountain range
JUZA	star
JAMB	leg armor; pillar; door part
JAOB	measure
JOAB	(David's) captain
JOAD	philosopher; Tom : Grapes of Wrath (Steinbeck)
JORD	Odin's wife; Thor's mother
JADE	gem; horse; exhaust
JAKE	Jacob; rube; money; satisfactory; ginger
JANE	woman; false hair; cloth; - Eyre; Lady — Grey
JAPE	deride
JAVE	Jehovah
JEFE	chief; leader
JETE	ballet jump
JIBE	sneer; agree; coincide; shift course
JIVE	dialect (dance, jazz)
JOIE	— de vivre (zest for life)
JOKE	jest; laughing stock
JOLE	jowl; cheek
JOSE	Carmen lover
JOVE	god; Jupiter; Zeus
JUBE	chancel screen; lozenge
JUDE	name; NT book, author; Jew: Ger.; — the Obscure (Hardy)
JUGE	judge: Fr.
JUKE	partridge call; — box; sociological name (with Kallikak)
JULE	name: Julian; Julius
JUNE	month; beetle; — moon, bride
JUPE	skirt
JURE	de — (by law)
JUTE	fiber plant; Corchorus; Low Ger.
JEFF	rope; nickname; Mutt and —
JIFF	instant
JAGG	pendant; tooth; slash
JOUG	iron collar; pillory
JUNG	young: Ger.; Carl Gustave (psychologist)
JETH	Hindu month
JHVH	Jehovah; God; Tetragrammaton
JHWH	Jahweh; God; Tetragrammaton
JOAH	record keeper
JOCH	yoke, measure: Ger.
JOSH	make fun; banter
JAMI	mosque
JATI	caste
JIBI	extinct bird
JITI	Rajmahal creeper
JOGI	yogi; ascetic
JOLI	pretty, nice: Fr.
JOTI	astrologer; astronomer
JUSI	fine P.I. fiber
JACK	flag; tool; card; fruit; raise
JERK	grab; twist; spasm; soda man; dullard; beef
JINK	prank
JOCK	John; jockey; hobo
JONK	jonquil
JOOK	perch; slumber
JUCK	partridge call
JUNK	ship; trash; scrap
JAAL	goat
JAEL	Sisera's killer; Heber's wife
JAIL	prison; gaol
JARL	Norse chief; earl
JEEL	pool; marsh
JELL	solidify; mature
JERL	boat joint
JILL	girl; sweetheart; Jack and —
JOEL	prophet, OT book
JOLL	move clumsily; knock
JOWL	jaw; cheek; wattle; gambler (Dickens)
JERM	Levantine boat
JHUM	cultivation method
JOOM	cutivation method
JAIN	sect (Indian)
JANN	genii
JAUN	palanquin
JEAN	name; cotton cloth
JINN	demon; spirit
JOAN	lass; cap; — of Arc, the Maid, la Pucelle
JOHN	name; saint, evangelist; cop; man; Bull (England); Long — Silver (Stevenson)
JOIN	mix; unite; coalesce
JUAN	John; Don —; Don Giovanni
JAKO	parrot
JATO	jet-assisted take-off
JOBO	hog plum; gumbo limbo
JODO	Buddhist paradise (Gokaruku)
JUDO	self-defense art
JUNO	goddess; Jupiter's wife, Hera; stately woman; missile
JEEP	vehicle; automobile
JUMP	leap; bounce; move; headstart; — the gun
JEER	scoff; taunt
JOAR	durra; millet
JOUR	day: Fr.
JUAR	durra; millet
JASS	card game; jack
JESS	strap on hawk leg
JEWS	harp
JOMS	Vikings; Norse colony

JOSS Chin. deity
JEST joke
JILT betray in love
JOLT shake; hard blow
JUST fair; virtuous; exact(ly)
JACU bird
JADU magic
JEHU (chariot) driver; prophet, king (Israel)
JESU name: Jesus
JOCU dog snapper
JUJU Afr. magic, charm
JHOW tamarisk shrub
JEUX cards, hands, games: Fr.
JINX hoodoo; bad luck
JYNX wryneck; charm
JADY gemlike
JAWY talkative
JOEY coin; clown; odd-job man; young kangaroo; Pal (O'Hara character)
JOKY jocular
JOSY nickname
JOZY Josepha; Josephine
JUDY name; Punch and —; Judith; Kipling character
JULY (5th Roman) month
JURY (court) panel; committee; grand —; hung —
JAZZ dance; music; banter
JEUZ chief Benjamite
JUEZ judge, juror: Sp.

KADA measure
KAFA Ethiopian
KAHA proboscis monkey
KAKA parrot
KALA bird
KAMA love god; desire; river
KANA Japanese writing
KAPA cloth(es)
KARA river
KASA grass
KAVA pepper shrub, root; gum resin; vein
KAWA pepper shrub, root; gum resin; vein
KELA measures
KETA dog salmon
KINA quinine
KIVA ceremonial chamber
KOBA antelope
KOLA caffeine nut; jackal; river; city; bay (Murmansk)
KONA Hawaiian storm; weight
KORA water cock; Hottentot dialect
KOTA P.I. fort; Dravidian language
KUBA carpet; measure
KUFA round boat
KULA measure; gift exchange
KUSA ceremonial grass
KALB de — (general)
KERB gutter part
KNAB nibble
KNOB lump; hill; antler; handle
KNUB waste silk
KTKB chess move
KTQB chess move
KAID chief; alcalde
KEID star
KELD spring; fountain
KIDD William (privateer)
KIND sort; species; gentle
KURD Sunnite Mohammedan; Iranian
KADE tick
KALE cabbage
KAME hill
KANE god
KATE bird; Shaks. shrew; Greenaway
KELE weight
KERE read(ing substitute)
KIBE chilblain crack
KILE measure; weight
KINE cattle
KIPE basket
KITE hawk; rogue; flying toy; banking fraud
KIVE brewer's vat
KLEE Paul (painter)
KNEE joint; bend(ing)
KOAE red-tailed bird
KOBE Honshu port
KOME Greenland division
KORE Persephone; Demeter's daughter; chaos (Maori myth.)
KUGE Jap. courtier
KUKE prince; cherry
KURE Jap. city; Hawaiian isle
KYKE fashion spy
KYLE sore; ulcer; farmer
KAIF languor; hemp
KEEF hemp; languor
KEIF hemp; languor
KERF cut; notch
KIEF hemp; languor
KIFF languor
KOFF Dutch sailboat
KANG — Hsi (Chinese emperor)
KING monarch; ruler; chief; chessman; card
KNAG spur; knot
KRAG rifle
KUNG public
KAPH letter
KATH astringent
KISH powder; basket; measure; Saul's father
KITH acquaintance; — and kin
KOCH cook: Ger.; Robert (bacteriologist)
KOPH Heb. K, Q, 100
KUSH Ham's son; country
KYAH partridge
KADI judge
KAKI bird; tree
KALI glasswort; carpet; evil genius; Agni's tongue; Siva's wife
KAMI language; deity
KARI gum tree
KASI tile work
KATI weight
KAVI Java language
KAWI Java language
KAZI Moslem judge
KEPI military cap
KERI read(ing substitute)
KIKI castor oil plant
KIRI paulownia tree; knobkerrie (missile)
KIWI flightless bird; apteryx; non-flyer
KIYI herring; cisco; yelp
KOBI Japanese reserve duty (term)
KOJI Jap. yeast cake
KOLI low-caste tribesman
KOMI Soviet republic; Zyrians
KOPI N.Z. tree (karaka)
KORI bustard; low weaver
KUEI disembodied spirit
KUKI Burma Mongol
KULI low-caste Indian
KURI Lezhgian tribesman

KWEI disembodied spirit
KAIK village
KECK vomit; show disgust
KEEK fashion spy
KELK fish roe
KIAK canoe
KICK hit; die; object(ion); excitement; -back
KINK twist; loop; cramp
KIRK church
KONK conk
KUNK measure
KURK church: Scot.
KYAK canoe
KAIL tree; ibex; kale
KARL Charles; – Marx
KEAL cabbage
KEEL ship bottom; navigate; ocher; guinea fowl
KELL Gaul; net; film
KIEL ocher; ruddle; seaport; – Canal
KILL slay; veto; creek
KOEL cuckoo
KOHL eye shadow; horse
KOIL cuckoo
KRAL hut; village
KUHL eyelid cosmetic
KASM measure
KHEM chief god (Min)
KLAM weight
KLOM weight
KULM crane; heron
KAAN inn; title
KAHN banker; test
KAIN tribute
KARN stone heap
KAUN resthouse; lord; title
KAWN resthouse; lord; title
KEEN sharp; acute; bewail
KERN soldier; peasant; grain; type part; Jerome (composer)
KHAN resthouse; lord; title; Agha —
KILN (burn in) oven
KIRN harvest feast
KLAN Ku Klux —
KRAN coin
KUAN pottery; official
KWAN coin; weight
KAGO conveyance
KAIO fruit
KALO taro root
KANO painting school
KARO plant
KAYO knock out
KENO lotto (game); prefix: empty
KIBO Afr. peak (Kilimanjaro)
KIHO peacock butterfly
KILO measure; -gram, -meter; prefix: 1000
KINO gum (catechu); prefix: moving
KOKO bird; palm; tribe; executioner (Mikado)
KOLO folk dance
KOSO tree; cusso; Panamint Indian
KOTO Jap. zither
KOZO paper mulberry
KROO Liberian Negro
KAPP measure
KEEP tend; retain; preserve; last
KELP seaweed, iodine source
KEMP fur refuse
KEUP measure
KIPP peak (Glacier National Park); gymnastic feat
KLIP rock; cliff
KLOP hard sound
KNAP summit; rap; talk; bite; button
KNIP bite; crop; rap
KNOP button; finial; stud
KOOP purchase; bargain
KAIR fiber
KEIR bleaching vat
KERR physicist
KHAR weight
KHOR watercourse; gorge
KIER bleaching vat
KNAR knot; burr
KNOR knot (wood); gnarl
KNUR gnarl; knot; wood ball
KTKR chess move
KTQR chess move
KUAR month
KYAR coconut fiber
KAGS convict (Dickens)
KAIS island
KERS cress
KEYS House of (Isle of Man legislature); cays; Florida —
KHAS special; noble
KIDS star (Auriga)
KISS touch gently; caress; sweetmeat
KOSS measure
KRAS tahr (goat)
KRIS dagger; stab
KVAS sour beer, cider (Russ.)
KAAT shrub; weight
KANT change course; Immanuel, philosopher
KEET guinea fowl
KELT Celt; cloth; trout
KENT Eng. county, duchy; Lear's follower
KEPT retained; lasted
KHAT measure
KHET mortal body; measure
KHOT farmer; contractor
KILT Scot's skirt
KIST chest; installment; measure
KMET Slav; tenant; mayor
KNIT looped, tie(d); unite; contract
KNOT tie; loop; hitch; sandpiper; problem; blemish; stud; Gordian —
KNUT king; son of Magnus
KOPT Copt
KTKT chess move
KYAT weight; Burmese money
KADU tribe
KAGU bird
KAHU harrier; bird
KAPU forbidden; taboo
KIKU chrysanthemum
KIVU tsetse fly
KOBU seaweed food (kelp)
KUDU Afr. antelope
KUKU N.Z. fruit pigeon; kukupa
KULU old woman (Kipling)
KIEV Ukrainian city
KNEW understood; was aware
KNOW understand; recognize; -how; nothing (party)
KATY Catherine; -did
KAZY Moslem judge
KNEZ Slavic prince

LAMA priest; llama; brown; Dalai, Panchen, Tashi —
LANA wood; flannel

LARA Byron poem
LATA jumping disease
LAVA fluid rock; obsidian's source; red
LEDA mollusk; mother of Castor, Pollux, Helen, Clytemnestra; wooed by Zeus as swan
LENA firewood: Sp.; river; Conrad heroine
LIDA Alida
LIJA unicorn fish
LILA deity manifestation
LIMA city; bean, yam; mollusk
LINA measure; Caroline
LIPA fat
LIRA money; lyre; hairlike ridge
LISA fem. name; nickname
LOJA bark (quinine)
LOKA sphere; universe
LOLA fem. name
LOMA fringe; lap; hill
LORA thong; strap
LOTA water pot; burbot genus
LOWA bush quail
LOXA pale bark: quinine
LUBA Bantu; Bashilange
LULA name; Louisa
LUNA moon goddess; silver
LURA brain opening
LYRA glockenspiel; constellation
LAMB amateur speculator; Charles — (Elia), essayist (roast pig)
LIMB leg; arm; member
LOBB go heavily; tennis stroke; till
LAIC secular
LAID put down; calmed
LAND ground; debark; state: Ger.
LARD fat; stuff
LAUD praise
LEAD metal; element; plummet; bullets; color; guide; command
LEND make loan; grant; — an ear
LEUD feudal tenant
LEWD lecherous; obscene
LIED fibbed; song: Ger.
LIND Jenny (singer, Swedish Nightingale)
LOAD burden; measure
LOOD weight
LORD ruler; Jehovah; Jesus; duck; planet
LOUD noisy; showy; vulgar
LABE city
LACE cord; flavor; netting
LADE load; dip
LAKE sea; pool; red (cochineal)
LAME cripple(d); halt; plate; fabric
LANE (fixed) route; throat
LATE dead; tardy
LAVE pour; bathe
LAZE idle(ness); tribesman
LENE smooth; consonant
LESE — majesty (disrespect)
LETE quadrille set
LICE insects (louse)
LIDE March (month)
LIFE existence; vivacity; biography
LIKE as; similar(ly); love; prefer; probable
LILE little
LIME calcium oxide (mortar); snare; caustic; linden (tree); amber; citrus fruit
LINE thin mark; cable; cord; wire; piping; row; direction; cover; align; track; flax
LIRE coins; read: Fr.
LITE suffix: mineral, rock
LIVE exist; continue; vital; alert
LOBE projection; ear part
LODE ore deposit; vein; load
LOGE theater box
LOKE Loki; surprise!
LOME Togo seaport
LONE single; — Star
LOPE go; move; gait
LORE history; learning
LOSE miss; forfeit; fail; forget
LOTE lotus (poetic); weights
LOVE affection; like; Cupid; Eros; zero
LUBE machine oil
LUCE fish, pike; Adriana's servant; Henry (editor); Clare (writer, stateswoman)
LUGE lodge; small sled
LUKE name; evangelist; Paul's companion; author Acts; -warm
LUNE crescent; hawk leash
LUPE Samoan fruit pigeon; Velez (actress)
LURE entice; decoy; trumpet
LUTE cement; bricklayer's tool; Apollo's musical instrument; jar ring
LUXE elegance; de —
LYME bloodhound
LYRE harp; constellation
LYSE undergo lysis
LEAF plant part; sheet; tea
LEIF Ericson (explorer)
LIEF gladly; freely
LOAF bread; idle
LOOF luff; sponge gourd
LUFF sail nearer wind
LUIF loof
LANG auld — syne; Fritz
LING fish; burbot; hake
LONG lengthy; extended; yearn; - John Silver (Stevenson); Huey - (La. politician); — time no see
LUNG air bladder; iron —
LURG marine worm
LAKH 100,000; coin
LASH (whip) stroke; tie; eye part
LATH strip; slat
LEAH fem. name; Laban's daughter; Jacob's wife
LECH slab; capstone; river
LITH prefix, suffix: stone

LOCH lake, bay: Scot.
LOSH wash leather
LOTH averse, reluctant
LUGH Celtic light god
LUOH white Nile Negro
LUSH luxurious; drunkard
LARI money; sea birds
LASI tribe
LAZI tribesman
LEHI prophet
LETI island off Timor
LEVI Jacob's, Leah's son; tribe
LIII 53; Claudius reign
LITI medieval peasants
LOCI places, sites
LODI city; Napoleon victory
LOKI god of discord; Aesir; Balder slayer
LORI lemur; Afr. Negro
LOTI Pierre (writer; Viaud)
LUDI Roman public games
LURI Lake Albert Negro
LVII 57; Nero reign
LXII 62; Nero reign
LACK need
LANK thin; lean(ness)
LARK bird; frolic; yellow
LAUK exclamation
LAWK surprise!
LEAK loss; ooze; crack
LEEK plant (onion, liliaceous); — green (Wales emblem)
LICK tongue; stroke; whip; conquer; bit
LINK (chain) loop; connect; join; torch; measure
LISK flank; loin
LOCK gate (canal, dam); tuft; wool; fasten(ing), grapple; tie up; -out (labor)
LONK black-faced sheep
LOOK observe; appear(ance); eye(wink); care
LUCK chance; event; fortune
LURK lie in wait; skulk
LUSK lazy (fellow)
LAEL Gershonite's father
LEAL loyal: Scot.
LEIL faithful, loyal (Land of the —)
LILL small pin; loll; Lillian
LOLL droop; lounge; sprawl
LULL (temporary) quiet
LIAM O'Flaherty: "Informer"
LOAM clay; soil
LOOM auk; appear(ance); weaver's frame
LYAM bloodhound
LAHN river
LAIN reclined
LAON Fr. city
LAUN ceramic sieve
LAWN fabric; grass plot; bishopric
LEAN be supported; incline; thin
LEON country, city; Ponce de (explorer)
LIEN claim; attachment; garnishment
LIIN measure
LIMN portray; delineate
LINN waterfall; linden
LION cat, king of beasts; celebrity
LLYN lake; pool
LOAN lend
LOIN body part; hips; meat cut
LOON diving bird; lout
LORN forsaken; bereft
LOUN loon; lout
LOWN calm; quiet; dolt
LUNN Sally (teacake)
LYON Fr. city; bean
LAGO lake
LALO composer
LAZO lasso
LENO (cotton, silk) fabric
LERO Dodecanese isle
LETO mother of Apollo, Artemis
LEVO prefix: left
LIAO Manchuria river
LIDO Venice beach
LIFO inventory method
LINO measure
LOBO timber wolf
LOCO (render) mad; weed
LOLO Caucasian Chinese
LORO monk parrot; fish
LOTO pot; game
LUDO game; pachisi
LAAP secretion; insect
LAMP light; bulb
LAPP N. Scandinavian
LARP secretion; insect
LEAP jump, skip; — year
LERP secretion; insect
LIMP halt; flaccid; loose
LISP speech defect
LOOP noose; catch; aerial stunt; Chicago area
LOUP half mask; Skidi Indian; river; fish
LUMP mass; swelling; barge; like it or — it
LAIR resting place
LEAR learning: Scot.; king; father of Goneril, Regan, Cordelia
LEER sly gaze; oven; loin
LEHR oven; Lew (comedian)
LEIR sea god (Lear)
LIAR prevaricator; plant
LIER rester; layer
LOIR dormouse; river
LOUR frown; lower; scowl
LAIS hetaera
LAOS country
LARS Porsena (conqueror)
LASS girl; sweetheart
LAWS rules; principles
LEES dregs
LENS eye part; glass (optical); herb
LESS shorter; fewer; inferior; minus
LIAS geol. period
LISS (fairy) fort; release; peace; fleur-de-lis
LOIS name; Timothy's grandmother
LOOS Anita (writer: Gentlemen Prefer Blondes)
LORS exclamation: lord!
LOSS forfeiture; bereavement; waste; defeat; — leader
LOTS tracts; quantities; very much; chances
LUBS of Lubeck (city)
LUES syphilis
LYAS geol. period
LACT prefix: milk
LAET freedman
LAIT milk: Fr.; cafe-au-
LAST block; final(ly); endure; measure

LEET court; list
LEFT departed; blow; — of center (Liberals)
LENT fasting period; slow; made loan
LEST for fear that
LETT Latvian, Balt (Riga man)
LIFT ra(i)se; exalt; steal; elevator
LILT (sing) lively tune
LINT raveling, fiber (of linen); netting
LIST strip(e); roll; register; enter; inclination; careen
LOFT attic; warehouse floor; golf stroke
LOOT plunder; booty
LOST not won; misplaced; confused; ruined; — cause
LOUT boor; bumpkin; dolt
LUFT air: Ger.; -waffe
LUNT light; smoke; Alfred (actor)
LUST sensual desire
LATU gold coins
LIEU place; stead
LIMU edible seaweed
LUAU feast; cook-out
LULU barn owl; name; Louisa
LXIV 64; Nero reign
LLEW Celt deity (Gwydion's son)
LWOW Polish city
LANX platter
LYNX wildcat; fur; constellation
LACY netlike
LADY title; bird
LAKY red
LAZY idle
LELY Dutch painter
LEVY assess; seize; tax
LILY flower; Turk's-cap; pure; white
LIMY viscous
LINY streaky
LIVY Roman historian; Titus Livius
LOGY heavy; dull
LORY parrot; touraco
LOWY banlieue; suburb
LUCY fleur-de-lis; fem. name; camera lucida; Lemonade — (Mrs. Hayes); — Stone, suffragist

LUNY crazy (man)
LINZ Austrian city
LITZ braided wire
LODZ Polish city

MABA Negro; tree
MAHA monkey; deer
MAIA goddess; crab; star
MAJA crab
MALA evil(s), wrong(s): Lat.; jaw
MAMA mother; goddess
MANA magic power; Chin. letter
MARA demon; aborigine; Naomi
MASA corn meal
MATA Hari (spy)
MAYA weaverbird; (Mexican) Indian; magic; Buddha's mother
MEDA secret Indian sect
MEGA prefix: great
MELA festival; prefix: black
MESA flat hill; oakwood color
META goal post; river
MICA isinglass (silicate)
MILA measure
MIMA woman actor
MINA weight; money; myna; watchman
MIRA star
MOHA millet; delusion
MOLA sunfish genus
MONA monkey; Lisa (La Gioconda, da Vinci)
MORA default; short syllable; Spartan army; stool
MOTA Moslem marriage
MOXA cautery wormwood
MOZA manservant
MUGA silk; moth
MURA Brazil Indian
MUSA banana genus
MUTA change; Moslem marriage
MYNA talking bird: grackle
MYRA name; ancient city
MYSA buffalo (Kipling)
MYXA plum (geiger) tree; sebesten
MEDB Conchobor's wife; goddess; Queen Mab
MOAB kingdom; language; Lot's son
MARC residue; name; weight
MAID servant; — of Orleans
MAND grass
MARD spoil
MAUD plaid; rug; name; Muller; Whittier, Tennyson heroine
MEAD drink; meadow; lake; Margaret, anthropologist
MEED reward
MELD announce (score); merge
MEND repair; improve
MILD calm(ly); soft; tame
MIND intellect; brain; memory; wish; mood; plan; tend; dislike
MOED festivals (Mishnah)
MOLD fungus; humus; die, matrix; shape; mix
MOOD humor; temper; verb form
MUDD measure; doctor of Booth (Lincoln assassin)
MUID measure
MUND protection right
MACE staff; spice; weight; coin
MADE successful; created; constructed
MAGE magician
MAHE island
MAKE produce, create; cause; reach; type; identify
MALE man(ly); tribe
MANE hair; in the morning: Lat.
MARE blues; sea; moon area; horse; shanks' —
MATE companion; match; tea; check-
MAZE labyrinth; daze; perplex
MEDE ancient Asian
MELE Hawaiian poem; chant
MENE – tekel upharsin (handwriting on the wall)
MERE fen; lake; boundary; war club; bare; only; simple; mother: Fr.
MESE Greek mus. term
METE measure; allot
MICE rodents (mouse)

MIDE Ojibway secret order
MIKE Michael; Mick; microphone
MILE measure; distance; 320 rods, 1,609.3 meters
MIME drama; act; actor; clown; smith (Nibelungs)
MINE possessive pronoun; dig; pit; rich source; explosive
MIRE bog; (stick in) mud
MISE levy; stake; tax; — en scene
MITE arachnid; parasite; small (coin)
MIXE Mexican Indian
MODE manner; fashion; drab; a la —
MOKE donkey; dolt
MOLE nevus; birthmark; pier; burrow(ing animal); Mossi language
MOME buffoon; -rath
MOPE be dull, listless (person)
MORE greater; additional; St. Thomas (Utopia)
MOSE Moses
MOTE speck; particle
MOUE pout; grimace: Fr.
MOVE impel; shift; excite; act; depart(ure); play
MULE equine hybrid; spinning jenny; slipper
MURE thrust against wall
MUSE meditate; goddess
MUTE silent; dumb; muffle
MIFF quarrel; offend
MOFF Caucasian silk
MUFF handwarmer; bungle
MAGG bird; chatter
MANG bat (Kipling)
MENG mix
MIGG marble (duck)
MING Chin. dynasty
MONG among; barter
MORG measure
MUNG grass
MAGH month
MASH crush; brew; mixture; hammer; flirt
MATH mowing; monastery; school course
MEAH wall tower
MESH net; netting; entangle
MICH me: Ger.
MOTH lepidopterous insect; -ball; -eaten; gypsy —; page (Shakespeare)
MUCH great (deal); far; —Ado (Shaks.)
MUSH meal; hasty pudding; flattery; proceed!
MUTH measure
MYTH (religious) legend; fiction
MABI tree
MADI Negro
MAGI caste; priests; wise men; kings of Orient; Melchior, Gaspar, Balthazar
MAHI river
MAKI lemur
MALI caste; nation; river
MANI peanut; prefix: hand
MARI prefix: sea; husband: Fr.; native
MAUI Polynesian hero
MCII 1102
MEDI prefix: middle
MIDI south(ern France)
MIII 1003
MIMI nickname; opera heroine
MLII 1052
MOJI Jap. seaport
MOKI N.Z. raft
MOTI elephant (Kipling)
MVII 1007
MXII 1012
MUNJ tough grass; twine
MACK coat
MARK sign; aim; stamp; money; observe; evangelist; easy —; — time
MASK disguise; screen; domino
MAWK maggot
MEEK mild; submissive
MICK Irishman
MILK nutritious fluid; sap; white; exploit; drain
MINK weasel-like animal
MIRK dark(ness)
MOCK jeer; taunt; sham; — apple, turtle
MONK ascetic; friar; bird; fish; spot; ferret
MOSK Moslem temple; Masjid
MUCK (rid of) manure; mess
MULK freehold land
MURK (make) gloomy
MUSK odor; aromatic secretion (of deer, ox, etc.)
MAAL measure
MAIL coin; tax; armor; post
MALL mallet; game; bird; assembly (place)
MARL clayey soil; fertilizer; fiber
MAUL hammer; bruise; mangle
MEAL grain; pulverize; repast
MELL (beat with) hammer; teacher (Dickens)
MERL blackbird
MEWL whimper; miaou
MILL grind(er); quern; box; John Stuart (economist)
MOIL toil; trouble; spot
MOLL Mary; girl; — Flanders (Defoe)
MULL muslin; ointment; ponder; humus
MYAL cultic
MAAM madam
MAIM disfigure; mutilate
MALM limestone
MARM ma'am; school-
MEUM carrotlike herb, spicknel; mine: Lat.
MIAM hut
MUMM mask; disguise
MAAN city
MAIN conduit; first; river; Spanish —
MANN man: Ger.; Horace (educator); Thomas (writer)
MAON Nabal's home
MAUN must
MEAN intend; denote; base; unkind; middle
MEIN Chin. noodles; chow —
MIAN sir; title
MIEN manner; bearing; air
MOAN lament
MOON satellite; crescent; month; Diana;

Cynthia; languish
MORN A.M.; dawn; East
MOWN cut down; trimmed
MACO cotton
MADO fish
MAJO dandy; shrub
MAKO shark
MALO loincloth
MAMO bird
MANO grindstone; hand: It.
MAPO goby (fish)
MARO ship name: Jap.
MAYO Indian; physicians, clinic (Rochester)
MAZO de la Roche (novelist; Jalna)
MEIO measure
MEMO note; statement
MENO prefix: month
MERO grouper (fish)
MIAO Chinese aborigine
MICO marmoset
MILO name; grain; sorghum; Venus (Melos)
MINO Jap. straw coat
MIRO tree; wood robin
MOGO stone hatchet
MOHO bird; honey eater
MOIO measure
MOJO tree; majagua; voodoo charm; Indian
MOKO Maori tattoo; -moko (lizard)
MOMO owl
MONO monkey; Indian; prefix: single, one
MORO finch; P.I. Moslem tribe
MOTO movement: It.; con —
MOXO Arawakan Indian
MOYO measure
MOZO manservant: Sp.
MUSO Chibchan Indian
MYXO slime mold
MUMP beg; mumble; cheat
MAHR marriage settlement
MEER sea: Ger.
MOHR gazelle; bezoar
MOOR heath; anchor; Moslem; Moroccan; blacka-
MUIR moor (Scot.)
MAAS river
MAIS but: Fr.
MANS Chinese aborigine; Le — (city; auto race)
MARS war god; planet
MASS rite; service; bulk; populace; mob, assemble
MENS mind: Lat.
MESS banquet; meal; muddle; disorder; botch
MEWS (royal) stables
MIAS orang-utan
MISS fail(ure); omit; want; girl; maiden
MONS mountain: Lat.; city (Belgium; WW I battle)
MORS deity; death
MOSS bryophyte; lichen; green; rose; Hart (writer)
MUSS mess; rumple; row
MAAT goddess
MALT barley; beer
MART market; nickname
MAST pole; brown; nuts
MATT lusterless
MEAT flesh; kernel; food
MEET encounter; face; combat; fulfill; fit
MELT liquefy
MENT falcon-headed god
MILT spleen; fish gland; nickname
MINT herb; menthol; bonanza; coin; — julep
MIST dim; haze; gray
MITT glove; hand
MOAT trench
MOLT shed (hair)
MONT mountain: Fr.; — Blanc (peak, Alps)
MOOT arguable; ring gauge
MORT nickname; woman; salmon; the kill; dead: Fr.
MOST greatest; almost
MOTT clump of trees; James, Lucretia (abolitionists)
MUNT sash bar
MUST be obliged to; necessity; new wine; stum; staleness; frenzy
MUTT cur; stupid one; — and Jeff
MYST Greek priest
MAFU stable boy
MAKU Indian
MANU prefix: hand; Laws (Hindu code book)
MARU ship name: Jap.
MASU salmon
MENU bill of fare
MEOU cat's cry; measure
MERU fabled mountain
MITU curassow; bird
MCIV 1104; First Crusade, conquest of Acre
MLIV 1054; Catholic Church Schism
MMIV 2004
MUAV geol. epoch
MXIV 1014; Brian Boru defeats Danes
MEOW cat's cry; measure
MANX pert. to Isle of Man; cat
MARX Karl (economist)
MCIX 1109
MINX pert girl
MLIX 1059
MMIX 2009
MXIX 1019
MANY numerous
MARY female name; queen: sister of Lazarus, Martha; Virgin; Lady
MATY (assistant) servant
MAZY perplexing
MINY of a mine
MIRY boggy; filthy
MITY parasite-infested
MIXY confusedly mixed
MOBY — Dick (whale; Melville)
MOLY magic herb (Homer)
MOSY moldy; rotten
MAAZ Judah's descendant
METZ city, former fort

NAGA snake
NAHA city
NAIA cobra
NAJA cobra
NALA hero
NAMA Hottentot; herb
NANA nurse; Aztec hero's wife; Zola novel; dog: Peter Pan (Barrie)
NAPA leather; wine region; city; river
NASA space-travel agency
NATA Nana's hero
NEMA eelworm; prefix: thread
NEPA water scorpion; needle bug
NERA Tiber tributary
NEVA river (Leningrad)
NINA goddess (Ea's daughter); ship (Pinta, —, Santa

Maria); girl: Sp.
NIPA palm; juice; mat; atap
NOLA fem. name; tune
NONA fate goddess; prefix: ninth
NORA Helmer (Ibsen heroine)
NOTA insect backs; — bene (N.B.)
NOVA star: new, temporary
NOXA harmful thing
NUBA Nubian; Berberi language
NUDA ctenophore; Beroida
NUMA Pompilius (Roman king)
NAAB river
NIMB nimbus; halo
NUMB deaden(ed); helpless
NAID worm
NARD plant; ointment
NEED compulsion; lack; want
NEJD kingdom
NKVD Soviet secret police
NUDD Brythonic god, king
NAHE river; near: Ger.
NAME title; reputation; clan; cite
NANE own; none
NAPE neck back
NARE Loki's son
NASE promontory; nose: Ger.
NATE born
NAVE hub; church part
NAZE promontory
NETE Greek mus. term
NEUE new
NEVE snow; firn
NICE good; kind; pleasing; delicate, dainty; quimper color; Riviera port
NIDE pheasant's nest
NIFE earth's core
NIKE victory goddess (Samothrace); missile
NILE river; green, blue
NINE number (of Muses); baseball team
NIUE Savage Island language
NODE knob; knot; orbit point; joint
NOME city (Alaska)
NONE not one; 9th hour
NORE Thames estuary
NOSE proboscis; smeller; scent; search; front; touch; — out (defeat); -dive
NOTE sign; tone; fame; heed; memo; IOU; record; see
NOVE nine: It.
NUDE naked; art work; color
NUPE Nigeria Negro
NAIF naive; of true luster
NEIF serf; native; fist
NEUF nine, new: Fr.
NIOG coconut palm
NOGG egg drink
NACH after: Ger.
NASH soft; humorist
NATH star
NESH soft; juicy; dainty
NIGH near(ly); direct
NISH Yugo. city
NOAH patriarch (Ark builder)
NASI prince; patriarch
NAZI fascist; Hitlerite
NERI Blacks: It.
NETI eulalia (thatch grass)
NGAI spiritual power
NIDI breeding places
NISI unless: Lat.
NODI knots; difficulties
NOLI — me tangere
NORI seaweed food
NOZI of Yanan tribe
NUCI prefix: nut
NABK shrub
NAIK leader
NARK informer; tease
NECK body part; violin part; isthmus; pet
NICK notch; moment; cheat; cut; Old — (devil); — Carter (detective)
NOCK notch (in bow)
NOOK corner; retreat
NUBK shrub
NAEL weight
NAIL fasten(er); claw; seize; expose
NEAL male name; novelist
NEIL male name
NELL Ellen; Helen; Little — (Dickens girl)
NIEL alloy
NILL refuse; negate
NOEL Christmas; carol; — Coward
NOIL combing (wool fiber)
NOLL Oliver (Cromwell); head; noddle
NOYL fiber knot
NULL nil; void; code filler
NURL wood knot; to mill
NAAM distrain
NEEM tree; Margosa
NORM type; standard; integer
NEIN no: Ger.
NEON gas(eous) element; lamp
NGAN measure
NOON midday; meal; acme
NORN demigoddess (Urth, Skuld, Verthandi)
NOUN speech part; name; substantive
NABO shrub
NAIO tree
NATO international (Western) alliance; treaty organization
NEBO wisdom god; Moab mountain (Moses died)
NEMO nobody: Lat.; prefix: glade; Captain (Verne hero)
NERO emperor; fiddler; Agrippine's son; — Wolfe (Stout)
NINO boy: Sp.
NITO climbing fern
NOIO noddy tern
NOLO — contendere
NONO ninth: It.
NUZO Chibchan Indian
NAIP native
NEAP wagon pole; tide
NEEP turnip
NOAP bullfinch
NOUP steep promontory
NATR weight
NEAR close(ly); approach
NEER never; kidney
NEIR kidney
NOIR black: Fr.; bet
NAIS nymph
NAOS star
NESS cape; promontory; suffix
NEWS intelligence; tidings
NIAS Ind. Ocean island(er)
NIBS personage (VIP); in Peter Pan

(Barrie)
NILS Bohr (physicist)
NOBS knave, Jack (card, cribbage)
NOUS mind; reason; wit; we: Fr.
NUNS sisters; veiling, fabric
NUSS nurse
NAST cartoonist
NAUT sea mile
NEAT tidy; trim; straight
NEST (make a) home
NETT undeductible
NEWT salamander; eft
NEXT nearest; following
NOTT Norse night (Dag)
NOWT neat cattle; doit
NUIT night: Fr.
NABU god; mountain
NAPU ruminant
NIOU measure
NOSU Lolo; Chin. Caucasian
NOIX edible gland
NAGY Hungarian premier
NARY not one
NAVY fleet; blue; tobacco; — yard
NIXY undeliverable mail
NIZY fool
NOSY fragrant; prying
NOWY having curvature

OBIA Ashanti religion
OBRA works: Sp.
OCHA weight
OCRA vegetable; gumbo
OCTA prefix: eight
ODEA theaters; halls; galleries
OFFA Angles' hero (Beowulf)
OHIA timber tree; apple
OKIA Moroccan money
OKRA vegetable; gumbo
OLEA shrub; olive
OLGA fem. name
OLLA jar; meat dish; -podrida (medley)
ONCA ounce
ONZA Sp. ounce (1/16 libra); coin
OOAA Hawaiian bird
ORCA killer whale
ORNA measure
ORRA oddly; laborer
OSSA bones; Mt. (Olympus)
OTEA Great Barrier Island
OTRA other: Sp.
OXEA sponge spicule
OREB Medianite defeated by Gideon
ODIC pert. to ode, od
OLIC chem. suffix
OTIC of the ear; auditory
OBED David's grandfather
ODED prophet or his father
OHAD Simeon's son
OLID smelly; fetid
OOID egg-shaped
OORD coin (double doit, ¼ stiver)
ORAD mouthward
OSID suffix: sugar
OVID poet (Metamorphoses); P.O.N.; Naso
OXID oxygen compound
OBOE woodwind; chanter
OESE bacteriologist's wire
OGEE arch; molding
OGLE gaze (amorously)
OGRE giant; monster
OHNE without: Ger.
OIME alas
OISE Fr. river
OKEE evil spirit
OKIE migratory worker
OLPE oil flask; pitcher
ONCE one time; if ever; former(ly)
ONDE wave: Fr.; wavy (Her.)
OOZE exude; slime; liquor
OPIE Eng. painter
ORFE fish; yellow ide
ORLE shield border; fillet
ORNE measure; river (Caen)
OSTE prefix: bone
OTOE Sioux Indian
OUSE Great — (river)
OWSE tan liquor
OEUF egg: Fr.
OLAF (Vi)king
OATH appeal; pledge; vow; curse
OKEH all right, O.K.
OLPH bullfinch
OPAH fish
OUCH exclamation
OUGH exclamation
OMEI Buddhist mountain
OMNI prefix: all
OMRI king of Israel
OZNI Gad's son
OMSK Siberian city
OBOL 1/16 drachma (coin)
ODAL land; vine
ODEL vine; land ownership
ODYL alleged force
OE'L eye: Fr.; — de boeuf
OHEL Zerubabbel's son
OPAL birthstone (Oct.); girasol
ORAL spoken; of the mouth
OREL Russian city
OVAL egg-shaped; elliptic; arena
OXYL oxygen radical
ODUM tree (iroko)
OGAM Irish alphabet
OGUM Irish alphabet
OLAM infinity; — haba (life after death)
ONYM technical name (biol.)
OVUM germ cell; egg
OXIM chem. compound
OZEM David's brother
OBAN coin
ODIN one-eyed Norse god: Frigg's husband, Thor's father
OLAN Wang Lung's wife (Pearl Buck: The Good Earth)
OMAN Arab. state; sultanate; Muscat
OMEN presage; portent; sign
ONAN Indian; Judah's son
OPEN plain; frank; undefended; uncertain; bare; start; unfold; public; — sesame
ORAN seaport
OREN Judah's descendant
OVEN (bake in) stove; kiln
OWEN (Welsh) name; socialist; zoölogist
OXAN gas
OXEN bovines; draft animals
OCTO prefix: eight
ODIO hatred: It.
OENO prefix: wine
OHIO Buckeye state
OKRO plant; stew; soup; gumbo
OLEO margarine
OLIO medley; olla-podrida
OMAO thrush

ONTO upon; wise to
ORDO order: Lat.; feast list
ORLO smooth surface; plinth
OSLO city (Norway); Christiania
OTHO Roman emperor
OTRO other, another: Sp.
OTTO name; palindrome; perfume; Ger. ruler
ODER river
ODOR smell; repute
OGOR early Turkic man
OLOR swan genus; Cygnus
OMAR Khayyam; tentmaker; caliph
OMER measure; sheaf; undertaker (Dickens)
ONER ace; blow; individual
OSAR glacial ridges; eskers
OSER dare: Fr.
OVER above; across; beyond; again; surplus; ended; Roger and —
OWER debtor
OXER hedge (fox hunting)
OYER hearing (law); — and terminer
OAKS horse race; trees
OBUS howitzer shell
OCHS Adolph (publisher)
ODDS inequality; advantage; at —; -on
OFFS cricket-field sides
ONES individuals
ONUS burden; duty
OONS mild oath
OPUS work
ORAS Danish money
OTIS bustard genus; general; inventor (elevator)
OTUS giant slain by Apollo
OURS possessive pronoun
OVIS sheep genus
OYES court crier's cry
OAST kiln
OBIT death notice
OINT apply oil
OKET ounce
OMIT leave out; neglect
OONT camel; mole
OUST eject; discharge
OAHU (Hawaiian) island
OGPU Soviet police body
ORDU Turk. military district, army corps
OBEX brain matter
ODAX rock whiting (fish)
OLAX tree
ONYX cameo stone; quartz; gem
ORYX antelope; gemsbok
OAKY oaklike
OARY oarlike
OATY full of oats
OBEY submit; comply
OHOY ahoy; call
OILY unctuous; bland; suave
OKAY approve; all right
OLAY palm
ONDY wavy (Her.)
ONLY alone; but; single; exclusively
OOFY rich (Eng. slang)
OOZY muddy; slimy
ORBY revolving
ORGY carousal; Saturnalia, Bacchanalia
ORLY Paris airport
OYEZ court crier's cry

PABA vitamin
PACA rodent
PAGA rice
PAHA hill
PALA weight; antelope; vine; rice
PANA city
PAPA father; Pope; potato: Sp.; baboon; clay
PARA coin; weight; river; city (Belem)
PASA raisin
PATA painting; turban; sword
PAWA weight
PEBA armadillo; Indian
PECA coin
PEDA pastoral staffs
PEGA remora fish
PELA wax (secreting insect)
PERA Istanbul district
PESA coin
PEVA Peru Indian
PICA type size; magpies
PIKA little chief hare
PIMA Ariz. Indian; cotton
PINA pineapple; silver cone
PIPA toad; measure
PISA city (leaning tower)
PITA fiber; flax; hemp; brocket (deer)
PLEA excuse; prayer; request; pretext; allegation
PODA suffix: foot
POHA gooseberry (jelly)
POLA Yugo. city (Pulj)
POMA rosa (rose apple)
POOA pua hemp
PROA Malay outrigger
PSHA exclamation
PUCA goblin; specter
PUJA worship. festival
PUKA rare N.Z. tree
PUMA cougar; catamount
PUNA high Andes; wind; sickness (soroche)
PUPA chrysalis; snail; instar
PUYA pineapple genus
PYLA brain opening
PLEB freshman cadet; common man
PARC park; oyster farm: Fr.
PYIC purulent
PAID recompensed; discharged; satisfied
PARD chum; leopard
PEND hang; be delayed
PHAD star
PHUD bullet sound; exclamation
PIED variegated; Piper; -a-terre
PLED pleaded
PLOD trudge; drudge
POND lake; pool; weight
POOD weight
PRAD horse
PROD reminder; goad; horse; prodigy
PUND weight
PUUD weight
PACE step; speed; peace: It.
PAGE young attendant; call, summon; leaf
PALE wan; pallid; ashy; picket; stake; beyond the —
PANE glass; panel
PAPE bunting (bird)
PARE cut off, peel
PATE head; paste
PAVE cover firmly; — the way; jewel setting
PEKE (Pekinese) dog
PELE fire goddess
PENE (hammer) head
PERE father, priest: Fr.;

— Goriot (Balzac)
PETE strongbox; Peter
PICE coin; weight
PIKE fish; weapon; pierce; highway; farmer; gamble; Zebulon (explorer; peak)
PILE hair; heap (up); awn; atomic —
PINE tree; conifer; evergreen; yearn; mourn
PIPE tube; flute; cask (measure); -dream; — down
PISE building material
PODE suffix: foot
POKE thrust, prod; pry; sack; potter; herb
POLE rod; tail; terminal: axis, battery; — Star; Polish, Polack
POME fruit; ball; globe
PONE corn bread; writ
POPE pontiff; Holy Father; — Joan (game); Alexander (poet); bird
PORE gaze; ponder; opening
POSE posture; affectation; baffle; propound
POTE poker; stick
POWE weight
PUCE flea: Fr.; eureka red
PUKE cloth; vomit
PULE cheep; whimper
PUME Yarura(n language)
PURE unmixed, chaste; sheer; free; Simon —
PYLE Ernie (journalist); Howard (artist)
PYRE funeral pile, fire
PELF booty; riches
PIFF bullet sound; exclamation
POOF exclamation
POUF puff; ottoman; bang!
PUFF blow; pastry; distend; hair roll; adder; powder —
PANG agony
PEAG money
PHAG comb. form: eating
PING (bullet, striking) sound
PLUG stop(per); plod; shoot; spark —; horse; praise
PONG sound; improvise
PRIG precisian; steal; thief; fop
PROG (steal) food; forage
PUNG (drive) box sleigh; mah jong term
PASH hurl; smash
PATH track; route
PISH reject; nonsense!
PITH marrow; kernel; gist
POOH pshaw!; — Bah (Mikado); Winnie (bear, Milne)
POSH slush; elegant
PRAH canoe
PTAH god
PUGH pshaw!; fish prong
PUSH shove; thrust; strive; -button
PADI rice
PAHI ship
PALI slope; coral parts; Buddhist language
PANI madam: Polish
PASI low-caste Hindu
PARI weight; prefix: equal
PEAI medicine man
PEDI prefix: foot
PERI fairy; elf; beauty
PFUI exclamation
PICI birds (woodpeckers)
PIKI maize bread; pik
PILI nut; grass; hairs
PIPI astringent; mollusk
PULI coins
PURI Indian yellow
PACK bundle, cosmetic paste; cards; crowd; animal(s)
PANK weight
PARK (common) grounds; green; deposit; Hyde, Central, etc.
PEAK point; top; summit
PECK measure; nip; bite; kiss
PEEK sly glance; pry; chirp
PENK minnow
PERK lift up; preen; cocky; percolate
PICK tool; scratch; choose; rob; eat; best
PINK color (red); ship; cut; hunter's coat; carnation; in the — (healthy)
PISK nighthawk
POCK pustule
POLK Cossack regiment; James Knox (President)
POOK hobgoblin; disk
PORK meat; swine; — barrel
PUCK sprite; Robin Goodfellow; Shaks. character; hockey disk
PULK (Cossack) regiment
PUNK touchwood; tinder; conch; tramp; bad
PAAL measure
PAIL bucket
PALL cloak; covering; cloy
PAUL click; detent; Apostle; Bunyan; Revere; — VI (Pope)
PAWL click; detent; tent
PEAL ring; loud sound; fish
PEEL pare; tower; spade
PEUL Fulah (Sudanese)
PHIL nickname; prefix: loving
PILL medicine tablet
POIL raw silk thread
POLL head; register, survey; cut off; Mary; parrot; vote
POOL pond; puddle; game; stake; fund; Thames
POUL Russ. coin
PULL drag; influence
PURL knitting stitch; beer; murmur; spin; swirl
PYAL veranda
PALM tree; measure; hand part; paddle; conceal; grease the —
PERM elec. unit; hair wave
PLIM swell; swollen
PLUM fruit (damson; greengage); tree; raisin choice job
POEM verse creation
PRAM carriage
PROM (college) dance, ball
PAAN town
PAIN ache; trouble; forfeit
PAON peacock blue
PAUN betel leaf
PAWN chessman; pledge
PEAN panegyric; praise;

fur
PEEN hammer head
PENN William (Penna. founder)
PEON laborer
PERN honey buzzard
PHAN measure
PHON loudness measure
PIAN tumor
PIEN arris (sharp edge)
PION dig; excavate
PIRN reed; bobbin; nose ring
PLAN design; scheme
POON tree (mastwood)
PUAN latex
PACO alpaca
PAGO -Pago (city)
PAHO prayer stick
PAJO prayer stick
PALO pole, wood: Sp.
PASO measure
PATO Muscovy duck
PAVO peacock; constellation
PECO black tea
PEDO child
PEHO morepork (bird)
PELO hair: It.
PEPO pumpkin; squash; melon; cucumber
PERO but: Sp.
PESO coin; Sp. dollar
PETO wahoo (fish); Henry IV figure
PHAO wolf (Kipling)
PHOO disgusting!
PICO peak; game; weight
PINO pine tree
PIRO Tanoan Indian
PISO weight
PITO fiber; flax; hemp; brocket (deer)
POCO slightly; old-clothes man
POGO springy stick
POLO game; Marco —
POMO California Indian
PORO Sierra Leone secret society
PRAO canoe
PROO slow up! (horse call)
PUNO Pacific trade wind; city (Peru)
PYRO prefix: fire, fever
PALP appendage; feeler
PAUP walk idly
PEEP chirp; bird; peer slyly; Bo —; jeep
PIMP procurer; bawd; maquereau
PLAP fall loudly
PLOP sound of fall
PLUP sound of (soft) fall
POMP pageant(ry); splendor
POOP deck; cabin; dickey; exhaust; tire
PREP prepare; student
PROP support; shore; theater equipment
PULP pith; tissue; paper; magazine
PUMP force; draw out; slipper
PAAR sand
PAIR couple; brace
PARR young fish; skegger; Catherine (Henry VIII wife)
PEAR fruit, tree
PEER gaze; equal; nobleman
PEOR Bib. mountain
PEUR fear: Fr.
PIER mole; dock; pillar
PIRR wind gust; whiz; gull
POOR indigent; scanty; feeble; lowgrade; lean; ill; hapless; cod (fish)
PORR push; poke; kick
POUR (make) flow; for: Fr.; emit; — le merite
PURR cat's sound
PAAS Easter
PAIS country: Fr.
PARS part: Lat.
PASS opening; go through; by; license; abstention; condition; amatory gesture
PESS hassock
PHOS phosphorus
PIUS Pope: X (St.; Sarto); XI (Ratti); XII (Pacelli)
PLUS and; more; extra; — fours
POBS porridge; pap
PONS bridge: Lat.; — asinorum; Lily (singer)
POUS measure
PRES near: Fr.
PUSS cat; lip; face
PACT agreement
PANT gasp; yearn
PART portion; duty; separate; role; split; go
PAST tense; ago; after
PATT stalemate(d)
PEAT darling; turf; fuel
PEET darling; turf; fuel
PELT skin; hurl; strike
PENT confined; -house
PERT bold; lively; sandpiper
PEST plague; insect; nuisance
PHIT bullet sound
PHOT light unit
PHUT (bullet) sound; OT people
PIAT magpie; antitank gun
PICT British aborigine
PIET magpie
PINT measure
PIOT magpie
PIST attention!; track
PITT statesman (Commoner, Chatham); diamond
PLAT plait; map; plot; fish
PLET three-lash whip
PLOT tract; ground; press (soap); scheme; intrigue
POET writer of verse, artist
POLT knock; trump; club
PONT ferry(boat); bridge: Fr.
POOT disgusting!
PORT harbor; haven; wine; blue-red; left side; tune; demeanor
POST pillar; advertise; mil. station; mail; inform; record
POTT paper size; editor (Dickens)
POUT sulk(iness); fish
PRAT buttock
PRET measure
PRUT exclamation; river
PUNT (propel) flatboat; kick; bet
PUTT golf stroke
PYAT magpie
PYET magpie
PYOT piebald; chatty
PATU weapon
PEAU skin: Fr.
PEGU Burmese language;

city
PELU hardwood tree
PERU country
POKU antelope
PRAU swift canoe
PUDU Chilean deer
PUKU Afr. antelope
PULU tree fern
PURU of Arawakan
PHEW exclamation
PLEW beaver skin
PLOW implement; till; cut; stars
PROW ship's bow; stem; beak
PLEX form a network
PNYX Greek voting site
PREX (college) president
PRIX price: Fr.; — fixe (table d'hôte)
PALY wan; heraldic design
PAVY peach
PEAY medicine man
PEVY lumberman's hook
PIAY medicine man
PIKY full of fish
PILY pilelike
PINY pinelike; peony
PIPY tubular; weepy
PITY sympathy; mercy
PIXY impish sprite
PLAY frolic; act; drama; contend; sport; game
PLOY make column; frolic; coup
POGY menhaden; trout
POKY shabby; dull; bonnet
POLY herb; Teucrium; prefix: many
PONY small equine (Shetland, polo); glass (1 oz.); translation
PORY porous; permeable
POSY flower; nosegay; poem
PRAY ask; beseech; please
PREY victim; pillage; booty
PUKY nauseated
PULY whining; complaining
PUNY weak; slight
PUXY ill-tempered
PHIZ physiognomy; face

QUAB fish
QAID alcaide
QUAD type; four; -rangle, -ruplet, etc.
QUID cud; essence; pound; — pro quo
QUOD prison; — erat demonstrandum (Q.E.D.)
QERE read(ing substitute)
QUAE — vide (which see)
QUAG morass
QUNG So. Afr. Bushman
QOPH Heb. K, Q, 100
QERI read(ing substitute)
QUAI pier
QUEI measure
QUAN money
QUIP witty sally; jest
QUAR fill; choke
QAIS island
QUAS sour beer, cider (Russian)
QKKT chess move
QQKT chess move
QUAT squat
QUIT abandon; yield; stop; free
QUAY pier
QUIZ test; odd one; hoax

RABA river
RACA reproach; fool
RADA legislature
RAGA state of nirvana
RAIA ottoman; fish
RAJA prince; fish
RAMA Indian; Vishnu incarnation; bull (Kipling)
RANA frog; prince; Aegir's wife
RARA — avis (rare bird)
RASA essence; tabula —
RATA tree; chestnut; rate; pro —
RAYA broadbill
REBA weight
REJA screen, grille: Sp.
RENA rockfish
RHEA Cybele; mother of the gods; Gaea's daughter; Cronos's wife; ostrich; satellite; grass
RHIA China grass
RIGA Latvian city, gulf
RIMA fissure; breadfruit; child heroine (Hudson)
RIPA river bank
RITA cosmic order (Vedic); Rio —; fem. name
RIVA shore: It.
RODA Nile island
ROKA mafura (tree)
ROMA Rome: It.
ROSA shrub genus; name; sub —; Bonheur (artist)
ROTA roster; curia tribunal; round; hurdy-gurdy
RUGA stomach membrane
RUPA body form (Buddhism)
RUSA deer; sambar; grass; oil
RUTA herb genus; rue
RAAB river
RHOB juice; jelly
ROUB measure
RUMB compass point
RAAD assembly; fish
RAID attack; foray
RAND border; ridge; strip; So. Afr. gold mine
READ interpret; learn; study; understand
REDD make tidy; free of; scold
REED woody grass; pipe; mouthpiece; Walter (doctor, hospital)
REND tear; rupture; bark trees
RIDD Lorna Doone's rescuer
RIND bark; peel; Vali's mother, Odin's wife
ROAD (rail)way; track; anchorage
RODD crossbow
ROED filled with roe
ROOD crucifix; measure
ROUD fish
RUDD carplike fish
RYND millstone support
RACE run; contest; people; speed; Cape —; rat-
RADE elated
RAGE fury; storm; fad
RAKE incline; tool; collect; roue; —'s Progress
RALE rattling sound
RAME branch
RAPE herb; ravish
RARE underdone; thin;

uncommon
RASE rub; demolish
RATE censure; ratio; charge; estimate; rank; tax
RAVE rant, rage; enthusiasm; rod
RAZE scrape; demolish
REDE interpret; counsel
REKE rick; pile
RESE shake; rush
RETE network
REVE (muse in) dream: Fr.
RICE cereal; use ricer; Elmer (playwright)
RIDE be borne; float; endure; manage; mount; journey
RIFE abundant; prevalent
RILE irritate; vex
RIME frost; (make) rhymes; chink; rung
RINE hemp; ditch
RIPE mature; fit; tipsy
RIRE to laugh: Fr.
RISE climb; grow(th); begin; emerge(nce); thrive; retort
RITE ceremony; liturgy
RIVE tear; split; — droite (right bank), — gauche (left bank)
ROBE gown; mantle; Douglas novel
RODE anchor rope; measure; was borne; cross
ROKE vapor; smoke
ROLE actor's part
ROME city (Eternal); Church; beauty (apple)
RONE brushwood
ROPE cord; cable; noose; bind; chain
ROSE stood up; got up; flower tree; wood; red; pink; window; Abie's Irish —; Eng. emblem
ROTE surf noise; routine
ROUE dissolute man; rake
ROVE wander; ramble; draw through an eye
RUBE Reuben; rustic; yokel
RUDE rough; boorish; vulgar
RULE law; guide; reign; method; control; — Britannia; ruler; line
RUNE Teutonic sign; magic
RUSE trick; deceit; slip
RUTE measure
RYME water surface
RYPE ptarmigan
RAFF Raphael
REEF shoal; lode; reduce sail
RIFF Berber; Kabyle; ripple
ROOF cover; house; top
RUFF collar; bird; fish; plait; trump
RANG sounded
RING gird; arena; prizefighting; gang; atomic order; sound (bell); Vienna landmark; Nibelungen cycle (Wagner)
RONG Sikkimese language
RUGG pull
RUNG wheel spoke; hooped
RAKH hayfield
RASH hasty; careless
RATH chariot; fort; temple; early; mome-
RESH Heb. letter, 200; plant
RICH wealthy; vivid; full; fragrant; fat
ROCH Saint (14th cent.)
RUKH fabled bird; jungle
RUSH haste(n); attack; red (mace); cattail
RUTH pity; grief; name; OT book, heroine (Moabitess); wife of Boaz
RABI crop; physicist
RAGI grass
RAKI spirits
RAMI branches
RANI princess; wife
RATI weight
RAVI tribesman
REKI Baluchistan nomad
REMI Gaul people; prefix: oar
RENI It. painter; prefix: kidney
RIFI Riffs
RIGI Swiss mountain
RODI Medit. island
ROMI Gypsy wife
RORI Bantu tribe
ROTI roasted: Fr.
RACK framework; clouds; gait; torture
RAIK weight; measure
RANK luxuriant; gross; fetid; grade; array
RECK heed; concern
REEK cloud; exude; smell
RICK pile (up); haystack
RIKK tambourine
RINK skating arena
RISK peril; hazard; subject of insurance
ROCK stone: Gibraltar; cliff; staunch support; diamond; candy; sway, lull; — the boat
ROOK bird; cheat; dupe; chessman (tower)
RUCK crowd; rake; wrinkle
RUSK bread; biscuit; Dean (statesman)
RAIL bird; scold; paling
REAL coin; true; genuine; very
REEL wind(er); dance; waver; sway
RIAL coin
RIEL Canadian (Indian) rebel
RILL (run in a) brook
ROIL disturb; muddy; vex
ROLL wrap; trill; drumbeat; rotate; list; bank-
ROOL crumple; ruffle
ROTL Afr. weight
RULL to wheel; trundle
RYAL coin
RYEL coin
REAM 500 (paper) quantity; bevel; enlarge
REEM ox; unicorn
REIM oxhide; strap
RHUM alcoholic drink
RIEM oxhide strap
ROAM wander
ROOM space; apartment; lodge; — and

board
RAIN shower; scratch; — check
RANN verse, stanza; kite (Kipling)
REIN strap; check; direct; kidney
RHIN Rhine: Fr.
RIEN nothing: Fr.; — ne va plus
ROAN horse; yellow-red
ROON treasure; darling
RUIN destroy; destruction; violate
RYAN peak, Idaho
RALO measure
REDO make over
RENO Nev. city ("biggest little"; divorce, gambling)
RIVO stream: It.
ROJO redskin: Sp.
ROTO ragged: Sp.; printing
RAIP rope
RAMP inclined way; rear
RASP grate; file
REAP cut; harvest
REPP silk or wool fabric
RISP metal bar
ROMP girl; gambol, frolic
ROUP a cold; hoarseness
RSVP please reply: Fr.
RUMP sirloin part; remnant; — Parliament
REAR back; raise; — admiral
RIER oil cask (whaling)
ROAR loud sound; laugh
ROER hunting gun
RUER repenter
RUHR Ger. industrial area
RAIS chief (Nepalese)
RATS bah!
REIS money; (boat) captain; effendi (state officer)
REMS river
REUS defendant: Lat.
REVS rotations per minute
RHUS sumac genus
RIIS Jacob (journalist)
RISS glaciation stage
ROOS Ger. painter
ROSS rough bark; seal; island; navigator; Harold (editor)
RUSS Russian; Slav
RAFT collection; float
RANT scold; rave; frolic
RAPT engrossed; rapture
RECT element (philos.)
REFT cleft; rift; deprived
RENT torn; schism; let, lease; payment; income
REST pause; stop; peace; prop; stay; rely; mus. sign; remainder; set; found
RIFT split; divide; cleft
RIOT tumult; success; act, squad
RIST engrave; scratch
RKKT chess move
ROOT underlying source; rhizome; base; dig; applaud; plant; eradicate
ROUT defeat; tumult; mob; the brant; snare
RQKT chess move
RUNT small animal, man
RUST oxydize; corrode; inaction; reddish-brown
RYOT Indian peasant
RAHU demon
RAKU -ware
RIMU red pine; imou pine
RURU N.Z. morepork
ROUX (soup, sauce) thickener; physician
RACY smart
RELY trust; depend
RILY turbid; irritated
RIMY frosty; rhyming
ROEY of mottled grain
ROKY misty; hoarse
ROPY viscous; stringy
RORY O'More (Irish novel)
ROSY blushing; optimistic
ROWY streaked
ROXY name: Roxana; Rothafel (impresario); theater
RUAY weight
RUBY gem; corundum; bird; name; Oswald killer
RANZ — des vaches (Alpine melodies)
RAZZ chaff; ridicule
RYAZ coin

SABA fiber; kingdom; island
SAGA legend; story; goddess; weight
SAHA measure
SAKA era; Scythians
SALA dining room: Sp.
SAMA fish; trance-inducing music
SANA Yemen's capital; fiber
SAPA grape juice
SARA native
SASA fencer's cry
SAVA Yugo. river
SAYA outer skirt
SEBA Bib. country; Ham's grandson
SELA Dead Sea town
SERA antitoxins; blood parts; whey; evening: It.
SETA caterpillar's hair; spine
SHEA tree; butter
SHOA Abyssinian
SHUA Abraham's son
SIDA herb; shrub; hemp
SIKA Jap. deer
SIMA igneous rock
SINA drug; mountain (Moses)
SITA Ramachandra's wife (Sanskrit Ramayana)
SIVA Hindu deity; cosmic dancer (Nataraja)
SKUA bird; great —; jaeger
SODA carbonated water; Vichy; drink; sodium compound (bicarbonate)
SOFA couch; divan
SOGA grass rope: Sp.; Bantu
SOIA food plant
SOJA bean; Glycine
SOKA drought blight
SOLA herb (topee source); alone; holla!
SOMA vine; drink; body
SORA bird; rail
SOYA bean; dill; fennel
STOA portico; poikile (Zeno)
SULA genus; booby;

gannet
SUPA P.I. tree: lamp oil
SURA Koran section; deva
SUSA Elam city (Esther story)
SYRA Aegean island
SCAB crust; strikebreaker
SCOB fabric defect
SERB Servian (Yugo)slav
SHAB paltry guy
SLAB slice; road
SLEB nomadic Arab
SLOB slovenly one
SLUB twisted wool roll
SNAB hill part; girl
SNIB escape logging work
SNOB social climber; game
SNUB rebuke; slight; stumpy
SORB wild apple; Slav
STAB pierce; trial
STIB sandpiper (dunlin)
STUB stump; penpoint; short, stocky; extirpate; ticket part; bump
SWAB mop; lout
SWOB sponge; wipe; mop
SAIC Near East ketch
SPEC speculation
SYNC synchronize
SADD dam; waste matter
SAID before-mentioned; Port —, city; name
SAND grit; silica; polish, smooth; red-yellow; George, novelist (Dudevant)
SARD carnelian; gem; Sardinian
SAUD Ibn (king)
SCAD fish; large amount
SCUD run fast; wind-driven clouds; skim; flea
SEED fertile germ; progeny; decay; plant; extract
SEID tribe; lord; chief; Mohammed's descendant
SEND transmit; dispatch; propel; swing; enthrall
SHAD fish
SHED cast off; abandon; drop; hut; shelter
SHOD wearing shoes
SIND river; Pakistan province; are: Ger.
SKID clog; slide; — Road, Row
SLED vehicle, snow or ice
SLID glided; slipped
SNED lop; prune
SNOD trim; snug; plausible
SOLD vended; persuaded; cheated
SOUD pay
SPAD nail
SPED hastened
SPUD scrape(r); potato; dig
STAD town
STOD Danish speech
STUD breeding stock; knob; stump; dot; poker
SUDD Nile waste; dam
SULD measure
SURD irrational; mute
SWAD mass; soldier
SYED Moslem chief
SYUD Moslem prince; title
SABE know
SADE letter; Marquis
SAFE secure; box
SAGE herb; wise; Russell — (financier)
SAKE purpose; beer
SALE bargain; auction; willow; salted: Fr.
SAME identical
SANE rational
SATE gratify; glut
SAVE rescue; avoid; lay by; but; — face
SAXE Saxony; blue
SEME (sprinkling) pattern
SERE wither(ed); Negroid
SEVE wine delicacy: Fr.
SHEE Irish fairyfolk
SHOE foot covering; crakow; wheel drag; tire
SHUE Tibetan deer
SICE number 6 on die
SIDE region; part(y); oblique; aspect; support; lateral
SIME monkey
SINE math. ratio; without: Lat.; — qua non; — die
SIRE father; beget; king
SISE six (dice)
SITE location; scene
SIVE sickle; knife
SIZE bulk; quality; glue; filler; — up
SKEE ski
SKYE Isle; dog, terrier
SLEE sly
SLOE blackthorn; plum; blueblack
SLUE swamp; twist; lot
SMEE pintail duck; widgeon; Peter Pan pirate
SNEE cut; snick(er) —
SOIE silk
SOKE jurisdiction
SOLE pelma (bottom); flatfish; single; only
SOME various; any; somewhat; part
SORE painful; vexed; sensitive; deer
SPAE prophecy
SPEE Graf — (ship, admiral)
STYE eyelid swelling
SUKE Susan; teakettle
SUPE stage extra; supercharge
SURE safe; firm; certain
SYCE groom
SYKE fountain (Her.)
SYPE ooze
SAUF safe: Fr.; — conduit
SELF identity; ego; one
SERF slave; peasant
SOUF sigh
STOF measure
SURF swell of sea; foam
SANG Hindu group; herb; weight; did sing
SARG Toni (puppeteer)
SCUG squirrel: Brit.
SHAG hair; tobacco; bird; rascal; dance step
SHOG shake; jog
SIEG victory: Ger.
SING vocalize; warble; tell
SKAG boat; keel part
SKEG keel part; plum; tear
SLAG dross; lava
SLOG hit (hard); slug; slam
SLUG snail; idle; metal

spacer; small drink; bullet; strike
SMOG fog and smoke; haze
SMUG tidy; neat; priggish
SNAG stump; cut; obstacle; tangle
SNIG chop off; drag; pilfer
SNUG cozy; trim; Shaks. character
SONG poem (music); pittance
STAG deer; men's party; warn
STOG stall in mud
SUNG chanted; Chin. dynasty
SWAG bag; booty; sway; sag
SWIG gulp; hoist; tackle
SAAH measure
SADH holy man
SAHH measure
SAMH bread plant
SAPH giant (Philistine)
SASH casement; scarf; belt
SEAH measure
SECH such
SETH banker; Adam's son; Osiris' evil brother
SHAH ruler
SHIH weight; measure
SIGH lament(ing sound)
SIKH Hindu soldier
SINH hyperbolic function
SISH slushy ice
SOPH 2nd-year student
SOSH jag; drunk; dash
SUCH of this kind; same
SADI poet
SAFI Afghan
SAKI monkey; Munro
SARI Hindu garment
SATI queen of the gods
SEBI prefix: tallow
SEMI half
SERI betel; Indian
SESI black-fin snapper
SETI river; pharaoh
SHRI glorious; holy; Lakshmi (goddess)
SIDI Moslem title; Negro
SIMI Dodecanese isle
SIRI betel
SISI porkfish
SODI Gaddiel's father (spy)
SOLI single performances; prefix: sun, alone
SORI clusters; spores
SUFI mystic ascetic
SUGI Jap. cedar
SUJI wheat; semolina
SUSI fine cotton
SACK dismiss; plunder; wine; bag; gown; sad —
SANK descended
SARK Channel island
SAUK Indian; Mont. river
SAWK measure
SECK unprofitable (rent)
SEEK ask; try; hunt
SEIK Hindu sectarian
SHIK Arab. Turkoman
SIAK latex
SICK urge (dog); ill; weak
SILK fiber; thread; -worm
SINK fall; droop; conceal; basin
SOAK absorb; sot
SOBK evil deity
SOCK beat; wind cone; stocking
SOOK Moslem market; hog call
SOUK Moslem market
SUCK draw in; bleed; drink
SULK mope; be sullen
SUNK immersed; overcome
SAAL hall: Ger.
SAIL canvas; rigging; journey; travel
SAUL tree; king (son of Kish; — of Tarsus (Paul)
SEAL otarian; pinniped; fur; fasten; brown; ratify; stamp
SEEL shut eyes of; blind
SEIL rope: Ger.
SELL vend; betray; persuade; hoax; — short
SHUL synagogue
SIAL earth's outer part
SILL beam (door, window)
SIOL great Irish clan
SKAL health toast
SKIL candlefish; beshow
SOIL earth, ground; land; stain; pollute
SOOL pull, tousle about
SOUL spirit; inspirer; force; psyche; person
SAIM grease
SALM star
SAUM weight
SCUM dross; refuse; rabble
SEAM fold; crevice; join; ornament; measure
SEEM look; appear
SEIM Polish assembly
SEJM Polish assembly
SHAM deceit; fake
SHEM Noah's son; Semite
SHIM leveling slip; shingle; knife
SIAM Thailand; Anna's king (The King and I)
SIUM water parsnip
SKIM scoop off; scud; brush
SLAM bang; criticize; grand —
SLIM slight; scanty; sly; slender
SLUM dilapidated district
STEM shaft; trunk; stock; axis; dam; check; derive; turn skis
STOM prefix: mouth
STUM grape juice; must; renew wine
SUUM hum; — cuique
SWAM floated
SWIM move in water; float; teem
SWUM swim participle
SAAN Bushmen
SAIN consecrate; tree
SAWN sawed; cut
SCAN examine; measure poetry
SCON teacake
SEAN John
SEEN observed
SEIN poss. pronoun, be, being: Ger.
SENN Swiss herdsman
SEWN stitched
SHAN Thai
SHEN Christian God (China)

SHIN leg, calf front; run; climb
SHUN avoid; abstain (from)
SIGN symbol; signal; subscribe; ratify; hire
SINN — Fein (Irish society)
SION purple seaweed; Zion
SKEN squint
SKIN hide; pelt; peel; fleece; — and bones
SKUN skinned
SOON promptly; willingly
SOWN scattered; seeded
SPAN stretch; team; measure; dog
SPIN whirl; twist; aerial stunt; — a yarn
SPUN twisted; whirled
STEN weight; gun
STUN stupefy; daze
SUAN — pan: Chin. abacus
SUNN hemp: fiber plant
SVAN Caucasian
SWAN constellation; dive; — song
SACO weight; river
SADO carriage; island; river
SAGO palm; starch
SAHO language
SAPO soap; toadfish
SCIO prefix: sky
SEGO herb; bulb; lily; Utah state flower
SEMO Sancus (deity); Dius Fidius
SERO prefix: thin; late pupil
SHOO scare away; begone!
SILO fodder pit; ensile
SINO prefix: Chin.
SIPO liana
SITO prefix: grain
SKEO fisherman's hut
SLOO swamp
SOCO heron; bittern
SOHO exclamation; London district
SOLO song; (fly) alone
SOSO middling; passably
SOTO Hernando de (explorer)
STLO WW II battle site
SUMO Ulvan
SALP marine animal
SAMP maize
SCAP skull
SCOP bard; poet
SCUP pan fish; porgy
SEEP ooze; small spring
SEIP seep; ooze
SHAP silk yarn
SHIP vessel; send; —of state
SHOP store; buy; buying place; talk —; window-
SIMP simpleton
SKEP basket; measure; beehive
SKIP jump; escape; mess; captain; -tracer
SLAP strike; — bang
SLIP slide; err(or); escape; pier; leash; garment; memo; cut
SLOP slush; gush; mash
SNAP seize; break; click; shut; photo; vigor; easy task; — out
SNIP cut; shred; slip
SNUP snap up cheaply
SOAP cleanser; detergent; money; soft —; -box; — opera
SOUP broth; stew; — and fish; duck —; step (up); explosive; fog
STEP pace; foot rest; rank; act; dance; crush; — on it
STOP halt; discontinue; arrest; close; instrument part; period
SUMP dig pit; tank; cistern
SWAP barter; exchange
SWOP trade
SHOQ tree (tanning); chogak
SAAR river; region
SADR tree
SAER tenant
SAIR savor
SAUR prefix, suffix: lizard
SCAR rock; cicatrix; mar(k); fish
SCUR horn tissue
SEAR burn; dried up; gun-lock catch
SEER prophet
SEHR very: Ger.
SEIR Bib. mountain (Hor), Edom (Esau's home)
SHER tiger
SHIR cook; gather; tiger
SHOR salt lake; Tatar tribe
SIER pintado (fish)
SKIR fly; scurry; skim
SKYR sour curdled milk
SLUR pass over; mumble; defame; stigma; glide (mark)
SMUR mist; cloud
SNUR snort
SOAR fly high; glide
SOIR evening: Fr.
SOUR acid(ify); tart; disagreeable
SPAR mineral; mast; gaff; box
SPIR prefix: coiled
SPUR point; goad; kick; otter track; ridge
STAR sun; heavenly body; asterisk; hummingbird; excel
STER suffix: agent
STIR agitate; rouse; ado; jail
SUER prosecutor; suitor
SAIS groom; city; know: Fr.
SANS without: Fr.; — culotte (radical); — gene
SASS sauce
SEIS six: Sp.
SEPS snake; lizard
SESS soap frame bar
SIRS gentlemen
SISS hiss; shame!; girl
SORS lot: Lat.; divination
SOSS hog call for food
SOTS yeast
SOUS coins; under: Fr.
SPES (goddess of) hope
SUDS lather; froth; beer
SALT sodium chloride, NaCl; sailor; season; — away; — Lake City; — Sea
SART Iranian Turk
SCAT buffet; scatter; begone!; tax; skat
SCOT Celt; Highlander; tax; — free
SCUT rabbit's tail; fur

SEAT chair; fundament; site; membership; install; hot —
SECT group; denomination
SEIT measure
SEPT social unit; screen; seven: Fr.
SERT Sp. painter
SETT tool; paving stone
SEXT canonical hour (noon); organ stop; sixth
SHAT saline lake
SHOT missile; pellet; guess; range; marksman; film record; long —; big —
SHUT close; refine
SIFT screen; separate; bolt
SILT sediment; scum; drift
SIST stay; delay; summon
SKAT card game; star
SKIT comedy sketch; jest
SKYT move fast; dart; slip
SLAT lath; slab; sheep's hide; flap
SLIT cut; slash; opening
SLOT (cut) opening; bolt; deer; track; — machine
SLUT slattern; harlot
SMIT struck; destroyed
SMUT soot; coal dust; plant disease; obscenity
SNOT wick end; blow nose
SOFT giving way; easy; light(ly); mild; tractable
SOOT powdery carbon smudge
SOPT Dog Star; Isis
SORT type; kind; quantity; classify
SPAT mollusk; gaiter; snap; tiff
SPET spit; barracuda
SPIT land point; rod; impale; expectorate; — and image
SPOT stain; point, place; fish; small amount; espy
SPUT boiler plate
STAT photocopy
STET let it stand!
STOT stumble; stutter
STUT horsefly
SUET hard fat
SUIT costume; card set, legal action; please; (out)fit
SUNT babul: gum tree; pod; were: Lat.
SURT Frey's slayer
SWAT hit (hard); river, state (Pakistan); Sultan of — (Ruth)
SWOT hard work; grind; hit
SYRT quicksand
SAHU spiritual body
SHLU Moroccan Berber
SHOU Tibetan deer
SUKU Bantu
SULU Moro
SUSU blind dolphin; Congo
SHIV bit of husk; fluff; blade
SKIV sovereign (coin)
SLAV Eastern European
SPIV slacker: Brit.
STEV stanza
SCAW promontory
SCOW flat-bottomed boat
SHAW thicket; pshaw; playwright (George Bernard)
SHEW show: Brit.; -bread
SHOW exhibit(ion); reveal; appear(ance); 3rd place; no — (airline term)
SKEW twist; swerve; distort(ed); slant(ing)
SLAW cabbage
SLEW killed; twist; swamp; large number
SLOW dilatory; tardy; inert; boring; hinder
SMEW merganser; duck
SNOW ice crystals; white hair; cocaine; — goose; TV spots
SPEW eject; scatter; gush
STEW boil; steep; hash; worry; study; oyster bed
STOW pack; hide; hold; skiing resort
SWOW I — (oath)
SPEX spectacles
STYX Hades river; nymph: daughter of Oceanus, Tethys
SAGY wise
SARY sorry
SEXY sexually appealing
SHAY chaise; carriage
SIDY pretentious
SIZY viscous
SKEY yoke bar
SLAY kill; overwhelm
SLEY weaver's reed
SORY vitriolic earth
SPAY deer; castrate
SPEY river
SPRY nimble; brisk; smart
STAY rope; fasten; prop, endure; wait; remain; stop(ping); — put
SUKY Susan; teakettle
SUSY name: Susan; Susanna
SUZY name: Susanna
SWAY oscillate; veer; rule
SIZZ hiss(ing sound)
SUEZ canal; seaport
SWIZ swindle

TAHA bird
TALA tree; basin; ruin
TAMA Indian
TANA shrew; rabbi; police station; lake (Blue Nile)
TAPA bark; cloth
TARA fern; goddess; palm
TAWA tree
TCHA (rolled) tea
TECA teak; Indian
TEDA Negro Berber
TELA tissue; web; banana port
TEMA musical theme; Arab
TERA Buddhist monastery
TESA Indian buzzard
TEWA N.M. Indian
THEA tea source; name
TINA fem. nickname
TIZA ulexite mineral
TOBA Tatar; Chaco Indian
TODA Ceylon aborigine
TOGA Roman garb; gown; senatorship
TOLA weight
TOMA Liberian Negro

TOOA hero; beefwood
TORA hartebeest; law (of Moses); Pentateuch
TOTA grivet monkey
TOXA sponge spicule
TSIA tea
TUBA saxhorn; tree; nut; fish poison; palm sap
TUFA porous rock
TULA metal; niello; city; Toltec ruins
TUNA fish; pear; opuntia
TUZA pocket gopher
THEB measure
THOB rationalize
TOMB grave; monument; bury
TURB crowd; clump
TALC soapy mineral
TLAC coin
TEND serve; incline
THUD dull sound; blow
TIED bound; knotted; drawn
TIND kindle
TOAD amphibian; anuran; fawn
TOED stepped (gingerly)
TOLD narrated counted
TROD walked track
TUND pound bruise
TACE steel splint
TAKE acquire, seize; scene part; receipts
TALE story; — of Two Cities; count
TAME gentle; subdue
TANE Polynesian god
TAPE band; tie; Indian; record; red —; ticker —
TARE vetch; allowance (weight)
TATE wool; hair lock
TAVE Octavia
TCHE fruit tree; Chin. flute
TELE prefix: far, complete
TENE suffix: ribbon
TETE head: Fr.; — a tete; hairdo
THEE you
TICE lure; yorker (bowled ball)
TIDE ocean's rise, fall; season; drift; endure; current; help
TIGE rifle steel pin; dog
TIKE child
TILE ceramic slab; drain pipe; domino; tessera slate
TIME period moment; credit term; speed rate; meter, rhythm Father —; space —
TINE tooth; prong; pain; grass
TIPE rabbit trap
TIRE fatigue bore; wheel covering; rubber shoe
TOBE cotton cloth; future
TODE (haul with) sled
TOLE entice told; tinware
TOME book; papal letter
TONE pitch, accent; Wolfe (Ir. rebel)
TOPE drink; shark; stupa; orchard
TORE ripped; geom. surface
TOTE carry; haul; total
TREE wood, plant; family —; boot, shoe —
TRUE factual; loyal; align
TUBE cylinder; tunnel; subway; radio, TV part; Audion (DeForest)
TUKE fabric; canvas
TULE bulrush cattail
TUNE song; pitch; harmony
TUTE tutor
TWEE bird's cry
TYEE chief
TYKE dog, child
TYNE Eng river
TYPE kind, sort; class(ify); printer's letter; use typewriter, produce copy
TYRE Phoenician city; Sur
TEFF grain plant
TIFF (petty) quarrel
TOFF dandy
TREF homestead
TUFF volcanic rock
TURF sod; grassy ground; peat racing
TANG spur, flavor; sound seaweed; dynasty
TEGG sheep in 2nd year
TEIG Teague; Thaddeus; Timothy
TENG measure
THUG assassin; hoodlum
TIGG swindler (Dickens)
TING sound; Chin. pottery
TOAG Indian
TONG secret society
TOUG horsetail standard
TRIG trim; sound; prim; math. course
TUNG tree; oil
TWIG discover; branch; beat
TANH math. term
TASH fabric
TATH dung
TECH technical school
TETH Heb. T, 9
TOPH drum; porous rock
TOSH bath(tub)
TUSH tooth; Georgian; pshaw!
TABI sock
TALI gold piece; weight
TARI coin; goddess
TAXI (ride a) cab; prefix: arrangement
TCHI measure
TELI low (merchant) caste
THAI Siamese
TIKI god; first man; image
TIPI wigwam
TITI monkey; tree; petrel
TOPI antelope; pith hat
TORI moldings
TSHI Gold Coast language
TUPI Amazon Indian
TURI Pathan tribesman
TUWI P.I. dyewood tree
TYBI 1st Egypt. spring month
TEBJ Negro Berber
TACK hook; rope; course; attach
TALK speak; converse; conference; empty words; dialect; — turkey
TANK basin; store; war vehicle panzer
TASK labor; assignment; take to - (censure)
TEAK tree; dark
TECK readymade tie
TICK parasite; mattress; count; tic
TOCK hornbill
TONK (cow bell) clang; honky-; game
TOOK seized; caught;

endured; supposed
TOSK Albanian
TREK migrate; journey
TRUK islands (Carolines)
TUCK draw up; fold (in); eat; Friar (Robin Hood)
TUNK rap; thump; game
TURK Mongoloid; Seljuk; Ottoman; Osmanli; horse
TUSK long tooth
TAAL lake; volcano; language
TAEL weight; coin
TAIL end; cue; follow; high-
TALL high; incredible
TEAL duck (blue)
TEEL sesame
TEIL linden tree; lime
TELL inform; discern; chat; William (Swiss hero)
TEYL linden; lime tree
TILL until; plow; cultivate; tray, cash box
TOIL work; drudge(ry); snare
TOLL tax; lure; sound
TOOL instrument; polish; dupe
TUEL furnace
TEAM group; yoke
TEEM abound
TERM phrase; word; condition; time, period
THEM pronoun
TIAM language
TRAM trolley; gauge
TRIM shear; adjust; adorn; rebuke; defeat; neat
TURM troop; company
TUUM thin: Lat.
TAEN taken
TAIN plate
TARN lake
TAUN measure
TAWN tawny
TEAN tone: Scot.
TEEN 13–19; injury; pain
TERN gull; threefold; ship
THAN in comparison with; conjunction
THEN at a time; therefore
THIN lean; dim; rare; dilute; — ice
TIEN sky: Chin.; — Chu (Lord of Heaven); your(s): Fr.
TION suffix
TMAN U.S. Treasury agent
TMEN Treasury agents
TOON tree (dye); mahogany
TORN ripped; damaged
TOWN city; hamlet; — hall; man about —
TRIN one of triplets
TSIN Chin. dynasty
TSUN measure (1/10 ch'ih)
TUAN measure; sir; title
TURN bending; corner; revolve; reverse; change; shape; act; movement
TWIN double; match; — Cities
TAJO trench
TANO Indian
TARO rootstock; poi; elephant's ear
TAXO prefix: arrangement
TECO Indian
THEO prefix: god
THIO prefix: brimstone
TIAO Chin. money
TINO Sambal language
TIRO amateur; novice
TITO Yugo. leader (Broz)
TOCO toucan
TODO bustle; stir; ado
TOGO Afr. republic; Jap. admiral and statesman
TOHO halt! (to dogs)
TOKO Chin. store; flogging
TOPO prefix: place
TORO N.Z. tree
TOTO baby (animal); all
TRIO set of 3; So. Amer. Indian
TSAO Chin. state
TUNO rubber tree; gum
TYLO dog (Maeterlinck)
TYPO printing error
TYRO beginner; novice
TYTO barn owl; Strix; Aluco
TAMP fill up; pound down; tool
TARP canvas; sailor; hat
TEAP ram
TERP prehistoric mound
TOOP measure
TORP croft; Swed. small farm
TOUP Malay lugger
TRAP snare; mouth; net; catch; clothe; basalt; — shooting
TRIP move; slip; journey; (mis)step
TROP too much: Fr.
TROT jog; gait; race; translation; fishing line
TRYP parasite in blood (sleeping sickness, nagana, surra)
TUMP drag slain deer
TURP turpentine
TYMP blast furnace stone
TYPP yarn count unit
TAAR tambourine
TAHR goat
TAIR goat
TARR tease
TAUR Taurus (bull)
TEAR drop; weep, rip; glass defect
TEER golfer; mix colors
TEHR wild goat
THAR goat
THOR thunder god (Thursday); Midgard slayer; Odin's son; missile
TIAR crown; shrub
TIER row; layer; pinafore
TOUR trip; circuit; — de force
TSAR emperor; dictator
TYER binder
TYRR Odin's son; war god
TZAR emperor; dictator
TAOS Indian
TAPS lights-out signal; bugle call
TASS Soviet News Agency
TEES river (North sea)
TEMS sieve; sift
TEOS Ionian city
TESS Theresa; Hardy heroine
THIS pronoun, demonstrative
THOS jackal genus
THUS in this way; hence
TIBS — eve (never-never)
TOGS clothes
TOPS most superior
TOSS throw; fling; change
TRES very: Fr. three: Sp.
TRIS prefix: thrice
TACT diplomacy; perception

TAFT President; Republican; rower's seat; -Hartley Act
TAIT marsupial
TAKT beat(s); tempo
TART sour; pastry; harlot
TATT knot lace
TAUT snug; tense
TEAT nipple
TENT cloth shelter; pup —; wine; frame
TEST shell; cupel; examination; try
TEXT (literary) substance; topic; Scripture passage; type
THAT so; which; pronoun; connective; that's —
TILT cover; incline; tip; joust; sport
TINT color; shade; tinge
TOAT plane handle
TOFT — and croft (house)
TOGT trading enterprise
TOLT writ; isolated peak
TOOT sound horn; carousal
TORT wrongful act
TOUT tip(ster); praise; all: Fr.; — a fait; — de suite
TRET weight allowance
TRIT prefix: third
TUFT crest; clump; tassle
TWIT taunt; yarn snarl
TABU forbidden
TAKU Indian
TAPU taboo
TASU measure
TATU Indian; armadillo; tattoo
TCHU exclamation
TEJU lizard
THOU 2nd pers. pronoun
TIBU Negro-Berber
TIOU Indian (Tonikan)
TOHU -bohu (confusion)
TOLU balsam (rose odor)
TORU N.Z. tree
TULU Dravidian Indian
TUNU rubber tree; gum
TUTU N.Z. shrub; poison; ballet skirt
THAW melt; unbend
THEW muscle; sinew
TROW believe; fishing boat
TRIX fem. suffix
TAKY taking
TAVY Octavia
THEY pronoun; people; men
TIDY (make) neat
TINY small; -tim (herb); Tim (Dickens)
TIVY huntsman's cry
TOBY cigar; mug; dog; rob
TODY green — (bird)
TONY nickname (Anthony); stylish
TORY conservative
TOTY low-caste worker
TOWY like flax fibers
TRAY salver; platter; old dog
TREY three(spot)
TROY weight system; Ilium, Ilion (Troas); city
TUNY melodious
TUPY Amazon Indian
TYPY typical
TYTY farmer of God's Little Acre

UEBA measure
ULLA grass; paper pulp
ULNA elbow bone; ell
ULUA cavalla; fish; caranx
ULVA sea lettuce; laver
UNCA 8th note
UPLA cow dung; fuel
UREA chemical compound
URFA Turkish city (Edessa)
URGA Outer Mongolia
URIA Bathsheba's husband auk
URNA measure
URSA bear; stars: — Major, Minor; Great, Little Bear (Dipper)
URVA mongoose
USHA Bana's daughter; sorceress
UTIA rodent
UVEA iris layer
UDIC Caucasian language
UVIC grapelike; acid
UDAD sheep
USED accustomed; secondhand
UVID moist; wet
ULME elm
UNBE cease to be
UNDE waving wavy (Her.)
UNIE unicorn fish
URDE key shaped (Her.)
URGE prod; impel; impulse
USEE future user
UANG beetle
UTUG horsetail standard
UMPH grunt
URTH Norn; Wyrd (with Verthandi, Skuld); Weird Sister
UTAH state; Indian; Deseret (Mormon)
UTCH "I"
UBII Teutonic tribe
UNCI hooks, claws
UTAI no songs (yo-kyou)
UZAI Palal's father
UNUK star; — al Hay
UDAL land
UNAL land
URAL -Altaic; mountains; hypnotic
UVAL grapelike
UZAL Shem's descendant
ULAM Gilead's descendant
URIM — and Thummim (sacred instruments)
UTUM small owl
ULAN lancer; — Bator
UPON prep.: above; against
URAN lizard; Indian
USUN ancient North Chin.
UZAN weight
UZUN ancient North Chin.
ULLO Indian shell money
ULMO muermo; hardwood
UMBO shield boss; shell beak
UNCO strange; very: Scot.
UNDO untie; unfasten; ruin
UNIO mussel
UNTO to; for; toward
UPDO upswept hair
UPGO ascend
URAO trona (mineral)
UBER over: Ger.
UFER fir pole; shore: Ger.
ULLR chief god; Sif's son; Thor's stepson
USAR salt; grass
USER employer
UTOR to use: Lat.
UNIS Etats — (USA)
UPAS tree (juice); arrow poison

UPIS Artemis, Nemesis
URBS (capital) city
URUS wild ox
USAS dawn godess
USES law of — (beneficiary)
USUS user, use: Lat.
UTAS 8 day feast; Jap. songs
UNIT single thing; basic amount; one; monad
UNAU sloth
URDU Hindustani language
ULEX spine shrub (furze)
UGLY badlooking; unpleasant; plug-
UNDY waving, wavy (Her.)
UPSY daisy
URDY key shaped (Her.)
UREY Nobel physicist
UNTZ weight

VARA measure
VASA ducts; Swedish dynasty
VEDA sacred Hindu books
VEGA meadow
VELA membranes; soft palates; the Sails (Argo constellation)
VENA vein: Lat.
VERA tree; measure; name
VETA mountain sickness
VICA Pota (goddess)
VIDA feminine of David
VIGA rafter; log
VILA fairy; New Hebrides
VINA harp; guitar; wines
VIRA Bantu
VISA endorse(ment); -vis
VITA life: Lat.
VIVA salute (long live); — voce (spoken aloud)
VOLA palm (hand, foot)
VOTA Roman festivals
VERB action word
VELD So. Afr. grassland
VEND Slav; sell; sale
VERD green(-leafed)
VOID empty; vacuum; cancel
VADE leave; — mecum
VALE valley; - of tears; farewell: Lat.
VANE weathercock; feather; blade
VARE weasel
VASE vessel
VICE sin; fault; vise; proxy; — versa
VIDE see: Lat.; for example; quae —
VILE base; evil; odious
VINE creeping plant
VIRE feathered arrow
VISE tool; clamp; endorse
VITE quick, lively: Fr.
VIVE — le roi!; long live!: Fr.
VOCE voice: It.; sotto —
VOLE rodent; slam (cards)
VONE robot bomb
VOTE ballot; suffrage; voice; enact; propose; Ingrian Finn
VANG rope
VOOG lode cavity
VUGG lode cavity
VACH goddess
VOTH Ingrian Finn
VUGH lode cavity
VAGI nerves
VALI Odin's son; viceroy
VARI lemur; prefix: diverse
VENI prefix: vein; —, vidi, vici (I came, I saw, I conquered)
VERI centipede
VIII 8 (Augustus reign)
VILI brother of Odin; Ve
VITI East African
VLEI marsh; lake; creek
VOLK people: Ger.; workmen (So. Afr.)
VAAL river
VAIL inventor
VALL valley
VEAL calf; meat
VEIL screen; facial garment; cloistered life
VIAL vessel
VILL village; township
VIOL string instrument
VEHM medieval tribunal
VAIN empty, idle; futile; proud
VEIN channel; streak; blood vessel
VULN wound (Her.)
VASO vase: It.; prefix: blood vessel
VELO speed unit
VENO prefix: vein
VETO prohibit(ion); no
VIBO gulf (Italy)
VINO palm liquor
VIVO spirited
VOTO So. Amer. Indian
VTWO robot bomb
VAMP sock; shoe part; fireman; ghost; flirt
VEEP vice-president
VAIR fur
VEER shift (course); waver
VIER striver; four: Ger.
VOIR see: Fr.
VANS race of gods
VEPS Finnish tribe (Chud); Dog Star (Isis); Horus
VISS weight
VAST huge (space)
VELT measure
VENT hole; let out; issue
VERT green (Her.); veer; convert
VEST waistcoat; clothe; empower
VINT card game
VOET measure
VOGT medieval official
VOLT sideways gait; fencing leap; elec. unit
VASU deity (Vishnu); nephew
VAYU wind god
VEAU veal, calf: Fr.
VIEW sight; see; aim; opinion; scene
VAUX village; fort (Verdun battle)
VADY vade mecum; summons
VARY alter; differ
VERY true; same; extremely; light signals; flare
VILY fairies
VINY entwining
VLEY marsh; swamp; creek

WAHA lake trout
WAKA canoe
WAWA gibbon
WEGA star
WEKA flightless bird
WETA wingless locust
WHOA stop!; opp. of giddap
WEBB Beatrice Potter (writer)
WAAC fem. soldier
WRAC women's army corp

WADD mineral
WAFD Egyptian
WAND rod; staff; magic —
WARD (safe)guard; parry; district; charge; Artemus (Browne)
WEED plant; tobacco; remove
WELD unite; junction
WEND Slav; go; travel
WILD rough; savage; mad; eager; unruly; wilderness
WIND turn; coil; flowing air; mere talk
WOAD herb
WOLD upland plain
WOOD timber; forest; Grant (painter); Leonard (general)
WORD term; news; promise; order; phrase
WURD Norn; Urth
WYND alley; small court
WYRD Norn; Urth
WABE tree
WADE pass; demon; Hampton
WAGE carry on; -earner; pay, salary
WAKE track; arouse; vigil; island
WALE streak; texture; ridge; welt
WANE ebb; lessen
WARE merchandise; beware
WATE sea demon
WAVE billow; swell; undulation, flutter; signal; — length; navy woman
WERE be (past tense); prefix: metamorphosed human
WESE we shall
WEVE contraction
WHEE whistle sound
WIDE broad; far; lax; astray
WIFE spouse; marry
WILE trick; guile; lure
WINE fermented juice
WIPE rub off; beat
WIRE cable; snare
WISE sage; learned
WIVE marry; act as wife
WNZE weight
WOKE stirred; roused
WORE had on (clothes); tired
WOTE Ingrian Finn
WOVE entwined; spun
WAFF flapping; paltry
WAIF stray
WAKF trust fund
WAQF trust fund
WARF warp
WELF ducal family
WERF farmyard
WOLF canid (dog); Lupus; larva; devour; dissonance; cry —; flirtatious man
WOOF crossthreads; texture; weft; bark
WRAF air force; aviatrix
WUFF gruff bark sound
WUKF trust fund
WAAG monkey
WAEG bird; kittiwake
WANG weight; meadow; prince
WEGG Silas (ballad seller: Dickens)
WHIG U.S., Brit. party
WIGG peruke; long hair
WING alar appendage; faction; annex; fly
WONG field; meadow
WRIG wriggle
WAGH interjection
WASH bathe; laundry; tint
WISH desire; request
WITH prep.: including, and
WYCH -hazel; — elm
WABI Indian; tree
WADI valley; river; oasis
WALI prefect
WEKI fern
WERI aweto (caterpillar)
WALK go on foot; path; pass, base on balls; — the plank
WAUK wake: Scot.
WEAK feeble; pliable; light
WEEK time unit; sennight; squeak
WELK (gather) snail; Lawrence (musician)
WICK part of candle, lamp
WILK (gather) snail
WINK blink; signal labor; mental
WORK product; act; operate; function; needlework
WAIL lament
WALL barrier; fence; enclose; knot; Berlin —
WAUL wail
WEAL body politic; stripe
WEEL fish basket, trap; pool
WELL (water) pit; shaft; eddy; flow; rightly; very; sound, healthy
WIEL whirlpool
WILL volition; choice; decree; bequeath; testament
WOOL (sheep) fleece; down
WARM hot; genial; newly made; heat; — Springs
WHAM exclamation
WHIM fancy; caprice
WHOM pronoun
WORM crawler; maggot; screw; insinuate
WURM glacial period
WAIN wagon; Charles's —
WARN caution; give notice
WEAN withdraw; alienate
WEIN wine: Ger.
WHEN whereas; how soon
WHIN gorse; restharrow; rock; winch
WHUN gorse; restharrow
WOON Burmese governor
WORN used (as clothing); shabby; tired
WREN bird; navy woman; architect
WYNN timber truck; Ed (actor, Perfect Fool)
WACO city
WHOO exclamation
WHYO gangster; footpad
WAMP eider
WAPP rope guide
WARP threads; twist; falsify
WASP yellow jacket; hornet; fem. flyer: WW II
WEEP cry; bend; leak
WHIP lash; urge; defeat
WHOP dash; beat; bump
WISP torch; shred; flock; brush; ignis fatuus
WRAP cloak; blanket; coat
WAER dam
WAHR true: Ger.
WEAR be clothed in; impair; endure; deteriorate

WEIR dam; fish trap
WHIR fly; hurry; buzz
WAYS wise; — and means
WELS sheatfish
WIES Ys
WIGS — on the green (fray)
WAFT float; flag; whiff
WAIT attend; defer; serenader; lie in —
WALT Whitman
WANT lack; desire
WART protuberance; -hog
WAST were
WATT inventor, elec. unit (volt-ampere); hare
WEET bird; cry of bird
WEFT yarn; mist; (weave) web
WELT ridge; wale; strip; sew; beat; universe: Ger.
WENT departed
WEPT cried; Jesus —
WERT were: archaic, poetic
WEST wind; painter, author; occident; go —; Mae —
WHAT interrogative; pronoun; what's —
WHET sharpen; excite; edge
WHIT bit; jot; dull sound
WILT droop; lose spirit
WIST know; knew; measure
WONT custom; contraction
WORT plant; (pot)herb
WRIT legal order; Holy —
WHAU why; tree
WIDU Moslem ablution
WUDU Moslem ablution
WUZU Moslem ablution
WHEW whistle; exclamation
WROX rot
WADY valley; river; oasis
WAKY alert
WANY diminished
WARY watchful
WAVY fluctuating; undulating
WAXY viscid; pliable
WHEY milk serum; thin; pale; curds and —
WILY artful; subtle
WINY vinous; drunken
WIRY tough; sinewy
WHIZ hum; bargain; corker

XEMA arctic gull
XINA nickname: Christina
XOSA Kaffir
XOVA Opata; Pimian Indian
XIPE -totec (Aztec god)
XIII 13; Augustus reign
XENO guest; prefix: foreign
XERO prefix: dry
XMAS Christmas
XXIV 24; Tiberius reign

YABA bark; cabbage tree
YAKA Bantu
YAMA first mortal (Judge of Dead)
YANA tribe
YAPA leaf mat
YAVA weight
YAYA copa, lancewood (tree)
YETA Jap. outcast
YIMA Avestan demigod
YMCA welfare organization
YNCA Quechuan Indian (ruler); Inca
YOGA mental discipline
YUCA cassava; manioc
YUGA Hindu age cycle
YUMA Indian (Calif.); city
YWCA welfare organization
YARD 3 feet; grounds; enclosure; spar
YELD barren; milkless
YOND past; beyond
YAGE plant
YAJE plant
YALE university; lock; Eli, Elihu —; myth. antelope
YARE prompt; ready
YATE eucalyptus
YIPE howl; cry
YITE bird (yellowhammer)
YOKE join; link; slavery
YORE ancient (times); long ago
YULE Christmas
YANG honk; male or positive principle
YEGG safecracker; tramp
YEAH yes
YHVH God, Yahveh, Tetragrammaton
YHWH God, Yahweh, Tetragrammaton
YODH Hebrew Y, 10
YOGH Middle English G, Y
YAGI antenna
YAKI cayman
YALI mansion
YATI ascetic; devotee
YETI abominable snowman
YENI So. Amer. tanager
YOBI Jap. military service
YOGI ascetic; yoga disciple
YUKI Cal. Indian
YANK jerk; New Englander; Union soldier; American
YARK yerk
YELK yolk
YERK wrench; kick; trump
YOLK egg yellow; essence
YORK city; archbishopric; Imperial (apple); Sgt. Alvin (WW I)
YARL Norse chief; earl
YAWL (sail)boat
YELL cry; cheer
YOWL howl(ing); yell
YPIL tree (brown dye)
YARM scream; wail
YIRM fret; whine: Scot., Ir.
YARN spun wool; story
YAWN openwide; gape; chasm
YEAN to lamb
YGUN antisub gun
YIRN whine; grimace; smirk: Scot., Ir.
YUAN dynasty; money
YAHO tribesman
YEDO Tokyo
YESO plaster of Paris; gypsum
YAMP herb; tuber
YAPP (bookbinding) style
YAUP yap; yawn
YAWP yap; yawn
YELP shrill bark
YOOP sobbing sound
YOUP yelp; scream; yawn
YARR growl; snarl; herb
YEAR time period; twelve month; leap —; calendar, fiscal —
YIRR growl; snarl: Scot.
YMER myth giant
YMIR rime-cold giant
YOUR poss. pronoun
YSER river
YAWS skin disease

YEAS yes votes
YELT gilt (sow)
YUFT Russ. leather
YUIT Asian Eskimo
YURT Kirghiz tent
YABU Afghan pony
YALU river (Korean War)
YARU Hades; heaven
YUTU Peru tinamou; bird
YUNX woodpecker genus
YOKY coupled

ZAMA Hannibal's defeat
ZARA city; Judah's son
ZAZA opera (Leoncavallo)
ZETA Greek Z, 7
ZIPA Chibcha chief
ZIRA measure
ZITA Austrian empress
ZIZA Rehoboam's son
ZOEA crab larva
ZOLA author (J'accuse: Dreyfus case; Nana)
ZONA girdle; shingles
ZUPA Yugo. district
ZUZA weight
ZYGA rowers' benches; brain fissures
ZIMB Ethiopian fly
ZINC metal; element; color
ZOIC pert. to animals
ZEND — Avesta (holy text)
ZOID organic body cell
ZEKE Ezekiel
ZEME (abode of) spirit; fetish
ZONE area; band; partition
ZYME ferment
ZARF holder for cup
ZING sharp thrill; vim
ZACH name
ZUPH Samuel's ancestor
ZATI bonnet monkey
ZEMI (abode of) spirit; fetish
ZUNI Indian; reservation
ZWEI two: Ger.
ZEAL ardor; enthusiasm
ZOLL measure
ZOOM buzz; climb; approach suddenly
ZAIN horse
ZEIN protein
ZION Israelites; heaven
ZOON developed compound animal
ZENO philosopher (Stoic, Cynic); emperor
ZERO nothing; cipher; nullity; — hour; Japanese plane
ZOBO mongrel yak
ZOGO sacred object
ZARP policeman
ZOAR town; Bela; city of Lot
ZIPS Czech.
ZOAS symbolic figures (Blake)
ZEUS chief god; Jupiter; Hera's husband; son of Cronus, Rhea
ZANT fish
ZEST orange peel; relish; gusto
ZOOT — suit: extreme style
ZEBU ox; Brahman bull
ZENU Afr. sheep
ZULU Bantu; Kaffir; ship; artificial fly
ZANY clown(ish)
ZIZZ whirring sound